SOUTHEAST
ASIA
HANDBOOK

SOUTHEAST ASIA HANDBOOK

SECOND EDITION

CARL PARKES

MOON
PUBLICATIONS INC.

SOUTHEAST ASIA HANDBOOK
SECOND EDITION
Published by
Moon Publications, Inc.
P.O. Box 3040
Chico, California 95927-3040, USA

Printed by
Colorcraft Ltd., Hong Kong

© Text copyright Carl Parkes 1994.
All rights reserved.
© Maps copyright Moon Publications, Inc. 1994.
All rights reserved.
© Photos copyright Carl Parkes unless otherwise noted.
All rights reserved.

Library of Congress Cataloging-in-Publication Data
Parkes, Carl, 1951-
Southeast Asia Handbook/Carl Parkes.—2nd ed.
p. cm.
Includes bibliographical references and index.
ISBN 1-56691-002-1
1. Asia, Southeastern—Guidebooks.
I. Title.
DS520.9.P37 1994
93-30740
CIP

Please send all comments,
corrections, additions,
amendments, and critiques to:

**SOUTHEAST ASIA HANDBOOK
MOON PUBLICATIONS, INC.
P.O. BOX 3040
CHICO, CA 95927-3040, USA**

Printing History
1st edition—August 1990
2nd edition—July 1994

Editor: Mark Morris
Assistant Editor: Sheri Wyatt
Copy Editors: Mark Arends, Asha Johnson, Deana Corbitt, Nicole Revere, Valerie Sellers
Production & Design: Nancy Kennedy, Dave Hurst
Cartographers: Bob Race, Brian Bardwell
Index: Mark Arends

Cover Art: Indonesian batik in Yogyakarta. Photo by Carl Parkes.
Photography: All photos by Carl Parkes unless otherwise noted.
Illustrations: All illustrations by Terra Musick unless otherwise noted.

Distributed in the U.S. by Publishers Group West
Printed in Hong Kong

Dedicated to Terra

ACKNOWLEDGMENTS

Writers write alone, but they survive only with generous doses of help and encouragement. Top marks at Moon Publications go to senior editor Beth Rhudy, editor Mark Morris, and art director Dave Hurst, all of whom labored well beyond the call of duty. The superb maps are credited to Bob Race, Brian Bardwell, and Annie Hikido. Gratitude is also given to sales director Donna Galassi, Taran March, Bill Dalton, and other Moonbeams who helped realize the book.

Support has also been provided by all the tourist offices in Southeast Asia, though special thanks must be awarded to Peachy Villanueva (Philippine Department of Tourism, San Francisco), Catherine Remedios (Hong Kong Tourist Association, San Francisco), and Sumonta Nakornthab (Tourism Authority of Thailand, Bangkok). I am also indebted to the people of Southeast Asia who took me into their homes and left me with memories to last a lifetime.

Special thanks to Laurie Fullerton for her updating work on the Philippines section.

Contributions From Readers

I would also like to thank the many readers who wrote to me about their travel adventures:

America: Susan Brown (NY), Burl Blackburn (VA), Alan Cartledge (AZ), Frank Cotter (MN), Rhys Evans (CA), Leigh Fox (GM), Steve Gilman (GA), Stephan Hammond (CA), Celeste Holmes (CA), Harry Hunter (WA), Martin Offenberger (CA), Dan Moody (CA), Jan Morris (KY), James Patterson (CA), Micheal Newman (LA), William Ring (CA), Yancey Rousek (CA), Claudia Siegel (NJ), Jefferson Swycaffer (CA), and Micheal Triff (GA).

Asia: Philip Drury (China) and Bruce Swenson (Japan).

Australia: Martin Ellison (Darlinghurst), Cas Liber (Elizabeth Bay), Kevin Mulrain (Sydney), Morgana Oliver (Wodonga), Catherine Spence (Mona Vale), and Keith Stephans (Noose).

Austria: Herber Walland (Graz).

Canada: Bob Cadloff (Quebec), Bruce Moore (BC), and Lenny Morgan (BC).

Germany: Ralf Neugebauer (Lubeck) and Wolfgang and Mosgit (Brey).

Netherlands: Maarten Camps and Claantie van der Grinten (Ryswyh), Rick Dubbeldam (Sas Van Gert), Erik van Velzen (Zoetermeer), and Herbert Walland.

Spain: Sevvy (Madrid).

United Kingdom: Alan Cummings, Linda Grace (Oxford), Mark Gregory (Leeds), David Host (Bulkington), John Maidment (Southbourne), Anthony Maude (Canterbury), Peter Moorhouse (Seathwaite), Tim Prentice (Kent), Nick Slade (Flackwell Health), Lois Tadd (Chesham), and David Veale (Fishbourne).

Many other people have helped whom I do not list; some have been mentioned in the text, while others I cannot name for fear of compromising their positions.

A Personal Note

Finally, I would like to extend my deepest gratitude and sincerest love to all my friends in San Francisco and throughout the world: Terra Muzick (my best friend), David (Norton) Ashby, Wayne (Riceman) Avila, John Kaeuper, Jim (Jimbo) Pire, Unforgettable Amy Pieh, Radio King Nick Marnell, Dean (Wolfman) Bowden, Linda and her geeky "Nerd," Hysterical Ellen and Handsome Dave, Cathy Doerr and Romantic Rambler, never-forgotten Lee and Pam Winick, Deke3!, Lovely Rita and Eric, Beam-me-up Scotty, Sexy Lynn, Dara and Significant Other (currently it's Roger), Helena (Bo-Leee-Ness) Havelock, Trixie and Trudi (call me), Susan Robinson, Rich and Rens, Jerome (Tatoo) Deltour, Ed and Pat Samarin, Steve Levin and Samba 86, Crazy Harry, Mark and Christine Hardeman, Chris Burt and Fab Toby, Karen Carlson (we'll always have Tahoe), Mark T. Larsen (Dick Butkus), Bill Bodewes in Amsterdam, Gary Flynn Down Under, Joe and Nancy from Japan, Rachael in Singapore, Pete the Giant Zimmie, Terri "The Terror" (just kidding) Gomes, Gail Davis, Nicole, Stephanie, Diana Sawiki-Bruno-Coley, Genevive Yuen, Nam Chu, Brenda, June, Vera, Nina, Joel Halpern, Party Marty, Escola Josephine and Brazilian Beat Chalo, Hugh Linton, Donna (Nip) Nakashima, Samba Annie, Bob Nilsen, Richard and Fran Reynolds, Hazel and mighty cool Rick, Vince, brother-in-law Stan (intelligent, handsome, and incredibly *rich*), my beautiful sister Claudia, Healthy Heath and Krazy Kev, and my loving parents.

CONTENTS

MAPS

MAP SYMBOLS

━━━ PARKWAY (EXPRESSWAY)	★ POINT OF INTEREST / SIGHTSEEING ATTRACTION	·········· TRAM / CABLE CAR	
─── MAIN ROAD	■ POINT OF INTEREST / RESTAURANT	┼┼┼┼ RAIL ROAD	
── MINOR ROAD	● HOTEL / ACCOMMODATION	───── FERRY	
- - - UNPAVED RD.	▲ MOUNTAIN	I. ISLAND	
·-·-· FOOT PATH	☂ SACRED TREE	RD. ROAD	
─ ─ INTERNATIONAL BORDER	⛰ WATERFALL	N.P. NATIONAL PARK	
·—·—· STATE BORDER	O CITY	GH GUESTHOUSE	
═ BRIDGE	o TOWN	☁ WATER	
┼-·-┼ TUNNEL	o BOAT STOP		
▨ PARK, OPEN SPACE, OTHER		TEMPLE	

CHARTS

ABBREVIATIONS

A$—Australian dollars
APEX—advance-purchase excursion fare
B—Thai *baht* (currency)
B$—Brunei dollars
BSB—Bandar Seri Begawan
d—double
GH—guesthouse
GPO—General Post Office
HK—Hong Kong
HK$—Hong Kong dollars

HKTA—Hong Kong Tourist Association
Jl—Jalan (street)
K—Burmese *kyat* (currency)
KK—Kota Kinabalu
KL—Kuala Lumpur
km—kilometers
km/h—kilometers per hour
M$—Malaysian dollars
MTPB—Malaysian Tourism Promotion Board

MTR—Hong Kong public transit
no.—number
PAL—Philippines Airlines
R.—river
Rest.—restaurant
RTW—round-the-world fare
s—single
S$—Singapore dollars
UB—Myanma Airways

IS THIS BOOK OUT OF DATE?

Travel books are a collaboration between author and reader. Every effort has been made to keep this book accurate and timely, but conditions change quickly in a region as dynamic as Southeast Asia. Please let us know about price hikes, new guesthouses, closed restaurants, transportation tips, map errors, and anything else that may prove useful to the next traveler. A questionnaire in the back of this book will help us find out who you are and what improvements might help the next edition of this book. Send your comments to:

Southeast Asia Handbook
Moon Publications
P.O. Box 3040
Chico, CA 95927-3040, USA

INTRODUCTION

I would rather be ashes than dust—
I would rather my spark should
burn out in a brilliant blaze
Than it should be stifled in dry rot.
I would rather be a superb meteor,
Every atom of me in magnificent glow,
Than a sleepy and permanent planet.
Man's chief purpose is to live, not to exist:
I shall not waste my days trying to prolong them.
I shall use my time.

—Jack London

The use of traveling is to regulate imagination by
reality, and instead of thinking how things may be,
to see them as they are.

—Samuel Johnson

If the doors of perception were cleansed
every thing would appear to man as it is, infinite.

—William Blake

OVERVIEW

Borneo and Bali, Mandalay and Macau, Sulawesi and Zamboanga—names that fire the imagination. In a world gone increasingly dull, Southeast Asia remains a land of magic and mystery, adventure and romance, far-flung destinations still strange and exciting in a Westernized world.

Travel with an open mind and you'll find many magical moments: sunrise on a volcano above a sea of swirling clouds, saffron-robed monks slowly encircling a gold-encrusted pagoda, old women burning incense and finding their fortunes in a smoky temple, sinewy fishermen setting sail from blazing white beaches, tribal villagers who don't believe that man has walked on the moon, river journeys through the heart of darkness. This is a land blessed with an incredibly rich tapestry of races, languages, natural wonders, histories, cultures, and peoples, ranging from the rulers of international banking empires to isolated tribes just emerging from Stone Age lifestyles.

Much of Asia's strong imagery derives from writers and adventurers who recorded their own journeys of discovery and inner exploration. Marco Polo's early records were followed by the verses of Conrad, Verne, Hesse, Maugham, Gurdjieff, Malraux, Fleming, Ginsberg, and Watts. Today a new generation of writers, Theroux, Iyer, Hansen, Krich, and the Blairs, continues to explore and examine the Brave New World of modern Asia.

And what a strange, surprising place it is. Both exotic and contemporary, Southeast Asia is no place for sentimental colonialism or quaint desires that unspoiled paradises will remain forever lost. The lament, "You should have been here last year," becomes a traveler's fraud when you consider that Southeast Asian cities are some of the most highly developed and technologically advanced in the world and that most Asians prefer Hollywood and holograms to meditation and mantras. The collision of East and West is modern reality but also, at times, just as fascinating and revealing as the relics of empire and history.

To see the real Asia—the Asia that lies just underneath the Western veneer—you must travel with wide eyes and an open mind. Avoid spending money just to isolate yourself against what appears to be an alien culture. Treat the residents and other travelers as you would have them treat you. Don't measure people by Western standards or your own cultural values. Keep a cool heart but an optimistic attitude. Remain open to chance encounters with travelers, shopkeepers, students, and monks. The success of your journey ultimately lies in your hands. Have a great adventure.

DACCA

CHINA

GUANGZHOU

MACAU
HONG
KONG

MANDALAY
PAGAN

HANOI

HAIPHONG

AKYAB

BURMA
(MYANMAR)

CHIANG
MAI

LAOS

LUANG
PRABANG

HAINAN
ISLAND

VIENTIANE

PROME

UDON THANI

RANGOON
(YANGON)

PHITSANULOK

THAILAND

HUE
DANANG

KORAT

QUI NHON

BANGKOK

PATTAYA

CAMBODIA VIETNAM

PHNOM
PENH

NHA TRANG

CAM RANH

HO CHI
MINH CITY

KO SAMUI

PHUKET

SONGKHLA

SOUTH CHINA SEA

HAT YAI

KOTA BARU

BANDA
ACEH

PENANG

KUALA TRANGGANU

BRUNEI

MEDAN

MALAYSIA

IPOH

KUANTAN

SARAWAK

KUALA
LUMPUR

KUCHING

SIBOLGA

MALACCA

SINGAPORE

SUMATRA

PONTIANAK

BUKITTINGGI

KALIMANTAN

PADANG

INDIAN OCEAN

JAMBI

BANJARMASIN

PALEMBANG

BENGKULU

INDONESIA

0   500 km

JAKARTA

JAVA

BOGOR

CIREBON

BANDUNG

SURABAYA

YOGYAKARTA

MALANG

BALI

© MOON PUBLICATIONS, INC.

SOUTHEAST ASIA

PACIFIC OCEAN

PHILIPPINE SEA

VIGAN

LUZON

BAGUIO

MANILA

NAGA

LEGASPI

VISAYAS

EL NIDO

ILOILO CEBU
CITY

PALAWAN

PUERTO
PRINCESA

PHILIPPINES

MINDANAO

ZAMBOANGA

DAVAO

KOTA KINABALU

SABAH

SULU ARCHIPELAGO

CAROLINE ISLANDS

TARAKAN

MANADO

GORONTOLA

SAMARINDA

BALIK PAPAN

BIAK

SULAWESI

AMBON

JAYAPURA

IRIAN JAYA

UJUNG
PANDANG

INDONESIA

NUSA TENGGARA

FLORES

DILI

TIMOR

SUMBAWA

SUMBA

KUPANG

AUSTRALIA

HIGHLIGHTS OF SOUTHEAST ASIA

Where to go and what to see is often a difficult decision since few Westerners are familiar with the history, geography, or tourist attractions of Southeast Asia. Sadly, few people contemplating a vacation in the region could even name or find a country on a globe in this unknown corner of the world. Southeast Asia is located east of India, south of China, north of Australia, and west of the South Pacific. The region is as wide as the United States and stretches across the equator from the latitude of New Orleans as far south as that of Bahia, Brazil. It's formed by almost a dozen countries, each with distinctive histories, archaeologies, topographies, flora, fauna, peoples, cultures, traditions, handicrafts, cuisines, political landscapes, and economic promises.

Despite the amazing number of possibilities, travel destinations familiar to the general public are largely limited to Hong Kong (because of its reputation as a shopping mecca), the tropical paradise of Bali (an island in Indonesia, not an independent country or a movie soundtrack), Singapore (credit goes to historical novels and the Singapore girl), and Thailand (promotional campaigns and word of mouth). A fine beginning, but there's more—far, far, more—to Southeast Asia than just this short list.

The following thumbnail sketches will provide quick glimpses of the major attractions found in this book. Further descriptions are provided at the beginning of each chapter under "Sightseeing Highlights." But to really make an intelligent decision on where to go and what to see, you'll need to diligently study maps to become familiar with the geography and conduct an organized reading campaign of travel guidebooks, background histories, and armchair travelogues to fire up your imagination.

Far too many travelers begin a long and expensive journey without even spending a single evening at the local library or bookstore. Often the only advance reading consists of a few destination pieces in the Sunday travel sections or a travel agent's promo brochures. Without some advance research, the trip quickly becomes a confusing trail of shrines, ruins, lectured commentaries, and strange customs, without any real understanding of it all. It is absolutely essential that you prepare yourself with a thorough examination of these pages, plus some of the general background reading suggested below and specific books listed under each country. A well-rounded reading program, together with the following thumbnail sketches and suggestions for travel themes, will point the way to a successful vacation.

Brunei

The small but immensely rich oil sultanate on the northern coast of Borneo is primarily a stopover between the Malaysian states of Sabah and Sarawak. Ruled by Sultan Hassanal Bolkia—the world's richest man according to Forbes magazine and the Guinness Book of World Records—Brunei is one of Southeast Asia's more intriguing destinations because of its curious marriage of oil, Islam, and Western materialism.

Burma (Myanmar)

Burma, also called Myanmar, is a country forever frozen, where timelessness and the search for Buddhist nirvana fly in the face of Western efficiency and capitalistic wealth. One of the world's most isolated and exotic countries, Burma is well worth a visit despite recent political turmoil, primitive internal transportation, decrepit hotels, and an official policy that limits visitors to two-week visits. As of this writing, the government admits tour groups but bars independent travelers from visiting the country. This policy may be relaxed if democratic forces are allowed to share power with the military dictatorship that has ruled the country since the 1950s.

Tourists are confined to several designated areas that are considered safe for foreigners and of historical significance. Yangon (formerly Rangoon), a crumbling city with a faded colonial atmosphere, is chiefly known for the world-famous Shwe Dagon Pagoda, though it's also amazing to see what four decades of neglect will do to a modern metropolis. The dusty and somewhat undistinguished town of Mandalay offers a handful of magnificent temples and monasteries. Travelers jaded by archaeology and old temples will enjoy the splendid natural environment and ethnic minorities of Inle Lake.

Certainly the highlight of any visit to Burma is the deserted city of Pagan, where an awesome sprawl of pagodas and temples forms one of the world's premier archaeological sites. The country is primitive, untamed, and extraordinarily memorable—"Quite unlike any land you will ever know," said Kipling, who also wrote, "In all the world there is no place like Burma."

Hong Kong

Until this "borrowed place on borrowed time" is returned to the Chinese in 1997, the densely packed and vibrant colony of six million citizens will remain a focal point of Asian tourism and an important stopover between the Far East and Southeast Asia. Recent events in China have raised the stakes in this British colony, chiefly known for its shopping bargains and urban vitality.

However, anyone seduced by Hollywood's image of Suzi Wong or the tourist hype of floating junks will be in for a shock. Hong Kong is one of the world's most congested, frantic, and high-pressure cities. If you like the pace of New York, you'll love Hong Kong. But don't be alarmed! Almost completely overlooked by most visitors are the peaceful countryside, isolated villages, and outer islands where life continues at a more leisurely pace. Most visitors stay only three days and spend over 60% of their time partaking of Hong Kong's number-one attraction—shopping. Much better is to stay a week and discover the real Hong Kong.

Indochina

The latest additions to the Southeast Asian circuit are the three countries of Indochina (Vietnam, Cambodia, Laos), which are now cautiously opening their doors to the outside world. Independent travelers can now freely visit all three countries. Group tours to Vietnam can be easily and quickly arranged with travel agencies in Bangkok. Cambodia's troublesome political climate has held tourism to a minimum, although brief visits to the world-famous site of Angkor Wat can be arranged through the same agencies. Tours to both Vietnam and Cambodia remain very expensive, but independent tourism on a shoestring level has finally arrived. Laos is open to both group tours *and* budget travelers. Primitive transportation and limited accommodations make Indochina a difficult yet immensely rewarding destination. Current travel conditions can be checked with travel agencies and backpackers in Bangkok.

Indonesia

Indonesia is a country of incredible beauty and boundless diversity. Stretching across one-seventh of the globe between Malaysia and Australia, this sprawling 13,000-island archipelago encompasses mind-stupefying extremes: 5,000-meter-high snowcapped mountains of Irian Jaya, sweltering lowland swamps of eastern Sumatra, open eucalyptus savannahs of Timor, lush rainforests of West Java; with lava-spewing volcanos the whole length. The most complex single nation on Earth, each of Indonesia's 6,000-plus inhabited islands has customs, native dress, architecture, dialects, ethnology, and geography all its own. This is a country where magic, mystery, and the promise of real adventure still live.

And what choices! Bali, the tropical island east of Java, is rightfully considered the national highlight despite some modernization and the inroads of mass tourism. Ignore the doomsayers: Bali remains an enchanted island of stunning beauty. Running a distant second in terms of visitor arrivals is the sweltering but historically rich island of Java. Highlights include the cultural capital of Yogyakarta, a climb to the summit of Mt. Bromo, and the ancient monuments of Borobudur and Prambanan.

The gigantic island of Sumatra—fifth largest in the world—is chiefly known for idyllic Lake Toba and the relaxing town of Bukittinggi. Rounding out Indonesia's leading travel destinations is the Tana Toraja region of southern Sulawesi. Beyond these four popular destinations—Bali, Java, Sumatra, and Sulawesi—are the jungle-covered island of Kalimantan, the spicy Moluccas, Nusa Tenggara with its dragons and textiles, and the remote land of Irian Jaya. It's easy to understand why Indonesia is ranked by many veteran travelers as one of the world's most fascinating destinations. Visitors are presently limited to 60 days per visit, but there's no limit on how many times you can leave the country and return for further explorations.

Macau

Just a short boat ride from Hong Kong, the tiny Portuguese colony of Macau is a sleepy world of cobbled streets, color-splashed mansions, and romantic cafes. Hong Kong's greatest attraction just might be the delightful Iberian outpost of Macau. Don't miss it.

Malaysia

The land of Kipling and Maugham, tigers and *stengahs*, is also one of Southeast Asia's most affluent and Westernized countries. While this modernization has watered down some of the country's exotic appeal, it has also brought a well-ordered transportation system, clean restaurants, and excellent hotels that charge among the lowest rates in the region. Malaysia, thus, is a delightful change after the poverty and rigors of travel in other Asian countries. Although the country offers few impressive temples or historic monuments, a great deal of traditional culture survives through the spectacular festivals of the Indian, Chinese, and Malay communities. Malaysia is also a land of great natural beauty, from expansive national parks to the world's oldest rainforest.

Consider the country as three distinct worlds. The west coast of peninsular Malaysia is characterized by modern cities, expressways, and a hard-working Chinese population intent on improving its financial standing. Penang is by far the most fascinating stop on the west coast, though the historic town of Malacca, the modern capital of Kuala Lumpur, the Cameron Highlands, and Taman Negara National Park are also worth visiting. On the other hand, the east coast of peninsular Malaysia remains a relatively undisturbed and traditional land where Malays, rather than Chinese, control the economy, where the call of Islam is stronger than that of Confucianism, and where a leisurely lifestyle is prized over material possessions. Tioman Island and the beach resort of Cherating are recommended. Sabah and Sarawak, the two states on the northern coastline of Borneo, are suited for those travelers who enjoy long river trips, ethnological explorations, vast caves, tremendous national parks, and mountain climbing. Malaysia might be the best surprise in Southeast Asia.

Philippines

The undiscovered paradise of Southeast Asia. Blessed with over 7,000 sun-drenched islands, this tropical wonderland has just about everything required for a superb vacation: exquisite white-sand beaches, unparalleled scuba diving, volcanos for mountaineers, baroque cathedrals, outstanding nightlife, and the wildest festivals in Asia. The Philippines is also an outstanding travel bargain, with some of the region's lowest prices for hotels, restaurants, and transportation.

But what really sets the Philippines apart from the rest of Asia is its people, whose warmth and enthusiasm are legendary throughout the East. Seldom will you meet such hospitable souls, so ready to smile, joke, laugh, and meet friends. If you believe the most important travel experience is to make friends and learn about people rather than just tour temples and museums, then the Philippines is your country. Despite the additional airfare needed to reach the islands, and the recent political troubles (which rarely touch the Western visitor), the Philippines remains *the* best rest-and-relaxation destination in Southeast Asia.

Singapore

The futuristic metropolis of Singapore comes as a surprise to most visitors. Rather than some romantic port of the Third World, Singapore impresses the traveler with its soaring architecture, luxurious hotels, air-conditioned shopping centers, industrial parks, highly disciplined population, and lack of crime. Though city planners have largely bulldozed the mysterious East into oblivion, the new city is indisputably one of the cleanest and safest places in the world—an ideal place to shop, recover from the hardships of travel in Indonesia, and enjoy the best food in Southeast Asia. Highly recommended is the Singapore Zoo, Jurong Bird Park, colonial architecture, and remaining Malacca terrace houses.

Thailand

If I had to nominate one country in Southeast Asia that offers the best mix of exoticism, history, facilities, beaches, food, and people, it would have to be the Royal Kingdom of Thailand. Tourism has soared in recent years for good reasons: superb archaeological sites, expansive national parks, glittering temples that rank among the finest in Asia, outstanding beaches, exuberant nightlife, great food, friendly people, and a society where Western influence has not yet triumphed over local custom.

Most visitors begin their tour in the capital city of Bangkok. Despite its stifling heat and unbearable traffic, Bangkok ranks as the most fascinating city in Southeast Asia. To properly explore the temples, museums, shopping centers,

HISTORICAL AND ARCHITECTURAL ATTRACTIONS IN SOUTHEAST ASIA

COUNTRY	LOCATION	ATTRACTIONS
Thailand	Bangkok	Wat Pra Keo, Grand Palace, Wat Po, Marble Temple
	Sukothai	Thailand's original 15th-century capital
	Ayuthay	Thailand's second capital; well restored
Burma	Rangoon	Schwedagon Pagoda; Southeast Asia's single best monument
	Pagan	12th-century lost city; mysterious and expansive
Indonesia	Yogyakarta, Borobudur, and Prambanan	Buddhist/Hindu monuments
	Bali	Gunung Kawi, Goa Gajah, Kerta Gosa, Tanah Lot
Malaysia	Penang	Peranakan architecture; old world atmosphere
Singapore	Singapore	Peranakan and colonial architecture, Chinatown
Cambodia	Angkor Wat	Southeast Asia's finest architectural site

and restaurants would take months, if not years. Within a 200-km radius of Bangkok are several well-developed beach resorts, the world's tallest Buddhist monument, the legendary Bridge on the River Kwai, and the splendid ruins of Ayuthaya. Central Thailand has several historic cities which once served as ancient capitals. Chiang Mai in the north serves as both cultural and artistic center of Thailand, as well as a convenient base for trekking into the mountains and touring the infamous Golden Triangle. Northeast Thailand offers outstanding Khmer monuments, plus the rare opportunity to get somewhat off the beaten track. South Thailand is a wonderland of pristine beaches and well-developed resort islands such as Ko Samui and Phuket. If you have time for only one country in Southeast Asia, make it Thailand.

SPECIAL-INTEREST TOURING

Another approach to travel is to specifically seek out those destinations or activities that carry the strongest appeal. Far too many visitors find themselves wandering from country to country, unsure of where to go or what to see. Remember that travel can be a craft done well or badly, conscientiously or with a general disregard for detail, but like most things, it is much more satisfying if you do it properly. Imagine Southeast Asia as a colossal gallery that can only be sensibly explored selectively. Mash too many experiences together and you end up with an unsatisfying mess. Find a few themes and follow them. It doesn't really matter what they are—just don't spread yourself too thin.

A well-thought-out itinerary begins with a logical travel plan followed with flexibility and a sense of spontaneity. What kind of a traveler are you and what are your interests—history, art, culture, dance, people, beaches, sports, nightlife? If you enjoy history and museums, you should focus on those countries, such as Thailand, Burma, and Indonesia, where museums and archaeology are the major attractions. Most importantly, do your background reading *before* you go. Music, dance, and performing-arts aficionados should concentrate on places where traditional theater and festivals still survive. Top choices are Yogyakarta, Bali, and Chiang Mai. Shopping—always one of the top attractions—is best conducted in the handful of towns which specialize in local crafts. Or would you prefer a total escape at a beach resort? The list is almost endless—educational tours, study programs, cultural minorities, adventure travel, restaurants, nightlife—but research and

PERFORMING ARTS VENUES IN SOUTHEAST ASIA

COUNTRY	LOCATION	THEATER	PERFORMANCES
Thailand	Bangkok	National Theater	Classical theater, ballet
Burma	Rangoon	Karaweik	Dance, music, puppets
Malaysia	Kuala Lumpur	Central Market	Malay and Chinese theater
	Kota Baru	Gelanggang Seni	Traditional Malay arts
Philippines	Manila	Cultural Center	Drama, dance, music
	Manila	Pistang Pilipino	Filipino dance revue
Singapore	Singapore	Hotels	Multicultural dance shows
Indonesia	Jakarta	Taman Ismail Marzuki Theater	Comedy, dance
	Yogyakarta	Dalem Pujokusuman	Ramayana theater
	Bali	Ubud	Balinese dance and drama

planning are essential for a successful and rewarding journey.

The following section is designed to help you ferret out those attractions and activities worth special consideration. I've included a short list of personal favorites but suggestions for future editions of this book will be highly appreciated. Send your list of top tens to Southeast Asia Handbook, Moon Publications, P.O. Box 3040 Chico, California USA 95927-3040, and I'll publish the results.

History And Architecture

While an endless procession of decaying old temples or ruined cities may not appeal to everyone, most visitors enjoy visiting a limited cross section of the more impressive monuments and historical sites. Each country offers a selection of architectural gems, but Thailand, Burma, and Indonesia offer the richest range when measured by antiquity and artistic merit. Singapore, Malaysia, and Macau are best for colonial architecture and 1930s domestic architecture. Though largely Westernized, Hong Kong has a handful of colorful Chinese temples and some outstanding modern architecture. Filipino churches are more intriguing than might be expected, since they often combine both Spanish and Asian architectural themes. Quick walking tours are given for most historical neighborhoods, but visitors with limited time should concentrate on the following sites.

Performing Arts

Travelers who enjoy dance and drama will be thrilled with Southeast Asia's extraordinarily rich bounty of performing arts: Hindu ballets on Java, Buddhist/animist dance troupes in Bangkok, shadow plays on Bali, Christian passion dramas in the Philippines, Islamic martial arts in Malaysia, Chinese street opera in Singapore, puppet theater in Burma. Local theater and dance-dramas are recommended both as great entertainment and windows into the histories, cultures, and value systems of the people. Performances can be either tourist-oriented or authentic spectacles intended for the local population. Though tourist performances are sometimes dismissed as mere contrived ripoffs, they're well advertised, reasonably priced, and often employ the finest dancers, musicians, and actors from the local community. However, anyone who would like to really understand Southeast Asian theater must also search out local performances. Here you'll experience the real Asia, complete with sweating crowds, old women cracking peanuts, kids running up and down the center aisle, and a dozen other distractions that make the performance so memorable.

The major drawback to authentic theater is that performances are often difficult to find. Outside a handful of towns which have developed strong theatrical traditions (see the "Performing Arts Venues in Southeast Asia" chart), you'll need to conduct an organized search by scanning English-language newspapers and magazines, inquiring at local tourist offices, and asking everyone from taxi drivers to waitresses. Your best chances are on temple grounds during religious festivals. Even in such sacred settings, high-brow classical theater is often wedged between blasting rock 'n' roll bands, reruns of old Hollywood films, and slapstick comedies heavy with sexual innuendo. Venues are subject to changes and last-minute cancellations.

Festivals

A highly recommended travel theme is the religious, ethnic, and national celebrations of Southeast Asia. No matter their size or importance, festivals generally guarantee a colorful

MAJOR FESTIVALS OF SOUTHEAST ASIA

MONTH	FESTIVAL	LOCATION	PERFORMANCE
January	Thaipusam	Hindu communities	Hindu parade of penance
	Independence Day	Burma, Rangoon	Parades on 4 January
	Sinulog, Ati Atihan	Philippines	Carnival in the tropics
February	Chinese New Year	Chinese communities	Dragons and firecrackers
	Union Day	Burma, Rangoon	Ethnic celebration
March	Moriones	Philippines	Easter Passion plays
April	Buddhist New Year	Thailand and Myanmar	Water-throwing festival
	Ching Ming	Chinese communities	All Souls Day
	Tin Hau Birthday	Hong Kong	Decorated fishing boats
May	Buddha Enlightenment	Thailand and Myanmar	Temple processions, fairs
	Bun Festival	Hong Kong	Floating children parade
June	Independence Day	Philippines, Manila	Parades on 12 June
	Kandazan Harvest	Malaysia, Sabah	Tribal festival
	Dayak Festival	Malaysia, Sarawak	Dayak music and dance
July	Buddhist Lent	Thailand and Myanmar	Monks ordination
	Candle Festival	Thailand, Ubon	Parade of giant candles
August	Independence Day	Singapore	Parades on 9 August
	Independence Day	Indonesia	Parades on 17 August
	Independence Day	Malaysia	Parades on 31 August
	Hungry Ghosts	Chinese communities	Chinese opera
September	Mooncake Festival	Chinese communities	Lanterns and foods
	Boat Festival	Burma, Inle Lake	Elaborate boats
October	Cheung Yeung	Chinese communities	Moon Watching Festival
	Asian Arts Festival	Hong Kong	Asian Performing Arts
	MassKara	Philippines, Negros	Masked celebration
	Thimithi	Hindu communities	Firewalking
	Deepavali	Hindu communities	Festival of lights
November	Loy Kratong	Thailand, Sukothai	Festival of lights
	Golden Mt. Festival	Thailand, Bangkok	Temple fair
	Elephant Round Up	Thailand, Surin	Pachyderm polo
December	Christmas	Philippines	Passion plays

DACCA
CHINA
GUANGZHOU
MANDALAY
PAGAN
INLE LAKE
MACAU
HONG KONG
ARAKAN
LAOS
HANOI
CHIANG MAI
CHIANG SAEN
LUANG PRABANG
BURMA (MYANMAR)
VIENTIANE
RANGOON (YANGON)
THAILAND
SI SATCHANALI
SUKOTHAI
PAKSE
AYUTHAYA
HUE
PIMAI
BANGKOK
KORAT
CAMBODIA
QUI NHON
ANGKOR WAT
VIETNAM
PETCHBURI
PHNOM PENH
HO CHI MINH CITY
KO SAMUI
PHUKET
HAT YAI
KOTA BARU
PENANG
SOUTH CHINA SEA
BANDA ACEH
MALAYSIA
BRUNE
IPOH
KUALA LUMPUR
MEDAN
MALACCA
SARAWA
LAKE TOBA
KUCHING
SUMATRA
SINGAPORE
NIAS
BUKITTINGGI
KALIMANTAN
PADANG
PALEMBANG
INDIAN OCEAN
BENGKULU
INDONESIA
JAKARTA
JAVA
SOLO
BANDUNG
YOGYAKARTA
BALI
MOON
0
500 km

**HISTORICAL AND
CULTURAL ATTRACTIONS
OF SOUTHEAST ASIA**

parade filled with floats, exotically costumed participants, the exhibition of valuable religious icons, traditional dance and drama, food stalls, charlatans, hucksters, and rare opportunities to photograph without the risk of offending somebody's sense of privacy. Religious celebrations predominate. Those listed in the "Major Festivals of Southeast Asia" chart are worth planning into your itinerary even if it involves additional time and expenses. Festivals are described in greater detail in each chapter. Chinese and Hindu festivals are detailed in the Singapore chapter.

Approximate dates are indicated despite festival dating being an inexact science in Southeast Asia. National celebrations, such as independence days, are dated by Western calendars and fall on the same date annually. However, religious and agricultural festivals are dated by lunar calendars and change year to year, consequently floating around the calendar from month to month. Exact dates should be confirmed with national tourist offices.

Shopping

While shopping might seem to be somewhat of an artificial theme for travel, visitors who understand the markets and enjoy bargaining will find Southeast Asia one of the world's great emporiums. Each country produces a unique range of goods: jewelry and masks in Bali, shell-work and baskets in the Philippines, batik and leatherwork in Java, pewter in Malaysia, puppets in Burma, silks and silverware in Thailand. The trick is to know what to buy and where to buy it. Unlike in Western countries where distribution networks efficiently spread products across dozens of markets, handicrafts in Southeast Asia tend to be sold only near the points of origin. Of course, many Thai products are available in Bangkok and Filipino handicrafts are sold in Manila, but villages where the handicrafts are originally produced generally offer the highest-quality product at the lowest prices.

The "Art and Handicraft Centers in Southeast Asia" chart will help point you toward the best places to shop. Shopping directly from the producer has several advantages. You'll be able to watch the craftsman in action and gain a greater appreciation for the work. You can also request custom jobs and negotiate prices. Perhaps most important is that money spent goes directly into the artist's pocket rather than to the middlemen.

Hotels

Southeast Asia has the finest hotels in the world. Surveys conducted by the world's press and *Institutional Investor,* a magazine sold to international bankers, have shown with remarkable consistency that Southeast Asia offers the world's greatest hotels when measured by comfort, new architectural concepts, and above all,

ART AND HANDICRAFT CENTERS IN SOUTHEAST ASIA

COUNTRY	LOCATION	HANDICRAFTS
Thailand	Bangkok	Silks, brassware, clothing, antiques, gems
	Chiang Mai	Silverwork, jewelry, imitation antiques
Burma	Pagan	Lacquerware
Malaysia	Kota Baru	Batik, embroidered fabrics, kites
Philippines	Sagada	Weavings
	Bontoc	Woodcarvings
	Cebu City	Shellwork
Indonesia	Jakarta	Antiques, modern batiks
	Bali	Masks, silverwork, painting, stonework
	Yogyakarta	Batiks, leatherwork, clothing, puppets
	Sulawesi	Tribal artifacts, textiles, woodcarvings

TOP HOTELS OF SOUTHEAST ASIA

HOTEL	CITY	FEATURES
Oriental	Bangkok	19th-century ambience with 20th-century comforts
Regent	Hong Kong	Darth Vader-style with incredible lobby views
Peninsula	Hong Kong	Oriental classic with impeccable service
Shangri La	Bangkok	Stunning modern architecture
Regent	Bangkok	Elegant lobby facing the Bangkok Sports Club
Mandarin	Hong Kong	Perfect service and outstanding restaurants
Manila	Manila	MacArthur's favorite and popular coup refuge
Raffles	Singapore	The classic hotel of colonial Asia
Bela Vista	Macau	Seedy and memorable, a real gem
E & O	Penang	Another classic constructed by the Sarkie brothers
Strand	Rangoon	Fabulous and funky, the classic of classics

service. The Oriental in Bangkok has remained in first place since the annual survey began in 1961. Among the 10 "Great Hotels of the World" described in *Travel and Leisure* are the Oriental, the Regent, and the Mandarin in Hong Kong. *Euromoney* adds to the list the Shangri-La in Singapore and the venerable Peninsula in Hong Kong. Readers of *Condé Nast Traveler* magazine recently voted the Peninsula, the Regent, the Oriental, and the Mandarin among the world's top-10 hotels.

Perhaps even more intriguing are the authentically old hotels that stand as relics of another era, with their 10-foot ceilings, paddle fans, peacock chairs on the veranda, and French doors that open onto grassy lawns. Although some of these hotels are now somewhat tattered around the edges, they evoke the mystery of what the Orient was a century ago, in the days of Conrad and Kipling.

Restaurants

Your journey through Southeast Asia could also follow a gastronomic theme. Though Southeast Asian food seems vaguely Chinese to most Westerners, a surprising amount of individuality occurs between the cuisines of each country. Top award goes to the food of Thailand, a spicy and pungent mixture of curries, coconut creams, and tiny chilies that should be cautiously removed from each dish. Indonesia is known for its peanut sauces, barbecued meats, and spicy Padang buffets. Hong Kong and Singapore restaurants serve the regional cuisines of China, including fresh Cantonese fish and elegant Mandarin duck. The Philippines, Burma, and Macau offer their own specialties. Southeast Asia's biggest surprise is perhaps the overlooked and underappreciated food of Malaysia. Though largely confined to home cooking and available only from small street stalls, Malay cuisine is a wonderful mixture of spicy Indonesian peanut sauces, rich Thai coconut milks, and fiery Indian curries with fresh vegetables and succulent meats. I'm getting hungry just writing about it!

Dining choices in Southeast Asia range from five-star hotel restaurants to simple food stalls on the side of the road. First-time visitors sometimes dismiss hawker food as unclean and assume that any meal served on a rickety aluminum table must be inferior to that of a first-class restaurant. Nothing could be further from the truth. If a steady queue of Mercedeses waiting for noodle soup is any indication, hawker food provides stiff competition for many of Asia's finer restaurants. In fact, street food should be your first choice for several reasons. Large congregations of food stalls in a singular location ensure a greater array of food than in any single restaurant. Secondly, since there is virtually no overhead, prices are kept low—a filling and delicious meal can be served for less than US$2. But perhaps most importantly, food stall dining is a great way to meet people, make friends, and gain some insight into Asian lifestyles.

FOOD CENTERS IN SOUTHEAST ASIA

COUNTRY	LOCATION	VENUE	SPECIALTIES
Singapore	Singapore	Hawker centers	Chinese, Indian, and Malay
Malaysia	Penang	Street stalls	Chinese and Nonya specialties
	Kuala Lumpur	Chinatown	Alfresco dining, Malay dishes
	Kota Baru	Night market	Wonderful sweets
Thailand	Chiang Mai	Night market	Oyster omelettes, soups, seafood
Indonesia	Bali	Kuta Beach	Fresh seafood, thick coffee
	Solo	Street stalls	Unique Solo specialties
Hong Kong	Kowloon	Temple Street	Clams in black-bean sauce, beer
	Causeway Bay	Lockhart Road	Chinese, Thai, Buddhist cafes
Macau	Macau	Restaurants	Portuguese-Chinese dishes, wine
Philippines	Sagada	Guesthouses	Vegetarian dishes, great coffee

Although restaurants and street stalls are found throughout Southeast Asia, certain towns have developed reputations as international food meccas. The food capital of Southeast Asia can be summarized in one word: Singapore. Here you will find some of the world's most delicious cuisines, from Chinese soups to Indian curries, served at rock-bottom prices from licensed hawker centers. Other great food centers, night markets, and clusters of street stalls are listed in the "Food Centers in Southeast Asia" chart. Readers are invited to send in their favorites, along with recommended dishes.

Nightlife
Each country in Southeast Asia offers something of interest for night owls. Manila and Bangkok are generally considered the entertainment capitals of Southeast Asia, though Hong Kong and Singapore offer a good assortment of hotel discos and British pubs. Nightlife is almost nonexistent in the conservative Muslim nations of Malaysia and Indonesia, except for in a handful of tourist stops such as Bali and Penang. Aside from the four cities mentioned above, nightlife in Southeast Asia is somewhat disappointing for several reasons. Public bars so familiar to Westerners are relatively rare; Asians prefer their socializing at home or in cafes. Almost all of the nightclubs and pubs popular with Westerners are owned and operated by Westerners. Discos are plentiful in luxury hotels but most

should be avoided since they're expensive, pretentious, and almost identical in atmosphere to their Western counterparts. Much better are those clubs that offer live entertainment, usually by Filipino musicians. You'll quickly discover that Filipinos are the premier musicians in Southeast Asia and that the best clubs hire Filipino bands. Bottom line for nightlife: try the Philippines and Bangkok.

Beaches
History, culture, and the performing arts may be rewarding themes for travel, but relaxing on an Asian beach is unquestionably a far more popular pastime. And what a great place for escape . . . stunning sands, crystal-clear waters, water sports, and glorious sunsets. Beach resorts are plentiful in all price ranges, from luxurious developments with first-class facilities to isolated beaches where the cost of lodging and food hardly breaks US$10 per day. Twenty dollars a day almost guarantees a clean and comfortable bungalow with a private veranda, barbecued fish dinners, and a bottle of rum. Even short-term visitors who generally limit their vacations to Hawaii or Mexico should consider a holiday in Southeast Asia since higher airfares are largely balanced by the lower costs of food and accommodations.

Selecting a beach without some background research can be a difficult task since Southeast Asia offers scores of resorts in varying states of

NIGHTLIFE IN SOUTHEAST ASIA

COUNTRY	CITY	LOCATIONS	ENTERTAINMENT
Thailand	Bangkok	Patpong, Soi Cowboy	Bachelor bars
	Pattaya	Beach Road	Transvestite revues
	Phuket	Patong Beach	Singles discos
Philippines	Manila	Ermita	Bachelor bars, folk music
	Olongapo	Magsaysay Avenue	Live rock 'n' roll
	Angeles	Fields Avenue	Bachelor bars, live shows
Hong Kong	Hong Kong	Kowloon	Brit pubs, live bands
	Hong Kong	Wanchai	Sailor bars, yuppie clubs
	Hong Kong	Lan Kwai Fong	Expat clubs, delis, discos
Singapore	Singapore	Orchard Road	Jazz bars, Brit pubs
Indonesia	Bali	Kuta Beach	Aussie bars and discos

development. One key to finding the perfect hideaway with the proper mix of primitivism and comfort is to consider the evolutionary cycle of Southeast Asian beach resorts. Virtually all of today's leading resorts—Phuket, Kuta, Ko Samui, Boracay, Puerto Galera, Batu Ferringhi—began as deserted beaches favored by independent travelers who lived in simple grass shacks and survived on fish and rice. Discovering the financial incentives of tourism, local villagers soon constructed guesthouses and cafes. Increasing numbers of travelers quietly tiptoed down, hoping that nobody else would discover their secret paradises. But word leaked out and soon the trickle became a rush as planeloads of land speculators and hotel operators joined the deluge. Within a decade what was once an idyllic stretch of sand had become an international clone of Waikiki or Mazatlán.

Although this sounds discouraging—and it is hard to deny that the hippie trails of the '60s have surrendered to mass tourism of the '90s—all is not lost. Even today, all over Southeast Asia, a small number of adventurous backpackers are sitting on deserted tropical beaches, being welcomed into the homes of villagers, and exchanging smiles with friendly children.

What's the perfect resort? Opinions differ, but for this author it begins with a long and wide stretch of thick, clean, powder-white sand. Water should be warm, clear, and aquamarine blue. The ocean floor should be flat and sandy. The wind should blow with enough velocity for windsurfing and sailing but not so hard as to ruin sunbathing. Behind the beach should stand a forest of palm trees interspersed with hiking trails and isolated villages. Beaches fitting this description are relatively plentiful in Southeast Asia. However, facilities that harmonize with the environment are often lacking. Imagine a major resort being developed without any sort of zoning, government controls, or centralized planning.

Tragically, many of Southeast Asia's most promising beach resorts have transformed themselves into not tropical paradises but travelers' ghettos of dilapidated guesthouses or touristy nightmares of faceless high-rises and noisy bars. Perfect resorts are neither backpackers' slums nor Asian Waikikis. They are locally developed, owned, and operated so that profits return to the people rather than the New York Stock Exchange. Guesthouses are clean, spacious, and constructed from natural materials such as bamboo and palm fronds. Restaurants serve local fare, such as fish and vegetables, rather than pseudo-French or American fast food. Nightlife should include traditional entertainment and folk music along with the inevitable discos and video bars. Traffic and noise is minimized by limiting local traffic to service vehicles only. Cars and motorcycles are kept well away from the beach and residential areas. I've saved the best for last: Lanterns and candles are used rather than electricity . . . a radical idea now proving successful at several resorts.

BEACH RESORTS OF SOUTHEAST ASIA

COUNTRY	LOCATION	DESCRIPTION
Thailand	Ko Samui	Peaceful paradise; well developed
	Phuket	The Waikiki of Southeast Asia; noisy but fun
	Ko Samet	Exceptional sand; primitive facilities
Malaysia	Tioman Island	Spectacular natural setting; mediocre beaches
	Cherating	Romantic and rural; simple bungalows
Philippines	Puerto Galera	Beautiful topography but poorly developed
	Boracay Island	Tranquil and stunning; intelligently planned
	El Nido	Outstanding diving; difficult to reach
	Panglao	Fine beaches; great potential
Indonesia	Kuta, Bali	Noisy, raucous, and commercialized
	Gili Trawangan, Lombok	Small, remote, beautiful

The "Beach Resorts of Southeast Asia" chart includes both highly developed destinations and upcoming beaches popular with world travelers. None are secret destinations since it is not the intention of this author to accelerate commercial development or ruin tropical hideaways. The more remote beaches are hinted at in this book but you'll need to read between the lines.

Scuba Diving

The world's fastest-growing sport is quickly gaining popularity in Southeast Asia, where tropical waters host outstanding coral reefs, colorful marinelife, and sunken ships. Dives can be arranged with shops located in large Asian hotels or in advance from international tour operators such as See and Sea Travel Service (50 Francisco Street, Suite 205, San Francisco, CA 94133, tel. 415-434-3400). More operators are listed below and in *Skin Diver* magazine.

Philippines: Southeast Asia's top dive destination remains the Philippines, despite unscrupulous fishing practices and devastating typhoons, which have damaged some of the more accessible coral gardens. Diving is most spectacular off the north coast of Palawan and at the

DIVING DESTINATIONS IN SOUTHEAST ASIA

COUNTRY	LOCATION	COMMENTS
Thailand	Similan	National park; accessible from Phuket
	Phuket	Major resort; good beaches; mediocre diving
Philippines	El Nido	Superb diving; full facilities
	Batangas	Near Manila; several land-based resorts
	Cebu	Mactan Island; full facilities
	Bohol	Great beaches; limited facilities
Malaysia	Tioman	Spectacular island; limited diving
	Sabah	Best in Malaysia
Indonesia	Jakarta	Thousand Islands; luxurious resorts
	Bali	Excellent corals and wrecks
	Flores	Remote and untouched; Indonesia's best?
	Sulawesi	Vast coral gardens; popular with Japanese

MOUNTAIN CLIMBS IN SOUTHEAST ASIA

COUNTRY	MOUNTAIN	LOCATION	METERS	COMMENTS
Burma	Kyaiktiyo	Mon	1,102	Easy; 2-day trek
Malaysia	Kinabalu	Sabah	410	Easy; 2-day trek
Philippines	Mayon	Luzon	2,422	Difficult; 2-day trek
	Apo	Mindanao	3,143	Moderate; 3-4 day trek
Indonesia	Merapi	Central Java	2,911	Difficult; 1-day trek
	Bromo	East Java	2,300	Easy; 3-4 hours
	Ijen	East Java	2,800	Moderate; 2-day trek
	Agung	Bali	3,142	Difficult; 1-day trek
	Rinjani	Lombok	3,726	Moderate; 2-day trek
	Tambora	Sumbawa	2,821	Difficult; 3-day trek
	Keli Mutu	Flores	1,731	Easy; 2-3 hours

widely proclaimed Tubbataha Reef in the Sulu Sea. Organized dive expeditions are necessary to reach these destinations, though independent divers can find good offshore corals near Cebu and Bohol. The Department of Tourism in Manila distributes a useful brochure entitled *Philippines, A Diver's Paradise,* which lists dive resorts, shops, operators, and packagers.

Thailand: Diving in Thailand revolves around the Similan Islands some eight hours north of Phuket. Dives can be easily organized with dive shops in Bangkok and Phuket.

Malaysia: Dives off the east coast of peninsular Malaysia include the offshore islands of Tioman and Kapas. Arrangements can be made through the Tanjung Jara Hotel near Kuala Dungun and Tioman Island Resort. Malaysia's most spectacular diving, however, is found in Sabah near Kota Kinabalu and at Sipadan Island in the southeast. Contact Borneo Divers at the Tanjung Aru Beach Hotel or Hyatt in Kota Kinabalu.

Indonesia: The vast archipelago of Indonesia offers endless dive possibilities, although the diving industry remains quite undeveloped. Thousand Islands near Jakarta boasts professional facilities but diving is mediocre because of dynamiting and silting. Bali, the tropical island famed mostly for its arts and crafts, offers surprisingly good diving off the north coast around Menjangan and at the submerged maritime wreck east of Karangasem. Hotels in Nusa Dua organize dives. Indonesia's two most promising dive locations are the 62,000-hectare marine reserve at Flores and the gigantic coral gardens off Manado in North Sulawesi. Contact Dive Indonesia, Borobudur Intercontinental Hotel, Shop 34, Jakarta, or Jakarta Dive School, Jakarta Hilton, Jalan Subroto, Jakarta.

Volcano Climbing

Much of Southeast Asia lies along the Asian Ring of Fire, an active volcanic belt which stretches from Japan to Australia. As a result, the region is blessed with dozens of volcanic peaks and some of the world's most adventurous climbing. Highlights include the perfectly shaped cone of Mayon in the Philippines, the snow-capped and highly revered Kinabalu on Borneo, and Mt. Apo near Davao on Mindanao.

But it is the explosive peaks which form the backbone of Indonesia that guarantee the toughest, most threatening, and most spectacular challenges east of the Himalayas. Those located near tourist centers can be scaled with the aid of porters and professional guides. Others situated on remote islands are dangerous—not to mention highly volatile—and should only be attempted by experienced mountaineers. As of this writing, Southeast Asian climbing expeditions are rarely organized by adventure travel companies, although this seems likely to change in the future.

Trekking

The great rainforests and remote tribal areas of Southeast Asia often surprise hikers expecting

TREKKING IN SOUTHEAST ASIA

COUNTRY	LOCATION	COMMENTS
Thailand	Chiang Mai	Tribal villages; popular but memorable
	Khao Yai	National park; 12 trails; limited wildlife
	Phu Kradung	National park; profuse vegetation; chilly
Malaysia	Taman Negara	National park; original rainforest; wildlife
	Sarawak	Belaga to Bintulu; Ibans and logging
	Sarawak	Mulu National Park; tremendous caves
Hong Kong	Lantau	Lantau Trail; 70 km in 12 sections; camping
Philippines	Sagada	Limestone canyons, caves, villages; superb
	Bontoc	Amazing rice terraces; dozens of good hikes
	Lake Sebu	Remote tribal homeland; beautiful topography
Indonesia	Java	Ujong Kulon National Park; wildlife reserve
	Java	Kaliurang; trails at base of Mt. Merapi
	Java	Baluran National Park; wildlife reserve
	Bali	Ubud; hiking through rice fields, art villages
	Sumatra	Lake Toba; pleasant, easy, one-day hikes
	Sumatra	Bukittingi; canyons, lakes, nature reserves
	Sulawesi	Tana Toraja; rich ethnological region
	Kalimantan	Kapuas to Mahakam rivers; 1-2 months

the crowds and commercialization of Nepal. Despite an obvious tourist infrastructure in regions with strong cultural appeal, Southeast Asia largely remains virgin territory for determined hikers. As in Nepal, trekking comes in all forms. Easy one-day hikes across rolling hills are plentiful in almost all countries. Moderately difficult hikes lasting several days are popular in the tribal areas of northern Thailand and central Luzon. Hiking along marked trails is very popular in the national parks of Malaysia and Thailand. Extremely challenging treks lasting several weeks or months can be made across Borneo and the islands of Indonesia. The "Trekking in Southeast Asia" chart describes several of the more popular treks. In most cases, guides can be hired in local villages. Longer journeys through remote regions will require professional assistance and patience. Need

RIVER JOURNEYS IN SOUTHEAST ASIA

COUNTRY	RIVER	COMMENTS
Thailand	Kok	Golden Triangle; 5 noisy hours to Chiang Rai
	Chao Phya	Bangkok canals; fast and exciting longboats
Burma	Irrawaddy	Mandalay to Pagan; 1 day; timeless journey
Malaysia	Skrang	Sarawak; Iban tribal area; commercialized
	Rejang	Sarawak; Iban tribal area; changing quickly
Philippines	Pagsanhan	Luzon; whitewater and falls; touristy but fun
Indonesia	Siak	Sumatra; slow, cheap boat to/from Singapore
	Alas	Sumatra; whitewater rafting with Sobek
	Kapuas	Kalimantan; longest river in Indonesia
	Makaham	Kalimantan; 2 months, Samarinda to Apo Kayan

some inspiration? Read Eric Hansen's superb *Stranger in the Forest.*

River Journeys

What could be more romantic than slowly drifting down a muddy river, past simple villages and golden temples, pretending to be Conrad or Kipling? Such fantasies are still possible in Southeast Asia, though you should also be prepared for onboard Rambo films and flashy discos. The "River Journeys in Southeast Asia" chart is not exhaustive; readers are invited to make further suggestions. As with other areas in adventure travel, the vast archipelago of Indonesia provides the largest number of opportunities. My personal favorite, however, is the Irrawaddy in central Myanmar, where, for a few dollars, you can slowly drift down the muddy river, past simple villages and golden temples.

Other Themes

The above list mentions the more obvious travel themes, but it could be expanded to include hobbies, professional and career interests, environmental concerns, billboard art, modes of transportation, steam engines, antique motorcycles, psychic phenomena, religious retreats, art-deco architecture, language studies, etc. Further possibilities are described below under "Adventure and Alternative Travel."

PRACTICAL INFORMATION

PLANNING YOUR TRIP

Routes

By studying the introduction and "Sightseeing Highlights" sections of each country, you should be able to plan an itinerary composed of the best mixture of history and recreation. A well-planned route that addresses the issues of sights, time, and budget can easily save hundreds of dollars and avoid the hassles of back-tracking, wasted opportunities, and unnecessary expenses. A map will help to orient yourself. The basic overland route runs between Bangkok and Bali, through Malaysia and Singapore. Tramped since the hippie days of the '60s, today it's a busy path firmly networked with hotels, restaurants, and other facilities for value-minded overlanders.

To add those remote and exotic destinations located off the familiar trail, you'll need to include side trips to Burma (Myanmar), the Philippines, and the outer islands of Indonesia. Burma can be reached on an inexpensive roundtrip ticket from Bangkok or visited as a stop en route to India. The Philippines can be easily reached on roundtrip tickets from Bangkok or Hong Kong, although more adventurous travelers might consider entering or exiting Manila from Kota Kinabalu. Because Indonesia's outer islands such as Kalimantan and Sulawesi are so time-consuming to properly explore, these are often considered separate journeys starting from Singapore.

After touring Southeast Asia, you'll want to continue your Asian odyssey through the Indian subcontinent, north to Japan, or eastward through the South Pacific. Two popular options from Bangkok include a flight to India or Nepal via Myanmar, or a flight to Japan via Hong Kong. Options from Bali include a direct flight to Australia, an overland journey across Nusa Tenggara followed by the short flight from Timor to Darwin, or a return flight to Singapore with stops in Sulawesi or Kalimantan. No matter what route, it's a grand adventure through one of the world's great regions.

From America: Planning your route also depends upon your point of origin. Southeast Asia is an important link in any round-the-world journey, whether beginning from the United States, Australia, or Europe. Americans have two fascinating choices. The northern Pacific loop includes stops in Japan, Korea, Taiwan, and Hong Kong before continuing into China or down to Bangkok. This ticket—usually on Korean Air or China Air—costs US$500-650 from budget travel agencies in San Francisco and Los Angeles. The second option is the southern Pacific loop, which includes stops in the South Pacific, New Zealand, and Australia before arriving in Bali. This ticket—usually standby on UTA—costs about US$1000 from the same agencies. A popular and relatively inexpensive itinerary begins with the northern Pacific loop, travels through Southeast Asia, and is followed by the UTA ticket across the South Pacific back

SAMPLE TIMETABLES FOR SOUTHEAST ASIA

COUNTRY	2 MONTHS	3 MONTHS	4 MONTHS	6 MONTHS	8 MONTHS
Thailand	1 month	1 month	1 month	6 weeks	2 months
Malaysia	2 weeks	2 weeks	2 weeks	2 weeks	1 month
Singapore	1 week	1 week	1 week	1 week	1 week
Hong Kong	1 week	1 week	1 week	1 week	1 week
Burma		1 week	1 week	2 weeks	2 weeks
Philippines		3 weeks	3 weeks	1 month	2 months
Indonesia			1 month	2 months	2 months

to the States. This outstanding trip covers Japan and northeast Asia, Southeast Asia, Australia, New Zealand, and the South Pacific for under US$2000 in total airfares.

From Australia: Travelers from Australia often fly direct to Bali or Singapore, although dozens of routes are far more intriguing. Timor is an inexpensive and adventurous gateway from Darwin. From Timor, you can island-hop by plane or public bus across Nusa Tenggara to Bali. Another possibility is the short flight from Cairns to Port Moresby in Papua New Guinea, followed by flights to Jayapura on Irian Jaya, the Moluccas, Sulawesi, and finally Bali.

From Europe: Europeans have the choices of overlanding, direct flights to Bangkok, or inexpensive charters that include stops in the Middle East or India. Budget agencies listed under "Getting There," below can advise on exact routings and current prices.

Time

Allow as much time as possible. The two most common mistakes for first-time travelers to Asia are overpacking their bags and trying to cram too many destinations into their schedule. With only two or three weeks, it's much better to visit a single place such as Thailand or Bali than to attempt the if-it's-Tuesday-it-must-be-Singapore tour. Travelers with an open schedule will find that Southeast Asia divides itself into convenient boxes which correspond to the length of visa. For example, Thailand, the Philippines, and Indonesia grant most nationalities a two-month stay. This is just about an ideal amount of time to spend in each country. Burma grants two weeks. Most visitors spend about a week in

Singapore and Hong Kong. Figured together, allow six to eight months to properly explore Southeast Asia. But if you only have a month or three, study the "Sample Timetables for Southeast Asia" chart for possible options.

Costs

The basic rule for estimating costs is that time and money are inversely related. Short-term travelers must spend substantially more for guaranteed hotel reservations and air connections. Long-term travelers willing to use local transportation, budget hotels, and streets stalls can travel almost more cheaply in Southeast Asia than anywhere else in the world. Expenses vary widely, but many budget travelers report that land costs average about US$20-25 per day or US$500-800 per month. Total costs can be divided into four main categories: airfare, local transportation, accommodations, and food.

Airfare: Airfare takes a big chunk of everybody's budget, but you'll be surprised at how many kilometers can be covered per dollar with some planning and careful shopping. Roundtrip airfare from the United States or Europe should average under US$1000. Figure on US$500-800 for additional flights around the region. The best strategy for independent travelers on an extended vacation is to buy a one-way ticket to Southeast Asia and onward tickets from travel agencies along the way. Located in nearly every large town and city in Southeast Asia, these discount agencies offer some of the world's lowest prices because of fierce competition and the unwillingness of local agents to follow fares suggested by international consortiums. Unless you're on a tight schedule, roundtrip tickets and fixed-stop tickets are not advised since your travel plans will change en route and changing tickets is also a hassle. Note, however, that some countries will refuse entrance to anyone entering by air without an onward ticket. Details below.

Local Transportation: Trains, buses, taxis, and other forms of internal transportation are ridiculously cheap by Western standards. For example, a two-day train ride from Singapore to Bangkok costs under US$40; a bus from Bali to Jakarta costs US$25; a taxi from the airport to most hotels in Manila costs US$2.

Accommodations: While air tickets and ground transportation costs are rather fixed, eating and sleeping expenses can be carefully controlled. Hotels are available in all price ranges, depending on the country, size of city, and level of comfort. Industrialized countries such as Thailand and Malaysia are, quite naturally, more expensive than less-developed countries such as Indonesia and Burma. On the other hand, it's also possible to spend over US$100 for a luxury hotel in Indonesia or less than US$5 for a backpackers' dorm in Singapore. Secondly, hotels in large cities are generally more expensive than those in smaller towns. Probably the most important pricing factor is comfort. Shoestring travelers who don't mind simple rooms with common bath and minimal furniture can sleep for under US$5 in most towns. Some of these places are desultory and noisy Chinese hotels located near the train or bus terminals, but others are clean and friendly guesthouses filled with Western backpackers. This informal network of guesthouses is the ideal solution for long-term travelers since they're great spots in which to relax, meet other people, and exchange travel information. Many have dormitories under US$2.

Guesthouses come under different names, depending on the country, and offer varying degrees of cleanliness, but most are a vast improvement over the sterility of large international hotels. Travelers who want better rooms with decent furnishings and private baths should figure on US$6-10 per day. Prices jump to US$10-15 with air-conditioning. While not a necessity at breezy beach resorts or in the hills, a/c becomes almost a necessity in hot and smoggy cities such as Bangkok. Moderately priced hotels in the US$25-40 range usually include hotel restaurants, lounges, TV, room service, and other standard amenities. Southeast Asia's top-end hotels are considered some of the finest in the world. Although recommended for an occasional splurge, it must be said that the cheaper the hotel, the more intriguing the people you'll meet and the more memorable the travel experience.

Food: Another old axiom encourages one to sleep rough but eat well. A great deal of money can sensibly be saved by staying in guesthouses rather than flashy hotels. The tragedy is that many travelers extend this bare-bones philosophy to dining, refusing to spend an extra 50 cents to enjoy a far superior meal. This is hardly recommended since surviving on a steady diet of fried rice and noodle dishes is not only monotonous and detrimental to your mental health, it deprives you of one of life's great travel experiences . . . food! Finding good food at bargain prices is the same anywhere in the world. Avoid those places signposted "We Speak English" or displaying credit card stickers. Instead, search out cafes filled with local customers, not groups of tourists. Don't be shy about road stalls and simple cafes; as mentioned above, these often provide the tastiest food at rock-bottom prices. By carefully patronizing a selection of local cafes and quality street stalls, it's surprisingly easy to enjoy three outstanding meals for less than US$10 a day.

Weather

Heat and rain can raise hell with your vacation plans. Southeast Asia is an equatorial land with a tropical climate. Temperatures perpetually hover between hot and excruciatingly hot, depending on whether it's the so-called "cool" winter season from November to March or the hot summer months from March to June. High temperatures and a humidity factor of almost 100% can be quite a shock for Westerners accustomed to more moderate climes, but there's little you can really do about it except stay out of the midday sun and escape into an air-conditioned hotel or restaurant. On the other hand, if you have control over your travel schedule, the best time to visit Southeast Asia—especially Thailand and Burma—is during the cooler winter months.

Monsoons, not temperature, are the most important weather factor in Southeast Asia. Derived from the Arabic word *mansim* (seasonal

CLIMATES AROUND SOUTHEAST ASIA

	JAN.	FEB.	MAR.	APR.	MAY	JUNE	JULY	AUG.	SEPT.	OCT.	NOV.	DEC.
BURMA												
Rangoon	hot . . . . extremely hot . . . . . monsoon . . . . hot											
HONG KONG												
Hong Kong	cool . . . . warm . hot . . monsoon . . . . warm											
INDONESIA												
Jakarta	rainy . . . . hot . . . . rainy											
Bali	rainy . . . . hot . . . . rainy											
Sumatra	rainy . . . . hot . . . . rainy											
Maluku	hot . . . . rainy . . . . hot											
MALAYSIA												
K. Lumpur	warm . . . . . hot . . . . monsoon											
Kota Baru	warm . . . . . hot . . . . monsoon											
Kuching	monsoon . . . . hot . . . . monsoon											
PHILIPPINES												
Manila	hot . . . . extremely hot . . . . monsoon . . . . hot											
SINGAPORE												
Singapore	warm . . . . rainy											
THAILAND												
Bangkok	hot . . . . extremely hot . . . . monsoon . . . . hot											

winds), monsoons are created by the differences in annual temperature trends over land and water. From May through September, winds from the southwest bring heavy rains to most of Asia lying north of the equator. In winter they reverse, bringing cool, dry air across mainland Southeast Asia and carrying rains to Indonesia and the northeast coastlines of mainland countries. The dividing line is formed by the equator. Best time to visit countries north of the equator (Burma, Thailand, Philippines, Hong Kong) is from November to March when the dry monsoons sweep down from China. Countries south of the equator are driest March to November. Monsoons flood streets and ruin holidays on the beach, but they're no cause for real alarm. For many seasoned travelers, the violent but brief rains of summer bring the real drama of Asia, providing an opportunity to witness nature in all her uncontrolled fury.

Luggage

Overpacking is perhaps the most serious mistake made by first-time travelers. Experienced vagabonders know that heavy and bulky absolutely guarantees a hellish vacation. Travel light and you'll be *free* to choose your style of travel. With a single carry-on pack weighing less than 10 kilos you can board the plane assured that your bags won't be pilfered, damaged, or lost by baggage handlers. You're first off the plane and you can cheerfully skip the long wait at the baggage carousel. You grab the first bus and get the best room at the hotel. Porters with their smiling faces and greased palms become somebody else's problem.

First consideration should be given to your bag. The modern solution to world travel is a convertible backpack/shoulder bag with zip-away shoulder straps. Huge suitcases that withstand gorilla attacks and truck collisions are best left to group tours and immigrant families moving to a new country. Serious trekking packs with outside frames are only suitable for the genuine backpackers they were designed for. Your bag should have an internal frame, a single-cell, lockable compartment without outside pockets to tempt Asian thieves. A light, soft, and functional bag should fit under an airplane seat and measure no more than 18 x 21 x 13 inches. Impossible, you say? It's done every day by thousands of smart and experienced travelers who know they are the most liberated people on the road.

Second consideration is what to pack. The rule of thumb is that total weight should never exceed 10 kilos (22 pounds). Avoid vagabondage by laying out everything you *think* you'll need and then cutting the pile in half. (To truly appreciate the importance of traveling light, pack up and take a practice stroll around your neighborhood on the hottest day of the year.) Take the absolute minimum and do your shopping on the road. The reasons are obvious: Asia is a giant shopping bazaar filled with everything from toothpaste to light cotton clothing, prices are much lower than back home, and local products are perfectly suited for the weather.

Half of your pack will be filled with clothing. Minimize your needs by bringing only two sets of garments: wash one, wear one. A spartan wardrobe means freedom, flexibility, and variety, plus it's great fun to purchase a new wardrobe when the old clothing no longer comes clean. Give some serious thought to what you *don't* need. Sleeping bags, parkas, bedding, and foul-weather gear are completely unnecessary in Southeast Asia. Experienced travelers buy their umbrellas when it rains and sweaters when it gets chilly.

Then pack everything into individual plastic bags. Plastic compartmentalization keeps your bag neat and organized, and possibly even dry when the *banca* capsizes in the Philippines! Here's a handy list of suggested items:

- Two pairs of long pants, one casual, one formal
- One stylish pair of shorts
- Two short-sleeved shirts with pockets
- Two pairs of underwear and socks
- Modest bathing suit
- One pair of comfortable walking shoes
- Sandals or rubber thongs
- Mini towel
- Medical kit
- Sewing kit
- Two small padlocks
- Swiss Army knife
- *Southeast Asia Handbook*

TRAVEL FORMALITIES

Travel Documents

Travel documents essential for travel in Southeast Asia include a valid passport and the necessary visas. American passports are issued by the U.S. State Department at offices located in most major cities and through state courts and certain post offices. Europeans and Australians can obtain passports from their respective governments. Allow plenty of time for processing, especially during the spring and summer months.

Visas are stamps placed in your passport by foreign governments that permit you to visit that country for a limited time and for a specified purpose, such as tourism or business. Visas are issued by embassies and consulates located both at home and in most large Asian cities.

The good news is that visa requirements are being eased throughout Southeast Asia. Most countries now permit visa-free entry for a limited time. For instance, Indonesian immigration officials stamp a two-month permit into your passport upon arrival. Visas are also unnecessary for short visits to Singapore, Hong Kong, Macau, Brunei, and Malaysia. The situation is stickier in Thailand, which grants only 15 days, and the Philippines, which gives only 21 days upon arrival. If you're planning on staying longer in either Thailand or the Philippines, you should pick up a visa *before* arrival since extensions after arrival are either prohibited or time-consuming to obtain.

Whether to get your visas prior to departure or on the road depends on what countries you intend to visit, how long you wish to stay, and your approximate dates of arrival. Travelers on short vacations can obtain the necessary visas in advance from consulates, travel agents, or visa agencies, which charge about US$10 per visa. On an extended trip, it's much better to pick up your visas as you travel. For example, most travelers get their Thai visa in a neighboring country shortly before crossing the border. This also circumvents the problem of visas with limited validities (unused visas often expire in six to 12 months; see below). Visas can be obtained in person from embassies located in most Asian capitals, but it's much faster to let a travel agent or visa service do the necessary paperwork.

PHOTOGRAPHY IN ASIA

Dragging heavy camera equipment around Southeast Asia has a series of drawbacks: It adds weight and bulk to your pack, the paranoia factor rises, film is often expensive, you become a target for thieves, and you will inevitably offend a few people by taking their photos. On the other hand, there are several good reasons to bring your camera: Photography can be an exciting and creative hobby, your visual senses are sharpened while searching for photos, and more than anything else, your travel memories are forever saved to be shared with friends and family. Finely crafted slide shows are an excellent way to recapture that once-in-a-lifetime Asian odyssey.

Those travelers who are ambivalent about photography or want to avoid a full-sized camera outfit can opt for a small but high-quality auto-focus camera such as those made by Canon and Minolta. These lightweight cameras cost about US$100 and take acceptable photos, but they lack interchangeable lenses and offer little creative control. Rather than be disappointed with your results, consider purchasing a high-quality 35mm camera with three interchangeable lenses at a cost of US$600-800. An excellent choice would be an Olympus OM2 or the Minolta Maxxam 7000, which offers all the features found on the cheaper models (autofocus, autowind, etc.) together with interchangeable lenses. Three lenses are recommended. The standard 50mm lens seems necessary, but it's really the least useful or interesting option. A 28mm wide-angle lens is highly recommended for landscapes, architecture, and groups of people. This small, lightweight, and very inexpensive lens is perhaps the single most useful of the three, but you might consider buying a wide-angle zoom lens such as a 24-50mm or a 28-75mm. Your third lens should be a zoom telephoto such as a 75-150mm or 90-250mm, which will prove invaluable for candid people photos and dramatic compression shots.

Because of its deep color saturations, the film of choice for most professional photographers is Kodachrome ASA 64 slide film. If you're an average photographer who carries a camera every day but shoots judiciously, figure on using two or three rolls of film per week. A sensible plan is to bring 20-30 rolls along and purchase additional film in Hong Kong and Singapore, where prices are the lowest. Elsewhere in Southeast Asia, Kodak film is either fairly expensive or difficult to find. Allow two weeks for processing from Asian capitals (the Kodachrome lab is in Australia). You'll also need a small flash, extra batteries, and a few filters. All this adds about three kilos to your pack.

Pack all your film in a film-shield pouch and then hand-carry everything through the airport X-ray machine. Despite their claims to the contrary, some Asian airports have their X-ray machines turned up too high; the result is fogged film. While taking photos in Southeast Asia, keep in mind that the extreme heat and glaring sun can fool your camera's automatic exposure control. Overexposed photos can be avoided by shooting in the softer light of the early morning and late afternoon. *Get close!* The single biggest problem with most amateur photographers is that they stand too far away. *Be quick!* Most Asians don't mind if you take a quick and nonobtrusive photo of them, but it becomes a painful intrusion when the photographer takes too much time. Use a telephoto for people pictures and be prepared. Before you even raise the camera to your eye, you should set your exposure and prefocus before quickly snapping the picture and moving on. Speed and discretion will avoid most problems, but when in doubt you should ask permission first. A final suggestion: hold the temple photos down to a minimum—it's the people pictures that capture the real meaning of Southeast Asia.

Wasting half a day wrestling with disgruntled consulate officials just isn't worth the modest service charge.

Additional Documents
International Health Certificates: Under the International Health Regulations adopted by the World Health Organization (WHO), a country, under certain conditions, may require from travelers an International Certificate of Vaccination against yellow fever. WHO has recently elimi-

nated the special page for cholera vaccinations. Southeast Asia is a relatively healthy place, but you should check with your doctor on current certificate requirements.

International Student Identity Card: The green-and-white ISIC card can help qualify you for discounts on airlines and at hotels throughout Asia. Eligible students can obtain cards from STA and Council Travel offices. Fake cards are sold at discount agencies in Bangkok, Hong Kong, and Penang.

ENTRY REQUIREMENTS FOR SOUTHEAST ASIA

(for U.S. passport holders)

COUNTRY	VISAS	LENGTH	EXTENSIONS
Brunei	None	1 week	1 week
Burma	Required	2 weeks	None
Hong Kong	None	1 month	1 month
Indonesia	None	2 months	None
Macau	None	20 days	None
Malaysia	None	30 days	30 days
Philippines	None	21 days	38 days; optional 60-day visas
Singapore	None	2 weeks	None
Thailand	None	15 days	None; optional 12-month visa

International Driver's License: Anyone contemplating renting a car or motorcycle should obtain an International Driver's License from a local automobile association. Fail to do this and you'll be subjected to Asian driving exams, extra fees, or outright refusal on your rental.

International Youth Hostel Card: Though invaluable in Europe and expensive Asian countries such as Japan, the IYHF card is of limited use in Southeast Asia. Contact any youth hostel office for a card and their *International Youth Hostel Handbook* to Africa, America, Asia, and Australasia.

GETTING THERE

Southeast Asia can be reached from North America, Australia, and Europe on dozens of airlines at all possible prices. Airline tariffs vary widely and substantial savings can be made by using legal loopholes and the services of a well-trained travel agent. To both novice travelers and professionals in the field, airfares and routings seem a disorganized mess. Much of the confusion and controversy revolve around the International Air Transport Association (IATA), a trade association of over 100 of the world's scheduled airlines, which attempts to enforce airfares agreed to bilaterally by national airlines and their respective governments. Fortunately, their efforts are frustrated by the realities of

modern ticketing, which say that empty seats should be filled no matter the demands of a price-fixing cartel.

Do-it-yourself travelers can benefit by learning some of the tools of the travel trade. First, read the local newspapers and then call airline, cruise, student, and discount-travel agencies for ticket and tour information. Contact all the national tourist offices for more information. Serious travelers can plan their itinerary and discover obscure air routes by studying the *Official Airline Guide* at the library. Then call an experienced travel agent. Even the most independent of travelers can save money and countless hours by letting a travel agent do the actual booking.

Another consideration is that many countries require travelers to show a ticket out of the country at the point of immigration. This could be an onward plane ticket or a miscellaneous charge order (MCO). But the best option is to purchase the cheapest ticket and get a refund later on. To save time and hassles it's quickest to buy your onward ticket with cash or traveler's checks from a major carrier with offices in major cities.

Full-fare Air Tickets
First, Business, Economy, APEX: Ticket prices vary enormously depending on dozens of factors, including type of ticket, season, choice of airline, flexibility, and experience of the travel agent. It's confusing, but since airfare comprises

**AIRLINE COMPANIES'
TOLL-FREE NUMBERS**

Cathay Pacific . . . . (800) 233-2742

Garuda . . . . (800) 332-2223

Malaysian. . . . . (800) 421-8641

Northwest. . . . . (800) 225-2525

Philippines . . . . (800) 435-9725

Singapore. . . . . (800) 742-3333

Thai . . . . (800) 426-5204

United . . . . (800) 241-6522

a major portion of total travel expenses, no amount of time getting it right is wasted. The rule of thumb is that price and restrictions are inversely related; the cheaper the ticket, the more hassles such as penalties, odd departure hours, layovers, and risk of last-minute cancellations. First class and business are designed for travelers who need maximum flexibility and comfort and are willing to pay the price. Economy is cheaper than business and you avoid advance-purchase requirements and cancellation charges. Advance-purchase excursion (APEX) fares—the airlines' main method for deep discounts—are about 25% less than economy but loaded with restrictions concerning advance payment, length of stay, and cancellation penalties. Read the fine print *very* carefully. Super-APEX is similar to APEX but even cheaper. Quantities are limited and sell out quickly; buy them early. APEX and super-APEX tickets are recommended for visitors with limited time who need guaranteed air reservations.

Mileage Tickets: Mileage tickets permit the traveler to pay the fare from A to B and make unlimited stops en route. For example, the ticket from San Francisco to Bangkok costs US$1061 and permits 9,559 miles. One possible routing is San Francisco-Tokyo-Seoul-Taipei-Hong Kong-Manila-Bangkok. Tickets are good for one year and a mileage surcharge is tacked on for travel beyond the allotted distance. Though mileage tickets are practical for certain routes, significantly less expensive tickets covering similar stops are sold by student and discount travel agencies.

Circle-Pacific: Circle-Pacific fares are another tempting piece in the puzzle of international airfares. Scheduled on major international airlines, these tickets allow you to circle the North Pacific, Southeast Asia, and South Pacific for about US$2020 in economy class. Restrictions are a problem, however, since they're limited to four stopovers, cost US$50 per extra stop, demand 14 days advance purchase, carry cancellation penalties, have a six-month expiration, and charge US$50 for each reissuance. Worse yet, only those cities served by the principal carrier and partner are possible stopovers. This eliminates most of the smaller but vitally important connections such as Singapore-Jakarta. Circle-Pacific fares are sold in North America by United (tel. 800-JET-AWAY), Northwest (tel. 800-447-4747), and Canadian (tel. 800-426-7000).

Budget and student travel agencies also put together circle-Pacific tickets, often at much lower prices than the airlines. Sample routings and prices from budget agencies are listed below.

Round-the-World: Another variation of APEX are the RTW tickets sold by several international carriers. RTW tickets cost US$2784 in economy class and allow unlimited stopovers on a combination of carriers. Tickets are good for one year but stops are limited to major cities served by the airlines. Contact the above airlines for further information. You should also contact student and discount agencies regarding their cheaper and less restrictive RTW tickets.

Bargain Tickets

The cheapest tickets to Asia are sold by wholesalers who take advantage of special rates for group tours by purchasing large blocks of unsold seats. Once an airline concludes it can't sell all of its seats, consolidators are offered a whopping 20-40% commission to do the job. They then hand most of the commission back to the clients in the form of reduced ticket prices. Known on the retail level as "bucket shops" (a term derived from European stock exchanges when business was conducted with buckets), consolidators originally only booked passage on Third World and communist carriers such as Korean Air and Aeroflot. Today they market 20-60% of all international tickets on virtually every airline from Northwest to Qantas. Tickets obtained from consolidators are legal and, in most cases, completely trustworthy. The ad-

CIRCLE-PACIFIC AND ROUND-THE-WORLD FARES

CIRCLE-PACIFIC

USA-Hong Kong-Bangkok-Singapore-Jakarta-Bali-Hawaii-USA **US$1299**

USA-Tahiti-Auckland-Noumea-Sydney-Jakarta-Singapore-Bangkok-Hong Kong-Taipei-USA
US$1499

ROUND-THE-WORLD

USA-Hong Kong-Bangkok-Bombay-London-USA **US$1299**

USA-Tahiti-Auckland-Noumea-Sydney-Jakarta-Singapore-Amman-Vienna-USA **US$1699**

USA-Tahiti-Cook Islands-Fiji-Auckland-Singapore-Bangkok-Kathmandu-Delhi-Amman-Vienna-USA
US$1999

USA-Dublin-Europe-Athens-Cairo-Nairobi-Bombay-Delhi-Kathmandu-Bangkok-Singapore-Jakarta
Bali-Hawaii-USA **US$2099**

---

vantages are obvious: cheap tickets (prices average 25-40% less than economy fares), plenty of choice, and guaranteed reservations on first-class airlines. The drawbacks: buckets rarely provide travel counseling, they keep you guessing about which airline you'll fly, tickets often carry penalties (see below), and routings can be slow and byzantine. Try to get the cheapest ticket, on the best airline, with the least number of unnecessary stops.

Sources For Bargain Tickets

Where do you purchase these cheap tickets? Consolidators don't deal with the public, but rather sell their tickets through student bureaus, independent travel agents, and travel clubs. In fact, you can buy consolidator tickets from almost everyone except the consolidators themselves and the airlines. Roundtrip prices currently average US$500 from the West Coast to Tokyo, US$550/US$650 low season/high season to Hong Kong, and US$750 to Bangkok, Singapore, and Manila. Roundtrip surcharges for East Coast departures are US$150-200. Current fares are advertised in the Sunday travel sections of major newspapers such as the *New York Times, Los Angeles Times,* and *San Francisco Examiner.* Advance planning is essential since the best deals often sell out months in advance.

Make a note of the following penalties and restrictions. Peak fares are in effect from June to August (add US$50-100) and tickets purchased less than 90 days in advance are subject to an additional US$50-150 surcharge. Flight cancellations or changes made more than 30 days in advance after the ticket has been issued usually cost US$50, but cancel your flight within 30 days of departure or any time after the ticket has been issued and you'll forfeit up to 25% of the published fare!

International Youth Hostel Federation

This group and their associated American Youth Hostels (AYH) also provide budget travel information and discounted tickets. Few AYH hostels are located in Southeast Asia, but travelers heading to Japan will find a superb network of budget accommodations. Membership is $25 per year. American Youth Hostels, P.O. Box 37613, Washington, D.C. 20013, tel. (202) 783-6161.

Council Travel

This excellent travel organization, a division of the Council on International Educational Exchange, has 27 offices in the U.S. and representatives in Europe and Australia. Prices are low and service reliable since they deal only with reputable airlines to minimize travel problems. Best of all, Council Travel sales agents are experienced travelers who often have firsthand knowledge of Southeast Asia. Council Travel also sells the Youth Hostel Association Card, the International Student Identity Card (ISIC), the Youth International Educational Exchange

STA (STUDENT TRAVEL ASSOCIATION) OFFICES

COUNTRY/CITY	ADDRESS	PHONE
UNITED STATES		
West Hollywood	7204 Melrose Avenue, Los Angeles, CA 90046	(213) 934-8722
Westwood	920 Westwood Boulevard, Los Angeles, CA 90024	(213) 824-1574
San Diego	6447 El Cajon Boulevard, San Diego, CA 92115	(619) 286-1322
San Francisco	166 Geary, Suite 702, San Francisco, CA 94108	(415) 391-8407
Berkeley	82 Shattuck Square #4, Berkeley, CA 94704	(510) 841-1037
Cambridge	1208 Massachusetts Avenue, Cambridge, MA 02138	(617) 576-4623
Boston	273 Newbury Street, Boston, MA 02116	(617) 266-6014
New York	17 East 45th Street, New York, NY 10017	(212) 986-9470
ENGLAND		
London	74 Old Brompton Road, London SW7 3LH	01-937 9962
London	117 Euston Road, London NW1 2SX	
Bristol	25 Queens Road, Bristol BS8 1QE	0272-294399
Cambridge	38 Sidney Street, Cambridge CB2 3HX	0223-66966
Oxford	19 High Street, Oxford OX1 4AH	0865-240547
AUSTRALIA AND NEW ZEALAND		
Melbourne	220 Faraday Street, Carlton 3053	(03) 347-6911
Sydney	1A Lee Street, Railway Square	(02) 519-9866
Brisbane	Northern Security Bldg, 40 Creek Street	(07) 221-9629
Adelaide	55A O'Connell Street, North Adelaide 5006	(08) 267-1855
Cairns	Raging Thunder Travel, 88 Lake Street 4870	(070) 513-912
Perth	426 Hay Street, Subaico 6008	(9) 382-3977
Auckland	64 High Street, Box 4156	(9) 390-458
Christchurch	223 High Street	(3) 799-098

Card (for nonstudents under 26), plus travel and health insurance. Their larger offices:

San Francisco . . . . (415) 421-3473
Los Angeles . . . . (213) 208-3551
Seattle . . . . (206) 632-2448
Chicago . . . . (312) 951-0585
Boston . . . . (617) 266-1926
New York . . . . (212) 661-1450

Budget Agencies In Europe
Trailfinders: Travelers in England should contact the nation's largest budget travel agency: 194 Kensington High St., London W8 7RG, tel. 01-938-3939.

Council Travel: Council Travel has 10 offices in Europe, including London (tel. 071-437-7767),

Paris (tel. 1-45631987), Lyon (tel. 78370956), and Dusseldorf (tel. 211-329088). Same services as above.

Globetrotter Travel: Swiss and German travelers can try Okista, SSR, Asta, Ontej, Unitra, Artu, Alternativ Tours, Asien-Reisen, or Globetrotter Travel Service. Globetrotter, the largest student travel agency in Germany, also distributes a useful travel magazine, *Travel Info*. A few Globetrotter addresses:

Rennweg 35, 8001 Zurich
   tel. (01) 211-7780
Neuengasse 23, 3001 Bern
   tel. (031) 211121
Falknerstrasse 1, 4001 Basel
   tel. (061) 257766

Rutligasse 2, 6003 Luzern·
tel. (041) 221025
Merkurstrasse 4, 9001 Gallen
tel. (071) 228222
Stadthausstrasse 65, 8401 Winterthur
tel. (052) 221426

Couriers

Aside from working as a travel agent or hijacking a plane, the cheapest way to reach Southeast Asia is by carrying urgent mail for one of the following courier companies. Roundtrip tickets from the West Coast average US$250-400 to Taipei, US$350-500 to Tokyo and Hong Kong, US$400-550 to Singapore, and US$450-600 to Sydney. Courier flights are also available to Bangkok, Malaysia, Manila, and even Vietnam. Standby couriers who need less than seven days' notice can fly roundtrip to Southeast Asia for about US$100-150. Some of the courier companies even let you accumulate frequent-flyer miles!

Anyone can do this, and it's perfectly legal (no drugs or guns are carried, just stock certificates and registered mail), but there are several restrictions: you're limited in most cases to carry-on luggage and length of stay averages only one to four weeks. Departures are available from Los Angeles, San Francisco, and New York.

The best source for current information on courier flights is an extremely helpful monthly newsletter from Travel Unlimited, P.O. Box 1058, Allston, MA 02134. $25 per year.

Last-minute Travel Clubs

Travel clubs are clearinghouses which sell leftover space on airlines, cruises, and tours at 15-50% discount. Most specialize in cruise discounts and charge an annual membership fee of US$20-50. **Warning:** most are honest but some travel clubs are fraudulent scams operated by the same people who sell time-share condos and commodity futures. Proceed with caution. Contact:

Worldwide Discount	(305) 534-2082
Discount Travel	(215) 668-2182
Moment's Notice	(212) 486-0503
Stand Buys	(800) 255-0200
Vacations to Go	(800) 624-7338

Tour Operators

There are several good reasons to consider an organized tour. They allow you to see the high-

---

TELEPHONE NUMBERS FOR COURIER FLIGHTS

In Northern California, call:

TNT Skypack	(415) 692-9600
MicomAmerica	(415) 872-0845
Jupiter Air	(415) 872-0845
UTL Travel	(415) 583-5074
Crossroads	(408) 434-6446

In Los Angeles, call:

TNT Skypack	(310) 410-1419
MicomAmerica	(310) 670-5123
DIF Travel	(310) 851-2572
Crossroads	(310) 643-8600
UTL Travel	(310) 645-4301
Way To Go	(213) 466-1126
Polo Express	(310) 410-6822

In New York, call:

Now Voyage	(212) 431-1616
Discount	(212) 655-5151
Courier	(800) 922-2359
Jupiter Air	(718) 341-2095
Halbart	(718) 656-8279

---

lights of Asia without the hassles of language difficulties, transportation delays, and the time wasted finding suitable accommodations. Often there is no cheaper way to get airfare and hotels, since large tour operators buy in bulk and can pick up sizable discounts from airlines and hotels. Don't dismiss tours for fear of simply being shepherded around—the "If it's Tuesday, this must be Bangkok" syndrome. Simple packages often include only transportation and hotels, leaving you free to independently wander around in each town. Other more expensive tours include bus tours, dining, and entertainment, but you're never under any obligation to follow the crowd. Finally, tours often bring about a feeling of togetherness and sharing.

Dozens of packagers and tour operators such as American Express, Thomas Cook, and Olson sell tours to Southeast Asia, but you should carefully read the fine print and check on what's included in the price. Probably the most important factors are the experience of the guides and the general emphasis of the package.

Rather than trying to see all of Southeast Asia at breakneck speed, it's better to limit yourself to a few highlights or perhaps just a single destination. Ask your agent about the quality and location of the hotels, what kinds of meals are included, how large the group will be, and cost of insurance and penalties for cancellation. One good choice is Travcoa (tel. 800-992-2004), which for almost 40 years has organized tours to the Orient, China, and Southeast Asia. Upcoming plans include visits to Angkor Wat, Laos, Vietnam, and Burma, besides their 46-day US$9000 tour of Southeast Asia. If none of these package tours seems appealing, investigate the special-interest tours and adventure packages described below. Here are a few companies to call:

Abercrombie and Kent . .	(800) 323-7308
Jetset Tours	(800) 453-8738
Olson Travelworld.	(800) 421-2255
Pacific Delights	(800) 645-2424
Globus Gateway	(800) 221-0090
Maupintour	(800) 255-4266
Odyssey Tours	(800) 654-7975

Freighters

Freighters are working cargo ships which accept a limited number of passengers on their long journeys. This form of transport allows you to visit remote and untouristy ports at a leisurely pace, mix with the few other passengers, plus dine with the captain at night. Costs average US$80-100 per day rather than the US$200-300 rate charged by luxury liners, although these savings must be balanced by the longer voyages. Facilities are simple but comfortable. Passengers must be flexible, since ports of call may change without notice and delays are not uncommon.

The biggest drawback is the scarcity of passenger freighters which travel to and from Southeast Asia. Services may multiply with the rising popularity of freighter travel, but for the present, only Chilean Lines (65-70 days; US$5500-6000), Lykes, and Pace Lines offer service from the West Coast to the Orient. Contact Freighter World Cruises (tel. 818-449-3106) or TravLtips (tel. 800-872-8584) for information and reservations. Both publish freighter newsletters, as does the Freighter Travel Club of America, Box 12693, Salem, Oregon 97309. Another excellent resource is Ford's Freighter Travel Guide, available from Ronald Howard, 19448 Londelius Street, Northridge, CA 91324, tel. (818) 701-7414.

GETTING AROUND

By Air

A large number of both international and domestic airlines serves just about every city and town in Southeast Asia. The variety of aircraft is rather amazing. One day you will be jetting across the South China Sea in a Boeing 747 with smiling hostesses and free-flowing liquor, and on the next it's a WW II-vintage DC-3 to a tropical island or a remote mountain village. Major Asian carriers are considered some of the finest in the world in terms of safety records, service, and food, as shown by a 1989 readers poll in Condé Nast Traveler, which placed Singapore Air in first, Thai International sixth, and Cathay Pacific 10th. Flying obscure airlines is also fun, especially across the remote islands of Indonesia.

Airfare around Southeast Asia need not be any more expensive per kilometer than airfare in the West. Discount tickets are sold in almost every major city from student and budget travel agencies. First check prices at an STA Travel office before doing comparison shopping among competing agencies. Examine tickets and restrictions carefully before handing over your money! Prices tend to be lowest in Bangkok, Hong Kong, Penang, and Singapore and slightly higher in Manila and Jakarta. Don't believe agents who claim they have the lowest prices in all of Southeast Asia. Tickets are cheapest in the city of origin, so buy your tickets from Bangkok in Bangkok and your tickets from Singapore in Singapore.

Luxury Cruise Ships

Perhaps 80% of the world's luxury cruises do the popular tourist routes through the Caribbean, Mexico, Alaska, and Hawaii, but a growing number of companies offer deluxe cruises through Southeast Asia.

The following companies will send colorful brochures, but bookings must be made through independent travel agents or a nationwide agency such as Travel of America (tel. 800-358-2838 nationwide, 800-228-8843 in California).

Royal Viking Line: Their "Captain's Pacific Journey" tour sails from San Francisco through the South Pacific to Australia, Africa, India, Phuket, Singapore, Bangkok, Hong Kong, and Tokyo. 95 Merrick Way, Coral Gables, FL 33134, tel. (800) 422-8000 (U.S.), tel. (800) 448-4785 (Canada).

Pearl Cruises: Sponsors a variety of tours, including a 20-day "Bangkok, Bali and Beyond" series from Bangkok to Singapore via Kuala Lumpur, Jakarta, Bali, and Pulau Sepa. 1510 S.E. 17th St., Fort Lauderdale, FL 33316, tel. (800) 556-8850.

Renaissance Cruises: Past sails have included three super-luxury cruises from Singapore to Bali (20 days from US$7000), Nusa Tenggara (14 days from US$5000), and Hong Kong (22 days from US$7000). 1800 Eller Drive, Box 35307, Fort Lauderdale, FL 33335, tel. (800) 525-2450.

Cunard Lines: Cunard sails through Southeast Asia on their *Sea Goddess II, Sagafjord,* and *Vistfjord* from autumn to spring. 555 Fifth Ave., New York, NY 10017, tel. (800) 221-4770.

Princess Cruises: Fall departures on their *Island Princess* and *Pacific Princess.* 10100 Santa Monica Blvd., Los Angeles, CA 90067, tel. (800) 568-3262.

Seabourn Cruise Line: Their 14-day Singapore-Bangkok-Singapore Cruise stops at some of the finest islands in Southeast Asia: Ko Samui, Tioman, and Penang. 55 Francisco St., San Francisco, CA 94133, tel. (800) 351-9595.

Exploratory Cruises

The most extraordinary of all Southeast Asian cruises are those on-board smaller vessels or private yachts which sail the more remote regions.

Abercrombie and Kent: This well-known operator conducts dozens of land-based tours plus Indonesian voyages on the 96-passenger *Explorer,* purchased in 1992 from defunct Society Expeditions. 1520 Kensington Rd., Oak Brook, IL 60521, tel. (800) 323-7308.

Windstar Cruises: First major cruise line to commit to year-round operations in Southeast Asia. Inaugural voyages from Singapore in early 1994. Beautiful rigged ships. 300 Elliot Ave. West, Seattle, WA 98119, tel. (800) 258-7245.

P & O Spice Island Cruises: Indonesia's only luxury minicruiser, the MV *Island Explorer,* operates across the islands of the Lesser Sun-

---

RESPONSIBLE TOURING

Before selecting a tour company, you might want to consider the following guidelines suggested by the Center for Responsible Tourism. If your prospective tour group or travel agent fails the test, investigate the Adventure Travel and Alternative Travel groups described later in the text.

1. Does the tour organizer demonstrate a cultural and environmental sensitivity? How are local people and culture portrayed in advertising brochures?
2. Who benefits financially from your trip? What percentage of your dollar stays in the country you visit rather than ending up with an international hotel chain, airline, or travel agency?
3. Is a realistic picture of your host country presented, or a sanitized version packaged for tourists?
4. Will you use local accommodations and transportation or be assigned to tourist facilities that prevent a real understanding of the environment?
5. Does your travel itinerary allow adequate time for meeting with local people? If it doesn't go!
6. Has the tour operator or travel agent mentioned anything beyond what's listed in the glossy advertisements? Ask about the social, economic, and political realities of Southeast Asia.

---

das (Bali, Lombok, Sumbawa, Flores, Savu, Sumba) for 10 months of the year and cruises Jakarta, Krakatau, Ujung Kulon, and South Sumatra during December and January. Twin share cabins cost US$3300 for 10-day Bali to Kupang, and US$2800 for nine days from Jakarta. In America call Abercrombie and Kent at (800) 323-7308.

Oceanic Society Expeditions: In conjunction with Friends of the Earth, this nonprofit organization sponsors educational ecotours and dive trips to a limited number of Asian destinations. Fort Mason Center, Bldg. E, San Francisco, CA 94123, tel. (800) 326-7491.

Sea Trek: Travelers bored with luxury ships should check out Sea Trek. Beginning from Bali, their traditional tall-masted Bugis schooners sail across the Lesser Sundas and off to the Moluccas and Sulawesi. Rates average US$100-130 per day—the least expensive and most adventurous sailing in the archipelago. Passage can be booked through American adventure-travel operators (try Adventure Center and Overseas Adventure Travel) or write to Sea Trek, Herengracht 215, 1016 BG Amsterdam, Holland.

Ocean Voyages: This very special organization arranges charters for individuals and groups on every type of vessel from sleek yachts to superb classic sailing ships. The possibilities are amazing: Pacific crossings, snorkeling in the warm Indonesian seas, high-performance yachting onboard the *Singha* in Thailand, a magnificent square-rigger off the coast of New Guinea, the famous 72-foot *Storm Vogel* from Phuket, and luxurious yachts between Manila and Hong Kong. All are captained by professionals who have spent years sailing and studying anchorages, local histories, anthropology, and marine ecology. Mary Crowley can also help with charters in the South Pacific, the Caribbean, and the Mediterranean. 1709 Bridgeway, Sausalito, CA 94965, tel. (415) 332-4681.

Local Ships

While luxurious ocean liners and exploratory cruises are expensive, plenty of budget seagoing adventures are still available to the Southeast Asian traveler. Prices are lower than air travel, and if you've got the time, you'll meet a fascinating cross-section of travelers and locals who will often share their food, tell you about their countries, and invite you to visit their villages. Ocean transport is a superb way to visit remote islands and experience a side of Asia rarely explored by most visitors. Ships range from rugged steamers straight out of a Joseph Conrad novel to luxurious cruisers equipped with private cabins, dining rooms, and entertainment centers. Shoestring travelers can sail for under US$10 per day. Spend US$25 per day and you'll get an air-conditioned cabin plus three meals in the first-class dining room. First-class ocean transport is one of the great undiscovered travel bargains in Southeast Asia.

Indonesia: Pelni, the national shipping agency of Indonesia, has recently replaced its notorious collection of rustbuckets with sleek new ships constructed in Germany. Recommendations on specific ships and routings are described in the Indonesia chapter. Services in addition to Pelni and the exploratory cruises mentioned above include scuba-diving expeditions and tall-masted schooners such as those operated by Sea Trek and Ocean Voyages.

Thailand: Several private companies now offer cruises through Thailand. Pansea, which started offering yacht cruises on a majestic ketch in 1986, now sails from Phuket between November and April, from Ko Samui between July and October, and from Singapore to the islands off Malaysia's east coast in May and June. Contact Thai International Tours, 942/38 Rama IV Road, Bangkok 10500, tel. 235-4100, or Asia Voyages, #05-11 Orchard Towers, 400 Orchard Road, Singapore 0923, tel. 732-7222. Another cruise choice is the *Seatran Queen,* a larger and more conventional ship which sails through the Andaman Sea near Phuket, around Ko Samui, and from Bangkok to Ko Samet. Contact Seatran Travel, 1097/157 Metro Trade Center, New Phetburi Road, Bangkok 10400, tel. 251-8467, or Trans Global Tours, tel. (800) 367-8792 in the U.S.

Singapore: The Singapore Tourist Promotion Board and local port authority have established Singapore as a major cruise hub with the construction of a US$20-million terminal at the World Trade Center. Popular five-to-eight-day cruises to Penang, Malacca, Langkawi, Medan, and Phuket on the revamped *Ocean Pearl* and *Coral Princess* can be booked through Jetset Travel in Singapore. Also of interest is the *Cruise Muhibah* of Feri Malaysia, which plies between Singapore and Borneo throughout the year. Contact Searo Feri Agencies, 19 Keppel Road, Singapore 0200, tel. 225-9938, or a sales agent listed below.

Malaysia: The Malaysian government operates a modern and luxurious cruise ship between Port Klang (the terminus for Kuala Lumpur), Singapore, Kuantan, Kuching, and Kota Kinabalu. Prices are reasonable; a one-way three-day cruise in a standard cabin from Kuantan to Kota Kinabalu costs under US$75. Contact Feri Malaysia, Menara Utama UMBC, Jalan Sultan Suleiman, Kuala Lumpur 5000; Feri Malaysia in Kuantan; Malaysia Shipping in the Kuching Hotel; Harrisons and Crosfield in Kota Kinabalu; Searo Feri in Singapore.

Car And Motorcycle Rentals

Car rentals are available in most Southeast Asian countries from Avis, Hertz, and local operators at prices comparable to American rates. As with rental agencies throughout the world, you must be careful about hidden charges such as taxes, drop-off fees, and insurance, so that the irresistible bargain doesn't become an expensive luxury. To economize on car rentals you should rent from local agencies rather than big-name operators, keep the car for a least a week or longer, share the expenses with two or three other people, and demand unlimited mileage.

Motorcycles can be rented in dozens of locations including Chiang Mai, Ayuthaya, Kanchanaburi, Pattaya, Ko Samui, and Phuket in Thailand; Penang in Malaysia; Bali, Yogyakarta, and Lombok in Indonesia; and Manila in the Philippines. Rates average US$5-8 per day with discounts for longer rentals. Driving conditions are relatively safe in the less congested towns but only experienced riders should ride on Bali or in the larger cities. Anyone contemplating renting a car or motorcycle is strongly advised to pick up an International Driver's License from any AAA office before leaving for Asia. Some countries require an International Driver's License or insist on a time-consuming and expensive licensing ordeal.

ON THE ROAD

Money

Smart travelers bring a combination of cash, traveler's checks, and a credit card. Each has its own advantages and disadvantages depending on the circumstances. Cash is king in countries such as the Philippines and Burma where the national currency is weak and dollars are in demand. Stash a few U.S. twenties in your pack for emergencies.

Some of your currency should be in the form of traveler's checks. TCs often bring better exchange rates than cash, plus they can be quickly refunded if lost or stolen. To speed the refund process you must keep an accurate list of serial numbers and a record of when and where you cashed each check. Traveler's checks are safe and convenient but certainly not free. Banks and companies that issue traveler's checks make their profit by charging a one-percent fee when you purchase the checks and a hefty amount on the float. This double whammy can be minimized by purchasing traveler's checks from institutions that sell checks without the standard service charge. The float can be minimized by leaving most of your funds in your home bank and making periodic withdrawals or money transfers through a large international bank. Large-denomination checks such as hundreds are easier to carry and cash than a massive pile of ones and twenties. Exchange rates are best at licensed money changers and banks rather than in hotels or at the airport. One sensible strategy is to cash a single traveler's check on arrival at the airport and search out the best exchange rates after reaching the city.

Smart travelers also bring credit cards for several reasons. First, they're invaluable for major purchases such as airline tickets and electronic equipment. Many of the cards now include an insurance policy on plane tickets and purchases—an important benefit in case of disputes over fraudulent or nondelivered merchandise. Credit cards save money by letting you enjoy an interest-free loan until the bill arrives. Major credit cards also allow you to cash checks and obtain cash advances throughout Southeast Asia. This saves some money since cash advances are normally converted into dollars at the interbank foreign-exchange rate, the wholesale rate used by international banks. But you must balance this against the hefty fees. American Express offers check-cashing privileges and cash advances in Hong Kong and Manila, but they charge a stiff US$80 transfer fee from San Francisco for the first US$2000. Visa and MasterCard give cash advances, but in most cases these are regarded as loans with interest accruing from the moment of the loan.

Bank Transfers

Most major banks have extensive international money-transfer operations which will wire money from your home account to their Asian representative. Before leaving on your vacation you should open an account at an institution such as Bank of America or Citicorp and request a list of their representatives in Southeast Asia. Funds can be transferred by telex or mail. Telex transfers are fast and convenient but expensive because of service charges (US$10 per transaction), the telex charge (US$20 each way), the one-percent commission on traveler's checks, and the currency spread. Mail transfers take two or three weeks but avoid telex charges. Another option is to open a managed account at a large stock-brokerage firm and use their services. The secret to travel money management: keep your money working in a money-market account, search for the lowest fees for transfers of funds, and demand commission-free traveler's checks.

Mail
The most dependable way to receive mail is at large post offices via poste restante, a French term which means general delivery. Instruct your friends to capitalize and underline your last name to prevent your mail being misfiled under your first name. You will need to show your passport and pay a small fee when you pick up your mail. Letters are held for several months before being returned to sender. Mail should not be sent to embassies since they deal only with official correspondence. Neither is American Express recommended since the company's mail services are being cut back. Mailing packages home is best done from major cities, where post offices sometimes provide packing services. Packages are limited to 10 kilos; above that you'll need to use private shipping firms. Use registered mail for important documents and keep all receipts to help trace missing parcels.

Telephone
Phone calls can be made quickly and relatively inexpensively from international phone centers located near general post offices in most Asian cities. Long-distance rates average US$8-12 for the first three minutes. As in Western countries, foreign telephone companies often have special rates at night and on weekends. Phone calls should not be made from hotels since most tack on outrageous surcharges. When the surcharges are prohibitive, it's best to place calls from a public telecommunications center or make a short call and have your friends call you back.

Dialing To Southeast Asia
Phone calls and faxes can be made by utilizing the International Direct Distance Dialing system from AT&T or other direct-dial services from smaller operators. To call overseas you must dial, in sequence, 011 (the international access code), the country code, the city code, the local telephone number, and then push the # sign to speed the call. For example, to call Bangkok you push 011 (international access code), 66 (country code for Thailand), 2 (Bangkok area code), and finally the local phone number. Remember that the most dependable method for reserving a hotel room is to send a fax, *not* to attempt a long-distance phone call.

Health
Southeast Asia is a surprisingly healthy place. With some predeparture planning and sensible behavior on the road, it is very unlikely that you will lose even a single day to sickness. Pretrip details involve five simple steps. First, lay out your itinerary and decide how much time you'll be spending in remote tropical areas. This information is vital to make decisions on immununizations, malaria pills, and medical supplies. Secondly, contact a doctor who specializes in travel medicine for a general checkup and immunizations. Health conditions and treatments change yearly, but current recommendations can be checked by calling the Centers for Disease Control (CDC) in Atlanta (tel. 404-639-2572 for general information and 404-332-4555 for malaria tips). Another source of information is *Health Information for International Travel,* published annually by the CDC and sold by the U.S. Government Printing Office (tel. 202-783-3238). More up-to-date facts are published by the CDC in their biweekly "Blue Sheets."

SOUTHEAST ASIA COUNTRY CODES

Brunei	673
Burma	95
Cambodia	855
Hong Kong	852
Indonesia	62
Laos	856
Macau	853
Malaysia	60
Philippines	63
Singapore	65
Thailand	66
Vietnam	84

VACCINATION REQUIREMENTS AND MALARIA PROPHYLAXIS IN SOUTHEAST ASIA

COUNTRY	VACCINATIONS		MALARIA PROPHYLAXIS	
		Area of Risk	Chloroquine Resistance	Recommended Regimen
Brunei	Yellow Fever	None	None	None
Burma	Yellow Fever	Rural only	Confirmed	A
Cambodia	Yellow Fever	All	Confirmed	B
Hong Kong	None required	None	None	None
Indonesia	Yellow Fever	Rural only	Confirmed	B
Laos	Yellow Fever	All	Confirmed	B
Macau	None required	None	None	None
Malaysia	Yellow Fever	Rural only	Confirmed	A/B
Philippines	Yellow Fever	Rural only	Confirmed	A/B
Singapore	Yellow Fever	None	None	None
Thailand	Yellow Fever	Rural only	Confirmed	A
Vietnam	Yellow Fever	Rural only	Confirmed	B

Explanation of codes:

A Routine weekly prophylaxis with Mefloquine alone. Malaria transmission is largely confined to rural areas rarely visited by Western travelers.

B Routine weekly prophylaxis with Mefloquine, *plus* carry Fansidar. Chloroquine or doxycycline is adequate for most urban areas and popular tourist sites. Fansidar should be taken promptly in the event of a febrile illness but *only* when professional medical care is not readily available.

Your doctor will provide you with the International Certificate of Vaccination, a small yellow booklet on which you must record all your immunizations. This card is occasionally demanded by immigration officials. The only vaccination currently required for travel in Southeast Asia is for yellow fever, and only for visitors arriving from infected areas. Cholera and smallpox vaccinations have been dropped. Your vaccination records for tetanus/diphtheria, typhoid, measles, and polio shots should be checked by your doctor and reboosted if necessary. A dose of gamma globulin helps the immune system and is particularly effective in the short term against hepatitis A. Most international travelers do not need any additional immunizations.

After a general check-up and necessary immunizations, discuss the issue of malaria with your doctor. *Malaria is the most serious health risk in Southeast Asia*. The estimated risk of contracting the disease varies markedly from area to area, so different precautions must be taken by each traveler. Visitors on short vacations who limit their programs to big cities and major tourist sites have little to worry about. Travelers who plan to get off the beaten track or camp out near equatorial lakes are under *serious* threat of contracting malaria unless proper medical procedures are rigidly followed. Travelers in high-risk areas should remain well covered, wear dark clothing, use mosquito nets, purchase insect repellents which contain deet (diethylmetatoluamide), and faithfully follow the recommended regimen of malarial pills.

Malaria is now receiving special attention because of the spread of *Plasmodium falciparum* strains, which resist many common malaria prophylaxis. Pills and dosages needed to ward off malaria depend on where you'll go and how long you'll stay. The CDC recommends a weekly dosage of Mefloquine, sold in the U.S. under the trade name of Lariam. Introduced by Roche Laboratories in 1990, Mefloquine is a new antimalarial which has proven effective against both chloroquine- and Fansidar-resistant *P. falciparum* infections. Chloroquine, once the most popular weekly malarial pill, is no longer recommended. Fansidar (pyrimethamine/sufadoxine) should also be avoided in most cases. Consult your doctor.

The final two steps for predeparture planning are to pack a small medical kit and to consider purchasing medical insurance. Keep your kit to the minimum since most medical supplies are sold very inexpensively throughout Southeast Asia. Short-term travel-insurance policies covering medical emergencies, trip cancellations, and flight insurance are sold by STA, other student travel groups, and private companies such as Cigna Travel Guard (tel. 800-826-1300), Access America (tel. 800-284-8300), and International SOS Assistance (tel. 800-523-8930). Before buying one of these short-term policies, read the fine print for exclusions and check your personal insurance plan to see if overseas medical treatment and evacuation are covered. No need to pay twice for the same services.

Behavior

Asian value systems regarding dress, social behavior, religion, authority figures, and sexuality are much more conservative than those of the average Westerner. Remember that visitors, travelers, and tourists in Asia are generally tolerated solely for their economic benefit and little else. Begin by checking all superiority attitudes at home. Open yourself up to the help and advice of Asians. Don't be in a hurry; rather, learn to enjoy the concept of "rubber time." Resist criticizing religious practices you don't understand and be cautious about admitting atheism. Western individualism and high-powered personalities are disliked in the East. Rather, Southeast Asians admire the person who goes with the flow, not the nonconformist. Announcing that you are an independent traveler brings pity rather than admiration as it does in Western societies. "Where are your friends?" is a common question put to solo travelers. Most important, control your emotions, since Asians respect those with a "cool heart." Losing your temper accomplishes absolutely nothing—your meal will never be served, you won't get that important train reservation, and your visa won't be extended. It's much better to smile, ask for some suggestions, and keep your sense of humor.

A clean and conservative appearance is absolutely necessary when dealing with border officials, customs clerks, local police, and petty bureaucrats. A great deal of ill feeling has been generated by budget travelers who dress immodestly. When in doubt, look at the locals and dress like they do. Aside from at beach resorts, you should never wear skimpy shorts, halter tops, low-cut blouses, or anything else that will offend the locals. Long slacks and a collared shirt are recommended for men in Asian cities. Women should keep well covered. Swimwear is only acceptable on the beach. If you're really an outrageous and flamboyant type of individual, go ahead and be yourself (Asians accept eccentric behavior from town crazies and oddball Westerners), otherwise, dress conservatively and try to blend in local society.

Since many Asians believe the head the home of the soul, it's considered impolite to touch anyone's head or physically stand over anybody. On the other hand, the feet are considered the lowest parts of the body, which makes it grossly disrespectful to place your feet on tables or point them at anyone. When sitting on a bare floor, tuck your feet carefully under your body or at least point them away from your host. The left hand is also unclean and should not be used to eat, receive gifts, or shake hands. Aggressive stances such as crossing or waving your arms are also considered boorish.

WARNINGS

Theft

Theft can be a problem in Southeast Asia. Losing your passport, air ticket, traveler's checks, and cash can be a devastating experience. Each country and each city seems to have its own peculiar type of thief—razor-blade artists on Bangkok buses, the hooked-pole trick in Kuta, trapdoor thieves in Manila—but with a certain amount of caution you can hold the damage down to a minimum. First, bring as few valuables as possible. Leave the jewelry, flashy camera bags, and other signs of wealth at home. To speed up the replacement of valuable documents, keep a duplicate copy of all

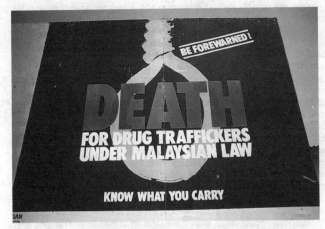

Just say no to drugs while traveling in Southeast Asia.

valuable papers separate from the papers themselves. Immediately report any theft to the local police and obtain a written report. Check the security of your hotel room and ask for a room with barred windows and a private lock. Valuables should be checked in the hotel safe and an accurate receipt obtained. Be cautious about fellow travelers, especially in dormitories. Keep your pack in full sight whenever possible. Be cautious about pickpockets in crowds, on buses, during festivals, and at boat harbors. Finally, try to maintain a balance between suspicion and trust. Most Asians are honest, so don't get paranoid about everybody who wants to show you around or practice their English. Meeting the people will almost certainly provide your most cherished moments while on the road.

Drugs
Unless you care to spend the next 20 years of your life in an Asian prison, don't mess with drugs in Southeast Asia. In 1986 the Malaysian government *executed* two Australians on drug-smuggling charges. There are plenty of drugs floating around—from grass to mushrooms and smack—but hundreds of foreigners are arrested and thrown into prison each year. Beware of scams. Organized drug raids of budget travelers' hotels are conducted by local police who haul suspects down to jail and demand stiff fines. Taxi drivers often sell drugs to travelers and turn them in for the reward the and return of the drug! Drugs are not worth the risk.

The Black Market
Many travelers supplement their dwindling funds by buying goods in country A and selling them for a profit in country B. This works well when you're going from a country with low prices such as Hong Kong or Singapore to a country where imports are restricted or highly taxed, such as India. However, since all the countries of Southeast Asia (except Burma) are relatively open with modest trade barriers, smuggling is rarely very lucrative. Remember that smuggling is illegal and, to some degree, risky; you must carefully weigh any economic benefit against the risk.

Asian Bureaucracy
Dealing with immigration officials, ticket clerks, and tourist officials is much smoother if you dress properly and keep your emotions under control. As mentioned above, you must never lose your cool no matter how slow, mismanaged, or disorganized the situation. Yelling and table pounding will only screw things up for you—in fact, Asian paper pushers *enjoy* slowing things up for the obnoxious foreigner. Smile, be polite, try some humor, and then firmly ask for their help and suggestions. Stubborn bureaucrats can suddenly become extraordinarily helpful to the cool tourist who knows how to play the game. Small tips discreetly slipped to the proper official will also speed things up. Bribery may seem anathema to most Westerners, but in Eastern societies it's considered a normal and perfectly acceptable way of con-

ducting business. If the request seéms high, it's perfectly OK to negotiate for a lower rate!

AIDS

Love and lust in Southeast Asia have taken an ugly turn since authorities first detected AIDS in 1984. According to a government survey released in 1992, Thailand alone has over 300,000 HIV-positive cases, while several thousand people had developed AIDS-Related Complex. The World Health Organization (WHO) reckons that AIDS could infect over five million Southeast Asians by the year 2000.

Unlike in the Western world, heterosexual sex—not gay sex or intravenous drug use—is the most common source of AIDS in Southeast Asia. The scourge has moved from the prostitution industries of Thailand and the Philippines to all other countries. Former Thai Population and Community Development Association (PDA) head Mechai Viravaidhya estimates that 50% of the prostitutes in Thailand now carry the virus, and that up to 10% of the male population are infected. WHO recently reported over 200 HIV-positive cases in Singapore, 200-300 new cases each month in Malaysia, a rapid rise in the once-untouched countries of Vietnam and Cambodia, and a frightening increase in Indonesia, Burma, and Laos.

The eerie quality of the raging epidemic is its invisibility. Most of those infected with AIDS have not yet developed symptoms and continue to engage in prostitution, unwittingly infecting their customers. Southeast Asia's sex-for-money trade will continue growing into the mid-1990s. And so will AIDS. Sexually active Westerners and Thais alike would do well to practice the only proven form of safe sex: complete abstinence.

Women Travelers

Should women travel alone in Southeast Asia? I have talked to dozens of solo women travelers and the general agreement is that most of Southeast Asia is a great place for the female traveler. Crime rates are lower than in the West, plus the Buddhist societies of Thailand and Burma as well as the Chinese societies of Hong Kong and Singapore have always placed great emphasis on respect for females. Problems of harassment are limited to conservative Muslim areas such as rural Malaysia and Indonesia. Female travelers in these regions should keep well covered, travel with a companion, and avoid getting into potentially dangerous situations.

ADVENTURE AND ALTERNATIVE TRAVEL

ADVENTURE TRAVEL

Almost 30 years ago a small English company began organizing truck journeys from London to Nepal, spawning an industry now encompassing over 100 companies which specialize in off-the-beaten-track destinations. Most of the trips still revolve around the big favorites such as trekking in Nepal and animal safaris in Africa, but a growing number are now directed toward Southeast Asia. All emphasize small groups, experienced guides, and the importance of low-impact travel. Costs average US$100-150 daily exclusive of airfare.

Some expeditions are rather mundane and can be easily accomplished by the independent traveler at far lower cost. Others, such as isolated river journeys, are virtually impossible to attempt without professional assistance. Adventure-travel companies fall into three categories: wholesalers who organize and promote their exclusive journeys, retailers who market a wide variety of wholesalers, and mixed vendors who sell both in-house expeditions and third-party trips. Contact the following for catalogs and detailed trip dossiers before booking through your local travel agent.

American Companies

Over 20 companies throughout the world organize adventure tours to Southeast Asia and gladly mail thick catalogs and detailed trip dossiers. Call everybody and enjoy their temptations.

Mountain Travel-Sobek: The largest adventure-travel operator on the West Coast offers over 140 different worldwide trips organized both in-house and by outside agents. Their 90-page catalog includes descriptions, photos, and day-by-day itineraries. 6420 Fairmount Ave., El Cerrito, CA 94530, tel. (510) 527-8100, (800) 227-2384, fax (510) 525-7710.

Adventure Center: One-stop source for American companies and English adventure-travel operators such as Explore, Encounter Overland, and Dragoman. Experienced and dependable. 1311 63rd St., Suite 200, Emeryville, CA 94608, tel. (510) 654-1879, (800) 227-8747, (800) 228-8747 in California.

Overseas Adventure Travel: The largest adventure-travel company on the East Coast specializes in cultural and natural journeys throughout Asia, including a two-week excursion to Thailand. Guide credentials are very impressive. 349 Broadway, Cambridge, MA 02139, tel. (617) 876-0533, (800) 221-0814, fax (617) 876-0455.

Wilderness Travel: Owner Bill Abbott states that almost 80% of his customers are repeats or referrals from past clients, a great record which speaks highly of this California-based operation. Southeast Asian tours include a cultural tour of Indonesia, expeditions to Borneo and New Guinea, and a 22-day journey from Thailand to Nepal. 801 Allston Way, Berkeley, CA 94710, tel. (800) 368-2794, (510) 548-0420, fax (510) 548-0347.

InnerAsia: *Very* first-class organization with unique treks in Nepal, Bhutan, India, and Indonesia. Recent additions include extremely rare visits to Laos, Cambodia, Vietnam, and the Arakan region of Burma, plus side trips to Thailand. 2627 Lombard St., San Francisco, CA 94123, tel. (415) 922-0448, (800) 777-8183.

Geo Expeditions: A 20-day cultural excursion to the historic capitals of Thailand and Burma. Box 3656, Sonora, CA 95370, tel. (800) 351-5041, fax (209) 532-1979.

Backroads Bicycle Touring: Bicycle journeys in northern Thailand from Chiang Mai to the Golden Triangle. 1516 Fifth St., Berkeley, CA 94710, tel. (510) 527-1555, (800) 245-3874, fax (510) 527-1444.

Asian Pacific Adventures: Standard vacations and an unusual biking tour on Phuket in southern Thailand. 826 South Sierra Bonita Ave., Los Angeles, CA 90036, tel. (213) 935-3156, (800) 825-1680 outside California.

All Adventure Travel: This retailer sells adventure-travel tours from all the leading operators such as Bolder Adventures, Journeys, and Asian Pacific Adventures. Box 4307, Boulder, CO 80306, tel. (800) 537-4025.

Creative Adventure Club: Alternative travel adventures to Southeast Asia, including jeep safaris in northern Thailand and the Asian Express from Singapore to Bangkok. Request a sample copy of *Adventures* magazine from this small but highly original tour group. Box 1918, Costa Mesa, CA 92626, tel. (714) 545-5888, (800) 544-5088.

European Companies
Explore: Traditional tours and adventure-travel programs, including Thailand trekking, the Malay Peninsula, and an unusual schooner voyage through Indonesia's Nusa Tenggara. 7 High St., Aldershot, Hants, England, GU11 1BH, tel. (0252) 319448.

Encounter Overland: Europe's most experienced adventure-travel operator offers the classic 11-week overlander from London to Kathmandu and a 30-day journey from Bali to Bangkok. 267 Brompton Rd., London SW5 9JA.

Exodus: English adventure operator with a 24-day volcano-climbing expedition in Indonesia and several treks through Borneo. 9 Weir Rd., London SW12 OLT, tel. (01) 675-5550.

Dragoman: Small company with overland expeditions across Africa, Asia, and South America plus a three-week Southeast Asian extension. 10 Riverside, Framlingham, Suffolk IP13 9AG, England, tel. (0728) 724184.

Australian Companies
World Expeditions: Australia's largest adventure-travel company sponsors three Thai excursions, including a tropical sail from Pattaya to Ko Samet. Third floor, 377 Sussex St., Sydney, NSW 200, tel. (02) 264-3366.

Intrepid Travel: Southeast Asian adventures including river rafting, trekking in Khao Sok National Park, and research expeditions to new regions. 801 Nicholson St., North Carlton 3054, Victoria, tel. (03) 387-3484, fax (03) 387-9460.

Specialized Companies
Some of the best tours are arranged through American agencies that specialize in specific regions rather than the entire world. Additional operators are described in the Indonesia chapter.

Absolute Asia: Ken Fish and Sandy Ferguson, in conjunction with a Thai-based company, operate an amazing range of personalized tours to some of the most remote and untouched regions in Thailand, Laos, Cambodia, and Vietnam. Recent excursions include an Issan and

Laotian Explorer, trekking in northern Thailand, and the world's first kosher tour of Thailand, with kosher meals and synagogue visits! 155 West 68th St., Suite 525, New York, NY 10023, tel. (800) 736-8187, fax (212) 595-9672.

Bolder Adventures: Rusty and Marilyn Staff are first-person experts who organize tours to both familiar and remote destinations in Thailand. With the help of local contacts and experienced professionals such as the author of the best-selling independent guide to Thailand (not me, the other guy), Rusty and Marilyn take you to national parks and ancient capitals. Box 1279, Boulder, CO 80306, tel. (800) 397-5917, fax (303) 443-7078.

Himalayan Travel: Sales agent for one of Thailand's largest alternative tour operators, with trekking and rafting in the Golden Triangle, elephant safaris near Mae Hong Son, and bicycle tours in the north. Also, conventional tours, beach resorts, and discount rates at better hotels. 112 Prospect St., Stamford, CT 06901, tel. (800) 225-2380, fax (203) 359-3669.

Scuba Diving
Detailed descriptions of diving possibilities are given under each country, but professional assistance can be obtained from the following dive operators. More dive groups are listed in *Skin Diver* magazine.

See and Sea Travel Service: One of America's largest and most respected dive operators leads groups to the Philippines, Indonesia, and Thailand. The owner, Carl Roessler, strongly urges all divers to try his live-aboard dive cruises rather than the typical land-based dive. 50 Francisco St., Suite 205, San Francisco, CA 94133, tel. (415) 434-3400, (800) 348-9778.

Tropical Adventures: A dive wholesaler representing over 35 fully outfitted live-aboard boats throughout the world, including the 147-foot *Island Explorer* in Indonesia and the 98-foot *Fantasea* in Thailand. 111 Second St. N, Seattle, WA 98109, tel. (206) 441-3483, (800) 247-3483, fax (206) 441-5431.

Poseidon Ventures Tours: Live-aboard options include the 100-foot MV *Tropical Princess* in Indonesia and the MV *New Lady of the Sea II* in the Philippines. 359 San Miguel Dr., Newport Beach, CA 92660, tel. (714) 644-5344, (800) 854-9334, fax (714) 644-5392.

RESPONSIBLE TOURISM

Tourism, some say, broadens the mind, enriches our lives, spreads prosperity, dissolves political barriers, and promotes international peace. While concurring with most of these sentiments, others feel that mass tourism often destroys what it seeks to discover; it disrupts the economy by funneling dollars into international travel consortiums rather than local enterprise; exploits the people, who find themselves ever more dependent on the tourist dollar; and reinforces cultural stereotypes rather than encouraging authentic dialogue between peoples. Responsible tourism is a movement that attempts to address both the virtues and the vices of mass tourism by making each traveler more sensitive to these issues. The fundamental tenet is that travel should benefit *both* the traveler and the host country, and that travelers should travel softly and thoughtfully, with great awareness of their impact on the people and the environment.

Spearheading this movement is the Center for Responsible Tourism (P.O. Box 827, San Anselmo, CA 94979, tel. 415-258-6594), a Christian group that holds annual conferences on the impact of mass tourism, publishes a thought-provoking newsletter, and offers workshops on how to lead a responsible tour. Visitors are encouraged to seek out low-impact and locally based travel experiences by patronizing cafes, guesthouses, and pensions owned by indigenous people. Their guidelines:

1. Travel in a spirit of humility, with a genuine desire to meet and talk with the local people.
2. Sensitize yourself to the feelings of your hosts.
3. Cultivate the habit of listening and observing, rather than merely hearing and seeing.
4. Realize that other people's concepts of time and thought patterns may be dramatically different from—not inferior to—your own.
5. Seek out the richness of foreign cultures, not just the escapist lures of tourist posters.
6. Respect and understand local customs.
7. Ask questions and keep a sense of humor.
8. Understand your role as a guest in the country; do not expect special privileges.
9. Spend wisely and bargain with compassion.
10. Fulfill any obligations or promises you make to local people.
11. Reflect on your daily experiences; seek to deepen your understanding of the people, the culture, and the environment.

ALTERNATIVE TRAVEL

Perhaps the most important and certainly the most captivating travel book published in recent years is Arthur Frommer's *New World of Travel.* As the doyen of American travel writing states in his introduction, "After 30 years of writing standard guidebooks, I began to see that most of the vacation journeys undertaken by Americans were trivial and bland, devoid of important content, cheaply commercial, and unworthy of our better instincts and ideals." Frommer's book carefully details the alternatives to conventional travel: vacation resorts that stretch your mind and change your life; political travel to widen your world view; selfless vacations for international volunteers; overlanding; low-cost language schools. He also includes a gold mine of information on budget travel and ways to meet the people. As he so eloquently writes, "Travel in all price ranges is scarcely worth the effort unless it is associated with people, with learning and ideas. To have meaning at all, travel must involve an encounter with new and different outlooks and beliefs. It must broaden our horizons, provide comparative lessons, show us how those in other communities are responding to their social and industrial problems."

The following section attempts to expand on his guidelines and suggestions for alternative travel in Southeast Asia. Travel books are collaborations between authors and readers. While I've tried to include a broad selection of alternative-travel groups and organizations, correspondence from readers is an essential ingredient for future editions. Please write and let me know about new travel groups, clubs, and programs that deserve to be mentioned. I'll study the information, contact the organization, and pass along my impressions. Send your letters, comments, and suggestions to Carl Parkes, *Southeast Asia Handbook,* Moon Publications, P.O. Box 3040, Chico, CA 95927-3040 USA.

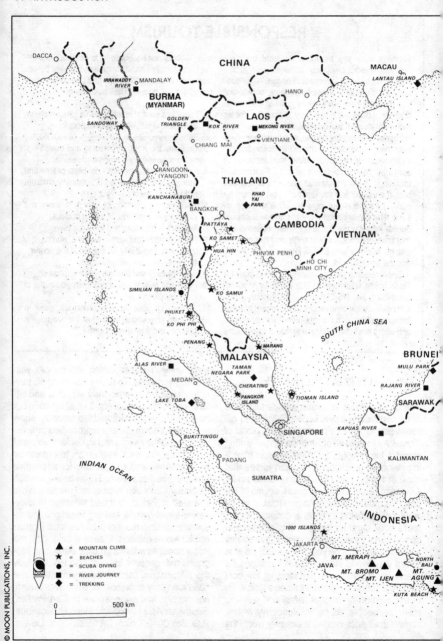

MOUNTAIN CLIMB = ▲
BEACHES = ★
SCUBA DIVING = ●
RIVER JOURNEY = ■
TREKKING = ◆

0   500 km

© MOON PUBLICATIONS, INC.

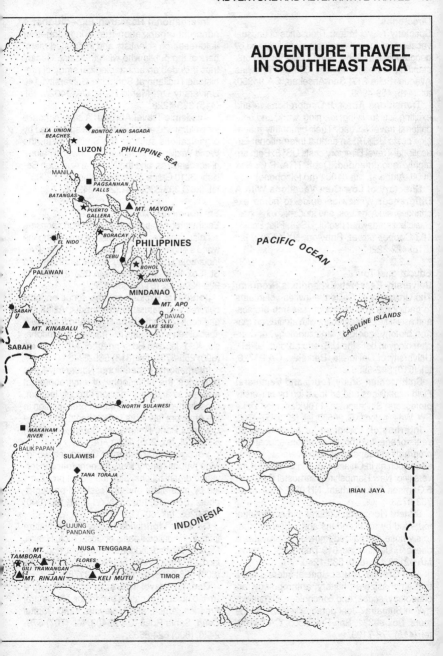

ADVENTURE TRAVEL IN SOUTHEAST ASIA

LA UNION BEACHES
BONTOC AND SAGADA
LUZON
PHILIPPINE SEA
MANILA
PAGSANHAN FALLS
BATANGAS
PUERTO GALLERA
MT. MAYON
EL NIDO
BORACAY
PHILIPPINES
PACIFIC OCEAN
CEBU
BOHOL
PALAWAN
CAMIGUIN
MINDANAO
MT. APO
SABAH
DAVAO
MT. KINABALU
LAKE SEBU
CAROLINE ISLANDS
SABAH
NORTH SULAWESI
MAKAHAM RIVER
BALIK PAPAN
SULAWESI
TANA TORAJA
IRIAN JAYA
UJUNG PANDANG
INDONESIA
MT. TAMBORA
NUSA TENGGARA
GILI TRAWANGAN
FLORES
MT. RINJANI
KELI MUTU
TIMOR

Directories

Specialty Travel Index: Thousands of unusual vacation listings indexed both by activity and by geographical location. Send US$8 for two outstanding 150-page catalogs. 305 San Anselmo Avenue, Suite 217, San Anselmo, CA 94960, tel. (415) 459-4900.

Transitions Abroad: Comprehensive and exciting lists for living, learning, work, and educational travel abroad. Their bimonthly magazine costs US$18; an annual International Educational Travel Directory costs US$8. Both are highly recommended. Dept. TRA, P.O. Box 3000, Amherst, MA 01004 (no telephone).

Directory of Low Cost Vacations With A Difference: Worldwide guide to home exchanges, study groups, and student exchanges. Basic but somewhat useful. US$8. Pilot Books, 103 Cooper Street, Babylon, NY 11702, tel. (516) 422-2225.

Educational Tours

University Research Expeditions Program: The University of California invites volunteers to participate in a variety of research projects and assist field researchers with studies on marine biology, zoology, anthropology, and archaeology in both the U.S. and abroad. UREP, University of California, Berkeley, CA 94720, tel. (510) 642-6586.

Smithsonian Study Tours and Seminars: Field expeditions and art tours led by university professors. Smithsonian, 1100 Jefferson Drive SW, Washington D.C. 20560, tel. (202) 357-4700.

Interhostel: Designed for adults over 50 years of age, Interhostel sponsors educational programs in cooperation with overseas universities such as in Chiang Mai and Bangkok. University of New Hampshire Interhostel Program, 6 Garrison Ave., Durham, NH 03824, tel. (800) 733-9753.

Distant Horizons: Cultural and educational tours led by art historians and museum curators whose specialized knowledge provides a deeper understanding. 619 Tremont St., Boston, MA 02118, tel. (800) 333-1240.

Joel Greene Tours: Special-interest tours that emphasize art history, anthropology, archaeology, scuba, and conchology. Conchology? In Sumatra? Joel personally leads all the tours. Box 99331, San Francisco, CA 94109, tel. (415) 776-7199.

International Research Expeditions: A nonprofit organization that brings together field-research scientists and interested members of the public who wish to assist. Recent trips included an archaeological study of prehistoric Thailand at Songkhla University. 140 University Dr., Menlo Park, CA 94025, tel. (415) 323-4228.

Academic Travel Abroad: A clearinghouse for cultural and educational tours sponsored by organizations such as the Smithsonian, the World Wildlife Fund, museums, university alumni associations, and the National Audubon Society. 3210 Grace St., Washington, D.C. 20007, tel. (202) 333-3355, fax (202) 342-0317.

Environmental Tours

Earthwatch: This nonprofit institution sponsors scholarly field research aimed at preserving the world's endangered habitats and species. Projects cost US$800-2500. 680 Mount Auburn St., Box 403N, Watertown, MA 02272, tel. (617) 926-8200, fax (617) 926-8532.

Journeys: Explorations that focus on local cultures and natural environments. Asian expeditions concentrate on Nepal and India, with specialized excursions in Thailand and Indonesia. 4011 Jackson Rd., Ann Arbor, MI 48103, tel. (800) 255-8735, fax (313) 665-2945.

International Expeditions: Nature travel that promotes the philosophy of environmental awareness and conservation through tourism. Closely involved with rainforest preservation in the Amazon; few tours to Southeast Asia. One Environs Park, Helena, AL 35080, tel. (800) 633-4734, fax (205) 428-1714.

Voyagers International: Organizes worldwide natural-history tours for nonprofit conservation organizations, plus individual programs led by naturalists and professional photographers. Box 915, Ithaca, NY 14851, tel. (800) 633-0299, fax (607) 257-3699.

Questers Worldwide Nature Tours: Nature tours to the national parks of Costa Rica, Hawaii, Mexico, Trinidad, Indonesia, Malaysia, and Thailand. 257 Park Ave. S, New York, NY 10010, tel. (800) 468-8668, fax (212) 473-0178.

Geostar Travel Tours: Small outfit with a limited number of nature expeditions to Central America, Africa, and Malaysia. 1240 Capital Court, Santa Rosa, CA 95403, tel. (707) 579-2420, (800) 624-6633.

Select Tours: Premier travel programs to Southeast Asia in conjunction with some of the finest land operators in the region. A small company with unique offerings to remote locations. P.O. Box 210, Redondo Beach, CA 90277, tel. (213) 343-0880, (800) 356-6680, fax (213) 318-2325.

Nature Expeditions International: Journeys to Africa, India, and treks through the rainforests of Borneo. P.O. Box 11496, Eugene, OR 97440, tel. (800) 869-0639.

Special-interest Tours

Close Up Expeditions: Small group photographic travel adventures designed to meet the needs of shutterbugs. Tours are led by professionals to Thailand and Burma. Lyon Travel Services, 1031 Ardmore Avenue, Oakland, CA 94610, tel. (510) 465-8955.

Trains Unlimited: Railroad-enthusiast tours to South America, Europe, and South Africa. Future plans include a visit to the steam locomotives in the Philippines. 235 West Pueblo Avenue, Reno, NV 89509, tel. (702) 329-5590, (800) 359-4870.

Valour Tours: Military tours for veterans to the battlefields of Europe and the Pacific Theater. Southeast Asian programs include Bataan day in Manila and the Leyte landing. Box 1617, Schoonmaker Building, Sausalito, CA 94965, tel. (415) 332-7850.

Victor Emanuel Nature Tours: A specialized operator with birding expeditions to Indonesia and Borneo. P.O. Box 33006, Austin, TX 78764, tel. (800) 328-VENT.

Archaeological Tours: Specialized tours led by distinguished scholars such as the director of Burmese studies at Northern Illinois University. 30 East 42nd St. #1202, New York, NY 10017, tel. (212) 986-3054, fax (212) 370-1561.

Big Five Expeditions: Nature and photography tours to Africa, India, and Indonesia. 2151 E. Dublin-Granville, Suite 215, Columbus, OH 43229, tel. (800) 541-2790, fax (605) 898-0039.

Reality Tours

Augsburg College: The Center for Global Education coordinates global education and foreign-policy seminars which examine the problems of international development from the perspective of the poor and disenfranchised. Travel groups have studied health care in Nicaragua,

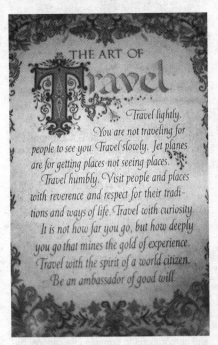

THE ART OF *Travel*

Travel lightly.
You are not traveling for
people to see you. Travel slowly. Jet planes
are for getting places not seeing places.
Travel humbly. Visit people and places
with reverence and respect for their tradi-
tions and ways of life. Travel with curiosity.
It is not how far you go, but how deeply
you go that mines the gold of experience.
Travel with the spirit of a world citizen.
Be an ambassador of good will

women of color in El Salvador, and land reform in the Philippines. 731 21st Avenue S, Minneapolis, MN 55454, tel. (612) 330-1159.

Global Exchanges: People-to-people political tours to learn firsthand about pressing issues confronting Third World nations. Meetings are arranged in the Philippines with labor organizers, peace activists, farmers, environmentalists, and government leaders concerned with land reform and the American bases. 2940 16th Street, Suite 307, San Francisco, CA 94103, tel. (415) 255-7296.

Institute of Noetic Sciences: Alternative tours that seek to harmonize the human-potential movement with spiritual healings. Tours led by Bruce Carpenter include Bali, the Feminine Path of Healing, and a nature/healing tour of Malaysia. 475 Gate 5 Rd., Sausalito, CA 94965, tel. (415) 331-5650.

Food First: Reality tours that offer firsthand experience of the economic and political realities of the poor in the U.S. and abroad. Past groups have visited Haiti, Nicaragua, and the Philippines in conjunction with the Center for Global

Education. 145 Ninth Street, San Francisco, CA 94103, tel. (415) 864-8555.

Global Volunteers: This nonprofit organization conducts three-week volunteer work experiences in rural communities in Africa, Asia, the South Pacific, and in a small tropical hamlet in Central Java. 375 E. Little Canada Rd., St. Paul, MN 55117, tel. (800) 487-1074.

Study Abroad

Council on International Educational Exchange: America's foremost organization concerned with international education and student travel, CIEE and its travel subsidiary, Council Travel, are an excellent source of information on study and work abroad. Ask for *Work, Study, Travel Abroad* for US$13, *Volunteer* for US$9, and the free booklet *Basic Facts on Study Abroad.* Undergraduate programs on Indonesian culture and language are given in Bandung, on Chinese studies in Hong Kong, on Thai culture in Chiang Mai. 205 East 42nd Street, New York, NY 10017, tel. (212) 661-1414.

Institute for International Education: The largest educational-exchange agency in America works closely with the U.S. government, World Bank, universities, private foundations, and corporations to promote international development. Their reference books are expensive but extremely comprehensive. 809 United Nations Plaza, New York, NY 10017, tel. (212) 883-8200.

World Learning: The oldest organization of its kind in the world, World Learning promotes world understanding through homestays, language training, and graduate study programs. Semester abroad programs are given in Bali and Chiang Mai. College Semester Abroad, School for International Training, Kipling Road, Brattleboro, VT 05301, tel. (800) 451-4465.

University of California: Semester abroad programs at Chulalongkorn University in Bangkok and at the Indonesian Dance Institutes in Bali and Bandung. Education Abroad, UCSB, Santa Barbara, CA 93106, tel. (805) 961-4139.

Southeast Asian Universities: Applications can also be made directly to universities abroad, although the response rate is rather dismal. Try Dr. Mathana Santiwat, Academic Affairs, Bangkok University, 40/4 Rama IV Road, Bangkok 10110; International Students Program, Mahidol University, Nakhon Pathom 73170; Dr. Thomas Lee, International Studies Program, Chinese University, Shatin, New Territories, Hong Kong. Further suggestions are appreciated.

Elderhostel: A nonprofit organization that offers those over 60 years of age a broad array of inexpensive, short-term academic programs hosted by educational institutions around the world. Southeast Asian destinations include homestays in Bali and cultural studies in Thailand. Highly experienced. 75 Federal St., Boston, MA 02110, tel. (617) 426-8056.

Working Abroad

Teaching English: One of the few opportunities for working in Southeast Asia is teaching English in Hong Kong or Bangkok. Pay is very low (US$3-8 per hour) when compared to Japan or Korea (US$10-25 per hour), but you'll have an opportunity to study the culture, attempt to learn the language, and develop friendships with the people. Jobs in Hong Kong can quickly be picked up at the Traveller's Hostel in Chungking Mansions. Teaching opportunities in Bangkok are limited to universities and teacher's colleges, private English-language schools, and fly-by-night operations run from somebody's house. Universities located throughout the country pay about US$400 per month plus a small housing allowance. Private English-language schools such as the American University (AUA) and YMCA pay well but the competition is keen. Fly-by-night language schools which advertise in the guesthouses on Khao San Road are the lowest-paying jobs.

Habitat for Humanity: An ecumenical, grassroots, Christian volunteer organization which builds homes for the poor and homeless throughout the world, including the Philippines. Good enough for Jimmy Carter, good enough for you. Habitat and Church Streets, Americus, GA 31709, tel. (912) 924-6935.

Worldteach: A social-service program of Harvard University which has placed over 500 volunteers in Africa, Central America, and throughout Thailand. Volunteers teach English, help run health clinics, and stay overseas from nine to 12 months. A highly regarded, professional organization. Harvard Insitute for International Development, One Eliot St., Cambridge, MA 02138, tel. (617) 495-5527, fax (617) 495-1239.

Homestay Programs

Servas: The world's largest homestay program is designed for thoughtful travelers who wish to build world peace and international understanding through person-to-person contacts. Travelers' fees are US$55 annually, while hosts contribute US$15 per year. Servas has thousands of host families in Europe and America but only a handful in Asia. 11 John Street, Room 407, New York, NY 10038, tel. (212) 267-0252.

Hospitality Exchange: A small but spirited homestay group useful in America and Western Europe. Hosts tend to be college-educated professionals in their mid-forties perhaps acting on cooperative values fostered in the sixties. Membership is only US$15 but you must be willing to be both a host and a traveler! 4908 E. Culver #2, Phoenix, AZ 85008, tel. (602) 267-8600.

ENVIRONMENTAL AND HUMAN-RIGHTS ORGANIZATIONS

Rainforest Issues

Southeast Asia's rainforests, once the most bountiful on the planet, are disappearing at an alarming rate. Unless the destruction is stopped, most will be gone or seriously damaged by the year 2010. Saving the rainforests is an immensely complicated task, but you can help by supporting the following organizations. Also: don't buy tropical-hardwood products such as rosewood and mahogany furniture; join the worldwide outcry against the destruction of indigenous tribal homelands by writing directly to the governments involved; and tell the World Bank to stop funding rainforest-killing development projects. Write to your congressman, corporate executives, and the editor of your local newspaper. Most importantly, remain concerned while you travel through Southeast Asia; tourism is the world's biggest industry and the discriminating traveler thus has powerful leverage against the despoliation of the environment.

Rainforest Action Network: RAN and the World Rainforest Movement is a worldwide network of concerned citizens who hope to crystallize concern and devise campaigns to stem the destruction of the tropical rainforests. Membership includes a monthly newsletter which covers battles to protect the forests and a quarterly report drawn from its worldwide affiliates. Membership is

---

SAVE THE WILDLIFE

As Asian rainforests are destroyed by man, the first casualties are wildlife. Rainforests are home to 90% of the world's primates, such as monkeys and orangutans; 80% of the world's insects; and half of the world's plants. According to the U.S. Academy of Sciences, a four-square-mile patch of forest will hold 125 different mammals, 400 species of birds, and hundreds of reptiles and amphibians. The region's endangered species include famous animals such as the orangutan, the Asian elephant, the Sumatran rhino, and the Philippines eagle, plus less-well-known animals such as Ridley's leaf-nosed bat, the flat-headed cat, and the violin beetle; an international study lists 166 endangered species in Southeast Asia. The end of the rainforests will bring wildlife destruction comparable only to the mass extinction that wiped out the dinosaurs 65 million years ago.

Spreading the message has largely been the work of rainforest groups, plus the efforts of the World Wildlife Fund and Friends of the Earth. But you, as a traveler, can also help by refusing to purchase animal goods made from protected or endangered species. The United States is the world's largest consumer of wildlife! Travelers often don't realize that seemingly innocuous products made from hides, shells, and feathers—and on sale in public markets in Asia—are often illegal and life-threatening souvenirs. Regulations are complex, but prohibited products include *all* sea-turtle items, Philippine crocodile hides, pangolin (anteater) leather from Thailand and Indonesia, most wild bird feathers, and all ivory products. Just as destructive is the purchase of coral items, since coral collection is directly responsible for the near-complete destruction of sea beds in many Southeast Asian countries. Prohibited items will be seized by customs officials, and you will risk a substantial fine: when in doubt, don't buy!

US$25/year. 450 Sansome St., Suite 700, San Francisco, CA 94111, tel. (415) 398-4404.

Nature Conservancy: An international agency that protects habitats through acquisition and purchase of rainforest land, a "debt-for-nature" swap which raises money for local environmental organizations. 1815 North Lynn Street, Arlington, VA 22209, tel. (703) 841-5300.

Rainforest Alliance: A small nonprofit organization dedicated to saving the forests with public-awareness programs, research into the timber industry, and publication of a quarterly newsletter. Membership is US$20/ year. 295 Madison Avenue, Suite 1804, New York, NY 10017, tel. (212) 599-5060.

Sahabat Alam Malaysia: The most influential of all rainforest-preservation groups in Southeast Asia, SAM also works to stop the logging in Penan ancestral lands in Borneo. Unfortunately, they rarely respond to letters. Membership is US$25/year. 43 Salween Road, Penang 10050, Malaysia.

Human Rights

Violations of human rights are not confined to any particular country or political system but are found throughout half the countries in the world, including those of Southeast Asia. Jailing of political dissidents, torture of those who speak out for human freedoms, press censorship, intimidation of the judiciary, manipulation of religion and nationalism to control the population—all these are widespread problems throughout the region. Important issues are briefly discussed in the text, but further details can be obtained from the following organizations.

Amnesty International: An independent worldwide movement working for the release of all prisoners of conscience, fair and prompt trials for political prisoners, and an end to torture and executions. Amnesty International has documented the torture of political dissidents in Burma, examined the gross violations of political and religious freedoms in Indonesia, and the "salvaging" of innocent civilians in the Philippines. They regularly publish country reports and an annual report which summarizes the human rights situation in over 135 countries. 322 Eighth Avenue, New York, NY 10001, tel. (212) 807-8400.

Asia Watch: A widely respected nonprofit organization which promotes the legal and moral obligation of the U.S. government to demand human rights worldwide. Asia Watch and its affiliate organization, Human Rights Watch, send missions to countries where abuses take place, and expose to public view the discrepancies between what Asian countries claim and their actual practices. Membership US$40/year. 36 West 44th Street, New York, NY 10036, tel. (202) 371- 6592.

Senate Report on Human Rights: The United States Senate's annual report on human rights covers in great detail the issues of individual liberties (torture, arbitrary arrest, and denial of fair trail), civil liberties (freedom of speech, press, and religion), and political rights (fair and open elections, international supervision of human-rights violations). Most libraries will have a copy.

Survival International: The human rights of threatened tribal peoples from South America to Borneo are served by this English organization. Their booklet, *Pirates, Squatters and Poachers—The Political Ecology of the Native Peoples of Sarawak,* is highly recommended. 310 Edgware Road, London W2 1DY, tel. (01) 723-5535.

Cultural Survival: The economic, social, and cultural rights of indigenous peoples and ethnic minorities throughout the world are defended by this outstanding organization. Their authoritative *CS Quarterly* is included in the US$25 annual contribution. 11 Divinity Avenue, Cambridge, MA 02138, tel. (617) 495-2562.

SOURCES OF TRAVEL INFORMATION

Before leaving on your journey, it's important to read about and study the countries you'll be visiting. Begin by quickly surveying the "Sightseeing Highlights" in each chapter of this book for a look at the major attractions. Visit your library and check out a few of the books recommended below. Then mail a form letter requesting information to all the national tourist offices listed under each chapter. Both the quality and quantity vary widely; the offices of Hong Kong, Singapore, Thailand, and Malaysia are excellent sources, but those of Indonesia, the Philippines, and Burma have little to offer.

You might also contact the embassies and national airlines of each Southeast Asian country, since both often have better information than the tourist offices. Travel sections in major newspapers are another source of current travel news. Call the adventure and alternative-travel organizations listed above for their free catalogs and brochures. Useful U.S. government agencies include the Citizens Emergency Center (tel. 202-647-5226) for the latest travel advisories and emergency assistance, the Bureau of Public Affairs (tel. 202-647-6575) for travel government publications and telephone numbers of overseas embassies, and Desk Officers (tel. 202-647-4000) for specific information on each country.

Travel agents experienced with Southeast Asia are a godsend but as rare as whale's teeth; student travel agencies are your best hope. Best of all, seek out and talk with other travelers who have been to Southeast Asia. Then read, read, read.

Travel Newsletters, Magazines, And Clubs
Great Expeditions: Detailed, concise articles on off-the-beaten-track destinations. Geared to the young and adventurous traveler. Highly recommended. US$18/six issues. Free sample. P.O. Box 18036, Raleigh, NC 27609, tel. (800) 743-3639.

International Travel News: Big, opinionated, and highly informative monthly magazine with dozens of honest travel articles. Recent stories have included coverage of ceremonies in Indonesia, adventure in New Zealand, and the Italian Riviera, plus columns on cruises, readers' tips, and seniors abroad. An excellent deal. US$14/12 issues. 2120 28th Street, Sacramento, CA 95818, tel. (916) 457-3643.

Condé Nast Traveler: Outstanding writing, photography, and graphics plus hard-hitting commentary and authoritative advice make this the finest travel magazine on the market. Covers Europe, America, and Africa—but not much on Southeast Asia. US$15/12 issues. Box 52469, Boulder, CO 80321, tel. (800) 777-0700.

Globetrotters Club: England's leading club for independent/budget/world travelers. Membership includes a handbook, six annual newsletters, and a list of over 1,200 members who occasionally accept homestays. Monthly meetings are held in New York, Southern California, and in London at 52 St. Martin's Lane. Volunteers are encouraged to organize monthly travel slide shows in their communities. US$14/year, US$5 initiation fee. BCM/Roving, London WC1N 3XX, England.

Consumer Reports Travel Letter: A 12-page monthly newsletter with dependable advice on airline and hotel discounts, auto rentals, coupon books, rail travel, and a limited number of destinations. Overpriced but very professional. US$37/12 issues. Subscription Department, Box 51366, Boulder, CO 80321.

Travel Bookstores
Bookstores located in major cities carry a mind-boggling selection of travel guides, maps, accessories, and literature. For rare, out-of-print editions contact Cellar Books at (313) 861-1776, Oriental Book Company (no catalog; visit them at 1713 East Colorado Boulevard, Pasadena, CA 91106, tel. 818-577-2413), and Oxus Books (121 Astonville Street, London SW18 5AQ, tel. 01-870-3854). The following bookstores offer catalogs:

Book Passage	(800) 321-9785
Easy Going	(415) 843-3533
	(800) 233-3533
Phileas Fogg's	(800) 233-FOGG
	(800) 533-FOGG
Complete Traveller	(212) 685-9007
Back Door Press	(206) 771-8308
Travel Books Unlimited	(301) 951-8533
Globe Corner	(800) 358-6013
Forsyth Travel	(800) 367-7984

TELEPHONE NUMBERS FOR PUBLISHERS SPECIALIZING IN SOUTHEAST ASIA

American Publishers

Contact the following private companies for their latest catalogs:

Moon Publications	(800) 345-5473
Hippocrene	(718) 454-1391
Humanities Press	(800) 221-3845
Globe Pequot Press	(800) 243-0495
Third World Resources	(415) 835-4692
Intercultural Press	(207) 846-5168
Lawyers Human Rights	(212) 629-6170
Greenwood Press	(203) 226-3571
Waveland Press	(312) 634-0091
Schenkman	(802) 767-3702
Anima	(717) 267-0087

University Presses:

Yale	(203) 432-0940
Cornell	(800) 666-2211
Columbia	(914) 591-9111
University of California	(800) 822-6657
University of Hawaii	(800) 234-5467

BOOK CATALOGS

A small number of publishers specialize in books on Southeast Asia.

Asian Publishers
Many of the best books on Asia and Southeast Asia are published overseas and rarely distributed in the West. Contact:

Oxford Press: 18th floor, Warwick House, Taikoo Trading Estate, 28 Tong Chong St., Quarry Bay, Hong Kong.

Times Editions: Times Centre, 1 New Industrial Rd., Singapore 1953.

Graham Brash: 36 C Prinsep St., Singapore 0718.

R. Ian Lloyd Productions: 18A Tanjong Pagar Rd., Singapore 0208.

Select Books: 19 Tanglin Rd. #03-15, Tanglin Shopping Center, Singapore 1024.

Institute of Southeast Asian Studies: Heng Mui Keng Terrace, Pasir Panjang, Singapore 0511.

Asia Books: 5 Sukumvit Rd. Soi 61, Bangkok 10112.

D.K. Books: 90/21-25 Rajaprarob, Makkasan, GPO 2916, Bangkok 10400.

White Lotus Press: GPO Box 1141, Bangkok 10501.

Either I am a traveller in ancient times, and faced with a prodigious spectacle which would be almost entirely unintelligible to me and might, indeed, provoke me to mockery or disgust; or I am a traveller of our own day, hastening in search of a vanished reality. In either case I am the loser.

—Claude Lévi-Strauss, Tristes Tropiques

"Are you a god?" they asked. "No." "An Angel?" "No." "A saint?" "No." "Then, what are you?" Buddha answered, "I am awake."

—Buddha

Between the Idea and the Reality . . . Falls the Shadow.

—T.S. Eliot

SUGGESTED READINGS

♦ Buruma, Ian. *God's Dust: A Modern Asian Journey*. New York: Farrar, Straus and Giroux, 1989. Buruma examines a familiar dilemma—can the nations of Southeast Asia modernize without losing their cultural identities?—with great wit, insight, and a sharp sense of humor. His observations on the decline of Burma, the confused Filipino sense of history, and the monstrous contradictions of contemporary Singapore make this an excellent resource for all visitors contemplating travel to Southeast Asia.

♦ Eames, Andrew. *Crossing the Shadow Line*. Vermont: Hodder and Stoughton, 1986. Young and talented Andrew Eames spent two years of his life probing the remote corners of Southeast Asia, from northern Thailand's Golden Triangle to an adventurous sail on Makassar schooners between Bali and Irian Jaya. A great tale spiced with prodigious amounts of humor and pathos. Highly recommended.

♦ Fenton, James. *All the Wrong Places*. New York: Atlantic Monthly Press, 1988. James Fenton, journalist, poet, and critic, is one of the new breed of travel writers: jaundiced, self-indulgent, hard-hitting, and more concerned with personal impressions than scholarly dissertation. The result is a mesmerizing book full of great perception, especially his observations of the Philippines.

♦ Iyer, Pico. *Video Night in Kathmandu*. New York: Vintage, 1988. Iyer's incongruous collection of essays uncovers the Coca-colonisation of the Far East in a refreshingly humorous and perceptive style. His heartbreaking accounts of decay in the Philippines, brothels in Bangkok, and cultural collisions in Bali form some of the finest travel writing in recent times. Highly recommended.

♦ Kirch, John. *Music in Every Room: Around the World in a Bad Mood*. New York: McGraw Hill, 1984. An offbeat look at both the pains and the pleasures of contemporary Asian travel. Lively, opinionated, and immensely readable.

♦ Nelson, Theodora, and Andrea Gross. *Good Books For The Curious Traveler—Asia and the South Pacific*. Boulder: Johnson Publishing, 1989. Outstanding in-depth reviews of over 350 books including almost 50 titles to Southeast Asia. Written with sensitivity and great insight. The authors also run a service that matches books with a traveler's itinerary. Write to Travel Source, 20103 La Roda Court, Cupertino, CA 95014, tel. (408) 446-0600.

♦ Reimer, Jo, and Ronald and Caryl Krannich. *Shopping in Exotic Places*. Virginia: Impact Publications, 1987. Step-by-step guide to the secrets of shopping in Southeast Asia. Detailed descriptions of shopping centers, arcades, factory outlets, and exclusive boutiques in Hong Kong, Singapore, Thailand, and Indonesia.

♦ Richter, Linda. *The Politics of Tourism in Asia*. Hawaii: University of Hawaii Press, 1989. A scholarly study of the complex political problems that confront the tourist industries in Thailand, the Philippines, and other Asian destinations. Filled with surprising conclusions about the impact of multinational firms and the importance of targeting grass-roots travelers rather than upscale tourists.

♦ Schwartz, Brian. *A World of Villages*. New York: Crown Publishers, 1986. A superbly written journal of a six-year journey to the most remote villages in the world. Filled with tales of unforgettable people and lands of infinite variety and beauty.

SUGGESTED READINGS

♦ Shales, Melissa, editor. *The Traveler's Handbook*. Connecticut: Globe Pequot Press, 1988. Fifth edition of the award-winning guide, which puts together the contributions of over 80 experienced travelers, all authorities in their particular fields. Practical suggestions on climate, maps, airfares, internal transportation, backpacking, visas, money, health, and theft.

♦ Simon, Ted. *Jupiter's Travels*. New York: Doubleday, 1980. Fascinating account of a 63,000-km motorcycle journey (500cc Triumph Tiger) from Europe, down the continent of Africa, across South America, Australia, and India. And what does Ted do now? Raises organic produce in Northern California!

♦ Theroux, Paul. *The Great Railway Bazaar*. New York: Houghton Mifflin, 1975. One of the world's best travel writers journeys from London to Tokyo and back on a hilarious railway odyssey. Rather than a dry discourse on sights, this masterpiece of observation keeps you riveted with personal encounters of the first order. Highly recommended for everyone!

♦ Various authors. *Culture Shock*. Singapore: Times Books. A series of practical guides to the rules of Asian etiquette, customs, and recommended behavior for every visitor to Asia. Lightweight and well distributed; excellent books to purchase and read while on the road. Highly recommended.

♦ Various authors. Insight Guides. Singapore: APA Publications. Superb photography and a lush text make this the best set of background guides to Southeast Asia. Read before traveling.

♦ Bloodworth, Dennis. *An Eye for the Dragon*. New York: Farrar, Straus and Giroux, 1970. The former Far East correspondent of the *Observer* incisively examines the comedies and tragedies of Asia, from the fanatic wranglings of Sukarno to racial tensions in Malaysia. Bloodworth makes history and politics—often dry and dull subjects—fascinating and memorable.

BRUNEI

If you go only once around the room,
you are wiser than he who stands still.

— Estonian proverb

I travel light; as light,
That is, as a man can travel who will
Still carry his body around because
Of its sentimental value.

— Christopher Fry,
The Lady's Not for Burning

Follow the first rules of a frequent traveler: Don't
overpack; leave all that excess emotional baggage at home.

— *Letter in* Condé Nast Traveler

INTRODUCTION

The tiny but wealthy country of Brunei, a 500-year-old sultanate situated on the north coast of Borneo between the Malaysian states of Sabah and Sarawak, offers an impressive mosque, river journeys, and untouched rainforests outside the capital city of Bandar Seri Begawan. Since Brunei hardly needs tourist income, the country has remained one of the least touristy in Southeast Asia. Residents are warm and friendly and quick to display traditional Malay hospitality. Best of all, Brunei has remained a physically beautiful country since oil wealth has helped preserve the rainforests and traditional ways of life. Hospitable people, unspoiled jungle, and the curious marriage of oil, Islam, and Western materialism make Brunei one of the more unique destinations in Southeast Asia.

HISTORY

Brunei has a strange, almost tragic history. When Magellan's ships landed at Brunei in 1521, Spanish conquistadors reported finding a rich and powerful Islamic sultanate which controlled most of Borneo and the trading routes from Indonesia to Manila. Brunei's golden age centered on two rulers, Sultan Bolkiah and Sultan Hassan, who mastered empires whose splendor rivaled that of any power in Southeast Asia. But the following centuries saw its influence diffused among hereditary chieftains—the Pengirans—who resorted to piracy and the sales of large tracts of Borneo to foreign nationals. By the early 19th century Brunei had been reduced to an emasculated shell, ruled by corrupt sultans who lived off taxes and slave auctions and plagued by roving bands of pirates who preyed on shipping merchants and upriver villages. Into this desperate situation sailed an English adventurer named James Brooke, the first of Sarawak's White Rajahs. Brooke forced the weakened sultanate to disgorge vast areas of Borneo as reward for his suppression of piracy and headhunting. His brilliant campaigns brought peace to North Borneo but also bankrupted the sultan, who could no longer rely on taxes, piracy, and revenue from slave auctions. By the time the sultanate appealed to Britain for protection in 1888, the once-powerful empire was little more than a small and powerless trading post situated on equatorial swampland.

Political change followed the discovery of oil at the first Seria oilfield in 1929. During the postwar

BRUNEI

SOUTH CHINA SEA

MUARA

JERUDONG

BANDAR
SERI
BEGAWAN

TUTONG

BUNUT

KLUDANG

LIMBANG

LABU

LUMUT

LAYONG

BANGAR

KUALA   SERIA
BELAIT

SINOKOH

BARAM

BADAS

BENUTAN

BARAM RIVER

LIMBANG RIVER

MIRI

LABI

BELAIT RIVER

MALAYSIA

0   20 km

TUTOH RIVER

MOUNT MULU
(2,371 m)

© MOON PUBLICATIONS, INC.

decolonization period, in 1963 the British urged Sultan Omar Ali Saifuddin to try democracy and join the new nation of Malaysia. Although Omar was intrigued with the concept of a united Malaysia, he declined the invitation because of his brief experiment with parliamentary elections in 1962. Omar had allowed free and open elections based on a 1959 constitution, but after 54 of 55 seats were won by the opposition Brunei People's Party (reputedly an antimonarchist and pro-Indonesia coalition) Omar suspended the constitution and refused to seat the winners. The subsequent civil rebellion was crushed by British Gurkha troops from Singapore who imprisoned or deported about 300 political dissidents. Although the monarchy was saved, this traumatic experiment sealed the political forum and ended the sultan's venture into democracy. Ironically enough, the following year saw the Brunei Legislative Assembly approve the country's entry into Malaysia. This bold move was reversed after objections from British

Petroleum and Shell Oil, two international consortiums who apparently didn't want to see the country's enormous oil profits being funneled to Kuala Lumpur.

In 1967 Sultan Omar voluntarily abdicated the throne to his son, Hassanal Bolkiah. Politely enduring a 15-year power struggle with his father, Hassanal finally asserted his rights by marrying his second wife, Mariam (a former hostess with Royal Brunei Airlines), and granting her status equal to that of his first wife, Raja Isteri Saleha. Although furious about the marriage, Sultan Omar lost the ensuing political maneuvering and eventually resigned himself to a largely ceremonial role. Brunei became a sovereign and independent country in 1984. Omar died in September 1987.

The tiny country received some unwanted publicity in 1987 when it was revealed during the Iran-Contra hearings that Hassanal had contributed US$10 million to the Contras. In a somewhat comical footnote, it was revealed that the money was returned to the sultan after Oliver North and Elliott Abrams mixed up the digits and deposited the funds in the wrong Swiss bank account.

GOVERNMENT

Brunei is an autocratic monarchy ruled by Sultan Hassanal Bolkiah, the 29th ruler of the dynasty. Plucked at age 21 from Britain's Sandhurst Royal Military Academy, Hassanal in his younger days enjoyed a playboy lifestyle filled with race-horses, polo, and excursions to London while his father continued to rule the tiny country. After taking control of Brunei in the early 1980s, Has-sanal gave up his racy image and settled down to the business of running the country. Brunei today is a hereditary autocracy ruled by Has-sanal, who serves as head of state, head of the Islamic religion, prime minister, and minister of defense. Though the absolute statesman of Brunei, Hassanal has proven himself to be a surprisingly progressive ruler who has made some remarkable changes in his government, such as splitting up ministerial positions and forming a cabinet no longer dominated by the royal family. As a result, Brunei now more close-ly resembles a modern parliamentary state than an autocratic monarchy, though it's unclear how much real power is shared between the sultan and his cabinet. Hassanal has also allowed the formation of political parties, including the Na-tional Democratic Party (PNDB), which supports the nationalization of Brunei Shell and gently encourages the sultan to step down from his position as prime minister. Blatant criticism isn't tolerated, however, and the government is quick to shut down political parties who criticize the sultan's absolutism or demand open elections.

Another taboo subject is the personal wealth of Sultan Hassanal, the world's richest man ac-cording to *Forbes* and the *Guinness Book of World Records*. The exact extent of his per-sonal fortune is unknown since the division be-tween the Bolkiah family's private assets and the public purse is one of Brunei's most closely guarded mysteries. Yet it hardly strained his pocketbook when he spent over US$600 mil-lion in 1984 to construct and furnish his 1,788-room riverside palace. It now serves as resi-dence to his extended family of about 30 people,

including his two wives, six daughters, three sons, three brothers, and their families.

ECONOMY

The postage-stamp-sized country of Brunei—more properly called Negara Brunei Darus-salam—is a paradox unlike any other country in Southeast Asia. With a population of just over 200,000, Brunei boasts a staggering per-capita income of US$22,000, one of the highest in the world and second in Asia only to Japan. Most citizens—aside from ethnic Chinese who have little hope of gaining citizenship—are provided with free education, health care, and interest-free loans for buying homes, cars, or making a pilgrimage to Mecca. As a result, there are al-most half as many cars as people, making for surprising rush-hour traffic jams in one of the world's smallest capitals! Brunei has no nation-al debt, no trade deficit, and levies no income tax except on 30% of corporate profits. Unem-ployment is rare because of the manpower shortage. Symbols of success and conspicu-ous consumption are everywhere: fleets of Mer-cedeses, air-conditioned shopping centers, color televisions and microwave telephones in re-mote longhouses, and an international airport larger than in Hong Kong.

This tremendous wealth is based almost en-tirely on the oil and gas reserves discovered near Seria by the Royal Dutch Shell Group in 1929. While relatively small in total world pro-duction, Brunei produces a great deal of oil on a per-capita basis. Hydrocarbons account for 96% of all exports, with the balance in rubber, timber, and jelutong, an ingredient for making chewing gum. So complete is the domination of oil and its attendant welfare state that local wags have dubbed Brunei the "Shellfare State." Gross domestic product from oil alone is breath-taking—US$15,000 yearly per person. Perhaps more staggering are Brunei's foreign reserves of US$20 billion, which generate about US$7000 yearly per person. Brunei has no fi-nancial worries about the future; even if the wells ran dry tomorrow, its gigantic foreign-ex-change reserves would generate enough in-vestment income to support the entire popula-tion of 250,000 people. Fabulous wealth from oil . . . no wonder Brunei has been dubbed the Kuwait of Southeast Asia.

PRACTICAL INFORMATION

TRANSPORTATION

Getting There From Sarawak

Both MAS (Malaysia Airline) and Royal Brunei Airlines fly daily from Kuching to Bandar Seri Begawan. The overland journey from Miri can be made in a single day with an early start. Travelers in a hurry can take a share taxi for about M$30. Buses are cheaper but slower since they are delayed longer for border formalities. Six buses leave Miri daily for Kuala Belait, the first town in Brunei. The bus crosses the wide Baram River and the narrow but congested Belait River. Brunei customs and immigration are located just before Kuala Belait. Delays at river crossings, especially the time-consuming ordeal at the Belait River, can be avoided by taking your gear off the bus and walking to the front of the line. Take the motorized boat or ask a car driver for a lift and then hitchhike from the opposite side. Buses from Miri to Kuala Belait take about 2½ hours. Buses from Kuala Belait to Bandar Seri Begawan leave several times daily, take 2½ hours, and sometimes race along the beach past monkeys and oil platforms to avoid the rough road. Hitching is recommended as an easy way to meet rich Bruneians who sometimes offer a place to stay in the expensive city of Bandar Seri Begawan. Traveler's checks can be changed in Kuala Belait.

Getting There From Sabah

Both MAS and Royal Brunei Airlines fly daily from Kota Kinabalu to Bandar Seri Begawan. Since there are no roads from KK and BSB (two popular abbreviations for the capitals of Sabah and Brunei, respectively), overland travelers must use a combination of bus and water transport. There are two different routes from KK to BSB. Both are time-consuming and somewhat expensive, although the journey is a fascinating adventure along the coastline once roamed by pirates, smugglers, and headhunters.

Labuan Island Route: Buses and taxis directly to Labuan leave from the bus stand on Jalan Balai Polis in Kota Kinabalu. Otherwise, take the bus to Beaufort and then continue up to

Mempakol and Menumbok by taxi. Boats make the 45-minute crossing from Menumbok to Labuan daily at 1030 and 1600. Ferries in the opposite direction from Labuan to Menumbok leave at 0800 and 1300. Taxi drivers in Beaufort usually know the latest schedules and will deliver you in time for the boat. Launches from Labuan to Bandar Seri Begawan leave twice daily, take two hours, and cost M$15. You will most likely find yourself stranded for a night in the expensive and charmless town of Labuan.

Sipitang-Lawas Route: The road west from Beaufort passes through Sipitang and Merapok before grinding to a halt in the one-horse town of Lawas. Ferries from Lawas to Bandar Seri Begawan leave twice daily, take two hours, and cost about M$25. Accommodations in Sipitang and Lawas include the Government Resthouse for M$30 and a handful of cheaper but grubbier hotels. Boat schedules should be double-checked with taxi drivers in Beaufort.

TRAVEL PRACTICALITIES

Visas

Visas are not required for citizens of Belgium, Britain, Canada, Denmark, France, Germany, Japan, Netherlands, Sweden, Switzerland, and most ASEAN countries for social visits of less than 14 days. Visa-exemption status is granted with a valid passport, confirmed onward ticket, and sufficient funds. Other nationalities can obtain visas from Brunei diplomatic missions in Washington, New York, London, Singapore, Tokyo, Kuala Lumpur, Bangkok, Manila, and Jakarta, or from British High Commissions and embassies where there are no Brunei diplomatic missions. Visas *cannot* be obtained in Sabah or Sarawak. Travelers who need visas should pick them up in an Asian capital.

Tourist Information

There is no national tourist office in Brunei except for a small visitor's information booth at the airport for maps and instructions on etiquette. Proper dress is a serious matter here in Brunei. The Economic Development Board in the State Secretariat Building is listed as the official tourist office but most travelers find the public-relations officer at the customs wharf much more helpful. This office is located in room 13 on the second floor of the white building at the southwest corner of Jalan MacArthur and Jalan Sungai Kianggeh.

Money

The Brunei dollar is convertible at par with the Singapore dollar. Exchange rates are approximately US$1=B$2.10. Malaysian currency units are about 40% cheaper than Brunei dollars and merchants will consequently only accept Malaysian money at deep discount. Traveler's checks can be changed at banks located in most larger towns.

Telecommunications

The dialing code for Brunei is IDD access code followed by 673 and then the appropriate area code. The area code for Bandar Seri Begawan is 2, 3 for Seria and Kuala Belait, 4 for Tutong, 5 for Temburong. International phone calls can be made 24 hours a day from most hotels and from the telecommunications counter at the General Post Office.

Background Reading

The government publishes a Malay-language newspaper called *Pelita.* English periodicals include the weekly *Borneo Bulletin* published in Kuala Belait and newspapers from Singapore

and Malaysia. Summaries of current political and economic conditions can be found in the *Asia Yearbook* published by the Far Eastern Economic Review and *Asia and Pacific Review* from Asiaweek.

Two books have recently been issued about Sultan Hassanal. *By God's Will: A Portrait of the Sultan of Brunei,* by Lord Chalfont, is a public-relations effort to improve the sultan's image, while *The Richest Man in the World: The Sultan of Brunei,* by James Bartholomew, is a somewhat scandalous look at the inner workings of the monarchy.

Holidays

Brunei celebrates an array of Islamic holidays. All are movable feasts dated by the Islamic calendar, which advances about 10 days in each Western year. Muslim holidays include Hari Raya Haji to commemorate the sacrifice of Abraham, the first day of the Muslim New Year, the first day of Ramadan, the anniversary of the revelation of the Koran, and Hari Raya Puasa at the end of Ramadan. Muslim religious celebrations are generally private religious observances or family gatherings without any kind of dramatic display. Chinese, Hindu, and Christian holidays are also observed together with a handful of state celebrations which occur on fixed dates. The best of these include Chinese New Year in February or March, National Day on February 23, Armed Forces Day on May 31, the Birthday of the Sultan on July 15, and Boxing Day on December 26.

TRAVEL

BANDAR SERI BEGAWAN

Brunei's capital city, often called simply Bandar or BSB, is a low-rise and surprisingly clean town that makes for a pleasant change from the urban messes that dominate most of Borneo. The national wealth of Brunei is reflected in the modern government buildings, manicured lawns, fountains, and lines of air-conditioned cars that briefly clog the streets at rush hour. Bandar is compact enough that most attractions can be reached on foot. Buses around BSB and to outlying destinations leave infrequently from the terminal behind the Brunei Hotel. Unmetered taxis are available and bargaining is essential. Figure on about B$2 per kilometer or B$15 to the airport.

Omar Ali Saifuddin Mosque

The highlight of any visit to BSB is a tour of this magnificent mosque, which ranks as one of the most impressive pieces of modern architecture in Southeast Asia. Set in the middle of a reflecting lagoon, this Saracenic wonder is capped by a vast golden dome speckled by millions of gleaming fragments of Venetian gold-leaf mosaic. No expense was spared during its construction in 1958. The exterior walls are cut from Hong Kong granite, interior walls and floors are inlaid with the finest Italian marble, the stained-glass windows and chandeliers were imported from England, and luxurious Persian prayer carpets are stacked up like sacks of potatoes waiting for the next call to prayer. Outstanding views of the city can be enjoyed from the 44-meter minaret served by an elevator. The mosque is open to non-Muslims Saturday to Wednesday 0800-1200 and 1300-1600, closed Thursday and Friday. Entry rules and dress regulations are strictly described at the front gate.

Kampong Ayer

Brunei's 400-year-old Malay water village, the world's largest community built on stilts, is actually a series of 28 separate *kampongs* connected by concrete footbridges and piping systems for sewage, running water, and electricity. Most of the houses are equipped with TVs which blast forth reruns of "Dynasty" or kung-fu videotapes imported from Hong Kong. A few remaining brass and silverware shops still remain. The floating village adjacent to the mosque can be easily toured on foot. Villages across the river can be toured inexpensively with ironwood water buses which leave from the main wharf and charge less than B$1 to cross the river and then circumnavigate the village. Water buses are most plentiful in the early morning and late afternoons. Private boats charge B$20-30 per hour, depending on your bargaining abilities.

Churchill Museum, Aquarium, History Museum

Former Sultan Sir Omar Ali Saifuddin's admiration for England led to the development of this small museum, certainly one of Asia's strangest memorials to British colonial rule. Unlike most countries in Asia, Brunei resisted the retreat of British forces after WW II. Adjacent to the collection of Churchill memorabilia is the Hassanal Bolkiah Aquarium and Brunei History Museum, open daily except Tuesdays 0900-1200 and 1400-1700. All three attractions are located on Jalan Sultan, several blocks back from the central park.

Brunei Museum

Brunei's National Museum on the banks of the Brunei River is located in Kota Batu, the original capital some three km from the center of BSB. Inside the air-conditioned building is a wide range of poorly labeled artifacts ranging from Chinese ceramics to Malay artwork. Much of the museum is dominated by Shell Petroleum, which has mounted the world's largest oil-industry display, but the real highlights are the outstanding displays of Kenyah, Murut, Dusun, and Kadayan ethnic art. Although the Kenyah reside in the Baram River region in Sarawak and not in Brunei, the museum's collection of Kenyah artwork is considered the finest in Borneo, especially the pieces by Trusau, who also created much of the work displayed in Kuching's Sarawak Museum. The museum is open daily 1000-1730, closed Mondays and Friday

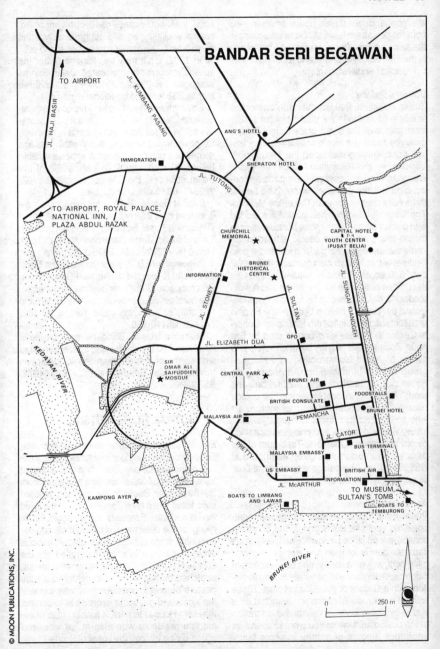

BANDAR SERI BEGAWAN

TO AIRPORT

JL. HAJI BASIR

JL. KUMBANG PASANG

ANG'S HOTEL

IMMIGRATION

SHERATON HOTEL

JL. TUTONG

TO AIRPORT, ROYAL PALACE,
NATIONAL INN,
PLAZA ABDUL RAZAK

CHURCHILL
MEMORIAL

CAPITAL HOTEL
YOUTH CENTER
(PUSAT BELIA)

BRUNEI
HISTORICAL
CENTRE

INFORMATION

JL. STONEY

JL. SULTAN

JL. SUNGAI KIANGGEH

GPO

JL. ELIZABETH DUA

KEDAYAN RIVER

SIR
OMAR ALI
SAIFUDDIEN
MOSQUE

CENTRAL PARK

BRUNEI AIR

BRITISH CONSULATE

FOODSTALLS

BRUNEI HOTEL

MALAYSIA AIR

JL. PEMANCHA

JL. PRETTY

JL. CATOR

MALAYSIA EMBASSY

BUS TERMINAL

US EMBASSY

BRITISH AIR

INFORMATION

JL. McARTHUR

TO MUSEUM,
SULTAN'S TOMB

KAMPONG AYER

BOATS TO LIMBANG
AND LAWAS

BOATS TO
TEMBURONG

BRUNEI RIVER

0   250 m

© MOON PUBLICATIONS, INC.

afternoons. Buses depart hourly or when filled from the downtown terminal. Other attractions in the same neighborhood include the Mausoleum of the Fifth Sultan of Brunei and a disappointing, overpriced handicraft center.

Sultan's Palace

Sultan Hassanal Bolkiah may rule one of the smallest countries in the world, but his 1,788-room palace on the banks of the Brunei River is believed to be the largest royal residence in the world, having displaced the 1,400-room Vatican in the *Guinness Book of World Records*. Further upstaging the pope's modest digs are the 16 acres of marbled floors, three full acres larger than the entire Vatican. The Moorish-Islamic-styled palace is studded with golden domes, cavernous banquet halls, a throne room, a private mosque, a heliport, an immense underground parking lot, and a polo field set within landscaped gardens that cover over 300 acres. Formally opened in 1984 as the private residence for the sultan and his extended family, the Istana Nurul Iman was designed by "Lucky" Leandro Locsin—the Filipino architect responsible for the Philippine Cultural Center in Manila—and constructed by Enrique Zobel—polo player, bank director, and owner of Ayala Construction. A Japanese group did the landscaping, American Dale Keller did the interiors, and Bechtel built the roads. According to local diplomats, the palace receives an unending stream of merchants who sell the world's finest antiques, jewelry, luxury Western goods, and priceless paintings by old and modern masters. Total cost of the palace and interiors has been estimated at US$600 million. The palace is open to the public on 15 July, the Sultan's birthday.

Accommodations

Pusat Belia Youth Center: This government-operated youth hostel is one of the only reasonably priced places in town. Facilities include separate dorms for men and women, a swimming pool, a gym, a library, and an inexpensive cafeteria. Admittance is generally limited to visitors with a student or youth-hostel card. Those without proper identification are admitted on a space-available basis, solely at the discretion of the custodian. Unless you want to spend an enormous amount of money in some fancy

hotel, you should dress neatly, be very polite, control your temper, and act graciously when given a bed. The center was closed to the public in 1992, but it may be reopened after the current residents are relocated. Jalan Sungai Kianggeh, tel. 23936, B$10 for the first three nights, B$5 for each additional night.

Government Resthouse: This government-operated resthouse is the only budget alternative to the Pusat Belia. Admittance is reserved for government officials, but Westerners are sometimes given rooms on a space-available basis. Jalan Sungai Kiangaeh, south of the Pusat Belia near the Chinese temple, tel. (02) 223571, B$10 single or double.

Capital Hostel: BSB's least expensive hotel is located near the civic center on a small street just behind Pusat Belia. All rooms are a/c with TV and fridge. Jalan Berangan off Jalan Tasik Lama, tel. (02) 223561, B$75-140.

Princess Inn: BSB's alternative to the Capital Hostel is located in the Seri Commercial Complex across the river beyond the mosque. The hotel provides pick-up from the airport and free shuttles into town. Jalan Tutong, tel. (02) 241128, B$110-160.

Sheraton Utama: Bandar's most luxurious hotel has 170 a/c rooms and suites furnished with all the standard amenities for business travelers. Jalan Bendahara, tel. (02) 244272, B$240-300.

ATTRACTIONS OUTSIDE BSB

Brunei has good beaches, waterfalls, and relatively untouched jungle within a few hours' journey of the capital city. Both Avis and Sharikat Yuran rent small Japanese cars and jeeps from B$100 per day. Buses to the following destinations leave when filled from the terminal behind the Brunei Hotel. Service is unpredictable. Hitchhiking, on the other hand, is quite simple and dependable since residents are always curious about Westerners. Hitching is signaled with the downward wave of the hand rather than an outstretched thumb, which is considered a rude gesture here in Brunei. Another way to meet the locals and get some exercise is to contact the Hash House Harriers, a running club of expatriate residents who also make weekend scuba-diving trips off the coast of Brunei.

Murara
Brunei's most popular beach, 28 km east of BSB, is where oil workers and their families gather on weekends to sunbathe, drink beer, and socialize with other visitors. The beach is mediocre, but pleasant walks can be made around the tip of the peninsula.

Limbang
Limbang is a Malaysian town located in the slice of land wedged between two sections of Brunei. There is little of interest here except for upriver trips to Iban longhouses and seedy brothels which have earned it a racy reputation. Limbang is an amazing mix of Christian tribalists and Muslim hedonists. Many of the prostitutes live in hotels nicknamed "embassies," such as the Thai embassy, Filipino embassy, and so on. Most Western travelers only visit the town briefly en route to Sabah. The two most popular routes to Sabah via Labuan Island or with direct boat to Lawas are described above. For a more leisurely journey, speedboats leave Brunei several times each morning for the 30-minute voyage to Limbang. Boats from Limbang to Punang in Sarawak depart daily except Sundays several times before noon. Taxis shuttle boat passengers to Lawas, where public transportation continues east toward Kota Kinabalu. The Borneo Hotel has singles from M$18 and doubles from M$25. Boat trips into the interior can be arranged at Limbang Trading, next door to the Borneo Hotel. Get further travel tips from the MAS, which flies daily from Limbang to Lawas in Sabah and Miri in Sarawak.

Bangar
Bangar is a small town located on the banks of the Temburong, a muddy river flanked with a handful of Murut longhouses. Oil wealth has brought cars and television to most longhouses, but the sheer absence of visitors has allowed the Muruts to retain their tradition of hospitality.

Most longhouses can be reached by taxis, which charge about B$1 per kilometer. Bring food and presents. Accommodation in Bangar is limited to a government resthouse which charges B$10 per night. Boats from BSB to Bangar leave several times each morning, cost M$6, and take about an hour. Bangar can also be reached by bus from Limbang. As relations improve between Malaysia and Brunei, it becomes more likely that the road from Bangar to Sabah will be completed. This would immensely simplify overland transport from BSB to Kota Kinabalu.

Lake Meribun
This remote and beautiful lake is a birdwatcher's paradise and a popular picnic spot for Bruneians on weekends. Facilities include a small campsite on the island and boat rentals for fishermen. Tasik Meribun can be reached by busing to Tutong and then hitching inland to the lake.

Labi Falls
Other popular interior destinations are the pond and waterfall near Kampong Labi in the Belait District. The small pond called Luagan Lalak is located just beyond Bukit Puan. The road continues through Labi and ends at the Chinese store where a narrow path continues up to Labi Falls. Because of the oil wealth, Brunei hasn't logged its rainforests into oblivion and much of the jungle near Labi is original growth. Jungle paths can be hiked to nearby longhouses and Murut villages where English is rarely understood but the hospitality is genuine. Labi can be reached by bus from Tutong. Hitching is easy.

Kuala Belait
Upriver journeys can be arranged here in the last oil town on the western edge of Brunei. Stranded travelers can choose from the Sea View and Sentosa Hotel, where a/c rooms go for B$130-180.

*I never travel without my diary. One should always have
something sensational to read in the train.*

—Oscar Wilde,
The Importance of Being Earnest

*A traveler has a right to relate and embellish his
adventures as he pleases, and it is very impolite to refuse
that deference and applause they deserve.*

—Rudolf Erich Raspe,
Travels of Baron Munchausen

*Order some golf shoes. Otherwise, we'll never get out of
this place alive. You notice these lizards don't have any
trouble moving around in this muck—that's because they
have claws on their feet.*

—Hunter S. Thompson,
Fear and Loathing in Las Vegas

BURMA (MYANMAR)

Of the gladdest moments in human life, methinks,
is the departure upon a distant journey into unknown
lands. Shaking off with one mighty effort the fetters
of Habit, the leaden weight of Routine, the cloak
of many Cares and the slavery of Home,
man feels once more happy.

—Richard Burton, *Journal*

The man who wishes to wrest something from Destiny
must venture into that perilous margin-country where
the norms of Society count for nothing and the demands
and guarantees of the group are no longer valid. He must
travel to where the police have no sway, to the limits of
physical resistance and the far point of physical
and moral suffering.

—Claude Lévi-Strauss, *Tristes Tropiques*

Pasteurized and homogenized cultures are not what take
us abroad.

—Pico Iyer, *Video Night in Kathmandu*

INTRODUCTION

Burma is one of the most isolated and exotic countries in the world, a land of gentle charm where timelessness and the quest for Buddhist nirvana fly in the face of Western efficiency and capitalistic wealth. The Burmese government recently opened some new areas and extended the seven-day visa to 15, but progress has come slowly to this intriguing land. Burma remains primitive, untamed, and extraordinarily memorable—"quite unlike any land you will ever know," said Kipling, who also wrote, "in all the world there is no place like Burma."

This is a destination for travelers rather than tourists, and a country best seen in retrospect. Only *after* the ordeal of rushing around, packing and unpacking, waiting for transportation, and dealing with one of the world's most medieval bureaucracies can you begin to love the country. Yet your recollections of magnificent temples and delightful people will captivate you as no other country in Southeast Asia possibly could. How much can you absorb in just two weeks? Only enough to know that you *must* return.

Myanmar What?

Burma has officially changed its name to Myanmar (pronounced Mee-en-ma), the name of the capital from Rangoon to Yangon (meaning "End of the Enemy"), and that of the historical center from Pagan to Bagan. The predominant nationality and official language are now called Myanmar, though the national airline has—for inexplicable reasons—been renamed Myanma Airways (without the *r*). Tourist Burma is now called Myanmar Travel and Tours, often abbreviated as MTT.

Government authorities say the changes are meant to better reflect Burma's ethnic diversity and provide Romanized spellings more phonetically in tune with local pronunciations. Minorities claim that Burmanising place-names is yet another historical distortion by the military junta.

The name changes imposed by the ruling regime were briefly adopted by the international press, but most newspapers, magazines, and wire services now use the older terminology, partly to avoid confusion among the public but also as a sign of nonrecognition of the Burmese

BURMA (MYANMAR)

INDIA

BANGLADESH

MYITKYINA

CHINA

BHAMO

CHINDWIN RIVER

SHAN HILLS

MINGUN
SAGAING
MAYMYO
MANDALAY
AVA   AMARAPURA

VESALI
MT. POPA
PINDAYA
SHWENYAUNG
MYOHAUNG
MEIKTILA
THAZI
HEHO   TAUNGGYI
MRAUK – U
KALAW
INLE LAKE
AKYAB
PAGAN

ARAKAN

IRRAWADDY RIVER

LAOS

BAY OF BENGAL

SALWEEN RIVER

MAE HONG SAN
CHIANG MAI

PROME

SANDOWAY

PEGU

MAE SOT

THAILAND

BASSEIN
RANGOON
TWANTE
SYRIAM   MOULMEIN

GULF OF MARTABAN

THREE PAGODAS PASS

KANCHANABURI

ANDAMAN SEA

TAVOY

GULF OF THAILAND

MERGUI

0   100 km

MERGUI

RANONG

© MOON PUBLICATIONS, INC.

dictatorship. This book will continue to use the original spelling, though the "Destination Names" chart will help decipher MTT publications and revised airline schedules.

THE PHYSICAL SETTING

Shaped somewhat like a hexagonal kite with a dangling tail, the heartland of Burma is a hot dry plain surrounded by rugged mountains on three borders and the Bay of Bengal to the south. This ring of mountains is the most important element affecting the climate; it has also served to keep Burma both politically and culturally isolated from the outside world. The central basin is divided into the fertile rice-growing region of lower Burma, which includes Rangoon, and the dry, almost desertlike region of upper Burma. To the north is a confusing knot of mountains that soars to over 6,000 meters. Mountains on the west run from China down to the southwest corner of Burma, where they disappear under the sea and reappear as the Andaman Islands. Burma's main transportation link is the Irrawaddy (Sanskrit for "River of Refreshment") River, popularized by Kipling as the "Road to Mandalay" and the "River of Lost Footsteps."

Rich tropical forests cover over half of Burma: rhododendron forests in the far north above 2,000 meters and monsoon teak at lower elevations. With some 80% of the world's teak reserves, Burma is a major exporter of valuable hardwoods. However, in a drive to increase foreign earnings, the Burmese National Timber Corporation has dramatically overcut the forests and recklessly sold logging licenses to the Thais. Large areas have been stripped by roving tribes who employ destructive slash-and-burn agricultural methods. After they burn the trees and plant their crops, the soil becomes leached of minerals, making it almost impossible for orig-

DESTINATION NAMES	
Former Name	**New Name**
Akyab	Sittwe
Burma	Myanmar
Bassein	Pathein
Irrawaddy River	Ayeyarwady River
Maymyo	Pyin Oo Lwin
Moulmein	Mawlamyine
Pagan	Bagan
Rangoon	Yangon

inal forest growth to return. The bottom line: marketable teak may be gone in 20 years.

Wildlife includes elephants, tigers, Malayan bears, gaur, *banteng,* white tapirs, the Asiatic two-horned rhinoceros, and the wild peacock, which has been designated Burma's national symbol. Snakes such as the deadly Russell viper and the Asiatic king cobra are plentiful in the dry zone around Mandalay and Pagan. Keep your eyes open while wandering around those ruins.

The central plains of Burma are extraordinarily hot during most of the year. Temperatures in Mandalay and Pagan during the summer months from March to June can soar to over 45° C (115° F), making your vacation feel like a week in Dante's Inferno. The only possible escapes from the heat are the hill resorts of Maymyo and Inle Lake. Winter months are usually clear, but freezing winds occasionally blast down from the north. Summer monsoons drench the coastal regions with over 5,000 mm (200 inches) of rain while the central region, protected by the rain shadow of the Arakan Mountains, receives only 500 mm (20 inches). Temperatures drop to more tolerable levels during the monsoons, although humidity hovers constantly near 100%. Best time to visit Burma

RANGOON'S CLIMATE

	Jan.	Feb.	March	April	May	June	July	Aug.	Sept.	Oct.	Nov.	Dec.
Avg. Maximum C	32°	33°	36°	36°	33°	30°	29°	29°	30°	31°	31°	31°
Avg. Maximum F	90°	92°	96°	96°	92°	86°	84°	84°	86°	88°	88°	88°
Rainy Days	0	0	1	2	14	23	26	25	20	10	3	1

SIGHTSEEING HIGHLIGHTS

Main Destinations

Rangoon: Rangoon's top attraction is the magnificent Shwedagon Pagoda, considered by many the world's greatest Buddhist monument. A twilight visit to this stunning pagoda is an unforgettable experience. Rangoon has little else of exceptional interest although it's amazing to see what 40 years of neglect will do to a city.

Mandalay: Many visitors make this dry and dusty town their second stop. Mandalay served as the final Burmese capital during the 18th and 19th centuries and, to a certain degree, still retains the easygoing charms of an earlier day. Several fascinating temples and monasteries are worth visiting, although not everybody is impressed with the modern developments.

Pagan: It would be difficult to find anyone not awestruck by the magnificent ruins of this 12th-century empire. With some 5,000 stupas and temples strewn across the dusty plains of central Burma, Pagan stands as one of the world's premier archaeological sites. A must-see for any visitor to Burma.

Inle Lake: That being said, those travelers jaded with archaeology and old temples might prefer the splendid natural environment of Inle Lake. This idyllic resort is perhaps one of the most beautiful places in Southeast Asia and an area of great cultural interest thanks to the various ethnic groups.

Secondary Destinations

Pegu: Eighty km north of Rangoon is the old Mon capital, with its fabulous Shwemawdaw Pagoda—almost as impressive as the Shwedagon. Together with several other temples in the region, Pegu makes for an outstanding day-trip from Rangoon.

Vicinity of Mandalay: Popular side trips from Mandalay include the great pagoda at Mingun and Ava, Sagaing, and Amarapura, sleepy towns that briefly served as the capitals of upper Burma during the 18th century. Although much of the secular architecture was pulled down when the capitals were moved, dozens of fascinating temples, pagodas, and monasteries are still standing. Finding the time to visit these towns can be problematical.

Maymyo: About two hours east of Mandalay, this former British hill station is known for its picturesque location, brisk climate, fascinating market, and nostalgic colonial hotel complete with rare roast beef and proper English tea. Maymyo is usually a one-night side trip from Mandalay and can be fit in with some rushing around.

Mount Popa: This dramatic mountain 50 km from Pagan serves as Burma's center for *nat* worship. Popa can be a day-trip from Pagan or a brief stopover between Pagan and Thazi.

Vicinity of Inle Lake: The former British hill station of Kalaw, known for its bracing weather and colonial architecture, is located directly on the road between Taunggyi and Thazi. Two hours north of Kalaw are the famous Pindaya Caves, with some 10,000 Buddhas.

New Destinations

Much of Burma has been closed to western visitors for over three decades. Before 15-day visas began in 1989, Burma had a variety of destinations ranging from legal to off-limits. Legal places such as Pagan and Mandalay were easy to reach but difficult to enjoy with so little time. Vaguely off-limits destinations such as Bassein and Prome could be reached with little problem. Officially discouraged destinations such as the Holy Rock at Kyaiktiyo and the sleepy port of Moulmein were fascinating but difficult to reach without aid from sympathetic Burmese. Off-limits destinations such as border regions controlled by insurgency groups could only be reached from Thailand. The extended visa policy has opened up Rakhine (Arakan) State and several historic towns near Mandalay.

Rakhine: Until its capture by the Burmese in the late 1700s, Rakhine (formerly called Arakan) was an independent kingdom with a distinct language and culture. Today it's a magical land with untouched ruins, spectacular landscapes, and a special sense of destiny. Top attractions are the ancient capitals around Myohaung and the beach resort of Sandoway.

Monywa: The Thanboddhay Pagoda, one of the Burma's most famous sites, is located in the ancient town of Monywa some 135 km west of Mandalay. Myanmar Travel and Tours has opened a hotel here.

the perils of
independent travel

is during the cooler winter months. Be sure to bring along a sweater or a light jacket.

HISTORY

Surrounded by towering mountain walls that encircle the country like an iron horseshoe, Burma has always been an isolated and insular region. During the early Christian Era, four separate races migrated down the river valleys from Tibet to settle in different parts of Burma. The first major group was the Pyu, a mysterious race that settled in south-central Burma near the present-day town of Prome. It's thought the Pyus practiced a syncretic form of Theravada Buddhism that included Brahmanic Hinduism, *naga* worship, and animism. Leaving almost no records behind, the Pyus were destroyed in 832 when Chinese from Nanchao plundered the capital and deported 3,000 slaves to Yunnan. The next major group were the Mons, who were firmly entrenched in the Pegu region of southern Burma prior to the arrival of the Burman people sometime in the 7th, 8th, or 9th centuries. Other Mon groups scattered over to Thailand and Cambodia and established the earliest empires in these nations. The Mons were a highly civilized and cultured race of people who had a profound influence on the Burman people in Pagan. The third major group to migrate into

Burma was the Burmans themselves, who fled the Tibetan plateau to escape Chinese raids for human sacrifices. The Burmans settled in the central valley of Upper Burma at Pagan. The last group to emigrate was the Shans (Tai or Thai), who fled the Mongol invasions of China's Nan Chao district in the 9th, 10th, and 11th centuries and eventually settled in the hills on the Thai-Burma border. From the moment of their arrival these four Mongoloid-Chinese races waged almost continual warfare against each other, with brief periods of peace and unity.

The Kingdom Of Pagan (1044-1287)
Burma's first and greatest empire was centered along the banks of the Irrawaddy in the dry and dusty plains of central Burma. Pagan blossomed under the leadership of King Anawrahta, an ambitious leader who conquered the Mons at Thaton and transported the entire Mon court of artists, philosophers, and religious leaders back to his isolated capital. The Mons made profound contributions to Burmese culture; their craftsmen and architects taught the Burmese their refined skills; Mon Buddhist leaders spread Theravadism and the Pali language; Mon architects helped erect thousands of temples and stupas which stand today as the greatest archaeological wonders in Southeast Asia. Pagan remained the region's major cultural and military power until an envious Kublai Khan demand-

ed tribute and threatened to march his armies on Pagan. Rather than face the wrath of Khan, the people abandoned the city.

Other Kingdoms

With the decline of Pagan, Burma split into three different kingdoms whose histories are a dizzying kaleidoscope of constant warfare. The Shans ruled upper Burma from their capital at Ava in the vicinity of Mandalay. The Burmans to the south founded the kingdom of Toungoo in the foothills of central Burma. The Mons established their kingdom at Pegu near modern-day Rangoon, where they conducted international trade with the Muslim empire at Malacca and constructed impressive temples which still stand today. During the 16th century, the Burmese conquered the Shans and captured Pegu from the Mons. The capital was moved around the country until a powerful Burmese king named Alaungpaya ("Future Buddha") reorganized Burmese forces and destroyed the Mons at Pegu. During his brief but important eight-year reign (1752-1760), Alaungpaya founded the powerful Konbaung dynasty which ruled Burma from Arakan to Tenasserim until the British completed their takeover in 1885.

British Occupation

Territorial conflicts between the British in India and local Burmese armies led to the first British-Burmese war in 1824. The Burmese provinces of Assam, Rakhine (Arakan), and Tenasserim were annexed by the British, while Burmese-British relations continued to deteriorate under the cruel reign of Pagan Min (1846-1853). After European traders protested the extortionate behavior of Burmese officials in Rangoon, a British force was sent up the Irrawaddy River to depose the religious-minded but temperamental Mindon Min (1853-1878). This led to the expansionist governor-general Lord Dalhouse annexing all of lower Burma, including Rangoon, in 1852. Under British rule, the rich Irrawaddy delta was cleared of its mangrove forests and carved into extensive rice plantations; it soon became one of the world's most productive rice-growing regions. But as in much of colonial Asia, the wealth was absorbed by British firms and Indian moneylenders while the indigenous peoples descended into abject poverty. Though King Mindon of Ava attempted to modernize what little remained of his medieval country, upper Burma fell to superior British forces on 1 January 1886. Burma now belonged to the British.

During the early 20th century, children of wealthy Burmese were sent abroad to receive liberal educations in London. Proselytized on the benefits of capitalism and democracy, they returned home to become the future political leaders of independent Burma. Early organizations pressing for freedom included the Young Men's Buddhist Association (YMBA) and the Thakins (Thirty Comrades) led by Aung San, U Nu, and Ne Win. These leaders organized student and worker strikes while moving their political ideology toward socialism, fascism, and radical philosophies popular in Japan during the 1930s. Aung San, the political activist considered the father of modern Burma, eventually moved to Japan, where he received military training from sympathetic Japanese leaders.

Japanese forces entered Burma in December 1941 accompanied by the Thakins, who were given token control of the country. The Japanese promised an Asian Co-Prosperity Sphere based on equality and brotherhood. Though initially welcomed by the Burmese, the Japanese quickly alienated the local population with their insulting behavior and sadistic treatment. Political leaders were manipulated and thousands of innocent civilians were murdered by the dreaded *kempatai*. Casualties were enormous; the Rangoon Cemetery holds over 27,000 soldiers and civilians killed by the Japanese through forced labor, torture, and starvation. The Burma Theater gave rise to Allied heroes such as "Vinegar" Joe Stilwell, Chennault and his Flying Tigers, and an American Army division called Merrill's Marauders. *Stilwell and the American Experience in China* by Barbara Tuchman has the full story. Eventually the war turned against the Japanese. When all seemed lost, Burmese patriots made overtures to underground British forces who later granted immunity from postwar prosecution.

Independence was granted to the Burmese at exactly 0420 on 4 January 1948—an auspicious hour chosen by Burmese astrologers. It was a painful and chaotic birth. The charismatic Aung San quickly took control by eliminating his rivals and expelling the communists from the Executive Council. He was then murdered by gunmen hired by a Burmese right-wing politician. Shocked and in disarray, the Burmese government named U Nu as his successor. What followed was near-complete economic and political collapse. The countryside erupted into warfare as the communists, Karens, and dissident followers of Aung San declared war against the newly formed Burmese government. In an attempt to appease the warring ethnic groups pressing for independence, U Nu established separate and semiautonomous states for the various minorities. But warfare and banditry continued. In 1962 General Ne Win led a coup d'état against the democratic government of U Nu. Ne Win's military dictatorship succeeded in slowing the open revolution but at high cost: the constitution was suspended, all industry was nationalized, and total censorship was imposed. By the mid-1970s a modest degree of peace had been achieved in the countryside.

Ah, Yes, A Kind And Gentle Land
But 1988 was the year that Burma finally exploded. Early rumblings were felt in the fall of '87 after the government declared large-denomination bank notes worthless. Burma's black market was the target; ordinary people were the victims when they awoke to discover their money fit only for lighting cheroots. The wave broke in March 1988 after a minor student brawl escalated into the first major antigovernment demonstrations since 1974. Dozens of protesters were massacred by the dreaded Lon Htein secret police. Forty-one people suffocated inside a police van. During a second wave of violence on 21 June, an estimated 100-120 students and monks were cut down by the secret police. Universities were closed, army reinforcements were sent to Rangoon, and students occupied the Shwedagon. On 23 June, Ne Win announced his resignation as party chairman, a tactical ploy which allowed honorable retreat from a desperate situation.

Incredibly, Sein Lwin—the man responsible for the brutality of March and June as de facto chief of the Lon Htein—was appointed the country's chief of state and party leader. Popular outrage was immediate. By early August hundreds of thousands of Burmese from all walks of life were marching through Rangoon. True to form, Sein Lwin responded with unprecedented brutality. Soldiers shot unarmed demonstrators and, in one of the worst incidents, massacred nurses and doctors inside the confines of the Rangoon General Hospital. Reliable diplomatic observers estimate that 1,000-3,000 people were killed. The brutal repression finally ended on 12 August. On 13 August Sein Lwin resigned and was replaced by Dr. Maung Maung, a Western-educated lawyer who promised real reforms. But the demonstrations grew larger. Over 500,000 people marched in Rangoon on 24 August, clapping and cheering in the belief that the country was about to return to democracy. People Power had arrived in Burma. The dream died on 18 September when the Burma Army seized control of the government and, once again, ordered troops to fire on demonstrators. The military government quickly declared martial law and consolidated its position.

GOVERNMENT

Since the republican-parliamentary form of government fell to the military forces of Ne Win in 1962, Burma has remained a single-party socialist government run by a prime minister and his nine-man cabinet. Political power rests with the National Unity Party (NUP) and the State Law and Order Restoration Council (SLORC), which follows Ne Win's "Burmese Way to Socialism"—an isolationist and xenophobic political philosophy which combines the Marxist and Fabian thinking popular during the 1930s. Ne Win's Road to Socialism has been a Road to Nowhere. Like the leaders of Singapore and Indonesia, Ne Win has remained in power for more than two decades. But unlike them he has driven his country to the brink of economic collapse, a stunning accomplishment considering that Burma is rich in gems and timber and was once the world's leading rice exporter. "Everything in this country is sliding down into a pit," says a Burma observer, "the only question is whether the pit has a bottom."

Ne Win is also one of the world's most idiosyncratic leaders. This self-proclaimed Buddhist and devoted family man has been married five times, including a marriage to the granddaughter of King Thibaw, the last monarch of Burma. Ne Win, in fact, believes himself a descendant of the old Konbaung Dynasty. In a country without any national parks, his love affair with golf has

Karenni culture week

brought the country over 25 golf courses. Even more bizarre is his abiding belief in the powers of astrology, mysticism, and numerology. It is said he personally ordered the introduction of odd 45- and 90-*kyat* banknotes since both numbers are divisible by nine, his lucky number. The renaming of Burma to Myanmar was done under the belief that an indigenous term would prevent wholesale Westernization. The decision was announced on 27 May, an auspicious day since two plus seven equals nine. Finally, Ne Win's astrologer once told him he would only reach nirvana if he married a girl from Arakan, shot his own image in the mirror, and bathed himself in blood. He's assumed to have completed all three rituals.

Insurgency Groups

Aside from the medieval form of government, Burma's other great political challenge is the bewildering array of insurgency groups that control most of the border areas. Burma nationalists claim these conflicts are a legacy of British colonial rule when the country was divided into ethnic enclaves and governed in the classic divide-and-rule pattern. Attempts have been made to solve this perplexing problem. Aung San formulated a unity-in-diversity policy which granted the minorities a certain degree of self-rule in return for joining the political union. U Nu convened a nationalities seminar in Rangoon to discuss the problem, but before any agreement could be worked out, Ne Win seized power and

jailed all the participants. The Old Man then abolished the federal constitution and forced through another which denied minority self-rule. Burma today is a divided country where government troops control the interior plains (and keep major tourist areas open), while rebels hold much of the mountainous countryside. Burma insurgency groups fall into three ideological groups: revolutionary, separatist, and warlord gangs.

Revolutionary groups seek to overthrow the Burma government and establish a completely new system of government. This includes the 10,000-man Communist Party of Burma (CPB), which controls much of the Sino-Burma border.

Separatist movements seek autonomy within a Burma framework and a return to a modified version of the old federal constitution. This includes the 11,000-man Kachin Independence Army (KIA), Burma's most powerful anticommunist rebel force. The Kachins are known for their long and distinguished history of warfare, having served under the British in Mesopotamia in WW I and with U.S. resistance forces during WW II. The KIA controls most of north Burma and much of the country's lucrative jade trade. Somewhat smaller but more familiar to Western observers is the 4,000-man Karen National Liberation Army (KNLA), which operates along the southern Thai-Burma border. The KNLA is a Christian, anticommunist, pro-Western political group that funds its revolution with a 5% tax on all smuggled goods.

THE ONLY GAME IN TOWN

Burma's closed-door polices have given rise to the world's strongest black market. The parallel economy is the only one that works. Perhaps 60-80% of the national economy is tied up in the black market. Corporation 24 (Burma has 23 government corporations) provides everything from dusty bottles of Johnny Walker and 555 cigarettes to Lacoste pullovers and warm cans of Coke. The problem exists because the country's state-owned enterprises operate in a closed market and have little incentive to compete with foreign goods in terms of quality and price. Distribution problems have left not one single item made by a government factory readily available on the open market. Fuel shortages and reduced rations force drivers to wait in day-long lines or purchase black market petroleum at 90 kyat (roughly US$13 at official exchange rates) per gallon. Production of consumer goods is regularly halted for lack of such basic materials as rolling paper for cigarettes and hops for beer. That's why Mandalay beer is so hard to find! Lack of spare parts keeps many factories closed or operating at less than 20% of capacity. Hunger is rare and few people go without their daily meals, but the shortage of even the most basic consumer goods is downright depressing. Never has a country so highly prized foreign-made ballpoint pens.

Most of the smuggling is conducted by rebel groups, but much is managed by high-ranking military and government officials, often with hilarious results. For example, several years ago the government banned all vehicles over 25 years old and forced more than 10,000 vintage cars and trucks off the roads. At the same time they allowed Burma's force of 4,000 merchant marines to legally import one car a year and re-sell it on the black market. The result has been that a reconditioned 1978 Toyota pickup truck fetches the equivalent of US$18,000 on the black market. Burma's hottest career opportunity: joining the merchant marines.

Warlord gangs function as opium smugglers with few political goals. This category includes the notorious Khun Sa and his 3,000-man Shan State Army (SSA), which controls the area east of the Salween near the Golden Triangle. In early 1986 the nine noncommunist groups of the National Democratic Front (Kachin, Karen, Shan, Mon, and others) met to forge a unified alliance with the Communist Party of Burma. In 1987 they gave up their previous demands for separation. But ideological differences between the Marxist-Leninist CPB and the democratically oriented NDF, plus problems with discipline and organization, make it appear unlikely that the rebels will pose any serious threat to the professional and highly disciplined 186,000-man Burma Army.

ECONOMY

Thirty years after embarking on its misguided road to socialism, Burma has joined North Korea and the Philippines on Asia's short list of foreign-debt defaulters. Ne Win's dead-end policies have led to nothing but economic collapse. Per-capita income of less than US$200 is somewhere between that of Botswana and Bangladesh. An unmanageable US$4.2-billion foreign debt gobbles up some 90% of export earnings while foreign reserves are barely enough to run the country for two weeks. With its vast reserves of teak, minerals, and oil, Burma is potentially one of Asia's richest countries. And yet, a country once able to feed most of Southeast Asia now faces the specter of its first food shortages since WW II. The Burma government was recently forced to reappraise its backward economic policies and ask the United Nations to classify it as a "Least Developed Country." Sadly, permission was granted. Burma has devolved into Southeast Asia's wounded isolation patient.

It must also be said that Burma's economic failure has spared the country the horrors of uncontrolled development. You won't find faceless high-rises, industrial pollution, or gaudy billboards filling the countryside. Burma is free from McDonald's, Hiltons, and flashing signs urging you to Drink Coke. Pure, peaceful, and perhaps the most untouched country in the world, but at a heavy price. Public transportation is often in creaky American-made buses that began life on the Burma Road during WW II. Hotels are still rich in colonial atmosphere but the elevators are busted and the showers have lives of their own. The retreat from the West has preserved family and religious traditions,

OPIUM TRADE AND KHUN SA

Burma's leading export isn't teak, gems, or oil . . . it's opium. The Golden Triangle—an isolated area of 75,000 square miles wedged between Burma, China, Laos, and Thailand—annually produces an estimated 1,000 tons of opium and over 50% of the world's illicit heroin supply. Most of this opium is exported through Thailand to the West where the profit potential is mind-boggling. One square mile of poppy field produces almost 2,000 kilos of raw opium. This sticky goo is heated in water, distilled with lime fertilizer and ammonia to produce morphine, and then fused with acetic anhydride to produce heroin. It is then smuggled by truck to Chiang Mai, where it brings US$15,000 a kilo. Heroin wholesales for over US$200,000 a kilo in the West *before* being cut six times by street dealers. The final tally: one kilo of raw Burmese opium eventually brings US$2.5 million; a single square mile of Burmese land can yield heroin worth US$50-200 million. Small wonder the hilltribes refuse to grow peanuts.

The mastermind of Burma's opium industry is Khun Sa (a.k.a. Chang Chi-fu), a half-Chinese half-Shan warlord widely regarded as one of the world's most prolific drug dealers . . . right up there with the Mafia and the Medellin cartel. Khun Sa first came to the attention of the world's press in 1967 when he launched the Opium War and wrestled control of the lucrative trade from the remnants of Chiang Kai-Shek's Nationalist Chinese Army. After being captured by Burma forces and thrown in a Rangoon prison, his private army (the Shan States Army) kidnapped two Soviet doctors as hostages for Khun Sa. By 1978 Khun Sa controlled 70-80% of Burma's opium trade. Capturing this outlaw has proven difficult. The U.S. government once offered US$25,000 for his head, but Khun Sa countered by offering payments for the murder of Americans in Chiang Mai. Dozens were evacuated. Khun Sa is something of a public-relations whiz, having repeatedly offered to sell all his opium to the U.S. government for US$500 million. So far no American president has taken him up on his bizarre proposal. Khun Sa is also a media manipulator who frequently meets with the press, including a 1989 visit by Tom Jarrell and the ABC-TV crew for "20/20" magazine.

but it has given new and painful meaning to the phrase "shared poverty." Burma's fascination sadly comes at the cost of human suffering and widespread deprivation.

Demonetization

Another of Burma's unique economic crises are the periodic recalls of printed money. Every few years the government declares certain banknotes worthless! The demonetization of 1985 was followed by another in 1987 in which the 25-, 35-, and 75-*kyat* banknotes were scrapped. All across the country Burmese woke up to find 80% of their currency declared null and void. Although these measures were designed to punish black marketers and wealthy Chinese entrepreneurs, the brunt of the burden fell on the poor farmer who discovered his nest egg was worth nothing. After the most recent demonetization, the government introduced notes of 45 and 90 *kyat* and compensated government officials and bank savers. But the psychological effects were permanent. Few Burmese today have any faith left in their printed currency.

THE PEOPLE

An ethnographical map of Burma shows a bewildering patchwork of peoples divided into dozens of ethnic groups speaking a veritable tower of babble. Two-thirds of Burma's 40 mil-

LANGUAGE

The people of Burma speak over 80 different languages divided into the three linguistic classes of Tibeto-Burman, Mon-Khmer, and Thai-Chinese. The Burmese alphabet has 32 consonants, eight vowels, and four diphthongs. It's a tonal language similar to Thai or Chinese, and like Chinese and Thai, it can easily trip up the beginning student. The script is a curious but delightful track of bubbles taken from the Pali script of South India. English is widely understood by educated Burmese and older citizens who remember the days of the Raj. However, simple courtesies such as special forms of address are always appreciated. *U* (pronounced "oo") is the respectful term for uncle. *Maung* refers to young males but can also be an expression of humility. *Ma* is used for all females up to middle age. *Daw* is used for adult women regardless of marital status.

how are you?	*maa yeh laa?*
I'm fine	*maa bah dai*
good morning	*min ga la baa*
thank you	*kyai zoo tin baa dai*
goodbye	*pyan dor mai*
excuse me	*kwin pyu baa*
do you understand?	*kin bar nar lai tha laa*
I don't understand	*chun note nar ma lai boo*
where is . . . ?	*. . . beh mah lai?*
bus stop	*bas car hmat tine*
railway station	*bu dar yon*
police station	*yeh sa khan*
hospital	*say yon*
how much?	*bah lout lai*
too much	*myar dai*
drinking water	*thow yea*
beef/chicken/fish	*ah meh tar/beh tar/ngar*
mutton/pork/rice	*seik tar/wet tar/san*
1, 2, 3,	*tit/nit/thone*
4, 5, 6,	*lay/ngar/chak*
7, 8, 9, 10,	*kun nit/shit/ko/ta sair*
100	*ta yar*

eyes, Tamil women in brightly colored saris, Chinese with light skin and Asiatic eyelids. Go to Inle Lake and the people change dramatically: Shans dressed in winding turbans and baggy blue pants, Karen women with rough-hewn dresses of red or white, Paduangs with heavy necklaces of brass rings. The far north and extreme west are home to the rebellious Kachins, the Wa, and the Naga. Burma is an ethnological mother lode, rich in racial groups that haven't yet been subjected to tour groups or wholesale Westernization. You'll find the broadest spectrum of peoples around Inle Lake.

Burmans

Burmans have been called the "Irish of Asia" because of their lively and genial but sometimes contentious nature. The term "Burman" traditionally has referred to the predominant ethnic group, while "Burmese" means all peoples living within national boundaries. (The 1989 law which changed Burma's name also changed the nationality from Burmese to Burma.) Like the Javanese in Indonesia and the Tagalogs in the Philippines, Burmans hold most of the nation's political and economic power, a situation resented by the less powerful minority groups. Burmese males typically wrap themselves in a plain or checkered *longyi* (like a *sarong*) tied directly in front and don a Western T-shirt or a short, tight-fitting jacket of Chinese design known as an *ingyi*. On formal occasions, men add a *gaungbaung* or turban of brightly colored strips of silk wrapped around a small wicker basket balanced on the head. Ladies prefer flowered *longyi* tied seductively on the hip. In sharp contrast to the Hindu society of India, Burma Buddhist society is remarkably free of class and caste distinctions. Burmese women enjoy equal opportunities to education and full property rights and are surprisingly liberated. They maintain almost complete control of family money matters and have considerable initiative in choice of a partner. Maiden names are kept after marriage.

Indians

Burma, especially Rangoon, has a sizable Indian population that, like the Chinese, has suffered from racial intolerance and government-approved discrimination. In an act of economic self-interest, British colonialists in the 19th and 20th centuries encouraged hundreds of thou-

lion residents are Burmans. The remainder are either Indian, Chinese, or belong to a half-dozen minority groups. Walk down the street in Rangoon and the kaleidoscopic range hits you: Burmans with dark brown skin and almond-shaped

FESTIVALS

Burma's Buddhist festivals follow the lunar calendar and take place on full-moon nights during the dry season. National holidays are fixed on the Gregorian calendar and take place on the same date each year.

January
Independence Day: 4 January. Burmese independence is celebrated in the wee hours of the morning—an annoyance for diplomats required to be on hand for the celebration. Rangoon holds a military parade. *Zat pwes* (special festivals that combine music, dance, and dramatics) and sporting events take place throughout Burma.

February
Union Day: 12 February. This state holiday honors the ethnic groups of Burma. A week-long celebration of dance, drama, and sporting events at Royal Lake in Rangoon. One of the best in Burma.

March
Farmers' Day: 2 March. This socialist holiday honors the working classes.

Resistance Day: 27 March. Armed Forces Day. Thousands of Burmese patiently wait near the Shwedagon for an early-morning military parade. No photography allowed.

Shwedagon Festival: Full moon of the final month in the Buddhist calendar. Marks the enshrinement of eight sacred Buddha hairs in the Shwedagon more than 2,500 years ago. Offerings of sticky rice are made to monks and Buddha images. Plenty of *zat pwes*.

April
Thingyan Festival: Full moon of the first month. Buddhist New Year and water-throwing festival. Buddha images are devoutly sprinkled with water while everyone else (especially foreign visitors) is mercilessly drenched with squirt guns, water buckets, and hoses.

May
Birth, Death, and Enlightenment of Buddha: Full moon of the second month. The holiest of all Buddhist holidays. Priests perform temple rituals while thousands of pilgrims carry candles and circle the Shwedagon.

June
Mount Popa Nat Festival: Full moon of the third month. *Nats* are honored at their headquarters at Popa. Look for *nat kadaw,* a trance dance performed by possessed villagers.

---

sands of Indians to emigrate to Burma. By the turn of the century, Burma had over a million Indian residents and Rangoon had become a predominately Indian city. Included in the mass migration were the Chettiars, a hereditary group of moneylenders who used their centuries of moneylending techniques to entrap the less wily Burmese. Indian agents went into the villages and loaned money at exorbitant interest rates. After spending their cash on parties and *pwes* (festivals) the Burmese were forced to surrender their land titles to the Indians. By 1945 over 60% of the rice lands had foreclosed into Indian hands. Unaccustomed to loan-sharking by the Indians and aggressive mercantilism by the Chinese, the Burmese people descended into abject poverty. By WW II they had become landless peasants ruled by the British, the Indians, and the Chinese. This intolerable situation changed quickly after independence when Indian-held land was nationalized and thousands of Indians fled westwards. By the late '60s Rangoon's Indian population had fallen from 500,000 to below 100,000. A three-tiered citizenship law now limits the political power of non-Burmans.

Minority Groups
Shan: Burma's second-largest racial group is the fiercely independent Shan, who live in the mountain ranges between Burma and Thailand.

Karen: Although their traditional homeland is in Karen state, many of Burma's three million Karens have moved to the delta area of lower Burma and integrated with the Burmans. Relations between the two groups have never been good. In earlier times the Karens were drafted as slaves by Burman armies. After WW II they went on the warpath to claim a sovereign Karen state. Today their rebellion is led by the Karen National Liberation Army (KNLA) and funded by smuggling taxes rather than drugs. Karens are

FESTIVALS

July
Dhammasetkya: Full moon of the fourth month. Commemorates Buddha's first sermon after his enlightenment. Marks the beginning of Buddhist Lent. A popular time for young men to enter the Buddhist priesthood. During the *shin pyu* (ordination ceremony) the young monk must surrender his garments, have his head shaved, and then wash his cranium with saffron. He is then interviewed by a senior monk and given his yellow robes, begging bowl, and other utensils. The ceremony brings great honor to the young man's mother. Monkhood lasts from a few days to several months.

August
Taungbyon Nat Festival: Full moon of the fifth month. A seven-day orgiastic festival of dancing, drinking, and music in Taungbyon, about 20 km north of Mandalay.

September
Inle Lake Boat Festival: Full moon of the sixth month. A spectacular sporting and religious event held in Yaunghwe. Five Buddha images from the Paung Daw Pagoda are placed on a royal *karaweik* barge and ceremonially pulled around the lake by Intha leg rowers. Boat competitions and *zat pwes* follow. An international event attended by tourists and tribes from the Shan States.

October
End of Buddhist Lent: Full moon of the seventh month. The Festival of Lights. Celebrates the time thousands of lights helped guide the Buddha back from heaven after teaching his mother. Also marks the end of the rainy season when young monks traditionally return to their homes.

November
Tazaung Daing Festival: Full moon of the eighth month. Temples and homes are illuminated with votive candles and handmade lanterns. Unmarried women in Rangoon gather at the Shwedagon to weave new robes for the monks.

December
Nat Festivals: Full moon of the ninth month. Almost every village in Burma honors the spirits. Trance dances are performed by transvestites and *nat kadaws* (spirit wives), professional prophetesses considered married to the insatiably polygamistic *nats* who possess them.

Tibeto-Burman speakers. Major subdivisions include the lowland Pwo, the Sgaw near the Thai border, and the Bwe in the highlands. Other colorful subgroups include the Kayah ("Red Karen"), Karenni ("Black Kâren"), and the Paku ("White Karen"), terminologies which refer to the dress colors for unmarried females. It's back to black after marriage. Karen religion is a mix of Theravada Buddhism, spirit worship, and Christianity introduced by a 19th-century Baptist missionary named Reverend Judson. Their eager acceptance of Christianity made the Karen early allies of the British but estranged them from the Buddhist Burmans who have since regarded them with suspicion. Interestingly, Karen religious folklore includes a seven-day creation, a great flood, and a sacred book. These biblical parallels have led some religious ethnologists to speculate that the Karen are one of Israel's 10 lost tribes.

Padaung: Burma's most famous ethnic minority is the 5,000-strong Padaung, who live about 100 km south of Inle Lake. The Padaung are chiefly known for their "giraffe-necked" women who stretch their necks with elaborate piles of brass rings. X-rays taken by *National Geographic* revealed that the necks didn't stretch but rather the shoulder blades were forced down into the ribcages. The practice has mercifully ended, although older women must still wear the rings. Padaungs occasionally visit the Taunggyi market.

Kayah: The Kayah ("Red Karen" or Karenni) in Kayah state consider themselves distinct from the Karens despite common racial and linguistic characteristics. Kayah are often visited by trekking groups originating from Chiang Mai or Mae Hong Son. You'll be shown copies of old agreements with the British which guaranteed them autonomy from Burma rule.

Kachin: Though closed to Westerners since WW II, Kachin state in the far north must be a fascinating place with dozens of Kachin subtribes such as the Jingphaw, Maru, Atsi, and

Lashi. The Kachins have a long and distinguished history of warfare. They first served with British forces in Mesopotamia during WW I and later with U.S. resistance forces during WW II. Today they're Burma's most powerful noncommunist rebel group. The 8,000-man Kachin Independence Army (KIA) has grown wealthy from its control of Burma's lucrative jade trade.

Wa: When Queen Victoria sent a survey party into northeastern Burma in 1900, two members lost their heads to this notorious group. Heads taken in battle were posted on bamboo posts as magical protection against evil spirits and to ensure bountiful rice harvests. Bearded travelers should remember that heads with enormous beards or long hair are considered extra powerful by the Wa! The Wa are considered so fierce that the Kuomintang used them to fight the communists, the Burmese Communist Party hired them to fight the Rangoon government, and the Americans hired them as fearless mercenaries. And the payment? The Americans purchased their entire opium crop.

Naga: This remote and rarely visited group along the Burma-India border was once known for their animistic beliefs, headhunting, and human sacrifice. Today they have formed two rebel armies which demand autonomy within the Sagaing Division.

PRACTICAL INFORMATION

GETTING THERE

Air

Land entry to Burma is prohibited except from Mae Sai in northern Thailand. Visitors arrive by air at Rangoon's Mingaladon Airport. Rangoon is served from Bangkok by Thai International (Mondays, Thursdays, and Saturdays), Myanma Air (daily), Bangladesh Biman (Mondays), and Royal Nepal (Wednesdays). Thai also flies from Singapore, Calcutta, Dacca, and Kathmandu. Other airlines serving Rangoon include Aeroflot (Wednesdays from Vientiane) and Air China (Wednesdays from Kunming). Tradewinds flies twice weekly from Singapore, plus Myanma Air flies twice weekly from Hong Kong.

Each airline has its peculiarities. Thai is more expensive but they reconfirm onward tickets, an important consideration for visitors on tight schedules. Myanma Air is less expensive and their early arrivals give independent travelers first crack at internal train and plane reservations. Myanma Air (UB) cannot guarantee onward reservations and in-flight service is minimal to say the least—lunch will be warm Coke and bologna sandwiches on white bread. Bangladesh Biman is cheaper but flights are often overbooked, delayed, or completely canceled. Bumped travelers are often given extensions in Burma. Two popular options from Bangkok are a Bangkok-Rangoon-Bangkok route and a Bangkok-Rangoon-Calcutta ticket for US$180-240.

Land Routes

Burma's lack of road transport has long been the missing link in the overlanders' dream of a continuous land bridge from Istanbul to Singapore. The present government's isolationist policies make it doubtful that land routes will be completed anytime soon but attempts have been made in the past. Roads constructed during WW II included the Imphal Road, the famous Burma Road which briefly supplied the armies of Chiang Kai-shek, and Stilwell's 400-km Ledo Road from northern Burma to India. All roads were abandoned after the war and have (presumably) returned to jungle. Roads still open include connections to Ranong and Three Pagodas Pass west of Kanchanaburi. Smugglers also cross the border at Mae Sot near Tak and up the river from Mae Hong Song. Despite land entry being risky, many travelers have visited rebel camps and tribal villages just across the border. Exciting, adventurous, very dangerous.

In 1993 the road from Mae Sai in northern Thailand to Kengtung (172 km from the border) was officially opened to tourists. The seven-hour journey is made by jeeps. Details at end of this chapter.

GETTING AROUND

Air

State-owned Myanma Airways Corporation (UB) operates air services between Rangoon, Mandalay, Pagan (airport at Nyaung O), Lake Inle (air-

MYANMA AIR TIMETABLE

Morning Flights	Depart	Arrive	Fare
Rangoon-Pagan	0645	0815	US$75
Pagan-Mandalay	0835	0905	US$35
Mandalay-Heho	0935	1005	US$35
Heho-Rangoon	1020	1145	US$75
Rangoon-Mandalay	0645	0905	US$110
Mandalay-Rangoon	0935	1145	US$110

port at Heho), and the state of Rakhine. The central loop is served by a Fokker F-28 jet, which flies clockwise in the morning. The counterclockwise loop was cancelled several years ago due to lack of Western passengers. The service will probably be reinstated when tourism returns to healthy levels. Be prepared for problems. UB is an extraordinarily disorganized airline. Schedules are changed and flights canceled without notice. Obtaining a seat on the cuff can be difficult since most flights are filled with government officials and groups. Fares are inordinately expensive unless you can figure out how to pay with black-market *kyat*—a difficult task after independent travel ended in 1989. Burma's outdated fleet of Fokker Friendships is also dangerous. In October 1987, 49 people including 36 foreigners died in an air crash near Pagan. A wing and a prayer.

BURMA TRAIN SCHEDULE

(prices in *kyat*)

Route	Dep.	Arr.	Ord.	1st	Upper
Rangoon-	0600	2000	44	88	110
Mandalay	1815	0835			
	2100	1130			
Mandalay-	0600	2000	44	88	110
Rangoon	1815	0815			
	2100	1130			
Rangoon-	0600	1700	36	72	99
Thazi	1815	0530			
	2100	0830			
Thazi-	0845	1945	36	72	99
Rangoon	2100	0815			
	2400	1130			

Train

The following information on local travel has been retained in the event that independent tourism returns to Burma. Trains in Burma are slow and crowded but cheaper than planes and more comfortable than buses. The only useful line is from Rangoon to Mandalay. An express leaves twice daily at 0600 and 1815, arriving in Mandalay about 14 hours later. Since the countryside is rather dry and monotonous, it's best to take the night train and save the day for sightseeing. There is *only* one class worth considering: upper class with reclining seats. Ordinary class condemns you to wooden seats so hard that you will sleep on the floor. First class is (barely) cushioned seats permanently fixed in an upright position. Both are nightmares. Remember: take upper class with reclining seats.

Visitors going to Pagan can take a train to Thazi and continue to Pagan on a crowded Datsun pickup. It's a journey you'll never forget. Inle Lake (Taunggyi) can be reached with the direct 2100 train marked Shwenyaung or by express train to Thazi and then a rugged seven-hour truck ride to Taunggyi. All tickets must be purchased from the tourist office in Rangoon. You might also try purchasing a ticket directly at the train station with unofficial *kyat*. Soft drinks and inedible fried chicken are sold on the train. Bring along bottled water and other snacks. Train windows should be kept closed while leaving Rangoon unless you enjoy buckets of water thrown by laughing schoolkids.

Buses And Minitrucks

Tour groups are shuttled between tourist sights and towns in large and comfortable buses. Independent travelers must travel on Datsun pickups. These are nightmares on wheels, packed to the gunwales with cargo and passengers, racing at reckless speeds. Ordinary buses used on other routes are crowded, uncomfortable, and subject to frequent breakdowns. Buses connect most tourist destinations but *only* the shorter routes such as Thazi-Pagan (four to five hours) or Thazi-Inle Lake (five to seven hours) can be recommended. Longer journeys such as Mandalay-Pagan (10-14 hours), Mandalay-Inle (12-15 hours), or Pagan-Inle (10-12 hours) will waste precious time and almost certainly ruin your week in Burma.

city bus at Mandalay Hill

Chartered Jeeps

Five-passenger jeeps can be hired by the week for about US$300-500 depending on your bargaining abilities and the black-market price for gasoline. Jeeps are illegal and problems with overcharging and breakdowns have been reported. However, they save time and avoid the hassles with tourist officials. Be sure to settle all details in advance, including sites visited and total costs such as black-market gasoline. Check the condition of the jeep and make clear that the driver is responsible for all repairs. Drivers can be found around the budget hotels in Rangoon.

Water Transport

The river voyage by paddle wheeler from Mandalay to Pagan is one of the great delights of any visit to Burma. Boats depart Sundays and Thursdays at daybreak, stop briefly at a few small Burma villages to unload vegetables, and arrive at nightfall in Pagan. One of Southeast Asia's premier travel experiences.

Further travel downriver to Rangoon is possible though time-consuming. Prior to the closure of Burma to independent tourism, this was a do-it-yourself budget trip that cost only a few dollars. Today it's tightly controlled by Burma Tourism and included in several of their tours. Other boat trips include the nighttime journey from Rangoon to Bassein, the shuttle service between Rangoon and Syriam, and a boat from Mandalay to Mingun.

VISAS

Visas and onward tickets are required of all travelers. The Burmese government currently grants 15-day/14-night visas, a dramatic improvement over the pre-1971 situation when visitors were only given 24-hour transit visas, and pre-1989 when only seven-day visas were issued. Despite the increased cost and continuing hassles, the two-week visa makes Burma a much more enjoyable destination.

Visas can *only* be obtained from authorized agents of Myanmar Travel and Tours (MTT), who subcontract out much of their work to smaller travel agencies (often located in backpackers' enclaves such as Khao San Rd. in Bangkok). Burmese embassies and consulates throughout the world no longer issue visas directly to individual travelers but rather refer all requests to authorized representatives of MTT.

Visas are issued to independent travelers and visitors prebooked on package tours operated by Myanmar Travel and Tours. MTT tours sold by high-end operators in Bangkok such as Diethelm cost thousands of dollars, but inexpensive two-day tour packages are available from discount agencies in Bangkok for US$100-200. This somewhat extortionate fee includes little more than a 14-day visa and two nights' accommodations in Rangoon—the Burmese government's solution to shoestring travelers who once milked the black market for an almost-free holiday in Burma. Visitors can then make their own itinerary and travel independently the remaining 12 days.

Visa Extensions

Travelers to Burma are limited to 15 days/14 nights with no possibility of extension. A visitor who overstays his visa for a legitimate reason can pick up a Permit to Stay from the Burmese Immigration Office on Strand Road. Valid excuses for missing your departure flight include bus delays, fully booked internal flights, transportation breakdowns (very common in Burma), and documented illness. Other strategies for longer stays include reconfirming departures on the 14th day or arriving at the airport without a confirmed seat.

Bumped visitors usually spend another day in Rangoon, but one- and two-week extensions are granted during the busy tourist season from November to January. Gifts such as packs (not cartons) of cigarettes for immigration and airline officials also work wonders. Visitors who overstay their visas more than a few days can face problems at the airport, though departure officials are very receptive to small tips.

Meditation Visas

Special two-month visas are granted for Buddhist studies. It's no school holiday, but those seriously interested in Buddhism can write to the following meditation centers: **Mahasi Meditation Center,** 16 Thathana Yeiktha Rd., Rangoon; **International Meditation Center,** 31 Inya Myaing Rd., Rangoon; **Chan Mye Yeiktha Meditation Center,** 655 Kaba Aye Pagoda Rd., Rangoon; **Mogok Meditation Center,** 82 Natmauk Rd., Rangoon.

TOURS VS. INDEPENDENT TRAVEL

Escorted Tours

As noted above, Burma can be visited by independent travelers or with an organized tour, whether a grand 15-day excursion or a budget two-day package. Myanmar Travel and Tours offers over a dozen different excursions lasting from five to 15 days. Tours purchased in America and Europe cost US$200-300 per day and include all accommodations, meals, transfers, domestic transportation, and services of English-speaking guides. Prices do not include visas or airfare between Bangkok and Rangoon. Tours use air transportation between major points and chartered buses for shorter journeys. Sample prices in U.S. dollars are shown in the "Tours in Burma" chart.

Expensive, high-end tours can be booked from travel agencies in Bangkok such as Diethelm

Travel (tel. 252-4041) at 544 Ploenchit Rd. and Arlymear Travel (tel. 236-9317) at 109 Surawong Road. Both are dependable and experienced. The official representative for MTT in Bangkok is Skyline Travel Service (tel. 233-1864) at 491/39 Silom Plaza, 2nd Fl., Silom Road.

Budget two-day visa/hotel packages cost US$100-200 and can be booked at over a dozen travel agencies near Khao San Rd. in Bangkok. Inexpensive multiday tours are also available from the same agencies. For example, a nine-day tour of Rangoon, Mandalay, and Pagan, including roundtrip airfare from Bangkok, visa, accommodations, and airport taxes, costs US$550-800 depending on the travel agency. After subtracting the extras (visa, air tickets, airport connections), land costs on MTT tours purchased from these budget agencies in Bangkok average US$40-75 per day, not an unreasonable amount when you consider the average hotel room in Burma now ranges from US$25 to US$40. Not cheap, but not as expensive as Bhutan or Antarctica.

Tours can also be booked overseas through officially approved operators and travel agencies. In America, contact EastQuest (tel. 800-638-3449), Journeyworld (800-635-3900), or Travcoa (800-992-2004). The Ministry of Trade in Rangoon has also established a Myanmar National Tourist Office in America (tel. 919-493-7500) at 2514 University Dr., Durham, NC 27707. They arrange both group tours and individual packages at stratospheric prices.

These new policies have made Burma somewhat more expensive but also have opened new areas such as Monywa near Mandalay, the hanging rock at Kyaiktiyo, and several historical and recreation areas in Rakhine (Arakan) state near the Bangladesh border, though the last region was closed in 1992 after violent political disturbances. Other intriguing areas, such as Kayah state, the far north, and border areas with Thailand, remain closed to tourists. Shan state and its capitol of Kengtung opened to tourism in 1993. First-time visitors usually limit their sightseeing to Rangoon, Mandalay, Pagan, and Inle Lake.

Independent Travel

Independent travel briefly ended in 1989 but returned in 1993 after the government saw arrivals plunge from over 40,000 to under 3,000 annual visitors. Travelers need to carefully plan their 15 days in Burma. To enjoy your short vacation it's important to limit yourself to just a handful of destinations besides Rangoon. To try to see everything will make you feel like being shot out of a cannon. You'll *see* the views but *touch* nothing as your time is reduced to a confusing nightmare of packed trains, hellish bus rides, and harrowing plane flights. All you remember is packing and unpacking in dazed confusion while fighting Burma's notorious bureaucracy. Sick, overheated, tired, miserable, and angry, you will almost certainly end up disliking Burma and the Burmese people.

On the other hand, visitors who limit themselves to a few favorites will remember Burma as a lovely and magical place with warm people and intriguing sights. You should also expect the unexpected. Transportation delays and equipment breakdowns are commonplace. Trains grind to a stop and don't move for 24 hours. Jeeps blow a head gasket on the way up to Maymyo, buses drop their transmissions en route to Pagan, paddle wheelers get stuck on sandbars, and flights are routinely delayed or canceled. That's the time to just relax and look forward to your next trip to Burma.

If you can afford the tariff, flights are recommended, since bus rides between Mandalay, Pagan, and Inle Lake are long and miserable ordeals guaranteed to ruin your vacation. In fact, the best way to see Burma's four major destinations in just two weeks is to fly all the important connections. There are several problems with this. Internal flights are expensive and/or completely booked up by tour groups and government officials who have priority over independent travelers. It is also impossible to buy Myanma Airways tickets with confirmed seat reservations from overseas offices. Independent travelers must take their chances when it comes to air travel.

An independent journey through Burma requires some special travel skills. From the airport you should go directly to the tourist office to book all possible plane, train, and bus transport, and then reconfirm international departures at the airline office. Visit Shwedagon Pagoda that afternoon but leave further sightseeing in Rangoon for your last day. From Rangoon, you can proceed to Mandalay, Pagan, or Inle Lake by air, taxi, or train. The night train to Mandalay is comfortable, but *only* in upper class with recliners. Train and plane reservations should be reconfirmed with the tourist office in Mandalay, Pagan, or Inle Lake. They also sell hotel vouchers.

Costs

All visitors must exchange US$200 upon arrival at the airport. Prior to 1989, Burma could be easily toured—with the help of some black-market transactions—in seven days for under US$100, not including the roundtrip air ticket from Bangkok. Those days appear to be history, though Burma need not be prohibitively expensive for creative travelers.

Tour and Visa: Budget travelers should first contact a discount travel agency near Khao San Rd. in Bangkok and purchase the 15-day visa and air ticket to Burma. After arrival in Rangoon, you are, essentially, an independent tourist.

All visitors to Burma, whether backpackers or wealthy tourists on a luxury tour, are strongly urged to bring liquor and cigarettes and sell these items on the black market to obtain *kyat* at free-market exchange rates. More details on the black market and currency forms can be found below under "Airport Arrival and Customs" and "Burma's Black Market."

Hotels: Aside from internal flights, the most expensive component of any visit to Burma is accommodations. All budget guesthouses were closed down in 1989, forcing visitors to billet in government-approved hotels, which cost US$20-30 per night. These hotels, however, can be incredibly cheap if you can pay with black-market *kyat* (obtained from your liquor and cigarette import business) rather than official *kyat*. See "Currency Declaration Form" below for tips on how to avoid having your currency form stamped by the hotel staff.

Air Travel: Bangkok-Rangoon-Bangkok currently costs US$180-240 depending on the airline, Myanma Airways being the least and Thai International the most expensive options. Transportation that officially requires currency-form stamps includes all internal flights, the express train from Rangoon to Mandalay, and the boat ride from Mandalay down to Pagan. Other transportation forms, such as local buses and minitrucks, are stamp-free. Air tickets are almost impossible to keep off your currency form. Current airfares are found in the "Airfare" chart.

AIRFARES

Rangoon-Pagan	US$75
Pagan-Mandalay	US$35
Mandalay-Heho	US$35
Heho-Rangoon	US$75
Rangoon-Mandalay	US$110

Train: Officially, all travelers should purchase train tickets from an MTT office, though tickets can often be purchased stamp-free directly at the train station. Burmese lounging around the train station are often happy to help purchase your ticket if the station clerk appears reluctant. The Rangoon-Mandalay Express costs US$30-40 at official rates, but only a tenth the total with black-market *kyat*. Local transportation remains an inexpensive if torturous affair.

Meals: Meals from local cafes and night markets are inexpensive and stamp-free.

Total Costs: Costs for an independent traveler average US$200 for a roundtrip air ticket from Bangkok, US$20 for the visa, US$20-40 per day for hotels, plus varying charges for food and internal transportation. Travelers report that, on the average, they must pay official *kyat* half the time, but can use free-market *kyat* during the remainder of their visits.

AIRPORT ARRIVAL AND CUSTOMS

The following description of airport arrival and the black market is directed toward independent travelers. While much of this information is irrelevant to group tours, it will prove valuable to the independent visitor.

Rangoon's Mingaladon Airport is your introduction to the wonders of Burmese bureaucracy. Minibuses whisk you from the plane to the terminal, where health officials check health cards of passengers arriving from infected areas. You must then fill out the Customs Declaration and Currency Control forms described below. Customs formalities are slow but in most cases you can clear entrance procedures in about 30 minutes. Traveler's checks can be cashed at the People's Bank in the lobby. Visitors not on group tours should reconfirm outbound flights, if possible at the airport. Visitors are given vouchers for the mandatory US$200 exchange.

Taxi vouchers are sold at the Myanmar Travel branch office. Authorized hotels and prices are posted on their blackboard. Taxi fare can be spread across four separate currency forms. Go directly to the tourist office in downtown Rangoon and make all necessary plane and train reservations. Keep your taxi for sightseeing. Find a hotel (if you're spending the night), reconfirm departure flights, and head directly for Shwedagon Pagoda. Overnighters should remain at Shwedagon until sunset and then attend the evening dance performance at the Karaweik Restaurant.

Customs

All visitors to Burma are allowed to bring in one carton of cigarettes, one bottle of alcohol, one bottle of perfume, and personal effects. All valuables must be noted on a Customs Declaration Form, which is returned to customs officials on departure. Don't alter or lose this form. Although this procedure is designed to discourage black marketeering, the system is full of holes. Customs inspections are often very cursory or completely skipped depending on the mood of customs officials. Departure inspections are equally brief.

Currency Declaration Form

All foreign currency brought into Burma must be declared on a Currency Control Form. This paper will be stamped whenever you: 1) change money, 2) purchase hotel room vouchers, and 3) purchase transportation coupons from Myanmar Travel. Other expenditures such as food, souvenirs, and cabs are not recorded on this form and should be paid for with black-market money. Currency Control Forms are rechecked when you leave Burma to confirm that enough money was legally exchanged to pay for all recorded purchases. In reality this is almost impossible, since adding and rechecking all the entries is confusing and time-consuming.

Though the form was devised to stop black-market currency dealings, illegal transactions continue since Burmese services are *much* cheaper when paid for with black-market *kyat* than with *kyat* obtained at official rates. For example, a K700 flight is US$100 when paid with official *kyat* but less than US$10 when paid for with black-market money. The same savings also apply to trains, buses, and hotels.

After obtaining some black-market *kyat* (see below), the challenge becomes how to pay for your hotels and transportation without having your currency form stamped. This is fairly easy since the Burmese government can't possibly control everything. Solutions include cash tips to the front-desk clerk, a pack of cigarettes or ballpoint pens, or having one member of your group pay for and accept all the stamps in his/her currency declaration form. The other members politely claim that their wealthy friend is treating everyone to a free vacation. Hotel owners forget to stamp your currency form if you agree to stay for several days. It also helps that many Burmese citizens see profits in helping visitors sidestep all the red tape. This allows budget travelers to stay at first-class hotels with black-market currency almost as cheaply as staying at budget hotels with legal currency. Stamp-free train and bus tickets are available from local entrepreneurs for a slight surcharge.

And when you finally leave Burma, your currency form has become such a mess of hieroglyphics and doodlings that most inspectors simply give it a quick glance and then wave you through. The form should roughly balance out, but exact accounting now seems less important. Excess *kyat* up to 25% of your receipts can be reexchanged at the airport for foreign currency.

BURMA'S BLACK MARKET

Burma's amazing black market has an insatiable appetite for all goods, including cigarettes and liquor, perfume, clothing, medicines, books, watches, flashlights, hand lotion, calculators, batteries, aspirin, toothpaste, and nylons. All can be easily sold or traded. Black marketeering carries some risk, but with a degree of caution it's fun, profitable, and provides needed goods to the Burmese people.

Determining The Black-market Rate

Black-market exchange rates have steadily increased over the years from K20 per dollar in the early 1980s to K80-150 per dollar in the early 1990s. While over 10 times the official rate, it will probably be significantly higher when you arrive. Ask around and don't sell anything

(especially to your cab driver) until you have determined the current rate. For example, cigarettes and whiskey bring only K500 at the airport but over K3000 by the time you arrive at the tourist office. Taxi drivers offer the worst rates since they have first shot at their captive audience. It's best to ask the cabbie for his final offer but refuse to sell until you have checked with the black marketers waiting outside the tourist office. Don't sell until offers have peaked.

With that conversion rate in mind (60:1, 80:1, 100:1) it then becomes a straightforward mathematical exercise to figure out the correct value of any goods you have brought into Myanmar. For example, if the black-market rate is K100 to the dollar, a US$2 ballpoint pen should bring a *minimum* of K200 (100 times 2). That doesn't even include a charge for your services! That 100:1 conversion rate also means that the US$25 spent on cigarettes and liquor in Bangkok should bring a minimum of K2500 in Rangoon. This conversion rate can be applied to everything from T-shirts to goods purchased at the Diplomatic Store.

Liquor And Cigarettes

There are many safe and semilegal ways to obtain black-market *kyat,* but the easiest is to bring along a liter of Johnny Walker Scotch and a carton of 555 cigarettes. JW Black is better than Red. Both can be purchased in the duty-free shops at the Bangkok airport and immediately sold in Rangoon to cab drivers, hotel employees, and young men outside the tourist office. There is little risk in this transaction.

The Diplomatic Store

Another way to pick up currency is through the Rangoon Diplomatic Store near the tourist office. Imported cigarettes, liquor, and other goods can be purchased upstairs and easily resold. Foreign visitors can change traveler's checks downstairs, walk up to the third floor, and purchase 10 cartons of Indian Duya cigarettes for US$50 and a liter of Stolichnaya vodka for US$5. A lady piles it all into a wicker basket and carries it downstairs where it is immediately turned over to your contact. Agree on all prices in advance. At 100 *kyat* per dollar, your 10 cartons of cigarettes should bring a *minimum* of K5000.

Although technically illegal, the Diplomatic Store gambit has been going on for over a

TOURS IN BURMA

5 DAYS	8 DAYS	12 DAYS	12 DAYS	14 DAYS	14 DAYS	15 DAYS	15 DAYS
Rangoon	Rangoon	Rangoon	Rangoon	Rangoon	Rangoon	Rangoon	Rangoon
Pagan	Pagan	Mandalay	Bago	Pagan	Bago	Mandalay	Heho
Mandalay	Mandalay	Pagan	Heho	Mandalay	Heho	Maymyo	Kalaw
Rangoon	Inle Lake	Mt. Popa	Taunggyi	Akyab	Taunggyi	Pagan	Pindaya
	Taunggyi	Thazi	Inle Lake	Rangoon	Inle Lake	Pindaya	Taunggyi
	Bago	Rangoon	Pindaya	Mrauk-U	Pindaya	Inle Lake	Inle Lake
	Rangoon		Mandalay	Vesali	Mandalay	Taunggyi	Mandalay
			Pagan	Rangoon	Mingun	Bago	Mingun
			Rangoon		Pagan	Rangoon	Pagan
					Mt. Popa		Ngapali
							Sandoway
							Rangoon
US$1175	US$1775	US$1995	US$1995	US$2295	US$2295	US$2495	US$2495

decade. Remember, however, that there are few opportunities to spend a large amount of currency in Burma.

TRAVEL PRACTICALITIES

Tourist Information
Myanmar Travel and Tours is located in Rangoon at 77 Sule Pagoda Road near the Sule Pagoda. Branch offices are located in Mandalay, Pagan, Taunggyi, Sittwe, and Sandoway. Burma Travel arranges all tours to Burma. Prior to 1989, independent travelers were forced to book all internal transportation and budget accommodations from that agency's offices. Although they're disorganized and hopelessly lost to the needs of foreign visitors, it's a *big* mistake to get angry and lose your temper with tourism employees. They understand the shortcomings of Burma bureaucracy but still dislike rude behavior from foreign visitors. Treat them with respect and humor and suddenly doors are unlocked, hotel rooms are vacant, and reserved seats magically appear.

Currency
The unit of currency is the Burma *kyat* (pronounced chat) which is divided into 100 *pya*.

The official exchange rate is about 6.8 *kyat* to the dollar. The black-market rate varies from 60 to 100 *kyat*. This enormous spread is nothing less than government robbery. Rather than playing fair with visitors and giving them an honest exchange, the government coolly confiscates over 80% of your money. The only way to fight back is to skip Burma or use the black market. Excess *kyat* up to 25% of the unused balance on your currency form may be reconverted back to dollars at official rates when you leave the airport. Only American Express is accepted, though Visa will also be accepted in the near future.

Health
Burma is the only country in Southeast Asia where visitors *should* worry about their health. Nausea and diarrhea combined with high heat and primitive tourist facilities can quickly make your two-week vacation an unforgettable ordeal. Eat and drink with extreme caution! Only bottled water, soft drinks or Mandalay beer should be consumed. Keep the diet simple and safe. Avoid dairy products, uncooked vegetables, rich sauces, and spicy dishes. Do not assume that the best hotels or restaurants serve safe food. Use malaria pills and bring along a strong antidiarrheal such as Pepto-Bismol.

SUGGESTED READINGS

Visitors with limited time should read (in the following order) *Golden Earth* by Lewis, *Stillwell and the American Experience in China* by Tuchman, and *The Burman, His Life and Notions* by Shway Yoe.

◆ Bixler, Norma. *Burma: A Profile*. New York: Praeger, 1971. One of the best general surveys published. Light and easy reading.

◆ Bouchaud, Andre, and Lewis Bouchaud. *Burma's Golden Triangle: The Opium Warlords*. Hong Kong: Asia 2000, 1988. Two French journalists tell of drug dealing in the Golden Triangle and the separatist struggles of the Karens, Karennis, and Kachins.

◆ Bunge, Frederica. *Burma: A Country Study*. Washington, D.C.: United States Government, 1983. A well-organized general study strong on political and military analysis.

◆ Cady, John. *The United States and Burma*. Cambridge: Harvard University Press, 1976. A detailed history that, despite the title, has little to do with the United States. Cady is a former diplomat and professor who authored several books on Burma including *A History of Modern Burma*. Serious and authoritative history.

◆ Collis, Maurice. *The Land of the Great Image*. New York: Alfred Knopf, 1943. Collis was a civil-service worker who during the 1920s and '30s wrote eight historical-biographical novels set in Burma, including *Siamese White, The Lords of the Sunset* about the Shans, and the title piece about a Portuguese Jesuit priest in 17th-century Arakan.

◆ Khaing, Mi Mi. *The World of Burmese Women*. London: Zed Books, 1984. The author concludes that Burmese women are less oppressed than women elsewhere. Other titles by this well-known Burmese social scientist include *Burmese Family* and *Cook and Entertain the Burmese Way*.

◆ Lewis, Norman. Golden Earth. London: Eland Books, 1952. Lewis traveled through Vietnam and Burma in the '50s shortly after the Communists took China. His descriptions of Burmese people, life, and customs are wonderful. One of the great travel books on Southeast Asia. A personal favorite. Highly recommended.

◆ Orwell, George. *Burmese Days*. London: Penguin, 1982. A sad and biting recollection of Orwell's term as a police official in Mandalay during the 1920s.

◆ Shway Yoe (Sir James George Scott). *The Burman, His Life and Notions*. New York: Norton, 1963. Although this quirky cultural guide was written over a century ago, it remains a landmark achievement filled with remarkable insight and understanding of the Burmese people. A classic.

◆ Trager, Frank. *Burma from Kingdom to Republic*. New York: Praeger, 1966. Trager has been writing scholarly books on Burmese politics and economics since the '50s, when he served in Rangoon for American aid programs. Comprehensive but heavy going.

◆ Tuchman, Barbara. *Stilwell and the American Experience in China*. New York: MacMillan, 1971. America's premier historian successfully ties together the legends of Stilwell, Chiang Kai-Shek, Mountbatten, and others. Her most important work. Exciting and well written. Highly recommended.

SUGGESTED READINGS

◆ U Maung Maung. *General Ne Win*. New York. A revisionist attempt to portray Ne Win as a national hero. Authored by Burma's former chief justice responsible for the constitution, which gave absolute power to Ne Win. U Maung Maung became Burma's first civilian president in August 1988; he lasted nine days before being ousted by the military.

◆ Various authors. *Burma*. Singapore: APA Publications, 1990. The best guide available to Burma. Somewhat hefty for traveling but highly recommended as predeparture background reading. Superb photography.

RANGOON (YANGON)

This decaying colonial city of 3.5 million—one of Asia's most fascinating relics—is probably best described by what it does *not* have: traffic jams, fast-food restaurants, freeways, smog, hordes of tourists, flashy discos, or businessmen in three-piece suits. More than any other city in Asia, Rangoon still reflects the Romance of the East as evoked by the writings of Conrad and Kipling. There has been little effort to improve or even maintain its appearances since the British left in 1948. Everything rests in a fine state of decay. Palm trees poke through the sidewalks, patches of jungle threaten to swallow much of the city, and buildings have remained unpainted for over four decades. Rangoon's infamous platoon of old taxis has now been replaced with modern Japanese cars, but many of the buses are still antiquated wrecks held together with wire and glue. In all the world there is no place like Burma.

ATTRACTIONS

Burma considers all temples and pagodas to be sacred no matter their condition. Western visitors are expected to respect Buddhist tradition by dressing conservatively. *Shorts are inappropriate when visiting Buddhist shrines.* Long pants and a clean shirt should be worn by males. Women must keep well covered. Sandals are better than shoes since footwear must be removed before entering every temple. A shoulder bag for slippers, camera, and water bottle is useful.

Shwedagon Pagoda

This "Great Pyramid of Fire," which rises like "a sudden hope in the dark night of the soul," is perhaps the most impressive Buddhist shrine in the world. A must-see for every visitor to Burma. Located on top of Singuttara Hill about five km north of the city center, this volcano of gold rises dramatically above the shores of Royal Lake to dominate the entire city. Shwedagon is the spiritual heart and soul of Burma—a magical fantasy land of countless shrines, pagodas, and holy images that never fail to dazzle the endless streams of pilgrims. Buddhists believe this highly venerated stupa enshrines eight sacred hairs of the Buddha plus relics of three Buddhas that preceded him. Shwedagon is best visited in the late afternoon or early evening, when temperatures drop and pilgrims begin to circle the shrine. Independent travelers can charter a taxi or ask the tourist office to draw the character of the appropriate public bus.

Note: numbers in parentheses refer to the "Shwedagon Pagoda" map and legend.

Southern Stairway (1): Shwedagon is usually approached up a stairway flanked by a pair of grinning *leographs* or *chinthes,* Burma mythological offspring from lions and dogs. Shoes must be checked before climbing the stairway filled with stalls of nirvana goods, headdresses, religious tomes, packages of gold leaf, *thanaka* cosmetics, and marionettes.

The Pagoda (2): At the top you leave the gloom and plunge into one of the world's most

RANGOON (YANGON)

TO AIRPORT

MAHA PASAN CAVE ★

KABA AYE PAGODA ★

INYA LAKE HOTEL

KABA AYE PAGODA RD

INYA LAKE

RANGOON UNIVERSITY ■

PROME RD.

ARMY CLUB ★

MAHASI MEDITATION CENTER ●

★ NIGHT MARKET

KEMENDINE TRAIN STATION

CHAUK HTAT GYI PAGODA

KEMENDINE

BURMA KITCHEN ■

NGA HTAT GYI PAGODA ★

BAMBOO HOUSE ■

★ KOE HTAT GYI PAGODA

RESISTANCE PARK ★

SHWEDAGON PAGODA ★

KANDAWGYI HOTEL ●

ROYAL LAKE

KARAWEIK RESTAURANT

THAI EMBASSY ■

ZOO ★

MUSIC AND DRAMA SCHOOL ★

THANADA HOTEL ●

SAKANTHA HOTEL ●

TRAIN STATION

AUNG SAN ST.

MARKET ★

ANAWRAHTA ST.

DAGON HOTEL ●

MAHABANDOOLA ST.

DIPLOMATIC STORE ■

SULE PAGODA ●

THIDA JETTY (TO SYRIAM) ◆

TOURIST BURMA ■

YWCA ●

YMCA ●

MORTON STREET JETTY (TO BASSEIN) ◆

GARDEN GH ■

MUSEUM ■

MERCHANT ST.

STRAND HOTEL ■

0   1 km

BURMA AIR ■ ■ GPO

BOTATAUNG PAGODA ★

STRAND RD.

RANGOON RIVER

© MOON PUBLICATIONS, INC.

brilliant spectacles. Here is the Shwedagon, a Buddhist fantasyland of dazzling golden spires, mysterious images of Buddha, and cheerful *nats,* extraordinary temples of imaginative design, all the magic and mystery conjured up by the Orient. During the cooler parts of the day, hundreds of saffron-clad monks and devotees constantly circle the central pagoda in clockwise fashion. Dominating the spectacle is the magnificent golden pagoda soaring over 100 meters into the clear blue sky. Burmese royalty over the last five centuries has donated tons of gold and thousands of precious stones. Today the pagoda is entirely sheathed in gold leaf and studded with a remarkable 20,912 bricks of *solid* gold. The tip is set with over 10,000 diamonds, rubies, and sapphires, topped by a gigantic 76-carat diamond.

Temple of the Konagamana Buddha (3): Each of the four stairways leads directly to pavilions dedicated to one particular Buddha. While most Westerners are familiar with Gautama (the historical Buddha), Burmese also believe in four previous Buddhas and a future Buddha whose arrival will mark the end of the world. This particular temple is dedicated to the second Buddha.

Planetary Post for Mercury (4): To the left is a small but popular astrological post. Burmese believe that each week has eight days astrologically aligned with eight corresponding planets and animals. This odd number is accounted for by Wednesday being divided into Bohddahu (Wednesday morning) and Rahu (Wednesday afternoon). Burmese seek out and make offerings at their planetary prayer post, since fate is influenced by the day of birth. If born on a Wednesday morning, this is your post.

Chinese Prayer Pavilion (5): The 28 small gold images inside and above the north wall represent previous incarnations of the Buddha. Female monks lounge around, including one dynamic old lady who presents flowers to tourists. A good place to relax and do some people-watching.

Planetary Post for Saturn (6): Dedicated to visitors born on Saturday.

Student Commemorative Monument (7): The plaque across the blazing hot marble slabs relates in four languages the 1920 student revolt against British rule. Nearby pagodas hold exquisite alabaster Buddhas.

Nat Glass Case (8): Bo Bo Gyi (Guardian Nat of Shwedagon) stands on the right, and Thagyamin (King of the Nats) on the left. Most of the humanlike figures at Shwedagon each represent one of Burma's 37 *nats.*

Arakanese Pavilion (9): A wooden structure noted for its well-carved but badly blackened roof.

Reclining Buddha (10): Hall with an eight-meter Buddha and the Tine Burma Clinic, which advertises "Medical advice and treatment given free of charge every Sunday."

Chinese Merchants Pavilion (11): This photogenic collection of Buddha images facing different directions was donated to the temple by wealthy Chinese merchants.

Mai Lamu and King of the Nats (12): Two mythical figures credited with establishing Shwedagon over 1,000 years ago. Located atop each other on the pagoda walls. Difficult to spot.

Temple of the Kassapa Buddha (13): The pavilion directly in front of the western stairway is dedicated to a previous incarnation of the Buddha.

Two Pice Pavilion (14): Named after the two-*pice* contribution collected from each pilgrim who climbed the western staircase.

Western Staircase (15): A long and grand staircase which leads down to Army Park. Indian palm readers here speak English and tell fortunes for 25 *kyat.*

Planetary Post for Jupiter (18): Dedicated to visitors born on Thursdays under the sign of the Rat.

Planetary Post for Rahu (19): Dedicated to those born on Wednesday afternoons under the sign of the Tuskless Elephant.

Pagoda of the Eight Weekdays (20): Eight niches hold eight *nats* riding tigers, elephants, *garudas,* and other mythological animals. Each niche corresponds to day of birth, ruling planet, and animal associated with your birth sign.

Maha Gandha Bell (21): Across the burning tiles is an enormous 23-ton bell (cast 1779), which ranks as the third-largest bell in the world after the monsters in Moscow and Mingun. Maha Gandha was once seized as war booty but dropped in the Rangoon River when the overloaded boat capsized. The British failed in their attempts to raise the bell from the river bottom. Permission was given to Burmese who attached bamboo floats and successfully raised the bell.

SHWEDAGON PAGODA

NOT TO SCALE

ENTRANCE

© MOON PUBLICATIONS, INC.

SHWEDAGON PAGODA

1. southern stairway
2. Shwedagon Pagoda
3. Temple of the Konagamana Buddha
4. Planetary Post for Mercury
5. Chinese Prayer Pavilion
6. Planetary Post for Saturn
7. Student Commemorative Monument
8. Guardian Nat of Shwedagon
9. Arakanese Pavilion
10. Reclining Buddha
11. Chinese Merchants Pavilion
12. Mai Lamu and King of the Nats
13. Temple of the Kassapa Buddha
14. Two Pice Pavilion
15. western staircase
16. small pavilion
17. small pavilion
18. Planetary Post for Jupiter
19. Planetary Post for Rahu
20. Pagoda of the Eight Weekdays
21. Maha Gandha Bell
22. Assembly Hall
23. Miracle Buddha
24. northwest corner pagoda
25. Wish-granting Spot
26. Chinese Prayer Hall
27. Buddha's Footprint Pavilion
28. northern stairway
29. Library of the Zediyingana Society
30. Sandawdwin Pavilion
31. Temple of the Gautama Buddha
32. Planetary Post for Venus
33. Mahabodi Pagoda
34. gilded pagoda
35. Kannaze Pavilion
36. Shin Itzagona Pavilion
37. Naungdawgyi Pagoda
38. carved pavilion
39. Maha Tissada Bell
40. Planetary Post for the Sun
41. Replica of the Hti
42. Replica of the Lotus Bud
43. Tawagu Buddha
44. Temple of the Kakusandha Buddha
45. eastern staircase
46. Planetary Post for the Moon
47. U Nyo Pavilion
48. Hintha Prayer Pillar
49. Planetary Post for Mars
50. Bodhi Tree with Buddha
51. Shwedagon Museum

Assembly Hall (22): Public lectures on Buddhism are given here.

Miracle Buddha (23): The image crammed into a tiny little cubicle is considered among the most powerful at Shwedagon.

Northwest Corner Pagoda (24): Over the wall is a miniaturized replica of the Shwedagon which reputedly contains relics of the four previous Buddhas. Photos look like aerial shots.

Wish-granting Spot (25): A popular place for pilgrim photos. Ceremonies often involve the induction of a young man into the priesthood, complete with friends and parents attired in Pagan-period costumes.

Chinese Prayer Hall (26): A modern structure erected after the disastrous fire of 1931.

Buddha's Footprint Pavilion (27): Note before entering the life-size plaster figures of black Indians who appear to be running while stretching licorice. Enclosing the interior footprint is a *naga* filled with sacred water. Most amazing is the Buddha image illuminated by a psychedelic neon halo. Andy Warhol meets Siddhartha in this collision of Burma piety and Hollywood glitz. Wait until you see the neon halos in Mandalay!

Northern Stairway (28): This rarely used staircase passes the Martyrs Mausoleum of Aung San. Convenient for classic photos of the Shwedagon Pagoda with towering palms.

Library of the Zediyingana Society (29): Books delving into Burma religion are stored inside.

Sandawdwin Pavilion (30): At one time this building encased a sacred well. It now appears to be filled.

Temple of the Gautama Buddha (31): Dedicated to Gautama, the historical Buddha who will dominate world history until the arrival of the fifth and final Buddha.

Planetary Post for Venus (32): Dedicated to visitors born on Fridays under the sign of the Pig.

Mahabodi Pagoda (33): An unattractive building which replicates the original Indian structure near Varanasi. A better copy stands in Pagan.

Gilded Pagoda (34): Topped with a golden *hti*.

Kannaze Pavilion (35): Holds a 200-year-old Buddha image and a "miracle-working stone" . . . but only for those strong enough to lift it!

Shin Itzagona Pavilion (36): Dedicated to an alchemist whose wild but ultimately futile experiments resulted in his two false eyes—one from a goat and one from a bull. Don't miss this delightful little temple slightly off the beaten track.

Naungdawgyi Pagoda (37): The spot where the eight hairs of Buddha were first enshrined is marked by this large and unattractive pagoda.

Maha Tissada Bell (39): The 42-ton "Great Sweet Voice" was cast in 1841 by King Tharrawaddy. Like the Maha Gandha Bell, this enormous bronze bell was stolen by foreigners (this time the Portuguese) and dropped in the Rangoon River, but it was later rescued by the Burmese.

Planetary Post for the Sun (40): Dedicated to those born on Sunday under the sign of the *garuda* (called *galon* in Burma).

Replica of the Hti (41): Sacred umbrellas that top pagodas are called *hti*.

Tawagu Buddha (43): Only males can visit the miracle-granting image tucked away in an upper niche of the pagoda. Admission tickets available at the front office.

Temple of the Kakusandha Buddha (44): Honors the first Buddha. Finest of the four veneration halls. Note the palm turned upward instead of downward as with most Buddhist images.

Eastern Staircase (45): This colorful passageway, packed with pilgrims, palm readers, and vendors of religious paraphernalia, leads down to the Karaweik Restaurant on the banks of Royal Lake.

Planetary Post for the Moon (46): Dedicated to visitors born on Mondays under the sign of the Tiger.

U Nyo Pavilion (47): Well-carved wood panels relate Buddhist *Jataka* legends.

Hintha Prayer Pillar (48): Topped by a sacred bird which represents the ancient Pegu Dynasty.

Planetary Post for Mars (49): Dedicated to those born on Tuesdays under the sign of the Lion.

Bodhi Tree with Buddha (50): A good place to escape the sensory overload of Shwedagon. Views of Rangoon now blocked by trees.

Shwedagon Museum (51): Holds a small but worthwhile collection of silver Buddha images and replicas of pagodas.

Sule Pagoda

None of the following attractions compare with Shwedagon, but they give you a reason to wander the streets and watch the people. Sule

religious rites at Shwedagon

Pagoda was made city center when the British laid out Rangoon's grid-street system in the 19th century. The tallest structure in town, this eight-sided pagoda serves as a sort of Piccadilly Circus, drawing a steady stream of pilgrims, fortune-tellers, and spirit mediums who believe it home of the Shwedagon guardian *nats*. The exterior has been marred with unattractive shops but the interior is set with four Buddhas blazing with neon halos.

National Museum

Burma's major museum is limited in scope but worth visiting for its historical, ethnological, and archaeological exhibits. Many of the finest artifacts were taken by the British following the third Anglo-Burmese War in 1886 but returned to Rangoon in 1964. Centerpiece of the museum's collection is King Thibaw's famous Lion Throne, which dominates the center of the first floor. Surrounding the throne are glass cases guarding beautiful swords, rifles, and royal regalia gilded with gold and encrusted with pre-

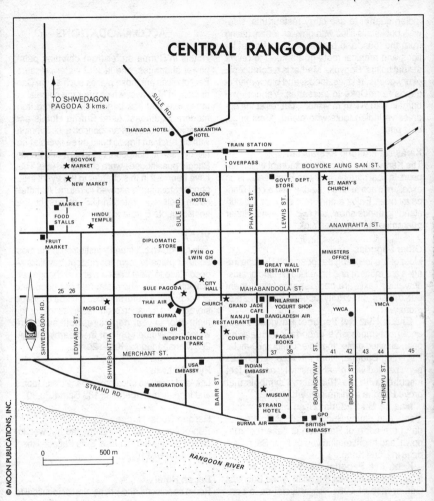

CENTRAL RANGOON

TO SHWEDAGON PAGODA 3 kms.

SULE RD.

THANADA HOTEL

SAKANTHA HOTEL

TRAIN STATION

OVERPASS

BOGYOKE AUNG SAN ST.

★ BOGYOKE MARKET

★ NEW MARKET

GOVT. DEPT. STORE

■ ST. MARY'S CHURCH

DAGON HOTEL

MARKET

FOOD STALLS

HINDU TEMPLE ★

PHAYRE ST.

LEWIS ST.

ANAWRAHTA ST.

FRUIT MARKET

DIPLOMATIC STORE

PYIN OO LWIN GH

MINISTERS OFFICE

■ GREAT WALL RESTAURANT

25 26

SULE PAGODA

★ CITY HALL

MAHABANDOOLA ST.

SHWEDAGON RD.

EDWARD ST.

★ MOSQUE

SHWEBONTHA RD.

THAI AIR

TOURIST BURMA

GARDEN GH

INDEPENDENCE PARK

CHURCH

★ GRAND JADE CAFE

NANJU RESTAURANT

COURT ★

■ NILARWIN YOGURT SHOP

BANGLADESH AIR

PAGAN BOOKS

YWCA

YMCA

MERCHANT ST.

37 39

41 42 43 44 45

USA EMBASSY

INDIAN EMBASSY

IMMIGRATION

BARR ST.

★ MUSEUM

BOAUNGKYAW ST.

BROOKING ST.

THEINBYU ST.

STRAND RD.

STRAND HOTEL

BURMA AIR

GPO

BRITISH EMBASSY

0   500 m

RANGOON RIVER

© MOON PUBLICATIONS, INC.

cious gems. In the left rear corner is a scale model of the Mandalay Royal Palace, worth studying since the original was tragically destroyed in WW II. Stairs hidden in the northwest corner lead upstairs to rooms filled with archaeological and anthropological artifacts. Free of charge; open Tues.-Fri. 1000-1500.

Botataung Pagoda

This modest and unimpressive pagoda near the Mandalay Jetty is unique among Burma stu-

pas. Rather than being constructed with a traditional solid core, the interior has been hollowed out with a series of meditation alcoves filled with dusty display cases. Many valuable Buddha relics, statuettes, and ancient inscriptions were uncovered when the original pagoda was bombed in WW II.

Bogyoke Market

Rangoon's largest and liveliest market is worth a quick look. From the tourist office, tour the

Indian quarter to see curry restaurants, sidewalk bookstalls filled with physics tomes dating from the '50s, and buskers selling herbal lotions and magical roots guaranteed to revive sexual spirits. Bogyoke Market is a cornucopia of dry goods, textiles, foods, and black-market goods from Coke to cassettes. Vendors will bargain with Western visitors, but resist the aggressive Indian touts who plead, "Best price, best price."

Karaweik Floating Restaurant
The Karaweik, a concrete restaurant which appears to float surrealistically on Royal Lake, is an excellent place to finish the day with a cold Mandalay beer. Enjoy a drink and stay for the outstanding dance show, but skip the awful dinner guaranteed to make you sick.

Other Pagodas
Most of the following pagodas and Buddha images are modern and have little historic or artistic value. Taxis are necessary to reach them but drivers cheerfully accept black-market money.

Chauk Htat Gyi Pagoda: Rangoon's second-most-impressive pagoda is actually an open-air shed protecting an enormous 70-meter Reclining Buddha. Note the face, which has been painted with great sensitivity, and the feet inscribed with the 108 sacred symbols that prove Buddha's enlightenment.

Mae La Mu Pagoda: Filled with *nat* monuments and gaudy Buddha statues, this pagoda in the north of Rangoon is deserted, run-down, and might remind you of Tiger Balm Gardens in Hong Kong.

Kaba Aye Pagoda: A modern and nondescript pagoda built for the Sixth World Buddhist Conference of 1954. An artificial cave constructed in the 1950s to accommodate over 10,000 conference visitors stands nearby. Ordinations and Buddhist seminars are held here.

Nga Htat Gyi Pagoda: An enormous Buddha sits inside.

Koe Htat Gyi Pagoda: A modern pagoda with a 20-meter Buddha.

Ah Lain Nga Sint Pagoda: A somewhat intriguing pagoda constructed about 30 years ago in a wedding-cake style with five Chinese towers, Muslim-style minarets, and a messy museum with plaster elephants and antique radios.

ACCOMMODATIONS

Hotels in Burma suffer from chipping paint, power shortages, and lack of water pressure. Best choices are those places such as the Candacraig in Maymyo, which offer the colonial atmosphere that has largely disappeared from modern Southeast Asia. Burma Hotels and Tourism Services has announced a joint venture with an Austrian firm to build three five-star hotels by 1994 in Rangoon, Mandalay, and Pagan. Budget guesthouses were closed in 1989. They have been left in this chapter in the event independent tourism is allowed to return. All hotels quote their room rates in U.S. dollars; budget hostels quote Burma *kyat.*

YMCA
This run-down but friendly institution is the most popular place in town for budget travelers. A good place to meet travelers and exchange current information. The restaurant has good food at low prices. Useful services include baggage storage and advance room reservations for the night prior to your departure. Both sexes are welcome. Women only at the nearby YWCA. 263 Mahabandoola, K80-120.

Pyin Oo Lwin
Low-end travelers once enjoyed the clean rooms and friendly management; 183 Barr, K60-90.

Garden Guest House
Run-down and poorly maintained but well located near the tourist office. Sule Pagoda Road, tel. 71140, US$10-20.

Dagon Hotel
Room conditions and prices almost identical to those of the Garden Guest House. Closer to the train station but noisy from street traffic. 256 Sule Pagoda, US$10-20.

Sakantha Hotel
Reasonably clean and conveniently located for those who need to catch an early train to Mandalay. Railway Station, tel. 82975, US$36-45.

The Strand Hotel
Constructed to compete with the Raffles in Singapore and the Oriental in Bangkok, this grand

THE ARTS OF BURMA

As in other Indianized countries in Southeast Asia, Burmese art received its source of inspiration from older Indian traditions. Prior to the rise of Pagan in the 11th century, the 7th-century Pyu kingdoms of Halin and Sri Kshetra created Indian-derived sculpture of Mahayanic images, funerary urns, and great cylindrical stupas. The western Mons in the lower Irrawaddy also constructed heavy and graceless temples with narrow, fretted windows and interior frescoes of Theravada inspiration. After the Chinese destroyed the Pyu in 832, Burman immigrants began to settle near Pagan. It was here, during the reign of King Anawrahta, that captive Mon architects and craftsmen constructed a magnificent empire of 5,000 pagodas and temples filled with images and frescoes.

Pagan and the Golden Age of Burmese Arts ended in 1287. The succeeding four centuries were periods of warfare; Burmese arts did not emerge from this period of political instability until the kingdom of Ava was established in 1636. This was the second chance for Burmese arts. After the defeat of the Thais in 1767, royal Siamese dancers were brought back to Ava, where Thai classical *khon* and *lakhon* were used to form the basis of modern Burmese dance. The final century of the Konbaung Dynasty (1783-1885) witnessed a resurgence of architecture, sculpture, and *zat gyi* (masked dance-drama) sponsored by the courts of Amarapura and Mandalay. Artistic creation died when British colonial rule ended state sponsorship and royal patronage.

Burmese Theater

Burmese dance-drama, marionette plays, spirit-medium dances, and classical masked dance are among Southeast Asia's most charming and likeable forms of the performing arts. Best are the *zat pwes* held during temple festivals and village fairs.

Starting in the evening around 2100 and finishing just before sunrise, this "people's theater" combines unrestrained dance and melodramatic action with Punch-and-Judy comedy and exuberant music. Among the 100 performers who parade across the stage are a dozen clowns who keep the audience howling with their wild antics. Stories are taken from Buddhist Jatakas, which recount early incarnations of Buddha, or from Indian epics such as the Ramayana. Stories set in classical periods of Burmese history are also popular. But rather than the serious retelling of old Buddhist or Hindu legends, Burmese theater is extraordinarily lively, warm, and full of good humor, and reflects the friendly personality of its people. If you enjoy the Burmese disposition, then you will love their theater. Dramatics are backed by a Burmese *saing* orchestra similar to Indonesian *gamelan* but with an additional circle of nine tuned drums and a 13-stringed harp. Although the music is atonal and based on the pentatonic scale, it ranks second only to Indonesian *gamelan* in terms of beauty and appeal.

Unfortunately, with only a 15-day visa and the disorganized state of Burma's tourist industry, it can be very difficult to find a performance. You must ask everyone from hotel employees to cigarette salesmen. Performances are generally held on temple grounds under a full moon night during the dry season from October to May. Visitors interested in *zat pwe* should arrange their visits to coincide with a full moon and then look for the makeshift bamboo stages on the grounds of Buddhist temples. Nightly dance performances in Rangoon's Karaweik Restaurant are touristy but nevertheless highly recommended for the superb costumes and outstanding technique. Burmese puppet shows can be seen in Pagan.

old dame remains one of Southeast Asia's most famous hotels despite the complete 1993 renovation by Adriaan Zecha, the Indonesian-born millionaire known for his deluxe hotels such as the Amanpuri in Bali and the Amandari in Phuket. Zecha and his partnership with Swissbel Hotels Asia also control the Inya Lake and Thanada hotels, giving them a near-complete monopoly over hotel rooms in Rangoon. No more chipping paint, broken bathroom fixtures, erratic showers, scampering rats, amusing lost-and-found cabinets, sneering waiters, and other

colonial curiosities . . . only a modern 159-room reconstruction of the last vestige of Kipling's East. 92 Strand, tel. 81533, US$200-300. Rooms cost US$10-21 prior to "restoration." Why can't they leave anything alone?

Kandawgyi Hotel

Previously used as the British Boat Club and Natural History Museum, the Kandawgyi is the finest hotel in Rangoon. Standards tend to high since it's the training center for the Burmese Hotel and Tourist Corporation. The Veranda

Bar is a popular gathering point for wealthy Burmese and foreign diplomats. Individual lakeside bungalows are luxurious. Kennedy Drive, Royal Lake, tel. 80412, US$35-60.

Inya Lake Hotel
An overpriced and sterile white elephant built by the Russians. So isolated that only tour groups are exiled up here. Kabe Aya Pagoda, tel. 50644, US$80-120.

RESTAURANTS

Burmese meals are centered on rice with side dishes of curried fish, chicken, or vegetables. The national side dish is *ngapi,* a strong-smelling fish paste that is an acquired taste like Korean *kim chi* and Filipino *balut.* Try the thick fish-and-noodle soup (*mohinga*), clear vegetable soup (*hingyo*), and rice cooked with coconut milk, a Burma delicacy. Outstanding Burmese food is only found in households. Restaurant fare is often a disappointing mix of bland curries, mysterious soups, and some of the foulest soft drinks in the world. You haven't lived until you have experienced Vimto and the dreadful orange tea of Burma. Mandalay beer is fairly good on a hot day . . . if the brewery isn't broken down, out of hops, or short on bottle caps.

Strand Hotel Restaurant
Decent Western meals and daily specials are inexpensive if you pay with black-market *kyat.* The food is nothing special but the atmosphere makes this one of Rangoon's great experiences.

Karaweik Restaurant
This ferroconcrete replica of an old Burmese boat is certainly one of Rangoon's most distinctive structures. Unfortunately, the food is awful and overpriced and will most likely make you sick. The nightly cultural show is outstanding. Skip the dinner, see the show.

Kandawgyi Hotel Restaurant
Some of the best food in Rangoon is served inside the cafeteria-style dining room. The sterile atmosphere is occasionally relieved with performances of Burmese music and dance.

Bamboo House
Considered by many the best Burmese restaurant in Rangoon. Inconveniently located at 3 Thapye Nyo Street northwest of the Shwedagon Pagoda. Taxis are necessary.

YMCA
Budget Chinese and Indian dishes are served buffet style on the main floor.

Palace Restaurant
Perhaps the best Chinese restaurant in Rangoon. Szechuan or Hokkien specialties are expensive but portions are generous. 84 37th Street near Merchant.

Nilarwin Yogurt Shop
Conveniently located near the center of town and a good place for fruit shakes and dairy products. A hangout for Burmese searching for Western goods.

Indian Restaurants
Most Indian restaurants in Rangoon are located on Anawrahta just west of Sule Pagoda. Try the cheap *biryani* and fresh *roti.*

ENTERTAINMENT

Karaweik Restaurant
Outstanding Burmese cultural shows are given nightly at 2000. The first-rate revue includes dancing, singing, instrumental selections, and an amazing display of rattan ball. Unless you are fortunate enough to stumble across a festival or *zat pwe* this will probably be your only opportunity to witness traditional Burmese dance. Highly recommended.

State School Of Music And Drama
Public performances of traditional Burma drama are given weekends at 1400 during the rainy season. The public can watch rehearsals during the school year from October to June. Myanmar Travel and Tours has details.

Festivals
The tourist office has schedules for upcoming celebrations. Theater performances and pup-

pet shows are given on full-moon evenings at Shwedagon.

SHOPPING

Burma has relatively little to offer the shopper aside from a few handicrafts such as lacquerware, Shan shoulder bags, and antique puppets. Like elsewhere in Asia, handicrafts are least expensive at the point of origin. You can save a bundle by using black-market currency or swapping your shirts, cassettes, and ballpoint pens. Among the better buys are lacquerware tables and chests from Pagan. Shan shoulder bags are cheapest in the Inle Lake region. *Longyi* collectors may want to pick up and then wear the Burmese sarong while traveling around the country. Males wear solids or plaids; ladies wear colorful splashes of tropical flowers. The Burmese will love you for it. Whackin' great cheroots are sold by toothy ladies at incredibly low prices. Pay for one and you get a month's supply. Most of the old 19th-century wooden puppets once sold at Shwedagon have now been purchased by antique dealers from Bangkok. Burma's most famous products are precious gems such as rubies, emeralds, and sapphires. Westerners can legally buy precious stones only at the Diplomatic Store in Rangoon. Prices are high, and unless you are an expert gemologist, *don't buy gems in Burma.* Street stones are just clever Japanese synthetics that convincingly scratch glass.

Where To Shop
Bogyoke Market: Burma's largest marketplace has a good selection of handicrafts sold by aggressive touts. Bring Western goods for trading and bargain firmly.

Diplomatic Store: This government-operated store near the tourist office has a poor selection of overpriced handicrafts. Shop first in Pagan and Inle and leave the Diplomatic Store for last-minute purchases. Best buy here? Stolichnaya at US$5 per liter.

Other Markets: Rangoon's Chinese market is at the intersection of Lanmadaw and Mahabandoola. The Indian Market is on 26th Street just off Anawrahta. Both are worth a quick look, although there isn't much worth buying.

Shwedagon Pagoda: The bizarre bazaar on the southern stairway is packed with bronze Buddhas, tattoo instruments, newly manufactured puppets, and other religious paraphernalia. Probably the most intriguing shopping opportunity in Burma.

PRACTICALITIES

Tourist Information
The main office of Myanmar Travel and Tours (the former Tourist Burma) is at 77 Sule Pagoda Road in the center of Rangoon. Myanmar Travel arranges tours, distributes maps, and changes money. Transportation vouchers and hotel permits are no longer sold here. Employees are helpful to those Westerners who treat them with respect and maintain a sense of humor, but they make life miserable for those who lose their tempers. Open 0800-2000 Monday-Friday; Saturdays until noon. The cold-water jug is a lifesaver on hot days.

Diplomatic Offices
Visas can be obtained from most foreign diplomatic missions in Rangoon, but this is not recommended because time is wasted and visas are priced the same as in other countries.

Communications
The GPO is located at the corner of Strand and Aung Kyaw Road. Mail service is not reliable. Overseas calls can be made from the Central Telegraph Office at the corner of Pansodan and Mahabandoola Street. Service is understandably erratic in a country with 40 million people and only 75,000 telephones.

Burma has two English-language newspapers, the *Working People's Daily* and the *Guardian*. Both are published by the Peoples Printing and Publishing Works and carefully monitored by the Press Scrutiny Agency. A few minutes reading through one of these papers reveals much about the Burmese mindframe.

Myanmar Broadcasting has three English-language radio programs which compete with foreign broadcasts such as the BBC. Television has been introduced. Burma is six hours *and 30 minutes* ahead of Greenwich mean time!

Rangoon is 30 minutes behind Bangkok standard time. Not that it really matters, but you might want to set your watch back.

Medical Services

Emergency medical attention is given at the Diplomatic Hospital (tel. 50149) on Kyaikkasan Road near Royal Lake. Doctors can extend visas. Travelers interested in bringing medical supplies to Burma should contact the Christian Guest House in Bangkok off Silom Road at 123 Saladaeng, Soi 2.

Bookstores

U Ba Kyi's Pagan Book House in the narrow alley at 100 37th Street has a surprisingly good selection of books for sale. He trades for books on Burma or travel in Southeast Asia. Other bookstores include Theingi Maw Book Shop at 355 Maung Taulay Street and the street stalls on Sule Pagoda Road.

GETTING AROUND

Taxis

Chartered taxis are a great way to tour Rangoon, but beware of drivers charging outrageous fares. Taxis should cost K30-40 per hour and not the K100-125 asked by drivers at the YMCA. Taxi fare to the airport is K90-110; city center to Shwedagon is K15-20. Public taxis are unmarked and in extremely short supply. Flagging one down is nearly impossible. Keep the taxi that picks you up at the airport. Taxis also wait outside the better hotels.

Buses

Myanmar Travel and Tours will explain local bus routes and write out the numbers in Burmese script. Rangoon buses at rush hour are the most crowded vehicles I have ever been crammed into . . . even worse than the minibuses near Malang on Java.

VICINITY OF RANGOON

PEGU (BAGO)

Pegu, ancient capital of Burma and storehouse of Burma culture, is a fascinating side trip from Rangoon. The city was established by King Byinnya, who had transferred his Talaing capital from Martaban in 1365. Hamsawaddy kings during the next three centuries erected dozens of monuments which survive today as the city's major monuments. In 1541 the Toungoo Dynasty annexed Pegu to create Burma's second capital before the city was visited in the 16th century by Europeans who described it as the most impressive city in Asia. Constant warfare bankrupted the dynasty. Pegu was razed by the ruler of Toungoo in 1599 but enjoyed another brief era of glory as a 17th-century Mon kingdom before being finally destroyed by King Alaungpaya in 1757. Pegu today is a modestly sized town with some of the more impressive monuments in Burma.

Attractions

Shwemawdaw Pagoda: Soaring to over 110 meters and loftier even than Rangoon's Shwedagon, Pagan's magnificent "Great Gold God Pagoda" is among the most venerated and impressive monuments in Southeast Asia. Mythological *chinthe* guard the cool passageways filled with religious souvenirs and fading murals. As at Shwedagon, the terrace is crowded with pilgrims who pray at the planetary posts and make offerings to *nat* and Buddha images. Shwemawdaw alone makes the journey to Pegu worthwhile.

Kalyani Sima: All of the following are located about three km east of Shwemawdaw. Trishaws can be hired but it's an interesting walk through town and across the Pegu River. Continue one km further and then walk north of the main road. Reconstructed Kalyani Sima now serves as a Buddhist ordination hall for hundreds of monks. Pali and Mon tablets to the east are inscribed with histories of Burma's trading policies with Sri Lanka and India.

Shwethalyaung Buddha: Constructed in 994 by King Migadippa, this enormous image was abandoned to the jungle until being uncovered in 1881 by British engineers. Many consider the 55-meter reclining image the most lifelike and beautiful in the country.

Mahazedi Pagoda: The great stupa to the north was constructed in 1560 to enshrine a replica of the Buddha's tooth brought from Sri Lanka. Badly damaged by earthquakes but recently reconstructed. Good views from the top.

Shwegugale Pagoda: 64 Buddha images encircle the dark interior.

Kyaikpun Pagoda: Constructed in 1476 by King Dhammazedi, this quartet of 30-meter seated Buddhas represents the four historical Buddhas; to the north is Gautama, Konagamana faces south, Kakusandha is east, and the destroyed image of Kassapa once faced to the west. Located four km south of Pegu, about 100 meters off the road to Rangoon.

Shwegugyi Pagoda: This cluster of ruined monuments was originally built by Dhammazedi after the original prototype in Bodgaya. Located in Payathonzu Village about one km farther toward Rangoon.

Accommodations

In 1991 Myanmar Travel and Tours opened the Shwewatan Hotel to foreign visitors who wish to overnight in Pegu. Most travelers simply tour Pegu on a day visit, but figure on US$25-35 for a room with private bath. Trishaws can also be hired here.

Getting There

Pegu is 80 km east of Rangoon. It's best to organize a group and hire a taxi from Rangoon. Be sure to agree on the price and all attractions to be visited. Trains depart hourly from Rangoon. Buses leave every 30 minutes from Edward Street. Tourist officials will write the bus number down in Burmese. Pegu can also be visited on the train back from Mandalay. The station isn't signposted but passengers will point out where to jump off the slowly moving train. Trishaws can be hired at the train station. There are no legal hotels in Pegu.

SYRIAM AND KYAUKTAN

Syriam was a major European trading post during the 15th and 16th centuries. The city was established by a Portuguese adventurer named De Brito who established a small kingdom here. After his gang of mercenaries sacked Pegu in

pilgrim at Shwedagon

1599, it appeared that the Portuguese were about to establish a colonial outpost in lower Burma. But reinforcements from Goa were not forthcoming, and Syriam fell to the Burmese in 1613. Sentenced to death, it is said that De Brito survived for three days after a sharpened stake was driven through his vital organs.

Syriam today is little more than a sleepy backwater blessed with Burma's largest oil refinery and the People's Brewery. Top draw is the hilltop Kyaik Khauk Pagoda. From Rangoon, take buses 9 or 12 down Bogyoke Aung San Road and ask to be let off at the Thida Jetty in the Pazundaung Creek. Ferries depart every 45 minutes. The last ferry leaves Syriam at 1800.

Twenty km south of Syriam and situated on a small island is the Kyauktan Pagoda (Ye Le Paya Pagoda), with temple murals and sacred catfish kept fat by devout pilgrims. Buses from Syriam take 45 minutes.

OTHER DESTINATIONS

Within striking range of Rangoon are several towns and monuments rarely visited by Westerners. Most are legal to visit but you'll need the assistance of sympathetic Burmese to reach or spend much time in these places.

Bassein
Chiefly known for the Shwemokhpaw Pagoda and umbrella-painting industry. Steamers depart daily at 1630 from the Morton Street Pier and arrive in Bassein the following morning at 0800. Steamers leave Bassein at 1630 and arrive in Rangoon the following morning.

Twante
A small town known for hand-fashioned pottery. Ferries leave from the Mawtin Street Pier two km west of the Strand. Allow three hours.

Kyaiktiyo
Burma's most popular pilgrimage center is the holy rock at Kyaiktiyo, about 160 km east of Rangoon. It's a five-hour hike up the winding trail to the golden-sheathed, hti-capped boulder which hangs precariously over the edge of a deep canyon. This trek is only possible during the dry season and best attempted on full-moon evenings from October to May. The summit has sleeping huts, shrines, and restaurants. Kyaiktiyo is currently off-limits.

Moulmein
Kipling probably was referring to the Kyaikthanlan Pagoda when he wrote "By the old Moulmein Pagoda, looking lazy at the sea," but given his powers of imagination it is possible that he wrote the lines while having tea aboard his tramp steamer. Other attractions include the Uzina Pagoda, Hapayon Cave, and Kawgaun Cave. South of Moulmein is a large Allied war cemetery and the beach resort town of Amherst popular with the British in colonial days. Moulmein is currently off-limits. Burma Air flies to Moulmein in 40 minutes. Trains leave Rangoon daily at 0600 but it is unlikely you'll be sold a ticket. Hotels are closed to foreigners but friendly Burmese have reportedly put up visitors.

MANDALAY

Burma's second-largest city is one of the most romantic place-names in the English language. Whether it was Kipling's famous verse about those flying fish on the Road to Mandalay or that old Bob Hope movie, this sprawling city has an image that most tourist-promotion departments would kill for. Mandalay is the cultural heart of Burma, where the most refined dance and music traditions survive and where Burmese is spoken in its purest form. Although much of the city was destroyed during WW II, surviving monasteries and temples stand as some of the finest wooden structures in the country. Nearby attractions include several former capitals with splendid secular and religious architecture, tremendous pagodas, and a British hill resort with a fascinating market and a nostalgic colonial hotel. Some complain about the hot climate and are disappointed with the monotonous modern architecture, but most visitors leave satisfied with their brief look at Burma's northern city.

HISTORY

Mandalay takes its name from Mandalay Hill, which according to legend was climbed by the Buddha, who pointed across the plains and prophesied that a magnificent city would be built on the 2,400th anniversary of his birth. Much of the region remained a deserted plain until about 2,400 years later when King Pagan Min (1845-1852) established the capital of his Konbaung Dynasty in nearby Amarapura. Dynamic but headstrong and fond of grandiose construction projects, Pagan Min financed his building mania by killing his rich subjects, collecting their fortunes, and forcing the remainder of his citizenry to work on his mad projects. British irritation with the bloody reign of Pagan Min resulted in the systematic dismemberment of lower Burma.

Following the embarrassing fiasco of the second Anglo-Burmese war, Pagan Min was de-

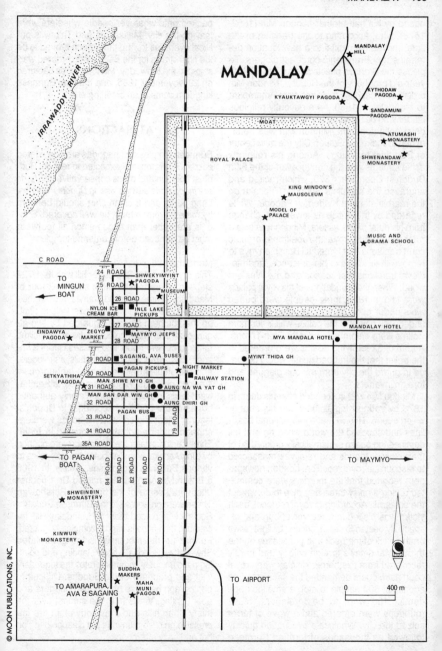

posed by his half-brother Mindon Min (1852-1878), who, according to the tradition of the time, moved his capital to a new location determined by Brahmanic court astrologers. To please the Brahmin priests and fulfill the 2,400-year-old prophecy of the Buddha, Mindon Min ordered his capital transferred from Amarapura to Mandalay in 1860. As a devoutly religious leader who believed he had truly reached Buddhist enlightenment, Mindon Min was determined to make his Golden City the new center of Buddhist teachings. Among his religious achievements was the convocation of the Fifth Buddhist Council in 1879, which recited and engraved the complete Buddhist Tripitaka on the marble slabs at Kythodaw Pagoda. While regarded by the British as a welcome change from his nutty predecessors, Mindon was also a ruler plagued by royalist rebellions, archaic court traditions that forced all British envoys to remove their shoes in his presence, and medieval traditions that scandalized the Western world. When the foundations of his royal palace were laid in 1858, three people were buried *alive* under each gatehouse, plus one more under each corner of the palace wall. Four more victims were entombed under the Lion Throne. A total of 52 terrifying deaths were ordered in the belief that the trapped spirits would continue to guard the city from ruinous plagues and foreign invaders.

Mindon Min was succeeded after his death in 1878 by young King Thibaw and his strong-willed queen. Thibaw made international headlines and shocked the world when he and his domineering queen systematically ordered 80 of their closest friends and relatives massacred to discourage royal rebellion. London newspapers reported that the murders were committed during a noisy three-day *pwe* to drown out the screams. According to royal protocol, each victim was placed in a red velvet bag and respectfully beaten to death; princes by light blows on the back of the neck and princesses on the throat. Mandalay's foreign colony had hardly recovered from this horrific display when royal court astrologers demanded the sacrifice of an additional 600 people to stop a smallpox epidemic; 100 were to be foreigners. Mass roundups were ordered and a wave of terror seized the city. Wholesale evacuation quickly followed as thousands of terrified Burmese

packed onto whatever paddle wheelers were leaving the city. Massacres and Thibaw's political overtures toward the French proved to be the final straws for the British, who ordered warships up the Irrawaddy. Mandalay was captured on 29 November 1885, and the final Burmese kingdom came to an crashing end.

ATTRACTIONS

Burmese temples and pagodas are considered sacred. All visitors are expected to respect Buddhist tradition and dress conservatively. *Shorts are inappropriate when visiting Buddhist shrines.* Long pants and a clean shirt should be worn by males. Women must be well covered. Sandals are better than shoes since all footwear must be removed before entering temples.

Mandalay Hill

This dry and dusty 236-meter hill with its 1,729 steps is where most visitors start their tour of Mandalay. Three covered stairways wind their way up to the summit, though most visitors climb up the southern staircase guarded by two gigantic *chinthe*. This long but relatively easy climb takes about two hours and passes Buddha images, dozing monks, souvenir stalls, astrologers, and beautiful Burmese women languorously smoking cheroots. Halfway up are the Pershawar Relics, perhaps the world's only authentic bones of the Buddha. According to Buddhist legend, after his cremation his bones were enshrined under eight stupas located in India. Three centuries later the chambers were opened by King Ashoka, who distributed the holy relics to various Buddhist strongholds. Finally, in 1908 a British Museum curator named Dr. Spooner uncovered some of the bones in Pershawar. These were presented to the Burmese Buddhist Society who placed them on Mandalay Hill. Incredibly, the shrine is almost completely ignored. Further up the mountain is the gold-plated Shweyattaw Buddha, whose standing and pointing pose uniquely commemorates the legendary visit and prophecy of the Buddha. Difficult to photograph because of cramped quarters and poor lighting. Views from the summit over the misty Shan hills and Irrawaddy plain are impressive on crisp mornings but disappointing on hot and hazy afternoons.

Kyauktawgyi And Sandamuni Pagodas

Constructed in 1878 by King Mindon, Kyauktawgyi is chiefly noted for its seated Buddha carved from a single block of Sagyin marble so monstrous that 10,000 men labored almost two weeks to drag it here from the banks of the Irrawaddy. King Mindon himself instructed the sculptors as to the shaping of the face but as one writer put it, "His pious zeal was greater than his artistic talent for the image, like the building which shelters it, is exceedingly ugly." You will, however, be impressed by the psychedelic neon halo. Fabulous. Surrounding the shrine are the 80 disciples of Buddha, 20 on a side.

The whitewashed pagoda of Sandamuni was constructed over the graves of the royal family members killed during the palace rebellion of 1866. Spread across the pagoda grounds are some 1,774 stone monoliths inscribed with commentaries on the Buddhist Pali Canon.

Kythodaw Pagoda

Built in 1857 by King Mindon, the central pagoda is modeled after the Shwezigon in Pagan and surrounded by a collection of 729 stone slabs inscribed with the complete Buddhist Tripitaka. After Mindon's Fifth Great Buddhist Council of 1879 corrected the sacred Pali texts, a team of 2,400 monks spent six months reciting the entire canon in a nonstop marathon. Afterward it took stonecutters another six years to carve the world's largest book of man-sized pages protected by individual pagodas. The foyer is now modernized with coin-operated puppet machines where for a few *pya* you can listen to a calliope melody as the puppets gyrate.

Atumashi Monastery

European visitors of the 19th century described this monastery as the most magnificent building in Mandalay. Although the pagoda, its four sets of priceless Tripitaka, and its colossal figure of Gautama tragically burned down in 1892, the sculpted foundations and stairways still hint at the former magnificence of the building. Photos of the pagoda prior to its destruction can be seen in the nearby Shwenandaw Kyaung Monastery.

Shwenandaw Monastery

This magnificently carved wooden monastery is all that remains of King Mindon's Royal Palace, which was destroyed during WW II. Shwenandaw originally served as the apartment of King Mindon and his chief queen until his death in 1878. His successor, King Thibaw, considered the building haunted by Mindon's ghost and ordered it disassembled and moved to the present location in 1880. Today it's considered Burma's single most outstanding example of 19th-century woodcarving and a must-see for all visitors to Mandalay. Supporting the monastery are dozens of fantastically carved *nagas*. Embellishments surrounding the doors and windows are masterpieces of the woodcarver's art. Inside the cool and dark interior are legions of antique clocks and religious art donated by pilgrims.

State School Of Music And Drama

This Performing Arts School on East Moat Road occasionally sponsors public performances. Visitors are welcome to visit the facilities during regular school hours. Myanmar Travel and Tours has details . . . maybe.

Royal Palace

King Mindon's Center of the Universe was constructed in 1859 and served as the final capital for the Burmese kings. By all accounts this Golden City was a magnificent city-within-a-city. Among the famous buildings was the Glass Palace and its Water-Feast Throne, a richly decorated monastery where King Thibaw served his priesthood, and an observatory tower where Queen Supayalat helplessly watched British troops enter Mandalay. During British occupation the palace served as Fort Dufferin. Great efforts were made by Lord Curzon to protect this absolutely unique example of old Burmese palace architecture. But tragedy struck on 20 March 1945, when, despite all possible precautions, British air raids against Japanese emplacements ignited fires which completely leveled the palace. Today all that remains are the massive walls, dilapidated towers, a poorly restored tomb of King Mindon, and a scale model of the former palace. There is little reason to go inside the walls.

Shwekyimyint Pagoda

This pagoda northeast of Zegyo Market was established in the 12th century by Prince Minshinzaw, the exiled son of Pagan's King

Alaungsithu (1112-1167). As such it significantly predates the founding of Mandalay in the 19th century. The central Buddha image enshrined by Prince Minshinzaw is noteworthy, but the adjacent rabbit warren of pagodas, plaster tableaux, and antiquated mechanical games is modern and somewhat garish.

Eindawya Pagoda

The outstanding proportions and brilliant glaze of this pagoda make it the finest religious edifice in Mandalay. Eindawya was constructed in 1847 by King Mindon to mark the site where he resided before ascending the throne. Inside is a beautiful Buddha image cut from chalcedony, a sparkling combination of quartz and opal. This beautiful pagoda is also difficult to find. Follow the unmarked lane that runs west from the market, or walk down 26th toward the river and turn left at the big yellow building.

Setkyathiha Pagoda

This pagoda is known for the five-meter bronze Buddha cast in 1823 at Ava and taken to Mandalay in 1884 during the third Anglo-Burmese war. Even more impressive than the image is the wild electronic halo which alternately spins clockwise and counterclockwise before radiating outwards. This mind-blowing display wins the *Southeast Asia Handbook* Award for Best Special Effects. The courtyard is also worth a wander to see the tableaux telling of the birth, temptations, and enlightenment of the Buddha, and a *bodhi* tree planted by U Nu. To the right of the south gate is an immense reproduction of the hanging golden rock at Kyaiktiyo.

Monasteries And Traditional Crafts

Visitors interested in 19th-century Burmese woodcarving should ask their trishaw driver to stop at the Shweinbin Monastery south of 35th Road and Kinwun Monastery across the Shweta Canal near 41st Road. This neighborhood is a beehive of traditional Burmese handicrafts. Most cottage industries operate from private homes but trishaw drivers know the locations. The hereditary occupation of gold-leaf production is especially interesting to watch. After being melted down, the gold is pounded into extremely thin sheets, pressed between oiled bamboo paper, and sold to worshipers who press the micro-thin leaves onto images of the Buddha.

Star Wars *meets the Buddha*

Other traditional crafts include ivory carving, silk weaving, puppet carving, production of musical instruments, and Buddha-image carving near Maha Muni Pagoda. Other outlying areas for traditional crafts include Amarapura for silk weaving, Ywataung near Sagaing for silversmiths, and Kyithunkyat near Amarapura for bronze- and brassworkers.

Maha Muni Pagoda

Also known as the Arakan Pagoda from its area of origin. Burmese believe the principal image to be one of only five exact likenesses made during Sakyamuni's lifetime. So highly revered is the image that gold leaf applied by pilgrims has almost completely obliterated all detail—Buddha becomes the Blob. Visitors are welcome to take photographs. Stacked somewhat haphazardly in the outer courtyard are six famous bronze Khmer sculptures which originally guarded the entrance to Angkor Wat. First hauled off to Ayuthaya by the Thais in 1431, the magical images were then taken to Pegu by the Mons in 1564, hauled off to Arakan in 1600, and finally delivered to Mandalay in 1784. Devotees believe the images can cure illnesses when rubbed on the appropriate spot. Gastrointestinal problems seem common. The courtyard also has inscription stones, a five-ton gong, and a curio museum filled with life-sized statues of Burmese kings.

ACCOMMODATIONS AND RESTAURANTS

Budget
The following guesthouses were closed in '89, but they may reopen when independent tourism returns to Burma. Mandalay's five guesthouses are simple hotels with small Chinese-style rooms and partitions that don't quite reach the ceiling. All cost K21 single and K36 double. Four of the guesthouses are located at the intersection of 80th Street and 31st Road near the train station and the night market. Facilities are almost identical but the Aung Dhiri Guest House (sign says Aung Thi Yi) is perhaps a touch cleaner. The Man San Dar Win, Aung Na Wa Yat, and Man Shwe Myo guesthouses are clustered nearby. The Myint Thida Guest House on 29th Road between 73rd and 74th Street is another possibility.

Moderate
Mandalay Hotel: Mandalay's top hotel has 60 rooms with private baths, a strangely deserted restaurant which serves mediocre Western food, and an upstairs bar that is positively grim. Burma Travel and a moneychanger are located in the lobby. Tour groups stay here. US$45-60.

Mya Mandala Hotel: This friendly hotel just around the corner from the Mandalay has 50 spacious a/c rooms with attached bathrooms, an outdoor patio, and a comfortable restaurant with bland food. US$25-35. Mya Mandala also has a pool and a lounge where you can watch Burmese TV on Sunday afternoons.

Restaurants
Hotel food in Mandalay is disappointing. For something more authentic and far tastier try the night market next to the train station. Inexpensive food stalls are also found on 26th Street adjacent to the Zegyo Market. Other popular spots include the well-named Nylon Ice Cream Bar, Olympia, and the Orient Cafe near city center. This string of cafes forms Mandalay's "restaurant row." Travelers waiting for the Pagan boat should search out the cozy cafe at the top of the dirt path.

TRANSPORTATION

From Rangoon By Air
Burma Air flies from Rangoon to Mandalay daily at 0645 and 1300. Tickets must be purchased from the tourist office in Rangoon. Complimentary transportation is provided from Mandalay Airport to the tourist office where hotel and transportation arrangements must be made. The tourist office also provides luggage-storage facilities for day-trippers, but bags should be locked to guard against theft. Trishaw drivers wait just outside the hotel.

From Rangoon By Train
Express trains depart Rangoon at 0600, 1815, and 2100, arriving in Mandalay about 14 hours later. Reclining seats in upper class are far more comfortable than those in first or second class. The night express allows an extra day of sightseeing in Mandalay. Visitors who intend to visit Pagan or Inle Lake and then return to Rangoon by train should purchase their Mandalay-Rangoon train tickets as soon as possible. First try the tourist office in Rangoon, second their office in Mandalay. Train reservations are difficult if not impossible to arrange both in Pagan and Inle. Train arrivals in Mandalay are routinely met by tourism officials who double-check passports. Trishaw drivers wait just outside the station. They charge honest rates.

From Pagan
Burma Air flies daily at 0835. Alternatively, you can take the 1400 Datsun truck to Thazi and then catch the evening train up to Mandalay. Buses from Nyaung U take 10-12 exhausting hours.

From Inle Lake
Burma Air flies daily at 1440. Buses leave from Taunggyi at around 0400 and take 10-12 tough hours.

Getting Around

Mandalay is surprisingly spread out—don't even think about walking around. Combined with the extraordinary heat the only practical way to see the sights is with hired trishaw or horse-drawn *tonga*. A full-day visit to the three main pagoda areas at the base of Mandalay Hill and several others near the center of town should cost 60-80 *kyat*. Buses are also possible: bus 1 to the Mahamuni Pagoda, buses 4 and 5 to Mandalay Hill, and bus 8 to Mahamuni Pagoda, Amarapura, and Ava.

VICINITY OF MANDALAY

AMARAPURA

Located near Mandalay are three ancient cities—Amarapura, Ava, and Sagaing—which once served as capitals for the final Burmese dynasty. Founded by King Bodawpaya in 1783 to succeed Ava, Amarapura ("City of Immortals") served as capital of upper Burma until 1850 when King Mindon moved to Mandalay. As was customary, most of the important wooden monasteries and royal palaces were disassembled and hauled off to the new location. Today, little of Amarapura's royal architecture remains intact, although the two surviving pagodas are worth visiting.

Attractions

Royal Palace Ruins: Most of Amarapura's wooden palace was transferred to Mandalay or subsequently pulled down by the British for road construction. Still standing are the four corner pagodas, a dilapidated watchtower, a rectangular record office, the masonry treasury, and a pair of royal tombs where King Bodawpaya and his grandson King Bagyidaw are buried.

Patodawgyi Pagoda: Constructed in 1820 by King Bagyidaw just outside the city walls, this well-proportioned stupa is one of the largest of its kind in Burma. Marble panels on three lower terraces are illustrated with scenes from the Jataka tales; good views from the upper terraces.

U Bien Bridge: This two-century-old bridge was constructed by mayor U Bien with teak planks salvaged from the royal city of Ava. The 1.2-km hike across the Taung Thaman lake is hot and tiring but the pagoda on the opposite side is worth the effort.

Kyauktawgyi Pagoda: This impressive replica of the Ananda Pagoda at the far end of U Bien Bridge was constructed in 1847 by King Pagan Min. An immense Buddha cut from green Sagyin jade dominates the interior, which is adorned with frescoes of Burmese nobility, Europeans, zodiac charts, and religious symbolism.

Silk Weaving: Amarapura is Burma's center for cotton and silk weaving. Visitors can watch *longyi* weaving in private homes or at the State Cooperative on the main street.

Getting There

Bus 8 to Amarapura and Ava leaves Mandalay from in front of the Shwekyimyint Pagoda. Buses from the corner of 84th and 29th are another possibility. Get off the bus when you see the palace walls on your left and the pagoda on your right. Better yet, organize a group and hire a taxi for the day to tour all three destinations.

AVA

After the destruction of the Kingdom of Pagan, Ava emerged as the new capital of the Burmese kings. Formerly known as Ratnapura ("City of Gems"), Ava was founded in 1364 by King Thadominbya and remained the capital of upper Burma for almost 400 years. During this turbulent era, Ava was attacked and conquered in turn by the Mons from Pegu and the Burmans from Toungoo. After a disastrous earthquake in 1838 leveled most of the city, the capital was shifted to Amarapura. Today most of the wooden architecture has rotted away and the palace grounds have been plowed for crops, but a few sights are worth visiting.

Attractions

Royal Palace: The Nanmyin Watchtower or "Leaning Tower of Ava" bears testimony to the destructive power of the 1838 earthquake, which almost completely leveled the city. This 27-meter campanile and some city walls are all that remain of King Thadominbya's royal palace.

Maha Aungmye Bonzan Monastery: Constructed in 1818 of stone rather than teak, this outstanding building has fortunately survived the fires and earthquakes that typically destroy wooden monasteries. Note the multiple roofs and wealth of ornamentation on this masonry monastery.

Judson Memorial: The Reverend Adoniram Judson and his wife Ann were American Baptist missionaries in the late 1800s who compiled the first Anglo-Burmese Bible and converted a large number of Burmese to Christianity. Both were briefly held prisoner in Ava. Ann eventually died from fever; Judson was tortured but eventually released to complete his translation work.

Getting There
Take bus 8 from either Mandalay or Amarapura and get off just before the Ava Bridge. Walk down to the Myitnage River and take the ferry that crosses to Ava. Another ferry crosses the Irrawaddy from Ava to Sagaing.

SAGAING

Founded in 1315 as a Shan capital, Sagaing served as the capital of upper Burma for 60 years. Unlike Amarapura and Ava, Sagaing remains a living city filled with hundreds of pago-

VICINITY OF MANDALAY

das, stupas, caves, and monasteries that attract thousands of monks. Sagaing is typically visited on an organized day tour, although it is possible to overnight in a Buddhist monastery.

Attractions
Thabyedan Fort: Burmese forces mounted their final resistance here against British forces during the third Anglo-Burmese War. This dilapidated fort is located just across the Ava Bridge.

Sagaing Hill: Most of Sagaing's active monasteries are located on this hot and dusty hill. Best views are from Soon U Ponya Pagoda just behind the town of Sagaing.

Kaungmudaw Pagoda: Considered the most famous pagoda in Sagaing, this gigantic breast-shaped pagoda was built by King Thalun in 1636 and modeled after the Indian-style Mahaceti of Sri Lanka. Surrounding the hemispherical 46-meter pagoda are 160 *nats* and the foundations of 812 stone oil lamps which at one time illuminated the huge dome. Kaungmudaw is located 10 km outside of town and can be reached with local jeeps.

Hsinmyashin Pagoda: The so-called Pagoda of Many Elephants, located between Sagaing and Kaungmudaw, was built in 1492 and extensively restored after the 1955 earthquake.

Ywataung: A small village of silversmiths also situated between Sagaing and Kaungmudaw.

Tupayon Pagoda: Constructed in 1444 by King Narapati, this uncompleted pagoda features a distinctive wedding-cake design of three circular stories marked by closed windows and anvil niches for Buddhist images. Located on the western side of Sagaing.

Aungmyelawka Pagoda: This sandstone pagoda was built in 1783 by King Bodawpaya, who had it fashioned after the Shwezigon Pagoda in Pagan. Located on the riverfront near the Tupayon.

MINGUN

Mingun is home to the world's largest uncracked bell and the world's greatest brickwork foundation, which, if completed, would have supported the largest pagoda in the world. Both were the ideas of King Bodawpaya, the mad king who conquered Arakan in 1785 to bring back the venerated Mahamuni and 20,000 slaves to work his megalomaniac building projects. Bodawpaya began his reign of terror with the slaughter of all possible rivals, including the royal family, his generals, their families, and all their servants. He later punished a traitor by killing every single living thing in the village—human beings, animals, fruit trees, and standing crops. His disastrous and costly campaigns against the Siamese were financed by tax collection so ruthless that his tax records became known as the Doomsday Book.

Attractions

Mingun Bell: Cast in 1790 at the insistence of King Bodawpaya, this iron monster weighs almost 90 tons and is nearly five meters across, second in size and weight only to the cracked bell of Moscow. After completion, the tyrannical king ordered the bronzesmith killed to prevent him recreating his masterpiece. Crawl inside and let one of the local boys give it a good ring.

Mingun Pagoda: Convinced that he was the reincarnation of the Buddha, Bodawpaya began construction on his monstrous pagoda in 1790. Some 20,000 Arakanese slaves worked on his mad project until 1797 when the project was abandoned due to economic and political exhaustion. Nothing on this scale had been attempted since the Egyptian pyramids, and as with the monuments of the pharaohs, the drain on human manpower was so great that society cracked. Entire villages fled into the jungle to escape forced labor. An earthquake in 1838 rent the gigantic cube with fantastic fissures and collapsed the upper section into the treasure vault filled with thousands of gold and silver images, precious stones, and even a soda machine which the crazy king had imported from England. The present pagoda is only one-third the intended size but even in this ruined state it remains a very impressive pile of rock. A pair of ruined *chinthe* guard the entrance.

Settawya Pagoda: Inside the small building, about 10 minutes south of the pagoda, is a Buddha footprint and an attractive seated Buddha backed by a gold-leaf standing Buddha.

Mingun Pagoda Model: This scale model just beyond the Settawya shows what the pagoda would have looked like if completed; enormous but not terribly graceful.

Hsinbyume Pagoda: The layout of this lovely pagoda is based on Buddhist cosmology which places the mythical Mount Meru in the center of seven waving chains of mountains. Hsinbyume lacks detailed carvings and has little of artistic interest, but it's kept nicely whitewashed and offers some good views from the top. The path south from the bell to this pagoda is home to some amazing old Buddhist nuns who collect alms, smoke cigars, and cheerfully pose for photographs.

Getting There

Riverboats leave Mandalay's 26th Street pier hourly until early afternoon. Boatmen sell tickets on board, so it is not necessary to buy the expensive ticket from the tourist office. Mingun is a full-day trip, so start early and remember that the last boat returns to Mandalay at 1600. The one-hour boat ride is a crowded, hot, but fascinating journey past graceful sailboats and immense rafts made of teak. A short stop is made at a muddy village before finally reaching Mingun. Walk straight ahead through the tea stands and Buddhist infirmary to the big bell. Mingun Pagoda is to the left. About 200 meters farther south is the Settawya Pagoda and finally the scale model of the pagoda. The Hsinbyume Pagoda is about 300 meters north of the bell.

MAYMYO (PYIN OO LWIN)

Located on the edge of the Shan Plateau about 67 km northeast of Mandalay, this former British hill station is a great place to escape the searing heat of the lowlands and relax in an old English hotel. Maymyo was established in 1886 by Colonel May of the 5th Bengal Infantry Regiment as a summer retreat for British colonials stationed in Mandalay. Despite 40 years of neglect, Maymyo retains the broad avenues, carefully tended vegetable gardens, and classically designed churches favored by the British. Sightseeing highlights include a fascinating morning market attended by Shan tribespeople, miniature stagecoaches which serve as local taxis, and a timeless atmosphere little changed from the days of Kipling.

The Burma Road

Maymyo is also the beginning of the famous Burma Road, which once served as supply route between the Americans and the beleaguered forces of Chiang Kai-shek. With the invasion of China by the Japanese in the 1930s and the retreat of Chiang's forces to Kunming, the Americans decided to construct a road to supply Chiang's resistance movement against Japanese forces. Winding 800 km through some of the world's densest jungle, the Burma Road took three grueling years and the services of some 40,000 laborers to complete before being seized by the Japanese. The Allies then began an airlift of military hardware across the Hump, a treacherous line of 6,000-meter mountains which eventually claimed over 600 planes and the lives of some 1,000 pilots. One ridge became so littered with wreckage that pilots nicknamed it Aluminum-Plated Mountain. Allied forces in 1944 constructed the Stilwell Road, which connected northern Burma to Ledo in India. Both the Stilwell and Burma roads were abandoned after the war and have presumably returned to jungle. Paul Theroux's *Great Railway Bazaar* has an amusing account of his attempt to travel the Burma Road.

Attractions

Maymyo Market: Each morning dozens of ethnic groups from the Shan states can be seen shopping in this fascinating bazaar. Among the sights are farmers in distinctive fan-shaped hats, young monks collecting alms, and turbaned ladies shopping for English produce such as cabbages, cauliflower, and ripe strawberries.

Stagecoaches: Lined up just alongside the bazaar are a half-dozen miniature coaches that resemble transport of the American Wild West. These 19th-century carriages can be hired to tour outlying attractions for about K30 per hour. Maymyo also has some amazing buses constructed entirely of wood.

Botanical Gardens: This 432-acre garden is located about one km south of town.

Waterfalls: Pwe Kauk Waterfall is located about eight km north of town and is fairly easy to reach. The more spectacular Anisakan Waterfall is 10 km west on the road to Mandalay.

Accommodations

Candacraig Hotel: This colonial-style hotel is one of the best reasons to visit Maymyo. Originally constructed in 1906 as a chummery for the staff of the Bombay-Burmah Trading Company, it has been ungraciously renamed the

a whackin' great cheroot

Maymyo Inn by the tourist office, although everyone continues to call it the Candacraig. Located about five blocks up the hill from the center of town. For a few extra *kyat* you can enjoy a roaring fire in the evening and try their British dinner of meat and potatoes. Large rooms with comfortable beds cost US$25-35.

Nann Myaing: Try this alternative hotel only if the Candacraig is filled.

YMCA: The YMCA is occasionally open to Westerners. US$10.

Getting There

Jeeps leave Mandalay hourly between 0700 and 1500 from the intersection of 83rd and 27th. Allow three hours to wind through the 22 hairpin turns and several stops for radiator water and snacks. These vintage jeeps are completely packed, so it's best to try and sit up front for extra legroom. Jeeps returning to Mandalay leave from the main road just down from the clock tower.

PAGAN

The mysterious and magnificent ruins of Pagan comprise one of the world's great archaeological sites. Although most of the original 5,000 monuments have been reduced to great piles of rubble, the remaining 50 or so temples still bear witness to the amazing construction frenzy that seized this area during the 11th and 12th centuries. Pagan is one of the wonders of the world and the major highlight for any visit to Burma.

HISTORY

The traditional date of the foundation of Pagan is 849, but the actual Golden Age began in the 11th century after King Anawrahta (1044-1077) ascended the throne and became the 42nd ruler of the Pagan Dynasty. Considered the greatest of all Burmese kings, Anawrahta conquered and united most of Burma while seeking a new religion to replace the decadent Tantric practices and Ari *naga* worship popular at the time. Tradition has it that Shan Arahan, a Buddhist monk from the Mon capital of Thaton, visited Anawrahta in the 11th century and converted him to Theravada Buddhism. Impressed by the logical rationalism of his newfound religion, Anawrahta requested a copy of the Tripitaka from the Mon king of Thaton. After King Manuha refused to share his sacred books with the northern barbarians, an angry Anawrahta sacked Thaton and hauled 30 elephant-loads of the Tripitaka back to Pagan. For good measure he also dragged along Manuha and his entire retinue of Mon architects, artisans, scholars, linguists, theologians, and the entire population of 30,000 souls. So impressed was Anawrahta with Mon culture and spiritual traditions that he quickly adopted their alphabet, religion, and artistic models.

Anawrahta's son, King Kyanzittha (1084-1112), intensified construction of Mon-style monuments during Pagan's so-called Golden Age of Monument Builders. Over the period of 28 years, Kyanzittha undertook the restoration of the Mahabodi Temple at Bodgaya and constructed his architectural masterpiece, the Ananda Temple. Kyanzittha's successor, Alaungsithu (1112-1167), continued building works of merit and authored the famous quadrilingual inscription at the Kubyaukgyi Temple. The discovery in 1911 of this Rosetta Stone of Burma inscribed in four languages (Pyu, Mon, Burmese, and Pali) helped provide the key to understanding the Pyu language and the chronology of the early Pagan kings. Temple construction continued with Narapatisithu but ended after King Htilominlo constructed his magnificent Gawdawpalin Temple.

After two centuries of continuous existence—a remarkably long period by medieval standards—the Pagan Dynasty collapsed from internal exhaustion and corrupt monarchies. This was epitomized by the final king, Narathihapati (1256-1287), who pompously described himself on the Mingalazedi Pagoda as "supreme commander of 36 million soldiers, the swallower of 300 dishes of curry daily, and the possessor of 3,000 concubines." Construction of his Mingalazedi Pagoda gave rise to the Burmese proverb, "the pagoda is finished and the great country ruined." But the final blow came when Kublai Khan, emperor of China, sent envoys to Pagan demanding tribute. Rather than returning a suitable acknowledgment of submission, Narathihapati foolishly seized and beheaded the Chinese ambassador, an act of arrogance that enraged the Great Khan, who ordered his powerful armies to march on Pagan. As preliminary battles were being witnessed by Marco Polo himself, the terrified Narathihapati abandoned his once-great city and fled south to Bassein.

ATTRACTIONS

Buddhist monuments in Pagan fall into two basic styles: pagodas and temples. Pagodas (also called stupas, *chedis, zedis, ceityas,* and *dagobas*) are solid, bell-shaped structures raised on series of terraces and crowned by golden finials known as *hti*. These serve as monuments of commemoration and each usually entombs a relic of the Buddha such as a sacred hair or a piece of bone.

BURMA
1. Buddhist rites humor; **2.** lady with brooms, Mandalay;
3. female monks at Shwedagon (all photos this page by Carl Parkes)

BURMA
1. golden winking wonder, Shwedagon Pagoda, Rangoon; **2.** monks as tourists
(all photos this page by Carl Parkes)

The earliest pagodas were based on medieval Indian forms and the heavy styles favored by the Mons. Burmese architects elaborated on the basic design and turned the simple terraced plinths into virtual sacred mountains resembling the Buddhist Heaven of Mount Meru. Although pagodas seem monotonously similar to most visitors, Pagan offers a fascinating range of styles from the simple forms of Bupaya and Ngakyawena to the grandiose monuments of Shwezigon and Mingalazedi.

Pagan's other basic architectural style is that of its temples, hollow structures which permit the pilgrim to enter a dark and cool in-terior and meditate before the image of the Buddha. You will be surprised at how much Pagan's temples with their towering transepts and moody corridors resemble the Gothic cathedrals of medieval Europe. The word "temple" as used in a Christian context is somewhat inappropriate since in Theravada Buddhism the Buddha is not considered a god to be "worshipped" but rather an enlightened being who is "honored" for his teachings. Or as Norman Lewis writes somewhat cynically in his *Golden Earth*, "Like most peoples who incline themselves before images, Buddhists insist with the gravest emphasis that they are not wor-

the author and friends

shipping the material object, but the great principle it represents."

Early temples were designed in a Mon style with dark hallways and small narrow windows. Burmese architects adopted the false ribbed arch from preceding Indian styles rather than the true corbelled arch. They later expanded the interior and added larger windows to let the light fall on the Buddha image. A fascinating variety of temple styles can be seen in Pagan: those based on North Indian models such as Ananda, others from Central India such as Mahabodi, and those based on South Indian styles such as Gawadapalin and Sulamani. Pagan also boasts a handful of unusual structures, such as the Pitakat Taik Library and Upali Thein Ordination Hall, which simulate in stone the architectural forms of wood.

Murals and terra-cotta tiles are also worth special attention. Many temple interiors are covered with superb murals which represent a treasure house of classical Burmese art. Some are reminiscent of eastern Indian Buddhist manuscript styles, others show delightful scenes of everyday Burmese life complete with bored clerks, laughing children, and lusty courtesans. Many of the finest murals have been tragically painted over by less talented artists, completely whitewashed out of existence, or stolen and sold to foreign art collectors. Those temples with original murals are often locked to guard against such vandalism, but a young villager or groundskeeper with the key will admit you for a small fee. Another strategy is to join a tour or at least keep an eye out for their bus.

The beautiful exterior walls fitted with glazed terra-cotta tiles often depict the Buddhist Jataka tales, stories of previous incarnations of the Buddha. Tiles come in two styles: the enameled green tiles which show Chinese influence such as those at Ananda and Shwezigon, and the red baked clay tiles of South Indian influence such as those at Petleik Pagoda. Repeated heavy gilding and repainting has destroyed many tiles but those at Mingalazedi and in Minnanthu are still in good condition.

MONUMENTS AT PAGAN VILLAGE

All Burma temples and pagodas are considered sacred. Visitors are expected to respect Buddhist tradition and dress conservatively. Shorts are inappropriate when visiting religious shrines. Males should wear long pants and a clean shirt; females should keep well covered.

Before exploring the ruins, visit the Pagan Museum for a useful introduction to the architecture and sculpture of the region. The Rangoon tourist office sells the *Pictorial Guide to Pagan* and the *Tourist Burma Map of Pagan*. The entrance fee into the Pagan Archaeological Zone is US$10. Visitors with only a day or two should limit themselves to the important monuments near Pagan village. Travelers with more time can get farther afield with either bicycle or

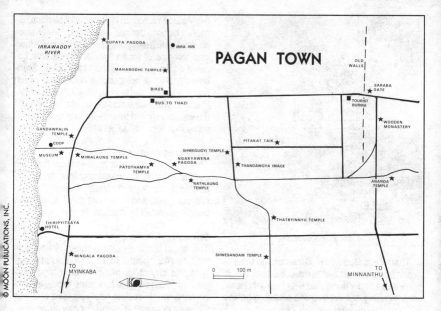

PAGAN TOWN

horse-drawn cart. Bullock carts are romantic, but as Sir George Scott wrote, "The unlucky passenger shortly discovers that there are bones in parts of his body where previously he had imagined all was soft."

Bicycles are the perfect answer: cheap, comfortable, and fast. Carefully check the bike's condition. All of Pagan's monuments can be reached by bicycle except for those south of Myinkaba because of the sandy roads. No matter what, sunsets should be enjoyed from the pinnacle of either Gawadapalin, Thatbyinnyu, or Dhammayaungyi temples. Less ambitious visitors might substitute a cold drink on the veranda of the Thiripyitsaya Hotel.

Saraba Gateway

The following monuments are described in a clockwise fashion starting from the tourist office. Saraba Gateway, the only surviving relic of the 9th-century city built by King Pyinbya (846-878), is flanked by a pair of masonry shrines holding sibling *nats*. To the left is Min Mahagiri, nicknamed Mr. Handsome, and to the right is his sister Shwemyethana, also known as Golden Face. Both died tragically (or possibly incestuously) in a fire and remain among the most pop-

ular of Burmese spirits. An attractive monastery lies to the left of the path leading to the Ananda Temple. This rarely visited building features some superb woodcarvings, which the young monks will be delighted to show you. Have a cup of tea with the old abbot.

Ananda Temple

Pagan's most famous monument is one of the region's few active Buddhist temples. Ananda was constructed by Kyanzittha in 1091 in the shape of a perfect Greek cross bisected by four gabled vestibules. The overall effect is of a gigantic white wedding cake standing atop the red soil of Pagan. Rising above the diminishing terraces is a golden spire or *sikhara* adapted from the temples of India, and then a bell-shaped pagoda of Burmese design. No one is allowed to climb this temple. Enshrined at the end of each corridor are four colossal standing Buddhas with hands raised in the pose of dispelling fear. Lighted mysteriously from concealed apertures in the vaulted ceiling, each represents one of the four previous Buddhas; Gautama is at the west. The western sanctum enshrines a life-sized statue of Kyanzittha and the monk Shin Arahan who converted the king

Ananda by Kyanzitha

to Theravada Buddhism. Ornamenting the exterior base are glazed terra-cotta tiles which have been badly disfigured with heavy-handed whitewashing, but check those squatting griffins with multiple penises.

Thatbyinnyu Temple
This 61-meter monument is the tallest temple in Pagan and an excellent place to view the sunset. Thatbyinnyu was built during the 12th century by King Alaungsithu, who was responsible for many of the Mon-style temples in Pagan. Despite the heavy mass of two cubes piled on top of each other, the architect also created a soaring effect with his use of corner stupas mounted on the terraces and the flamboyant arch-pediments that point skyward. Hidden in the circumambulatory corridor around the central mass is a narrow set of stairs that leads up to the Buddha image seated on the upper floor. Another set of stairs leads to the uppermost terrace, where the sunsets are spectacular.

Shwesandaw Pagoda
Somewhat of a side trip from the central area, this whitewashed pagoda was built by King Anawrahta soon after his conquest of Thaton in 1057. Of all stupas in Pagan, the Shwesandaw is the most perfectly balanced with its five diminishing terraces that complement the cylin-

drical stupa resting on an octagonal platform. Bisected by well-defined stairways, the terraces have an eerie resemblance to the Central American temples of Incan and Mayan design. Located on the grounds is the 11th-century **Shinbintalyaung,** a nondescript brick shed which houses an 18-meter recumbent image of the Buddha. The image has been defaced but note the well-preserved tree-of-life fresco surrounded by Balinese-style figures.

Thandawgya Image
This six-meter Buddha located back from the central area was constructed from brick and plaster in 1284 by King Naráthihapati. The roof has collapsed and it appears that his belly has been excavated by treasure hunters.

Shwegugyi Temple
This small but finely proportioned temple was built by Alaungsithu in 1131 in a surprisingly light and airy style. Mounted on a high brick platform, this little gem has some exquisite stucco carvings, including finely molded birds on the west doorway. The interior has a pair of inscribed stone slabs which poetically tell the history of the temple.

Pitakat Taik Library
Although this building is often overlooked by visitors to Pagan, it has great historical and architectural significance. After King Anawrahta conquered the Mon kingdom of Thaton he brought back 30 elephant-loads of prized Buddhist scriptures, an event that established Pagan as one of the more important cultural and political powers in Southeast Asia. The precious scriptures were stored in this library. Significantly, this building replicates in stone the styles which were commonly built of wood and have long since disappeared.

Nathlaung Temple
This badly deteriorated temple, dedicated to Vishnu, remains the only surviving Hindu sanctuary in Pagan. The outer wall has 10 niches holding seven of the avatars of Vishnu. Three images in poor condition are found in the cool interior, which once held a Vishnu riding his *garuda* prior to its removal to Berlin's Dahlem Museum.

Patothamya Temple

This small 11th-century temple is typical of Mon-influenced architecture—single storied and set low to the ground with dark corridors dimly lit by narrow windows. Patothamya is kept locked to protect the mural paintings with Mon inscriptions.

Mimalaung Temple

Built by King Narapatisithu in 1174, this small square temple is surmounted by multiple roofs which have been insensitively reconstructed with ferroconcrete.

Gawadapawlin Temple

Constructed by Narapatisithu (1174-1211) in an architectural style similar to that of Thatbyinnyu, this massive temple was badly damaged during the disastrous 1975 earthquake, which struck 225 of the 2,217 Pagan monuments officially registered by the Burmese archaeological department. Afterward the Burmese government embarked on a project to fortify the monuments with funds provided by the U.N. Development Program. European earthquake engineers who studied the problem recommended that the bonding capacity of the old mortar be strengthened by cement injection and steel ties. You can see the startling results on the reconstructed *sikhara,* which soars to 55 meters. Another popular place for sunsets despite the obnoxious electronic loudspeaker.

Bupaya Pagoda

Once used as a navigation aid for passing ships, this stupa stands on the banks of the Irrawaddy above circular rows of crenellated terraces. The antiquity of this pagoda is indicated by the bulbous shape, as opposed to the tall and tapering forms of later periods. It is, however, a complete re-creation, since the original structure collapsed into the river during the 1975 earthquake. Boats can be hired below to cross the Irrawaddy.

Mahabodi Temple

Constructed by Nantaungmya (1124-1174) after the original in Bodgaya, this unique Guptaperiod temple is typical of Central Indian styles rather than traditional Burmese designs. Some intriguing statuary lies scattered among the weeds in the back yard.

MONUMENTS TOWARD NYAUNG U

The following monuments are located along the paved road that connects Pagan with the village of Nyaung U. A three- or four-hour bicycle journey can be made from Pagan to Nyaung U, stopping at Upali Thein, Htilominlo, Shwezigon, and Sapada Pagoda before returning on the southern paved road past Kubyaukgyi Temple. The sense of isolation and complete stillness makes this a powerful and memorable travel experience.

Upali Thein Ordination Hall

Similar to the Pitakat Taik, this attractive Buddhist hall has great importance since it replicates in stone the wooden architecture from the 13th century. Influenced by South Indian prototypes, the exterior design and treatment of carved stone somewhat resembles the 7th-century seaside temples of Mahabalipuram. Interior frescoes from the early 18th century are kept locked to prevent vandalism.

Htilominlo Temple

This impressive temple was erected by King Nantaungmya to commemorate his ordination into the Buddhist priesthood. Of special note are the decorative friezes and exquisite stucco carvings which survive on the false exterior columns. Several are capped by strange creatures set with bulging eyes and dangling tongues, mythological animals which inexplicably resemble those in Bali. Four Buddha figures of recent construction face the cardinal points on the ground floor, although inscribed horoscopes found at the east entrance are more intriguing.

Shwezigon Pagoda

This golden stupa is one of Burma's most venerated since it enshrines a cornucopia of Buddha relics, including the Buddha's frontlet bone obtained by King Anawrahta, his collarbone from Sri Kshetra, and a duplicate of the Tooth of Kandy from Sri Lanka. Anawrahta began construction of this temple to fuse indigenous *nat* worship with his newfound faith. The project was finished by subsequent kings after Anawrahta was gored to death by a mad bull in 1077. Important artistic features include the enameled plaques around the terrace which depict Jataka tales and the four Gupta-style Buddhas standing in the entrance chambers. Also note the *nat* images riding mythical animals in the building at the northeast corner. As at other famous pagodas in Burma, the grounds are filled with weird and wonderful oddities that range from the sublime to the ridiculous. Toward the east are a revolving coin-toss *hti,* which grants wishes to pilgrims with good aim, and several gaudy dioramas which show the Buddha calmly facing raging animals and earthly temptations.

Sapada Pagoda

This modest brick stupa is considered a landmark in the history of Buddhism. During the 12th century a Burmese monk named Sapada from Bassein journeyed to Sri Lanka for ordination into the Sinhalese form of Theravada Buddhism. Afterward he returned to Pagan to establish the pure form of Buddhism and construct this pagoda. The most distinctive feature is the cubical relic chamber mounted above rather than buried beneath the bell.

Kubyaukgyi Temple

Featuring a distinctive spire of Indian Gupta style, the chief features of this small 13th-century temple are the outstanding frescoes painted on the interior walls. Because many were stolen by German art collectors in the late 19th century, the interior is kept locked to protect the remaining frescoes. Local attendants might have keys, although you can still peer through the steel bars for a partial view.

MONUMENTS TOWARD MINNANTHU

Roads from Pagan village to Minnanthu are unpaved but passable by bicycle. It's a strange but memorable journey to pedal out here on a hot afternoon.

Dhammayangyi Temple

Constructed during the short but bloody reign of King Narathu (1167-1170), this massive shrine is chiefly known for its outstanding exterior brickwork. The floor plan of this temple is similar to Ananda's, but the interior circumambulatory passage has been mysteriously blocked with brick. Note the unusual set of double Buddhas in the west entrance. This temple is very popular

for sunsets, but finding your way to the top can be difficult. Children playing at the entrance will show you the narrow and claustrophobic stairway located at the southeast corner of the ground floor. Take careful note of the route or risk getting lost on the way back down. Forget the way and the kids will laugh at you.

Sulamani Temple

Constructed in 1181 by King Narapatisithu, this important temple heralded the final period of temple construction. The monument consists of two stories ornamented with parapets and stupas with four porches facing the cardinal points. The exterior lacks the impressive brickwork of Dhammayangyi, but 18th-century frescoes located on the interior of the southern walls are fascinating. The requisite Buddhas are there, but it is the ordinary scenes of everyday Burmese life that project such warmth. Note that almost everyone seems to be smiling behind the protective wire screen.

Minnanthu Village

The following four temples are located just east of Minnanthu village, about 20 minutes by bicycle beyond Sulamani. Allow an hour to pedal here from Pagan. The road is well marked and you won't have any problem with heavy sand. These modest little temples are chiefly known for their superb interior frescoes, which are always locked. The village of Minnanthu has a small lake to the left and a group of houses to the right. Stop here and ask for the young girl who keeps the keys to the temples. Mg Aung Lin, a popular guide, and the girl with the temple keys both expect a small tip or present.

Lemyethnat Temple: This neglected temple immediately on your left has a shocking example of priceless frescoes carelessly splattered over with whitewash.

Payathonzu Temple: This triple temple farther to the right features vaulted corridors joined together by narrow passageways. Each little gem is capped by a *sikhara* modeled after Orrisian prototypes. The interior vaults are covered with exquisite and well-preserved frescoes of Mahayanist and Tantric character. Extraordinary mythical monsters, animals, and human figures are cleverly woven among floral motifs.

Thanbula Temple: Constructed in 1255 by the wife of King Uzana, this small shrine features some outstanding murals in the circumambulatory corridor.

Nandamannya Temple: This final temple contains the finest frescoes in Minnanthu. Behind the temple is a subterranean monk's retreat which welcomes visitors.

MONUMENTS TOWARD MYINKABA

The following temples are located on both sides of the road which parallels the river. Bicyclists can follow the dirt road as far as the Nanpaya Temple, but beyond that the sand becomes too thick.

Mingalazedi Pagoda

Although this pagoda was constructed in 1284 just a few years before Pagan was abandoned, the basic shape is almost identical to that of the Shwezigon constructed two centuries earlier. Mingalazedi is chiefly noted for the outstanding terra-cotta tiles embedded on the steep terraces. Some of these unglazed tiles have been stolen or badly defaced by art collectors, but a large number are still extant in fine condition. The groundskeeper will unlock the gate for you and there is no admission charge.

Kubyaukgyi Temple

Constructed in 1113 by Rajakumar, son of Kyanzittha, this small Mon-style temple is noted for the frescoes that cover the inner sanctum and surrounding corridors. The central mural relates the 547 Jatakas in nine rows, of which Buddha's descent from Tavatimsa is considered the most important. Orthodox Theravada paintings predominate, but a 10-handed Mahayana bodhisattva is also painted on the outer porch. Note, too, the unusual stone windows cut with geometrical designs. Kubyaukgyi is where the Myazedi stone was discovered, the Rosetta Stone of Burma which enabled linguists to decipher the ancient Pyu language. Kubyaukgyi is kept locked but someone in Myinkaba village can provide the key for a small tip.

Myinkaba Village

On your left as you enter the village is a small lacquerware store which sells ice-cold drinks and "instant antique" terra-cotta tiles. Myinkaba has an active lacquerware industry and is a good place to trade your Western goods for lacquerware.

Manuha Temple

In 1057 King Anawrahta conquered the southern capital of Thaton and brought back King Manuha and his royal court. Manuha was exiled south to Myinkaba, where he was allowed to build this temple in 1059. The exterior is dull, but some say that the claustrophobic interior with its cramped Buddhas is an allegorical representation of the captive king's mental distress. Visitors can climb the narrow stairs in the rear and peer down on the sitting image. Although the story is intriguing, the temple is ugly and has little architectural or sculptural merit.

Nanpaya Temple

Located just behind the Manuha Temple is this well-preserved monument with distinctive arch pediments and Mon-style perforated stone windows. The interior has four stone pillars carved with outstanding hanging floral designs and rare bas-relief figures of Brahma holding lotus flowers. Archaeologists believe this temple may have been a Hindu shrine before being converted to Manuha's prison. Nanpaya is kept locked to prevent damage, but young boys usually have the key.

Abeyadana Temple

Visitors on bicycles will find the road too thick with sand to proceed south of Nanpaya. Abeyadana is a Mon-style temple constructed by King Kyanzittha to commemorate the loyalty of his wife Abeyadana. The northern porch, pierced by three entrances constructed from true rather than false arches, leads to the inner sanctum, which is filled with paintings inspired by Pagan's three major religions: Theravada Buddhism, Mahayana Buddhism, and Hinduism. Mahayanist figures of bodhisattvas cover the outer walls of the corridor while the inner walls are painted with small circular panels of Brahmanic gods and terrifying Tantric images. Porch panels illustrate Jataka scenes with Mon script.

Nagayon Temple

According to legend, this Mon-style temple was also constructed by King Kyanzittha on the spot where he was miraculously protected by a giant *naga* snake. The locked interior contains a huge standing Buddha flanked by two smaller Buddha images, plus a large number of niches filled with Buddha images. Unlike Abeyadana Temple (mentioned above), this temple contains mural paintings devoted solely to Theravada Buddhism.

Somingyi Monastery
Very few of Pagan's wooden monasteries have survived centuries of weather and fire. Somingyi, once a residential college for young monks, is a rare example of a brick monastery.

Seinnyet Ama Temple And Pagoda
The temple is of standard design with multiple terraces and a *sikhara* supported by a square basement. The embellished stupa has some finely carved lions on the second terrace. Both face each other within a walled enclosure.

East And West Petleik Pagodas
These two pagodas hold what are considered to be the finest existing terra-cotta plaques in Pagan. Constructed during the 11th century, the lower portions of both pagodas were buried under dirt and debris. When excavated in 1905, archaeologists discovered 550 Jataka plaques in excellent condition. These unglazed panels described and labeled in traditional Pali script are in far better condition than the glazed plaques at Ananda and Shwezigon. Vaulted corridors have been reconstructed to protect the plaques.

PRACTICALITIES

Accommodations
Budget Guesthouses: Prior to the political disruptions of 1988, almost a dozen inexpensive guesthouses lined the narrow road that bisects Pagan. Then, in a fit of politically motivated anger, the Burmese government demolished all the guesthouses and cafes, forcing the residents to relocate four km east to the dusty town of Nyaung U. The government claimed the reason was archaeological excavations, though most observers believe it was a misguided attempt to intimidate the locals prior to the 1989 elections.

Pagan today resembles a ghost town, Aung San Suu Kyi remains a prisoner, and the people of Burma suffer under the world's most repressive military dictatorship.

BURMESE PUPPETS AT PAGAN

Although *yokthe pwe* (Burmese marionette theater) has been popular since the 17th century, today it's lost favor with the Burmese and is rarely performed outside temple festivals. Foreign visitors are fortunate to have two marionette theaters in Pagan. Nightly performances are given at the Thiripyitsaya Hotel and at the Zawgyibyan Puppet Show in the residence of U Mg Hla near the Gawadapalin Temple. During the 45-minute show, the master puppeteer and his assistant manipulate 28 puppets hanging from a dozen strings, recite poetry, and extemporaneously add dialogue that ranges from humorous to bawdy. Taken from the Jatakas or the Ramayana, the stories include colorful characters, from heroic princes and their lovely princesses to Brahmanic priests, corrupt officials, and slapstick clowns. You will especially enjoy the flying sorcerers and the extraordinarily realistic galloping horses.

Irra Inn: This riverside hotel is a good compromise between basic guesthouses and the expensive Thiripyitsaya Hotel. Both Western and Burmese dinners are served with advance reservations. Irra Inn often forgets to stamp currency forms of visitors staying three or more nights. US$25-35.

Thiripyitsaya Hotel: This modern resort hotel has 36 a/c rooms overlooking the Irrawaddy River. The Thirip is a surprisingly luxurious hotel for Pagan, perhaps the best in Burma. Facilities include an outstanding restaurant open to hotel guests only, a veranda bar for sunsets, and an inviting pool covered with brilliant green algae. Nightly puppet performances in their claustrophobic showroom are highly recommended. US$60-80.

Shopping

Pagan is the lacquerware capital of Burma. Dozens of shops produce superb boxes, bowls, *sadaik* manuscript chests, and traditional objects such as *kunit* (betel-nut boxes), *lahpetok* (receptacle boxes divided into pie-shaped sections), *hseileik taung* (cheroot boxes), and *bu* (storage containers for *ngapi* fish paste). Lacquerware comes in a wide range of styles and qualities, but inferior items are usually made with a wooden base while the finer products are shaped over a fine bamboo frame and then covered with tree lacquer. After the bamboo skeleton has been woven it is wrapped with horsehair and then painted with a black lacquer resin from the *Melanorrhoea usitata* tree. It is then dried, sanded, and covered with a second layer of lacquer mixed with bone, rice husks, or cow dung. Finally the bowl is engraved and decorated with gold leaf. Pagan lacquer is famous for a unique style of incised decoration called *yun*, in which the carved patterns are filled with coloring matter of either red, yellow, or green. The entire process often takes several months and yet the bowls sell for only a few dollars! Several lacquerware factories are located in Pagan on the street running parallel to the main road, and in Myinkaba village. For an excellent introduction visit the **Pagan Lacquerware School and Museum** on the road to the Irra Inn.

TRANSPORTATION

Getting There From Rangoon

By Air: Myanma Airways flies daily at 0645 and takes 90 minutes. Pagan's airport is located in Nyaung-U about 10 km from Pagan. Free transportation is provided to the tourist office in Pagan.

By Train and Minitruck: Express trains depart at 0600, 1815, and 2100, arriving in Thazi 12 hours later. An official from the tourist office usually waits at the Thazi train station, although early arrivals may have to hang out until sunrise. Japanese minitrucks for Pagan leave from the bus terminal 150 meters distant when completely filled or when wealthy Westerners pay the fare differential. This train-and-minitruck combination is cheap and reasonably comfortable if you travel upper class on the train.

Getting There From Mandalay

By Air: Burma Air once flew daily at 1540 and arrived in Pagan just 30 minutes later, an inexpensive flight vastly preferable to the torturous bus journey. Unfortunately, this convenient flight was cancelled in 1991 due to the decline of tourism and, hence, lack of passengers. The service will probably be reinstated when tourism returns to healthy levels.

By Bus: An antiquated bus leaves at 0400 from 81st Street between 32nd and 33rd roads and takes a minimum of 10-12 hours. There is also a Japanese pickup truck leaving at 1200 from 83rd between 29th and 30th roads. Both are exhausting ordeals guaranteed to ruin your week in Burma.

By Riverboat: The river journey from Mandalay to Pagan is one of Southeast Asia's great travel experiences—a rare opportunity for adventure, floating past primitive villages closed to the outside world and populated by people who haven't seen Westerners in over two decades.

Prior to the events of '89 both ordinary and express boats were available. Ordinary boats left Mandalay daily at sunrise from the end of A Road and arrived in Pagan the following morning. Tickets sold on the boat cost K16 deck class and K31 in the cabin. Visitors were allowed to sleep onboard the night before departure to save the cost of a night's accommodation. These ferries stopped in the town of Pakkaku, where travelers usually stayed at the Myayatanar Inn. Pagan was a short two-hour ferry ride the following morning.

Express boats are all that's left now. These are somewhat faster but still incredibly memorable. These leave Mandalay twice weekly at sunrise and arrive in Pagan the same evening. Express boats are included in the cost of an organized tour. Otherwise the price of US$18 deck and US$30 cabin class includes breakfast, lunch, and high tea plus transfers. Exact departures and tickets for this express service are available from the tourist office in Mandalay.

Getting There From Inle Lake
A Datsun minitruck leaves Taunggyi at daybreak and takes eight-to-10 bone-crushing hours to reach Pagan.

Leaving Pagan
To Rangoon: Datsun pickups leave Pagan daily at 0330 and 1400 and arrive in Thazi four hours later. Both minitrucks will drop you at the Oasis Restaurant, where Sein Ngwe serves up some decent Chinese and Burmese food. You must then take a horsecart two km to the train station. Don't ask why, just repeat to yourself, "In all the world there is no place like Burma." Express trains back to Rangoon leave Thazi at 0900, 2115, and midnight.

It is important to have a reservation in upper class with a reclining seat or else you'll risk having to spend the night on the floor. This reservation can be made at the tourist offices in Rangoon or Mandalay. The Pagan Burma Travel can do this . . . if they like you. The best strategy is to make this reservation as soon as possible. Purchasing a Mandalay-Rangoon ticket from the tourist office in Rangoon is a straightforward way to guarantee your seat on the train.

MOUNT POPA

This 1,518-meter peak some 50 km from Pagan is the official home of Burma's *nats*—a collection of 37 magical spirits both feared and honored by Burma citizens. The dusty village of Popa situated at the base of the sugarloaf mountain has souvenir stalls, several basic but adequate restaurants, and hostels for pilgrims. Main attraction is the *nat* museum constructed in 1925, which holds 37 life-size *nat* statues sculpted from teak by a Mandalay craftsman. Thousands of Burmese gather here twice yearly to honor the spirits and attend the festivals. The one-

BUDDHA AND THE *NATS*

Burma is perhaps the most profoundly Buddhist country in the world. Over 85% of the population follows the precepts of Theravadism. Monks of all ages in all shades of yellow and orange robes are seen everywhere. Each morning some half-million monks silently walk the streets with their begging bowls, giving residents the opportunity to improve their karma. Another 100,000 have permanently joined the Noble Order of the Yellow Robe.

And yet there is more to Burmese religion than just monks and Buddhism. Underlying Burma's Theravadism is an animist substratum of nature spirits, ghosts, and departed ancestors who control the weather, health, luck, future, life, and death. The average Burmese honors the Buddha but keeps an abiding sense of fear and respect for the all-powerful 37 *nats*. As with the Chinese practice of ancestor veneration, the Burmese propitiate *nats* to prevent the great trouble they cause when ignored. And like the saints of the Catholic Church, *nats* boast magical powers that can be called on in time of need. Soothsayers, magicians, and mediums all invoke their spirits to cure disease and foretell the future. *Nats* are also similar to Thai *phi* in that most are derivations of historical figures (*dewas*) taken from ancient Hindu mythology. As in Thailand, small spirit houses are nailed to buildings and trees, while *nat* images, with oversized ears and bulbous noses, figure prominently in almost every Buddhist temple. *Nat* veneration continues to form the bedrock of Burmese religion, despite arguments against it made by King Anawrahta of Pagan in the 12th century, King Mindon in the 19th century, and U Nu and Ne Win in modern times.

hour climb to the summit passes the Min Mahagiri Shrine, dedicated to Mr. Handsome and Miss Golden Face, the two most beloved *nats* in Burma cosmology.

Popa can be visited on a side trip from Pagan (look for notices in the tourist office) or as a brief stop en route to Thazi. Accommodations are available in the monastery.

INLE LAKE REGION

One of the most picturesque spots in Southeast Asia, Inle Lake and the surrounding region is an outstanding alternative to the historical attractions of Pagan and Mandalay. Surrounded by lovely blue mountains, this idyllic lake is home to the Intha people, who live in stilted villages and farm floating islands created from mud and reed. The Intha are also known for their curious technique of rowing slender crafts with a single leg wrapped around the oar. Although Inle Lake and the leg-rowers are the most famous attractions in the region, there's more. The region also offers Taunggyi and Kalaw, two former British hill stations with cool weather and colorful markets visited by tribals from the Shan states. North of Kalaw are the famous Pindaya Caves filled with countless Buddhist images. Although most first-time visitors do the standard Rangoon-Mandalay-Pagan tour, Inle Lake remains a splendid off-the-beaten-track destination well worth an entire week.

Orientation

Place-names at Inle can be confusing. Taunggyi, the largest town in the region, has the main office of Burma Tourism, the largest marketplace, and the only first-class hotel. Heho airport is 25 km west of Taunggyi. The train terminus is at Shwenyaung, about 12 km north of the lake, almost midway between Taunggyi and Heho. Yaunghwe, situated on the northern shore of Inle Lake, has a small tourist office, money-exchange facilities, and a pair of inexpensive guesthouses. Yaunghwe is probably the most convenient place to stay if time is limited. Guesthouses in Yaunghwe were closed several years ago but may be reopened by the time you arrive. Ask around.

TRANSPORTATION

Getting There From Rangoon

By Air: Myanma Airways cancelled flights several years ago.

By Train and Minitruck: Express trains depart Rangoon at 0600, 1815, and 2100, and arrive in Thazi 12 hours later. A tourist official will meet you and direct you toward the Inle-bound minitruck. This Datsun leaves only when completely filled, making it necessary to wait or pay the fare differential. Visitors who wish to go directly to the lake and save two hours of unnecessary travel should get off at Shwenyaung and take a bus to Yaunghwe.

By Train: The 2100 express train from Rangoon arrives in Thazi at 0830 the following morning. The ordinary train direct to Shwenyaung isn't recommended since it takes a full day.

Getting There From Mandalay

Flights depart at 0935 and arrive just 30 minutes later. This short flight is reasonably priced and (if you can get a ticket) much more comfortable than land transport.

Datsun trucks leave at 0530 and 0800 from 25th Street between 82nd and 83rd and take a minimum of 10-12 hours. Another option is to take the train to Thazi and then minitruck up to Taunggyi.

Getting There From Pagan

Burma Air flies from Pagan to Mandalay daily at 0835 and from Mandalay to Heho at 0935. You must pay for both sectors—about US$70.

A Datsun minitruck leaves daily at 0330 and 1400 and reaches Thazi four hours later. You must then walk or take a horsecart to the Thazi bus terminus for another six-hour minitruck ordeal to Inle. It can be cold during the winter months; bring along a sweater or jacket. This is a long and miserable trip.

KALAW

This former British hill station, on the edge of the Shan Plateau about 70 km west of Taunggyi, is usually bypassed by visitors rushing up to Inle Lake. But with its cooler climate and fine old Tudor houses spread among the tall pine trees, Kalaw is an interesting stop for anyone with some extra time. The highlight of your visit will be the Kalaw Market with its Shan, Padaung, and Pa O people. This colorful bazaar rotates every five days between Taunggyi, Kalaw, Pindaya, Heho, and Aungban before returning to Taung-

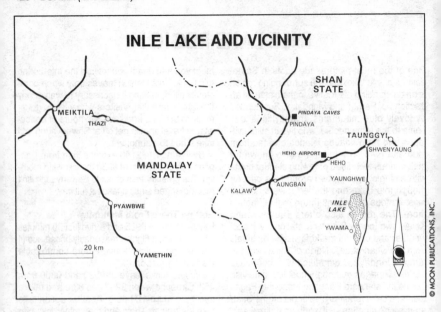

INLE LAKE AND VICINITY

SHAN STATE

MEIKTILA
THAZI

PINDAYA CAVES
PINDAYA

TAUNGGYI
SHWENYAUNG

HEHO AIRPORT
HEHO

MANDALAY STATE

YAUNGHWE

KALAW
AUNGBAN

INLE LAKE

PYAWBWE

YWAMA

0   20 km

YAMETHIN

© MOON PUBLICATIONS, INC.

gyi. Arriving in Kalaw on market day is pure luck, but exact schedules can be checked with the tourist office in the Kalaw Hotel.

Other attractions include the Thein Tong Pagoda overlooking the main road and the glittering Dama Yan Thi Pagoda near the market. Those interested in trekking to the nearby Padaung villages of Ta Yaw, Shwe Mine Phone, and Pein Ne Pin should ask at the tourist office.

Accommodations at the colonial Kalaw Hotel cost US$30-40. Or stay at the rustic Pineland Resthouse in the center of town.

PINDAYA CAVES

This small town about 45 km north of Kalaw is known for its limestone caves filled with thousands of gilded Buddha images. The scenic road from Kalaw via Aungban passes Pa O and Danu villages before arriving in Pindaya, which is chiefly inhabited by Taungyos. Entrance to the caves is from the ridge overlooking the lake and can be reached by hired jeep or via the covered walkway. Northwest of Pindaya are the Padah Lin Caves, with Neolithic wall paintings of bison, elephants, and human figures.

Accommodations are limited to the Pindaya Guest House toward the caves, with standard rooms at US$25-35. The tourist office in Kalaw may know of cheaper accommodations.

Public buses to Pindaya via Aungban leave from Kalaw, although service is sporadic and time-consuming. Much faster are chartered jeeps for US$25, which travel Kalaw-Pindaya and then on to Yaunghwe before nightfall.

TAUNGGYI

Spread across the wooded foothills above Inle Lake is the cool and colorful hill town of Taunggyi. This former British hill resort was founded in the 19th century by Sir James George Scott who, under his pseudonym of Shway Yoe, wrote his classic work *The Burman, His Life and Notions*. Situated at a bracing 878 meters, Taunggyi is the capital of Shan state and is an important economic pipeline for goods smuggled from Thailand.

Attractions
Chief draw is Taunggyi Market, held once every five days. This colorful bazaar with its fascinating

mix of hill tribes in traditional costumes is one of the most authentic in Burma. An excellent introduction to some of the 30 tribes of the Shan Plateau can be found at the Shan State Museum near the Taunggyi Hotel. Except for the these ethnological attractions and a few colonial reminders there is little else of interest in Taunggyi.

Accommodations

Visitors who prefer to stay in Taunggyi rather than down by the lake at Yaunghwe can choose from three hotels. The top-end Taunggyi Hotel has spacious standard rooms with attached baths at US$40-55. The tourist office and moneychanging facilities are located here.

Budget hotels include the fairly clean San Pya Guest House on the main street and the scruffy May Kyu Guest House on a side street one block south of the market. Both were closed several years ago but may reopen in the future.

YAUNGHWE

This small town at the northern end of Inle Lake has a few simple restaurants and a branch office of the tourist office. This is also the main launching point for boat tours of the lake.

Visitors with limited time will find Yaunghwe much more convenient than Taunggyi. Yaunghwe, one of some 200-odd Intha settlements constructed around the lake, has a few pagodas worth visiting and a small museum just north of the Bamboo Lodge. The tourist office at the boat pier southwest of the market sells guesthouse vouchers, makes limited transportation reservations, and arranges the only legal boat tours of the lake. They also change money. Prior to their closure several years ago, accommodations included the Inle Inn and the Bamboo Inn. Both are several blocks to your left from the bus stop and may be reopened with permission of the Burmese government. Two popular restaurants for both food and minitours of the canals include the Friendship and Sunflower.

INLE LAKE

Inle Lake—one of the most dazzling and magical places in Asia—is inhabited by the Intha ("Sons of the Lake"), a Mon people who migrated here centuries ago from the southeastern regions of Burma. This clever and relatively prosperous race of people literally farms the lake by cultivating floating gardens and fishing with enormous conical traps. To a large degree, their brilliant concept of manufacturing land has made them famous. First the rubbery tubes of water hyacinths and rushes are woven together into gigantic mats. Incredibly fertile mud is then dredged from the bottom of the lake and dumped on the mat to form instant land. When the layer of humus is deep enough to allow farming but not so heavy as to sink, the floating garden is towed to the owner's home and pegged to the lake floor with long bamboo staves, thereby disproving Will Rogers' axiom, "Buy land, they ain't making it anymore."

These remarkable people have also developed an eccentric method of fishing while rowing with one leg wrapped around the oar. Although this storklike style of rowing appears peculiar and overly dramatic, it effectively leaves one hand free for holding the net while maneuvering through the water hyacinths. When the fisherman spots a sizable shoal of fish in the shallow and crystal-clear water, he drops the huge trap and pushes it home with his leg. The ensnared fish are then speared at his leisure through a hole in the top of the cage.

Touring The Lake

The only authorized method of touring the lake is by a tourist-office boat. Almost every morning around 0800 a boat leaves for the five-hour tour including stops for lunch, shopping, and sightseeing. The boat holds 10 people and costs K1000, or K100-120 per person when filled. Tickets should be purchased in advance from the tourist office at the pier in Yaunghwe.

The boat trip passes floating gardens, wildlife, leg rowers, and fishermen before reaching the picturesque village of Ywama, where once every five days a small but colorful floating market is held along the largest canal. This is certainly the best day to visit Ywama (although the tourist office claims this market to be a daily event). Also located in this Burma Venice is the modest but highly revered Phaung Daw U Pagoda with its five tiny and shapeless Buddha images which, according to legend, were brought from Malaysia by King Alaungsithu in the 12th century. Having proved their miraculous powers, they are now transported around the lake on a gilded royal barge each fall during the annual Karaweik Celebration.

Besides being successful farmers and fishermen, the Intha are also talented craftsmen who produce famous Shan shoulder bags, thick Shan *longyis,* conical hats called *khamouts,* and delicate silverware sold at the market and Myanmar Travel and Tours souvenir shop. An alternative to the Inle Lake tour, which can be expensive without a full boatload of passengers, is a canoe trip down the canals near Yaunghwe. More details from the tourist office or the Inle Inn.

KENGTUNG

In May 1993 the Burmese government officially opened the town of Kengtung to foreign visitors. Off-limits to tourists for over 40 years, Kengtung has long been known as the unofficial capital of the opium-growing Golden Triangle.

Attractions
Kengtung, a tranquil town of 30,000 famed for its rightly preserved Buddhist culture, boasts several Buddhist monasteries, the oldest of which dates from the 14th century. Although the magnificent 85-year-old palace of the traditional rulers was destroyed by the government in 1991 (a symbol of Shan nationalism), most of the monasteries and temples are still standing.

Also visit the Catholic Mission where three Italian nuns have lived continuously for over 60 years.

Transportation
Kengtung is 172 km from Mae Sai in northern Thailand. Pickup trucks from the border checkpoints at Mae Sai first stop in the Burmese border town of Tachiliek to pick up visas at the immigration office. Visas cost $18 and processing takes about an hour.

The truck ride takes about seven hours and passes magnificent hills tragically stripped of trees by the government and local hilltribes.

Bangkok Airways intends to start air service from Chiang Rai to Kengtung sometime in 1995. Perhaps.

The glamour of the East had cast its spell upon him; the mystery of lands in which no white man had set foot since the beginning of things had fired his imagination; the itch of travel was upon him, goading him to restlessness.

—Hugh Clifford,
The Story of Exploration

Travel can hardly ever fail to wreak a transformation of some sort, great or small, and for better or for worse, in the situation of the traveller.

—Claude Lévi-Strauss,
Tristes Tropiques

Every man carries within himself a world made up of all that he has seen and loved; and it is to this world that he returns incessantly, though he may pass through, and seem to inhabit, a world quite foreign to it.

—Chateaubriand,
Voyage en Italie

HONG KONG

*He who travels far will often see things far removed from
what he believed was Truth. When he talks about it in
the fields at home, he is often accused of lying, for the
obdurate people will not believe what they do not see
and distinctly feel.*

—Herman Hesse,
Journey to the East

*We are all guilty of crime, the great crime of not living life
to the full. But we are all potentially free. We can stop
thinking of what we have failed to do and do whatever
lies within our power.*

—Henry Miller

*Why do people travel? To escape their creditors. To find a
warmer or cooler clime. To sell Coca-Cola to the Chinese.
To find out what is over the seas, over the hills and far
away, round the corner, over the garden wall.*

—Eric Newby,
A Traveller's Life

INTRODUCTION

Once described by the queen's foreign secretary as a "barren rock with hardly a dwelling upon it," Hong Kong today is a land of startling juxtapositions: old and traditional lifestyles set slapdash against the dynamic world of modern commerce; an exotic backdrop for Hollywood movies; a highly urbanized environment of Eastern lifestyles and Western conveniences; a Chinese city of soaring skyscrapers constructed over the ruins of a colonial outpost; one of the world's most intense, high-strung, frustrating, and fascinating destinations.

As you probably know by now, in July 1997 the territory will cease to be a British Crown Colony and revert back to Chinese rule. Until then, it will remain an essential Asian destination and one of the world's most popular vacation spots. First of all, Hong Kong is a shoppers' paradise of Chinese craft stores, quality boutiques, and factory outlets overflowing with the trendiest jeans and the latest high-tech wonders. For roaming gourmets with a sense of adventure, Hong Kong offers a wide range of Oriental and Occidental restaurants which serve everything from snake soup to chauteaubriand. There're temples and *tao* and *tai chi* for those in-

terested in Chinese culture. Walking tours described in the text are memorable excursions through the living history of the colony. Sightseeing possibilities beyond the urban core range from rural villages and hiking trails to smoky temples and giant water slides. Finally, Hong Kong is also an easy place to explore, since many of its citizens speak English and public transportation is well organized.

But visitors lured by Hollywood's image of Suzi Wong or the standard tourist hype will be in for a shock. In today's Hong Kong, Chinese junks are powered by noisy diesel engines and the rickshaw "boys" only serve as photographers' models. And Suzi plays the stock market while waiting for her exit visa. Nothing stays the same. Locked in a perpetual state of demolition and massive reconstruction, Hong Kong is a place where the national bird is the construction crane and the national anthem the clatter of the jackhammer. "It'll be a great city when they finish building it."

Situated on little more than 1,000 square km, Hong Kong is both highly urbanized and extraordinarily *crowded,* with some neighborhoods packing over 150,000 residents per square kilometer,

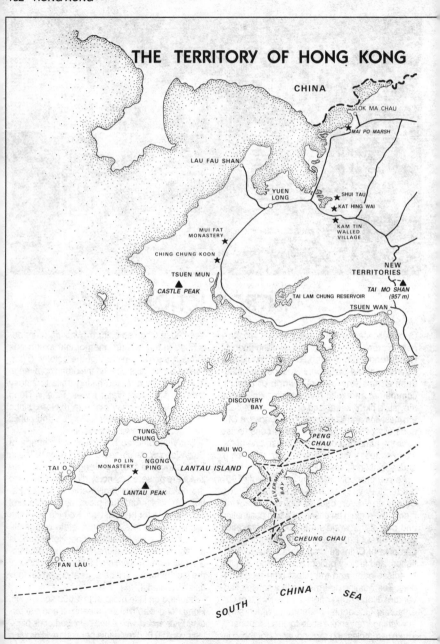

THE TERRITORY OF HONG KONG

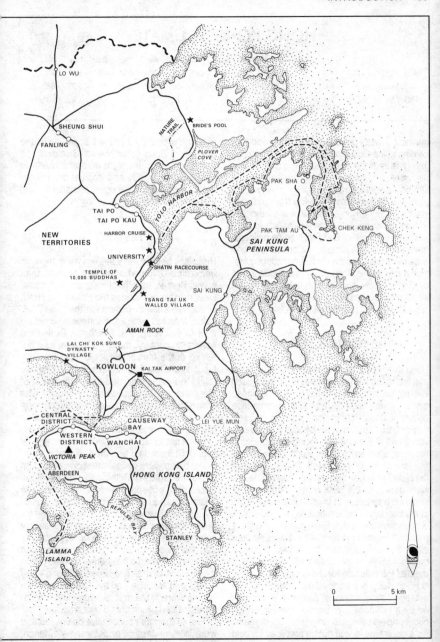

HONG KONG'S CLIMATE

	Jan.	Feb.	March	April	May	June	July	Aug.	Sept.	Oct.	Nov.	Dec.
Avg. Maximum C	18°	17°	19°	24°	28°	29°	31°	31°	29°	27°	23°	20°
Avg. Maximum F	64°	62°	66°	75°	83°	84°	88°	88°	84°	81°	73°	68°
Rainy Days	4	5	7	8	13	18	17	15	12	6	2	3

the most densely populated area in the world according to the *Guinness Book of World Records*. The initial impact is an overwhelming dose of people, neon, and noise. Walking down a street is like being sucked into the vortex of a tornado plunging into a volcano. If you like New York then you'll love Hong Kong. And as in any other city with six million people crammed into housing projects and concrete office towers, some residents have forgotten the importance of courtesy and good manners. Even the most diplomatic of guidebooks has called Hong Kong "the rudest place on Earth." Crowds, heat, and noise are the flip side to the excitement and vitality of this "borrowed land living on borrowed time."

THE PHYSICAL SETTING

Hong Kong has a land mass of 1,062 square km and lies at the same latitude as Mexico City and Hawaii. Located only 145 km from the Chinese city of Canton and 65 km from the Portuguese colony of Macau, Hong Kong's geographic setting of harbor and hills indisputably compares with those of Rio and San Francisco as among the most spectacular in the world. Over 80% of the land is rocky wasteland, though some of the New Territories and outlying islands have a stark beauty in the brisk winter months. Most visitors are surprised to learn that less than 20% of the total land area is urbanized and over 80% is open farmland and national parks. Hong Kong means "Fragrant Harbor," a term derived from either the incense factories that once clustered on the shores or the British opium ships that created the rationale for the colony.

Hong Kong is a tropical, monsoonal country with two distinct seasons. Winters are dominated by a northeastern monsoon which brings cool temperatures and an agreeable dryness. It's a good time to visit but be prepared for cold weather, especially if you're just getting off the plane from Bangkok or Manila. Sweaters can be picked up in the night markets. Summer brings high humidity and tropical monsoons. Watch the TV and take cover at signal 8. Best time to visit Hong Kong is spring or fall.

HISTORY

Historians believe early settlers were migrants from north China who stopped here on their way to Borneo, the Philippines, and Indonesia. Later migrations included the Hakka and Hoklo who established their farms in the New Territories, followed by the Cantonese who set up their fishing villages at Aberdeen. During the early 16th century, the great commercial potential of the harbor attracted both the Portuguese and the English. In 1557 the Chinese rulers in Peking awarded the trading post of Macau to the Portuguese and a century later allowed the Europeans to establish a mercantile settlement near Canton. It was a profitable but problematical arrangement. The soaring popularity of tea forced the English to import a great deal of Chinese leaf and the Chinese government, being wary of the intentions of foreign devils, began demanding silver as payment. Faced with a deepening trade imbalance, the British proposed an immensely dirty but incredibly profitable solution: sell opium to China's two million drug addicts. Although an unsavory occupation, a certain degree of respectability was maintained by holding opium auctions in Calcutta and letting private British traders export the drugs to China. The history of Hong Kong shows that Noriega and the Colombian drug barons weren't the first to appreciate the advantages of a syndicated drug cartel.

Two of the most successful opium runners were William Jardine and James Matheson,

MAN MO TEMPLE, HOLLYWOOD ROAD

Man Mo Temple

Scottish merchants who were religious in a strict Calvinist way but completely indifferent to moralistic reflections. With the efforts of the Scots and other British merchants, opium exports to the Chinese soon soared to over 50,000 chests per year. Alarmed at the reversal of their economic fortunes, the government in Peking sent an aggressive anti-opium general to clean up the situation in Canton. He promptly dumped thousands of opium chests into the ocean, an act of economic outrage which touched off a series of Opium Wars and treaties which gave the British their foothold in Hong Kong. Looking for a trading post outside Chinese or Macanese control, a young British captain named Charles Elliot annexed the rocky and unwanted island of Hong Kong. In an ironic twist of fate, Elliot discovered his policies so accommodative and his barren rock so worthless that he was ultimately banished to a desolate Texas outpost! The British proceeded to take Hong Kong in slow but steady bites. In 1842 the Chinese were forced to sign the Treaty of Nanking, which awarded Hong Kong Island to the British in perpetuity. The Convention of Peking in 1850 ceded the Kowloon Peninsula and a final treaty in 1898 gave Britain a 99-year lease on the New Territories. A government opium monopoly was established in 1913 and the trade remained legal in Hong Kong until 1946.

While enjoying a measure of prosperity during the 1920s, Hong Kong was actually the poor stepsister to Shanghai, that glittering yet doomed metropolis whose strategic location on the Yangtze River was immeasurably superior to that of her southern cousin. Hong Kong's fortunes changed dramatically with the arrival of WW II. After a short struggle at the now-demolished Repulse Bay Hotel in 1941, the Japanese invaded and with little resistance conquered Hong Kong. Treatment by the Japanese was so harsh that over one million Chinese fled back into the rural safety of China and Hong Kong's population fell to less than 500,000. Mao's triumph in 1947 sent waves of refugees back to Hong Kong, including the wealthy industrialists of Shanghai with their financial expertise and vast sums of capital. Hong Kong re-exploded during the '50s and grew from less than one to over five million residents. Tremendous strains were placed on social services, sanitation, and housing as thousands were forced to live as squatters on barren hillsides and in decaying tenements more suited to cattle than human beings. The British government eventually began an ambitious housing program and, within a single generation, the poor and desperate refugees had carved an economic miracle few people thought possible.

GOVERNMENT

Hong Kong is British territory headed by a governor appointed by the Queen who is in turn assisted by the Executive Council (Exco) and

SIGHTSEEING HIGHLIGHTS

The average visitor stays only 3.4 days in Hong Kong and spends over 60% of the time on Hong Kong's number-one attraction—shopping. Much better: stay a week and discover what makes Hong Kong the most visited city in Southeast Asia. It's not surprising that with so little time most first-time visitors are confused by local geography and place-names. A quick look at the four general areas (Kowloon, Hong Kong Island, New Territories, Outlying Islands) and townships in each area will help you get a handle on the place.

Kowloon

This densely packed neighborhood of high-rise buildings and rushing crowds is the territories' leading hotel and restaurant area.

Tsimshatsui: This is where you'll find most of Kowloon's hotels, nightlife, and restaurants. Gourmets will love the culinary treats, whether dining at roadside stalls or in five-star restaurants. Tsimshatsui (pronounced Chim-Sa-Choy) also has a modest museum and an impressive new cultural center. The biggest draw, however, is the shopping. A good place to start is on Nathan Road, a tree-lined neon strip so packed with shops that it's been nicknamed the Golden Mile; it's a shopping zone where even the deepest of credit cards can run aground in a single afternoon. Bargainers will find lower prices in the night markets of Mongkok and the small factory shops hidden inside Kaiser Estates.

New Tsimshatsui: Directly east is New Tsimshatsui, a landfill project now blanketed with expensive hotels and vast shopping centers. A memorable experience is walking the waterfront promenade as lights blink on at sunset.

Yaumatei and Mongkok: Fifteen minutes north of Tsimshatsui is Yaumatei, a less touristy neighborhood of working-class shops, historic temples, and the famous jade market. Of special note is a walking tour through side streets that still exude some of the flavor of old China. Mongkok, a densely packed neighborhood north of Yaumatei, offers craft stores, brothels, and less expensive hotels. Top pick up here is the Temple Street night market, a nightly happening that typifies what is most exotic and exciting about the territory.

Beyond Kowloon: More sights are located north of Boundary Road, the geographic boundary that separates Kowloon from the New Territories. Temple aficionados will enjoy the architecture of Wong Tai Sin, considered by many Hong Kong's most impressive temple. Also of interest are the Sung Dynasty Village in Lai Chi Kok and seafood restaurants in Lei Yue Mun.

Hong Kong Island

Hong Kong is a geographic term that confuses both locals (who can't decide whether to spell it "Hong Kong" or "Hongkong") and visitors who mix up Hong Kong (the entire territory) with Hong Kong (the island). The mountainous and highly urbanized *island* of Hong Kong is divided into several townships with distinct histories and personalities.

Central: The economic and political capital of Hong Kong offers a botanical garden, trendy nightlife

the Legislative Council (Legco). Important matters are first fleshed out by the governor and Exco before being handed down to Legco for further discussion and approval. There are no political parties except for a handful of special-interest groups and boards such as the Urban Council (Urbco) and Regional Council (Regco), which take care of mundane tasks like garbage collection and health services. It has been said that real power in Hong Kong resides with the Jockey Club, Jardine and Matheson, the Hong Kong and Shanghai Bank, and the governor—*in that order*. Hong Kong lacks political motivation or nationalist fervor. There's no national anthem, pledge of allegiance, or large standing

army. Despite the recent events in China, the ideals of representative government such as freedom of speech and press are still dismissed as hopelessly idealistic, eccentric, or totally impossible. Recent elections attracted so little interest that less than 20% of the population registered to vote and less than a quarter of those turned out on election day.

Under the terms of the Joint Agreement signed a few years ago by Britain and China, Hong Kong becomes a Chinese possession at exactly midnight on June 30, 1997. Together with the Basic Law this agreement supposedly allows Hong Kong to keep its capitalist system for 50 years with a promise of local autonomy as

SIGHTSEEING HIGHLIGHTS

in the area called Lan Kwai Fong, and some of the world's most striking modern architecture. Looming over the glass-and-steel statuary is Victoria Peak, perhaps the island's best place to escape the crowds and survey the dazzling panorama.

Western: Situated just 15 minutes west is the Western district, a traditional neighborhood of Chinese drugstores, old teahouses, snake restaurants, ginseng emporiums, elderly gentlemen dressed in silk pajamas, and other reminders of old Hong Kong. A highly recommended walking tour is fully described in the text.

Causeway Bay: Causeway is the main hotel, dining, and shopping area for visitors who want to stay on Hong Kong Island rather than in Kowloon. Hugging the landfilled harbor are chic department stores, luxury hotels, and literally hundreds of restaurants with cuisine from Thai to Tunisian. Causeway Bay's other attractions include the weird and wonderful sculptures at Aw Boon Haw and the racetrack in Happy Valley.

Wanchai: The boozy nightlife-and-restaurant area first made famous by Suzi Wong and the movie of the same title is now much less sinful and exotic; most of the girlie joints have been replaced with yuppie bars and Filipino discos. The Wanch has several excellent middle-priced hotels and is conveniently located between Causeway Bay and Central and within easy walking distance of the new convention center.

South Side of Hong Kong Island: Mere minutes from the hustle and bustle of Central you'll find the famous floating community of Aberdeen and expatriate towns of Stanley and Deepwater Bay. Hong Kong's most popular and crowded beaches are located over here. The south side also offers Southeast Asia's largest leisure complex and several country parks with spectacular sea views from wooded hiking trails.

New Territories

North of Kowloon are the New Territories, a hard and rocky land of planned cities firmly rooted in the 21st century and small villages clinging to lifestyles little changed from past centuries. You can explore a temple with more than 10,000 Buddha images or visit protected marshlands filled with various species of migratory birds. A circular day-trip by public bus gives a quick glimpse into this land between.

Outlying Islands

Almost completely unknown to the average visitor are the 236 outer islands. All are unhurried places of peaceful walks, Buddhist temples, and wide-open spaces . . . near nirvana after the noise and confusion of Hong Kong. The major islands are linked to Hong Kong and Kowloon by ferries of all types and sizes. Best of the lot is Cheung Chau, a delightful Mediterranean island with great charm and character. Lantau, the largest island in the territory, offers superb hiking opportunities and several relatively untouched villages. A third stop could be made at Lamma just south of Hong Kong Island. All have hotels for overnighters or could be quickly visited on day excursions.

---

a "special administrative region" within the People's Republic of China. In this one-country but two-system arrangement the Chinese have promised that private property, ownership of enterprise, rights of inheritance, and foreign investment will be protected by law and that Hong Kong will remain a free port and international financial center with unrestricted foreign exchange and securities markets.

But what will really happen? Optimists point out the logical reasons for Hong Kong's continued existence, such as the US$6 billion annual foreign trade conducted through this capitalistic outpost by the Chinese government. As their economic lifeline to the outside world, it would seem foolish to kill the goose that lays

the golden egg. But some doubt the Chinese will honor their promises after their actions in Tibet and the massacre at Tiananmen. The great remaining flaw is that the *kowtow* Basic Law does not even envisage a democratically run Hong Kong; the Chinese will only allow one-third of the post-1997 legislature to be directly elected. Visa applications have soared in recent months despite Britain's highly restrictive immigration policy that refuses citizenship to most residents. Hong Kong's lease on life is running short and political hormones are starting to flow. Citizenship in Western countries takes so much money that the joke goes: Vietnam has its boat people but Hong Kong will soon have its yacht people. There is only one conversation here: What are you going to do when the Communists come?

ECONOMY

As the second leading economic power in Asia after Japan, Hong Kong is a testament to what purely unregulated, unbridled, and untamed capitalism can do. The complete lack of natural resources—except for its excellent harbor and energetic work force—makes the economic miracle of Hong Kong all the more remarkable. The economy continues to grow at 6-10% yearly or about three times the rate of most Western countries. Gross Domestic Product is well over US$6000 per year, 10 times higher than in China. This is a textbook value-added economy that imports raw goods and exports finished products. It's also in many ways more of an industrial miracle than postwar Japan since it lacks both a hinterland from which raw materials could come and a large population to absorb most of its products. Business is religion and Mammon its only god. Marx would have called the citizens of Hong Kong unrepentant petit bourgeois, but unlike Christians, Muslims, or Marxists, the Chinese of Hong Kong have never suffered shame in the pursuit of wealth.

Hong Kong's economy is almost completely unencumbered with vague socialist programs. There are few import or export duties. Incorporation is so easy that one could register a business in the morning and be making profits by lunchtime. The tax code is a modest booklet with few of the complexities that plague other nations. Consumer goods are untaxed except for a few luxuries such as cigarettes and perfume. Funded by the income from property sales, license plates, and gambling, the government of Hong Kong does not interfere with or subsidize declining industries but allows market forces to settle the fate of businesses that can't compete. All this laissez-faire economics has forced local entrepreneurs to move quickly from plastic flowers and transistor radios in the '50s to workstation computers and industrial robots in the '90s.

Hong Kong's economy, like the skyline itself, has changed radically in recent years. Many of the British-controlled *hongs* who once sold opium to the Chinese are now controlled by Chinese millionaires who sell their high-quality products back to the British. The Hong Kong and Shanghai Banking Corporation may still represent British economic power in the Orient, but its dominance is being challenged by Chinese and American banking firms. Jardine Matheson shocked the economic community a few years ago when it yanked its headquarters from Hong Kong to Bermuda. Americans are now, in fact, the driving force behind new industries and products, pumping in over US$1 billion in fresh capital—twice that of the Japanese and eight times that of the British. Demographics have also changed. With 16,000 American expatriates compared to Britain's 14,000, it appears that Hong Kong 1997 will be an American rather than British economic outpost being turned over to the new masters in Beijing.

THE PEOPLE

Hong Kong's 5.6 million residents include 1.3 million on Hong Kong Island, 2.8 million on the Kowloon Peninsula, and the remainder in the New Territories and outlying islands. Average population density is a modest 5,170 people per square kilometer, but the density in Shamshuipo soars to over 165,000 people per square km—a world record according to Guinness. Chinese comprise 98% of the population. Most are descended from Chinese refugees but locally born. Cantonese is the most common Chinese dialect but you might even hear Chinglish, a local slang that combines Chinese and English.

Most Hong Kong residents are Cantonese from the southern province of Guangdong. A tough and hardworking people with a lively sense of humor and a healthy zest for life, the Cantonese are considered the culinary geniuses of the Chinese world. The next largest group are the Shanghainese, who emigrated to Hong Kong in large numbers after the fall of Shanghai. Bringing along their factories (literally) and financial expertise, these wealthy industrialists quickly rose to the top of the economic ladder in Hong Kong. The Chiu Chow (Teochew in Singapore) emigrated from the mainland coastal cities of Shantou and Xiamen on China's southern coast. In earlier times they dominated the wholesale drug traffic but today they have

HONG KONG'S VANISHING PEOPLES

Hong Kong's minority groups include the fishermen and farmers who wandered down from southern China in the 14th century. First on the scene were the Puntis who claimed the most fertile farming lands in the New Territories. Soon afterwards the Hakka (a term that means "Guest People") arrived to become the largest group in the region. The Hakka's matriarchal society permitted women to engage in construction and other work traditionally reserved for Chinese males. Most Hakkas have now integrated into mainstream society, though some elderly Hakka women still dress in their traditional black pajamalike suits (*samfoo*) and wear distinctive hats framed by black curtains. Another group still to be seen in Hong Kong is the Tanka (called the egg people since they once paid their taxes in eggs), who live in junks moored in typhoon shelters at Aberdeen, Causeway Bay, and Yaumatei. Long discriminated against in precommunist China and refused permission to live on land or intermarry with the local population, these hardy seafolk are now moving into housing projects and abandoning their lives on the sea. The Hoklo are another group of fishermen from southern China.

Hakka collecting alms

moved into more ordinary occupations. Recent arrivals include Vietnamese boat people who fled their homeland after the floodgates were opened in the '70s.

RELIGION

Although the Chinese outnumber all other races on Earth, their religious beliefs are perhaps the least understood. Often described as a combination of Buddhism mixed with the social teachings of Confucianism and Taoist mysticism, their real religion involves ancestor veneration and the appeasement of malevolent spirits with countless rituals designed to divine and influence the future. The more philosophical concepts of Confucianism and Taoism complete the picture. This cross-pollination of religious beliefs can be confusing to visitors and even to the Chinese themselves, who care little for philosophical introspection. Look carefully and you'll notice that Chinese temples often have statues of the Buddha standing next to Taoist gods behind Confucian heroes! Chinese see no moral conflict in burning incense for Buddha while following the philosophical precepts of Confucius and having last rites performed by a Taoist priest, since all serve to fulfill certain feelings of piety and superstitious belief.

Popular Folk Gods

Mythological evolution has created over 600 gods which Chinese believe influence both the present and the future. Most Chinese homes have a special area that holds a statue of their favorite god or goddess such as Kuan Yin, the popular Buddhist Goddess of Mercy worshipped from Japan to Sri Lanka, or Tin Hau, the influential Goddess of the Sea who calms the waters and brings good luck to fishermen. Less important but just as significant are nature spirits who inhabit natural objects such as ancient trees, irregular rocks, or animal bones. These spirits

lips sealed with tar

have traditionally protected villages from disease and invasion. But few gods are more popular than Tsao Kwan, the highly honored Kitchen God who keeps an eye on the household and reports all activities to the Jade Emperor once a year. With the family's luck or misfortune decided by his heavenly dossier, the Chinese unabashedly resort to bribery such as dabbing the image's lips with honey (opium in earlier days) to ensure a favorable review. Like many other Chinese deities, the Kitchen God is powerful but not so all-knowing that he cannot be influenced by human beings—a belief that lies at the root of most Chinese ritual.

Confucianism

This guide to morality and good government is based on the philosophies of the Chinese sage who lived during 6th century B.C. in feudal China. Raised in great poverty, Confucius rose

to became a minor government official before resigning in protest over the anarchy and corruption that gripped the country. After studying the ancient masters, he formed his own philosophical system that emphasized obedience to both parents and righteous rulers. Political authority was considered a mandate from heaven, a philosophical belief which, quite understandably, strongly appealed to the rulers of imperial China. Confucianism was soon elevated to the status of state religion and used to maintain domestic order and preserve tradition. Candidates for government jobs were required to take civil-service exams based on Confucian ideas until the technological progress of the West caused many intellectuals to blame Confucianism for the backwardness of China. Today it survives only in the noncommunist Chinese states of Taiwan, Hong Kong, and Singapore.

Confucius, however, was no metaphysician; he said little about his own religious beliefs and never claimed divinity. Although he reluctantly accepted the concept of ancestor worship (or veneration, depending on your perspective), he refused to discuss the question of life after death and insisted that prayers for special favors were useless. Confucianism, then, is not a religion in the Western sense since it has no clergy and does not teach the worship of a god or the existence of a life after death.

Taoism

While Confucianism provided an ethical social framework for Chinese society, Taoism and Buddhism provided the religious foundations. Originally a reaction movement against the logic and conformity of Confucianism, Taoism ranks as the second major belief system in traditional Chinese thought. On a practical level it follows the doctrines of nonbeing and emphasizes the importance of action in harmony with nature. On a mystical and magical level it extols communications with spirit mediums, levitation, and immortality through magic. This bizarre aspect mainly appeals to elderly and superstitious Chinese who pack the Taoist temples hoping for miracles. Taoism is still practiced in Hong Kong, but many educated Chinese feel that it has degenerated into a superstitious folk religion operated by mercenary priests.

PRACTICAL INFORMATION

GETTING THERE

Hong Kong is an important gateway to Asia whether coming from America, Europe, or Australia. Discount tickets are sold by wholesalers who advertise the latest fares in the Sunday travel sections of major newspapers such as the *New York Times, Chicago Tribune, Los Angeles Times,* and *San Francisco Examiner* and *Chronicle.* Discount tickets are also sold in Bangkok, Penang, and Singapore, but they're more difficult to locate in Manila and Jakarta.

Airport Arrival

Kai Tak International Airport is served by over 35 carriers who schedule over 1,000 flights each week. Plans are being made for a second airport on Lantau Island. Whether your plane approaches from the east or scrapes the rooftops on the western landing, the final descent to Kai Tak Airport is always dramatic. After immigration and customs formalities, stop at the Hong Kong Tourist Association (HKTA) counter just outside the customs gate for maps, brochures, and their weekly magazine. The Hong Kong Hotel Association will check hotel vacancies at their member hotels. This doesn't include super-budget dorms or hostels. Checking on vacancies is a sensible idea in the late afternoon or evening when most hotels are fully booked.

Deak International operates the money-changing operations and levies a 5% service charge—rip-off situation. Rates are computed by Reuters and posted on a TV monitor. Departure tax is an outrageous HK$150 for adults but free for children.

Getting To Your Hotel

Kai Tak Airport is approximately 20 minutes from Kowloon and 40 minutes from hotels on Hong Kong Island. Cheap, fast, and comfortable KMB Airbuses to most hotels leave every 15 minutes 0700-2300. Airbus A1 costs HK$9 to Kowloon hotels such as the Ambassador, the Peninsula, the Regent, the YMCA, and Chungking Mansions. Airbus A2 costs HK$14 to Central and Wanchai hotels such as the Mandarin, the Hilton, the Marriott, the Furama, and Harbour View International House (the YMCA). Airbus A3 costs HK$14 to hotels in Causeway Bay such as the Excelsior, Lee Gardens, the Ramada Inn, and the Park Lane Radisson. Airbus A4 costs HK$9 to hotels in the Mongkok area of Kowloon. A computerized tape message announces the stop in various languages—a nicely surrealistic introduction to Hong Kong. Taxis cost HK$35-40 to Kowloon hotels and HK$65-75 to hotels on Hong Kong Island. This includes the HK$20 Cross-Harbor Tunnel surcharge. Taxi fares can be double-checked in the *Getting To Your Hotel* leaflet.

LOCAL TRANSPORTATION

Hong Kong's unusual geography and dense population have brought about one of the world's most efficient and colorful transportation systems. In fact, some of the ferries, streetcars, and funiculars—not to mention the man-powered rickshaws—have become tourist attractions in themselves. Because of low fares and the government's policy of discouraging private car ownership almost everybody uses public transport, something you'll notice at rush hour when all systems are standing room only.

Water Transport

Star Ferry: Some of Hong Kong's leading tourist attractions are the green-and-white ferries which began linking the island with Kowloon in 1898. Since then they've starred in almost every movie made about the colony. All of these historic workhorses, including *Twinkling, Celestial,* and *Golden Star* (the latest addition) operate daily between 0630 and 2330. The first-class section upstairs costs HK$1 and is preferred by photographers, but the downstairs section allows one to peer into the chugging engine room. The Star Ferry connects Tsimshatsui with Central in just eight minutes. The company's new Tsimshatsui-Wanchai service provides a convenient transport link to the Hong Kong Convention Center.

Walla Wallas: After the ferries stop, late-night barflys are left with either the MTR (which ends at

FESTIVALS

Hong Kong has over 20 annual religious and state festivals that range from subdued family affairs to riotous street celebrations. Chinese festivals common to both Hong Kong and Singapore are fully described in the Singapore chapter. Note that religious festivals that follow the lunar calendar are very difficult to date on the Western calendar. Exact dates can be confirmed with the Hong Kong Tourist Association.

January
Hong Kong Arts Festival: One of Southeast Asia's largest and most important cultural events. Two weeks of concerts by orchestras, dance companies, and internationally known drama groups. Entertainment is Western rather than Oriental; you might be more interested in the October Asian Arts Festival.

February
Chinese New Year: Moon 1, Day 1. Celebrated at nearly all temples. See the Singapore chapter for more details and information on the meaning of "Moon 1, Day 1."

Birthday of the God of Wealth: Moon 1, Day 2. Nearly all Chinese keep the images of the Kitchen God and the God of Wealth in their homes. People celebrate their birthdays by replacing the images and visiting temples to check on their financial luck for the coming year. The Wong Tai Sin Temple in Kowloon is packed with people shaking fortune-telling sticks and tossing fortune-telling blocks.

Lantern Festival: Moon 1, Day 15. Chinese New Year is traditionally ended with children's lantern contests and illuminated processions throughout Hong Kong. The Society for the Advancement of Chinese Folklore hosts cultural shows at Sung Dynasty Village, Tiger Balm Gardens, Edinburgh Place, the Landmark, and many public parks. Ancestral halls in the New Territories are hung with lanterns by villagers to whom a son was born during the previous year.

March
Birthday of Hung Shing Kung: Moon 2, Day 13. Known as the deity who rules the Southern Seas, the Dragon King is honored with celebrations at several Hung Shing Kung temples such as Ap Lei Chau in Aberdeen, Tai O on Lantau, and Kau Sai in the New Territories.

Birthday of Kuan Yin: Moon 2, Day 19. Celebrated at the Buddhist Ku Tung Temple in Fanling. See the Singapore chapter.

floating child at Bun Festival

HONG KONG TOURIST ASSOCIATION

April
Ching Ming Festival: Spring Solstice, often 2 or 3 April. An Ancestor Remembrance Day held twice yearly at Hong Kong cemeteries. Best seen (not photographed) at cemeteries in Aberdeen and Wo Hop Shek near Fanling.

Birthday of Pak Tai: Moon 3, Day 3. Pak Tai is the long-haired Ruler of the North who defeated the Demon King in Chinese mythology. Offerings are made at Stanley, Cheung Chau, and Mong Tseng Wai in the New Territories.

May
Birthday of Tin Hau: Moon 3, Day 23. With over 40 temples dedicated to the Queen of Heaven and Protector of Seamen, Tin Hau is unquestionably the most popular deity in Hong Kong. Celebrations in her honor include Chinese opera, rocket competitions, giant parades of floral shrines called *fa paau*, and huge fleets of gaily decorated boats. Temple celebrations are staggered over a two-week period. The HKTA has the schedule.

FESTIVALS

Vesak: Moon 4, Day 8. Buddha's birthday is celebrated with great reverence at the Po Lin Monastery on Lantau Island.

Birthday of Tam Kung: Moon 4, Day 8. Tam Kung, God of Weather and second patron saint of the boat people, is honored at the Shaukeiwan Tam Kung Temple on Hong Kong Island. One of Hong Kong's larger celebrations.

Cheung Chau Bun Festival: Date selected by divination. Held on Cheung Chau Island, this great Buddhist-Taoist festival honors Pak Tai, the ferocious warrior god, with Chinese opera, vegetarian feasts, and a parade of "floating children" surrealistically supported by concealed steel frames. The six-day festival is climaxed with the distribution of thousands of pink and white sweet buns mounted on 30-meter-high bamboo and paper towers that serve as talismans against sickness and bad luck. A decade ago the towers were climbed by young men who picked the buns, but the tradition was abandoned after one of the towers collapsed.

June
Dragon Boat Festival: Moon 5, Day 5. Exciting and highly popular boat races are held off Hong Kong's East Tsimshatsui Waterfront in the first week of June. Entries come from over 100 local teams and two-dozen overseas groups from Rome, Nagasaki, and Chicago.

July
Enlightenment of Kuan Yin: Moon 6, Day 19. Celebrated at Pak Sha Wan in Hebe Haven.

August
Festival of the Hungry Ghosts: Moon 7, Day 15. Hong Kong's largest festival is celebrated with free opera in *matshed* (bamboo) theaters. An outstanding opportunity to watch Chinese opera. See Singapore for background notes.

Food Festival: This month-long culinary extravaganza is another highly successful creation of the Hong Kong Tourist Association. Food bazaars and dining tours are held throughout the territory for both locals and visitors alike. Lan Kwai Fong in Central sponsors a two-day street carnival.

September
Mid-autumn or Moon Festival: Moon 8, Day 15. The HKTA has the locations of officially sponsored carnivals held in public parks.

Birthday of the Monkey God: Moon 8, Day 16. The Monkey God shows himself to believers twice monthly on the first and the 15th, but the day after the Mid-autumn Festival is considered especially propitious. Trance mediums under the influence of the monkey demonstrate their invulnerability by cutting tongues, piercing cheeks, drinking boiling oil, and walking across fire. Held at the Sau Mau Ping Temple near Kwun Tong in Kowloon.

October
Birthday of Confucius: Moon 8, Day 27. Celebrated at the Confucius Hall Middle School on Caroline Hill Road in Causeway Bay.

Cheung Yeung Festival: Moon 9, Day 9. The second annual Ancestor Remembrance Day is held in all cemeteries. Also the a day for climbing hills, a tradition taken from a Han dynasty fable.

Asian Arts Festival: Two weeks of Asian dance, music, and theater. A rare opportunity to see some of the best performing-arts companies in Southeast Asia.

0100), public buses (which run all night long), or water taxis which operate throughout the night on a demand basis. Named for either their coughing engine or the Washington town where the original craft was built, walla wallas leave from the left of the Star Ferry on Kowloon side and to the right of the Star Ferry on Hong Kong side.

Outlying Islands Ferries: Over 85 double-decker ferries link Hong Kong with the principal outer islands like Cheung Chau, Lamma, and Lantau. Most departures are from the Outlying Districts Ferry Pier on Hong Kong Island, a 10-minute walk west of the Star Ferry. Ferries to Macau depart from the Macau Ferry Terminal in Central and from another pier in Shamshuipo, north of Mongkok. The China Ferry Terminal is located in Kowloon at China Hong Kong City.

MTR
The 60-km underground is the quickest and easiest way to cross the harbor and reach distant shopping districts. Hong Kong's MTR carries a staggering number of people each day: over 50,000 passengers per kilometer route as com-

porters with Tai Pan

HKTA

pared to only 2,100 for San Francisco's BART or 5,000 for London's underground. The MTR operates daily 0600-0100. Fares range HK$3-10 depending on distance. The HK$20 MTR Tourist Ticket allows travel without having to purchase individual tickets. As a bonus, the last journey is provided free regardless of remaining ticket value. The HKTA publication, *MTR Tourist Guide,* describes how to reach over 40 tourist attractions using buses, trams, and the MTR.

Buses And Trams

Double-decker Buses: Hong Kong's lumbering streetcars operate to most destinations daily from 0600 to midnight. China Motor Bus runs services on the island while Kowloon Motor Bus operates the cream-and-red coaches in Kowloon. Destinations are painted on the front. Exact fare should be deposited in the metal boxes next to the driver.

Hong Kong Island Tram: This 86-year-old institution, which chugs along the north side of the island, is one of the more fascinating trips in Hong Kong. Best seat is up front on the top deck. Enjoy this ride while you can—these time machines won't last much longer. A special antique tram, restored to its original 1920s condition, runs between Whitty Street and North Point via Happy Valley. This tram can be hired for private parties by calling Hong Kong Tramways at 891-8765.

Victoria Peak Tram: This century-old funicular railway leaves every 10 minutes between 0700 and midnight from the terminus on Garden Road just behind the Hilton Hotel. A Swiss company has recently refurbished the system and installed new cars that double the passenger-carrying capacity.

Other Transport

Taxis: Hong Kong's 15,000 red taxis charge a HK$10 flagfall plus 95 cents for every 500 meters after the first two kilometers. Pay only the fare shown on the meter plus surcharges of HK$4 for each piece of luggage, HK$20 for the Cross Harbour Tunnel, and HK$5 for the Aberdeen Tunnel.

Train: The Kowloon-Canton train, which departs every 15 minutes from the Hung Hom Terminal in Kowloon, is an excellent way to explore the New Territories. Popular stops include Shatin (10,000-Buddha Monastery and Shatin Racetrack), University Station (Tolo Harbor Cruise and University Museum), Tai Po (carpet factory), and Fanling. Visitors bound for China should take one of the four daily expresses to Guangzhou.

Rickshaws: The old boys and their colorful contraptions still gather at the ferry concourse in Kowloon and on Hong Kong side. Though the HKTA finds the sight of old men hustling tourists rather depressing, and few visitors are willing to pay HK$50 for a ride around the block, you might want to pay their HK$10 modeling fee. Be prepared to bargain firmly and don't attempt candid photos unless you're using a very long lens—these guys are *quick*. Rickshaw licenses are no longer being issued.

HONG KONG TOURIST OFFICES

Australia	55 Harrington St., Sydney, N.S.W. 2000	(02) 251-2855
Canada	347 Bay St., #909, Toronto, Ontario, M5H 2R7	(416) 366-2389
France	38 Avenue George V, 75008 Paris	(01) 4720-3954
Germany	Weisenau 1, 6000, Frankfurt am Main	(069) 722841
Italy	Piazza Dei Cenci 7/A 00186 Roma	(06) 6869112
Japan	Toho Twin Tower 4th fl., 152 Yurakucho, Chiyoda-ku	(03) 3503-0731
New Zealand	POB 2120, Auckland	(09) 520-3316
United Kingdom	125 Pall Mall, London, SW1Y 5EA	(071) 930-4775
U.S.A.	333 N. Michigan Ave., #2323, Chicago, IL 60601	(312) 782-3872
	590 Fifth Ave., 5th fl., New York, NY 10036	(212) 869-5008
	10940 Wilshire Blvd., #1220, Los Angeles, CA 90024	(310) 208-4582

TRAVEL FORMALITIES

Visas

All visitors must have a valid passport and sufficient funds for onward travel. Visas are not necessary for most visitors. Citizens of 26 countries including those of America and Western Europe are automatically granted a one-month stay on arrival. Commonwealth subjects are granted 90-day visa-free stays and British citizens get six months. Extensions can be applied for at the Department of Immigration (tel. 824-6111) in Wanchai, 7 Gloucester Road, 2nd floor. Anyone who intends to work or study in Hong Kong should obtain a visa prior to arrival.

Tourist Information

The well-organized and well-funded Hong Kong Tourist Association (HKTA) has offices at the Kai Tak Airport, the Star Ferry Terminal in Kowloon, and in the basement of the Jardine House (formerly the Connaught Centre) in Central. The HKTA offers a deluge of maps, magazines, and brochures including *Places of Interest by Public Transport, Central and Western District Walking Tour, Yaumatei Walking Tour,* and *Visitors Guide to Chinese Food in Hong Kong.* Some are free, some aren't. Upcoming cultural shows are listed in their magazine, *Hong Kong.*

Other useful publications include the gossipy rag, *Hong Kong Tatler,* and the *TV and Entertainment Times,* which lists upcoming arts events in addition to boob-tube delights. Better libraries include the Urban Council Public Library at City Hall in Central and the British Council Library at 255 Hennessy Road in Wanchai.

Maps

The best map available is the *Hong Kong Official Guide Map* published by the Survey Office of the Buildings and Lands Department. Highly recommended for hikers and backpackers are the *Countryside Series* of topographic maps published by the same group. These show hiking trails, campsites, and youth hostels throughout the colony. The *Map of Hong Kong Territory and Kowloon* from Universal Publications is also useful. Nobody has done a Nancy Chandler-style map of Hong Kong . . . yet.

Money

The Hong Kong dollar (HK$) currently trades at about 7.8 to the U.S. dollar. Currency can be changed at banks, licensed money changers, franchised airport stalls, or in hotels. Finding the best rate is imperative, since service charges and exchange commissions vary anywhere from one to eight percent. Sidewalk money changers generally charge a stiff eight-percent fee to compensate for high rents and risks such as counterfeit notes, holdups, and losses from currency fluctuations. Banks usually offer the best rates despite their three-percent spread between buying and selling prices. *Beware of money changers who offer exceptionally good exchange rates.* Signs posted with misleading rates and deceptive sales gimmicks are commonplace here in Hong Kong. "No charge on buy orders" or "no buying commission" doesn't mean that exchanges are commission-free, only that you should expect a hefty "buying commission." The situation is tricky, but unless you have money to burn, *always* check exactly how much you will get before handing over your money by asking "How many Hong Kong dollars will I get for this traveler's check?"

Post Offices
Kowloon's most convenient post office is located on Middle Road just behind the Ambassador Hotel. The GPO is at 405 Nathan Road just north of Jordan Avenue. The Hong Kong Island GPO is in Central next to the Star Ferry. Both GPOs are open Monday-Saturday 0800-1800.

Telephones
Local calls are free from private phones and cost HK$1 from public phones. All local phone numbers were changed in January 1990. Seven-digit numbers dropped the district prefixes and six-digit numbers absorbed the district prefixes to create seven-digit numbers.

International phone calls can be made from hotels and from one of a dozen Hong Kong Telecom offices. In Kowloon the most convenient office is just next to the post office on Middle Road. The cheapest way to call overseas is with an IDD (International Direct Dialing) phone, from which you dial 001, then the country code, followed by the area code, then the local number. To call Hong Kong from abroad, dial 001 (IDD access code), 852 (country code for Hong Kong), then the local number. On Hong Kong Island try the GPO in Central. Some useful numbers:

Directory Assistance	1081
Emergency	999
International Calls	010
Police Hotline	527-7177
Hong Kong Telecom	732-4336
Post Office (HK Island)	523-1071
(Kowloon)	388-4111
Ambulance (Kowloon)	713-5555
(HK Island)	576-6555
Immigration	824-6111
HKTA	722-5555
HKTA Hotline	801-7177
HK Ferry Company	542-3081
Airport	769-7531

International Clock

Hawaii	-17
California	-15
New York	-12
Europe	-8
Israel	-6
Thailand	-1
Japan	+1

Travel Agencies
Budget Agencies: Budget tickets, visas, and hotel discounts are available at Hong Kong Student Travel offices: 1021 Star House in Kowloon (just opposite the Star Ferry), tel. 721-3269; 1812 Argyle Centre at 688 Nathan Road in Kowloon, tel. 390-0421; 30 Queen's Road in Central, tel. 810-7272; and 11/F Circle Plaza, 499 Hennessy Road in Causeway Bay, tel. 833-9909. Another excellent place for cheap tickets is the Traveller's Hostel on the 16th floor of Chungking Mansions. Other budget agencies pass out flyers on the sidewalks and advertise in the local newspapers, but remember that fraud is a problem in Hong Kong; it's better to pay slightly more at a reputable company.

China Travel: Travel arrangements for China can be made through travel agents or directly from the official representatives, China International Travel Service (CITS) and China Travel Service (CTS). CITS exists to help foreigners, while CTS also assists overseas Chinese.

CITS Hong Kong offices: Main Office, South Seas Centre, 6th floor, 75 Mody Rd., Tsimshatsui East, tel. 732-5888; Central Branch, Swire House, Room 1018, 11 Chater Rd., Central, tel. 810-4282; Causeway Bay Branch, Causeway Bay Plaza, Room 1104, 489 Hennessy Rd., Causeway Bay, tel. 836-3485.

CTS Hong Kong offices: Central Branch, China Travel Bldg., 2nd floor, 77 Queen's Rd., Central, tel. 521-7163; Kowloon Branch, Alpha House, 27-33 Nathan Rd., 1st floor, tel. 721-4481; Mongkok Branch, 62-72 Sai Yee St., 2nd floor, tel. 789-5970.

Visas for China can be obtained from most travel agencies in about 24 hours. The cheapest visas are available from the Ministry of Foreign Affairs of the PRC (tel. 835-3657), China Resources Bldg., 26 Harbour Rd., 5th floor, Wanchai, Hong Kong Island. Single-entry visas valid for 90 days cost about HK$90 and require two days to process.

HONG KONG
1. street scene in Hong Kong (Carl Parkes); **2.** Tin Hau Festival (HKTA);
3. Hau Wang Festival (HKTA)

HONG KONG
1. Cheung Chau child; **2.** Bun Festival beauty; **3.** Bond Centre;
4. Chinese opera performer applying makeup (all photos this page by HKTA)

BASIC CANTONESE

please/thank you.	*cheng nay/um goy*
yes/no	*hai/mmmhai*
hello/how are you?	*wai/nei how ma?*
good/very good	*hoe/hoe hoe*
what is ycur name?	*gwai sing a?*
how much money?	*gay dough cheen?*
too expensive	*tie gwai*
very expensive.	*ho gwai*
very cheap	*ho peng*
make it cheaper.	*peng di la*
never mind.	*mgan yow*
1, 2, 3	*yaht, yee, sam*
4, 5, 6.	*sei, ng, look*
7, 8, 9, 10	*chat, baht, gau, sup*

Express trains from Hong Kong to Canton take three hours and depart from the main train station at 0818, 0903, 1228, and 1428. Tickets can be purchased at CTS or directly at the train station. A jetcat departs from China Hong Kong City in Kowloon daily at 0815 and takes three hours. Express trains and jetcats both cost about HK$160. An overnight ferry departs from China Hong Kong City at 2100 and arrives in Canton the following morning—a good way to save the cost of a night's accommodation and arrive ready to tackle the mayhem of Canton.

Abercrombie and Kent: A great source for tours to China, Vietnam, and Cambodia. 27F/Tai Sang Commercial Building, 24-36 Hennessy Road, Wanchai, tel. 865-7818.

Travel Agents—Tips

Most of Hong Kong's travel agencies are honest but you must watch out for dishonest bucket shops that peddle worthless or highly restricted tickets. Chinese New Year seems to bring out the worst offenders! Carefully read the terms and conditions of your ticket before leaving a deposit. Check all dates and times and make sure the ticket is endorsed with an "OK." Never pay for a ticket until you have received it. Bait-and-switch techniques are standard practice with many agencies that collect your money and then casually inform you that all flights are filled for the foreseeable future. Refunds are rarely given. Allow plenty of time for discount tickets since inexpensive flights are often filled despite ads in the *South China Morning Post.* Recheck all visa and health regulations for each country you intend to visit. Travel agents couldn't care less if you're legal or not. Be careful when using independent agencies for China trips since many overcharge for their visas.

Special Tours

Hong Kong has some rather unusual tours such as the four HKTA outings, each of which takes a different approach to the New Territories. Their Housing Tour and Home Visit program allows you to visit two large public-housing estates and the Wong Tai Sin Temple, the best Chinese temple in Hong Kong. The Land Between Tour is a relaxing way to explore some new areas without having to wrestle with public transportation. The HKTA Heritage Tour visits four restored architectural sites including an ancestral hall, an 18th-century walled village, and a 2,000-year-old burial chamber. And finally, their Mai Po Marsh Tour is an easy way to visit the protected wetland habitat in northwestern New Territories.

Hong Kong is also a good place to learn something about Chinese arts, crafts, and customs. Introductory lectures and demonstrations on acupuncture can be arranged through the Chinese Medicine & Acupuncture Centre in Kowloon. Kung fu lessons are given through the YMCA and the Hong Kong Chinese Martial Arts Association at 687 Nathan Road in Kowloon. Chinese cooking lessons are offered by the Home Management Centre in Causeway Bay and Chopsticks Cooking school in Kowloon. Mandarin and Cantonese can be studied at the Translanguage Centre in Wanchai. The picturesque San Miguel brewery on Castle Peak Road and the Carlsberg brewery in Tai Po accept groups by special arrangement. Visits can also be arranged to the *South China Morning Post* and Asia Television in Kowloon. The HKTA publication *Associations and Societies in Hong Kong* can suggest other special-interest groups.

KOWLOON

Legend relates that after Emperor Ping of the Sung Dynasty counted eight dragons on the hills of Hong Kong and then added one more for his Imperial Self, Kowloon became known as Gau Lung ("Nine Dragons"). Situated at the southernmost tip of the Kowloon Peninsula and seven minutes by ferry from Hong Kong Island, this is where most of the territory's hotels, shopping centers, and restaurants are found.

Kowloon is also one of the world's most crowded cities, with over two million people packed into just 12 square kilometers, a population density almost 20 times greater than that of most Western cities. No matter what hour of the day or night you leave your hotel, it will seem that a large percentage of Kowloon's population is also out there, mixing, moving, and shoving in unison, making it almost impossible to go in any direction other than that of the majority. Westerners accustomed to giving way to the other person should quickly abandon that courtesy and learn to walk Hong Kong-style: charge straight toward oncoming pedestrians and avoid direct eye contact. Just before collision, rotate your shoulder *away* from the other person and make a modest brushing contact. After some practice you should be handling the crowds with ease.

ATTRACTIONS

Kowloon's best diversion is people-watching: bargaining with the vegetable vendor, washing clothes in aluminum pots, eating noodles, burning hell notes at the temple, pulling tourists into dimly lit bars, or tearing down a building less than 10 years old. Kowloon is made up of several distinct neighborhoods. Tsimshatsui has the tourist hotels and restaurants, Tsimshatsui East offers super-luxury hotels and expensive nightclubs, Yaumatei is the place for temples and walking tours, and Mongkok is known for its nightlife and street markets.

Tsimshatsui
First stop at the Hong Kong Tourist Association (HKTA) in the Star Ferry terminal for maps, brochures, and their weekly magazine. This well-organized branch office also posts schedules for upcoming festivals and free cultural performances. International newspapers are sold out front.

Railway Clock Tower: Aside from this nostalgic reminder, the final traces of the historic Kowloon-Canton Train Station were torn down two decades ago for a quartet of modernistic buildings that form the cultural heartland of Hong Kong.

Hong Kong Cultural Centre: One of the most controversial pieces of architecture in Hong Kong, opened in 1989, the ski-sloped Centre includes a 100-seat concert hall, a 1,750-seat theater, an arts library, two restaurants, and a cinema where an international film festival is held every April. The windowless architecture practically guarantees bad *fung shui,* though the *Flying Frenchman* statue in front makes a welcome diversion.

Hong Kong Museum of Art: Hong Kong's latest addition to the culture scene was opened in 1992 after the closure of the Museum of Art in the Central District. The six interior exhibition galleries display Chinese antiques, historical photographs, contemporary art, and the renowned Xubaizhai Collection donated by a local art connoisseur.

Hong Kong Space Museum: Inside the golf-ball-shaped hall are two halls with interactive exhibits and a planetarium with seven daily shows.

Across Salisbury Rd. you might find Mr. Chan Chong-chi, the Taoist from Yunnan who has been weaving grass crickets in the same location since 1946.

Shopping Centers: Shoppers could spend weeks exploring the vast Ocean Terminal/Ocean Center/Harbour City shopping complex. Back on Salisbury Rd., enjoy the views from the rooftop restaurant of the YMCA or sip afternoon tea in the Peninsula Hotel.

Tsimshatsui East: Along the waterfront promenade past the impressive Regent Hotel (the lobby with the best *fung shui* in town) you'll find the evil-looking New World Centre, where free cultural shows are given every Friday at 1800. The face of Kowloon changed forever with the

BUSES TO ATTRACTIONS IN KOWLOON

DESTINATION	FROM	BUS NO.
Airport	Major Hotels	A1
Kaiser Estates Factory Outlets	Star Ferry	5C
Lai Chi Kok Amusement Park	Star Ferry	6A
Lei Cheng Uk Tomb and Museum	Star Ferry	2
Mongkok Night Market	Nathan Rd.	2, 6, or 7
Railway Station	Star Ferry	5C
Sung Dynasty Village	Star Ferry	6A
Yaumatei and Jade Market	Nathan Rd.	2, 6, or 7
YMCA (Waterloo Road)	Star Ferry	7

opening of Tsimshatsui East, a gigantic landfill project blanketed with many of Hong Kong's most luxurious hotels, restaurants, and nightclubs.

Hong Kong Science Museum: The neighborhood's latest addition is the HK$350-million museum with 500 hands-on exhibits on Science Museum Road.

Kowloon Park: Return to Nathan Rd. and walk north up to the HK$30-million Kowloon Mosque constructed a decade ago to serve the religious needs of Hong Kong's 50,000 Muslims. Open to the public on Mondays 0900-1100. Also in the park are the Chinese Gardens, an indoor Olympic-sized swimming pool, and the Hong Kong Museum of History, with a small, disappointing collection of pre-European photographs.

Yaumatei

Typhoon Shelter: Walking remains the single best way to make contact with any city, especially in a neighborhood as colorful as Yaumatei. It's impossible to get lost but useful maps and descriptions are given in the HKTA publication entitled *Yau Ma Tei Walking Tour.* From Nathan Road, walk down Jordan and up Ferry Street to the protected harbor just north of a decrepit housing project. This bobbing collection of junks and sampans is home to over 400 Tanka people who patiently wait their turn for public housing. Someone will offer you a personalized boat tour that might include a brief stop at a floating brothel known as a "one-girl sampan."

Walking the Streets: Yaumatei's cross web of side streets offers a quick look at traditional

Chinese enterprise. Several mah-jongg and ivory shops are located on Canton Street opposite the lively fruit and vegetable market. Not far away is the Chung Kee Marble Factory at No. 630 and an art-deco youth club at No. 601 which served as a prisoner-of-war holding station in WW II. On Battery Street look for metal shops, woodcarvers, and factories that continue to manually print the old-style wedding invitations. Reclamation Street is home to Chinese herbalists, traditional wine shops, and incense makers, while stores on Shanghai Street still sell traditional bridal gowns although hardware stores seem more successful. Saigon Street has a few remaining street barbers and fortune-tellers while funerary stores filled with paper models of cars and boats are found on Ning Po Street. While not as glamorous as the fancy bank buildings in Central or the modern shopping centers in Kowloon, the streets of Yaumatei seem to have an important connection with the past.

Yaumatei Jade Market: This famous outdoor market is located at the north end of Battery at Kansu Street. Years ago the dealers would spread their wares on the sidewalk and negotiate prices with hand signals hidden under the protective cover of newspapers. Today the jade dealers have moved into organized cubicles and much of the romance has been lost. It's still worth a quick stop between 1000 and 1300 but be forewarned: much of the jade is fake.

Tin Hau Temple

Originally built on the waterfront over 100 years ago, this complex actually comprises 4 separate temples dedicated to various gods.

Fook Tak Temple: The temple on the far left honors a half-dozen deities plus Kuan Yin, the Buddhist Goddess of Mercy. Also known as Kwun Yum or Kuan Iam in Macau, Kuan Yin is a Sinofied adaptation of a deity originally worshipped by Tibetan Mahayana Buddhists. Some say that she was originally a male god who mysteriously changed sex when adopted by the Chinese. Kuan Yin is certainly the most beloved

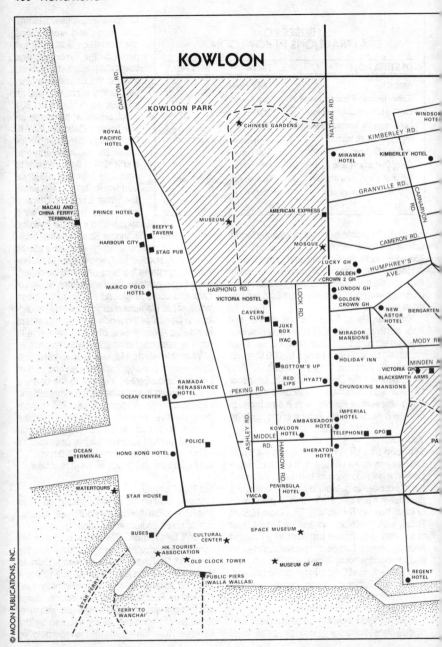

KOWLOON

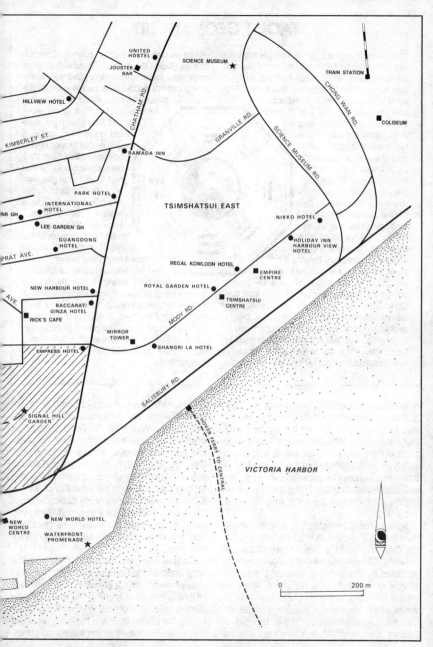

UNITED HOSTEL

JOUSTER BAR

SCIENCE MUSEUM ★

TRAIN STATION

HILLVIEW HOTEL

CHATHAM RD.

CHONG WAN RD.

COLISEUM

KIMBERLEY ST.

GRANVILLE RD.

SCIENCE MUSEUM RD.

RAMADA INN

PARK HOTEL

TSIMSHATSUI EAST

INTERNATIONAL HOTEL

AR GH

NIKKO HOTEL

LEE GARDEN GH

HOLIDAY INN HARBOUR VIEW HOTEL

GUANGDONG HOTEL

PRAT AVE.

REGAL KOWLOON HOTEL

EMPIRE CENTRE

NEW HARBOUR HOTEL

ROYAL GARDEN HOTEL

T AVE.

TSIMSHATSUI CENTRE

BACCARAT/ GINZA HOTEL

MODY RD.

RICK'S CAFE

MIRROR TOWER

EMPRESS HOTEL

SHANGRI LA HOTEL

SALISBURY RD.

SIGNAL HILL GARDEN ★

HOVER FERRY TO CENTRAL

VICTORIA HARBOR

NEW WORLD CENTRE

NEW WORLD HOTEL

WATERFRONT PROMENADE ★

0   200 m

TAOIST GEOMANCERY

Chinese mythology teaches that people's fortunes and futures can be determined by natural and artificial landscapes, which range from the design of their homes to the placement of their tombs. Since some Chinese believe that mysterious energies race over the face of the Earth and malevolent dragons dwell below the ground, they feel that disturbing the Earth runs the risk of upsetting these spirits. It sounds far-fetched to most Westerners, but prior to high-rise construction or excavations for funeral plots, highly skilled *feng shui* (wind and water) geomancers are called in to determine the proper alignment which will successfully balance the ancient principals of yin and yang. Using both intuition and a compass engraved with ancient trigrams derived from the *I Ching*, Hong Kong geomancers attempt to balance the relationship between landscapes and their resemblance to both mythical and actual animals.

Many Chinese scoff at this emotional concept of the universe and mock the geomancers as charlatans, but almost without fail their services are employed on major construction projects. Consider this: the Regent Hotel was designed with an enormous glass atrium after an influential geomancer announced that the local sea dragon would be displeased if he was walled in. The famous bronze lions in front of the Hong Kong and Shanghai Bank were placed in that exact spot by a geomancer. Modern office buildings often have their main entrances in the *rear* on the advice of geomancers. Fish tanks in corporate offices are thought to ensure good *feng shui*. Many people believe that the new headquarters for the China Bank in Central was designed with sharp angles to cast bad *feng shui* on nearby competitors.

Among the more obvious displays of *feng shui* are the eight-sided mirrors placed outside of windows to deflect evil spirits. Called *pat kwa*, you'll see them on shop fronts, hanging from balconies, or stuck on spirit trees. The power of these mirrors is considered so great that some believe that Bruce Lee died because his *pat kwa* was destroyed in a typhoon.

---

of all Buddhist bodhisattvas, those compassionate beings who attained nirvana but delayed entrance into heaven to help humanity. Her serene and feminine image, found in almost every Hong Kong temple, is so popular with both the Buddhists and the Taoists that all three possible days for commemorating her are celebrated: her birthday in the second moon, her enlightenment in the sixth, and her death in the ninth.

Shing Wong Temple: The second temple from the left is dedicated to Shing Wong (a.k.a. the City God) and the Ten Judges of the Underworld. Chinese believe that the dead must be escorted by Shing Wong through the underground to the courts of punishment, where he pleads for mercy and attempts to intercede on their behalf. Meanwhile, relatives of the deceased ceremonially burn paper replicas of houses, cars, and TVs to make sure that the

departed has the comforts of home in the afterlife. Despite these efforts and the intercession of Shing Wong, it is the Ten Judges of the Underworld who ultimately consider the plaintiff's sins and then impose various punishments. Often depicted with human torsos and animal heads, these 10 judges can be seen on the altar running the full width of the far wall. Also on the side walls are 10 murals which depict the gruesome and sometimes humorous penalties meted out to sinners. Only after seven weeks of punishment does the soul become eligible for reincarnation.

Tin Hau Temple: The third temple from the left is dedicated to Tin Hau, the Taoist Queen of Heaven and Protector of Fishermen. The scarlet interior is filled with one of the most comprehensive collections of gods in Hong Kong. Dominating the center altar is a large statue of Tin Hau draped in heavily embroidered red robes.

More than 50% of Hong Kong's temples are dedicated to Tin Hau, the immensely popular goddess who rules the sea and weather. The legend began when she once used her supernatural powers to rescue her family's junk from a storm. Afterward she dedicated her life to rescuing seafarers from maritime disasters before an early death . . . while still a virgin. What a story! Tin Hau was formally declared Queen of Heaven by the Ching Dynasty (1644-1911). Clay figures to the left represent General Favourable Wind Ear and Tin Hau's Bookkeeper, who holds a huge pencil and a paper pad to record people's virtues and sins. To the right is General Thousand Li Eye holding an ax and Tin Hau's Guardian of the Seal cradling a yellow box. To the left is an altar to Shing Wong and another to Kuan Yin. To the right are the images of the God of Wealth and the black Taoist God of Justice. Mounted on the side wall (to the right as you face Tin Hau) are three long shelves displaying 60 identical Tan Sui gods that represent years of the 60-year Chinese calendar. Each doll is carefully wrapped in red paper so that only the head and shoulders are displayed. Devotees place spirit money issued by the Bank of Hell under the deity dedicated to the year of their birth.

Shea Tan Temple: The temple on the far right is dedicated to a dozen gods, besides being a favorite gathering spot for fortune-tellers, palmists, and face readers. In the front courtyard you'll find a carved tombstone of the District God who guards the health and prosperity of local residents and four other rocks that keep evil away.

Temple Street Night Market

Cheap clothing, copy watches, sidewalk charlatans, snake carvers, free opera, acrobatics, and great food at low prices make this one of Kowloon's great attractions. Nothing happens during the day but there's plenty of action shortly after sunset. The market starts on Temple Street just two blocks off Jordan and continues north almost to Waterloo. At Kansu Street it seems to dead-end at a large concrete car park . . . but keep walking! Around the corner are several palmists (some advertise, English Spoken), amateur Chinese opera, and a fortune-teller whose trained bird predicts the future. Nearby an old man sells false teeth with a sign warning, Not Photo—Each $20. The market continues up

Temple past denim merchants, noodle stalls, and sidewalk chefs who provide great theater with their pyrotechnic displays. The market ends in Mongkok where dozens of street stalls serve some incredibly cheap and tasty Mongolian hot pots, fried clams, and oysters in black bean sauce. This is Hong Kong at its very best.

Bird Lane

In a city where tiny apartments preclude most pets, people lavish affection on miniature songbirds in delicate cages. The best place to hear the birds is the short Mongkok lane called Hong Lok Street, an alley two blocks west of Nathan Rd. and just south of Argyle Street. Arrive before 0600 and find a seat around the corner in the Wan Loi tea shop.

Sung Dynasty Village

Daily cultural shows in this replica of a 12th-century Sung Dynasty village include a traditional Chinese wedding performed without enthusiasm at breakneck speed, a kung-fu demonstration, and a fairly clever monkey act. Bored craftsmen demonstrate calligraphy, read palms, and carve ivory. This artificial attraction is open daily 1000-2030; admission is HK$100. Take bus 6A from the Kowloon Star Ferry terminal to the terminus at Lai Chi Kok Amusement Park. Chinese Opera at Lai Chi Kok has been replaced with third-rate cabaret singers.

Wong Tai Sin Temple

This large and extremely elaborate structure built in 1973 is probably the most impressive religious monument in Hong Kong. Wong Tai Sin, Taoist God of Healing, is said to have discovered the secret of changing cinnabar into the drug of immortality. Since he is also the God of Good Fortune, this magnificent temple is constantly jammed with Chinese who wish to learn their fortunes. Exit the MTR terminal and you immediately bump into the stalls of fortune-tellers, palmists, and other occultists. Past the incense-burning pits you'll find the main foyer, where dozens of Chinese shake the *chim* until a single bamboo stick falls out. Numbers on the sticks are interpreted by soothsayers. It's all done in a relaxed and fun-loving manner; only young girls appear serious about it. Inside the main temple (closed to visitors without special permission) is a painting of Wong Tai Sin. The adjoining buildings and Chinese gardens on the left are remarkable examples of traditional Chinese architecture. Take the MTR to the Wong Tai Sin Station.

ACCOMMODATIONS

Accommodations in Kowloon range from the budget dormitories of Chungking Mansions to the eye-popping spectacles in Tsimshatsui East. Hotels in Hong Kong are quite simply some of the finest in the world. They're also in short supply. Despite a building boom which increased the room count to over 35,000 by 1992, occupancy rates perpetually hover between 90% and 95%. Arriving without a reservation—especially in the late afternoon or evening—can be a big gamble. It's also tricky during the peak months from March to June and September to December. Vacancies at member hotels can be checked at the airport with the Hong Kong Hotel Association.

All rooms in member hotels are a/c with private baths, telephones, and TV. There is little price differential between single and double rooms. Prices quoted below in the text are for the least-expensive standard rooms. Superior and deluxe rooms are 15-30% higher. All rooms except for dorms and budget guesthouses are subject to a 10% service charge and a five-percent government tax, which goes to the tourist office. Kowloon hotels are found in several neighborhoods.

Tsimshatsui: Hong Kong's leading tourist enclave has several luxury hotels, dozens of middle-priced hotels, and most of Hong Kong's inexpensive dormitories and hostels. All are located right in the heart of the action near the shopping centers, nightclubs, and restaurants.

Tsimshatsui East: Hong Kong's newest tourist spot is a high-tech wonderland of super-luxurious hotels, spectacular shopping centers, and nightclubs so large that you need a map to find the bar. Hotels here are among the best in the world.

Yaumatei and Mongkok: North of Jordan Street is where the locals shop, eat, and party, the place to try if you want to save some money and experience the *real* Hong Kong. Hotel prices are moderately lower because Yaumatei and Mongkok are 20-30 minutes from Tsimshatsui.

Budget

Hong Kong is a tough place for budget travelers since over 85% of all rooms are in the high-price bracket, 10% in the medium range, and less than five percent are hostels or guesthouses, often filled with a semipermanent group of travelers who teach English, study Chinese, and make pocket change as models or actors. Dormitory beds cost HK$30-45 depending on how many beds per room; you pay more to avoid that sardine feeling. Tiny, tiny, airless rooms slightly larger than a shoebox cost HK$100-150.

Guesthouses and dorms are concentrated in or around Chungking Mansions, well located near the shopping centers and nightclubs. Hong Kong Island has almost nothing cheap except for an isolated youth hostel and a few guesthouses in Causeway Bay.

Although Chungking Mansions is the first place most budget travelers check, other inexpensive hostels and dormitories are located within a few blocks. Most are identical in terms of size, space, cleanliness, and price. In other words, they're cramped, claustrophobic, somewhat dirty, and overpriced.

Chungking Mansions: For over a decade this dilapidated complex has served as an accommodations center for legions of budget travelers. Somehow these decaying dormitories, hostels, minihotels, doll factories, rug weavers, and Indian restaurants have escaped the wrecker's ball, but every year sees new rumors about its imminent demise.

Five separate towers, designated A, B, C, D, and E, are served by ridiculously small and slow elevators festooned with plastic signs advertising what's upstairs. Listings change frequently, but the Traveller's Hostel on the 16th floor of A block remains a useful starting point. Dorms cost from HK$30 and rooms from HK$75. This noisy, dirty, crowded place may not suit everybody, but it remains a good place to meet other travelers and exchange information. If you stay in the Traveller's Hostel, avoid the room next to the obnoxious television and be prepared for all-night parties. The accompanying chart lists some of the (slightly) better dorms and hotels in Chungking Mansions. Names, prices, and cleanliness change quickly, so inspect a few places before taking a room. A walk down the stairwell will teach you more about Hong Kong than any possible

CHUNGKING MANSIONS
(prices in HK$)

HOTEL	BLK	FLR	DORM	S	D
Traveller's Hostel	A	16	40	90	140
Park Guest House	A	15	—	80	120
New Asia	A	8	—	100	130
Tom's	A	8	—	90	130
Double 7	A	7	—	95	120
Chungking House	A	5	—	190	250
Carlton	B	15	—	90	120
Columbia	B	12	—	90	120
Happy	B	10	—	90	120
Travelers Friend	B	6	30	90	120
Centerpoint	C	3	—	110	150
Boston	D	10	—	90	120
Rainbow	D	9	—	90	120
New Humphrey	D	3	—	75	105
Holiday	E	6	—	75	105

guided tour! Ask for a discount if you plan to stay for several days. In the fall of 1993, almost 80% of the guesthouses were closed by government officials who cited the overcrowding and potential fire hazard. Most guesthouses intend to comply with the stiffened laws and seek relicensing. Rates are expected to climb dramatically.

Mirador Mansions: This big, rambling, collapsing building (similar to Chungking Mansions) has several popular guesthouses and dormitories. Try the Garden Hostel on the 3rd floor of F block, Mini Guesthouse on the 7th floor of F block, or the Kowloon Guesthouse on the 10th floor of D block. Man Hing Lung Guesthouse on the 14th floor has been highly recommended by several travelers. Enter on Mody Street and wander around until you spot the lift. Or walk the stairs for a slice of real life. 58 Nathan Road. HK$35 dorms, HK$100-280 rooms.

London Guest House: This reasonably clean but very small dormitory is a popular alternative to the Chungking dives. Rooms are with fans; the more expensive have windows. 66-70 Nathan Road, 5th floor, tel. 369-1782. HK$40 dorm, HK$100-280 rooms.

Golden Crown: All rooms in this well-located guesthouse are air-conditioned, a real lifesaver during the hot summer months. Singles, doubles with two small beds, and family suites are available. One of the cleanest and most comfortable places for low-budget travelers. Golden Crown Mansion, 66-70 Nathan Road, 5th floor, tel. 369-1782. HK$40 dorm, HK$100-250 rooms.

Golden Crown 2: Another branch of the highly successful Golden Crown. Dorms with eight beds are cheaper than those with four. 4 Humphreys, 2nd floor, tel. 739-5084. HK$50 dorm.

Lucky Guest House: Small but friendly dorm with only three or four bunks per room. Popular with working Brits. 4 Humphreys, 5th floor, tel. 367-0342. HK$40 dorm.

International Youth Accommodation Center (IYAC): Another old-time favorite. Slightly off the beaten track at 21A Lock Road. HK$40 dorm.

Victoria Hostel: One of the newest and cleanest additions to the budget scene in Hong Kong has hot showers, color TV, cooking facilities, and visa services for China. Recommended. Lucky Guesthouse, in the same building on the third floor, is also recommended. 33 Hankow Rd., 2nd floor, tel. 376-0621, fax 369-9046, HK$40-60 dorms, HK$150-300 a/c rooms with TV.

Victoria Guesthouse: Another good choice tucked away on a less hectic side street near several popular restaurants and British pubs. 4 Minden Ave., 2nd floor, tel. 368-7181, fax 369-9046, HK$40-60 dorms, HK$150-300 a/c rooms with TV.

Lee Garden Guesthouse: A friendly manager named Charlie Chan (love it!) and clean, well-decorated rooms make this a popular spot to escape the high-rise hovels of Chungking and Mirador. 36 Cameron Rd., D Block, 8th floor, tel. 367-5972, HK$200-280.

Star Guesthouse: A clean and friendly guesthouse also managed by the inimitable Charlie Chan. All rooms are a/c with private bath and TV; probably the best value in the upper-budget

KOWLOON ACCOMMODATIONS

HOTEL	SINGLE	DOUBLE	ADDRESS	PHONE
SUPER LUXURY	**(HK$)**	**(HK$)**		
Peninsula	2500-3750	2700-4000	Salisbury	366-6251
Ramada Renaissance	1950-3150	1950-3150	8 Peking Road	375-1133
Regent	2000-3000	2000-3000	Salisbury	721-1211
Shangri La	2250-3400	2450-3600	64 Mody	721-2111
LUXURY				
Holiday Inn G Mile	1200-1500	1500-1900	46-52 Nathan	369-3111
Holiday Inn Harbour	1750-2900	1750-2900	70 Mody	721-5161
Hyatt Regency	1750-2400	1750-2400	67 Nathan	311-1234
Miramar	1200-2200	1200-2200	130 Nathan	368-1111
New World	1400-1700	1400-1700	22 Salisbury	369-4111
Nikko	2000-2650	2150-2750	67 Mody	739-1111
Omni Hongkong	1500-2750	1500-2750	Harbour City	736-0088
Omni Marco Polo	1650-1900	1650-1900	Harbour City	736-0888
Omni Prince	1500-1650	1500-1650	Harbour City	736-1888
Regal Kowloon	1100-2000	1100-2000	71 Mody	722-1818
Royal Garden	1400-2200	1400-2200	69 Mody	721-5215
Sheraton	1400-2400	1400-2400	20 Nathan	369-1111
MODERATE				
Ambassador	1500-2500	1600-2500	26 Nathan	366-6321
Empress	900-1250	1000-1400	17-19 Chatham	366-0211
Guangdong	1050-1500	1050-1500	18 Prat	739-3311
Hillview	900-1200	900-1200	13-17 Observatory	722-7822
Imperial	950-1150	950-1150	30-34 Nathan	366-2201
International	650-1050	750-1250	33 Cameron	366-3381
Kimberley	800-1200	800-1200	28 Kimberley	723-3888
Kowloon	1050-1200	1200-1250	19-21 Nathan	369-8698
New Astor	1050-1200	1250-1400	11 Carnavon	366-7261
Park	1200-1650	1250-1650	61-65 Chatham	366-1371
Ramada Inn	1050-1450	1050-1450	73-75 Chatham	311-1100
Royal Pacific	1250-2400	1250-2400	China HK City	736-1188
Windsor	900-1200	1000-1400	39-43 Kimberley	739-5665

BUDGET

HOTEL	SINGLE	DOUBLE	DORM	ADDRESS	PHONE
Garden Hostel	—	—	50	58 Nathan F 3/F	721-8567
Golden Crown GH	130	160	40	66 Nathan 5/F	369-1782
Golden Crown 2 GH	110	160	50	4 Humphreys 2/F	739-5084
Kowloon GH	80	110	—	58 Nathan D 10/	366-1090
London Guest House	100	250	35	66 Nathan 5/F	369-1782
Lucky Guest House	—	—	40	4 Humphreys 5/F	367-0342
Mini GH	80	100-250	—	58 Nathan F 7/F	367-2551
United Hostel	—	—	50	119 Chatham 2/F	367-4536
YMCA Salisbury	600	950	100	Salisbury	369-2211

price range. Recommended. 21 Cameron Rd., 6th floor, tel. 723-8951, HK$280-340.

United Hostel: Run-down place with a large sitting room and kitchen facilities. Roomier than Chungking and Nathan Road dorms. Grand View Mansion, 119 Chatham Road, 2nd floor, tel. 367-4536. HK$50 dorm.

STB Hostel: The Hong Kong Student Travel hostel is located in Mongkok, 30 minutes by foot north of Kowloon. Rooms are large, very clean, and fully air-conditioned. Other services include hot showers, lockers, and a budget travel service. STB Hostel is somewhat isolated but ideal for visiting the night markets and shops along Upper Nathan Road. Take the MTR or any bus going north up Nathan Road. Great Eastern Mansion, 255-261 Reclamation Street, 2nd floor, tel. 710-9199, fax 385-0153. HK$60 dorm, HK$250-350 rooms.

YMCA And YWCA

Kowloon's two YMCAs are excellent value. Air-conditioned double rooms with private bath, phone, and color TVs start from just HK$450. Room reservations should be made several months in advance; include one day's rental with your request. The HKTA at the airport can check vacancies.

Salisbury YMCA: Located adjacent to the Peninsula Hotel on one of the most expensive pieces of real estate in the world, this great old lady features a swimming pool, a sauna, tennis courts, a library, and a roof-garden. 41 Salisbury Road, tel. 369-2211, fax 739-9315, HK$600-950.

YMCA International House: This modern and clean hotel is much easier to get into than the Salisbury branch. Facilities include a fast-food cafeteria, an inexpensive restaurant, an exercise room, and a sauna. Dorms with fans are for men only. It's a great place and well worth the slight transportation hassle. Take the MTR or any bus going north up Nathan Road. 23 Waterloo Road, tel. 771-9111, fax 388-5926. HK$125 dorm, HK$420-540 rooms.

Moderate Accommodations

Many of the best hotels in the HK$400-500 range are found in Yaumatei and Mongkok, two neighborhoods about 20- to 30-minutes' walk from Tsimshatsui. Hotels are located within easy walking distance of the Temple Street Night Market, the Jade Market, Chinese emporiums, dozens of other department stores, and countless restaurants. And it's less touristy than Tsimshatsui—much more of the real Hong Kong. All rooms are air-conditioned, with telephones and color TV, and they are far more spacious than the claustrophobic guesthouses in lower Kowloon.

Caritas Bianchi Lodge: There's little atmosphere in the lobby and the rooms are heavy with vinyl, but it's clean, cheap, and perfectly acceptable if you just need a simple room at a reasonable price. 4 Cliff Road, tel. 388-1111, fax 770-6669. HK$440-580.

Salvation Army Booth Lodge: Cheerful, modern, and spotlessly clean. Although the Christian atmosphere may not appeal to everybody, this is easily one of the best low-priced hotels in Hong Kong. 11 Wing Sing Lane, tel. 771-9266, fax 385-1140. HK$400-500.

Bangkok Royal: The gloomy lobby might put you off, but the rooms are perfectly adequate plus their restaurant serves some great Thai food. Hidden away in a small street near the Jordan MTR station. 2-12 Pilkem, tel. 735-9181, fax 730-2209, HK$420-700.

Luxury Accommodations

Peninsula: Constructed in 1928 in a colonial old-world style, this 60-year-old Hong Kong landmark is consistently voted one of the world's top-10 hotels. The Pen offers several outstanding restaurants, a beautiful lobby famous for afternoon tea and people-watching, plus a fleet of nine Silver Shadows for airport pick-up. A 30-story addition with 132 rooms was completed in the spring of 1994. Salisbury Road, tel. 366-6251, fax 722-4170, HK$2500-4000.

Regent: This ultra-elegant hotel was voted the second finest hotel in the world by the U.S. financial magazine *Institutional Investor;* the same survey put the Peninsula in tenth! Strategically located on the waterfront with a magnificent glass-walled lobby, the Regent is perhaps the most spectacular hotel in Asia. Worth visiting if only to daydream yourself a millionaire. Salisbury Road, tel. 721-1211, fax 739-4546. HK$2200-3000.

Tsimshatsui East Hotels: Many of Hong Kong's newest and most luxurious hotels are situated just east of Tsimshatsui. All the big names are here: the **Shangri La,** managed by the West-

YAUMATEI AND MONGKOK

MONGKOK

STB HOSTEL

NATHAN RD.

WATERLOO RD.

YMCA

WATERLOO RD.

RECLAMATION RD.

FERRY ST.

NIGHT MARKET ENDS

YAUMATEI MTR

HOT POTS

KING'S HOTEL

BOOTH LODGE HOTEL

CARITAS BIANCHI LODGE

TIN HAU TEMPLE

JADE MARKET

CAR PARK

PALM READERS/OPERA

KANSU ST.

0   200 m

YAUMATEI TYPHOON SHELTER

YAUMATEI

SAIGON ST.

CANTON ST.

BATTERY ST.

NANKING ST.

EATON HOTEL

NATHAN HOTEL

FORTUNA HOTEL

NIGHT MARKET BEGINS

GALAXIE HOTEL

FORTUNA COURT HOTEL

GASCOIGNE RD.

MAJESTIC HOTEL

CHUNG HING HOTEL

JORDAN RD.

JORDAN ROAD BUS TERMINAL

JORDAN RD.

JORDAN MTR

PARK

SHANGHAI ST.

TEMPLE ST.

PARKES ST.

BOWRING ST.

PRUDENTIAL HOTEL

SHAMROCK HOTEL

BANGKOK ROYAL HOTEL

AUSTIN RD.

RITZ HOTEL

FUJI HOTEL

CANTON RD.

NATHAN RD.

KOWLOON PARK

CAFE ADRIATICO

JUNGLE PUB

TIBET PUB

© MOON PUBLICATIONS, INC.

YAUMATEI AND MONGKOK ACCOMMODATIONS

HOTEL	SINGLE (HK$)	DOUBLE (HK$)	ADDRESS	PHONE
Bangkok Royal	420	700	2-12 Pilkem	735-9181
Booth Lodge	400	500	11 Wing Sing Lane	771-9266
Caritas Bianchi	440	580	4 Cliff	388-1111
Chung Hing	650-750	700-800	21-30 Saigon	752-7178
Eaton	1000-1400	1000-1400	380 Nathan	782-1818
Fortuna	950-1400	950-1500	355 Nathan	385-1011
Fortuna Court	800-1050	900-1150	3-5 Chi Woo	780-4321
Galaxie	500-700	700-750	30 Pak Hoi	780-7211
Ginza	650-750	700-800	29 Chatham	369-9103
King's	500-550	700-750	473 Nathan	780-1281
Majestic	1000-1400	1000-1400	348 Nathan	781-1333
Nathan	650-950	750-1000	378 Nathan	388-5141
Prudential	800-1500	800-1500	222 Nathan	311-8222
Ritz	950	1050	122 Austin	369-2282
Shamrock	650-750	750-900	223 Nathan	735-2271
STB Hostel	60 (dorm)	250-350	255 Reclamation	710-9199
YMCA Int'l House	420	540	23 Waterloo	771-9111

in Hotels, the Taiwanese-owned but Japanese-managed **Nikko,** and the elegant **Regal Kowloon.** The smaller **Royal Garden** is recommended for its tasteful interiors and stylish facilities.

RESTAURANTS

Hong Kong has an estimated 6,000 licensed restaurants and possibly another 10,000 noodle shops, teahouses, and *dai pai dong* (roadside hawkers) that altogether serve some of the best Chinese food in the world . . . including China. The selection is dazzling, though finding a good restaurant is somewhat different than back home. Rather than the simple and unpretentious places with cheap but great food, in Hong Kong it's often the glitzy neon palaces with elaborate menus that excel. Dining is casual to the extreme. Even in the better places you might see diners spit out bits of bone, spill sauces on the tablecloth, and slurp soups with abandon, since many feel the more succulent the food the richer the sounds of eating should be. Afterward, diners don't linger but quickly abandon a scene of almost unbelievable gastronomic carnage.

Although Western fast food is very popular (McDonald's is just the sanitized version of a *dai pai dong*), the culinary glory of Hong Kong is the vast array of Chinese cuisines. See the Singapore chapter for descriptions and suggested dishes. Most restaurants in Hong Kong serve Cantonese food, the style most familiar to Westerners. Some have special English-language menus but these are often highly abbreviated and limited to tourist dishes such as sweet-and-sours and other concoctions buried under piles of cornstarch. The ideal solution is to have a Chinese friend interpret the menus, as the freshest dishes and daily specials are often marked only in Chinese script. Otherwise, pick up a copy of the HKTA brochure entitled *Visitor's Guide to Chinese Food in Hong Kong,* which suggests restaurants and specific dishes. The photographs are very useful.

Chinese Restaurants

A good place to start is the fixed-menu "businessmen's lunch" in a hotel restaurant. These three- to four-course lunches often cost HK$88, a sum considered auspicious since the sound of "8" in Cantonese is strikingly similar to that for "prosperity." Doubling the sound makes your lunch more expensive but also increases your prosperity! Hotel restaurants are pricey but often serve great food since they can afford to employ the best chefs. Dozens of less expensive restaurants are tucked away on the back streets of Mody, Hart, Prat, Cameron, and Granville roads. Trust your instincts and patronize those restaurants packed with locals.

Lychee Village: Dependable Cantonese food served in a hectic restaurant. All the standard items plus steamed whelk in sweet-and-sour sauce, roast pigeon, shark's-fin soup, deep-fried snake in the winter, and cold seafood soups in the summer. Anything that shows its back to the sky is fair game for a Cantonese cook—experiment with caution. 9 Cameron Road. Expensive.

North China: Upscale restaurant for northern dishes: Peking duck, clay-baked Beggar's Chicken, Mongolian hot pot, handmade noodles in rich gravies, spicy prawns, yellowtail steamed in wine. Similar to most other northern restaurants, North China is decorated in typical Pekinese fashion and fits all the stereotypes with red brocade, tasseled lanterns, and heavy dark furniture carved with dragons. Some of the waiters speak English and can help guide you through the menu. Request the soup with Peking duck; otherwise it goes to the kitchen help. 7 Hart Avenue. Peking. Moderate.

Golden Red Chiu Chow: Simple surroundings but a good place to try hearty and simple Chiu Chow specialties: braised goose in dipping sauce, suckling pig, fried carp in black bean sauce, steamed pigeon with ham. Chiu Chow (Teochew in Singapore) food tends to be strong and earthy. Big favorites also include shark's-fin and bird's-nest soups. Meals often start and end with a tiny cup of Iron Maiden, a muddy, bitter, and highly charged tea which aids digestion. Prat Avenue. Moderate.

Minden Row Restaurants: Great spots for cheap, fast, and delicious Chinese food. Try a takeaway order of oysters in black bean sauce and an ice-cold Tsingtao beer—best in Hong Kong! In the alley just behind Holiday Inn. Cantonese. Inexpensive.

Other Cheap Eats: Check the buffets listed in the local newspapers, businessmen's lunch specials, and "happy hours" with complimentary snacks at luxury hotels. Kowloon also has a number of continental and Asian restaurants with menus dedicated to the proposition that visitors do not want to eat Chinese all the time.

Dim Sum Restaurants: One of Hong Kong's most popular dining experiences is dim sum, served in nearly all Cantonese restaurants from early morning until late afternoon. Interior decorations are often a chaotic frieze of frenzied dragons and monumental phoenixes emblazoned in garish reds and golds. Ignore the outrageous decor and deafening pandemonium to enjoy these Asian petits fours. See the "Singapore" chapter for more information.

Asian Restaurants

Mayur: With one of the largest Indian communities outside the subcontinent, it's little wonder that Hong Kong can boast some of the best Indian restaurants this side of Bombay. North and South Indian specialties such as tandoori breads, mutton curries, and salted *lassis* are served at the Mayur. Strange but true, Szechwan food is also served. BBC Building, 25-31 Carnarvon Road, 13th floor. Moderate.

Indian Cafes: Chungking Mansions has a great selection of inexpensive Indian restaurants. Those on the ground floor are OK, but better messes include the Umar E Khyam on the 7th floor of A block, Taj Mahal Club Mess on the 3rd floor of C block, and Sheri Punjab Restaurant on the 3rd floor of C block. Inexpensive.

Sawadee: Reasonable prices, friendly service, and outstanding dishes such as Tom Yam Kung (coconut soup with prawns) and Pla Pae (steamed freshwater fish) make Sawadee a local favorite. Hillwood Road. Moderate.

Satay Indonesian: Popular for fast, informal dinners of *nasi goreng, gado gado,* or spicy *satay*. Mody Road. Indonesian. Moderate.

Manila Restaurant: Of all of Asia's diverse cuisines, Filipino food is probably the least known and appreciated. Although Filipinos make up the largest number of expatriates living in Hong Kong—some 40,000 at last count—there are precious few Filipino restaurants here. Visitors curious about Filipino dishes such as pork *adobo,* crispy *pata,* and spicy *sinigang* soup can try the Mabuhay or Manila on Minden. However, no *lugaw*. 9 Minden Avenue. Moderate.

Cafe Adriatico: A chic, upmarket restaurant with Filipino/Spanish cuisine. Kimberley Road. Expensive.

Temple Street Night Market

Without a doubt the cheapest and most adventurous eating in Kowloon is at the Temple Street Night Market. The exact location is noted on the "Yaumatei and Mongkok" map. Start on Temple Street (clothes, cassette tapes, fake watches), walk around the car park (fortune-tellers, opera singers, acrobats), past the Tin Hau Temple (old men playing checkers and practicing *tai chi*), and keep walking north.

Toward the end of the road (almost to Waterloo Road) you'll find dozens of food vendors who serve dishes such as oysters or snails in black bean sauce and Indonesian *satay* with peanut sauce. For a real treat try a bubbling hot pot, an Asian-style fondue which offers an unlimited variety of meats and seafoods boiled in an open cauldron then dipped in Eight Generals' Sauce. Find a vendor, sit down, and point to whatever looks best. Eaten as much for the fun as for the food. If you miss this night market and food show, you've missed one of the highlights of Hong Kong.

NIGHTLIFE

Kowloon nightlife is focused on hotel discos, formal nightclubs with cabaret singers, rock and jazz nightclubs, seedy Suzi Wong bars, and a handful of British-style pubs that cater to both locals and visitors. Hong Kong nightlife is *very* tame when compared to Bangkok's Patpong or Manila's Ermita district; bachelors looking for female companionship should save their money. While most discos are pretentious joints best avoided, several of the British-style pubs and jazz/rock nightclubs are friendly watering holes which can be highly recommended. Legal drinking age in Hong Kong is 18. Clubs stay open all night and are often at their peak between midnight and the early morning hours.

Pubs, Nightclubs, And Discos

Blacksmith Arms: A cozy place with friendly management; the best pub in Kowloon. Stop by for happy hours. 16 Minden Avenue.

Rick's Cafe: A very hot, jumping nightclub decorated in a *Casablanca* motif. Features terrific local bands, pop groups from Southeast Asia, and jazz musicians from the States. Some of the Filipino groups will knock your socks off. Highly recommended. 4 Hart Avenue.

Cavern: One of the liveliest and least pretentious discos in Kowloon. Heavy with Beatles memorabilia. Hankow Road.

Juke Box Disco: Another lively late-night club which attracts a good mix of locals and visitors. Weekend minimums include two drinks. Action starts late and doesn't let up till sunrise. Recommended. Hankow Road just across from the Cavern.

Ned Kelly's: This long-running and very friendly nightclub has Dixieland music popular with the middle-aged sing-along crowd. 11A Ashley.

Waltzing Matilda's: Good name, but both branches are tacky and should be avoided. 9 Cornwall and 22 Cameron Road.

Bar City: A mindless supermarket of phony discos; one of the worst nightlife centers in Asia. Do local trendies really enjoy this? Basement of the New World Centre.

Hostess Nightclubs

Wealthy visitors might enjoy the large and lavishly decorated hostess bars filled with Chinese and foreign ladies who talk, pour drinks, and inflate your ego while deflating your pocketbook. Charges include covers, minimums for hostesses (billed every 15 minutes), escort fees, and very expensive ladies' drinks. Check all prices in advance and pay for drinks when served since bills can escalate quickly and final tabs in the *thousands* are not uncommon. One sensible alternative is the *Yum Sing—Night on the Town Tour* coupon book sold by the HKTA. Their reasonably priced Deluxe Tour includes a hostess club coupon good for two standard drinks and one hour with a hostess.

Volvo Nightclub: The most popular and expensive club in Kowloon claims to be the largest Japanese-style hostess club outside Japan. This massive 70,000-square-foot dance lounge decorated in baby pink boasts 1,000 hostesses and a full-sized replica of a Rolls-Royce which transports customers to their table. Tsimshatsui East.

China City: Somewhat more restrained in its approach, this nightclub comes complete with an aviary filled with lovebirds. Tsimshatsui East.

Girlie Bars

Compared to Manila and Bangkok, Hong Kong's sex and sin industry is sedate, discreet, and expensive. Westerners venturing out to Mongkok,

FLOATING SLEEVES AND PAINTED FACES

Chinese opera, a sometimes bewildering combination of high-pitched singing, clashing music, and stunning costumes, is an artistic form of expression with no real counterpart in the West. That alone makes it worth watching at least once. To compensate for the stark simplicity of the staging, costumes are brilliant and unbelievably elaborate—heavy embroidered gowns, superb makeup, and amazing water sleeves that float expressively without support. Although the dissonant music irritates most Westerners, it can at times be ravishingly melodic and completely haunting.

Stories taken from ancient Chinese folklore are told with symbolic gestures but few props. Role identification is linked to makeup, which ranges from the heavy paint worn in Peking-style opera (derived from older masked drama) to the lighter shades favored by the Cantonese. The more complicated a character, the more complex the makeup: a red face indicates courageous character, black a warrior's face, blue is cruelty, white face indicates an evil personality, purple is used for barbarian warlords, yellow for emperors. Costumes and movement are also highly stylized. The more important characters wear larger headdresses and express themselves with over 50 different hand and face movements.

Cantonese opera is the most common genre, followed by highly refined Peking opera, considered the classic version. Soochow opera with its lovely and soft melodies is rarely performed. Hong Kong's 10 Cantonese opera troupes occasionally perform in the streets during temple fairs and religious festivals. Regularly scheduled performances are also given around town—check with the HKTA.

Hong Kong's red-light district (look for the *yellow* lights), must be accompanied by a Chinese friend to gain admittance. Easier to visit are the handful of bars in lower Kowloon which have transcended sleaze to become classics of camp.

Bottom's Up: This sophisticated and long-running topless club was featured in the James Bond film *Man with the Golden Gun*. Popular with everybody from single males to cautious couples, this intimate club seems entirely safe . . . maybe *too* safe.

Red Lips: This relic of the '50s is known for its aging hustler-waitresses who still remember the days of Suzi Wong . . . if not Suzi herself. Watch out for the old nag on the sidewalk who won't take no for an answer. Kowloon has dozens of other girlie bars but ask about hidden charges and big minimums.

Chinese Theater-Restaurants

For something less depressing and more kitsch, try one of the set dinners and elaborately staged shows at a Chinese theater-restaurant. Best described as a throwback to the '50s, these cabaret shows feature anything from Chinese folk music to Cantonese new-age rock. Cover charges of HK$100-200 include both the show and a fixed meal. Ordering a la carte can be dangerous to your wallet. Convenient showcases include the Golden Crown Nightclub at 66 Nathan Road just to the left of the Chungking Mansions entrance and the Ocean City Nightclub on the 4th floor of the New World Centre.

CULTURAL ENTERTAINMENT

Chinese Festivals: Hong Kong's most authentic cultural performances are found at Chinese festivals such as the Festival of the Hungry Ghosts in the fall and the Cheung Chau Bun Festival in the late spring. The HKTA has exact dates.

Chinese Cultural Shows: Much easier to locate and almost as fun are the free weekly cultural shows sponsored by the HKTA. These twice-weekly one-hour shows offer some of Hong Kong's most outstanding Cantonese and Peking opera troupes, Chinese magic, acrobatics, Chinese instrumental music, Fukien string puppets, shadow puppets, traditional martial arts, and Chinese folk dancing. Free shows take place every Friday evening at 1800 in the New World Centre in Tsimshatsui. These highly recommended shows are within easy walking distance of Kowloon hotels. Performances are also held Thursdays at noon in the Cityplaza Shopping Center in Tai Koo Shing on Hong Kong Island. Allow plenty of time to get there.

Other Shows: Upcoming cultural shows are listed in the HKTA newspaper *Hong Kong.* Strange and amateurish street opera is performed nightly at the Temple Street Night Market near the Tin Hau Temple. Photography *not* permitted. The Asian Arts Festival in October is an outstanding opportunity to see many of Southeast Asia's best performing arts.

SHOPPING AREAS IN KOWLOON

Nathan Road: Shopping is the first thing most people think about when you mention the name Hong Kong. And most people begin their shopping excursions on Nathan Road in Tsimshatsui. Shops along the so-called Golden Mile range from the expensive boutiques in Park Lane Shoppers Boulevard to the budget emporiums inside Chungking Mansions. Smaller streets and alleys branching left and right are lined with stores selling everything imaginable, from laser toys to sable furs.

Harbour City Shopping Complex: Comprised of Ocean Terminal, Ocean Centre, and Ocean Galleries, this multitiered complex with its 200-odd stores ranks as one of the world's biggest shopping centers. Best of all, it's completely air-conditioned; a great escape from the horrors of sidewalk shopping. The famous Amazing Grace Elephant Company sells home decorative items and ceramic pachyderms.

East Tsimshatsui: Dozens of immense and futuristic shopping complexes including Houston Centre, Wing On Plaza, Tsimshatsui, Empire, and Peninsula centers. Also elegant restaurants and fancy nightclubs.

Chinese Arts and Crafts: Some of Hong Kong's most intriguing shopping takes place inside the stores operated by the People's Republic of China. A great place for inexpensive arts and handicrafts, but forget those funky clothes! Three locations in Kowloon: the Star House just across from the Star Ferry, in the New World Shopping Center in Tsimshatsui, and the main outlet at 233 Nathan Road in Yaumatei. Highly recommended.

Other Chinese Emporiums: Other Chinese emporiums worth checking include China Products (488 Hennessey Road and 73 Argyle Street), Yue Hwa (301 Nathan Road), and Chung Kiu (530 Nathan and 17 Hankow roads).

Temple Street Night Market: Hong Kong's cheapest goods are sold from temporary stalls set up nightly 2000-2300 in Yaumatei and Mongkok. It's a wonderland of inexpensive men's clothing, copy watches, factory rejects, and manufacturer's seconds; check the quality carefully. You might also see Chinese opera, fortune-tellers, and street dentists selling wooden denture sets. What a scene!

Tung Choi Market: Known in Cantonese as Nui Yan Kai (Ladies Street), this alley near the Mongkok MTR terminal is known for rock-bottom prices on ladies' wear and female accessories.

Jade Market: Each day 1000-1400, jade traders set up their stalls under the flyaway in Yaumatei. Many of the trinkets are little more than soapstone passed off as jadeite or nephrite. Unless you really know your jade, do your shopping at a quality jewelry store or at China Products.

Kaiser Estates Factory Outlets: Factory outlets are one of Hong Kong's more famous shopping experiences. Most are either connected to the factories that produce the goods or simply sell goods purchased from the factories. First stop should be the three large blocks of buildings in the factory complex called Kaiser Estates. Take a bus, taxi, or walk to Hung Hom just beyond the train station. Prices have risen sharply in recent years (group shopping tours are responsible), but bargains can still be found on silk clothing, carpets, shoes, brass, and furniture. Double-check all merchandise; much is excess stock, over-runs, and quality-control rejects. Most outlets have twice-yearly sales during summer and near New Year's. More information can be gleaned from the HKTA publication *Factory Outlets in Hong Kong* and Dana Goetz's *The Complete Guide to Hong Kong Factory Bargains.*

SHOPPING TIPS

Hong Kong's number one attraction isn't the temples, scenery, or even restaurants . . . it's the shopping. Staggering but true—Hong Kong's three million annual visitors spend 65% of their time and over a *billion* U.S. dollars per year on shopping. The shopping scene has changed in recent years. While good values and outstanding variety are still found in Hong Kong, inflation, high rents, and rising wages have sharply forced up prices. Locally produced goods such as clothing and watches are still cheap, but Japanese electronics and other imported items are often cheaper back home. Any possible savings should be carefully weighed against warranty and service problems, the hassles of shopping (crowds, hot weather, language barriers), and the attitude problem of many shopkeepers who, despite efforts of the HKTA, remain indifferent to the point of rudeness. Far too many shopkeepers continue to operate on the theory that tourists are fools who deserve to be cheated. And remember that refunds are rarely given for faulty, counterfeit, or unconscionably overpriced merchandise.

It is strongly recommended that you price all possible purchases at home before going to Hong Kong. Visitors from high-tariff countries such as New Zealand will love the prices, but visitors from low-tariff countries such as the U.S. will find prices on many goods *higher* in Hong Kong. Prices vary considerably from store to store, so it's important to shop around and compare prices. Try different districts such as Kowloon and Causeway Bay. Also recommended is J. Morgan's booklet *How Not To Get Ripped Off Buying Cameras in Hong Kong.*

Prices can also be gauged by understanding local price fixing. Almost everything sold in Hong Kong has a "manufacturer's suggested retail price," which, as you might expect, is high enough to make the merchant rather than the customer happy. It does, however, serve as a useful starting point. There are three ways to determine this price: call the product's "sole agent" (phone numbers are listed in the HKTA brochure *Official Guide to Shopping*), check the HKTA brochure *Shopping in Hong Kong* for its abbreviated price lists, or simply ask the merchant to show you the manufacturer's suggested retail price list. Most will be happy to do so. Then ask what kind of discount is offered. It boggles the mind, but there's also a "manufacturer's recommended discount rate" on many items such as camera equipment and watches. Bargaining can now begin after you have determined the manufacturer's suggested retail price and the manufacturer's suggested discount rate.

Duty-free Goods—A Reminder
Hong Kong is a duty-free port where most products except for alcohol, tobacco, perfumes, and cosmetics can be imported without duties. The savings can then in theory be passed to the customer. This does not mean that goods will necessarily be duty-free when taken home! For example, Americans are allowed to bring back articles totaling US$400 free of duty but must pay 10% duty on the next US$1000 and varying rates of duty after that. Anyone planning on big shopping sprees should check their country's customs regulations and read the U.S. government publication *Know Before You Go.*

Bargaining
Bargaining is acceptable almost everywhere except in major department stores and exclusive boutiques. Assume the role of a tough negotiator and know exactly what you want and how much to pay before you enter a store. Bargaining in Hong Kong is tough. Don't be afraid to demand extras and boldly challenge extravagant claims. Don't be surprised if the once-friendly atmosphere turns decidedly hostile; only then do you know that you have reached a fair price.

Methods Of Payment
You should change traveler's checks into local currency before shopping. With all the varying rates of exchange and hidden service charges it makes sense to ask, "How many Hong Kong dollars will I get for my traveler's check?" Retail stores which accept traveler's checks do so only at poor rates. Credit cards often carry additional (and illegal) service charges of up to eight percent. Check with the sales staff on credit-card policies before starting negotiations.

Deposits, Receipts, And Refunds
In general, deposits paid for custom-made orders such as tailored suits, shoes, or unusual jewelry designs are not refundable. *Never leave*

MOVIES ABOUT HONG KONG

The World of Suzi Wong: Based on Richard Mason's best-selling novel published in 1957, Ray Stark's story of the love affair between Wanchai prostitute Nancy Kwan and American William Holden is the best Hong Kong flick to date. Although the novel takes place in the Wan-

PARAMOUNT PICTURES CORPORATION

scene from The World of Suzy Wong

chai District, much of the movie was filmed near the Man Mo Temple on Hollywood Road.

Love is a Many Splendored Thing: The only film worse than the 1986 dud *Tai Pan* is this 1955 melodrama starring William Holden and Jennifer Jones. Portraying a Eurasian doctor torn between family duty and modern love, Miss Jones managed to come up with the single worst Chinese accent ever attempted. Other problems included the lovely theme song, which was played *ad nauseam,* and the sappy dialogue, which must have mortified Han Su-Yin.

Enter the Dragon: Bruce Lee's masterpiece starts with a few good shots of junks in the harbor. Any suggestions on more films to be included in the next edition?

---

a deposit unless you are absolutely sure you intend to make a purchase. Accurate and honest receipts should be obtained. Purchase receipts should specify brand name, model, and serial number, and describe all contents such as gold quality, stone descriptions, origin of fur, etc. Prices should be honestly listed. Phony receipts intended for customs officers are easily available but they rarely work as planned. Receipts should be obtained whenever you ship a package back home. Insurance against loss or damage is also a good idea. Remember that *goods once sold are not returnable or refundable.*

Guarantees

All electronics and other high-end products such as watches should be purchased with a worldwide or international guarantee. Local retailer guarantees valid only in Hong Kong are next to worthless after you have returned home. What are you gonna do, write 'em a letter? Beware of phony guarantees. Authentic international guarantees should list the name of the authorized sole agent in Hong Kong, date of purchase, address of the shop, and the model and serial number. Double-check these numbers to make sure they match the equipment.

Warnings

Fraud is still a problem in Hong Kong. Reconditioned cameras are sold as new merchandise, expensive watches are filled with inferior clockworks, Carter watches are sold as Cartier, Siekos sold as Seikos, phony pearls, plastic jade, glass rubies, and synthetic diamonds (can *you* tell the difference?), camel bone sold as ivory, instant antiques sold with "certificates of authenticity," gold bracelets cut with cheaper metals, even bootleg Nikon cameras and Gucci shoes. The HKTA recommends that you patronize those establishments that belong to the HKTA and display their red-junk logo. Bona-fide members of this organization have promised to maintain ethical standards and promptly rectify any justified complaints. Fraud victims should contact the Consumer Council or the Royal Hong Kong Police in Wanchai.

The End Of The Elephant

Hong Kong serves as the center of the worldwide ivory trade. Despite laws aimed at preventing the import of poached ivory into Hong Kong, legal loopholes and large-scale smuggling still allow merchants to bring in a tremendous amount of ivory. Most of this is carved into bracelets, baubles, and Chinese landscapes. It all looks rather romantic in the shop window but remember this: it is a simple and terrible fact that to get the ivory of an elephant, the elephant must die. African elephants are being slaughtered in record numbers and ivory is the reason why. In 1979 the total elephant population of Africa was estimated at 1,300,000. Today less than 750,000 remain. Some 70,000 elephants are killed each year to meet the worldwide demand for ivory. At present rates, the African elephant will be an extinct species in less than 10 years and one of the world's most beloved and majestic creatures will have been exterminated for a few bracelets and bangles. Despite worldwide protests and ivory import bans by most Western countries, poached ivory is still being sold in Hong Kong. It takes both dealers and customers to kill elephants. The single best way to help stop the slaughter is not to buy ivory.

HONG KONG ISLAND

One hundred and fifty years ago, Hong Kong was just a "barren island with hardly a house upon it," unwanted and unloved by the first British colonialists. A century later it was given the title "Pearl of the Orient" by travel writers who also awarded the misnomer to Bangkok, Singapore, and god-only-knows how many other Asian cities. But Hong Kong today more closely resembles New York than anything vaguely Oriental. From almost every vantage point overlooking the harbor, you see only the Occidental—shorelines blanketed with tall buildings, office blocks forming windswept canyons, smokestacks in Kowloon, hundreds of ships moored in the harbor, highrise housing estates, and winding city streets that follow early contours now erased by successive land reclamations. Don't be misled. Hong Kong is a Chinese city populated by Chinese people who have only taken on the more obvious and convenient Western traits.

What you see and remember largely depends on where you stay and what neighborhoods you explore. Central, Hong Kong's financial district, offers some historic government buildings, striking modern architecture, and great panoramas from Victoria Peak. The Western District, on the other hand, is a neighborhood filled with strange sights and medieval insanitariness—one of the last places to see what's left of old Hong Kong. A highly recommended three-hour walking tour is described below. Wanchai has sailor bars, singles nightclubs, yuppie watering holes, and a handful of moderately priced hotels located near the new convention center. Causeway Bay is where most of the luxurious hotels, chic shopping centers, and restaurants are found. The south side of the island has the floating village of Aberdeen and wealthy residential neighborhoods such as Stanley and Repulse Bay.

CENTRAL AND WESTERN DISTRICTS

Around The Ferry Building
Step off the Star Ferry and you have arrived in Central (formerly called Victoria), Hong Kong's center of finance and government. Central is a curious mixture of a few remaining colonial structures and space-age skyscrapers thoughtfully connected with elevated walkways.

Rickshaws: Immediately outside the ferry are some of the last rickshaw "boys" in the territory. Nineteenth-century Hong Kong had over 7,000 rickshaws but today fewer than 20 old men hang on to licenses that expire forever on their deaths. Short rides around the block cost about HK$50; photos of you lounging in a rickshaw cost HK$20.

Tourist Information: The HKTA in the basement of Jardine Centre (formerly called Connaught Centre or the House of a Thousand Assholes) distributes free information on sightseeing, shopping, and local transport.

Central's largest bus terminal is hidden underneath the adjacent Exchange Building.

Culture: Both the Landmark Shopping Center and the City Hall Complex are used for cultural performances; schedules from the HKTA.

Statue Square: Across the street and wedged between the Italianate Legislative Council (one of the few buildings spared by the wrecker's ball) and the exclusive Mandarin Hotel is Statue Square, packed with thousands of Filipino housekeepers on Sundays. The statue of the Queen has been replaced with a representation of the first manager of the Hong Kong and Shanghai Bank, an ironic but completely appropriate symbol of modern Hong Kong.

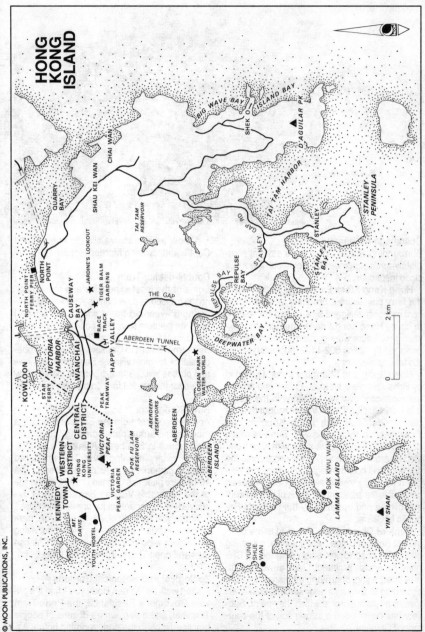

© MOON PUBLICATIONS, INC.

*the view from
Victoria Peak*

HONG KONG TOURIST ASSOCIATION

Space-age Architecture

Surrounding Statue Square are several completely amazing pieces of architecture worth a close inspection.

Hong Kong Stock Exchange: To the right of the ferry pier soars a brooding, almost iridescent monolith designed by architect Remo Riva to house Hong Kong's newly merged stock exchanges. Tours during trading hours can be arranged by calling 522-1122, but watch out for the talking elevators.

Hong Kong and Shanghai Bank: Designed by British architect Norman Foster and among the most controversial buildings in the world, this US$1-billion Darth Vader monolith is as closely identified with Hong Kong as the Transamerica Pyramid is with San Francisco or the World Trade Towers are with New York. Visitors are welcome to ride the escalator to the first floor and note that high technology has now given us totally visible elevator guts! A classic contrast is the adjacent old Bank of China Building, owned and operated by the People's Republic of China.

Bank of China: Down the road is the communist Bank of China headquarters, a soaring glass-sheathed rocket ship designed by Chinese-American architect I.M. Pei with countless threatening, sharp-angled triangles which, according to *fung shui* geomancers, cast ill will toward all institutions at which they point. Subtlety has never been a strong suit of the communist Chinese.

Almost as impressive are the cubist Bond Centre and towering Marriott Hotel.

Double-decker Tram

Some of the least expensive and most fascinating transports anywhere in Asia are the lumbering 85-year-old trams which slowly travel from the western town of Kennedy to the eastern town of Shau Kei Wan. The 30-minute journey from Western to Causeway Bay will probably suffice for most visitors. Best seats for views and photos are upstairs, front row, center. Pay the driver the posted fare on the way *out.*

Hong Kong Park

Across the street from the Bank of China is a modernistic urban park boasting the largest greenhouse in Southeast Asia and a HK$21-million aviary housing over 100 feathered species gathered from Asian rainforests. The 10-hectare park was opened in 1991 on the site of the venerable Victoria Barracks (now destroyed—a major defeat for preservationists).

Flagstaff House: Also located on park grounds inside Hong Kong's oldest surviving colonial-style building is a museum of Chinese teaware, open Thurs.-Tues. 1000-1700.

Zoological And Botanical Gardens

A short walk up Garden Road you'll find the private Governor's Residence, the Peak Tram Terminal, and a park where dozens of people practice *tai chi* in the early morning hours. Associated with the metaphysical principals of Taoism, this sport of shadow boxing is popular with Chinese grandmothers keeping arthritis at bay, business executives loosening up before hitting the market, and young men impressed with the defensive possibilities. Legend has it that this ancient toning technique developed from combat between a bird and a snake, both of which used 108 synchronous movements to get to the same place.

You might also see somebody playing mahjongg, a game which uses slamming ceramic tiles in something akin to open warfare. Almost identical to gin rummy, the object of the game is to match the tiles in straights or sets of three. The Botanical Gardens house over 300 species of birds including flamingos, cranes, and a colony of endangered Palawan peacock pheasants.

Victoria Peak

Views from the summit of this 1,305-foot peak are some of the world's most spectacular. It's like the Holy Grail: if you miss it you have missed Hong Kong.

Victoria Peak can be reached by taxi, public bus 15 leaving from underneath the Exchange Square, or an open-topped bus which leaves every 15 minutes from the Star Ferry terminal, but nothing compares with a ride in the recently renovated Peak Tram. Built in 1888, this 72-passenger relic (perfectly safe) is actually a funicular railway pulled by 5,000-foot steel cables which leaves every 10 minutes from the terminal behind the Hilton Hotel, lurches up the hillside at impossible angles, and stops nonchalantly before reaching the site of the old Peak Tower which was demolished in 1993. New facilities will open in 1995. In the meantime, circumnavigate the peak in 45 minutes along Harlech and Lugard roads.

Then walk up Austin Road to Victoria Peak Gardens. The perfect time to arrive is late afternoon for the captivating sunset. Like New York, Hong Kong takes on a mysterious beauty when viewed from a distance, a galaxy of lights that hide all the blemishes.

One can return to Central by tram or bus or walk down through the exclusive housing districts of the midlevels. Alternatively, walk south from the peak all the way down to Aberdeen via Pokfulam Reservoir. This is a terrific hike, but bring along the *Hong Kong Island Map—Countryside Series No. 1.* Tram fare is HK$10 one-way, HK$16 return.

Western District Walking Tour

This is old Hong Kong, an undeveloped neighborhood of winding alleyways, street merchants, herbal shops, snake restaurants, and aging temples. The HKTA sells a useful guide called *Central and Western Walking Tour* but the following three- to four-hour tour covers much the same ground with a few variations.

Alleys and Eggs: Beginning from the Star Ferry, walk down Des Voeux Rd. past the cheap clothing stalls on both Li Yuen East and Li Yuen West streets. Central Market isn't recommended for those with weak stomachs! Other small alleys quickly follow. Wing On ("Cloth Alley") is a covered bazaar filled with fabric stalls. Wing Wo has jewelry stores. Farther on is Wing Sing ("Egg St."), with a few difficult-to-find dealers selling all manner of salted and preserved chicken and duck eggs. Wing Lok has herbal medicine stores while Man Wa Lane is lined with chop carvers who will quickly carve your name in Chinese characters. Mercer St. is home to the Gold and Silver Exchange.

Snakes and Urns: Snake restaurants on Bonham Strand East are active only during the winter months. Visit the snake shop at 127 Bonham and photograph the magnificent urns at the tea shop at the corner of Possession Rd. and Queen's Rd. West.

Western Market: At the intersection of Connaught Rd. Central and Morrison St. stands the Western Market, a late-Victorian/Edwardian redbrick building constructed in 1906, declared a historical monument in 1990, and completely renovated in 1992.

Ginseng and Incense: Return to Bonham Strand West for deteriorating buildings filled with wholesale ginseng dealers. Visitors are graciously ignored but welcome to browse and smell. Turn left on Des Voeux West to glance inside incense stores and preserved-food shops where old ladies glare at passersby. Sidewalk barbers no longer operate on Sutherland Street.

The Far West: Continue walking several blocks farther and turn left on Western Street. Two blocks straight up is a lively fruit-and-vegetable market—good photographic possibilities. This is as far west as the walking tour goes. Continue back to Central via the upper roads.

WESTERN AND CENTRAL DISTRICTS

HK MACAU FERRY

● VICTORIA HOTEL

★ HARBOUR BLDG.

SHIN TAK ★ BLDG.

POOR MAN'S NIGHTCLUB

CONNAUGHT RD. CENTRAL

SHEUNG WAN MTR ■

CHINA MERCHANT HOTEL ● ● EMERALD HOTEL

WING LOK ST.

EGG STREET ★

CLOTH ALLEY ★

CONNAUGHT RD. WEST

SNAKE SHOPS ★

★ CHOP CARVERS

BONHAM ST. WEST

DES VOEUX WEST

WELLINGTON ST.

GINSENG SHOPS ★

TEA SHOP ★

★ DRIED FISH SHOPS

POSSESSION POINT ★

QUEEN'S RD. WEST

HOLLYWOOD RD.

★ CAT STREET (ANTIQUES)

★ COFFIN MAKERS

HOLLYWOOD RD.

■ ANTIQUES

★ MAN MO TEMPLE

★ WESTERN ROAD MARKET

LADDER STREET ★

WESTERN DISTRICT

HONG KONG ISLAND

N

0   250 m

© MOON PUBLICATIONS, INC.

Hong Kong Hollywood: Ambitious hikers may enjoy a side trip up to the University of Hong Kong for fine views, prewar architecture, and a small museum with pottery and porcelain. Less-determined visitors can simply return toward Central on Queen's Rd. West (slightly tricky to find; just keep walking) past stores selling Chinese wedding dresses and paper funeral effigies. Turn right on Hollywood Rd. and walk past the coffin carvers and shops selling Korean

chests, Thai brass noodlecarts, Japanese hibachis, Chinese porcelains, and lacquered rosewood furniture.

Man Mo Temple: Eventually you'll find Man Mo Temple situated at the corner of Hollywood and Ladder St., the oldest and most famous religious site on Hong Kong Island. Inside the interior, often cloaked in a smoky haze of burning joss coils, are mysterious figures of deities and Taoist gods, gigantic hanging incense coils, and

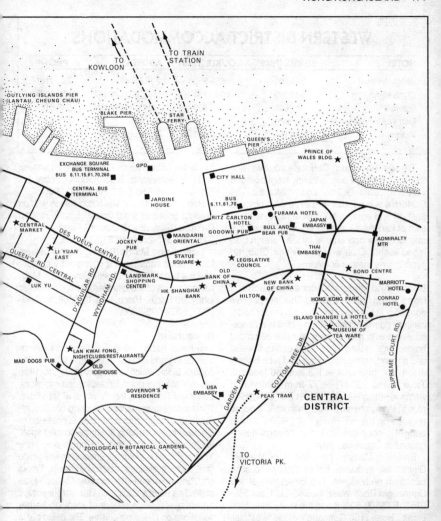

a pair of sedan chairs used to carry Emperor Kwan and Emperor Man in annual ceremonies—an exotic and strange world far removed from the hustle and hype of contemporary Hong Kong. Photography is permitted but small donations to benefit the local hospital are appreciated.

This neighborhood might look vaguely familiar—it was used in the film *The World of Suzi Wong*. Suzi's hotel is the building just to the

right and slightly up Ladder Street. Ironically, the book was written in and based on imaginary events in Wanchai's old Luk Kwok Hotel, torn down and replaced with a businessman's hotel in 1991. Is nothing sacred?

Antique Shops: A few steps downhill is Upper Lascar Row or Cat Street. Once possibly a brothel area, today the street is filled with expensive antique stores and funky junk stores. Massive Cat Street Antiques is below on Lok Ku Road.

WESTERN DISTRICT ACCOMMODATIONS

HOTEL	SINGLE (HK$)	DOUBLE (HK$)	ADDRESS	PHONE
Bangkok Royal	550-600	650-950	2-12 Pilkem	735-9181
China Merchants	750-1000	900-1150	160 Connaught W.	559-6888
Emerald	600	800	152 Connaught W.	546-8111
Man Wui Youth Hostel	50 (dorm)		Mt. Davis	817-5715
Victoria	1750-2150	2000-2400	Connaught C.	540-7228

Trendy Terminus: Conclude your walking tour in Lan Kwai Fong, a trendy neighborhood with chic cafes, bistros, and nightclubs. The California is a popular and expensive place to dust off and enjoy a tall cool drink. One block east of Lan Kwai Fong is the candy-striped former icehouse now shared by the Foreign Correspondents Club and the Fringe Club, an avant-garde theater company.

Budget And Moderate Accommodations
Hong Kong Youth Hostel: This inexpensive dormitory at the top of Mt. Davis in the far northwestern corner of Hong Kong Island is a peaceful place with great views, but like all official hostels, it's closed 1000-1600 during the day and a membership card is required. The biggest drawback, however, is the isolated location. Take buses 5B, 47, or 77 from central and watch for the YHA sign; tel. 817-5715, HK$25 plus YHA membership fees. Then walk about 45 minutes up the hill. Hong Kong Island's other budget places are limited to several guesthouses in Causeway Bay.

Emerald: Many of the hotels in the Western District are midrange hotels catering to businessmen on budgets. The Emerald is at 152 Connaught Road West, tel. 546-8111, fax 559-0255, HK$600-800. It and the new China Merchants Hotel (160 Connaught Road West, tel. 559-6888, HK$750-1150) are modern, clean, and much less expensive than the five-star hotels in Central. Additional charges include a 10% service charge and five-percent government tax.

Luxury Accommodations
Mandarin Oriental: The Mandarin has for over two decades been consistently named one of the 10 best hotels in the world. A two-year remodeling program has completely refurbished this hotel, known for its European-style service and fine restaurants. 5 Connaught Central, tel. 522-0111, fax 810-6190, HK$2000-2800.

Hong Kong Hilton: The Hilton comes with an outdoor pool and great views from the rooftop Chinese restaurant. 2 Queen's Road, tel. 523-3111, fax 845-2590, HK$1800-2600.

Hong Kong Marriott: Hong Kong's newest luxury hotel consists of a seven-story podium and a 41-story tower of reflective glass. Magnificent views of Victoria Harbor from the tiered lobby. 88 Pacific Place, tel. 810-8366, fax 845-0737, HK$2000-2600.

Restaurants
Lan Kwai Fong: Hong Kong's most fashionable dining and entertainment area sits in a little square block which once served as the 19th-century starting point for sedan-chair carriers. Lan Kwai Fong is a trendy world of fern bars, Western restaurants, and watering holes, a refreshing change from a nonstop succession of Chinese cafes. Among the more popular spots is Beverly Hills Deli, Hong Kong's only New York-style deli with kosher specialties like gefilte fish, cheese blintzes, matzo-ball soup, Texas chili, and American cheesecake. Kosher Texas chili? The nearby California Restaurant serves hamburgers, huge orders of fries, and other variations on California cuisine. The salad bar is pushed aside on weekends for late-night dancing. Further on is the '50s Restaurant, Cafe Luneta, and the European-styled Seasons.

Luk Yu Teahouse: Too trendy? Just a block away at 24 Stanley is the venerable Luk Yu Teahouse which serves dim sum in an old-world atmosphere of marble-backed chairs, brass spittoons, and elaborately carved partitions. A classic.

Poor Man's Nightclub: One of Hong Kong's most memorable experiences is dining al fresco

CENTRAL DISTRICT ACCOMMODATIONS

HOTEL	SINGLE (HK$)	DOUBLE (HK$)	ADDRESS	PHONE
Hong Kong Marriott	2000	2600	88 Pacific Place	810-8366
Hong Kong Hilton	1800	2600	2 Queen's Road	523-3111
Furama Intercontinental	1650-2250	1650-2250	1 Connaught C.	525-5111
Mandarin Oriental	2000	2800	5 Connaught C.	522-0111
Ritz Carlton	2400-3400	2600-3800	2105 E. Queensway	526-5031

in the parking lot near the Macau Ferry. Surrounding the denim and handicraft merchants are a dozen-plus food stalls famous for Mongolian hot pots, escargot in black bean sauce, and delicious seafood specialties. The atmosphere is touristy and prices higher than at the Temple Street Night Market, but the carnival-like atmosphere and outstanding food make this a real Hong Kong highlight.

Snake Restaurants: During the cooler winter months, you might want to visit the snake restaurants on Jervois and Hillier streets. A live snake is brought to your table, split open with a sharp knife, and then drained of its blood, which is mixed with wine to make an aphrodisiac bile. The snake meat is boiled into soup.

Nightlife
Bull and Bear: Central is a beehive of traditional English-style pubs that cater to expatriate bankers and the young *hongsters* working the financial district. Of the half-dozen pubs on Hong Kong side, I'd recommended the cozy and friendly Bull and Bear, where you'll find all the necessities: darts, dark ale, oak beams, and suitably warm barmaids. Lambeth Walk.

Godown Pub: This popular place serves as an English restaurant until 2000 when the chairs are pushed aside to make room for dancing. Live jazz with the Victoria Jazz Band every Wednesday evening 2130-0100. Middle-aged clientele. Located in the basement of the Sutherland House but the entrance is on Club Alley. Walk down the steps past the photos of Madonna, Michael Caine, and Eartha Kitt.

Jockey Pub: A sterile and uninviting pub popular with Chinese yuppies. Swire House.

Lan Kwai Fong Nightclubs: Hong Kong's two hottest nightlife scenes are in Wanchai and here at the top of D'Aguilar Street in Upper Central. The half-dozen nightclubs, discos, and delis are filled with Chinese trendsetters and expatriates who stumble down from the midlevel homes. Both the cavernous videotheque known as the Underground (formerly Disco Disco) and the well-named 1997 charge HK$65-90 admission for entrance and two drinks. Deserted before midnight but then packed until sunrise. California's HK$85 cover on Wednesday, Friday, and Saturday includes dancing and two drinks. At the top of the street (use the back entrance) is Mad Dogs, a traditional Scottish-style pub with upstairs drinking and downstairs dancing.

Shopping
Landmark Shopping Center: Three floors of first-class boutiques surround a central fountain area in perhaps the most elegant shopping complex in all of Hong Kong. Cultural performances are given in the afternoons; schedules at HKTA. Queen's Road Central above the MTR terminal.

Lane Crawford: This elegant and very expensive department store has a good selection of jewelry, clothes, and antiques. The place to shop when money is no object. 70 Queen's Road Central.

Chinese Arts and Crafts: These Chinese-owned stores are "must" shopping for most foreign visitors. Check the arts-and-crafts section for inexpensive cloisonné, jewelry, fabrics, wooden masks, and beautiful carpets. 24 Queen's Road East. Also try the Chinese Merchandise Emporium at 92 Queen's Road.

Lanes and Alleys: Between Queen's and Des Voeux roads are several narrow lanes filled with small shops selling cheap clothes and odd souvenirs. Li Yuen East and Li Yuen West are overflowing with inexpensive stockings, copy handbags, and sportswear, while Wing On Street (Cloth Alley) is crammed with dozens of fabric merchants. Bargain hard and watch for pickpockets.

Cat Street and Hollywood Road: Many of Hong Kong's leading antique stores are located here. Don't expect great bargains; local demand for quality antiques has dramatically forced up prices in recent years.

Poor Man's Nightclub: Dozens of tables filled with cheap clothing, shrink-wrapped electronics, and tourist souvenirs. Prices are surprisingly low. Afterwards, enjoy Mongolian hot pot or a seafood specialty at the dozen food stalls. Just beyond the Macau Ferry Terminal.

CAUSEWAY BAY AND WANCHAI

Once filled with the *godowns* of British opium merchants, the Causeway Bay and Wanchai districts are now known for their exclusive department stores, outstanding restaurants, lavish nightclubs, businessman hotels, and the new Hong Kong Convention Center. Sightseeing highlights aren't ancient temples or historic architecture (most has been torn down) but rather the tremendous activity on the sidewalks, people-watching, discovering the latest restaurant, shopping in the street markets, and relaxing over cocktails at happy hour.

Wanchai

Queen's Road East: Take the tram from Central and alight near the Wesley Hotel. Walk up Queen's Road East past rattan and wooden furniture shops, stores with enormous bags of rice, dried fish, lanterns, instruments for Chinese brush calligraphy, temple furnishings, and incense sticks to the Hung Shing Temple. Then ride the glass bullet elevator to the top of Hopewell Center, Hong Kong's second tallest after the new Bank of China. Great views from the rooftop restaurant. Back down on street level, continue walking east to the Wanchai Post Office, one of Hong Kong's last remaining protected buildings. Temple enthusiasts may also want to visit the Pak Tai Temple on Stone Nullah Lane off Queen's Road East and the Chai Kung Temple on Tik Loong Lane. The latter is plastered with thousands of lucky mirrors donated by pilgrims cured of illnesses. Turn left down Wanchai Road and wind your way past Southern Playground to Hennessey Road.

modern architecture in Hong Kong

HONG KONG TOURIST ASSOCIATION

Lockhart Road: Wanchai, once the home of Suzi Wong, has curiously enough become the art capital of Hong Kong Island. The Arts Centre houses several art galleries and auditoriums. The adjacent Hong Kong Academy for Performing Arts houses the 1,188-seat Lyric Theatre, the Drama Theatre, and the Studio Theatre. The Museum of Chinese Historical Relics on the first floor of the Causeway Centre displays cultural treasures from mainland China. The magnificent new Hong Kong Convention Centre features extensive conference facilities and a pair of first-class hotels.

Causeway Bay can be reached by walking either past the restaurants on Lockhart Road or along Hennessey with its tailor shops, cafes, and discount electronics stores.

Causeway Bay

Aw Boon Haw Gardens: This Chinese version of Disneyland is a kitsch amusement park filled with atrocious Chinese pagodas and bizarre cement figures depicting Chinese mythology and morality in graphic realism. Tiger Balm Gardens (the old name) was constructed in 1935 by inventors of the Asian version of Ben Gay. Memorable scenes include sinners being sawed in half and boiled in oil. Tacky but worth visiting if only to tour the restored ground floor of the family residence, which contains one of the world's great jade collections. Open daily 0900-1600. Free.

Noon Day Gun: This is the famous recoiling three-pound Hotchkiss immortalized by Noel Coward, who penned, "In Hong Kong they strike a gong and fire off a noon day gun." Today it's still fired at noon, a traditional salute begun by Jardine and Matheson to announce the arrival of important *taipans*. Use the underground tunnel to avoid the traffic.

Typhoon Shelter: The crowded anchorage across from the Excelsior is home to both luxury yachts of the Royal Hong Kong Yacht Club and a large colony of floating sampans. Boats can be hired for tours and sampan dinners.

Victoria Park: The enormous green lung across the overhead walkway served as center for many of the demonstrations after the Tiananmen massacre. Facilities include tennis courts, lawn bowling, swimming pools, and exercise par courses. Exit the park via the underpass.

Tin Hau Temple: Causeway Bay's oldest shrine, constructed over 250 years ago but rebuilt in 1868, is dedicated to the Goddess of the Sea.

Tung Lo Wan Road: One of the few streets in Causeway Bay with a sense of history. Explore the alleys and reconstructed Lin Fa Kung Temple on Wun Sha Street, constructed in 1863. Jones Street boasts a row of old homes called Perfection Place. Aw Boon Haw Gardens (Tiger Balm Gardens) can be reached by walking up Tai Hang Road or catching bus 11 from the Morton Terrace Bus Terminal.

Horse Racing At Happy Valley

Horse-racing season from October to May annually attracts thousands of Chinese who place their bets and test their luck a few blocks back from Causeway Bay. Visitors are welcome to make independent wagers or join the HKTA special horse-racing tours that visit Happy Valley and the ultra-modern Shatin racetrack in the New Territories.

Locals are apparently completely nuts about horse racing. Consider this: each race day an estimated two million residents bet over HK$60 million—six times the average at New York's Belmont Park Racetrack. Bets exceed HK$150 in the cheap seats and over HK$800 in the member stands. Almost 20 Hong Kong newspapers are devoted solely to racing news.

The century-old Jockey Club, an exclusive organization which controls the racing and lottery market in Hong Kong, is reputedly the world's richest gambling cartel, bringing in over HK$25 billion a year. Even the criminals do big numbers. A major racing scandal several years ago revealed that many races were fixed and that the overseas assets of some jockeys involved ran into the *billions* of Hong Kong dollars.

Budget Accommodations

Budget accommodations in Wanchai/Causeway Bay are limited to a few hostels and Chungking-like high-rises.

Leishun Court: Hong Kong Island's answer to Chungking Mansions is the smaller version located off Leighton Rd. behind Heison Mansion. Several guesthouses, with small but acceptable rooms, have recently opened on the lower floors. Fuji Guesthouse (tel. 577-9406), Villa Lisboa (tel. 576-5421), and Cannes House (tel. 890-2736), all located on the first floor, have both fan and a/c rooms with common or private baths. 116 Leighton Rd., HK$150-360.

Phoenix Apartments: Small but reasonably priced rooms are found in the building adjacent to the upscale Lee Gardens Hotel. Many serve the short-time trade with circular beds and horizontal mirrors, but are otherwise good value for budget travelers. 70 Lee Garden Hill Rd., HK$160-320.

Nobel Hostel: Three locations with 50 a/c rooms equipped with TVs, towels, and Chinese tea. Right in the heart of Causeway Bay. 9 Kingston Street, Clarke Mansion, Flat 2A 2/F; 6 Cleveland Street, Newtown Mansions, Flat B, 8/F; 37 Paterson Street, Paterson Building, Flat C1 7/F; tel. 576-6148, HK$250-300 single, HK$300-350 double. Go directly to the main office on Paterson Street, above the Daimaru Department Store.

Moderate Accommodations

Harbour View International House: Despite the confusing name, this is actually a cleverly disguised but perpetually filled YMCA. The Hong

WANCHAI AND CAUSEWAY BAY

TO KOWLOON

TO HUNG HOM

WANCHAI

WANCHAI FERRY PIER

WANCHAI MTR

NEW WORLD HARBOUR VIEW HOTEL

GRAND HYATT

HK CONVENTION CENTRE

ACADEMY FOR PERFORMING ARTS

YMCA

HK ARTS CENTRE

CHINESE CONSULATE & MUSEUM

FLEMING RD.

MALAYSIA EMBASSY

HUA LONG LODGE

IMMIGRATION

ADMIRALTY MTR

ISLAND CAVERN NIGHTCLUB

JOE BANANAS

LUK KWOK HOTEL

O'BRIEN RD.

HARBOUR HOTEL

ARSENAL ST.

JAFFE RD.

LOCKHART RD.

WHARNEY HOTEL

MAKATI INN

CENTURY HOTEL

INDIAN EMBASSY

FENWICK

ONE FOR TWO NIGHTCLUB

QUEENSWAY RD.

MARRIOT HOTEL

CROSSROADS CLUB

EVERGREEN HOTEL

NEPTUNE CLUB

STRIP JOINTS

WANCHAI MTR

WESLEY HOTEL

NEW HARBOUR HOTEL

LUARD RD.

CONRAD HOTEL

JOHNSTON RD.

ISLAND SHANGRI-LA HOTEL

WANCHAI RD.

QUEEN'S RD. EAST

0   250 m

HOPEWELL CENTRE

© MOON PUBLICATIONS, INC.

Kong Hotel Association at the airport will call on vacancies. Reservations should be made well in advance by mailing one night's lodging. 4 Harbour Road, tel. 802-0111, fax 802-9063, HK$700-1000 single or double.

Harbour Hotel: An excellent location and reasonable prices make this new hotel a good choice for mid-level travelers. 116-122 Gloucester Rd., Wanchai, tel. 574-8211, fax 572-2185, HK$550-900.

Luxury Accommodations
Park Lane: Completely renovated and considered one of the better mid-priced hotels. 310 Gloucester Road, tel. 890-3355, fax 576-7853. HK$1200-2000.

New World Harbour View: Facilities in the space-age 864-room hotel on top of the Hong Kong Convention Center include Hong Kong's largest outdoor swimming pool and a fleet of Mercedes Benzes. 1 Harbour, tel. 802-8088, fax 802-8833, HK$1800-3000.

Grand Hyatt: Like most other hotels in Hong Kong, this Asia flagship property was opened on a date deemed auspicious by *fung shui* geomancers. Some 70% of all rooms have harbor views. 1 Harbour, tel. 588-1234, fax 802-0677, HK$1800-2900.

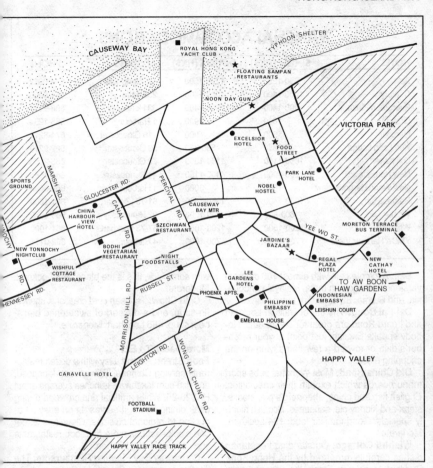

Restaurants On Lockhart Road

Lockhart Road between Wanchai and Causeway Bay is probably the single best place in Hong Kong to find a good, cheap, and informal restaurant. Start your search at the intersection of Lockhart and Arsenal Street, then walk east along Lockhart toward Causeway Bay.

Happy hour is an ideal time to try those wild-looking but actually very tame Suzi Wong bars. Terrific neon. Lockhart has everything imaginable from Szechwan to Shanghai and Cantonese to Thai. The best strategy is to try a place that looks popular and serves a cuisine that sounds intriguing. The following restaurants are listed in walking order from Wanchai to Causeway Bay.

American: Strange name but serves excellent northern dishes such as Mongolian hot pot, Peking duck, sizzling prawns, and thick soups. 23 Lockhart. Peking. Moderate.

Saigon Beach: Vietnamese specialties prepared by Chinese chefs. Try Saigon hot pots, spring rolls with fish sauce, glass noodle salads, rich noodle dishes. 66 Lockhart. Inexpensive.

Chili Club: One of the better Thai cafes in Hong Kong. Try the spicy *tom yam kai* (coconut soup) or beef in peanut sauce. 68 Lockhart. Inexpensive.

WANCHAI ACCOMMODATIONS

HOTEL	SINGLE (HK$)	DOUBLE (HK$)	ADDRESS	PHONE
Asia	950-1250	1250-1500	1A Wang Tak	574-9922
Century	1000-1400	1000-1400	238 Jaffe	591-6000
Evergreen Plaza	1000-1400	1000-1400	33 Hennessy	866-9111
Grand Hyatt	1800	2900	1 Harbour	588-1234
Harbour	500	900	116 Gloucester	574-8211
Hua Long Lodge	450-650	500-750	53 Gloucester	529-9219
Luk Kwok	1050-1150	1150-1300	72 Gloucester	866-2166
New Harbour	900-1000	900-1150	41 Hennessey	861-1166
New World Harbour View	1800	3000	1 Harbour	802-8088
Ramada Inn	1050-1400	1050-1400	61-73 Lockhart	861-1000
Wesley	600-800	800-1000	22 Hennessey	866-6688
Wharney	1200-1500	1200-1500	57-73 Lockhart	861-1000
YMCA Harbour View	700-1000	700-1000	4 Harbour	802-0111

SMI: A simple cafe with almost 100 different versions of curry from India, Malaysia, Indonesia, and Burma. 85 Lockhart. Inexpensive.

Dai Pai Dong: The street stalls at Lockhart and Luard Road are great for cheap eats. Nobody speaks English; just point at your neighbor's dish or toward a few items lying on the chopping block.

Old China Hand: Most Wanchai pubs sport menu boards which explain their specialties: English fish and chips, shepherd's pie, steaks, steak-and-kidney pie, sausages, Scottish nightly specials. Good familiar food. 104 Lockhart. Moderate.

Wishful Cottage: Outstanding vegetarian dishes carefully prepared by the Hong Kong Buddhist Association. One of the older and more authentic restaurants in Causeway Bay. 336 Lockhart. Moderate.

Bodhi Vegetarian Restaurant: Bean-curd specialties taste exactly like chicken and meat in this terrific restaurant. The creative, highly descriptive menu is worth a close look. 388 Lockhart. Inexpensive.

Yaik Sang: This longtime favorite is known for lemon chicken, roast goose, double-boiled soups, and salted beggar's chicken. 454 Lockhart. Cantonese. Moderate.

Szechuan Lau: Fiery treats like hot-and-sour soups, smoked duck, prawns sautéed in chili sauce, eggplant with garlic. If you like your food with some kick, this is the place. 446 Lockhart. Moderate.

Chiu Chow: Try bean-curd creations, shark's-fin soup, and a dessert of sweetened bird's-nest soup. 485 Lockhart. Moderate.

More Places To Eat

Food Street: A short alley with a dozen restaurants serving Chinese, Taiwanese, Japanese, and dim-sum takeaway. Lunches average about HK$20-25. While artificial and crowded during peak dining hours, it serves as an easy introduction to regional cuisines. Cleveland Street one block east has more fast-food restaurants such as Vegi Food Kitchen.

Causeway Bay Floating Restaurants: The floating sampans in Causeway Bay provide an unusual if touristy dining experience. Organize a group of eight to 12 people, bring a few bottles of wine, and walk down to the typhoon shelter just opposite the Excelsior Hotel around 1900 or 2000. Use the tunnel under the road. Expect to be accosted by insistent sampan ladies who ask HK$120-150 for ride and dinner on board one of the sampans. Pay on return. No service during rain or typhoons. Touristy but most visitors enjoy it . . . except for those awful floating orchestras.

Russell Street Food Stalls: Causeway Bay's night market is rather inelegant but it's a real slice of life. Russell Street just off Percival.

CAUSEWAY BAY ACCOMMODATIONS

HOTEL	SINGLE (HK$)	DOUBLE (HK$)	ADDRESS	PHONE
Caravelle	700-800	800-950	84 Morrison	575-4455
China Harbour View	1000-1250	1250-1750	189 Gloucester	838-2222
Excelsior	1400-2150	1400-2150	281 Gloucester	576-7365
Lee Gardens	1250-1650	1250-1750	Hysan	895-3311
Nobel Hostel	250-300	300-350	9 Kingston 2A 2/F	576-6148
New Cathay	550-650	5550-700	17 Tung Lo Wan	577-8211
Park Lane	1200-2000	1200-2000	310 Gloucester	890-3355

Girlie Bars

The Wanch achieved lasting fame from Richard Mason's *The World of Suzi Wong* and the memorable movie starring William Holden and the lovely Nancy Kwan. During the '50s and '60s it was a hotbed of wicked nightclubs packed with sailors in need of drink, drugs, and girls. Massage parlors offered all varieties from Japanese to French with rooms upstairs by the hour.

But the end of the Vietnam War saw the sinful side of Wanchai flicker, fade, and die. Today it's filled with office buildings, modestly priced hotels aimed at the business traveler, and a few trendy nightclubs. Even Suzi's old hotel, the Luk Kwok, has been torn down and replaced with a conventioneer's hotel.

And yet, a dozen strip joints hang on. Happy-hour specials are a cheap way to check it out; beers cost HK$15-25 and hostess drinks (colored water) are about HK$45. The elaborate Tonnochy Nightclub, a popular hostess club halfway to Causeway Bay, is geared for affluent tourists and businessmen with unlimited expense accounts. See the descriptions and warnings under "Kowloon Nightlife."

Nightclubs And Bars

Most of the girlie bars and strip joints in Wanchai have given way to discos, English-style pubs, and singles bars, which are, together with Lan Kwai Fong, about the best in Hong Kong.

Joe Banana's: A friendly and inexpensive nightclub popular with expatriates who want to mingle rather than be suffocated with loud music. Good vibes and great selection of beers. Highly recommended. No cover. 23 Luard Road.

Island Cavern Nightclub: First-class club with live rock bands, occasional reggae, and samba shows. One of the few Hong Kong clubs to hire cutting-edge rock groups. Cover on weekends is HK$45-80. Fenwick at Jaffe Road.

Makati Inn: Although this homey upstairs club is a little run-down, it's a popular rendezvous spot for expatriates and their Chinese girlfriends. No cover and drinks are cheap. Luard between Jaffe and Lockhart Road.

Filipino Discos: Hong Kong has over 20,000 Filipino housemaids who pack the Wanchai discos on their nights off (try Sundays). Live music by bands from Manila. Three of the more popular are Crossroads, Neptune, and One for Two at Luard and Lockhart Road.

Dickens Bar: This pretentious and plastic pseudo-British pub is best visited for the Sunday afternoon jazz concert. Basement of the Excelsior Hotel.

Shopping

Department Stores: Causeway Bay is one of Hong Kong's best shopping districts. Some say that prices are lower than in Kowloon but bargaining might be necessary. Shopping is anchored around five large, luxurious, and expensive Japanese-linked department stores and hundreds of small electronics, clothing, and souvenir shops. Trendy Lane Crawford is here.

Chinese Emporiums: Try the main branch of China Products located towards the end of Yee Woo near Victoria Park or the smaller outlet near Mitsukoshi. Great arts and crafts.

Jardine's Crescent: Once a street market for *hong* employees, this bustling side street is a great place for inexpensive ladies' clothing. Ad-

BUSES TO ATTRACTIONS ON HONG KONG ISLAND

FROM CENTRAL

DESTINATION	TERMINAL	BUS
Aberdeen	Central	7
Aberdeen	Exchange Square	70
Airport	Major Hotels	A2
Aw Boon Haw	Central	11
Ocean Park	Exchange Square	70
Ocean Park	Admiralty MTR	71M
Repulse Bay	Exchange Square	6 or 61
Repulse Bay	Admiralty MTR	61M
Stanley	Exchange Square	6 or 260 (express)
Victoria Peak	Exchange Square	15
Zoo	Connaught Rd.	3 or 12

FROM CAUSEWAY BAY

DESTINATION	TERMINAL	BUS
Aberdeen	Moreton Terrace	72 or 76
Airport	Major Hotels	A3
Ap Lei Chau	Moreton Terrace	92
Ocean Park	Moreton Terrace	92
Shau Kei Wan	Yee Woo St.	2

jacent Jardine's Bazaar has stalls selling sportswear, factory rejects, vegetables, dry goods, and Chinese provisions.

SOUTH SIDE OF HONG KONG ISLAND

Around The Island By Bus

The south side of the island has been referred to as Hong Kong's Riviera. A bit of an exaggeration perhaps, but there's enough of interest to make for an enjoyable day-trip.

Self-guided tours by public bus are easy, plus they give the flexibility necessary to stop, look, and listen. Begin at the Exchange Square Bus Terminal in Central. Buses 6 or 260 will reach Stanley quickly via the shortcut but it's better to take bus 2 to Shaukeiwan and then bus 14 to Stanley. Sit on the left side for the views. Alternatively, you could take the streetcar tram from Central to the final stop at Shaukeiwan. Check

out the junk builders at waterfront, then backtrack two stops to Nam On Lane and take bus 9 to Shek O, perhaps the best beach on the island.

Continue on to Stanley with bus 14, and visit the market, beach, and temple in Stanley. Then take buses 6 or 73 to Repulse Bay or on to Aberdeen for the floating community, boatbuilders, and monstrous housing projects. Visitors short on time can reach Central in 20 minutes with bus 6 or 61, but a slower and much prettier ride is bus 7 along the western coastline.

Stanley Village

This residential enclave of Stanley is best known for its weekend market where locals and visitors reputedly find some of the best clothing bargains in Hong Kong. Check carefully, since many of these designer-name fashions are over-runs and seconds.

The Tin Hau Temple at the end of the street was built in 1767 and, like almost all temples in Hong Kong, is dedicated to the Goddess of the Sea. The skin hanging on the wall is from a tiger supposedly shot by a Japanese soldier. Stanley also has a small beach popular with windsurfers and a prison used as an internment camp by the Japanese during WW II.

Repulse Bay

Named after the famous battleship, this exclusive residential neighborhood boasts one of Hong Kong's better beaches—except on weekends when its fully packed and trashed out. Repulse Bay is where Hong Kong fell to the Japanese. The biggest draw was once the Repulse Bay Hotel, an unprofitable structure destroyed in 1982 despite the impassioned pleas of preservationists. The reconstruction Verandah Restaurant offers Bamboo Bar and an expensive restaurant called Spices. Nostalgia and the traditions of the past carry little appeal in Hong Kong.

Ocean Park And Deep Water Bay

Southeast Asia's largest entertainment complex has dolphin shows, an aviary with 3,000 birds, cable cars, the world's largest oceanarium, roller-coaster rides, a Shark Tunnel with 40 species of sharks, a butterfly house, a greenhouse complex, and the world's longest outdoor escalator (no kidding), which climbs the hill from the Middle Kingdom. The Kingdom is a new craft village which presents 13 dynasties in life-size settings, a vast improvement over the Sung Dynasty Village in Kowloon. Admission is a stiff HK$140, but this includes both Ocean Park and the Middle Kingdom. A special Ocean Park bus leaves every 30 minutes from the Admiralty MTR station. Avoid weekends.

Deep Water Bay is an exclusive residential area where Jennifer Jones swam in a chilly scene from *Love is a Many Splendored Thing*. One assumes that the beaches and waters were cleaner back then. In Chinese, Hong Kong means "Fragrant Harbor," a singularly apt description of the polluted waters that befoul the territory.

Aberdeen And The Boat People

Once upon a time some 40,000 Tanka boat people lived aboard their junks and sampans moored in the fishing village of Aberdeen. As poor refugees from China's Fukien Province, the Tanka were the untouchables of Chinese society, an inferior people routinely denied the right to live on land or marry mainlanders. Tankas worshipped their own gods, celebrated their own festivals, and lived in conditions considered by tourists as picturesque.

Today these people are taking factory jobs, sending their children to public schools, and moving to the modern housing estates that rise behind Aberdeen like gigantic concrete mushrooms. If you take a boat tour, look for the shrine images carved to honor ancestors. On the 49th day after the death of a family member, professional mediums communicate with dead souls who wander homeless in the afterworld. The deceased laments his condition and asks for a few necessities, like money or a Mercedes. The deceased will also be asked about his preference of carved wooden image—riding a tiger, depicted as a young man, seated on a throne, etc. The image is then carved and mounted on the family altar to house the soul after it has finally passed through purgatory.

Sampan tours are offered (even insisted on) at HK$30-50 per hour, but time seems to be running out for this "tourist attraction." Ignore the arm-tugging sampan ladies and walk over the bridge to Ap Lei Chau, where boatbuilders construct crafts according to age-old designs. As with most traditional boatbuilders, blueprints and master designs are unknown.

Floating restaurants across the way have architecture as gaudy as the food is awful, but you might take advantage of the free water shuttle to have a quick look around. Immense housing projects and monstrous power stations behind the city have brought energy to the people and ruined whatever aesthetics Aberdeen once had. Back in town there's a Chinese wedding-gown shop filled with *red* dresses, a shrine dedicated to Hung Shing, the weather-prediction god, mah-jongg stores, and a McDonald's.

The sole cause of man's unhappiness is that he does not know how to stay quietly in his own room.

—Blaise Pascal, *Pensées*

You do not see that the Real is in your own home,
And you wander from forest to forest listlessly.
Here is the truth!
Go where you will, to Banaras or to Mathura,
If you do not find god in your own soul
The world will be meaningless to you.

—Kabir

All travel is circular.

—Paul Theroux, *The Great Railway Bazaar*

NEW TERRITORIES

The New Territories are formed by the land north of Kowloon to the Chinese border and the outlying islands of Lantau, Lamma, and Cheung Chau. Although much of the peninsular region has given way to monstrous housing projects accommodating Hong Kong's ever-growing population, you can still find some pleasant rural scenery, isolated beaches, simple fishing villages, and old fortress towns that date back hundreds of years. The attractions below are listed in clockwise order.

Getting Around By Bus

To tour the New Territories in a single day you'll need an early start and plenty of change for the buses. Try the clockwise loop from Kowloon through Yuen Long, Kam Tim, Fanling, and Taipo. Buses are listed below. A pricier but easier alternative is the HKTA The Land Between tour, which avoids the standard route by cutting through the interior. Another recommended transportation option is the Tolo Harbor Ferry, which leaves University Station Harbor (Ma Liu Shui) daily at 1500.

Youth-hostel Accommodations

The Hong Kong Youth Hostels Association maintains several inexpensive facilities in the New Territories. Some hostels are open year-round, others on weekends only. Beds cost HK$25, tent camping is permitted, and YHA membership cards are required. Advance reservations and memberships from: YH Association, Shek Kip Mei Estate, Block 19, Room 225, Shamshuipo, Kowloon, tel. 788-1638, fax 788-3105.

Sze Lok Yuen Youth Hostel: This hostel can be reached in about two hours from Kowloon. First take the MTR from Kowloon to the Tseun Wan MTR station, followed by bus 51 to Tai Mo Shan Road. Walk 40 minutes until you see the YH sign on the right side. Most visitors climb nearby 957-meter Tai Mo Shan, Hong Kong's highest peak, in the early morning hours. Bring very warm clothing.

Bradbury Lodge: Formerly called the Wayfoong Hall, this YHA hostel at the base of Plover Cove Reservoir on Ting Kok Rd. has been completely renovated by local hostel authorities. Take the train to Tai Po Station, then bus 75K to Tai Mei Tuk. The hostel is 200 meters south in a beautiful setting.

Bradbury Hall: Sai Kung Peninsula is home to both Bradbury Hall in Chek Keng and Pak Sha O Youth Hostel. Take bus 92 from Kowloon (Choi Hung Estate terminal) to Sai Kung, bus 94 to Pak Tam Au, then the path toward Check Keng village. Alternatively, take a bus or train to the Ma Liu Shui (see "University and Tolo Harbor," below), and then the Tolo Harbor ferry out to either Chek Keng for Bradbury Hostel or to Lai Chi Chong for Pak Sha O Hostel. Both require a one-hour hike.

Pak Sha O Hotel: Pak Sha O is situated on the northeastern edge of Sai Kung Peninsula, facing Tolo Harbor and Mirs Bay. Take bus 94 from Sai Kung to Ko Tong village, followed by a hike to the hostel. The last word in isolation.

ATTRACTIONS

Planned Cities

After a series of devastating fires destroyed vast areas of squatters' huts in the 1950s, the Hong Kong government began building public housing in the city core and throughout the New Territories. Early attempts were little more than highrise slums, but the government persisted to become the world's largest landlord. Today over 50% of Hong Kong's population lives in the New Cities of the New Territories. Tours of these cities can be arranged through the HKTA, though it's easy enough to simply wander around the planned communities of Tsuen Wan or Shatin.

Tsuen Wan's Sam Tung Uk Folk Museum, the largest folk museum in Hong Kong, highlights the culture of the Hakka people with displays of clothing, farming instruments, and a small-scale reproduction of a typical Hakka community.

Ching Chung Kong Temple

This impressive temple an hour's drive from Kowloon is known for its ancestral halls filled with precious relics, Taoist gods, and countless photographs of departed ancestors. One of the few temples where pure Taoism is still prac-

BUSES TO THE NEW TERRITORIES

DESTINATION	FROM BUS TERMINAL	BUS
Clear Water Bay	Star Ferry	5 to terminus, then 91
Kam Tin Walled Village	Jordan Rd.	68X to Yuen Long, then 54
Laufaushan	Jordan Rd.	68X to terminus, then 55
Miu Fat Monastery	Jordan Rd.	68X direct
Plover Cove	Jordan Rd.	70 to Tai Po, then 75K
Sai Kung	Star Ferry	5 to terminus, then 92
Shatin	Jordan Rd.	70
Tai Po	Jordan Rd.	70
10,000-Buddha Monastery	Jordan Rd.	71 to Shatin

CIRCLE THE NEW TERRITORIES BY BUS

FROM	TO	BUS
Jordan Rd. Terminal	Yuen Long (East)	68X
Yuen Long (West)	Kam Tin	54
Kam Tin	Tai Po	64K
Yuen Long (West)	Sheung Shui	76K
Sheung Shui	Fanling, Tai Po	70
Tai Po	Jordan Rd. Terminal	70

ticed, Ching Chung Kong is dedicated to Lui Tung Bun, one of the eight Taoist Immortals who spread the mystical doctrine throughout China. You'll find his gold-leaf, bearded image in the rear of the temple. Only images of Taoist Immortals are displayed on the altars.

This temple also serves as a residence for elderly Chinese who lack relatives to support them. Like Wong Tai Sin, it's a modern but strikingly beautiful structure built in traditional Chinese style with finely carved woodwork and imperial yellow- and blue-tile roofs. Entrance is made through an imposing *pai lau* gateway flanked by Chinese dragons. Surrounding the temple are hundreds of *pun joi* trees similar to Japanese bonsai. Sunday morning services are worth attending, and, if you missed breakfast, vegetarian meals are available on the first floor.

Ching Chung Kong is located in Lam Tei on Castle Peak Road about 1.5 km beyond Tuen Mun. Take the MTR to Tsuen Wan Station and then bus 66M to the last stop. Alternatively, from the Jordan Road Bus Terminal take bus 68 to the Miu Fat Monastery, have a look around, and then backtrack two stops with bus 63.

Mui Fat Monastery

This HK$60-million three-story temple is considered one of the great temples in Hong Kong. Decorations include more than 10,000 sculptures of Buddha as well as Chinese and Thai paintings.

Yuen Long

Only people touring the New Territories by bus need stop here. Bus 68X from the Jordan Road Bus Terminal will drop you at the Yuen Long West Bus Terminal. You must then walk down the street to the Yuen Long East Bus Terminal to take either bus 76K for Sheung Shui, bus 54 to Kam Tim, or bus 55 to Laufaushan.

Laufaushan

Hong Kong's oyster capital in the northwest corner of the New Territories is a scruffy but intriguing fishing village with a handful of good oyster restaurants. After getting off the bus, walk through the narrow street to the bay where fishermen work amid mountains of oyster shells. Cultivation begins when floating oyster eggs attach themselves to 36-cm-long cement poles embedded in the seabed. They're edible in five

YOUTH HOSTELS IN THE NEW TERRITORIES

HOSTEL	ADDRESS	PHONE
Bradbury Hall	Chek Keung, Sai Kung Peninsula	328-2458
Bradbury Lodge	Plover Cove, Ting Kok Rd.	656-8323
Pak Sha O	Pak Sha O, Sai Kung Peninsula	328-2327
Sze Lok Yuen	Tai Mo Shan, Tsuen Wan	488-8188

years if they survive a steady diet of cadmium, mercury, and waste from nearby pig farms.

Restaurants along the narrow road serve tasty oyster dishes. Raw oysters should be avoided, but fried dishes are safe, tasty, and supposedly excellent for your sexual appetite.

Kam Tin Walled Village

East of Yuen Long are several walled villages settled by the Tang family during the 17th century. Each is surrounded by brick walls and entered through narrow passages wide enough for only a single person. Watchtowers, parapets, and gun slots complete the scene. Streets are laid out in geometric fashion with narrow lanes separating communal households. Kat Hing Wai (also called Kam Tin) is the largest village but it's become highly commercialized in recent years. Costumed ladies at the entrance demand payment for both admission and photographs; refuse and they spit at you! Beyond the gates are modern buildings and souvenir stalls selling tourist junk.

Adjacent villages are less touristy but outsiders are unwelcome except in Shui Tau, north along the road from Kam Tin. Other fortress towns in the New Territories include Tsang Tai Uk (see "Shatin," below), Sam Tin near Lok Ma Chau, and Sam Tung Uk located in Tsuen Wan.

Sheung Shui

Top draw in this modern city is the Man Shek Tong Ancestral Hall, constructed two centuries ago by the Liu clan. Much of the original architecture was lost in the '30s when it served as a public school. Difficult to find without some help.

Fanling And The Egrets

Fanling is a completely nondescript town promoted for unknown reasons by the HKTA in their *Luen Wo Market* brochure. Skip the boring market and instead walk west from the train station to the Fung Ying Sing Koon Temple. On Sundays, dozens of people come here to shake the *chims* and have their fortunes told by soothsayers. Others come to burn paper money for departed ancestors.

Thousands of white egrets, Chinese pond herons, and *swinhoes* nest in the trees of the protected Yim Tso Ha Egretry between March and September. Take bus 69K from Fanling or sign up for the HKTA tour of Tai Po Marsh. Pat Sin Leng Country Park and the Bride's Pool near Luk Keng are also nearby.

Tai Po

Organized tours to this modern city usually visit the dismal Tin Hau Temple on Ting Kok Road and then drop by the Tai Ping Carpet Factory to learn about modern carpet production. The factory is located beyond the temple where the road curves to the right. The Hong Kong Railway Museum on On Fu Road records colorful local rail history.

University And Tolo Harbor

The Chinese University Museum features an art gallery with calligraphy, Han bronze seals, and jade flower carvings.

Cruises of Tolo Harbor leave twice daily from the harbor at Ma Liu Shui, about 15 minutes by foot from University Station. The four-hour morning ferry does not stop for sightseeing, but the afternoon ferry at 1500 makes six brief stops and a 45-minute layover in Tap Mun. Both youth hostels on the Sai Kung Peninsula can be reached with this ferry. Kung fu movies are filmed at the Shaw Brothers Studios near Clearwater Bay.

Shatin

This mind-boggling metropolis of some 500,000 people sports the Shatin Racecourse, one of the world's most luxurious racetracks. Even the stables are air-conditioned! Tours organized by the HKTA include transportation, meals, racing guides, and entry to the members' enclosure. Races are held from May to September.

A BREATH OF FRESH AIR

Hiking the country parks of the New Territories is a delightful way to escape the noise and congestion of urban Hong Kong. Routes that avoid the urbanized sections can be planned with the *Countryside Maps* published by the Survey Office. These highly recommended maps show hiking trails, youth hostels, campsites, old forts, bus terminals, and all ferry routes. Sold at the Government Publications Centre in the Central GPO and in Kowloon at 382 Nathan Road near Kansu Street, Sheet 4 (the most useful map) covers the youth hostels and hiking trails around the Sai Kung Peninsula. Local authorities advise that you select a route to match your ability, don't hike alone, listen to weather forecasts, and bring water bottles, a good map, flashlights, and some first-aid supplies.

Trail choices are almost limitless, but the MacLehose Trail is considered the most ambitious hike. Named after a former governor of Hong Kong, the trail runs laterally across eight country parks and stretches more than 100 km from Sai King to Tuen Mun. It's been divided into 10 stages, the first two being scenic hikes from High Island Reservoir to remote Tai Long village. The ridgewalker is rewarded with panoramic views form Neele Hill to Tai Mo Shan, Hong Kong's highest mountain.

Tsang Tai Uk, a walled village at the northern end of Lion Rock Tunnel Road, was built in 1840 by a wealthy quarryman of Hakka origins. Walk south across the bridge, continue past the intersection, and look left.

Temple Of 10,000 Buddhas

Top attractions in the New Territories are the temple complexes west of Shatin. From the railway station, walk through the underpass and follow the small signs to the right; don't take the obvious concrete steps that only lead to somebody's house! Exactly 506 steps later (go ahead, count 'em) you'll reach the main temple crammed with 13,000 miniature clay Buddhas. Statues on the lower levels are now covered with thick wire mesh to prevent theft.

The temple was founded shortly after WW II by Yuet Kai, a Shanghai philosophy professor who penned almost 100 books on Buddhism before his death in 1965. A Christ-like image of Yuet is displayed between a pair of gilded Buddha statues. For something really bizarre, continue up to the upper temple to see his gilded corpse preserved under glass.

The whole place is something of a low-end Aw Boon Haw Gardens with its pagodas, garish statues of Buddha disciples, and assorted gods riding blue lions and white elephants. Views from the hill encompass the housing projects and Amah Rock, which, some say, resembles a woman with child on back.

OUTLYING ISLANDS

Beyond the heat and crowds of Kowloon are 236 rocky islands that form the remainder of the New Territories. Lantau, Lamma, and Cheung Chau are the most popular and Cheung Chau is the best. In any event, the outlying islands are much more peaceful and interesting than the peninsular New Territories.

All can be reached by ferries, including air-conditioned hovercrafts and interisland junks. Most ferries leave from the Outlying Districts Ferry Pier in Central. Departures are hourly 0600-2000. Call the Hong Kong and Yaumatei Ferry Company at 542-3081 for departure schedules. Whatever you do, don't go on weekends, when it seems like half of Hong Kong's population is trying to escape the city.

CHEUNG CHAU

Shaped like a dumbbell with hills on the bells and a town in the waist, this attractive little island is the best choice for visitors with limited time. The somewhat Mediterranean atmosphere (use your imagination) has also made this island popular with locals and expatriates who value the lower rents and unhurried pace of life. Motorized vehicles except for a few service vehicles that race around with trolleys of Cokes or squealing pigs are banned on Cheung Chau. Development has arrived with new resort projects and condominium complexes, yet the island still retains some traditions, such as the clan associations and trade guilds that dominate the local economy.

The central waist is a densely populated village with winding alleys and a handful of good restaurants that face the crowded harbor. The northern bell is being developed with condominiums and has little of interest. The scenic southern bell can be walked in three or four hours along a well-marked path. Cheung Chau is 12 km west of Hong Kong and can be reached in one hour by air-conditioned ferry.

The Town

The *praya* (waterfront) is a constant hive of activity where you might discover a junk unloading baskets of fish or a Chinese funeral in full progress. Waterfront cafes and inexpensive food stalls south of the pier provide a grandstand view of everything likely to happen. The Cheung Chau Fire Station across from the air-conditioned Amigo Cafe (try their excellent coffee or beef in spicy pepper sauce) has one of the few motorized vehicles allowed on the island, a two-stroke miniature fire truck only two meters long. But it's slow—in a real emergency the firemen get up and run! Nearby you'll find a small bookstore and Citicorp Bank, which cashes traveler's checks. Wander through the alleys of Cheung Chau for more discoveries: bakery shops selling miniature egg tarts called *dun tat,* stonemasons fashioning Chinese gravestones for the island's thriving funeral business, fish-processing factories with their distinctive smells, dim-sum restaurants packed in the early mornings but deserted in the afternoons. The Village Tree Inn next to the post office is a popular social center in the evening. Cheung Chau even has its own floating restaurant; from the pier take the sampan with the yellow flag.

The North

The Pak Tai Temple constructed in 1783 honors the Master of Weather and Emperor of the Dark Heaven. Sometime in the late spring, Pak Tai is paraded around town during the famous Bun Festival before being returned to his corner sedan chair for another 12 months. The temple is decrepit and nothing special but the female temple attendant is enthusiastic about all the garish oddities. Note the well-carved solid granite pillars of dragons clutching pearls in their mouths. Photographs of floating children from the spectacular Bun Festival can be seen in the Temple Association Headquarters down the street on the left. Boatbuilders to the north fashion junks without blueprints.

Southern Bell Walking Tour

Walk south past the sterile concrete shopping centers and take the path up the first hill. Soon you'll pass a series of planned villages built by the Round Table Association, then an ice factory stuck in a weedy inlet. The nondescript village of

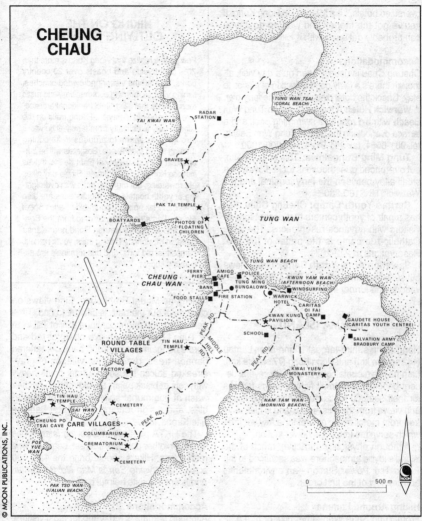

CHEUNG CHAU

RADAR STATION

TAI KWAI WAN

TUNG WAN TSAI (CORAL BEACH)

GRAVES

PAK TAI TEMPLE

BOATYARDS

PHOTOS OF FLOATING CHILDREN

TUNG WAN

TUNG WAN BEACH

FERRY PIER

AMIGO CAFE

POLICE

CHEUNG CHAU WAN

BANK

TUNG MING BUNGALOWS

KWUN YAM WAN (AFTERNOON BEACH)

WINDSURFING

FOOD STALLS

FIRE STATION

WARWICK HOTEL

CARITAS OI FAI CAMP

KWAN KUNG PAVILION

GAUDETE HOUSE (CARITAS YOUTH CENTRE)

SCHOOL

SALVATION ARMY BRADBURY CAMP

ROUND TABLE VILLAGES

TIN HAU TEMPLE

PEAK RD.

MIDDLE HILL RD.

PEAK RD.

ICE FACTORY

KWAI YUEN MONASTERY

TIN HAU TEMPLE

SAI WAN

CEMETERY

PEAK RD.

NAM TAM WAN (MORNING BEACH)

CHEUNG PO TSAI CAVE

CARE VILLAGES

COLUMBARIUM

POE YUE WAN

CREMATORIUM

CEMETERY

PAK TSO WAN (ITALIAN BEACH)

0   500 m

© MOON PUBLICATIONS, INC.

MOON

Sai Wan and an unimpressive Tin Hau Temple overlook a bay of junks.

The Cave of Cheung Po Tsai at the southern tip is not worth the effort to locate. Return instead to the American-built CARE Village and hike along Peak Road to secluded Italian Beach. Although considered the best beach on the island, you might feel strange with the hundreds of Chinese gravesites looking down on you.

Farther on is a crematorium, a columbarium, and expensive condominium complexes built in a pseudo-Spanish style.

Peak Road eventually passes several Christian churches and youth centers before reaching Tung Wan Beach. Windsurfers are available at the Cheung Chau Activities Center on Afternoon Beach. Both of these crowded and dirty beaches have lost their intimacy to condos and oversized hotels. Like they say in Hong Kong: If you've got the money and want to do it, you can probably get away with it.

Accommodations

Cheung Chau is usually seen on a day visit, although there's a fairly good selection of places to stay. Check the hotel displays near the ferry pier.

Warwick Hotel: A modern hotel on Tung Wan Beach with big rooms, a swimming pool, and a terrace overlooking the beach. Tung Wan Beach, tel. 981-0081, fax 981-9174, HK$800-1000.

Tung Ming Bungalows: This small, clean, but overpriced guesthouse is tucked away in a small alley between the ferry terminal and the Warwick. HK$180-280.

Caritas Youth Camp: Cheung Chau also has a pair of youth centers that accept foreign visitors with advance reservations. The large Catholic-run camp is the better of the two. Reservations at 242-2071.

Salvation Army Youth Camp: Great views but surly management. Call 332-4531 for reservations and further information.

LAMMA ISLAND

Hong Kong's third-largest island after Lantau (142 square km) and Hong Kong (77 square km). Lamma is a mountainous island with several decent beaches and small fishing towns famous for their seafood restaurants. Also good hiking and views from the hills. The island is blessedly free from motor traffic except for a few vehicles which serve the immense power station.

Although physically attractive, much of the island's idyllic atmosphere was sacrificed to the Po Lo Tsui Power Station—an environmental horror show of the first order.

Hiking Around Lamma

From Yung Shue Wan either hike or hire a bicycle. Paths lead south past the popular beach at Hung Shing to the fishing village of Sok Kwu Wan, where a dozen seafood restaurants line the waterfront. From Sok Kwu Wan, take a *kaido* (motorized sampan) across to Aberdeen or walk back to Yung Shue Wan for the HYF Ferry to Central.

Hikers may want to scale the 353-meter summit of Yin Shan (Shan Tei Tong), known to colo-

---

HIKING ON THE OUTLYING ISLANDS

Few people realize that Hong Kong is more than 70% countryside and boasts over 20 country parks. All offer the visitor uncrowded beaches, fishing villages, farming communities, and rustic monasteries that still reflect traditional architecture and age-old lifestyles. Hiking trails on the islands vary in difficulty from family-style walks through grasslands to arduous treks cutting through forest plantations. Botanists will be surprised at the wide variety of plant life that thrives in Hong Kong's unique climate. Single-day hikes are rewarding, but multiday treks with overnighting at youth hostels and monasteries are also possible. Pick up the *Countryside Series Sheet No. 3—Lantau and Islands* map from the Central GPO or at 382 Nathan Road near Kansu Street in Kowloon. All hiking trails, youth hostels, campsites, old forts, and bus terminals are accurately shown.

---

nialists as Mount Stenhouse. Fine views on clear days but the path is difficult to find. Time permitting, you might continue to Mot Tat Wan or Tung O, keeping an eye open for red and purple bougainvilleas, green bamboo, tattered banana trees, dragonflies, villages of gray-streaked stucco houses, laundry poles heavy with sets of black pajamas, old men doing their wash at communal spigots, fields of vegetables, and a sign reading, Helicopter Landing Site Keep Clear.

The HKTA publication *Outlying Islands* has details on other points of interest, beaches, and restaurants. Hikers should bring the 1:20,000 scale *Countryside Series Map No. 3—Lantau and Islands* and its helpful booklet.

Accommodations

Although Lamma is a day-trip for most visitors, accommodations are available both at the main village of Yung Shue Wan and at Hung Shing Ye Beach.

Man Lai Wah Hotel: Just below the ferry pier is a small, decent hotel with a/c rooms and private baths. Main St., Yung Shue Wan, tel. 982-0220, HK$250-350.

Lamma Vacation House: Another good spot is south of the pier, across from the seafood

Cheung Chau

cafes. 29 Main St., Yung Shue Wan, tel. 982-0427, HK$200-250 weekdays, HK$375-450 weekends.

Wing Yuen Hostel: Lamma's least expensive hostel offers big discounts for long-term weekly or monthly rentals. Hung Shing Ye Beach, tel. 982-0222, HK$160-200 weekdays, HK$300-420 weekends, HK$2000 monthly.

Concerto Inn: Lamma's most expensive hotel. Hung Shing Ye Beach, tel. 836-3388, HK$500-900.

Han Lok Yuen Hotel: Located on the steep hill overlooking the beach. Hung Shing Ye Beach, tel. 982-0608, HK$300-420.

Transportation

Ferries to Yung Shue Wan on Lamma Island leave 12 times daily from the Central Harbor Pier adjacent to the Outlying Islands Ferry Pier in Central on Hong Kong Island. *Kaidos* leave every two hours from Aberdeen Harbor. The best plan is to ferry from Central to Yung Shue Wan, hike for an hour down to Sok Kwu Wan, then take a ferry or *kaidos* back to Central or Aberdeen.

LANTAU ISLAND

Lantau is twice the size of Hong Kong Island but has only 16,000 inhabitants, the territory's largest and least-densely populated island. Blessed with a rugged landscape of stark beauty and wide-open spaces, Lantau serves as a kind of safety valve for Hong Kong's overcrowded citizens.

Getting Around

Like on the other outlying islands, some of the peace and tranquillity has been lost to condo complexes and vacation resorts, but most of the island remains rugged and wild—an amazing change from the neon jungle of Kowloon. Although the island easily deserves a few days of leisurely exploration, day-trippers can get a quick impression by taking a very early ferry from the Outlying Districts Pier in Central. Alternatively, first visit Peng Chau Island and continue by small boat across the narrow straits to the Trappist Monastery. From here it's a one-hour walk to Silvermine Bay. Buses leave Silvermine for Po Lin Monastery, where most sightseers spend the entire day, returning in the early evening to Silvermine Bay for the return ferry. It's almost impossible to include Cheung Chau in the same day.

Hiking On Lantau

More than 50% of Lantau is a country park of scraggly mountains, lonely valleys, and remote beaches. Literally dozens of trails have been laid out for the weekend explorer. Those with more time and determination might try the 70-km Lantau Trail. Starting at the main port town of Mui Wo (also called Silvermine Bay), this challenging trail is divided into 12 sections of varying difficulties. The first six sections follow a sky-

FUNERALS ON CHEUNG CHAU

Although Chinese religion seems to be a mix of Buddhism and the nonstop pursuit of money, ancestor worship and spirit propitiation actually form the bedrock of their beliefs. Cheung Chau is a likely place to see a traditional Chinese funeral because of the island's large number of cemeteries. Whether relatives of the departed or professional mourners, everyone will be immaculately dressed in white robes. The procession and a small orchestra of Chinese oboes and crashing cymbals follow the immense clover-shaped coffin through the streets to the distant graveyard. Sites are selected by *fung shui* geomancers. Paper objects such as hell notes and car replicas are burned in the temple to symbolically ensure the dead receive some material comforts in the hereafter.

Thus laid properly to rest, the dead become focal points for the living. Twice annually, thousands of Chinese return to the gravesites to consecrate offerings and socialize with friends. The rituals continue after the body has completely decomposed, when the bones are exhumed and cleaned with soap and sandpaper. The entire skeleton is reconstructed by the eldest son, who then places the remains into a large ceramic urn. Bones must be carefully arranged with the foot bones on bottom and skull on top. The urn is then reburied in a smaller and

grandfather bones

less costly spot or taken home to the family shrine. Few seem concerned that these "grandfather urns" are purchased by visitors and later converted into lamps or flower pots! Traditional funeral practices are changing almost as rapidly as the skyline of Central. Permanent plots in private cemeteries have become so expensive (HK$150,000 and up) that over 65% of the dead are now cremated in the territory's 22 crematoriums.

line ridge trail over rugged mountains before finishing at the fishing village of Tai O. Smaller bits and pieces of this trail can be sampled from the Po Lin Monastery. The next six stages circle the island counterclockwise, hugging the coastline back to Silvermine Bay.

All of the trails, campsites, information boards, and youth hostels are carefully labeled on the *Countryside Series Map—Lantau and Islands*, available from the Government Publications Office. Hiking trails have also been graded in difficulty. It is not necessary to do the entire trail—day visitors might just do one small section starting from Silvermine Bay or Po Lin Monastery.

Peng Chau Island

The Lantau ferry pauses at Peng Chau, a tiny and picturesque C-shaped island across a narrow channel from Lantau. Peng Chau retains some of its pre-industrial charm, although modern houses are now replacing traditional struc-

tures as commuters discover the island. Places of interest include a Chinese cemetery and porcelain factories that supply ornamental goods for Hong Kong emporiums. Beaches are small and secluded. Motorized sampans called *kaido* leave from the small pier for the Trappist Monastery on Lantau.

Trappist Monastery

An isolated monastery operated by the Trappist Cistercian Order, one of the strictest in all Catholicdom. Originally established in 1644 by a French cleric living in Peking, the order was moved to Hong Kong in the 1950s for political reasons. Monks keep complete silence while working the vegetable farms and dairy operations that supply some of the finest restaurants in Hong Kong. Try the vegetarian restaurant. Visitors seriously interested in overnights should write to Trappist Haven, Lantau Island, P.O. Box 5, Peng Chau, Hong Kong.

Silvermine Bay

Lantau's main commercial center and transportation hub is named after the old silver mines in the northern part of the valley. There is little of interest here except for a few bars and restaurants. Buses leave from the terminal near the pier.

Po Lin Monastery

Southeast Asia's largest Buddha image has recently been installed at the highly commercialized monastery atop Ngong Ping Plateau. Visible from Macau almost 70 km away, the 16-meter 250-ton statue was constructed in Nanjing and transported to Hong Kong in 219 segments. The basic design and exhibition halls have been modeled after the Temple of Heaven in Beijing.

Overnight accommodations are available in the monastery and youth hostel. Vegetarian meals are served in the monastery.

There's plenty to do up here: watch the sun rise from Lantau Peak, rent a pony for the day, learn about tea production at nearby Lantau Tea Gardens, hike the Lantau Trail. A rougher trail leads down to Tung Chung, an ancient farming community near Buddhist temples and an old fort constructed by Chinese troops at war with the Europeans.

Po Lin, also known as Precious Lotus Monastery, can be reached with bus 2 from Silvermine Bay to Shum Wat Road Circle. A minibus continues up the mountain.

Tai O Village

Tai O is home to a large colony of Tanka boat people whose converted junks form three-story apartment complexes permanently anchored in the muddy bay. The Kwan Ti Temple is dedicated to the God of War and Righteousness, who protects the poor from the rich. Bus 1 leaves Silvermine Bay every 30 minutes for Tai O.

Accommodations

Campsites: Almost a dozen free campsites operated by the government are located across Lantau. Exact locations are shown on the *Countryside Series Map—Lantau and Islands.*

Po Lin Monastery: Dormitory accommodations and three vegetarian meals cost HK$150. Avoid weekends, when half of Hong Kong overruns the mountain. Po Lin, Ngong Ping, tel. 985-5610.

Lantau Tea Gardens: A pleasant alternative to the dorms. Po Lin, Ngong Ping, tel. 985-5161, HK$180-300.

Davis Youth Hostel: The morally less fit might stay at the youth hostel near Po Lin Monastery. Youth hostel membership is required and facilities are open weekends only. Po Lin, Ngong Ping, tel. 985-5610, HK$25.

Trappist Haven Monastery: Several other Buddhist monasteries welcome guests who come for spiritual purposes. Visitors willing to abide by the rules (early rising, periods of silence, courteous behavior) may contact the Trappist monastery in Tai Shui Hang just across from Peng Chau Island. Advance reservations are required from Trappist Haven, Lantau Island, P.O. Box 5, Peng Chau, Hong Kong, or call 987-6286.

Mui Wo Hotels: Over a half-dozen modestly priced hotels are located in Lantau's main town near the ferry pier. None are as romantically located as the facilities near Po Lin, but a stay might be necessary if you miss the last ferry back to Hong Kong Island.

SUGGESTED READINGS

◆ *Another Hong Kong*. Hong Kong: Emphasis, 1989. A guidebook that offers step-by-step walks through the New Territories and Outlying Islands.

◆ Baker, Hugh. *Ancestral Images*. Hong Kong: South China Morning Post, 1979. Reprints of newspaper articles originally published during the late 1970s in a local newspaper. Quirky and highly personalized descriptions of almost everything from Chinese gods to zombies. Hardback sequels include *More Ancestral Images* and *Ancestral Images Again*.

◆ Bloomfield, Frena. *The Book of Chinese Beliefs*. London: Arrow Books, 1983. A brief survey of ancestor worship, *fung shui*, exorcisms, fortune-telling, and other matters of the occult. This easy-to-read and inexpensive little book is an excellent introduction to the mysteries of Chinese religions.

◆ Cameron, Nigel. *Hong Kong: The Cultured Pearl*. Hong Kong: Oxford University Press, 1978. The first half is history but it is the critical second half that holds your interest. Like many other resident writers, Cameron has an obvious love-hate relationship with the place.

◆ Clavell, James. *Tai Pan*. New York: Atheneum and Dell, 1966. Historical fiction based on the founding of Hong Kong. Clavell's *Noble House* describes the wheelings and dealings of Hong Kong *hongs* during the 1960s. Clavell's other Asian-based novels include *Shogun*, set in feudal Japan, and *King Rat*, staged in Singapore during WW II.

◆ Collis, Maurice. *Foreign Mud (Anglo-Chinese Opium War)*. London: Faber and Faber, 1946. The classic retelling of the messy circumstances that led to the founding of Hong Kong. Reprinted by Graham Brash.

◆ Elegant, Robert. *Dynasty*. New York: McGraw-Hill, 1977. Chinese power in Hong Kong during the 20th century. Elegant is a scholar on things Chinese and has written a number of nonfiction books including *China's Red Master, Mao's Great Revolution* and the Time-Life publication *Hong Kong*, an honest look at the author's final days in Hong Kong, where he resided for over 25 years.

◆ *Hong Kong*. Singapore: APA Productions, 1981. Outstanding photographs and a well-written text. This profusely illustrated book is highly recommended for predeparture reading.

◆ Hughes, Richard. *Hong Kong: Borrowed Place—Borrowed Time*. London: Andre Deutsch, 1968. Although written over 20 years ago, this modern classic remains witty and full of genuine insight.

◆ Mason, Richard. *The World of Suzi Wong*. Glasgow: Collins, 1957. Caucasian businessman falls in love with Wanchai bar girl, one of the great love stories of Southeast Asia. The novel was penned in the Luk Kwok Hotel during the 1950s and later made into the classic movie, which forever sealed the image of Hong Kong.

◆ Morris, Jan. *Hong Kong*. London: Viking, 1988. The famous chronicler of British imperialism has written a marvelously evocative and informative travel companion. Highly recommended.

VIETNAM

*Travel is not really trade; it's communication between
people. Just as travel promotes understanding,
understanding promotes peace.*

—Lars-Eric Lindblad

*Let the tourist be cushioned against misadventure.
Your true traveler will not feel that he has had his money's
worth unless he brings back a few scars.*

—Lawrence Durrell,
Spirit of Place

*One who has hotel reservations and speaks no French
is a tourist.*

—Paul Fussell,
Abroad

INTRODUCTION

Vietnam. The name alone evokes unforgettable images: a young girl running down a country road, an execution on the streets of Saigon, helicopter evacuations on the roof of the American Embassy, Tank no. 843 crashing through the gates of the Presidential Palace, boatloads of refugees fleeing for the political freedoms and economic promises of the West.

Despite two decades of peace, it seems that many Westerners still think of Vietnam as a war rather than a country, a misconception fueled by international agendas and Vietnam's reticence to reveal itself to the outside world. As a result, Vietnam remains one of the world's final enigmas, a land we claim to understand but, in reality, know almost nothing about.

Memories of the war and fears of the unknown have long held tourism to a bare minimum. Fortunately—and for good reasons—this seems to be changing.

Vietnam is a destination considered by many veteran travelers among the most beautiful in all of Southeast Asia. The country offers over 2,000 km of magnificent coastline almost completely untouched by mass tourism. There are misty rainforests in the west and north where you find minority tribes and remote hill stations constructed out of old French villas peeling behind coconut palms and rubber plantations. There are exquisite temples and remains of an ancient Cham civilization, narrow streets illuminated by oil-lit lamps that remind you of the Indochina of your dreams, and, most importantly, some of the most hospitable and cultured people you will ever meet.

Twenty years after the end of the war, Vietnam has healed its wounds and learned to forgive and forget. Westerners ready to return the favor should include Vietnam in their travel plans.

THE PHYSICAL SETTING

The Land
Arched like a two-headed Chinese dragon, Vietnam stretches over 1,600 km from the border of China to the Gulf of Thailand in the far south. Vietnam is roughly the size of Japan or California. Endowed with great physical beauty and surprising geographic diversity, the country vaguely resembles a pair of roundish rice baskets balanced at the ends of a long and narrow bamboo pole.

The principal physiographic features are the 1,200-km Annamite (Troung Son) Cordillera, which dominates the interior, and the two alluvial deltas formed by the Red River (Son Hong) in

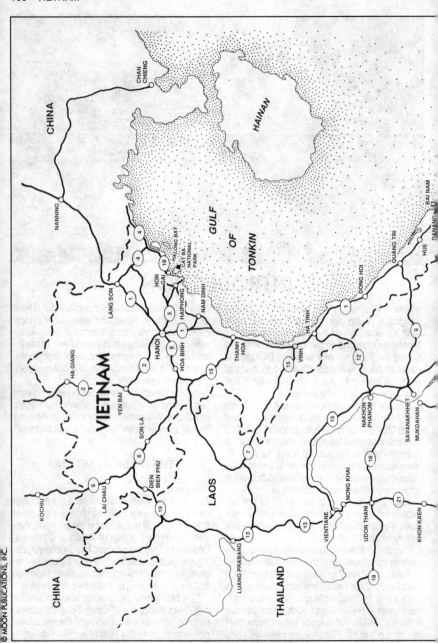

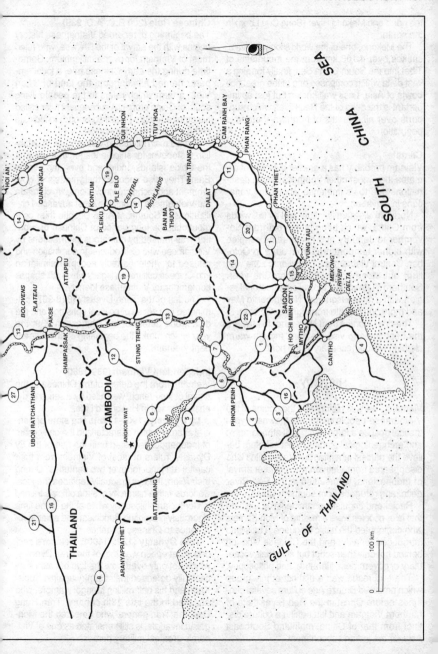

the north and Mekong River (Song Cuu Long) in the south.

The Mekong, one of the world's longest rivers, snakes over 4,100 km from the mountains of Tibet into the South China Sea, finally forming a vast delta which comprises one of the great rice bowls of Asia. Less well known but just as important is the delta of the Red River, which supports over nine-tenths of northern Vietnam's population.

Climate

Vietnam probably has a greater diversity of climates than most other Southeast Asian destinations due to its immense length and variations in elevation.

Northern Vietnam is influenced by the winds from China, which bring bitter cold from November to January and heavy rains coupled with higher temperatures from June to October. Central Vietnam is a transitional zone with light but steady rains throughout the year. Southern Vietnam is a typical subequatorial region with a dry season from November to May and monsoon climate from June to October.

The drier months from November to May are the best times to visit Vietnam, though warm clothing will be necessary in the north.

HISTORY

Vietnam's earliest history and the origins of the Vietnamese people remain somewhat hypothetical despite a large number of ethnographic and archaeological studies. Most scholars believe the earliest inhabitants were Negritos who disappeared from Vietnam with the later arrival of Indonesians, who settled in the Red River delta, and refugees from southern China.

Racial and linguistic characteristics indicate that later peoples were a mixture of Mon-Khmers who contributed the basic language, Thais who introduced tonality, and the Chinese who left behind not only their script but also their vocabulary of government, literature, and philosophy.

The end result was a distinct ethnic group which practiced Bronze Age culture several centuries before Christ in the Red River delta of northern Vietnam and left behind a culture distinct from that of China, mainland Southeast Asia, or the Indian subcontinent.

Chinese Rule (200 B.C.-A.D. 939)

The beginning of recorded Vietnamese history begins with the arrival of the Chinese, who ruled most of Vietnam for over a millennium. Sometime during the early Chinese rule, a local emperor named his kingdom the land of "Nam Viet," a term which refers to the people living south of China proper. A subsequent ruler called his empire Annam ("Pacified South") to indicate complete Chinese domination.

China's main interest in Vietnam was to establish a stopover for ships engaged in trade with the Spice Islands, India, and even the Middle East. They also imposed their models of government and technical innovations, which made the Vietnamese among the most advanced civilizations in Southeast Asia. Despite their contributions, the long period of Chinese occupation was marked by numerous insurrections by Vietnamese who disliked foreign domination and refused to wholeheartedly accept assimilation into Chinese culture—a legacy which still shapes contemporary Vietnamese identity.

The fall of the Tang Dynasty (618-907) culminated in a series of political uprisings and the disastrous defeat of the Chinese in 939, the year which marks the beginning of an independent Vietnam.

Independent Vietnam (939-1860)

Vietnam, from the defeat of the Chinese to the arrival of the French, was ruled by a series of dynasties based in Hanoi and Hue.

Ly Dynasty (1009-1225): The state of general anarchy which characterized the early years of independence lasted until the rise of the Ly Dynasty, rulers of most of Vietnam from their capital at Hanoi for over two centuries. During their reign, the Lys gradually replaced the local warlords with a hierarchy of state officials trained in Confucian philosophy while at the same time vigorously promoting Buddhism and a fierce resistance to Chinese influence.

Tran Dynasty (1225-1400): Vietnam's second great epoch was that of the Tran Dynasty, which not only overthrew the Lys but also successfully defended their country against Kublai Khan and his half-million Mongol warriors, who attacked in the late 13th century. Tran Hung Dao, the Tran general who defeated the Mongolian invaders, is still venerated as one of Vietnam's greatest military heroes.

SIGHTSEEING ATTRACTIONS

Despite Vietnam's great attractions, the disadvantages are just as plentiful. Whether you arrive as an independent traveler or on an escorted tour, Vietnam can be an expensive and frustrating destination. Group tourists are often charged unreasonable rates for rudimentary hotels, uninspired food, inadequate air and land transport, and an absence of reliable financial and communication systems. Just as disturbing is the apparent greed of tourist authorities and Vietnamese citizens who seem determined to mine, without conscience, the pocketbooks of the foreign tourist. Even sightseers with minimal expectations of comfort and convenience will find Vietnam a challenging destination.

And yet tourism continues to boom, as thousands of Europeans, American veterans, and Vietnamese expatriates arrive to discover the mystique of Asia's final frontier. The bottom line is that jaded travelers, who despair of ever finding any place fresh or unspoiled, will find Vietnam a sparkling revelation, limited in amenities but full of the qualities that their absence encourages.

Saigon (Ho Chi Minh City)

Most visitors arrive in the vibrant former capital of South Vietnam, renamed Ho Chi Minh City (HCMC) after the war, though everyone still calls it Saigon. The city itself is a startling study in contrasts between the poverty of socialism and the heady spirit of capitalism which seems to infect every nook and cranny of the city.

Vietnam's largest city and principal seaport still shows some of the old French-colonial charm in its faded architecture, long tree-lined avenues, and sidewalk cafes that serve up cafe lattes and croissants. More contemporary attractions include an informal "war tour" of the museums and other public buildings which figured so prominently in the American conflict. Saigon also offers religious shrines, excellent shopping, and all sorts of nightlife from seedy nightclubs to splashy cabarets. Saigon is a very wild place.

Vung Tao

Two hours southeast of Saigon is a popular seaside resort with a fairly good stretch of sand plus inexpensive restaurants, cafes, and colonial villas converted into hotels and guesthouses. A convenient side trip from Saigon, Vung Tao also has a temple consecrated to the whale cult and other oddities such as a 30-meter statue of Christ erected by the Americans in 1971.

Mekong Delta

The vast alluvial delta of the Mekong River offers a great deal to the traveler: beautiful scenery, friendly people, and an almost complete lack of Western tourists. Visitors can spend a few days in the villages nearest Saigon, such as Mytho, Vinh Long, and Cantho, or make a longer excursion to the more remote and almost completely untouched villages of Long Xuyen, Chau Doc, and Rach Gia, all located toward the Cambodian border.

Dalat

A highlight of any visit to Vietnam, Dalat is an old French hill station nestled amid rolling hills, pine-covered valleys, and lakes in the central highlands some 300 km northwest of Saigon. Dalat's bracing temperatures and quiet beauty guarantee a welcome relief from the heat and noise of Saigon.

Sights around town include some old French-colonial cathedrals, seminaries, and romantic old villas, many of which have been converted into cozy hotels. Outside town are natural attractions such as the Valley of Love and the Lake of Sorrows.

Nha Trang

Nha Trang is an important seaport known for its six-km white-sand beach and warm waters popular with scuba divers and fishermen. The town has a vaguely Mediterranean feel and one of the better beaches located within an urban area in Vietnam, plus Buddhist pagodas, a Christian cathedral, a limited amount of war nostalgia, and ancient Cham towers.

Hoi An

Visitors who enjoy the timeless atmosphere of old towns should visit this crumbling village, 32 km south of Danang. Once a major trading port, Hoi An is now a sleepy fishing port blessed with fine Chinese temples and one of the largest arrays of prewar architecture in Vietnam. Highly recommended.

Danang

Danang, Vietnam's fourth-largest city, is perhaps best known abroad as the seaport where American Marines first landed in March 1965 to secure an air base and initiate the American conflict. Danang is

SIGHTSEEING ATTRACTIONS (continued)

also the former homeland of the Chams, who once controlled Vietnam from Hue to Vung Tao. The Cham Museum provides a good introduction.

Other attractions include the Marble Mountains and the famous Vietnam-era resort of China Beach.

Lang Co Beach
Several dazzling beaches are located about 35 km north of Danang and just beyond Hai Van Pass, the rugged limestone karst which once formed the physical barrier between ancient Vietnam to the north and the Champa Kingdom in the south.

Lang Co Peninsula is highly recommended to all lovers of tropical beauty. The sparkling 10-km beach is wonderfully set between the emerald-blue waters of the South China Sea and an idyllic lagoon which washes up toward the mountains—perhaps the most spectacular beach in Vietnam.

Hue
Hue is Vietnam's artistic, cultural, and historical center, having served as the imperial capital of the Nguyen kings for almost 150 years. The town's main attractions are the baroque tombs of the Nguyen emperors, the remains of the old Imperial City, and its superbly romantic location on the banks of the Perfume River.

Demilitarized Zone (DMZ)
The DMZ, which once served as the boundary between North and South Vietnam, is defined by the Ben Hai River, which follows the 17th parallel.

Among the most famous sites are the battlefield at Khe Sanh; Vinh Moc Tunnels, where hundreds of

Vietnamese lived during the war; Doc Mieu Base, former headquarters for American electronic surveillance; Con Thien Firebase, the primary base for an elaborate military barrier designed to detect enemy incursions across the DMZ; Truong Son National Cemetery; Camp Carroll; and Hamburger Hill, scene of a terrible 1968 battle in which 241 Americans died in less than one week.

Most of the war memorabilia has been dismantled and hauled away by Vietnamese scrap collectors, though American veterans and anyone else intrigued by the war will enjoy a visit to the DMZ.

Hanoi
Hanoi, the capital of the Socialist Republic of Vietnam, is a decrepit but atmospheric city of tree-lined boulevards, narrow alleys mercifully free of traffic, and weathered colonial buildings still unchanged from the days of the French. The major attractions—Ho Chi Minh's Mausoleum and an assortment of religious shrines—are secondary to the timeless ambience found in the streets of the Old City.

Halong Bay
Halong Bay and Cat Ba National Park are undoubtedly Vietnam's most magnificent natural marvels. Centerpiece of the movie *Indochine,* Halong Bay is a stunning combination of over 1,000 limestone islets rising dramatically from an iridescent sea—a visual wonderland comparable only to Guilin in China.

The beaches are disappointing and facilities are simple by Western standards, but visitors with sufficient time will find Halong a welcome change from the urbanized destinations in Vietnam.

Le Dynasty (1428-1776): The decline of the Tran Dynasty was followed by yet another Chinese invasion and a Ming-directed administration which ruthlessly exploited the hapless country. Hatred of Chinese occupation forces led to the rise of Emperor Le Loi, who established the Le Dynasty and drove the Chinese from Vietnam. For his remarkable military accomplishments, Le Loi is also honored as one of Vietnam's great heroes in the ongoing struggle against Chinese hegemony.

The Le Dynasty also pursued a policy of territorial expansion which drove the Chams from southern Vietnam and integrated Saigon into a unified nation shortly before 1700.

Nguyen Dynasty (1802-1883): Vietnam after the Le Dynasty was carved up into two divisions which lasted until 1802, when Emperor Gia Long established the Nguyen Dynasty—the final Vietnamese dynasty—from his royal capital at Hue. Gia Long captured Hanoi and, once again, re-unified the country under a single ruling family. Today, the Nguyen era is regarded as the artistic culmination of modern Vietnamese history.

French Rule (1860-1954)
France's role in Vietnamese history was an outgrowth of the rising hostility of Vietnamese Mandarins against Catholic missionaries who were having great success in the Buddhist

country. After the execution of 25 European priests and 30,000 Vietnamese Catholics between 1848 and 1860, French forces attacked Saigon and forced Emperor Tu Duc to cede three southern provinces and create the French colony of Cochin China. In 1883, Vietnam was formally divided into the French protectorates of Tonkin (North Vietnam), Annam (Central Vietnam), and Cochin China (South Vietnam), though the entire region was simply known as French Indochina.

French rule improved the physical infrastructure and brought a degree of stability to the country, though ill-conceived policies devastated the peasantry, who fell farther into debt and servitude. As elsewhere in Southeast Asia, heavy-handed policies of the colonial masters led to the rise of revolutionary movements such as the Indochina Communist Party, established in 1930 by Ho Chi Minh.

The defeat of French colonial forces at Dien Bien Phu in 1954 marked the end of the First Indochina War, while a joint French-Vietnamese conference in Geneva the same year divided Vietnam along the 17th parallel into two countries. An all-Vietnamese election scheduled for 1956 to unify the country was never approved by either the U.S. or South Vietnam, as it was believed the vote would have gone to the communists in the north.

The American Conflict (1954-75)

The withdrawal of the French was countered by the arrival of the Americans, who assumed responsibility for the survival of South Vietnam by providing financial aid and military advice for the anticommunist government. In 1954, a Roman Catholic Confucian named Ngo Diem returned from his self-imposed exile in the U.S. to become president of South Vietnam. Although the situation was stable for several years, the insurgency waged by the underground Viet Minh (called the Viet Cong by the Americans) and an unhappy military elite led to the overthrow of Diem in 1963. Nine changes of government followed before the military regime of Nguyen Ky and Thieu seized control in 1965.

South Vietnam continued to deteriorate. Buddhist priests opposed to Thieu's government were soon burning themselves in public spectacles that shocked the viewers of American television and galvanized the world on the troubles of a distant Asian land. The U.S. government responded on 7 March 1965 by sending 3,500 Marines to the beaches of Danang in an effort to protect an endangered airfield. By July the number had reached 75,000 and by early 1968, over 500,000 American soldiers were stationed in Vietnam.

The Vietnam War reached a climax with the Tet Offensive of February 1968, when the Viet Minh attacked more than 100 cities and military bases in the south. Although the offensive was a devastating military defeat for the communists, it was an important psychological victory which convinced many Americans that total victory in Vietnam would require unacceptable sacrifices. Chicago rioted, Watts burned, Lyndon quit, and the Americans withdrew from Vietnam shortly before Tank no. 843 crashed through the gates of the Presidential Palace. The Vietnam War was soon over.

Reunified Vietnam

Victory by the Viet Minh did not signal better days but rather a period of political revenge, in which tens of thousands were exterminated or sent off to reeducation camps, and a period of economic collapse which has made Vietnam among the world's poorest countries. No matter your feelings about the war, the reunified government of Vietnam has mismanaged the country, repressed human rights, alienated the most important segments of its population, created over a half-million political and economic refugees, and, finally, inflicted on the nation one of the world's most disastrous economic models.

Twenty years of failure seems finally to be having an effect on the rulers of Vietnam, who announced a policy of economic *doi moi* (new life) in 1991.

Recent changes on a social level are even more startling: today, you can purchase war-era Zippos in Hanoi, listen to the Doors wail in Saigon's Apocalypse Cafe, or sign up for the annual surfing contest at China Beach.

President Clinton, perhaps reluctant to expose himself to criticism that he is soft on Vietnam, is expected to grant full recognition to Vietnam in the near future, a formality which will improve tourism but, more importantly, allow American investors to enter what is expected to be one of the new economic tigers of Southeast Asia.

THE PEOPLE

Vietnam is the world's 12th-most-populous country, with about 70 million people who primarily reside along the coast and in the lowland provinces of the Red and Mekong river deltas. Overall population density of 200 people per square km and urban density of over 1,000 people per square km make Vietnam among the world's most densely populated agricultural countries. The problem is exacerbated by high birth rates and the fact that over 50% of the population is under 20 years of age.

Vietnamese

An estimated 85% of the population are ethnic Vietnamese (Viet Kinh), who were Sinicized during the 1,000 years of Chinese rule but who have successfully maintained their cultural and ethnic identity. Ethnolinguistic studies indicate that the Vietnamese are a mixture of migrants from southern China, Mon-Khmers, and Thais from the west, and Malayo-Indonesians who arrived over two millennia ago. Originally residing in the Red River delta of northern Vietnam, the Vietnamese progressively moved south to populate central Vietnam around A.D. 1000 and the Mekong River delta in the 17th century.

Chinese Vietnamese

Vietnam's largest ethnic minority are the Chinese (Viet Kieu), who number about four million and primarily live in southern urban areas such as the Cholon District in Saigon. Most have adopted Vietnamese nationality but retain their ethnic identity through language, school systems, and social organizations arranged around their dialect and provincial origins.

Successful at commerce, banking, and finance, Chinese Vietnamese have long been Vietnam's most energetic but persecuted minority. Government persecution after the Viet Minh victory forced almost two million Chinese to flee Vietnam between 1975 and 1990—a full one-third of the Chinese population. Some say the exodus was seen by the government as an easy way to confiscate the wealth of the emigrants and purge the country of its ethnic minority.

Fortunately, the Vietnamese government now recognizes their importance in the national economy and encourages the return of overseas Chinese who are largely responsible for the economic miracle of the south.

Montagnards (Highland Peoples)

Vietnam's 54 ethnic minority groups—called Montagnards by the French—total roughly eight million people or about 13% of the national population. Most of these minorities dwell in the northern mountains near the Chinese border and in the Central Highlands, which comprise about 75% of Vietnam's land area.

Centuries of isolation ended abruptly in the 1940s, when Vietnamese revolutionaries established their resistance bases in highland areas and recruited minority soldiers for their war of national liberation. Other highland groups such as the Montagnard FULRO guerrillas were enlisted by the U.S. military and the South Vietnamese government in the war against the Viet Minh. Today, most have returned to their simple lives as mountain farmers who use slash-and-burn techniques to raise rice, vegetables, and a bit of opium.

The highland groups are often grouped according to their ethnolinguistic roots and geographic locations. Major groups in the northern mountains include the Thai (Black, Red, and White Thai), who number almost one million, the Nung, who have been considerably influenced by Viet culture, and smaller groups such as the Hmong, who share cultural roots with the hilltribe peoples of northern Thailand.

Central Highland groups such as the animist Jarai and Raday are often seen in the marketplaces of Dalat and Bon Me Thout, the capital of Dac Lac Province.

Minorities in the far south include the Chams, who were driven from the coastal homelands by the Vietnamese in the 16th century, and the Mon-Khmers, who are descendants of the Khmer civilization that once stretched from the South China Sea to Angkor.

PRACTICAL INFORMATION

A State Of Flux

Special note must be made about travel restrictions and conditions in Vietnam. All writers discussing travel details about a rapidly changing country such as Vietnam are at the mercy of government agencies, which often make sudden changes in the rules and regulations. For example, the first edition of this book stated that all visitors to Vietnam must sign up with an organized tour arranged through Vietnam Tourism. Six months later this restriction was dropped and independent tourism became a viable option. In early 1993, the Vietnamese government dropped the permit system for outlying provinces; visitors can now travel freely except in military zones and other restricted areas. It is also anticipated that the American government will soon lift the remaining limits on organized travel to Vietnam.

Another problem is that the rules are interpreted throughout Vietnam by different officials in various ways. Government officials and policemen often view the fining of Western tourists as a convenient way to supplement their meager incomes. While it's best to follow the rules, everyone should also be prepared to bargain down bribes while understanding the motivation behind the shakedown.

For these reasons, the following advice on visas, permits, transportation, money, and other travel details is subject to change and should be confirmed with travel agencies that specialize in Vietnam, especially the budget outfits on Khao San Road in Bangkok.

As always, your best sources of current information will be other travelers who have just returned from Vietnam. Final details can be ironed out after arrival in Saigon.

GETTING THERE

By Air

Bangkok is the most convenient embarkation port for flights to Saigon. Thai International, Air France, and Bangkok Airways fly twice daily to Saigon for US$180 one-way and US$360 roundtrip. Other services include Philippine Airlines from Manila, MAS from Kuala Lumpur,

Cathay Pacific from Hong Kong, Garuda from Jakarta, Singapore Airlines from Singapore, and JAL from Tokyo.

Travel to Saigon on Vietnam Airlines (Hang Khong, known among connoisseurs as "Hang On Vietnam") is a frightening experience best left to those unable to fly on airlines with better safety records.

Air services are also available from Bangkok to Hanoi, but most travelers fly to Saigon and then overland to Hanoi before flying on to Laos or back to Bangkok. Travel agents on Khao San Road charge about US$350 for a visa and airfare for Bangkok-Saigon and Hanoi-Vientiane.

Airport departure tax is US$6.

By Land From Cambodia

Land access is now possible from Cambodia, depending on the political situation. Buses depart daily from Phnom Penh in the early morning and take about 12 hours to reach Saigon. Travelers must have the proper endorsements on their visas or run the risk of being turned back at the border. Exit and entry stamps can be changed in Phnom Penh. See the Cambodia chapter for details.

Buses from Saigon to Phnom Penh leave from 155 Nguyen Hue Blvd., adjacent to the Rex Hotel, daily at 0600 except on Sunday. Travelers whose visas state their point of exit as Saigon or Hanoi airports can change this at several Saigon travel agencies, such as Ann Tourist on Ton That Tung St. and Vacation Planners on Tran Nhat Dvat Street.

By Land From Laos

Several American tour companies are now using land connections between Laos and Vietnam. As of this writing, these border crossings were not open to independent travelers, though this may change in the near future. Check with other travelers, tourist offices, guesthouse owners, and budget travel agencies on Khao San Road in Bangkok. All visitors must have proper visas and the necessary entry and exit permits.

Highway 9: The most popular route is on Highway 9 from Savannakhet in southern Laos through Khe Sanh in central Vietnam and then to the coast just north of Hue. This exciting option makes it possible to tour northeast Thailand, southern Laos, and Vietnam before continuing overland across Cambodia and back to Bangkok.

Highway 7: Another possible land route is from the Plain of Jars in northeastern Laos to Vinh in Vietnam via Highway 7. This route has been open for several years though only group tours have been allowed.

Highway 6: Certainly the most fascinating and ultimately useful route is between Luang Prabang and Hanoi via the famous battleground of Dien Bien Phu in northwestern Vietnam. This intriguing land crossing would allow you to transit the entire length of Vietnam without having to backtrack or skip a large portion of the country—a complete circuit of Indochina from Nong Khai to Laos and northern Vietnam, including the vast length of coastal Vietnam.

By Land From China
Highway 1 from Hanoi to southern China is expected to open to Western travelers in the near future. It now appears possible to exit Vietnam to China with the proper exit visa (Lang Son) plus a travel permit for Lang Son, obtained from travel agencies in Hanoi. You'll also need a visa for China.

To enter Vietnam overland from China (from Nanning, capital of Guangxi Province), you'll need a Vietnamese visa marked "Huu Nghi Quan" ("Friendship Gate"). Travel agents in Hong Kong can help with the details.

By Sea
When the U.S. eased restrictions on the marketing of tours to Vietnam in 1992, cruise lines were among the first travel companies to take advantage of the new policy. The following companies offer cruises along the coastline of Vietnam, with optional extensions to China and Southeast Asia.

Pearl Cruises: The 400-passenger *Ocean Pearl* does a circuit from Hong Kong and Manila with six stops in Vietnam. Call (800) 556-8850.

Classical Cruises: Classical's German-constructed *Aurora 1* sails twice yearly between January and April from Hong Kong to Bangkok via six ports in Vietnam. Call (800) 252-7745.

Abercrombie and Kent: Travelers looking for a smaller ship might try the 96-passenger *Explorer,* which sails from Saigon to Hong Kong

SAMPLE TRAVEL TIMES BY BUS	
Saigon-Nha Trang	12 hours
Nha Trang-Danang	12 hours
Danang-Hue	3 hours
Hue-Vinh	14 hours
Vinh-Hanoi	14 hours

via Vung Tau, Nha Trang, Qui Nhon, Danang, Hue, Haiphong, Halong Bay, and the Hainan Straits. Call (800) 323-7308.

GETTING AROUND

Getting around Vietnam can be frustrating and time-consuming due to the sad state of the roads and the disorganized condition of buses and trains. Another problem is the government bureaucracy, which remains suspicious about Westerners freely wandering around the country. Bring along plenty of patience.

Fortunately, Vietnam has an extensive bus network which reaches every accessible corner of the country, and a dependable—if slow—train service from Saigon to Hanoi. Vietnam Airlines is the quickest way to get around, though routes are limited to major towns and flights are often booked weeks in advance.

Air
Vietnam Airlines operates daily flights between Saigon and Hanoi with three stops weekly in Danang.

Most other towns are only served once a week—a big problem for visitors with limited time. For example, Vietnam Airlines flies once weekly from Saigon to Dalat, Hue, Nha Trang, and Qhi Nhon. From Hanoi, Vietnam Airlines flies once weekly to Dien Bien Phu, Dalat, Hue, Nha Trang, Pleiku, and Vinh.

Reservations should be made as soon as you arrive in Vietnam and reconfirmed within 48 hours of departure. Tickets are payable in U.S. dollars, but traveler's checks are sometimes accepted. Overbooked flights are common, though cancellations and no-shows allow most travelers to sign the waiting list and make their flight. Flights generally leave mornings before 0700.

Pacific Airlines, a new service inaugurated in 1993, flies many of the same routes as Vietnam Airlines at the same price, but with better planes and better service.

By Bus

Buses and minibuses serve most major destinations in Vietnam. Service is slow since less than 20% of the nation's roads are surfaced and many of the bridges destroyed during the war are still down. Be prepared for breakdowns and impromptu stops for engine repairs. On the other hand, overland travel is the best way to see the country and experience Vietnam off the beaten track.

The best roads are in the south, while those in the north are dismal to nonexistent. For this reason, many travelers take a bus from Saigon to Danang or Hue and continue by train up to Hanoi.

Bus stations are usually located on the outskirts of town and departures are in the early-morning hours from 0400 to 0600. Minibuses with reserved seating and a/c now serve many of the more important destinations. Advance booking of express buses and minibuses is recommended whenever possible. Prices are low despite the fact that foreign tourists are sometimes charged an extra fee over local rates.

See the "Sample Travel Times by Bus" chart for an idea of what to expect.

By Train

The Reunification Express, which connects Saigon to Hanoi, is a slow and densely crowded service that passes through some of the most amazing scenery in all of Southeast Asia.

Choices include ordinary trains, which have hard wooden benches and take 68 hours, express trains (TN2 and TN4), which have padded couchettes and take 58 hours, and a so-called special express (TBN8), which covers the 1,730 kilometers in about 48 hours, provided the train isn't derailed or struck by a typhoon.

Train travel is an outstanding way to go, but fares are not cheap, since Western visitors are charged about four times the official rate. This makes train travel almost as expensive as air transport. For example, Saigon to Hanoi on the express train with sleeper costs US$130 while the airfare is US$150.

Some travelers have reportedly been able to buy train tickets at Vietnamese rates with the aid of local contacts. A student ID purchased in Bangkok can also help obtain lower rates.

Car Rental

Cars with drivers are a sensible option for groups who wish to travel from Saigon to Hanoi in relative comfort. Cars rented from Vietnam Tourism are very expensive, but from smaller outfits in Saigon the cost can be quite reasonable. For example, a seven-day tour of South Vietnam and the Central Highlands costs about US$350, while a 16-day journey from Saigon to Hanoi is US$500-600. Split among four travelers this is a great way to explore the country. Guesthouses in Saigon can locate the cheaper car-rental agencies.

Local Transportation

Local transportation in major cities is provided by old Russian Volga taxis, tricycles known as *cyclos* which cost about US$.50 per hour, and bicycles rented from guesthouses and rental shops.

ORGANIZED TOURS

American tour operators are now permitted to book trips into Vietnam, though visas must be obtained at overseas Vietnamese embassies and American airlines are still prohibited from flying directly into Vietnam.

Most American, European, and Australian tour companies rely on Asian-based operators that have been running tours into Vietnam for several years—such as Tour East, Diethelm Travel, and the East-West group in Bangkok. In turn, these Bangkok-based tour operators sell packages put together by Vietnam Tourism or Saigon Tourism, the official representatives for promoting tourism in the country.

Tours organized by Vietnam Tourism range from three to 21 days in length and cost US$100-125 per day including internal transportation, accommodations, guides, and a limited number of meals.

Less expensive tours at US$25-35 per day can be arranged with private tour companies in Saigon such as Ann Tourist, Youth Tourist Centre, Far East Tourist, Peace Tours, and Vacation Planners. These tours include a car or minibus with driver and whatever permits may be required. Passengers select and pay for their

THAI TOUR OPERATORS

Air People Tour & Travel	183 Rajadamri Rd.	tel. (662) 254-3921	fax 255-3750
Diethelm Travel	140 Wireless Rd.	tel. 255-9150	fax 256-0248
Exotissimo Travel	21/17 Sukumvit Soi 4	tel. 253-5240	fax 254-7683
MK Ways	57/11 Wireless Rd.	tel. 254-5583	fax 280-2920
Vista Travel	244 Khao San Rd.	tel. 282-9339	fax 281-3216

own hotels and restaurants. Obviously, the cheapest tours are sold in Saigon, not in Bangkok or abroad.

See the "American Tour Operators" chart for the phone numbers of U.S. firms arranging tours to Vietnam.

Thai Tour Operators

Bangkok now has dozens of travel agencies which book tours directly with Vietnam Tourism or act as agents for the officially recognized outlets. The largest concentrations of budget agencies are on Khao San Road and around the Malaysia Hotel, while upscale operators are found on Sukumvit and Silom roads. Prices vary sharply and it pays to shop around. Major operators are listed in the "Thai Tour Operators" chart.

INDEPENDENT TRAVEL

Independent travel is now permitted in Vietnam despite the usual hassles with internal transportation and obtaining services at local, not tourist, rates.

The rule that all visitors must enter on a group tour was dropped several years ago. Today, most travelers pick up their visa and air tickets from a budget travel agency on Khao San Road in Bangkok and are on their way within a few days.

The most popular package sold by travel agents includes a Vietnamese visa, an air ticket to Saigon, overland transport to Hanoi, and a flight to Vientiane, all for about US$350. Those who wish to include Cambodia can fly to Siem Reap or Phnom Penh and then continue overland to Saigon.

The Vietnamese actually love independent travelers, viewing them as easy sources of extra cash through penalties, permits, and all sorts of fines. The vagueness of Vietnamese laws

regarding tourism and the poverty of most government officials has created a cottage industry of ongoing fines and bribes.

Visitors should not uniformly accept these shakedowns. Keep calm and smile, insist on your innocence, and ask for a reduction in the fine. Most fines in the US$45-200 range can be talked down to US$10-20, a sizable sum in a country where the average monthly income is just US$15.

TRAVEL FORMALITIES

Visas

All visitors to Vietnam must have a visa—arranged by travel agents or tour operators, or obtained directly from a Vietnamese embassy. Visas are good for 30 days and cost US$50-100, depending on the travel agency or whether you obtain your visa directly from a Vietnamese diplomatic office.

The Vietnamese Embassy in Bangkok at 83/1 Wireless Rd., tel. 251-7201, grants visas during office hours, 0830-1100 and 1300-1600. Other Vietnamese diplomatic offices are located in Phnom Pehn, London, Paris, Berlin, Jakarta, Rome, Tokyo, Vientiane, Kuala Lumpur, and Manila.

As of this writing, travel agencies in the U.S. obtain their visas from the Vietnamese embassies in either Canada or Mexico, but a Vietnamese embassy is expected to open in Washington, D.C. after restrictions are relaxed by the Clinton administration.

Visas should be obtained on separate pieces of paper rather than stamped directly into your passport.

Allow about three weeks to obtain a visa in the U.S. or Australia and a few days in Bangkok. Tour operators listed above can obtain visas for a reasonable service charge.

AMERICAN TOUR OPERATORS

Abercrombie and Kent	(800) 323-7308
Advantage Travel	(800) 882-2098
Adventure Center	(800) 227-8747
All Adventure Travel	(800) 537-4025
Asian Pacific Adventures	(800) 825-1680
Bolder Adventures	(800) 397-5917
Bryan World Tours	(800) 255-3507
Diva Worldwide	(415) 777-5351
InnerAsia	(800) 777-8183
InterPacific Tours	(800) 221-3594
Mountain Travel Sobek	(800) 227-2384
Orient Flexi-Pax Tours	(800) 545-5540
Overseas Adventure Travel	(800) 221-0814
South Sea Travel	(800) 546-7890
TTS Tourism	(206) 721-3928
Travcoa	(800) 992-2004
Wilderness Travel	(800) 368-2794
Wings of the Worlds	(416) 482-1223
Zegrahm Expeditions	(800) 285-4000

Your visa should be obtained *before* you enter Indochina to avoid lengthy delays and other bureaucratic hassles.

Recent reports indicate that visas are *sometimes* granted on arrival at the Saigon airport. This formality should be confirmed with a Vietnamese diplomatic office prior to departure for Vietnam.

Visa Extensions

Visas can be extended at Immigration Police offices in Saigon and Hanoi. Technically, visa extensions are only granted with the purchase of a tour, though travel agents in Saigon and Hanoi are able to work around this rule. Many of the budget guesthouses in Vietnam are now affiliated with travel agencies that obtain visa extensions at reasonable cost—a sensible option which avoids much of the bureaucratic red tape which strangles the Vietnamese tourist industry.

Two-week extensions cost US$10-20 and the process can usually be repeated several times for a total travel time of up to two months.

It is advisable to bring along six passport-size photos and make several photocopies of your

visa, passport, and entry/exit card to show—and leave—with immigration officials and police. Whenever possible, hand over these photocopies rather than the original documents; Vietnamese officials often hold passports in an attempt to extort extra payments from tourists.

Entry And Exit Stamps

Vietnamese visas include your points of entry and exit, usually the airports in Saigon or Hanoi. Travelers intending to enter or exit the country overland from Cambodia or Laos should be sure to obtain the correct entry and exit stamps at the Foreign Ministry offices in Saigon and Hanoi if they decide to change travel itineraries after arrival in Vietnam.

Airport Arrival And Customs

All visitors must fill in a detailed customs report which must be shown to customs officials when they leave the country. Customs forms and currency declarations are rarely checked on departure, but it's a good idea to keep currency-exchange receipts and other records in order. Also see "Changing Money."

Photographers should note that the X-ray machines in Vietnam are antiquated and all film should be hand-carried through customs. The same rule applies on departure.

Police Registration

All visitors not on an organized tour must register with the Immigration Police within 48 hours of arrival in Vietnam. Registration is usually done through Vietnam Tourism or private agencies which operate in Saigon and Hanoi. Check with your hotel or guesthouse owner.

Internal Travel Permits

Foreigners in Vietnam are no longer required to obtain internal travel permits. This restriction was dropped in early 1993, after complaints by potential investors trying to check out Vietnam's emerging economy, and due to the fact that almost nobody was checking these permits.

Visitors, however, are barred from some border areas, military zones, and other areas the government deems sensitive.

Tourist Information

Vietnam Tourism offices located in nearly every major tourist destination can help with private guides, car rentals, and escorted tours, but are useless for independent travelers.

You may, however, need to contact Vietnam Tourism for information on visa extensions and other paperwork. Provincial tourism offices located outside the main towns can also help with travel arrangements.

MONEY

The unit of currency is the *dong,* though the U.S. dollar is widely accepted throughout the country.

American dollars, most European currencies, and traveler's checks can be exchanged at banks, hotels, shops, and money vendors who work on the streets of Saigon and Hanoi. Black-market rates from independent vendors are somewhat higher, but perhaps not worth the risk due to rip-offs and legal consequences.

Changing Money
Exchange rates have risen dramatically from 900 *dong* per dollar in 1989 to over 12,000 *dong* in early 1994. Vietnam's steep inflation rate hardly affects Western visitors since most hotels, guides, and taxi drivers in major tourist destinations quote their rates in dollars and not *dong.* On the other hand, *dong* are the accepted form of currency outside Saigon and Hanoi, where it can be difficult or impossible to exchange traveler's checks. *This chapter quotes rates in dollars* to sidestep problems with the declining *dong.*

Receipts should be retained for reexchange on departure from Vietnam and to satisfy customs officials who sometimes check currency-declaration forms.

Reexchange may be impossible at the airport; spend *all* your *dong* prior to departure.

One strategy is to bring along a handful of American dollars and cover any shortages with traveler's checks.

Credit Cards
Visa and MasterCard are accepted by larger hotels and restaurants in Vietnam. Cash advances on Visa cards can be obtained from Vietcombanks in Saigon and Hanoi. Due to the Trading with the Enemy Act, credit cards issued in the U.S. cannot be honored in Vietnam until full diplomatic relations are established. This

formality will hopefully be completed during the Clinton administration.

Costs
On a local level, Vietnam is one of the best travel bargains in Asia. Budget travelers who can obtain local rates can easily travel for under US$15 per day, including hotels, food, and transportation.

Unfortunately, tourist prices in Vietnam are linked to what the traffic will bear. For example, a hotel room in Saigon that costs US$20 for the Western visitor costs a Vietnamese just US$3, a US$80 plane ticket sold to a Westerner costs just US$10 for a Vietnamese citizen, and train tickets for Westerners are subject to a 400% tourist tax. Essentially, you will be overcharged for almost everything you buy.

The Vietnamese government has a no-apologies policy of grabbing as much Western money as possible. This rip-off mentality also applies to private citizens who feel justified charging up to 10 times the local rate to wealthy Western visitors. And since few prices are written down outside the main tourist centers, a journey through Vietnam quickly becomes an adventure in trying to guess and obtain the local rate.

No matter the length of your journey, it's important to negotiate and set prices before ordering meals or venturing forth on a *cyclo* or in a taxi. Written agreements regarding prices and services often prevent misunderstandings.

Accepting the unfair prices charged throughout Vietnam will only perpetuate the situation and make it more difficult for the next traveler to obtain local prices. Both tourists and travelers should attempt to pay local prices while realizing that modest surcharges are inevitable throughout Vietnam.

OTHER PRACTICALITIES

Health
Vaccinations are not required for entry to Vietnam, but immunizations against cholera, hepatitis, typhoid, tetanus, and polio are recommended. The most serious health risk is malaria, which remains widespread outside the major cities. Malaria tablets such as Mefloquine or Halfan are recommended for anyone venturing off the beaten track.

Food is relatively safe, but drink only bottled water or soft drinks.

AIDS is a major problem among the estimated 10,000 prostitutes in Saigon and the government-supervised brothels in Hanoi.

Time
Vietnam is seven hours ahead of Greenwich Mean Time. Noon in Vietnam is 0100 in New York, 2200 in San Francisco, 0500 in London, and 1500 in Sydney.

Government Hours
Government offices are open Mon.-Fri. 0800-1200 and 1300-1630. Banks are open the same hours, plus Saturdays 0800-1200. Museums are open Tues.-Sun. 0900-1200 and 1300-1630.

Telecommunications
International calls and faxes are best made from the better hotels in Saigon and Hanoi. Calls can also be made from general post offices, but delays are common and connections can be poor. Mail service appears fairly reliable.

The International Access Code for Vietnam is 84.

Crime
Vietnam is a very poor country with more than its fair share of beggars, pickpockets, and con artists. Drive-by thieves on motorcycles and bag snatchers in trains are also common. Although Vietnam is actually much safer than your hometown and armed robbery is virtually unheard of, anyone who leaves bags unattended at the train or bus station should kiss them goodbye. Whenever possible, valuables should be stored in hotel safe-deposit boxes.

Don't trust strangers with stories about inexpensive gems, rare antiques, old Zippos, and other collectibles that will fetch great prices back home. *All* are fakes.

SOUTHERN VIETNAM
SAIGON (HO CHI MINH CITY)

Saigon—renamed Ho Chi Minh City (HCMC) in 1975—is the heart and soul of the new Vietnam, the economic engine that drives the rest of the country. Visitors expecting to discover a sleepy colonial relic or Vietnam War leftover will find Saigon a complete surprise. This is a city on the *move*—one of the most energetic and madcap destinations in Southeast Asia.

Saigon offers plenty of formal attractions, from French-colonial architecture to ancient pagodas, but the chief interests in this city of four million are the sharp contrasts between East and West, and the all-encompassing love of *song voi,* or living quickly. Flashy discos, cafes serving angel-hair pasta, and armies of cruising motorcycles are the essential experiences of Saigon, not the socialist ideology of the north.

Saigon is also a place where you must clear your mind of all preconceptions. First, Americans need fear nothing aside from the incessant curiosity and overwhelming goodwill offered by almost every resident of the city. There is nothing to fear from government officials and local denizens who, at times, seem to love the foreign visitor more than their rulers in the north. Saigon has a mind-frame far removed from hardship and war: this vibrant city is among the most peaceful yet exciting in the East.

There are problems, of course: decaying hotels, dismal restaurants, and an ungodly number of beggars working the streets. And yet, despite these hassles and headaches, Saigon remains a completely sassy town, where girls flounce around in lovely *ao dais*—the traditional tight-fitting dress unequaled throughout the East—where young kids shout "Hello Mister You American?" and where the black market flourishes as strongly as back in 1968. Here in Saigon, everyone is on the make and on the take.

Hold on to your wallet. Saigon is a very *wild* place.

ATTRACTIONS IN CENTRAL SAIGON

Saigon is divided into 12 districts, including the central *quan* of Saigon which gives the metropolis its name. The following sights are grouped into three sections: "Central Saigon," "Cholon" (the Chinese district), and "Around Saigon."

A walking tour of central Saigon can be completed in a single day starting from the Saigon Floating Hotel. *Cyclos* are unnecessary but a rented bicycle is a great way to reach the attractions listed below under "Attractions Around Saigon."

Saigon River

Across from the floating hotel (towed from Australia) is a statue honoring Tran Hung Dao, a Vietnamese general who opposed the Mongol invasion of Kublai Khan in the 13th century.

Ferries across to several popular floating restaurants leave from piers just south of the hotel.

Dong Khoi Street

Dong Khoi ("Simultaneous Uprising") St.—the Fifth Avenue of Saigon—was called Rue Catinat during the French era and Tu Do ("Freedom") St. during the Vietnam conflict, when it served as a nightclub and brothel area for American soldiers. Shaded by large trees, the boulevard has many grand old sites such as the renovated Majestic Hotel (renamed the Cuu Long), Maxim's Restaurant, Caravelle Hotel (Doc Lap), which once operated as the U.S. press-corps headquarters, and Continental Hotel, constructed in 1885 during the Belle-époque days and a star of the French film *Indochine.*

The street also has an inordinate number of beggars, con artists, wheelers and dealers, pickpockets, Amerasian hustlers, transvestites, and other varieties of shamsters. Be careful.

The nearby Rex Hotel (Ben Thanh), another old favorite of war correspondents and U.S. officers, offers good city views and cold beer from the terrace on the fifth floor.

Municipal Theater

This French-era building was once home to the South Vietnamese National Assembly but now functions as a concert hall. Nightly shows (2000-2400) run the gamut from Vietnamese theater and local acrobats to contemporary dance and cabaret.

City Hall

Constructed from 1901 to 1908 as the Hotel de Ville, this gingerbread yellow-and-white building now serves as the headquarters of the Ho Chi Minh City People's Committee.

Notre Dame Cathedral

Erected between 1877 and 1880 in a grassy central square, Notre Dame has survived a great deal of history to become one of Saigon's most famous landmarks. Masses are held weekday mornings and Sundays at 1600 and 1800.

The adjacent **General Post Office** was completed in 1888.

U.S. Embassy

Several former embassies are situated a few blocks north of the cathedral.

Top draw is the former U.S. Embassy, chiefly remembered as the site of frantic rooftop helicopter evacuations and the dramatic finale to the Vietnam War on 30 April 1975. Today, the building contains the offices of Vietnam's State Petroleum Authority and the grounds are frequently cleaned for American and European film crews working on *Rambo*-like epics.

Visitors are admitted through a side door, though there's little to see except for a plaque which commemorates the Tet Offensive of 1968 and the decisive events of 1975.

Military Museum And History Museum

Le Duan Boulevard leads to the Military Museum, with tanks and planes in the front compound, and the History Museum (former National Museum), filled with an outstanding range of artifacts which illustrate the evolution of Vietnamese culture. The Military Museum is disappointing but the History Museum is highly recommended for its extensive collection of Dong Son, Funan, Cham, Khmer, and Vietnamese relics.

Both museums are open Tues.-Sun. 0800-1100 and 1300-1600.

Saigon Zoo And Botanical Gardens

Although decimated by the war and poorly maintained since reunification, the zoo and gardens are lively scenes on weekends when they provide a welcome escape from the heat and noise of Saigon.

Reunification Hall

Originally the residence of the French governor-general and later the presidential palace of Diem, this reconstructed administrative center is where Viet Cong tanks crashed through the iron gates on 30 April 1975 to end the American experience in Vietnam.

Guided tours visit the banquet room, state chambers, cabinet hall, underground command post, and reception rooms on the upper floors. Highly recommended. The hall is open daily, except Sunday afternoons, 0800-1000 and 1300-1700.

War Crimes Museum

Constructed on the site of the old Information Service Office of Saigon University, Saigon's most famous Vietnam War-era sight includes replicas of the infamous "tiger cages" from Poulo Condo Island, American tanks and helicopters, displays on the massacre at My Lai, grisly photos of the effects of napalm and Agent Orange, a guillotine used by the French to execute South Vietnamese dissidents, and some crudely rationalized propaganda. A place for strong stomachs and a sense of historical judgment.

The museum is open Tues.-Sun. 0730-1145 and 1330-1645.

Xa Loi Pagoda

Saigon's best pagodas (temples) are in Cholon, though this modern pagoda on Ba Huyen Thah Quan St. played an important role in the history of the Vietnam War. It was here, on 11 June 1963, that a Buddhist monk named Thich Quang Du from Hue assumed the lotus position, poured gasoline over himself, and committed suicide through self-immolation. The unforgettable image made front-page headlines around the world, electrified the American public, and signaled the beginning of the end for the Diem regime.

The Austin car which transported the monk to Saigon is now displayed in a pagoda in Hue.

TAY NINH BUS TERMINAL

TO CU CHI TUNNELS AND TAY NINH

CONG HOO ST.

SAIGON
(HO CHI MINH CITY)

HOANG VAN THU ST.

CHAINS FIRST HOTEL

STAR HILL HOTEL

CHAINS FIRST HOTEL

CACH MONG THAN ST.

HUONG LO 2 ST.

HUONG LO 14 ST.

TAN BINH HOTEL

THUNG KIAT BLVD.

GIAC LAM PAGODA

LAC LONG QUAN ST.

AN VUONG ST.

NGUYEN TRI

NGUYEN TRI ST.

AMUSEMENT PARK

KY HOA HOTEL

HOA BINH THEATER

GIAC VIEN TU PAGODA

BINH THAI ST.

STADIUM

QUAC TU PAGODA

SEE "CHOLON" MAP

BA HAM ST.

3 THANG 2 BLVD.

NGUYEN CHI THANH BLVD.

HUNG VUONG BLVD.

HUNG VUONG ST.

TO MIEN TAY BUS TERMINAL AND MEKONG DELTA

LO HAU GIANG BLVD.

CHO QUAN CHURCH

BINH TIEN ST.

TO CON GIUOC

© MOON PUBLICATIONS, INC.

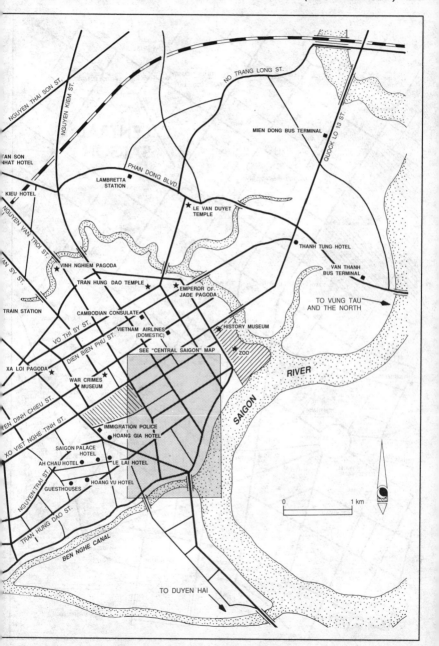

CENTRAL SAIGON

Map labels:

FOUNTAIN

TO ZOO AND HISTORY MUSEUM

TO AIRPORT

VO VAN TAN ST.

FORMER U.S. EMBASSY
FRENCH CONSULATE

FORMER BRITISH EMBASSY

TON DUC THONG ST.

WAR CRIMES MUSEUM

XO VIET NGHE TINH ST.

NGUYEN THI MINH KHAI ST.

CHU MAN TRINH ST.

THAI VAN LUNG ST.

LE DUAN BLVD.

HAN THUYEN ST.

HAI BA TRUNG ST.

NAM KY KHAI NGHIA ST.

NOTRE DAME CATHEDRAL

GPO

NGUYEN DU ST.

MADAME DAI'S

REUNIFICATION HALL

DONG KHOI ST.

ORCHID HOTEL

LY TU TRANG ST.

THI SAC ST.

DON DAT ST.

LE THANH TON ST.

REVOLUTIONARY MUSEUM

CITY HALL

SAIGON TOURIST

VIETNAM AIRLINES (INTERNATIONAL)

MUNICIPAL THEATER

EMBASSY HOTEL

PHNOM PENH BUSES

CONTINENTAL HOTEL

CARAVELLE HOTEL

APOCALYPSE NOW

TON DUC THANG MUSEUM

CHUA CONG

LIBRARY

HUONG DUONG HOTEL

REX HOTEL

MOSQUE

SAIGON HOTEL

TRUNG TRUC ST.

NORFOLK HOTEL

LE LOI ST.

BONG SEN HOTEL

HINDU TEMPLE

POST OFFICE

KIM DO HOTEL

MONDIAL HOTEL

PALACE HOTEL

STATUE

SAIGON FLOATING HOTEL

BEN THANH MARKET

HUONG SEN HOTEL

VIETNAM TOURISM

HUE BLVD

DONG KHOI HOTEL

RIVERSIDE HOTEL

STATUE

BOAT CRUISES

LE LAI ST.

HUNH THUC KHANG ST.

MINIBUS OFFICE

MAXIM'S

PHAM NEU LAO ST.

HAI VON HOTEL

MAJESTIC HOTEL

TRAN HUNG DAO ST.

BEN THANH BUS TERMINAL

VINH LOI HOTEL

HAM NGHI BLVD.

TAN DUC THANG ST.

SAIGON RIVER

VINH LOI HOTEL

TO CHOLON

ART MUSEUM

KY CON ST.

CALMET ST.

NGUYEN THAI BINH ST.

VIETNAM BANK

PHO DUC CHINH ST.

FORMER U.S. EMBASSY

MEKONG RIVER BOATS

THAI BINH DUONG HOTEL

FOREIGN EXCHANGE BANK

NATIONAL BANK

YERSIN ST.

NGUYEN CON TRU ST.

PHUNG SONG TU TEMPLE

DUONG DUONG ST.

BEN NGHE CANAL

HO CHI MINH MUSEUM

0   250 m

Revolutionary Museum

Once known as the Gia Long Palace, this neo-classical building currently houses a permanent collection of memorabilia devoted to the national struggle for unification. The building is connected to the Reunification Hall by a network of underground concrete bunkers.

Ben Thanh Market

Saigon's Cho Ben Thanh—once the main railway terminal—is the largest and most popular of some 35 markets throughout the city. The market was constructed in 1914 by the French as Halles Centrales and renovated several years ago by city officials, though the clock remains permanently fixed at half past one. Inside you'll find a surprising range of imported goods from Japanese televisions to French perfumes, plus excellent food stalls and souvenir shops.

Phung Song Tu Temple

A small but attractive temple constructed shortly after WW II by Fukien Chinese to honor Ong Bon, guardian spirit of happiness and virtue. Highlights include the wonderfully illustrated doors and multiarmed image of Kwan Yin, Buddhist goddess of mercy.

Dan Sinh Market

Just around the corner from Phung Song Tu Temple on Nguyen Con Tru St. is an informal market which specializes in American, Chinese, and Russian war surplus, such as dog tags and military hardware. Most of the goods are fake, though authentic memorabilia occasionally passes through the market. Buy with caution.

ATTRACTIONS IN CHOLON

Cholon, Saigon's Chinatown, is home to some half-million Vietnamese of Chinese descent who live and work in the liveliest section of town. Cholon ("Big Market") offers a large number of unique pagodas, superb restaurants, plenty of hotels, and excellent shopping in a half-dozen markets.

The following walking tour takes a half day. The second attraction described below—a temple in the northwest section of Cholon—is worthwhile for temple aficionados but can otherwise be skipped to save time.

Markets

An excellent place to start any tour of China-town is in colorful and vibrant **Binh Tay Market** near the Cholon bus terminal. Binh Tay essentially serves as a wholesale marketplace filled with fruits and vegetables imported from the Mekong River delta. Bring your camera and plenty of film.

Another market worth visiting (exact location unknown) is the very modern **An Duong Market.** Constructed by Chinese investors to signal the return of Chinese power, the shopping emporium is a wonderful place to watch Vietnamese schoolgirls, hand in hand in their pure white *ao dais,* take their first thrilling ride up Vietnam's only functioning escalator.

Khanh Van Nam Vien Pagoda

Constructed by the Cantonese from 1939 to 1942, this is one of the few temples in Vietnam dedicated to Taoism and Lao Tse, its founder. Aside from the usual collection of Chinese deities, the temple features several yin-yang emblems and graphic instructions on breathing exercises and proper diet.

Services are held mornings from 0800 to 0900.

Cha Tam Church

Constructed around the turn of the century, Cha Tam (Van Lang) is chiefly noted as the final refuge of President Diem and his brother Nhu, who fled the Presidential Palace during a coup attempt in 1963. The pair negotiated their surrender at the church but were quickly murdered by soldiers on the ride back to the palace. News of the assassination was welcomed by the military, religious leaders, and most citizens of Saigon, who considered Diem a dangerous and deranged despot, better dead than red.

Quan Am Pagoda

Constructed by Fukien Chinese in the early 19th century and dedicated to the goddess of purity and motherhood, Quan Am is among the oldest and most artful temples in the city. Noteworthy features include the traditional ceramic figurines mounted on the roof, front doors decorated with golden lacquered panels, and a broad array of images drawn from Taoist and Buddhist mythologies.

CHOLON

SU VAN HANH ST.

NGO GIA TU BLVD.

TRAN PHU BLVD.

HUNG VUONG BLVD.

AN DUONG VUONG BLVD.

TO CENTRAL SAIGON

TO CENTRAL SAIGON

TRAN HUNG DAO BLVD.

HANH LONG HOTEL

TRAI PHUONG ST.

DONG KHANH HOTEL

HOA BINH HOTEL

DONG KINH HOTEL

KINH TAU HU CANAL

VINH VIEN ST.

HAO HAO ST.

DAO DUY TU ST.

NGO QUYEN ST.

PHU DO 1 HOTEL

BA HAT ST.

NHAT LO ST.

NGUYEN KIM ST.

BAT DAT HOTEL

ARC EN CIEL HOTEL

STADIUM

PHU THO HOTEL

GOLDSTAR HOTEL

LY THUONG KIET BLVD.

NGHIA AN HOI QUAN PAGODA

TAM SON HOI QUAN PAGODA

NGUYEN CHI THANH BLVD.

PHUOC AN HOI QUAN PAGODA

QUAN AM PAGODA

THIEN HAU PAGODA

3 THANG 2 BLVD.

THU DO HOTEL

TRUONG THANH HOTEL

TRUONG MAI HOTEL

PHENIX HOTEL

HAI THUONG LAN ONG BLVD.

GPO

HA TON QUYEN ST.

CHA TAM CHURCH

NGUYEN THI NHO ST.

CHOLON BUS TERMINAL

HAU GIANG BLVD.

PHAN VAN KHOE ST.

BINH TAY MARKET

KHANH VAN NAM VIEN PAGODA

TRANG TRI ST.

TO MIEN TAY BUS TERMINAL

PHUNG SON PAGODA

500 m

0

© MOON PUBLICATIONS, INC.

Phuoc An Hoi Quan Pagoda

Another temple erected by the Fukiens and considered one of the most beautifully decorated in Saigon. Dedicated to Quan Cong, a deified Chinese general closely associated with his sacred red horse, the temple is noted for its ceramic rooftop decorations and profuse use of carved wood and gilded figurines.

Thien Hau Pagoda

Constructed by the Cantonese from 1825 to 1830 and among the most elaborate temples in Saigon, this enormous complex is dedicated to Thien Hau, goddess of the sea and protector of fishermen. Of special note are the rooftop friezes, considered the most complex and richly ornamented in all of Vietnam.

Tam Son Hoi Quan Pagoda

A simple and peaceful temple constructed in the 19th century by Fukien immigrants and dedicated to Chua Thai Sanh, the goddess of fertility. For this reason, the temple is chiefly visited by young women and couples who pray for children.

Nghia An Hoi Quan Pagoda

Among the excellent carvings is a magnificent golden wooden boat which hangs over the entrance and the enormous red horse of General Quan Cong on the left. Chinese believe safe journeys can be insured by praying to the horse and ringing the bell that hangs around its neck.

ATTRACTIONS AROUND SAIGON

The following sights are scattered around the perimeters of Saigon and are best reached by rented bicycle, *cyclo,* or taxi.

Emperor Of Jade Pagoda

Saigon's most spectacular temple was constructed around the turn of the century by Cantonese Buddhists who dedicated the colorful site to the Emperor of Jade, the supreme god of the Taoists. Inside the wildly decorated sanctuary are dozens of effigies constructed of wood and reinforced paper, which encompass almost the entire religious pantheon of Buddhism, Taoism, and Confucianism.

Among the deities is the King of Hell, the Buddha of the Future, the Goddess of Mercy, a Chinese general who defeated the Green Dragon, the God of Lightning, and of course the Emperor of Jade, flanked by his four guardians. A thick haze of incense smoke completes the surrealistic scene.

Vinh Nghiem Pagoda

The newest and largest temple in Saigon was completed in 1971 with the aid of the Japanese Friendship Association, which accounts for the vaguely Japanese flavor of the architecture. Although this pagoda lacks the historical or artistic significance of others in Saigon, it compensates with some outstanding statuary in the central chapel and on each level of the eight-story tower.

Le Van Duyet Temple

Le Van Duyet was a court eunuch and military leader credited with crushing the Tay Son rebellion in the early 19th century. This temple, dedicated to his memory, contains his tomb and his rather strange collection of memorabilia: a stuffed and moth-eaten tiger, spears, ethnic artifacts, and some of his personal effects.

Giac Vien Tu Pagoda

A Buddhist temple constructed in 1771, this pagoda is considered by many to be among the best-preserved religious sites in the country. Dedicated to the veneration of Emperor Gia Long, this lavishly decorated temple is filled to the brim with over 100 images of divinities and spirits both inspired and demonic. The cast of characters—combined with the darkness and heavy waves of smoke—make this everything you want in the mysterious East.

Giac Lam Pagoda

Giac Lam, the oldest temple in Saigon, is architecturally similar to Giac Vien Tu and perhaps temple overkill for some visitors, but it's worth the trip. Giac Lam is one of the country's purest examples of traditional Vietnamese religious construction and boasts a number of unique features: superb blue-and-white porcelain plates which decorate the roof; hardwood columns engraved with *nom* characters—the Vietnamese script used prior to the introduction of the Roman alphabet in the 17th century; and friendly monks often happy to practice their English with foreign visitors.

ACCOMMODATIONS

Hotels in Saigon include budget guesthouses, old French-colonial hotels in varying states of decay or renovation, hotels constructed during the American era, and another 15 projects scheduled to open within the next few years. Most visitors stay in central Saigon rather than in hotels near the airport or in Cholon.

All of the larger hotels are owned by Saigon Tourism or other government agencies, while smaller hotels are privately operated or joint ventures between Saigon Tourism and outside investors.

Many hotels have been renamed since the events of 1975 but are still called by their old Vietnam War-era titles. Hotel name changes include the Caravelle (new name is Doc Lap Hotel), Continental (Hai Au), Rex (Ben Thanh), Majestic (Cuu Long), Miramar (Bong Sen), Lotus (Huong Sen), Palace (Dong Khoi), Liberty (Que Huong), Champagne (Vinh Loi), and Arc En Ciel (Thien Hong) in Cholon.

Budget Accommodations

Prices for midrange and luxury hotels are on par with international levels but budget hotels and guesthouses are more expensive than their counterparts in Bangkok or Jakarta. Figure on spending US$5-15 for a simple room with fan and bath that elsewhere in Asia would cost half that amount.

The reason for overpriced rooms in Saigon (and elsewhere in Vietnam) is that many owners double or triple the rates for Westerners. Request the least expensive room and bargain for discounts. Whenever possible, ask for room rates in *dong*. Unfortunately, most hotels in Saigon quote their prices in dollars, not *dong*.

Hoang Vu Hotel: A backpacker's favorite located a few blocks west of the Ban Thanh Market and just beyond the new Le Lai Hotel. The hotel has a decent cafe, rents bicycles, and offers both fan-cooled and a/c rooms. 265 Pham Ngu Lao St., tel. 396522, US$5-15.

Nearby budget hotels, which handle the overflow, include the Prince, Vien Dong (recommended), and several adjacent guesthouses.

Dong Khoi Hotel: Good location in central Saigon with rooms inside the French-era hotel that are large, somewhat seedy, perhaps a/c, and with a degree of colonial atmosphere. 8 Dong Khoi St., tel. 294046, US$8-20.

Youth Center (Thanh Doan TP): Clean dormitory beds and friendly management in a handy location just behind the Notre Dame Cathedral. 1 Pham Ngoc Thach St., tel. 523288, US$3-10.

Saigon Hotel: Facilities at this moderate hotel include two restaurants, car rentals, visa services, and a travel agency. Convenient site just opposite the mosque in central Saigon. 41 Dong Du St., tel. 299734, US$18-45 a/c with private bath and color TV.

Cholon Hotels: Cholon has several dozen hotels which mostly cater to Chinese businessmen and Vietnamese expatriates back home on holiday. Most charge US$5-10 for clean rooms with fan and US$10-15 for a/c rooms with private bath.

The **Truong Thanh** is centrally located but rooms facing the street can be noisy. Other hotels similarly priced are shown on the Cholon map. 117 Chau Van Liem St., tel. 556044, US$3-15.

Moderate To Luxury Accommodations

Most of following hotels were constructed in the '60s or '70s but renovated in recent years. Almost all belong to the Saigon Tourist hotel chain and charge similar prices payable only in U.S. dollars. Tour groups are usually billeted in the Rex, Caravelle, Palace, Majestic, or Continental hotels. Remember that American-issued credit cards cannot be honored until full diplomatic relations are established between the two countries.

Majestic (Cuu Long) Hotel: A waterfront hotel with swimming pool, breezy Sky Bar on the fifth floor, and 120 a/c rooms with TV and private bath. The more expensive rooms face the river while budget rooms front an inner courtyard. Recommended for the large rooms, river views, and lively Cyclo Bar. 1 Dong Khoi St., tel. 295515, fax 291470, US$35-80.

Bong Sen (Miramar) Hotel: A narrow six-story 85-room hotel right in the heart of central Saigon. Nothing special but cheaper than most renovated places in downtown. 117-123 Dong Khoi St., tel. 299744, fax 298076, US$30-95.

Rex (Ben Thanh) Hotel: One of Saigon's most famous hotels features a very small swimming pool on the sixth floor, restaurant and outdoor "buvette" on the fifth, and an ornately decorated reception hall with heavy furniture and pseudo-Roman columns on the ground floor. 141 Nguyen Hue, tel. 292186, fax 291469, US$35-80.

Continental (Hai Au): This venerable hotel once served as the favorite watering hole of foreign correspondents and diplomats stationed in Saigon during the Vietnam War. Much of the atmosphere from Graham Greene's novel *The Quiet American* remains despite complete renovation a few years ago. The hotel was featured in the film *Indochine*. 132 Dong Khoi St., tel. 294456, fax 290936, US$85-150.

Saigon Floating Hotel: Formerly moored on Australia's Great Barrier Reef, this US$70-million mobile hotel has become one of Saigon's major sights since its arrival alongside Hero Square in 1990. Rates are high and rooms are small, but this is one of the few hotels in Vietnam with complete business facilities, including interpreter services, international direct dialing, and satellite television. P.O. Box 752, tel. 290783, fax 290784, US$220-340.

FOOD

Vietnamese cuisine offers a wide variety of fine dishes which combine the flavors of China and ingredients more typical of Thailand. Among the popular dishes are *pho*, a delicious soup of noodles and beef, *ho tieu*, another soup made with fish and aromatic herbs, and the national dish of *cha gio*, spring rolls made from crab and pork mixed with prawns and mushrooms.

Other specialties include *nem chua*, fermented pork; *bo bay mon*, a seven-course Chinese beef dish; *chan chua*, tamarind soup; and *cu lao*, beef soup.

Soups and noodle dishes purchased at street stalls or in small cafes should cost well under US$1. A full meal in a simple cafe should cost under US$2. Even the best restaurant in Saigon or Hanoi should be able to put together a full dinner for under US$10. The only exceptions are those restaurants serving European dishes or with live entertainment.

Warning

As in other emerging countries with primitive sanitation facilities, it is wise not to drink the water or consume ice. Bottled water and boiled tea are safer options, though few travelers seem to suffer from stomach disorders in Vietnam.

Western visitors should not pay substantially higher rates than the Vietnamese for identical food and service, though overcharging is common in cafes without formal menus. Snacks such as cashews and crackers which are brought to the table unsolicited will be added to the bill unless immediately returned to the waiter. All prices should be checked before ordering and the final bill should be scrutinized for mysterious last-minute additions and surcharges.

Food Stalls And Cafes

Hotel restaurants are expensive and often a bit bland, but street stalls and simple cafes are plentiful, cheap, and safe to experience despite their spartan setups. Cafes (*nha hang*) are often unnamed but simply identified by their street address, such as Nha Hang 69, or "Restaurant 69."

Pham Ngu Lao Street: Central Saigon's largest collection of food stalls is located just west of Ben Thanh Market and on the same street as the backpacker's center at Hoang Tu Hotel. Inexpensive.

Apocalypse Now: Wins best prize for creativity, plus decent food and inexpensive beer. Situated just off the main drag of Dong Khoi, this is an excellent place to hang out and pick up current travel tips from other backpackers. It's also a place to listen to the Doors wail about "The End" and try an Apocalypse Whiskey—bourbon and Chinese herbs soaked with a large cobra. 42 Dong Du Street. Inexpensive.

Givral Patisserie: A government-owned cafe with excellent cakes, pastries, and reasonably priced entrees just across the street from the Continental Hotel. Another backpacker's favorite. 2 Le Loi Street. Inexpensive.

Lam Son Restaurant: A French-style cafe with both Vietnamese and European dishes at low prices. Good atmosphere. Located near the Caravelle Hotel and just across the street from the Municipal Theater. Le Loi Street. Inexpensive.

Nha Hang 95 Dong Khoi: The former Imperial Bar on former Tu Do St. is a pleasant place to relax and watch the parade while enjoying a sizzling steak and an ice-cold beer. 95 Dong Khoi Street. Moderate.

Bordard Cafe: Another time-warp cafe with '60s decor and reasonably good food. Convenient location in central Saigon. 131 Dong Khoi Street. Moderate.

Restaurants

Choices include hotel restaurants and a limited number of privately owned operations.

Rex Hotel: A great escape from the crowds with fine views over Saigon is in the fifth-floor restaurant and open-air cafe in the Rex Hotel. 141 Nguyen Hue Boulevard. Moderate.

Palace Hotel: Some of Saigon's finest panoramic views can be enjoyed from the restaurant on the 15th floor. 56 Nguyen Hue Boulevard. Moderate.

Madame Dai's: Owned and operated by one of Saigon's more famous personalities, Suzi Dai's "La Bibliothéque" serves French cuisine in her private law library, now heavy with old-world ambience. The memorable atmosphere—not to mention the personal service of the Paris-trained lawyer—compensate for the tasty but underspiced food. Ask her about cats, her now-useless law books, her antique ceramics. Conversation is best attempted in French. 84 Nguyen Du Street. Expensive.

Maxim's: Saigon's premier restaurant features a massive menu and live music in a '60s time-warp setting. The place is pricey—figure on US$15-20 per person—but most visitors consider Maxim's a worthwhile splurge. 13 Dong Khoi Street. Expensive.

PRACTICALITIES

Tourist Information

Government-operated tourist information centers include Vietnam Tourism at 69 Nguyen Hue Boulevard and Saigon Tourist at 49 Le Thanh Ton Street. Both agencies essentially exist to book expensive tours and provide little assistance or useful information to independent travelers.

Immigration Police

Rules on police registration and other bureaucratic hassles change frequently, but as of this writing all independent travelers are required to register within three days of arrival with the Immigration Police at 161 Nguyen Du Street. This formality is often completed with the help of Vietnam Tourism, guesthouse owners, or local tour companies.

Consulates

Most European and Asian countries maintain embassies in Hanoi and consulates in Saigon. The most useful reps for independent travelers are the Cambodian Consulate at 41 Phung Khac Khoan St. and the Laotian Consulate at 181 Hai Ba Trung Street. Both offices are open Mon.-Sat. 0800-1100 and 1400-1700.

Visas take about a full week to process. This formality is best completed by guesthouse owners and local travel agencies who understand the paperwork requirements and byzantine mindframes of local bureaucrats.

Money

U.S. dollars, European currencies, and traveler's checks can be cashed at the highest legal rates at the Foreign Trade Bank at 29 Ben Chuong Duong St. and at any branch of Vietcombank. Exchange facilities are also provided at most hotels, a slew of licensed foreign banks, and at legal exchange windows on Dong Khoi Street. Facilities are also found at the Saigon airport.

The official exchange rate is almost equal to black-market rates. American dollars converted on the black market bring somewhat higher returns, but be cautious when offered outlandish rates by young men working the streets. All are con artists who pass fake *dong* or simply grab your money and run.

Post And Telecommunications

Postal, telex, telegraph, and fax services are available at the General Post Office across from the Notre Dame Cathedral and from the post office branch on Le Loi Boulevard. Most hotels provide the same services for modest charges.

Mail service is fairly reliable, but international phone calls are unrealistically pegged at US$15-25 for the first three minutes.

TRANSPORTATION

Saigon is 300 km from Dalat, 445 km from Nha Trang, 965 km from Danang, 1,071 km from Hue, and 1,710 km from Hanoi.

Airport Arrival

Saigon's Tan Son Nhat Airport, eight km northwest of city center, has a Vietcombank branch with exchange facilities, a post office, airline reservation offices, and Vietnam Tourism and Saigon Tourist information counters.

Cameras and film should *not* be sent through the high-powered X-ray machines. Be prepared for an inordinate amount of paperwork. Keep your sense of humor.

Taxis into town which cost US$5-8 can be shared among several passengers. *Cyclos* waiting outside the airport are a cheaper option at about US$2 but are suitable only for travelers with little baggage.

Airline Offices

The Vietnam Airlines international booking office at 116 Nguyen Hue Blvd. acts as the general sales agent for all airlines serving Saigon. The office is open Mon.-Sat. 0730-1100 and 1300-1600.

Reservations can also be made directly at the offices of Malaysian Airlines at 116 Nguyen Hue Blvd. and at Air France in the Caravelle Hotel at the corner of Dong Khoi and Le Loi streets.

Other important airlines include Thai International, Garuda, and Lufthansa, all located at the airport. Cathay Pacific is at 49 Le Thanh Ton, Aeroflot at 4 Le Loi, Pacific Airlines at 76 Le Thanh Ton, Philippine Airlines at 4 Le Loi, and Singapore at 6 Le Loi.

Getting Around Saigon

Most of Saigon can be explored on foot but outlying sights can be quickly reached by *cyclo* or by a bicycle rented from any number of hotels or guesthouses. *Cyclos* charge about US$.50 per hour and bikes cost under US$2 per day. Taxi charters for up to four passengers cost US$30-45 per day.

Another option is to purchase a bicycle in Saigon, use it during your travels in Vietnam, and sell it for 70-80% of the original cost in Hanoi.

Public buses to Cholon leave from the Ben Thanh Bus Terminal near the Ben Thanh Market and from Le Loi St. just opposite the Hoang Tu Hotel. Cholon-bound buses also leave from the southern end of Nguyen Hue Blvd. near the river.

Train

The ticket office at the Saigon Railway Station is open daily 0700-1100 and 1300-1500. Tickets for the Reunification Express, which links Saigon with Hanoi, should be purchased several days in advance. Western visitors are charged four or five times the official rate, which makes train travel almost as expensive as, but certainly

safer and more scenic than, domestic air travel. Try your student ID or ask a willing Vietnamese to purchase your ticket.

Trains heading north leave daily at 1000 and 1700.

Buses From Saigon

Saigon has two major bus terminals on the outskirts of town.

Mien Tay Bus Terminal: All buses to points south of Saigon leave from this terminal, situated 10 km west of central Saigon in a suburb called An Lac. The terminal can be reached by city bus leaving from the Ben Thanh Bus Terminal in central Saigon.

Ordinary buses to most destinations leave throughout the day until about 1600. Express buses leave twice daily at 0430 and 1500. Tickets for express buses can be purchased several hours in advance directly at the bus terminal or a day in advance by having a Vietnamese speaker call the station office at 55955.

Mien Dong Bus Terminal: All buses to points north of Saigon leave from this terminal situated six km north of downtown on National Highway 13. The terminal can be reached by *cyclo* or city bus from Ben Thanh Bus Terminal. Express tickets can be reserved a day in advance by calling the station office at 94056.

Principal destinations (and travel times): Vung Tau (three hours), Dalat (seven hours), Nha Trang (11 hours), Qui Nhon (18 hours), Pleiku (22 hours), Danang (26 hours), Hue (30 hours), and Hanoi (52 hours).

Express Minibuses

Saigon also has an increasing number of privately owned minibuses which serve all the principal tourist destinations. The office at 39 Nguyen Hue Blvd. is centrally located and very popular with independent travelers. Hotel and guesthouse owners can help find other outlets.

Buses To Cambodia

Buses to Phnom Penh leave from 115 Nguyen Hue Blvd., adjacent to the Rex Hotel, daily at 0600 except on Sunday.

Travelers whose visas state their point of exit as Saigon or Hanoi airports can change this formality at Saigon travel agencies, such as Ann Tourist on Ton That Tung St. and Vacation Planners on Tran Nhat Dvat Street.

VICINITY OF SAIGON

CU CHI TUNNELS

The tunnels of Cu Chi are the famous subterranean creation of the Viet Cong, used during their wars of resistance against French and American forces. The 200-km system of tunnels contained living areas, kitchens, hospitals, printing presses, munitions compounds, and underground street signs designed to help NLF forces find their way. At their greatest expansion, the tunnels stretched from downtown Saigon almost to the borders of Cambodia. When discovered by the Americans, the tunnels were gassed and bombed from above, then brazenly explored by tunnel commandos—a terrifying assignment graphically depicted in the film *Platoon*.

Today, tourists are given a short video presentation and description by local volunteers and then invited to crawl around the claustrophobic maze. Most of the tunnels are now closed and far too narrow for Western tourists, though several segments have been widened to allow passage for hefty foreigners.

Aboveground attractions include a rusting American M41 tank being eaten by weeds and a firing range where for a few dollars you can fire M-16s or AK-47s while pretending to be Rambo, the dimwitted movie idol surprisingly popular in Vietnam. Even the guides find this behavior strange.

Transportation

Cu Chi, 40 km northwest of Saigon city center, can be reached by organized tour, rental car, or public transportation, and is usually combined with a visit to the Cao Dai Cathedral in Tay Ninh. The tunnels are several kilometers outside the town of Cu Chi but are served by motorcycle taxis.

The easiest solution is to organize a party of four passengers and hire a car for the day. Car rentals cost US$30-40 per day—a sensible and cost-effective alternative to overpriced tours or creaky buses.

Buses to Cu Chi leave Saigon from the Mien Tay Bus Terminal in Cholon and the Tay Ninh Terminal in Tan Binh District.

An intriguing alternative is to hire a bicycle and take it on the bus to Cu Chi, riding from town to tunnels. This option gives you freedom of movement plus the opportunity to explore a bit of Vietnamese countryside.

CAO DAI CATHEDRAL

Tay Ninh, a provincial capital 95 km northwest of Saigon, is home to an indigenous and eclectic religion called Cao Dai which holds services in one of the most remarkable cathedrals anywhere in Asia.

Constructed from 1933 to 1955 in Long Hoa, a small village four km east of Tay Ninh, this rococco fantasy neatly combines Western and Eastern influences into a stunning and completely surrealistic piece of architecture. Cao Dai is Disneyland on the Mekong—a truly unique creation as intriguing as the religion itself.

The Cao Dai sect was founded in 1928 as a mystical synthesis of Confucianism, Buddhism, Taoism, Hinduism, Christianity, and Islam. Among its more esoteric beliefs is the theory that Shakespeare, Lenin, Joan of Arc, Victor Hugo, and other luminaries were Cao Dai messengers capable of communicating with the spiritual world. The equally varied architecture reflects these psychic leaps of logic.

Services are held daily at 0600, 1200, 1800, and 2400. Visitors are welcome to observe from the cathedral balcony and take photographs with permission.

Accommodations

Several hotels open to foreigners are located on the main street of Tay Ninh. Rooms should cost under US$5.

VUNG TAO

Vung Tao—the "Bay of Boats"—is an immensely popular beach resort some 110 km southeast of Saigon.

Known as Cape Saint Jacques during the French era, Vung Tao has a number of beach-

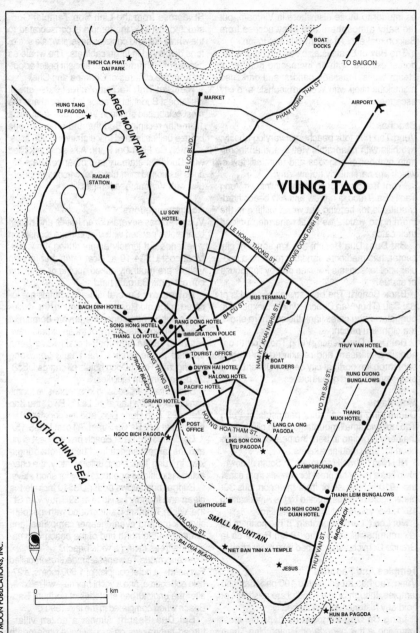

THICH CA PHAT DAI PARK

HUNG TANG TU PAGODA

LARGE MOUNTAIN

RADAR STATION

LU SON HOTEL

BOAT DOCKS

TO SAIGON

MARKET

PHAM HONG THAI ST.

AIRPORT

LE LOI BLVD.

VUNG TAO

LE HONG THONG ST.

TRUONG CONG DINH ST.

BUS TERMINAL

BA CU ST.

BACH DINH HOTEL

SONG HONG HOTEL

RANG DONG HOTEL

THANG LOI HOTEL

IMMIGRATION POLICE

QUANG TRUNG ST.

NAM KY KHAI NGHIA ST.

BOAT BUILDERS

TOURIST OFFICE

DUYEN HAI HOTEL

HALONG HOTEL

PACIFIC HOTEL

VO THI SAU ST.

THUY VAN HOTEL

RUNG DUONG BUNGALOWS

THANG MUOI HOTEL

FRONT BEACH

GRAND HOTEL

POST OFFICE

HOANG HOA THAM ST.

LANG CA ONG PAGODA

LING SON CON TU PAGODA

CAMPGROUND

NGOC BICH PAGODA

SOUTH CHINA SEA

THANH LEIM BUNGALOWS

LIGHTHOUSE

NGO NGHI CONG DUAN HOTEL

HALONG ST.

SMALL MOUNTAIN

THUY VAN ST.

BACK BEACH

BAI DUA BEACH

NIET BAN TINH XA TEMPLE

JESUS

HUN BA PAGODA

© MOON PUBLICATIONS, INC.

0   1 km

es inferior to those elsewhere in Vietnam, but the salty atmosphere and easy access from Saigon make this a worthwhile excursion.

The Bay of Boats is also something of a hedonist escape, with an increasing number of steam baths, massage parlors, and darkened nightclubs filled with Western tourists and city escapees.

Beaches

Vung Tao has four beaches of varying quality, two hills with panoramic views, and an inordinate number of pagodas and temples, few of which are particularly noteworthy.

Front Beach: Just opposite downtown Vung Tao is Bai Truoc, a narrow and silty beach hardly suitable for bathing but worth visiting in the morning to watch the local fishermen unload their catch.

Bai Dua: Dua Beach, two km south of city center, has mediocre sand but remains a popular spot for sunsets from the nearby lighthouse or statue.

Back Beach: The best stretch of sand is at Bai Sau (Thuy Van Beach), where inexpensive bungalows and cafes flank the southern end of the eight-km beach.

Bai Dau: Dau Beach, Vung Tao's fourth option, is a pleasant and relaxing palm-fringed spot three km north of city center. Decent sand plus several good guesthouses.

Mountains

Dominating the triangular peninsula of Vung Tao are two small mountains worth climbing in the early morning to beat the heat or late afternoon for spectacular sunsets.

Nui Nha ("Small Mountain"): South of downtown lies a rocky hill great for sunsets from either the 1910 lighthouse or from the enormous 30-meter figure of Jesus erected by the Americans in 1971. No, you're not in Rio de Janeiro.

Nui Lon ("Large Mountain"): The northern hill is circumnavigated by the 10-km Route de la Grande Corniche and capped by a radar station.

Temples And Pagodas

Vung Tao has an estimated 100 pagodas and temples, though only a handful are aesthetic or hold any historical significance.

Lang Ca Ong Pagoda: Perhaps the most intriguing is this pagoda on Hoang Hoa Tham St. across from the Linh Son Temple. Constructed in 1911, the temple is consecrated to the whale cult and contains several whale skeletons displayed in large cabinets. The whale as "Savior of Fishermen" is an ancient belief adopted from the cultures of Champa and Chela.

Niet Ban Tinh Xa Temple: Niet Ban—one of the largest Buddhist temples in Vietnam and the most celebrated shrine in Vung Tao—features a 12-meter reclining Buddha and an enormous bronze bell estimated to weigh over 5,000 kilos.

Thich Ca Phat Dai Park: A hillside park filled with Buddhist statuary and other concrete images fashioned after historical personages. Popular with Vietnamese tourists.

Accommodations

Vung Tao has several dozen hotels and beach bungalows packed with Vietnamese tourists on weekends but largely empty during the week. Most cost US$4-10 at local rates, but foreign visitors are routinely asked double or triple the correct tariff. Bargain hard.

Downtown: Several midrange hotels are located in the old Russian Compound, the exclusive neighborhood once the private domain of Soviet oil workers. Many of these expats have returned home and their hotels have been opened to the public. The Thang Loi, Song Huong, and Rang Dong hotels all charge US$8-28 depending on facilities.

Budget travelers seeking less expensive rooms can check the Da Lan at 14 Le Loi Blvd., the Sao Mai at 93 Tran Hung Dao, and the popular International at 242 Ba Cu Street. All cost US$5-15.

Back Beach: Back Beach has the best sand and the largest selection of beachfront bungalows in Vung Tao. Most, unfortunately, are characterless cubicles adequate only for short stays.

Budget bungalows under US$10 include the clean and friendly La Rose at 39 Thuy Van St., the Youth Tourism Campground with inexpensive rooms and even cheaper campsites, and Bimexo on the north end of the beach with casuarina trees facing a wide beach.

An enormous Taiwanese-funded resort called Fairyland—a hotel complex of 1,500 rooms, a 27-hole golf course, and a yacht marina—will radically alter the undisturbed stretches of northern Back Beach when completed in the late 1990s.

Bai Dua Beach: Almost a dozen villas-turned-bungalows on a cozy cove underneath the spreading arms of the Christ statue. All cost US$8-24.

Bai Dau Beach: Somewhat isolated but very quiet and set with a half-dozen villas in varying states of collapse and renovation. This is the cheapest, and in many ways, the most relaxing place in Vung Tao. A dozen-plus private villas have decent fan-cooled rooms with common bath from US$5. Best bets are the Nha Nghi My Tho at 47 Tran Phu St. and the Nha Hang 96, back from the water.

More expensive hotels with a/c rooms and private baths from US$15 include the Nha Nghi 29 on the waterfront and the Nha Nghi 28 at 126 Tran Phu Street.

Practicalities

The Vung Tao Tourist Office at 59 Tran Hung Dao Blvd. can help with local tours and transportation schedules. Tours can also be arranged through OTAS in the Pacific Hotel at 4 Le Loi Street. Con Dau Tourism at 450 Truong Cong Dinh St. has information on the nearby archipelago known as "Devil's Island" during the French era.

Traveler's checks can exchanged at the Vietcombank at 27 Tran Hung Dao Boulevard. The Immigration Police are at 14 Le Loi St. near the International Hotel.

Transportation

Vung Tao is three hours southeast of Saigon. Buses leave from the Mien Dong and Van Thanh bus terminals in Saigon daily until about 1500. Perhaps more convenient are the express minibuses which depart hourly from the halt at 39 Nguyen Hue Blvd. in central Saigon. Marriage taxis—enormous old American cars—are an alternative from Saigon.

Minibuses back to Saigon leave from the square on Tran Hung Dao Blvd., from Ly Tu Trong St., and from 21 Tran Hung Dao Boulevard.

THE MEKONG DELTA

The vast alluvial delta of the Mekong River offers a great deal to the traveler: beautiful scenery, friendly people, and almost a complete lack of Western tourists. Traditionally the rice basket of not only Vietnam but many other regions in Southeast Asia, the Mekong Delta is a surprisingly prosperous area where the markets are piled high with fresh produce and the people seem satisfied with their relatively high standard of living.

Visitors can spend a few days and visit the villages nearest Saigon, such as Mytho, Vinh Long, and Cantho, or make a longer excursion to the more remote and almost completely untouched villages of Long Xuyen, Chau Doc, and Rach Gia, all located toward the Cambodian border.

Travel is best completed during the dry season from November to April. Heavy monsoons from June to October make transportation difficult though not impossible.

As banks with exchange facilities are in rare supply, visitors should bring along sufficient *dong* or American currency.

Accommodations

All of the following towns have simple but adequate hotels that cost US$2-10, depending on whether you pay the local or tourist rate. Fortunately, the notion that Western tourists are uniformly wealthy and deserve to be overcharged isn't common in the delta.

Transportation

Transportation is somewhat slow around the region due to the large number of rivers which must be crossed by ferry, but roads are in good condition and buses operate frequently between almost every possible village and hamlet. Plus the scenery is wonderful.

Buses to towns in the Mekong River Delta depart from the Mien Tay Bus Terminal in western Saigon.

Principal destinations (and travel times): Mytho (two hours), Vinh Long (three hours), Cantho (four hours), Long Xuyen (five hours), Bac Lieu (six hours), Chau Doc (six hours), Rach Gia (seven hours), and Camau (eight hours).

A relaxing alternative to the bus is the passenger ferry, which departs Saigon daily in the afternoon from the pier on Ton Duc Thang St. at the end of Ham Nghi Blvd. in Saigon. The boat reaches Mytho in 6-8 hours, Cantho in 15-18 hours, and Chau Doc on the Cambodian border in 30-36 hours.

MYTHO

Mytho (My Tho), the provincial capital of Tien Giang Province, is a small but prosperous agricultural town 71 km southwest of Saigon. A popular stop en route to the deeper delta, Mytho can also be visited on a day-trip from Saigon.

The Tien Giang Provincial Tourist Office is on Hung Vuong St. at the north end of town.

Attractions

Like most towns in the Mekong Delta, Mytho has few important pagodas or historical sights, but it is situated among some of the most beautiful countryside in Vietnam. Spend your time exploring the country or taking a boat ride rather than searching for history or religion.

Sights in Town: The Central Market and yellow-and-white Mytho Church are worth visiting, but avoid the horrid tourist traps known as Vinh Trang and Quan Thanh pagodas. Both are sad spectacles completely devoid of character or authenticity—deplorable and wretched amusement parks whose only purpose is to squeeze dollars from unfortunate victims of escorted tours.

Island of the Coconut Monk: Thirty minutes by boat from Mytho is the island of Con Phung, former home of a charismatic monk who founded a religion which fused Christianity and Buddhism. The rather unusual triumvirate of this syncretic faith included Jesus, Buddha, and the Virgin Mary.

Although the colonial outpost is now largely abandoned to the weeds, the strange history of the site and the wonderful ride from the southern end of Trung Trac St. make this the highlight of Mytho.

Accommodations

Several hotels are located in the southeast corner of town. Clean and inexpensive hotels include Khach San 43 at 43 Ngo Quyen St. and the Rach Gam at 33 Trung Trac Street. The Song Tien (former Grand) Hotel is a midpriced hotel with both fan-cooled and a/c rooms. The best budget spot is the Lien Doan Lao Dong Tien Giang at the corner of 30 Thang St. and Le Loi Blvd. Rooms here cost under US$5.

Transportation

Buses from the Mien Tay Bus Terminal in Saigon terminate at the Mytho bus halt several kilometers west of town. Minibuses and *cyclos* continue into town.

VINH LONG

Vinh Long is the next riverside town reached by most visitors heading through the Mekong Delta. Once a Khmer stronghold, Vinh Long later figured in the spread of Christianity throughout the delta and was the site of heavy fighting during the Vietnam conflict.

The Cuu Long Provincial Tourist Office on Thang 5 St. can help with transportation to nearby ruins and boat journeys down the Co Chien River.

Attractions

Sights in Town: The influences of Catholicism and newer sects are seen at the cathedral, the Catholic seminary, and Cao Dai church near the bridge. Also visit the market.

Khmer Temples: Most of the Mekong Delta was populated by Khmers until Vietnamese colonizers arrived to construct a network of canals in the 17th and 18th centuries. Khmer ruins are visible four km from town adjacent to a small lake called Ba Om and south of town near the village of Tra Vinh.

Accommodations

The Cuu Long Hotel, on the river near the market, and the An Binh Hotel, behind the bus terminal, are inexpensive and fairly clean hotels.

Transportation

Vinh Long is 148 km from Saigon and 70 km southwest of Mytho. The bus terminal is in the center of town near the market and the post office and within walking distance of the hotels.

CANTHO

Cantho (Can Tho), the capital of Hau Giang Province, is the largest and most commercially successful city in the Mekong Delta. The town has an airport, a busy shipping industry, and a university that conducts agricultural research.

Hau Giang Provincial Tourist Office is on Chau Van Liem St. near the southern end of the riverside market.

Attractions

Sights around town include the Central Market on the banks of the Hau Giang (Bassac) River, the Vang Pagoda on Hoa Binh Ave. in the center of town, and a contemporary Khmer-Buddhist sanctuary known as Munikangsyaram Pagoda. Other activities include a visit to the Orchid Gardens northwest of town and a boat ride along the Hau Giang River.

Accommodations

As you might expect, the commercial and transportation center for the Mekong Delta has a large number of hotels in all price ranges. Hoa Binh Hotel, on Hoa Binh Blvd. and just opposite the Munikangsyaram Pagoda, is very cheap if somewhat noisy.

Tour groups and mid-level travelers often stay in the Quoc Te (International) Hotel facing the river and one block north of the marketplace. Rooms here cost US$8-10 with fan and US$12-25 with a/c. Probably the best deal in town. Hau Giang Hotel on Nam Ky Khan Nghia St. is in the same price range.

Transportation

Cantho is 165 km from Saigon and 32 km from Vinh Long. The bus terminal is two km northwest of town near the ferry halt. Cantho can also be reached by passenger boat from Saigon.

DALAT TO NHA TRANG

The southern third of Vietnam includes the deltas, coastline, and highlands that lie between the southernmost extension and Qui Nhon in south-central Vietnam.

The South is quite different from the North—differences which range from social and psychological to political and economic. Much of these contrasts can be attributed to the superior economic conditions in the South, its long history of foreign involvement, and its preferable climate. The North is regularly ravaged by typhoons and has a wet, bitterly cold winter, while the South is blessed with a pleasant tropical climate more conducive to pleasure than work. In addition, the North is much more densely populated, causing serious land shortages and forcing northerners to work harder and then conserve their savings with tightfisted determination.

Furthermore, travelers and even the Vietnamese themselves report significant personality differences between the peoples. Southerners are considered to be friendly, funny, easygoing, open-minded, and adventurous, while northerners sometimes come across as uptight, traditional, and conservative.

Although these differences sharpen as you slowly travel from Saigon north toward Hanoi, the beauty of Vietnam and the essential goodness of the people also make the journey one of the better travel experiences in Southeast Asia.

DALAT

First stop for many travelers from Saigon is the delightfully cool mountain resort of Dalat, 300 km north of the city.

Dalat was founded in the early 1920s by the French, who were enchanted with the region's temperate climate, its pine forests and waterfalls, its alpine vistas and tropical lakes. Inspired by nature and anxious to escape the searing heat of Saigon, they fashioned a romantic piece of Europe 1,500 meters above sea level, a summer retreat rife with exquisite colonial villas, blooming gardens, and broad residential streets overlooking verdant valleys.

Today, Dalat is the honeymoon capital of the South, flush with romantically named hideaways such as the Valley of Love and Lake of Sighs, filled with ducks and tiny sailboats.

Dalat has plenty of attractions but perhaps the greatest draw is simply watching Vietnamese tourists and honeymooners carry on their lives and courtships in such an incongruous place—a taste of France in the mountains of Vietnam.

Dalat has got it all—superb scenery, pleasant climate, colonial atmosphere, cozy cafes, and a broad range of hotels and guesthouses.

Xuan Huong Lake

The centerpiece of Dalat is this lovely lake created in 1919 by flooding the west end of the

DALAT

TO LAT VILLAGE (6 km)

TUNG LAM

TO ANCROET FALLS (10 km)

★ VALLEY OF LOVE

CHIEN THANG LAKE

■ DALAT CEMETERY

NGUYEN CONG TRU ST.

PHU DONG THIEN VUONG ST.

MILITARY ACADEMY ●

■ NUCLEAR RESEARCH CENTER

■ DALAT UNIVERSITY

TO LAKE OF SIGHS (2 km)

★ DOMAINE MARIE CONVENT

LINH SON PAGODA ★

MAI HOC DE ST.

HAI BA TRUNG ST.

PHAN DINH PHUNG ST.

★ FLOWER GARDENS

GOLF COURSE

XUAN HUONG LAKE

GRAND LYCEE YERSIN ■

QUANG TRUNG ST.

CAM LY WATERFALL

SEE "CENTRAL DALAT" MAP

HOANG VAN THU ST.

OLD RAILWAY STATION ■

LE THAI TO ST.

HOANG HOA TAM ST.

LAM TY NI PAGODA ★

POST OFFICE ★

TOURIST OFFICE ★

PALACE HOTEL ●

TRAN HUNG DAO ST.

VILLAS ●●●

★ GOVERNOR-GENERAL'S RESIDENCE

DALAT CATHEDRAL ★

DALAT HOTEL ●

DINH II VILLA ●

DU SINH CHURCH ★

PASTEUR INSTITUTE ★

VILLAS ●

LE HONG PHONG ST.

MINH TAM VILLA ●

★ BAO DAI SUMMER PALACE

KHE SANH ST.

SU NU PAGODA ★

0   1 km

THIEN VUONG PAGODA ★

TO SAIGON (308 km) AND PHAN RANG (101 km)

HWY. 20

MINH NGUYET CU SY LAM PAGODA ★

© MOON PUBLICATIONS, INC.

valley. Around the lake is a 64-hectare golf course, laid out by the French in 1925 but abandoned after reunification in 1975; the Dalat Flower Gardens, which date from 1966; and the Palace Hotel, overlooking the south end of the lake.

French Quarter

A surprising amount of old French-colonial atmosphere survives in the streets and lanes between the town square and Phan Dinh Phung St., and near the bridge spanning the Cam Ly River. More spectacular French villas are located southeast of the lake along Tran Hung Dao Street.

French Governor-general's Residence

Many of the French-colonial villas in Dalat are now owned by the Provincial Tourism Authority, which rents them to visitors, including this impressive house open to the public daily 0730-1100 and 1330-1630.

Bao Dai Summer Palace

The 25-room summer residence of Vietnam's last Nguyen emperor, Bao Dai (reigned 1926-45), stands in a large park about two km from city center. Constructed in 1933 and designed by a French architect in the then-popular art-deco style, Dai's retreat is well preserved and worth visiting to view the period interior furnishings and watch the antics of Vietnamese tourists. Open daily 0730-1100 and 1330-1630.

Attractions Outside Town

The following sights are worth visiting if only to see how Vietnam markets its tourist attractions and the impact of clearcut logging on the once-dense forests. All can be reached by bicycle, rented motorcycle, or motorcycle taxi.

Cam Ly Falls: Three km west of downtown are some badly commercialized falls surrounded by souvenir shops and food stalls. Waterfalls located farther afield are usually less crowded and less commercially exploited.

Valley of Love: An artificial lake formed in 1972, with horse rides and boat rentals.

Lake of Sighs: A well-named natural lake with horses, boats, and small cafes.

Tribal Villages: Dalat is centered amid a number of small villages inhabited by various animist minorities who sometimes visit the weekend market in Dalat. Local officials discourage visits to these villages, which, in most cases, are fairly Westernized and lack the allure of other more remote villages.

Budget Accommodations

Dalat has almost 100 guesthouses, villas, and hotels spread across town and in the hills. Most have now opened their doors to Western visitors, but the more popular places are often filled on weekends and double or triple their rates for tourists. Hotel touts at the bus terminal can help you find a place in your price range.

Plenty of inexpensive hotels are found near the Central Market and in the old French Quarter just above the market. Prices are subject to negotiation.

The two most popular backpackers' guesthouses are the Mimosa Hotel at 170 Phan Dinh Phung St. and the nearby Cam D. Hotel. Both charge US$5-10 for clean rooms and are located a few blocks west of the Hoa Binh Hotel, shown on the map of "Central Dalat."

The Modern Hotel facing the roundabout is reasonably priced and conveniently located but somewhat noisy on weekends. A half-dozen inexpensive guesthouses line Nguyen Chi Thanh St., up the stairway and one block west of the Central Market.

Another street filled with small budget guesthouses is Phan Bai Chau, northwest of the market and just past the cinema. Inexpensive choices north of Hoa Binh Square include the Phu Hoa, Phuoc Duc, and Vinh Quang hotels. All have rooms from US$3-10.

Moderate Accommodations

By far the most memorable option is to stay in one of the old French chalets overlooking the lake.

Private Villas: The largest concentration is on Tran Hung Dao St. just south of the lake and near the Pasteur Institute on Le Hong Phong Street. Some can be rented through the tourist office but a more direct and possibly cheaper approach is to simply knock on the door and inquire about rooms.

An entire villa should cost US$10-25 per day, depending on the size and amenities such as meals. Top-end places are priced accordingly.

Dinh II Villa: The former governor-general's residence described above is quite imposing but overrun with Vietnamese tourists who romp

CENTRAL DALAT

VINH QUANG HOTEL

NGUYEN VAN TRAI ST.

TO LAT VILLAGE

TO GUESTHOUSES

PHUOC DUC GUESTHOUSE

TANG BAT HO ST.

PHAN BAI CHAU ST.

LOCAL BUSES

PHU HOA HOTEL

HOA BINH HOTEL

TRUONG CONG DINH ST.

HOA BINH SQUARE

CINEMA

NHA KHACH GUESTHOUSE

TO MIMOSA AND CAM DO HOTELS

CENTRAL MARKET

VIETNAM AIRLINES

DUY TAN ST.

THUY TIEN HOTEL

ANH DAO HOTEL

THANH BINH HOTEL

HAI SON HOTEL

KHAI NGHIA NAM KY ST.

NGUYEN CHI THANH ST.

LE DAI HANH ST.

NGUYEN THI MINH KHAI ST.

TO FLOWER GARDENS

THANH THUY RESTAURANT

CAFES

GUESTHOUSES

NGUYEN THAI HOC ST.

XUAN HUONG LAKE

0   100 m

KHAI NAM ST.

DALAT BUS TERMINAL

TAXIS

PALACE HOTEL

TO LAKE OF SIGHS

TOURIST OFFICE

POST OFFICE

DALAT HOTEL

HUONG VAN THU ST.

TO PASTEUR INSTITUTE AND VILLAS

DALAT CATHEDRAL

TO VILLAS AND SAIGON

© MOON PUBLICATIONS, INC.

through the common areas during the day. 12 Tran Hung Dao St., tel. 2092, US$40-80. Reservations can be made at the tourist office.

Dalat Hotel: Another old villa constructed in 1907 in a convenient location adjacent to the cathedral. The colonial elegance has faded somewhat but renovations are planned. 7 Tran Phu St., tel. 2863, US$30-75.

Palace Hotel: The finest hotel in Dalat includes two dozen large and well-appointed rooms, tennis courts, and outstanding views from the restaurant which overlooks the lake and valleys. 2 Tran Phu St., tel. 2203, US$50-95.

Restaurants

The high elevation and moderate climate of Dalat allow the cultivation of a wide range of produce and fruit, probably the greatest selection anywhere in Vietnam. Depending on the season, the market will be filled with anything from fresh strawberries to ripe avocados, not to mention persimmons, cherries, and crisp apples.

Budget Cafes: Restaurant prices are quite reasonable due to competition and the fact that most of the produce and fruit is locally grown. The least expensive options are the food stalls behind the Central Market and the small cafes which line the road heading down to the lake.

Lakeside Restaurants: Certainly the most memorable meals in Dalat are available in the villas, which offer panoramic views, and in the small cafes and elevated restaurants on the shores of Xuan Huong Lake. Among the restaurants with lake views are the Thanh Thuy on the north side near the bus terminal, Xuan Huong at the western edge, and Thuy Ta overlooking the lake below the Palace Hotel.

Practicalities

Tourist Information: The Long Dong Provincial Tourist Office, near the post office and opposite the Dalat Hotel, helps arrange tours and rents chalets but is otherwise useless for most visitors. A better bet is the Youth Tourism Company near the Central Market, which assists campers and sponsors treks into the countryside.

Banks: Currency and traveler's checks can be exchanged at several banks near the Central Market and at the Palace Hotel.

Post and Telecommunications: The General Post Office near the Dalat Hotel also provides international telephone and fax services.

Transportation

Dalat is 300 km northeast of Saigon and 110 km from Nha Trang.

Air: Vietnam Airlines flies three times weekly from Saigon to Dalat Airport, 30 minutes south of the city. The office is on Truong Cong Dinh St. just across from the Rap 3/4 Cinema.

Bus: Dalat has two bus terminals. Long-distance buses to Saigon and Nha Trang depart from the Dalat Bus Terminal (Ben Xe Dalat), near the lake and fountain roundabout. Buses to destinations within the province leave from the Provincial Bus Terminal (Ben Xe Hoa Binh), behind the cinema.

Minibuses to Saigon and Nha Trang leave from both terminals. Most travelers find minibuses faster and more comfortable than public buses. Departures are from 0500 to 1200.

PHAN RANG

Phan Rang and its sister city of Thap Cham are small seaside towns chiefly visited for their Cham towers and isolated Cham villages situated in the dry, almost desertlike landscapes of south-central Vietnam. The region is also famed for its production of table grapes.

Phan Rang is a minor destination though it provides a convenient layover point between Saigon or Dalat and Nha Trang. A small tourist office is located in the Huu Nghi Hotel.

Attractions

Champa was a Hindu-influenced empire which rose around present-day Danang in the late 2nd century and expanded southward to Nha Trang and Phan Rang by the 8th century. Ruled by a series of kings who adopted Hinduism as their religion and employed Sanskrit as the court language, the Cham Empire fell in the 17th century to Vietnamese forces during their southward march toward Saigon.

Po Klang Garai Towers: Phan Rang's claims to fame are the four Cham towers constructed during the 13th century on a boulder-strewn hill some seven km west of town on the road to Dalat. The heavily renovated towers, two km beyond the village of Thap Cham, can be reached by bicycle, *cyclo,* or any bus heading toward Dalat. Train arrivals can see the towers from the train station in Thap Cham.

Po Ro Me Towers: Another set of Cham towers is situated 10 km south of Phan Rang and five km west of Highway 1. These brick towers were constructed by King Po Ro, the final ruler of an independent Champa, who died a prisoner of the Vietnamese in 1651.

Accommodations

Phan Rang has several hotels about 500 meters south of the main bus terminal. Nuu Nghi Hotel on Huong Vuong St., about 200 meters east of the main road, is the main tourist stop, but rooms are overpriced at US$20-35.

More reasonable are the Thong Nhat Hotel, on the main road in the north end of town, and the budget Phan Rong Hotel, at the south end of the main road and one block past the pink Chinese pagoda. Both should cost under US$10 for fan-cooled rooms or US$15-20 with a/c.

Transportation

Phan Rang is 344 km north of Saigon, 82 km east of Dalat, and 105 km south of Nha Trang. The long-distance bus terminal 500 meters north of town has regular connections with Saigon, Dalat, and Nha Trang. The local bus terminal is on the main road in the south end of town.

The nearest train station is at Thap Cham, about five km west of town. Trains take about 10 hours from Saigon.

NHA TRANG

Nha Trang, a prosperous fishing town of 250,000 people, is known for its collection of restored Cham towers and the six-km white-sand beach which flanks the eastern edge of the seaport.

Perhaps the cleanest municipal beach in South Vietnam, the sands of Nha Trang were immensely popular during the war era with American servicemen stationed at nearby Cam Ranh Bay and later the favorite spot of Soviet sailors who occupied the sprawling naval complex until a few years ago.

Today, Nha Trang is chiefly visited by domestic tourists and a handful of Western travelers who enjoy the long palm-fringed beach and vaguely Mediterranean flavor of the seaside town. Deserted beaches, diving, sportfishing, and historical ruins are the highlights of Nha Trang.

Beaches And Islands

Nha Trang's lovely beach is complemented by a half-dozen nearby islands surrounded by aquamarine, almost transparent waters, which provide some of the best scuba diving in the country. Western dive operators are just now beginning to explore the nearby reefs and islands such as Bamboo (Hon Tre), Ebony (Hon Mun), and Salangane (Hon Yen), a major source of bird's nests for soup and an important sportfishing area.

Po Nagar Cham Temple

Vietnam's more accessible examples of Cham architecture are the four Brahman sanctuaries which rise from a rocky hill two km north of Nha Trang, just beyond the two bridges which cross the Cai River. Flag down a bus or enjoy the walk.

The 23-meter North Tower was constructed in 817 to honor Po Nagar (Thien Yana, or "Mistress of the Kingdom"), the mythical goddess who introduced weaving and new agricultural techniques to the Chams. Today the tower enshrines a black stone image of the goddess—female counterpart to Shiva—and her associated animal. The statue was decapitated during the French era and the original head is now displayed in the Guimet Museum in Paris.

The Central Tower, reconstructed by King Jaya Indravarman in the 12th century, contains a Hindu lingam (phallic symbol) and serves as a fertility temple for childless couples.

More statuary is exhibited in the Cham Museum of Danang.

Long Son Pagoda

A gaily decorated pagoda founded in the 19th century but heavily reconstructed in recent years, the interior sanctuary features murals depicting stories, Chinese dragons which wrap around the columns, and several finely illuminated images of the Buddha.

Behind the pagoda sits an immense white Buddha which contemplates all of Nha Trang from its elevated position. The nine-meter Buddha was constructed in 1965 to commemorate those monks who committed self-immolation and called worldwide attention to the human-rights abuses of the Diem regime.

Pasteur Institute

Nha Trang's Pasteur Institute was founded in 1895 by Dr. Alexandre Yersin, a French mili-

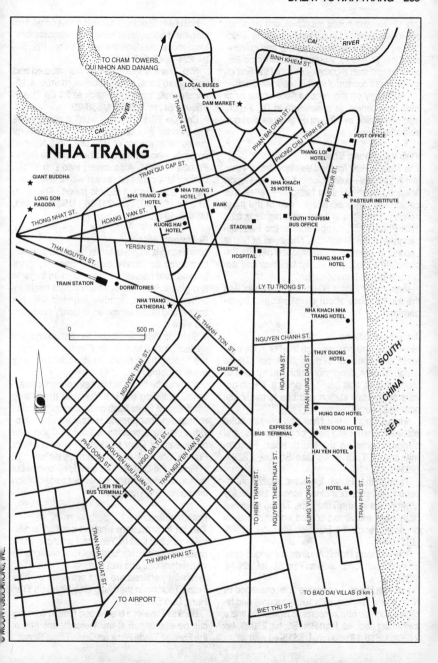

NHA TRANG

TO CHAM TOWERS,
QUI NHON AND DANANG

CAI RIVER

BINH KHIEM ST.

LOCAL BUSES

DAM MARKET ★

2 THANG 4 ST.

PHAN BAI CHAU ST.

PHONG CHU TRINH ST.

POST OFFICE

THANG LOI HOTEL

PASTEUR ST.

TRAN QUI CAP ST.

GIANT BUDDHA ★

LONG SON PAGODA ★

NHA TRANG 2 HOTEL ●

NHA TRANG 1 HOTEL ●

NHA KHACH 25 HOTEL ●

PASTEUR INSTITUTE ★

THONG NHAT ST.

HOANG VAN ST.

BANK ●

KUONG HAI HOTEL ●

STADIUM ■

YOUTH TOURISM BUS OFFICE ●

YERSIN ST.

HOSPITAL ■

THAI NGUYEN ST.

THANG NHAT HOTEL ●

TRAIN STATION ▬

DORMITORIES ●

NHA TRANG CATHEDRAL ★

LY TU TRONG ST.

0   500 m

NHA KHACH NHA TRANG HOTEL ●

LE THANH TON ST.

NGUYEN CHANH ST.

NGUYEN TRAI ST.

CHURCH ■

HOA TAM ST.

TRAN HUNG DAO ST.

THUY DUONG HOTEL ●

SOUTH CHINA SEA

HUNG DAO HOTEL ●

EXPRESS BUS TERMINAL ■

VIEN DONG HOTEL ●

PHU DONG ST.

NGUYEN HUU HUAN ST.

NGO GIA TU ST.

TRAN NGUYEN HAN ST.

HAI YEN HOTEL ●

TO HIEN THANH ST.

NGUYEN THIEN THUAT ST.

HUNG VUONG ST.

HOTEL 44 ●

LIEN TINH BUS TERMINAL ■

TRAN PHU ST.

TRAN NHAT DUAT ST.

THI MINH KHAI ST.

TO AIRPORT

BIET THU ST.

TO BAO DAI VILLAS (3 km)

CAI RIVER

© MOON PUBLICATIONS, INC.

tary doctor and noted microbiologist who had previously assisted Louis Pasteur in Paris. Credited with the introduction of rubber and quinine-producing trees to Vietnam, Yersin also discovered and then recommended that the French government construct the hill resort at Dalat.

The library on the second floor of the back wing now serves as a museum to Dr. Yersin, who was buried by request on institute land outside Nha Trang.

Vinh Van Phong Beach

The *Master Plan for the Development of Tourism in Vietnam*—a six-volume 1,000-page report financed by the United Nations—called this completely deserted beach "one of the most beautiful sea sites in Asia—of a higher quality than Phuket and comparable to the beautiful beaches in the Seychelles and even of Sierra Leone." A great recommendation despite the complete absence of tourist facilities and access by public transportation.

Vinh Van Phong is 60 km north of town. Ask the tourist office about directions and transportation.

Accommodations

Most hotels are on the beach road or in the center of town just north of the train station. Those which accept *dong* are much cheaper than tourist hotels that demand dollars. *Cyclo* drivers at the train station and bus terminal can help find budget places.

Vien Dong Hotel: New and very popular place with swimming pool, bicycle rentals, and budget rooms on the fourth floor. Recommended. 1 Tran Hung Dao St., tel. 22291, US$10-25.

Thang Nhat Hotel: Excellent beachfront location and spacious clean rooms. Like many other hotels in Nha Trang, the Thang Nhat has both inexpensive fan-cooled and moderately priced a/c rooms. 18 Tran Phu Blvd., tel. 22966, US$10-25.

Thuy Duong Hotel: Another low-priced hotel on the beach road. 36 Tran Phu St., tel. 22534, US$6-22.

Hai Yen Hotel: An upscale hotel managed by Khanh Hoa Tourism, with 106 a/c rooms and facilities such as tennis courts, a nightclub, and a swimming pool. 40 Tran Phu St., tel. 22828, fax 21902, US$8-12 with fan, US$15-40 with a/c.

Hotel 44: Spacious colonial mansion with an elegant if somewhat run-down atmosphere. Most rooms overlook the sea. 44 Tran Phu St., tel. 22445, US$15-35.

Nha Trang 2 Hotel: Newly constructed and very clean hotel with spacious rooms. A 10-minute walk from the beach at 21 Le Thanh Phuong St., tel. 22956, US$8-20.

Cau Da Villa: The final word in elegance is this colonial villa constructed in the 1920s as the summer retreat of Bao Dai, final Nguyen emperor, who threw parties here until he fled to France in 1954. Also called Bao Dai Villas, today it is a capitalist retreat with a seedy but memorable French Gothic mood. Tran Phu St., tel. 22449, fax 21906, US$5-10 fan, US$25-40 a/c.

Restaurants

Nha Trang is famous for its seafood specialties, such as locally caught lobsters, giant prawns, and horseshoe crabs cooked in garlic and ginger. More adventurous diners might try butter-fried frogs, noodles sautéed with pig brains, and rabbit simmered in locally produced red wine.

Seaside cafes and open-air restaurants are perfect places to point and order and watch the fishing fleet return to town in the early evening hours.

Many of the better hotels have decent restaurants, including the Hai Yen and the Thang Nhat, known for its fresh crabs and spicy rocket shrimp. Another popular restaurant which provides tableside cooking is the Lac Canh, one block east of Dam Market. This spot offers French, Chinese, and Vietnamese dishes.

Finally, the Cau Da Villa serves elaborate but reasonably priced meals in its restaurant, which overlooks Nha Trang Bay.

Practicalities

Tourist Information: Khanh Hoa Tourism on the grounds of the Hai Yen Hotel arranges tours, rents cars and boats, and provides services for visa extensions and exit permits.

Similar services are also provided by Nha Trang Tourism in the Hung Dao Hotel on Tran Hung Dao Street.

Banks: Traveler's checks and foreign currency can be exchanged at the Vietcombank and at the Foreign Trade Bank on Quan Trung Street.

Post and Telecommunications: The post office is on Tran Phu Street. International phone calls can be made from the GPO and telecommunications office on Le Thanh Ton St., 100 meters from the beach.

Transportation

Nha Trang is 105 km from Phan Rang, 110 km from Dalat, 238 km from Qui Nhon, and 445 km from Saigon.

Air: Vietnam Airlines flies four times weekly from Saigon and Hanoi and twice weekly from Danang. Their office is at 82 Tran Phu Boulevard.

Train: Trains heading north leave four times daily and take 10 hours to Qui Nhon and 40 hours to Hanoi. Express trains take 10 hours to Saigon. The ticket office at the train station is open daily 0700-1400.

Bus: Express buses leave from the Lien Tien Bus Terminal in the southwest section of Nha Trang and from another terminal on Le Thanh Ton St. near the Hung Dao Hotel. Long-distance bus services are also available from the centrally located Youth Tourism office just north of Yersin Street. Advance booking is recommended.

Local buses leave from the halt on 2 Thang 4 Street.

QUI NHON TO HUE

QUI NHON AND VICINITY

Qui Nhon, the capital of Binh Dinh Province, is a convenient spot to break the long journey between Nha Trang and Danang. The town was once the center of the Cham kingdom and later one of four primary deep-water ports used by the American military—the others being Saigon, Danang, and Cam Ranh Bay, 50 km south of Nha Trang.

Vietnamese nationals associate the town with the famous Tay Son Rebellion of 1771-88, during which the Tay Son brothers brilliantly defended their country against Chinese aggression and briefly united Vietnam. The brothers are now revered as among the greatest of all national heroes.

Attractions

Qui Nhon itself offers little of great interest aside from walking along the beach and visiting the market in the early morning hours. Most attractions are located well outside town and are difficult to reach without private transportation.

Lon Khanh Pagoda: Qui Nhon's main religious shrine was founded by a Chinese merchant around 1710 but the present building dates from 1946. Noteworthy features include several large Buddha images and photographs of the monks who committed self-immolation in Saigon to protest the Diem regime.

Cham Towers: Thap Doi are two Cham towers with distinct arching roofs situated three km west of town toward Highway 1. Cham ruins are also located at Cha Ban some 26 km north of Qui Nhon. Thap Duong Long ("Towers of Ivory") are eight km from Cha Ban.

Quang Trung Museum: A small museum dedicated to the most famous of the three Tay Son brothers (Quang Trung) is found 48 km west of Qui Nhon on Highway 19 in the direction of Pleiku.

Accommodations

Several decent hotels are near the bus terminal and within walking distance of the train station. Most accept *dong* and are therefore quite inexpensive.

Nha Khach Ngan Hang Dau Tu: Two blocks down the street from the bus terminal is a budget hotel with fairly clean rooms. 399 Tran Hung Dao St., tel. 22012, US$3-10.

Qui Nhon Peace Hotel: Just down the road from the first hotel. Similar facilities and prices. 266 Tran Hung Dao St., tel. 22900, US$3-10.

Viet Cuong Hotel: About 100 meters south of the train station and north of the bus terminal is a simple place with small but acceptable rooms. 460 Tran Hung Dao St., tel. 22434, US$3-10.

Qui Nhon Tourist Hotel: As the name implies, this hotel is geared toward tourists and therefore demands payment in dollars. The hotel is overpriced but has some of the few a/c rooms in town and faces the best stretch of

QUI NHON

SOUTH CHINA SEA

VIET CUONG HOTEL
BUS TERMINAL
TO TRAIN STATION AND HWY. 1
PHAN DIN PHUNG ST.
MAI XUAN THOUNG ST.
BACH DANG ST.
THANH BINH HOTEL
NHA KHACH NGAN HANG DAU TU HOTEL
SAIGON HOTEL
DONG PHUONG HOTEL
QUI NHON PEACE HOTEL
NHA KHACH HUU NGHI HOTEL
TRAN CAO VAN ST.
1 THANG 4 ST.
STADIUM
BANK
OLYMPIC HOTEL
CHURCH
TRAN HUNG DAO ST.
TANG BA HO ST.
LON KHANH PAGODA
LE LOI ST.
CENTRAL MARKET
PHAN BOI CHAU ST.
TRAN BIN TRANG ST.
TRAN PHU ST.
HONG PHONG ST.
HAI BA TRUNG ST.
LINH ST.
POST OFFICE
NGUYEN TRAI ST.
MOON
MINI HAI HA HOTEL
EXPRESS BUSES
QUI NHON TOURIST HOTEL
DIN BO
NGUYEN HUE ST.
TOURIST OFFICE
ZOO
CITY BEACH

0   100 m

© MOON PUBLICATIONS, INC.

sand within the municipality. 12 Nguyen Hue St., tel. 32401, US$25-35. Vietnamese citizens pay US$4-6.

Saigon Hotel: New hotel catering to tour groups and affluent travelers. Best in town. Tran Hung Dao St., tel. 22404, US$20-30.

Transportation

Qui Nhon is 238 km north of Nha Trang and 304 km south of Danang.

Train: The Qui Nhon train station is about 1.5 km northwest of city center. Travelers intending to visit Qui Nhon must take one of the slower trains—express services do not stop here. For this reason, most visitors arrive by bus or chartered taxi.

Bus: Long-distance buses leave from the bus terminal on Tran Hung Dao St., about one km northwest of city center, and from the Ex-

press Terminal near the Qui Nhon Tourist Hotel. Departures to Nha Trang and Danang are in the early morning around 0500.

QUANG NGAI AND MY LAI

My Lai

The massacre at My Lai—a small hamlet near the provincial capital of Quang Ngai—will always be remembered as among the most unfortunate incidents of the Vietnam War. My Lai also signaled a turning point in the war, when many Americans began to question the morality of the Indochinese conflict.

The incident began on the morning of 16 March 1968 soon after paratroopers of the 23rd Infantry Division landed near the village of Son My. Under the command of Lt. William

Calley, their assignment was to investigate the earlier deaths of six soldiers who had stumbled across Viet Cong landmines. Instead, Calley and his soldiers proceeded to massacre some 347 unarmed men, women, and children before killing the livestock and torching the village.

Almost every command level of the American Army then became involved in an elaborate plan designed to coverup the crime. The ruse worked until the story was reported by Seymour Hersh in the *New York Times* on 13 November 1968—a full eight months after the massacre.

Although Calley was court-martialed and personally convicted of almost 109 murders, Nixon granted a presidential pardon after Calley had served just three years of his sentence. Calley later committed suicide.

Today, the site is commemorated with a large memorial, a small museum, and a few small graves. No less moving are the comments in the visitors' book, many of which are from returning GIs.

Accommodations

My Lai: A small guesthouse surrounded by flowers is located in My Lai, though most visitors simply pause for an afternoon or spend the evening in Quang Ngai.

Quang Ngai: Khach San So 1 Hotel across from the bus terminal and Khach San So 2 Hotel two blocks northwest are inexpensive places which accept payment in *dong*.

Nha Khach Uy Ban Thi is a better spot but demands payment in dollars and is overpriced at US$20.

Song Tra: Most visitors are forced to overnight at this high-rise hotel on the northern outskirts of town. To nobody's surprise the hotel is owned by Quang Ngai Tourism. Quang Trung St., tel. 21663, US$20-30.

Transportation

Quang Ngai is 174 km north of Qui Nhon and 130 km south of Danang.

The bus station is conveniently located in the center of town just off Highway 1. The train station is about three km west.

The turnoff to My Lai, 14 km northeast of Quang Ngai, is indicated by a plaque one km north of town. My Lai can be reached by motorcycle taxi from town.

HOI AN

Hoi An is an ancient city and a living museum nestled on the banks of the Thu Bon River, 28 km south of Danang. The town features some of the best-preserved architecture found anywhere in Vietnam.

Originally a seaport during the Champa era, Hoi An (then called Faifo) served as a thriving port of call for traders from all parts of the world from the 16th to 18th centuries. Portuguese traders and Jesuit missionaries, who arrived after expulsion from Japan, were followed by waves of Chinese entrepreneurs who fled their homeland after the fall of the Ming Dynasty. Japanese merchants also arrived to construct their homes and temples, take Vietnamese wives, and conduct business.

Home to a vibrant, international community of merchants, Hoi An sparkled as one of Vietnam's more important trading centers until the silting of the Thu Bon River forced the community to pull up roots and move north to Danang. The town then went into decline.

Today, Hoi An sleeps on, an undisturbed piece of history largely spared the destruction which has befallen so much of ancient Vietnam. This fact alone makes Hoi An one of the best destinations in central Vietnam.

Hoi An's ancient homes and Chinese assembly halls are concentrated near the riverfront on Tran Phu or Nguyen Thai Hoc streets. A small tourist office is on Tran Hung Dao St. near the Hoi An Hotel.

Japanese Covered Bridge

A convenient start for your walking tour is the famous landmark constructed in the 17th century to connect the Chinese quarters with the Japanese settlement on the south bank.

Quang Dong Assembly Hall

Many of the Chinese groups which fled their homeland after the fall of the Ming Dynasty erected elaborate assembly halls to aid their compatriots and honor Quan Cong, a talented general of the Three Kingdoms period, and Thien Hau, goddess of the sea and protector of fishermen.

Unlike most other assembly halls in Hoi An, Quang Dong served the economic and religious needs of all Chinese citizens regardless of their region of origin.

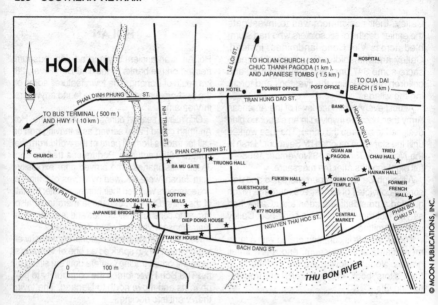

Nguyen Thai Hoc Street

Many of the fine old homes erected by wealthy Chinese and Vietnamese merchants have opened their doors to visitors for a small admission charge, including the Tan Ky House at number 101 and the Diep Dong Nguyen House at number 80. All reflect the wealth and refined taste of their owners, who utilized both Chinese and Japanese architectural styles.

Tran Phu Street

Among the highlights on this ancient street are the private homes at numbers 74, 77, and 148, plus several assembly halls erected by Fukien, Hainanese, and Cantonese traders.

Many of the elongated homes now function as cotton mills filled with superb old looms that click and clack throughout the day.

Quan Cong And
Quan Am Pagodas

A pair of interlinked pagodas—founded in the 17th century but reconstructed in modern times—are found at the east end of Tran Phu St. just opposite the Central Market.

French Architecture

Colonnaded and shuttered homes of French inspiration flank the entire length of Phan Bai Chau St. just east of Cam Nam Bridge.

Hoi An Church

Many of the European traders, colonial administrators, and foreign missionaries who once lived in Hoi An are buried in the grounds of this modern church.

Chuc Thanh Pagoda

The oldest pagoda in Hoi An is in the north end of town some 800 meters past the church. Chuc Thanh (also called Phuc Thanh) was founded in 1454 by a Buddhist monk from China.

Phuoc Lam Pagoda

A 17th-century pagoda about 400 meters north of Chuc Thanh.

Accommodations

Hoi An Town Guesthouse: Simple place with inexpensive rooms and shared bathrooms. 92 Tran Phu St., no phone, US$5-8.

Hoi An Hotel: Restored colonial-style building situated amid trees and gardens. 6 Tran Hung Dao St., tel. 4373, US$10-22.

Tourist officials have announced plans to construct a new hotel, which will probably demand payment in dollars.

Transportation

Hoi An is 28 km south of Danang, near the mouth of the Thu Bon River.

Buses from both the main and local bus terminals in Danang take about an hour to reach Hoi An, passing through lovely scenery of ricefields and swaying palms.

DANANG AND VICINITY

Danang is situated in a region rich with history—both ancient and contemporary. Vietnam's fourth-largest city (population 400,000) rose to prominence in the 2nd century A.D. as the primary port of the Chams, the brilliant Hindu empire which once stretched all the way from Hue in the north to Vung Tao in the south. During the mid-18th century the city was the focus of struggles between Vietnamese and Spanish forces, who ostensibly wished to end mistreatment of Catholic missionaries by the government of Emperor Tu Duc. By that time, Danang had superseded Hoi Fa as the primary seaport and commercial center between Hanoi and Saigon.

The French began their colonial experience here in August 1858 when French forces fired at Danang's coastal defenses and landed troops to seize the town they subsequently renamed Tourane, a term which roughly described the soup-tureen-shaped bay to the north.

But for Americans, Danang will always be remembered as the site where 3,500 American soldiers landed on 8 March 1965 to signal the official arrival of combat troops—not advisers— into the Vietnam War. During the next decade, Danang grew to become the world's largest Marine base, the "Rocket City" where hundreds of thousands of Americans got their first look at the exotic land of Vietnam.

The fall of Danang to the Communists in 1975 shocked the world with its desperate scenes of panicked refugees trying to board the last planes and ships out of town. Four weeks later, the first rockets fell on Saigon.

ATTRACTIONS IN TOWN

Despite all the history, Danang offers a limited number of attractions within the city limits. Visitors interested in Cham ruins or beaches must make day-trips from the city.

Cham Museum

A useful introduction to the culture and artistic styles of the Chams is provided in this open-air museum founded in 1916 by the École Française D'Extrème-Orient as the world's finest repository of Cham art. The complex includes a number of rooms arranged around different periods and regions of origin, including chambers filled with outstanding sculpture from My Son, Tra Kieu, Dong Duong, and Thap Mam. Indian and Khmer influence is obvious in the later periods.

The museum is open Tues.-Sun. 0800-1100 and 1300-1700.

Cao Dai Church

Danang's Cao Dai Church, second largest in the country, is less striking than the sect's headquarters in Tay Ninh but nevertheless worth visiting to see the elaborate interior and the mystical symbols on which the religion is based. Services are held daily at 0600, 1200, 1800, and 2400.

Danang Cathedral

Constructed by the French in 1923, this pink sandstone edifice with its stained-glass windows and Gothic moodiness is now home to a community of some 4,000 Catholics. Masses are held daily at 0500 and 1700.

American Legacies

Visitors intrigued with signs of colonial occupation and the Vietnam War are often surprised at the near-complete lack of evidence throughout the country. The vestiges are here, though often repainted, renamed, and converted to more utilitarian uses.

American Consulate: Once dubbed the "White Elephant" by U.S. personnel stationed in Danang, this decrepit brick building now houses a small theater and desultory War Crimes Museum which local authorities intend to move soon to another location.

American Navy Club: Now the Seamen's Institute—a curious name for a bar.

Third Marine Amphibious Headquarters: Now a Vietnamese military training center called Nguyen Ai Quoc Academy, named after one of the noms de guerre of Ho Chi Minh.

Danang International Airport: Once among the most active airbases in the world, today the enormous airfield shows little evidence of its turbulent history aside from a few abandoned batteries and rusting carcasses of destroyed jets. According to folklore, most of the scrap was sold to the Japanese, who melted it down and reforged it into automobiles then sold to the Americans—a farfetched tale retold with great relish by many local Vietnamese.

French-era City Hall: The provincial headquarters of the local Communist party.

American Press Center: A shrimp cannery.

ACCOMMODATIONS AND FOOD

Danang has over a dozen hotels, which seem to overcharge less than their counterparts elsewhere in Vietnam. Those which accept *dong* are near the train station and in the north end of town.

Danang Hotel: Inconveniently located in the north end of town, but rooms are clean and low priced—probably because of the location. Take a *cyclo* or motorcycle taxi from the train station or bus terminal. 3 Dong Da St., tel. 21179, US$4-8 fan, US$15-25 a/c.

Marble Mountain Hotel: Newer hotel with clean fan and a/c rooms at fair prices. 5 Dong Da St., tel. 23258, US$6-20.

Khach San Duong Sat 29: Danang's cheapest hotel near the train station has 200 barebones dorm beds in the four-story structure, also called the Railway Hotel. 59 Haiphong St., tel. 22905, US$1-3.

Hai Van Hotel: Another decent and lowpriced hotel with fairly clean fan-cooled and a/c rooms. Recommended. 2 Nguyen Thi Minh Khai St., tel. 21300, US$6-20.

Song Han Hotel: Modern if somewhat characterless hotel with a restaurant, a nightclub with live music and tiny hostesses, and 40 a/c rooms in three classes. 36 Bach Dang St., tel. 22540, fax 21109, US$12-25.

Hai Chau Hotel: Excellent location near the center of town and clean a/c rooms make this one of the most popular hotels in Danang. Unfortunately, the hotel is often booked out, prices have risen sharply in recent years, and Westerners must pay triple the rate for Vietnamese. 215 Tran Phu St., tel. 22722, US$15-30.

Phuong Dong (Orient) Hotel: Vietnam Tourism books tour groups into this centrally located hotel with a/c rooms and rooftop restaurant offering great views over Danang. 93 Phan Chu Trinh St., tel. 21266, US$22-38.

Thai Binh (Pacific) Hotel: Another overpriced and poorly maintained hotel used by Vietnam Tourism. 80 Phan Chu Trinh St., tel. 22137, US$22-38.

Dien Luc Hotel: An upscale if cheaply constructed hotel just across from the Cao Dai Church. All rooms are a/c; breakfast included. 37 Haiphong St., tel. 21864, US$28-45.

Peace Hotel: New hotel near the north end. All rooms a/c. 3 Tran Quy Cap St., tel. 23984, US$22-35.

Bach Dang Hotel: Danang's newest and largest hotel in a central location with views of the river. 50 Bach Nang St., tel 23649, US$28-50.

Restaurants

Danang is known for its seafood and locally produced beer, sensibly called Danang Export.

Riverside Restaurants: Certainly the most enjoyable spots to dine are the simple cafes and restaurants facing the Han River along Bach Dang Street. Thanh Lich Restaurant at 48 Bach Dang is somewhat expensive but serves an impressive array of Vietnamese and French specialties. Other riverside choices include the Kim Dinh at 7 Bach Dang and the venerable Seamen's Institute—the former American Navy Club—which hangs right over the water.

City Center: Tu Do (Freedom) Restaurant at 180 Tran Phu St. near the Hai Chu Hotel is generally considered the best in town, with excellent food, friendly staff, and ice-cold beer. Nearby and less pricey places include the Kim Do at 174 Tran Phu and the Thoi Dai at 171.

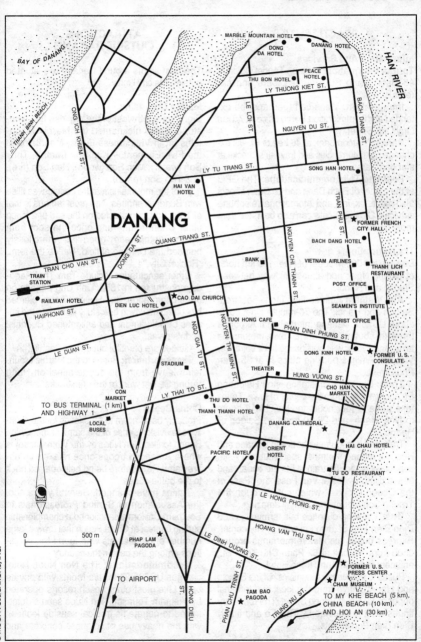

PRACTICALITIES

Information And Services

Tourist Information: Danang Tourist Office at 48 Bach Dang St. arranges tours and car rentals.

Immigration: Visas can (perhaps) be extended at the Immigration Police office at 7 Tran Quy Cap Street.

Banks: Vietcombank at 46 Le Loi St. will exchange most currencies and traveler's checks at standard rates.

Post and Telecommunications: The GPO at the corner of Bach Dang and Le Duan streets also has telex, fax, and international telephone services. Overseas calls can also be made from most hotels.

Transportation

Danang is 108 km south of Hue, 130 km north of Quang Ngai, and almost midway between Saigon and Hanoi.

Air: Vietnam Airlines flies Mon.-Sat. from Saigon and Hanoi. The 70-minute flight costs about US$85. Danang International Airport is three km southwest of town. Taxis, motorcycle taxis, and *cyclos* wait outside the front entrance. Vietnam Airlines booking office is at 35 Tran Phu Street.

Train: Danang train station is on Haiphong St. about 1.5 km from the center of town. Trains take three to four hours to Hue, 14-18 hours to Nha Trang, and 26-30 hours to Saigon or Hanoi.

Train and bus journeys between Danang and Hue are among the most spectacular in Asia, especially when the train skirts the ocean and buses climb over Hai Van Pass, the "Pass of the Ocean Clouds," which cuts through the Truong Son Mountains. Simply amazing.

Bus: The long-distance bus terminal is at 8 Dien Bien Phu St., two km west of city center. Express buses also leave mornings around 0500 from the halt at 52 Phan Chu Trinh St., adjacent to the Thanh Thanh Hotel.

Buses to the Marble Mountains, China Beach, and Hoi An leave from the local bus terminal opposite 80 Hung Vuong Street. The road continues west to become Ly Thai To and finally Dien Bien Phu streets.

ATTRACTIONS OUTSIDE DANANG

The best sights around Danang are situated outside the city limits.

Marble Mountains

Eight km southwest of the city rise five limestone peaks nicknamed the Marble Mountains or, in Vietnamese terms, Mountains of the Five Elements—Kim Son (metal), Thuy Son (water), Moc Son (wood), Hoa Son (fire), and Tho Son (earth).

All of the mountains feature eerie caves filled with Buddhist shrines. The most famous is that of Thuy Son, constructed on the site of a much older Cham shrine and once the spot from which Vietnamese guerrillas mercilessly bombed the Danang airfield. Hence the term, "Rocket City."

Other sanctuaries include Tam Thai Pagoda, constructed in 1852, Linh Ung pagoda on the eastern edge, and Huyen Khong, pierced by chambers which gracefully illuminate the images of Sakyamuni and enlightened Buddhist bodhisattvas.

Guides are plentiful but bring a flashlight.

Transportation: Buses to the Marble Mountains leave from the bus terminal on Hung Vuong St. just west of the train tracks.

China Beach

Probably best known to Americans for the short-lived television series of the same name, China Beach (called Non Nuoc by the Vietnamese) is where American troops once relaxed on abbreviated R&R before being helicoptered back to the battle zones.

Things have changed. Several years ago, the Association of Surfing Professionals in Southern California sanctioned a championship surfing contest at China Beach that drew a large number of contestants who found the conditions among the best in the country.

Accommodations: The Non Nuoc Hotel charges US$25-34 for a/c rooms with private bath. Like most other beach resorts operated by Vietnam Tourism, Non Nuoc seems determined to negate its tropical seaside location with the heavy use of colorless concrete and restaurants placed as far away from the sea as possible. Nevertheless, the place is often filled with domestic visitors and foreign tour groups. Call 21470 to check on vacancies.

Transportation: China Beach is one km from the Marble Mountains and can be reached in 20 minutes with buses from the terminal on Hung Vuong Street.

Cham Ruins

Vietnam's largest collection of Cham ruins is located at My Son, 72 km southwest of Danang, and at Dong Duong, 62 km from Danang. Although both sites were heavily damaged during the war, several dozen monuments still stand as testimony to the unique creativity of the Chams.

Both sites are extremely isolated and almost impossible to reach with public transportation. The only feasible option is to arrange a car and driver through your hotel or the tourist office in Danang.

Lang Co Beach

Some of the most dazzling beaches in central Vietnam are located about 35 km north of Danang and just beyond Hai Van Pass, the rugged limestone karst which once formed the physical barrier between ancient Vietnam to the north and the Champa Kingdom in the south.

Lang Co Peninsula is highly recommended to all lovers of tropical beauty. The dazzling 10-km beach is wonderfully set between the emerald-blue waters of the South China Sea and an idyllic lagoon which washes up toward the mountains. The spectacular peninsula is dotted with palm trees interspersed with tiny villages inhabited by friendly fishermen. Lang Co is among the most spectacular beaches in Southeast Asia and should not be missed.

Accommodations: Vietnam Tourism recently opened Lan Co Seaside Resort, but a much better option is to find a homestay in one of the villages which hug the coastline. This may require some ingenuity since many locals are unaccustomed to Westerners and are afraid to offend Vietnamese tourism officials. When the situation loosens, Lang Co will rank up there with Ko Samui and Kuta—but decades before the onslaught of tourism.

Transportation: Situated almost exactly midway between Danang and Hue, Lan Co village can be reached by bus from either town. Alternatively, take a nonexpress train to the Lang Co train station and find a *cyclo* out to the beach. *Cyclo* drivers may know about homestays.

HUE AND VICINITY

Hue, the famed imperial capital of the Nguyen kings, once was the cultural, religious, and historical center of central Vietnam and is among the highlights of any visit to the country.

The city has dozens of pagodas, temples, and mausoleums superbly situated on the banks of the romantic Perfume River. Hue is also reasonably small and intimate—a relaxing diversion from the larger cities of Vietnam.

HISTORY

Hue, in many senses, is a country unto itself. The city was founded in the spring of 1601 by Lord Nguyen Hoang (1524-1613), who erected the Phu Xuan Citadel and Thien Mu Pagoda, which still stands on the left bank of the Perfume River. King Nguyen was the first in a series of 10 kings who fought the Chams and attempted to control the south from Hue to Saigon.

It wasn't until 1802 that the 10th Nguyen ruler crushed the Tay Son uprising, unseated his rival in Hanoi, and proclaimed himself Emperor Gia Long—the formal beginning of the Nguyen Dynasty, which lasted 143 years until the abdication of Emperor Bao Dai in 1945. Brilliant and ruthless, the Nguyen Dynasty for the first time in Vietnamese history united the country from the borders of China to the southern reaches of the South China Sea. Despite its brevity, some scholars consider this era the golden age of Vietnamese creativity, during which 13 emperors constructed more than 300 palaces, temples, mausoleums, libraries, and theaters in and around the Imperial City.

Vietnamese revisionist historians sometimes claim that Nguyen kings were national traitors who in 1884 sold their country to the French and that Hue should be considered secondary in importance to more contemporary and revolu-

HUE

TO AN HOA BUS TERMINAL (500 m) AND HANOI

TO AN HOA BUS TERMINAL

TRIEU QUANG PHUC ST.

HUONG SEN RESTAURANT

NGUYEN TRAI ST.

DINH TUEN HOANG ST.

BACH DONG ST.

FORBIDDEN PURPLE CITY

TO THIEN MU PAGODA (3 km)

LE DUAN ST.

MIEU TEMPLE ★

★ THAI HOA PALACE

9 URNS ★

MAI THUC LOON ST.

IMPERIAL MUSEUM ★

DIEU DE PAGODA ★

CHIEU UNG PAGODA ★

NGO MON GATE ★

★ MILITARY MUSEUM

CHI LONG ST.

PERFUME

TRAN HUNG DAO ST.

DONG BA BUS TERMINAL

PHU XUAN BRIDGE

RIVER

TRANG TIEN BRIDGE

TRAIN STATION

NHA KHACH CHINH PHU ★

HO CHI MINH MUSEUM ★

SONG HUONG RESTAURANT

NHA KHACH 18

PERFUME RIVER HOTEL

BAO QUOC PAGODA ★

NHA KHACH HUE

★ QUOC HOC SCHOOL

LE LOI ST.

TOURIST OFFICE

MORIN HOTEL

HUE HOTEL

GPO

BEN NGHE GUESTHOUSE

NGO QUYEN ST.

VIETNAM AIRLINES

KINH DO HOTEL

TU DAM PAGODA ★

NUA THU HOTEL

THUAN HUA HOTEL

NGUYEN HUE ST.

DINH PHUNG ST.

DONG DA HOTEL

HUE CITY TOURISM VILLAS

DONG DA ST.

BANK

PHAN CHU TRINH ST.

MUNICIPAL THEATER

BA TRIEU ST.

NOTRE DAME CATHEDRAL ★

HUNG VUONG ST.

AN CUU BUS TERMINAL

AN DINH PALACE ★

TO DANANG

0   500 m

tionary landmarks such as Dien Bien Phu and the Ho Chi Minh Trail. Fortunately (especially for architectural conservationists), Hue's status appears to have been upgraded in recent years, as Vietnamese historians reassess the Nguyen Dynasty and delineate the specific roles of each individual king.

Hue was invaded in 1833 by the French and in 1945 by the Japanese, who demanded the resignation of Bao Dai, the final Nguyen king.

Americans remember Hue as the scene of some of the fiercest and most senseless fighting of the entire war. During the Tet Offensive of 1968, Viet Minh forces seized and held the Imperial Citadel for 25 days and massacred perhaps 3,000 Vietnamese civilians, including children, old women, medical personnel, schoolteachers, and missionaries. An estimated 10,000 people died during the battle.

Subsequent American firepower destroyed many monuments in the Citadel, though a great deal survived the tragic episode.

SIGHTS IN HUE

The Imperial City

The Imperial Citadel (Dai Noi) of Hue was constructed in the early 19th century as an almost exact copy of the Forbidden City in Beijing, with an outer wall (Kinh Thanh) enclosing the Yellow City (Hoang Thanh) and the Forbidden Purple City (Tu Cam Thanh). Today it is the major attraction in Hue and among the country's most memorable sights.

Ngo Mon Gate: The richly decorated main entrance is fronted by nine holy cannons, a flag tower which defiantly flew the Viet Minh flag during the 1968 siege, two auxiliary gateways used by common citizens, and the Golden Water Bridge, once reserved exclusively for the emperor.

Thai Hoa Palace: Directly beyond the gate lies the Palace of Supreme Peace, the most significant and best-preserved structure in the Imperial City, constructed in 1805 as the ceremonial quarters and reception room for visiting diplomats.

Forbidden Purple City: Beyond the Red Gate lies the fabled Forbidden Purple City which, unfortunately, has almost completely disappeared over the last century from an onslaught of typhoons, floods, fires, termites,

thieves, and firepower provided by French, American, and Viet Minh forces.

The most impressive buildings which have survived the elements and artillery are located west of the royal enclave.

Nine Dynastic Urns: Cast in 1835 and weighing an estimated 2,000 kilos each, these elaborate creations symbolize the divinity of individual Nguyen dynasties and, on a less noble note, were featured in the French film *Indochine*. Some of the recent restorations were financed by the film company.

Mieu Temple: North of the urns is the impressive "Temple of Generations," constructed in 1821 to honor the earliest of the Nguyen emperors.

Museums

As you might expect, Hue has several museums which illustrate the city's history. Although the exhibits here are poorly labeled, the **Hue Imperial Museum** should be visited for its striking architecture and modest collection of ceramics, furniture, and bronzeware.

The nearby **military museum** has the standard array of weapons, tanks, and missiles in the central courtyard. Both museums are open 0830-1700.

Thien Mu Pagoda

This small but well-situated temple on the banks of the Perfume River, four km southeast of Hue, has an elegant worship chamber and a rather curious sight—the Austin car that carried a 73-year-old Buddhist monk named Thich Quang Duc from Hue to Saigon, where he immolated himself on 11 June 1963 and electrified the world. Malcolm Browne's historic photo of the event is mounted on the front windshield.

The adjacent 21-meter octagonal tower is the unofficial symbol of Hue and among the most famous structures in Vietnam.

Right Bank Attractions

The Imperial City, museums, and royal mausoleums (described below) are probably enough for most visitors, but true culture vultures might explore the sights hidden amid the right bank in modern Hue.

Bao Quoc Pagoda: Founded in 1670 by a Chinese Buddhist monk but renovated in the late 1950s, Bao Quoc features images of Buddhas past, present, and future enshrined on the central altar.

Ho Chi Minh Museum: Small assortment of photographs and personal items less impressive than the counterpart museum in Hanoi. Ho attended nearby Quoc Hoc School along with other notables such as General Giap and President Diem.

Notre Dame Cathedral: A simple single-spired church which combines European architectural styles with Vietnamese elements.

ROYAL MAUSOLEUMS

As the political and spiritual center of the Nguyen Dynasty, Hue features a large number of pagodas and royal mausoleums spread across a wide area south of city center. Most follow a standard arrangement of a paved courtyard flanked by stone figures of elephants and military mandarins, a stele pavilion engraved with the biography of the deceased king, a central temple dedicated to the king, and auxiliary houses constructed by the king for his royal retinue of concubines, servants, and guardian soldiers.

The tombs and pagodas are best reached by rented bicycle, which provides an opportunity to see the countryside. Many are badly damaged or architecturally redundant, making it unnecessary to view the entire selection. Hurried visitors can sign up for a tour or rent a car. The most romantic options are boats rented from docks in the center of town near the bridge. Bargain hard.

All are open daily 0800-1700 and charge a small admission fee.

Tu Duc Tomb
An architectural masterpiece constructed in the mid-19th century around lakes, pine-covered hills, and pavilions used for relaxation and meditation. Emperor Tu Duc was apparently quite a character: over 100 wives and concubines (but no children), 50 chefs who prepared his daily meals of 50 courses, and hundreds of slaves forced to construct his pleasure palace seven km south of Hue.

Dong Khanh Tomb
Just 500 meters from the tomb of Tu Duc is a small but completely unique mausoleum con-

structed in 1889 for the nephew and adopted son of Emperor Tu Duc.

Khai Dinh Tomb
Majestically situated on the slopes of Chau Mountain 10 km south of Hue, this royal mausoleum was constructed from 1920 to 1931 as the final monument of the Nguyen Dynasty. Khai Dinh is a contemporary ferroconcrete creation noted for its rather sinister staircase of dragons, ceiling murals, and frescoes made from thousands of ceramic and glass fragments.

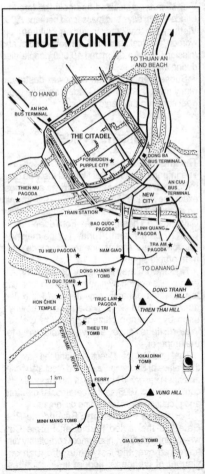

HUE VICINITY

TO THUAN AN AND BEACH

TO HANOI

AN HOA BUS TERMINAL

THE CITADEL

FORBIDDEN PURPLE CITY

DONG BA BUS TERMINAL

AN CUU BUS TERMINAL

THIEN MU PAGODA

NEW CITY

TRAIN STATION

BAO QUOC PAGODA

LINH QUANG PAGODA

TU HIEU PAGODA

NAM GIAO

TRA AM PAGODA

DONG KHANH TOMB

TO DANANG

TU DUC TOMB

DONG TRANH HILL

HON CHEN TEMPLE

TRUC LAM PAGODA

THIEN THAI HILL

THIEU TRI TOMB

KHAI DINH TOMB

0   1 km

FERRY

VUNG HILL

MINH MANG TOMB

GIA LONG TOMB

PERFUME RIVER

The overall effect is quite impressive but reflects the gaudy excesses and Eurocentricities of the final Nguyen kings.

Minh Mang Tomb

Minh Mang, 12 km south of Hue, is perhaps the most impressive royal mausoleum in the region. Constructed from 1840 to 1843, the complex is renowned for its harmonious architecture, elaborate decorations, and glaring stone dignitaries set in a majestic site amid peaceful ponds and tributaries of the Perfume River.

ACCOMMODATIONS AND FOOD

Hue has about 20 hotels (*khach san*) and guesthouses (*nha khach*) situated along or near Le Loi St., which skirts the right bank of the Perfume River. Most demand dollars and are overpriced.

Ben Nghe Guesthouse: Best bet for budget travelers. Ben Nghe St., tel. 3771, US$5-10.

Nha Khach Hue: Clean and comfortable with fan and some a/c rooms. Near the train station. 2 Le Loi St., tel. 2153, US$5-12.

Nha Khach Chinh Phu: Former palace with spacious rooms, grand hallways, romantic ambience. Recommended. 5 Le Loi St., tel. 2234, US$15-25.

Nha Khach 18 Le Loi: A well-located if somewhat seedy guesthouse operated by Hue Tourism. 18 Le Loi St., tel. 3720, US$8-18.

Hue City Tourism Villas: Excellent alternatives to the riverside guesthouses are the three cozy villas owned and operated by Hue City Tourism. The a/c rooms are large, clean, and have private bathrooms. Ly Thoung Kiet St., tel. 3889, 3679, US$16-24.

Morin Hotel: Renovated colonial-style building, once part of Hue University. Operated by Hue Tourism. 2 Hung Vuong St., tel. 3039, US$4-8 fan, US$8-15 a/c. Recommended.

Huong Giang (Perfume River) Hotel: Older semiluxurious hotel. 51 Le Loi St., tel. 2122, fax 3424, US$24-50.

Hue Hotel: Hue's newest and finest hotel, in a wonderful location right over the river. Superb views from top-floor rooms. 49 Le Loi St., tel. 3391, fax 3394, US$24-50.

Restaurants

Hue offers a number of specialties peculiar to the north: *banh khoi* (deep-fried prawns, pork, and bean sprouts wrapped in a crepe), *banh thit nuong* (meat and vegetables) dipped in *nuoc leo* (spicy peanut and sesame sauce), and *ram* (rice pancake stuffed with pork). Huda 22 is a mild locally produced beer.

Huong Sen Restaurant: Popular spot elevated in a lotus pond in the Imperial Citadel. Serves both Vietnamese and Western dishes. 42 Nguyen Trai Street. Moderate.

Song Huong Floating Restaurant: Central location just downstream from the Trang Thien Bridge. Pleasant ambience. 32 Le Loi Street. Moderate.

Huong Giang (Perfume River) Hotel: Surprisingly good Vietnamese food and outstanding views from its fourth-floor location. 51 Le Loi Street. Moderate.

PRACTICALITIES

Information And Services

Tourist Information: Hue Tourist Office at 51 Le Loi St. and Hue City Tourism at 18 Le Loi St. sell package tours and arrange rental cars with drivers and guides. Neither office has much information for independent travelers.

Banks: The Industrial & Commercial Bank at 2 Le Quy Don St. is open Mon.-Sat. 0800-1130 and 1300-1600. The Huong Giang and Hue hotels also change money.

Post and Telecommunications: The GPO on Hoang Hoa Tham St. offers international phone and fax services.

Transportation

Hue is 108 km north of Danang, 166 km from Dong Hoi, 368 km from Vinh, 664 km from Hanoi, and 1,071 km north of Saigon.

Air: Vietnam Airlines flies twice weekly from Hanoi and Saigon to the Phu Bai Airport, 20 km south of city center. Vietnam Airlines's booking office one block from Dong Ba Market at 16 Phan Dang Luu St. is open Mon.-Sat. 0700-1100 and 1330-1700.

Train: Hue railway station is at the southwestern end of Le Loi Street. Both express and ordinary trains depart several times daily for Hanoi and points south. The booking office is open daily 0700-1700. Advance reservations for sleepers are recommended.

Bus: Hue has three bus terminals. The An Cuu Station at 43 Hung Vuong St. serves destinations to the south. Buses north leave from the An Hoa Station at the northwest corner of the walled citadel. Buses to destinations near Hue leave from the Dong Ba Station on Tran Hung Dao St. near the bridge.

Most departures are in the mornings 0500-0600.

QUANG TRI AND THE DMZ

QUANG TRI

Highway 1 north from Hue passes through a series of small towns and along a lovely coastline before arriving at the Demilitarized Zone (DMZ), which formed the legal separation between South and North Vietnam from 1954 to 1975. Most visitors head straight across the DMZ and overnight in Vinh, a reconstructed town which provides a useful break on the long journey to Hanoi.

Quang Tri, 59 km north of Hue, served as a citadel city until the spring of 1972, when battles between the Viet Minh and South Vietnamese forces almost completely obliterated the town. The main points of interest are the nearby Vietnam War sites such as Khe Sanh and former American bases now reduced to iron scraps scattered amid a lunar landscape.

Accommodations
A guesthouse operated by a local People's Committee is located near the bus terminal on Le Duan Street.

DONG HA

The provincial capital of Dong Ha serves as a useful base from which to explore the Demilitarized Zone and war sites to the west. The town has been reconstructed since the war in standard fashion and has little of interest aside from a few surviving blockhouses once used by French and then American military forces.

Highway 9 To Laos
Dong Ha, near Quang Tri, is located at the intersection of Highway 1 and Highway 9, which leads west to Khe Sanh and the border of Laos. The two-lane asphalt road was constructed by the Americans during the war and has been recently upgraded to provide dependable access to landlocked Laos.

The crossing is now open to Western travelers who have obtained the proper entry or exit permits from both Vietnamese and Laotian officials. As of this writing, only members of escorted tours have been granted permission to cross at this border.

Accommodations
Both Nha Khach Dong Ha on Tran Phu St. and Dong Truong Son Hotel three km outside town accept Western visitors for US$10-18 per night.

KHE SANH

Khe Sanh, a remote valley 62 km west of Dong Ha, was the site of one of the most famous battles of the entire Vietnam War. Today a barren plateau surrounded by low hills and tropical vegetation, Khe Sanh marks the spot where the North Vietnamese attempted to inflict the final blow against the Americans—not unlike Dien Bien Phu, which drove the French from Vietnam.

But unlike the French at Dien Bien Phu, American forces were prepared for the assault with an enormous amount of weaponry and firepower. The 77-day attack, now thought to be an elaborate diversion against the upcoming Tet Offensive, made worldwide headlines and was followed by millions of Americans on the nightly news. When the smoke finally cleared and Highway 9 was reopened, 248 Americans and an estimated 10,000 Vietnamese had lost their lives.

Khe Sanh was abandoned by the Americans in July 1968 after General Westmoreland reassessed his positions and decided that Khe Sanh held no further strategic importance.

Khe Sanh today shows few signs of battle since most of the military hardware was removed or blown up by the departing Americans. Aside from a handful of American veterans who witnessed combat here, few visitors make the journey to Khe Sanh or other nearby war memorials such as Camp Carroll, the Rockpile, Con Thien Firebase, the Ho Chi Minh Trail, and Hamburger Hill in Ashau Valley.

Accommodations
An inexpensive guesthouse is in Khe Sanh town just west of the bus terminal.

Transportation
Buses to Khe Sanh town leave several times each morning from the bus terminals in Hue and Dong Ha. The battle site is located 2.5 km north of town. Since the widely scattered war sites listed above are difficult to reach by public transportation, most visitors hire a car with driver and guide in Hue.

WAR SITES NEAR THE DMZ

The Demilitarized Zone (DMZ), which once served as the boundary between North and South Vietnam, is defined by the Ben Hai River, which follows the 17th parallel.

The following sights can be visited on daytrips from Dong Ha, though a better idea is to charter a taxi from Hue and hire a guide who can provide historical backgrounds.

Warning: The entire region was heavily bombed and now resembles some sort of eerie moonscape, complete with a terrible number of live ordnance and mines which continue to kill impoverished peasants in frightening numbers. Anyone touring the region should keep to established paths and never touch any of the mines and bombs which still lie scattered around the battlefields. Anything—ordnance, mines, or shoes—left untouched by scavengers is extremely deadly.

Vinh Moc Tunnels
The tunnels of Vinh Moc, just north of the DMZ near the village of Ho Xa, comprise a remarkable testimony to the sacrifice and tenacity of the Vietnamese in their struggle during the war. Although the 2.8-km labyrinth of underground passages has been compared to the tunnels of Cu Chi near Saigon, there is really no comparison.

This is the real thing—an unadulterated and completely untouristed subterranean world once home to some 1,200 villagers who farmed above ground during the day and lived their lives at night in the elaborate complex of passageways and chambers.

Vinh Moc is 13 km east of Highway 1. The turnoff is six km north of the Ben Hai River.

Doc Mieu Base
Once the headquarters for American electronic surveillance, Doc Mieu is now a vast expanse of nothing more than craters filled with rainwater and scattered remnants such as combat boots and live mortars.

Con Thien Firebase
Con Thien once served as the primary base for the so-called McNamara's Wall, the elaborate military barrier designed to detect enemy incursions across the DMZ. This place is extraordinarily dangerous—even desperate Vietnamese scrap collectors refuse to venture into this no-man's land.

Truong Son Cemetery
Formerly a Vietnamese Army base but today a national cemetery and memorial dedicated to the tens of thousands of Viet Minh soldiers who died at the DMZ and along the Ho Chi Minh Trail. Many of the headstones are simply labeled *Liet Si*, Unknown Martyr.

Camp Carroll
Once a major American military installation with enormous 175-mm cannons, Camp Carroll today is a quiet spot of weeds and craters. Most of the war architecture, including the concrete bunkers and cannons which once shelled Khe Sanh, has been dismantled and hauled away by Vietnamese scrap collectors.

The Rockpile
Former American Marine lookout overlooking old artillery batteries.

Aluoi And Hamburger Hill
Sixty-five km south of Khe Sanh is a lovely valley that was once a major war zone. Among the more infamous battle sites are those at Cunningham, Erskine, Razor, and Hamburger Hill, scene of a terrible 1968 battle in which 241 Americans died in less than one week.

NORTHERN VIETNAM

Vietnam north of the DMZ but south of Hanoi is a kind of shadowy transition zone between the capitalist South and the socialist North, a land caught in the middle of ideological struggles and tempted to go in either direction.

North-central Vietnam is also one of the country's poorest and most crowded regions. Here, peasants eke out an existence from thin soil and produce only enough food to avoid starvation. The region has some fine beaches and a fair number of monuments which mark the southern expansion of Vietnamese empires, but most visitors bypass this coastal stretch in their hurried journey to Hanoi and the impressive landscapes of the far north.

A few towns are described below in the event that you have enough time or interest to break the journey between Hue and Hanoi.

DONG HOI TO THANH HOA

DONG HOI

Dong Hoi is the provincial capital of Quang Binh Province and an active fishing port heavily damaged during the Vietnam conflict.

Attractions
Dong Hoi is known for its remains of an ancient citadel erected in the early 17th century and for its aromatic wines, distilled from wild strawberries which survive amid the encroaching sand dunes.

Phong Na Caves, 45 km northwest of Dong Hoi, are the premier attraction in the province and widely considered one of the greatest natural wonders of Vietnam. Approached via an underground river, the caves include a series of grottoes once used as Cham religious sanctuaries in the 9th and 10th centuries.

Accommodations
Dong Hoi has one guesthouse patronized by domestic tourists and two modest hotels just east of Highway 1. All accept Western tourists but sometimes demand payment in dollars.

Most Western visitors are required to stay in the four-story Hoa Binh Hotel, where a/c rooms with private baths cost a stiff US$25-30.

VINH AND VICINITY

Nghe Tinh Province is known throughout Vietnam as the birthplace of several national poets and the father of modern Vietnam, Ho Chi Minh.

The city has variously been destroyed by French aerial bombing in the 1950s, a series of devastating fires in the '60s, and massive naval bombardments from American warships in the '70s. Vinh was almost completely rebuilt with East German assistance after the war in a uniformly depressing style of monolithic socialist architecture. Quang Trung Street, Vinh's main thoroughfare, looks like an Orwellian nightmare on the verge of collapse.

Despite the dreary architecture and utter poverty which grips most of the province, Vinh is a useful stop on the hard journey from Hue to Hanoi.

A tourist office is on Quang Trung St. just north of the Rap 12/9 Cinema.

Attractions
There is nothing of interest in Vinh aside from contemplating the cruel joke which East German architects have sprung on the town.

Ho Chi Minh House: Ho Chi Minh was born in Chua (Kim Lien), 14 km northwest of Vinh, but raised in the nearby village of Sen. Both villages have modest museums and memorials in his reconstructed homes.

Cua Lo Beach: This beach, 20 km east of town, is somewhat narrow but offers clean sand and a complete absence of tourists aside from a few Vietnamese day-trippers. Accommodations at the Cua Lo Hotel. The tourist brochures promises "sun-basking, sea crabs, and Phuc Trach shaddocks." Let me know what you find.

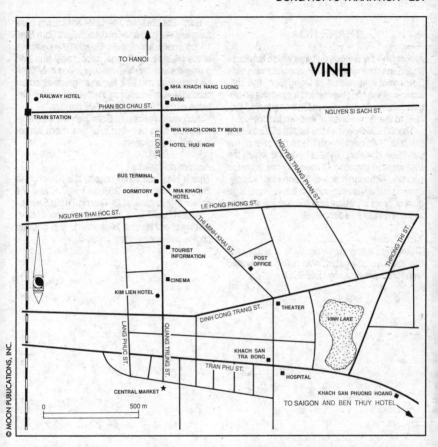

Accommodations

Next to the train station is a survivable hotel with inexpensive rooms. One km east down Phan Boi Chau St. are several more hotels in somewhat better condition. Bus arrivals might try the adjacent dormitories or Nha Khach Luong across Le Loi Street.

Budget travelers often stay at the friendly Ben Thuy Hotel about two km from city center. Clean rooms cost US$6-10.

Closer to town is the Khach San Tra Bong and Khach San Phuong Hoang, where acceptable rooms with attached baths cost from US$5.

Vinh's luxury spot is the monolithic Kim Lien Hotel, which opened in 1990 on Quang Trung St., across from the market and about three blocks south of the bus terminal.

Transportation

Vinh is 368 km north of Hue, 197 km from Dong Hoi, and 291 km south of Hanoi. The train station is in the northwest section of town, three km from city center. Vinh is served by both ordinary and express trains from Hue and Hanoi.

The bus terminal is centrally located a few blocks north of the central market. Express buses to Hanoi and Hue depart around 0500.

THANH HOA

Among the mysterious cultures which fascinate historians and archaeologists concerned with Southeast Asia is that of Dong Son, the civilization of the Ma River which forged the elaborate bronze drums uncovered from north Thailand to the far reaches of eastern Indonesia.

Thanh Hoa served as the capital of Vietnam in the late 14th century and was the site of the Lam Son Uprising (1418-28), during which the Vietnamese expelled Chinese forces from the country. Although much of Thanh Hoa was destroyed in the Vietnam conflict, this remains a region of great historical and cultural significance to the Vietnamese people.

Attractions

Thanh Hoa's only surviving signs of history are the massive city gates, now being excavated with funds provided by UNESCO.

Sam Son Beach: The chief attractions near town are the long and fine beaches at Sam Son, 16 km southeast of town. Beyond the beaches is the Ham Rong Bridge, repeatedly bombed during the war by the Americans and only finally destroyed in 1972 by laser-guided "smart bombs"—a precursor to the technological displays of the 1991 Persian Gulf conflict.

Accommodations at Sam Son include simple beachside guesthouses and more elaborate concrete chalets.

Accommodations

Thanh Hoa has three hotels, the Khach San 25A and Khach San 25B on Hwy. 1, and the newer tourist hotel at 21 Quang Trung Street.

Khach San Thanh Hoa, in the center of town just west of National Highway 1, is a popular choice with rooms from US$6-8.

HANOI

Hanoi—capital of the Socialist Republic of Vietnam—is a decrepit but romantic city of broad tree-lined boulevards, narrow shophouses, sleepy public squares, misty lakes, and French-era legacies such as colonial villas, universities, museums, hotels, and an opera house. Unlike its brash and commercialized sister city in the south, Hanoi still feels completely authentic, a time-warp destination as yet unchanged by the advent of mass tourism.

Hanoi will strike some as dirty and poor and with far too many rats. The city certainly needs some repairs and a touch of paint, but unlike most other destinations in Southeast Asia, Hanoi retains a timeless charm little altered from the colonial days of the French. There is also the novelty of visiting a place just opening up to the outside world after decades of severe isolation.

HISTORY

Founded in 1010 at the beginning of the Ly Dynasty (1010-1225), Hanoi served as the capital of northern Vietnam until 1400, when the Ho Dynasty temporarily transferred the royal city to Than Hoa. The Le Dynasty restored Hanoi's primary diplomatic status in 1428. The city later served as a regional capital after Emperor Gia Long, founder of the Nguyen Dynasty, moved his royal entourage down to Hue. Western traders, diplomats, and missionaries arrived in the early 17th century, though Hanoi remained independent until 1882, when the city fell into the hands of the French.

Pleased with the cooler climate and convenient location on trade routes to China, the French declared Hanoi their Indochinese capital in 1902 and began a construction program which has left the city with much of its rich architectural legacies. Despite widespread destruction during the Vietnam War, older neighborhoods remain museum pieces of weathered shophouses and colonial villas, which taken together form a striking monument to colonial rule.

The French abandoned Hanoi after their defeat at Dien Bien Phu in 1954; the Geneva Conference in the same year partitioned the country into North and South. Hanoi was heavily bombed during the Vietnam War, though obvious signs of destruction are difficult to spot within the city limits.

Today the city appears to be slowly awakening from a long slumber as entrepreneurs cautiously open small businesses and other services aimed at domestic consumers and the burgeoning tourist trade.

ATTRACTIONS IN CENTRAL HANOI

Not a city of major monuments or great historical ruins, Hanoi displays its charms in the familiar: narrow streets, small shops, old men fixing bicycle tires on the sidewalks, children dressed for school, the smile of a young girl.

Vietnam Tourism conducts tours but the only way to really experience Hanoi is to walk or hire a bicycle. The following walking tour starts in the center of town near the hotels and then winds around toward the sights in northwestern Hanoi.

Hoan Kiem Lake
Named after a legendary incident from the 15th century, a Vietnamese tale of magical swords similar to King Arthur's Excalibur, Hanoi's Lake of the Restored Sword features a somewhat dilapidated Tortoise Tower on a small southern islet and the Jade Hill Pagoda constructed on a northern spit in the early 19th century. The lake is popular with joggers, lovers, and tai chi practioners in the early morning hours.

Old Quarter
Dong Kinh Nghia Thuc, the rabbit warren of narrow alleys situated between Hoan Kiem Lake and Long Bien Bridge, is the most memorable district in Hanoi and among the most evocative urban sights in Vietnam.

The neighborhood originated several centuries ago as an interlinked series of villages set up by guilds to provide handicrafts and consumer goods for the royal court. Even today, many of the streets are defined by their particular crafts and continue to specialize in particu-

CENTRAL HANOI

THE CITADEL

TO HO CHI MINH MAUSOLEUM

★ DONG XUAN MARKET

HANG CHIEU ST.

TO WEST LAKE AIRPORT, HAIPHONG, AND HALONG BAY

TO CHUONG DUONG BRIDGE

RED RIVER

PIANO BAR   ● CHA CA CAFE

HANG BUOM ST.

★ OLD QUARTER

BAT DAN ST.

RESTAURANT 22

● PHUNG HUNG HOTEL

CAU GO ST.

PHUNG HUNG ST.

HAN BONG ST.

HOAN KIEM LAKE

★ NGOC SON TEMPLE

BACH DANG ST.

TRAN QUANG KHAI ST.

NAM PHUONG HOTEL
PHU GIA HOTEL   ●

● BINH MINH HOTEL

TRAN HAN ST.

● DONG DO HOTEL

★ ST. JOSEPH'S CHURCH

TRANG THI ST.

HOAN KIEM GUESTHOUSE

NATIONAL LIBRARY ■

● GPO

■ BANK

ROSE HOTEL ●
● DONG LOI HOTEL

★ HANOI HILTON

AUSTRALIAN EMBASSY

VIETNAM AIRLINES (INTERNATIONAL)

BODEGA HOTEL

● PULLMAN METROPOLE HOTEL

● RAILWAY HOTEL
RAILWAY STATION

★ AMBASSADOR'S PAGODA

SOFIA HOTEL ●

DAN CHU HOTEL ●

REVOLUTIONARY MUSEUM

HAI BA TRUNG ST.

MUNICIPAL THEATER ★

★ HISTORY MUSEUM

KHACH SAN 30 ● CAPITAL HOTEL

■ IMMIGRATION POLICE

QUANG TRUNG ST.

LY THUONG KIET ST.

PHAN CHU TRINH ST.

LE THANH TONG ST.

TOYOTA SERVICE STATION

CAMBODIAN EMBASSY

● HOA BINH HOTEL

FRENCH EMBASSY

TRAN HUNG DAO ST.

LAOTIAN EMBASSY

● HOA KIEM HOTEL

DUONG LE DUAN ST.

TRAN BINH TRANG ST.

● BOSS HOTEL

VIETNAM AIRLINES (DOMESTIC)

LE VAN HUU ST.

0   250 m

● NHA TRO DORMS

KIM LIEN BUS TERMINAL

THIEN QUANG LAKE

PO HUE ST.

LENIN PARK

TRAN NHAN TONG ST.

BAY MAU LAKE

RESTAURANT 202 ■
TOURIST INFORMATION (TO SERCO)

TO HIEN THANH ST.

● BICYCLES

© MOON PUBLICATIONS, INC.

lar items such as shoes, jewelry, gold, or papier-mâché offerings used in funerals.

Hanoi's so-called 36 Streets District is quite remarkable. Largely erected in the late 19th and early 20th centuries, the neighborhood features hundreds of "tube houses" constructed in an super-elongated style and decorated with red-tiled roofs and bricks held together with sugarcane juice, sand, and lime. The result is a vernacular alchemy of traditional Vietnamese styles mixed with grander French touches such as wrought-iron balconies, windows with louvered wooden shutters, and plaster-relief friezes of flowers and birds.

Tragically, shophouses are now being torn down at a furious pace to be replaced with the same modern concrete cubicles which mar most other cities in Southeast Asia. Architectural conservationists have sounded the alarm but it appears unlikely that they will have any more luck in Hanoi than they had in Singapore's Chinatown.

A hopeful note is provided by the French-era Dong Xuan Market in the northern section of Old Hanoi, whose recent restoration retained the old facade and modernized the interior.

Revolutionary Museum

Vietnam's long history of struggles against Chinese, Japanese, French, and American forces is recounted in a series of rooms arranged chronologically inside the former French Customs House. Displays retell the defeat of Chinese Mongol forces in 938, Japanese atrocities during WW II, the 1954 French defeat at Dien Bien Phu, the American antiwar movement of the 1960s, plus a guillotine, torture devices, and gruesome execution photos best avoided by the squeamish.

History Museum

Formerly the Louis Finot Museum under the supervision of the École Francaise d'Extrème Orient, Vietnam's leading historical museum features a dazzling if somewhat confusing series of exhibits chronologically arranged around particular dynasties and historical episodes. Highlights include presentations on prehistoric and Neolithic man, bronze Dong Son drums and funerary urns, Cham relics, the Funan culture of the Mekong Delta, Buddhist statuary and bodhisattvas, weapons used in the Tay Son Re-

volt, displays on the Nguyen Dynasty, and the struggle for national unification.

The museum is open Tues.-Sun. 0800-1200 and 1300-1600.

Municipal Theater

A magnificent Beaux Arts-style building constructed by the French in 1911 as a replica of the Paris Opera House. From this spot, Viet Minh forces announced in 1945 the success of their August Revolution and the liberation of Vietnam from colonial occupation.

Cultural performances are held most evenings 2000-2400.

Hanoi Hilton

Hoa Lo Prison is the grim, high-walled structure where hundreds of captured American POWs were incarcerated and mercilessly tortured during the war. Today a prison for common criminals and Vietnamese political dissidents, Hoa Lo remains a profoundly disturbing monument to the atrocities of modern warfare and the refusal of the Vietnamese government to honor the accords of the Geneva Convention.

Ambassador's Pagoda

Originally constructed as a guesthouse for ambassadors to the court of the Le Dynasty, the Quan Su Pagoda was subsequently destroyed then rebuilt in 1942 as the official center of Buddhism in Hanoi. Interior details include fine stone sculptures and a mural which recounts the enlightenment of Sakyamuni, the historical reincarnation of the Buddha.

ATTRACTIONS IN NORTHWESTERN HANOI

Rather than a neighborhood of ancient history, northwestern Hanoi recounts contemporary events and the legacies of Ho Chi Minh. The following walking tour follows a counterclockwise route from central Hanoi and finishes at the Temple of Literature near the Fine Arts Museum.

Army Museum

First stop might be this museum fronted by a Soviet-built MiG-21 which triumphs above a jumbled graveyard of wrecked B-52s and F-111s—thereby setting the tone for subsequent

NORTHWEST HANOI

WEST LAKE

THUCH BACH LAKE

QUAN THANH PAGODA ★

THUY KHUE ST.

HOANG HOA THAM ST.

PHAN DINH ST.

HOANG DIEU ST.

PRESIDENTIAL PALACE ★

HO CHI MINH HOUSE ★

HOANG VAN THU ST.

HO CHI MINH MAUSOLEUM ★

HUNG VUONG ST.

NATIONAL ASSEMBLY

ONE PILLAR PAGODA ★

HO CHI MINH MUSEUM ★

DIEN BIEN PHU ST.

DOI CAN ST.

LE HONG PHONG ST.

THE CITADEL

LA THANH HOTEL ●

TRAN PHU ST.

CHINESE EMBASSY ●

ARMY MUSEUM

KIM MA BUS TERMINAL ■

BURMESE EMBASSY ●

FINE ARTS MUSEUM ★

KIM MA ST.

NGUYEN THAI HOC ST.

STADIUM

HAI YEN HOTEL ●

MAI ANH HOTEL ●

GUESTHOUSE ●

TEMPLE OF LITERATURE ★

DONG LOI HOTEL

GIANG VO HOTEL ●

THANG LONG HOTEL ●

CAT LINH ST.

HANG BAT ST.

QUOCK TU GIAM ST.

GIANG VO ST.

SAO MAI HOTEL ●

GIANG VO LAKE

0   500 m

■ EXHIBITION HALL

TRAIN STATION

© MOON PUBLICATIONS, INC.

rooms and displays. Perhaps the most poignant revelation is that the American experience formed but a small blip in the 2,000-year history of struggle against outside forces.

The museum is open Tues.-Sun. 0800-1200 and 1300-1600.

Ho Chi Minh Mausoleum

Set on a great boulevard of waving flags and guarded by no-nonsense soldiers is the imposing granite edifice and final resting place of Ho Chi Minh. Modeled after Lenin's tomb in Moscow, this lotus-shaped polygonal structure

seems alien to the delicate sensibilities of the Vietnamese people and perhaps even Uncle Ho himself, who almost certainly would have preferred a simpler monument to honor his modest lifestyle.

Visitors must first register at the nearby office and deposit their bags before marching in double file to the mausoleum. Inside, Chairman Ho lies embalmed and painted by Soviet technicians to resemble a waxy Vietnamese mummy—despite his specific wishes to be cremated and treated like an ordinary citizen. Above the glass sarcophagus towers a gigantic hammer and sickle, one of the last places in the world to view the symbol of a fallen ideology.

The mausoleum is open Tue.-Sun. 0800-1200.

Ho Chi Minh House

Ho's simple house stands just north of his mausoleum. Ho was born near Vinh on 19 May 1890 into a poor but scholarly family of aristocratic lineage that despised colonial control of Vietnam. He later attended Quoc Hoc College in Hue before leaving for further studies in France and subsequent travels in England, North Africa, and America. During his stay in Paris, Ho studied the works of Marx and joined the French Socialist Party, embracing the radical communist ideology which proved quite popular during the Depression era of the 1930s. Less idealistically, Ho also worked at the Carlton Hotel in London as an assistant pastry chef.

In 1923, Ho moved to Moscow, where he was trained as a communist activist and socialist spy later assigned to an outpost in Canton. His travels from China were varied: Buddhist monk in Thailand, subversive activist in Hong Kong, exiled Vietnamese patriot sentenced in 1930 to death in absentia by the French.

It was not until the early 1940s that the modest village activist assumed the pseudonym by which he is now known—Ho Chi Minh. Ho returned to Vietnam in the 1940s to lead the national struggle for unification until his death in 1969 in the simple house within the former governor's residence.

Presidential Palace

Constructed by the French in 1906 as national headquarters for the governor-general of Indochina, this building is now used for official receptions and other state functions. Rather than living here after his arrival in Hanoi, Ho chose to reside in the nearby servant quarters described above.

West Lake

Just north of the Presidential Palace lies an enormous freshwater lake once encircled by magnificent palaces and pavilions constructed by the early kings of Hanoi. All were destroyed in various feudal wars, but visitors can enjoy the views and tour the Quan Thanh and Tran Quoc pagodas. Tran Quoc, the oldest religious sanctuary in Hanoi, was established in 1639 and completely rebuilt in 1842.

One Pillar Pagoda

Chua Mot Cot, perhaps the most curious structure in Hanoi and among the most ancient and revered monuments in Vietnam, was established in the early 11th century but reconstructed in 1954 after being burned to the ground by departing French troops. The curious name is derived from the singular pillar which supports the little lotus-shaped temple, which symbolizes the sacred blossom rising from the Sea of Sorrow and provides hope in the Buddhist universe.

Ho Chi Minh Museum

Adjacent to the One Pillar is an impressive museum opened in 1990 to commemorate the centenary of Ho's birth. Although the exhibits are labeled in Vietnamese and finding an English-speaking guide can be difficult, the chronological arrangement and historical photographs help you understand the life of Vietnam's most famous patriot.

The museum is open Tues.-Sun. 0800-1200 and 1330-1600.

Fine Arts Museum

Once the French Ministry of Information but today a Vietnamese propaganda museum filled with contemporary socialist-realism art, plus there's a small collection of handicrafts on the second floor.

Temple Of Literature

Van Mieu is considered the most important temple complex in Hanoi and among the finest surviving examples of traditional architecture in Vietnam.

The center was founded in 1070 during the reign of Ly Thanh Tong as the national headquarters for the study of Confucianism and as the spiritual center of the Red River delta.

Van Mieu is divided longitudinally by gateways into five courtyards entered through the Van Mieu Gate at the southern end. The Poetry Balcony above the gate is followed by two large and now-empty squares which were once filled with wooden hostels for students and teachers. Van Mieu's most important artifacts are the 82 stone stelae arranged inside the third courtyard and inscribed with the names and academic records of the laureates who passed the triennial examinations. Beyond this courtyard lie the Dai Thanh ("Great Success Gate") and a series of temples which honor the Chinese philosopher.

ACCOMMODATIONS

If the Western concept of tourism is foreign to Vietnam, then Hanoi has a long way to go before it can offer the standards of service and comfort found elsewhere in Southeast Asia. Most of the following hotels are in rudimentary condition and overpriced by any conceivable benchmark. On the positive side, hotel staffs are often friendly and facilities are slowly improving as more tourists arrive in the nation's capital.

The best neighborhood for visitors is central Hanoi, where most of the moderately priced hotels are located, not in the outskirts of town where Vietnam Tourism often attempts to shuttle Westerners on packaged tours.

Budget Accommodations
Many of the cheaper hotels are reluctant to accept Westerners or take payment in *dong,* though this restriction seems to have loosened in recent years. Budget travelers with student IDs purchased in Bangkok can often pay in *dong.*

Trang Tien Hotel: Very popular and well located guesthouse in the center of town near the Bodega Cafe. 35 Trang Tien St., US$7-15.

Dong Loi Hotel: Several low-end hotels are just across from the train station, including this renovated place with both fan-cooled and a/c rooms. Overpriced, but one of the few hotels near the train station which accepts foreigners. Le Duan St., tel. 55721, US$8-18.

Other Railway Station Hotels: Some travelers have reportedly had luck at the nearby Railway Hotel (Khach San Ga), Khach San 30, Khach San Chi Long, and Railway Service Company Hotel (Khach San Cong Nhan Duong). All cost US$2-5.

Dong Do Hotel: The first choice for many budget travelers for its clean rooms and Ann Tourist Offices, visa extensions, air tickets and travel tips. 27 Tong Duy Tan St., tel. 233275, fax 256569, US$10-35

Hoan Kien Guesthouse: Spotless rooms and friendly management make this one of the best choices in Hanoi. 76 Hai Ba Trang St., tel. 268944, US$20-25 a/c.

Sofia Hotel: Good location and reasonable prices makes this a popular choice near Hoan Kiem Lake. The Sofia is scheduled for renovations and prices may soon rise dramatically. 6 Hang Bai St., tel. 53069, US$8-24.

An Uong Dach San Guesthouse: Excellent little spot behind a restaurant and very near the larger Bodega Hotel shown on the map of central Hanoi. Recommended for its location, cozy courtyard, and friendly vibes. 37 Trang Tien St., tel. 53448, US$4-12.

Phung Hung Hotel: Budget travelers who wish to stay near the Old Quarter might try this simple but adequate hotel just east of the Citadel. The Phung Hung has both fan-cooled and a/c rooms at reasonable prices. 2 Duong Thang St., tel. 52614, US$6-14.

Nha Tro Dorms: Open all night and one block north of the Kim Lien Bus Terminal is a rudimentary hotel useful for late bus arrivals. Each rooms has six beds fitted with mats, not mattresses. 100 Duong Le Duan St., tel. 52405, US$2-4.

Moderate Accommodations
Several acceptable hotels in the US$25-50 range are conveniently located in the center of town near Hoan Kiem Lake.

Rose Hotel: New and comfortable hotel with a/c rooms and decent restaurant. Overpriced, but well located just a few blocks from the train station. 20 Phan Boi Chau St., tel. 254438, fax 254437, US$25-45.

Bodega Hotel: Good-value hotel situated above a popular cafe with clean a/c rooms. Friendly managers. Recommended. 57 Trang Tien St., tel. 59842, US$15-20.

Phu Gia Hotel: Older hotel with decent rooms in a fine location near Hoan Kiem Lake and the Old Quarter. Rooms on the upper floors offer lakeside views. 136 Hang Trong St., tel. 55493, US$20-45.

Dan Chu Hotel: Faded, old colonial-style hotel up the street from the Municipal Theater. Constructed in the late 19th century and once called the Hanoi Hotel, the Dan Chu is overpriced but all rooms are a/c and breakfast is included. 29 Trang Tien St., tel. 253323, fax 266786, US$42-55.

Luxury Accommodations
Aside from the Pullman, luxury hotel is a contradiction in terms here in Hanoi.

Thang Loi Hotel: Situated in a wonderful location overlooking West Lake (four km from city center), this Cuban-built hotel features all the standard Cuban amenities: a waterless swimming pool, broken a/c units in each room, large mosquitoes, dry rot, and crumbling concrete walls. Tour groups are often exiled out here. Yen Phu St., tel. 268211, fax 252800, US$45-70.

Tayho Hotel: Another horrendous white elephant completed in 1991 but appearing to have existed since the days of Khrushchev and black-and-white television. This reincarnation of Soviet politburo architecture is located several kilometers outside town and should be avoided at all costs. Nguyen Tai St., tel. 232380, fax 232390, US$45-70.

Pullman Metropole Hotel: The only luxury hotel in Hanoi worth considering is the former Thong Nhat, recently refurbished at a total cost of over US$10 million. Originally constructed in 1911 and now comparable with the Peninsula in Hong Kong and the Raffles in Singapore, the 300-room Metropole also features a swimming pool, a French bistro, and a business center. 15 Ngo Quyen St., tel. 266919, fax 266920, US$155-340.

RESTAURANTS

Western restaurants are located in all hotels and, unlike the rooms, meals are reasonably priced. However, the best meals are found in streetside stalls in the Old Quarter and small coffee shops in the tourist district.

Dishes to try include *pho* (spicy chicken soup), *cha* (barbecued pork), *ban cuon* (egg rolls filled with minced meats), *nem* (crab and egg pancakes), and *com* (sticky rice).

Central Hanoi Restaurants
Sofia Restaurant: Downstairs restaurant and second-floor cafe with Vietnamese and Western dishes at reasonable prices. 6 Hang Bai Street. Moderate.

Bodega Cafe: Another popular spot for light snacks, drinks, pastries, and ice cream. 57 Trang Tien Street. Inexpensive.

Restaurant 202: Many members of the diplomatic community consider Nha Hang 202 the best restaurant in town, with a wide selection of both Vietnamese and European dishes. Four blocks east of Lenin Park in the south side of Hanoi. 202 Pho Hue Street. Moderate.

Old Quarter Restaurants
Many of the least expensive but best restaurants are located north of the lake in Old Hanoi.

Restaurant 22: More properly called the Quang An, this upstairs cafe is an expatriate favorite for its extensive Vietnamese, Chinese, and international specialties. Located two blocks northwest of Hoan Kiem Lake. 22 Hang Can Street. Moderate.

Piano Bar: Decent food, pleasant atmosphere, and live music make this one of the most popular late-night destinations in Hanoi. Situated just across from the train tracks. 50 Hang Vai Street. Moderate.

LaVong's Cha Ca Cafe: A real Vietnamese family-dining experience; serves one daily fish specialty plus rice brandy and Saigon beer. Great fun. 14 Cha Ca Street. Inexpensive.

NIGHTLIFE

Hanoi is a very sleepy town where most cafes and nightclubs are closed by 2100 or 2200. What little nightlife exists is almost exclusively limited to clubs in the major hotels.

Municipal Theater: Entertainment inside this replica of the Paris Opera House ranges from traditional music to revolutionary theater.

Water Puppets: Water puppetry is a folk art unique to northern Vietnam and one of the best entertainments offered in Hanoi. As implied by the name, the performance involves a number of large wooden puppets which are manipulated under the water with long bamboo poles by puppeteers who stand partially submerged behind a bamboo curtain. Performances are held weekly in the Hoan Kiem Lake Theater, established in 1956 by Ho Chi Minh himself.

Circus: Vietnam's amateunsh but highly entertaining State Circus performs seasonally near the entrance of Lenin Park. Recommended.

Hotel Nightclubs: For a glimpse into the future, check out the hotel discos and ballrooms packed every weekend with young and trendy Vietnamese. Western residents in Hanoi often join the private clubs at the Australian and Swedish embassies.

PRACTICALITIES

Tourist Information
Vietnam Tourism at 54 Nguyen Du St. exists solely to sell tours and rent cars and not to aid independent travelers. Hanoi Tourism (TOSER-CO) at 8 To Hien Thanh St. is friendlier and can help with visa extensions, police registration, and changes in departure endorsements.

Additional services are provided by other state-controlled agencies such as Saigon Tourism and the Center for Trade and Tourism at the corner of Hang Khay and Ba Trieu streets.

Many travelers prefer the service and lower prices at privately owned travel agencies such as Ann Tourist Office in the Dong Do Hotel, Ecco Vietnam Tours at 50 Ba Trien St., Especen Tours at 79 Hang Trong St. and Pacific Tours at 58 Tran Nhan Tong Street.

Immigration Police
As of this writing, all visitors to Vietnam who initially arrive in Hanoi must register within three days with the Immigration Police at 89 Tran Hung Dao Street. This formality is usually completed with the help of your hotel manager or Hanoi Tourism.

Travel permits are no longer required in Vietnam.

Banks
Cash and traveler's checks can be exchanged at the highest legal rate at the Bank of Foreign Trade at 47 Ly Thai To Street. Rates in hotels are very poor and the black market rate is only slightly higher than bank rates.

Post And Telecommunications
The General Post Office on Dinh Tien Hoang St. also provides international telephone, telex, and fax services at incredibly high rates, though mail service appears reliable. The GPO is open daily 0630-2000.

Embassies
Hanoi is the capital of Vietnam and has all possible embassies and consulates. The most useful are the Cambodian at 71 Tran Hung Dao St., the Chinese at 46 Hoang Dieu St., the Laotian at 22 Tran Binh Trong St., and the Thai at Khu Trung Tu Street. Americans are expected to soon reoccupy the old U.S. Embassy at 21 Tuin Street.

TRANSPORTATION

Hanoi is 103 km from Haiphong, 165 km from Halong, 420 km from Dien Bien Phu, 658 km from Hue, and 1,710 km from Saigon.

Air
Hanoi's Noi Bai Airport, 35 km north of city center, is served by taxis for about US$15-20 and a local bus for US$2-3 which leaves from terminal front gate. From city center, the airport can be reached by taxi or an ordinary bus departing in the early morning from the international Vietnam Airlines office.

X-ray machines in Vietnam are *not* film safe and all film should be hand-carried through customs.

Hanoi is served by most Asian-based international airlines such as Thai International, Cathay Pacific, Philippine Airlines, Malaysian Airlines, Singapore Airlines, and Garuda.

Vietnam Airlines has two offices, including a domestic office at 60 Quang Trung St. and an international office at the corner of Trang Thi and Quang Trung streets, which handles reservations and ticketing for all international airlines. Thai International, Air France and Aeroflot are adjacent to the Vietnam Airlines international office at 1 Quang Trung Street.

The US$5 international departure tax is payable in either dollars or *dong*.

Train
The ticket office at the Hanoi train station is open daily 0730-1130 and 1330-1630. Tickets should be purchased one day in advance. Beware of pickpockets.

Several express trains leave daily for Saigon and points en route. Trains also head east to the port city of Haiphong and northwest to Pho Lu and across the border to Kunming in China. Train service to China was discontinued after border disputes in 1979 but is expected to resume within a few years.

The main problem with train travel is that Westerners are charged five or six times the official Vietnamese rate, an outrage which makes trains almost as expensive as air transportation. This surcharge can be avoided by showing an international student ID, insisting on payment in *dong* not dollars, or asking a cooperative Vietnamese to purchase your ticket.

Despite the surcharge, trains are in almost every respect superior to buses: there's room to stretch your legs, opportunities for conversation, and better scenery since trains typically pass through countryside rather than along crowded roads.

Bus

Hanoi has several bus terminals which serve different destinations. Long-distance buses usually leave mornings around 0500. Tickets should be purchased a day in advance. Kim Lien Bus Terminal near Lenin Park serves points south of Hanoi such as Sam Son Beaches (five hours), Vinh (eight hours), and Saigon (54 hours).

Kim Ma Bus Terminal near the Ho Chi Minh Museum in northwestern Hanoi serves destinations to the west such as Hoa Binh (two hours), Son La (18 hours), and Dien Bien Phu (24 hours).

Long Bien Bus Terminal on the east bank of the Red River serves points northeast of Hanoi such as Halong Bay (five hours) and Lang Son (12 hours) on the border with China.

Buses to Halong Bay also leave from the Toyota service station on Le Thanh Tong St., about 100 meters south of the Municipal Theater.

Minibuses to Haiphong (two hours) leave from the fountain at the north end of Hoan Kiem Lake.

THE NORTHEAST COAST

HAIPHONG

Haiphong, Vietnam's second-most-important port and third-largest city, is often bypassed by visitors heading directly to the natural wonders of Halong Bay. Yet, Haiphong is a worthwhile stop for unhurried visitors. Admittedly, Haiphong's outer districts are little more than industrialized sprawl, but the surprising amount of colonial architecture which survived the Vietnam War and the general dilapidation of the waterfront area impart a rich and memorable atmosphere to the downtown districts.

History

Haiphong port was established in 1888 by the French, who occupied Vietnam until their departure from the same port on 15 May 1955. As a primary conduit for Soviet arms during the Vietnam War, the city was subjected to heavy bombing by the Americans, who mined the harbor in May 1972 and finalized the conflict with the Christmas attack of 1973. The city has since recovered with a healthy construction boom and the rehabilitation of many of the outlying factories.

Attractions

Haiphong Tourism at 15 Le Dai Hanh St. arranges tours, rents cars, and will organize private boat excursions to Halong Bay and Cat Ba National Park.

Colonial Architecture: Haiphong's real charm is found in the French-era warehouses on the Cam River waterfront, the Catholic churches, and other colonial buildings located in the center of town on Dien Bien Phu St. and a few blocks south on Tran Hung Dao Street. Top draw is the former Haiphong Opera House, now the Municipal Theater.

Markets: Shops opposite the colonnaded opera house and down Cau Dat St. sell all kinds of local handicrafts at reasonable prices. Cho Sat, Haiphong's largest market, is in the western district near Tam Bac River.

Du Hang Pagoda: Haiphong's most ornate temple is dedicated to Le Chan, the valiant female warrior who fought with the Trung sisters against their Chinese overlords. The pagoda is one km south of the opera house.

Hang Kenh Pavilion: A small communal house famed for its superb range of woodcarvings. One km south of the train station near Hang Kenh public park.

Do Son Beach

Northern Vietnam's most popular beach resort offers fine sand, waving palms, pine-clad hills, and a good selection of moderately priced hotels once patronized exclusively by French colonialists and high-ranking Vietnamese. Do Son is

21 km southeast of Haiphong. Buses depart from Lach Tay Street.

Accommodations include the 120-room Do Son Hotel run by Haiphong Tourism, which costs US$20-30, and a half-dozen seaside bungalows favored by expats from Hanoi.

Haiphong Accommodations

Haiphong has almost a dozen hotels in the low-to-moderate price range. Most accept Westerners but usually demand payment in dollars.

Hoa Binh Hotel: Decent budget spot just opposite the train station. 104 Luong Khanh Thien St., tel. 46907, US$8-12.

Hotel de Commerce: Formerly the Huu Nghi, this old French-era hotel ajacent to Haiphong Tourism has been renovated and now includes a/c rooms with private bath. 62 Dien Bien Phu St., tel. 47206, US$14-28.

Ben Binh Hotel: Large and clean rooms in a fine location near the river make this a good alternative to hotels on Dien Bien Phu Street. 6 Ben Binh St., tel. 57260, US$18-28.

Transportation

Haiphong is 103 km southeast of Hanoi.

Bus: Buses from the fountain at the northern end of Hoan Kiem Lake in Hanoi take about three hours to Haiphong. Buses back to Hanoi depart from the halt near the Municipal Theater. Buses south to Thai Binh leave from Tran Nguyen Han Street.

Boat: One of the best reasons to visit Haiphong is to take the four-hour ferry ride to the town of Hon Gai on Halong Bay through a surrealistic landscape of spellbinding limestone mountains and emerald green waters. Ferries depart three times daily from the municipal dock on Ben Binh Street.

HALONG BAY

Halong Bay, considered by many to be the most spectacular landscape in Vietnam, is a watery wonderland of ethereal limestone formations which rise abruptly from perfectly placid waters, isolated coves, breathtaking grottoes, and thousands of misty islets fantastically carved in the shapes of tigers, unicorns, and sea dragons. Ancient junks and simple sampans gliding through placid waters help complete the timeless scene.

A unique aquatic terrain which resembles some sort of Chinese ink painting, Halong is actually the remnant of an ancient seabed which has eroded into the bizarrely sculpted topography found from Vietnam to Guilin.

Halong and its junks almost stole the show from Catherine Deneuve in the French film *Indochine.*

Boat Tours
Beaches around Halong Bay are disappointing, being both rocky and badly polluted from nearby coal mines. For this reason, the only sensible activity is to hire a boat and spend the day touring around the 1,500-square-km region.

Among the more spectacular grottoes are Hang Hanh, which extends almost two km inside a limestone karst; Hang Dau Go, nicknamed "Cave of Wonders" by 19th-century French tourists; and Hang Trinh Nu or "Cave of Virgins," monikered after an old Vietnamese folk story.

Boats can be rented from most hotels and less expensively from independent operators at the boat quays in Bay Chay and Hon Gai, the two towns in Halong Bay. Independent travelers can inquire at larger hotels about joining a tour group.

Perhaps the most authentic and certainly the cheapest way to sail through Halong is with the ordinary ferry which departs mornings from the dock in Hon Gai and arrives four hours later in Haiphong.

Bai Chay Accommodations
Halong's main port is in Hon Gai but most hotels are in Bai Chay, a surprisingly large town three km west and a short ferry crossing from Hon Gai. Buses from Hanoi pass through Bai Chay en route to Hon Gai.

Adjacent to the ferry dock is the Bach Dang Hotel, which costs US$25-35, and the Van Hai Hotel, with clean and comfortable rooms for US$10-15. The Nha Nghi Cong Doan is a state owned "Workers' guesthouse" with rooms from US$4-6.

Two km west toward Hanoi is the modern Post Office Hotel, the older Bach Long, the renovated Hoang Long, and finally the elegant, colonial-style Ha Long Hotel with a/c rooms and sports facilities. All are operated by Quang Ninh Tourism and charge US$25-35 per double room.

Several more hotels are under construction.

Hon Gai Accommodations
Hon Gai Floating Hotel, near the ferry dock, and Khach San Hai Au, about one km west, both charge US$5-15 for small but decent rooms.

Transportation
Hon Gai is 165 km from Hanoi and 62 km from Haiphong.

Bus: Buses from Hanoi take about five hours to reach the tourist office in the hotel district of Bai Chay.

Taxi: Taxis from Hanoi take three hours and cost US$40-80 return depending on the model of car. Charters are found outside major hotels, near the Vietnam Airlines office, and perhaps least expensively from the Toyota service station on Le Thanh Tong Street.

Boat: The finest way to reach Hon Gai port is by ferry from Haiphong. Ferries depart Hon Gai three times daily for Haiphong.

CAT BA NATIONAL PARK

Cat Ba, the largest island within Halong Bay, is famed for its superb beaches and isolated coves, primeval forests and freshwater swamps, and rich diversity of wildlife including hornbills, wild cats, and migratory waterfowl down from China.

A small portion of the island was declared a national park in 1986 to protect the fragile ecosystems and endangered wildlife.

Accommodations

Most island residents live along the southern coastline in or around the town of Cat Ba. Several small hotels and an upscale resort are located in town and one km from the Cat Ba dock.

Transportation

Cat Ba is 30 km east of Haiphong and 20 km south of Hon Gai. A ferry departs Haiphong daily around 0600 and takes three or four hours.

NORTHWESTERN VIETNAM

The region northwest of Hanoi comprises an isolated and wildly beautiful land almost completely unexplored since WW II.

The reason for this fortuitous state is that northern Vietnam was kept firmly off-limits to Western visitors until early 1993, when French president Mitterrand make his dramatic visit to the battle site at Dien Bien Phu. After his departure, tourism officials abandoned their discredited system of travel permits and declared the entire north open to Western travelers for the first time since the late 1930s.

Today, the far north provides a unique chance to visit a sleeping land of superb scenery and untouched villages whose inhabitants are *amazed* to see you.

Northern Vietnam's most popular route is west from Hanoi to Hoa Binh and Son La before reaching Dien Bien Phu, site of the decisive 1954 battle between the North Vietnamese and the French.

The road from Dien Bien Phu into Laos is theoretically open to Western visitors, though as of this writing only escorted tours have been able to obtain the necessary permits. Travelers must have a Laotian visa and the proper exit endorsement from authorities in Saigon or Hanoi.

This border crossing will become immensely convenient for independent travelers as restrictions are slowly lifted. Guesthouse owners and travelers in Hanoi can help with current details.

Westerners are now permitted to depart Vietnam via the town of Lang Son near the Chinese border. Be sure your visa shows Lang Son as your approved departure point, and double check current requirements on travel permits to the Lang Son district.

HOA BINH AND VICINITY

Hoa Binh lies in a valley once inhabited by the Lac Viet peoples, who created Dong Son culture and the famous bronze drums now found in museums throughout the world. Hoa Binh can be a day-trip from Hanoi or a convenient stopping point en route to Dien Bien Phu.

Attractions

All of the following sights are located outside Hoa Binh and are best reached by tour or chartered taxi.

Chua Thay Pagoda: Also known as Thien Phuc Tu ("Heavenly Bliss") Pagoda, this impressive temple complex features three sections filled with images of Buddhas, Vietnamese heroes, and a 12th-century herbalist to whom the temple is dedicated. Chua Thay is 40 km southwest of Hanoi in the village of Sai Son.

Tay Phuong Pagoda: A hillside temple chiefly famed for its collection of 74 wooden effigies of enlightened monks, considered the finest examples of 17th-century woodcarving in Vietnam. The temple is six km southwest of Chua Thay Pagoda in the village of Thac Xa.

Huong Son ("Perfume Mountain"): A superb wonderland of pagodas, shrines, and religious sanctuaries nestled in a spectacular region of limestone mountains and tropical jungle. An important Buddhist pilgrimage center, Huong Son is widely considered among the most beautiful destinations in the north. The mountain is 60 km southwest of Hanoi and can be toured by boats up the Yen Vi River.

Accommodations

The Hoa Binh Hotel is about two km west of city center on the road to Dien Bien Phu, near a reconstructed Muong minority village. Hotel guides can arrange visits to nearby minority villages. Simple rooms cost US$2-6.

Transportation
Hoa Binh is on the banks of the Hac Giang River some 75 km southwest of Hanoi. Buses from Hanoi's Kim Ma terminal take two hours.

SON LA

Son La, two-thirds of the distance from Hanoi to Dien Bien Phu, is the capital of the province of the same name and home to many of Vietnam's ethnic minorities.

Attractions
French Prison: Son La was administered by the Black Thai ethnic minority until the beginning of the 20th century, when the French established control and brutally put down a series of anticolonial revolts. Many of the revolutionaries were executed in the small prison constructed in 1908 on a small hill in the center of town.

Minority Villages: Son La lies near mountainous villages inhabited by ethnic minority groups such as Tai, Hmong, Tay, Zao, and Muong. Many of these peoples have integrated into Vietnamese society and abandoned their traditional lifestyles. Excursions to minority villages in the Mai Chau Valley can be arranged at the Son La Guesthouse.

Accommodations
A small guesthouse is located in the center of town near the main market.

Transportation
Son La is 310 km northwest of Hanoi on the southern banks of the Nam La River. Buses from Hanoi's Kim Ma Bus Terminal take 14-18 hours over increasingly rough roads, often impassable during the rainy season from June to October.

DIEN BIEN PHU

Dien Bien Phu was the site of the catastrophic defeat of the French which signaled the end of their colonial empire in Southeast Asia and laid the seeds for subsequent American involvement.

The Indochinese Waterloo began in 1952 when General Giap occupied the remote village of Dien Bien Phu in an elaborate ruse to lure the French into a vulnerable strategic position, with colonial supply lines drawn extremely thin. In 1953 Giap drove into Laos, skirted the French forces on the Plain of Jars, and reached the outskirts of Luang Prabang before pulling back to avoid the summer monsoons. In French eyes, Giap had proven that the Viet Minh could move into Laos with relative impunity and that Dien Bien Phu was a vital barrier from which to block Communist moves into Laos, then a close ally of the French.

In late 1953, French General Henri Navarre proposed that Dien Bien Phu be occupied as a mooring point from which to defend Laos and penetrate the rear guard of the Viet Minh, possibly on a straight march into Hanoi. Despite warnings from other French commanders that Dien Bien Phu would become a "meat grinder" of French battalions rather than a mooring point, Navarre ordered French troops dropped into the valley starting in November 1953. By early 1954 the stage was set: the French had 10,000 combat-trained troops hemmed in a closed valley almost impossible to resupply aside from a massive airlift operation; the Vietnamese had over 50,000 experienced troops and a frightening amount of heavy artillery emplaced in carefully camouflaged positions. It was no contest.

The Viet Minh attacked in March 1954 and by late April it was apparent that the French would soon suffer one of the worst defeats in modern military warfare. On the afternoon of 7 May 1954, the Viet Minh's red flag went up over the French command bunker. A world away on the following morning, nine delegations assembled around a horseshoe-shaped table at the old League of Nations building to settle the question of French authority in Vietnam. On 20 July 1954, members at the Geneva Conference agreed that Vietnam should be divided along the 17th parallel pending elections to determine the future of the country. Nine years of warfare had wiped out almost 95,000 French-colonial troops and an estimated 250,000 Viet Minh.

Dien Bien Phu made international headlines in February 1993 when French President Francois

Mitterrand made a pilgrimage to the battleground and later had an official dinner with Giap in Hanoi. Later that year, Pierre Schoendorffer, a former prisoner of the conflict and now a French film director, released his award-winning *Dien Bien Phu*.

Attractions

Dien Bien Phu today is a quiet valley with little signs of the conflict aside from a small museum and several plaques which show the progress of the battle. The 2,242 French colonial troops who perished and were buried under the rice paddies are commemorated with a simple memorial.

Dien Bien Phu is also home to several minority tribes such as Tai, Hmong, Phu La, and Coong, who often visit the market on weekends and can sometimes be visited on organized treks. Best of all, the entire valley is almost completely untouched by tourism.

Accommodations

Western visitors first arrived in Dien Bien Phu in early 1993, shortly after the visit of French president Mitterrand. Travelers have reportedly been able to stay at a simple guesthouse and a small hotel operated by municipal authorities.

Transportation

Dien Bien Phu is 110 km from Son La and 420 km from Hanoi. Most travelers overnight in Son La and complete the bus journey to Dien Bien Phu the following day.

The guest is always right—even if we have to throw him out.

—Charles Ritz,
New York Times

You can define a good flight by negatives:
you didn't get hijacked,
you didn't crash,
you didn't throw up,
you weren't late,
you weren't nauseated by the food.
And so you are grateful.

—Paul Theroux,
The Old Patagonian Express

I have found out that there ain't no surer way
to find out whether you like people or hate them,
than to travel with them.

—Mark Twain,
Tom Sawyer Abroad

CAMBODIA

*Before the fall of Sihanouk, Cambodia was the last paradise,
the last paradise.*

—Helicopter pilot,
Victory in Vietnam

*Angkor is not orchestral; it is monumental. It is an epic poem
which makes its effect, like the* Odyssey *and* Paradise Lost,
*by the grandeur of its structure as well as by the beauty of the
details. Angkor is an epic in rectangular forms imposed upon
the Cambodian jungle.*

—Arnold Toynbee,
East to West

*I have lived seventy-eight years without hearing of bloody
places like Cambodia.*

—Sir Winston Churchill,
The Struggle for Survival

INTRODUCTION

Life has returned to Cambodia. The Vietnamese occupation army which drove the Khmer Rouge from their "Killing Fields" has packed up and gone home. Kampuchea has been renamed Cambodia in a literary effort to eradicate the painful images created by the Khmer Rouge during their five-year reign of terror. And, after a long gestation period criticized by almost everyone connected with Asian politics, United Nations-supervised elections in May 1993 finally settled the question of who will run the country and be formally recognized by the international community.

Today, thousands of tourists cautiously venture back each year to visit Phnom Penh and the famed ruins at Angkor, considered among the world's greatest archaeological achievements.

And yet some people still say "don't go," including the American State Department, which offers stern warnings about political dangers, and travelers who complain that Cambodia is unbearably hot, accommodations are dismal and overpriced, and you can't escape the rat-tat-tat of machine-gun fire late at night. Others warn you about depressing economic conditions, the sorry state of the capital city, and a life-threatening malaria epidemic which strikes a third of the population.

Should you go?

By anyone's standards, Cambodia is hardly a typical tourist destination. For one thing, a civil war still rages between Cambodian troops and Pol Pot's outlaw Khmer Rouge on the borders of Thailand and Laos. Diplomatic protection—for what it's worth—is minimal since the present government is helpless to protect tourists who stray off the approved path and venture into unsecured territories: everywhere but Phnom Penh and (perhaps) Angkor. And most of Cambodia remains economically and psychologically devastated by the terror of the Khmer Rouge, who refuse to surrender and lay down their arms.

But, encouraged by improved travel connections and the lure of an untouched land, visitors now arrive in the greatest numbers since the mid-1960s, when over 30,000 tourists ignored the impending dangers and made the journey to Cambodia. According to recent government statistics, almost 10,000 Western travelers now manage to visit Cambodia each year and few problems are reported by those who stick to the primary destinations of Phnom Penh and Angkor.

Cambodia is adventure travel at its most adventurous.

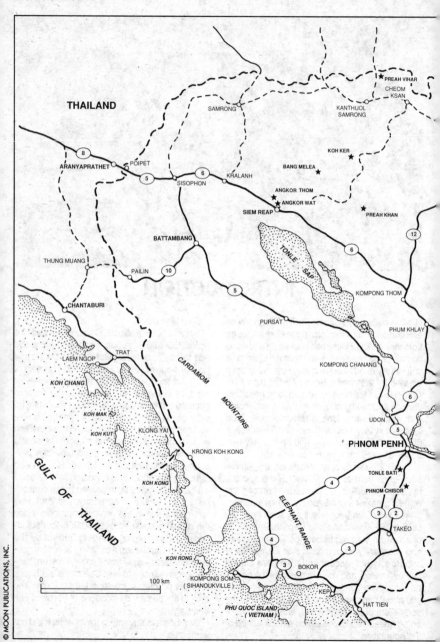

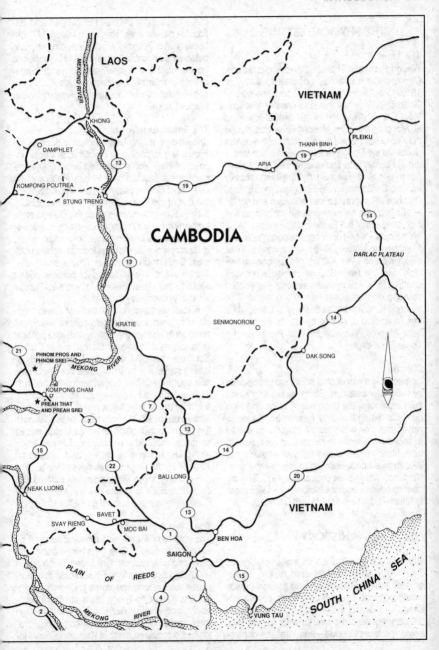

THE PHYSICAL SETTING

The Land

Wedged between Thailand, Vietnam, and Laos, Cambodia is a sparsely populated country of 181,035 square kilometers—about the size of Great Britain or half the land area of Vietnam. Most Cambodians live in the central low-lying alluvial plain along the Mekong River and around the Tonle Sap ("Great Lake"). North of the central plains are the Donggrek Mountains, which form a natural barrier with Thailand, while the southern perimeter is delineated by the romantically named Cardamom and Elephant mountains. Cambodia is separated from Vietnam and southern Laos by the densely forested mountains and high plateaus of the Eastern Highlands.

Cambodia's two dominant geographical features are the Mekong River, which rises in Tibet and traverses over 500 km of Cambodian territory, and the Tonle Sap, an immense but very shallow lake which ranks among the richest sources of freshwater fish in the world. The Mekong is navigable all the way to Laos, while the Tonle Sap is served by ferries which connect Angkor Wat with Phnom Penh via the Tonle Sap River.

Climate

Cambodia is a monsoonal country characterized by two major seasons. Strong prevailing winds from the southwest bring heavy rains and high humidity during the rainy season from June to November. Travel is possible though you should expect daily afternoon rains. Summer months from March to June can be overwhelming to Westerners unaccustomed to the searing temperatures, which often soar above 40°C. The dry and somewhat cooler season from December to March is the best time to visit Cambodia.

HISTORY

Cambodia's importance in the evolution of Southeast Asian culture and history is far greater than its limited size and political power would suggest. Lying on the trade routes between China and India, Cambodia has been the center of several powerful empires—Angkor being the most famous—and later the center-piece of struggle between European and nationalist movements. The tragic history of Cambodia continues today with the ongoing struggle between democratic forces of a U.N.-supported government, the Vietnamese desire to control events in their troublesome neighbor, and the communist war of insurgency waged by the Khmer Rouge.

The Funan Empire

Knowledge of Cambodian history prior to the Funan era is limited to Neolithic artifacts uncovered near Tonle Sap and Bronze Age implements excavated near Phnom Penh and the seaport of Oc Eo. Historical records begin with the rise of the Funan Empire in the 1st century A.D. until its incorporation into the Chenla state in the 6th century. Centered along the lower reaches of the Mekong and Tonle Sap rivers, and prosperous owing to its location on the east-west trade route between China and India, Funan eventually extended its political power south to the Malay Peninsula and east across most of present-day Vietnam.

Funan was among the earliest Asian kingdoms to embrace the Hindu culture which still profoundly shapes the history, art, and political landscapes of not only Cambodia but all of Southeast Asia. Although populated by indigenous peoples and by immigrants from Indonesia and southern China, Funan accepted much of its knowledge of religion and political organization from Indian merchants and theologians who arrived about 2,000 years ago. By the 5th century, Funan civilization used an Indian-based script, worshiped a pantheon of Hindu gods along with Mahayana deities, and created art inspired by the Gupta movement of India.

Eventually, these Hindu elements merged with original designs to create the first true Cambodian empire and the cultural godfather to Angkor.

The Chenla Empire

The empire of Funan was slowly displaced by the rising powers of Chenla, a Hindu-based dynasty originally located near Stung Treng and in southern Laos near Wat Phu. Diplomatic marriages subsequently gave rise to Chenla strongholds at Kampong Thom, in the center of Cambodia, and Angkor Borei in Takeo. Although rarely visited by Westerners, architectural prototypes discovered north of Kampong Thom inspired many of the innovative forms embraced by Khmer builders.

Chenla survived as a united dynasty until the 7th century, when disputes between feuding families led to the creation of "Land Chenla" near the Tonle Sap and "Water Chenla" on the lower Mekong. The Water Chenla empire is famed for its use of hydraulic techniques for cultivation, a sophisticated system later exploited in the complex and highly successful systems of Angkor.

The rise of Srivijaya in southern Sumatra, and new trade routes which favored Indonesian over Cambodian entrepôts, eventually made Chenla a vassal state of the Sailendra dynasty on the island of Java. Several of Chenla's rulers spent time at the Sailendra court, including Jayavarman II, who returned to Cambodia around 800 to establish the civilization of Angkor. The political connections between Java and Cambodia explain many of the architectural and sculptural similarities between the two civilizations.

The Khmer Empire

Cambodia's most famed empire was that of the Khmers, founded in 802 by King Jayavarman II at his capital of Angkor just north of the Tonle Sap. Renowned for its brilliant achievements in art and architecture, Angkor was also an immensely powerful nation which, between the 9th and 13th centuries, controlled most of Southeast Asia from Burma to Indochina, from China to Malaysia.

The introduction of Mahayana Buddhism, which undermined the prestige of the king, combined with the extravagance of the throne, which bankrupted the nation's elaborate irrigation system, finally led to the decline and fall of the Angkor civilization in the 13th century. Angkor fell to the Siamese in 1431. More details under "Angkor," below.

French Rule

The next 500 years—from the fall of Angkor to the arrival of the French in 1863—was an undistinguished period marked by Siamese control and the flight of Cambodian power to various capitals. In 1863, after a series of devastating battles between Siamese and Vietnamese forces, the French seized Cambodia to counter British and Thai expansion up the Mekong River. Their rule was benign. Although the French did little to develop the country, private-sector investors developed vast rubber estates while the government ensured the survival of the Cambodian state by supporting the king in a splendor unequaled since Angkorian times. It was this support of the Cambodian throne which stifled any nationalist activity comparable to that of Vietnam.

The Japanese seizure of Indochina in WW II left the French in nominal control; in 1941 they crowned the 18-year-old schoolboy Prince Norodom Sihanouk the final king of Cambodia. In March 1944, Japanese forces ousted the French and persuaded Sihanouk to declare independence. The French returned after the war and in 1946 abolished the absolute monarchy, though Sihanouk remained titular head of state. Dien Bien Phu was the site of the 1954 defeat of French forces in Vietnam. The withdrawal of French colonial forces from Cambodia led to the complete independence of Cambodia on 9 November 1953 and the triumphant return of Sihanouk to Phnom Penh. Sihanouk abdicated in 1955—absolute monarchies being no longer popular in Asia—but he has remained the principal political leader to the present day.

The Khmer Rouge

Sihanouk may have enjoyed an almost semidivine status with the Cambodian peasantry, but his intractable problems with both right- and left-wing political forces led to his downfall in March 1970 and the seizure of the government by Army Commander Lon Nol. Lon Nol immediately abolished the monarchy, proclaimed a republic, and started his war against the communist rebels—nicknamed the Khmer Rouge or "Red Khmers" by the deposed Sihanouk.

The Khmer Rouge seized Phnom Penh on 17 April 1975 and soon began one of the world's most horrific reigns of terror. To finalize their goal of a Maoist-style agrarian society, Pol Pot and his Khmer Rouge evacuated the cities and forced entire populations into slave labor. Currency was abolished, newspapers outlawed, postal services halted, and the Cambodian calender was reset to "Year Zero." During their 44-month rule, the Khmer Rouge murdered over a million people in an orgy of death unmatched since the days of Adolf Hitler. But statistics are misleading: the percentage of population slaughtered by the Khmer Rouge is an unchallenged world's record.

The Present Scene

To stop the reign of terror largely ignored by the outside world, Vietnamese forces invaded and took Phnom Penh on 7 January 1979. Vietnam's occupation of Cambodia was condemned by the United Nations and unpopular with many Cambodians, who have traditionally disliked the Vietnamese, but nobody else seemed willing to put an end to the holocaust of the Khmer Rouge. Resistance to Vietnamese rule was organized by the Khmer Rouge from their bases on the Thai border and several other groups such as the Sihanuouk National Army (ANS), headed by Sihanouk, and the anticommunist Khmer People's National Liberation Front (KPNLF), headed by Son Sann, a former prime minister under Sihanouk.

After 11 years of occupation and under considerable pressure from the Soviet Union, the Vietnamese withdrew from Cambodia in September 1989, leaving behind a Vietnamese-installed caretaker government under the control of President Heng Samrin and Prime Minister Hun Sen. Although an imposed government will never be popular, most outside observers and many Cambodians appreciate the efforts of the Vietnamese to stop the Khmer Rouge and feel that Hun Sen has been a fair and essentially effective leader.

In October 1991 a peace agreement signed in Paris established a framework for peace and brought in the United Nations Transitional Authority in Cambodia (UNTAC), which has since proved to be the largest and most costly peace-keeping operation in U.N. history. Elections were held in May 1993.

In September 1993, Norodom Sihanouk, one of this century's most resilient political survivors, became king of Cambodia for the second time. Sihanouk named his son, Prince Norodom Ranariddh, as prime minister. Hun Sen, who had led the Vietnam-installed governent, was named the No. 2 official.

The U.S. reestablished formal diplomatic relations in October 1993.

THE PEOPLE

Prior to Pol Pot's time and the holocaust of the Khmer Rouge, Cambodia had an estimated population of over eight million. This number dropped to around five million by the late 1970s but has since rebounded to about seven million due to a high birth rate and the return of refugees from Thailand. Exact numbers of killed or refugees are impossible to know, but it is believed about 2 million refugees fled the country and have been held in refugee camps unless repatriated or accepted by foreign countries. Overall population density is low except in the south-central region near Phnom Penh, where it's actually quite high.

Khmers

Cambodian (Khmer) stock accounts for over 90% of the total population—a strikingly high homogeneity unique in Southeast Asia and the source of Cambodia's strong sense of national identity. The Khmers belong to the Mon-Khmer ethnolinguistic group, which migrated into the fertile Mekong delta from southern China, the Korat Plateau in northeastern Thailand, and perhaps even from Indonesia prior to the Angkorian period. Influenced over the centuries by Indian and Javanese kingdoms, the Khmers have intermarried with successive waves of immigrants from Thailand during the 10th to 15th centuries, Vietnamese from the 17th century, and Chinese in the 18th and 19th centuries. Despite this racial admixture, Khmer stock remains the dominant feature of Cambodian society.

Chinese

Prior to 1975, Cambodia's most important racial minority were the Chinese, who controlled the national economy and maintained their high degree of ethnic distinctiveness despite widespread intermarriage with local Cambodians. As in Thailand, the Chinese were able to integrate into Cambodian life without the racial tensions and government discrimination promoted in other Southeast Asian nations. In fact, many of the leading political figures in Cambodian society are of partial Chinese extraction.

All this changed in 1975 when the Khmer Rouge initiated a ruthless campaign to rid Cambodia of all foreign influence, including the Vietnamese, the West, and the Chinese, who abandoned the economic engines of the country. The result is a society without the entrepreneurial talents of the Chinese, who now comprise less than 3% of the population.

Vietnamese

Cambodia's most controversial minority is the Vietnamese, who have traditionally lived in the lower Mekong River delta and make up less than five percent of the population. Mistrust and animosity between the Cambodians and the Vietnamese have now reached a point where many diplomats fear race riots and "Vietnamese bodies floating down the Mekong," according to an American envoy. It has happened before: in 1970, an anti-Vietnamese pogrom supported by the Lon Nol regime saw thousands of Vietnamese murdered by Cambodian soldiers and dumped in the Tonle Sap River.

Ethnic hatred of the Vietnamese, combined with familiar anti-Western diatribes, have been skillfully exploited by the Khmer Rouge in recent years. Ousted from power by the Vietnamese army, they have driven home the centuries-old fear of political and cultural domination by the Vietnamese and widespread concerns about the influx of Vietnamese immigrants drawn by Cambodia's economic boom. While it appears that all Vietnamese occupation soldiers have returned home, the Khmer Rouge continue their relentless attack against "the despicable *Yuon*" (a pejorative Khmer term for the Vietnamese) and often raid remote villages in search of Vietnamese victims. Racial tension between the Cambodians and the Vietnamese —not the Khmer Rouge—is considered by many experts to be the primary threat to peace inside Cambodia.

Cham Muslims

Cambodia also has about 100,000 Cham Muslims, also known as Cham Malays or Khmer Islam, living north of Phnom Penh along the Mekong River. Many are descended from the people of the royal kingdom of Champa in Vietnam, who were driven into Cambodia by the Vietnamese in the 15th century. Others arrived by invitation of the Muslim-Khmer king Chan, who ruled central Cambodia in the mid-17th century.

Cham Muslims were horribly persecuted during the Pol Pot regime, when, according to some experts, half of their population was exterminated and over 80% of their mosques destroyed. The survivors regard Chur Changvra near Phnom Penh as their spiritual center and follow their traditional roles as cattle traders, silk weavers, and butchers (Theravada Buddhism prohibits most Khmers from slaughtering, though not consuming, animals).

Ethnic Minorities

Cambodia's Khmer Loeu, or Upland Khmers, traditionally lived in the forested hills of the northeast until the Vietnam War forced many down to the plains and into more sedentary lives. Today, the surviving groups not assimilated into modern Cambodian society include the Saoch in the Elephant Mountains, the Pear in the Cardamom Mountains, the Brao along the Lao border, and the Kuy in the far northwest. Like other tribes in Southeast Asia, these peoples are animist, seminomadic farmers who practice slash-and-burn agriculture.

PRACTICAL INFORMATION

GETTING THERE

Air Transportation

Land access is now possible from Thailand and Vietnam, but most visitors arrive by air at Pochentong Airport, 12 km outside Phnom Penh.

From Bangkok: There are now over 30 weekly flights to Phnom Penh from Bangkok. Major carriers include Thai International, which departs daily at 1100 and arrives at 1210; Cambodia International Airlines, which departs daily at 1230 and three times weekly at 1600; and Bangkok Airways, which departs daily at 0900 and 1400. All charge US$280 roundtrip or US$140 one-way. Travel agents on Khao San Rd. can probably beat these prices. Several airlines have requested permission to fly direct from Bangkok to Siem Reap, the town near the ruins of Angkor.

From Vietnam: Vietnam Airlines and Cambodia International fly daily from Saigon to Phnom Penh for about US$70 one-way. Both airlines fly twice weekly from Hanoi to Phnom Penh for US$150 one-way.

From Other Cities: Phnom Penh can also be reached by major carriers from Hong Kong, Kuala Lumpur, Singapore, Manila, and Vientiane.

Land Transportation

Depending on the political situation, land access is permitted from both Thailand and Vietnam. Before considering an overland journey from Bangkok to Cambodia, read the "Warning" below under "Independent Travel."

From Thailand: The border crossing at Aranyaprathet opened in early 1993 and, as of this writing, remained opened to visitors with Cambodian visas. Travelers can reach Aranyaprathet from Bangkok by bus or train and continue to Siem Reap or Phnom Penh by bus or truck. Most travelers head directly to Siem Reap and spend a few days exploring Angkor before continuing down to Phnom Penh and east to Vietnam.

Train lines from Poipet (the Cambodian border town) to Phnom Penh are being reworked and service may be resumed by 1994.

From Vietnam: Travelers can also make the 245-km journey from Saigon to Phnom Penh on Route 1, via the border crossings at Moc Bai (Vietnam) and Bavet (Cambodia). The bus ride takes anywhere from eight to 15 hours depending on border delays, ferry delays, and bribes, which must be paid to almost every official between Saigon and Phnom Penh. This is a much safer journey than the overland route from Bangkok.

All travelers heading to Cambodia from Saigon must have a Cambodian visa and a proper exit endorsement on their Vietnamese visa. Travelers whose Vietnamese visa lists "Saigon" or "Hanoi" as their departure point must get an extra stamp which states "Moc Bai" as the permitted exit port. These stamps can be picked

---

SIGHTSEEING HIGHLIGHTS

Despite the hassles, high costs, and political turmoil, the lure of ancient Cambodia remains as strong as ever.

Angkor Wat
Cambodia's chief attraction is the dazzling 1,000-year-old ruins of Angkor, hidden away in tropical jungles some 300 km northwest of Phnom Penh. Constructed by the Khmers before the 12th century, Angkor is widely considered the premier architectural attraction in Southeast Asia and among the wonders of the world.

Phnom Penh
Also of note is the capital, Phnom Penh, whose religious and artistic monuments were largely untouched by the Cambodian holocaust. Phnom Penh has an excellent museum which provides a good overview of Khmer history and arts, a moving memorial to the horrific reign of the Khmer Rouge, and a lazy atmosphere quite refreshing after the cacophony of Bangkok.

Kep
Tourist officials are also hoping to reopen Kep, a beach resort left over from French colonial days and largely unvisited since the tourist heyday of the 1950s.

KAMPUCAMBODIAN CONUNDRUM

Perhaps only the former Yugoslavia could compete with Cambodia as the world's leading nightmare for cartographers.

The word Cambodia is the English version of Kambuja, an ancient term which means "Sons of Kambu." According to Khmer traditions, Kambu was an Indian ascetic who married a goddess and founded the kingdom of Chenla, the precursor empire to that of the Khmers.

Cambodians themselves transliterate Kambuja to Kampuchea, while the English-speaking world says Cambodia and the French call it Cambodge. The Cambodians prefer to call their country Kampuchea, but negative perceptions created by the Khmer Rouge—who insisted on calling the country Kampuchea—have brought the term Cambodia back into official favor.

The four decades since independence in 1953 have witnessed many different terms for the "Sons of Kambu":

1953—Kingdom of Cambodia: The official title adopted after independence from France. Cambodia at the time was a monarchy under the rule of Norodom Sihanouk.

1970—Khmer Republic: Cambodia was renamed by the government of army marshall Lon Nol after the overthrow of Sihanouk and the abolition of the monarchy.

1975—Democratic Kampuchea: The term used by the Khmer Rouge after their victory over Lon Nol in April 1975.

1979—People's Republic of Kampuchea: Vietnamese occupation forces renamed the country with suitably socialist overtones.

1989—State of Cambodia: The present name, although given the ongoing political conditions this could change at any moment.

Surprisingly, there has been little talk of renaming the country the Kingdom of the People's Democratic Kampuchean State of Khmer Cambodia.

up in Saigon at the Foreign Ministry or the Saigon tourist office.

Buses leave Saigon early each morning from the halt adjacent to the Rex Hotel. The bus heads across Vietnam to Moc Bai, where immigration officials collect passports and check for the proper exit endorsement. After passing through Cam-

bodian immigration, the bus continues west to Phnom Penh. The journey costs about US$5.

Buses from Phnom Penh to Saigon depart early mornings from the intersection of Ok Nga Sou and 211 streets.

From Laos: Route 13, which heads north from Stung Treng to Khong and Pakse in southern Laos, is currently closed to Western visitors.

Sea Transportation

Cambodia's main maritime port is at Sihanoukville (formerly Kompong Som), at the terminus of Route 4, some 180 km southwest of Phnom Penh. Western visitors are not allowed to enter Cambodia via Kompong Som, though this may change if peace returns and restrictions are relaxed.

Reportedly, Thai tourists have been able to take boats from Trat Province to Koh Kong (Kong Island) and continue to Phnom Penh by bus or truck.

GETTING AROUND

Air Transportation

Cambodia Airlines flies from Phnom Penh to several towns in Cambodia but most Westerners take one of the twice-daily flights to Siem Reap (Angkor), which cost US$50 one-way and US$90 roundtrip.

Reservations should be made as far in advance as possible, since most flights are overbooked or suddenly filled with diplomats on holiday. Travelers without reservations can arrive early at the airport, sign the waiting list, and hope for no-shows and cancellations. Airport officials sometimes collect an extra US$30 from passengers without reservations.

Other destinations possibly served by Cambodia Airlines include Stung Treng in the north, Battambang toward the Thai border, and the port town of Sihanoukville.

Land Transportation

Despite roads ranking among the worst in Asia, a steady stream of buses and trucks hauls passengers around Cambodia while trying to avoid running into the Khmer Rouge. As of this writing, Western visitors are taking Route 5 from the Thai border to Phnom Penh, Route 6 from Phnom Penh to Siem Reap, and Route 1 from

Phnom Penh to Saigon. The situation is extremely volatile and should be checked with local tourism officials and diplomatic representatives before leaving Phnom Penh.

Taxis can be hired in Phnom Penh at the Hotel Cambodiana and from several of the government ministries for US$25-50 per day.

TRAVEL PRACTICALITIES

Visas

Visas are required for all visitors to Cambodia. Visas can be obtained from Cambodian diplomatic offices in Saigon, Hanoi, Vientiane, and other countries which recognize the Vietnamese-installed government of Hun Sen. This limited list of diplomatic offices will probably expand after the 1993 elections legitimize the Cambodian government and bring official recognition by the United Nations.

At present, Cambodian visas are best obtained from tour operators and travel agents in Bangkok. Agencies on Khao San Rd. take about a week to book air passage to Phnom Penh and arrange for visas, which are picked up on arrival at Pochentong Airport. If the land crossing is open, travel agents will also book train tickets to Aranyaprathet and arrange Cambodian visas.

Independent travelers can also try the Cambodian Embassy in Bangkok, which is expected to reopen sometime in 1994.

Visas are also relatively easy to obtain at the Cambodian Consulate in Saigon. The consulate is open Mon.-Sat. 0800-1100 and 1400-1700.

Visas are issued for different periods of time— from one week to one month—depending on which embassy does the paperwork and the latest policy handed down from Phnom Penh. The price of the visa also varies from US$8 to US$25, depending on the consulate.

Travelers should check carefully with several travel agents before booking tours or paying for visas. Many agencies charge exorbitant fees which triple or quadruple the price of visas.

Extensions: Visas are sometimes extended by the Ministry of Foreign Affairs at the intersection of 240 St. and Quai Karl Marx in Phnom Penh.

Travel Permits

Travel permits are generally required for all travel outside Phnom Penh. Permits for Siem Reap are issued by the General Directorate of Tourism at the intersection of 232 St. and Achar Mean Boulevard.

Permits for all other provinces require a letter of approval from the Ministry of Foreign Affairs, which is then turned over to the Ministry of the Interior, which issues the permit.

Recent visitors report that the travel permit system was scrapped in late 1993 and that permits are no longer required for travel *anywhere* in Cambodia.

Tours

Cambodia is presently open to both tour groups and independent travelers who make their own arrangements in Bangkok.

Most packages sold by Western travel agents include Vietnam or Laos in the tour itinerary, though a minimum five-day side-trip from Bangkok makes sense for rushed visitors. All Cambodian tours visit Phnom Penh and Angkor. Tours over seven days also visit Tonle Sap (the "Great Lake" near Siem Reap) and several attractions near Phnom Penh such as Udong, Khaki, and Tonle Bati.

The most critical detail is the number of days at Angkor Wat. Almost unbelievably, several of the most famous and highly advertised Western tour wholesalers sell packages which include just a single day at the ruins. This is criminal. Angkor Wat is an immense place with dozens of worthwhile temples that demand a *minimum* of three days and two nights. Do not purchase the 24-hour stop being sold by many agents.

Tours to Cambodia are priced from Bangkok and include roundtrip airfare to Phnom Penh and the connecting flight to Siem Reap, all hotels and meals, sightseeing coaches, and guide services. Figure on US$200-250 per day. Recommended tour operators are listed in the Vietnam and Laos sections.

Sample tours and prices:
```
5 Days/4 nights . . . . . . . . . . US$1050
7 Days/6 nights . . . . . . . . . . US$1375
9 Days/8 nights . . . . . . . . . . US$1750
```

Independent Travel

Although the Khmer Rouge remains the most powerful armed force in the country, independent travelers continue to enter the country and visit Phnom Penh and Angkor Wat. The safest and most sensible route is to fly from Bangkok to

Phnom Penh. The cheapest but most dangerous route is to go overland from Bangkok to Angkor via the border towns of Aranyaprathet and Poipet.

Warning: Western Cambodia is in a state of political turmoil and extremely dangerous due to Khmer Rouge terrorism on the Thai-Cambodia border. The outlaw terrorist Khmer Rouge has recently murdered dozens of Cambodian farmers of Vietnamese ancestry, kidnaped and threatened to kill U.N. employees, and certainly has no fear of Western tourists who are stupid enough to wander through their territory.

Visitors should not proceed unless they understand all the risks and have checked the latest situation with the U.S. State Department and travelers, travel agencies, and diplomatic missions in Bangkok.

Money

Cambodia's unit of currency, the *riel,* is subject to wild fluctuations in the official exchange rate. For example, the 1990 exchange rate of 150-200 *riels* per dollar had risen to 1000-1200 *riels* just three years later. The *riel* is expected to continue its steady decline.

The American dollar serves as an alternative currency, accepted and quoted by most hotels and restaurants in the country. Travelers are advised to bring along a fistful of small-denomination American bills, which are easy to exchange and gladly accepted as payment for most services. Thai *baht* are accepted by some establishments.

Prices in this chapter are quoted in U.S. dollars, rather than unstable *riels.*

Black Market

Cambodia's black market for hard currency is illegal but conducted quite openly from shops and markets in Phnom Penh. Rates for U.S. greenbacks are somewhat higher than the official exchange rate.

Climate

Cambodia has three distinct seasons. The rainy season from June to October is the worst time to visit, while the hot season from March to June will make you think you have died and gone to hell. The best times to visit are the dry and cooler months from November to March.

Health

Inoculations are not required, though it is smart to arrive immunized against typhoid, cholera, hepatitis, rabies, polio, tetanus, and tropical diseases as prescribed by your doctor. All visitors should take malaria pills and stay well covered after dark. The World Health Organization estimates that one-third of all Cambodians have malaria.

Avoid unsterilized water, ice, and uncooked vegetables and fruits which cannot be peeled.

Medical facilities in Cambodia are primitive. Aside from major life-threatening emergencies, all treatments should be undertaken in Bangkok.

Business Hours

Government offices are open Mon.-Sat. 0730-1200 and 1400-1800. Banks are open the same hours on weekdays only.

SUGGESTED READINGS

♦ Chandler, David. *The Tragedy of Cambodian History.* New Haven: Yale University Press, 1992. Chandler writes about Sihanouk: "Anyone trying to form a judgment about his years in power must also confront his disdain for educated people, his impatience with advice, his craving for approval, his fondness for revenge, his cynicism, and his flamboyance." The best book about Cambodian politics from 1945 to 1979.

♦ Coedes, George. *Angkor.* Singapore: Oxford in Asia, 1986. Originally published in French in Hanoi in 1943, few guides to Angkor have since equaled the scholarship and insight of this modern-day classic. Visitors are advised to purchase this book in Bangkok prior to departure.

♦ Madsen, Axel. *Silk Roads: The Asian Adventures of Andre and Clara Malraux.* New York: Pharos Books, 1989. Prior to the publication of his classic novel of revolution, *Man's Fate,* the 24-year-old Malraux and his young wife traveled to Cambodia to steal temple ruins and make a quick profit selling the treasures to Western museums. Malraux failed but later organized an anti-colonial newspaper in Saigon and eventually served as the French Minister of Culture under Charles de Gaulle.

♦ Mazzeo and Antonini. *Monuments of Civilization: Ancient Cambodia.* New York: Grosset & Dunlap, 1978. The best coffee-table book yet produced on Angkor Wat. Includes a fine introduction by Han Suyin and detailed floor plans of each monument.

♦ Ngor, Haing, with Roger Warner. *A Cambodian Odyssey.* New York: MacMillan, 1987. Haing Ngor is the Cambodian refugee who later served as the principal actor in *The Killing Fields.* An unforgettable look at the Khmer Rouge and their reign of terror from 1975 to 1979.

♦ Parmentier, Henri. *Guide to Angkor.* Phnom Penh: EKLIP, 1959. A small booklet not comparable to Coedes's but often available as a reprint in Phnom Penh.

♦ Sihanouk, Norodam. *My War with the CIA.* New York: Pantheon, 1973. The most important figure in modern Cambodian politics relates the assassination attempts and CIA-backed coup which finally toppled his government in March 1970. A seriously unbalanced but highly entertaining book, much like the author himself.

PHNOM PENH

Prior to the arrival of the Khmer Rouge in 1970, Phnom Penh was nicknamed "Paris of the East" for its wide, tree-lined boulevards laid out by the French, croissants and cafe latte, and its elegant villas which recalled a more peaceful era. But four years of occupation and enforced abandonment by the communists tragically left Phnom Penh a sad relic ripped with deep scars: potholed streets, not a single telephone, and dynamited buildings from the National Bank to the Catholic cathedral.

Much has changed in recent years. Yes, sanitation is still poor, most of the colonial architecture is in a sad state of disrepair, and there are serious problems with almost everything from electricity supplies to garbage collection. But the Parisian-style boulevards are now swept clean, dozens of new shops have opened up (English-language schools seem popular), and people come across as genuinely hospitable and anxious to tell their stories. Phnom Penh even has traffic jams.

Impressions are once again favorable. Most visitors who tour both Saigon and Phnom Penh prefer the slower pace and friendlier atmosphere of the Cambodian town, though the avalanche of investment funds and unbridled capitalism is quickly changing the once-sleepy character of the capital.

For the present, Phnom Penh remains strangely suspended between the horrors of the past and the promise of the future, a time-warp town waiting for the curtain to rise on the next act.

ATTRACTIONS

Although sometimes considered simply a connection to Angkor, Phnom Penh offers several worthwhile sights that deserve a good look.

Finding your way around the sprawling city can be time-consuming and somewhat confusing due to the odd street nomenclature imposed in 1979 by the Vietnamese. Larger streets and boulevards have been assigned socialist names (Karl Marx Quay, Lenin Blvd.) while smaller streets running north-south are odd-numbered and streets running east-west are even-numbered.

Phnom Penh's neighborhoods include the former European Quarter around Wat Phnom, the Chinese Quarter near the Central Market, the Khmer Quarter near the Royal Palace, and the New Quarter to the west of Boulevard Achar Mean.

The best way to reach outlying sights is on a *samlor* or cyclo, which costs about US$.50 for most rides or US$1 per hour. Some drivers speak fair English and tell interesting tales. Tours usually begin with a ride along the riverfront esplanade, continue past the bronze dogs staring out over the Mekong River, and then stop at the Royal Palace.

Royal Palace

Cambodia's Royal Palace and auxiliary buildings form the finest collection of traditional architecture left in Phnom Penh. Most of the original buildings were erected in the late 19th century by the French but reconstructed in modern materials in the 20th century.

The Royal Palace in the northern compound has been closed to the public since its November 1991 reinstatement as the residence of Prince Sihanouk but may be reopened in the near future. Fortunately, the Silver Pagoda in the southern courtyard is still open.

Prior to the return of Sihanouk, the grounds of the Royal Palace were entered through the Chan Chaya Pavilion, an elegant hall that was once the performance venue of classical Cambodian dancers.

Several noteworthy buildings are inside the northern courtyard, but certainly the most impressive is the Throne Hall, inaugurated 1919 by King Sisowath as the replacement for a wooden hall constructed in 1869. Adjacent to the Throne Hall is the Royal Treasury and the Napoleon III Villa, presented to the king of Cambodia in 1867.

Silver Pagoda

Also called Wat Pra Keo or "Temple of the Emerald Buddha," the Silver Pagoda in the southern compound is named after the 5,000 silver blocks (six tons of pure silver) which make up the magnificent floor. To the rear is a famed 17th-century "emerald" Buddha, actually carved from jade or

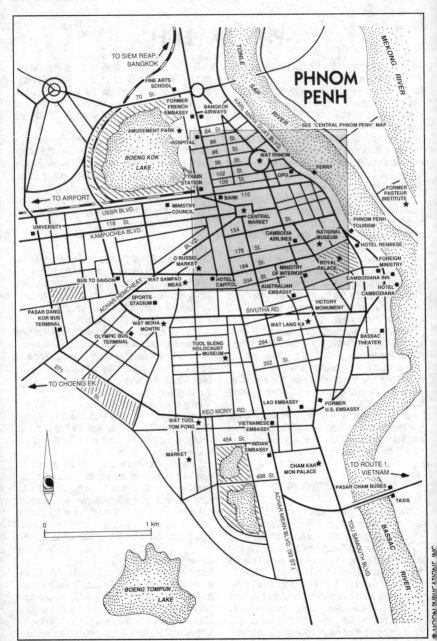

green crystal, and a 90-kg solid-gold Buddha studded with almost 10,000 diamonds.

Also of interest are the *Ramayana* murals on the courtyard walls and a dozen smaller structures including a royal *mondop* or library, footprints of the Buddha, and stupas dedicated to King Ang Duong (reigned 1845-59), King Norodom (1859-1904), King Suramarit (1955-60), and one of Prince Sihanouk's daughters.

The Silver Pagoda is open daily except Monday, 0700-1100 and 1400-1700.

National Museum

The blood-red Khmer-style building which houses the National Museum of Khmer Art, or Musée des Beaux Arts, was designed by a French architect from 1917 to 1920 to form the centerpiece storehouse of Khmer art in Cambodia.

Displayed inside the museum are masterpieces from the pre-Angkor periods of Funan and Chenla (5th-9th centuries), the Indravarman period (9th-10th centuries), the classical Angkor period (10th-14th centuries), and the post-Angkor period (15th-20th centuries). Among the more strikiٖng pieces are images of Hindu deities recovered from Bangkor Borei, the pre-Angkorian statue of Harihara from Kompong Thom, and a bronze Vishnu discovered in the West Baray at Angkor Wat.

The museum is open Tues.-Sun. 0800-1100 and 1400-1700.

Wat Ounalom

Cambodia's most important temple dates from the 1443 construction of a monastery which eventually became the center of the national Buddhist order. In 1975 the Khmer Rouge seized Phnom Penh and executed many of the 500 monks who once lived at the temple. The Khmer Rouge also executed the supreme patriarch and destroyed many of the auxiliary buildings, including a famous library which once held the complete works of the Cambodian Buddhist Institute.

Wat Ounalom has been restored and once again functions as national headquarters for the Buddhist *sangha*.

Tuol Sleng Holocaust Museum

Tuol Sleng—once just a neighborhood high school—was seized in 1975 by the Khmer Rouge and converted into the largest detention and torture center in the country. During its four years of operation, almost 20,000 Cambodians passed through the school to be eventually murdered by the Khmer Rouge. Fewer than 10 prisoners survived. Those who died during torture were tossed into mass graves on the school grounds, while those who survived the tortures were shipped outside town to the infamous extermination camp of Choeung Ek, now known as the Killing Fields.

The exact number of deaths at Tuol Sleng is a matter of public record because the Khmer Rouge, like the Nazis, were meticulous record keepers who carefully numbered and photographed all their victims. Photos mounted on the wall include several unfortunate Westerners such as Michael Scott Deeds, an American who fell into Khmer Rouge hands in 1978 while sailing the Gulf of Thailand. Deeds was executed two days before Vietnamese forces liberated the country.

Inscribed in the remembrance book is a fitting summary: *"Auschwitz sur le Mekong."*

Tuol Sleng is at the intersection of 113 and 350 streets. The museum is open daily 0800-1100 and 1400-1700.

Wat Phnom

According to legend, Phnom Penh takes its name from a rich Khmer lady named Penh who constructed this hilltop monastery in 1372 after her miraculous discovery of four Buddha images inside a floating tree. The present stupa, which dates from the late 1880s, has been reconstructed almost a half-dozen times.

Also on the 30-meter *phnom* ("hill") are shrines dedicated to Vietnamese spirits and the Hindu god Vishnu.

English Street

An excellent place to chat with residents is along 184 Street, where dozens of English-language schools serve the needs of local students.

Buddha Factories

Shops around Wat Prayuvong near the Victory Monument produce Buddhas to replace those destroyed by the Khmer Rouge. Most are on the eastern side of Tou Samouth Blvd. about 300 meters south of the monument.

Markets

Phnom Penh has several markets worth visiting for shopping and photography.

Central Market: This art deco-style market sells foodstuffs, checkered scarves called *kramas,* household goods, a small selection of silver and gold jewelry, old coins, and fake antiques.

O Russei Market: Popular for its food stalls and hundreds of small shops which sell local jewelry and black-market household supplies.

Tuol Tom Pong Market: The market just south of Wat Tuol Tom Pong is Phnom Penh's best place for both real and fake antiques, plus carved wooden furniture and miniature Buddhas.

Choeung Ek Genocide Center

From 1975 to 1979 the murderous Khmer Rouge slaughtered almost 20,000 Cambodians at the extermination camp at Choeung Ek some 14 km southwest of Phnom Penh. The memorial stupa erected at Choeung Ek is filled with the skulls of Cambodians exhumed from mass graves dug in the once-peaceful orchards and ricefields. Remains also include those of the six Americans, three French, two Australians, and one Briton caught in the national nightmare.

Estimates of the toll inflicted by the Khmer Rouge run around one million, though the current Cambodian government reckons the actual figure at over three million with another half million either wounded or orphaned. Perhaps more frightening than these grim statistics is the fact that many of the Khmer Rouge leaders still exist in the Thai jungle or have quietly integrated themselves into the present government.

The Killing Fields of Choeung Ek can be reached by motorcycle taxi for about US$5 roundtrip.

ACCOMMODATIONS

Phnom Penh has over a dozen hotels and guesthouses perpetually packed with United Nations employees, international relief volunteers, and the handful of tourists who visit Cambodia annually. Space can be a problem since the city has only 2,000 rooms, though new hotels coming onstream by 1995 will push the total to about 5,000 rooms.

Prices are high but expected to fall with the withdrawal of U.N. peacekeeping forces. Some of these government-run hotels charge less for rooms on the upper floors to compensate for broken elevators.

Budget Accommodations

Hotel Capitol: The budget travelers' favorite has relatively inexpensive rooms and friendly managers who can help with current travel information. This hotel is near the O Russei Market and a local bus stop. 107 St., US$8-12.

Moderate Accommodations

Hotel Le Royal: A colonial-era hotel constructed in 1910 and the favorite of foreign correspondents during the war. Formerly called the Phnom and the Samaki, the Royal has gone to seed but still has some charm. Many of the events depicted in the film *The Killing Fields* took place here, though the Railway Hotel in Hua Hin (Thailand) substituted in the film. Facilities include a pool and a restaurant. Achar Mean Blvd., tel. 24151, US$25-50.

Hotel Sukhalay: A small and unassuming hotel with temperamental air-conditioning, water-soaked walls, rock-hard pillows, and a pleasant cafe where the drink of choice is five-star Hennessy *cognac et soda.* This seven-story hotel was also a favorite of pre-1975 journalists. Achar Mean Blvd., tel. 26140, US$18-45.

Hotel Santhiphep: Another old but reasonably priced hotel in the center of town. Facilities include a restaurant and both fan-cooled and a/c rooms. Achar Mean Blvd., tel. 23227, US$12-35.

Hotel Asia: A popular mid-priced hotel in the center of town near the Central Market and other tourist hotels. Like many other hotels operated by local government agencies, the Hotel Asia is scheduled for renovation and will probably raise room rates on completion. 136 Achar Mean Blvd., tel. 22751, US$22-45.

Hotel Renakse: Just opposite the Royal Palace is a lovely French colonial building converted into a hotel in early 1992. The Renakse has a good restaurant, travel services provided by Naga Diva Tours, and clean a/c rooms with private bath. Recommended. Lenin Blvd., tel. 22457, US$35-50.

Luxury Accommodations

Hotel Monorom: Western tour groups are usually billeted in the Cambodiana, the Orchid, or this six-story hotel conveniently located near the post office, a bank, the train station, and Phnom Penh Airways. The Monorom has a ground-floor restaurant and a sixth-floor terrace cafe with superb views over the city. Hopefully, the elevator will be repaired by the time you arrive; otherwise insist on huge discounts for upper-floor rooms. 89 Achar Mean Blvd., tel. 26149, US$40-65.

Hotel Cambodiana: Phnom Penh's top-end choice is this riverside complex with 280 rooms, three restaurants, three bars, a swimming pool, tennis courts, CNN news, and a health center—an amazing touch of luxury on the banks of the Tonle Sap. The Cambodiana was originally designed for guests of Prince Sihanouk, but construction halted after Lon Nol's 1970 coup and the Khmer Rouge failed to appreciate its money-making potential. The Sofitel hotel group currently runs the hotel. 313 Karl Marx Quay, tel. (855) 23-26288, fax (855) 23-26290, USA tel. (800) 221-4542, US$180-240.

RESTAURANTS AND NIGHTLIFE

Restaurants

Phnom Penh hotels may be overpriced, but local cafes and French-style restaurants serve good food at rock-bottom prices.

Cafe No Problem: Owned and operated by a local Frenchman, this lovely colonial mansion on

---

CINEMA CAMBODIA

Several films and documentaries available on videotape will help you understand the recent tragedies of Cambodia.

The Killing Fields: Directed by Roland Joffe and based on Sydney Schanberg's *The Life and Death of Dith Pran,* this powerful film won an Academy Award for its depiction of the Cambodian holocaust. Schanberg returned and screened the film in Phnom Penh in 1989 during the ill-fated Cambodian Conference in Paris.

Swimming to Cambodia: Spalding Gray, America's famed monologist, used his experiences from the filming of *The Killing Fields* to explore the social and political undercurrents of contemporary Southeast Asia.

Year Zero and *Year Ten:* Two superb documentaries that retell Khmer Rouge horrors in 1979 and a follow-up program released in 1989. Directed by David Muroe and distributed by Central Independent Television.

---

the north side of the National Museum has become Phnom Penh's most popular hangout for expatriates and budget travelers. The food is tasty and reasonably priced, plus there's a pub and a billiards room. 178 Street. Inexpensive.

Tonle Sap Floating Restaurants: Several good cafes are moored on the Tonle Sap opposite the Royal Palace near the remains of the Chruoy Changvar Bridge. Specialties include Khmer-style frogs' legs, spicy crabs, steamed lobster, buffalo steaks, and local delicacies such as fried baby eels, crispy rice birds, and crunchy crickets. Karl Marx Quay. Moderate.

Boeng Kak Lake Cafes: Two popular open-air restaurants are in the amusement park on the shores of Boeng Kok Lake. A good spot for seafood dishes and sunset dining but bring along your bug spray. Moderate.

International Restaurant: Some locals claim that this cafe on the ground floor of the Hotel Pailin serves the best food in town. Quite popular with expatriates and U.N. employees. 219 Achar Mean Boulevard. Moderate.

Restaurant Thmor Da: Several good cafes have recently opened one block west of Achar Mean Blvd., near the intersection of 128 (Kampuchea-Vietnam Blvd.) and 107 streets. This place is clean, well lit, and recommended by many locals for its Cambodian-style soups and salads. 128 Street. Moderate.

Hotel Sukhalay: Everyone seems to enjoy a breakfast of croissants and French pastries at this venerable hotel.

Central Market: Dozens of food stalls operate until nightfall on the western side of the Central Market. All other markets in Phnom Penh have food stalls open during the day, but be cautious about consuming iced drinks and raw vegetables or fruits which cannot be peeled. Inexpensive.

Train Station Night Market: A lively night market sets up every evening between the train station and USSR Boulevard. Inexpensive.

Nightlife

Nightlife in Phnom Penh is limited to a handful of hotel discos which open and close with the seasons and dance companies attempting to revive the ancient forms of Khmer drama.

Fine Arts School: Phnom Penh's École des Beaux Arts operates two campuses. The main campus near the National Museum teaches ar-

CENTRAL PHNOM PENH

86 St.

88 St.

90 St.

BOENG KAK LAKE

NATIONAL LIBRARY ■

HOTEL LE ROYAL ●

92 St.

HOTEL WAT PHNOM

★ WAT PHNOM

POST OFFICE

FERRY

FERRY

TONLE SAP RIVER

102 St.

106 St.

108 St.

TRAIN STATION

NIGHT MARKET ★

110 St.

■ MARKET

QUAY KARL MARX BLVD.

■ BANK

● PHNOM PENH AIRWAYS

118 St.

■ CUSTOMS

TO AIRPORT

● HOTEL DOSIT

HOTEL MONOROM ●

HOTEL APSARA

126 St.

130 St.

POST OFFICE ●

HOTEL SUKHALAY ●

KAMPUCHEA BLVD.

● HOTEL ASIA

★ CENTRAL MARKET

136 St.

HOTEL SANTIPHEP ●

● BLUE HOTEL

■ LOCAL BUSES

WAT OUNALOM ★

HOTEL PARADIS ●

HOTEL PAILIN ●

HOTEL PACIFIC

PHNOM PENH TOURISM ★

154 St.

ACHAR HEMCHEAY BLVD.

LENIN BLVD.

CAFE NO PROBLEM ●

172 St.

HOTEL NEAKPEAN ●

CAMBODIA AIRLINES ■

13 St.

ENTRANCE ●

174 St.

HOTEL MITTAPHEP ●

● HOTEL ORCHID

178 St.

NATIONAL MUSEUM ★

19 St.

41 St. (TOU SAMOUTH BLVD.)

51 St.

WAT KOH ★

63 St.

ENGLISH STREET

ROYAL PALACE ★

O RUSSEI MARKET ■

180 St.

ACHAR MEAN

184 St.

SILVER PAGODA ★

BICYCLES ■

LOCAL BUSES ■

182 St.

■ MINISTRY OF CULTURE

200 St.

● HOTEL CAPITOL

208 St.

111 St.

107 St.

105 St.

BLVD.

214 St.

220 St.

★ WAT SAMPAO MEAS

143 St.

125 St.

115 St.

113 St.

228 St.

GENERAL DIRECTORATE OF TOURISM ★

232 St.

VICTORY MONUMENT ★

244 St.

0   200 m

MOON

© MOON PUBLICATIONS, INC.

chitecture and archaeology, while the auxiliary campus on 70 St. concentrates on dance and drama. Performances for tour groups can be arranged by contacting the school or the Ministry of Information and Culture at 395 Achar Mean Boulevard.

Hotel Cambodiana: Abbreviated forms of Khmer dance are often given in Phnom Penh's leading hotel.

Boeng Kak Lake: Lakeside cafes in this amusement park are excellent spots to hear Khmer singers belt out Madonna hits and Cambodian love ballads.

Hotel Monoram: Live bands entertain until midnight in the nightclub on the sixth floor.

Hotel Le Royal: The place for live rock, disco, and Vietnamese taxi dancers.

INFORMATION AND SERVICES

Tourist Information

The two government agencies in Phnom Penh which handle tourism essentially exist to sell travel permits, rent cars, and book tours to Angkor. Neither have much printed information or can advise on independent travel.

The Directorate General of Tourism (DGT), also called Cambodia Tourism, is at the intersection of 232 St. and Achar Mean Boulevard. Phnom Penh Tourism is across from Wat Ounalom at the intersection of Lenin Blvd. and Karl Marx Quay.

Both offices are open Mon.-Sat. 0800-1100 and 1400-1700.

Currency Exchange

Currencies and traveler's checks from the United States, Britain, France, Australia, Canada, Germany, and Switzerland can be exchanged at the Banque du Commerce Exterieur du Cambodge (Foreign Trade Bank) in Phnom Penh. Other banks with exchange facilities include the Bank of Commerce of Kampuchea at 26 Achar Mean and the State Bank on Son Ngoc Minh Boulevard.

Exchanging traveler's checks, however, can be a difficult and time-consuming task. Bring along cash and use the black market.

Money wired to these banks can only be picked up in *riels*. Advances on Visa cards are possible at the Foreign Trade Bank.

International Telephone

International calls are best made from the Hotel Cambodiana in Phnom Penh, which operates a private satellite service for IDD calls and international faxes. Phone calls can also be made from the General Post Office on 13th St. and the Post & Telephone office on Achar Mean Blvd. across from the Hotel Monorom.

Diplomatic Offices

The Vietnamese Embassy at Achar Mean Blvd. and 436 St. is open weekdays and Saturday mornings 0730-1100 and 1400-1700. Vietnamese visas require two photographs and take two days to process.

The Laotian Embassy on Keo Mony Rd. a few blocks east of Achar Mean Blvd. will only grant visas to those on escorted tours.

It is expected that most Western nations will recognize the government of Cambodia after the May 1993 elections and open diplomatic offices somewhere in Phnom Penh. Until then, most Western diplomatic offices have established themselves in the Hotel Cambodiana.

The Thai Consulate is on Tousamouth Blvd., near 380 street.

TRANSPORTATION

Air Transportation

Phnom Penh is now served by a half-dozen international and private airlines, including the national carriers of Cambodia, Vietnam, Laos, Thailand, Malaysia, and Singapore.

The Cambodia Airlines booking office at 62 Tou Samouth Blvd. is open Mon.-Sat. 0700-1000 and 1400-1700. This office also represents Aeroflot, Vietnam Airlines, and Lao Aviation.

Thai Airways, Cambodia Airlines, and Silkair (from Singapore) have an office at No. 16, 106 Street, near the river.

Bangkok Airways is at No. 61B, 214 Street.

Transindo Tours at 16 Achar Mean Blvd. is an agent for Bangkok Airways, which flies daily between Bangkok and Phnom Penh.

Phnom Penh Airways in the Hotel Dosit on 118 St. flies daily to Singapore.

Pochentong International Airport, 12 km west of downtown Phnom Penh, can be reached by taxi or buses from O Russei Market.

Buses Around Cambodia

Buses to destinations north, west, and east of Phnom Penh depart from the Olympic bus terminal on 199 St. adjacent to the Olympic Market. The location is shown on the "Phnom Penh" map.

Buses heading south and southwest depart from Pasar Dang Kor bus terminal on Keo Mony Blvd. adjacent to Dang Kor Market.

Until the political situation calms down, Western visitors are discouraged from taking buses toward the Thai border and other regions controlled by the Khmer Rouge.

Buses To Saigon

Buses to Saigon depart at 0600 from the southwestern corner of Ok Nga Sou (182 St.) and 211 streets. Permission to use the buses depends on the political situation in eastern Cambodia, but this route now appears secure and travelers are generally allowed to overland to Vietnam.

Train

Trains to Kompong Som and Battambang depart every other day around 0600. Daily service will begin with the completion of a second rail line. Battambang takes perhaps 15 hours and the ride is free on the flatbeds in front of the engine; they double as minesweepers. A better option is on top of one of the coaches *behind* the engine.

Westerners are rarely permitted to take trains around Cambodia but this might change in the next few years.

River Transportation

Government-run ferries depart from the two adjacent ferry docks just east of Wat Phnom. Ferries north up the Mekong River to Kompong Cham, Kratie, and Stung Treng leave from the northern dock between 102 and 104 streets. Ferries to Siem Reap leave from the same dock and take two days to Angkor.

Boats to Vietnam leave from the ferry landing on the east side of Monivong Bridge, which crosses the Bassac River.

Western visitors are usually prevented from boarding boats in Cambodia, except for the fascinating journey to Siem Reap.

Local Transportation

Taxis can be hired in Phnom Penh at the Hotel Cambodiana and from several of the government ministries for US$25-50 per day. City transportation is also provided by cyclos, man-powered rickshaws operated by English-speaking guides.

ATTRACTIONS NEAR PHNOM PENH

Most of the following sights can be done in a single day from Phnom Penh. Westerners are permitted to take buses to the following destinations.

Buses to destinations north and west of Phnom Penh depart from the Olympic bus terminal on 199 St. adjacent to the Olympic Market.

Buses heading south and southwest depart from the Pasar Dang Kor bus terminal on Keo Mony Blvd. adjacent to Dang Kor Market.

Buses going east to Koki Beach leave from the Olympic bus terminal and from the eastern side of Monivong Bridge.

KOKI BEACH

Koki Beach is a simple but immensely popular weekend escape some 14 km east of Phnom Penh on the banks of the Mekong River. Sundays bring hundreds of families who rent shaded sections of platform at the edge of the river and then eat and drink until sundown.

Transportation
The beach is just off Hwy. 1 en route to Vietnam. Take a taxi or bus from the halts on the east side of the Bassac River adjacent to the Monivong Bridge.

TONLE BATI AND TA PROHM TEMPLE

Tonle Bati
Tonle Bati is a large recreational waterpark 35 km south of Phnom Penh. The resort is deserted during the week but packed on weekends with families down from the capital.

Wat Ta Prohm
The principal reason to visit Tonle Bati is to see this remote temple, perhaps constructed by King Jayavarman VII (ruled 1181-1201) over the site of a 6th-century Khmer shrine. To cover his bases, Jayavarman consecrated the temple to both Buddha and the Hindu god, Brahma.

The highly complex plan involves a great variety of buildings enclosed within two concentric galleries and a central sanctuary of five chambers encasing statuary or Hindu lingams. Among the sculpture which has survived the elements and vandalism of the Khmer Rouge are images of the Hindu god Preah Noreay and bas-reliefs which relate parables from the life of the king and his consorts.

Transportation
Ta Prohm is 35 km south of Phnom Penh and three km west of Highway 2. Any bus from Pasar Dang Kor bus terminal going down Hwy. 2 toward Takeo will pass the access road.

PHNOM CHISOR

Phnom Chisor is a hilltop temple complex some 55 km south of Phnom Penh. The principal sanctuary was constructed in the early 11th century and originally known as Suryagiri in honor of the Hindu god Brahma. Phnom Chisor and two other Khmer temples situated on the lower plains—Sen Thmol and Sen Ravang—were later converted, as indicated by the Buddha images now enshrined in the interiors.

All of the temples have been badly damaged by the elements and perhaps the Khmer Rouge, though the sense of isolation makes this a worthwhile extension from Ta Prohm.

Transportation
Take a bus 55 km south from Phnom Penh to the turnoff marked by Prasat Neang Khamu, the so-called and wonderfully entitled Temple of the Black Virgin. Phnom Chisor and its auxiliary temples are four km east of Prasat Neang Khamu.

UDONG

Udong (also spelled Oudong) served as the capital of Cambodia from 1618 to 1866 under a series of important rulers including King Ang Douong (reigned 1845-55) and his son, King Norodom.

Over the centuries, each dynasty erected temples and continued construction of the royal palace. Prior to the arrival of the Khmer Rouge, noteworthy structures included Viharn Preah Chaual Nipean and its immense reclining Buddha; Tan San Mosque, maintained by Cham Muslims; and Viharn Preah Ath Roeus, dedicated by King Sisowath and known for its nine-meter Buddha. Several other memorial stupas were once located on the twin hills just south of the old capital.

Almost unbelievably, most of these temples, stupas, and palaces were destroyed by the Khmer Rouge during their horrendous reign of terror. Today, Udong is chiefly visited for its surviving structures and memorial to the more than 1,000 people who were murdered by the Khmer Rouge and dumped into mass graves.

Transportation
Udong is 40 km northwest of Phnom Penh just off Route 5, which leads to Tonle Sap and Battambang. Take a bus five km past the Prek Kdam ferry to the roadblock, then continue four km south to Udong.

SOUTH-COAST TOWNS

KEP

Once Cambodia's premier beach resort and home to many of its ruling elite, Kep was, prior to its destruction by the Khmer Rouge, the favorite escape of French colonialists and wealthy Cambodians who came to gamble, yacht, water-ski, and dive in the warm waters. Even Prince Sihanouk maintained a residence on the hill, still visible but in ruins.

Kep today is a largely deserted place where weeds poke through the old casino and the Kep Hotel stands empty. Investors are talking about fixing the place up, but at present there's little here but a few remaining villas and armed teenage guards who patrol the former resort.

Transportation
Kep is 155 km south of Phnom Penh and 18 km southeast of Kampot, where Route 3 reaches the ocean. Take a bus to Kampot and continue by truck, or take a train to Damnak Chang Aeu, a few kilometers northeast of Kep.

KAMPOT

Kampot, five km from the ocean, is a scenic town which largely escaped mass destruction by the Khmer Rouge. The town was evacuated during the late 1970s but has since been re-populated with over 15,000 residents who work as fishermen and farmers in the nearby ricefields. Tourism authorities in Phnom Penh have announced plans to promote both Kampot and Kep as alternative escapes for Western visitors.

Accommodations
Several inexpensive hotels survived destruction by the Khmer Rouge, including the Phnom Kamchai and the Phnom Khieu in the center of town near the market, and the Kampot Province Hotel on the banks of the Tuk Chou River.

Transportation
Kampot, 150 km south of Phnom Penh, can be reached in about five hours by buses from Pasar Dang Kor bus terminal.

ANGKOR

Angkor—the colossal and powerful center of the ancient Khmer empire—is the cultural and spiritual heart of the Cambodian people and one of the world's great architectural achievements.

Situated seven km north of Siem Reap, the widely scattered monuments have tantalized Western travelers since 1858 when Henri Mouhot, a French naturalist, stumbled across the ruins and then wrote an account of his voyage and discovery. Today, monuments of the Khmer civilization continue to amaze thousands of visitors who manage to break through the bureaucratic webs and political turmoils which still ensnare the Khmer nation.

SIEM REAP

The town of Siem Reap ("Siamese Defeated") serves as the base for visits to the 100-plus monuments which constitute the empire of Angkor. Siem Reap was badly damaged and largely abandoned during the Khmer Rouge era but has rebounded since the flight of the Khmer Rouge and return of tourism to the region.

Tourist Information
Angkor Tourism, the government agency which supervises local tourism, maintains an office near the Grand Hotel d'Angkor in the north end of Siem Reap. The office primarily deals with group tours but also helps independent travelers with details on budget guesthouses and local transportation.

Angkor Conservation, the government agency responsible for the restoration and protection of the monuments, is 1.5 km north of Siem Reap on the road toward Angkor Wat. The agency trains guides and stores thousands of statues in its guarded compound.

Visitors can view the statuary but only with written permission from Angkor Tourism. Those who have toured the collection consider it among the most impressive array of Asian art in all of Southeast Asia.

Admission Fees
To the outrage of Western visitors, Angkor Tourism continues to charge each visitor a stiff fee to tour the monuments. Protests to the Directorate General of Tourism have been unsuccessful to date, though the fee may be reduced in the near future.

Some travelers have reportedly been able to dodge the fee collectors at the three roadblock checkpoints.

Current fees are US$15 for Angkor, US$10 for the Bayon, and US$5 for Bantei Srei.

Safety
Certainly the most disturbing aspect of any visit to Angkor is the sporadic gunfire which still erupts nightly just outside Siem Reap and sometimes during the day in the vicinity of the monuments. Local guides claim the source is government troops shooting at birds (right), but the presence of Khmer Rouge forces remains a fact of life in war-torn Cambodia.

The biggest dangers are teenage soldiers and government guides who occasionally rob tourists, and unexploded landmines still scattered in the fields near the ruins. Visitors should stay on well-marked paths.

Accommodations
Many of the old French-constructed hotels, including the venerable Auberge Royale and the Hotel Air France, were destroyed by the Khmer Rouge in the late 1970s, but Thai and Cambodian entrepreneurs are now renovating the surviving structures and constructing new facilities for the anticipated upturn in tourism. Siem Reap now has four hotels which essentially cater to group tours and a handful of small guesthouses and homestays.

Budget Guesthouses: Budget guesthouses, on the road that parallels the Siem Reap River and one block east, can be located through *samlor* drivers or at the Bayon Restaurant, Siem Reap's backpackers' hangout. Another great place to gather information about homestays and how to avoid the dreaded "temple pass" is at the Sanapheap ("Equality") Cafe, across from the Grand Hotel and five minutes east of the river.

All of the dozen-plus homestays charge about US$5 for small but adequate rooms. You'll need to bargain.

MONUMENTS OF ANGKOR

© MOON PUBLICATIONS, INC.

Grand Hotel d'Angkor: Constructed by the French in 1928 as the first hotel near Angkor, Siem Reap's faded grand dame is now managed by the Aseana hotel group, which intends to restore the venerable hotel to its former glory. Facilities include a restaurant, a tour agency, bicycle and motorcycle rentals, and 65 rooms with fan or a/c. All visitors who stay here must pay for the infamous "temple pass." US$45-65.

Villa Apsara: Just opposite the Grand Hotel and on the banks of the Siem Reap River are renovated bungalows used by tour groups and visiting dignitaries. US$30-55.

Hotel de la Paix: Thai investors have renovated this old French hotel which now caters to tour groups and midrange independent travelers. The hotel is in the center of town a few blocks east of the river. US$20-45.

Getting There

Air: Cambodia Airlines's twice-daily flights from Phnom Penh to Siem Reap cost US$50 oneway and US$90 roundtrip. Several airlines have announced plans for direct flights from Bangkok.

Land: Travelers coming overland from Thailand can reach Siem Reap from Aranyaprathet in about a day of hard bus travel. A bus or truck from Phnom Penh takes about two days to cover the 311-km journey via Kompong Thom and Route 6.

Boat: Ferries from Phnom Penh's Pasar Cha Ministry of Transport landing, situated on Karl Marx Quay at 102 St., take two days to reach Phnom Krom, a small Tonle Sap town about

ANGKOR WAT AND ANGKOR THOM

© MOON PUBLICATIONS, INC.

10 km south of Siem Reap. This is an amazing trip up the Tonle Sap River and across the length of the immense Tonle Sap, Southeast Asia's largest freshwater lake.

Local Transportation

Monuments around Angkor are difficult to tour without hired transportation. Tour groups are taken around by car or minibus, depending on the size of the group. Independent travelers can reach the monuments with a rented bicycle or motorcycle, or hired car, which costs around US$40 per day with driver.

THE MONUMENTS

Angkor has an estimated 300 monuments widely scattered throughout the jungle in all directions from Siem Reap. Three days are necessary to visit the three most important sites: the Bayon and Baphuon, which essentially comprise the ancient city of Angkor Thom, Ta Prohm and Preah Khan just outside the city walls, and Angkor Wat to the south of the former capital.

Many visitors first visit the Bayon and Baphuon, two immense temple complexes which face east and are best toured in the fine light of the early morning hours.

Ta Prohm and Preah Khan, outside the perimeter of Angkor Thom, can be visited as side trips between Angkor Thom and Angkor Wat.

Angkor Wat, which faces west, is best visited and photographed in the late afternoon, though several visits are necessary to really appreciate the amazing spectacle.

History

Between the 9th and 13th centuries, Southeast Asia from Burma to Indochina and from China to Malaysia was controlled by a powerful Khmer empire centered just north of the Tonle Sap River.

Angkor's original capital was established in 802 by a Khmer king named Jayavarman II, who made Hinduism the state religion and crowned himself the reincarnation of Shiva. Jayavarman's concept of a god-king—perhaps a combination of Saivite concepts of divinity and older megalithic beliefs—set the style for succeeding rulers who, at times, considered themselves the earthly representatives of Shiva, Vishnu, and ultimately, the Buddha.

Although chiefly noted for its wondrous architecture and sculpture, Angkor was also an immense technological achievement from which central Cambodia derived its agricultural prosperity. By creating an elaborate and highly sophisticated system of lakes, channels, and irrigation canals which radiated from Tonle Sap, the Khmer empire grew into one of the wealthiest and most powerful empires on the face of the earth. Utilizing its vast resources and tens of thousands of slaves, Khmer kings initiated a 400-year building spree which left the world with splendid baroque palaces, towering monuments, royal mausoleums, vast lakes, magnificent highways, and hundreds of immense temples bursting with diamonds, rubies, and gold.

Bantai Srei and the Bakheng—mystical mountains along the lines of Borobudur—were constructed in the 10th century. King Suryavarman II constructed his masterpiece, Angkor Wat, in the early 12th century, though the immense effort and cost almost bankrupted his nation.

It was left to Angkor's final great king, Jayavarman VII, to revitalize the empire and construct his magnificent royal city of Angkor Thom. Breaking all previous Khmer traditions, Jayavarman placed himself under the patronage of Mahayana Buddhism and adopted as his patron deity one of the Buddhist bodhisattvas.

Angkor declined after the reign of Jayavarman, but today the enigmatic faces of Lokesvara, Buddhist Lord of the World, still smile and gaze wondrously over the four directions of the world.

Cosmic Symbolism

Angkor was not only a city but, more importantly, an immense representation in stone of Hindu cosmology whose mythological symbolism was intended to preserve spiritual harmony between the gods and mankind.

All major monuments at Angkor can be visualized as magical mandalas that represent the Hindu-Buddhist universe: the central shrines symbolize Mt. Meru, the celestial paradise of both Hindu and Buddhist deities; the gates and cloisters depict the successive outer envelopes of cosmic reality; moats represent the seven oceans which form concentric rings around the holy mountain.

And, similar to Borobudur in Java, causeways and staircases carry the pilgrim on a journey through the mythological worlds of mankind toward the realm of the supreme god.

Angkor Wat

The most spectacular and best preserved of Angkor's temples is the self-contained universe of Angkor Wat, erected by Suryavarman II (reigned 1112-52) to honor himself and the Hindu god Vishnu. Angkor Wat is approached from the west along a magnificent road lined with colossal balustrades carved like cosmic serpents.

Recently restored by the Archaeological Survey of India, the complex rises in three concentric enclosures behind the western gate, which is almost as large as the central shrines. An entire day can be spent wandering around the terraces and pinnacles studying the Hindu deities, bullet scars, and row of Buddhas ungraciously decapitated by the Khmer Rouge.

Perhaps the most spectacular creation is the kilometer-long relief sculpture in the open colonnaded gallery which tells of Hindu epics, Suryavarman's earthly glory, celestial dancing maidens called *apsaras,* fish and flowers, ghastly *makara* demons, arabesque plants, and Vishnu presiding over a tug-of-war between the armies of Khmer good and evil—an appropriate symbol of contemporary Cambodian life.

Phnom Pakheng

Those walking from Angkor Wat to Angkor Thom may want to climb this 65-meter hill for excellent views over the Angkor plains. Highly recommended at sunset.

Angkor Thom (Royal City)

The final and most baroque creation of the Khmers was the Royal City of Angkor Thom, which consists of the central temple, the Bayon, a secondary and older temple called the Baphuon, and several elaborate terraces and victory towers enclosed within ancient city walls.

Though several of the structures are older, the building frenzy of Angkor Thom reached its pinnacle during the reign of King Jayavarman VII (1181-1200), greatest of all Khmer constructionists and the final ruler before the Khmer empire collapsed into economic and spiritual ruin.

Although much of the city has disappeared into the jungle, Angkor Thom once ranked among the most colossal cities anywhere on earth: a million people spread across an area of 10 square kilometers, 12 kilometers of massive walls and wide moats which protected the population against foreign marauders, and two immense artificial lakes (the Western and Eastern Barays) far vaster and more sophisticated than anything seen before in Asia. Angkor Thom was a planned city of greater complexity and spaciousness than any in medieval Europe—larger and perhaps more populous than the whole of ancient Rome.

The Bayon

Focal point and mystic center of the royal city is the temple-mountain of the Bayon, chiefly noted for its 54 powerful four-sided Towers of Faces. Each of the 216 countenances bears the same blank image: Jayavarman as the reincarnation of the Buddha, eyes closed and with an enigmatic and disturbing smile.

The Bayon also features over 1,200 meters of stupendous bas-reliefs carved on the outer walls of the central sanctuary and inner walls of the laterite enclosure. Symbolic differences between the two series of reliefs are noted by the first terrace carvings, which depict realistic tableaux of common life and historical events, and the inner walls, which relate the epic worlds of gods and legends.

And yet, the Bayon's great achievement appears not in its sheer size or hastily carved murals, but in the stupendous architectural arrangement that represented the universe and kingdom—religion and state combined in a single symbol.

The Baphuon

The temple-mountain of King Udayadityavarman II (reigned 1050-66) predates Angkor Wat and the Bayon and, as such, once represented one of the most colossal works of man in the world.

Today, however, it is difficult to appreciate the past splendor since most of the complex has collapsed into a vast accumulation of stone and chaotic ruin. The blame lies with the inadequate technical skills of Khmer architects who erected the monument on an unsteady artificial hill and employed primitive support structures rather than the corbeled arches then known to the Western world.

Royal Enclosure And Phimenakas

From the Baphuon, walk past the moats and through the southeastern gate of the Royal Enclosure into the immense rectangular yard which once formed the heart of the ancient Angkor empire.

Centerpiece of this forbidden city is the now-dilapidated Phimenakas, the pyramidal "Palace of the Winds" constructed by Rajendravarman (reigned 944-968) but later used and embellished by all subsequent kings.

Terrace Of The Elephants

Dominating the eastern wall of the Royal Enclosure, some 200 meters north of the Baphuon, is a 350-meter-long terrace once used as a royal audience hall and review stand for public ceremonies. Constructed by Suryavarman I, the terrace derives its name from the bas-reliefs of elephants and rows of life-sized lions and winged garudas which once supported the royal pavilion.

Terrace Of The Leper King

Anchoring the northeastern corner of the Royal Enclosure is a seven-meter platform richly carved with dancing *apsaras* and bands of mythological animals which frequented the subterranean slopes and upper elevations of Mt. Meru, Hindu center of the universe.

Perhaps constructed as a cremation tower for Angkorian aristocracy, the platform is surmounted by a mysterious and completely sexless image believed to represent either Shiva, the Hindu god of death, or Yasovarman, founder of Angkor. The original now resides in the courtyard of the National Museum in Phnom Penh.

In any event, the naked and lichen-embalmed image conveys a surrealistic impression of advanced leprosy.

Ta Prohm

The remainder of the widely scattered monuments at Angkor are a long hike from Angkor Thom, but visitors with enough time might follow the Avenue of Victory to the following temple just south of the Eastern Baray.

All of the mystery and romance associated with Angkor is epitomized by this 12th-century temple, which has graciously been allowed to disappear into the jungle. Consumed by gigantic trees and split by destructive vines, Ta Prohm is one of the last great unrestored sanctuaries in the East, an amazing journey back to a lost world.

Ta Prohm was constructed by King Jayavarman VII (ruled 1181-1200) to honor his mother, represented here as Prajnaparamita, the reincarnation of perfect wisdom. A stele discovered at the site indicates the former glory and sheer immensity of the project: 566 stone dwellings, 39 major sanctuaries, 18 chief abbots, 2,740 priests, 2,202 assistants, and 615 dancing girls engaged in service to the priests.

The highly complex plan involves a great variety of buildings enclosed within a series of concentric galleries. The chief structures include several libraries and a central sanctuary of five chambers encasing statuary or Hindu lingams.

All these monuments have collapsed into magnificent ruins; one of the real highlights of Angkor.

Some men go skimming over the years of existence to sink gently into a placid grave, ignorant of life to the last, without ever having been made to see all it may contain of perfidy, of violence, and of terror.
　　　　　—Joseph Conrad, *Heart of Darkness*

To many people holidays are not voyages of discovery, but a ritual of reassurance.
　　　　　—Philip Adams, *Australian Age*

Countries, like people, are loved for their failings.

　　　　　—F. Yeats Brown, *Bengal Lancer*

LAOS

You do not yet see that the Real is in your own home,
And you wander from forest to forest listlessly.
Here is the Truth!
Go where you will,
to Vientiane or to Luang Prabang,
If you do not find god in your own soul
The world will be meaningless to you.

—Kabir

I'm convinced that to maintain one's self on this earth
is not a hardship, but a pastime,
if we will live simply and wisely.

—Thoreau

Travelers are fantasists, conjurers, seers—
and what they finally discover is
every round object is a crystal ball:
stone, teapot, the marvelous globe of the human eye.

—Gladys Parrish

INTRODUCTION

The tiny landlocked nation of Laos—one of the remnants of "Old Asia"—recently opened its borders to visitors from the outside world. An isolated region long called the "Land of a Million Elephants," Laos is now attempting to change its image from the Albania to the Shangri-La of Southeast Asia; it's a herculean though nonetheless conceivable task, thanks to the nation's central location, peaceful atmosphere, and almost completely untouched range of attractions.

Problems remain with rudimentary tourism facilities, overpriced government-controlled services, and the fact that most of the country remains off-limits or difficult to reach, but more than any other destination in Southeast Asia, Laos retains a remarkable feeling of serenity and timelessness. The time to visit is *now*.

THE PHYSICAL SETTING

The Land

Laos is among the most mountainous countries in Asia; over 90% of the land is low-lying but rugged forest-clad mountains. Slightly larger than Great Britain, the nation is comprised of two physiographic zones. Northern Laos in-

cludes several mountain ranges, the politically important Plain of Jars, and the Annamite Cordillera, which creates a formidable barrier between Laos and Vietnam. Southern Laos is characterized by the Mekong River, which traces the western perimeter, and the Boloven Plateau, situated at an average elevation of 1,100 meters.

The confusing knot of mountains which dominates much of the country and the primitive state of the roads make land travel extremely time-consuming. A prime example is Route 13, which connects Vientiane with Luang Prabang, the ancient capital 140 km to the north. Despite the fact that these are the two most important destinations in the country, Route 13 is little more than a rough dirt path so poorly maintained that scheduled bus service has never been attempted. Fortunately, the road is now being paved and bus service may soon be started. In the meantime, most internal transportation is provided by Lao Aviation.

Climate

Laos is a subequatorial and monsoonal country with a wet season from June to November and dry season the remainder of the year.

Rainfall during the monsoon season is heaviest in the higher elevations such as the Bolovens Plateau, which receives over 400 centimeters of annual precipitation.

The summer months from March to June are dry but extremely hot. Most visitors find the best travel season to be the cooler months from November to February, and not the hot season from March to June or the rainy season from June to November. Be prepared for cold weather in higher elevations such as the Plain of Jars and the Bolovens Plateau near Pakse.

HISTORY

The history of Laos is a record of almost continual tragedy. For centuries, the tiny country has been a pawn in the hands of more powerful neighbors, who coveted it for its strategic location between China to the north, Vietnam to the east, and Thailand to the southwest. Despite the gentle nature of the people, Laos has historically served as a mountainous battleground between warring Siamese and Vietnamese kingdoms, and more recently between the Americans and the Vietcong, who constructed much of their Ho Chi Minh Trail inside the national boundaries.

Prehistory

Though documentary records are nonexistent prior to the founding of the Lan Xang Kingdom in the 14th century, linguists and archaeologists believe that the Lao people began to migrate from southern China toward the Mekong River basin prior to the 10th century. The original inhabitants, Kha, were slowly displaced by the Tai peoples who filtered down and settled into Thailand, Burma, and Indochina.

The migratory process accelerated in the 13th century after Mongol invasions of southern China by Kublai Khan and widespread slave raids by the Han Chinese. Laos was raided by the Lanna Thai kingdom of Chiang Mai during the 11th century and by the Khmers during the 12th and fell under the suzerainty of the Sukothai Empire during the 13th century.

Lan Xang Kingdom

Recorded history and the unified nation of Laos began in 1353 under the leadership of Fa Ngum,

a Lao prince who was raised in the Khmer courts of Angkor and married a Khmer princess for political gain. Considered the father of modern Laos, Fa Ngum was a visionary politician and talented warrior who, from 1353 to 1371, conquered most of present-day Laos and extended his Indo-Khmer civilization across the Mekong into north and northeastern Thailand. Fa Ngum also brought in Khmer missionaries from the empire of Angkor who introduced Theravada Buddhism as the state religion.

Fa Ngum—ruler of one of the largest territories in Southeast Asia—named his expansive holdings the Kingdom of Lan Xang, an epiphanous term which translates to "Kingdom of a Million Elephants." His widespread empire proved a resounding success. Aside from a half-century of Burmese rule (1574-1637), Lan Xang dominated Laos until 1713, when it split into the three separate kingdoms of Vientiane, Luang Prabang, and Champassak.

Other great leaders of the Lan Xang period included Samsenthai, who succeeded Fa Ngum and organized the nation along Siamese political lines, and Setthathirat, who is revered for bringing the Emerald Buddha to Vientiane in 1547 and successfully defending Laos from foreign aggression by Siamese and Burmese forces.

The Golden Age of Lan Xang occurred during the 60-year reign of King Souligna Vongsa, an enlightened leader who promoted Buddhism and established Vientiane as a center of regional intellectual brilliance. The death of Souligna in 1694 plunged the nation into a period of chaos and political domination by Vietnamese despots. In 1713 Laos split apart into three rival kingdoms and the glorious empire of Lan Xang ceased to exist.

The French Era

The fall of Lan Xang was followed by rule from three disparate kingdoms with divided loyalties. Luang Prabang under Souligna's grandson was chiefly aligned with China, Vientiane (properly called Vieng Chan) under Souligna's nephew was influenced by the Vietnamese empire at Hue, and Champassak in the south was largely controlled by the Siamese. However, the Siamese eventually proved their mettle by annexing Vientiane in 1826, Champassak in 1846, and Luang Prabang in 1885.

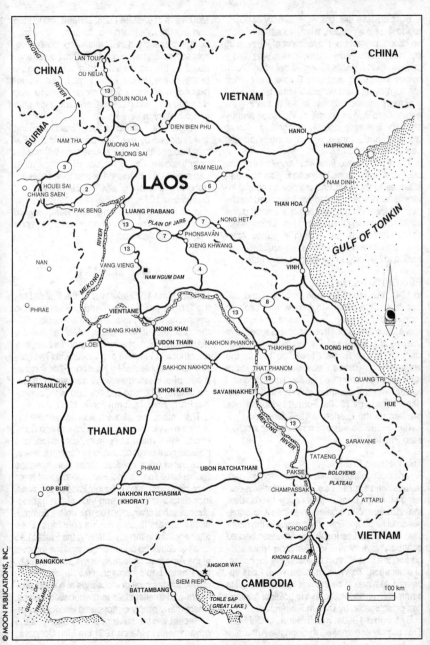

But Siamese designs were directly opposed to those of the French, who had established a so-called "protectorate" over most of Vietnam by the mid-19th century. Laos, in fact, was also a pawn in the territorial struggles between British forces expanding east from Burma and French forces moving west across Vietnam.

Events moved quickly. In 1886, the French established a vice-consul in Vientiane and by 1893 the Siamese officially recognized Laos as a French protectorate. French annexation was completed in 1907.

The French paid little attention to Laos except as a buffer zone between British economic zones to the west and their own colonial interests in Vietnam. Not much happened for the next 50 years; Laos remained a sleepy place almost completely unknown to the outside world. French diplomats stationed in Vientiane, however, considered themselves extraordinarily fortunate to be living in the land of lotus eaters.

Rise Of The Pathet Lao

In 1941, the Japanese took Indochina and, before their defeat in 1945, proclaimed Laos an independent nation. But France's refusal to leave Laos and grant true independence led to the rise of several anti-French movements, including the Lao Issara ("Free Lao") under the leadership of Prince Petsarath and the more radical Pathet Lao ("Lao Nation"), which joined forces with the communist Viet Minh of Vietnam in the early 1950s. Formal independence granted by the French in 1953 was soon followed by the defeat of French forces at Dien Bien Phu in 1954.

The Vietnam Era

A series of coalition governments—rightist, neutralists, and Pathet Lao representatives—attempted to run Laos until the early 1960s when the Vietnam War spilled over into the once-peaceful kingdom. From their bases in the northeast, the Pathet Lao fought the American-backed coalition government in Vientiane while supporting the Viet Minh in their struggle for national unification. To Western observers, Laos appeared destined to be the first "domino" to fall to communism, according to the political analogy first promulgated by Dwight Eisenhower.

By the mid-1960s, much of the Ho Chi Minh Trail supply line snaked through the Annamite Mountains of eastern Laos. Determined to stop communist Vietnamese forces, American bombers stationed in Thailand conducted secret saturation bombings of Pathet Lao strongholds in the northeast and along the entire length of the Ho Chi Minh Trail. It was an unprecedented campaign: more tonnage was dropped on Laos than on Germany during the entire history of WW II.

Despite the horrific onslaught, and a secret war financed by the CIA, Laos fell to the Pathet Lao shortly after the American withdrawal from Vietnam. On 23 August 1975, the Pathet Lao marched into Vientiane and took final control of the Kingdom of a Million Elephants. On 2 December 1975, the 600-year-old monarchy was abolished, opposition coalition leaders were ousted from the government, and Kaysone Phomvihane was appointed premier.

GOVERNMENT

Following the 1975 takeover by the Pathet Lao, the former pro-Western and U.S.-supported government was replaced by the People's Democratic Republic of Laos, which followed a Marxist-Leninist philosophy modeled loosely after those in Vietnam and Cambodia. The government was headed by Kaysone Phomvihane, a son of a Vietnamese civil servant from Savannakhet who had led the Laotian Communist Party since its formation in 1955.

The Pathet Lao takeover was quite unlike the communist victories in South Vietnam and Cambodia. After years of venality, corruption, and political games manipulated by foreign powers, Laotians of many political stripes welcomed the Pathet Lao. Their bloodless coup showed them capable of imposing uniquely Laotian solutions, including a tolerance and lack of the aggressiveness that characterized the violent communist takeovers in neighboring countries. Even after abolishing the royal family, the Pathet Lao didn't execute the prince or demand the removal of the American diplomatic corps. Unfortunately, the Pathet Lao's homegrown solution also included the removal of thousands of political prisoners and intellectuals to reeducation camps, where many simply disappeared without a trace.

Recent events have markedly changed the government. In March 1991 the Fifth Congress of the Lao People's Revolutionary Party (LPRP) voted for pro-market reforms and installed new leaders committed to *chin thanakan amai,* or "new thinking." The hammer-and-sickle motif was removed from the state emblem. By August 1991, even the hardline Kaysone had publicly announced the abandonment of a pure communist government in favor of a free-market economy, though he ruled out any real challenge to the party's monopoly on power. In November 1991, the U.S. agreed to upgrade relations and send an ambassador to Vientiane for the first time since the Pathet Lao took power in 1975.

Kaysone died in November 1991. His replacement, President Nouhak Phoumsavan, has been a Politburo member since the ruling LPRP was founded in 1955 and he was appointed the country's finance minister. Although also a hardline communist and close friend of Vietnam, Nouhak supports free-market reforms and has mounted a campaign to upgrade the country's relations with the outside world, particularly China and Thailand. The government is now headed by Nouhak, a secretary-general who serves as prime minister, and the LPRP, which is organized much like other communist parties, with a Central Committee headed by the Politburo.

ECONOMY

Laos is one of the world's poorest countries, with a gross national product ranked in the bottom 10 and an average annual income of just US$160. Over 80% of the population are farmers who primarily raise rice, cotton, maize, and cash crops such as coffee, tobacco, and cardamom. Opium is an important source of income in the Laotian portion of the Golden Triangle. The depressing wages in the public sector—government employees in Vientiane consider themselves lucky to make US$20 per month—has brought widespread corruption to every level of Lao society.

Much of the blame must be laid on the Pathet Lao who, after their victory in 1975, set about imposing a Stalinist system on the devastated economy: they collectivized farms, nationalized the tiny industrial base, and centralized control of prices and all other facets of the wounded economy. Their bloody campaign against intellectuals and political dissidents, combined with a mass exodus of the Laotian elite across the Mekong River to Thailand, stripped Laos of those who were most capable of restoring the economy and running the government. Since 1975, over 300,000 Laotians—roughly a tenth of the population—have fled to Thailand or emigrated to the United States.

However, the economy now seems to be improving, at least in Vientiane, where motorcycles, blue jeans, and consumer products from Thailand have flooded the local markets. Despite some recent crop failures and the abrupt loss of massive amounts of aid from the former Soviet Union, foreign economists estimate that the economy now grows at about 7% per year and that the inflation rate has dropped from stratospheric levels to just under 10%. Recent economic reforms have brought substantial foreign aid from United Nations agencies and major investments in the garment industry from Thai, Hong Kong, and Taiwanese companies. The deficit problem is finally being addressed. Overwhelming poverty still grips the countryside, but Laos now has an emerging entrepreneurial class in the urban areas and farmers welcome the opportunity to market their crops in a postsocialist economy.

THE PEOPLE

The people of Laos are divided by language, culture, and ethnographic background into four main cultural groups, which are subdivided into over 60 minority tribes which generally live in extremely isolated locations.

Lao Loum
The principal ethnic group in Laos accounts for about two-thirds of the national population and comprises most of the Laotians you will meet during your travels. The Lao Loum (also Lao Lum and Lao Lu) arrived from southern China sometime before the 10th century and slowly displaced the Lao Theung from the lowland valleys along the Mekong and its tributaries.

Lao Loum speak Laotian Tai, which is closely related to Thai, and are ethnically indistinguishable from the Lao Thais who inhabit the Issan Plateau of northeastern Thailand.

Lao Thai

Perhaps a subset of the Lao Loum, the Lao Thai are tribal minorities who have resisted assimilation into mainstream Lao society, chiefly by living in the highlands rather than the lowlands favored by the national majority.

The Lao Thai are divided into several groups conveniently distinguished by the color of the female dress: Red Tai, White Tai, and Black Tai. Lao Tai villages are often included with tours of southern Laos.

Lao Theung

The Lao Theung, better known as the Mon and Khmer, or Mon-Khmer, are seminomadic tribals who live mainly on mountain slopes throughout Laos. Although composed of perhaps some 60 ethnic groups, the lowland Lao often call them simply Kha, a derogatory term which translates as "Slave" and refers to their traditional role within ancient Lao society.

The more important subsets include the Khamu, who practice swidden agriculture and are mostly animists living in the north; the Akha, Alak, and Ta-Oy, who reside on the Bolovens Plateau in the south; and the Lamet, who are thought to be descendants of the earliest inhabitants of the country.

Lao Sung

The Lao Sung, or "High Lao," are tribal groups identical to the famous hilltribes of northern Thailand. Most migrated to Laos from southern China during the 18th and 19th centuries and today live in villages above 1,000 meters. Principal groups include the Hmong (formerly known as the Meo), the Yao (also called the Mien), the Lisu, and the Lahu. The Akha are often included in this group.

The Hmong are the largest group within the Lao Sung and certainly the most well-known to the outside world, chiefly because over 100,000 Hmong now live in the United States. The Hmong were originally recruited as mercenaries by the French colonialists in the final days of their struggle against the Pathet Lao. The Americans via the CIA subsequently trained and equipped thousands of Hmong to fight the Laotian communists under the command of their chief, a colorful rebel named Vung Pao who later fled to Thailand with his six wives and 29 children. Today, the remaining Hmong mainly survive by growing opium and exporting their product on horseback to the markets of Chiang Mai.

PRACTICAL INFORMATION

VISAS AND TRAVEL PERMITS

Visas

All visitors to Laos must have visas and enter the country with an organized tour. Be sure to obtain the correct visa with the proper endorsements.

Transit Visa: This seven-day visa is granted to passengers in transit from Thailand, Vietnam, Cambodia, Burma, Russia, and other destinations linked by air with Vientiane. This visa is *not* recommended, since extensions are prohibited and visitors are confined to Vientiane Prefecture.

Business Visa: Thirty-day business visas can be obtained from Lao embassies or consulates when accompanied by a letter of invitation from a recognized Lao company, citizen, foreign mission, volunteer agency, or travel service which represents Lao Tourism. Permission must also be obtained from the Ministry of the Interior in Vientiane.

Non-immigrant Visa: A 30-day visa granted to short-term volunteers and other professionals approved by the Ministry of the Interior. This visa also requires a letter of invitation and can be extended once for an additional 30 days.

Tourist Visa: This is the most common type of visa. Tourist visas are valid for 15 days and are only extended by the Department of Immigration in Vientiane (Thanon Talat Sao, off Lane Xang Avenue) in exceptional circumstances (transportation problems, illness, etc.) or when accompanied by a letter of endorsement from a government agency.

Tourist visas are granted to visitors who book a package tour through a travel agency registered with Lao Tourism. The agency which arranges the tour also obtains your visa from the nearest Lao embassy, which must in turn reconfirm the tour with the Ministry of the Interior in Vientiane. Do not contact a Laotian embassy; you'll just be given a list of approved travel agents.

Travel agents in Bangkok can obtain visas in about two days while those in Nong Khai are somewhat slower. Approved agents are also located in Chiang Mai, but your best bet is to contact an agent in Bangkok.

Lao embassies occasionally issue tourist visas to individuals not on tours, but it is extremely difficult to convince embassy officials without official approval from a government agency in Vientiane.

Lao Embassies

Visas are arranged by tour companies, though travelers who wish to *attempt* to obtain tourist visas can contact the diplomatic offices listed in the "Lao Embassies" chart.

Visa Restrictions

Laotian visas carry some tricky restrictions.

Entry Points: Unless you request otherwise, all tourist visas are automatically stamped "By Air—Wattay," which requires the visitor to both enter and exit the country by air at the Vientiane airport. While this is no problem for those on organized tours, travelers who intend to enter or exit the country via Nong Khai in northeastern Thailand should request a "Land Entry" stamp or, at least, avoid the "By Air" endorsement.

Limited Access: Business visas and transit visas are *not* recommended, since travel access is restricted to Vientiane Prefecture.

Visa Fees: Tourist visas obtained from Laotian embassies cost only US$12. Officially recognized agents charge additional fees to cover their expenses, but beware of unscrupulous agents who charge over US$100 for the visa alone. A Laotian visa plus one night's hotel room in Vientiane should cost under US$100, especially if the hotel is in the budget or moderate price class.

Visa Extensions: Many tourist visas are now valid for the full 15 days and extensions are no longer necessary. However, in the event that your visa is valid for only three days, you must immediately report to the Immigration Office of the Ministry of the Interior (Ministere d'Interier) in Vientiane on Thanon Talat Sao, opposite the Morning Market. The extension process takes 24 hours and requires three passport photos and completion of several forms.

Travel Permits

Travel to all provinces outside Vientiane Prefecture requires travel permits, which are

LAO EMBASSIES

Australia. . . . . 1 Dalman Crescent, O'Malley, Canberra, ACT 2606.
Cambodia . . . . 111 214th St., Phnom Penh, tel. 251821.
Germany . . . . 1100 Berlin Esplanade 17, Berlin.
Thailand . . . . 193 Sathorn Tai Rd., Bangkok, tel. 2254-6963, telex LAOEMB. TH.
U.S.A.. . . . . 2222 S St. NW, Washington D.C., 20008
Vietnam . . . . 40 Quang Trung St., Hanoi, tel. 52588.

checked by local police when boarding domestic flights or long-distance buses or river ferries. Travel permits cost US$45 per province and can be obtained by any travel agency in Vientiane.

In most cases, travelers are *not* required to travel in a group or be accompanied by guides. However, it is wise to have all necessary permits with correct travel itineraries before leaving Vientiane; travelers with incomplete or incorrect travel permits can be bumped from flights or deported.

The most economical option is to obtain your travel permits in Vientiane, find the cheapest way to get to your destination, and then hire a local guide (if necessary) on arrival for about US$10 per day. Regulations change frequently: The most accurate advice is from fellow travelers and guesthouse owners in Vientiane.

As of mid-1993, travel permits were issued for Luang Prabang, Xieng Khwang (Plain of Jars), and the following provinces or towns in southern Laos: Savannakhet, Saravan, Champassak, and Attapu.

Provinces expected to open by the mid-1990s include Luang Nam Tha (Golden Triangle), Hua Phan (Vietnamese border), and Phong Sali (Chinese border).

Obviously, at US$50 a provincial pop—plus airfares and overpriced hotels—Laos can be an expensive destination.

Thai Visas

Visitors returning to Thailand who intend to stay more than 15 days can obtain Thai visas at the Thai Embassy in Vientiane on Thanon Phon Kheng, northeast of the Anousavari (Pratuxai) Monument. The application costs 300B and requires three passport photos. The embassy is open weekdays 0900-1200 and 1400-1600.

TOURS

Independent Travel

The Laotian government does not encourage independent tourism and requires all visitors to enter the country on organized tours. Some of these restrictions are purely mercenary, while others stem from unfortunate incidents such as the 1990 theft of Buddha images from caves near Luang Prabang and backpackers who inadvertently wandered into a political rehabilitation camp north of Vientiane.

These government-imposed restrictions make Laos a relatively expensive destination compared to other countries in Southeast Asia. Costs, however, can be minimized by taking the cheapest and shortest tour from Bangkok, then striking out on your own, or booking onward tours with an officially recognized travel agency in Vientiane.

For example, travel agents on Khao San Rd. in Bangkok sell two-day tours of Vientiane (visa and hotel only) for about US$100. You must purchase your air ticket separately or, less expensively, enter the country from Nong Khai in northeastern Thailand.

Upon arrival in Vientiane, you can extend your visa to 15 days (if necessary), obtain the required travel permits, attempt to board the bus or boat to Luang Prabang, and then return to Vientiane on a boat down the Mekong. This is the cheapest possible tour of Laos.

Travelers barred from boarding the bus to Luang Prabang can purchase a short tour of Luang Prabang for US$150-250 (including return air) and spend a few extra days exploring the Luang Prabang region.

Other destinations cost US$250-500 depending on the distance from Vientiane. South-

SIGHTSEEING HIGHLIGHTS

Budget travelers with 15-day visas usually limit themselves to the primary destinations of Vientiane and Luang Prabang, plus side trips to nearby caves and a river journey down the Mekong. Visitors on organized tours can include 'the Plain of Jars in northern Laos, and Pakse and Champassak in the south.

Vientiane

First stop for all visitors is Vientiane, a somnolent market town masquerading as the nation's capital. Formally called Vieng Chan by Laotians (Vientiane is a French-imposed term), Vientiane offers some bucolic charm but little of great interest aside from a handful of temples, French baguettes, and a sleepy atmosphere that entices (or bores) most visitors.

Luang Prabang

Laos's cultural highlight is this unsullied and sleepy village of great historical and artistic interest, 35 minutes by air north of Vientiane. The town of 50,000 is a treasure trove of splendid temples remarkably well preserved considering the political disruptions and benign neglect of recent years. Side trips from Luang Prabang include Pak Ou Caves—an ancient retreat packed with Buddha images—and journeys of varied lengths down the Mekong River.

Plain Of Jars

One hour by air from Vientiane lie several small and undistinguished towns in an eerie landscape covered with bomb craters and several hundred stone funeral urns. The landscape is beautiful and the region offers a fascinating historical connection with the Vietnam War, though the unimpressive jars and steep cost of an organized tour have held tourism to a bare minimum.

Pakse

Southern Laos opened for tourism in early 1992 and by late 1993 the government allowed foreign visitors in a half-dozen towns. Pakse, the largest town in the south and center of a former kingdom, chiefly serves as the jumping-off point for visits to the famed pre-Angkor Khmer ruins of Wat Phu, located near Champassak.

Champassak

The archaeological site of Wat Phu, eight km from Champassak, is considered the premier religious shrine in Laos and among the most impressive Khmer monuments outside Cambodia.

Bolovens Plateau

Adventure-travel groups often head directly to this plateau to enjoy jungle trekking, waterfalls, visits to tribal villages, and a spectacular river journey down the Kong River to Attapu Valley, the newest region to open in Laos.

---

ern Laos—around Pakse and Champassak—is a popular but expensive excursion due to the additional airfare from Vientiane. While somewhat pricey, these tours include domestic air transportation, local jeeps, all hotels and meals, and guide services.

Lao Tourism

All tours in Laos are ultimately handled by state-run Lao National Tourism (LNT) but booked through agents authorized by the organization. LNT sets base fees which are marked up by authorized agents to cover their expenses and profits. Contact LNT: P.O. Box 2912, Setthathirat Rd., Vientiane, tel. 3134, telex 4348 MICOM LS.

Recognized agents are located in America, Europe, Australia, Thailand, and Vientiane.

Lao Tour Operators

Travelers can contact the following agencies for onward travel. Once again, prices vary and visitors should check several agencies.

Lao National Tourism is the most expensive and least organized agency. In addition to the following agencies, the government has announced plans to allow several more privately operated tour companies to open in the next few years.

Lani Guesthouses: Neither of the two budget guesthouses in Vientiane are official agencies, but their commissions are reasonable and they can advise on the possibilities of independent travel to most destinations. See "Vientiane" for addresses and phone numbers.

Vientiane Tourism: Operates the same tours as LNT but at somewhat lower prices and with

TOURS OF LAOS

TOUR	ITINERARY	DURATION	PRICE
LA01	Vientiane–Luang Prabang	5 days	US$900-1200
LA02	Vientiane–Luang Prabang–Plain of Jars	6 days	US$1200-1600
LA03	Vientiane–Luang Prabang-Pakse-Saravan	8 days	US$1800-2200
LA04	Vientiane–Luang Prabang-Plain-Pakse-Saravan-Khong	9 days	US$2200-2600
LA05	Ubon-Khong-Pakse-Tataeng-Attapu-Saravan	11 days	US$2400-2800

less hassle. Sithan Neua Building IIA 101, Thanon Luang Prabang, P.O. Box 2511, Vientiane, tel. 4417, fax 5448, telex SPIMEX 4310.

Transindo Travel: Organized outfit with both upscale and budget tours. 16 Fa Ngum Rd., P.O. Box 70, Vientiane, tel. 3626, telex 4314.

14 April: Conducts budget independent tours to Luang Prabang but only official tours to other provinces. 29/3 Pang Kham Rd., P.O. Box 2947, Vientiane, tel. 2979, telex 4335.

Thai Tour Operators

The following travel agencies were official agents of Lao National Tourism as of this writing, but the list is revised on an annual basis. Agencies are located on Khao San Rd. (Banglampoo), Silom Rd., Sukumvit, and near the Laotian Embassy in Bangkok.

Costs vary widely and it is highly recommended that you check several agencies to find the lowest price. The least expensive tours are arranged by budget outfits rather than the major operators, and by authorized agents rather than nonlisted agencies who simply contact an authorized agent and add their commission. The cheapest agencies are on Khao San Road.

Vista Travel: Vista Travel is the official representative for Lao Tourism in the Banglampoo neighborhood. All other travel agencies go through Vista and add their commissions. 24 Khao San Rd., tel. 281-0786, fax 280-0348.

Inter Companion Group: Sells reasonably priced tours which include overnight accommodations in Nong Khai and one night's stay at the Mekong Guesthouse in Vientiane. 86 Rambuttri Rd., Banglampoo, tel. 282-9400, fax 282-7316.

Thai Indochina: Convenient for visitors staying near the Malaysia Hotel. 79 Pan Rd., 4th floor, Silom, tel. 233-5369, fax 236-4389.

Pangkaj Travel: Official outlet at 625 Sukumvit Rd., Soi 22, tel. 258-2440, fax 259-1261.

Exotissimo Travel: One of the more established firms in a convenient location near Nana Complex. 21/17 Sukumvit Rd., Soi 4, tel. 253-5240, fax 254-7683. Branch office: 755 Silom Rd., tel. 235-9196, fax 233-4885.

Diethem Travel: The most highly regarded (and expensive) travel agency in Thailand. Kian Gwan Bldg., 140/1 Wireless Rd., tel. 255-9150, fax 256-0248.

American Tour Operators

All of the tour operators mentioned in the Vietnam chapter also conduct tours into Laos, usually in combination with a visit to Vietnam and Cambodia. Below are two tour operators specializing in Laos.

Bolder Adventures: Bolder offers a 16-day tour of Vientiane, Luang Prabang, Plain of Jars, Pakse, and Wat Phu for US$2800-3200 from Bangkok. They also sell comprehensive Indochina programs and can help with customized journeys throughout the region. Call (800) 397-5917.

Absolute Asia: Almost a dozen programs from five to 12 days which include hotels, meals, guide services, and transportation from Bangkok. Call (800) 736-8187. See the "Tours of Laos" chart for sample programs and prices.

GETTING THERE

Air Transportation

Visitors on organized tours generally fly into Vientiane, though land access from Nong Khai (Thailand) is a cheaper option.

Air from Thailand: Both Thai International and Lao International fly from Bangkok to Vientiane for US$100 one-way and US$190 roundtrip. Thai International uses Boeing 737s, while Lao struggles along with Soviet-built Antonov-24 turboprops. Thai Airways on Silom Rd. in Bangkok is the agent for Lao International.

Bangkok Airways, in conjunction with Lanna Tours (a subsidiary of Diethelm Travel), has announced plans for weekly charters from Chiang Mai to Luang Prabang—the back-end approach to Laos.

Air from Vietnam: Vietnam Airlines and Lao International connect Hanoi with Vientiane twice weekly for US$90 one-way. The twice-weekly flight from Saigon to Vientiane stops in Pakse, where disembarkation is permitted with a visa and a travel permit.

Air from Cambodia: Lao International has two return flights a week from Phnom Penh to Vientiane, with a stop in Pakse, for US$130 one-way.

Departure Tax: US$5 is collected on international flights and 550 *kip* on domestic departures.

Land Transportation

Vientiane can also be reached by bus and boat from Nong Khai in northeastern Thailand. Visitors should obtain a visa in Bangkok or confirm that travel agents in Nong Khai are currently obtaining visas for Laos.

"By Land" Stamp: Travelers intending to enter or exit Laos via Nong Khai should ask their travel agents to stamp "By Land" rather than "By Air" in their passports. Travelers with "By Air" stamps who wish to leave Laos by boat should obtain from the Lao Aviation office in Vientiane a "telegram" confirming that all flights are fully booked—a normal procedure even if the flights are empty.

From Nong Khai: Ferries leave every day 0800-1630 from the Thai town of Nong Khai for the official border post at Tha Dua, 25 km from Vientiane. Buses continue from Tha Dua to Vientiane.

When the Lao-Australian bridge across the Mekong is completed in late 1994, travelers will probably be allowed to walk across the bridge, complete entry formalities, and take a bus to Vientiane. Local tour operators have announced plans to conduct organized tours directly from the guesthouses and hotels in Nong Khai.

From Pakse: In 1993, the Laotian government began allowing visitors on organized tours to enter and exit Laos via the Thai town of

Chommeck, 76 km east of Ubon Ratchathani. From Chommeck, the road continues 52 km east to Pakse, from where the highway heads south to Champassak and Wat Phu.

At present, only recognized tour operators who have obtained written permission from the Ministry of the Interior in Vientiane are allowed to use this land entry. When this border opens to independent travelers, southern Laos will become a reasonably priced option to the north.

Other Land Crossings: The government also intends to open the border at Savannakhet from the Thai town of Mukdahan and allow visitors on organized tours to enter Laos from several points in Vietnam, including Danang, Vinh, and perhaps Dien Bien Phu.

GETTING AROUND

Laos is a mountainous country with no railway, one seasonally navigable river (the Mekong), and some of the worst roads in the world.

Air Transportation

Lao Aviation International connects Vientiane with Luang Prabang (US$40 one-way), Sayabuli (US$30), Xieng Khwang (US$55), Sam Neua (US$55), Savannakhet (US$60), Luang Nam Tha (US$60), Saravan (US$80), and Pakse (US$95). Other scheduled destinations include Sayaboury, Oudomxay, Honeisay, and Thakhek.

On domestic flights, Lao Aviation uses a patchwork of Soviet-built twin-prop Antonovs, Chinese-built 17-seater Y-12s, and two French ATR42s of more recent vintage.

Most flights are booked by your tour company, though independent travelers are allowed to book their own flights with a valid travel pass issued by the Department of Commerce.

Tourists are given priority over locals when booking flights but are charged double the local rate. Departures are often delayed for weather reasons or canceled due to lack of spare parts from their Russian and Chinese suppliers. Soviet-built ME8 army helicopters substitute when all the planes are down.

Land Transportation

Roads in Laos, to put it mildly, are terrible. For example, the 230-km journey from Vientiane to

Luang Prabang takes 35 minutes by air but any-where from 12 hours to several days on tortuous mountain roads. Conditions are slowly improv-ing, however, with the aid of the World Bank and the Asian Development Bank, which have allocated US$40 million to upgrade Route 13, the main north-south artery. When completed in 1995, it will be possible to drive all the way from Singapore to Beijing through Malaysia, Thai-land, and Laos.

Most of the road from Vientiane to Luang Pra-bang is now sealed and passable, except during the rainy season from June to November, when landslides often close portions of the road for several days.

The official rule is that foreign visitors are not allowed to board interprovincial buses or trucks without a valid travel permit. Those with the permit are *sometimes* allowed to take buses from Vientiane to Luang Prabang, depending on the mood of the local police and govern-ment officials.

Intercity transportation is provided by *tuk tuks*, motorcycles, and ancient taxis of Soviet or Eastern European origins. Sample fares from the morning market in Vientiane to the Aus-tralian Club are K800 by shared taxi, K900 by *tuk tuk*, K240 by motorcycle, and K3000 by private taxi.

Taxis chartered in Vientiane, Luang Prabang, Pakse, and Savannakhet cost US$10-15 per day. Self-drive jeeps can be hired for US$20-35 per day. Bicycles provide a popular way to get around Vientiane and Luang Prabang.

River Transportation

The Mekong River is navigable from Luang Pra-bang down to Savannakhet, though larger boats can only complete the journey during the rainy season from June to November.

The most popular journey is downriver from Luang Prabang to Vientiane, a three-day sail which costs US$6-8. The trip passes Tha Deua and Paklay in the Golden Triangle before reaching Chiang Khong at the Thai border and finally Vientiane; a romantic interlude once de rigueur with hippie backpackers in the late 1960s.

TRAVEL PRACTICALITIES

Money

The unit of currency is the *kip* (K), which ex-changes at about 800 *kip* to the dollar. The pre-vious multiple-exchange-rate system has been abolished and there is no black market. The *kip* is nonconvertible, so exchange all *kip* back into *baht* before you leave Laos.

According to Stan Sesser in the *New Yorker,* the daily exchange rate is determined by a bank employee who wanders through Vientiane's Morning Market to determine how many *kip* the shopkeepers are offering per dollar.

Thai *baht* and U.S. dollars are widely ac-cepted throughout Laos, but traveler's checks can only be cashed in Vientiane and Luang Pra-bang. The best strategy is to bring along plenty of small-denomination Thai *baht.*

Prices in this section are quoted in dollars since the American greenback is more stable than the devaluating *kip.*

Health

Hospitals and medical facilities in Laos are poor and the country presents more health risks than westernized countries such as Thailand. No in-oculations are required but immunizations against tetanus, polio, hepatitis, rabies, typhoid, and cholera are recommended.

Malaria is common in Laos and all visitors are strongly advised to take malaria pills and stay covered after dark.

Only bottled water should be drunk and all food, especially fish and seafood, should be well cooked to guard against liver flukes (opisthorchiasis).

Business Hours

Government offices are open weekdays 0800-1700 but often closed 1200-1400 for lunch. Banks are open 0800-1200 and 1400-1600.

Museums and other state-regulated tourist attractions are open Tues.-Sun. 0800-1130 and 1400-1630.

Laos is seven hours ahead of GMT; noon in Vientiane is 0100 in New York, 1500 in Syd-ney, and 0500 in London.

VIENTIANE

The national capital and administrative center of Laos was constructed by the French on the site of Lan Xang, the ancient empire which once extended from southern China to northern Thailand.

Vientiane is a modern and unassuming town without the awe-inspiring sights of other Asian centers, but a welcome sense of peace pervades this tranquil oddity perched on the banks of the muddy Mekong.

ATTRACTIONS

Vientiane—a capital of no special beauty—can be easily toured on foot or with a rented bicycle in just a few hours. Perhaps the best activities are simply watching people in the markets and contemplating the jarring contrast between old Vientiane and the sudden influx of stereos from Japan, pop music from Thailand, and other icons of the Western invasion.

The following temples are described as a walking tour starting from the Lao Tourism office in the center of town.

Revolutionary Museum
A distinctive white building filled with a fascinating collection of memorabilia about the fall of the "imperialists" and the victory of the people's revolution.

Open Tues.-Sun. 0800-1130 and 1400-1630.

Wat Mixai
Lao *wats* incorporate the same basic elements as those in Thailand, though architectural terminology differs. The main ordination hall which contains the principal Buddha image is called a *sim* rather than a *bot* as in Thailand. Secondary chapels attached to the *sim* are *hor sang pra* rather than *viharns*. Also, stupas in Laos are called *that* (pronounced tat) and not *chedi,* while *chofas* are *sofas* and *nagas* are *nyaks*.

Wat Mixai features a veranda which encompasses the entire *sim,* constructed in the 19th-century Bangkok style.

Wat Hai Sok
A reconstructed temple in the Bangkok style with a soaring peak and multilayered, uneven-numbered roofs.

Wat Ong Teu
Originally constructed around 1500 by King Setthathirat but rebuilt in the 19th and 20th centuries, Wat Ong Teu is famed for its immense Buddha which dominates the *sim* and for its facades, wooden doors, and windows magnificently carved with Ramakien and Mahabharta legends. The *wat* is also home to the largest monastery in Laos.

Wat Impeng
Like most all temples in Laos, this *wat* was constructed several centuries ago but subsequently destroyed by the Thai, Burmese, or Chinese armies which have periodically ransacked Vientiane. The present-day replacement features exquisite woodcarving and mosaic filigree.

Wat Chan
Inside this reconstructed *sim* sits a remarkable bronze Buddha, moved here from the original temple after its destruction by Thai forces in 1827. Also note the solitary Buddha in the "Calling Rain" *mudra* on the courtyard stupa.

Presidential Palace
The former royal palace now serves as the reception hall for President Nouhak Phoumsavan, who replaced Kaysone Phomvihane after his death in December 1992. Closed to the public.

President Nouhak, along with many other Pathet Lao leaders, lives in Kilometer 6, an American-style suburb on the edge of Vientiane, complete with ranch homes built by the United States during the Vietnam War.

Wat Sisaket
Among the most important religious sites in Laos, Wat Sisaket was constructed in 1818 and was the only temple to survive the Siamese destruction of 1827. Inside the main

sanctuary are over 2,000 Buddha statues encased in small niches and another 300 images sculpted in classic Lao style. Wat Sisaket is also noted for its interior Jataka murals and flowered ceilings inspired by Siamese prototypes in Ayuthaya.

Residence of the head of the Buddhist *sangha* in Laos, Wat Sisaket is both an important religious site and an officially designated museum which charges an admission fee to tourists. Open Tues.-Sun. 0800-1130 and 1400-1630.

Wat Pra Keo

Wat Pra Keo (also spelled Phra Kaew and Pha Kaeo but never Paw Cow) was originally constructed in 1565 as the royal temple of Lao monarchy and to house the Emerald Buddha, presently installed in Bangkok's Wat Pra Keo.

The present structure, which dates from 1936-54, features exquisite examples of Lao wood sculpture and a superb assortment of Buddha images in all possible styles and schools: Lao, Khmer, and Thai. Among the more outstanding statues are Laotian interpretations of the famous walking Buddha from Sukothai, a 16th-century door carved with Hindu erotic images, multi-armed Khmer deities, and a stone Dvaravati-style Buddha considered to be the oldest image in the country. The courtyard has a stone urn helicoptered down from the Plain of Jars. Wat Pra Keo, now a national museum, is open Tues.-Sun. 0800-1130 and 1400-1630.

That Dam

Vientiane's so-called Black Stupa perhaps dates from the Lanna Period (12th-14th centuries) due to its resemblance to Chiang Saen-era stupas. Local mythology claims That Dam to be the abode of a powerful seven-headed dragon which protects Vientiane from Siamese invaders.

Markets

Vientiane's best are the misnamed Morning Market (Talat Sao), which is jammed throughout the day, Talat Khua Din for produce and flowers, and Talat Tong Khoun Thum, an evening market which locals claim is best visited in the morning.

Anousavari Monument

Vientiane's oddest landmark is this Oriental-baroque monstrosity, constructed from American cement intended for a new runway at the airport. Also called the Pratuxai or Victory Monument, it resembles an ill-proportioned version of the Arc de Triomphe topped by an astonishing wedding-cake structure of Byzantine spires and Gothic gargoyles.

Visitors can pay a small admission fee and climb to the top, where Vientiane seems to quietly disappear beneath the tropical foliage.

Pra That Luang

According to legend, Pra That Luang (Great Sacred Stupa) was erected in 1566 by King Setthathirat over an older site which contained a relic of the Buddha. Now considered Vientiane's most important religious site and a symbol of Lao sovereignty, the 31-meter stupa provides a rare example of Lao art largely unaffected by Thai styles, which typically dominate most Laotian architecture. The overall effect, however, is less impressive than at Wat Pra Keo or Wat Sisaket.

Pra That Luang, four km northeast of city center, is open Tues.-Sun. 0800-1130 and 1400-1630.

ACCOMMODATIONS

Vientiane now has over 25 hotels and guesthouses concentrated in the city center and south of town on the banks of the Mekong. Most hotels cost US$20-40 for a/c rooms with private bath, while guesthouses charge US$8-12 for simple but adequate rooms with common facilities.

Visitors usually stay initial nights in prebooked hotels but are free to move to less expensive quarters the following days.

Budget Accommodations

Compared to Thailand, Laotian guesthouses and budget hotels are overpriced—though rates may fall with increased competition and more lenient government policies.

Lani 1 Guesthouse: Clean and quiet guesthouse conveniently located near city center; popular with long-term visitors, volunteer workers, and American tour groups. Offers both fancooled and a/c rooms. Recommended. 281 Thanon Setthathirat, tel. 4175, US$8-22.

Lani 2 Guesthouse: Another well-priced clean guesthouse with a popular cafe and up-to-

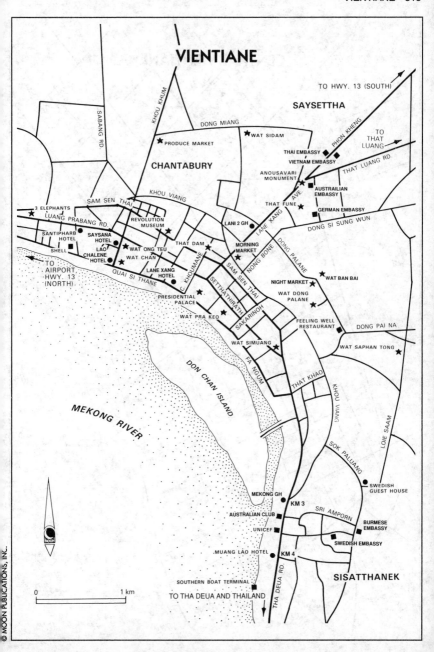

CENTRAL VIENTIANE

VIENGLATY MAI RESTAURANT
LANI 2 GH
NONG BONE RD.
BUS STATION
KHUA DIN MARKET
GALLIENI
SAKARINOH
CATHOLIC CHURCH
SAYLOM
TALAT SAO
MORNING MARKET
KHOU TIANG
LE CLUB
IMMIGRATION
SAYLOM
POST OFFICE
SAM SEN THAI
FRANCE EMBASSY
SETTHATHIRATH
MAHOSOT
U.S. MOVIE THEATRE
LANE XANG AVE.
WAT PRA KEO
U.S.A. EMBASSY
MAHOSOT HOSPITAL
THAT DAM
PANG KHAM
PHAY NAM
HOTEL EKALAT METRO
AEROFLOT
WAT SISAKET
ASIAN PAVILION HOTEL
MINISTRY OF FOREIGN AFFAIRS
CHANTA KHOUMANE
HANDICRAFTS
PRESIDENTIAL PALACE
FA NGUM
SWIMMING POOL
TELEPHONE
LAO RADIO
MOSQUE
NAM PHOU RESTAURANT
KY HUONG
STADIUM
LAO TOURISM
LANE XANG HOTEL
KHOUN BOULOM (KHOU VIANG)
REVOLUTIONARY MUSEUM
FIRE STATION
LE SOURIYA RESTAURANT
PANG KHAM
VIENTIANE TENNIS CLUB
SYRI GH
SAMSENTHAI HOTEL
LAO AVIATION
SANTISOUK RESTAURANT
MANH THATOURATH
SETTHATHIRATH
BANK
LAO GALLERY
WAT XIENG NGUN
SAIGON
HAIPHONG
HENG BOUN
WAT MIXAI
PHAY NAM
PHNOM PENH
TOURANH
NOKGO KHOUMANE
BOATS TO LUANG PRABANG
DU PUTS
HANOI
WAT HAI SOK
FRANCOIS NGIN
MIXAI CAFE
MEKONG RIVER
ANOU HOTEL
LANI 1 GH
WAT ONG TEU
CHAO ANOU
WAT CHAN
CHANH
FA NGUM
SAYSANA HOTEL
NIGHT MARKET
BAN TAVANH RESTAURANT
WAT IMPENG
LAO CHALENE HOTEL
SIHOM
SOVIET CULTURAL CENTER
IMPENG
LUANG PRABANG
WAT BANG LONG (VIETNAMESE)
HANLE DISCO
VIENTIANE TOURISM
SAM SEN THAI
KHOUN BOULOM

0   200 m

© MOON PUBLICATIONS INC.

date travel tips. 268 Thanon Saylom, tel. 2615, US$8-22.

Mekong Guesthouse: Also called the Sai Khong, this backpacker's favorite offers Vientiane's least expensive rooms in a somewhat inconvenient location, three km from downtown. Tours booked on Khao San Rd. often include the first night here. Proprietor Porn—information source on independent travel around Laos—also operates the riverbank Mexiai House. Tha Deua Rd. Km 3, tel. 5975, US$5-8.

Syri Guesthouse: Friendly family-run homestay with travel tips, bicycle rentals, and hearty breakfasts. Good location near the stadium and noteworthy temples. Quartier Chao Anou, tel. 2394, US$6-10.

Lao Chalene Hotel: Large rooms, excellent restaurant, and low prices make this one of the better bargains in downtown Vientiane. The former Inter Hotel needs some cleaning but otherwise represents good value in a handy location near the night market. Thanon Chao Anou, tel. 2881, US$10-20.

Moderate Accommodations

Many of the following hotels are 1950s relics renovated by consortiums of Lao, Thai, and Chinese investors. Newer luxury hotels scheduled to open by 1995 include the Premier, Le Parasol, and Champa Lane Xang.

Asian Pavilion: Formerly the Vieng Vilay, all rooms in this refurbished hotel include a/c and private bath. Good midrange hotel. 379 Thanon Samsenthai, tel. 3287, US$18-36.

Samsenthai Hotel: Centrally located hotel with clean rooms and brightly polished wooden floors. 15 Thanon Manh Thatourath, tel. 9456, US$16-36.

Anou Hotel: Another refurbished hotel that reminds you of Bangkok luxury in the 1950s. Facilities include Raja Tours, a small cafe, and a cabaret "animated by a Famous Live Band." 1 Thanon Heng Boun, tel. 3324, fax 3660, US$12-15 fan, US$22-40 a/c.

Lane Xang Hotel: Vientiane's venerable hotel is a disastrous combination of Soviet esthetics and management skills donated by the Laotian government. Facilities in this government-run monstrosity include the standard stuff; tour groups now stay at the nearby Premier International Hotel. Thanon Fa Ngum, tel. 3672, fax 5448, US$38-52.

RESTAURANTS

Lao Cafes

Lao dishes are best found in markets, street stalls, and small sidewalk cafes rather than restaurants, which usually serve Chinese or Thai fare.

Morning Market: Start your day with a bowl of steaming-hot Lao noodles or *khao ji pate,* French bread stuffed with Laotian pate. Inexpensive.

Night Market: Vendors in the night market behind Nong Chan pond serve Lao specialties

---

LAO FOOD

Similar to Thai cuisine, Lao meals revolve around heaps of glutinous rice, steaming vegetables, and freshwater fish spiced with lemongrass, chilies, tamarind, coconut milk, and other aromatic herbs such as marijuana, sold in the Morning Market as a cooking ingredient.

Staples: Fish (*paa*), chicken (*kai*), duck (*pet*), pork (*muu*), beef (*sin wua*), and vegetables (*phak*).

Condiments: As in Thailand, meals are often consumed with side dishes such as fish sauce (*nam paa*), hot chili sauce (*jaew*), and raw chilies (*mak phet*).

Rice and Noodles: Accompanying every Lao meal will be glutinous rice (*khao nio*), white rice (*khao jao*), flat rice noodles (*foe*), or thin white wheat noodles (*khao pun*).

POPULAR LAO/THAI DISHES

laap: raw meat marinated in lemon and
    chili; the national dish of Laos and
    northern Thailand
laap kai: raw marinated chicken
laap sin: raw marinated beef
phaneng kai: chicken stuffed with
    peanuts and coconut
kai ping: grilled chicken
kaeng kalami: cabbage-fish soup
tom yam paa: fish and lemongrass soup
paa beuk: giant Mekong catfish
kung ping: sautéed prawns
lao lao: white wine made from
    fermented rice
fanthong: red *lao lao*

such as *kai ping* and *laap* (also called *lab* and *larb*). Inexpensive.

Mixai Cafe: The Haan Kheuang Deum Mixai is a friendly spot with decent food, great sunsets over the Mekong, and cold beer which seems inordinately popular with Western travelers and volunteers. Inexpensive.

Street Stalls: Vientiane's center for sidewalk cafes and late-night snacks is on Thanon Chau Anou, opposite the cinema and near the Lani 1 Guesthouse. Inexpensive.

French-Lao Restaurants

When the French departed Laos in 1953, they left behind their language, their legislative protocols, and best of all, their cuisine. Vientiane is a place where you can find baguettes and *pain au chocolat* along with fried rice and *tom yam kung*.

French and French-Lao restaurants are pricey by local standards (US$6-8) but reasonable when compared to overpriced hotel restaurants.

Santisouk: Also known as La Pagode, this outstanding and popular teahouse features an extensive French menu and tasty pepper steaks. Conveniently located near the Syri and Lani 1 guesthouses on Thanon Nokgo Khouman. Inexpensive.

Le Souriya: Vientiane's classiest French restaurant offers upscale cuisine and fine wines in an elegant setting; owned by a former Hmong princess from Xieng Khouang. Thanon Pang Kham. Moderate.

Nam Phou: The best European food in Laos and a longtime favorite of diplomats and expatriates. Also called the Mekhala Inthavong. Nam Phou Place. Moderate.

PRACTICALITIES

Tourist Offices

Vientiane has several government-run and privately operated tourist information centers, but better travel tips are scribbled in the guesthouse notebooks in Banglampoo, Nong Khai, and Vientiane. Try the Lani and Mekong guesthouses.

Lao National Tourism: LNT primarily exists to sell tours and not to disseminate travel information. Thanon Setthathirath, P.O. Box 2912, tel. 3134, telex 4348 MICOM LS.

Vientiane Tourism: A private tour company which sells the same LNT tours at identical

prices. Thanon Luang Prabang, tel. 4417, fax 5448, telex SPIMEX 4310.

Immigration

In the event that your visa is valid for only three days, you should apply for an extension at the Immigration Office of the Ministry of the Interior (Ministère d'Intérieur) on Thanon Talat Sao, opposite the Morning Market. The process takes 24 hours and requires three passport photos and completion of several forms.

Banks

Traveler's checks in U.S. dollars can be cashed at La Banque pour le Commerce Exterieur Lao on Thanon Pang Kham, the Joint Development Bank opposite the Morning Market, and the Lane Xang Hotel. Most travelers find it easier to bring along a thick wad of *baht* or American bills in small denominations.

International Telephone

Overseas calls can be made around the clock from the office on Thanon Setthathirat and from the Burapha Business Center on Thanon Fa Ngum. Many hotels also have international phone services, but first check the service charges.

The country code for Laos is 856. To phone or fax, press 011 (the international access code), 856 (country code), and then the local telephone or fax number.

TRANSPORTATION

Air

Wattay Airport, three km west of city center, can be reached from Vientiane by taxi for about US$4, *samlor* for US$2, motorcycle taxi for US$1, or least expensively by public bus marked "Phon Hong" from the Morning Market.

To reach Vientiane from the airport, take a taxi or bus from the road just outside the terminal.

Exchange rates at the airport service counter are poor, and visitors are advised to exchange money (if necessary) at a bank or the free market in town.

Bus

Most buses leave from the Morning Market, though travel permits are required for destinations outside Vientiane Prefecture. Nam Ngum Dam, described below, is within legal range.

Boat To Thailand

Ferries depart from Tha Deua, 20 km south of Vientiane, to Nong Khai (Thailand) every 15 minutes 0800-1130 and 1400-1630 daily except Sundays. Tha Deua pier can be reached by taxi for US$5 per carload or by public bus from the Morning Market.

Mekong River Boats

Boats to the north depart from the north jetty near the Mixai Cafe. Boats heading south leave from the south jetty, about five km from city center.

VIENTIANE TO LUANG PRABANG

Nam Ngum Dam

Laos's leading export isn't timber, opium, or political refugees, but rather electricity generated from this massive Soviet-built hydroelectric dam, 92 km north of Vientiane toward Luang Prabang on Highway 13. The reason is that little electricity is required for Lao factories and so almost 80% of the output passes via high-tension lines across the Mekong to Thailand. Exported power brings in over US$50 million per year, almost half the country's hard-currency income. Travel permits are not required to visit this lake.

Attractions: Travelers usually visit the market in the village of Ban Thalat then cross the bridge and continue another four km to the dam. Boats here cruise past the submerged tree trunks and islands once used as rehabilitation centers for prostitutes, drug dealers, and political dissidents. Most of these folks have left the country or moved back to Vientiane and, perhaps, resumed their old jobs.

Boat tours cost US$3-5 depending on your bargaining abilities. There's also an ordinary ferry which heads to Huay Mo on the northern shore, from where minitrucks continue north to Vang Vieng, Kasi, and Luang Prabang.

Accommodations: Nam Ngum is usually a day-trip from Vientiane, though Lao Tourism and Vientiane Tourism operate simple bungalows at the lakeside and on one of the islands. Ban Thalat homestays are also possible.

Transportation: Buses from the Morning Market take about three hours to reach the lake. Visitors with private transportation can reach the lake via Highway 10, a more scenic alternative which passes through Ban Koen and Ban Thalat.

Vang Vieng

Vang Vieng—150 km north of Vientiane and midway to Luang Prabang—is a picturesque region blessed with waterfalls and Buddhist caves rarely visited by outsiders. Most of the residents are Hmong or Yao hilltribe groups traditionally considered enemies of the Laotian government.

Political problems, hijacked buses, and missing tourists have kept this region off-limits for over a decade, though road construction and the presence of foreign advisers are slowly opening the area to the outside world. Current conditions can be checked at Vientiane guesthouses.

NORTHERN LAOS

LUANG PRABANG AND VICINITY

Luang Prabang—the historic, religious, and artistic capital of Laos—lies in a superb location on a promontory at the confluence of the Mekong and Khan rivers. Still exuding a dreamlike atmosphere not unlike some Indochinese Shangri-La, Luang Prabang with its royal palaces, wondrous caves, and gilded temples remains the real reward of any visit to Laos.

Attractions

The easygoing provincial town of Luang Prabang, and its 30 intact temples clustered together around Mount Phousi (Phu Si), can be leisurely toured in about two days on foot or in a single day with a rented bicycle.

Tours arranged by Lao Tourism usually visit the Royal Palace Museum, Wat Chom Si on Mount Phousi, Wat Xieng Thong, Pak Ou Caves, and several nearby villages.

Royal Palace Museum

Luang Prabang's major attraction is the former palace of Savang, converted into a national museum soon after the disappearance of the king. The well-maintained Khmer-style residence provides useful insight into regional history and the quirky collection habits of the final ruler of the 600-year-old dynasty.

The most significant image of the numerous 15th- to 17th-century Buddha statues is a golden reproduction of the highly venerated Pra Bang, a 50-kilogram statue of Ceylonese origins brought to Luang Prabang in 1353 by King Fa Ngum. Pra Bang's arrival marks the introduction of Buddhism in Laos and inspired Fa Ngum to rename the city from Xieng Thong to Nakhon Luang Prabang—"Great City of the Big Buddha."

Other historical and religious images include Luang Prabang-style standing Buddhas carved from marble, Khmer bronze drums from Wat Visoun, and outstanding friezes removed from local temples and presented to the king for safekeeping.

The queen's reception room to the left holds a strange but fascinating collection of state gifts for the final monarch: teacups from Mao, medals from Lyndon Johnson, a rifle from Brezhnev, a boomerang from Australia, even a moon rock from the Apollo 11 lunar mission. Also note the portraits of the royal family donated by a Soviet artist in 1967 and a photograph of the ethereally beautiful Queen Khamphoui; she gazes down wistfully from the walls.

The museum is open to tour groups and solo travelers as permitted by Lao Tourism. Independent travelers generally will need to hook up with an organized tour.

Wat Mai

Also called Wat Souvanna Phommaram, this five-roofed royal temple ranks among the most impressive edifices in Luang Prabang and is also the holiest, as it once served as residence for the Supreme Patriarch of the Lao Buddhist *sangha* (priesthood). Dominating the exterior facade is a magnificent golden bas-relief which recounts the legend of Vessantara—penultimate reincarnation of the historic Buddha—while the interior central beam retells the mythological Hindu origins of Ravanna and Hanuman.

Mount Phousi

Mount Phousi is not only a magnificent site for panoramic views and sunsets over the Mekong but also the cultural and symbolic centerpiece of ancient Luang Prabang. Most temples are of modern origins and rather unspectacular aside from their superb locations and agreeable senses of benign neglect.

Wat Chom Si: This gold-spired stupa constructed in 1804 is now the starting point for a lovely candle-lit procession which initiates the Buddhist-Lao New Year.

Wat Tham Phousi: A small cave temple which enshrines several Buddhist images.

Wat Pra Buddhapat: Another minor temple famed for its life-size three-meter-long footprint of the Buddha. "Pat" and "bat" and "bath" and "phat" are Pali variations of the word for "footprint." Hence Buddhapat: "Footprint of the Buddha."

Wat Xieng Thong

Luang Prabang's crowning architectural achievement and among the most striking monuments

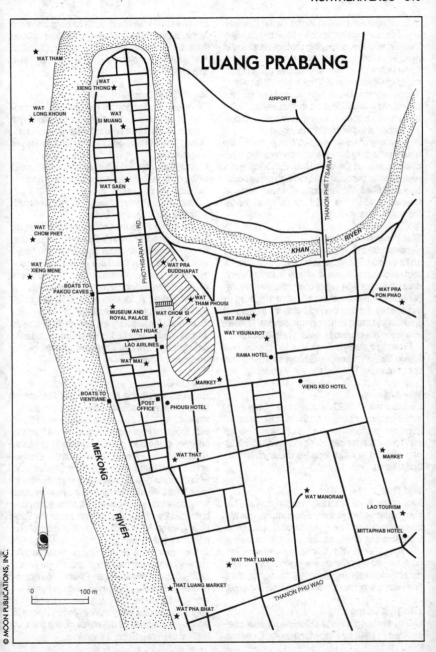

LUANG PRABANG

WAT THAM

WAT XIENG THONG

WAT LONG KHOUN

WAT SI MUANG

AIRPORT

WAT SAEN

PHOTHISARATH RD.

KHAN RIVER

THANON PHET/SARAT

WAT CHOM PHET

WAT XIENG MENE

WAT PRA BUDDHAPAT

WAT PRA PON PHAO

BOATS TO PAKOU CAVES

WAT THAM PHOUSI

MUSEUM AND ROYAL PALACE

WAT CHOM SI

WAT AHAM

WAT HUAK

WAT VISUNAROT

LAO AIRLINES

RAMA HOTEL

WAT MAI

MARKET

VIENG KEO HOTEL

BOATS TO VIENTIANE

POST OFFICE

PHOUSI HOTEL

MEKONG RIVER

WAT THAT

MARKET

WAT MANORAM

LAO TOURISM

MITTAPHAB HOTEL

WAT THAT LUANG

THAT LUANG MARKET

THANON PHU WAO

WAT PHA BHAT

0   100 m

© MOON PUBLICATIONS, INC.

in Southeast Asia is Wat Xieng Thong ("Golden City Temple"), constructed in 1559 by King Setthathirat with low, sweeping roofs overlapping in delicate yet complex patterns. One of the few religious sites to survive successive raids of marauding Chinese and Thai tribes, Wat Xieng Thong represents the high point of Lao creativity with its magnificent interior mosaics, richly decorated wooden columns, and coiffured ceiling embellished with dharma wheels.

Auxiliary chapels behind the primary *sim* house an extremely rare bronze reclining Buddha displayed in the 1931 Paris Exhibition and a royal funeral sanctuary carved with erotic sculpture and filled with a grand 12-meter wooden hearse, used for the 1959 cremation of the father of the final sovereign.

Wat Visunarot (Visoun)

Reconstructed in 1898 as a replica of the original 1513 version, Wat Visoun is chiefly noted for its vast collection of museum-quality Buddhas which date back over 400 years and collectively represent one of the finest arrays of religious art in the country. Among the highlights are the largest Buddha in Luang Prabang and several famous images in the classic pose of "Calling for Rain."

Fronting the *sim* is Thak Mak Mo (nicknamed Melon Stupa), a curious Sinhalese-style stupa constructed in 1504 by Queen Visounalat.

Wat Aham

Constructed in 1823 by a relative of the king, Wat Aham later served as the residence of the supreme patriarch of the Lao Buddhist *sangha.* Today the temple sleeps on, visited for its pair of spirit shrines located under courtyard bodhi trees.

Wat That

Like many *wats* in Luang Prabang, Wat That was constructed in the 15th century, heavily damaged during foreign invasions, restored at the beginning of this century, and renovated in the early 1990s. With its multilayered roof, *sim* richly carved with *Ramayana* legends, and pillars ornamented with *nagas,* Wat That serves as a fine example of traditional Luang Prabang style.

Wat That Luang

Luang Prabang's royal mausoleum was constructed in 1818 by King Manthaturat for ashes of royal family members such as King Sisavang Vong, father of the final sovereign, now interred inside the golden stupa. Someday, perhaps, the ashes of King Savang Vatthana will rest in this temple.

Right Bank Temples

Temples situated across the Mekong—accessible by ferries from the pier opposite the Royal Palace Museum—are modest structures best visited for their timeless settings and senses of remoteness.

Wat Xieng Mene: Small temple constructed in the early 20th century, about one km north of the old royal cemetery.

Wat Chom Phet: Peaceful hilltop retreat with scenic views over the Mekong.

Wat Long Khoun: Once a royal retreat for kings of the Lan Xang Dynasty, Wat Long Khoun includes an older section in the back, which dates from the 18th century, and contemporary additions from the late 1930s. Some of the modern woodcarving is outstanding.

Wat Tham: A limestone cave temple complex filled with ancient Buddhas carved in Lao, Thai, and Burmese styles, as were the stupas and religious decorations which adorn exterior balustrades. Bring a flashlight to explore the unlit caves.

Pak Ou Caves

Some 25 km up the Mekong River lies one of the wonders of northern Laos: enormous limestone cliffs and a pair of sacred caves studded with thousands of wooden and gilded Buddha images, some dating back hundreds of years. According to legend, the caves were discovered in the 16th century by King Setthathirat, who commanded local artisans to fill them with their finest works, though most of the images were donated by devotees or monks. Many are carved in the distinctive Lao attitude of the Buddha "Calling for Rain": hands downward and palms turned inward.

The lower cave, Tham Thing, is reached by a stairway which continues left around the caves to the upper caves, Tham Phum. Both complexes once served as meditation retreats for monks who shared their quarters with powerful guardian spirits. Today the caves are visited in April by thousands of devotees during the Lao festival of Pimai. Bring a flashlight.

GONE TO THE NORTH

Luang Prabang was established in 1353 by Fa Ngum as the royal capital of the first Lao Kingdom, Lan Xang, more romantically called the "Land of a Million Elephants." Previously the city served as a seat of early Thai-Lao kingdoms and a trading conduit between China and southern empires.

Luang Prabang remained the center of the Lan Xang Kingdom until 1563 when King Settathirat transferred the capital to Vieng Chan (Vientiane). Despite the move and subsequent fall of the Lan Xang Kingdom in 1694, Luang Prabang remained the source of monarchical power and spiritual headquarters well into the 20th century.

The French arrived in the late 19th century and took control of Luang Prabang after a succession of territorial treaties with the Siamese. Unlike in Vientiane, where the French imposed grand boulevards and pseudo Arcs de Triomphe, Luang Prabang was left alone as a sleepy escape for lotus eaters.

The Japanese occupation of Laos ended in 1945 with the arrival of French paratroopers, who once again declared Luang Prabang and Laos a French protectorate. However, French experiences in Vietnam and their ongoing problems with Algeria forced them to grant full sovereignty in 1953.

Luang Prabang remained a royal city until the Communist Pathet Lao takeover in 1975 and the elevation of Kaysone Phomvihane to the position of Prime Minister. The Pathet Lao immediately abolished the monarchy in Luang Prabang and established the Lao People's Democratic Republic (LPRP), which continues to rule the impoverished nation.

The main drama of modern Luang Prabang centers around the fate of Savang Vatthana, the final king in a line of rulers that dates back to the empire of Lan Xang. Educated in Paris, Savang had a penchant for *Remembrances of Things Past* by Marcel Proust, and a classic white Ford Edsel that still sits in the royal palace garage. The king was also a devoted patron of Buddhism and a national patriot who cried over the terrible fate of his country.

Savang was initially named an "advisor" to the new Communist regime, but the government, fearing a coup built around the king but organized by insurgents in Thailand, sent the royal family into internal exile in Sam Neua Province in 1977. Sometime in the early 1980s the royal family (king, queen, and Crown Prince Vongsavang) perished in the jungle, though no one knows the details of their deaths, which the government only officially acknowledged to the outside world in 1989.

Curiously, the death of the final monarch has never been reported to the Laotian people, who are still told the great Lao-Orwellian euphemism: the king has "gone to the north" for "seminars."

Xang Hai: The upstream journey passes itinerant gold panners, yellow mats spread with Lao watercress, and the village of Xang Hai (20 km upriver), where villagers use oil drums placed over charcoal fires to brew *lao lao*, a potent but very tasty moonshine whiskey distilled from fermented rice. Most boats stop for a quick shot, but it's best to drink *lao lao* straight (no chaser) and not diluted with unfiltered water.

Transportation: Boats from the pier in Luang Prabang take about two hours to the caves, one hour down, and charge about US$20 for the 10-person longtail. Permits from Lao Tourism are required, though they are rarely checked.

Mekong River Journey

Before the Vietnam conflict spilled across the border, a downriver journey from Luang Prabang to Vientiane was on every backpacker's itinerary. Today, a large and reasonably comfortable passenger ship departs twice weekly for Vientiane and charges US$6-8 for the two- or three-day sail. The upriver journey usually takes four days. Travelers should bring along extra food and water.

Lao Tourism's attitude about this boat seems to change each season. Foreigners are sometimes allowed to take the boat but only with an official permit. At other times, tourists are expressly forbidden to use the service and those apprehended at random downriver stops are forced to pay penalties or risk deportation.

Independent travelers should check current restrictions and weigh the rewards against the risks.

Accommodations

Luang Prabang's four hotels will soon be joined by a few budget places affiliated with guesthouses in Vientiane.

Rama Hotel: A modern three-story hotel with clean fan-cooled rooms and cafe. Madame Sayavong rents bicycles and runs a "discotheque" with live bands on weekends. Thanon Visunarot, tel. 7105, US$8-12.

Vieng Keo Hotel: Acceptable alternative when the Rama is filled. All rooms include fan and private bath. Thanon Setthathirat, US$6-10.

Phousi Hotel: Just south of Phousi hill is a renovated hotel with garden restaurant and both fan-cooled and a/c rooms. Tour groups are usually sent here or to the Mittaphab. Thanon Setthathirat, US$25-40.

Mittaphab Hotel: Luang Prabang's top-end choice, located on a small hill at the edge of town, has a swimming pool and a restaurant with both Lao and Western dishes. All rooms are a/c with private bath. Thanon Phu Wao ("Kite Hill"), P.O. Box 50, tel. 7233, US$35-50.

Practicalities

Lao Tourism: Lao Tourism in the Mittaphab Hotel arranges package tours around Luang Prabang, issues travel permits for other provinces, and provides guides for about US$5-8 per day. The office has very little information for independent visitors.

Bank: Travelers checks can be exchanged at the bank near Wat Mai and in the Mittaphab Hotel.

Post Office: The GPO on Thanon Phothisarath is unreliable and packages should only be mailed from Vientiane or Thailand.

Telephone: Vientiane can be called from several of the hotels but international calls cannot be made from Luang Prabang.

Transportation

Luang Prabang is 230 km north of Vientiane.

Air: Lao Aviation daily flights from Vientiane cost US$40 one-way and US$78 return. All passengers should have travel permits.

Road: Lao Tourism does not currently grant permission to travel overland due to political problems with Hmong rebels near Vang Vieng. However, the government intends to reopen the road to Western visitors when it feels the route is safe for tourists. Independent travelers can check on the latest conditions at guesthouses in Vientiane and, in the event that overland travel is permitted, take a bus from the Morning Market to Luang Prabang.

The basic route is from Luang Prabang to Thalat (two hours), ferry across Nam Ngum reservoir (two hours), and a bus or minitruck to Vang Vieng (one hour), where most travelers overnight. Buses the following day take another 12-15 hours to reach Luang Prabang.

River: Several ferries depart weekly from Vientiane's north jetty and take about four days to reach Luang Prabang. Larger boats can only complete the journey with high waters during the rainy season. Fares are US$6-8 per person and passengers should bring along extra food and water.

PLAIN OF JARS

The Plain of Jars is situated in Xieng Khwang (also spelled Xieng Kuouang and Xiang Khoang) Province some 200 km northeast of Vientiane and 130 km southeast of Luang Prabang.

This remote and rarely visited region is famed for its mysterious stone urns scattered across the valley near the town of Phonsavan and the horrific bombing inflicted during the Vietnam War. Authorities estimate that almost a half-million tons of bombs were dropped here during Nixon's secret war against the North Vietnamese army and the rebel forces of the Pathet Lao. In the end, American bombers dropped over two million tons of bombs on Laos—more than the U.S. dropped during WW II—only to watch the Pathet Lao move south from the Plain of Jars and take Vientiane in 1975.

The Plain of Jars can only be visited with an organized tour. Visitors generally fly into the main town of Phonsavan, see the jars and war memorials in the afternoon, and return to Vientiane the following day. Side trips to caves used as cover during the bombing raids and to the Vietnamese border are also possible.

The high cost of this tour and the unspectacular array of jars makes this region less popular than other destinations in Laos. And yet the refreshing scenery and the simple fact that Westerners haven't toured the province in several decades make Xieng Khwang Province a worthwhile stop for sophisticated travelers.

PHONSAVAN

The main town in Xieng Khwang province lies in a lovely valley pocketed with thousands of craters which impart a moonlike effect among the rolling ricefields. Phonsavan was declared the provincial capital by the new government in Vientiane shortly after the annihilation of the previous capital of Xieng Khwang.

Revolutionary Museum
Phonsavan (population 6,000) itself offers little of interest aside from the weekly market and a brief visit to a small Revolutionary Museum, three km south of town near the Hotel Plaine de Jarres.

Most of the military memorabilia has been moved to the Revolutionary Museum in Vientiane but the remaining assortment of flags, uniforms, cluster bombs, and photographs will interest those intrigued with local military history.

The museum is locked and only open to tour groups with special permission.

Plain Of Jars
Scattered across the plains 12 km southeast of Phonsavan are over 300 immense 2,000-year-old stone urns whose origins and purposes remain an enduring enigma. Some believe the sandstone vessels once served as funeral encasements for nobility and members of the royal court, but according to Lao legend they were constructed by giant ancestors for the production and storage of potent rice-based *lao lao,* the same fire water widely consumed today. The second story rings truer.

Group tours are also taken to a cave once used by the Pathet Lao as a military headquarters. Some have speculated that the cave once served as a kiln for the production of the urns, though it seems more likely the urns were carved from solid pieces of sandstone and hauled down to the valley.

Surprisingly, most of the jars appear relatively intact despite the enormous number of bombs jettisoned by American B-52s returning from raids on the Ho Chi Minh Trail. The Plain of Jars was also bombed to deter southern moves by the Pathet Lao and, some say, simply as a dumping ground for excess ordnance. Whatever the reasons, visitors are advised to take care when walking around the fields; undetonated bombs are still a major problem here.

The Lao air force has recently constructed a huge base on the Plain of Jars, as the former headquarters near Vientiane was considered geographically unsuitable.

Accommodations
In an effort to promote tourism the government has recently constructed several small hotels which cater almost exclusively to the group tours which arrive every few days. All are simple places with fan-cooled rooms and small cafes.

Hotel Plaine de Jarres: An older hotel three km south of town with a friendly staff but rudimentary facilities. Route 4, US$5-10.

Phou Phieng Xieng Khouang: A new hotel one km east of town with panoramic views across the valley and somewhat dependable water and electricity service. Route 7, US$5-10.

Plain of Jars Hotel: Newly opened hotel in the center of town. Thanon Phonsavan, US$5-10.

Transportation

Lao Aviation flies daily from Vientiane to the Phonsavan airstrip for US$120 return. Soviet-built helicopters sometimes substitute when planes are canceled due to heavy cloud cover. The flight takes 50 minutes.

Western visitors are not allowed to take trucks or buses from Vientiane or Luang Prabang to the Plain of Jars due to the terrible conditions of the roads and ongoing political problems with Hmong rebels.

XIENG KHWANG

Some tours also visit the former provincial capital of Xieng Khwang, home to an ancient kingdom which predated even the Lan Xang Dynasty of Luang Prabang.

Famed for its succulent oranges and peaches, moderate climate (elevation 1,000 meters), and distinctive style of religious architecture, Xieng Khwang was almost completely destroyed by American bombers in the early 1970s, then reconstructed and renamed Muang Khoune by the Pathet Lao.

Attractions

Xieng Khwang today has little of great interest aside from its outstanding location in a magnificent valley and the tremendous amount of war material (bomb casings, tank parts, fuselages) cleverly incorporated into local construction projects. Tours usually visit a small hillside shrine and the ruined remains of several 16th-century temples.

Accommodations

Xieng Khwang (population 10,000) has several simple hotels geared to local visitors and Lao businessmen but, until government approval, tourists are not allowed to overnight in Xieng Khwang.

Transportation

Xieng Khwang is usually visited on a full-day jeep tour from Phonsavan, about 40 km north.

MUANG KHAM AND VICINITY

Western travelers are also allowed to visit the town of Muang Kham, 53 km east of Phonsavan and almost halfway to the Vietnamese border.

Attractions

Devastated during the war, Muang Kham has since been rebuilt with an ingenious combination of wood, mortar, and the war debris which lies scattered from the Plain of Jars to the Ho Chi Minh Trail.

Muang Kham itself has little aesthetic appeal but the drive on Route 7 from Phonsavan is superb, passing through splendid valleys surrounded by towering limestone karsts. Organized tours usually stop at several war sites and a Hmong village where bomb casings serve as picket fences.

Tam Phiu Cave: About five km north of town is one of the most poignant reminders of the futility of war: a large cave where perhaps hundreds of innocent Laotians were killed during an American bombing raid in March 1968. The cave now serves as a memorial to the tragedy.

Nong Het: Nong Het (Haet) is a booming trade town on the Vietnamese border, some 60 km from Muang Kham. Improved relations with the Vietnamese and a lull in Hmong rebel activity have opened up this region, along with the provincial capital of Sam Neua in Hua Phan Province.

Lao and Vietnamese tourism officials have also announced plans to open the land crossing at Nong Het (Barthelemy Pass) and in Hua Phan Province to Western visitors, a useful connection which would allow an overland circumnavigation of Indochina: Bangkok-Phnom Penh-Saigon-Hanoi-Vientiane-Bangkok.

Transportation

Once again, Soviet-built jeeps are the usual form of transportation for Western visitors on escorted tours. Buses from Phonsavan reach Muang Kham in a few hours but Westerners are usually barred from these buses.

SOUTHERN LAOS

Officially opened for tourism in 1992, southern Laos remains almost completely unexplored despite its great natural beauty and a famous temple constructed by the Khmers. The region is blessed with lush valleys and remote plateaus which provide some of the newest opportunities for adventure travel in Southeast Asia.

Southern Laos appears to be a prime target for government-approved tourism. Provinces now open to group tours include Savannakhet, Saravane, Champassak, Sekong, and Attapu, including virtually every possible town and natural attraction in the lower third of the country.

Best of all, visitors can now enter Laos by land via the northeastern Thai town of Ubon Ratchathani. This direct route makes tours of the south less expensive and time-consuming than before.

Southern Laos Tours

New tours are being introduced almost monthly, but as of this writing, the most intriguing is an 11-day "Southern Lao Adventure Trek" which flies from Bangkok to Ubon Ratchathani and continues by road the following morning to the Thai-Lao border. This tour costs from US$2200 from Bangkok.

After crossing into Laos, passengers cruise along the Mekong to the stunning Khmer ruins of Wat Phu and then head south for a two-night stay on Khong Island. The largest of some 4,000 islands situated at the southern extremity of Laos near the Cambodian border, Khong Island is known for its colonial-era buildings constructed by the French, its great natural beauty, and rare freshwater dolphins which inhabit the Mekong during the winter months.

The fourth day is spent in Pakse, an old Lao kingdom, then it's overland to Saravane Province and the rarely visited tribal villages near Tataeng. The scenery here is among the most spectacular in Indochina.

An early departure on the sixth day heads to the river at Ban Phom, from where boats head downstream through the magnificent Attapu Valley, an unforgettable gorge which separates the Annimite Mountains on the Vietnamese border with the Bolovens Plateau to the west. Sights in Attapu include a 15th-century temple and several tribal villages.

The next three days are spent at Tad Lo Lodge in Saravane, with a visit to Tad Lo Waterfalls—the highest in Laos—plus an elephant trek and an excursion to marshes inhabited by the near-extinct Lao crocodile. Obviously, southern Laos is best considered an adventure-travel destination, with a brief look at history and ethnology.

Shorter tours which concentrate on the south include a four-day "Tad Lo Lodge Excursion" (Bangkok-Ubon-Pakse-Saravane) priced from US$700 and a seven-day "Khong Island and Tad Lo Excursion" (Bangkok-Ubon-Pakse-Khong Island-Saravan) priced from US$1200.

Independent Travel

As of this writing, independent travel is not permitted in southern Laos. The situation may change; latest details can be picked up on Khao San Rd. in Bangkok.

Independent travel will probably be arranged through travel agents who will sell the least expensive package tour in order to legally obtain a visa from the Laotian Embassy. Travelers will then need to arrange their own transportation and lodgings in the south.

PAKSE (PAKXE)

Pakse, the first destination reached from northeastern Thailand, is the largest town in southern Laos and an important commercial crossroads between Vietnam, Cambodia, Laos, and Thailand.

Pakse served in the early 20th century as the regional headquarters for French occupation forces who left behind a handful of faded colonial buildings, and later as a Lao kingdom under the extravagant tutelage of Prince Boun Oum of Champassak. The prince was exiled to France shortly after the Pathet Lao seized Vientiane in 1975.

Pakse chiefly serves as the launching point for visits to the famous temple complex of Wat Phu and excursions to the natural wonders of the Bolovens Plateau.

Lao Tourism has a small office near the main jetty.

Attractions

Pakse has a lively market and two curious pieces of architecture.

Boun Oum Palace: Constructed in the late 1960s by the last prince of Champassak, Pakse's so-called People's Palace lords over the city as a monument to royal megalomania and the sheer madness of unrestrained extravagance.

Prince Oum, the final royal ruler in southern Laos, initiated the 1,000-room six-story monstrosity in 1968, but construction stopped with his banishment in 1975. Visitors are shown around his enormous ground-floor ballroom, dozens of unfinished stairways which lead nowhere, and the sixth-floor casino with outstanding views over Pakse and, in the opposite direction, the Bolovens Plateau. No wonder so many Laotians despised their royalty and supported the Pathet Lao.

Wat Luang: Adjacent to the Xe Dong River is the oldest temple in Pakse, constructed in 1830 but almost completely renovated in 1990. The central *sim* features well-carved doors below a reconstructed exterior plastered with all the gaudy touches so loved by rural Buddhists.

Ban Saphay: A small village 11 km north of Pakse known for its production of *ikat* silk weavings and a small temple that possibly dates from the Angkor period.

Accommodations

Hotels in Pakse are in the center of town near Wat Luang and the bus terminal.

Pakse Hotel: Older place with both fan-cooled and a/c rooms with private bath. US$5-10.

Champa Vilay: Somewhat cleaner hotel with simple rooms and small cafe. Thanon Souvannah Hongkham, US$5-10.

Souksamran: New hotel with a highly recommended restaurant. All rooms include private bath. US$6-15.

Sala Champa Hotel: A 30-room French-colonial hotel magnificently furnished with period furniture; the best in town. US$12-35.

Transportation

Air: Daily Lao Airways flights from Vientiane cost US$100 one-way and US$180 return.

Bus: Most visitors now arrive by bus from the Thai border town of Chommeck, 76 km east of Ubon Ratchathani and 52 km east of Pakse.

All travelers must have a Lao visa and be affiliated with an organized tour.

CHAMPASSAK

Champassak—the nearest town to the Angkor ruins of Wat Phu—served as a Cambodian outpost from the 10th to 13th centuries and was ruled by the Lan Xang Empire from the 15th to 17th centuries. After the fall of Lan Xang, Champassak remained an independent Lao kingdom loosely affiliated with Vientiane until the victory of the Pathet Lao in 1975.

Today the town is the jumping-off point for visits to Wat Phu.

Accommodations

Most visitors tour Wat Phu and then continue south by road to Khong Island or return to Pakse and head east to the Bolovens Plateau.

Champassak Hotel: The only hotel currently open to Western visitors is located by the pier and the Morning Market (which, like all "Morning Markets" in Laos, operates all day). US$5-10.

Transportation

Champassak is 34 km south of Pakse and eight km north of Wat Phu.

Bus: Buses from Pakse take one hour and terminate at the pier just opposite Champassak.

Boat: More pleasant options are longtail boats from Pakse, which take two hours to Champassak and then continue south to Wat Phu.

WAT PHU

The archaeological site of Wat Phu, eight km south of Champassak, is the most impressive Angkor-period structure in Laos and among the most significant pieces of architecture in Indochina.

History

Although its early history remains murky, some historians surmise that Wat Phu was an important religious site in the 6th-century Chen La empire of the Chams, who, from their nearby base at Sresthapura, ruled most of the lower Mekong until the rise of the Khmers. Sresthapura (Cesthapoura), now an army base, is five km north of Wat Phu.

Archaeologists believe that the present temple complex was begun in the late 11th century by Khmer King Suryavarman II, who later constructed his far more elaborate Angkor Wat in Cambodia. As such, Wat Phu predates and possibly served as the prototype for the architectural culmination of the Khmer civilization.

According to legend, the Hindu-Khmer king situated his temple at the foot of 1,400-meter-high Phu Pasak mountain because of the presence of a hilltop stone lingam, the symbol of Shiva and centerpiece of the Hindu-Khmer pantheon. Today, nobody can find the lingam and it takes great imagination to see the mountain as some enormous phallus.

Even after the Khmers moved their capital to Angkor, Wat Phu (also spelled Wat Phou and Wat Pou) remained an important religious sanctuary financially maintained by the Khmers until the last days of their Cambodian empire. The hillside temple was swallowed by the jungle after the fall of Angkor but rediscovered in 1866 by a French explorer named Francis Gaunier.

Some say that the Emerald Buddha enthroned in Bangkok is merely a copy, and that the true image lies buried in the jungle near Wat Phu.

The Complex

Wat Phu is approached via a pair of complementary reservoirs which symbolize earthly domains and, more practically, collect water for local irrigation projects.

Beyond the reservoirs, a long processional walkway—once flanked by undulating *nagas* and statues of other mythical animals—leads to the summit and its remarkably intact pavilions, libraries, and sanctuaries carved with superb images of the major themes of Hindu mythology: divine *asparas,* Vishnu dancing on the Sea of Milk, Indra mounted on his three-headed elephant, and Kala, the Hindu god of time and death.

Wat Phu has suffered from centuries of neglect and the devastating effects of a monsoonal climate. Renovations funded by UNESCO and the United Nations Development Program will disassemble the collapsing complex stone by stone and rebuild it over a concrete base and an underground drainage system. The US$10-million project will be completed by the year 2000.

Transportation

Wat Phu, eight km south of Champassak, can be reached by chartered jeep or public boat. Wat Phu is referred to locally as Muang Kao, or "Old City."

KHONG ISLAND

Don Khong and Don Khone are two of the thousands of islands formed in the confusing onrush of the Mekong at the Cambodian border.

Unlike the upper Mekong, which seems a lethargic mess of narrow and slow-moving waters, the Mekong here can be over five km wide or, at other times, a narrow series of charging rapids.

Tours arranged by Lao Tourism and sold by travel agents spend a few days exploring the islands and rapids of the Mekong.

Attractions

Boat tours to rapids crashing through narrow cataracts are the main activities in the Khong Island region. Also, keep an eye out for rare freshwater dolphins, which often play in the waters during the rainy season.

River Falls: French expeditions moving upriver in the 1860s discovered that the Mekong was impassable at several points due to a series of unnavigable cascades near the island of Don Khone. The situation become so desperate that French engineers were brought in to construct a railway line from the southern to the northern tip of Don Khone.

The rusting hulks of abandoned locomotives still litter the railyards near Ban Khone bridge.

Visitors today are taken to see the cataracts of Li Phi Falls, due west of Ban Khone Thai town, and Khong Phapheng Falls ("Voice of the Mekong"), east of Don Khone near the town of Ban Thakho.

Accommodations

Tours usually spend the night in the town of Muang Khoune on Don Khong Island, just opposite Ban Hat Sai Khoun on Route 13. Choices include an old government resthouse and a rehabilitated hotel to the left of the pier.

Transportation

Khong Island is 150 km south of Pakse on Route 13. Tour groups are taken here by bus, though a more scenic alternative would be a boat chartered in either Pakse or Champassak. Route 13 continues southeast to the Cambodian border; the crossing was closed as of this writing.

SARAVANE

Saravane, the capital of Saravane (Salavan) Province, serves as access point to the lovely, almost ethereal, beauty of the Bolovens Plateau and a river journey down the Kong (Xekhong or Sedone) River gorge to magnificent Attapu Valley. One of the more spectacular regions in Southeast Asia, Saravane will probably become a major focus of adventure travel in the next decade.

Saravane town itself was largely destroyed during the war and has little of interest aside from the market and a handful of colonial-era buildings which survived the bombing raids.

Accommodations
The old French town lacks formal accommodations and most visitors head directly to Tataeng Lodge or Tad Lo Lodge on the Bolovens Plateau.

Transportation
Lao Aviation flies twice weekly from Vientiane via Savannakhet for US$80 one-way. Buses from Pakse take a full day on the southern route through Bolovens Plateau or the northern route through Souvanna Khili and Khong Sedone.

BOLOVENS PLATEAU

Spread across the borders of Saravane and Champassak provinces is an immensely fertile plateau rich with coffee, tea, and cardomom plantations developed by French plantation owners around the turn of the century. In fact, the route from Pakse to Paksong is referred to as the "Coffee Road," though finding a good cup of coffee around here is almost impossible.

The principal towns on the plateau are Paksong, 175 km east of Pakse, and Tataeng (Tha Teng), some 40 km south of Saravane.

People
The Bolovens Plateau is both a beautiful region and an ethnological gold mine inhabited by over a dozen ethnic minorities, most of whom arrived in the late 1960s seeking safety from American air strikes on the Ho Chi Minh Trail to the east.

Among the larger racial groups are Katou, Tayoi, Ngai, and Suk, along with traditional stocks of lowland Lao Loum—the principal ethnic group in Laos—and Mon-Khmer descendants called Lao Theung, seminomadic inhabitants of the Annamite Mountains to the east.

Attractions Near Paksong
Principal sights near the agricultural center of Paksong include several waterfalls, gorges, and villages of rarely visited tribal groups set amidst some of the most spectacular landscapes in Southeast Asia.

Tad Phan Waterfall: A 130-meter waterfall—one of the longest in Asia—is located southeast of Paksong on the road to Pakse, near a downriver hydroelectric dam which provides much of the power for southern Laos.

Ban Houei Houne: A Katou village known for its traditional *ikat* weavings produced with old backstrap looms. Tours are also taken to several other remote villages inhabited by ethnic minorities who fled their traditional homelands in the Annamite Mountains during the heavy bombardment of the Vietnam War.

Attractions Near Tataeng
The small farming community of Tataeng, 40 km south of Saravane, is known for its bracing climate, temperate fruits, and remote villages inhabited by cultural minorities who still follow traditional lifestyles.

Ban Khian: The standard tour of this section of the Bolovens Plateau usually includes a visit to an Alak village and then the downriver boat trip to Attapu. Ban Khian's residents are Austro-Indonesian animists who live in grass-thatched huts arranged in circles and follow social beliefs which invoke spirits, shamans, and animal sacrifice.

Kong River: Adventure-travel tours of southern Laos leave Tataeng early in the morning and head due east to the town of Ban Phom, from where boats sail downriver through a magnificent gorge to fabulous Attapu Valley. Many consider this among the most scenic water journeys in Southeast Asia.

Accommodations

Several lodges have been constructed by Lao Tourism for group tours visiting the Bolovens Plateau.

Tataeng Chalet: Travelers making the river journey to Attapu usually overnight here in these government bungalows. Independent travelers who make it here would probably be charged US$5-10.

Tad Lo Resort: A highly recommended resort near Saravane at the summit of the highest combination falls in Laos: upper Tad Lo and lower Tad Hang. Remote and beautiful, Tad Lo Resort is an excellent place to relax, swim in the river, and explore the plateau by rented jeep or on elephantback. US$8-20.

ATTAPU

The newest region to open in southern Laos is the superbly remote and geographically stunning valley in the "Emerald Triangle" intersection of Laos, Vietnam, and Cambodia.

Attapu served as the center of the Attapu Dynasty from the 15th century until political changes and military challenges from the Cambodians brought about the empire's fall in the 18th century. As elsewhere across Laos, Attapu's proximity to the Ho Chi Minh Trail brought saturation bombing during the Vietnam conflict; evidence of the war legacy is everywhere.

Attractions

Attapu was largely destroyed in the late 1960s, though some evidence of its rich historical past survives in the nearby Muang Khao or "Old City."

Wat Sathathrat: This temple was founded by a northern Lao king who discovered Attapu in the 15th century and established his new fiefdom near the Cambodian border. Wat Sathathrat has been reconstructed several times in contemporary style.

Villages: Groups often visit several traditional villages inhabited by lowland Lao Loum or various highland Lao Theung groups such as Akha, Taoy, and Alak.

Accommodations

Lao Tourism puts up Western visitors in a government guesthouse.

Transportation

A fairly decent road connects Attapu with Pakse to the west and Saravane to the north. Most tours include a downriver boat trip through the gorge that separates the Annamite Mountains from the Bolovens Plateau, then a bus ride back to Pakse or Saravane, depending on the itinerary.

SAVANNAKHET

The commercial center and provincial capital of Savannakhet lies on the banks of the Mekong just across from the Thai town of Mukdahan.

The town has become quite prosperous due to its strategic location on Route 9—the highway that leads from Thailand to Danang in Vietnam—and its large community of Chinese traders who, as elsewhere in Asia, dominate the economy.

Attractions

Savannakhet is rarely visited by Westerners, since land access from Thailand is prohibited and the town offers little of great interest aside from its riverside location and a few monuments constructed by a vassal kingdom of Vientiane.

That Inheng: Savannakhet's oldest religious structure is this weathered 16th-century stupa constructed by a contemporary of King Setthathirat.

River Journey: Longtail boats can be hired at the pier for day-long excursions on the Mekong.

Accommodations

Although Westerners rarely visit Savannakhet, Lao Tourism has renovated four old hotels for use by group tours. All visitors must have travel permits.

Santipharb Hotel: Acceptable hotel with small restaurant and both fan-cooled and a/c rooms. Thanon Tha Dan, US$5-15.

Mekong Hotel: An old French-constructed hotel with some charm and large rooms with attached facilities. Thanon Tha Dua, US$6-18.

Transportation

Air: Lao Aviation flies daily from Vientiane for US$60 one-way and US$110 return.

Bus: Independent travelers with permits are sometimes allowed to take buses from Vientiane down Route 13 to Savannakhet. Check with the guesthouses in Vientiane.

Boat: Certainly the most memorable way to reach southern Laos from Vientiane is on the passenger boat that departs weekly and takes two days to reach Savannakhet. Permission must be obtained in advance from Lao Tourism.

The modern reader of travelers' tales is a cautious fellow, not easily fooled. He is never misled by facts which do not assort with his knowledge. But he loves wonders. His faith in dragons, dog-headed men, bearded women, and mermaids is not what it used to be, but he will accept good substitutes.

—H.M. Tomlinson,
The Face of the Earth

*He who travels fastest travels alone,
but he who travels best travels with a companion,
if not always a lover.*

—Paul Fussell,
Abroad

It's not worthwhile to go around the world to count the cats in Zanzibar.

—Paul Theroux,
The Great Railway Bazaar

MACAU

Travel, for too long, has been trivialized in the popular press and by the promoters of popular tours; it deserves better. It is an enduring subject of human concern, the essential requisite for a civilized life, perhaps the most effective tool for reducing foolish national pride and promoting a world view.

—Arthur Frommer,
New World of Travel

Travel broadens the mind.

—Anonymous

Everybody in the world is a little mad.

—Joseph Conrad,
The Shadow Line

INTRODUCTION

A plaque outside the entrance to Monte Fortress proclaims "Stop! Take heed! Consider briefly the beautiful history of our country. Enter proudly and hold your head up high because you are a citizen of that country." Since those words were engraved in 1622, Macau has grown from an Iberian outpost on the southern coast of China into a modern city with industrialized parks and housing estates. And yet, to a surprising degree, it remains a sleepy Portuguese town of cobbled streets and color-splashed architecture—a delightful land of grand mansions, magnificent churches, and romantic cafes. Hong Kong's greatest attraction? Macau.

PHYSICAL SETTING

Macau is located on the southeastern coast of China some 100 km south of Canton and 60 km east of Hong Kong. Over 90% of the population lives on the peninsula with the remainder residing on the southern islands of Taipa and Coloane. The land is hilly with little arable acreage; much of the reclaimed land has been covered with housing projects, casinos, and recreation areas. The climate is subtropical and monsoonal, with cool-dry winters and hot-wet summers. Eighty percent of the total annual rainfall occurs during the summer rainy season, when the southwest monsoon blows up from the Indian Ocean bringing typhoons and high humidity. Winters can be very cold. Best times to visit are early spring and late fall, when the days are sunny but cool.

HISTORY

Shortly after Columbus made landfall on the Americas and well before other European nations arrived in strength, the Portuguese successfully exploited the navigational discoveries of Prince Henry to secure trading posts at Goa (1510), Malacca (1511), the Moluccas (1521), and Macau (1557). Macau was their final link in the chain of ports which allowed them to control trade between Europe and Asia by circumventing the Middle East and breaking Venice's iron grip on the Asian spice trade. Macau was founded after the Chinese ended direct trade between Japan and China. Recognizing the great potential for profit, Portuguese merchants soon began trading Chinese silks and porcelains for silver from Nagasaki and spices from India.

MACAU

At the time it was a long and perilous journey through pirate-infested waters. Chinese authorities awarded Macau to the Portuguese in 1557 for clearing the waters. Yet many feel that Macau became a Portuguese possession not from diplomacy or military campaigns but from the efforts of a Jesuit priest named Francis Xavier, the St. Paul of the Far East. Xavier had previously converted thousands to Christianity during his sojourns in Goa and Indonesia. Intrigued by reports of China and Japan, the saint left Malacca in 1549 for the Japanese city of Kagoshima, where he worked until 1552. Yearning to bring the gospels to China, Xavier sailed to the island of Sheungchuen (80 km southwest of Macau), where he made a temporary base while awaiting final approval from Chinese authorities. Xavier died on the island from tropical fever on 2 December.

The period from 1557 to 1640 was a time of prosperity for Macau but decline for Portuguese power in Asia. Against all odds, the citizens of

MACAU'S CLIMATE

	Jan.	Feb.	March	April	May	June	July	Aug.	Sept.	Oct.	Nov.	Dec.
Avg. Maximum C	20°	20°	21°	23°	28°	29°	31°	31°	30°	28°	25°	20°
Avg. Maximum F	68°	68°	70°	73°	82°	84°	88°	88°	86°	82°	77°	68°
Rainy Days	4	5	7	8	13	18	17	15	12	6	2	3

Macau resisted the Spanish Crown and supported the Portuguese monarchy, an event now heralded by the inscription over the Senate entrance, "City of the Name of God, There is None More Loyal." But loyalty wasn't enough. Coveting the prosperity and privileged location, both Dutch and English forces initiated a series of sea raids on the outpost. A renowned Dutch attack in the 17th century was barely repulsed by a motley crew of Portuguese sailors, Jesuit priests, and African Bantu slaves. Portuguese influence in Macau finally ended in 1638 after the Portuguese were expelled from Japan. With the heart of their lucrative China-Macau-Japan trade cut out, the Portuguese only survived through markets in Indochina and their Chinese trade monopoly. This lucrative trade arrangement ended in 1685 when the emperor declared all Chinese ports open to foreign ships. Macau continued along as an opium trading post and foreign residence until 1847, when the British established the free-trade port of Hong Kong. Macau's coffin was finally sealed when the harbor silted up and traders moved across to the British colony. Since then, this sleepy Iberian backwater has survived on a mix of gambling, light industry, and tourism.

GOVERNMENT

Macau is a Portuguese territory administered by an appointed governor and his 17-member Legislative Council. The Portuguese have controlled Macau for over 430 years as their last overseas outpost . . . but not for long. According to the Sino-Portuguese Joint Declaration signed in 1987, Macau will revert to Chinese rule on December 20, 1999, just two years after Britain hands over Hong Kong. This bilateral agreement states that Macau will become a Special Administrative Region with the same self-rule and freedoms guaranteed to Hong Kong. A

Basic Law (a mini-constitution of sorts) will be promulgated by the Chinese in 1993-1994. Beijing also agreed to several amendments designed to satisfy Portuguese concerns about preserving their dignity.

Few believe this will be enough. With little economic or political interest in Macau, the Portuguese have repeatedly threatened to leave their colony. More telling were the events in Tiananmen in June 1989, which cast serious doubt on the future of the oldest remaining European settlement in Asia. Many of those who once expressed their passionate support of the student movement in Beijing have now been cowed into an eerie silence. Retaliation is expected. The bottom line on Macau's future is that Beijing will do exactly whatever it wants.

ECONOMY

Macau's biggest industry is gambling. Over 80% of this revenue is generated by the Macau Tourism and Amusement Society (STDM), a government syndicate which operates Macau's five casinos and racetracks. Each year almost four million Hong Kong Chinese flock here to test their luck. Macau's remaining one million visitors include Japanese, North Americans, Southeast Asians, and Europeans. Macau also produces garments, toys, artificial flowers, fireworks, and electronic goods. Most of these companies are owned and operated by the Chinese, an economy situation that accounts for much of the local diffidence to events in China.

PEOPLE

Almost 95% of Macau's 500,000 inhabitants are Chinese. The remaining citizens are Portuguese, European, and Macanese. Most follow Chinese religions, but some 25,000 Catholics are served by nearly 60 Portuguese and Chinese priests

*view over
central Macau*

in a dozen churches and cathedrals. The most politically powerful group besides the Portuguese administrators are the Macanese, locally born citizens descended from mixed Chinese-Portuguese marriages. Educated in local Portuguese schools and fluent in the Portuguese language, this community has traditionally served as intermediaries between the Chinese and non-Chinese-speaking Portuguese administrators. Though some 85% of Macau's civil service are local recruits, Macanese fill nearly all positions that require fluency in Portuguese.

While most consider themselves more Chinese than Portuguese and seem reluctant to leave Macau for emotional and economic reasons, they also feel very fortunate to possess Portuguese passports. This so-called "Portuguese parachute" will give some 3,000 public servants the option to leave Macau before 1999. The Portuguese government has also granted citizenship rights to about 100,000 local residents, a policy in sharp contrast with that of Britain, which has refused similar rights to some three million people born in Hong Kong.

PRACTICAL INFORMATION

GETTING THERE

Until the airport is completed in 1994, the only way to reach Macau is by sea. Ferries leave several times hourly from the Macau Ferry Terminal in the Shun Tak Centre, Central, a 15-minute walk west of the Star Ferry terminal. Departures are so frequent that advance reservations are only necessary on weekends and holidays. Round-trip tickets should be purchased to avoid delays on the return voyage. Ferries also depart nine times daily from the China Hong Kong Terminal in Kowloon. A HK$22 departure tax is included in the ferry ticket price. There is a 20-*pataca* tax on departures from Macau. The tax is included in the price of your ticket.

Arrival

Ferries from Hong Kong pass through the crowded harbor and then continue past Lantau and Cheung Chau before turning in to the channel leading to the crowded Macau Ferry Terminal.

First impressions of Macau are uniformly disappointing—an ugly landfill of faceless concrete structures and sterile gambling emporiums. Don't be discouraged! The terminal branch of the Macau Tourist Office has free brochures and maps. Change money if necessary but note that Hong Kong dollars are welcome here. You should also buy a return ticket. Self-drive cars and Mokes are available.

Taxis and public buses wait outside. Buses 3 and 3A go down Ribeiro Avenue to the inner harbor and Floating Casino area, where Macau's budget accommodations are located.

GETTING AROUND

Local Transport

Visitors with limited time could take an organized tour or charter a taxi, but neither option is recommended in a town as compact as Macau. It's much better to slowly walk the back alleys and quiet neighborhoods. Day visitors should take a taxi to the center of town and then *walk* before returning to Hong Kong that evening.

Taxis: Macau has over 500 licensed and fully metered taxis identified by their distinctive cream-colored tops. Flagfall is 6 *patacas* for the first 1,500 meters and 4 *patacas* for each subsequent kilometer. There is also a 6-*pataca* surcharge to Taipa and 12 *patacas* to Coloane. No surcharge on return trips.

Buses: Over 10 different bus and minibus lines run from 0700 till midnight. Fares are just 90 *avos*. Buses to Taipa and Coloane depart from Ave. Infante D'Hernique. Best views from the open-roofed buses.

Mokes, Pedicabs, and Bicycles: Visitors looking for a good time might consider hiring a Moke on arrival at the Macau Ferry Terminal. These small, rag-topped jeep-like vehicles are great fun on sunny days and reasonably priced when shared by a group. Pedicabs are a relaxing way to tour the Praia Grande (seaside

SEA TRANSPORT TO MACAU

TYPE	DURATION	DAILY	DEPARTURES	OW FARES	PHONE
Jetfoils (Central)	55 min.	42 times	0700-0300	HK$75-110	859-3111
Jetfoils (Kowloon)	55 min.	9 times	0700-1900	HK$75-110	859-3111
Hydrofoils	75 min.	22 times	0800-1800	HK$65-75	540-1882
Catamarans	70 min.	14 times	0800-1800	HK$65-75	540-1882
Hover Ferries	65 min.	10 times	0800-1800	HK$60-75	542-3081
High-Speed Ferries	100 min.	5 times	0800-2300	HK$50-70	815-3043

BUS ROUTES IN MACAU

3	Ferry Terminal - Downtown - Ave. Rebeiro - Floating Casino - China Gate
3A	Ferry Terminal - Downtown - Ave. Rebeiro - Floating Casino
5	A Ma Temple - Floating Casino - China Gate
9	Lisboa Hotel - Bela Vista Hotel - A Ma Temple - Floating Casino - China Gate
11	Lisboa Hotel - Taipa
21	Lisboa Hotel - Taipa - Coloane - Coloane Village
21A	Lisboa Hotel - Taipa - Coloane - Checc Van and Hac Sa Beach

perimeter loop) but are useless on hills and cobblestoned roads. Besides that, you really feel like a TOURIST. Rickety bicycles can be hired but they're not allowed on the bridges to Taipa or Coloane.

Into China

Tours into China can be arranged from agencies or from China Travel Service (tel. 782331) in the Hotel Beverly Plaza. Independent travelers can obtain visas from CTS. One-day tours visit the birthplace of Sun Yat-Sen, a local commune, and a fishing village. Other programs include a four-day Pearl River delta tour from Macau to Guangzhou. Visitors with a penchant for adventure can now Moke into China for about HK$500 per day. Temporary licenses good for 15 days are issued at the Gongbei border. Drivers must take a driving test, hold an international driving permit, be over 21, and deposit 3,000 *patacas* if under 35. Buses to China leave opposite the floating casino.

TRAVEL FORMALITIES

Visas

Visas are not required for residents of the United States, Canada, Australia, New Zealand, Germany, England, France, and most other European nations.

Other nationals from countries which have diplomatic relations with Portugal can obtain visas on arrival in Macau: HK$160 for individuals, HK$80 for tour-group members. Nationals of countries without diplomatic relations with Portugal must obtain visas in advance from an overseas Portuguese consulate. The Portuguese Consulate in Hong Kong is at 1001 Exchange Square Two, 10th Floor, Central, tel. 522-5488.

Tourist Information

Tourist offices are located at the Macau Ferry Terminal, and most conveniently on the third floor of the Macau Ferry Terminal Building in Central. Purchase your ferry ticket and then

MACAU TOURIST OFFICES

COUNTRY	ADDRESS	PHONE
Australia	449 Darling St., Balmain, Sydney, N.S.W. 2041	(02) 555-7548
Canada	1530 West 8th Ave., Suite 304, Vancouver V6H3V9	(604) 736-1095
France	7 rue Scribe, 75009 Paris	742-5557
Germany	Kaiserstrasse 66-IV, 6000 Frankfurt am Main	(0) 69-234094
Portugal	Avenida 5 de Outubro 115 5th Fl., 1000 Lisbon	797-9348
United Kingdom	6 Sherlock Mews, Paddington St., London W1M3RH	(071) 224-3390
U.S.A.	3133 Lake Hollywood Dr., Los Angeles, CA 90068	(213) 851-3402
	70A Greenwich Ave. #316, New York, NY 10011	(212) 206-6828

FESTIVALS IN MACAU

Macau celebrates Chinese festivals, Catholic holidays, and special events such as the Macau Grand Prix. All together it adds up to over 25 official and semiofficial public holidays. Most of the religious festivals are movable feasts dated by the lunar calendar. Exact dates should be confirmed with the Macau Tourist Office. Chinese festivals are described in the Singapore and Hong Kong chapters. Only unique or exceptionally popular festivals are listed below.

February
Chinese New Year: While it's a quiet family affair in Hong Kong, the Macanese celebrate the new moon with fireworks, revelry, and nonstop gambling. At midnight the STDM director ritually places the first bet at the roulette wheel and then steps aside for the gamblers who throw money away at a furious rate, since many believe this the luckiest day of the year.

Catholic procession: "Our Lady of Passos"

March
Feast of Our Lord of Passos: A candle-lit procession in which the image of Christ is slowly paraded from the Church of St. Augustine to the Macau Cathedral. One of the finest festivals in Macau.

April
Easter: Macau's 25,000 Christians celebrate with special masses in the Macau Cathedral.

Birthday of A Ma: The namesake of Macau (known as Tin Hau in Hong Kong) is honored by thousands of pilgrims, who bring offerings of food and incense to her temple near Barra Point. Taoist priests enter trances and perform magic rituals and self-mutilation.

Procession of Our Lady of Fatima: A Christian festival that commemorates the miraculous appearance of the Virgin Mary to three shepherd children over 80 years ago. Church dignitaries and veiled children carry images of the Virgin Mary through the streets.

June
Camoes Day: The famous Portuguese poet is honored with a military parade and pilgrimage to his grotto. The governor holds a party at his residence. Also known as Portugal Day.

Feast of St. Anthony: A procession starts from the Church of St. Anthony.

Feast of St. John the Baptist: A small statue of the patron saint of Macau is taken from the Senate Chambers chapel and paraded around the City Square.

October
Republic Day: This public holiday marks the founding of the Portuguese Republic on 5 October 1910.

November
Macau Grand Prix: One of the world's premier motoring events. For over 40 years, movie stars and royalty have come to Macau to watch the world's fastest cars race through the winding Guia circuit. Other events include the Classic Car Event for nostalgia buffs, a Super Car Challenge, and the Motorcycle Grand Prix. Hotel reservations must be made well in advance.

December
Procession of Immaculate Conception: This procession of clergy, bishops, and church members slowly winds through the cobbled lanes of Macau.

---

take the escalator upstairs for brochures, maps, and a copy of *Macau Travel Talk,* which lists upcoming festivals and cultural events.

Macau's Visitors Information Center is located at 9 Largo do Senado. An exuberant group of Portuguese runs the place!

Maps
Maps provided by the Macau Tourist Office are pretty useless. Unless you enjoy getting lost (not half bad in Macau!) you should buy either the *Map of Macau and Zhuhai* by Universal Publications or *Map of Macau* by Jor-

nal VA Kio. Both are both well worth the extra *patacas*.

Note that Macau has adopted the official form of Romanized place names. Among the most common with former spellings in brackets are: Beijing (Peking), Guangdong (Kwangtung), and Guangzhou (Canton).

Currency

The legal currency of Macau is the *pataca* (M$), which is divided into 100 *avos*. The "Macau dollar" is pegged at 100 to 103 Hong Kong dollars, with a permissible variation of up to 10 percent. There is no currency black market. The Hong Kong dollar circulates freely in Macau and all merchants gladly accept HK dollars at par with the *pataca*. **Important:** the *pataca* is *not* acceptable in Hong Kong. Be sure to change remaining *patacas* back to HK dollars or expect to be murdered by the money changers in Hong Kong. Exchange facilities are located at major banks and the Macau Ferry Terminal.

Telephone

Phone calls are free in Macau.

Directory information. 3001
Fire 999
Police. 999
Ambulance 999
Department of Tourism 6397-1115

ATTRACTIONS

Southeast Asia's most romantic collection of historic churches, villas, and temples is situated within a cameo-sized country so compact that determined walkers can visit most of the highlights in a single day. The following tour begins with a walk through the southern section and then moves north to the Chinese border. Visitors with limited time should start center stage with the Leal Senado, St. Paul's, and Old Protestant Cemetery, then walk south along the Praia Grande. The northern area is somewhat industrialized and less inviting than the central or southern sections.

SOUTHERN PENINSULA

The Praia Grande

Long the favorite subject of painters and poets, this elegant esplanade is flanked to the left by a row of banyans spreading their canopies out towards the sea and to the right by a procession of colored stucco houses with balustraded balconies, carved architraves, frilled ironwork, and inked shutters. Many of the old buildings have been pulled down and replaced with modern structures, but enough remains of this "Gateway to the Mirror Bay" to make for a worthwhile walk. About a kilometer down the road are some unusual fishing nets, manually lowered into the ocean and then raised with a few small fish.

Government House

Just beyond the statue of Jorge Alvares is the rose-pink Government House. This regal residence was constructed in 1849 by Jose Tomas Aquino, the Portuguese architect who also designed the Governor's Residence, St. Lawrence's Church, and the Hermitage of Penha Hill. The symmetrical pink-and-white exterior with white stucco trim is centered on a veranda supported by Corinthian columns. The interior has a grand staircase and a reception hall decorated with ornately carved furniture and hand-painted blue tiles. Closed to the public but the exterior makes for a great photo . . . if you've got a wide-angle lens.

Bela Vista Hotel

Constructed in the late 1800s by the English captain of the HK-Macau Ferry, this green-and-white Victorian mansion with its wonderful views and timeless atmosphere represents what is best about Macau: the unhurried pace, a natural elegance, an appreciation for simpler times. The Bela Vista was completely renovated by the Mandarin Oriental Hotel group in 1993 and now ranks as among the most exclusive small-scale hotels in Southeast Asia.

Penha Hill And Bishop's Palace

The immense Bishop's Palace and adjacent Chapel of Our Lady of Penha at the top of Penha Hill were originally constructed in 1622, when Macau reigned as the center of Asian Catholicism from Japan to India. Dedicated to Notre Dame de France, the Protectress of Sailors, the original chapel once served as a point of pilgrimage for sailors about to make the perilous journey back home. It featured in several of George Chinnery's paintings. Both buildings were restored in 1935 and painted an unimaginative gray. Just beyond the the parking lot is a replica of the Grotto of Lourdes. Back down the road is a souvenir stall with a hand-painted sign declaring, "From here we can see the nice view of China." Perhaps . . . but the views from Monte Fortress are better.

Governor's Residence

Macau's head of state currently resides in the Palacio de Santa Sancha, constructed in 1849 by Macau's leading architect, Tomas de Aquino. A very stern set of guards keeps the public away; there is little reason to hike up here to peek through the front gate. The best views are from the Praia Grande or the balcony of the Bela Vista. Continue walking along the waterfront or cut through the winding streets.

Barra Fort And
Pousada De Sao Tiago

This small fort served as Macau's most important defensive position from its construction in 1629 until the Japanese closed their doors to foreign trade a few years later. The fort was manned while the harbor silted up and business moved across to Hong Kong, but was abandoned and fell into ruins after WW II.

A decade ago the Macau Tourist Department hired Nuno Jorge, a local Macanese architect, to design a *pousada* (Portuguese Inn) inside the stone walls. With great imagination and sensitivity the old fort was gutted, renovated, and successfully converted into Macau's finest hotel, the Pousada de Sao Tiago. Visitors can enter through the cavelike street entrance and visit the Chapel of St. James, dedicated to the patron saint of the Portuguese army. Portuguese and Macanese specialties are served on the second level in the Garden Terrace Restaurant.

Temple Of Goddess A Ma

Situated beneath Barra Hill, this shrine is dedicated to the Chinese goddess of the sea, known as A Ma in Macau and Tin Hau in Hong Kong. Chinese believe the temple has great *fung shui* from its auspicious location: backing the hills where protective dragons live and facing the open sea for good fortune.

Macau takes its name from this temple. Portuguese sailors first called the area "A Ma Gao" (Bay of A Ma) but later shortened this to Ma Gao or Macau. To the left of the main courtyard is a statue of Tin Hau dressed in the costume of a Chinese bride with strings of glass beads hanging over her face. To the rear is perhaps the most famous feature of the temple: a carved and brightly painted rock with bas-reliefs of a Fukien junk which, according to legend, carried the goddess from South China to Macau, where she climbed up Barra Hill and then ascended into heaven. The main prayer hall was completely reconstructed with fire-resistant concrete after being gutted in 1988. Inside stands another image of Tin Hau dressed as a Chinese bride on her throne.

Exit through the circular Moon Gate and then look back over the beautiful tiled roofs. Continue up the serpentine walk (Path of Enlightenment) past the small third temple to the final temple dedicated to Kuan Yin, the Buddhist Goddess of Mercy.

Maritime Museum And Bay Cruise

Berthed alongside the small museum are several vessels including an ornate number used in the film *Tai Pan*. All can be boarded and toured. The museum operates a special cultural tour on weekends and Watertours of Hong Kong sails a Chinese junk named *Bauhinia*.

CENTRAL MACAU

Church Of Saint Lawrence

Macau was established by the Portuguese in 1557 as a trading post and religious center for the Jesuits and Augustinians, who constructed their European-baroque churches with funds donated by the Portuguese Crown. Many of the

tropical Iberian architecture

original structures were ravaged by fire and then insensitively reconstructed in modern styles—but not the Church of Saint Lawrence. With its finely proportioned European towers painted in a Mediterranean scheme of cream and white, this is easily one of Macau's most beautiful churches. Note the Oriental features such as the terracotta panels and Chinese-tiled roof. The front entrance is kept locked but visitors can gain access by walking to the rear and ringing the buzzer. The caretaker will open the gate and let you inside the church with its aquamarine ceiling and modernistic stained-glass windows.

Seminary And Church Of Saint Joseph

This confusing maze of classrooms and chapels was founded in 1728 by the Jesuits as their base of Chinese operations. St. Francis Xavier's humerus bone was kept here before being moved to the namesake chapel on Coloane Island. The Roman Renaissance Church of Saint Joseph is across the seminary courtyard (look for the curving staircase). Macau's most famous citizen and resident historian, Father Manuel Teixeira, works here with his extensive collection of religious art and history books. Priest, benefactor, and walking encyclopedia of Macau's past, Teixeira has almost single-handedly preserved the heritage of Portugal in Asia by publishing over 100 works in Portuguese and English-language brochures on the A Ma Temple, St. Paul's Church, and the Bela Vista Hotel.

Dom Pedro V Theater

This yellow-and-white gem was originally constructed in 1859 in a neo-classical style similar to that of other European theaters. Inside to the right (check for a side door) of Asia's first Western playhouse is a small theater with plush seats and heavy curtains decorated in red and gold. Much of the historical interest and architectural detail was lost during some heavy-handed restorations. The theater is currently used by the Club de Macau (a private men's club) and closed to the public, although you might be able to sneak in for a quick peek: turn right and avoid the club hostess.

Church Of Saint Augustine

This baroque-style church was originally built in 1586 by Spanish Augustinians from the Philippines and reconstructed in 1814. The facade is plain but the interior features a tremendous baroque altar displaying a life-sized statue of Jesus, a highly revered image solemnly paraded through the streets during Lent. Note the exceptionally lurid diorama of Christ carrying the cross and an urn which holds the right arm of Antonio Coelhos and the ashes of Maria Basos, his 12-year-old bride who died giving birth. Someone might tell you the famous story. Beyond the church is the restored Sir Robert Ho Tung Cultural Center and Library.

Leal Senado

Facing the Largo do Senado (main town square) is the 18th-century Loyal Senate, a classically

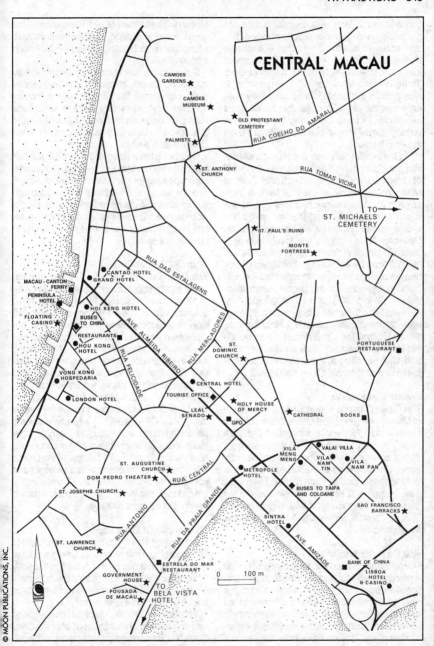

CENTRAL MACAU

CAMOES GARDENS ★
CAMOES MUSEUM ★
★ OLD PROTESTANT CEMETERY
RUA COELHO DO AMARAL
PALMISTS ★
★ ST. ANTHONY CHURCH
RUA TOMAS VICIRA
TO → ST. MICHAELS CEMETERY
★ ST. PAUL'S RUINS
MONTE FORTRESS ★
RUA DAS ESTALAGENS
● CANTAO HOTEL
● GRAND HOTEL
MACAU - CANTON FERRY ★
PENINSULA HOTEL ■
FLOATING CASINO ★
● HOI KENG HOTEL
BUSES TO CHINA ■
RESTAURANTS ●
● HOU KONG HOTEL
AVE. ALMEIDA RIBEIRO
RUA MERCADORES
ST. DOMINIC CHURCH ★
PORTUGUESE RESTAURANT ■
VONG KONG HOSPEDARIA ●
RUA FELICIDADE
● CENTRAL HOTEL
TOURIST OFFICE ◆
● LONDON HOTEL
LEAL SENADO ★
★ HOLY HOUSE OF MERCY
GPO ■
★ CATHEDRAL
BOOKS ■
● VALAI VILLA
VILA MENG MENG ●
VILA NAM TIN ●
● VILA NAM PAN
ST. AUGUSTINE CHURCH ★
DOM PEDRO THEATER ★
RUA CENTRAL
● METROPOLE HOTEL
ST. JOSEPHS CHURCH ★
◆ BUSES TO TAIPA AND COLOANE
SAO FRANCISCO BARRACKS ★
RUA ANTONIO
RUA DA PRAIA GRANDE
● SINTRA HOTEL
AVE. AMIZADE
ST. LAWRENCE CHURCH ★
■ BANK OF CHINA
■ ESTRELA DO MAR RESTAURANT
0   100 m
GOVERNMENT HOUSE ★
TO BELA VISTA HOTEL
POUSADA DE MACAU ★
LISBOA HOTEL & CASINO ●

© MOON PUBLICATIONS, INC.

proportioned building with a simple facade and delicately carved interior details of wood, tile, and stone. Above the front lobby entrance, a Portuguese inscription gives the full and proper name for Macau: "City of the Name of God. There is None More Loyal." The term "loyal" was applied to the Macanese after they defiantly flew the flag of Portugal through 60 years of Spanish occupation during the early 17th century. Small rooms on either side are used for art exhibitions.

Up the central staircase is a pair of wrought-iron gates surmounted by a sculptured bas-relief of Queen Leonor, who founded Santa Casa de Misericordia, the oldest medical welfare institution in Asia, surrounded by adorning fans and a pair of angels. Beyond the iron gates is a walled garden with busts of Camoes (left) and Governor Amavel (right) and lovely blue-and-white tile friezes of flowers, dolphins, and cherubs. Walk up the staircase to the Senate Chamber, decorated in traditional Iberian fashion with heavily paneled walls and large wooden chandeliers. Open 1100-1200 and 1500-1600.

The adjacent Senate Library was built in the early '20s and designed after a Northern Portuguese library. The first chamber is plain but the two inner chambers with their wooden balconies and teak paneling are masterpieces of Portuguese woodcarving. Open 1300-1900.

Senate Square Area
The Santa Casa da Misericordia (Holy House of Mercy) still serves the needs of the colony's few remaining lepers as the oldest Christian charity on the China coast. Take a break from all this culture: relax around the fountain or try some Chinese food at Restaurant Long Kei or Macanese food at Cafe Safari. Then walk east, stopping at Kam Pec Casino where the game is electronic craps with digital timers. This so-called "Coolie's Casino" is scheduled for demolition.

Rua Da Felicidade
Macau's aptly named Street of Happiness was a notorious red-light and opium-den district until pressure from the United Nations cleaned the area up in the 1960s. Today the three-storied opium shops/teahouses and hotels/brothels have been converted into respectable establishments and Rua da Felicidade has become

Macau's "Restaurant Row." Farther on is the garish Floating Casino, with a claustrophobic interior but an elaborately carved exterior worth a photograph.

Return to the town square by systematically wandering the side streets filled with vegetable stalls, old women lounging in the sun, cranky rickshaw boys, streetside barbers, schoolkids in neat uniforms, and several Chinese herbalist stores which stand as masterpieces of prewar Chinese architecture.

Occupying three floors of 5 Rua de Outubro is Loc Koc Teahouse, a seedy-yet-authentic restaurant popular for early-morning tea, dim sum, and rice soups. The third floor is often filled with bird fanciers who gather under the high ceiling of wooden pyramid vaults trimmed with carved lintels—a rare example of turn-of-the-century Chinese architecture.

Church Of Saint Dominic
The facade of this beautiful 17th-century baroque church constructed by the Spanish Order of Dominicans features three tiers of Ionic columns with shuttered windows and surprisingly large doors. Inside the pastel interior is a multitiered altar that almost exactly reproduces the shape of the exterior facade. The soaring altar of cream-colored columns and fine statues buried amid baroque embellishments is considered one of Macau's great artistic masterpieces . . . see it without fail. To the left is Our Lady of Fatima, carried through the streets every May. Other works of art include several *santos* figurines with exquisitely carved ivory faces wrapped in gorgeous robes and set inside silver reliquaries. To the rear of the church is a small dusty museum with a disorganized collection of church sculpture. The church is often closed: ring the buzzer on the small gate to the right of the front entrance.

The Facade Of Saint Paul
This haunting wall is Asia's finest monument to Christianity and the most popular sight in all of Macau. Constructed by the Jesuits in the early 17th century, this sermon in stone successfully fuses Occidental and Oriental religious motifs as few structures have ever done.

The front of this architectural masterpiece was designed by an Italian Jesuit after the Gesu Church in Roman and constructed with the as-

sermon in stone

sistance of Japanese Christian artisans who had fled religious persecution in feudal Nagasaki. Since the chapel and its magnificent library were destroyed by a fire in 1835, the great wall has taken on a surreal ghostlike quality, with doors and windows that reveal nothing but open sky.

Top Tier: The center top pediment has a bronze dove (the Holy Spirit or Dove of Peace) surrounded by the sun, moon, and four stars. This spiritual and spatial arrangement symbolizes a fixed moment for the Immaculate Conception.

Fourth Tier: Just below is a bronze statue of Jesus surrounded by writhing vines and the nine instruments of the crucifixion. To the left are pincers, a hammer, a whip, a crown of thorns, and a lance. To the right is a Roman flag, a reed, three nails, and a ladder. Also left of center is an angel with the inscription INRI, to the right an angel with a pillar.

Third Tier: Enshrined centerstage is a bronze statue of the Virgin surrounded by Chinese peonies and Japanese chrysanthemums, symbolizing the blending of Occidental and Oriental faiths. Flanking the Virgin are six angels who pray, play music, and swing incense burners. To the left are three panels carved with the Fountain of Eternal Life, a Portuguese ship watched over by the Virgin, and a ghoulish figure of a woman's body and a devil's head (you guessed it . . . Temptations of the Flesh). To the right are three more panels with the Tree of Life, a

seven-headed dragon being killed by the Virgin, and finally an impaled skeleton/Grim Reaper (not as easy . . . Victory over Death).

Second Tier: This tier seems plain and unfinished when compared to the top three. Flanking the three large windows are four Jesuit saints: Borgia, Loyola, Xavier, and Gonzaga.

Bottom Tier: Inscribed over the main doorway is "Mater Dei" (Mother of God), while the Jesuit symbol N.S.I. (The Holy Name of Jesus) tops the other two doors. Note the floor decorations reminiscent of Florence.

Monte Fortress

During the 16th century both China and Japan forbid their own citizens to conduct foreign trade, leaving that unsavory activity to Western barbarians such as the Portuguese, who earned fabulous profits by controlling the silk, porcelain, and silver markets. The returns were so spectacular that even Portuguese priests invested their savings in merchant ships. Anxious for some of the action, other European powers made overtures to the Chinese and Japanese. In 1622 the Dutch sent an armed fleet to attack the poorly defended citadel of Macau. The city was miraculously saved when Jesuit priests ran up to Monte Fortress, primed the cannons, and made an incredibly lucky shot that landed directly on the enemy's powder supply. A motley crew of Portuguese soldiers, Jesuit priests, and drunken slaves then charged the bewildered Dutch, who turned and fled.

Today the fort serves as a weather station with the best views in Macau. To the west is St. Paul's, Chinese tenements, nigh-rise office buildings, and tropical vegetation. To the east is Hong Kong and north is China. Well-placed cannons remind you of that lucky shot.

Camoes Gardens

Luis Camoes was a famous Portuguese poet whose national epic *Os Lusiadas* tells of the tremendous achievements of 16th-century Portuguese explorers during the great Portuguese Age of Discovery. This short-lived but amazing episode is largely credited to Prince Henry the Navigator, whose mastery of navigational sciences made Portuguese mariners the best informed in the world. Local folklore relates that Camoes was banished to Macau (where he held the dismal post of Purveyor to the Dead in China) after he wrote a biting satire of Portugal's rich and powerful. Up the steps past the *Ficus microcarpa* and *Erthrina indica* flame trees is a bronze bust of Camoes with two stanzas from his famous work. The park is popular with old men who play checkers and fortune-tellers who set up their booths near the entrance.

Camoes Museum

This 18th-century building of whitewashed stone, elegantly curved windows, and green shutters is Macau's principal museum. The building was constructed in the 1770s by a retired merchant and later rented by the British East India Company as a residence for their president. Controlling most of the trade east of the Suez, the British East India Company was one of the richest commercial empires in the world until its charter was repealed in 1833 and private traders such as Jardine and Matheson moved into the lucrative opium business. The final chapter was written in 1841 when Hong Kong opened as a free port and almost all traders abandoned Macau for the new port. This building remained abandoned until being purchased by the Macau government for use as a museum in 1960. The house is an elegant piece of architecture, but the exhibits are unimpressive except for a few bronzes, a Chinese wedding bed, and a collection of opium pipes.

Old Protestant Cemetery And Church

This burial plot for both common sailors and distinguished politicians is situated next to the local headquarters of the British East India Company. Although the doorway dates the cemetery to 1814, the inscriptions of many of the tombstones are often much older, since Macau's Catholic government long refused a cemetery for the Protestants. This punitive measure forced the English to bury their dead outside the city walls until the British East India Company established this cemetery and moved many of the older graves here.

To the left of the entrance is a small Anglican Chapel whose interior seems extraordinarily plain after the elaborate Roman Catholic churches. A sloping path leads down to the well-tended cemetery with the tombstones of the artist George Chinnery, Henry Churchill (a distant relative of Winston Churchill), and Robert Morrison, who compiled the first Chinese version of the Bible. Also buried here are Thomas Beale, the opium king, and dozens of common sailors who died under tragic but sometimes peculiar circumstances. A careful reading of their epitaphs will make Macau's history come to life.

St. Michael's Cemetery

This fascinating Catholic cemetery dating from 1875 is well worth a brief stop. Surrounding the lovely green-and-white Chapel of St. Michael are tombstones capped with dramatic angels, benevolent Virgins, and assorted saints. Grandfather bones are picked clean and then arranged in the proper order to dry on the chapel's roof. Down to the right is a wall of traditional Chinese crypts embedded with somber photographs and festooned with bouquets of plastic flowers. Exorbitant land prices have led to some fairly strange burial practices in Macau and Hong Kong. Full-sized burial plots are rented for a limited time, the remains are then dug up, cleaned by a leading male relative, and finally transferred into the walled crypts.

NORTH MACAU

Restoration Row

About 20 years ago these three-storied yellow-and-red-bricked structures dating from the 1920s were threatened with demolition. Rather than tearing down these Palladian-style residences with their wide verandas and graceful balconies, the government purchased and carefully restored them—one of Southeast Asia's rare cases of architectural preservation. The National Library and National Archives are located here.

Lou Lim Ioc Gardens

Inspired by the traditional designs of Soochow, these peaceful gardens effectively combine classical European architecture with Chinese horticulture. The 19th-century gardens were laid out by a wealthy Chinese businessman whose Victorian home in the rear has been converted into a middle school. The park is maintained (poorly) by the Macau government.

Memorial Home Of Sun Yat-Sen

The Father of Modern China is remembered as the revolutionary hero of the 1911 Revolution,

Macau-Taipa bridge

which toppled the Ching Dynasty and established the modern Chinese republic. Born in 1866 in a small village 30 km north of Macau, Sun attended Oahu College in Hawaii, studied medicine in Hong Kong, and in 1892 returned to Macau to work at the Kiang Vu Hospital. During his brief stay he wrote, lectured, and organized demonstrations against the corrupt Ching Dynasty. Sun then returned to Hawaii and established his first revolutionary society. Sun later served as provisional president of the new Chinese republic and helped found the Kuomintang Party. Sun never lived in this mock-Moorish memorial home but it serves as a reminder of his important position in Chinese history. Unfortunately, the exhibits are meager and poorly exhibited with few English explanations. Open daily except Tuesdays 1000-1300.

College Of Perpetual Help

A pop classic by Carlos Marreiros. Much of Macau's outstanding modern architecture is the creation of young and talented Macanese architects who seem determined to explore new frontiers. Macau's other important modern works include the Walter Johnson-inspired bank by Antonio Bruno Soares, the Pousada de Sao Tiago by Nuno Jorge, Eddie Wong's interiors of Fat Sui Lau Restaurant, and his exterior treatment of Adam's Apple Restaurant. The juxtaposition of old Portuguese shophouses and energetic modern architecture is one of Macau's great surprises.

Guia Fortress

Situated on the highest point in Macau, this 17th-century fort was attacked by the Dutch in 1622 but successfully defended by the Portuguese and their battalion of African Bantu slaves. Inside you'll find a small chapel similar to 17th-century Portuguese hermitages with vaulted ceilings and buttressed walls. The Western-style lighthouse, oldest on the China coast, has been shining continuously since 1865.

Kuan Iam Tong Temple

This 400-year-old temple is Macau's finest showcase of traditional Chinese art and architecture. Dedicated to Kuan Iam (Kuan Yin), Buddhist Goddess of Mercy, this is also the territory's largest and wealthiest temple, an elaborate complex devoted to deities, *joss,* and ancestor veneration. Unlike most other Chinese temples, Kuan Iam Tong is purely Buddhist and not a combination of Buddhism and Taoism. The main temple is guarded by a pair of stone lions clenching granite balls in their mouths. Three turns to the left brings good luck. The interior holds images of past, present, and future Buddhas, plus statues of Kuan Yin, Tin Hau, and Marco Polo with his bulbous European nose and curly beard. To the right are banks of ancestor tablets, beautiful paintings, and bonsai trees carefully twisted into Chinese characters symbolizing long life. The rear courtyard has a stone table surrounded by four granite stools where, in 1844, the United States and China signed their first trade agreement. Forced into this embarrassing treaty after losing the Opium War to the British, the dispirited Manchu emperor refused to sign on Chinese soil.

Mong Ha Fortress

This fortress was built in 1868 overlooking the border to protect against invasion by the Chinese. The long and hot walk up to the summit passes the red-and-orange School of Tourism and Industry, designed by Lima Soares. The weedy old fortress at the top has little of interest except for the direct view of the Barrier Gate into China. To the west is the restored Municipal Market and several small fireworks factories.

Ling Fong Temple

This elaborate but rather dirty temple near the Chinese border is one of the better examples of traditional Chinese architecture in Macau. Rather than exclusively serving the Buddhist faith as Kuan Iam does, Ling Fong serves both Buddhist and Taoist traditions. The facade is carved with a series of bas-reliefs depicting mythological stories, while the interior has images of Tin Hau and her two military companions. The altars on the left hold Chinese deities of art, education, and gambling.

Barrier Gate

Before the door was opened to Western tourists, it was quite a thrill to come up here and peek through binoculars at the Chinese sentry and snap photographs of the forbidden country. Today there is little reason to visit this grubby district of housing complexes and industrial estates.

TAIPA ISLAND

Once an important trading post, Taipa faded into a sleepy backwater until the arching Macau-Taipa bridge was built in 1969. Buses to Taipa and Coloane leave from Ave. Infante D' Henrique. Taxis are about M$40. Near the bridge terminus is the curious and controversial Macau Monument (*Os Calhau,* or "Unformed Stones"), a jumble of falling walls carved in a hopelessly outdated version of social realism—a monument to bad taste and misguided political ambitions.

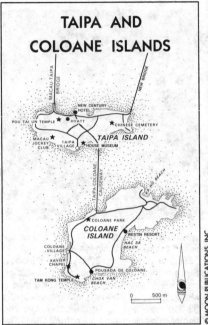

Taipa Village

This sleepy village of Portuguese homes and Chinese shophouses covered with tropical molding now has a few air-conditioned shopping centers surrounding the old Tin Hau and Pak Tai Temple. Eat at Ricardo's Restaurant, perhaps the best Portuguese cafe in Macau. A few fireworks factories still survive in the winding alleys and back streets. On the eastern hill is the century-old Church of Our Lady of Carmel; from there paths lead to the old Praia (waterfront) lined with restored Portuguese mansions and the Taipa Folk Museum, which recreates the living environment of early 20th-century Macanese families.

Macau Jockey Club

Horse races are held afternoons in the new facilities just west of Taipa. Unusual features of the course include an enormous television dish which transmits races to Taiwan and a giant screen to follow the action. Also of interest is the four-headed image of Buddha in the parking lot. It's modeled after images in Bangkok and, appropriately enough, Las Vegas. Farther afield is the cliffside United Chinese Cemetery and the Pou Tai Un Temple with its vegetarian dining room.

COLOANE ISLAND

Much less commercialized than booming Taipa, this tropical island is chiefly known for its relics of Western saints and Oriental martyrs.

Churches And Temples
The cream-and-white Chapel of Saint Francis Xavier has a silver reliquary with the humerus bone of the traveling saint, who died in 1552 on nearby Shangchan Island while awaiting permission to enter China. Except for the arm bone, his remains were returned to Goa by the Japanese Bishop, who was unable to return to Japan because of anti-Christian persecution. The relic was shuttled between the Macau Cathedral and St. Joseph's Seminary before being installed here in 1978. Other boxes in the side chapel contain the bones of Japanese Christians martyred in 1597 at Nagasaki.

On the outskirts of town is the Tam Kong Temple, known for its dragon boat carved from a whale bone almost two meters long.

Beaches
Cheoc Van, Macau's most popular beach, is often muddied by the Pearl River. Try Hac Sa Beach; dark sand but cleaner water. The Hac Sa Sports Complex to the rear is equipped with an Olympic-size swimming pool, a roller-skating rink, and an 18-hole golf course. Both can be reached on foot or by local bus.

PRACTICALITIES

ACCOMMODATIONS

Budget—Central Macau
Prepare yourself for low-end accommodations which are claustrophobic, overpriced, and often closed to Westerners.

Budget hotels are concentrated in Central Macau behind the Sintra Hotel and farther west near the Floating Casino. Budget accommodations in Central Macau cost M$150-180 and are relatively plentiful, but you'll have better luck down near the Floating Casino, where prices drop to M$50-120.

Note that budget hotels in Macau often call themselves *vilas, hospedarias,* or *pensaos* and are generally signposted in Roman script.

Nam Pan: Most of the guesthouses in the streets behind the Sintra Hotel are cramped and reluctant to take Westerners except for the Nam Pan, which has fairly large rooms, will take foreigners, and is probably the best in this neighborhood. 6 Ave. D. Joao, tel. 72289, M$150-180.

Vila Nam Tin: A clean and friendly spot with small rooms with double beds and attached bathrooms. Travia da Praia Grande, tel. 81513, M$150-180.

Vila Meng Meng: A friendly but somewhat overpriced pension on the second floor. 24 Rua Jose Lobo, tel. 89339, M$160-200.

Va Lai Vila: Friendly management and fairly clean rooms make this one of the better spots in this neighborhood. 44 Rua da Praia Grande, tel. 89446, M$180-260.

Budget—Floating Casino Vicinity
Budget travelers will find better guesthouses in the narrow streets on the west side of Macau. Over a dozen small and inexpensive hotels are located on Rua da Lorchas and in the nearby alleys. Conduct a quick search and inspect several hotels if you intend to stay several days in Macau.

From the ferry terminal, take buses 3 or 3A to the far end of Avenue Ribeiro.

Cantao Hotel: Cantao is well located but noisy from paper-thin walls and open ceilings between rooms. Friendly manager. Rua da Guimaraes 62, tel. 922416, M$60-75.

Vong Kong Hospedaria: Moving downscale is this less noisy dive just opposite the Floating Casino. The owner doesn't speak English but he won't get mad when you interrupt his mah-jongg game. Carved cubicles stand at the top of the tiled staircase . . . like a Charlie Chan movie set; you expect to find sultry women and old coolies smoking skinny pipes. 253 Rua da Lorchas, M$25-50.

Hoi Keng Hotel: Tucked away in one of the mazelike alleys is a decent place with slightly better rooms. 153 Rua da Guimaraes, tel. 572033, M$120-150.

Moderate

Several good-value hotels are located near the Floating Casino. Most are old and need repairs, though a few new hotels have recently been constructed. Prices below are weekend rates; ask for a 25-40% discount during the week.

Peninsula Hotel: A new 123-room hotel with clean a/c rooms and private bath. Highly recommended for midlevel travelers. Rua da Lorchas, tel. 318899, M$250-375.

Central Hotel: Macau's Central Hotel, infamous for prostitution and opium, was finally made respectable in the 1950s after pressure from the United Nations. Today, the hotel is safe and within easy walking distance of Macau's restaurants and sights, but rooms are in poor condition and badly need renovation. 26 Ave. Ribeiro, tel. 373309, M$220-280.

Grand Hotel: A clean and comfortable hotel that represents better value than the Central. 146 Ave. Ribeiro, tel. 579922, M$220-280.

London Hotel: Large quiet rooms with private bath in a rather strange location two blocks south of the Floating Casino. 4 Praca Ponte Horta, tel. 937761, M$200-240. Big discounts on weekdays.

Luxury

Macau's top-end accommodations range from standard cookie-cutter hotels to Portuguese *pousadas* and international resorts. Advance reservations are absolutely necessary on weekends, when Macau is flooded with Hong Kong gamblers. Most hotels grant 25-40% discounts during the week, when Macau is practically deserted, but it's usually necessary to ask. Tax and service charges are extra.

In addition to the following hotels, Macau has a Holiday Inn, a Hyatt Regency, a Mandarin Oriental, and the Westin Resort on Coloane Island. It's amazing what a new international airport will do for a territory.

Bela Vista: Perched on top of a small hill and approached from a street to the rear, this was once one of the great, seedy, romantic hotels of Southeast Asia. Rooms with sagging beds and chipping paint were priced under M$70 until the Mandarin Oriental Hotel group completely refurbished the BV in an effort to move it upscale. Very pretty but, like the Raffles in Singapore and the Strand in Rangoon, the colonial atmosphere is forever gone. 8 Rua Comedador Kou Ho Neng, tel. 573821, M$1400-2200.

Lisboa Hotel: Macau's largest hotel-casino complex is also a tourist landmark because of its Las Vegas-styled roofline. Rooms are large, air-conditioned, and equipped with color TVs; the favorite hotel for Chinese gamblers. Avenida da Amizade, tel. 577666, fax 567193, M$750-1200.

Pousada de Sao Tiago: This intimate Portuguese inn inside the ruins of the 17th-century Barra Fort is the finest hotel in Macau—a wonderful place for those who can afford the tariff. Facilities include a small swimming pool, a romantic restaurant, and 23 rooms furnished with Portuguese antiques and thick Chinese carpets. Located at the far southern end of the peninsula. Avenida da Republica, tel. 378111, fax 552170, M$1200-1800.

Hyatt Regency: This Mediterranean-style resort on Taipa Island makes up for its distant location with a fitness center, sports facilities, several restaurants, a disco, a gambling parlor, and first-class rooms. Free transportation is provided from the wharf and the Lisboa Hotel. Taipa Island, tel. 321234, fax 320595, M$1000-1400.

RESTAURANTS

Portuguese-Macanese cuisine is an exotic combination of traditional Portuguese dishes, Chinese cooking styles, and recipes from Portuguese colonies in Africa, India, and South America. Many dishes are hardy stews of meats and seafoods carefully blended with tomatoes, potatoes, and olives. Other specialties are fowl dishes sautéed in heavy oils and prodigious amounts of garlic.

Enjoy wine? Macau offers a good selection of Portuguese wines, ports, and brandies, from sweet Mateus to the drier Dao and Vino Verde, at *exceptionally* low prices. Be sure to bring a bottle back to Hong Kong. Many of Macau's budget Portuguese restaurants are owned and operated by Chinese chefs who prepare daily

A PORTUGUESE MENU

bacalhau: codfish; the favorite seafood of the Portuguese

bacalhau guizado: Portuguese-style codfish stew

bacalhau a bras: codfish shredded and mixed with egg, potatoes, and olives

cabrito: grilled lamb served with chucks of peppers and chilies

caldo verde: potato puree with green vegetables sautéed in olive oil

camoroes: prawns

camoroes biri-biri: large crustaceans, peppered and barbecued over an open fire

carangue jos: crab

carne: beef

coelho: rabbit

feijoada: a traditional Brazilian stew of pork, spicy sausage, rice, and black beans

galinha: chicken

galinha a africanan: African chicken. Strips of chicken are marinated and spiced, then charcoal-broiled or baked in a *tandoori* oven. The classic Macanese dish.

galinha a Portuguesa: chicken baked with potatoes, onion, and eggs, and spiced with saffron, in a rich but mild curry sauce

minche: minced meat baked and sautéed with potatoes and onions

peixe: fish

Portuguese chicken stew: chicken in a delicious coconut and curry stock

sopa: soup

sopa de mariscos: seafood soup

sopa a alentejana: vegetable-and-meat soup

---

specials in addition to the standard fare. An easy way to find the daily specials is to check the local newspaper. Macau's Restaurant Row is near the Floating Casino on Rua da Felicidade.

Henri's Gallery: Macau's classic restaurant is known for giant prawns in spicy sauce, African chicken, and fried rice with Portuguese chorizo. 4 Avenue Republica. Expensive.

Restaurant Fortaleza: The elegantly restored restaurant inside the Pousada de Sao Tiago serves French and Portuguese dishes such as roast sardines and braised rabbit. Expensive.

Estrela do Mar: This restaurant is known for seafood specialties, green vegetable soup, sautéed rabbit, and Brazilian *feijoada*. The cheaper alternative to Henri's. They also have a

budget branch near A Ma Temple. 11 Travessa do Paiva. Moderate.

Bela Vista: The food has been upgraded and prices raised, but the big draw remains the outstanding views from the terrace. Outdoor barbecues on weekends. Expensive.

Nova Koka: Not one of those Chinese-Thai-restaurants-for-tourists but a genuine Thai cafe for girls who work at the massage parlor across the road. Try the *tom yam kung* and the *homok talay,* a delicious seafood mousse. Slow in the evening but packed around 3 a.m. Rual Ferreira do Amaral. Inexpensive.

Fat Sui Lau: Despite the funny name and fancy decor, this popular restaurant serves tasty Portuguese dishes at reasonable prices. 64 Rua da Felicidade. The dozen other restaurants on the street represent the best collection of moderately priced restaurants in Macau.

Riguexo Cafe: This *very* basic cafe serves excellent home-cooked Portuguese meals. Lunches only. Difficult to find, no sign, upstairs and to the rear. 69 Sidonia Pais, Park 'n Shop center. Inexpensive.

More Cheap Eats: The Venda de Cobra snake shop on Rua da Felicidade does a landmark business during the busy winter months. Long Kei on Senate Square is popular for Chinese lunches. Cheap food stalls are found on Rua das Lorchas just opposite the Floating Casino. Bangkok Pochana Restaurant at 31 Rua Ferreira do Amaral near the Sintra Hotel is also crowded with Thai massage girls. Skip the nearly deserted Solmar on Praia Grande and proceed with caution at the Safari near the Senate. Both are surviving on past reputations and convenient locations.

Outlying Islands: Locals claim that Macau's two best Portuguese restaurants are Ricardo's on Taipa Island and Fernando's at Hac Sac Beach, Coloane Island. Macau's big Portuguese chefs often eat here. Moderate.

NIGHTLIFE

Perhaps it was the movie *Macau* or the writings of Ian Fleming that glamorized Macau as a sinful world of brothels, opium dens, and nests of international spies. Nothing could be farther from the truth. Except for some casino action, Macau is one of the sleepiest towns in Southeast Asia. Chinese come to gamble, but you'll probably wind up nursing a bottle of vino in a quiet Portuguese restaurant. Not half bad.

Crazy Paris Show: Try the nightly revue in the Hotel Lisboa only if you have an overwhelming urge to spend your *patacas* on Las Vegas-style dance. Nightly at 2030 and 2200; M$100 weekdays, M$120 weekends.

Paris Night Club: A low-key club in the Hotel Estoril with live entertainment and hostesses. Parisian clubs in a Portuguese colony?

Portuguese Folk Dancing: The Portas do Solo Continental nightclub and restaurant in the Hotel Lisboa has a short but lively dance show.

Massage Parlors: Raunchier nightlife is found in Macau's Thai-style nightclubs and massage parlors in the Lisboa, Sintra, and Estoril hotels. Services are similar but prices exorbitantly higher than in Bangkok or Manila. Massages cost from 150 *patacas* per hour.

GAMBLING

Macau's casinos, greyhounds, harness racing, and jai alai annually bring in over US$300 million. This money machine is controlled by Sociedade De Turismo e Diversoes de Macau (STDM), a government-licensed gambling syndicate which operates several hotels, runs the world's largest fleet of hydrofoils, and largely supports the government of Macau. Profits are funneled back into social and welfare projects such as low-income housing schemes, entertainment ventures, bridges, airports, and translating volumes of Portuguese laws into Chinese.

Casinos: This Vegas of the East isn't really much like Las Vegas or Monaco. Forget about extravagant architecture and a glamorous crowd dressed in tuxedos and sequined gowns— Macau's five casinos are utilitarian structures filled with gamblers dressed in soiled sweaters and sloppy sports jackets. Curious visitors might wander through the 24-hour Lisboa Hotel casino or try their luck at the luxurious Mandarin Oriental Hotel casino. Moving downscale is the ornately decorated Floating Casino and old Kam Pek Casino (scheduled for demolition), where upstairs gamblers use wicker baskets to lower their bets. Note the sign: "Only risk what you can afford to lose."

Macau's casinos offer Western games like blackjack, roulette, and slots (called "hungry tigers" by the Chinese), and Chinese games such as *fan-tan* and *dai sui*. The former is an extraordinarily simple and boring game played with a pile of porcelain buttons while the latter ("big and small") is an equally obvious game played with three dice. Both rely more on luck than skill.

A word of warning about Macanese poker. Local casinos are filled with professional card sharks who prey on Japanese tourists and Westerners who don't understand the unusual odds: rather than the standard deck, a 40-card deck is used with twos, threes, and fours removed; the fewer cards guarantee higher hands, encouraging amateurs to seriously overestimate the value of their hands. Poker is played for table stakes, making it easy for well-financed professionals with enormous arsenals of cash to easily force underfinanced amateurs to fold. Also, beware of the surly croupiers who encourage gamblers to make foolish bets and extort tips of HK$50-200 from winners.

Horse Racing: Macau's gambling possibilities include more than just casinos. Flat racing has returned to Macau after a half-century gap. Punters gather at the Macau Jockey Club on Taipa Island on weekend afternoons. Admission tickets can be purchased at the Lisboa Hotel; buses leave just opposite.

Greyhound Racing: Held in the open-air Canidrome five times weekly at 2000. Computerized totalisators handle all bets such as quinellas, trifectas, and six-ups.

For my part, I travel not to go anywhere, but to go.
I travel for travel's sake. The great affair is to move.

—Robert Louis Stevenson

MALAYSIA

*Travel is fatal to prejudice, bigotry, and narrow-mindedness,
and many of our people need it sorely on these accounts. Broad,
wholesome, charitable views of men and things cannot be acquired
by vegetating in one little corner of the earth all one's lifetime.*
—Mark Twain,
The Innocents Abroad

*A good traveler is one who does not know where he is going to,
and a perfect traveler does not know where he came from.*
—Line Yutang

*If you reject the food, ignore the customs, fear the
religion and avoid the people, you might better
stay home.*

—James Michener

INTRODUCTION

Perhaps it was the literature of Conrad or Maugham, Kipling or Wallace, or those old British films that formed our images of Malaysia: an exotic land of thick jungle and tropical rainforest filled with aboriginal headhunters, murderous pirates, man-eating tigers, and shaggy orangutans; a romantic crossroads of Asian trade lanes where White Rajahs sipped their evening *stengahs* on the edge of immense rubber plantations; an intoxicating colonial empire of ambitious traders, rugged planters, tin miners, sailors, government servants, and British administrators. While these early stories tell of a Malaysia now largely transformed by the West, the impression remains of a tropical hideaway full of adventure and excitement.

This reputation as an exotic destination attracts increasing numbers of Western tourists each year, yet Malaysia is also one of Southeast Asia's most affluent and progressive countries. The signs are everywhere. City youngsters are more interested in trendy fashions and progressive rock than top spinning or hand-stamped batik. A highway of American standards stretches along the West Coast from Singapore to the edge of Thailand. And the steel-and-glass city of Kuala Lumpur hardly differs from Munich or Los Angeles. While this modernization has watered

down some of Malaysia's primitive appeal, it has also brought a well-ordered transportation system, excellent hotels, clean restaurants, and (wonder of wonders) tap water you can safely drink. Malaysia is exotic but comfortable, a delightful change after the poverty and rigors of travel in other Asian countries. Although the country admittedly offers few impressive temples or historic monuments, a great deal of traditional culture survives through the spectacular festivals of the Indian, Chinese, and Malay communities. Malaysia is also a land of great natural beauty, from expansive national parks and river journeys in Borneo to tropical jungles and deserted beaches in Peninsular Malaysia. Beyond all these superb attractions, Malaysia has terrific food, classic architecture in the West Coast cities, and a unique multiracial community which makes the country a fascinating political and social destination.

THE ENVIRONMENT

The Land
Situated in the very heart of Southeast Asia, Malaysia is geographically divided into two basic areas: Peninsular Malaysia, the thin but bul-

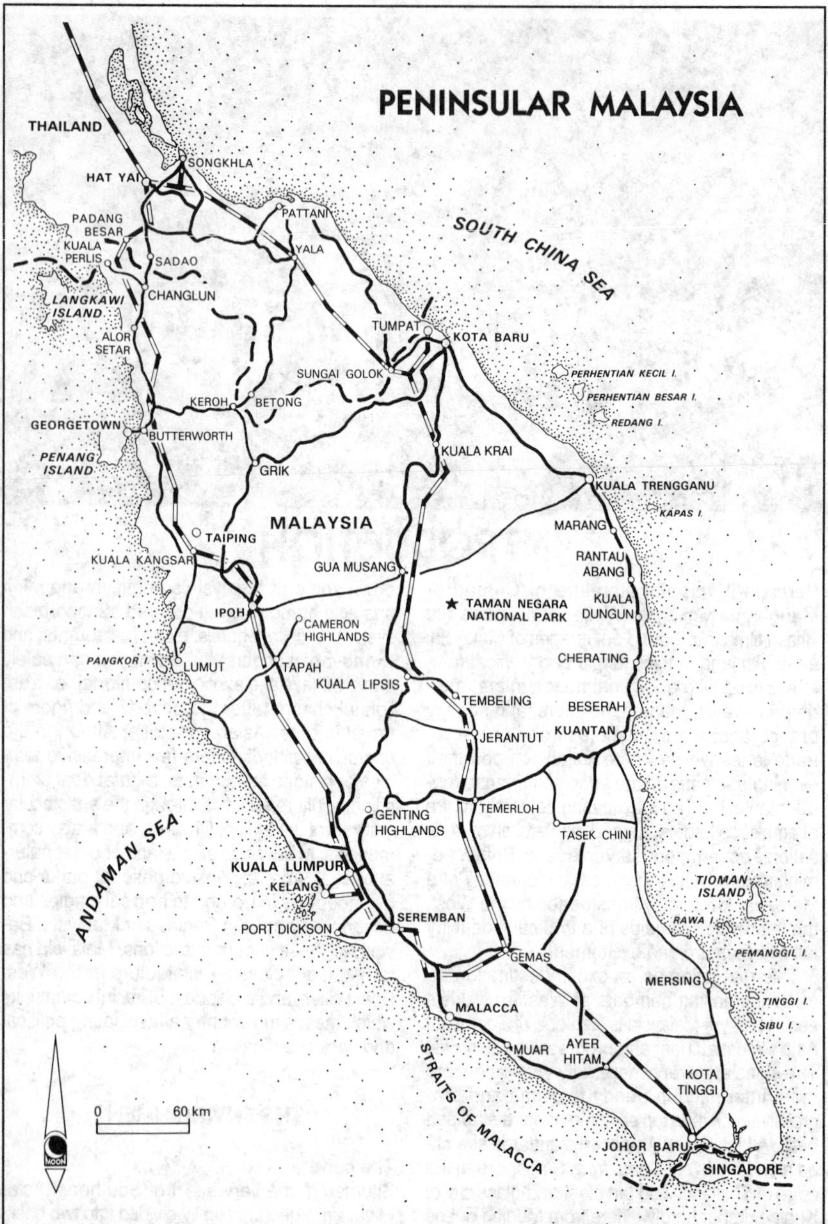

PENINSULAR MALAYSIA

THAILAND

HAT YAI
SONGKHLA
PADANG BESAR
KUALA PERLIS
SADAO
CHANGLUN
PATTANI
YALA

SOUTH CHINA SEA

LANGKAWI ISLAND
ALOR SETAR
TUMPAT
KOTA BARU
SUNGAI GOLOK

PERHENTIAN KECIL I.
PERHENTIAN BESAR I.
REDANG I.

GEORGETOWN
PENANG ISLAND
KEROH
BETONG
BUTTERWORTH
GRIK
KUALA KRAI
KUALA TRENGGANU
KAPAS I.

MALAYSIA
TAIPING
GUA MUSANG
MARANG
RANTAU ABANG
KUALA KANGSAR

★ TAMAN NEGARA NATIONAL PARK

KUALA DUNGUN

PANGKOR I.
IPOH
CAMERON HIGHLANDS
CHERATING

LUMUT
TAPAH
KUALA LIPSIS
TEMBELING
BESERAH

ANDAMAN SEA

JERANTUT
KUANTAN

GENTING HIGHLANDS
TEMERLOH
TASEK CHINI

KUALA LUMPUR
KELANG

TIOMAN ISLAND
RAWA I.

PORT DICKSON
SEREMBAN
GEMAS
PEMANGGIL I.

MALACCA
MERSING
TINGGI I.
SIBU I.

MUAR
AYER HITAM
KOTA TINGGI

STRAITS OF MALACCA

JOHOR BARU
SINGAPORE

0   60 km

MOON

© MOON PUBLICATIONS, INC.

RAINFALL IN MALAYSIA
(measured in millimeters)

	Jan.	Feb.	March	April	May	June	July	Aug.	Sept.	Oct.	Nov.	Dec.
Kuala Lumpur	168	145	213	302	179	129	112	132	167	270	259	225
Malacca	89	100	138	182	164	176	182	177	209	216	237	142
Penang	67	93	139	214	248	177	203	231	344	375	251	107
Kota Baru	171	60	85	845	116	134	152	164	192	298	677	588
Kuantan	318	167	155	175	189	163	157	177	226	276	326	590
Kota Kinabalu	139	66	71	118	209	317	273	262	305	336	297	240
Kuching	664	532	334	289	256	200	191	209	274	335	339	466

bous piece of land that fattens out like one of Popeye's arms before being joined by the Johor Causeway to the island nation of Singapore, and Insular Malaysia, almost 1,000 km to the east. East or Insular Malaysia includes Sabah and Sarawak, the two Malaysian states which share the tropical island of Borneo with the Indonesian state of Kalimantan. Most of the country, except for the alluvial plain on the West Coast of the peninsula, is mountainous and covered with tropical jungle. Although it appears to be a gigantic nation, Malaysia actually covers a total land area only slightly larger than New Mexico, or England without Wales.

Flora
As you might expect in a tropical land located between one and seven degrees north of the equator, the flora of Malaysia is luxurious and abundant. Dense tropical forests, estimated to be over 100 million years old, cover almost half the country. Among the 15,000 different species of plants which thrive in Malaysian jungles are over 5,000 kinds of trees, including prized hardwoods such as ebony, teak, and sandalwood. Among the most flamboyant flora are the flowering trees such as flame of the forest (Delonix regia) from Madagascar and the tulip tree (Spathodea campanulata) from West Africa.

Because of its immense forest reserves and aggressive logging policies, Malaysia is now one of the world's largest exporters of tropical hardwood. But as in Indonesia, Thailand, and the Philippines, the hardwood forests of Malaysia have been felled at a breathless—even reckless—pace. Environmental groups such as Friends of the Earth and senior officials in the Malaysian Forestry Department claim that, at present rates of logging, most of the country's tropical rainforests will be gone by the year 2020. Allocation of timber concessions is a jealously guarded source of political and economic patronage (Sarawak's minister of the environment is also the owner of several valuable logging concessions), and unless international diplomacy can turn the tide, it appears certain that Malaysia will end up like the Philippines, a once-timber-rich country stripped of trees and now forced to import finished wood products. (More information under "Sabah," below.)

Climate
Malaysia has a typical tropical climate with high temperatures, extreme humidity, and heavy rainfall during the two monsoon seasons. Total annual rainfall is relatively evenly distributed throughout the year, since the climate is somewhat moderated by the Indonesian island of Sumatra. The southwest monsoon from June to September brings intermittent but light rains to the West Coast of Peninsular Malaysia. The northeast monsoon from November to February brings heavy rains and strong winds to the East Coast. Roads and bridges are often washed out and week-long delays are commonplace. Check the weather forecasts and move to the

SUGGESTED TIMETABLES FOR MALAYSIA

AREA	2 WEEKS	3 WEEKS	4 WEEKS	8 WEEKS
Penang Island	1 week	1 week	1 week	1 week
Kuala Lumpur	2 days	2 days	2 days	2 days
Hill Resorts	3 days	3 day	3 days	3 days
Malacca	2 days	2 days	2 days	2 days
East Coast	—	1 week	2 weeks	2 weeks
Sabah/Sarawak	—	—	—	4 weeks

West Coast when rains become oppressive. Sabah and Sarawak are difficult to travel in during the monsoons from November to February.

HISTORY

Due to its important geographical position on the trade lanes between Asia and Europe, Malaysia has been inundated by waves of conquerors, traders, and colonialists during its long and complicated history. First on the scene were the dark-skinned and kinky-haired Negritos who still live in the jungles of Peninsular Malaysia. These indigenous people were driven from the lowlands into the interior forest by Proto-Malays from southern China who arrived several millenia before Christ. Deutero-Malays, a more advanced people, arrived next, bringing their Iron and Bronze Age culture to the peninsula before continuing southward toward the Indonesian archipelago. These groups eventually merged to form the modern Malay communities of Indonesia, the Philippines, and Malaysia. Malaysia entered recorded history during the early Christian Era, when much of Southeast Asia came under the influence of Indianized kingdoms such as the Dravidian states in Southern India and the Funanese Empire in the lower Mekong Delta. The decline and breakup of Funan in the 6th century led to the rise of the Mon Dvaravati Kingdom in Thailand and, more importantly to the history of Malaysia, the maritime empire of Srivijaya, centered near Palembang on Sumatra. Influenced by India but also the first empire with Malay roots, Srivijaya became immensely powerful in the 8th century by controlling the Straits of Malacca, the remarkably narrow channel which funnels most of the trade between China and India. This Islamic empire fell five centuries later to the Majapahit Empire of Java, an expansionist dynasty which exerted strong cultural and political influence over the Malaysian Peninsula while balancing the territorial ambitions of the Thais at Ayuthaya.

Malacca

Modern Malaysian history began in 1401 when Paramesara, a refugee prince-consort from Palembang, fled Sumatra to Singapore and then Malacca, a small *orang laut* village with excellent harborage and an outstanding location between China, India, and the Indonesian Spice Islands. Malacca blossomed and soon became the center of Eastern commerce, diffusing Islam throughout Southeast Asia while controlling the legendary spice route which stretched from the Malukus to Europe. Traders met to exchange Chinese silks, Japanese gold, Banda pearls, Malaysian tin, Ming potteries, exotic feathers, and highly prized spices such as cloves, mace, nutmeg, and sandalwood. Early sultans adopted sensible open-trade policies and held duties at attractively low levels, two smart moves which ensured continued vitality for the young port. But greed and the Christian desire to confront the rising tide of Islam attracted European powers, notably the Portuguese, who, under the leadership of Alfonso de Albuquerque, had established a string of economic and military outposts from Africa to the Malukus. Anxious to compete with the Arab traders who had monopolized the spice trade since the Middle Ages, the Portuguese took Malacca in 1511. Early profits were encouraging, but sky-high duties, repressive taxes, and ill-conceived conversion attempts outraged the local population, who abandoned the city for friendlier ports. The city later fell to the Dutch, though they ignored the port in lieu of Jakarta, and finally to the British, who regarded Malacca as the poor stepsister to Penang and Singapore.

The British

Anxious to protect their lucrative tea and opium trade with China, the British East India Company, led by the young and ambitious Sir Francis Light, established a free-trade port on the jungle-covered island of Penang in 1786. Penang remained the region's major trading port until 1819, when Raffles established Singapore after obtaining the tiger-infested island from the sultan of Johor. The superb geographical location of Singapore and Raffles's enlightened leadership made the island an overnight success. Thousands of Chinese immigrants, merchants, and traders flooded the young city, anxious to escape the horrors of feudal China and hopefully make their fortunes in the New China. Singapore, Malacca, and Penang were combined to form the British Straits settlement in 1826. Singapore was declared capital of the British interests in 1832.

The late 19th and early 20th centuries were a period of great change for Malaysia. The European industrial revolution fueled the growth of tin and rubber industries, two dangerous and difficult enterprises which held little appeal to the local Malays. To keep their economic machinery in proper running order and fill labor shortages in tin mines and on rubber plantations, British colonialists actively encouraged thousands of Chinese and Indians to emigrate to Malaysia. This self-serving act profoundly changed the racial composition and political history of the country. In addition, local sultanates foolishly battled between themselves, enabling British authorities to gradually extend their suzerainty over the war-torn peninsula. British rule failed to create a modern nation-state, but peace was established, the economy boomed, and Malay political power was protected against the encroaching mercantilism of the Chinese. By the 1920s, all of Peninsular Malaysia had fallen under British control.

World War II

In a lightning attack which completely surprised Allied commanders in Southeast Asia, the Japanese army landed at Kota Baru in December 1941. From there, they quickly drove their tanks and rode their bicycles toward Singapore, the so-called Gibraltar of the East. Impregnable Singapore fell to Japanese forces in only three months, an embarrassing debacle which forever smashed the myth of white superiority. Promising a Greater Asian Co-Prosperity Sphere, the Japanese occupied Malaya and immediately rounded up tens of thousands of Allied soldiers and civilians who were beaten, tortured, starved, and marched off to die in the construction of Siam's death railway. Malays were also mistreated, but the worst cruelty was reserved for the Chinese, executed in shocking numbers by the Japanese Kempetai before being dumped into mass graveyards. Many fled into the jungles where they formed resistance units sympathetic to communist and Maoist ideology. After Hiroshima and the defeat of the Japanese, these communist freedom fighters initiated a violent counterrevolution against British occupation forces. The struggle finally ended in November 1989 when legendary communist leader Chin Peng, who had led the party since the late 1940s, agreed to give up his armed struggle and leave his jungle stronghold.

Independence

British agreements to grant total independence to the Malays after WW II were complicated by divisions of political power between the Chinese and Malays. The former were 19th-century immigrants who by then almost completely dominated the Malaysian economy, the latter the indigenous peoples who intensely feared the power of the Chinese. Realizing that British departure would leave both economic and political control in the hands of the Chinese, the once-disinterested Malays organized themselves into a political coalition determined to preserve Malay rights and privileges. Political power was ultimately secured by the Malays, but economic control was left with the Chinese, an unsatisfactory but seemingly irreversible situation which continues to the present day.

Malaya was granted independence in 1957 and changed its name to Malaysia in 1963 after Sabah and Sarawak agreed to join the new republic, a strategic move which helped maintain a Malay racial majority against the Chinese-dominated island of Singapore. This marriage was aborted in 1965 when Singapore was ejected from the new coalition on the grounds of po-

SIGHTSEEING HIGHLIGHTS

Malaysia's Tourist Development Corporation divides the country into four specific regions: Kuala Lumpur/ Malacca, Penang/Langkawi, the East Coast, and Sabah/Sarawak. A better division would be West Coast, East Coast, and Sabah/Sarawak, since most travelers arriving from Singapore or Thailand are limited by time constraints to one or possibly two of the three.

West Coast

Malaysia's most highly developed region is characterized by modern cities, efficient expressways, and a hard-working Chinese population intent on improving their financial standing. Penang is the most fascinating stop on the West Coast, but other highlights include exploring the historic town of Malacca and the vibrant capital of Kuala Lumpur, relaxing at the former British hill resort of Cameron Highlands, and trekking through the rainforest of Taman Negara National Park.

Kuala Lumpur: Spruced up several years ago for an international travel symposium, the cosmopolitan city of Kuala Lumpur (KL) now resembles the futuristic but architecturally diverse city of Singapore. Highlights include the National Museum (perhaps the finest in all of Southeast Asia), Moorish architecture left behind by the British, spectacular modern architecture, and a vibrant Chinatown that becomes a fascinating street bazaar at sunset. Kuala Lumpur is a compact town that can be easily toured in a day or two.

Malacca: Melaka (Malaysian spelling), historical capital of Malaysia, has been occupied since the 15th century by Portuguese, Dutch, and British forces who left behind a selection of worthwhile forts and churches. Although the modern city has little charm, the old quarters' nostalgic architecture and sense of intimacy makes Malacca a worthwhile stop between Singapore and Kuala Lumpur.

Beaches: West Coast islands such as Langkawi and Pankor are attractive and have decent beaches, but hotel facilities, restaurants, and nightlife are much better on the islands of southern Thailand. On the other hand, Langkawi is recommended for those visitors who seek solitude and want to get somewhat off the beaten track.

Cameron Highlands: Offering a pleasant escape from the oppressive heat of the coastal lowlands, Cameron and other former British hill resorts are ideal places to relax, read a good book, and wander through tea plantations. Cameron is the largest and most scenic of Malaysia's four hill resorts.

Taman Negara National Park: Situated midway between the coasts and accessible from Kuala Lumpur, Singapore, or Kuantan on the East Coast, Malaysia's largest and most popular park offers river excursions, jungle trekking, and wildlife observatories. Tigers and wild elephants are rarely seen these days, although it's perhaps the easiest place in Asia to experience the wonders of a primeval tropical jungle.

Penang: This wonderfully eccentric and somewhat seedy old town is the premier tourist destination in Malaysia. Populated by Chinese, Tamils, and Malays, Penang is full of delightful character, charm, personality, great food, good beaches, romantic old hotels, elaborate temples, and fascinating architecture dating from the turn of the century. If you only have time for one stop on the West Coast, make it Penang.

East Coast

The East Coast of peninsular Malaysia remains a relatively undisturbed and traditional land despite a pair of major highways which now link it with the West Coast. This is where Malays, rather than Chinese, control the economy, where the call of Islam is stronger than that of Confucianism, and where a leisurely lifestyle is prized over material possessions. Large, modern towns such as Kota Baru, Kuala Trengganu, and Kuantan have little to recommend them, but the pristine beaches and sleepy fishing villages almost completely untouched by mass tourism are worth visiting. Two words of caution: Beaches are clean and untouristy, though not as spectacular as the hyperbole churned out by the local tourist office. Secondly, although the East Coast is an extremely relaxing destination, single women and travelers in search of an escapist holiday should note that a resurgence of fundamentalist Islam has dramatically affected the mood and tolerance level on the East Coast. This is especially critical in the conservative state of Trengganu, which is *not* the place to drink, find romance, or sunbathe in a skimpy bathing suit.

Tioman Island: Tioman is a large, lovely, densely forested island two hours by boat from Mersing. A first-class resort here has a golf course, plus a half-dozen inexpensive chalets strung along a fairly nice (but not great) beach. Restaurants are simple and nightlife is nonexistent, but the skin diving and jungle trekking are superb.

SIGHTSEEING HIGHLIGHTS

Cherating: Best choice for *kampong* atmosphere and privacy on the 710-km coastline that stretches from Singapore to Thailand is the secluded cove of Cherating. Club Med has constructed an outpost here but most visitors stay in simple wooden chalets set in a beautiful coconut grove. Cherating is the up-and-coming star attraction on the East Coast, undiscovered by mass tourism yet popular enough to be fun.

Leatherback Turtles at Rantau Abang: One of the most impressive natural phenomena of Southeast Asia is the annual arrival of leatherback turtles at Rantau Abang from May to September. Visitors to the beach wait patiently at seaside cafes for one of the immense *Dermochels coriacea* to struggle up the steep beach to bury her eggs in a shallow hole, an eerie and unforgettable experience. Accommodations range from inexpensive bungalows to some of the finest resorts on the East Coast.

Marang: Home to Malay customs and traditions, the East Coast is the ideal place to learn about Malay pastimes, arts, crafts, hobbies, sports, entertainments, value systems, and lifestyles. Most people live in small villages called *kampongs* and arrange their lives around the precepts of Islam. Although superbly idyllic and postcard beautiful, Malay *kampongs* are often difficult for Westerners to visit because of conservative attitudes and distrust of outsiders. Marang, however, one of the prettiest villages in Malaysia, is somewhat accustomed to curious outsiders and a reasonably good place to experience life in a Malay *kampong*. Marang has several sets of inexpensive bungalows.

Sabah And Sarawak

These two states on the island of Borneo are for those travelers who enjoy long river trips, ethnological explorations, vast caves, tremendous national parks, and mountain climbing to the highest summit in Southeast Asia. Like other isolated regions, the rarely visited states of Sabah and Sarawak are somewhat expensive and time-consuming to explore.

litical aggression. Racial tensions—always bubbling gently beneath the calm surface of Malaysian society—came to a boil in 1969 when 248 people died in racial riots and the government of Malaysia's first prime minister, Tunku Abdul Rahman, was toppled. This racial uprising also led to the creation of the New Economic Policy, a government program which seeks to restructure society and eliminate poverty among the indigenous Malays.

THE PEOPLE

Malaysia is a multiracial country with an estimated population of 18 million people. Eighty-two percent of the people live in Peninsular Malaysia, 10% in Sarawak, and 8% in Sabah. Malays comprise 48% of the population, the Chinese make up 35%, Indians 10%, and various indigenous tribal groups account for the balance. Although the largest racial group in the country, the Malays' less than 50% is a significant statistic in light of the political and economic equation. These races—Malay, Chinese, Indian, and tribals—have historically kept their distance from each other by following their own religions, doing different kinds of work, and living in separate communities. Incorporating this range of ethnic groups under one national flag has largely shaped Malaysia's political and economic structure, besides remaining an endless source of fascination to specialists on Asia.

Malays

Article 160 of the Malay constitution defines a Malay as a person who follows Islam, speaks Malay as the mother language, and conforms to Malay customs. Malays are of a mixed ethnic background, some having lived in the country for millennia while others are recent immigrants from Sumatra, Java, Sulawesi, Borneo, and other Indonesian islands. Malays, in fact, come from the same basic racial stock as people of the Philippines and Indonesia. A warm and extremely hospitable group with refined sensibilities and gracious manners, Malays typically live in rural villages and prefer the occupations of farmer and fisherman rather than urban businessman or entrepreneur.

Together with the Ibans, Kadazans, Melanaus, and other tribals living in East Malaysia, Malays constitute the Bumiputras, a government-recognized racial group. Being a "Son of

AFFIRMATIVE ACTION— MALAY STYLE

Malaysia faces several economic challenges. Most serious is the uneven distribution of income between West and East Malaysia, between urban and rural residents, and most dramatically, between Malays and Chinese. As in nearly all other countries in Southeast Asia, the economy of Malaysia is controlled by the Chinese. UMNO Baru and the Malay people are determined to change this equation through their New Economic Policy (NEP), an ambitious government program aimed at eradicating poverty and restructuring society through a more equitable distribution of the country's wealth. NEP's major goal is to increase Malay Bumiputra (literally "Sons of the Soil") ownership of shares in public limited companies. In 1971, foreigners owned 62% of the nation's corporate wealth, the Chinese controlled 36%, and the Bumiputra owned less than 4%. As a result of the NEP, foreigners today have seen their corporate equity slashed to 30%, the Chinese have increased theirs to 50%, and the Malays hold some 20% of Malaysian equity. Although a dramatic improvement over 1970 levels, it remains far short of the 30% promised to Malays by 1990. Even this 20% figure is questionable, since many businesses transferred from Chinese to Malay ownership are only transactions that paper over continued Chinese control. The NEP has also come under a great deal of criticism from foreign corporations and Chinese entrepreneurs who say it discourages individual enterprise and institutionalizes widespread racial discrimination against the Chinese. Critics also charge that the NEP has primarily benefited well-connected Bumiputra, helping few of the poor Malays who still work in the ricefields. Despite unending complaints and apparent shortcomings, the NEP has been extended past its 1990 deadline, since many powerful politicians believe it plays an important role as peacemaker between the races.

the Soil" has great advantages. Most government positions are given to Bumis, 80% of university openings are reserved for them, job priority is enjoyed even when a Bumi is less qualified than a Chinese, low-cost loans are plentiful for Bumi businesses, and most government licenses are, by law, awarded to them. Statistics show that Malays hold 80% of all government executive jobs, are granted 85% of all college scholarships, and receive 95% of all government land distributed to settlers. Malays can, at times, be somewhat defensive about their privileges, arguing that they were first in the country and were discriminated against by British colonialists who favored the Chinese and the Indians. Chinese, on the other hand, consider the Malays lazy, uneducated, and, perhaps worst of all, less than shrewd. Both Chinese and Indians resent the Malays' political domination and preferential treatment—especially the educational bias in favor of the Bumiputras—but largely accept these affirmative-action programs as necessary conditions for national peace and reconciliation.

Chinese

Malaysia's other large ethnic group is the Chinese, who arrived in large numbers in the late 19th century to work on the rubber plantations and in the tin mines. Between 1897 and 1927, when the disintegrating Manchu Dynasty could no longer enforce emigration restrictions, some six million Chinese fled the twin scourges of war and famine to find their fortunes in Southeast Asia. Most of Malaysia's Chinese emigrated from Kwangtung and Fukien provinces, from the towns of Amoy, Swatow, and Canton. Early immigrants settled into various lifestyle groupings: Babas, who descended from mixed Malay-Chinese marriages and developed a unique Sino-Malay culture; Straits Chinese who followed Chinese lifestyles modified by generations of life in Malaysia; and Straits-born Chinese who held to a culture as purely Chinese as possible. Together they formed microcosms of southern China as reflected in their various dialects, foods, marriage customs, funeral rites, and variety of religious and superstitious beliefs. Hokkiens became prosperous through trading and shopkeeping. Cantonese cleared the jungles, dug for tin, and tapped rubber. Rivalries between their various tongs (secret societies) were often violent and frightfully bloody, but peace was restored, and by the early 20th century the Chinese largely controlled the economy. Today they drive the Mercedes in Penang, own the stately mansions in Kuala Lumpur, and keep the wheels turning in the gambling casinos at Genting Highlands. While Malays might consider them usurious moneylenders and tight-fisted merchants,

Malay market day

Mandarin-speaking teachers were appointed to Chinese primary schools and the government banned Mandarin language courses from public universities. Discrimination is typically less obvious: a ban on the use of Chinese characters at a seafood festival in Johor State, university courses taught in Malay only, and the compulsory wearing of traditional Malay headdresses for non-Malay university graduates.

Indians

Malaysia's third-largest ethnic group was brought to the country by the British in the 19th century to work the rubber plantations. Most Indians are Dravidians from South India who speak Tamil, Telugu, or Malayalam, but Punjabis can be found in the larger cities working in railways, bureaucracies, and professional occupations. Most originally came from lower castes, economic and social classes which have largely disappeared in Malaysia through acculturation and intermarriage with locals.

Indigenous Peoples

Several other groups share Malaysia with the Malays, Chinese, and Indians. Largest of these *orang asli* ("original men") are the 40,000 Senoi or Sakai who live a seminomadic existence in the central foothills. Most are now Westernized and wear blue jeans rather than loincloths, though some continue to hunt with their traditional blowguns near the Cameron Highlands. The second-largest tribal group is the Jakun, Proto-Malays of the southern peninsula who have generally adopted a sedentary farming life. The northern regions of Peninsular Malaysia are home to Negritos or Semang, a short and kinky-haired people who continue their age-old nomadic hunting and gathering rituals, speak a Mon-Khmer language, and are respected by Malays for their prowess in witchcraft and magic. Sabah and Sarawak are ethnological gold mines of Land Dayaks, Sea Dayaks, Punans, Bajaus, Muruts, and dozens of other small groups.

most would agree that the economic miracle of Malaysia is largely due to the admirable work ethic of the Chinese.

Race is a thorny and complex issue here in Malaysia, but it boils down to this: the Malays control the political machinery and want more economic power, the Chinese control the economy and want more political power. As mentioned before, racial discrimination against the Chinese has become government policy supported by the New Economic Policy. But not everyone agrees that the Malays are an indigenous race; tribals roamed the peninsula long before the Malays arrived. Therefore, the Chinese claim, everybody's an immigrant—a line of logic that understandably infuriates the Malays.

Pragmatists to the extreme, Chinese generally accept Malay leadership in the political life of the country but deeply resent government meddlings in Chinese culture. The biggest clashes have revolved around the government's Bahasa Malaysia language policy, which seeks to unify the country by encouraging everyone to speak Malay. Tempers flared recently after non-

RELIGION

Islam is the state religion of Malaysia. Nearly all Malays are Sunni Muslims who follow the orthodox Shafie school of interpretation and five fundamental precepts of the Koran: profession

Hindu marriage

of faith, daily prayer, religious alms to support the poor, a fast during Ramadan, and a pilgrimage to Mecca. Islam in Malaysia has important political and economic significance. Symbolizing Malay supremacy over non-Bumiputras, it now permeates every level of society, culture, and political affiliation. UMNO maintains an image of an Islamic party in response to the nationwide increase of Islamic consciousness. Laws have been passed, an Islamic bank established, and a government-supported Islamic university now teaches traditional law. PAS, the opposition Party of Islam, which seeks to make Malaysia an Islamic state governed by an Islamic constitution and ruled by Islamic law, has made great strides in recent years. Although a radical party primarily supported by poor rural-based Malays, what began as the extremist Malaysian Islamic Youth Movement in the '70s has now gained respectability with the Malaysian middle class. No longer are *dakwah* (proselytizing Muslims) limited to nonconformist youth or students disappointed by economic inequality brought on by Western capitalism. The rise of right-wing Islam is most apparent on the East Coast where women wear black robes and remain veiled in *purdah*, while *dakwah* of the hard-line Darul Arqam community can be seen with their long black robes, green headgear, and trademark goatees hanging from their chins. And despite many middle-class Malays being disturbed by these developments, few dare speak out for fear of being labeled anti-Islam, infidel, or *murtad* (deviant within the faith). Travelers should remember that Islam is one of the five sensitive subjects whose special position must not be questioned and which are protected under the Sedition Act.

Under pressures from the ultraconservative PAS and Islamic student organizations, the legal trend in Malaysia has been one of gradual and officially sponsored adherence to the stricter tenets of *shariah* (Islamic) law. The Non-Islamic Religions Act of 1988—a measure which forbids conversion attempts on behalf of any religion except Islam—was used to arrest Christian missionaries who proselytize among Muslims. A major constitutional amendment the same year ended the rights of the civil bench to overrule a *shariah* court decision. Legislation has also been proposed to require Malay women to cover all but their hands and faces in public. Punishment administered by Islamic *shariah* courts seems extraordinarily harsh by Western standards: whippings for the consumption of alcohol, *khalwat* (close proximity between the sexes), and *zina* (illicit sex); the amputation of thieves' hands; the stoning to death of adulterers; the crucifixion of murderers. Worldwide press was given to a 1987 case in which a young man was whipped six times with a cane for drinking liquor and committing *khalwat* . . . in a Kota Baru restaurant. Islamic law currently applies to Muslims only, but political pressure to enforce *shariah* laws uniformly on all people has frightened both the Chinese and Indian communities.

FESTIVALS

The multiracial and multireligious nation of Malaysia celebrates a staggering number of festivals, from Indian *pujas* to Chinese celebrations of the dead. All offer the visitor an excellent opportunity to discover something of Malaysia's rich and varied culture. Some festivals are national affairs held throughout the country, while others are confined to individual states. Most are connected with either Islam, Buddhism, Hinduism, or Chinese social dictums. Among the most memorable are the birthdays of the sultans, a rare chance to see traditional Malay performing arts. State holidays are fixed by the Western Gregorian calendar. Most religious festivals tend to float around the calendar since they are moveable feasts based on cycles of the moon; exact dates can be checked with the tourist office. Chinese and Hindu festivals are described in greater detail in the Singapore chapter, Buddhist festivals under Thailand.

January
Birthday of the Sultan of Kedah: 25 January. Aside from Sabah, Sarawak, and Penang, each state in Malaysia has a sultan who celebrates his birthday with great pageantry. East-coast venues provide outstanding opportunities to experience traditional Malay culture. Performances during the week-long festivities usually include *wayang kulit* (shadow puppets), *makyong* (traditional theater performed by females), *nogo* dance, and demonstrations of *pencak silat* (martial arts). Kite-flying, top-spinning, and bird-singing competitions are also held.

February
Federal Territory Day: 1 February. Kuala Lumpur's founding is marked with parades, cultural shows, and athletic competitions.

Thaipusam: A masochistic Hindu festival celebrated at Batu Caves near Kuala Lumpur and in Penang. Probably the most spectacular Hindu festival in Southeast Asia, Thaipusam is more fully described under Singapore Festivals.

Chinese New Year: Family visits, firecrackers, and shouts of "*Gung Hay Fah Choy*" are essential to the Chinese community. See the Singapore chapter.

Chap Goh Meh: Hokkiens celebrate this festival on the 15th and final day of the Chinese New Year. Considered an excellent time to find a rich husband; you'll see lovely ladies dressed in extravagant gowns cruising around in flashy cars.

Chingay: Celebrated in Penang and Johor Baru 22 days after the Chinese New Year. Acrobats and temple volunteers carry temple idols and enormous flags through the streets.

Genggulang Day: Animist New Year's celebration held by the *orang asli* in South Perak.

March
Birthday of the Sultan of Selangor: 8 March. Festivities, cultural performances, and prayers are held in the capital city of Alam and the royal town of Klang.

Melaka Week: Food festivals, cultural events, and decorative competitions are held during this week-long celebration.

Panguni Uttiram: This Hindu festival honors the celestial marriage of Lord Shiva to goddess Parvati with vegetarian meals and all-night prayer vigils.

Birthday of the Sultan of Kelantan: 30-31 March. Celebrated in Kota Baru on the East Coast. A rare opportunity to watch traditional Malay sports and performing arts such as *wayang kulit, pencak silat,* top spinning, and kite flying. Poetry competitions are held in the evenings.

April
Birthday of the Sultan of Johor: 8 April.

Birthday of the Sultan of Perak: 19 April. Celebrated in both Ipoh and the royal town of Kuala Kangsar.

Birthday of the Sultan of Trengganu: 30 April. Another outstanding east-coast celebration.

Kelantan Kite Festival: Enormous kites of all shapes and sizes are decorated with colored and shimmering paper before being sent aloft.

Ching Ming: Chinese visit and clean up the elaborate tombs of their ancestors during this celebration of the dead. See the Singapore chapter.

Sri Rama Navami: Rama is honored during this nine-day Hindu festival.

May
Hari Raya Puasa: An Islamic holiday which marks the end of the fasting month of Ramadan. Muslims pray in mosques and attend religious discussions. Homes are opened to relatives and friends.

Vesak Day: An important Buddhist festival which celebrates the birth, death, and enlightenment of Lord Buddha. Picturesque lantern processions encircle most Buddhist temples.

FESTIVALS

Penang Boat Races: International boat competitions are held between sleekly decorated dragon boats manned by 24 oarsmen, a *taikong* helmsman, and a gong beater.

Puja Pantai: A big and noisy beach festival held five km south of Kuala Trengganu. Originally a pagan celebration to ensure a successful rice harvest, it now revolves around rock bands and thunderous disco.

Kota Belud Festival (Sabah): Bajau dances, blowgun competitions, and horse-riding demonstrations are held in Kota Belud, 77 km from Kota Kinabalu. Sipitang holds a similar festival.

Kandazan Harvest Festival (Sabah): Ritualistic celebration of the rice harvest held annually by the indigenous Kandazans of Sabah. An enormous amount of *tapai* (rice wine) is drunk.

Dayak Festival (Sarawak): The Dayaks of Sarawak get into the spirit of spring with ritualistic animal sacrifices, war dances, cockfights, blowgun competitions, and the liberal consumption of *tuak*.

Kapit Festival (Sarawak): Cultural performances and a regatta are held in Sarawak's Seventh Division.

June

Birthday of the Sultan of Melaka: 10 June.

Fiesta of Saint Peter: 29 June. Christian fishermen's festival held at a Portuguese settlement near Malacca.

Kelantan Giant Drums Festival: Teams of *rebana ubi* pounders challenge each other in Kota Baru. Judges award points for *lendik* (tone), *merdu* (sound), and *rentak lagu* (reverberation), in addition to the team's costumes and drum decorations.

July

Birthday of the Governor of Sarawak: 7 July.

Birthday of the Governor of Penang: 16 July.

Birthday of the Sultan of Sembilan: 19 July.

Lumut Sea Carnival: The port town for Pangkor Island sponsors a boat procession, water sports, and the crowning of the Pesta Queen.

August

Krishna Festival: This Hindu festival marks the eighth reincarnation of Vishnu with dance and drama recalling the adventures of the blue-skinned lover and hero of the Mahabharata.

Koran Reading Competition: Held in Kuala Lumpur and televised throughout Malaysia.

Festival of the Hungry Ghosts: Chinese believe that once a year the gates of hell are opened and hungry ghosts are freed to roam around. Offerings of food, incense, and entertainment are made to appease these straying, destitute, and possibly bothersome ghosts. Chinese street opera can be seen in most West Coast towns.

Hari Raya Haji: This Muslim holiday marks the occasion when pilgrims visit the holy black stone in Mecca.

Maal Hijrah: Islamic New Year's Day. Commemorates the journey of Mohammed from Medina to Mecca in 622.

Malacca Festival: Week-long celebration of kite flying, bird singing, top spinning, martial arts, boat races, windsurfing competitions, beauty pageants, and food fairs at the major hotels.

National Day: 31 August. Malaysia's independence is celebrated in Kuala Lumpur with parades, Chinese opera, traditional Malay dance, and Hindu drama.

September

Birthday of the Governor of Sabah: 10 September.

Birthday of the Sultan of Perlis: 25 September.

Firewalking Festival: Hindus race across beds of burning coals to prove their devotion.

October

Birthday of the Sultan of Pahang: 24 October.

Deepavali: Hindu festival celebrating the victory of Rama over Rawana, good over evil, wisdom over ignorance.

Moon Cake Festival: Marks the overthrow of the Mongol overlords in feudal China. Lanterns are lit, women pray to the goddess of the moon, and everyone enjoys heavy cakes made from egg and lotus seed.

Festival of the Nine Emperors: The nine kings of ancient China are honored with Chinese opera and some spirited firewalking. A grand procession is held on the ninth day of the ninth moon to commemorate the return of the gods to heaven.

Navarathri: Young Hindu girls dress up as the goddess Kali to honor their virginity. Hindu organizations in Kuala Lumpur stage Hindu dance and drama.

FESTIVALS

November

Mohammed's Birthday: Muslims celebrate Mohammed's birthday with prayers, religious lectures, and recitations of the Koran.

Kuan Yin's Birthday: The Chinese goddess of mercy celebrates her birthday four times a year. What kind of lady would celebrate her birthday four times yearly?

December

Penang Festival: December is carnival time in Penang. Highlights include decorated floats, an international film festival, Indian and Chinese theater, boat races, and sports competitions.

Feast of St. Francis Xavier: Catholics of Malacca honor their patron saint with a religious procession.

PRACTICAL INFORMATION

GETTING THERE

International Connections

Malaysian Airlines (MAS; tel. 800-421-8641) flies five times weekly from Los Angeles to Kuala Lumpur. Stopovers in Tokyo, Taipei, and Hong Kong cost US$50 extra. MAS also serves Kuala Lumpur from Australia, New Zealand, and Europe.

From Thailand

Air: Malaysia can be reached from Thailand by air, train, bus, or shared taxi. Both Thai International and MAS have direct flights from Bangkok, Phuket, and Hat Yai to Penang and Kuala Lumpur. The Phuket-Penang flight is reasonably priced and saves a full day of hard bus travel.

Train: The International Express operates daily between Bangkok and Butterworth, the terminus town just across from the island of Penang. The train then continues south to Kuala Lumpur and finally Singapore. Schedules change frequently; accurate departure times and fares can be checked with tourist departments or stationmasters in Thailand. The express is comfortable and offers good scenery, but some restrictions apply. For example, only first and second classes are available. In addition, supplemental charges for air-conditioning, superior classes, and sleeping berths make the express much more expensive than ordinary trains or buses.

Most ordinary trains from Hat Yai terminate at the border town of Padang Besar, from where you walk across to Malaysia. Trains and buses continue south to Butterworth and Kuala Lumpur.

In late 1993, direct train service from the Thai border town of Pandang Besar to the Malaysian town of Aru was resumed. The service had been terminated in 1987 due to smuggling. It is once again possible to take a train from Hat Yai to Butterworth, just opposite Penang Island.

Trains can also be taken from Hat Yai to the East Coast of Peninsular Malaysia. Ordinary trains leave Hat Yai each morning and terminate at the border town of Sungai Golok. Travelers then get off the train, follow the slowly shuffling crowds along the tracks into Malaysia, and continue into Kota Baru by train or on bus 29. More details on border crossings are found in the Penang and Kota Baru sections. A super-deluxe Orient Express was introduced in 1993.

Bus: Two types of buses cross from Thailand into Malaysia: ordinary nondirect buses which terminate at the border, and direct buses which cross the border and continue south to Penang or Kuala Lumpur. Whether going to the West or the East Coast, ordinary buses terminate at the border; you must then walk across and wait for a connecting bus. Nondirect bus connections on the West Coast are problematic, since buses terminate at the Thai town of Sadao, a full 20 km from the Malaysian town of Changlun. Neither buses nor taxis cross this no-man's land.

Crossing the border by bus on the East Coast is much easier, since public buses continue all the way to the border. As described above, you then walk across the border, have your passport stamped, and continue into Kota Baru by bus or train. Direct buses from Phuket, Ko Samui, Surat Thani, and Hat Yai to Penang or Kuala Lumpur are much more convenient. Although more expensive than nondirect transport, they save a great deal of time and eliminate hassles at border crossings. Direct buses can be booked through travel agents in the above origination or other large towns in southern Thailand.

Share Taxis: You can also cross the border by share taxi. These lumbering Mercedes are fast, comfortable, cozy, fun, and memorable, since you never quite know who your traveling companions will be: old ladies with shopping bags, traveling salesmen, shy schoolgirls, Koranic scholars, turbanned Sikhs. The Hat Yai-Butterworth taxi fare of about M$25 compares favorably with private buses. Share taxis leave Hat Yai from budget guesthouses and the train station.

From Singapore

Train: Almost a dozen trains leave daily from the Singapore train station on Keppel Road. Services range from slow ordinary trains to night expresses and the International Express to Bangkok. Departures change frequently; exact schedules can be checked at the Singapore Tourist Office or by calling the railway station at tel. 222-5165.

Bus: Buses for most Malaysian destinations leave Singapore from the open-air bus terminal at Lavender Road and Kallang Bahru, near the Little India district. Departure times, prices, and durations are listed at the end of the Singapore chapter ("Leaving Singapore"). Current schedules can be double-checked with the Singapore Tourist Office. A cheaper alternative is public bus 170 from Queen Street to Johor Baru. Buses fan out from the Johor Baru bus terminal to most Malaysian towns.

Share Taxis: Share taxis can be picked up at various budget hostels or through taxi services. These taxis are fast and comfortable, although the driving styles range from dangerous to suicidal.

From Indonesia

Air: Both Garuda and Malaysia Airlines serve Kuala Lumpur from Jakarta, Denpasar, and

TRAINS BETWEEN THAILAND AND MALAYSIA		
CITY	**IE**	**ORD.**
Bangkok	1515	–
Hat Yai	0705	–
Padang Besar	0900	0900
Alor Star	1051	1130
Butterworth	1225	1225
CITY	**IE**	
Butterworth	1340	
Alor Star	1510	
Padang Besar	1605	
Hat Yai	1640	
Bangkok	0835	

several towns in Sumatra. The most popular connection is the daily flight from Medan to Penang for about M$80. This ticket also satisfies the "ticket-out" requirements for the Indonesian visa.

Sea: The twice-weekly ferry *Gadis Langkasuka* from Belawan (the port for Medan in Sumatra) to Penang is about half the price of an air ticket. This boat service is sporadic and often canceled during monsoons. Ferry boats occasionally cross from Dumai in Sumatra to Malacca. A third alternative is the weekly cargo boat from Pekanbaru in Sumatra to Singapore. (Further details under "Singapore.")

GETTING AROUND

Air

Malaysia Airlines Systems (MAS) operates all international and domestic routes within the country. MAS flights within Peninsular Malaysia are rarely necessary, thanks to the country's excellent network of buses, trains, and taxis. Private Pelangi Air flies Twin Otters to less-frequented destinations such as Tioman Island. It's a different story over on Borneo (Sabah and Sarawak), where bus and taxi service ranges from dismal to nonexistent; here, MAS is often the only way to reach interior towns or bypass long stretches of the coastal highway destroyed by monsoons. Travelers bound for Borneo should note that it's significantly cheaper to fly there from Johor Baru than from Singapore.

MAS offers all the standard discounts such as advance-purchase, night fares, student prices, and family fares. Departure tax on international flights is M$15.

Train

Trains on Peninsular Malaysia present a wonderful alternative to crowded buses. Service is reasonably frequent, prices are moderate (comparable to a/c buses), and the scenery is superb. Trains are also safer, saner, and offer a great deal more legroom. Best of all, trains provide endless opportunities to meet people, wander around, gaze out the window, read a book, and simply enjoy the nostalgia unique to this kind of travel.

Peninsular Malaysia has two train lines: West Coast service from Singapore to Thailand and an East Coast line from Gemas to Kota Baru. Malayan Railways (Keretapi Tanah Melayu or KTM) sells a 10-day railpass for M$90 and a 30-day pass for M$190, not much of a deal because of the limited lines.

Trains come in several classes and types. Ordinary trains and mail coaches in second and third classes only stop at every station and are very slow. The Ekspres Sinaran and the Ekspres Rakyat (People's Express) in a/c or fan coaches are much faster and only slightly pricier than ordinary trains. Unless you have a great deal of time, these are the ones to take. Supplemental charges for sleeping berths are M$20 in first-class a/c, M$10 in first-class ordinary, M$8 in second-class lower berth, and M$6 in second-class upper berth. Seats and sleeping berths should be booked well in advance of holidays. Schedules change frequently but accurate timetables can be picked up from stationmasters in Singapore and Kuala Lumpur.

Malayan Railways offers several tours. Their Penang Rail Experience is a two- to four-night package with return fare, transfers, and accommodations in the deluxe Shangri-La Hotel. The Langkawi Express from Kuala Lumpur includes transportation to Langkawi and first-class accommodations. Train Tourama is a direct train-bus connection to Cameron Highlands.

Bus

Bus transport on Peninsular Malaysia is fast, frequent, and fairly comfortable on short hauls.

Most destinations are served by deluxe a/c coaches complete with smiling hostesses, complimentary soft drinks, and freezing air-conditioning. Ordinary buses serve most of the same routes, plus all the smaller towns off the beaten track. Dozens of bus companies operate in Malaysia but the largest is MARA, the Malaysian government service which usually operates from centrally located terminals.

Share Taxis

Another convenient way to travel around Malaysia is by share taxis, comfortable and fast Mercedes-Benzes which cost about the same as second-class trains or a/c buses. Share taxis from Johor Baru to Kuala Lumpur, Kuala Lumpur to Penang, or Penang to Kota Baru cost about M$25, can typically be found waiting near bus or train stations, and leave when filled with five passengers. They're extemely fast and exciting as drivers pass wildly on blind curves and roar through crowded streets at breathtaking speeds. Unless you have nerves of steel, it's best to sit securely in the back seat and ignore the driver's appalling lack of sense.

Car Rentals

Malaysia is probably the best country in Southeast Asia in which to hire a car, since roads are in excellent condition, destinations are well signposted, and driving habits (except for taxis and trucks) are reasonably civilized. All international rental firms such as Avis and Hertz are located here. Rental rates are reasonable, but drop-off charges should be carefully checked. Best prices are from Malay firms such as Siniat and Mayflower, which rent small cars with unlimited mileage and insurance from M$500 per week or M$1700 per month; a great deal for large parties. International Driver's Licenses are required and seatbelts are mandatory. Malaysian drivers use several unique signals. A right indicator signal means Do Not Overtake rather than Right Turn. A left indicator means Overtake With Caution, not Left Turn. Flashing headlights mean the oncoming driver is claiming the right of way. Be prepared to pull off the road if necessary.

Tours

Great Value Holidays, a tour group operated by the Malaysian tourist office, offers dozens of excursions throughout the country. Contact

MSL Travel (tel. 298-9722) at the Asia Hotel in Kuala Lumpur or the Hotel Merlin in Penang. Asian Overland Services specializes in adventure experiences with comfort. Contact AOS (tel. 292-5622) on Jalan Dewan Sultan Sulaiman Satu in Kuala Lumpur.

TRAVEL FORMALITIES

Visas

Visas are unnecessary for most visitors to Malaysia. Citizens of the United States, Australia, New Zealand, and most European nations are normally granted one-month visitor's permits upon arrival. The exact duration of this permit is solely at the discretion of the immigration officer. Two months are sometimes given on request. Three-month extensions can be obtained at state capitals and the immigration office in Kuala Lumpur.

Both Malaysia and Singapore expressly forbid the entrance of "hippies," a term loosely defined as any undesirable shoestring traveler who arrives wearing thongs, dirty shirts, weird Indonesian clothes, and long hair. Such characters were in earlier days refused entrance or, when apprehended on the beaches of Penang, hustled out of the country after having their passports stamped *SH* ("Suspected Hippie"),

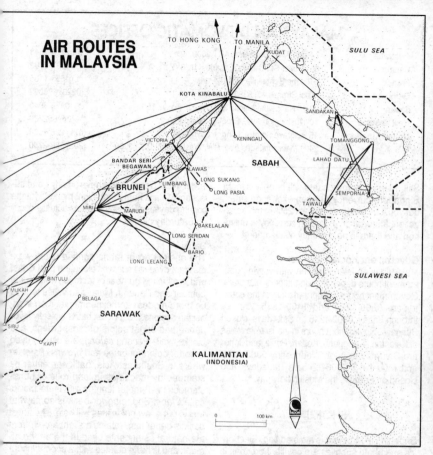

AIR ROUTES IN MALAYSIA

TO HONG KONG   TO MANILA   SULU SEA

KUDAT

KOTA KINABALU   SANDAKAN

VICTORIA   KENINGAU   TOMANGGONG

BANDAR SERI   LAHAD DATU
BEGAWAN   LAWAS   SABAH

BRUNEI   LIMBANG   LONG SUKANG   SEMPORNA

LONG PASIA   TAWAU

MIRI   MARUDI

BAKELALAN

LONG SERIDAN

LONG LELANG   BARIO

SULAWESI SEA

BINTULU

MUKAH

BELAGA

SIBU   SARAWAK

KAPIT

KALIMANTAN
(INDONESIA)

0   100 km

IT ("In Transit"). Malaysian immigration authorities are more tolerant these days, but it is sensible to arrive well dressed and carry enough money to prove your solvency.

Tourist Information

The Malaysia Tourism Promotion Board (MTPB) has a fairly good selection of maps and brochures in its offices located throughout the country.

Maps

Complimentary maps from the MTPB are fairly useful, but the APA and Shell maps of Malaysia are larger scale and more accurate. The Esso Map of Peninsular Malaysia includes small but useful city maps of Kuantan, Kuala Trengganu, and Kota Baru. Visitors to Kuala Lumpur should pick up Lani's Kuala Lumpur Discover Map, a superbly informative guide to the sights, restaurants, and nightlife of the capital city.

Currency

The unit of currency is the Malaysian *ringgit* (often called the Malaysian dollar), which is divided into 100 *sen* or cents. Over the past five years, the Malaysian *ringgit* has steadily declined in value versus the American dollar. As of this writing it's US$1=M$2.80. It's also declined vis-à-vis the Singapore dollar to where these two currencies are no longer interchangeable.

MALAYSIAN DIPLOMATIC OFFICES

Australia	7 Perth Ave., Canberra, ACT 2600	(06) 273-1543
Canada	60 Boteler St., Ottawa, Ontario K1N 8Y7	(613) 237-5182
France	2 Bis rue Benouville, 75116 Paris	4553-1185
Germany	Mittel Strasse 43, 5300 Bonn 2	(0228) 376803
Japan	20-16 Nanpeidai-Machi, Shibuya-ku, Tokyo 150	3476-3840
New Zealand	10 Washington Ave., Brookly, Wellington	(04) 852439
United Kingdom	45 Belgrave Square, London SWIX8QT	(071) 235-8033
U.S.A.	2401 Massachusetts Ave. NW, Washington, D.C. 20008	(202) 328-2700

Still, Malaysian merchants will happily accept Singapore currency at even exchange rates, but you'll be giving up at least 25% in the transaction. Importation of foreign currency is unlimited and there is no currency black market.

Government Hours

Malaysia is an Islamic nation with varying government hours depending on the particular state. Government hours throughout most of the country are 0800-1245 and 1400-1615 Monday through Friday, 0800-1245 on Saturdays, closed Sundays. Government hours in the Islamic states of Kelantan, Trengganu, Kedah, Perlis, and Johor are Saturday through Wednesday 0800-1245 and 1400-1615, 0800-1245 on Thursdays, and closed on Fridays, the Muslim holy day.

SHOPPING

Shopping in Malaysia is a mixed bag. Electronics and photo supplies are costlier here than in the duty-free ports of Hong Kong and Singapore, and traditional handicrafts are less plentiful than in Thailand or Indonesia. Handicrafts are of highest quality and lowest prices on the East Coast, but MARA government stores in

GOVERNMENT OFFICE HOURS IN MALAYSIA

Monday-Thursday	0815-1245, 1400-1615
Friday	0815-1200, 1430-1615
Saturday	0800-1245

larger West Coast towns have a fairly good selection. Malays name their night markets for the coming days, so Sunday markets actually occur on Saturday nights.

Batik

The ancient art of fabric printing using wax-resistant dyes still survives along the East Coast and in a limited number of factories near Kuala Lumpur and Penang. Malaysian styles tend to be more modern and experimental than Indonesian designs. East Coast batiks typically favor dense and bright colors of reds, greens, and blacks, while Penang *sarongs* are usually dyed in softer colors of blues and browns. As elsewhere in Southeast Asia, batik can either be stamped by machines in long rolls or hand-stamped in 12-meter lengths with metal blocks called *japs*. Shopping for batik is somewhat tricky, but a few guidelines will help. The finest batik is paper thin, retains a slight aroma from the natural astringents used in the aftertreatment, and is hand painted with a copper instrument called a *janting*. Don't buy batik printed on only one side; this has been mass-produced by a textile-printing process.

Songket

Malaysia's cloth of gold is a distinctive fabric made from fine silk or cotton interwoven with imitation gold or silver threads. Patterns are reproduced from Islamic designs of Arabic calligraphy and geometric designs of plant life such as the petals of the *chempaka* flower. Rarely seen in ordinary wear, *songket* shows up during religious ceremonies and *akad nikah* marriage ceremonies. As you might expect, this time-consuming craft is very expensive. Other deco-

MALAYSIAN TOURIST OFFICES

OVERSEAS OFFICES

Australia	65 York St., Sydney, NSW 2000	(02) 294441
Germany	Rossmarkt 11, 6000 Frankfurt Am Main, FDR	069 283782
Hong Kong	47-50 Gloucester Rd., Hong Kong	528-5810
Japan	3-4 Nihombashi-Hongokucho, Chuo-ku, Tokyo 103	(03) 279-3081
Singapore	10 Collyer Quay, Ocean Bldg., 0104	(02) 534-4466
Thailand	315 Silom Rd., Bangkok 10500	236-7606
United Kingdom	57 Trafalgar Square, London WC2N 5DU	(01) 930-7932
U.S.A.	818 West 7th St., Los Angeles, CA 90017	(213) 689-9702

DOMESTIC OFFICES

Ipoh	Capitol Building	(05) 532800
Johor Baru	Kompleks Tun Razak, Jalan Wong Ah Fook, 8000	(07) 223590
Kota Baru	Jalan Ibrahim	(09) 725533
Kota Kinabalu	Jalan Sagunting, Wisma Wing Onn Life, 88000	(088) 248698
Kuala Lumpur	Putra World Trade Center, Jalan Tun Ismail	(03) 293-5188
Kuala Lumpur	3 Jalan Hishamuddin	(03) 230-1369
Kuantan	Jalan Mahkota, Teruntum Complex	(09) 522346
Kuching	AIA Bldg, Jalan Song Tien Cheok, 93100	(082) 246575
Penang	10 Jalan Tun Syed Barakbah, 10200	(04) 619067
Kuala Trengganu	2243 Jalan Sultan Sainal Abidin, 20000	(09) 621433

ration techniques include gilded needlework used for military epaulettes and pressed gold-leaf designs called *telepuk*.

Pewterware

Malaysia enjoys a reputation for producing some of the finest pewterware in the world. Pewter is made from tin, with a token amount of antimony and copper added for strength. The resulting 97% alloy can be cast, hammered, and stretched into beer mugs, sake cups, and a wide range of kitchen implements. Malaysia's largest and most famous pewtermaker is in Selangor near Kuala Lumpur.

Silverware

Malaysia's finest silverwork comes from Selangor Pewter and from the town of Sireh near Kota Baru in the state of Trengganu. Currently out of vogue but fascinating nevertheless are silver chastity discs displayed in the National Museum.

Pottery

Malaysian pottery is hardly famous, though there is a surprisingly good selection. Chinese-style pottery in utilitarian designs is produced by Aw Eng Kwang Pottery at Air Hitam, 120 km north of Johor Baru. Peninsular Malaysia's most distinctive potteries are the stunning black pots of Perak made by the Labu people of Leng-

MALAYSIAN AREA CODES

Singapore	02
Kuala Lumpur	03
Penang	04
Ipoh	05
Malacca	06
Taiping	044
Seremban	067
Kuantan	075
Kuala Trengganu	076
Kota Baru	077

INTERNATIONAL CLOCK FOR MALAYSIA

San Francisco . . . . -16
New York . . . . -13
London . . . . -8
Paris . . . . -7
Sydney . . . . +3

gong, Kepala Bendang, and Pulau Tiga. Ochre pots are made in Kelantan, but the most sought-after potteries are those produced by the indigenous peoples of Sabah and Sarawak. Decorated with traditional tribal designs, the hand-applied decorations often feature Sarawak hunters, Murut dancers, and stylized dragons from the Kayah tribes.

A CAUTION

In Malaysia, *dadah* (drugs) mean death. Despite pleas for mercy from the Australian and British governments, two Australians caught with 180 grams of heroin at the Penang airport in 1983 were hanged for trafficking under Malaysia's strict drug laws. Ten foreigners have been executed since drugs became a hanging offense in 1975. Over 120 people (including 20 foreigners) are currently facing death and another 70 are serving long jail terms. While many were merely pawns in corporate drug-smuggling games, the Malaysian Dangerous Drugs Act demands the death sentence purely on the quantity of drugs found and not on culpability. There is little distinction between soft and hard drugs; holding a few joints is almost as serious as carrying large quantities of heroin. Drugs are sold by rickshaw drivers and hotel clerks, but remember that most drug busts are the result of tip-offs from dealers who pick up sizable cash rewards. When in Malaysia, just say no.

MOVIES FILMED IN MALAYSIA

South Pacific: Tioman, a beautiful island off the East Coast of Peninsular Malaysia, was used as a backdrop for the Rogers and Hammerstein musical. You'll recognize the distinctive twin mountains as you approach by hovercraft from Kuantan. Other scenes in *South Pacific* were filmed on nearby Malaysian atolls and on the Hawaiian island of Kauai.

Farewell to the King: Nick Nolte played the king of the Dayaks in this 1989 flick filmed in the rainforests of Borneo. Spectacular photography, but Nick's Dayak dialogues, subtitled for Westerners, are silly.

PENINSULAR MALAYSIA~ WEST COAST

The east and west coasts of Peninsular Malaysia are differentiated by their unique histories, peoples, cuisines, weather, architecture, crafts, religious traditions, political leanings, and cultural attractions. The East Coast is home to easy-going Malays who follow Islam and earn their livings as fishermen or farmers. Progress has arrived with the opening of new roads and discoveries of oil and natural gas, but much of the region remains a timeless world of sleepy fishing villages, deserted beaches, minarets, and colorful weekend markets filled with exotic fruits, smelly fish, woven baskets, and batik sarongs. West coast towns and cities, on the other hand, are mostly populated by hard-working Chinese who prefer more entrepreneurial pursuits like shopkeeping and trading. An enclave of energy and excitement, the pace of west coast life is cranked up several notches beyond typical Asian levels. While the east coast is more relaxing and has better beaches, the west offers more in the way of historical sights, religious architecture, vibrant night markets, and topographic variety.

SIGHTSEEING HIGHLIGHTS

As described above, the most important sights on the west coast are the futuristic city of Kuala Lumpur, the small historic town of Malacca, beaches at Pangkor and Langkawi, the relaxing hill resort of Cameron Highlands, Taman Negara National Park, and Penang, the premier travel destination in Peninsular Malaysia. Travelers with additional time might visit one or more of the following attractions.

Fraser's Hill
Deserted during the week, this small old British hill resort is packed on weekends, when wealthy businessmen arrive with their families to play golf and tennis and relax in luxury condos which have sprouted in the cool mountain air.

Ipoh
Ipoh's rich past is recalled through its stately colonial architecture, its magnificent Perak homes, and elegant Chinese shophouses in the old quarter. It's delightfully free of tourist hype and hustle (you'll be the only Westerner in town), and you can get a quick impression with a three- or four-hour walking tour starting from the bus or train station. Ipoh has dozens of hotels in all price ranges.

Kuala Kangsar
Perak State's old royal capital is famous for the Ubudiah Mosque, perhaps the most beautiful example of Islamic architecture in Malaysia. Other attractions include a small but informative museum and the magnificent Iskandariah Palace, constructed in a unique art-deco-Saracenic style. Kuala Kangsar is a worthwhile and relatively easy three-hour stop between Ipoh and Penang.

Taiping
One of the prettiest little towns on the West Coast, Taiping is an ideal spot to wander around, soak up the '30s atmosphere, enjoy some tasty Chinese food, check out the museum's ethnological artifacts, and experience Malaysia slightly off the beaten track.

Maxwell Hill
Bukit Larut is a small and unpretentious former tea plantation and hill station with pleasant hiking trails, flower gardens, romantic old bungalows, and spectacular views across the Straits of Malacca. Maxwell Hill is a good alternative to the more developed hill resorts at Genting Highlands and Cameron Highlands.

JOHOR BARU

Johor Baru (also spelled Johore Bharu and Johor Bahru) is the administrative and royal capital of the state of Johor. Situated just across the causeway from Singapore, this city of 750,000 people is one of the country's richest and most Westernized, a fact largely attributed to Sultan Abu Bakar. This strong-willed, English-educated maharaja established his capital at the small fishing village of Tanjung Petri in 1866, changed the name to Johor Baru (New Johor), initiated an ambitious building program, and then successfully kept the sultanate free of foreign domination and British economic exploitation during his 33-year reign. Most travelers simply race through Johor Baru en route to Malacca or Kuala Lumpur, but those with the time might walk along the waterfront to the following attractions.

Attractions

Istana Besar: Abu Bakar's Grand Palace was built in 1866 in Victorian English style, the favorite architectural motif of this admitted Anglophile. The palace, overlooking the sea, is set amid 50 hectares of lush tropical gardens with a Japanese teahouse and a small zoo. The north wing of the palace houses a throne room and a museum with collections of court dresses, weapons, the famous Ellenborough centerpiece, and other state regalia; open weekday mornings except Fridays 0900-1200. Reservations must be made in advance at the Johor State Tourist Office on the 2nd floor of Orchid Plaza, Jalan Wong Ah Fook, tel. (07) 223590.

Abu Bakar Mosque: This yellow Victorian building at the top of a small hill about a block beyond the Istana commands a panoramic view of the Johor Straits and Singapore housing projects. The foundation stone was laid in 1892 by Abu Bakar, who finished the architectural gem in 1900.

Bukit Serene: Located about three km east of downtown, the modern palace and residence of the present sultan of Johor is crowned by a 32-meter tower, Johor's most distinctive landmark.

Accommodations

Budget: Few Western visitors stay in Johor, although inexpensive hotels can be found near the train, taxi, and bus stations in the center of town. Chinese hotels in the M$15-20 range include the Nam Yang and Suan Fang on Jalan

Meldrum, a busy street parallel to the waterfront and east of the Singapore Causeway. On the same street is the clean Malaya Hotel at 20 Meldrum, tel. 221691, M$18-27, and the Hawaii Hotel at 21 Meldrum, tel. 226332, M$33-45.

Luxury: Johor has over a dozen hotels which cater to traveling Chinese businessmen. Top choice is the Holiday Inn located north of town in the Holiday Plaza (which bills itself as Asia's longest shopping complex) on Jalan Dato Sulaiman, tel. 323800, M$110 single, M$130 double. Closer to city center is Merlin Tower Hotel on Jalan Meldrum, tel. 225811, M$100 single, M$120 double.

Getting There From Singapore

Bus 170 leaves every 15 minutes from Queen Street, within easy walking distance from the budget dorms on Bencoolen Street. Alternatively, the Johor Baru Express leaves every 30 minutes from the terminus on Rochor Road. Singapore's main bus terminal for Malaysian destinations such as Malacca, Kuala Lumpur, Penang, and East Coast towns is located on Lavender Road at the far end of Little India.

Leaving Johor

As the transportation hub for Peninsular Malaysia, Johor has frequent departures of buses, taxis, trains, and planes. All are cheaper than similar transport from Singapore. Least expensive (besides hitching) are the buses which leave from the terminal on Jalan Datu Dalam. Ekspres Rakyat (Peoples Express) trains from the station on Jalan Campbell are about 10% more expensive than a/c buses but more comfortable on longer journeys. Call 224727 for departure information. Chartered taxis from the taxi stand on Jalan Trus are 30-50% more expensive than a/c buses or trains but convenient and *very* fast. The Johor Baru airport is 20 km north of town. Note that airfares to Sabah and Sarawak are 20% cheaper than flights from Singapore—the savings can be substantial. Malaysian Airlines System (MAS) operates an express bus service from Singapore to the Johor airport. MAS is located in the Aziza Building on Jalan Wong Ah Fook.

MALACCA

Few cities in Southeast Asia can match Malacca (Melaka in Bahasa Malaya) in history or antiquity. For hundreds of years, the Portuguese, Dutch, and British fought for Malacca's strategic position on the Straits of Malacca and its incalculable wealth generated from the Asian silk and spice trades. Malacca is also something of a paradox. Although six centuries of colonization, warfare, and political intrigue left behind a rich historical legacy, few impressive monuments remain aside from some colorful Dutch architecture. This is the legacy of conquerors who successively demolished their predecessors' heritage. The Portuguese dismantled Islamic mosques and royal palaces to build their military forts and churches. Then, nearly all Portuguese architecture was destroyed during subsequent Dutch assaults or pulled down when the British finally took Malacca. Still, the handful of surviving European buildings, Chinese temples, and old Malaccan terrace houses makes this city one of Malaysia's leading destinations.

HISTORY

At the beginning of the 15th century, Malacca was little more than a small cluster of fishing huts located at the confluence of a narrow muddy river. To the south was Temasik (ancient Singapore), a small but successful trading port ruled by Sumatran Prince Parameswara, who endured almost constant attack by hostile Thai and Indonesian forces who sought to control the Straits of Malacca and its lucrative spice trade. After final destruction by Thai forces, Parameswara took his Islamic court and fled north to a small fishing village of sea pirates and shady *melaka* tress. It was an inauspicious beginning. But this was the era of spices, when European consumers were willing to pay fabulous sums for Indonesian condiments used to flavor and preserve meats during their long, cold winters. Profits were enormous; 45 Spanish dollars of spice in the Malukus would bring over $1800 in Venice. This trade had long

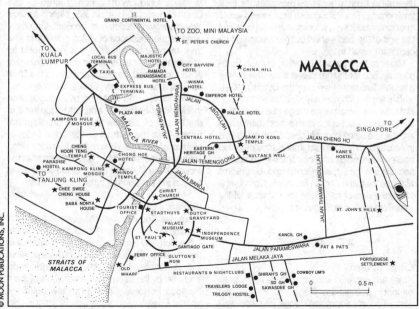

© MOON PUBLICATIONS, INC.

been controlled by Arab and Indian traders who stopped to rest, barter, and store their goods in Malacca between the monsoons. Paramesara organized the port, lowered taxes, built warehouses, and, with the blessings of the powerful Chinese court in Peking, turned Malacca into one of the world's great trading emporiums.

Mastery of the lucrative spice trade belonged to the nation that controlled the Malukus and held the Malacca Straits, a situation nicely described by Tome Pires: "Whoever is Lord of Malacca has his hands on the throat of Venice." To break the stranglehold of Arab traders and possibly convert some heathens to Christianity, the Portuguese sailed east while Columbus sailed west. Malacca fell to the Portuguese in 1511 when Alfonso de Albuquerque, governor of Portuguese India, sailed into Malacca with a fleet of 18 ships and 800 Portuguese soldiers. He found the ruling sultanate opulent and strongheaded, yet decadent and unable to protect its fragile empire. Albuquerque quickly took the city and massacred all who would not convert to Christianity; in a fit of rage, he then tore down all Muslim mosques and royal palaces. Most traders fled south to Johor or across the channel to Aceh, where they reestablished their trading port. The Portuguese then raised taxes to extortionate levels, a foolish act which marked the end of the port's short but glorious reign as center for Asian trade.

Malacca then passed between various European nations for the next several centuries. After a terrible five-month seige by the Dutch in 1641, which almost completely destroyed the city, Malacca was rebuilt in the image of a Dutch mercantile town. Most of the town's most memorable architecture dates from this period. But authorities in Amsterdam lost interest after discovering that trade winds would carry their spice ships directly from Java to the Cape of Good Hope. By the time Malacca fell to the English East India Company in 1824, the harbor had silted up and most of the trade had moved to Singapore.

ATTRACTIONS

Christ Church

Small and compact Malacca can be easily seen on foot in a single day. Begin your walking tour at the Tourist Information Center and then walk across to Malacca's "Red Square," a collection of salmon-colored buildings that forms the finest Dutch architecture in Malaysia. Finest of the assemblage is the bright red church built in 1753 for the Dutch Reform Church but now used by the Anglicans. The sanctuary bears many Dutch characteristics: massive walls of thick brick built over plinths of red granite, a roof of Dutch tiles, heavy roundheaded windows, and louvers topped with fan-shaped decorations. The interior is especially rich in detail: massive ceiling beams cut from a single tree, a collection of antique silverware behind the altar, handcarved pews, a brass Bible rest dated *Anno 1773*, and most striking, the old Portuguese, Dutch, and Armenian tombstones set into the floor. The small park in front holds the marble Queen Victoria Fountain and a beautifully proportioned clock tower donated by a wealthy Chinese merchant. Local Chinese who remember Japanese brutality during WW II were upset when the old English clock was replaced by a Seiko model. Trishaw drivers can be hired here.

The Stadthuys

Malacca's old city hall, constructed by the Dutch between 1641 and 1669, stands as their oldest surviving building in the East. Originally used as the residence of Dutch governors and their retinue, the Stadthuys is now used as government offices. Inlaid in the embankment walls are several memorial plaques to the United East India Company, Queen Victoria's Diamond Jubilee, the first king of Portugal, and the Makara Stone, an ancient Hindu relic in the shape of a stone fish with an elephant head—now the symbol of Malacca. Indonesian *prahus* and wily old sailors smoking *kreteks* sometimes hang out at the pier at the mouth of the Malacca River. Good Indonesian food in the cafe on the right.

St. Paul's Church

From Red Square, climb the steps to the top of Residency Hill, but don't take the path to the left, which only leads to the private residence of the governor. Residency Hill was once covered with Portuguese homes, churches, and shops, enclosed by the three-meter-thick walls of the A Famosa Fortress. One of the few buildings spared English destruction was St. Paul's, constructed in 1590 by Jesuit missionaries who had previously hosted famous Jesuit missionary St. Francis Xavier. Xavier's corpse was interred here for several months after his death near Macau; his crypt in the rear is covered with wire mesh and a marble statue of the saint stands in the front. After Malacca fell to the Dutch, St. Paul's was converted into a fortress and the roof was pulled down to allow for military extensions. In 1753 the hill was converted into a burial ground for Dutch notables. Among the 36 unbelievably large tombstones are Latin, Dutch, and Portuguese inscriptions describing the lives of the second bishop of Japan, the captain of Malacca, and various wives and children of local merchants. St. Paul's is also a popular spot for local artists to display their works and chat with Western visitors. The talkative and gregarious Francis Goh is a good source of local information.

Santiago Gate

This badly blackened stone gate is all that remains of the great 16th-century Portuguese fortress, A Famosa (The Famous). Soon after his conquest of Malacca in 1511, Albuquerque ordered the construction of the walled city as a bastion of Portuguese power and symbol of the nation's predominance in Southeast Asia. Hundreds of slaves and war prisoners tore down local mosques and Muslim tombs for the building brick used to construct a Portuguese castle, two palaces, five churches, and hundreds of homes. After being badly damaged in a Dutch attack, the gate was renovated and ironically replastered with the VOC Dutch crest, dated *Anno 1670*. The fort was finally demolished by the British, who only spared Santiago Gate (Gate of St. James) at the insistence of Southeast Asia's first architectural preservationist, Sir Stamford Raffles.

Malacca Historical Museum

Displayed behind the thick brick walls of a 300-year-old Dutch home are artifacts from every era of Malacca's turbulent past—ancient *batu hidup* stones which reputedly grow with age, the Islamic tombstone of Sultan Mansur Shah, Ming porcelain, Portuguese costumes, Dutch silverware, *nonya* wedding dresses, Malay *krises,* and English sepia-toned photographs. The history of Malacca is recreated here with a new Sound and Light Performance.

Independence Museum

Mementos of Malaysia's struggle for independence are exhibited inside the air-conditioned Malacca Club. The building was constructed in 1911 by local British planters who installed a library, a cabaret, several bars, and a billiards room. One of the early visitors was Somerset Maugham, who wrote "it is a spacious but shabby building: it has an air of neglect . . . in the morning you may find a couple of planters who have come in from their estates on business and are drinking gin-slings before starting back."

Peranakan architecture in Malacca

Malaccan Sultanate's Palace

The Malaysian government has reconstructed the palace of Sultan Mansur (1459-1477) from architectural descriptions in the *Malay Annals.* Exhibits are first class, especially the lifelike recreations of Malaccan court life and Malaysian weddings. The *Malay Annals* claimed that the Malacca sultans and local Chinese traders once measured their gold in *baharas,* each unit being approximately 200 kilos. It was a fabulous stash: Prime Minister Tun Mutahir had about a ton of gold and wealthy Chinese traders supposedly accumulated over 1,000 *baharas* of the precious metal! Even more intriguing, the enormous haul has never been found. Most think it unlikely that embattled Sultan Shah was able to remove such a staggering amount of gold, and Portuguese conquerors never admitted to finding such a fantastic cache. Further clues were unearthed in 1988 when foreign marine salvagers discovered Albuquerque's flagship, the *Flor de la Mar,* buried off the coast of Malacca. The ship sank in 1512, possibly carrying with it the plundered treasure of the Malaccan sultanate.

Dutch Graveyard

This old Protestant cemetery has several intriguing Dutch and English headstones that relate sad stories of death in the tropics; memorials to Lt. Harding, killed during the Naning War; Rachel Milne and her two children, dead from disease; and John Kidd, the doomed captain of the *Morning Star.*

Jalan Tun Tan Cheng Lock

Walk back to the tourist office and then cross the bridge to Malacca's old town, a crosshatch of narrow streets perhaps more fascinating than any historical attractions. Walk slowly to watch people: beaming Malay schoolgirls with heads tightly wrapped in white shawls, heavy Tamil women draped in polyester saris, serious young men on their way to the nearest mosque, Chinese shopkeepers anxiously peddling antiques, old *nonya* ladies dressed in the traditional *sarong kebaya,* pasty tourists being peddled around by sweating rickshaw drivers. The range of emporiums is equally fascinating: coffin carvers with shamrock-shaped repositories, Chinese herbalists who cure fatigue with shark's fin, Indian sari vendors, rubber mills ingeniously situated inside automobile garages, bird sellers up a cheerful alley. Walk across the bridge, immediately turn left, then walk right down Jalan Tun Tan Cheng Lock. Once known as Heeren Street and nicknamed Millionaires Row, this narrow alley is flanked by Peranakan ancestral homes dating from late 19th and early 20th centuries. Their opulent homes are often decorated with canopies of Chinese tiles, porcelain dragons and flowers, and elaborately carved double doors which open onto interiors furnished with blackwood chairs and other hardwoods fashioned after Chinese and Dutch designs. Two buidings are very special:

Baba Nonya Heritage House: This private home at 50 Tun Tan Cheng Lock offers a rare chance to tour an authentic Peranakan mansion. Originally constructed in 1896 by millionaire rubber planter Chang Cheng Siew, the Heritage House was opened to the public several years ago by William Chan. The 45-minute tour costs M$7 and begins daily at 1000, 1130, 1400, and 1530.

House of Chee Swee Cheng: The magnificent Chee House, located at 117 Tun Tan Cheng Lock, was designed by a Eurasian architect named Westerhout and constructed in 1906. The Dutch-style house incorporates Chinese and European elements in a classic example of Straits Chinese architecture. The house once served as the Dutch Embassy, but today it's the private residence for descendants of the founder of the Overseas Chinese Bank. Another elaborate '20s building decorated with carved deer stands three blocks farther west at 167.

Cheng Hoon Teng Temple

The Temple of the Green Merciful Clouds is one of the oldest and finest examples of traditional Chinese temple architecture in Malaysia. Designed in a typical southern Chinese style which emphasizes the roofline and formal arrangement of halls and courtyards, the temple has been the center of the Chinese community since founded over 300 years ago by Malacca's Kapitan China, a distinctive title and position created by the Dutch as the political boss of the Chinese trading community. The finely proportioned front entrance is flanked by a pair of guardian lions, which symbolize filial piety, and moon windows that open into the first courtyard. The wooden plank at the entrance is intended to force an automatic bow or *kowtow,* and not to keep out evil spirits as assummed by most Westerners. Inside the spacious main hall is a 75-centimeter solid bronze image of Kuan Yin, the idealization of womanhood and infinite piety in whose honor the temple is dedicated. To her left is an image of Ma Cho Po, Guardian of the Fishermen. To her right is red-faced Kwan Ti, God of War, Literature, and Justice. Also note the wooden support beams carved with jolly Chinese and fat Europeans dressed in East Indian Company uniforms. Perhaps the most striking are the beautiful lacquer tables and elaborate woodcarvings behind the altars. Halls behind the main temple are dedicated to Confucius and filled with ancestor tablets of all the Kapitans China who served as heads of the Chinese community in Malacca. The new headquarters of the Malaysian Buddhist Association is just across the street.

Kampong Kling Mosque

Before exploring the mosque, drop by the shop of Nam Tong and say hello to the friendly proprietor who folds, glues, and staples those paper creations which are burned at Chinese funerals. A souvenir from this shop is almost as intriguing as, and certainly much less expensive than, the antiques sold on Jalan Hang Jebat. Kampong Kling is a lovely little mosque and one of the few Westerners can visit without being harassed by indignant Muslims. Shoes must be taken off, shorts are not permitted, and women must be well covered. This Islamic house of worship was constructed in 1868 in a unique Sumatran-Chinese design with a distinctive tower shaped somewhat like a Chinese pagoda. The stunning interior resonates thanks to the profuse use of Portuguese and British glazed tiles which support the Victorian chandelier and wooden floral ceiling. The tasteful integration of Corinthian columns, Chinese tilework, and Islamic woodcarving makes this one of Malacca's architectural gems.

Sri Poyatha Vinayagar Moorthi Temple

The central altar of this colorful Hindu temple constructed in 1781 enshrines a black stone statue of Vinayagar (also known as Subramaniam), the Hindu deity represented by a human body with four hands and an elephant's head. The temple has been badly disfigured by an ugly wire fence, but the wild color combinations and *hantu tetek* (papier-mâché gods) make great photographs.

Other Attractions

China Hill: Bukit China, a huge Chinese graveyard hill about two km southeast of the tourist office, holds over 13,000 burial plots whose elevated location blocks the winds of evil and gives the spirits an unobstructed view of their descendants. As the oldest and largest Chinese graveyard outside China, this weedy hill offers great views and another sidelight into Malaccan history. The *Malay Annals* relates that in 1459 the Malaccan sultan accepted a Chinese bride from Emperor Yung Lo of the Ming Dynasty to cement economic agreements. In return, the sultan bestowed this hill to his young bride and her 500 handmaidens. This historic exchange ensured Malaccan safety and almost guaranteed great economic power. The modest temple at the base of the hill has a dirty but famous well which, according to legend, will ensure the return of any visitor who drinks its waters; it's more likely you will die from pollution.

Portuguese Settlement: Located about three km south of downtown, this small community of 500 Eurasians of Portuguese descent speaks a medieval dialect called Cristao (surprisingly similar to 16th-century Portuguese) and celebrates all the familiar Christian holidays such as Easter and Christmas. The Malaysian government has built a Portuguese Square with cafes serving authentic Portuguese meals and pitchers of ice-cold beer, but the highlight is the weekend cultural show featuring Portuguese songs and dances. The settlement itself resembles a low-income housing project. Take a taxi or bus 17.

Tanjung Kling: This quiet but nondescript beach 10 km north of Malacca has a handful of rudimentary hotels for travelers who would rather spend a few days at the beach, however narrow and polluted, than in a city hotel. Take bus 51 from the Malacca terminal and be prepared for an early-morning wake-up from the Muslim loudspeaker.

Mini Malaysia: Visitors with a strong interest in traditional Malay architecture can see 13 reconstructed examples of Malay homes in this theme park 14 km east of Malacca. Each state is represented: Malacca long-roofed house, Johore five-roofed house, traditional Kadazan house, Iban longhouse. Performances of Malay dance, top spinning, kite flying, and *pencak silat* are given in the central bandshell every Sunday afternoon. Nearby Air Keroh Recreational Forest offers log-cabin accommodations, the Malacca Village Resort with 160 luxury guest rooms, and the Malacca Zoo with two of the world's 7 surviving Sumatran rhinos. Take the bus labeled Air Keroh.

ACCOMMODATIONS

Budget

Malacca has several inexpensive hostels that cater to budget travelers, a clean and centrally located Chinese hotel, and a beach resort with several run-down but cheap shacks.

Bus arrivals are invariably met by hordes of frantic, shouting, pushing, sweating rickshaw drivers who desperately wave mimeographed sheets and photo albums of their hostels. Although a rude introduction to what is otherwise a pleasant town, the drivers are helpful and friendly, especially the character called Cowboy.

Most of the budget spots are located in modern but faceless building complexes down near the reclamation area. From the main bus station take bus 17 or 25 and ask the conductor to stop at the Road Transport Office on Jl. Parameswara. Otherwise, walk a block north to the local bus station and proceed directly to the pleasant beach at Tanjung Kling.

Trilogy Hostel: One of Malacca's two most popular travelers' centers is Trilogy, a modern and clean apartment building inconveniently located in a nondescript neighborhood. As their flier claims, there's free coffee, tea, lockers, cooking facilities, and travelers' information. Bedrooms and communal bathrooms are very clean. 223B Jl. Taman Melaka Raya, tel. (06) 245319, M$6 dorm, M$12-20 private room.

Shirah's Guesthouse: Another clean and friendly homestay that draws raves from its steady stream of visitors. Mansour, his wife, and their young daughter, after whom the guesthouse is named, run one of the best operations in the region. 229B Taman Melaka Raya, M$6 dorm, M$12-20 private room.

If filled, try the other nearby guesthouses such as Travelers Lodge, Sawasdee Guesthouse, Sunny's Inn, and Pat and Pat's, operated by a Portuguese/Malay and his American wife.

Cowboy Lim's: Malacca's most colorful trishaw driver opened his small hotel in the heart of the city's restaurant and nightlife district. Clean rooms, free tea, cooking facilities, and luggage storage. 168A Taman Melaka Raya, M$6 dorm, M$12-20 private room.

Kane's: This older rabbit warren of dorms and shoebox rooms is another possible crash pad for shoestring travelers. Although it needs a good cleaning, Mr. Frankie, the friendly proprietor, is an endless (sometimes nonstop) source of information. Take a rickshaw from the bus terminal. Visitors coming from Singapore can ask the driver to stop in front. Jl. Laksaman Cheng Hoe, tel. (06) 235124, M$12-20.

Eastern Heritage Guesthouse: For a change of pace, you might investigate this 1918 neoclassical building near Bukit China. Take the yellow bus from the main bus terminal. 8 Jl. Bukit China, tel. (06) 233026, M$6 dorm, M$12-20 private room.

Paradise Hostel: Declining birth rates have turned this old maternity ward into a large budget hostel with small uncomfortable rooms. Friendly Indian management but the vibes are all wrong: locals believe the place is haunted. 4 Jl. Tengkera, tel. (06) 230821, M$6 dorm, M$12-20 private room.

Chong Hoe: Although this isn't really a travelers' center with noticeboard and fruit smoothies, the Chong Hoe is highly recommended for its old atmosphere and great location just across from Kampong Kling Mosque; the cleanest and cheapest Chinese hotel in town. 26 Jl. Tukang Emas, tel. (06) 226102, M$15-25.

Majestic: This aging Chinese hotel with carved wooden swing doors and overhead fans has the potential to be a colonial classic; unfortunately, it falls somewhat short of the mark. The classic exterior and timeless bar are delightful throwbacks to an earlier age, but the less expensive rooms are hardly larger than shoeboxes. 188 Bunga Raya, tel. (06) 222455, M$22-40.

Tanjung Kling Beach Hotels

Some travelers prefer to stay out at the beach despite the uninspiring stretch of sand and the choppy waters of the Malacca Straits. Facilities are basic and it can be a hassle waiting for the bus, but it's a good place to unwind for a few days. Take any Pat Hup bus from Malacca's local bus terminal.

Tanjung Kling beach has a half-dozen hotels in all price ranges. The following are described in order coming from Malacca.

Melaka Beach Bungalow and Youth Hostel: Located nine km from town and three km before Tanjung Kling, this modern guesthouse is probably the best-value spot out at the beach. 7379 Spring Garden, tel. (06) 512395, M$6 dorm, M$25-35 private room with bath. Ask the bus driver to let you off at Spring Garden.

Shah's Beach Hotel: The most luxurious hotel at the beach offers 50 deluxe chalets, swimming pool, and upscale restaurant. Tanjung Kling, tel. (06) 511120, M$85-120.

Farther on are the Motel Tanjung Kling, with overpriced rooms from M$28, and some primitive shacks such as Yashico Hostel, with mattresses-on-the-floor rooms from M$10.

Moderate To Luxury

Ramada Renaissance: Malacca entered the major leagues several years ago when this 24-story hotel was constructed at the top end of town. Facilities include several restaurants, a health center, squash courts, the city's most popular disco, and a small pool on the ninth floor. Jl. Bendahara, tel. (06) 248888, fax (06) 249269, M$160-240.

Emperor Hotel: Providing some competition for the Ramada, this locally owned hotel promotes itself with discounted rooms, happy hours in the lounge, and special events in the disco. Jl. Munshi Abdullah, tel. (06) 240777, M$85-140. Discounts of 30-40% are sometimes available.

Tapa Nyai Island Resort: A relatively luxurious hotel complex has been constructed on the small island of Pulau Besar about 25 minutes by catamaran from Malacca. Facilities include a swimming pool, a tennis court, and Melaka-style bungalows known as *rumah melaka*. Pulau Besar, tel. (06) 236733, fax (06) 236739, M$120-160.

RESTAURANTS

Glutton's Corner

Malacca's most popular group of food stalls is on Jalan Taman, just opposite the massive land-

MALACCA ACCOMMODATIONS

HOTEL	SINGLE	DOUBLE	ADDRESS	PHONE (06)
LUXURY	**M$**	**M$**		
City Bayview	140-160	160-200	Bendahara	239888
Emperor	85-120	105-140	Jl. Munshi Abdullah	240777
Ramada Renaissance	160-200	200-240	Jl. Bendahara	248888
MODERATE				
Palace	45-60	60-80	201 Jl. Munshi Abdullah	225115
Majestic	25-30	30-40	188 Jl. Bunga Raya	222455
Midtown	60-90	80-100	Jl. Tun Sri Lanang	240088
BUDGET				
Chong Hoe	12-15	15-20	26 Jl. Tukang Emas	226102
Cowboy Lim's	12-15	15-20	168 A Jl. Taman Melaka	
Fastern Heritage GH	12-15	15-20	8 Jl. Bukit China	233026
Kane's	12-15	15-20	Jl. Cheng Hoe	235124
Paradise	12-15	15-20	4 Jl. Tengkera	230821
Shirah's GH	12-15	15-20	229 B Jl. Taman Melaka	
Trilogy	12-15	15-20	218 Jl. Parameswara	245319

fill project. Vendors are overly aggressive, but selection is outstanding and prices are kept low due to cutthroat competition. Try oyster omelettes at stalls seven or nine, sautéed crab with green onion, and fresh seabass steamed in fish stock. A full description of food stall specialties is found under "Penang."

Food Stalls

Inexpensive food stalls can also be found on Jalan Bendahara, opposite the decrepit Central Hotel, and near the produce market on Jalan Kee Ann. Upscale food stalls do business across from the Ramada.

Indian Cafes

Both the Sri Lakshmi Vilas and Sri Krishna Bavan are located at the south end of Jalan Bendahara. Madras Cafe just a block away on Jalan Temenggong smells of fresh *parathas* and thick mutton curries. The small cafe opposite has famous Hainanese mutton steamboat . . . reputedly an aphrodisiac.

Portuguese Square

Malacca's Portuguese Settlement, three km south of downtown, has four cafes that serve Portuguese seafood dishes with jugs of cold beer. Cultural performances are given every Saturday evening.

LEAVING MALACCA

Long-distance buses leave from the terminal on Jalan Kilang. Service is frequent and advance reservations are rarely necessary. The taxi stand is 50 meters up the road. Share taxis depart when filled, are fast, and cost about 50% more than a/c buses. Buses for Tanjung Kling leave just across from the taxi stand.

Malacca's train terminus is in Tampin, 40 km north of town; call 223091 or 411034 for schedules and fares. The airport is at Batu Berendam, about eight km from town. MAS flies to Kuala Lumpur, Singapore, and Pekanbaru on Sumatra.

The Malacca-Dumai (Sumatra) ferry leaves every Thursday morning at 1000, takes three hours, and costs M$80 one-way. Contact Atlas Travel Service, tel. 220777, at 5 Jalan Hang Jebat for tickets.

SEREMBAN

Serembah is the capital of Negri Sembilan (Nine States), the so-called Minangkabau state because of the concentration of settlers from western Sumatra. These peaceful and well-educated people follow a matrilineal society based on Sumatran *adat perpatih* laws; all property belongs to females instead of males. The term Minangkabau itself means "Buffalo Horns," perhaps from the feisty nature of the people, their legendary beginnings, or their magnificent homes with distinctive horn-shaped roofs.

Attractions

Seremban is rarely visited by Westerners but it's a pleasant enough place with several good hotels and a handful of worthwhile attractions.

Lake Gardens: Seremban's centrally located twin lakes are known for their weekend cultural performances, the imposing State Secretariat Building at the north end, and the modern Disneyesque mosque with nine columns representing the nine states of Negri Sembilan.

Taman Seni Budaya: The state government has constructed a handicraft complex and Minangkabau house about one km from the heart of Seremban. Admission is free.

Accommodations

The Tong Fong (tel. 06-723022) and Wang Seng (tel. 06-725669) hotels, both on Jl. Birch, have rooms at M$12-20. You might also try the International New Hotel (tel. 06-714957) at 126 Jl. Veloo, where rooms cost M$15-25.

A cleaner alternative is the Carlton Hotel (tel. 06-725336) at 47 Jl. Tuan, where rooms cost M$20-50. Top-end Tasik Hotel (tel. 06-730994) on Jl. Tetamu has a/c rooms for M$85-100.

PORT DICKSON

Port Dickson, a small town with 17 km of good beach stretching southward to the rocky headlands capped by the Cape Rachado Lighthouse, is one of Malaysia's more popular seaside resorts because of its proximity to Kuala Lumpur, although the sand and water don't compare with Langkawi or beaches on the east coast. Port

Dickson can be reached from Kuala Lumpur and Malacca by bus or taxi.

Attractions

Activities involve sunbathing, seafood dinners and sunsets in a small restaurant, and taking the weekend Linggi River Safari from the Ming Court. The 16th-century Portuguese lighthouse at Cape Rachado can be visited with advance permission from the Malacca Tourist Office.

Accommodations

A near-continuous line of beach chalets and hotels in all possible price ranges has been con-structed along the beach. Kenmuning Park, 4.5 miles south of Port Dickson, has dorms from M$10 and private rooms from M$25, while an inexpensive but run-down youth hostel is two km farther down the road.

Other choices include the Sunshine Rotary Club at Batu 6 (mile 6) for M$12-20, Si Rusa Inn at Batu 7 where super-deluxe rooms cost M$120-200, the Lido and Ming Court Hotel at Batu 8 for M$80-120, Pantai Motel at Batu 9 for M$25-40, and the top-end Pantai Dickson Resort at Batu 12 for M$180-220. These weekend prices are heavily discounted during the week.

KUALA LUMPUR

Romantically named after the muddy Kelang and Gombak rivers, Kuala Lumpur ("Muddy Estuary") has unfairly gained a reputation as just another faceless Southeast Asian city best avoided by Western travelers. While the metropolis admittedly has less to offer than Bangkok or Singapore, it is surprisingly rich with graceful architecture that reflects its ethnic diversity: Tudor edifices, Saracenic railway stations and office buildings, smoky Chinese temples filled with gigantic joss sticks, wildly painted Indian temples dedicated to multiarmed gods, gleaming Islamic mosques, and most unexpectedly, some of Southeast Asia's most impressive modern skyscrapers. KL, as the city is commonly called, also boasts an outstanding museum (perhaps the most exciting in Asia) and an exceptionally vibrant night market. Also intriguing is the way the city's divergent races live together with little outward signs of racial tensions.

Kuala Lumpur isn't a major destination. But to skip this clean, safe, modern, and aesthetically pleasing city is to miss a look at modern Malaysia.

HISTORY

Kuala Lumpur, one of the youngest cities in all of Asia, has a turbulent history that would rival that of any gunslingers' town of the American Wild West. The city was established in the 1850s when two mining chiefs, Raja Jumaat and Raja Abdullah, persuaded Chinese miners to prospect for tin in the Kelang Valley, a dozen km beyond the rich mines of Lukut. It was a treacherous undertaking: only 18 of the original 87 Hakka miners who poled up the Kelang River survived the first month's rigors. Enormous tin deposits were uncovered and a tremendous mining town constructed, but a devastating civil war between rival secret societies and contentious Malay chiefs almost leveled the young enterprise.

Into the desperate situation walked Yap Ah Loy, a ruthless but energetic Hakka who made his reputation as a fighting man before moving to Kuala Lumpur. There, he rose to the position of "Kapitan China" and restored order by offering 50 dollars in silver for each hooligan's head. Yap transfomed Kuala Lumpur—a filthy, disease-ridden mining camp with wide-open brothels, opium dens, and enormous gambling halls—into a thriving enterprise and the leading commerical center of the Malayan Peninsula.

Attracted by the economic vitality, the British government transferred their headquarters from Klang to Kuala Lumpur in 1880 and, under the leadership of Frank Swettenham, widened streets and constructed dozens of delightful Moorish-styled offices. Malaysians agitated for independence until 1957, when the Union Jack was lowered for the final time on KL's central *padang*.

ATTRACTIONS

Kuala Lumpur is compact; most of the following attractions are within easy walking distance of city center. The biggest challenge facing walkers is traffic—busy highways often divide attractions. Crossovers and walkways exist but are difficult to find! A good map is essential; unfortunately, maps from the city tourist office near the railway station and the national tourist office in the Putra World Trade Center are generalized and fairly useless. Best resource for self-guided discoveries is *Lani's Kuala Lumpur Discovery Map,* a highly personalized and accurate guide to sights, shops, and restaurants. The following attractions are described in a suggested walking order.

Moorish Architecture

After the young city, constructed of cut timber and dried *atap,* was destroyed several times by fire in the late 19th century, local architects turned to fire-resistant brick. Many of the famous buildings that have come to symbolize Kuala Lumpur—the State Secretariat, City Hall, the Railway Station—were designed by British colonial engineers between 1894 and 1910. These ambitious young men borrowed all the forms of romantic styles from English Tudor to Indian Saracenic.

The city's leading architect was A.C. Norman, a sensitive designer who looked to the Moghul traditions of North India for his inspiration. Another important draftsman was A.B. Hubbard, who had just been transferred from Northern India where he had become enamored of the artistry of Islamic designers. Needing to create an image which would reflect the Islamic faith of the Malays, Norman and Hubbard boldly fused golden domes, soaring minarets, graceful Islamic archways, and spiralling stairways into a remarkable series of buildings that now stands as Kuala Lumpur's greatest attraction.

Jame Mosque: A good place to begin your walking tour is at the red-and-white Masjid Jame (Friday Mosque) nestled within a grove of coconut palms at the exact point where the city was founded in the 1850s. Designed by A.B. Hubbard in 1909 and modeled after a North Indian mosque, this enchanting structure of arabesque domes and soaring minarets is both

modern Islamic architecture

the physical and the psychological center of the Islamic republic. It is a pity that none of Malaysia's modern multimillion-dollar mosques can approach the Jame for beauty and elegance. Well-dressed visitors are welcome to tour the gardens.

Information Department: Designed by A.C. Norman in 1909, this building originally served as the survey department. Today it's a public information center where you can buy government maps and rent movies from the National Film Library.

Old City Hall: Norman's Euro-Islamic City Hall was designed in 1897 and originally housed the town council. The new City Hall is on Jalan Raya Laut.

High Court: Also designed by Norman in 1909, this beautiful building is still used by the Malaysian High Court. The Islamic facade on the riverside is especially elegant in the late-afternoon sun.

Old Secretariat: Now called the Sultan Abdul Samad Building, this magnificently symmetri-

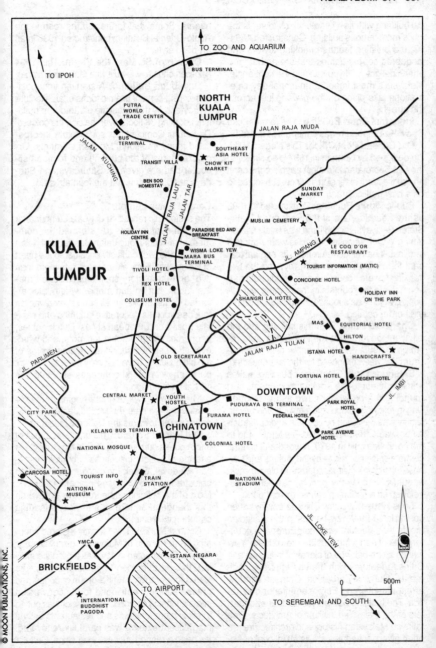

TO ZOO AND AQUARIUM

BUS TERMINAL

TO IPOH

NORTH KUALA LUMPUR

PUTRA WORLD TRADE CENTER

BUS TERMINAL

JALAN RAJA MUDA

JALAN KUCHING

SOUTHEAST ASIA HOTEL

TRANSIT VILLA

CHOW KIT MARKET

BEN SOO HOMESTAY

SUNDAY MARKET

KUALA LUMPUR

HOLIDAY INN CENTRE

PARADISE BED AND BREAKFAST

MUSLIM CEMETERY

JL. AMPANG

LE COQ D'OR RESTAURANT

WISMA LOKE YEW MARA BUS TERMINAL

TOURIST INFORMATION (MATIC)

TIVOLI HOTEL

REX HOTEL

COLISEUM HOTEL

CONCORDE HOTEL

HOLIDAY INN ON THE PARK

SHANGRI LA HOTEL

MAS

EQUITORIAL HOTEL

HILTON

JALAN RAJA TULAN

ISTANA HOTEL

HANDICRAFTS

JL. PARLIMEN

OLD SECRETARIAT

FORTUNA HOTEL

REGENT HOTEL

CITY PARK

CENTRAL MARKET

YOUTH HOSTEL

DOWNTOWN

PARK ROYAL HOTEL

JL. IMBI

PUDURAYA BUS TERMINAL

FURAMA HOTEL

FEDERAL HOTEL

KELANG BUS TERMINAL

CHINATOWN

PARK AVENUE HOTEL

NATIONAL MOSQUE

COLONIAL HOTEL

CARCOSA HOTEL

TOURIST INFO

TRAIN STATION

NATIONAL STADIUM

NATIONAL MUSEUM

JL. LOKE YEW

YMCA

ISTANA NEGARA

BRICKFIELDS

TO AIRPORT

INTERNATIONAL BUDDHIST PAGODA

0   500m

TO SEREMBAN AND SOUTH

© MOON PUBLICATIONS, INC.

cal building with its 41-meter clock tower is the city's most famous building. Constructed 1894-97, the building features flanking towers and lacquered copper domes that are a photographer's delight . . . if you can find the right angle. Malaysia's most important national-day celebrations take place on the *padang* just across the street.

Industrial Court Building: The former Loke Chow Kit Emporium was constructed in 1905.

Old General Post Office: This elegant building designed by Norman in 1897 is so similar to the Old Secretariat that most people consider it an architectural extension. It's now scheduled to be a new public library.

Public Works Building: Constructed in 1896 as the headquarters of the Federated Malay States Railways, this building was badly altered during WW II, when its pinnacles were removed and lost. It has since returned to its original elegant form with a central archway, and the two flanking towers now serve as a handicrafts museum. Note the fountain in the *padang* just opposite, which was supposedly purchased from a mail-order catalog.

Chartered Bank: Both this building and the adjacent Government Printing Office were restored in 1988. A Kuala Lumpur historical museum has been proposed for the latter building.

Selangor Club: This Tudor building makes a fine contrast to the Arabian monuments surrounding the *padang*. Known as the Spotted Dog in reference to the club's mascot, the private facility was designed by Norman and constructed between 1890 and 1910. The large wing to the north was built in 1970. A wonderful cultural contrast was once made by the Indians and Chinese who drank their *stengahs* and played cricket out front; today the *padang* has been redeveloped as a shopping center and car park.

Loke House: Wealthy Chinese *towkays* often constructed their new homes in the Palladian motifs then popular with their European counterparts. The former residence of Loke Yew strikes a fine balance of classical influence and Chinese features with the use of Greek pediments, Dutch-style gables, Chinese window arrangements, and European interior decoration. The building now serves as the headquarters of the Malaysian Institute of Architects. Free talks on Malaysian history and architecture are often given; schedules are listed in local newspapers. Somewhat farther up the road is the Anglo-Oriental Building, constructed 1936 in an art-deco style.

Church of St. Mary the Virgin: This 1894 Anglican church was built with Malaysian timber.

Dayabumi Building: A startling juxtaposition to 19th-century Islamic forms of architecture is provided by this exquisite ultramodern building. Looming 36 floors over the city, the colossal Dayabumi Complex has successfully incorporated many traditional Moorish elements. Organized tours of the building and rooftop helicopter pad are given on Saturdays and Sundays at 1000, starting at the fountain area.

Central Kuala Lumpur

The systematic rebuilding of Kuala Lumpur after the 19th-century fires transformed the commercial districts along Jalan Bandar and Jalan Petaling, the two roads still considered the heart of Chinatown. Early efforts were little more than two- and three-story shophouses sans ornamentation, but tin and rubber wealth later afforded Chinese *tokangs* all sorts of extravagant touches such as decorative columns and capitals based on European styles, Dutch gables, pepperpot and pineapple topknots, and whatever else seemed stylish at the time. Some of the old buildings have tragically been torn down, but many classic shophouses survived the 1980s building boom.

The following walking tour begins in the old market square near the Masjid Jame and proceeds south towards the National Museum.

Old Market Square: This unaltered block of shophouses surrounding the old clock displays a range of eclectic influences through its Venetian windows, Greek Ionic columns, Palladian balustrades, and Chinese Peranakan tilework. Most of the buildings date from the '20s, when this triangular square was the city's leading commercial district.

Central Market: This recently restored shopping center is one of Malaysia's great success stories. Constructed in 1935 as a produce market, this art-deco/neo-Egyptian building was slated for demolition until a group of concerned preservationists petitioned for its conversion into a shopping complex. The interior was gutted to allow room for shops and restaurants but the magnificent exterior was carefully renovated. It's been a roaring success ever since. Cultural performances are given on the riverside patio. This is the place to watch hip young Malaysians do exactly what hip young kids do everywhere else in the world: hang out at the mall. Neighboring Central Square is also being redeveloped into an upscale art and handicraft center.

Sze Ya Temple: Tucked away in a tight alley at a 45-degree angle, this Taoist temple was founded in 1882 by Mr. Yap, the Chinese warlord regarded as the founding father of Kuala Lumpur. Red and green paper figures plastered on the walls are akin to Chinese voodoo dolls in that people pound them to work off anger toward their enemies. The row of shophouses at 24-30 Jalan Hang Kasturi includes some of the best in the city.

Jalan Petaling: This is Chinatown: a fascinating neighborhood of old Chinese trading houses filled with scantily dressed men, pavement palmists who predict the future, restaurants that serve steaming bowls of python soup and iguana *satay*, tiny shops overflowing with Chinese wedding dresses, roast ducks strung up like little wagons, roadside hawkers peddling pirated cassettes and cheap shoes, 1920s coffeehouses filled with fat men watching cricket on TV, streetside barbers who clean ears for M$1, Chinese pharmacies pushing potions of deer antler and rhino horn. Jalan Petaling is even more amazing in the evening when the streets are closed to traffic and hundreds of merchants set up their portable stalls.

Sri Mariamman Temple: Kuala Lumpur's oldest and most important Hindu Temple was built in 1887 and reconstructed in 1965-72. Women at the entrance string flower garlands to be sold to worshippers of four-armed Murga, his two wives, and a beautiful six-armed goddess. Daily *pujas* at 1800; weddings on Saturdays.

Chan See Shu Yuen Temple: The elaborate Chan ancestral temple built in 1906 features ceramic glazed roof ornamentation of subjects from Chinese mythology and history.

Khun Yam Temple: Note the arched *pai lou* gateway with doric pillars and pagoda-shaped altar ovens used for burning holy papers. The production of hand-dipped incense is big business here.

Railway Station
Although it conjures up images of Arabian Nights, Kuala Lumpur's favorite landmark shel-

---

CULTURE CLASH IN KUALA LUMPUR

Anyone who wanders around central KL or spends any time in the Central Market will discover the underbelly of Malaysian society: the heavy-metal world of the *Kutus*. Literally meaning "lice" in Malay, *kutus* are young Malaysian rockers who have rejected the increasing Islamic fundamentalism of Malaysian society and embraced the rebellious signs of the Western world—punk music, black leather jackets, safety pins and chains. While not a remarkable form of rebellion elsewhere, *kutu* culture and their "decadent" rock music are considered a direct challenge to conservative Muslim lifestyles. Government bans against rock concerts (Michael Jackson was banned in 1988) have done little to change the tide. Today, *kutu* culture—and rock bands such as Search and Bumiputra Rockers—is immensely popular, adding another startling suprise to a visit to Malaysia.

---

ters a functional train shed modeled after old English glass-and-iron prototypes. This Moorish combination of domes, spires, turrets, and archways was designed in 1911 by British architects who drew their inspiration from Indian models. The interior holds a small cafe with mediocre food and a refurbished hotel with spacious doubles from M$40. Several other nearby buildings are worth visiting: the Malayan Railway Administration Headquarters, the contemporary National Mosque and gleaming Islamic Center open daily until 1800 for well-dressed visitors, and the National Art Museum, which is open daily 1000-1800. All government offices and religious buildings are closed Fridays 1215-1445.

National Museum
This is one of Southeast Asia's finest museums and main repository for the country's historic and artistic wealth. Unlike most other Asian museums, which display their goods under dusty and poorly labeled glass cabinets with little thought or creativity, Musium Negara is an ongoing circus of dioramas, changeable theme shows, and extraordinarily imaginative projects that bring Malaysian culture to life. There's something for everybody. The cultural gallery on the left offers a life-sized Malay wedding,

superb collections of Southeast Asian puppets and circumcision tools, a fascinating group of Islamic grave markers, an excellent Peranakan room, Malay games, and even Lat cartoons!

The history gallery to the right is filled with Srivijaya bronzes, the famous Trengganu stone, Martaban jars, and an "amok catcher" used to capture Malays run amok. The Gold Room to the extreme right is filled with dazzling objects from precious *krises* to curious modesty discs. Walk upstairs for changing exhibits, which might include Malaysian rock lyrics or live shadow theater. Directing this ongoing extravaganza is Dato Shahrum, the wonderfully innovative director who was awarded Asia's prestigious Magsaysay Award for his efforts. Do not miss this museum.

More Attractions

Lake Gardens: Kuala Lumpur's green-belt area features a national monument sculpted by the same artist responsible for the Iwo Jima Memorial (you'll notice the resemblance), Parliament House, Razak Memorial, and an orchid garden.

International Buddhist Pagoda: Located south of the city center and filled with replicas of Buddhas and pagodas, this modern stupa was modeled after the ancient pagodas of central India. Open daily 0700-2200.

Menara Maybank Building: This stunning 58-story banking center and *kris*-shaped wonder was constructed in 1988 by a local architectural firm. A coin museum is located on the ground floor.

India Mosque: Located in Kuala Lumpur's former red-light district, this Muslim Indian mosque is headquarters for the Jammah Tabligh, Malaysia's most fundamentalist Islamic missionary body. Their 30,000 missionaries wear *baju Melayu* or Pakistani attire with untrimmed moustaches and beards. The mosque is surrounded by Muslim paraphernalia shops, merchants peddling woven hairpieces, Indian street barbers, *sari* emporiums, and sidewalk portrait painters. Try the delicious Malay food stalls just opposite.

Batu Road: Now renamed Jalan Tuanku Abdul Rahman, this colorful street is filled with Indian restaurants and inexpensive hotels. Batu Road is closed to traffic and filled with hawkers' stalls on Saturday evenings.

Jalan Ampang: Kuala Lumpur's former millionaire's row has several impressive mansions converted into embassies and art galleries, including the seedy Bok House (Le Coq D'or Restaurant), worth visiting for the elaborately tiled bathrooms alone. Just opposite is the nostalgic Chan Chin Moo House and a path through a pretty cemetery to Pasar Minggu.

Jalan Bukit Nanas: Several fine Gothic and neo-Classical buildings are located on the road up Pineapple Hill: Old St. John's Church (built in 1886), St. John's Institution (1908), and the Convent of the Holy Infant Jesus (1912).

Attractions Near Kuala Lumpur

Batu Caves: This is probably the most popular side trip from the city. Inside a series of immense limestone caves some 13 km north of town are dozens of life-sized sculptures which depict the mythological exploits of Lord Muruga and other Hindu deities. Reached up 272 steps, the surrealistic cave figures are made even more bizarre by theatrical colored lights. Hindu mythologists will also enjoy the ground-level museum cave, which has another 200 garishly painted statues. Fairly sleepy during most of the year, Batu comes alive at Thaipusam, when nearly 100,000 Hindus gather to honor Lord Subramaniam. Batu Caves can be reached in 45 minutes on minibus 11 from Leboh Pudu or Jalan Semarang, or bus 70 from Puduraya Bus Terminal. Both pass some of the world's largest and ugliest open-pit tin mines.

Templar Park: Western visitors without the time or energy to trek the tropical rainforests of Taman Negara National Park can substitute this 1,200-hectare national park located 10 km beyond Batu Caves. Well-marked pathways wind through cascading streams, bathing pools, and tropical foliage. Templar Park can be reached in an hour with buses 66, 78, 83, or 95 from the Puduraya Bus Terminal.

National Zoo: Ideally you'd discover the rich animal life of the Malaysian tropical forest in its natural environment, but the only place to absolutely, positively see mousedeer (the size of a domestic cat), curious tapirs, tigers, dwarf crocodiles, and wooly orangutans is at the zoo. Hours are 0900-1700 daily but it's best to arrive for the early-morning or late-afternoon feedings. The zoo is 13 km northeast of the city and can be reached via buses 17 or 23 from Puduraya Terminal.

Genting Highlands: This hillside gambling resort has three expensive hotels with swim-

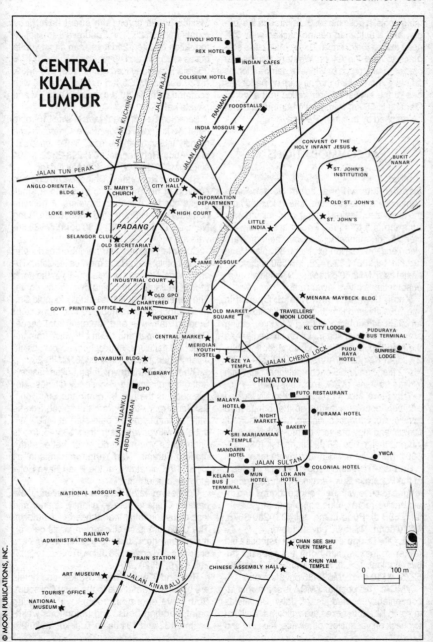

CENTRAL
KUALA
LUMPUR

JALAN KUCHING

JALAN RAJA

JALAN ABDUL RAHMAN

TIVOLI HOTEL
REX HOTEL
INDIAN CAFES
COLISEUM HOTEL

FOODSTALLS

INDIA MOSQUE

CONVENT OF THE
HOLY INFANT JESUS

BUKIT
NANAR

JALAN TUN PERAK

ANGLO-ORIENTAL
BLDG.

ST. MARY'S
CHURCH

OLD
CITY HALL

ST. JOHN'S
INSTITUTION

LOKE HOUSE

INFORMATION
DEPARTMENT

OLD ST. JOHN'S

ST. JOHN'S

HIGH COURT

PADANG

LITTLE INDIA

SELANGOR CLUB

OLD SECRETARIAT

JAME MOSQUE

INDUSTRIAL COURT

OLD GPO

GOVT. PRINTING OFFICE

CHARTERED
BANK

MENARA MAYBECK BLDG.

INFOKRAT

OLD MARKET
SQUARE

TRAVELLERS'
MOON LODGE

CENTRAL MARKET

KL CITY LODGE

PUDURAYA
BUS TERMINAL

MERIDIAN
YOUTH HOSTEL

DAYABUMI BLDG.

SZE YA
TEMPLE

JALAN CHENG LOCK

PUDU
RAYA
HOTEL

SUNRISE
LODGE

LIBRARY

CHINATOWN

GPO

FUTO RESTAURANT

JALAN TUANKU ABDUL RAHMAN

MALAYA
HOTEL

FURAMA HOTEL

NIGHT
MARKET

BAKERY

SRI MARIAMMAN
TEMPLE

MANDARIN
HOTEL

JALAN SULTAN

YWCA

NATIONAL MOSQUE

KELANG
BUS
TERMINAL

MUN
HOTEL

LOK ANN
HOTEL

COLONIAL HOTEL

RAILWAY
ADMINISTRATION BLDG.

CHAN SEE SHU
YUEN TEMPLE

ART MUSEUM

TRAIN STATION

KHUN YAM
TEMPLE

JALAN KINABALU

CHINESE ASSEMBLY HALL

TOURIST OFFICE

NATIONAL
MUSEUM

0   100 m

MOON

ming pools, a golf course, trails through the jungle, and a utilitarian casino packed with Chinese testing their karma. This is Malaysia's sole place to lose money on Western games like blackjack and craps or Chinese games such as *tai sai*. Experts claim that its gaming parlor has one of the lowest pay-out ratios in the world! Genting is 56 km from Kuala Lumpur and can be reached by bus from Puduraya.

ACCOMMODATIONS

Budget

Meridian International Youth Hostel: Kuala Lumpur's favorite travelers' hotel is located near the renovated Central Market, a 10-minute walk from the bus terminal. Prices are somewhat steep for dormitory facilities, but the rooms are clean and the location excellent. 36 Jalan Hang Kasturi, tel. (03) 232-1428, M$6.50 with youth hostel card, M$8.50 otherwise. The Indian owner sometimes offers lower rates.

Kuala Lumpur Youth Hostel: Opened in late 1989, this modern and clean four-story hostel offers 84 dormitory beds, TV lounge, dining area, and tour services. Not as convenient as the Meridian, but larger and more comfortable. 21 Jalan Kampung Attap, tel. (03) 230-6870, M$12 first night, M$8 each additional night with YH membership (M$30 extra per year).

Travellers' Moon Lodge: A centrally located and very popular guesthouse that brings rave reviews from budget travelers. Managers Fred, Cletus, and May are very willing with sightseeing and dining tips. 36 Jl. Silang, tel. (03) 230-6601, M$10 dorm, M$25-30 private room.

Sunrise Travellers Lodge: Five minutes east of the Puduraya Bus Terminal is another popular guesthouse with both budget dorms and inexpensive rooms, plus complimentary breakfast. 89B Jl. Pudu Lama, tel. (03) 230-8878, M$10 dorm, M$25-30 private room.

KL City Lodge: Not really a guesthouse but rather an inexpensive hotel just opposite the bus terminal. 16A Jl. Pudu Lama, tel. (03) 230-5275, M$10 dorm, M$25-35 private room.

YMCA: This popular YMCA is somewhat inconveniently located just off Jalan Brickfields in south KL. Both sexes are welcome. Call first to check on vacancies; otherwise, the Lido and

Mexico hotels across the street have good rooms from M$25. The Puduraya Terminal information counter, 2nd level, can direct you to buses 4, 33, 36, and 49 which reach the YMCA. 95 Jalan Kandang Kerbau, tel. (03) 274-1439, M$20 dorms, M$25 fan-cooled doubles with common bath, M$50 a/c doubles with TV and private bath.

Paradise Bed & Breakfast: A small 10-room hotel two km north of downtown. Operated by a friendly Indian "manageress." 319-1 Jalan Tuanku Abdul Rahman, tel. (03) 293-2322. M$24 single, M$29 double, breakfast included.

Ben Soo Homestay: Chinese Ben Soo has converted his mother's house into a small guesthouse for Western travelers. A genuine homestay. 61 B Front (2nd floor), Jalan Tiong Nam, tel. (03) 291-8096, M$8 dorm, M$20 private room.

Colonial: KL has two neighborhoods with cheap hotels: Batu Road (now called Jalan Tuanku Abdul Rahman or Jalan TAR) to the north of Masjid Jame and Chinatown to the south. The venerable Colonial is actually four old Chinese shophouses combined into a maze of winding hallways and teetering staircases. Rooms are small and clean but noisy from the open wall partitions. Atmosphere . . . of sorts. 43 Jalan Sultan, tel. (03) 238-0336, M$20-25.

Others in Chinatown: Jalan Sultan has several other cheap but *very* seedy Chinese hotels such as the Lee Mun and the Sun Kong. Ask for a room away from the street. Rooms with fan and common bath start at M$20, a/c doubles with private bath are M$35-45. In this price range you might do much better at the modern Furama, Nan Yang, or Mandarin, all located in Chinatown, or the Pudu Raya Hotel atop the bus terminal.

Coliseum: Jalan Tuanku has several inexpensive Chinese hotels—slightly cleaner and less claustrophobic than those in Chinatown. The Coliseum is chiefly known for its cafe on the ground floor, but the upstairs rooms are spacious and cheap. 98 Jalan Tuanku, tel. (03) 292-6270, M$20-25.

Rex and Tivoli: These two low-end hotels are popular alternatives to the busy Coliseum. Both have enormous rooms with chipping paint, sagging beds, and ubiquitous washbasins. 132 and 134 Jalan Tuanku, M$20-25.

KUALA LUMPUR ACCOMMODATIONS

HOTEL	SINGLE	DOUBLE	ADDRESS	PHONE (03)
LUXURY	**M$**	**M$**		
Equatorial	300-350	350-400	Jl. Sultan Ismail	261-7777
Federal	200-280	220-300	Jl. Bukit Bintang	248-9166
Holiday Inn Centre	300-400	350-450	Jl. Raja Laut	293-9232
Hilton	400-450	500-600	Jl. Sultan Ismail	242-2222
Concorde	250-300	300-350	Jl. Sultan Ismail	243-0033
Park Avenue	250-300	300-350	16 Jl. Imbi	242-8333
Park Royal	350-450	400-500	Jl. Sultan Ismail	242-5588
Regent	400-550	500-700	160 Jl. Bukit Bintang	241-8000
MODERATE				
Fortuna	150-180	180-200	87 Berangan	241-9111
Furama	90-120	100-150	Jl. Sultan Ismail	230-1777
Malaya	90-120	100-150	Jl. Hang Lekir	232-7772
Mandarin	65-90	75-100	2-8 Jl. Sultan	230-3000
Pudu Raya	90-120	100-150	Jl. Pudu Terminal	232-1000
Asia Kuala Lumpur	60-80	80-120	69 Jl. Haji Hussein	292-6077
BUDGET				
Ben Soo Homestay	8	20-25	61B Jl. Front, Tiong Nam	291-8096
Coliseum	20-25	20-25	98 Jl. Tuanku Abdul Rahman	292-6270
Colonial	20-25	20-25	43 Jl. Sultan	238-0336
Lee Mun	20-25	22-28	9 Jl. Sultan	238-2981
Lok Ann	25-30	30-40	118A Jl. Petaling	239-9544
Meridian Youth Hostel	9	–	36 Jl. Hang Kasturi	232-1428
Paradise B&B	24	29	319-1 Jl. Tuanku Abdul Rahman	293-2322
Rex	20-25	20-25	134 Jl. Tuanku Abdul Rahman	298-3895
Tivoli	20-25	20-25	132 Jl. Tuanku Abdul Rahman	
YMCA	20-40	25-50	Jl. Kandang Kerbau	274-1439

Moderate Accommodations

A double whammy of recession and hotel over-building in the mid-1980s has kept room prices in Kuala Lumpur among the lowest in Southeast Asia. There have been some spectacular bankruptcies. Many hotels give discounts by request to walk-in customers. Hotel charts in this chapter should serve as guidelines only; don't hesitate to ask for discounts if you plan to stay for several days. Rates in the following hotels are subject to 10% service charge and 5% government tax.

Pudu Raya Hotel: Facilities at this new 200-room tower just above the bus terminal include a restaurant, a health club, and a gym. Good location, great price. Puduraya Bus Terminal, 4th floor, tel. (03) 232-1000, M$90-120.

Furama: This high-rise hotel in the heart of Chinatown is another good choice for mid-priced accommodations. Jalan Sultan, tel. (03) 230-1777, M$90-150.

Station Hotel: Inside the famous train station is a newly refurbished hotel with spacious rooms, a Malaysian restaurant, and a cocktail lounge. All rooms are a/c with private bath. Jalan Sultan Hishamuddin, tel. 274-7433, M$80-100 single, M$120-180 double.

Luxury Accommodations

Shangri-La: Rated among the leading hotels in the country together with the Regent and Oriental. Three restaurants serve Japanese, Cantonese, and European fare. Other amenities include a health club, a semicircular pool, Club Oz, and the largest guest rooms in town. 11 Jalan Sultan Ismail, tel. (03) 232-2388, M$450-700.

Regent: KL's newest property boasts 542 luxurious guestrooms with panoramic views, five restaurants, four bars, and a beautiful swimming pool. 160 Jalan Bukit Bintang, tel. (03) 241-8000, M$400-700.

Carcosa Seri Negara: Special mention must be made of this spectacular pair of fully restored colonial mansions set on 450 acres of landscaped gardens, just five minutes from city center. Developed by Amanresorts (Amanpuri, Amandari, etc.), this splendid creation will hopefully inspire more renovation of KL's endangered colonial architecture. However, the place ain't cheap. Taman Tasik Perdana, tel. (03) 230-6766, fax (03) 230-6959, M$900-2800.

RESTAURANTS

Chinatown Night Market

Kuala Lumpur's most unique and memorable dining experience is at the inexpensive and delicious food stalls in Chinatown. Jalan Hang Lekir, at the eastern end of the street, has several popular stalls serving steamboat, chili crab, steamed prawns, and *bah kut teh* (pork ribs with rice). Futo House of Curry Laksa has M$2 claypots, or try the well-marked corner stall for delicious *lo han kuo,* an ice-cold drink made from boiled *longan* and sugar. Chinatown food stalls operate evenings only until about 2000. A full description of Malay dishes and food stall specialties is found under "Penang."

Pasar Malams

Malay food stalls are found on Jalan Masjid India two blocks north of the mosque, and at Chow Kit Market in the north end of town. The Pasar Minggu (Sunday Market) in Kampong Baru is held on Saturday evenings. It has good food and a worthwhile antique store but is otherwise disappointing. Saturday evenings are better spent on Jalan Tuanku Abdul Rahman, which is closed to traffic and packed with shoppers. Venues for other night markets change frequently; check the *Malay Mail* for current locations.

Indian Cafes

Kuala Lumpur's best inexpensive South Indian restaurants are in the Brickfields area near the YMCA. Most are banana-leaf coffeeshops serving vegetarian *murtabaks* or curried specialties at extremely low prices. The highly recommended Devi Annapoorna Restaurant on Lorong Maarof in Bangsar dishes up a tasty *sampoorna* vegetarian dinner for just M$10. This nonprofit venture is run by volunteers who turn the proceeds over to the Temple of Fine Arts.

Coliseum

This 70-year-old hotel and restaurant is considered a Malaysian institution for its M$12 sizzling, pepper, and sirloin steaks served on clean starched tablecloths by elderly Hainanese waiters. If walls could talk, they would whisper of British plantation barons, wealthy Chinese tycoons, and local politicians charting Malaysia's future over endless rounds of ass-kicking *stengahs.* 100 Jalan Tuanku Abdul Rahman. Inexpensive to moderate.

Le Coq d'Or

Once the lavish mansion of a wealthy Chinese merchant and now quite run-down, this grand old dame still evokes images of old Malaysia with its lofty ceilings, Italian marble statues, oil paintings in gilt frames, and airy dining rooms ventilated by fans powered by reconditioned DC-3 engines. Skip the *plat du jour* and try the beef fondue, chicken breast with cognac, steak á la Luciano, flaming crepes suzette, or the famous Bombe Alaska. 121 Jalan Ampang. Moderate to expensive.

Riverboat

This trendy bar and restaurant in the restyled Central Market serves Western dishes to the sounds of '60s rock music. It's hip and cool and a refreshing change from Asian cuisine. Moderate.

PRACTICALITIES

Airport Arrival

Kuala Lumpur's Subang Airport, located 22 km from city center, has all the standard facilities such as post office, left-luggage service, international phones, and a tourist information office open daily 0900-2300. Toll-free telephones are available in the arrival hall. Taxis operate on a coupon system and cost M$14-18 depending on the hotel. Private a/c buses leave every 45 minutes and cost M$8. Public bus 47 costs M$1.20, runs every 30 minutes, and stops at the Kelang Terminal in Chinatown.

Getting Around

Kuala Lumpur is fairly compact; public transportation is only necessary for cross-town journeys. Buses are cheap but routes are difficult to follow since bus maps are unavailable. Taxis are metered and cost a dirt-cheap 30 *sen* per mile with a 70-*sen* flagfall. Taxis carry a 20% surcharge for a/c and a 50% surcharge from midnight to 0600. Car-rental companies are located at the airport, in hotels, and in shopping complexes.

Tourist Information

The Malaysia Tourism Promotion Board (MTPB), tel. 293-5188, is inconveniently located on the 2nd level of the Putra World Trade Center in the north of town; open Monday-Friday 0830-1645, Saturdays 0830-1300. Much better is the new Tourist Information Office (tel. 03-243-4929) on Jalan Ampang in KL's Golden Triangle. Services include an information counter, MAS reservations, package tours, a phone and fax center, a restaurant, audio-visual shows, and cultural performances daily at 1530. Visitors staying near Chinatown can also check the KL City Tourist Office (tel. 03-238-1832) located on Jalan Sultan Hishamuddin near the famous train station.

KUALA LUMPUR PHONE NUMBERS

Directory	103
Information	108
Telegram	104
Emergency	999
Airport	776-1014
Railway	238-7197
Bus Info	230-0145
Taxi Info	230-0145

Best source for city directions is *Lani's Kuala Lumpur Discovery Map,* available from the tourist offices.

Other Information

Visas: Malaysian visas can be extended at the Immigration Office on Jalan Pantai Baru, tel. 757-8155. Most foreign diplomatic offices are open Monday-Friday 0900-1500, but a quick phone call might save a wasted trip.

Mail: The General Post Office in the Dayabumi Complex is open daily except Sundays 0900-1900.

Taman Negara Reservations: Get information and reservations from the Malaysia Tourist Information Complex (tel. 03-243-4929) at 109 Jalan Ampang.

Travel Agents: Get budget tickets from the youth travel bureau of MSL Travel located in the Asia Hotel Kuala Lumpur, 69 Jalan Haji Hussin, tel. 298-9722.

Package tours of Taman Negara, Sabah, and Sarawak; rafting expeditions; and scuba-diving adventures can be booked through Asia Overland Services, 35-M Jalan Dewan Sultan Sulaiman Satu, tel. 292-5637.

Language Instruction: Malay, Thai, Japanese, and Chinese language lessons at the YMCA are priced from M$120 per 10-week session.

International Telephone: Overseas calls can be made 24 hours daily from the Central Telegraph Office on Jalan Raja Chulan, and until midnight from Subang Airport. Towns within Malaysia and Singapore can be dialed directly from public phones.

Leaving Kuala Lumpur

By Air: Subang International Airport can be reached by taxi for M$15-18 or by bus 47, which takes 45 minutes, costs M$1.20, and leaves hourly from the Kelang Bus Terminal on Jalan Sultan Mohammed near Chinatown. Airport information is at tel. (03) 776-1014; MAS airport information, tel. (03) 746-4555. Departure tax is M$15 for international flights, M$5 to Singapore, M$3 domestic.

By Bus: Kuala Lumpur's Puduraya Bus Terminal near Chinatown is the departure and arrival point for most buses and taxis to Singapore and all West Coast destinations. Departures to Penang and Singapore are most frequent mornings before 0900. Call (03) 230-0145 for exact departure information.

The Kelang Bus Terminal on Jalan Sultan Mohammed serves sights near Kuala Lumpur, Selangor, and the airport. Buses to East Coast destinations leave from the Mara Bus Terminal on Jalan Medan Tuanku and from the car park opposite the Putra World Trade Center in the north of town. More East Coast buses leave from the Pekeliling Bus Station near the PWTC.

By Train: Trains leave from the station on Jalan Hishamuddin. Call (03) 238-7197 for exact departures and prices. Schedules and informa- tion on student discounts, 10-day railpasses, and the International Express to Bangkok can be picked up in the lobby.

Long-distance Taxis: Share taxis provide the fastest and most exciting way to get around Malaysia. Taxis leave from the Puduraya Terminal when filled. Fares are divided by the passengers and average about 50% more than an air-conditioned bus. Ignore the sidewalk touts and deal directly with the drivers inside the terminal.

TAMAN NEGARA

Straddling a range of mountains in the heart of Peninsular Malaysia that has never experienced glaciation, Taman Negara ("National Park" in Bahasa Malaysia) is one of the world's oldest tropical rainforests—over 130 million years old. Malaysia's premier park is isolated (the only link to the outside world is the Tembeling River), pristine (there are no roads in the park), and enormous (4,343 square km, large enough for six Singapores).

Highlights include the three-hour river trip to park headquarters at Kuala Tahan, hiking through the dense jungle on well-marked trails, and spending a night searching for wildlife from an elevated observation hide. Local fauna includes tapir, mouse deer, wild boar, and several cats, including civets and the elusive tiger, but sightings of larger game are rare. Birdlife is plentiful, however, and an evening at a salt lick will almost guarantee a sighting of smaller animals.

Jungle Walks

Despite the size of the park and endless possibilities for multi-day treks, most visitors limit themselves to the shorter trails, which lead out from park headquarters. Hiking paths are well marked and easy to follow with maps provided by local rangers. Many of the trails were originally mapped and marked by a 42-year-old Australian naturalist named Ken Rubeli, who has actively campaigned since 1974 to stop the construction of dams and roads in the park.

A popular half-day hike leads to the summit of Bukit Teresek and then on to the salt lick at Tabing. Guides will point out immense nest ferns that sprout from tree trunks, exquisite hanging necklaces of red flowers that smell like rotting flesh to draw insects, trilobite beetles protected by their reddish armor, and the sounds of the "perfect octave" bird. Leeches can be stopped by spraying your shoes with insecticide. From Bukit Teresek the trail descends to the Tahan River, where you can float downriver to Kuala Tahan while keeping an eye out for pesky *buntal* fish that nibble on fingernails and toenails.

South of Kuala Tahan are more salt licks and a bat cave where thousands of fruit bats hang from the ceiling and stare silently into flashlight beams. Taman Negara's most ambitious hike is to the summit of 2,187-meter Gunung Tahan, loftiest peak in Peninsular Malaysia. Guides are required on this grueling 10-day trek.

River Trips

Motorized canoes can be hired at park headquarters to explore several of the rivers peppered with rapids, waterfalls, and swimming pools. Prices start at M$60 for two-hour journeys on six-man boats.

One of the most popular trips is the upstream ride to the cataracts and natural pools of Lata Berkoh. Another three-hour canoe excursion goes up the Tembeling River to Kuala Terenggan, passing through seven sets of rapids expertly negotiated by the boatmen. Kuala Kenyam is 90 minutes farther through the huge primeval rainforest filled with chattering birds and *orang asli* settlements. Fishing for the fighting *Sceleropages formosus* is best during the months of February, March, July, and August. Equipment can be rented at park headquarters.

Wildlife Observatories

A wide variety of wildlife such as sambar, barking deer, wild boar, and various species of small cats can sometimes be seen and photographed from observation hides that overlook the half-dozen salt licks situated within the park. Hides are two-story structures on stilts equipped with bunk beds, gravity-fed toilets, and wide observation windows. Wild animals are best spotted at those hides farthest from park headquarters. Bring a sleeping sheet, drinking water, a powerful flashlight, high-speed film, and patience.

General Information

Reservations: Boat and room reservations should be made in advance at the Malaysia Tourist Information Complex (tel. 03-243-4929) at 109 Jalan Ampang in Kuala Lumpur. Visitors arriving without advance booking might not find room on the afternoon boat from Kuala Tembeling to park headquarters. A M$30 deposit is required to confirm.

Organized Tours: Fully guided adventure tours can be arranged from STA and Asian Overland Services in Kuala Lumpur.

What to Bring: A long-sleeved shirt, long pants, and bug repellent will help ward off the insects. Sneakers are fine for hiking. Don't forget swimwear, antibiotic ointment, antimalarials, a powerful flashlight, and high-speed film for best results in the low light beneath the jungle canopy. Food and other essentials can be purchased in the park grocery store. Camping equipment, sleeping sheets, and fishing rods can be rented from the same shop.

When to Go: Taman Negara is driest between March and September and closed during the rainy season from mid-November to February.

Accommodations

Most lodging is located in Kuala Tahan, a surprising jungle town with mown lawns, manicured gardens, generator-powered electricity, and several small restaurants. Facilities range from campsites priced at M$5 to modern brick chalets with double beds and private baths at M$40. Tents can be rented for M$3. The Asrama Dormitory is clean and costs M$10 per person in rooms with eight beds and shared

bath. Simple but adequate visitors' lodges have been built at Kuala Atok, Kuala Terenggan, and Kuala Kenyam, but certainly the most memorable places to stay are the elevated wildlife observatories at Tabing, Kumbang, and Cegar Anging.

Jerantut: overnighters in Jerantut can stay at the popular Chet Fatt Hotel (tel. 09-265805) on Jalan Diwangsa, where clean rooms cost M$15-25. A great information center.

Getting There

From Kuala Lumpur: First travel to Jerantut and then take a bus or taxi 16 km farther to the frontier town of Kuala Tembeling. Allow four hours for this journey. Riverboats leave Tembeling daily at 0900 and 1400 and reach park headquarters at Kuala Tahan about three hours later. An early start is essential from Kuala Lumpur. Share taxis and public buses leave from KL's Puduraya Bus Terminal direct to Jerantut. Public buses and taxis continue up the winding road to Tembeling.

From Singapore: A train departs Singapore at 2100 and arrives in Jerantut at 0630 the following morning. Continue up to Tembeling by public transport, or make advance arrangements and have the train stop directly at Tembeling Halt, the station between Jerantut and Kuala Lipis.

From Kota Baru: The morning train from Kota Baru misses the afternoon boat from Tembeling, so travelers coming from the north must spend a night in either Jerantut or Kuala Lipis.

From Kuantan: Take a bus or share taxi toward Kuala Lumpur and get off in the junction town of Temerloh. Buses from Temerloh to Tembeling take about two hours.

The Boat Ride: Riverboats leave Tembeling daily at 0900 and 1400, cost M$30 roundtrip, and take three hours to reach park headquarters at Kuala Tahan. The 60-km trip passes through thick jungle of huge *merbau* trees with immense root systems, liana water vines, kingfishers, hornbills, and several *orang asli* settlements on the southern banks.

HILL RESORTS

Peninsular Malaysia has four hill resorts that offer a refreshing break from the sweltering heat of the coast. Genting Highlands, 51 km from Kuala Lumpur, is a gambling resort with expensive hotels and a golf course geared to wealthy Chinese weekenders. Fraser's Hill, 105 km north of Kuala Lumpur, is a weekend resort popular with businessmen and school groups because of its proximity to Kuala Lumpur. The nine-hole golf course and the health club are the big draws here. The small resort of Maxwell Hill is located just outside Taiping. If you have time for only one hill resort, I'd recommend Cameron Highlands, some 200 km north of Kuala Lumpur. This is Malaysia's premier hill resort and a good place to relax away the rigors of overland travel.

FRASER'S HILL

According to legend, this small golf resort takes its name from an English adventurer who operated a mule train, a gambling hall, and an opium den up here around the turn of the century. When Bishop Ferguson-Davie of Singapore climbed the mountain in a fruitless search for the recluse in 1910, Fraser had disappeared but the bishop's discovery led to the establishment of the hill resort in the 1920s.

Fraser's Hill is relatively undeveloped and almost completely deserted except on weekends, when wealthy businessmen come here to play golf and tennis and hike along the jungle paths. A map with hiking trails, waterfalls, and other attractions can be picked up at the tourist information office near the Merlin Hotel. Fraser's is an excellent place for golf since greens fees are only M$8 and clubs can be rented from the pro shop. Bring some warm clothing since it gets chilly here at 1,524 meters above sea level.

Accommodations
FHDC Bungalows: Most of the bungalows and Tudor chalets at FH are operated by the Fraser's Hill Development Corporation, tel. (09) 382201. Doubles start at M$30-60 per night and are M$5 higher on weekends. Reservations are recommended on weekends and holidays and during the peak months of April, August, and December.

Merlin Hotel: Fraser's only international hotel has 109 rooms overlooking the golf course, which was constructed over a landfilled sluice and not, contrary to first impressions, across an abandoned tin mine. The Merlin has a comfortable coffee shop and a weekend disco, rents bicycles, and offers exchange services seven days a week. Jalan Lady Guillemard, tel. (09) 382274, M$130-200. Discounts given during the week.

Corona Nursery Youth Hostel: This privately run hostel at the far end of the golf course has several small but cheap rooms from M$7. High Pines Bungalows is another inexpensive possibility. The information office can help with directions; they'll also call about vacancies.

Gap Rest House: This old-world bungalow located a few kilometers down the road from FH is a great alternative to staying directly at the resort. Rooms with private baths from M$25. Highly recommended.

Getting There
First take a bus or taxi to Kuala Kubu Baru (KKB) 62 km north of Kuala Lumpur. Then take another bus or taxi the remaining distance to the resort. Buses for KKB leave regularly from Kuala Lumpur's Puduraya Bus Terminal. The twice-daily bus from KKB to Fraser's Hill departs at 0800 and 1200. The same bus returns from Fraser's to KKB at 1000 and 1400. Share taxis are also available at M$6. Alternately, you might take a public bus from KKB to the Gap and then try hitching the remaining eight km up to Fraser's Hill. Two inexpensive hotels in KKB and a rest-house at the Gap can put you up if stranded.

CAMERON HIGHLANDS

In 1885, a British government surveyor on a mapping assignment reported his discovery of "a fine plateau with gentle slopes shut in by lofty mountains." Soon after his favorable report, Indian tea planters and Chinese vegetable farmers settled in the valley and the British government constructed a road to serve its cool re-

CAMERON HIGHLANDS

MARKET

ARMY CAMP

WONG VILLA

BRINCHANG

KOWLOON HOTEL

MERLIN HOTEL

CLUBHOUSE

ORANG ASLI SETTLEMENT

SAM PO TEMPLE

CAMERON GOLF LINKS

G. PERDAN (1,576m)

YE OLD SMOKEHOUSE

2

G. JASPAR (1,696m)

12

BALA'S CHALETS

PARIT WATERFALL

G. BEREMBAN (1,841m)

3

11

TANAH RATA

5

GARDEN HOTEL

MOSQUE

7

HOTELS

CLOCK TOWER

8

CHURCH

BUS AND TAXI

PLAYGROUND

TOURIST INFORMATION AND MUSEUM

13

G. MENTIGA (1,563m)

ROBINSON WATERFALL

9A

BHARAT TEA ESTATE

14

9

POWER STATION

TO BOH TEA ESTATE 8 kms

0   1 km

TO TAPAH 52kms

GUNONG EMAS TEA ESTATE

© MOON PUBLICATIONS, INC.

CAMERON HIGHLANDS ACCOMMODATIONS

HOTEL	SINGLE (M$)	DOUBLE (M$)	ADDRESS	PHONE (05)
Bala's Chalets	10-25	25-50	Km 1 Main Road	941660
Federal	30-35	35-50	44 Main	941777
Merlin Inn	180-280	180-280	Tanah Rata	941205
Seah Meng	20-30	30-40	39 Main	941615
Ye Old Smokehouse	200-280	200-360	Golf Course	941214

treat. Today the Cameron Highlands is the largest and best organized of Malaysia's four hill resorts. Most visitors are immediately struck by the strong British flavor: Tudor lodgings, a wide green golf course, and manicured flower gardens. There's little to do but relax in the sun or hike through the thick jungle, but it's a welcome relief from the concrete towns of the lowlands. Cameron has three small towns but most visitors head directly for Tanah Rata, where most of the hotels and restaurants are located.

Attractions

Hiking: The tourist office shut down a few years ago but accurate maps showing hiking trails and tea plantations can be purchased for M$2 from shops in Tanah Rata. The muddy pools at Parit Waterfall and the more impressive falls at Robinson can be reached in less than 30 minutes. Allow a full day to climb Gunung Beremban via trail seven. While wandering the poorly marked trails you might come across groups of *orang asli,* Malaysia's original peoples who now dress in blue jeans and T-shirts but continue to hunt with traditional blowguns.

Tea Plantations: Several tea plantations welcome visitors to watch the various production processes such as drying, rolling, fermenting, and packing. All are very distant from town center and without private transportation; the only practical way to visit a plantation is by share taxi or the three-hour tour which costs M$15. Vegetable gardens and flower nurseries are also open to the public.

Golf: Cameron's famous 18-hole naturally air-conditioned golf course costs M$30 during the day and M$20 after 1400. Club rentals are M$10. The rough is so radical that ball boys follow you around, diving into the towering grasses to rescue lost balls.

Accommodations

Bala's Holiday Chalets: Cameron's favorite budget hostel is a confusing rabbit warren of tiny rooms, hidden bathrooms, lukewarm showers, and an expensive restaurant, but the views from the grassy patio can't be beat. A 20-minute walk up the road from Tanah Rata, tel. (05) 941660, M$6 dorm, M$10-50 rooms.

Tanah Rata: Cameron Highland's principal township has a half-dozen inexpensive hotels that charge M$15-40 for small rooms. The Federal and Seah Meng are two of the better choices.

Brinchang: This nondescript town five km beyond Tanah Rata also has several inexpensive Chinese hotels with rooms in the same price range. Brinchang is surrounded by ugly housing projects and has a depressing urban feel, but the Wong Villa has dorms for just M$4 and shared rooms for M$5.

Ye Old Smokehouse: This 20-room Tudor mansion just opposite the golf course is worth a photo even if you can't afford the tariff. Golf Course Road, tel. (05) 941214, fax (05) 941214, M$200-360.

Merlin Inn: Cameron's international-standard hotel has 60 rooms with private bath and color TV. Box 4, Tanah Rata, tel. (05) 941205, M$180-280.

Getting There

Cameron Highlands can be reached from Kuala Lumpur or Penang by bus or taxi to Tapah, from where buses leave hourly up the winding road to Tanah Rata. A direct bus from KL's Puduraya Bus Terminal departs at 0830 and arrives in Tanah Rata around 1300. Tapah's transportation center is in the Restoran Caspian, which serves good Muslim food and can help with onward connections.

Leaving Cameron
Bus tickets from Cameron can be purchased from Bala's or the Town House Hotel in Tanah Rata. Buses to Kuala Lumpur depart at 1430, to Butterworth (Penang) at 0800. Bus departures are more frequent from Tapah: Singapore at 1000, 2030, and 2100; Penang at 1000, 1100, 1200, 1300, and 1430; Malacca at 1000, 1115, and 1315; Hat Yai (Thailand) at 2330; Kuantan at 0930 and 2200. Restoran Caspian in Tapah sells tickets.

WEST CENTRAL

IPOH

Ipoh, capital of Perak State, is a predominately Chinese town of 500,000 residents. It's attractively situated on a limestone bed with twin limestone towers guarding its northern and southern extremities. The city was founded in 1884 after the discovery of immense tin deposits in the nearby Kinta Valley. Thousands of Chinese tin miners flooded the boomtown, which was later nicknamed "millionaires' town" after the numerous wealthy miners who built their mansions here in the early 20th century.

In recent years the tin industry has fallen on hard times but Ipoh still recalls its rich past through its stately colonial-style architecture, magnificent Perak homes constructed with gingerbread molding, and elegant double-story Chinese shophouses embellished with lovely Peranakan tilework. While the city lacks the historical and architectural attractions of other Malaysian destinations, it offers a memorable ambience and is refreshingly free of other tourists. Visitors with limited time can get a quick impression with a three- or four-hour walking tour starting from the train or bus stations.

Attractions

Railway Station: Constructed in 1917 by British architects, this elegant whitewashed building is now a nostalgic hotel with an immense dining room and reasonably priced lunch specials. A fine place for drinks before starting your walking tour, though Paul Theroux described it thusly: "It is the sort of hotel that has a skeleton in every closet and a register thick with the pseudonyms of adulterers."

Colonial Architecture: Several outstanding examples of British 1920s architecture can be found grouped together within a few blocks of the railway station. The Ipoh Town Hall immediately across the street features colonnaded wings projecting at 45 degrees from the Palladian facade. A small tourist office with a good collection of pamphlets and maps is reached through the rear entrance. City Hall is flanked by a modern state mosque and the colonial High Court. North along the multicolored sidewalk is the Ipoh Club, the rococo St. Michael's School, and finally the modest India Mosque.

Old Ipoh: Continue circling back around to explore the colorful streets of Jalan Sultan Yusof, Jalan Leech, and Jalan Treacher. Ipoh's old town comprises the small area west of the muddy Kinta River. Although progress is changing the character of the neighborhood, a great deal of remarkable Peranakan and Chinese shophouse architecture is still standing. Note the gigantic rococo scrollwork, pompous Palladian porticoes on narrow shops, and multihued Peranakan peacocks at Jalans Treacher and Panglima.

Tengah Mosque: This surprising little gem just across the Kinta River is also called Masjid Panglima Kinta. Jalan Hume has some more fine shophouses. From here you can explore Ipoh's new town with sidewalk shops, small restaurants serving famous Ipoh *kway toew,* and the well-named Bomba Fire Station on Jalan Sultan Idris Shah.

Attractions Near Ipoh

Kelly's Castle: This mysterious mansion buried under a tangle of jungle vegetation was constructed in the 1920s by a wealthy Scottish rubber planter named William Kelly Smith. In 1926, while construction was still in progress, Smith left for England and died unexpectedly in Lisbon. His uncompleted castle and vast estate were sold by his widow. Kelly's Folly is 12 km south of Ipoh just off the road to Batu Gajah in the Kinta Kellas Rubber Estate. Take the bus toward Batu Gajah and ask the driver to drop you off nearby.

Cave Temples: Several Buddhist caves are located just off the trunk road which runs north and south of Ipoh. The following caves can

IPOH

© MOON PUBLICATIONS, INC

be toured quickly if you spot them from the speeding bus.

Sam Po Cave Temple: Five km south of Ipoh on the east side of the road, Sam Po has two vegetarian restaurants, a turtle pond, and is one of the largest Buddhist monasteries in Malaysia.

Perak Tong Cave Temple: 6.5 km north of Ipoh on the east side of the road, this is a better stop with 40 Buddhist statues and over 100 murals ranging in size from miniatures to immense portraits of Chinese mythological deities more than 30 meters tall. New paintings are constantly added by visiting artists.

Accommodations

YMCA: Ipoh's YMCA is somewhat distant from the center of town but it's clean, friendly, and very quiet. Grab a taxi or take a bus from the city bus terminal. Rooms are air-conditioned with private bath. 211 Jalan Raja Musa Aziz, tel. (05) 540809, M$7 dorm, M$25-35.

Southeastern: This rough but adequate hotel is conveniently located near the bus and train stations. Jalan Leong Boon Swee, M$15-25.

Rex: Another simple but survivable Chinese hotel with clerks and furnishings from the '20s. Jalan Sultan Iskandar Shah near the Kinta River. 540093, M$10-20.

Embassy: Most of Ipoh's inexpensive hotels are located in the business quarter near the traffic circle at the south end of Jalan Chamberlain. This is also Ipoh's noisy nightlife and restaurant center so ask for a room away from the street. The Embassy is the first in a line of hotels which includes the Hollywood, the City, the Cathay, the Beauty, the Kowloon, and the Winner. 35 Chamberlain, tel. (05) 549496, M$25-50.

Station: This colonial relic in the north end of Ipoh has 34 enormous but musty a/c rooms each with private bath, separate sitting room, TV, and refrigerator. Tons of atmosphere together with the smells of mold. Club Road, tel. (05) 512588, M$70-120. Discounted rooms are M$46-75.

Excelsior: Ipoh's second-best hotel has 133 a/c rooms, a comfortable coffee shop, and small lounge with live entertainment. 43 Clarke Street, tel. (05) 536666, M$140-180 single or double.

Royal Casuarina: Ipoh's finest hotel is located five minutes outside town in a residential neighborhood near the race course. 217 rooms, 16 suites, huge swimming pool. 18 Jalan Gopeng, tel. (05) 505555, M$180-250.

Leaving Ipoh

Ipoh has three bus terminals located around the same intersection. Private operators will usually approach and help you find the next available bus. Buses to Kuala Lumpur, Butterworth, Singapore, and other interstate destinations leave from the terminal behind the big modern building. Bus offices are on the ground floor. Buses to Lumut (the town for ferries to Pangkor Island) leave hourly from the same terminal complex and from the smaller station across the road. Buses to Kuala Kangsar and Taiping leave from the local bus terminal.

PANGKOR ISLAND

Located 88 km southwest of Ipoh off the coast from Lumut, Pulau Pangkor (Pulau is Bahasa Malaysia for "Island") is an undeveloped jungle-clad island with long beaches and clear waters. Accommodation ranges from rudimentary shacks for students and budget travelers to expensive resorts for wealthy Malaysians and first-class travelers. Pangkor is popular with Malaysians who flock to the island on weekends, but Western visitors should be forewarned about some problems. First of all, beaches and waters are less pristine than those on Ko Samui or Phuket, and the inexpensive beach huts are uniformly depressing and rarely show the imagination or sensitivity that one finds at Thai beach resorts. What's worse is the uncollected trash that accumulates in large piles on the beach. Almost unbelievably, on my last visit I saw untreated sewage being dumped into large beachside pits. And finally, many Western women have reported being harassed by young men who have strange ideas about the morals of white ladies. Pangkor has potential to be a wonderful resort, but it still needs a great deal of improvement.

Attractions

Although the beaches have been marred with seaborne trash and unattractive huts, a day's excursion around the island can still be recom-

mended since the island is actually a stunning mix of thick jungle, deserted beaches, and idyllic Malay fishing villages. The entire island can be circled in four hours on funky bikes rented from the Pangkor Beach Club. Check the brakes (there are some terrifying hills on the east coast) and head north past the superb beaches of Telok Ketapang and Coral Bay, which can be reached by dirt path through strange trees. These two beaches are ideal spots for western women to escape Muslim voyeurs, provided you lie outside their lines of sight.

Privately owned Golden Sands Beach at the northwest corner charges a hefty M$30 admission charge for day-trippers; consequently it's the cleanest beach on the island. Pedal your bike over the steep hills to the commercial developments of the east coast to see the Chinese and Muslim cemeteries, boatbuilders, and an amazing house decorated with Heineken bottles.

The nondescript town of Sungai Pinang Besar has several good seafood restaurants. Continue through Pangkor Village past the immense jackfruit tree wrapped with protective coverings to the old Dutch Fort constructed in 1670 as an outpost to store tin and protect against Malay pirates. The abandoned fort has been carefully restored by Musium Negara. About 30 meters from the fort is a large boulder known as Batu Bersurat and inscribed *Ifcralo 1743*, with carvings of a tiger and a child. The rock is intriguing but nobody knows the exact meaning . . . tiger eats Dutch child?

Accommodations

Pangkor's guesthouses and hotels are concentrated on Pasir Bogak beach, across the island from Pangkor village.

Pangkor Anchor: Since the devolution of Sam Khoo's, Pangkor's most popular backpackers' stop has been the quiet and inexpensive set of bungalows operated by Mrs. Wong, chief information source on Pangkor Island. Pasir Bogak, tel. (05) 951363, M$12-20 for basic A-frame huts with mattresses on the floors.

D'Village Beach Resort: A tent complex with common bathrooms and cooking facilities is located at the north end of the beach. Pasir Bogak, M$8 per person, M$70-90 private chalets.

Pangkor Paradise Village: Another inexpensive but very rudimentary set of claustrophobic A-frame huts is scattered along the south

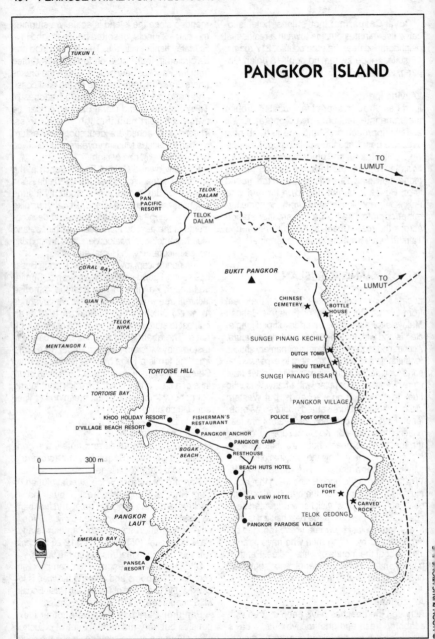

PANGKOR ISLAND

PANGKOR ISLAND ACCOMMODATIONS

HOTEL	SINGLE (M$)	DOUBLE (M$)	ADDRESS	PHONE (05)
Pansea	100-120	120-240	Pangkor Laut	951320
Pangkor Anchor	6	9-12	Pasir Bogak	951363
Rest House	20	20	Pasir Bogak	951236
Sam Khoo's Minicamp	6	8-12	Pasir Bogak	951164
Sea View	85	120	Pasir Bogak	951605

end of the beach. Nothing special, but very quiet. Pasir Bogak, tel. (05) 985872, M$12-18 huts, M$45-55 fan-cooled chalets.

Khoo Holiday Resort: Several years ago, Pangkor's original backpackers' homestay was redeveloped into an uncreative collection of towering concrete buildings that fail to inspire much love for old Sam. Motel 6 standards on such a lovely island? Come on, Sam. Pasir Bogak, tel. and fax (05) 951164, M$60-110 fan, M$80-150 a/c.

Sea View Hotel: The southern end of Pasir Bogak has several overpriced and poorly maintained hotels which face the beach. Best of the lot is this nondescript place that compensates with a pleasant restaurant. Pasir Bogak, tel. (05) 939159, M$85-120.

Tourist Complex Sri Bayu: This $2.5 million development includes a dormitory, 48 chalets, a swimming pool, tennis courts, and a small marina. Pasir Bogak, M$8 dorm, M$35-80 chalet.

Pan Pacific Resort Pangkor: All of the above accommodations are located on Bogak Beach, but the finest sand and amenities on Pangkor are at Telok Belanga (Golden Sands) Beach at the northwest corner. Facilities include a beautiful swimming pool with bar, a small golf course, water sports, and three restaurants. Six daily direct ferries from Lumut. Telok Belanga, tel. (05) 951399, fax (05) 951852, M$300-550.

Pansea Pangkor Laut Resort: Pangkor's other first-class resort is on Pangkor Laut, a 500-acre privately owned island just west of Pangkor. Managed by a French hotel corporation, the 120 individual bungalows and clubhouse have been designed in traditional Malay fashion with *atap* roofs and open-air verandas. The remaining 500 acres on the island have been left undeveloped except for hiking trails which lead across to aquamarine Emerald Bay. Day-use fee for nonresidents is M$30. Direct ferries leave four times daily from Lumut. Pangkor Laut, tel. (05) 951320, M$120-240.

Getting There

Ferries to Pangkor leave from Lumut, a small town served by bus and taxi from Ipoh, Taiping, Kuala Lumpur, Butterworth, and once daily from Cameron Highlands. Buses leave Ipoh hourly from the Lumut terminal and from the larger bus terminal across the street. Ferries from Lumut to Pangkor leave every 30 minutes 0800-1930, sail past Russian tankers, and stop briefly at Sungai Pinang Kechil before continuing to Pangkor. Stay on the boat until the last stop. Taxis can be hired for M$3 from Pangkor for the short ride to Pasir Bogak, where all of the inexpensive accommodations are located. Buses are infrequent. Lumut has two inexpensive hotels and money-changing facilities in case you get stranded.

KUALA KANGSAR

Perak State's former royal capital has enough outstanding architecture to make for a worthwhile three-hour stop between Ipoh and Penang. Leave your bags at the bus terminal and walk through the market, across the bridge, and along the muddy Perak River to the following sights.

Former Malay College: The long, hot walk is finally rewarded by a magnificent but crumbling colonial mansion which now serves as a local school. Everyone smiles at you as you wander around.

Muslim Cemetery: The royal burial grounds and small marble mausoleum at Bukit Chandan are lovely and informative; both ancient

KUALA KANGSAR

0   250m

© MOON PUBLICATIONS, INC.

and modern Muslim graves show a wide range of burial arrangements. Although nobody else will be there, visitors should be well dressed.

Ubudiah Mosque: Appearing like a vision from the Arabian Nights, this byzantine wonder is widely regarded as the most beautiful mosque in all of Malaysia. The Ubudiah was designed by an English engineer and constructed between 1913 and 1917 on orders of Idris Murshidul, the 28th Sultan of Perak. Across the road are a wonderful old Islamic school and elevated Perak homes with gingerbread moldings.

Iskandariah Palace: This magnificent Saracenic edifice was built in 1930 in an art-deco-Islamic style to replace the former palace, and underwent a major face-lift in 1984 for the coronation of the 34th sultan of Perak. It is unfortunately closed to the public. Views are best from the rear but decent photos are almost impossible.

Former Royal Palace and Museum: Situated down the road to the right, the elaborate Istana Kenangan (Palace of Memory) was constructed in traditional Malay style without the use of nails. Looks like a scene from *Alice in Wonderland*. Interior displays and interesting photographs relate Perak's colorful history.

TAIPING

Taiping's history goes back to the middle of the 19th century when the discovery of rich tin deposits attracted thousand of Chinese laborers to the fever-ridden mining camps of Larut. After warfare broke out between the rival secret societies of Hai San (Hakka) and Ghee Hin (Cantonese), British authorities stepped in and restored order; they wisely renamed the wild mining town Taiping, City of Everlasting Peace. Modern Taiping is an attractive little town of Peranakan shophouses and residences dating from the 1920s and '30s. Most visitors to Taiping spend the night up on Maxwell Hill.

Attractions
Lake Gardens: Taiping's most famous landmark is the garden laid out in 1890 over an abandoned tin pit by an Indian mine inspector named Captain Akwhi. A small zoo is located on the grounds of the 80-hectare park, as well as a prison where political troublemakers are held captive under the Internal Security Act.

State Museum: A small but well-presented collection of historical photographs and ethnological artifacts is displayed in Malaysia's oldest museum. Open daily 0900-1700; closed Fridays 1200-1430.

Ling Nam Temple: This Chinese temple on Station Street contains hundreds of gold-plated antiques imported from China during the last century.

Accommodations
Old Government Resthouse: Taiping's less expensive resthouse, located near the train station, has 10 rooms with private baths.

Jalan Setesen Taiping, tel. (05) 838482, M$12 double.

New Government Rest House: This beautiful Minangkabau-Roman resthouse on a hill overlooking the lake is a 45-minute walk from the station, so take a taxi. Jalan Sultan Mansor, tel. (05) 822044, M$24-36 double.

Other Budget Hotels: Taiping has over a dozen inexpensive Chinese hotels in the M$10-15 range, including the Wah Bee at 62 Jalan Kota and the Town Hotel on the same street.

MAXWELL HILL

Rising up directly behind the Taiping Lake Gardens, the former tea plantation of Bukit Larut is the oldest and least developed hill resort in Peninsular Malaysia. Maxwell is blessedly free of flashy casinos and trendy golf courses. What you find instead are hiking trails, flowers blooming in well-tended gardens, and a handful of fine old bungalows with superb views across Taiping to the Straits of Malacca. Access to the resort is along a one-way road which winds up the 1,372-meter hill through some 72 hairpin turns. Land Rovers leave hourly from the foot of the hill near Taiping Lake Gardens, make a midway stop at the Tea Garden House, and then continue up to the bungalows.

Accommodations

Accommodations are available at a number of bungalows and resthouses, including Rumah Rehat Bukit Larut (Maxwell Resthouse) at 1,036 meters and Gunong Hijau (Speedy Resthouse) at 1,113 meters. Both have singles from M$6 and doubles from M$8. Rumah Beringin (Watson Bungalow) at 1,036 meters and Rumah Cempaka (Hugh Low Bungalow) at 1,139 meters are M$60 for large eight-man cabins. Bookings can be made by calling the superintendent at tel. 886241 from the Land Rover station in Taiping.

PENANG

Penang Island, with its urban center of Georgetown, is Malaysia's most popular tourist destination. And for good reason. Unlike most other Asian towns, which have lost their distinctive identities through modernization and urban development, Penang has stayed wonderfully nostalgic by retaining its old architecture, narrow alleyways, extravagant temples, lively street markets, authentic ethnic neighborhoods, and, perhaps most importantly, its gracious sense of disorder. Much of the island is so unchanged from the late 19th century that you could imagine Conrad or Kipling sailing in on a broad-masted ship or sipping coffee in a small cafe. Penang is great. Don't miss it.

HISTORY

Penang opened to the outside world in 1786 when Sir Francis Light negotiated with the sultan of Kedah to make the island a tax-free and duty-free entrepôt for British traders. According to legend, the adventurer and visionary ex-navy man from Suffolk encouraged the clearing of the thick jungle by firing cannons filled with gold and silver coins into the island's undergrowth. Local Malays and Indian *sepoys* quickly cleared a small area on the Isle of Betel Nuts and erected a small wooden stockade on the present site of Fort Cornwallis. Georgetown's population grew rapidly and the city boomed as immigrants and traders arrived from China, South India, and Indonesia. But Light's policy of free trade failed to bring in enough revenue to support the adventure, and Penang began a slow but steady decline after Light's death from malaria in 1794. Penang had fallen on hard times by the time Raffles established Singapore in 1819. In 1826, the island was joined with Malacca and Singapore to form the Straits Settlement; six years later the capital was moved to Singapore. Penang sputtered along without much fanfare except for a brief revival during the rubber boom of the early 20th century. Most of the island's extravagant mansions and Peranakan shops date from this period.

Penang in the late 1960s lay smack in the middle of the hippie trail, the overland odyssey that stretched from Europe to Southeast Asia. Like Kuta and Kathmandu, Penang was a comfortable place to rest up, purchase a cheap air-

PENANG ISLAND

line ticket, enjoy some good food, and get high on cheap weed. Opium dens were commonplace. Batu Ferringhi, the main tourist beach on the island, enjoyed a near legendary reputation as an untouched stretch of sand where inexpensive bamboo huts could be rented for a few dollars and nudity rarely caused more than a shrug among the locals, who regarded the foreign invasion as just another colorful bit of local history. Those days ended in the early '70s after developers and international consortiums moved in to claim the beach and authorities began deporting longhairs from their grass shacks; passports were stamped with the acronym for "Suspected Hippie: In Transit."

Although Penang is less wide-open these days, it's far more liberal than most of Malaysia. Perhaps this is because it's the only state dominated by Chinese, who generally have a live-and-let-live attitude. Or maybe it's the politics: Penang is the only state controlled by the opposition Gerankan Party, a political phenomenon that continues to astonish most observers, who had expected UMNO to quickly recontrol the rebellious island. While hard to quantify, it seems that much of Penang's great appeal comes from its easygoing attitude toward Westerners, the immense likeability of its people, and its unique attractions, described below.

ATTRACTIONS

Street names in Penang are somewhat confusing since many are now being Malaysianized (street is now *leboh*, road is *jalan*, lane is *lorong*, avenue is *lebohraya*) and renamed (Rope Walk is now Jalan Pintal Tali, Northam Road is Jalan Sultan Ahmad Shah, Green Lane is Jalan Mesjid Negeri). Furthermore, the Chinese community uses another set of names which describes the streets in historical terms such as Noodle Maker Street, Malay Cemetery Street, and Bean Curd Street. When in doubt, try all three versions: English, Chinese, and Bahasa.

Fort Cornwallis And The *Padang*
A good spot to begin a walking tour of Penang is the central *padang* (parade grounds) surrounded by handsome late-Victorian memorials to Penang's colonial past. The Penang Tourist Association on Jalan Tun Syed Shed, tel. 366665, and the adjacent TDC office have glossy brochures and the useful publication *Penang for the Visitor*. Named after the governor of Bengal, Fort Cornwallis was built 1808-10, reputedly on the spot where Captain Light first landed. Protruding from the renovated fort are iron cannons retrieved by the British from pirates who took them from the Johor sultanate, once a Dutch protectorate. One cannon, the famous phallic Seri Rambai, is believed to bring fertility to childless women who place flowers in its big barrel. Next to the fort, traffic circles around the King Edward Circus Clock Tower donated to the city by a Penang millionaire in honor of Queen Victoria's Diamond Jubilee. The imposing lime-washed City Hall constructed in 1897 stands at the far end of the *padang*. The old High Court building and St. George's Church complete the British colonial arrangement of Military, Government, and Commerce—with Religion discreetly tucked away in the background.

St. George's Church
This magnificent neo-Greek edifice on Farquhar Street was built with convict labor between 1817 and 1810 as the oldest Anglican church in Southeast Asia. Designed by the artist-captain R. Smith, the Palladian structure of Doric columns and pillars cost the East India Company the sizable sum of 60,000 English pounds. The building has remained unaltered except for the gabled portico which overlays the original flat roof. A circular and curiously empty monument to Francis Light stands on the front lawn.

Penang Museum And Art Gallery
Inside the peeling building which once was the oldest English school east of the Suez is a marvelous collection of old photographs, etchings, and artifacts illustrating the tumultuous history of Penang. The Chinese bridal chamber and descriptions of *tong* warfare are intriguing, but the highlight might be the air-conditioned rooms which offer blessed relief from the sweltering heat. Open 0900-1700 daily, closed Fridays 1215-1445.

Cheong Fat Tze Mansion
Between 1860 and 1880 at least five mansions modeled after Ching Dynasty homes were constructed in Malaysia by wealthy Chinese merchants. Aside from the House of Tan Yeok Nee in Singapore, the sole surviving example of this imperial style of architecture is the Penang residence of Teo Tau Siat. Teo was a prosperous rice merchant who built separate courtyards and rooms for the sons and wives of his nine future generations. The complex is surrounded by 10-foot walls with two signed entrances which warn off curious visitors. Flanking the central chamber are two side halls with discolored walls which have taken on a wonderful patina from the elements. Note the porcelain shards and decorative plaster work which has

Padang Parade

been modeled under the gabled roof. A quick photo from the front lawn is OK, but visitors are not allowed inside the private residence with its ancestral hall, spiral staircase, courtyards supported by Corinthian iron pillars, and sitting halls embellished with ornamental screens.

Old Christian Cemetery

This Protestant and Roman Catholic cemetery shaded by lovely frangipani trees is where the body of Captain Light lies buried among other European settlers. Light's archaic tombstone is on the left as you enter from Farquhar Street.

Muntri Street

Malaysia's finest collection of Chinese shophouses with Peranakan details is found on Muntri and Stewart streets between Penang and Pitt roads. The lovely tilework, richly carved doorways, and extravagant decorative molding make this street one of Asia's architectural goldmines—a must-see for any visitor to Penang. Formerly the home to a thriving Eurasian community of Babas and Nonyas, this idyllic alley also features several superb Chinese-association buildings constructed on traditional Chinese floorplans—especially fascinating at dusk as the lights flicker on and residents socialize on the five-foot walkways. A public toddy shop, popular with Indian rickshaw drivers and budget travelers looking for a cheap buzz, is located on the right side of Pasar just before Pitt Street; it opens an hour before sunset.

Kuan Yin Temple

Constructed in 1800 by the Hokkien and Cantonese community on a site given to them in perpetuity by the British government, this small and unassuming temple is the spiritual heart and soul of Penang's Chinese community. Although the temple is relatively plain by Chinese standards, it seems perennially crowded with devotees who burn immense towers of incense and make offerings to Kuan Yin, the beloved Buddhist Goddess of Mercy. Puppet shows are given on her birthday three times yearly on the 19th days of the Chinese 2nd, 6th, and 9th moons.

Sri Mariamman Temple

Although Penang is essentially a Chinese city, it has always had a sizable community of Indians who originally immigrated to work as policemen, soldiers, clerks, and laborers on rubber plantations. Many settled on Queen Street near the government offices and inadvertently created an ethnic buffer zone between the colonial rulers and the Chinese merchants. These racially divided neighborhoods were identified by their street names: China Street for the Chinese, Chulia Street for the Southwest Indian Muslim traders, Acheh Street for Sumatran merchants, Malay Street for the indigenous Muslim population. Racial boundaries are now somewhat blurred, but to a surprising degree Little India still thrives along Queen and adjacent side streets. Religious centerpiece for the Hindu community is the

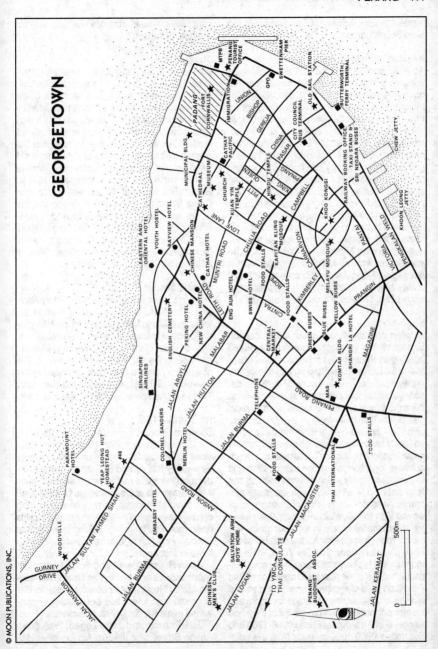

GEORGETOWN

© MOON PUBLICATIONS, INC.

modest temple built in 1883 and dedicated to Lord Subramaniam.

Kapitan Kling Mosque

As if to compete with the Chinese and Indian temples in the neighborhood, this arabesque monument was built in 1801 by Cauder Mohideen, Kapitan of the Indian-Muslim community. (Kapitan was the name given to the powerful headman through which the colonial administration governed the Chinese and Indian communities. Kling is slang for South Indians, particularly the Tamils.) This dome-shaped and ochre-painted mosque replaced an earlier attap structure erected in 1786 by the Havidars, Jemadars, and Indian Sepoys attached to the British East India Company. Well-dressed visitors are welcome to walk along the cool marble floors of the mosque, which serves the religious needs of Indian Muslims and Jawi Pekan, descendants of mixed Malay and Indian Muslim marriages. Nearby Acheh Street has a modest Malay Mosque with a curious Egyptian-style minaret kept locked and closed to the public.

Khoo Kongsi

Located up a small side street called Cannon Square stands the most elaborately decorated building in Penang and possibly the whole of Malaysia. Built in 1906 in the style of a miniature imperial palace, this clanhouse of the Khoo descendants literally drips with stucco dragons, ceramic flowers, and fantastic mythological guardians. It also symbolizes an important tradition in Chinese culture in which the extended family becomes a major element for the Chinese immigrant; this isn't a temple but headquarters for a *kongsi*—a clan organization and benevolent society which extends spiritual and financial help to all people with the same surname. Ancestor worship is inextricably interwoven with this Confucian concept as shown by the memorial tablets in the right room. The center room has an altar for the worship of the Khoo's tutelary deity, Tua Sai Yeah, while the room on the left contains plaques honoring distinguished living members and an image of Tua Peh Kong, God of Prosperity. Across the square is a dusty but finely carved stage for opera and theater performances. The interior of the Khoo Kongsi is open Monday-Friday 0900-1700 and Saturdays 0900-1300 by pass from the adja-

cent clan office. Photos of the shady exterior are best at sunset.

The Docks

Just south of the Butterworth-Penang ferry terminal is a series of jetties named after the Chinese clans which first settled here; the Chew Jetty opposite Armenian Street is populated by the Chew clan while the Leongs live on the jetty near Acheh Street. The piers are somewhat modernized with tin roofs and TV antennas but worth a visit for views of the city. Also note the used-car lots with cheap Austin Mini Coopers and the surviving *attap* house opposite Melayu Street. The financial district near Pantai and China Streets is also worth a visit to see the banks and trading companies housed in magnificent old stone buildings. Two of the best are the Commercial Banking Center on Pantai Street and the old Customs Building (Wisma Kastam) on China at Weld Street.

Komtar Tower

Penang's latest monument is the 65-story Kompleks Tun Abdul Razak, which bills itself as the tallest building in Malaysia. Within the US$115-million circular tower are several shopping centers, an office of the Malaysian Airlines System, and most of the island's government offices. The observatory on the 58th floor has spectacular views over Georgetown's sea of red-tiled roofs. Tours are given once daily in the early afternoon.

Residential Tour

Some of Penang's greatest architectural attractions are the magnificent Sino-colonial mansions constructed during the early 20th century by wealthy rubber and tin barons. Some have decayed in tropical mildew but others have been well maintained at great expense by local families. Most are located west of downtown and can be easily visited by trishaw or rented bicycle or on foot. The following walking tour starts at Penang Road and Campbell Street and takes three or four hours.

Jalan Hutton: Several attractive Peranakan shophouses stand on Nagore Lane just before the Merlin Hotel. Just opposite the Merlin is a large mansion which has been tastefully converted into a Kentucky Fried Chicken.

Jalan Anson and Jalan Logan: Walk down Anson Street past the Pro-Am Snooker Hall

Komtar view

and turn right on Logan Street. Alternatively, make a detour to visit the spacious Penang Buddhist Association. Several fine old homes grace shady Logan Street, such as the Salvation Army Boys' Home at number 8A and the Chinese Men's Club at number 34. Walk across Perak Street and along Dunn Street past a dozen identical bungalows dating from the 1920s with hanging reed curtains wrapped around the porches. Turn right on Peel and continue walking under the row of stately royal palms to Perak and Jalan Burmah.

Bangkok Lane: An exceptionally fine set of terrace houses stands on this small street.

Wat Chayamangkalaram: This Thai-style temple is chiefly known for its enormous 33-meter reclining Buddha, which combines Thai, Burmese, and Chinese religious motifs. The curious fusion is symbolized by the dual entrances with Buddhist *nagas* left, Chinese dragons right, and the interior, which has Buddha statues right and Chinese deities left. Visit the small Burmese temple just across the street and then walk down Burma Lane to the waterfront.

Gurney Drive: Bordered by swaying casuarina trees, this is an ideal spot to enjoy a late lunch from one of the hawkers who set up their portable stalls alongside the promenade.

Northam Road: East toward town is Northam Road, now renamed Sultan Ahmed Shah. Often dubbed Millionaire's Row, this is where wealthy Chinese merchants, rubber barons, and powerful colonial administrators built the most extravagant mansions in all of Penang. Some have kept their colonial nametags such as Woodville and Soonstead, while others have been rechristened with Chinese titles such as the magnificent Yeap Leong Huat Homestead. The equally impressive Runnymede, site of the former residence of Sir Stamford Raffles which was torn down in 1901, presently houses the 2nd Infantry Division of the Malaysian Army. Hopefully someone will save the abandoned Metropole Hotel before it collides with the wrecker's ball. Continue down Northam to end your tour with a cocktail inside the famous E & O Hotel.

Botanical Gardens

This 30-hectare garden at the end of Waterfall Road some eight km west of town has hundreds of exotic and indigenous plant species, plus a gaggle of inquisitive rhesus monkeys whose chatterings and unabashed begging are always amusing. Take City Council bus 7 from the Weld Quay Bus Terminal one block from the Ferry Building.

Penang Hill

Barely one year after Captain Francis Light arrived in Penang, he instructed his *sepoys* to build a trail to the top of Penang Hill, 830 meters above sea level. Finding the temperate climate more agreeable than the malarial lowlands, British colonialists constructed a hill resort complete with English bungalows and vegetable gardens. In 1923 a railway line was built to the peak, where spectacular panoramic views spread across Penang to the coastal stretches of the mainland. Sunsets are magical as the lights blink on and twinkle in steamy Georgetown. Trams leave every half-hour 0630-2130 from the terminus near the village of Ayer Itam. Take Green Bus 91 from the Jalan Prangin Bus Terminal near the Komtar building to Ayer Itam, where City Council bus 8 continues up to the tram terminus. From the summit it is possible to hike down Waterfall Road and reach the Botanical Gardens in about three hours.

Kek Lok Si Temple

Malaysia's largest Buddhist temple complex is dominated by the 30-meter Pagoda of 10,000 Buddhas, whose unique architectural style combines a Chinese base, Thai middle tiers, and a golden Burmese stupa on top. The resulting mishmash is inelegant but less irritating than the aggressive salesmen who work the continuous sprawl of souvenir shops that flank the long entrance walk. The only way to avoid the hustle is to arrive in the late afternoon after the busloads of tourists have returned to Georgetown. Take Green Bus 91 from the main terminal on Jalan Prangin near the Komtar building to Ayer Itam.

Around The Island

Penang is a beautiful island of tumbling waterfalls, miles of forest, idyllic *padi* fields, and quaint fishing villages of wooden Malay *kampung* houses elevated on rickety stilts. To do the 75-km circular route in a single day, an early start is recommended. A rented car or motorcycle is preferable to public buses since many of the fishing villages and beaches are located on side roads and inaccessible without private transportation. Bus travelers should begin with Yellow Bus 83 to the Snake Temple. The same bus continues on to Balik Pulau, where Yellow Bus 76 continues north to Telok Bahang. Blue buses return to Georgetown with a quick change in Tanjung Bunga.

Snake Temple: Dedicated to the Taoist deity Chor Soo Kong, the Temple of the Azure Cloud is known for its venomous Wagler pit vipers kept harmlessly dazed by the intoxicating fumes curling up from the burning joss sticks. This popular tourist stop is quite ordinary aside from the sleepy snakes.

Balik Pulau: After passing through industrial estates, the Penang Free Trade Zone, the turn-off for the notorious M$850-million white elephant Penang Bridge, the Penang International Airport, and spice plantations of clove and nutmeg, the bus lurches to a halt in the pleasant rural town of Balik Pulau. Yellow Bus 76 continues north past turnoffs for Malay fishing villages, durian plantations, freshwater pools at Titi Krawang, the Forest Recreation Park, an orchid farm, and the Penang Butterfly Farm, which claims the world's largest collection of lepidopterous insects.

Telok Bahang: The newly opened and immense five-star Penang Mutiara Hotel has dramatically changed the sleepy atmosphere of this small and mostly undeveloped fishing village situated at the northwest corner of Penang. Inexpensive accommodations (M$5) are available at Rama's Homestay off the main intersection toward the water. Rama's son will probably find you. Hikers might enjoy tramping through the Muka Head Forest Reserve. The trail starts at the beach and soon divides into two forks. The path right leads to the USM Marine Research Station and an hour later reaches the lighthouse and beach at Muka Head. The left trail winds through the forest to the public campsites at deserted Keracut Beach, also called Monkey Beach because of the colony of monkeys that comes down to play in the sand.

Batu Ferringhi

Penang's best beaches are found along the north shore about 15 km from Georgetown. The entire coastline is broken into a series of small coves with private beaches except for a singular stretch of sand nicknamed Batu Ferringhi (Foreigner's Rock). During the late '60s this was home to legions of hippie backpackers—until the infamous police raids of the early '70s forced the freaks northward to the more tolerant islands of Phuket and Ko Samui. Batu Ferringhi today only welcomes travelers with enough cash to afford the plush first-class hotels that overhang the beach. Some say the police did the freaks a favor: the coarse sand and murky water at Batu Ferringhi don't compare with the sand and sea at Thai beach resorts. Although the atmosphere is artificial and disappointing (there is little reason to day-trip out here from Georgetown), the jagged hills and the swaying palms over the beach remain quite attractive. Also, hotel rates have remained low from overbuilding and perennially high vacancy rates.

ACCOMMODATIONS

Budget

Travelers will be pleasantly surprised at the hotel situation in Penang. A dramatic increase in the number of luxury hotels has forced owners of older hotels to slash rates to fill vacant rooms. Amazing but true: many hotels in Penang's Chinatown are cheaper than they were a decade ago. And unlike most cheap Asian hotels that are either dumps, whorehouses, or concrete shoeboxes, Penang has a good selection of clean Chinese hotels with high ceilings, swishing ceiling fans, and, of course, old Chinese men sitting around in their underwear. Most of Penang's budget hotels in the M$15-20 range are located in Chinatown along Leboh Chulia and adjacent side streets, a 10-minute walk or M$3 rickshaw ride from the ferry terminal. Middle-priced hotels in the M$30-70 range are around the corner on Penang Road. Most of Penang's luxury hotels are located at Batu Ferringhi Beach.

Eng Aun and Swiss Hotels: Penang's two most popular budget hotels are simple, clean, and quiet since they are nicely situated back from the road. Other facilities include travel services and inexpensive restaurants with decent food and friendly vibes. The old men who hang around the office and sleep in the hallways are the owners. Both hotels are often filled by early afternoon, especially during the high travel season from November to March and during August. 380 and 431 Chulia Street, tel. (04) 612333 and (04) 620133, M$15-20.

New China Hotel: This quiet hotel tucked away on a less hectic side street is a good alternative to the busy Eng Aun and Swiss hotels. Rooms need cleaning but the owner is helpful and the ambience is suitably relaxed. 22 Leith Street, tel. 631601, M$6 dorm, M$15-20.

Other Chinatown Cheapies: A quick stroll along Leboh Chulia, Lorong Cinta (Love Lane), and Leboh Leith will uncover another two-dozen budget hotels of varying standards. Most charge M$15-20 for rooms with fan and common bath.

Couples should ask for a single room, which often has a bed large enough for two people. Super-budget travelers might try the M$5 dorms at the Tye Ann on Leboh Chulia or the Wan Hai around the corner on Love Lane.

Youth Hostel: Penang's official Asrama Belia is located in a large deteriorating building adjacent to the E & O Hotel. The hostel appears about ready to collapse but dorm beds are only M$5 and there's plenty of room to accommodate the overflow from Leboh Chulia. The reception office at the back of the second floor is difficult to find.

YMCA: Penang's coed Y is located about 20 minutes from Chinatown in a quiet residential neighborhood near the Thai Embassy. All rooms have attached baths. 211 Jalan Macalister, tel. (04) 362211, M$30-45.

Moderate

Penang Road Hotels: Penang's middle-priced hotels in the M$35-80 range are located on Penang Road between the waterfront and Chinatown. Most rooms are air-conditioned with private bath and basic Motel 6 furniture. A modest restaurant or a nightclub with painted ladies is often found on the ground floor. Room tariffs quoted in tourist brochures and listed on the hotel chart in this book are rarely demanded since intense competition has dramatically lowered walk-in rates; during my last visit, almost every hotel on Penang Road had a large banner hanging from the roof advertising room discounts of up to 50%. Comfortable a/c doubles were M$40-70 at the Peking, White House, and Federal, while the more luxurious Oriental and Continental had a/c doubles for just M$80-100.

Cathay Hotel: Similar but superior to the Eng Aun and the Swiss, this delightful old Chinese hotel has large and well-furnished rooms with air-conditioning, private baths, and hot showers. With an exterior paint job and a spacious lobby that evoke the 1920s, this is the hotel for couples looking for atmosphere at an affordable price. 15 Leith Street, tel. (04) 626271, M$40-60.

Luxury

Eastern and Oriental Hotel: Constructed in 1885 by the Sarkie Brothers of Raffles fame, Penang's Grand Dame is one of Southeast Asia's great colonial hotels. Although it needs some refurbishing, anyone who appreciates

CENTRAL GEORGETOWN

EASTERN AND ORIENTAL HOTEL

SULTAN AHMED SHAH

ENGLISH CEMETERY

YOUTH HOSTEL

CITY BAYVIEW HOTEL

CONTINENTAL

LIGHT

MALAYSIA

PEKING

CHINESE MANSION

FEDERAL

NEW CHINA

WALDORF

HIGH COURT BUILDING

AMBASSADOR

CATHAY

PENANG MUSEUM

TOWN HOUSE

MODERN

LUM FONG

LOVE LANE

TEONG WAH

ST. GEORGE'S CHURCH

ORIENTAL

MUNTRI STEWART

LUM THEAN

CHUNG KING

PENANG

FOOD STALLS

ENG AUN

WAN HAI

SWISS

PING SENG

KUAN YIN TEMPLE

YENG KENG

NOBLE

NAM WAH

TYE ANN

QUEEN

TODDY SHOP

FOOD STALLS

CHULIA

SRI MARIAMMAN TEMPLE

CAMPBELL

FOOD STALLS

CINTRA

ROPE

DAWOOD'S RESTAURANT

KIMBERLEY

FOOD STALLS

KAPITAN KLING MOSQUE

GREEN BUSES

CARNARVON

BLUE BUSES

PITT

KHOO KONGSI

YELLOW BUSES

MALAY MOSQUE

PRANGIN

0   100m

© MOON PUBLICATIONS, INC.

CENTRAL PENANG ACCOMMODATIONS

HOTEL	SINGLE	DOUBLE	ADDRESS	PHONE (04)
LUXURY	M$	M$		
City Bayview	160-200	180-240	25 Farquhar	633161
Shangri-La	240-300	260-400	Magazine	622622
Eastern & Oriental	150-200	200-250	10 Farquhar	630630
MODERATE				
Merchant	100-150	120-160	55 Penang	632828
Continental	100-140	120-160	5 Penang	636388
Federal	60-90	80-120	39 Penang	64114
Malaysia	100-120	120-150	7 Penang	633311
Oriental	80-100	100-120	105 Penang	6344211
Peking	35-50	40-60	50 Penang	29451
Town House	60-90	80-120	70 Penang	368722
Waldorf	45-60	50-80	13 Leith	626140
Cathay	40-50	50-60	15 Leith	626271
BUDGET				
Eng Aun	15-20	15-20	380 Chulia	612333
Lum Fong	15-20	15-20	108 Muntri	624124
Modern	20-30	25-40	179 Muntri	25424
New China	15-20	15-20	22 Leith	631601
Swiss	15-20	15-20	431 Chulia	620133
White House	25-40	25-40	72 Penang	22385
Youth Hostel	5 dorm		12 Farquhar	

nostalgic old-world atmosphere will love this waterfront hotel. 10 Farquhar Street, tel. (04) 630630, fax (04) 634833, M$150-250.

Shangri-La Hotel: Downtown Penang entered the modern age with the opening of this towering 18-story hotel in 1986. Swimming pool, health club, and business center, adjacent to the Komtar building. Jalan Magazine, tel. (04) 622622, fax (04) 626526, M$240-400.

Batu Ferringhi Hotels: Penang's most popular beach is lined with eight international hotels that have all the standard amenities, such as restaurants, swimming pools, and water-sports activities. Rooms at the Casuarina Beach Hotel, the Golden Sands, the Holiday Inn, the Pan Pacific, and the Rasa Sayang start at M$160, while the less luxurious Ferringhi Beach and Lone Pine offer rooms from M$100. The Penang Mu-tiara, a five-star hotel managed by the Mandarin Group from Singapore, offers rooms from M$240 on Ferringhi's only private beach. Budget rooms from M$15 are found at Ali's Guesthouse and the White House Hotel located in the village at the west end of the beach.

FOOD STALLS

Penang's multiracial population has given it one of Asia's most diverse and exciting ranges of foods. Rivaling Singapore in terms of affordability and variety, the city's food emporiums offer everything from Malaysian *nasi lemak* and Chinese *kuay teow* to Nonya *kerabu* and Indian *nasi kandar*. Most restaurants and food stalls serve the Chinese and Indian dishes described

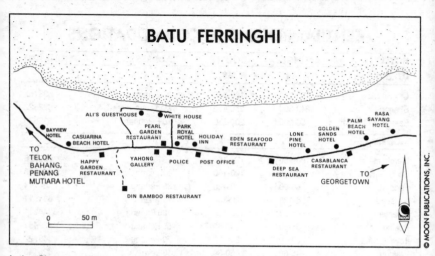

BATU FERRINGHI

BAYVIEW HOTEL
CASUARINA BEACH HOTEL
ALI'S GUESTHOUSE
WHITE HOUSE
PEARL GARDEN RESTAURANT
PARK ROYAL HOTEL
HOLIDAY INN
EDEN SEAFOOD RESTAURANT
LONE PINE HOTEL
GOLDEN SANDS HOTEL
PALM BEACH HOTEL
RASA SAYANG HOTEL

TO TELOK BAHANG, PENANG MUTIARA HOTEL

HAPPY GARDEN RESTAURANT
YAHONG GALLERY
POLICE
POST OFFICE
DEEP SEA RESTAURANT
CASABLANCA RESTAURANT
TO GEORGETOWN

DIN BAMBOO RESTAURANT

0   50 m

© MOON PUBLICATIONS, INC.

in the "Singapore" chapter, but the island's great culinary discovery is Malay cuisine, a wonderful mixture of spicy Indonesian peanut sauces, rich Thai coconut milks, and fiery Indian curries with fresh vegetables and succulent meats. Malay cuisine is typically limited to home cooking and therefore difficult to find but worth seeking out.

Penang has countless places to eat from simple cafes to expensive restaurants, but streetside food stalls provide the island's great culinary adventure. First-time visitors sometimes dismiss hawker food as unclean, assuming that any meal served on a rickety aluminum table at the edge of a busy street must be inferior to those in a first-class restaurant. Nothing could be further from the truth. If a steady queue of Mercedes-Benzes waiting for noodle soup is any indication, hawker food provides stiff competition for many of Penang's best restaurants. Hawker food is popular for several reasons. Large congregations of food stalls in a singular location ensure a greater array of foods than in any single restaurant. Secondly, since there is virtually no overhead, prices are kept low—a filling meal can be served for a M$2 to M$4 in most cases. But perhaps most importantly, food-stall dining is a great way to meet people; al fresco dining is one of Penang's great social events.

Ordering from a hawker stall can sometimes be confusing in Southeast Asia, but you won't have much trouble here in Penang. The simplest method is to wander around a group of stalls and point to whatever looks best. To aid both visitors and locals, many of the food stalls have put up plastic signs that list their specialties. Owners often speak some rough English and are often happy to explain their dishes to confused strangers. Conversations might be limited to baby talk, but you will probably find the people of Penang (including hawkers) both friendly and helpful . . . especially when they stand to make a small profit. Serious eaters should purchase *Hawkers Galore: A Guide to Penang Hawker Food*, which describes with color photographs the island's most popular street dishes.

Hawker Locations
Chulia at Carnarvon Road: Hawker food is sold throughout the day at several locations; most are within easy walking distance of Chinatown. This collection of food stalls is conveniently located in the middle of Penang's cheap hotel section. Unlike most of the other hawker areas, which operate evenings only, Carnarvon Road is best visited in the early morning. Try the tasty Malay breakfast called *nasi lemak*.

Kimberley at Cintra Road: Chinatown's largest collection of hawker stalls branches off from this intersection. More food stalls set up in the evenings on Tamil Lane, just off Penang Road one block north of Kimberley, and along Malabar Lane at Penang Road.

Komtar Building: Several popular hawker centers are located diagonally opposite and to the west of Penang's tallest building. The entire sidewalk in front of the GAMA Department Store on Jalan Brick Kiln is taken up with hawkers, as are those on the west side of Jalan MacAlister and farther afield on Lorong Selamat.

Gurney Drive: Because of its prime location next to the sea and its almost endless selection of stalls, Gurney Drive is considered the premier hawker center on Penang. Activity is minimal during the day but after sunset the mile-long promenade comes alive with countless hawkers who unload their portable furniture and fire up the woks. A rickshaw from Chinatown to Gurney Drive is M$4.

Night Market: Almost as popular as Gurney Drive is the roving night market which changes locations every two weeks. Local residents and the tourist office will know the current venue.

Toddy Shop

Toddy is palm wine made from the fermented juice of unopened fronds. Tappers climb the trees in the morning and sell the pungent beverage to shops which operate under a government license. The milky broth is popular with Indian rickshaw drivers and budget travelers who gather in the late afternoon at the toddy shop on Lorong Pasar, off Leboh Pitt near the Kuan Yin Temple. Bring your own cup and ignore the drug dealers.

PRACTICALITIES

Arrival

Airport: Penang's Bayan Lepas International Airport is 16 km south of Georgetown and 35 km from Batu Ferringhi Beach. Penang is served by flights from Kuala Lumpur, Singapore, Bangkok, Hat Yai, Medan, and Madras. The MTPB has a small information booth in the lobby. Airport taxis use a coupon system and cost M$15 to the city, M$23 to Batu Ferringhi. Yellow Bus 83 leaves hourly from the airport, costs M$2, and reaches Weld Quay in an hour.

Bus, Train, and Taxi: Most buses, trains, and taxis bound for Penang terminate in Butterworth, a small town just across the straits from Georgetown. The rebuilt Butterworth-Penang ferry opposite the terminal operates 24 hours. On arrival in Butterworth you can walk to most hotels in 15 minutes, or take a trishaw for M$4.

Getting Around

Bus: Penang has five bus companies which operate from three different terminals. Routes are displayed on signboards and ticket collectors can advise on fares and destinations. The Blue, Yellow, and Green buses all leave from Jalan Maxwell (now called Jalan Lim Chwee Leong) near the Komtar Building. Blue buses go to the north side of the island including Batu Ferringhi and Telok Bahang. Yellow buses go to the Snake Temple, Bayan Lepas, Air Itam, and Balik Pulau. Green buses go to Air Itam. City Council MPPP buses leave from the Leboh Victoria Terminal one street from the ferry terminal and go to various city destinations. Useful routes include MPPP Bus 7 to the Botanical Gardens, MPPP Bus 1 to Air Itam and Kek Lok Si Temple, and MPPP Bus 8 from Air Itam to the Penang Hill Railway.

Trishaws: Three-wheeled manpowered vehicles called *lancas* in Penang average about M$2 per kilometer or M$6-8 per hour. Some of the Tamil and Chinese drivers are very knowledgeable about sightseeing attractions, but rates should be agreed on before boarding.

Bicycles and Motorcycles: Bikes can be rented for M$5 daily from several of the budget hotels and bookstores on Jalan Chulia. Ambitious types can circle the island in a single day. Motorcycles cost M$20 daily from the same locations and from roadside stands in Batu Ferringhi.

Taxis: Penang taxis do *not* use their meters. Drivers are supposed to charge fixed rates based on city zones but most ask whatever they think they can get. Fares should be agreed on in advance. Short distances within the city are about M$3-6.

Other Information

Tourist Offices: The Penang Tourist Association, tel. (04) 366665, is on Jalan Tun Shed Barakbah near Fort Cornwallis. Useful publications include *Penang for the Visitor* and *This Month in Penang*. The poorly informed MTPB office, tel. (04) 619067, is in the same building. The Malaysia Immigration Office, tel. 615122, is on Leboh Pantai.

Foreign Consulates: Ten countries maintain consular representatives in Penang, but the most useful is the Royal Thai Consulate at 1 Ayeh Rajah Road, tel. (04) 23352. Take bus 7 or walk there in 45 minutes on the residential walking tour described above. The Indonesian Con-

A HAWKER MENU

ayam goreng: Malay-style fried chicken

ban chian koay: a sweet Indian pancake of rice flour, coconut milk, eggs, and sugar cooked in an earthenware pot. Ground peanuts and sesame are sprinkled on top.

cendol: a cold dessert made from pandan-flavored green noodles, palm sugar, and coconut milk. This weird-looking dish vaguely resembles green worm soup.

chok: thick rice porridge garnished with shredded chicken, spring onions, and sliced ginger. Although this dish sounds extremely boring, it can be superb when prepared by a talented cook.

curry kapitan: an Indonesian specialty of curried chicken with chunks of red onions, chilies, and yellow ginger sautéed in coconut oil, sugar, and lemon juice; best prepared in the Indian cafes across from the Sri Mariamman Temple

curry mee: Noodle soup made with curry paste, coconut milk, sliced clams, shrimps, and dried bean cake; sometimes garnished with cockles, pig's blood, and mint leaves; moderately spicy.

enchee kabin: marinated and deep-fried chicken served with rice and piquant sauce. This Nonya specialty fuses Malay sauces with Chinese cooking techniques.

gado gado: Indonesian salad of blanched vegetables such as potatoes, cabbage, beans, and sprouts covered with a rich and spicy peanut-coconut sauce. Prawn crackers (*krupok*) are also served.

Hainanese chicken rice: Singapore's classic dish of roast chicken, ginger, spring onion, and cucumber served with lightly oiled rice and garlic chili sauce is also very popular in Penang.

Hokkien prawn mee: rich and very spicy soup made from pork ribs, prawns, round rice noodles, and ground chilies. Exudes a great fragrance after being slowly stewed for several hours.

ice kachang: Malay snowcone made from colorful sweet red beans, corn, jelly, and fruit buried under thick syrup. Evaporated milk and ice cream are sometimes added. Delicious on a hot day.

ikan bilis: fried whitebait or anchovies served as an appetizer with *nasi lemak*. Crunchy, salty, strong, and addictive with daily intake.

ikan sadin: canned sardines in tomato sauce

kari ayam: curry chicken

kerang: fried cockles

kueh mueh: traditional Nonya desserts made from tapioca, glutinous rice, and sago, and flavored with *gula melaka*, coconut milk, or pandan juice. Tables filled with these vibrantly colored desserts are dazzling sights.

kuay teow: char (fried) *kuay teow* are flat white rice noodles fried in a black bean sauce together with eggs, clams, prawns, cockles, and bean sprouts. *Kuay teow* is the classic pasta dish of Penang.

laksa: thick rice noodle soup served in a tangy broth made from fish stock, onions, lemon grass, and tamarind juice. Penang or *asam* (sour) *laksa* has a sharp and slightly sour flavor in contrast to the creamy and mild Singapore version. *Laksa lemak* (also called *siam laksa*) is a sweeter, richer, and somewhat spicier version. Both are outstanding.

lok lok: Penang's version of the traditional steamboat. Hawker stalls display a variety of meats and vegetables on colored skewers which indicate price. Just walk up, select a stick, and drop it in the boiling water for a few seconds. The skewer is then dipped into a dish of rich spicy sauce and quickly eaten. *Lok lok,* sensibly enough, means "dip dip."

lontong: vegetables and fried rice cakes covered with coconut gravy. A simple but delicious Malaysian snack.

lor bak: deep-fried meat wrapped in a crispy vegetable skin. The same hawker stall will also serve deep-fried prawns, octopus fritters, crispy pigs' ears, hundred-year-old eggs, and fried stingray served with glutinous chili sauce.

mee: Chinese yellow wheat noodles can be prepared in literally hundreds of ways: *mee java* is noodles in a tomato soup (often made from Del Monte catsup), *mee rebus* is noodles with eggs and prawns in a tasty brown gravy, *mee goreng* is fried noodles without gravy, *mee siam* is fried rice vermicelli with chili in a thin gravy, *mee hoon* is threadlike white rice noodles in mixed sauces.

nasi: *Nasi* is Malay for "cooked rice." Rice can also be prepared in limitless ways: *nasi goreng* is fried rice, *nasi padang* is rice prepared in a cooking style associated with the Minangkabau people of Western Sumatra, *nasi kandar* is an Indian Muslim rice dish with a variety of curries.

nasi lemak: rice cooked in coconut milk and pandan leaves served with tasty tidbits such as prawn fritters marinated in tamarind juice, chilies with lime, sliced fruit, and crunchy anchovies. Just

A HAWKER MENU

point through the window to whatever looks inviting and it will be piled on the plate. This traditional Malay breakfast is now sold at hawker's stalls throughout the day.

ngau lam: dark and spicy noodle soup cooked with meats, vegetables, a generous dose of black pepper, and a dash of cloves. First decide which noodles you prefer: *mee, meehon,* or *kuay teow,* and then point out what ingredients you want in your soup. This can also be left to the discretion of the chef. A Chinese dish also popular with Malays.

o chien: oyster omelette cooked with onions and sweet potatoes

popiah: spring rolls stuffed with pork, prawns, fried bean curd, and beans. The *popiah* (thin pancake) is first spread with black bean, plum, or *hoi sin* sauce with chili before being carefully wrapped around the mixture. Very tasty.

rendang: spicy Indonesian curries served with beef or chicken

rojak: a spicy fruit-and-vegetable salad mixed with a black sauce of sugar, chilies, and *hoi sin.* The unripened assemblage is then garnished with ground peanuts and served in a takeaway plastic bag.

roti jala: traditional Malay pancakes made by swirling thin egg batter from a punctured can of condensed milk onto a sizzling griddle. The lacy creation is normally eaten with a mild chicken curry.

sambal: fiery chili sauce used in Malay and Indonesian cooking

satay: Skewers of chicken, beef, or lamb are first seasoned in a medley of spices and then slowly grilled over a charcoal fire. Malay *satay* is served with peanut sauce, while the Chinese version is made with pork and served with sweet potato-chili sauce.

sayor: Malay for "vegetables"

soto ayam: *soto* is soup, *ayam* is chicken. *Soto ayam* is spiced chicken soup with vegetables and potatoes.

sotong: cuttlefish

tahu goreng: deep-fried beancurd covered with pungent peanut sauce

tahu lemak: beancurd cooked in coconut-milk curry

telor goreng: fried eggs

udang sambal: prawns fried in *sambal* hot sauce

---

sulate is at 467 Jalan Burmah, tel. (04) 25162. Both consulates are open weekdays 0900-1200 and hopelessly disorganized. Let a travel agency pick up your visa unless you enjoy bureaucratic hassles and want to waste half a day.

General Post Office: Penang's GPO on Leboh Downing is open daily except Sundays 0800-1800.

Telephone: International phone calls can be made around the clock from the telegraph office on Leboh Downing and from the Penang International Airport daily 0800-2030. The Penang area code is 04.

Travel Agents: Penang's budget travel agencies sell almost every conceivable ticket at rock-bottom prices. Most are honest but some are fly-by-night operations that sell invalidated, stolen, or highly restricted tickets. Carefully inspect your ticket before handing over the money. Airline tickets should *never* be purchased from freelancers who work the streets and lobbies of budget hotels. Where are the cheapest tickets? Rule of thumb is that prices are lowest when purchased from point of origin:

airline tickets from Bangkok should be bought in Bangkok, from Singapore in Singapore, from Penang in Penang. This also makes it much easier to go back to the agent if you have problems. Happy Holidays Travel at 442 Chulia Street is an honest agency with good prices.

Drugs: Despite a recent crackdown, Penang is still a town with plenty of drugs. Opium dens operate on back alleys and trishaw drivers offer everything from grass to smack. Anyone thinking about getting high should consider the risks. Drugs are Malaysia's number-one social problem and in recent years the government has executed several travelers and over 100 Malaysians for possession of small quantities of drugs. In Malaysia, *dadah* (drugs) mean death.

Leaving Penang

Air: Penang's international airport can be reached by taxi in 30 minutes or in one hour by Yellow Bus 83 from the Pengkalan Weld Bus Terminal near the ferry. Departure tax is M$15 for international flights, M$5 to Singapore, and M$3 for domestic flights.

PENANG PHONE NUMBERS

Airport 830373
Ferry 315780
Flight Info 830371
GPO 619222
Hospital 375299
Immigration 615122
International 108
Malaysia Calls 101
Police 999

Bus: Penang's bus terminal is next to the ferry terminal in Butterworth. Most departures are in the morning before 0900 and in the evening 1800-2000. The bus to Kota Baru departs daily at 0830. For Tioman Island, take the 1600 bus to Johor Baru, the 0600 bus from Johor to Mersing, and the noon ferry to Tioman. Buses leave several times daily for Hat Yai, Krabi, Ko Samui, and Phuket in Thailand. Call MARA Transport at tel. 345021 for exact information on long-distance buses or contact their office next to the E & O Hotel. Travel agents on Jalan Chulia also sell tickets.

Train: Penang's railway station is located in Butterworth. For bookings or information, call the ferry terminal at tel. 610290, or the Butterworth station at tel. 347962.

Share Taxis: Malaysia's fastest and most hair-raising forms of transport are share taxis which leave next to the ferry terminal in Butterworth. Because they avoid delays at the border, share taxis provide a speedy way to reach Thailand. Fares are about 50% higher than those for non-a/c buses.

Sea: The ferry MS Selesa Express leaves Penang for Belawan (Medan, Sumatra) every Tuesday and Friday at 0800, takes 15 hours, and costs M$100 one-way or M$170 return in deck class. Cabins are M$10 extra. Reclining chairs and private cabins can be booked at the office adjacent to the tourist office. The same ferry serves Langkawi Island every other day at 0900, arrives seven hours later, and costs M$40 one-way.

Getting To Thailand

Air: You can fly or take the train, bus, or a share taxi from Penang to Thailand. There is little reason to fly from Penang to Hat Yai (unless you want to explore the deep south), but the Penang-Phuket flight is reasonably priced and saves two full days of very hard bus travel. Penang-Phuket-Bangkok is somewhat cheaper than a direct Penang-Bangkok ticket.

Train: No ordinary trains run from Butterworth to Hat Yai. Train travelers must take the thrice-weekly International Express. Except for the expensive International Express, crossing by train is a slow and frustrating experience. Most travelers take a bus or a share taxi.

Bus: Buses can be taken from Penang to Thailand, but you should only take a bus that goes *directly* to Hat Yai, Phuket, Krabi, or Ko Samui. Tickets are available from travel agents in Penang. Do not take a bus that terminates at the Malaysian border town of Changlun, since Sadao, the nearest Thai border town, is 20 km distant and can only be reached by hitchhiking.

Share Taxi: One of the best ways to reach Hat Yai is by fast and comfortable share taxi. These lumbering old Mercedeses make the crossing in record time since they avoid border formalities that delay train and bus travelers. Share taxis can be picked up just outside the bus terminal in Butterworth, leave when filled, and cost about 50% more than non-a/c buses. They can also be chartered from travel agents in Georgetown.

THE NORTHWEST

ALOR STAR

Northwest Malaysia is, for most visitors, a lush and green land glanced at from the window of their speeding bus or train. Alor Star, the provincial capital of Malaysia's richest rice-growing region, offers a hybrid Thai-Malay culture and some uniquely stylized architecture grouped around the Padang Besar.

Attractions

Most famous of the curious buildings is the Moorish-styled Masjid Zahir, which some consider the most beautiful mosque in Malaysia. The octagonal Balai Nobat (Hall of Drums), just opposite, holds the *nobat,* a Malay royal orchestra of drums, gongs, and *napori* trumpets. Constructed in 1898, the Thai-colonial Balai Besar down the road is now used for royal ceremonial functions such as the Sultan's Birthday. The State Museum on Jalan Bakar Bata has a small collection of artifacts from nearby archaeological excavations. The Wednesday market is held daily.

Accommodations

Most hotels are clustered near the bus and taxi stations. Best choice for low-end travelers is the Kuan Siang Hotel on Jalan Langgar, where rooms with shared bath are M$15-25. Proprietor Mr. Kim can help with transportation to Thailand, Langkawi, and points south.

LANGKAWI ISLAND

Still relatively remote and unspoiled, these sparkling islands in northwestern Malaysia are slowly catching on with Western visitors who prefer solitude over the more developed islands in southern Thailand. This sleepy archipelago of 99 islands has been romantically nicknamed the Legendary Islands after the colorful tales surrounding its history; one claims the islands were cursed for seven generations by a Malay princess unjustly executed for adultery.

In an effort to attract more visitors and promote tourism, the government has paved the roads, declared Langkawi a duty-free port, and provided low-interest loans for local chalet development. The 1990 opening of the Pelangi Beach Resort finally put the island on the map.

Today, increasing numbers of Malaysians and Singaporeans arrive from November to January and during April. Light monsoons sprinkle the island between July and October; better beach weather is found on the East Coast.

Government offices and banks on Langkawi follow Islamic hours: closed Friday, open half a day on Saturday, and Sunday is an ordinary business day.

Beaches And Other Attractions

Langkawi, from which the archipelago takes its name, is an enormous island twice the size of Penang. Organized tours of the island can be booked at the Pelangi Beach Resort, at Langkawi Island Resort in Kuah, and at the Semarak Beach Resort at Cenang Beach. This is probably the easiest and quickest way to see the island. Motorcycles cost M$20 per day from the Malaysia Hotel and Chuan Hin motorcycle shop in Kuah. Cycles are recommended for experienced riders since they provide the flexibility to explore the island at a leisurely pace without having to worry about public transportation. Buses circle the island several times daily, but schedules are erratic and service sometimes ends in the early afternoon. Taxis cost M$10 per hour or M$40 per day—a good deal for larger groups. The following tour goes counterclockwise from Kuah.

Kuah: Aside from a picturesque mosque and duty-free shops, not much of interest detains travelers in this little port town.

Durian Perangin Waterfall: The road north from Kuah passes through serene landscapes of ricefields, rubber plantations, coconut farms, and sleepy Malay villages tucked away under thick jungle. A small sign near Sungai Itau, some nine km from Kuah, marks the turnoff for the cascading falls best seen at the end of the monsoon season. The Telaga Hotsprings (Air Panas), 13 km from Kuah, were completely renovated in 1993. Facilities now include a 200-seat theater restaurant, redeveloped hot springs almost five

LANGKAWI ISLAND

© MOON PUBLICATIONS, INC.

times the former size, and a wide range of cultural displays.

Pantai Rhu: Pantai Rhu ("Casuarina Beach") on the north shore is where a Malaysian company once attempted to build a world-class resort and cash in on the expected tourist boom. The crowds never arrived and the collapsing hotel and other abandoned wreckage have badly disfigured the beach. This ill-conceived project has nearly ruined what was once a superbly idyllic destination.

Pantai Hitam: Langkawi's unimpressive Black Sand Beach is believed to be colored by floating streaks of tin oxides. The dock for the MS *Gadis Langkasuka* is in the adjacent town of Telok Ewa.

Telaga Tujuh: Although the term translates to "Seven Wells," it's really a freshwater stream cascading down through a series of seven bathing pools. Telaga Tujuh can be reached by motorcycle from Kuala Teriang village (watch out for dozing monitor lizards) or by boat from Kuala Teriang and Pantai Cenang.

Pantai Kok: Several inexpensive chalets have been constructed on what is possibly the most attractive beach on Langkawi. The approach along the unpaved path is almost as breathtaking as the long sandy beach interrupted by a few rocky outcrops. Kok Beach can be reached by taxi or motorcycle or on foot from Kuala Teriang.

Pantai Cenang: Langkawi's most popular beach offers a dozen bungalows in the M$15-40 range, plus the striking Semarak Langkawi Beach Resort for middle-market travelers. The two-km beach is beautiful and peaceful, except on weekends and school holidays when Malaysian tourists fill most of the chalets. Cenang also boasts the five-star Pelangi Beach Resort, a world-class escape managed by Singapore's Mandarin Hotel Group.

Pantai Tengah: Central Beach to the south of Cenang Beach also has a few bungalows for budget travelers.

Accommodations In Kuah

The ferry from Kuala Perlis arrives in the small port town of Kuah ("Gravy"), which takes its name from a legendary nuptial fight in which the gravy pot landed where the town grew up. Kuah is a convenient spot for accommodation and transportation but better beaches are found at Cenang, Tengah, and Kok. Taxis from the rickety pier can be hired directly to Cenang Beach or into town, where several hotels are located.

Malaysia Hotel: Kuah's most popular budget hotel is located at at the far end of town in Pokok Assam. The helpful proprietor, Mr. Vellu, rents motorcycles and bikes at reasonable rates. Take the bus or share a taxi from the pier past the Asia and Langkawi Hotels where rooms start from M$20 (M$12 with shared bath). 66 Pokok Assam, tel. (04) 788298.

Langkawi Island Resort: Langkawi's most luxurious hotel is south of the pier. Operated by the TDC, facilities include an amusement center with billiards, tennis courts, and a large swimming pool. Motorcycles, topper sailboats, windsurfers, and snorkeling equipment can be rented at high prices from the activities center. Kuah, tel. (04) 916209, fax (04) 916414, M$160-240.

Accommodations On Pantai Cenang

Langkawi's most popular beach now has over a dozen places to stay, ranging from budget guesthouses in the M$20-30 range to five-star resorts at top-end prices. To reach Cenang Beach

from Kuah, take a bus to the village of Temonyong or hire a taxi for M$8-10. The following spots are described from north to south.

Pelangi Beach Resort: This 280-room luxury *kampong* resort, one of Malaysia's finer beach resorts, includes all types of recreational activities such as trekking, golf, bicycling, scuba diving, windsurfing, yachting, and just relaxing on the expansive beach. Pantai Cenang, tel. (04) 911001, fax (04) 911122, M$280-460.

Beach Garden Resort: Just south of the Pelangi is Wolfgang Sauer's "Bistro and Beergarden" with small pool, excellent restaurant, and 12 attractive a/c chalets. Pantai Cenang, tel. (04) 911363, fax (04) 911221, M$130-160.

Budget Bungalows: Several less expensive places such as Beach Garden Resort, Grand Beach Motel, and Cenang Resort House are located just south of Wolfgang's resort.

Semarak Langkawi Beach Resort: This attractive resort features 16 thatched and fan-cooled chalets tastefully fashioned after traditional Malay architecture. Dinner is served in an open restaurant with a unique *bertam* roof woven in an intricate pattern. Pantai Cenang, tel. (04) 911377, M$65-250.

Sandy Beach Hotel: Perhaps the island's most popular resting spot for budget travelers, Sandy's has bicycles and boats for hire at reasonable cost and a small outdoor canteen for tasty Thai meals. Success, however, seems to have gone to the owners' heads, and they have let the quality slide in recent years. Pantai Cenang, tel. (04) 911308, M$30-40.

AB Motel: Four more budget spots with rooms for M$20-30 are just south of Sandy Beach near the rocky overpass to Pantai Tengah. Sri Inai, Samila, Suria, and the Delta are adequate, though the venerable AB Motel remains the best choice. Pantai Cenang, tel. (04) 911300, M$20-30.

Pantai Tengah

Tengah Beach, just south from Pantai Cenang, has several budget guesthouses and a few upscale hotels on a fairly decent beach.

Budget Chalets: Low-end choices include the Green Hill Beach Motel, Tanjung Mali Beach Motel, Sugar Sands, Sunset Beach Resort, and Charlie's. Pantai Tengah, M$20-35.

Langkawi Holiday Villa: The southern tip of Langkawi Island is now dominated by this 258-

room luxury resort with its two swimming pools, tennis courts, and convention facilities. Pantai Tengah, tel. (04) 911704, fax (04) 911504, M$220-360.

Pantai Kok

The second-most-popular beach on Langkawi is less developed and has cleaner sand and water than Pantai Cenang. Over a dozen bungalows and hotels are located between the north end of the bay, Teluk Burau, and the southern tip, known as Teluk Nibong.

Country Beach Motel: Dead center on the beach is an old favorite with a popular restaurant, motorcycle rentals, and both fan-cooled and air-conditioned rooms. Other nearby cheapies include the Mila Beach Motel, Dayang Beach Resort, Pantai Kok Motel, and the Coral Beach Motel. Pantai Kok, tel. (04) 911212, M$20-65.

The Last Resort: One of the better spots, operated by a Brit expat and his Malay wife, is at the north end of the beach near the luxurious Burau Bay Resort. Prices are slighter higher but the layout is less cramped than at other budget places. Adjacent Southern Cross Resort is also recommended. Pantai Kok, tel. (04) 911046, M$35-60.

Sheraton Langkawi Resort: The early 1990s saw a construction frenzy that brought Langkawi a half-dozen resorts, including this luxurious outpost at Teluk Nibong. Pantai Kok, tel. (04) 911901, fax (04) 911968, M$250-450.

Burau Bay Resort: Capping the north end of Pantai Kok is the less expensive alternative to the Sheraton, complete with a small pool and 150 individual cabanas nestled under a thick grove of trees. Pantai Kok, tel. (04) 911061, fax (04) 911172, M$180-250.

Pantai Rhu

The only developed beach on the north coast offers some of Langkawi's finest sand and perfect solitude but lacks much in the way of facilities. Hopefully, a few guesthouses will open up in the coming years.

Mutiara Beach Hotel: This heroic but doomed white elephant finally opened several years ago after a long financial struggle. Facilities include a swimming pool, restaurants, and endless water sports. Pantai Rhu, tel. (04) 916488, fax (04) 788489, M$140-220.

Getting There

Langkawi is 30 km off the coast from Kuala Perlis, 51 km from Kuala Kedah, and 109 km north of Penang.

From Penang: MAS flies daily from Penang, Kuala Lumpur, Singapore, and Phuket in Thailand. Additional air services are provided by Pelangi Air, Tradewinds, and Silk Air.

Langkawi International Airport, 20 km from Kuah but very close to the better beaches, is served exclusively by taxis which operate at fixed rates on the coupon system.

Daily high-speed catamaran service is provided on the *Selesa Express,* which departs Penang daily at 0900 and arrives several hours later at Teluk Ewa on Langkawi's north shore. This ferry (and ferries to Sumatra and Satun in Thailand) is operated by the unimaginatively named Kuala Perlis-Langkawi Ferry Service (tel. 04-625630) from their Penang office adjacent to the tourist office at Fort Cornwallis. They also have ticket offices in Kuah on Langkawi, Kuala Perlis, Kuala Kedah, Satun, and Medan.

Ferry service is often canceled during the July-Sept. monsoon season.

From Kuala Perlis: Overlanders from Penang or southern Thailand can take a public bus to Kangar, followed by a shared taxi to the port town of Kuala Perlis. Ferries leave Kuala Perlis hourly and cost M$10-12 depending on the speed of the boat and your bargaining abilities.

From Kuala Kedah: Hourly ferry service at similar fares is also provided from Kuala Kedah near Alor Star.

From Thailand

From Phuket: MAS and Thai International fly daily from Phuket to Langkawi.

From Hat Yai: Travelers can take bus or train from Hat Yai to the border town of Padang Besar and then continue by train down to Arau or by bus to Kangar, from where shared taxis can be hired for the quick ride to Kuala Perlis.

From Satun: As of this writing, daily boat service was provided by the Kuala Perlis-Langkawi Ferry Service from the small southern Thai town of Satun down to Langkawi. However, demand has been low and this service may be canceled in the near future. Check with the budget guesthouses in Hat Yai, Krabi, or Phuket before heading down to Satun. More information under "Satun" in the Thailand chapter.

PENINSULAR MALAYSIA~ EAST COAST

The charms of the East Coast are largely the result of geography. Isolated by the jungle-clad Barisan Mountains, which run the length of the peninsula, the East Coast is a land of small villages, verdant ricefields, and fleets of bobbing fishing boats moored in blue lagoons. Unlike the West Coast with its modern architecture and bustling cities filled with hard-working Chinese, the East Coast is a sleepy place where life moves at a delightfully slow pace. Most residents are laid-back Malays who follow Islam and make their livings from fishing or farming. Cross-peninsula highways have brought modernization, and oil rigs and petroleum refineries have marred some of the coastline, yet much of the East Coast remains an idyllic region of sun-drenched beaches, funky *kampongs* of stilted houses, and gentle people whose gracious lifestyles haven't changed much in recent times.

Two caveats: East Coast beaches are clean and untouristy but not as stunning or well developed as those in southern Thailand. Secondly, single women and travelers looking for an escapist holiday should note that fundamentalist Islam has dramatically affected the mood and tolerance level on the East Coast. Except for a few isolated beaches and offshore islands which offer some privacy from outraged locals, this is *not* the place to drink, find romance, or sunbathe in a skimpy bathing suit.

ATTRACTIONS

Top draws are the beaches, islands, villages, handicrafts, festivals, and the annual migration of the leatherback turtles. Four recommended destinations include Tioman Island, the beach at Cherating, turtles at Rantau Abang, and the fishing village of Marang.

Towns
Urban centers such as Kota Baru, Kuala Trengganu, and Kuantan are monotonous and dis-

appointing places with little of interest except for the colorful local markets. The best one is in Kota Baru, where dozens of brightly clad ladies sell their goods in a tiered emporium under wonderfully diffused lighting. To experience the best of the East Coast, avoid the towns and stay at the beaches or in the villages.

Beaches
The 710-km coastline from Thailand to Singapore is a nearly continuous stretch of sand interrupted only occasionally by rocky headlands or muddy estuaries which ooze their reddish waters into the turquoise sea. Although less impressive than the beaches of Thailand or the Philippines, many visitors love the sleepy pace and the lack of commercial development. These beaches are also far more attractive than the somewhat polluted beaches on the West Coast. About a dozen offer accommodations from simple bungalows in the M$5-15 range to international-class hotels with all the standard amenities, but for privacy and rural ambience I'd recommend the beach at Cherating. It's lovely, peaceful, and relatively undeveloped, with only a few dozen bungalows standing under the swaying palm trees. Marang to the south of Kuala Trengganu is also beautiful, although accommodations are limited to primitive bungalows.

Islands
Serious beachcombers will also want to visit several of the superb islands that sparkle in the sunshine off the coast from Mersing. As you will be told dozens of times, Tioman (largest and most famous of this 64-island archipelago) served as the backdrop for the 1950s film *South Pacific*. It has also been nominated by an obscure Swiss magazine as one of the world's 10 most beautiful islands. Accommodations range from an international-standard hotel with golf course to a dozen budget bungalows facing the crystal-clear waters. Beaches are fairly good and most visitors find a trek through the interior

jungle a fascinating experience. Tioman and other nearby islands such as Rawa, Sibu, and Tinggi can be reached by boat from Mersing. To the north and reached by fishing boats from Besut and Marang are the quiet and largely deserted islands of Kapas, Perhentian, and Redang. Most of these islands have simple huts or middle-priced bungalows.

Villages

Malay *kampongs* are worth a quick visit since they are perhaps the cleanest and most picturesque villages in all of Southeast Asia. Remember, however, that this is the Bible Belt of Muslim Malaysia; conservative residents place great importance on modest dress and proper behavior. Shorts and bathing suits are completely inappropriate when wandering around an Islamic village! Visitors who disregard local traditions and dress immodestly will find themselves subjected to hostile stares . . . or worse. Because of these conservative attitudes, only villages such as Marang, which are accustomed to curious outsiders, should be visited.

Turtles

Among the annual visitors to the beaches of the East Coast are the giant leatherback turtles that struggle ashore nightly during the summer months to lay their eggs on the beach at Rantau Abang. While the abusive treatment of these magnificent creatures by local schoolkids is sometimes shocking, this spectacle remains one of Southeast Asia's great natural phenomena.

TRANSPORTATION

A paved and well-maintained road skirts the coast from Singapore up to the Thai border just north of Kota Baru. Other useful roads include the east-west highway across the top of the peninsula and the newly completed central highway which parallels the railway line between Johor Baru and Kota Baru. A steady stream of local buses rumbles along the coastal road and independent travelers should have little trouble flagging one down. Transportation terminals in the larger towns are usually located on the main highway, at a strategic intersection, or adjacent to the central marketplace. Share taxis are also available for about 50% more than ordinary buses. Hitchhiking is

relatively easy (but not guaranteed) and a good way to meet a traveling salesman. Roads are flat and bicyclists will enjoy the lack of traffic. Cars can be hired in Kuala Trengganu, Kuantan, and Johor Baru. MAS flies from Kuala Lumpur to Kota Baru, Kuantan, and Kuala Trengganu.

PRACTICALITIES

Weather

Travel can be difficult or impossible during the monsoon season from November to January, when rivers flood and roads disappear under mountains of water. Read the newspapers carefully and travel the West Coast during monsoons.

Banking Hours

The Muslim weekend falls on Thursday and Friday in the states of Kelantan and Trengganu. Banks are open until 1130 on Thursdays, closed all day on Fridays, but open 1000-1500 on Saturdays and Sundays.

Festivals

Most East Coast celebrations take place from April to June. This is an excellent time to watch top spinning, kite flying, shadow-puppet plays, traditional dances, and boat races. Festivities also surround the birthday of the sultan of Kelantan in late March and the birthday of the sultan of Trengganu in late April. Cultural activities are sponsored weekly throughout the year at the cultural center in Kota Baru.

Shopping

Malaysia's best selection of handicrafts is found on the East Coast. Each state produces its own specialties. The Kelantanese of Kota Baru produce outstanding silver filigree work, gold-thread needlework known as *songket,* and some truly exquisite paper kites. Trengganu artisans are known for their colorful hand-stamped batik and woodcarvings of intricate figureheads for fishing boats. Each town has a number of handicraft shops, often located somewhat outside the city limits; tourist offices can advise on nearby handicraft villages.

Behavior And Dress Codes

The East Coast is the most conservative Muslim region in Malaysia and visitors must take

laid-back palm

this into account and act in accordance with Malay traditions. Some of the best beaches are now closed to Westerners, who have offended local sensibilities with immodest dress such as shorts and bathing suits. Beaches next to Malay *kampongs* are generally off-limits. Best locations for sunbathing without upsetting the locals are at Cherating, Telok Chempedak near Kuantan, and offshore islands such as Tioman. Shorts and halter tops are considered offensive dress in all urban areas, where visitors should wear long pants or full-length skirts. Women must be especially careful about this. Visitors to mosques must also be well covered. Public consumption of alcohol can be risky outside of protected tourist enclaves. There's more: smoking is discouraged, public displays of affection are considered scandalous, and it is inadvisable to show any disrespect toward the sultan. Possession of drugs can bring heavy fines, jail terms, or execution. While Muslim laws against indecency, alcohol, and close contact between persons of the opposite sex may seem harsh to Westerners on holiday, to disregard them could bring serious consequences.

MERSING

The small fishing town of Mersing is the departure point for boats to Tioman and other nearby islands. There is little of interest here except for a mosque overlooking the town and the small flotilla of fishing boats constructed with hulls in the distinctive style of Trengganu.

Accommodations

Most of Mersing's inexpensive Chinese hotels can be found by walking east toward the pier. Boredom can be relieved with a movie at the nearby Union Theater.

Embassy Hotel: A popular backpackers' hotel and rendezvous spot despite the loud TV and somewhat expensive dishes in the cafe. Friendly managers. 2 Jl. Ismail, tel. (07) 793545, M$16-25 fan, M$32-45 a/c.

Sheikh Tourist Agency: Sulaiman Aziz's place just opposite the post office toward the dock is another dependable backpackers' spot that doubles as a tourist agency. 1B Jl. Abu Bakar, tel. (07) 793767, M$6 dorm.

Mandarin Hotel: The third-best choice is the hotel just opposite the bus station, where fan-cooled rooms on the upper floors are inexpensive and quiet. 3 Jl. Sulaiman, tel. (07) 793344, M$12-25.

Mersing Merlin Inn: Mersing's top-end choice is two km outside town. Endau Rd., tel. (07) 791312, M$90-120.

Getting There

Avoid spending a night in Mersing by arriving in time to catch the noon boat to Tioman. An early bus from Kuantan and the 0900 bus from Singapore's Lavender Street bus terminus will arrive in time. An early start is essential from Kuala Lumpur since buses take about five hours. Most buses stop at the roundabout opposite the Restoran Malaysia, which sells bus tickets and tasty Indian food. To reach the ferry pier, walk east through Mersing to the boat offices.

TIOMAN ISLAND AND VICINITY

When James Michener described Bali Hai in his *Tales of the South Pacific* as an island paradise of sandy beaches, clear blue waters, and beautiful brown people, he never anticipated that moviemakers would one day search for the mythical island. The quest ended when Tioman was selected as the mysterious Bali Hai for Rogers and Hammerstein's hit musical *South Pacific*.

Located in the South China Sea off the eastern coast of Peninsular Malaysia, the teardrop-shaped and surprisingly undeveloped island achieved further fame when Geneva-based Magnum Press declared Tioman to be one of the world's 10 most beautiful islands. While Tioman certainly isn't in that rarefied class, it offers some fairly good beaches, clear waters filled with corals and colorful fish, and a spectacular jungle that climbs up soaring mountain walls.

ATTRACTIONS

West Coast Hike
Pulau Tioman, with its towering rock spires, thick jungles, and wealth of flora and fauna, provides ideal hiking opportunities for anyone interested in nature and wildlife.

The most famous rock formations are the twin peaks of Nenek Sri Mukut and Bau Sirau, which figured prominently in the film *South Pacific*. From the central pier at Tekek, hike south past Tioman Island Resort to a deserted stretch of beach which rates among the best on the island. A small trail just beyond the hazardous but scenic 18-hole golf course leads over the hill to another long, fine beach flanked by swaying palms and large boulders set in clear waters. Across the bamboo bridge and over a steep hill is a small Malay fishing village, Kampong Paya, where an unmarked track leads to the summit of Gunung Kajang.

The seashore path north of Tekek winds past the cool Mango Grove Cafe where the proprietor, Encik Amin, sells cold drinks and a selection of hand-painted batik beachwear. The trail continues past Ayer Batang Beach (where the best budget bungalows are located) and ends at Salang Beach about two hours farther north.

Cross-Island Hike
Tioman's most spectacular hike is the trans-island trail which starts near the mosque in Kampong Tekek and climbs over the mountains to Kampong Juara. The well-marked trail passes freshwater pools, waterfalls, and a rubber plantation. Allow two or three hours for this trek. Kampong Juara has several cafes and bungalows set on a beautiful beach.

Diving: Perhaps the most compelling reason to visit Tioman is to experience the underwater world. Waters immediately offshore have little to offer, but several of the nearby islands are rich in tropical fish and corals. Pulau Rengis, a minuscule island a few hundred meters offshore from the beach, is the easiest island to dive. Snorkelers can also view a coral-encrusted wreck of a Japanese warship near Mukut and explore the underwater caves around Pulau Cebeh. The reefs at Tulai, Sepoy, and Labas islands have also been recommended. Dives can be arranged through the Tioman Island Resort, Samudra Swiss Cottages on Tekek Beach, and Ben's Diving Center on Salang Beach.

ACCOMMODATIONS

Tekek Beach
Tioman's central beach is dominated by the beautiful Berjaya Imperial Beach Resort (former Tioman Island Resort), tel. (09) 445445, where standard a/c rooms with private baths are M\$125-150, superior rooms M\$175-250.

Slightly north of this international-class hotel is the attractive Samudra Swiss Cottages where doubles are M\$65-85. The owner serves a tasty dinner buffet and rents scuba gear at reasonable rates to divers with C cards.

To the north of the pier are a dozen unnamed bungalows with simple rooms in the M\$10-15

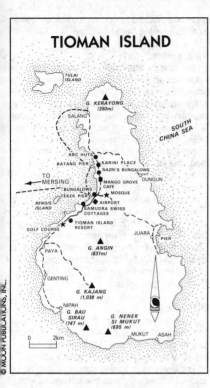

TIOMAN ISLAND

TULAI ISLAND

G. KERAYONG (390m)

SALANG

SOUTH CHINA SEA

ABC HUTS

BATANG PIER   KARINI PLACE

NAZRI'S BUNGALOWS

TO MERSING   MANGO GROVE CAFE   DUNGUN

BUNGALOWS   MOSQUE

TEKEK PIER   AIRPORT

RENGIS ISLAND   SAMUDRA SWISS COTTAGES

GOLF COURSE   TIOMAN ISLAND RESORT

JUARA PIER

PAYA   G. ANGIN (831m)

GENTING

G. KAJANG (1,038 m)

NIPAH

G. BAU SIRAU (747 m)   G. NENEK SI MUKUT (695 m)

MUKUT   ASAH

0   2km

© MOON PUBLICATIONS, INC.

range. Unfortunately, none of these bungalows have been built with any imagination and all are disappointing when compared with similar efforts at Thai beaches. Best of the group are the two large brown bungalows owned by Rahim and Rahman. Most travelers prefer the simpler and less expensive huts at Ayer Batang.

Ayer Batang

The fine white sand and sense of seclusion of Batang have made it the most popular backpackers' beach on Tioman. The A-frame huts are extremely basic with mattresses on the floor and no electricity but only cost M$8-10 depending on the season, how long you plan to stay, the mood of the owner, and your bargaining ability.

Nazri's Bungalows just south of the jetty is situated on good sand and offers water sports, but it's often filled because of proximity to the pier. North of the jetty is Tioman House, Kartini Place, Rinda House, and the recommended ABC Bungalows at the extreme northern end of the beach—worth the 20-minute walk. Bumboats from Mersing first stop at the Telek Jetty and continue up to the Ayer Batang Jetty on request.

Salang Beach

The small fishing village on the northwest corner of Tioman has excellent diving and an outstanding beach. Accommodations and diving gear are available at Ben's Diving Center, Bidin's Guest House, and Abidin Bungalows. Bumboats go to Salang with advance notice and a M$5 surcharge.

Juara

The settlement on the East Coast of Tioman has several inexpensive bungalows at M$4 per person, including Rahman's, Ali Awang's, and Sammy Hussein's Chalets.

GETTING THERE

Air

Tradewinds, a subsidiary of Singapore Airlines and Pelangi Air, flies daily to Tioman from Singapore and Kuala Lumpur for M$100. Alternatively, ICSA Transport offers a daily catamaran service from Singapore to Tioman for S$120 return.

Boat

Tioman is 43 nautical miles from Mersing and can be reached in two to five hours with several different types of boats. All depart Mersing 1200-1400, depending on the tides.

Cheapest and slowest are the fishing vessels called bumboats (appropriately nicknamed bumpboats), which cost M$15 and take four to five hours to reach Tioman. On a clear and sunny day this is a relaxing way to reach Tioman, but these unstable boats should *not* be taken during high winds or rough seas.

Faster motor launches cost M$23 and take 2¹/₂ hours including a mid-ocean transfer. Speedboats, hydrofoils, and hovercrafts booked from Mr. Froggy cost M$30 and arrive in about two hours, but speeding toward Tioman is dramatic overkill.

The Mersing Pier and ticket offices are located at the far end of town.

OTHER ISLANDS NEAR TIOMAN

Rawa Island

Rawa is the most developed of the islands that dot the waters near Mersing. Opened in 1971, Rawa has a capacity of 140 people and is run by a member of the Johor Royal Family. Activities include windsurfing, canoeing, fishing, sunbathing, and skin diving, though little remains of the coral beds.

Accommodations are available in chalets and bungalows built on stilts in the traditional style with palm-thatched roofs and wide verandas. Chalet doubles are M$45, bungalow doubles M$50, and four-man hilltop rooms cost M$65-95.

Boats to Rawa charge M$16 roundtrip and leave at noon from the Mersing pier. Day visitors may visit the island for an extra M$3 but are not allowed to camp, picnic, or bring food and drink. Rawa is pleasant during the week but crowded on weekends. Bookings can be made at the Rawa Safari office at the Mersing pier.

Besar Island

Larger and closer to the mainland than Rawa, this sparkling island has a few cheap bungalows at M$20-40 per person and several small resorts built in the traditional Malay style.

Radin's Besar Country Resort, to the left of the Kampong Busong Jetty, and Tunku Hassan's Besar Village Resort both have comfortable cottages at M$40 double. Besar Beach Club has rooms in the same price range.

Boats to Besar cost M$18 return. Like other nearby islands, Besar gets crowded on weekends and closes down during the monsoon season from November to January.

Tinggi Island

Pulau Tinggi's unmistakable conical silhouette once earned it the nickname of "General Hat's Island" from passing Chinese sailors. This is a magnificent volcanic peak of sheer granite walls plunging into a deep blue sea; the interior jungle is home to screeching monkeys, pythons, and brilliantly plumed birds that can be trained to mimic the human voice with extraordinary precision. The island is so beautiful that some say an image of Tinggi was superimposed over a scene filmed on Tioman for the movie *South Pacific.*

Across the water from Tinggi's main village is Thomas Chow's fishing platform, which provides basic accommodations in a thatched *attap* hut. The leading luxury choice is Smailing Island Resort, where fine huts on a superb beach cost M$50-100. Recommended. Boats can be chartered from the Tourist Boat Association at Mersing jetty.

Sibu Island

Some eight km west of Tinggi and reached in two hours from Mersing, the superb island of Sibu is a favorite destination for travelers who enjoy squeaky white sand, skin diving, and solitude.

The Sea Gypsy Village Resort located on an exquisite crescent-shaped beach has well-constructed A-frames at M$30 double and bungalows with private baths for M$40. Other choices include O & H Kampung Huts at M$15-20, Sibu Island Resort at M$50-70, and Sibu Island Cabanas at M$60-90.

EAST-CENTRAL

KUANTAN

Situated midway up the East Coast at the mouth of a muddy river, this gritty Chinese business town has little to offer most visitors, who head directly to the nearby beach resort of Telok Chempedak.

Attractions

Kuantan attractions include a Muslim dinner at a waterfront cafe, the night market on Jalan Mahkota, and a ferry ride across the river to a Malay *kampong*. Kuantan is also the center for Pahang's numerous cottage industries, such as woven silks, pandan-leaf baskets, wood pieces carved by *orang asli*, silver filigree jewelry, dara jade necklaces, and handpainted batiks. The handicraft center at Telok Chempedak has a good selection.

Attractions near Kuantan include Lake Chini, picturesque during the summer months when it is blanketed with a brilliant carpet of red and white lotuses, the Buddhist Cave at Sungai Lembing with its immense reclining image, the touristy fishing village of Beserah, and Chendor Beach, where loggerhead turtles lumber ashore during the summer months.

The Pahang State Tourist Office in the Kompleks Terantum, Kuantan's 22-story shopping and office complex, can help with transportation details.

Accommodations

Kuantan is a compact town and most of the hotels are within walking distance of the bus terminal. Just across the street are three inexpensive Chinese hotels. Both the Tong Nam Ah and the Tin Ah Hotels have small but ade-

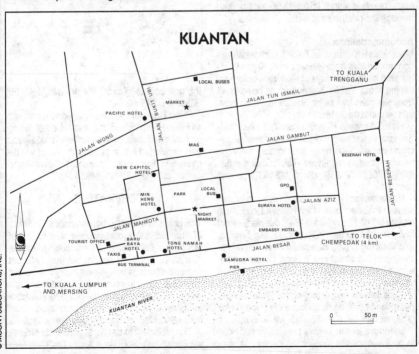

quate rooms for M$11-15. Ask for a quiet room in the rear. The larger Baru Raya Hotel to the left has marginally better rooms with fan and attached bath from M$25 double. Much quieter and with a touch of exterior charm is the Min Heng Hotel on Jalan Mahkota, where basic cubicles cost M$11.

TELOK CHEMPEDAK

Kuantan's big draw is the beach at Telok Chempedak, about five km north of town.

The road leading down to the beach is lined with gaudy Chinese restaurants, sleazy bars, and tourist shops selling T-shirts and cheap sunglasses: a discouraging introduction to what is otherwise a fairly pleasant place. Busloads of Malays picnic under the trees and patronize the handicraft stalls next to the parking lot. The small beach is often crowded on weekends because of its easy accessibility to Kuantan. Much more attractive and often completely deserted are the beaches at Methodist and Pelindong bays, reached with a leisurely 30-minute hike through the peninsula forest.

Accommodations

Most Western visitors at Telok Chempedak are conventioneers from Singapore or Kuala Lumpur who need a few days of relaxation before returning home. Telok Chempedak can be reached from Kuantan by taxi or bus 39 from the local bus terminal on Jl. Mahkota.

Hotel Asrama Bendahara: The best budget spot in the neighborhood is somewhat decrepit but perhaps more memorable than the nearby faceless high-rises. Telok Chempedak, tel. (09) 525930, M$8 dorm, M$16-20 private rooms.

Homestays: Unusual options are the homestays in the street behind the Hillview Hotel. Most charge M$12-16 single, M$18-24 double. Current favorites include the Sri Pantai, Taman Negara, and Pancing Caves Bungalows. Homestays at the top of the street are in good shape but the vandalized houses at the bottom of the road vaguely resemble a ghetto housing project.

Kuantan Hotel: A fairly good if somewhat overpriced hotel is just opposite the Hyatt. Telok Chempedak, tel. (09) 524755, M$40-60.

Samudra Hotel: Telok's best midpriced hotel is on the opposite side of the peninsula near

TIOMAN ISLAND

the golf course. Telok Chempedak, tel. (09) 505933, M$45-60.

Hyatt Kuantan: Another high-end resort with all the standard amenities, even a small wooden junk once used by Vietnamese refugees but now converted into a beach bar. What will the marketing director dream up next? Telok Chempedak, tel. (09) 525211, M$140-220.

CHERATING

This beautiful sweeping beach about 45 km north of Kuantan is the most popular stop for travelers on the East Coast of Peninsular Malaysia. The sand is nothing special but the idyllic setting and attractive bungalows make this an outstanding place to relax for a few days . . . or weeks. Cherating is also one of the few beaches in Malaysia where Westerners can wear swimsuits without fear of offending Muslim sensibilities.

The jutting hill to the north separates Cherating Beach from Southeast Asia's first Club Med,

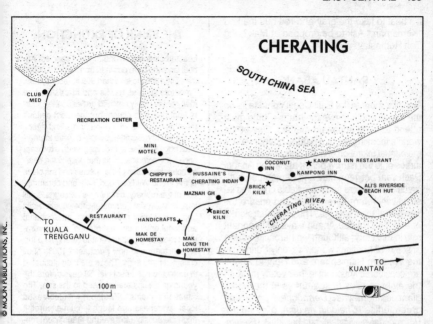

while an off-limits Vietnamese refugee camp is located across the Cherating River to the south. There isn't much to do here but loaf, wander around the beach looking for sand crabs, and perhaps inspect the old and collapsing brick kilns. Cherating is an idyllic and perfectly relaxing destination.

Accommodations

Cherating is quickly expanding as local entrepreneurs open new bungalows and restaurants on a near-weekly basis. Accommodations range from basic A-frames in the M$10-15 price range to a/c chalets with private baths for M$25-40. Many represent excellent value.

Mak Long Teh Homestay: Teh Ahmad, or Mak Long Teh, pioneered the idea of village accommodations for tourists over 20 years ago. Today, his family operates one of those wonderful travel experiences where you are allowed to enjoy authentic Malay hospitality in a romantic *kampong* home. Cherating, tel. (09) 503290, M$12-15 including meals.

Mak De Homestay: Another memorable homestay. Cherating, tel. (09) 511316, M$12-15 including meals.

Coconut Inn: A quick walk along the narrow road uncovers some real gems, but perhaps the best choice is this lovely Malay house facing the arching bay. Cherating, tel. (09) 503199, M$12-35.

Other Budget Chalets: Seaside Kampong Inn has decent rooms from M$12, brown Cherating Indah features individual porches and tables, older Hussaine's Bungalows has adequate rooms from M$10, while Ali's Riverside Beach Hut at the end of the road offers clean bungalows and views over the Cherating River.

Club Med: Club Med to the north was constructed on a public beach, technically open to day guests despite the heavy presence of guards. Facilities include a conference center, restaurants, and extensive sports facilities. Cherating, tel. (09) 591131, US$1000 per week.

Coral Beach Resort: Pahang's best international-class resort is 28 km south of Cherating at Balok Beach, ranked as one of the best windsurfing spots in Asia. Balok Beach, Sungei Karang, tel. (09) 587544, M$140-220.

Transportation

All buses between Kuantan and Kuala Trengganu roar past Cherating, but from Kuantan it's best to take the gray-and-red bus marked "Kemaman." Ask to be dropped at Mak Long Teh Homestay.

RANTAU ABANG

Not all visitors to the East Coast come to lie on the beach and improve their tans. Some must attend to more important matters. One of the world's most impressive natural phenomena is the annual migration and struggle of leatherback turtles onto the narrow beach at Rantau Abang. Each year between May and September, hundreds of these rare and remarkable creatures instinctively return here to nest and ensure the survival of their species. The 20-km stretch of beach near Rantau Abang plays an important role in this story; although leatherbacks spawn at some 12 locations worldwide, only Surinam in the Western Hemisphere and Rantau Abang are considered important in their yearly ritual. Of the eight species of sea turtles in the world, giant leatherbacks (*Dermochels coriacea*), green turtles (*Chelonia mydas*), olive ridleys (*Lepidochelys olivacea*), and hawkbills (*Eretmochelys imbricata*) are all known to nest in Malaysia. But leatherbacks are unquestionably the largest and most famous—the *Guinness Book of World Records* cites a monster which measured almost three meters and tipped the scales at over 1,000 kilos! In the reptile world only the estuarine crocodile and the Komodo dragon compare in sheer physical size.

Leatherback Spotting

Turtle watching is a rewarding but exhausting experience since the female turtle prefers nocturnal cover for her egging expeditions. Although it plays havoc on a good night's sleep, you must join the crowds and wait patiently in a seashore restaurant. Rantau Abang's beaches are divided and tendered to licensed egg collectors, who are authorized to collect entrance fees to their enclosed beaches. Fee collectors can be recognized by certified identification tags from the Fisheries Department. Turtle watching is free along the stretch of beach controlled by the government near the Rantau Abang Visitor's Center.

Turtles are most numerous in late August when the reptiles swim ashore from midnight to early morning. Relax with your *paratha* and

THE BRINK OF EXTINCTION

Leatherbacks are an endangered species. Annual landings have declined from over 10,000 in the early 1950s to less than 600 in recent years. Predators such as hawks and lizards capture many of the newly hatched turtles as they scurry from beach to ocean, but the most serious threat is man. As with rhino horns and tigers' paws, some misguided people believe leatherback eggs to be an aphrodisiac worth exorbitant prices. It's incredibly tragic that despite the near-complete extinction of the species and the pleas of the World Wildlife Fund, sale and consumption of the rubbery, pingpong-sized eggs is still legal in Malaysia! Fortunately, the situation isn't hopeless. Under pressure from international and local environmental groups, the government recently gazetted Rantau Abang as a turtle sanctuary and now purchases 100% of all collected turtle eggs. These are then incubated in protected sand nests for 56 days before the young hatchlings are released to the sea. The situation remains critical, but with increased local awareness and tough legal measures it might be possible to save the magnificent reptiles from extinction.

roti bakar until someone sounds the alarm. Everyone then races down the beach and gathers in the eerie darkness to watch the creature silently struggle up the steep beach. It is like a King Kong movie as the primeval dinosaur lumbers past the silent crowds, patiently digs a dummy hole to fool the predators, and then laboriously lays 50-100 eggs in her final hole. Tears of exhaustion slowly drip from her eyes. A licensed egg collector keeps the crowd quiet and prevents any possible disturbances while he gathers the eggs under the watchful eye of the Fisheries Department. After he departs, spectators take photos, kick sand, and ride the frightened animal.

Accommodations

Three inexpensive bungalows are located on the beach within walking distance of the turtles and the edifying Turtle Information Center, while a trio of better resorts is within a few kilometers.

Awang's Beach Bungalows: Pak Awang almost single-handedly started local tourism in

1959 when he constructed the first rustic dormitory at Rantau Abang. Pak arranges tours to nearby Pulau Kapas, Sekayu Waterfall, and the night market at Kuala Dungun. Despite its age, Awang's remains perhaps the most popular budget spot at the beach. Rantau Abang, tel. (09) 842236, M$10-15.

Ishmail's Bungalows: Similar facilities adjacent to Awang's. Rantau Abang, tel. (09) 842257, M$10-15.

Dahimah's Bungalows: A clean and quiet alternative to the tourist center is provided at this popular guesthouse one km south toward Dungun, on the west side of the Abang River. Recommended. Rantau Abang, tel. (09) 842166, M$10-15.

Merantau Inn: The middle price gap is filled by this older resort located a few kilometers south of the visitor center. Kuala Abang, tel. (09) 841131, M$45-80.

Rantau Abang Visitor Center: One km north of the Turtle Information Center is another decent place with very large chalets and a reasonably priced restaurant. Rantau Abang, tel. (09) 841533, M$65-90.

Tanjong Jara Beach Hotel: The top-end choice, six km south of the Turtle Center and 13 km north of Kuala Dungun, has 100 luxurious rooms spread across 76 acres. Best of all, the hotel has a seven-km beach stretching between two headlands virtually to itself. Mile 8 Jl. Dungun, tel. (09) 841801, M$160-380.

MARANG

Situated 15 km south of Kuala Trengganu on the estuary of a wide river, the splendid fishing village of Marang offers a rare opportunity to observe local Malay lifestyles and enjoy one of the finest beaches in the region. The setting is ridiculously picturesque: quaint little houses elevated on stilts surround a pure blue lagoon speckled with colorful fishing boats. Wide-eyed children smile shyly at the visitor while older residents go about their business of drying squid and fish in the blazing sun. Despite its superb location and fine beach, Marang remains almost completely untouched by tourism.

Attractions
Kampong **Walk:** Westerners are welcome to wander around the small village north of the river, but local customs must be observed. All visitors should remain well covered. Shorts and revealing tops are considered scandalous dress in the village and bathing suits can only be worn on the beaches directly fronting the tourist bungalows.

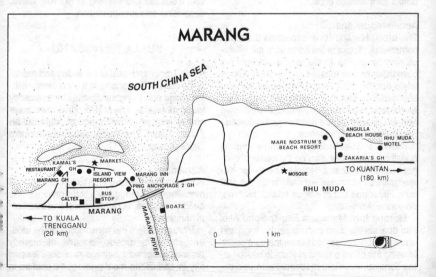

Kapas Island: Scattered offshore from Marang and Kuala Trengganu are several islands with pristine beaches and submerged coral beds rich with tropical marinelife. Kapas, six km from Marang, has a succession of deserted beaches joined at low tide, a bat cave, monitor lizards, and excellent snorkeling on the backside of adjacent Gemai Island. Kapas is a day-trip for most visitors, although you can sleep on the beach or stay in a basic chalet with attached bath for M$15-30. Bring food, drink, and mosquito net if you plan to camp out.

Accommodations at Primula Kapas Island Village Resort include 40 deluxe bungalows US$35-60. Facilities include a pool, a restaurant, and all types of sea sports. Contact the Pantai Primula Hotel in Kuala Trengganu for details.

Kapas can be reached by speedboat from the Beach House for M$10. The island gets crowded on Muslim weekends of Thursdays and Fridays.

Marang River: Day-long voyages up the muddy Marang can be arranged through most bungalows. Boats typically leave in the early morning and return by sunset with wildlife stops and lunch at Kuala Mesta some 50 km upriver. A five-man fishermen's boat costs M$40. Motorized self-drive boats are available at the riverbanks for the same price.

Accommodations

The broad Marang River separates the small commercial district to the north from the village of Kampong Rhu Muda to the south. Five guesthouses are located in the main village while another four beach resorts are two km south in Rhu Muda. Guesthouses out in Rhu Muda tend to be more expensive than in town and are geared toward middle-market families rather than budget travelers.

Kamal's Guesthouse: Marang's original guesthouse has been serving the needs of budget travelers for over a decade. The owner, Kamaruzaman, arranges excursions up the Marang River and out to Kapas Island. Marang, no phone, M$5-15.

Marang Inn: Managers Eric Tho and Alex Lee operate the most popular spot in town and one of the best guesthouses on the east coast. Marang Inn offers organized tours to nearby attractions, an excellent restaurant with free ba-

nanas ("while supplies last"), and wonderful locally made batiks. 132-133 Bandar Marang, tel. (09) 682132, fax (09) 628093, M$5-15.

Ping Anchorage 2 Guesthouse: Opened in 1992 by the guys from Marang Inn, this lovely home offers even more value. Friendly management, excellent food, and a genuine homestay atmosphere. Recommended. 190A Bandar Marang, tel. (09) 682132, M$5-15.

Angulia Beach House Resort: A reasonably attractive resort though individual chalets are overpriced and the place badly needs some landscaping. Bargain for a room. Km 20, Kampong Rhu Muda, tel. (09) 681322, M$25-75.

Mare Nostrum's Beach Resort: Better value is found at this adjacent resort. Note: both resorts in Rhu Muda are surrounded by protective fences and visitors are strongly advised to safeguard their valuables. Incidents of theft, rock throwing, and tire slashing by scandalized locals have been reported. Lot 313 Jl. Pantai, Marang, tel. (09) 681433, fax (09) 681579, M$12-50.

Transportation

Marang is 15 km south of Kuala Trengganu and 23 km north of Rantau Abang. From the south, take any bus heading north and get off in Rhu Muda, or near the bridge for Marang guesthouses. From Kuala Trengganu bus station, take a bus marked, Marang, or Kg. Rhu Muda, depending on your destination.

KUALA TRENGGANU

Kuala Trengganu, seat of the sultan and capital of the state of Trengganu, is a once-sleepy fishing village now being transformed by its recently found oil wealth. The MTPB office is inconveniently located at the far end of Jalan Sultan Zainal Abidin. The Trengganu State Tourism Office is near the GPO.

Attractions

Rather than impressive architecture or historical monuments, Trengganu's top draws are the nearby beaches, tropical islands, and traditional handicrafts.

Market: Before the construction of the modern shopping arcade, dozens of brightly dressed ladies sold their wares under the open sky in one of the most photogenic scenes in

KUALA TRENGGANU

all of Malaysia. Today the merchants do business in a well-organized but impersonal and dark market best experienced in the early morning hours—durians are downstairs, handicrafts upstairs. Jalan Bandar between the taxi stand and the market has some fine wooden buildings that have survived fire, monsoons, and urban development.

Old Sultan's Palace: This curious French-style *istana* was constructed in 1903 to replace the burned Green Palace. With its tapered roofs and wooden windows embellished with intricately carved Koranic inscriptions, the yellow palace is still used for royal ceremonies and as a secondary residence for Trengganu's 250-year-old sultanate. The State Mosque stands on the adjacent corner.

Duyong Besar Island: The estuary of the Trengganu River has several islands which are

home to Malay fishermen and boatbuilders who fashion both traditional and modern crafts. Boat-builder Abdullah Mudir uses dried *chengal* hard-wood to first construct the wall of the boat before its skeleton is wrapped around. In earlier days, an elaborate mast-guard carved in the form of a crane was placed in front as the appropriate talisman, but today most of his boats are constructed with modern designs. The Exeter Maritime Museum in Britain exhibits one of Abdullah's traditional boats.

Ferries to Duyong Besar cost 50 *sen* and leave from the jetty near the taxi stand. Boats can also be hired for upriver trips to Kampong Pulau Rusa, whose occupants are famous for the quality of their *songket* weavings.

Handicrafts: The people of Trengganu are well known for their outstanding handicrafts such as fabrics, brassware, and woodcarving.

Most are cottage industries practiced in private homes, although a small handicraft center is located in Kampong Rusila some 12 km south of Trengganu. The TDC (Tourism Development Corp.) has addresses for local craft homes.

Accommodations

Kuala Trengganu has two backpackers' hostels, plus a half-dozen hotels in the low to middle price range in the center of town.

Ping Anchorage Homestay: The best guesthouse in town offers a wonderful rooftop cafe, dorms and private rooms, and organized tours to all possible locations. The secret to enjoying Kuala Trengganu is to explore the countryside and nearby islands instead of hanging around the rather dull town. Also, don't miss the newly opened Istana Tengku Long, an old sultan's palace now converted into one of Southeast Asia's largest museums. 77A Jl. Dato Isaac, tel. (09) 620851, fax (09) 628093, M$5-25.

Awi's Yellow House: A rustic waterside guesthouse in a traditional village on the ship-building island of Duyong Besar. Guests often include artists and sailing enthusiasts who hang around for months while supervising construction of their boats. Mellow and highly atmospheric; a great spot to escape city life and *relax*.

From Kota Baru, get off the bus at the enormous new bridge that spans the Trengganu River. From Kuala Trengganu, take a Duyong bus from the local bus terminal or a ferry from the jetty. 3576 Duyong Besar, tel. (09) 631741, M$5-25.

Rex Hotel: Late arrivals might crash overnight at this acceptable place near the local bus terminal. Jl. Masjid, tel. (09) 622455, M$15-25.

Pantai Primula Hotel: Kuala Trengganu's only luxury hotel features all the standard amenities, such as a swimming pool and three restaurants facing a fairly good beach. Jl. Persinggahan, tel. (09) 622100, fax (09) 633360, M$140-280.

Transportation

Kuala Trengganu is 76 km north of Kuala Dungun and 142 km south of Kota Baru. A new transnational highway now connects Kuala Trengganu with Gua Musang (Taman Negara National Park) in the center of the country and Ipoh on the west coast. Express buses leave from the new terminal near the waterfront on Jl. Sultan Abidin. Local buses leave from the old terminal on Jl. Masjid. Share taxis leave from Jl. Sultan Ismail, at the waterfront near the jetty for Duyong Besar Island.

KUALA TRENGGANU TO KOTA BARU

Traveling north from Kuala Trengganu, the road leaves the coast and passes through a rich tobacco- and rice-growing region. Side roads reach the coastal villages of Merang (not Marang) and Besut, where boats depart for several beautiful and nearly deserted islands. Most have been declared protected marine parks to prevent fishing and coral collection within eight km of their shores. All have clean beaches and crystal-clear waters filled with varied marine life, sponges, and unique coral beds.

Access is by group tour or fishing boat from Merang, Besut, or Kuala Trengganu. Boat service is most frequent on the Muslim weekends of Thursdays and Fridays. Organized snorkeling and scuba dives can be arranged at the Pantai Primula Hotel in Kuala Trengganu.

Merang

Merang, another idyllic fishing village located on a long stretch of clean, white sand, is also the departure point for boats to Pulau Redang and other smaller islands.

Accommodations: Man's Homestay, some 500 meters north of town center, is a simple but acceptable place with helpful managers and decent rooms from M$10. More upscale is the Merang Beach Resort where A-frame chalets facing a great beach start at M$15. Both spots can help with boats to Redang Island.

Transportation: Merang is difficult to reach but served by daily direct buses from both Kuala Trengganu and Kota Baru. Alternatively, take a bus to the Penarik turnoff at Permaisuri, another bus to Penarik, and a share taxi to Merang.

Redang Island

Pulau Redang, 50 km from Trengganu and 30 km from Merang, is actually an archipelago of over 25 small islands known for its pure beaches, spectacular coves, and outstanding diving over vast expanses of coral beds. Long a secret of nature lovers, change arrived suddenly in 1993 with the construction of an immense resort

cheaper by the dozen

bitterly opposed by Malaysian environmental groups such as the Malaysian Nature Society. Redang Island Resort will ultimately cover almost 25% of the main island with a four-story 250-room hotel, dozens of chalets, and, almost unbelievably, an 18-hole golf course constructed over landfilled mangrove swamps! Incredible.

First port of call is the small but orderly fishing village of Kampung Puala Redang, where last-minute supplies are available from the general store. Activities include skin diving among the hard and soft corals, jungle hiking, and swimming in the crystal-clear bay at Teluk Dalam.

Accommodations: Accommodation on Redang is limited to camping at Teluk Kalong, the very expensive Redang Island Resort, or Dahlan Beach Chalets, owned and operated by a tour and dive operator from Kuala Trengganu.

Transportation: Boat service from Merang to Pulau Redang is very sporadic except on Thurs. and Fri., when local Malays charter boats for the two-hour journey. Otherwise, it's imperative to make advance reservations with Dahlan in Kuala Trengganu (tel. 09-627050) or risk having to charter an entire boat for about M$250. Camping Holiday in KL (tel. 03-717-8935) sponsors three-night stays for M$280; six scuba dives cost an additional M$280.

Kuala Besut

Kuala Besut, a rather run-down fishing village with lots of odor and little charm, is the departure point for boats to Pulau Perhentian Besar (the larger island) and Pulau Perhentian Kecil (the smaller).

Accommodations: The Kuala Besut Resthouse, one km south of town, is on an excellent beach but badly overpriced at M$60-80. A better bet is Bukit Keluang Beach Chalet (tel. 01-970943 or 09-976943), where decent rooms cost just M$10-15.

The chalet is located three km south of Kuala Besut and 14 km northeast of Jerteh, a large town on the main highway. From Kuala Trengganu, take a bus to Jerteh, then bus toward Kuala Besut, alight three km prior at Pengkalan Nyireh, and catch a final bus to the beach. From Kota Baru, take a bus to Pasir Puteh, another to Kuala Besut, and a third to Pengkalan Nyireh.

Perhentian Islands

The twin islands of Perhentian Besar and Perhentian Kecil, 21 km off the coast from Kuala Besut, are outstanding warm-water destinations long more popular than Redang due to their proximity to the mainland and easy access from Besut. But like Pulau Redang, Perhentian is due for some big changes as developers arrive to construct larger and larger resorts and transportation wizards dream of hydrofoils and, believe it or not, even an airport.

Still, Pulau Perhentian remains a place you wouldn't mind being shipwrecked for several weeks . . . if not months.

Accommodations: Nearly all organized accommodation is located on Perhentian Besar, though a few homestays and simple bungalows are found on the smaller island at Pasir Petani. Camping is free on both islands.

Perhentian Island Resort (tel. 01-333910 or 03-243-8011 in Kuala Lumpur) is a small, tastefully designed resort consisting of two dormitories priced from M$12 and 31 chalets M$40-70.

Twenty minutes away is the budget accommodation beach opposite the village of Kecil, where almost a dozen inexpensive guesthouses have sprung up in the last few years, including Abdul's Chalets, which proudly claims to be "where dreams become reality"—as opposed to Perhentian Island Resort, which boasts to be "where reality becomes fantasy." Apparently, somebody's been eating mushrooms again.

Transportation: Boats from Besut leave in the early morning, return in the late afternoon, and cost around M$15 one-way.

KOTA BARU AND VICINITY

Tucked away at the northeastern corner of the peninsula some 24 km from the Thai frontier, Kota Baru (also spelled Bahru and Bharu), the state capital of Kelantan State, is considered the heartland of traditional Malaysian culture. While the city is physically indistinguishable from most other Asian cities constructed of concrete and cinderblock, it remains the best place in Malaysia to see shadow puppets, kite flying, top spinning, and other Malay games. It is also somewhat of a handicrafts center with a handful of shops producing fine batiks, silverware, brasswork, and woodcarvings. The tourist office on Jalan Ibrahim just south of the clock tower is friendly and can help with directions to nearby handicraft villages.

Note that all banks and other government offices such as the tourist office in Kelantan State are closed on Thursday afternoons and Fridays but open Saturdays and Sundays. Thai visas can be obtained 0900-1600 Sunday-Thursday at the Royal Thai Consulate, tel. (09) 782545, at 4426 Jalan Pengkalan Chepa.

ATTRACTIONS

Sights in town are limited to several historic buildings clustered together near Merdeka Square, a few blocks south of the commercial center.

Central Market
A good place to begin your walking tour is at this modern market where scores of brightly clad women gossip, chew betel nut, and display their rambutans, mangosteens, pandan mats, and batiks in the open-air emporium. Con-structed like a theater with two stories of balconies that overlook the vegetable center court, this fabulous market is perfectly lit by the filtered sunlight which radiates through the glass ceiling. This is Malaysia's most colorful market . . . a photographer's dream.

Istana Jahar and State Museum
The superb craftsmanship of the Kelantanese is evident on this eclectic architectural marvel which harmoniously combines Dutch-Javanese and Asian styles. Originally the residence of the Sultans, this century-old building now serves as a State Museum with a small but worthwhile collection of royal costumes and regalia and a startling variety of swords and antique daggers. The museum is open daily except Wednesdays.

Istana Balai Besar
The Palace with the Large Audience Hall was built in 1844 and still serves as a venue for coronations and royal weddings. Inside is a Throne Room, the State Legislative Assembly Hall, and an elaborately carved Royal Barge used once in 1900 for a kingly pleasure cruise on the Kelantan River.

Merdeka Square
The State Mosque on the far side of the park was constructed in 1926 in a European-Saracenic style similar to that of the Abu Bakar Mosque in Johor Baru. The adjacent State Religious Council Building was built at the same time to foster Islamic development and progress in Kelantan. Also note the old Hong Kong and Shanghai Bank. Constructed in 1912 as the first brick building in Kelantan, it served as the head-

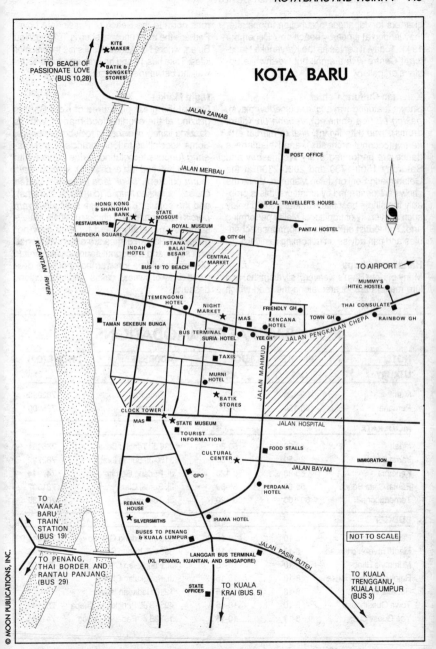

quarters for Japanese occupation troops after they landed at a nearby beach on 7 December 1941. Today, it serves as the Karyaneka Handicraft Centre with a small but worthwhile upstairs art gallery.

Kelantan Cultural Center

Shows featuring *wayang kulit* (shadow plays), *gasing uri* (top spinning), *rebana ubi* (giant drums), *wau* (kite flying), *silat* (a martial art), *kertok* (coconut orchestra), and Kelantanese dance are performed every Wednesday and Saturday 1500-1730 and 2000-2300 at the Gelanggang Seni on Jalan Mahmud. While the shows are performed by amateurs, this is probably the single best place in Malaysia to enjoy such a diversity of traditional Malay performing arts. The tourist office has performance schedules and can advise on upcoming festivals.

Handicraft Shops

Many of Kota Baru's weavers, silversmiths, and kite makers are located along the road which runs north to the Beach of Passionate Love. Perhaps the most unusual shop is Tukang Wau Bulan, where Nik Abdullah sells his technicolor kites. Take bus 10 and be prepared to do some walking between showrooms.

Night Market

One of the great pleasures of Kota Baru is grazing at the evening food market, with its dazzling variety of dishes at rock-bottom prices. Some specialties to look for include *nasi dagang* (unpolished glutinous rice served with coconut milk and fish or chicken), *kerutup ayam* (curry chicken), *solok lada* (steamed stuffed chilies), *gulai ikan tongkol* (curried bluefin tuna), and the popular Kelantanese specialty *ayam percik* (charcoal-grilled chicken). While Malaysians are generally noted for their fiery-hot recipes, Kelantan dishes are often sweetened with sugar and a coconut sauce called *lemak*. Dieters should be forewarned about the delicious array of sweets, cakes, and other caloric desserts.

KOTA BARU ACCOMMODATIONS

HOTEL	SINGLE	DOUBLE	ADDRESS	PHONE (09)
LUXURY	**M$**	**M$**		
Murni	100-120	120-200	Jl. Dato Pati	782399
Perdana	140-160	160-200	Jl. Mahmud	785000
MODERATE				
Indah	40-50	50-80	236 Jl. Tengku Besar	785081
Irama Baru	35-50	45-60	3180 Jl. Sultan Ibrahim	782722
Kencana	60-80	70-120	Jl. Padang Garong	747944
Pantai Cinta Beach	55-60	55-60	Jl. Pantai Cinta	781307
Temenggong	80-100	100-120	Jl. Tok Hakim	783130
BUDGET				
City Guesthouse	8-10	10-15	395 Jl. Padang Garong	741444
Ideal Traveller's House	8-10	10-15	3954 Jl. Kebun Sultan	742246
Mummy's Hitec	8-10	10-15	Jl. Pengkalan Chepa	787803
Rainbow Guest House	8-10	10-15	Jl. Pengkalan Chepa	787777
Rebana House	8-10	10-15	1218 Hadapan Istana	
Town Guesthouse	8-10	10-15	4959B Jl. Pengkalan Chepa	785192
Yee Guesthouse	8-10	10-15	1872B Jl. Padang Garong	741944

ACCOMMODATIONS

Kota Baru has a good selection of inexpensive hostels with dormitory accommodations and shared bathrooms in the M$4-6 range, plus cramped but adequate rooms for M$8-$12. All provide free tea, often have bicycles for loan or hire, and sport notebooks spread around the lobbies which provide useful tips for off-the-beaten-track destinations near Kota Baru.

Budget to upper-end hotels are listed in the hotel chart.

Ideal Traveller's House: Kang Sam Chuan's private home is probably the best spot in town since it's tucked away in a quiet neighborhood and well removed from the noise of Kota Baru. Also, the owners are helpful and it's conveniently located near the night market and bus station. Last time I stayed here the place was overrun with Italian "fruitarians"! 3954 Jl. Kebun Sultan, tel. (09) 742246, M$8-15.

Yee Guesthouse: Clean, comfortable, and well-located guesthouse run by Mr. Yee and Nasron, two of the friendliest people in town. Ask for a quiet room in the back. 1872B Jl. Padang Garong, tel. (09) 741944, M$8-15.

City Guesthouse: A spotlessly clean and modern guesthouse located in the shopping complex near Kentucky Fried Chicken. Often serves as an overflow for the Ideal, which fills by early afternoon. 395 Jl. Padang Garong, tel. (09) 741444, M$8-15.

Town Guesthouse: Town, somewhat outside town and cursed with a fairly grungy exterior, has decent rooms and a very popular rooftop cafe with views over the KB greenbelts. Ask for Anuar Yusoff. 4959B Jl. Pengkalan Chepa, tel. (09) 785192, M$8-15.

Mummy's Hitec Hostel: Mummy is certainly one of the most colorful characters you will meet in Malaysia. The cramped hotel on the outskirts of town offers good vibes . . . if you enjoy all-night parties in the living room. Ask to see her photo album. The Thai Consulate and the Rainbow Guest House, a hippie crash pad with little furniture but plenty of bad art, are located across the street. Take buses 4, 8, or 9 from the bus terminal. 4398B Jl. Pengkalan Chepa, tel. (09) 787803, M$8-15.

Rebana House: Enjoy Malay *kampong* life at this graceful little house just 10 minutes from

the bus terminal. The owner, world traveler and "Culture Man" Mr. Pok Jak, can help with travel and shopping advice. 1218 Hadapan Istana Kota Lama, no phone, M$8-15.

LEAVING KOTA BARU

Bus
The bus terminal for nearby destinations including most East Coast towns is located just opposite the night market. Buses to Kuala Trengganu and Kuantan depart every two hours. Buses to Penang and Kuala Lumpur leave from the two long-distance bus terminals on Jalan Hamzah in the south of town. Buses to Kuala Lumpur and Singapore leave from the Mara Bus Terminal on Jalan Pasir Puteh also in the south of town. Direct buses to Penang depart once daily at 1000. Buses to Kuala Lumpur, Johor Baru, and Singapore leave twice daily at 0800 and 2000. Schedules should be double-checked with the tourist office.

Train
The Kota Baru train station is located across the Kelantan River in Wakaf Baru. Take bus 19 or 27 from the central bus terminal. The train passes through some spectacular jungle and is useful to reach Taman Negara National Park, Kuala Lumpur, or Singapore. The single daily departure at 1100 arrives at 2000 in Jerantut, the stop for Taman Negara. Visitors going to the park must spend a night at the local resthouse in Jerantut and proceed the following morning to Tembeling Halt for the noontime boat trip to park headquarters. The train reaches Singapore the next day at 0500 or Kuala Lumpur at 0615 after a change of trains in Gemas. Schedules change frequently and exact departure times should be rechecked with the tourist office.

Getting To Thailand
Yellow Bus 29 departs hourly for the Malaysian border town of Rantau Panjang. You then follow the crowds and walk along the train tracks to the Thai border town of Sungai Golok. Be sure to have your passport stamped. Hat Yai in southern Thailand can be reached by rapid trains which depart twice daily at 1020 and 1330 Thai time. Exact train departure from Golok

should be double-checked at the Royal Thai Consulate in Kota Baru.

Ko Samui In 24 Hours

Take Yellow Bus 29 at 0815 to Rantau Panjang, change money, walk across the bridge to Sungai Golok, and have your passport stamped. The 1020 rapid train (1120 Malay time) arrives in Surat Thani at 2100. Take a bus or a taxi down to the harbor, where the night ferry to Ko Samui leaves at 2300. The ferry pulls into Samui at the crack of dawn.

VICINITY OF KOTA BARU

Beaches

The Kelantanese, true romantics at heart, have given the nearby beaches some unforgettable names. Pantai Cinta Berahu (Beach of Passionate Love) some nine km north of Kota Baru is superbly named, although it is highly unlikely you will witness any open displays of romance here in the heartland of Islamic Malaysia. Other well-named but ordinary beaches near Kota Baru include Pantai Kuda (Horse Beach), Pantai Bisikan (Whispering Breeze), and Pantai Irama (Beach of Melody). Pantai Dasar Sabak, 13 km from town, is where Japanese troops first stormed ashore to conquer Malaya and then ride their bicycles down to Singapore.

Wat Photiviharn

While Kota Baru's population might be predominately Muslim, the several Buddhist temples in the region include this one, which claims to hold the largest reclining Buddha in Southeast Asia. Not so, since the 70-meter image in Rangoon and the 46-meter statue at Wat Po in Bangkok are both larger than the 40-meter specimen at Wat Photiviharn. This temple is located in Kampung Jambu, 12 km north of Kota Baru towards Tumpat.

Kelantan River Trip

Bus 5 leaves Kota Baru at 0800 and arrives in Kuala Krai around 0930. The 1100 boat from Kuala Krai to Dabong takes two hours. From Dabong you can either return to Kuala Krai on the 1345 train or spend the night in the Government Rest House for M$15 and explore the nearby Gua Ikan (Fish Cave) on the main road about three km east of Dabong and Jelawang Waterfall across the river toward Jeli.

SARAWAK AND SABAH
SARAWAK

Borneo brings to mind the mysterious tropical island that framed the human dramas and adventure stories of Joseph Conrad: a world of impenetrable rainforests filled with vibrant flora and fauna, friendly yet dangerous natives fond of headhunting, a visionary white society that ruled Sarawak during the heady years of the White Rajahs. Time has passed and the realities of modern Borneo may not be quite as romantic as the legends of the past. In all but the most remote villages you will find teenagers wearing Rambo T-shirts, tribal families gathered around battery-operated TV sets, and small shops selling kung-fu videos, music cassettes, and electronic calculators. Despite these changes, Borneo remains a rugged land where you can explore upriver villages where several generations of families share a common household, climb through immense caves, and tramp across some of the finest national parks in all of Southeast Asia. The world of Conrad may be drawing to an end in the romantically named "Land of the Hornbills," but the lingering aura of mystery and adventure still makes Borneo a unique and memorable destination.

THE PHYSICAL SETTING

The state of Sarawak stretches some 700 km along the northwestern coast of the tropical island of Borneo, third largest in the world. Borneo is actually the old name for the island now parceled into four political subdivisions. Kalimantan is the Indonesian state, which comprises the lower two-thirds of the island. Brunei is an independent oil-rich sultanate wedged between the Malaysian states on the northern coastline. Both Sarawak and Sabah are former British Crown Colonies which merged with Malaya in 1963 to form the Federation of Malaysia.

Climate
Sarawak is a tropical country with two seasons. The northeast monsoon from November to February brings heavy rains which flood coastal towns and reduce most roads to muddy and impassable quagmires. The southwest monsoon during the summer months is less wet. Best time to visit Sarawak is from April to July, when the skies are clear and rivers remain high enough for journeys into the interior. Upriver journeys are difficult from July to November, when many rivers become too shallow for boats. Sarawak's best festivals (harvest celebrations) take place during May and early June.

ATTRACTIONS

Kuching
The economic and geographic isolation of Sarawak's capital city has helped Kuching retain some of its old charm and character. The city offers evocative architecture, a nearby beach resort and national park, and an outstanding museum where you can learn the fascinating story of the Brooke Dynasty, which ruled the state for over a century. Kuching is one of Malaysia's most romantic towns—an excellent introduction to Sarawak.

Skrang River
Only outside Kuching do the particular flavors of Sarawak begin to assert themselves. The nearest opportunity to see tribal people who still live in sprawling, stilt-raised apartments called longhouses is along the Skrang River, a five-hour bus ride from Kuching. A visit to a jungle-surrounded longhouse to experience communal living, war dances, ceremonial dresses, and peer at a dusty collection of skulls is perhaps the single greatest attraction in Borneo. Although the Skrang River has become somewhat commercialized in recent years because of its easy accessibility to Kuching, the longhouses are genuine, and traditional tribal lifestyles resume after the tourists have returned to their hotels. Overnight visits can be arranged by travel agents in Kuching.

SARAWAK, BRUNEI, AND SABAH

PHILIPPINES

SULU SEA

TURTLE ISLANDS

Sulu Sea

SIBUTU ISLAND

SULAWESI SEA

SANDAKAN

LAHAD DATU

GOMANTONG CAVES

SEMPORNA

TAWAU

KUDAT

MOUNT KINABALU (4,101 m)

SEPILOK ORANGUTAN SANCTUARY

MOUNT KINABALU N.P.

KOTA BELUD

PORING HOT SPRINGS

TAMBUNAN

SABAH

KENINGAU

KOTA KINABALU

PENAMPANG

PAPAR

BEAUFORT

MERAPOK

SIPITANG

LAWAS

LONG SEMADO

KALIMANTAN (INDONESIA)

LABUAN ISLAND

MEMPAKUL

BANDAR SERI BEGAWAN

LIMBANG R.

GUNUNG MULU N.P.

BAREO

LONG LELLANG

LIO MATOH

LUMUT

SERIA

BRUNEI

MARUDI

TUTOH R.

LONG MURUM

RUMAH KULIT

KUALA BELAIT

MIRI

BARAM R.

BUNUT LAKE

KEMANA R.

LONG AKAH

BELAGA

RAJANG R.

BALEH R.

NIAH CAVES N.P.

BATU NIAH

SMILIJAU N.P.

BINTULU

KAPIT

SARAWAK

KANOWIT

SOUTH CHINA SEA

SIBU

SARIKEI

KEMANA R.

SKRANG R.

BANDAR SRI AMAN (SIMANGGANG)

SEMATAN

LUNDU

KUCHING

BAKO N.P.

SERIKIN

100 km

© MOON PUBLICATIONS, INC.

Rejang River

When compared to the longhouses on the Skrang, those on the Rejang River are less touristy and more authentic but also more time-consuming and expensive to reach. Don't expect to find something from Conrad's *Heart of Darkness;* as Sarawak's commercial lifeline, the wide and muddy Rejang River is surprisingly busy with timber boats stacked with precious cargo and air-conditioned express boats that entertain passengers with the latest videos. Though the Rejang is firmly rooted in the 20th century, it remains the best river trip in east Malaysia.

Niah Caves

Niah National Park near Miri encompasses over 3,000 hectares of forest, vast limestone formations, and the Great Niah Cave, one of the most important archaeological sites in Southeast Asia. The forest department maintains a comfortable and inexpensive hostel here. Journeys are also possible up the Baram River to remote interior towns.

Gunung Mulu National Park

This recently opened park is known for its impressive landscapes and an extensive underground cave system, reputedly one of the largest and longest in the world. The river journey from Marudi to park headquarters takes a full day.

TRANSPORTATION

Getting There

Air: MAS has daily flights to Kuching from Singapore for M$180, from Johor Baru for M$150, and from Kuala Lumpur for M$240. Flights from Singapore to Kuching are priced the same whether purchased with Malaysian or Singaporean dollars. Recent weakening of the Malaysian dollar means you can save over 20% on tickets purchased in Malaysia with Malaysian *ringgit* rather than in Singapore.

Other discounts available from MAS include special night flights and advance-purchase tickets. For example, a 14-day advance-purchase ticket on a roundtrip flight from Johor Baru to Kuching is only M$250. Discounts are also given to students and groups of three or more who purchase tickets at least one week in advance.

Merpati flies weekly to Kuching from Pontianak (Indonesian Kalimantan). Visitors who intend to enter or exit Indonesia via Pontianak should double-check the latest visa requirements.

Getting Around

Land: Overland transportation is a slow and tedious affair in Borneo. Scheduled buses cover the entire stretch from Kuching to Brunei except for the short distance between Sarikei and Sibu. Most of the road is abominable. Although the trans-Sarawak highway was theoretically completed a few years ago, the Sibu to Bintulu section is often impassable during the rainy season except by four-wheel drive vehicles. It's a grinding ordeal of potholes, tangles of vegetation, collapsed cliffs, and sunken bridges. Boats substitute whenever the road is temporarily closed. The Kuching Tourist Office has a schedule of current bus departures.

Boat: Much of Sarawak is a flat, swampy, and monotonous coastline bisected by a network of muddy rivers which wind up to the interior (called the *ulu*). Before the arrival of aircraft, these rivers served as the region's sole communication and transportation network. Today each river can be explored with boats ranging from primitive dugouts to flashy cruisers.

In most cases, you will have to choose between regularly scheduled commercial boats and expensive private charters. Commercial boat service, both affordable and dependable, can be found on most rivers, especially along the lower reaches. Schedules are listed in the *Borneo Post.*

Chartered boats, on the other hand, are often your only choice during midweek in the deep *ulu.* Charters can be extremely expensive unless you share expenses with a large group of eight to 12 people. Worse yet is the amount of time wasted hanging around some dirty little town, waiting for the next boat. Bring a good book.

Air: MAS operates a network of services linking most urban centers in Sarawak. Prices are reasonable since flights are heavily subsidized by the Malaysian government. Current schedules can be checked in the *Borneo Post* or by calling MAS in Kuching at (082) 23790, in Sibu at (084) 26166, in Bintulu at (086) 31554, or in Miri at (085) 34544. Most flights are heavily booked and advance reservations are recommended. If you don't have a reservation, go to

END OF THE RAINFORESTS

The controversy surrounding the commercial logging of rainforests in Sarawak has intensified from a national to an international issue in recent years. Malaysia is the world's largest exporter of tropical-hardwood logs, most of which are harvested from Sarawak. Malaysia's largest state reaps almost M$2 billion yearly from hardwood exports. Almost 80% of the timber is sold to Japan, a small nation that consumes three times as much timber per head as Western Europe and eight times as much as the United States. Regardless of who ultimately consumes the timber, tropical rainforests remain an essential link in the world's ecosystem: they modulate our climate by precipitating rain; they provide plentiful sources of food and give us 40% of our medicines; they ensure stability of soil masses, and they provide refuge for millions of species of wildlife.

The situation in Sarawak has become increasingly grim since the late '70s when logging companies were awarded large concessions by government officials. The Malaysian environmentalist group, Sahabat Alam Malaysia (SAM), estimates that 76 hectares of Malaysian forest are cut down each hour, and that if commercial logging continues at the same rate, 30% of Sarawak's forest will be destroyed in the next 10 years. The long-term impact, they contend, will be ecological disaster. Reports from the World Bank, the United Nations, and international conservation groups such as the Rainforest Action Network estimate that the complete destruction of Southeast Asia's rainforests will be a fait accompli within 50 years. Even senior officials in the Forest Department concede that unless the political will is found to sharply curtail logging, Malaysia will end up like the Philippines—a country once rich with tropical forests, now forced to import timber.

Blame is usually laid on shifting agriculturalists (tribals who farm with slash-and-burn techniques) and international logging companies. Other factors include a soaring population that needs land and food, the necessity for developing countries to raise hard cash, and the simple fact that the logging industry provides jobs. Yet the environmental consequences remain monumental. Critics charge that the lack of effective controls stems from the thick tangle of political patronage that revolves around the granting of the state's 320 timber licenses. Most of Sarawak's largest logging concessions are held by senior government officials such as prime ministers and retired state governors. The conflict of interest is astounding: Sarawak's minister of the environment and tourism (whose job it is to protect the environment and encourage tourism) is also the owner of Limbang Trading, one of the largest and most successful logging consortiums in Sarawak. He's publicly stated that selective logging practices rather than large-scale reforestation projects will save the rainforests, a rationale that finds little support among environmentalists, who find natural reforestation a failed pipe dream. The bottom line is that so long as the political machinery is controlled by those who profit from logging, there is little hope for the rainforests of Malaysia.

Much of the world's press coverage about the Sarawak situation has centered on the struggle of the Penan tribespeople to save their ancestral homelands from indiscriminate logging. Under a scheme adopted by the state government, over one million acres of Sarawak's rainforests are to be cleared and replaced with rubber and cacao plantations. The nomadic Penans and other Dayaks such as the Kayans will then be resettled in townships and offered employment on these agricultural plantations. Understandably enough, the Penans are opposed to the plan. They have instead demanded that logging be completely halted in their homelands near the Baram River and that compensation be paid for land already cleared of forest. To dramatize their situation, human barricades have been formed to blockade the logging trucks, an action which found a great deal of sympathy and support from Malaysian public and international environmentalist groups. The Penans, clad in little more than loincloths and beads, then traveled to Kuala Lumpur to ask for government assistance in their struggle against the logging companies. The Malaysian government responded with the Forest Ordinance, which decreed stiff fines and lengthy jail sentences for anyone caught obstructing logging operations. In November 1987, the Malaysian government arrested 43 Penan leaders and placed Harrison Ngau, tribal activist and director of Malaysia's Friends of the Earth, under house arrest. In January 1989, in the largest demonstration to date, 125 tribespeople were arrested. Trials, fines, and imprisonment face the Penans of Borneo.

the airport and ask to be put on the waiting list. Overbooking is so common that most waiting-list passengers get seats.

TRAVEL PRACTICALITES

Visas And Special Permits
Both Sarawak and Sabah have their own immigration controls. Visitors arriving on international or domestic flights from Peninsular Malaysia are usually granted two-month visas. Shorter visas can be extended at immigrations offices in Kuching and Miri.

Special permits are technically required for several areas: to visit the longhouses above Kapit on the Rejang River, and to trek from Belaga to Bintulu. Both permits are free and available in Kapit, but they're never checked; few district officers seem to know anything about them. Permits are also necessary to visit the Painted Cave in Niah Caves National Park. All permits can be picked up from the Sarawak Museum in Kuching, the national park office in Miri, or, most conveniently, directly at park headquarters. The Painted Cave permit is unnecessary for anyone who hires a guide.

Costs
Travel in both Sarawak and Sabah is much more expensive than on Peninsular Malaysia. Most merchandise is imported and the cost of meals, transport, and other necessities is accordingly about 50% higher. The hotel situation is worse. Except for dormitories in Kuching and the national parks, rooms are about double the cost of their mainland counterparts. Budget travelers should be prepared to spend a minimum of M$20-25 for a basic double with fan and shared bathroom. Even at these inflated prices, rooms are often filled with oil drillers and refinery workers who live as semipermanent residents. Many of the cheaper hotels are brothels. A rough worksheet for a one-month visit: M$700-800 for transportation costs including return ticket from Singapore or Kuala Lumpur, M$750 for double rooms, and another M$300-400 for meals.

Time
Sufficient time should be allotted for sightseeing and the inevitable transportation delays. A minimum of one month is needed to travel over-land from Kuching to Kota Kinabalu with a journey up the Rejang River, visits to several national parks, a few days in Brunei, and the climb to the summit of Mt. Kinabalu. Two weeks is enough if you use air transport.

KUCHING

Kuching, provincial and administrative capital of Sarawak, is one of the more attractive and fascinating towns in Malaysia. Situated on the Sarawak River 32 km from the sea, Kuching has escaped rampant modernization and retained a degree of charm because of its historical and economic isolation from mainland Southeast Asia. An aura of past colonial splendor lingers on: Anglo-Oriental mansions slowly chip and fade in the tropical heat, ferns grow from roof gutters, and rows of Chinese shophouses fight a losing battle against time and the elements.

Kuching also shows change: modern subdivisions that uncannily resemble the urban sprawl of Los Angeles, Malay and Chinese yuppies who network at the San Francisco Grill House, and daily traffic jams of Toyotas and Nissans that clog downtown bottlenecks. Despite the contemporary culture, much of the town remains an open-air museum that recalls the colorful history of rule under the White Rajahs.

Attractions
Sarawak Museum: This internationally renowned museum is home to a staggering collection of Bornean archaeological and ethnological artifacts, as well as natural-history specimens gathered by the famous naturalist and co-founder of the theory of evolution, Sir Alfred Russell Wallace. Within its walls are Sarawak tribal weapons, indigenous tools, weavings, woodcarvings, burial paraphernalia, and other cultural oddities that form an excellent introduction to the flora, fauna, and tribal groups of Borneo. This fascinating and somewhat eclectic assemblage was masterminded by Rajah Charles Brooke, with encouragement from Wallace, who visited Sarawak in 1854-56. In 1880, Brooke commissioned his French valet to design the building, which, when completed in 1891, perhaps not surprisingly resembled a French chateau in Normandy style. Open daily except Fridays 0900-1200 and 1300-1800. Free.

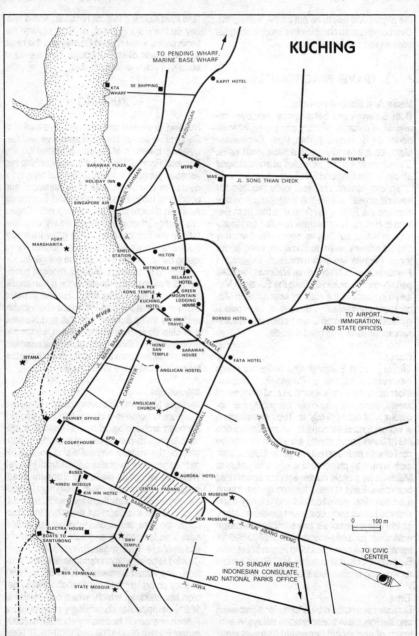

KUCHING

TO PENDING WHARF,
MARINE BASE WHARF

KTA WHARF

SE SHIPPING

★ KAPIT HOTEL

SARAWAK PLAZA

HOLIDAY INN

SINGAPORE AIR

JL. PADUNGAN

MTPB

MAS

★ PERUMAL HINDU TEMPLE

JL. SONG THIAN CHEOK

FORT MARGHARITA ★

JL. TUNKU ABDUL RAHMAN

JL. PADUNGAN

SHELL STATION

HILTON

METROPOLE HOTEL

SELAMAT HOTEL

TUA PEK KONG TEMPLE ★

KUCHING HOTEL

GREEN MOUNTAIN LODGING HOUSE

JL. MATHIES

JL. BAN HOCK

JL. TABUAN

SARAWAK RIVER

SIN HWA TRAVEL

BORNEO HOTEL

TO AIRPORT, IMMIGRATION, AND STATE OFFICES

ISTANA ★

JL. MAIN BAZAR

HONG SAN TEMPLE

SARAWAK HOUSE

JL. TEMPLE

ANGLICAN HOSTEL

★ FATA HOTEL

JL. CARPENTER

ANGLICAN CHURCH ★

TOURIST OFFICE

GPO

JL. McDOUGHALL

JL. RESERVOIR TEMPLE

★ COURTHOUSE

BUSES

HINDU MOSQUE ★

KIA HIN HOTEL

AURORA HOTEL

JL. INDIA

CENTRAL PADANG

JL. BARRACK

OLD MUSEUM ★

NEW MUSEUM ★

JL. TUN ABANG OPENG

SIKH TEMPLE ★

JL. MESJID

ELECTRA HOUSE

BOATS TO SANTUBONG

MARKET ★

BUS TERMINAL

STATE MOSQUE ★

JL. JAWA

TO SUNDAY MARKET, INDONESIAN CONSULATE, AND NATIONAL PARKS OFFICE

TO CIVIC CENTER

0   100 m

© MOON PUBLICATIONS, INC.

Downtown: The historic center along the waterfront near the Pangkalan Batu Boat Ferry has several fine survivors of former days. Constructed in 1874, the old Courthouse with its oversized veranda and landmark clock tower was designed to impress the people with its sense of permanence. The English Renaissance fortress known as the Square Tower originally served as a prison before being converted into a local dance hall. Constructed in an imposing Neoclassical style with Corinthian columns and ornamented friezes, Kuching's General Post Office is one of the few buildings erected by Vyner Brooke, the third and final rajah, who ceded Sarawak to Britain in 1946 despite protests by his subjects. Almost directly opposite is a graceful and distinctive three-story building nicknamed the Pavilion.

Kuching's best shopping venue is the Sunday market on Jalan Satok, packed with housewives, Chinese farmers, and tribal peoples. The market is in full swing on both Saturday nights and Sunday mornings 0600-1300.

Istana: Sarawak is divided by the Sarawak River into the south city, with the museum, hotels, and commercial and residential areas, and the north city with the new Petra Jaya Ministerial Complex and two historical landmarks constructed by Charles Brooke. The Istana features a style similar to British houses in Java during Stamford Raffles's governorship. The crenellated tower dates from the 1880s. The decaying Istana (also spelled Astana), or Palace, was the official residence for Charles, who succeeded his Uncle James and served as the second Rajah of Borneo from 1868 to 1917. Currently closed to the public, the complex serves as official residence of Sarawak's governor and can be seen clearly from the opposite riverbank.

Fort Margarita: Named after Ranee Margaret, wife of the second White Rajah, this fort was constructed in 1879 to guard against attack by maurauding bands of pirates. In later years it served as headquarters for the paramilitary Sarawak Rangers before being converted into a Military Museum. Ironically, the only occasion when the fort came under attack was on 19 December 1941, when the Japanese bombed Kuching. While the building is an outstanding example of British colonial architecture, the most famous sight is the six laugh-ing skulls kept hanging in the watchtower. Believed to have been collected in battle by an Undup warrior in the late 18th century, legend has it that laughter was heard coming from the skulls while in transit to the museum. Enter the room with caution. The old fort is reached by *tambang* ferry from Pangkalan Batu near the Sarawak Tourist Association Building.

Moderate Accommodations

Kuching has several luxury hotels and the standard collection of middle-priced Chinese lodgings, but only a limited number of budget hostels. Remember that "cheap" in Borneo means a double room in the M$25-35 range and not M$10-15 as on the Peninsula.

Anglican Hostel: Most budget travelers stay at this clean and comfortable hostel where spacious rooms with fans cost M$20 single and M$25 double. Larger flats which sleep four cost M$45. Tel. 082-414027. Located on the hill behind St. Thomas's Anglican Church.

Kuching Hotel: This Chinese hotel near city center is Kuching's other popular backpackers' spot. Adequate rooms with fan and common bath are M$20-30 single and M$25-35 double. 6 Temple Street, tel. 082-413985.

Selamat Hotel: This hotel and the adjacent Green Mountain Lodging House have clean a/c doubles from M$34. Special rates in the M$18-24 range are often given on request. 6 Green Hill Road, tel. 082-411249.

Luxury Accommodations

Holiday Inn: Kuching's first international hotel is located on the banks of the Sarawak River, within easy walking distance of sights and shopping. 320 rooms, swimming pool, fitness center. Jalan Tunku Abdul Rahman, tel. 082-423111, M$150-180 single, M$160-240 double.

Kuching Hilton: Kuching's newest hotel offers 322 rooms fronting the river, five food and beverage outlets, and sports facilities. Jalan Tunku Abdul Rahman, tel. 082-248200, M$180-240 single, M$200-280 double.

Holiday Inn Damai Beach: Sarawak's number-one beach resort is located on Santubong Beach, 32 km north of Kuching. Windsurfing, trekking, 18-hole Trent Jones golf course, and over 200 chalets and studios surrounded by beach and mountains. Tel. 082-411777, M$180-240 single, M$220-280 double.

KUCHING ACCOMMODATIONS

HOTEL	SINGLE	DOUBLE	ADDRESS	PHONE (082)
LUXURY	**M$**	**M$**		
Kuching Hilton	180-240	200-280	Tunku Abdul Rahman	248200
Holiday Inn Damai	180-240	220-280	Damai Beach	411777
Holiday Inn Kuching	150-180	160-240	Tunku Abdul Rahman	423111
MODERATE				
Aurora	100-120	125-140	McDougall	240281
Borneo	50-60	60-80	30 Tabuan	244121
City Inn	60-70	70-80	275 Abell	414866
Fata	60-70	70-80	Tabuan	248111
Liwah	110-140	120-150	Song Thian Cheok	240222
Longhouse	60-70	70-80	Abell	249333
Mayfair	90-110	100-140	45 Palm	421486
Metropole	40-60	50-80	22 Green Hill Road	412484
Palm	40-50	50-60	29 Palm	240231
BUDGET				
Anglican Hostel	20-25	25-30	Anglican Church	414027
Kuching	20-30	25-35	6 Temple Street	413985
Selamat	30-35	35-40	6 Green Hill Road	411249

General Information

Tourist Information: The Sarawak Tourist Information Center, in an old godown near the ferry pier, is the best source of information for travel in Sarawak. Ask for their Legacy Walk brochure. They also have a small kiosk at the airport.

The Malaysia Tourism Promotion Board (MTPB), tel. 246775, in the AIA Building on Song Thian Cheok Road, has glossy maps and pretty brochures but little practical information.

National Parks: Information and advance room reservations for Bako, Niah, and Gunung Mulu national parks can be made at the National Parks Office, tel. 248088, on Jalan Satok, one km west of city center. Reservations for Niah and Gunung Mulu can also be made in Miri.

Visa Extensions: Malaysian visas and Permits to Stay can be extended at the State Government Complex on Jalan Simpang Tiga, three km south of town en route to the airport. Immigration is open Monday-Friday 0900-1630 and Saturdays 0900-1200. Take blue CCL buses 6 or 17 from the bus stop near the State Mosque. Visas can also be extended at most other towns in Sarawak.

Indonesian Visa: The Indonesian Consulate on Pisang Road can be reached on buses 5A or 6. Most Indonesian towns are now visa-free entry points, but the situation for Pontianak seems to change with the seasons. Be sure to double-check the current status before flying from Kuching to Kalimantan.

Getting Around: Local buses are operated by the privately owned Chian Lian Long Motor Vehicle Company. Useful routes include Jalan Mosque to the State Government Complex on buses 6 or 17, Jalan Satok to the Police Marine Base Wharf via bus 17 or 19; Jalan Tunku Abdul Rahman to Bintawa Wharf with bus 16.

Maps: Large-scale maps (1:50,000 scale) useful for trekking or locating obscure longhouses can be purchased on the 2nd floor of the State Government Complex in the south of Kuching. The bookstore inside the Holiday Inn sometimes sells the two-part 1:500,000 scale map of Sarawak.

Tours: Kuching's top travel and tour agencies include Borneo Transverse, tel. 082-257784, 10B Wayang Street, and Interworld Travel Services, tel. 082-252344, on Green Road. Both can arrange comfortable and reasonably authentic visits to longhouses on the Skrang River as well as longer journeys up the Rejang and treks through Gunung Mulu National Park.

Leaving Kuching

Air: Kuching International Airport is 10 km south of town and can be reached by taxi for M$12 or bus 12A for M$1.

The MAS office, tel. 244144, on Jalan Song Thian, has a variety of flights and tickets including ordinary, discounted early-morning flights, and even cheaper advance-purchase tickets. MAS and small airlines such as Borneo and Hornbill Skyways fly to over 20 small towns in Sarawak and Sabah.

Merpati has flights every Friday to Pontianak and onward to Jakarta. Merpati tickets are sold at Sin Hwa Travel, tel. (084) 246688, at 8 Jalan Temple near the Kuching Hotel.

By Bus: Long-distance buses to points east such as Sri Aman and Sarikei are operated by the Sarawak Transport Company and leave from the long-distance bus terminal on Jalan Jawa near the river. Buses to Sri Aman leave at 0800 and 0930, cost M$13, and take three to four hours. Buses to Sarikei leave at 0745 and 1300, cost M$23, and take seven to eight hours.

No public buses serve Sarikei to Sibu. Instead, an express boat from Sarikei to Sibu departs hourly 0700-1530, costs M$6, and takes about two hours. The road from Kuching to Sibu is a real horror show, and there's little reason to travel overland unless you are going up the Skrang River. Since it is impossible to reach Sibu by bus in a single day, most travelers fly Kuching-Sibu or take one of the following boats.

By Boat: Both speedy launches and slow cargo boats sail from Kuching to Sibu. The *Pomas Hovermarine* departs daily at noon from Bintawa wharf six km east of town, costs M$25, and takes about four hours to reach Sibu. Tickets can be purchased one day in advance from the Tan Boon Tien Shell Station on Jalan Tunku Abdul Rahman. Take bus 16. The *Sibu Kuching*

Union Express departs daily at 0830 from the Police Marine Base Wharf, costs M$25, and takes about five hours to Sibu. Tickets are sold on the boat. Take buses 17 or 19.

Cargo passenger boats are slower and cheaper but more relaxing if you have the time. These take about 18 hours to reach Sibu with stops at various ports and cost about M$10 deck class. Check the local newspaper and the Sarawak Tourist Association for current schedules.

VICINITY OF KUCHING

Bako National Park

Sarawak's two most famous attractions are river journeys with longhouse visits and a few days spent exploring one of the region's national parks. Bako's 2,742 hectares are set on a sandstone plateau covered with open scrub and mangrove swamps thick with exotic vegetation such as epiphytic ferns, heath forests, and several species of carnivorous plants including bladderworts and giant pitcher plants. Wildlife includes silver leaf monkeys, water monitor lizards, and the bizarre long-nosed proboscis monkey, native only to Borneo.

Bako isn't as rugged as Gunung Mulu nor as famous as Niah Caves, but it's easy to reach from Kuching and offers over 30 km of organized trails from short walks to exhausting all-day treks. Maps and other details can be obtained at park headquarters.

Accommodations: Resthouses, equipped with cooking facilities and beds, sleep up to six people and cost M$20-30 per room. Hostels with five-man dormitory rooms cost M$2 per person. Reservations can be made at the National Parks Office in Kuching or you can just show up and take your chances.

Transportation: Bako, about 37 km from Kuching, can be reached via bus 6 to Kampong Bako, from where boats continue onwards.

Semonggok
Wildlife Rehabilitation Sanctuary

This animal refuge 22 km from Kuching is where orangutans, hornbills, and monkeys rescued from captivity are trained for reentry into the jungle. Permits must be obtained in advance from the National Parks and Wildlife office (tel. 082-248080) on Jalan Satok, one km west of

Kuching city center. Semonggok can be reached in 30 minutes with bus 6 followed by a 30-minute hike.

Santubong

Kuching's leading beach resort is located 22 km from Kuching at the mouth of the Sarawak River. The sand is rather ordinary (better beaches are west at Sematan) but the fishing village is picturesque and the overall setting quite spectacular.

Santubong was an important trading center from the 7th to 13th centuries, as shown by the Chinese and Hindu rock carvings and artifacts unearthed by archaeologists. Of the notable rock carvings located along the small river, Sungai Jaong, the most intriguing is the human figure carved spread-eagle with Kenyah headdress. This rock is situated up the road toward Kuching about two km beyond the *kampong*. Turn right after the second coconut farm and follow the stream about 200 meters, or ask locals for *batu gambir*.

A Sarawak Cultural Village has been erected to help preserve the states' rich cultural heritage.

Accommodations: Accommodations include the luxurious Holiday Inn Damai Beach (tel. 082-411777), which charges M$180-280.

Transportation: Boats to Santubong leave each morning at 0830 from the Pangkalan Panjang Long Pier in Kuching. Buses to the jetty terminal at Tanjung Embang leave from city center. Shuttle buses leave daily from the Kuching Holiday Inn.

SKRANG RIVER

Sarawak's classic adventure is visiting several Iban (Sea Dayak) or Bidayuh longhouses scattered upriver in the *ulu*. The area immediately near Kuching has several badly commercialized longhouses that can be quickly visited by frantic group tours.

Although the most pristine longhouses are those in the upper reaches of the Rejang River, visitors with limited time can still experience authentic longhouses on the nearby Skrang. Excellent two- and three-day tours organized by Borneo Transverse Tours begin with a four-hour drive through rubber and pepper plantations before the one-hour upstream journey in native longboats. The Skrang is much smaller than the Rejang and in many ways seems more mysterious with its hanging vines and harrowing rapids.

You will quickly discover that the Ibans are a warm and slightly outrageous group of people who perform their dances with what appears to be genuine enthusiasm. Iban hospitality revolves around singing, dancing, and the consumption of prodigious quantities of *tuak*. It's rude to refuse!

After a night in the longhouse, tours either return to Kuching the following morning or continue upriver to visit another longhouse. While package tours of the Skrang are somewhat expensive at M$250 and sound contrived to seasoned travelers, they avoid the hassles and offer a rare opportunity to experience Iban dance.

SRI AMAN

Formerly called Simmanggang, this backwoods town is where Charles Brooke spent some time before becoming the rajah of Sarawak. During his short tenure he constructed Fort Alice in 1864 to control the fierce Skrang Ibans.

As in most towns in Borneo, there is little of interest here except for arranging a journey up the Skrang River; self-guided river trips are possible but difficult. Public boats, most numerous on weekends and holidays, are the cheapest forms of transport. Otherwise, it will be necessary to charter a private boat or accept an invitation from a local Iban. The cost can be estimated by asking how many tanks of gas (each tank holds about 20 liters or five gallons) are required to reach the longhouse, then multiplying by the cost of the gas. It is customary to pay an additional M$25 one-way for the boatman and another M$15 for the bowman, who watches for dangerous rocks.

Accommodations: Travelers stranded in Sri Aman can stay at either the Alishan or Taiwan hotels on Jalan Council or the Sum Sum or Hoover hotels on Club Road. Rates range M$25-35 depending on hotel facilities and room size.

Transportation: Buses to Sarikei depart at 0730 and 1330. Boats from Sarikei to Sibu leave hourly until 1600.

SIBU

Situated 130 km from the sea on the right bank of the Rejang River, Sibu (formerly called Maling) is the second-largest town in Sarawak and gateway for journeys up the Rejang River. The Sarawak Tourist Association has a representative at the Sarawak Hotel.

Attractions

Most travelers spend the night in town and leave the following morning, but with a few extra hours you might visit the central market, where Hokkien shopkeepers bargain with Iban tribesmen over cassettes and polyester shirts, and then wander through the Chinese temple by the docks where Mr. Tan Teck Kong can explain the Buddhist and Taoist deities. Weekend visitors should visit Sungai Aup, seven km from Sibu, where both Ibans and Chinese enjoy the views and make offerings on the sacred hill.

Accommodations

Hotels in Sibu are mostly run-down and overpriced, but staying in one is a necessary evil before heading upriver the following day.

Hoover House: Sibu's cheapest and cleanest spot is a revamped colonial house adjacent to the Methodist Primary School. 22 Jl. Pulau, tel. 084-332491, M$10-12.

Miramar Hotel: Travelers turned away from the oft-filled Hoover House generally stay at this decent hotel down at the waterfront and near the night market. 47 Jl. Channel, tel. 084-332433, M$22-28.

New World Hotel: A midpriced hotel with a/c rooms, private baths, and TV. Good value. 1 Jl. Wong Nai Song, tel. 084-310313, M$35-50.

Leaving Sibu

To Kuching: The hovercraft leaves daily at 0700 from the Delta Wharf, costs M$25, and takes three hours. The ordinary launch leaves daily at 0830 from the same wharf, costs M$20, and takes five hours. The slow boat is a better way to enjoy the scenery. Purchase tickets on board.

MAS, located on Kampung Nyabor Road opposite the Premier Hotel, flies several times daily to Kuching. Airport taxi is M$6 or take bus 1.

To Bintulu and Miri: Although the Sibu-Bintulu road is paved, the bus ride remains a hellish ordeal of bumps, potholes, and other terrors. Buses leave daily at 0630 and 1230 and take about five hours to Bintulu. Since Bintulu is an expensive hole, most travelers take the daily 0630 a/c bus straight through to Miri in about eight hours. Buses to Bintulu and Miri do not leave from the central terminal on Jalan Channel but from the terminal on Jalan Khoo Peng Loong just down from Jalan Workshop.

MAS flights throughout Sarawak are limited in number and should be booked in advance before exploring the Rejang River. Cargo/passenger boats can be booked from Miri Sin Chiung Shipping on Jalan Jawan and from Siam Shipping on Main Bazaar.

Up The Rejang River: Speedy, ultramodern boats equipped with Rambo videos and blasting stereos depart hourly 0700-1300 from the Delta Wharf on Jalan Peng Loong and take five hours to reach Kapit. The gigantic twin diesels that move the flat-bottomed boats along at 35 km/h generate a dangerous wake and a thunderous roar loud enough to drown out Stallone as he blasts Russian Commies. Stops en route include Kanowit, the town where Charles Brooke built a fort to suppress headhunting, and Song, where dozens of Japanese lost their heads while promising the New Asia Co-Prosperity Sphere. The skeptical Ibans were delighted when British commanders gave permission to resume their headhunting.

REJANG RIVER LONGHOUSES

Travelers hungry for a bit of the Byronesque will discover a journey up the Rejang River—the same river that inspired Conrad to write *Lord Jim*—to be one of the most rewarding travel experiences in Sarawak. The main attractions are jungle trekking, local tribespeople, and a few days of residence in an Iban longhouse.

Enjoying the scenery and watching people barter in the Kapit Market is fun and simple, but visiting a longhouse is no easy task. In recent years, great numbers of visitors have arrived, walked up to a longhouse, and expected to be welcomed with open arms. While the Iban remain a warm group of people with a near-legendary reputation for hospitality, their patience has been pushed to the limit and some have become unenthusiastic about strangers knocking on their front doors. This is not to say that longhouse visits are impossible, but without a formal invitation it takes a great deal of guts to front up, smile, and walk in. Brave souls should first seek permission to enter, park their shoes at the door, and then ask to see the *tuai rumah* (headman) in Iban longhouses or *tua rumah* or *tua kampong* elsewhere.

Travelers' experiences vary dramatically. Sometimes you are completely ignored, meals are served to you in a lonely room, and items mysteriously disappear from your backpack. At other times you are welcomed as a long-lost relative who is feted with food and *tuak* before being wished a fond farewell by the entire village. Travelers determined to experience longhouse living should bring along small gifts such as beer, cigarettes, food, medicines like *tiga kaki,* shirts, batiks, large sealed containers, and Indonesian sarongs as gifts or for bartering. Presents should be given to the headman, who will distribute the goods evenly. Earplugs are also a good idea to muffle the grunting pigs, howling dogs, and crowing roosters that live underneath the floor.

Longhouses near Kapit are somewhat commercialized but more authentic examples can be visited up the river toward Belaga. Ask townspeople, boat drivers, and other travelers for recommendations, but double-check prices for transport, beer, and other luxuries before accepting anybody's "generous" offer.

KAPIT

Tiny Kapit is the final trading post of the mighty Rejang River, 250 muddy and winding kilometers up from the sea. No roads link Kapit with the outside world—the only feasible way to reach this back-of-beyond town is by riverboat. Kapit sits on a two-square-km clearing which forms a perfect place to relax and watch Ibans land their dugouts and sell their fruit, peppercorns, and cocoa to Chinese brokers, the commercial kingpins of the *ulu.*

Permits to travel beyond Kapit must theoretically be obtained from the Pejabat Am office on the first floor of the State Government Complex. Kapit has two banks which change money at poor rates. MAS is just opposite the jetty.

Attractions

Sights include Fort Sylvia, built by the Brookes in 1880, and a pair of waterfalls. Sungai Sera-

man is a one-hour hike across the Rejang River. Bukit Garam is 30 minutes by taxi and then a 45-minute hike. Try hitching on the weekends.

Kapit is also a convenient base for exploring nearby jungle and villages. Most travelers visit the longhouses on the Rejang River en route to Belaga, but closer longhouses are situated up the Baleh River. Try Rumah Temonggong Jugah and Long Agat, home of the late Temmonggong Koh. Both impressive longhouses have small museums in the headman's *bilek* (room), although they are now somewhat spoiled from tourists and commercial film crews. The perfect book to bring along is *Into the Heart of Borneo* by Redmond O'Hanlon, a humorous account of his 1983 journey up the Baleh to climb Mount Tiban and "re-discover the Borneo rhinoceros."

Accommodations

Like most other upriver towns, Kapit has several cheap hotels that double as brothels and a few midpriced places for traveling businessmen and a steady trickle of tourists.

Rejang Hotel: One of the few decent cheap hotels is about 300 meters down from the jetty near a traffic roundabout. The Rejang has a variety of rooms in all sizes, with varied decor, and available with or without fan, a/c, or private baths. 28 Jl. Temenggong Jugah, tel. (084) 796700, M$15-35.

New Rejang Inn: The owners of the Rejang opened a new annex in 1991 about 50 meters from the jetty. Rates are somewhat high but the rooms are clean, all with a/c, and include private baths, hot showers, and TV. 104 Jl. Teo Chow Beng, tel. (084) 796600, M$40-48.

Ark Hill Hotel: The lumber business has brought several new, good-value hotels to Kapit, including this clean spot just three blocks to the right of the jetty. All rooms are a/c with private bath. Recommended. 1 Jl. Tiga, tel. (084) 796168, M$35-45.

Hotel Meligai: Kapit's top-end choice, north of the jetty in the direction of the airport, features a lobby photo of the famous Iban chief, Temmonggang Koh. 34 Jl. Airport, tel. (084) 796611, M$55-80.

Transportation

MAS flies on Thurs. and Sun. from Kapit to Sibu and Belaga for M$50.

Boats downriver to Sibu leave hourly 0700-1300. Boats upriver to Belaga take about six hours and leave daily except during the July-Oct. dry season, when shallow waters and dangerous rapids prevent commercial boat service. Dugouts chartered during the dry season cost about M$200 per day, but this expense can be shared by a large group.

BELAGA

Kapit is now somewhat civilized. Belaga, on the other hand, is a real *ulu* town where most of the Kenyahs and Kayans go barefoot and sport tattoos. Sights include the elaborate carvings at Mr. Ong's shop and the hilltop tomb of the late Temenggong Matu Puso.

Belaga's three decrepit hotels are to the right of the Borneo Post sign. Best of a bad lot is the Sing Soon Hing Hotel, with fan-cooled rooms with private bath from M$20 and a/c rooms from M$30. The Government Rest House (Rumah Temuai) just before the Y has dorm beds for M$5 on a space-available basis.

Going Upriver

Permission for upriver travel should be obtained from the District Officer and police who usually write "not advised to proceed" on the permit. This technicality doesn't necessarily stop upriver travel, but it waives all government responsibility.

Ordinary express boats to upriver towns and longhouses are most plentiful on weekends and reasonably priced: Wong Jawa in two hours for M$10, Ukit in a full day for M$35. Scalpers may be your only choice during the week. Prices are determined by the number of gallons or tanks needed to reach your destination. One tank equals five gallons and costs about M$50. It takes two tanks to Long Murum or eight tanks to Ukit. Other passengers (including friends and relatives of the boatmen) should be expected to share the cost. Belaga can be reached from Kapit by twice-weekly MAS flights, ordinary boats when the river is high, or chartered dugout during the dry season.

Trekking From Belaga

An intriguing possibility when leaving Belaga is to hike over the watershed to Bintulu. This hike has been completed by hundreds of travelers and takes two to five days depending on the route. It also saves backtracking to Sibu and covers some new territory. Trekking agencies which offer guide services are now established in Bintulu, although guides are generally unnecessary. It's a good idea, however, to organize a group and share expenses.

The quick route involves a short boat ride, some hiking, and a jeep down to Bintulu for about M$50. A slower but more varied route is upriver to the Tiban Rapids where you alight and hike several hours along a good path to circumvent the rapids. A second boat costs about M$50 to the next longhouse, where you spend the night. Tubau, the town on the Kemana River midway between Belaga and Bintulu, can be reached by hiking over the hills or hitching a ride with logging trucks. You can stay in Tubau with Daniel Levoh or other teachers at the 7th Division boarding school. Boats that leave from Tubau to Bintulu take three hours and cost M$12.

BINTULU

The discovery of large natural-gas reserves near Bintulu in the late 1970s transformed the once-sleepy coastal village into a modern boomtown filled with pipe fitters and migrant laborers. Today, the economic expansion continues with the arrival of another immense liquefied-natural-gas plant at Kidurong (second largest in the world) and the enlargement of the deepwater port in the same region.

Attractions

Bintulu is a modern town with little of interest except for the remnants of a fishing village on the banks of the Kemana River, an attractive mosque opened in 1988, and the blue-roofed produce market down at the riverfront. The remainder of the attractions are outside of town, such as the Kemana River and Similajau National Park, 20 km north.

A small tourist information center and Similajau Adventure Tours are in the PDA Building on Jl. Sommerville.

Accommodations

Oil wealth has transformed Bintulu into one of Malaysia's more expensive towns.

Guesthouses: Bintulu's cheapest spots are bare-bones cubicles, perhaps acceptable for a single night. Most are located on the waterfront road near the jetty and bus terminal. Jl. Bazaar, M$15-20.

Capitol Hotel: Somewhat more expensive but certainly less depressing is this aging hotel a few blocks west of the bus terminal. Keppel Rd., tel. (086) 34667, M$15-40.

Kemana Lodging House Annex: Another budget choice is located near the airport but rooms must be booked at the Kemana Lodging House. 78 Keppel Road, tel. (086) 31533, M$15-30.

Plaza Hotel: Top-end choice for oil workers and businessmen is the luxurious L-shaped hotel just opposite the waterfront bus terminal. 116 Jl. Abang Galau, tel. (086) 335111, fax (086) 332742, M$160-280.

Transportation

Bintulu is about 360 km from Kuching. MAS flies several times daily from Sibu, Kuching, Miri, and Kota Kinabalu. The airport is incongruously located in the middle of town, a 10-minute walk from the hotels.

Bintulu's main bus terminal is in the center of town near the jetty and the Plaza Hotel, while another terminal is outside town just opposite King Siang Lodging. Buses to Batu Niah (Niah Caves) leave daily at 0730 and 1200, cost M$12, and take three hours. Buses to Miri leave five times daily 0600-0900, cost M$16, and take four hours. Buses to Sibu leave five times daily 0600-0900.

NIAH CAVES

North Borneo's famous limestone caves were discovered in the 1870s by British naturalist and explorer A. Hart Everett, but the real significance of the caves remained unknown until 1954, when anthropologists from Kuching's Sarawak Museum excavated evidence of man's existence in Borneo dating back some 40,000 years. The discovery of the skull of a young *Homo sapiens* startled the world's scientific community by challenging the theory that mankind's ancestors originated in the Near East and progressively migrated to the Far East. Later excavations of Chinese porcelains and stone tools from the Paleolithic and Neolithic periods led anthropologists to conclude that the caves were inhabited from 40,000 B.C. up to

A.D. 1400! The most spectacular discovery was the Painted Cave, an ancient burial chamber filled with red haematite rock paintings, spirit offerings, and elaborately carved Ships of the Dead complete with skeletal remains. The Painted Cave is open to visitors who hire a guide or have permits from the park ranger in Niah.

The caves are also a geological wonder. The Great Cave alone covers an area of over 11 hectares—large enough to fit 26 football fields—which makes it one of the largest single chambers in the world. Beyond the Great Cave is an intricate network of grottoes which extend right through the 394-meter limestone massif known as Gunung Subis. Guides cost M$30 for groups up to 20 people.

Just as fascinating is the collection of edible bird's nests which form the expensive ingredient in the Chinese delicacy, bird's-nest soup. Twice yearly in the spring and fall, licensed collectors scale rickety 60-meter bamboo poles to scrape the ceilings of the precious clumps of twigs and congealed bird saliva. And how precious! Top-quality first-regurgitation nests can command over M$1000 per kilo. Another unusual activity is the collection of bat and bird guano by native Ibans who sell the droppings as fertilizer to nearby pepper plantations.

The caves are approached by a four-km trek through dense jungle across an elevated plankway. Visitors are encouraged to wander off the path and explore the virgin lowland rainforest filled with long-tailed macaques, hornbills, and Rajah Brooke butterflies. Another outstanding natural phenomenon is the mad flight of millions of swiftlets and bats through the cave entrance at sunset.

Accommodations

The national park operates a Visitor's Hostel at Pangkalan Lobang, directly opposite the river and plankway to the cave entrance. Dorm beds cost M$3 per night. Bedding, cooking utensils, toilets, showers, and refrigerators are provided. Visitors should bring some food, since no restaurants exist in the park. Advance bookings from Kuching's Sarawak Museum or Miri's Forest Office are unnecessary during the week but advisable on weekends, when locals pack the hostel.

The town of Batu Niah, about three km from the Visitor's Hostel, has three hotels with rooms from M$20.

Getting There

From Bintulu: Buses directly to the Visitor's Center at Batu Niah leave Bintulu daily at 0730 and 1215, take three hours, and cost M$10. Buses from Bintulu to Miri will drop you at the park turnoff, but you must then walk, hitchhike, or take a taxi the remaining 13 km to park headquarters. A direct bus is best.

From Miri: Buses direct to Batu Niah leave Miri daily at 0700, 1030, 1200, and 1400, take three hours, and cost M$10. Taxis cost M$15. From Batu Niah you must either take a small boat to Pangkalan Lubang for M$2 or walk for 45 minutes.

MIRI

The administrative capital of the Fourth District is another boomtown with the standard assortment of air-conditioned hotels, karaoke clubs, seedy bars, and expensive restaurants.

Attractions

Most travelers simply pause long enough to make transportation connections to Brunei, Niah Caves, or Gunung Mulu National Park and obtain the necessary permits at the National Parks Office (tel. 085-36637) on Jl. Raja, the road behind the mosque toward Brunei. The Land & Survey Office sells detailed maps of Sarawak.

Pick up information on Gunung Mulu National Park at several tour agencies, such as the Malang Sisters Travel Agency (tel. 085-38141) on Jl. Halaman Kabor.

Accommodations

Most of the local hotels are expensive and often filled on a semipermanent basis with oil and timber workers.

Tai Tong Lodging House: Cheapest of the lot is this rudimentary Chinese hotel, near the riverfront and opposite the Chinese temple. 26 Jl. China, tel. (085) 34072, M$6 for a dorm bed in the hallway, M$25-35 for a private room with fan, M$45-55 a/c.

Fairland Inn: A well-priced hotel just behind the town square with clean a/c rooms and attached baths. Jl. Raya, tel. (085) 413981, M$35-45.

Hotel Plaza Regency: Miri also has a handful of expensive hotels such as the newish spot

just outside town on the road toward Brunei. 47 Jl. Brooke, tel. (085) 414458, M$125-175.

Transportation

MAS flies daily to Kuching, Bintulu, Kota Kinabalu, and several upcountry towns such as Marudi, Bareo, Long Lellang, Lawas, and Sibu.

Buses leave from the terminal behind the Park Hotel on Jl. Raja five times daily to Bintulu and Batu Niah (the town near Niah Caves), and twice daily to Sibu 0700-0800. Tickets can be purchased in advance from the Syrikat Bus Company across from the bus terminal.

Getting To Brunei

The Miri Belait Transport Company has six buses daily to Kuala Belait, the first town in Brunei. After crossing a few rivers and racing along the beach past monkeys and oil platforms, you pass through customs and immigration before arriving in Kuala Belait about three hours later. Delays at river crossings can be avoided by taking your gear off the bus and walking to the front of the line. Drivers often give rides to Western travelers, or you can cross the river by boat and then hitchhike. From Kuala Belait you should immediately take a bus to Seria and then onward to Bandar Seri Begawan. Traveler's checks can be changed at the bank in Kuala Belait. The entire stretch can be covered in a single day.

BARAM RIVER AND THE INTERIOR

Miri is the starting point for trips up the Baram River and the remote longhouses of the Kayan and Kenyah. The entire region is a cultural feast, more pristine than more-exploited areas such as the Skrang or the Rejang River.

Marudi

This Christianized trading post is a pleasant change from the red-light districts of the oil boomtowns.

Buses leave Miri hourly for Kuala Baram, the town toward Brunei at the mouth of the Baram River. Launches equipped with video machines and blasting stereos leave Kuala Baram at 0800, 1000, 1200, and 1400, and take about three hours to reach Marudi. The obnoxious kung-fu videos can't compare with the scenery viewed from the roof of the boat.

Most travelers stay at the Grand Hotel, where clean rooms are M$14 single or double; the manager is a good source of travel information. Visa extensions and permits for interior travel can be picked up from the district officer located in Fort Hose, constructed in 1901 and named after the last of the Rajah's Residents.

Upriver Towns

Multi-day river journeys are possible to the villages and longhouses scattered along the Baram and Tinjar Rivers. Hustlers in Marudi will ask "*Mau pergi ulu?*" (Going upcountry?), but expensive private charters should only be used as a last resort. Sarawak's seventh and newest national park is located at Logan Bunut, a picturesque lake on the Tinjar River a few km beyond the town of Long Teru. Regular launches up the Baram River to the town of Long Lama leave several times each morning, take four hours, and cost M$12.

Accommodations: Long Lama's hotels include the obvious Long Lama Hotel, where dirty rooms cost from M$15. Much cleaner and friendlier is the Telang Usan Hotel. Turn left, walk down to the bazaar, and follow the paved lane on the right.

Transportation: Local guide Yup Po Kiuk at the Yak Radio Shop leads expensive tours and can advise on nearby longhouses. An express boat from Long Lama to the 50-door Kayan longhouse at Long Miri costs M$5-7 and takes about two hours. Also served by ordinary river taxis are Long Akah and Long San, where the Christian Church has been completely carved with Kenyah art. Lio Matah is another day's journey upriver.

Interior Towns

MAS flies Twin Otters from Miri and Marudi to Bario and other interior towns. Flights are actually more economical than paying for chartered boats and getting ripped off by greedy boatmen.

The most popular upcountry destination is Bario, a small town set in the Kelabit Highlands near the Indonesian border. MAS flights are usually met by Ngimet Ayu, who operates a lodging house with rooms for M$10. The entire region is covered with hiking trails through valleys and across mountains dotted with longhouses. Guest books are filled with recent travelers' accounts and suggestions for treks.

One of the best hikes is west to Pa Umur to see their ancient stone called *batu narit,* to Pa Lungan, and to the large Murut settlement at Ba Kelalan. Visitors are welcome to stay in most longhouses but presents of food, canned sardines, frozen meat from Marudi, sweets, sugar, medicines such as panadol, and batik sarongs are expected.

GUNUNG MULU NATIONAL PARK

This park is famous for its extensive underground system of caves, rich flora and fauna, and magnificent topography of towering mountains and jutting limestone pinnacles. Mount Mulu Park caused a great deal of excitement among speleologists in 1980 when an expedition uncovered the world's largest cave, the Sarawak Chamber, which according to the *Guinness Book of World Records* is spacious enough to hold Carlsbad Caverns and Lav Verna Caves in France with room to spare. Other spectacular chambers include the Deer Cave, which boasts the world's largest cave entrance, and Clearwater Cave, which ranks as the longest cave in Southeast Asia at over 62 kilometers. All are filled with impressive stalactites and stalagmites (hanging down and rising upwards, respectively) and home to wildlife such as *Tadarida plicata* bats, snakes, white crabs, and swiftlets which find their ways in the dark by making clicking noises and listening for the echoes.

Both Deer and Clearwater caves are open to visitors but others such as the Sarawak Chamber and Windy Cave are closed for safety reasons. Guides are required to explore all caves and charge M$25-30 per group of up to 25 people. Other activities in the park include a three- to five-day hike to the summit of Gunung Mulu and visits to primitive Penan settlements.

Accommodations

The National Park Service operates two hostels which have 20 dorm beds at M$5 per person. Cooking facilities, drinking water, and blankets are provided. A small canteen sells basic supplies but extra food should be packed in. Permits and room reservations must be arranged in advance from the National Parks and Wildlife Office in Miri. Escorted tours can be arranged through Malang Sisters Travel Agency in Miri.

Getting There

Gunung Mulu's biggest drawback is the great expense involved in hiring boats to the park entrance and the guides required to explore the caves. Boat drivers and cave guides charge flat fees, which can be split between members of large groups. It's best to organize a group of eight to 10 people in Miri and then travel together while sharing expenses. Individual travelers and couples who cannot hook up with a large group will find Mulu prohibitively expensive.

To reach the park in a single day from Miri, you must either fly to Marudi for M$30 or take the 0600 bus to Kuala Baram and then the 0800 express boat up to Marudi for M$15. The noon express boat from Marudi costs M$12 and reaches Long Panai or Kuala Apoh several hours later, depending on the level of the river. From Kuala Apoh you must take either a commercial longboat or a private craft for another M$35 per person to the park. Taken together, the minimum cost to reach park headquarters from Miri is M$50-60—much higher without an organized group.

SABAH

Sabah, the former British Crown Colony, occupies the northeastern tip of Borneo, the isolated island famous for its dense jungles, tribes, wildlife, and soaring mountains. Nicknamed the Land Below the Wind (since it lies south of the Southeast Asian typhoon belt), Sabah is a wonderland for the outdoor adventurer. Its 1,448 kilometers of coastline are flecked with technicolor coral reefs and tiny archipelagos of tropical islands washed by the warm South China and Sulu seas. Dominating the terrain is 4,101-meter Mount Kinabalu, highest peak in Southeast Asia and one of Asia's most popular climbs. Sandankan's famous orangutan sanctuary attracts a steady stream of Western visitors.

Rivers snake past the tribal homelands of Kadazans, Bajaus, and Muruts, who cling to ancient customs while carefully stepping into the 20th century. Other peoples include Chinese merchants, Malay immigrants from the Peninsula, Filipinos from the Sulu Archipelago, and Indonesians up from Kalimantan.

Good beaches, clean seas, swift rivers, soaring mountains, profuse wildlife, friendly people, and large tracts of unspoiled jungle await the discerning traveler. Short of a trip to Africa or interior South America, Sabah is one of the world's best adventure-travel destinations.

And yet very few people come here. Apart from tourist centers such as Mount Kinabalu, it is unlikely that you will see more than a handful of Western visitors. Many are discouraged by the high cost of travel. The island isn't geared to tourism and exploring the state can be surprisingly expensive. Hotels, especially the first-class ones, demand high prices for rooms that elsewhere in Southeast Asia could command only half the amount. Aside from a few national parks with dormitories, budget travelers should expect to pay a minimum of M$20-30 per night for basic accommodations.

Food and transportation are also expensive. Hawker stalls in the cities are plentiful, but it is difficult to find a good meal in a comfortable restaurant for under M$15. Transportation is disproportionately expensive because of higher fuel costs and the need to import all vehicles. Religion is another factor; the collision of a conservative faith such as Islam and the hedonistic demands of international tourism is a troublesome one. Sabah has a great deal of beauty and the potential to be one of Asia's great tourist destinations, but you should be prepared for rugged conditions and bring along enough money to afford the adventure.

ATTRACTIONS

Kota Kinabalu

Completely destroyed during WW II, the capital of Sabah is a bustling commercial enclave with little charm or character. Top draw is the offshore group of islands, which offers good beaches and attractive coral beds. KK (the common abbreviation for Kota Kinabalu) is a convenient place for visas, permits, transportation arrangements, and one of Sabah's few places with good restaurants.

Mount Kinabalu

Sabah's most famous attraction is the immense sawtooth mountain which ranks as the highest peak between New Guinea and Myanmar. Kinabalu can be climbed in two days by almost anyone in good physical condition. The surrounding national park is a naturalist's wonderland of waterfalls, rivers, and spectacular flora and fauna such as bizarre pitcher plants and the famous rafflesia.

Orangutan Sanctuary

Sandakan, another nondescript town, boasts the Sepilok Orangutan Sanctuary—one of the world's few places where orangutans can be observed in their natural habitat.

Adventure Travel

River rafting, mountain climbing, and scuba diving on Sabah are among the finest in Southeast Asia. All the navigable rivers have recently been graded from Class I (easy) to Class VI (expert). Novices can try their luck on the Papar River (Classes I and II) and the Kadamaian River near Kota Belud (Classes II and III). Serious enthusiasts can challenge themselves on the Padas River, a Class-IV excursion through the spectacular Tenom Gorge. Contact Api Tours, tel. 221230, fax 212078, Lot 49, Bandaran Berjaya, Kota Kinabalu.

Scuba diving is also spectacular. Dive locations include Tunku Abdul Rahman (TAR) Marine Park near Kota Kinabalu and a tiny island called Sipadan, in the southeast of the state. TAR Marine Park is adequate for beginners, but experts compare the proliferation of marinelife and the towering coral walls of Sipadan to the Maldives and the best of Australia's Great Barrier Reef. Contact Borneo Divers, tel. 421371, fax 424566, Batu 3.5, Jalan Tuaran, Kota Kinabalu. Sabah has the potential to become the premier adventure-travel destination in Asia.

TRANSPORTATION

Getting There

Air: MAS flies daily to Kota Kinabalu from Singapore for M$346, from Kuala Lumpur for M$380, and from Johor Baru for M$301. Cheapest fares are 14-day advance-purchase tickets from Johor Baru, which cost M$260. To encourage airline traffic, MAS provides complimentary bus service from its office in Singapore to the Johor Baru airport. Economy night flights are offered from Kuala Lumpur. Group travel is another discount possibility. Groups of three or more people can save 50% off regular MAS airfares by purchasing tickets at least seven days in advance. MAS and Cathay Pacific fly twice weekly from Hong Kong to Kota Kinabalu for M$650.

MAS and Philippine Airlines fly daily from Manila to Kota Kinabalu for US$189. Visitors traveling south from the Philippines might find this an intriguing route: Manila to Kota Kinabalu, overland to Kuching in Sabah, Kuching to Pontianak by air, and finally down to Jakarta. Another unusual possibility is a flight from Zamboanga to Kota Kinabalu. This route is frequently canceled but when in service saves expensive backtracking from Mindanao. Check with PAL in Manila. MAS also flies daily from Kuching with a stop in Brunei.

Getting Around

Land: Buses, minibuses, and Land Rovers run along an asphalted road in much better condition than the coastal road in Sarawak. The so-called Trans-Sabah Highway from Sandakan to Tawau remains in terrible condition, but the good stretch from Beaufort to Sandakan is fast and comfortable. For example, the 400-km journey from Kota Kinabalu to Sandakan can be covered in a single day. Travelers coming from Brunei can reach Kota Kinabalu in two days then continue out to Kinabalu National Park. Most visitors then return to KK, although adventurous types can continue to Sandakan and then reach Kalimantan from Tawau.

Air: MAS operates Fokker F-27s and Britten Norman Islanders daily from Kota Kinabalu to Sandakan, Tawau, Labuan, and other small towns. Flights around Sabah are reasonably priced but often booked solid, especially on weekends and holidays. On the other hand, multiple bookings are so common that MAS often discovers its fully booked flights leaving with empty seats. Best strategy for filled flights is to simply arrive early at the airport and put your name on the waiting list; in most cases you'll fly.

VISAS AND PERMITS

Both Sabah and Sarawak have their own immigration controls, although the officials in Sabah seem more flexible about extensions.

Most Westerners are initially given one-month permits which can be easily extended at immigration offices in larger towns. Permits are unnecessary for interior travel. Permits and reservations for Kinabalu National Park must be made in advance at the parks office in Kota Kinabalu. A permit is technically required to visit the orangutan sanctuary near Sandakan, but this formality is rarely enforced.

KOTA KINABALU

Known as Jesselton prior to 1963, Kota Kinabalu is a relatively modern and undistinguished city constructed over the ruins of the original town destroyed during WW II. Lacking Kuching's charm or character, KK is also a destination plagued by bad luck: during the late 19th century it was pillaged and burned by pirates so many times that local inhabitants nicknamed their town Api! Api! ("Fire! Fire!"). Postwar reconstruction has created a faceless place, although it offers some good restaurants and is a convenient place to extend visas and make reservations for Mt. Kinabalu.

Attractions
State Mosque: This splendid example of contemporary Islamic architecture lacks the grace of older *masjids* but is nevertheless a worthwhile visit on Friday afternoons when the faithful gather for services. Situated south of downtown toward Tanjung Aru, the modernistic Arabian fantasy was designed in 1977 by an Italian architectural firm. Well-dressed visitors are usually allowed to enter. Take the red bus from Jalan Tunku Abdul Rahman.

Sabah Museum: KK's impressive repository for Sabah's ethnological treasures is located near the State Mosque in a trio of modern buildings modeled after Rungus and Murut longhouses. The various galleries display collections of tribal artifacts, contemporary handicrafts, dioramas on natural history, Chinese ceramics, and exhibitions which help introduce the peoples of the state. Also visit the science center, the art gallery, and the theater where the slide show *Sabah, The Land Below the Wind* is given twice daily. The museum is open daily except Fridays 1000-1800. Take the red bus from Jalan Tunku Abdul Rahman and get

off near the mosque, then climb the hill opposite the State Secretariat.

Tanjung Aru Beach: The satellite town of Tanjung Aru, eight km south of KK and 10 minutes from the airport, has a passable beach and Sabah's premier resort hotel, nicely set on 23 acres of landscaped gardens: Tanjung Aru Beach Hotel, tel. (088) 587111, M$380-650. Take the red bus signposted Beach from Jalan Tunku Abdul Rahman.

Tunku Abdul Rahman National Park: Just offshore from Kota Kinabalu are five attractive and popular islands with sheltered bays, clear waters, and protected coral beds. Pulau Gaya, the largest island of the group, has 20 km of graded nature trails through mangrove swamps and tropical forests filled with wild rattan, tristana trees, rhizophora with distinctive aerial roots, nibong palms used as *attap* for old-fashioned roofing, and exotic birds such as pied hornbills and megapodes. Api Tours runs a daily tour.

The most popular and developed island in the park is Pulau Sapi, which has a sandy beach and clear waters. Pulau Mamutik is a relatively unspoiled island with a 12-man resthouse for M$60 per night. Reservations can be made from the Sabah Parks Office in KK, tel. (088) 51591. Pulau Manukan is being developed for campers while Pulau Sulug remains the most distant and least visited of the islands.

Camping is permissible on all islands. Basic cooking and washing facilities are provided, but visitors should bring proper gear and food supplies. Gaya and Sapi islands are just offshore from downtown KK, while the last three are closer to Tanjung Aru.

All can be reached by shuttle boats from the Tanjung Aru Beach marina and by private charter from the jetty in front of the Hyatt Kinabalu. Boat service is frequent on weekends. Return fares are M$16-20 depending on the island.

General Information
Tourist Information: The Sabah Tourism Promotion Corporation, tel. (088) 211729, on Jalan Raya, can help with the latest transportation schedules and lists of upcoming festivals and weekly markets (*tamus*). The nearby Malaysian Tourism Promotion Board (MTPB) is also helpful.

National Parks: The Sabah Parks Office, tel. (088) 211585, is on Jalan Tun Fuad Stephens one block west of the tourist office. Room reser-

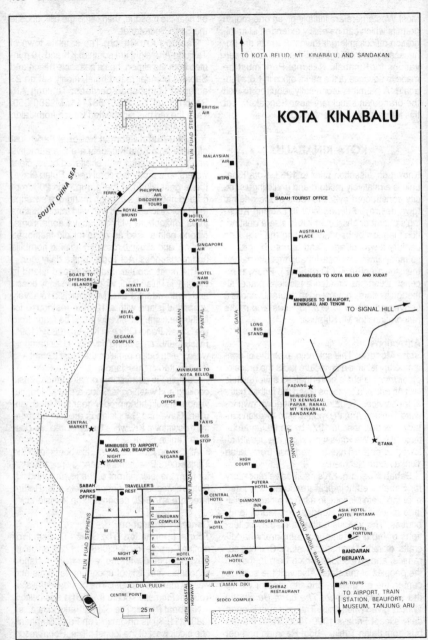

KOTA KINABALU

TO KOTA BELUD, MT KINABALU, AND SANDAKAN

SOUTH CHINA SEA

BRITISH AIR

MALAYSIAN AIR

MTPB

FERRY

PHILIPPINE AIR DISCOVERY TOURS

ROYAL BRUNEI AIR

SABAH TOURIST OFFICE

HOTEL CAPITAL

SINGAPORE AIR

AUSTRALIA PLACE

BOATS TO OFFSHORE ISLANDS

HYATT KINABALU

HOTEL NAM XING

MINIBUSES TO KOTA BELUD AND KUDAT

MINIBUSES TO BEAUFORT, KENINGAU, AND TENOM

TO SIGNAL HILL

BILAL HOTEL

SEGAMA COMPLEX

JL. HAJI SAMAN

JL. PANTAL

JL. GAYA

LONG BUS STAND

MINIBUSES TO KOTA BELUD

PADANG

MINIBUSES TO KENINGAU, PAPAR, RANAU, MT KINABALU, SANDAKAN

POST OFFICE

TAXIS

BUS STOP

JL. PADANG

CENTRAL MARKET

MINIBUSES TO AIRPORT, LIKAS, AND BEAUFORT

NIGHT MARKET

BANK NEGARA

HIGH COURT

ISTANA

SABAH PARKS OFFICE

TRAVELLER'S REST

JL. TUN RAZAK

PUTERA HOTEL

CENTRAL HOTEL

DIAMOND INN

ASIA HOTEL HOTEL PERTAMA

HOTEL FORTUNE

A
B
C
D
E
F
G
H
I
J

SINSURAN COMPLEX

K | L

M | N

PINE BAY HOTEL

IMMIGRATION

JL. TUNGKU ABDUL RAHMAN

BANDARAN BERJAYA

NIGHT MARKET

HOTEL RAKYAT

ISLAMIC HOTEL

RUBY INN

JL. TUN FUAD STEPHENS

JL. TUGU

JL. DUA PULUH

SOUTH COASTAL HIGHWAY

JL. LAMAN DIKI

SHIRAZ RESTAURANT

SEDCO COMPLEX

API TOURS

TO AIRPORT, TRAIN STATION, BEAUFORT, MUSEUM, TANJUNG ARU

CENTRE POINT

0   25 m

KOTA KINABALU ACCOMMODATIONS

HOTEL	SINGLE	DOUBLE	ADDRESS	PHONE (088)
LUXURY	**M$**	**M$**		
Capital	180-220	220-260	23 Haji Yaacub	53433
Hyatt Kinabalu	280-420	280-420	Datuk Salleh	221234
Jesselton	100-120	100-120	69 Gaya	55633
Shangri-La	120-150	150-160	Bandaran Berjaya	212800
Tanjung Aru Resort	380-650	380-650	Tanjung Aru Beach	58711
MODERATE				
Asia	40-50	50-70	68 Bandaran Berjaya	53533
Islamic	25-35	25-35	27 Perpaduan	54325
Kinabalu	70-80	80-90	59 Bandaran Berjaya	53233
Rakyat	30-45	30-45	Block I, Sinsuran	211100
Winner	65-75	75-85	9 Haji Saman	52688
BUDGET				
Cecilia B&B	12-20	20-30	413 Saga, Kampong Likas	35733
Likas Guest House	15-25	20-30	371 Likas, Kampong Likas	31706
Traveller's Rest	25-34	32-38	Block L, Sinsuran Complex	231892

vations at Kinabalu National Park should be made well in advance, especially during weekends when it seems like half the population of KK sets out to conquer the mountain. Guides are best hired directly at the park.

Visas: The immigration office on the 4th floor of the Government Complex just off Jalan Tunku Abdul Rahman can extend visas and permits in an hour. The Indonesian Consulate, tel. (088) 54100, is in the Wing On Life Building on Jalan Sagunting.

Travel Agencies: Discounted airline tickets are sold at several agencies in town, but prices never reach the rock-bottom levels of Singapore, Hong Kong, or Bangkok. Visitors traveling from Singapore to Manila via Borneo should purchase through tickets rather than try to piecemeal tickets together.

Adventure Travel Companies: Local travel agents can arrange tours into longhouse regions, river journeys, scuba diving, and overnight treks up Mt. Kinabalu. Scuba divers should contact Borneo Divers, tel. (088) 53074, on Tuaran Road. Whitewater trips are organized by Api Tours, tel. (088) 231230, in Bandaran Berjaya (on the map).

Another popular choice is Chris Perez's Borneo Tropical Adventures, tel. (088) 231892, Block L, 3rd Floor, Sinsuran Complex.

Budget Accommodations
Traveller's Rest: Kota Kinabalu is a difficult place to find clean and inexpensive accommodations. Chris Perez's place is noisy but centrally located near the parks office and night market. 3rd floor, Block L, Sinsuran Complex, tel. 231892, M$15 dorm, M$28-34 single, M$32-38 double.

Cecilia B&B: Several clean and quiet guesthouses geared to travelers are located in Kampung Likas, about six km north of city center. Take a minibus. Cecilia Chew and her husband Danny also operate a small, personalized adventure-travel company. 413 Jalan Saga, Likas, tel. (088) 35733, fax 236902, M$8-30 dorms and private rooms.

Moderate Accommodations
Hotel Rakyat: Perhaps the cleanest of KK's inexpensive hotels. Block I, Sinsuran Complex, tel. (088) 211100, M$35-60.

Islamic Hotel: The city's most popular travelers' hotel despite cleaner rooms at the Rakyat and better atmosphere in Kampong Likas. Several other moderate-priced hotels are found on Jalan Perpaduan. 27 Jalan Perpaduan, tel. (088) 54325, M$25-35.

Asia Hotel: KK has over a dozen hotels in the M$40-60 range for a/c doubles with attached baths. Some serve the short-time trade but most are reasonably clean and safe, such as the Asia off Jalan Tunku Abdul Rahman. 68 Jalan Bandaran Berjaya, tel. (088) 53533, M$40-70.

Luxury Accommodations

Hyatt Kinabalu: Located in the heart of town along the waterfront stands the city's premier business hotel. Facilites include several restaurants, the Bambaazon bar, and a swimming pool overlooking the South China Sea. Jalan Datuk Salleh Sulong, tel. (088) 221234, fax (088) 225972, M$280-420.

Tanjung Aru Beach Hotel: Overlooking the spectacular marine park, Kota Kinabalu's only resort hotel is now managed by Shangri-La International, one of the world's most prestigious hotel chains. Tanung Aru, tel. (088) 58711, fax (088) 217155, M$380-650.

Leaving Kota Kinabalu

Air: KK's modern airport in Tanjung Aru, eight km south of town, can be reached by taxi for M$10 or by red Putatan bus from Jalan Tunku Abdul Rahman. Taxis from the airport to town operate on the coupon system at fixed fares. MAS and other airlines fly to Singapore, Kuala Lumpur, Johor Baru, Manila, Hong Kong, Kuching, and Bandar Seri Begawan.

Bus: KK has three stops where buses, minibuses, Land Rovers, and share taxis depart for destinations in Sabah. Locations are shown on the map. Minibuses are somewhat more expensive than buses but are also faster and more comfortable. Departures for nearby towns such as Beaufort and Kota Belud are plentiful up until 1400. Service to distant towns such as Sandakan usually ends around 0800 or 0900. All three bus stops are centrally located near the Sabah Government Complex. Visitors going to Kinabalu National Park can take any bus or minibus bound for Ranau or Sandakan and get off at park headquarters.

Getting To Brunei

Overland travelers can reach Brunei from Kota Kinabalu in two ways. Land-and-water transportation is necessary since no roads connect Kota Kinabalu with Bandar Seri Begawan, the capital of Brunei. Neither route is easy but with an early start it's possible to reach Brunei in a single day.

Labuan Island Route: Buses and taxis directly to Labuan leave from the bus stand on Jalan Balai Polis in Kota Kinabalu. Otherwise, you can first go to Beaufort and then take a taxi up to Mempakol and Menumbok. From here, boats make the 45-minute crossing to Labuan daily at 1030 and 1600. Ferries from Labuan to Menumbok leave at 0800 and 1300. Taxis and bus drivers in Beaufort usually know the latest schedules and will deliver you in time for the boat. Launches from Labuan to Bandar Seri Begawan leave twice daily at varying times, take two hours, and cost M$15.

Sipitang-Lawas Route: The road west from Beaufort passes through Sipitang and Merapok before grinding to a halt in the one-horse town of Lawas. Ferries from Lawas to Bandar Seri Begawan leave twice daily at varying times, take two hours, and cost about M$25. To avoid getting stuck in Lawas, it's important to double-check schedules before leaving Beaufort. Lawas has a Government Resthouse for M$30 if you miss the last boat to Brunei.

PENAMPANG AND PAPAR

Kadazans, the members of the ethnic group which forms one-third of Sabah's population, make their homes in the towns near Penampang 13 km south of Kota Kinabalu. These agriculturalists are known for their handicrafts, harvest dances called *sumazau,* and ritualistic exorcisms known as *monogit.* Progress is changing the character of the region, although several small and beautiful Kadazan villages with palm-thatched houses elevated on stilts are still found in the countryside.

Sights in town includes historic St. Michael's Church, Kadazan graveyards, and the so-called House of Skulls, where spiritual ceremonies are held to appease the 42 skull spirits. Penampang holds its weekly market every Saturday morning.

Papar, a modern Kadazan village 38 km south of Kota Kinabalu, holds its *tamu* on Sundays. Buses to both towns leave Kota Kinabalu from the terminal behind the GPO.

BEAUFORT

Much of this quaint market town is constructed on stilts to escape the annual flooding of the Padas River. Reasons to visit Beaufort are to change money, attend the Saturday market, and catch the train to Tenom.

Trains leave Beaufort on weekdays and Saturdays at 0830, 1050, and 1355 and on Sundays at 0645, 0910, 1430, and 1540. The two-hour journey along the banks of the Padas River passes through spectacular countryside while crossing the Crocker Range into the heart of the Padas Gorge.

Back in Beaufort, the Padas Hotel north of the bus terminal has rooms from M$35.

LABUAN ISLAND

This Federal Territory near Sabah's westernmost point attracts local visitors with its skin diving and duty-free shopping. The island has played an important role in local history as a base for pirates in the 17th century, a pivotal settlement for British traders, and the scene of Japanese surrender at the end of WW II.

Sights include an orchid farm and the Commonwealth War Cemetery three km from the principal town of Victoria. Labuan, unfortunately, is somewhat dull and expensive—even by Borneo standards.

Many of the cheapest hotels such as the Kim Soon Lee, the Aurora, and Hotel Meriah are strung along Jalan Okk Awang, but even the smallest rooms cost a minimum of M$40. For most visitors, Labuan is simply a transit point between Sabah and Brunei.

TENOM

South of Kota Kinabalu lies Murut country, a timber territory inhabited by Murut tribals who have largely given up their traditional lifestyles

for jobs in timber factories. Blue jeans and T-shirts emblazoned with cheeky slogans are far more popular than tribal dress. The countryside of jungle and farmland is quite beautiful although most of the towns are commercial zones controlled by Chinese shopkeepers. The small enclave of Tenom has been spared the pell-mell development of other timber towns, but there is little to view except for rubber plantations and the Cocoa Research Center.

Undoubtedly the highlight of any visit is the train journey from Beaufort, as described above. Trains from Tenom to Beaufort depart at 0730, 1340, and 1500. The few remaining Murut longhouses several days' hike into the jungle can be reached with local guides.

Accommodations in Tenom include the Hotel Kin San and the adjacent Tenom Hotel, with fan rooms from M$20.

KENINGAU

The largest town and administrative center of the interior is home to both the Muruts and Kadazans who have migrated to the city for jobs. Some adventurous types have reportedly reached Indonesia from Pensiangan by private launch down the Sembakung River and then hiking across the unmanned border to Lumbis.

Perhaps the most remarkable scene around Keningau is the convoys of thundering lumber trucks which carry their cargo to the timber factories. Like Indonesia and the Philippines, Sabah is felling its tropical hardwoods at a breathless rate. Experts estimate that at current rates of depletion, over 80% of the original forests in Sabah will be completely logged in less than 20 years and, despite the claims of government officials, few hold any hope for natural regeneration or commercial replanting. The economy of Keningau and other timber towns continues to boom but the ecological rape of Sabah is not a pretty picture.

As with other boomtowns in North Borneo, most of the less expensive hotels are continually filled with migrant workers and government officials. The Government Resthouse costs M$12 when beds are available. Otherwise, check the Hiap Soon Hotel or Tai Wah for rooms under M$30.

TUARAN

Several towns famous for their *tamus* (weekly markets) are located slightly north of Kota Kinabalu. Throughout Sabah and generally on weekends, villagers and ethnic groups from the country meet at the nearest town to exchange vegetables, fish, chickens, cassettes, clothing, baskets, weavings, and hand-rolled cigarettes, while catching up on the latest gossip.

Tuaran, a small town 30 minutes north of Kota Kinabalu, has a lively market every Sunday morning. From Tuaran a visit can be made to the nearby Bajau fishing village of Mengkabong, constructed on stilts, where sampans remain the chief mode of transportation. Picturesque Mengkabong is worth a detour, although it has become so popular with group tours that some residents have become disturbingly aggressive about their salesmanship.

KOTA BELUD

Probably the most famous *tamu* in Sabah is the Sunday market held in Kota Belud, a sleepy town 77 km north of Kota Kinabalu. This weekly gathering is attended by not only Malay housewives and Chinese merchants but also Kadazans and Bajaus who occasionally turn up on their small horses fitted with bells and colorful caparisons for dramatic effect.

Aside from the famous Kadazan harvest festivals in late May, visitors and photographers will find this market to be one of Sabah's best introductions to tribal folkways. From Kota Belud, you can continue north to Kudat or backtrack to Tamparuli, where buses head east to Kinabalu National Park.

KUDAT

Borneo's northernmost town, over 240 km from Kota Kinabalu, is home to the Rungus, an indigenous subset of the Kadazan/Dusun people that forms the largest ethnic group in Sabah. Unlike most of their relatives in the Crocker Range, the Rungus continue to live their lives in longhouses and follow traditional lifestyles still relatively unaffected by modernization. Every

Sunday the womenfolk gather in Sikuati, 23 km away, to trade goods while wrapped in black knee-length sarongs, beaded necklaces, and heavy brass bracelets.

The rarely visited beaches at Bak Bak, 11 km north of Kudat, are some of the best in Sabah.

Kudat has several hotels in the M$30-35 range and a Government Resthouse for M$15 when space is available.

KINABALU NATIONAL PARK

Soaring 4,101 meters (13,445 feet) into the clear blue skies of northern Borneo, the sacred mountain of Kinabalu is the highest point between the Himalayas and the snowcapped massif of Mount Wilhelmina in Irian Jaya. The chief attraction is a two-day climb to the summit of the sawtooth mountain, still revered by native Kadazans as Aki Nabalu or "Home of the Departed Spirits."

Apart from the magnificent topography, the 767-square-km national park is home to an extraordinary range of flora and fauna, some found nowhere else in the world. Botanists claim that half the plants growing above the 1,500-meter level are unique to the mountain, although close relatives are found in the highlands of New Guinea, Australia, and New Zealand. Over 800 species of orchids and 500 species of birds live in the park. Among the more famous plants are the rare and endangered rafflesia, whose bloom can reach a meter in diameter, and the more common genus of bizarre carnivorous plants known as *Nepenthes* because of their pitcher-plant shapes.

The park also has something for history buffs: the Kundasang War Memorial, which honors the 2,400 Allied POWs who died on the 11-month death march from Sandakan to the foothills of Mount Kinabalu.

The Climb
The two-day trek can be accomplished by most people in good health, although it requires some preparation. Permission to climb Kinabalu *must* be obtained in advance from the park office in Kota Kinabalu. Guides are also required at M$60 each; this expense can be shared by joining a large group at park headquarters or di-

rectly at the gate checkpoint near the power station. Park officials in Kota Kinabalu encourage visitors to hire guides in advance but will also accept promises of joining a group at the park. Don't be concerned if your guide is a cheroot-smoking old lady! Porters at M$60 each are optional.

It is very important to remember that the weather is changeable and nighttime temperatures often fall below freezing—bring along proper raingear and an extra set of warm clothing packed in plastic bags. Other necessities include a flashlight, toilet paper, adhesive bandages, kerosene, and food. Mountain huts are equipped with bunks, mattresses, sleeping bags, blankets, kerosene stoves, and cooking facilities. Also attend the naturalist programs at park headquarters and read Susan Kacobson's *Kinabalu Park,* available at the headquarters.

The hike begins with a one-hour walk or a 15-minute drive from park headquarters at 1,585 meters to the power station at 1,890 meters. Security guards here check for the mandatory guide. Guideless hikers should arrive early enough to beat the guard or ask to join a registered group.

The first leg of the climb passes through montane and rhododendron forests to Carson's Falls, where water bottles can be refilled. The trail continues to the first shelter at 2000 meters and then through a zone of Low's pitcher plants, named after the British colonial officer who first climbed the mountain in 1851. The trail climbs past swaying bamboo forests, several sets of primitive huts, and finally the Layang Layang Camp, three hours from the summit at an elevation of 3,359 meters. Most exhausted hikers collapse here, but hardy types can continue another 90 minutes to the new huts at Laban Rata that complement the older huts farther up at Sayat Sayat. Fully equipped with hot water, heaters, and a restaurant, the Laban Rata Huts can accomodate over 70 persons in dormitories. Beds cost M$25 per person at Laban Rata Guesthouse but only M$4 at the Panar Laban, Gunting Lagandan, and Sayat Sayat huts.

The following morning it's up to the summit where, weather permitting, a spectacular sunrise and magnificent views are the final rewards. Since rainstorms and thick clouds often obscure views by 0900, some hikers hedge their bets

by booking two nights at Layang Layang or Sayat Sayat. The return hike takes about six hours. Anyone wishing to soak in the hot tubs at Poring Hot Springs that same evening must catch the last minibus to Ranau, which passes park headquarters around 1430.

Accommodations

Park Headquarters has a wide range of accommodations from inexpensive dormitories to comfortable but expensive bungalows. Room reservations must be made in advance at the Sabah Parks office in Kota Kinabalu. Weekends and holidays are extremely busy, but reserving a bed during the week is easy.

Dorm beds in the old hostel cost M$10 per person; those in the new hostel are M$15. Both hostels are equipped with bedding, cooking facilities, and fireplaces. Private cabins start at M$100 for a double. There are two restaurants and a provisions store with food, drink, hiking supplies, and equipment rentals.

Park rangers conduct daily walking tours of the nearby trails and give informative slide shows in the evenings. While a hike to the summit is the top attraction at Kinabalu National Park, a few days exploring the caves, waterfalls, and surrounding forests are also recommended.

Getting There

Any bus or minibus going to Ranau or Sandakan can drop you at park headquarters. Minibuses to the park leave three times daily before 1300 from the bus station on Jalan Balai Polis in Kota Kinabalu. Land Rovers are available for a few extra dollars. Both take about 2¹/₂ hours. Coming from the *tamu* in Kota Belud, you should transfer to a Sandakan-bound minibus in Tamparuli rather than return to Kota Kinabalu.

Poring Hot Springs

The main attraction of Poring, 43 km from park headquarters, is a series of hot sulphur baths first developed by Japanese soldiers during WW II. Both the hot- and cold-water baths are nicely set in landscaped gardens surrounded by tropical jungle interlaced with winding trails to waterfalls, caves, and bamboo forests.

Accommodations include the Poring Hostel for M$8 and more expensive cabins that average about M$20 when filled.

Poring is a great place to relax after conquering Mount Kinabalu, but to reach the springs the same evening you must catch the final Ranau-bound minibus, which passes park headquarters around 1430. Ranau, a small town on the KK-Sandakan highway, about 18 km south of the springs, is a transit point since most travelers head off immediately to the springs. Pickups to Poring are plentiful on weekends and holidays but somewhat scarce during the week. A charter taxi costs about M$15. Accommodation in Ranau includes the Ranau Hotel, where rooms start at M$24, and the Government Resthouse outside town.

SANDAKAN

Sandakan lies approximately 386 km from Kota Kinabalu, on the east coast of Sabah facing the Sulu Sea. Formerly the capital of North Borneo, Sandakan was completely destroyed by the Japanese during WW II but quickly rebuilt afterward by Chinese entrepreneurs. It served as center for the state's booming timber industry until the mid-'80s when overlogging finally exhausted the resource in the district: the devastation is painfully obvious on the bus ride from Ranau to Sandakan.

The National Parks Office, tel. (089) 42188, is on Jalan Leila near the Ramai Hotel three km west of town. No reason to visit this office, since permits are rarely checked for the orangutan sanctuary. The immigration office is on Jalan Leila near the long-distance bus terminal.

Sepilok Orangutan Sanctuary

Its name literally translating to people of the jungle, the humanlike orangutan was once hunted by the great British naturalist, Sir Alfred Wallace, who reported that the red-haired beasts were especially fond of . . . durians! Today the gentle animal is an endangered species largely because its natural habitat has been destroyed by logging. Sepilok, 22 km from Sandakan, contains one of the world's three orangutan sanctuaries designed to reintroduce into the jungle those animals captured in logging camps or kept illegally as pets. Other protected wildlife such as gibbons, macaques, Malay sun bears, and wild cats are also brought to Sepilok and eventually coaxed back into the jungle. The park is open daily 0900-1600; apes are fed once daily 0900-1030 from an elevated platform in the middle of the jungle. Orangutan spotting is strictly a matter of luck: sometimes a half-dozen young animals will appear for their breakfast of milk and bananas, while on other days attendance is zero. Other park attractions include jungle hiking through mangrove forests, waterfalls, swimming pools, and educational programs sponsored by park rangers.

Permits are unnecessary to visit the reserve. Sepilok can be reached on the bus marked Sepilok Batu 14, which leaves mornings from the bus terminal located at the waterfront at the west end of the fruit-and-vegetable market. Buses marked Sepilok Batu 16, 17, and 30 will drop you at the junction two km from park headquarters.

Turtle Sanctuary

This conservation park north of Sandakan is made up of three islands (Selingan, Bakungan, and Gulisan) and their surrounding coral reefs. Egg-laden green and hawksbill turtles come here between August and October to nest in the warm sand. Hatcheries are open to the public.

The Government Resthouse on Pulau Selingan has four-man chalets with private baths and cooking facilities for M$120 and more rustic cabins for M$30 per person. Reservations must be made at the National Parks Office in Sandakan.

Few travelers visit the sanctuary, since there is no regular boat service and only large groups can afford to charter a boat for the three-hour journey. Boat transfers and guided tours are best arranged through tour operators and the parks office.

Gomantong Caves

Sandakan's third major attraction is the enormous network of caverns famous for their edible bird's nests. Similar to the more accessible caves at Niah, thousands of swiftlets called *burong layang layang* spin their phlegm baskets inside the immense limestone cliffs. Harvests are conducted several times a year by skilled collectors of the Orang Sungeti tribe, natives of the nearby Kinabatangan River area.

Gomantong is situated on the other side of the bay about 32 km south of Sandakan and can be reached by boat across the bay and then a 16-km Land Rover ride—a difficult and expensive journey best arranged through travel agents.

Mandatory permits can be obtained from the Forestry Department in Sandakan.

Accommodations

The hotel situation in Sandakan is fairly grim for budget travelers. The Hotel Federal adjacent to the long-distance bus terminal on Jalan Tiga has rooms from M$38, the Hotel New Sabah and Gaya Hotel from M$48. Rooms get cheaper as you walk east down Jalan Tiga past MAS and the Chartered Bank. First on the right is Hotel Paris, where rooms start at M$21. Three blocks farther down Jalan Tiga is the clean and popular Hung Wing Hotel, with rooms on the upper floors for only M$15.

Certainly the best-value spot is Uncle Tan's (tel. 089-669516) at Batu 7 near the airport, where dorm beds cost M$15. Tan also runs very cheap tours to nearly islands and river camps.

LAHAD DATU

This prosperous Chinese town of 20,000 people receives the few visitors going from Tawau to Tarakan in Kalimantan. Boats can be chartered to explore the offshore islands near Semporna, an old Bajau town three hours south of Lahad Datu. Formed from an arc of land which once rimmed a volcanic crater, these stunning islands are inhabited by seafaring Bajaus who live over the water in pilehouses or in traditional Bajau boats called *lipa lipa*. The Semporna coral beds are reputedly some of the finest in Southeast Asia; contact Borneo Divers in Kota Kinabalu. The nearby Segama River and its Dismal Gorge was kayaked several

years ago by some Americans who barely survived the ordeal.

Lahad Datu has eight hotels in the M$25-40 price range and a Government Resthouse near the airport for M$12. Buses and minibuses for Lahad Datu leave from the bus terminal near the Federal Hotel in Sandakan. Allow five tough hours to Lahad Datu and eight hours to Tawau. MAS flies daily to Lahad Datu and Tawau.

TAWAU

Tawau, a small commercial center at the southeastern border of Sabah, mainly serves as a transit point for Indonesian Borneo. Visas can be picked up at the Indonesian consulate on Jalan Tuhara. Tawau has several hotels in the M$25-30 range on Jalan Stephen Tan, three blocks east of the bus terminal and near the central market.

Getting To Indonesia

Although time-consuming and expensive, it is entirely legal to enter Tarakan (Indonesia) from Tawau. Remember that Tarakan is *not* a visa-free entry point and all visitors *must* obtain a one-month visa in advance from an Indonesian consulate. It's best to pick up your Indonesian visa in Kota Kinabalu, since the Consulate in Tawau is somewhat disorganized and capricious about who deserves one. Bouraq flies twice weekly between Tawau and Tarakan. Boats from Tawau to Nunukan, a small Indonesian fishing town just across the border, cost M$25 and leave several times weekly. Another boat continues south to Tarakan.

The real meaning of travel, like that of a conversation by the fireside, is the discovery of oneself through contact with other people, and its condition is self-commitment in the dialogue.

—Paul Tournier, *The Meaning of Persons*

I shall always be glad to have seen it—for the same reason Papa gave for being glad to have seen Lisbon—namely, that it will be unnecessary ever to see it again.

—Winston Churchill

Fish & Visitors stink in 3 days.

—Benjamin Franklin

SUGGESTED READINGS

◆ *See the Third World While It Lasts.* Penang: Consumer's Association of Penang, 1985. A hard-hitting look at the social and environmental impact of tourism. Raises some important and disturbing questions about the effects of mass tourism on third-world countries. Photographs and reproductions of advertisements by Airlanka ("We've put a price on Paradise") and the Shangri-La Hotel ("Don't change your way of life just because you change countries") are alone worth the price.

◆ Hong, Evelyne. *Natives of Sarawak: Survival in Borneo's Vanishing Forest.* Penang: Institut Masyarakat, 1987. A well-argued and liberally illustrated insight into the cultural elimination of Borneo's Penan tribespeoples. Very important reading.

◆ Lat (Mohamad Nor Khalid). *Kampong Boy.* Kuala Lumpur: Straits Times Publishing, 1979. Lat's cartoons of *kampong* life, pop heroes, fat mothers worrying about their rebellious sons, disorganized weddings, comical circumcision rituals, and gentle ribbing of political leaders are hilarious and miraculously reveal the essense of being Malay. Highly recommended.

◆ Mahathir, Dr. Mohammed. *The Malay Dilemma.* Kuala Lumpur: 1970. Malaysia's controversial prime minister talks about race, religion, and politics in his book, which was internally banned for several years.

◆ Maugham, Somerset. *Collected Short Stories.* London, 1951. One of the world's great writers describes life in colonial Malaya during the '20s and '30s.

◆ Moore, Donald. *Where Monsoons Meet.* London: George Harrap, 1960. An anthology by various writers on riots, history, and tall tales such as "How to Speak to a Tiger." Used bookstores in Penang and Kuala Lumpur sometimes carry this amusing little paperback.

◆ Naipaul, V.S. *Among the Believers: An Islamic Journey.* London, 1981. A critical but revealing look at Islamic fundamentalism from the Middle East to Indonesia.

◆ Skeat, Walter William. *Malay Magic.* London: Macmillan, 1900. This anthropological classic describes Malaysian folklore, religion, magicians, fire charms, divination, and the black arts with great insight. Comprehensive but less captivating than the similar efforts on Burma by Shway Yoe. Dover republished this book a few years ago.

◆ Winstedt, Richard. *A History of Malaya.* Kuala Lumpur: Marican & Sons, 1982. A classic, but with a rather stuffy introduction. Widely available in the country.

THE PHILIPPINES

Diego Gutieres, first Pilot who went to the
Phillippinas, reports of many strange things:
If there bee any Paradise upon earth, it is in that
countrey, and addeth, that sitting under a tree, you
shal have such sweet smells, with such great content
and pleasure, that you shall remember nothing,
neither wife, nor children, nor have any kinde of
appetite to eate nor drinke.

—Henry Hawks (1572),
Navigations of English Nations

When I wish to be misinformed about a country,
I ask a man who has lived there thirty years.

—Lord Palmerston,
The Imperial Idea

Three hundred years in the convent and fifty years
in Hollywood.

—Anonymous

INTRODUCTION

The Philippines is the undiscovered paradise of Southeast Asia. Blessed with over 7,000 sun-drenched islands, this tropical wonderland has just about everything needed for a superb vacation: exquisite white-sand beaches fringed with gently swaying palm trees, unparalleled scuba diving, volcanos for mountaineers, classic baroque cathedrals, vast expanses of verdant ricefields, outstanding nightlife, and the most enthusiastic festivals in Asia. The Philippines is also an outstanding travel bargain since it offers some of the region's lowest prices for accommodation, food, and transportation. With all this, you might expect the country to be crowded with visitors and overrun with tour groups. Surprisingly, most of the country remains virtually untouched by mass tourism, giving adventurous travelers the opportunity to easily get off the beaten track.

But what really separates the Philippines from the rest of Asia is the people, whose warmth and enthusiasm are legendary throughout the East. Seldom will you meet such hospitable people—so ready to smile, joke, laugh, and make friends with Western visitors. Perhaps because of their long association with Spain, Filipinos are emotional and passionate about life in a way that seems more Latin than Asian. And because of their American ties, communication is easy since most Filipinos speak English, whether American slang or some home-grown pidgin. They're also a talented race of people. Music fans will be happy to learn that Filipinos, for reasons endlessly debated, are unquestionably Asia's most gifted singers, musicians, dancers, and entertainers. If you believe that the most important travel experience is to make friends and learn about people, rather than just tour temples and museums, then the Philippines is your country. Despite the extra airfare and a Westernized culture that makes the islands less exotic than other Asian destinations, those who take the time to discover the Philippines often consider it their favorite country in Southeast Asia.

ACTIVITIES

Beaches

Beaches are the number-one attraction in the Philippines. The possibilities are nearly endless—the country boasts a coastline twice the length of the United States's and dozens of

PHILIPPINES

PHILIPPINE SEA

SOUTH CHINA SEA

CAPE BOJEADOR
LAOAG
VIGAN
TUGUEGARAO
SAGADA
BONTOC
BANAUE
BAYOMBONG
SAN FERNANDO
BAUANG
BAGUIO
LINGAYEN
100 ISLANDS
ANGELES
OLONGAPO
LUZON
MANILA
LAKE TAAL
BATANGAS
LOS BANOS
DAET
NAGA
IRIGA
LEGASPI
CATANDUANES I.
CATARMAN
CATBALOGAN
ALLEN
MASBATE
ROMBLON I.
TABLAS
MARINDUQUE
PUERTA GALERA
CALAPAN
MINDORO
ROXAS

© MOON PUBLICATIONS, INC.

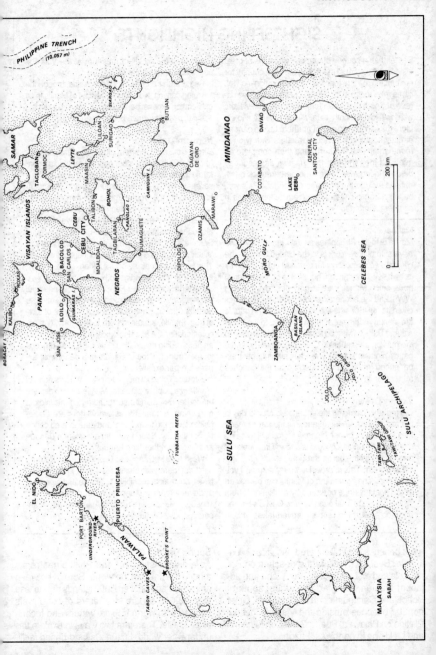

SIGHTSEEING HIGHLIGHTS

Rather than a country of monumental ruins or great historical attractions, the Philippines is a country for sunbathing, hiking, nightlife, and relaxation—a welcome relief to travelers burned out on an endless parade of Southeast Asian temples. First-time visitors with less than a month usually fly into Manila and explore the hilltribe regions of northern Luzon or head directly south to a beach. Travelers with two full months can see the north and then complete an overland loop through the Visayas as described below. Recommended off-the-beaten-track destinations include the beaches of northern Palawan, beautiful Camiguin Island, and remote tribal areas in southern Mindanao.

Manila

Manila is to the Philippines as the famed *New Yorker* version of New York is to the United States—the country's ecopolitical center distorted out of shape by its own self-importance. There's little of great interest here, since Manila was largely destroyed during WW II and the economic slump of recent years has taken its toll. Sunsets are stunning, and the people are friendly, but major sights are limited to the Malacañang Palace (Marcos's former digs, now open to the public), an elaborate Chinese cemetery, and a heady nightlife scene. The Philippines is best experienced in the countryside and on the beaches rather than in the cities.

Vicinity Of Manila

Corregidor: Guarding the entrance to Manila Bay is the rock where American and Filipino forces made their last stand against Japanese forces. Now being restored, the jungle-covered island will intrigue anyone moved by the heroic struggle.

Lake Taal: This impressive crater lake and volcanic cone one hour south of Manila can be viewed from Tagaytay ridge or toured by private boat from Talisay. Visits to Taal often include Cavite's historic bamboo organ, the relaxing seven lakes of San Pablo, and an excellent museum at the Villa Escudero coconut plantation.

Pagsanjan Falls: Running the rapids through the towering canyon two hours southeast of Manila is an exhilarating experience. Dozens of movies, including *Apocalypse Now,* have been filmed here.

Northern Luzon

Circle Route: Aside from along the beaches, perhaps the Philippines' most popular route is a counterclockwise circuit through northern Luzon. This seven- to 14-day journey through spectacular countryside visits the world-famous rice terraces at Banaue, limestone caves near the isolated village of Sagada, and a magnificent highway which winds along the mountain ridges from Bontoc to Baguio. Banaue's ancient manmade rice terraces have justifiably been ranked among the wonders of the world. This is also a great region for hiking, photography, and learning about indigenous hilltribes.

Sagada: One of the Philippines' most peaceful mountain towns sits in a limestone valley 30 minutes north of Bontoc. Sagada takes two full days of travel from Manila, but the superb topography, fine accommodations, and ethnological interests make this an outstanding destination. The rugged all-day bus journey from Bontoc to Baguio is a panoramic experience *par excellence.*

Baguio: This cool mountain city five hours north of Manila is a popular place for Manileanos to escape the lowland heat. The surrounding countryside is refreshing, but most Western visitors are disappointed with the traffic jams and deteriorated condition of the city. Spend your time exploring Banaue and Sagada rather than Baguio.

West Coast Beaches: Beaches near Bauang can't compare with those elsewhere in the Philippines, but their accessibility to Manila and high level of development will appeal to tourists on a tight schedule. Hundred Islands on Alaminos Bay is another popular destination.

great beaches both discovered and virtually unknown. Best bets include the beaches on Boracay Island just north of Panay, Cebu and adjacent Mactan, Panglao Island just south of Bohol, and Camiguin north of Mindanao. Other popular beaches outside the Visayas include El Nido on Palawan, Puerto Galera on Mindoro, and La Union in northwest Luzon.

Scuba Diving

As a dive destination, the Philippines ranks among the finest in the world. Spread between an archipelago of over 7,000 islands are no less than 28,000 square kilometers of coral reefs blessed with warm tropical waters and technicolor sealife. There are two ways to explore this underwater world. Luxurious land-based facili-

SIGHTSEEING HIGHLIGHTS

Southern Luzon

Legaspi and Mt. Mayon: Legaspi, gateway to the south, is a bustling town in the shadow of Mt. Mayon, the world's most perfectly formed volcanic cone, which unexpectedly erupted in 1993, killing over 60 Filipinos who were living on the slopes of the volcano. The area also offers hot thermal springs and the excellent beach at Rizal.

Other Volcanos: Mayon is the most famous of all Philippine peaks, but mountaineers can also challenge themselves on Mt. Isarog near Naga, Mt. Iriga a few kilometers to the south, and beautiful Bulusan in Sorsogon Province. The most infamous—and nonclimbable—volcano is Mt. Pinatubo, which erupted in June 1991 and forced the closure of American-run Clark Air Force Base.

Other Islands

Bohol: One of the prettiest but least visited islands in the Visayas is known for outstanding Spanish churches, crystalline beaches on nearby Panglao Island, and the eerie geological formations known as the Chocolate Hills. Travel logistics make Bohol an easy side trip from Cebu.

Boracay: The spectacular expanse of crystalline sand, clear waters, and swaying coconut palms have deservedly made Boracay the most famous beach resort in the Philippines. Facilities range from simple nipa-palm bungalows to first-class resorts with air-conditioned chalets, windsurfing, sailing, and entertainment from sunsets to folk music.

Cebu: Cebu City, economic and cultural hub of the Visayan Islands, is a convenient base for exploring the beaches, churches, and diving areas of the central Philippines. Visitors short on time can fly directly to Cebu and make side trips to Bohol, the nearby beaches on Mactan and Moalboal, and then continue west across Negros and Panay to Boracay. Cebu City has good restaurants, great festivals, lively nightlife, and historical attractions connected with the Spanish era.

Mindanao: Travelers not discouraged by the remoteness and political disruptions of Mindanao will discover Muslim townships little changed in generations, some of the country's last remaining stands of tropical forests, and isolated pockets of tribal culture. Camiguin, north of Cagayan de Oro, is a superb island with great beaches and few tourists. Lake Sebu, west of General Santos City in southern Mindanao, is the idyllic homeland of the traditional T'boli people. Islamic lifestyles continue near Marawi City and in the Sulu Archipelago. Davao and "exotic" Zamboanga are modern towns with little of charm or interest.

Mindoro: Puerto Galera on Mindoro Island is an immensely popular beach resort only five hours from Manila. Although haphazard development has ruined some of the region, scuba diving remains outstanding and the more remote beaches are still inviting.

Negros: Top draws are the ancient steam trains that haul cane on sugar plantations near Bacolod. Train enthusiasts come from all over the world to photograph and ride the rare German and British steamers.

Palawan: Long considered the final frontier of the Philippines, Palawan in recent years has been attracting increasing number of travelers who want to get off the beaten track and enjoy some of the best beaches and diving in the country. Highlights include topographic wonders near Puerto Princesa, underground caves near Port Barton, anthropological discoveries at Tabon, and the spectacular scuba diving at El Nido. Travel conditions remain primitive, but accommodations and restaurants are plentiful and cheap.

Panay: Spanish churches modified with Filipino designs are the highlights of Iloilo, capital of Panay. Other draws include the private and posh island resort of Sicogon and the annual Ati Atihan festival in Kalibo.

Samar and Leyte: Waterfalls and historical ties to WW II are the main attractions here. Frequent interisland buses and boats connect Samar and Leyte with Luzon and the lower Visayas.

---

ties have been established at several resorts, including La Union and Batangas on Luzon, Puerto Galera on Mindoro Island, Moalboal and Badian Island on Cebu, Panglao Island south of Bohol, and El Nido at the north end of Palawan.

More adventurous divers might prefer one of several specialized dive boats which provide accommodations and unlimited air supply while cruising from one dive location to another. Tours can be arranged through dive shops in Manila or with international dive organizations listed in the Introduction. A PADI, NAUI, or other C card is required. Certification programs have been established at most major dive areas. Rates are comparable to those of other dive destinations in the world. An excellent brochure entitled *Philippines,*

MANILA'S CLIMATE

	Jan.	Feb.	March	April	May	June	July	Aug.	Sept.	Oct.	Nov.	Dec.
Avg. Maximum C	29°	31°	33°	34°	33°	33°	31°	31°	31°	31°	30°	29°
Avg. Maximum F	84°	88°	92°	94°	92°	92°	88°	88°	88°	88°	86°	84°
Rainy Days	6	3	4	4	12	17	24	23	22	19	14	11

A Diver's Paradise, with a complete description of dive sites, resorts, shops, and licensed dive-boat operators, is available from the Philippine Convention and Visitors Corporation.

Mountain Climbing

Another natural attraction of the Philippines is the string of volcanic peaks spread across the archipelago. Mount Mayon (2,646 meters), considered the world's most perfectly formed cone, is an inspiring but dangerous climb best left to experienced mountaineers. Mayon's 1993 eruption killed over 60 residents, and for the foreseeable future, no one is allowed near the volatile crater. On the other hand, Mt. Makiling (1,144 meters), near Los Banos south of Manila, is an easy climb along well-marked trails.

Southern Luzon has three other volcanos which can be climbed by almost anyone in good physical condition. The four- to five-day climb to the summit of Mt. Apo (2,953 meters) near Davao City passes pools of bubbling mud, mountain ponds, waterfalls, and hot springs. Other mountains hiked on a regular basis include Kanlaon (2,465 meters) on Negros and Pulog (2,930 meters) in northern Luzon. Further information can be obtained from the Manila Tourist Office and from regional park headquarters.

Routes

Visitors with limited time should fly directly from Manila to the beach or island of their choice. Travelers with more time (six to eight weeks) might take a more leisurely approach with an overland journey through northern Luzon and then around the central Visayan Islands. The trip can be done in either direction starting from, and with a return to, Manila, with a combination of boats and public buses. The clockwise route first visits Legaspi and Mt. Mayon in southern Luzon before continuing south through Samar and Leyte to Cebu. Bohol can be toured

between Leyte and Cebu or as an easy backtrack from Cebu. The journey continues west across Negros and Panay to Boracay. Then it's north to Mindoro and the beaches at Puerto Galera before returning to Manila. More travel details under "Islands to the South."

THE ENVIRONMENT

Surrounded by the Philippine Sea to the east, the South China Sea to the west, and the Sulawesi Sea to the south, the 7,109 islands of the Philippines spill like a diamond necklace from northern Batanes to the Sulu Archipelago. This widely scattered archipelago is divided into four major groups. The largest and most important is Luzon, home to Tagalog-speaking Filipinos and site of Manila. The best beaches and diving are found in the Visayas, the string of islands situated between Luzon and Mindanao. To the south is the rarely visited but culturally rich island of Mindanao. To the west is snakelike Palawan, a remote destination almost a world unto itself.

Problems In Paradise

The rich volcanic soil and heavy rainfall of the Philippines have blessed it with an exotic and varied plant life, from flowering plants to hardwoods such as the Philippine mahogany. At one time, most of the country was covered with mangrove swamps and tropical forests filled with spectacular wildlife. But unchecked population growth and reckless logging have seriously depleted the once-plentiful tropical forests and killed most of the wildlife. Resource specialists chart a staggering rate of destruction. When independence was achieved in 1946, over 30 million hectares—almost three-quarters of the land—was covered with tropical hardwoods and drier *molave* forests. Last year it stood at less than five million hectares. Calling it among the highest rates of deforestation in the world, the Asian Development Bank estimates that at present levels the Philippines will be completely stripped bare in less than two decades.

The devastation has aroused the passions of both international environmentalists and the local Catholic Church, which recently ranked it as a more serious threat than political instability and economic stagnation. Loggers, of course, bear much of the blame, but deforestation is mostly due to skyrocketing population growth and destructive slash-and-burn farming techniques of the landless poor. Solutions have been proposed by environmental groups such as the World Wildlife Fund and Manila-based Haribon Foundation, but unless action is quickly taken the outlook for the Filipino environment is grim.

Nature On The Rampage

After a series of almost unbelievable natural disasters, the citizens of the Philippines must be wondering what Mother Nature has against their country.

The first disaster to make international headlines was the Baguio earthquake of July 1990, which killed hundreds and almost completely destroyed the local economy. Baguio is still recovering.

The June 1991 eruption of Mt. Pinatubo, considered the most devastating volcanic explosion of the 20th century, followed. After 600 years of lying dormant, Pinatubo roared to life, creating tremendous tidal waves of volcanic ash and mud that killed almost 800 people and forced over half a million to flee the region. The massive destruction caused Clark Air Force Base to close and nearby Subic Naval Base—also covered with ash—to be returned to the Philippine government in Nov. 1992.

In Feb. 1992 an earthquake caused widespread damage on Bohol; a late-1992 flash flood in southern Leyte almost wiped out an entire town.

Just when Filipinos were catching their breath, Mt. Mayon in southern Luzon unexpectedly erupted in early 1993, killing over 60 people farming the volcano's slopes. Mt. Mayon has been declared off-limits to Western tourists, although volcano aficionados are flocking to the nearby town of Legaspi to await further developments.

Climate

The Philippines is a tropical land with high temperatures and extreme humidity along with heavy rainfall during the summer monsoons. Temperature varies with altitude but not latitude; if it's hot in Zamboanga it will be just as uncomfortable in Manila. The country has three seasons. Winter months from November through February are hot and dry but pleasant. The extraordinarily hot summer months from March through June can be devastating to first-time visitors. Travel during the rainy season from June to October is difficult but enjoyable because of the green landscapes and cooler temperatures. Rainfall and typhoons hit the east coast during the summer months. Best time to visit the Philippines is during the dry and slightly cooler period from November to April.

HISTORY

Filipino history is unique in Asia. Early inhabitants of the archipelago were dark-skinned Negritos and brown-skinned Malays who had emigrated across land bridges from Indonesia and mainland Southeast Asia. Chinese, Indian, and Arab traders began arriving in large numbers sometime after A.D. 1000. Animism, the native religion of the lowland agriculturalists, fell in the 14th century to Islam, which arrived from Brunei and quickly spread north to Manila. Though the pre-Hispanic Philippines served as an important trading crossroads for Chinese and Indonesian merchants, it failed to develop into a unified nation with a sense of insular cohesion. Life remained loosely organized around tribal villages (*barangays*) ruled by hereditary chieftains (*datus*) who had rejected the Hindu and Buddhist cultural influences that dominated the balance of Southeast Asia. Expansive empires were never constructed; sophisticated economies never developed; great heroes and political leaders never rose to unify the vast archipelago.

This lack of an evocative past prior to the arrival of the Spanish is of great significance to modern Filipino history. Filipino scholars searching for their cultural identity are often frustrated by historical records which seem scant when compared to the other countries of Southeast Asia. The paucity of data has inspired some historians to romanticize the past and create false legends about mythological characters. More importantly, the lack of history has sapped national self-confidence and weakened the search for political unity.

All this was exacerbated by the arrival of Spanish *conquistadores* and American colonialists who brought with them their Western religion, artforms, political models, and value systems. This long and destructive period of foreign rule—the so-called 300 years in a Spanish convent and 50 years in Hollywood—has created an Asian contradiction: the Philippines, gateway to Asia, is essentially a highly Westernized country populated by a Christian majority that speaks English.

Spanish Rule

Filipino history, at least in written form, begins with the arrival of Ferdinand Magellan in 1521. Assigned by the Spanish Crown to discover a western route to the Spice Islands of Indonesia, the Portuguese explorer instead stumbled across the Philippines, where he befriended the raja of Cebu and converted hundreds of islanders to the Spanish faith. Considering his great feats of exploration and diplomacy, it is ironic that Magellan foolishly got involved in tribal politics and was killed by Lapu Lapu, a petty chieftain now immortalized as the first Filipino to resist foreign rule. Magellan's ship eventually returned to Spain loaded with valuable spices, thereby recovering the expense of the three-year expedition and successfully completing the first circumnavigation of the world.

Another Spanish explorer, Legaspi, annexed the islands in 1565 and named them "Filipinas" in honor of King Philip of Spain. Legaspi moved his army and capital from Cebu to Manila, where Spanish military and religious power continued to rule for 327 years. Catholic friars proceeded to convert most of the population to Christianity—except for the Muslims of Mindanao and the mountain tribals of northern Luzon. From an economic standpoint, however, the Philippines was a failure. Without revenues from the Sino-Mexican galleon trade—Chinese silks exchanged for Mexican silver via the trading entrepot of Manila—the colony would have collapsed long before the Americans took control in the early 20th century.

The Philippine Revolution

Spain continued to rule the Philippines without serious opposition until the late 19th century, when Filipino leaders began agitating for greater political control. The struggle for independence gained worldwide press in 1872 after several Filipino priests were brazenly executed by the Spanish authorities for leading a small revolt in Cavite. Three Filipinos soon emerged as leaders of the revolution. The most dynamic was Jose Rizal, the Filipino-Chinese national hero who founded the Propaganda Movement and inspired the masses with his passionate poetry. Andres Bonifacio formed the radical Katipunan Society, while Emilio Aguinaldo served as Bonifacio's revolutionary captain. The Spanish made their biggest blunder in 1896 when they publicly executed Rizal after a farcical trial, thereby creating the revolution's first martyr and inadvertently uniting the educated classes (*illustrados*) and the revolutionaries. Inspired by the martyrdom and fiery writings of Rizal, Bonifacio organized armed resistance against Spanish rule but was executed by Aguinaldo during a bitter power struggle. Aguinaldo eventually proved himself a figure of great power but also a ruthless leader who ambushed his rivals and made a long series of grave political blunders. His moment of glory arrived on 12 June 1898, when he unfurled a flag and declared his country a sovereign state. The Philippines had become Asia's first country to declare independence from European colonialism.

American Rule

Filipino independence seemed assured when the Spanish-American War erupted in 1898 and Dewey's warships steamed from Hong Kong to Manila under the war cry, "Remember the *Maine* and to Hell with Spain." But the promise of Filipino statehood proved short-lived. Despite the painful conflict of American democracy and colonial rule, and an American Senate which almost rejected the war prize, the Spanish-American Treaty of Paris ceded the Philippines, Puerto Rico, and Guam to the U.S. in return for $20 million. The Filipinos felt deeply betrayed. Fighting immediately erupted between American troops and Filipino rebels who rejected President McKinley's policy of Manifest Destiny. It was a horrible war in which over 200,000 Filipinos were killed. The revolution sputtered to an end in 1901 when Aguinaldo was captured and most of the educated *illustrados* joined the new government. Under McKinley's policy of benevolent assimilation, American leadership over the next five decades proved itself somewhat more enlightened than Spanish rule. Huge sums were spent on infrastructure and health. Perhaps most significant were the American ideals of political democracy and other less tangible manifestations such as dress, purchasing preferences, and hierarchy of social values. English was introduced as the medium of instruction in an attempt to bind together the disparate linguistic and religious groups. By the time the Americans left five decades later, American cultural imperialism—from language to mass marketing—was inexorably ingrained in Filipino consciousness.

World War II

The American timetable for Filipino independence was disrupted in December 1941, two days after Pearl Harbor, when Japanese forces bombed Clark Air Base and began their fateful march toward Manila. Filipino-American troops under the leadership of General Douglas MacArthur retreated to Corregidor island, where they mounted a valiant but futile last stand. MacArthur subsequently fled to Australia, where he proclaimed "I shall return," while the remaining 80,000 POWs endured the Bataan Death March, a five-day ordeal in which over 10,000 soldiers died from torture, starvation, and beatings. MacArthur fulfilled his promise on 20 October 1944, when he beached at Leyte to begin the reconquest of Luzon. Blinded by their nationalistic fervor, Japanese forces retreated to Manila's historic city of Intramuros and refused to surrender, a tragic decision that cost the lives of over 100,000 Filipino civilians and forced the near-complete destruction of Manila. Although the brutal Japanese occupation was deeply resented by most Filipinos, it also broke prewar colonial bonds and inspired the Filipinos to take their place in the new Asian consciousness.

The Marcos Era

America's colonial experience came to a close on 4 July 1946, when Manuel Roxas, the nation's first president, proclaimed Filipino independence. The ensuing two decades were a traumatic period of mounting political anarchy, economic chaos, and increasing concentration of wealth in the hands of a few. Leftist insurgencies flourished in central Luzon, while Muslim secessionist movements plagued the south. Into this firestorm came Ferdinand Marcos, a brilliant and charismatic lawyer who took the presidency in 1965. Marcos at first enjoyed widespread and genuine popularity as he constructed schools, roads, and telecommunications systems while attempting to deal with the Philippines' chronic social and economic problems. But corruption, lawlessness, and civil disorder worsened.

Legally barred from serving a third term, Marcos declared martial law in 1972, dissolved the congress, and rewrote the constitution. He also jailed hundreds of political opposition leaders, including Benigno Aquino, who had been considered a virtual shoo-in to win the 1973 presidential election. As the new supreme godfather, Marcos proceeded to establish a nation-strangling network of nepotism and cronyism that made his friends and relatives grotesquely rich. His wife Imelda was appointed governor of Manila, with a nonaccountable budget of US$200 million. Her brother became governor of Leyte, Marcos's cousin was made chief of staff of the armed forces, his golfing buddy was awarded control of the nation's largest construction company, and other cronies were given control of the sugar and coconut industries. The level of graft was breathtaking even by generous Filipino standards. By the time Marcos fled the country in 1986, he had become neither the longest-reigning nor the most dictatorial leader in Southeast Asia. He had, instead, become the world's biggest crook: the country was bankrupt, the people's standard of living had collapsed, and Marcos had salted away an estimated US$10 *billion* in Swiss bank accounts.

The Aquino Era

Political opposition to the Marcos regime galvanized after Benigno Aquino was assassinated by the Philippine military in August 1983. General Fabian Ver, a close friend and trusted ally of Marcos, was arrested and interrogated during a carefully staged ten-month trial which ended with the conviction of a lone dead gunman. The country exploded. Threatened by widespread political demonstrations, Marcos suddenly called for "snap" presidential elections to settle the question of national leadership. Benigno's widow, Corazon Aquino, a political neophyte with little experience and an election machinery that resembled a Filipino Woodstock, disproved the maxim that Filipinos lack the willpower to depose evil dictators. Despite widespread vote buying, intimidation by goons, and voter disenfranchisement that characterized the dirtiest election in Philippine history, Marcos lost the referendum and was forced to flee the country in February 1986. Left behind were his dialysis machines, Ouija boards, half-eaten tins of caviar, a collection of crystals and power pyramids, and a basement filled with Imelda's gowns, furs, and 3,000 pairs of shoes including disco sprinters equipped with rechargeable lights in the heels. With People Power versus the Forces of Evil as the theme, Marcos was the loser in a stunning victory that set off political reform throughout the rest of Asia.

GOVERNMENT

The Philippines is a constitutional republic with a presidency and a National Assembly comprised of a House of Representatives and a Senate. An extraordinarily complex constitution, which passed a few years ago, limits the president to a term of six years (whether the president can run for a second term still seems unclear), restricts presidential power, guarantees human rights, and attempts to legislate morality with restrictions on birth control and abortion. Corazon Conjuangco Aquino officially claimed the presidency by plebiscite in May 1987. She hails from a wealthy and aristocratic Filipino-Chinese family which controls Hacienda Luisita, one of the country's largest sugar estates, located in Tarlac north of Manila.

Aquino's miracle, engineered by the Filipino people and military forces commanded by Ramos, was a magical moment in Philippine history. But the housewife from Tarlac soon discovered that political honeymoons are difficult to sustain. Democracy was restored and a painfully long-winded "freedom" constitution passed, but economic problems centered on land reform and massive foreign debt continued to pile up. Marcos's vast fortune has eluded the Pres-

idential Commission on Good Government, and the anticipated flood of post-revolution foreign aid and investment has slowed to a trickle. Aquino has promised to end human-rights violations, but anticommunist vigilante groups and military death squads have led to an upsurge in abuses and political killings known as "salvagings." The country also remains divided by linguistics, religion, and the widening gap between rich and poor.

Although declining, another threat to national survival is the communist insurgency, which continues to smolder throughout the archipelago. An estimated 10,000 full-time members of the New People's Army (NPA), operating in 63 of the country's 73 provinces, continue to fight for socialism, the dissolution of sugar estates, nationalization of major industries, and land reform. Widespread poverty and sophisticated propaganda have kept them strong, but their momentum has slowed because of the arrest of top-level NPA officers. Other factors are the seizure of financial documents which revealed their funding sources, and a new military strategy which stresses winning the people's hearts rather than waging a purely battleground campaign. The NPA poses few problems for travelers to the Philippines.

The Ramos Era

On 11 May 1992, democratic elections brought new national leadership under the helm of Fidel Ramos, the former military leader who received critical endorsement from Corazon Aquino. In accepting President Ramos, Filipinos voted soundly against Marcos crony Eduardo Conjuangco in an obvious vote against authoritarianism. They voted strongly against Ramon Mitra, in a demonstration against the politics of patronage which dominates Philippine society, but voted in large numbers for antigraft crusader Miriam Santiago as they registered their contempt for corrupt public officials. The litany of losers perhaps told more about contemporary Filipino society than the election of a bespectacled West Point graduate who co-led the February 1986 revolt.

President Ramos won't find it easy. The Philippine government is almost broke and must spend 40% of its annual budget to finance its massive debt, not to mention dealing with ongoing power shortages and natural disasters such as droughts and the devastating eruption of Mt. Pinatubo.

Ramos, however, brings the possibility of great change to the Philippines. Ramos is a Protestant who seems serious about family planning and population control, pressing issues for a country with a 60% poverty rate, and he seems determined to finally raise tax rates for the wealthy elite. Ramos's three-tiered cabinet of military leaders, corporate technocrats, and professional politicians seems determined to pull the Philippines out of its economic malaise and return it to the legendary levels of the 1950s, when it was at the same economic level as Japan and Taiwan. Time will tell.

ECONOMY

News on the Filipino economy has improved in recent years. With the fall of Marcos and increased investments from local and foreign entrepreneurs, a sense of confidence has returned to the country. The economy is now growing at six to eight percent, a welcome reverse from the declining figures of the early '80s. Untapped potential has encouraged a massive influx of Taiwanese and Hong Kong capital. But the recovery faces serious obstacles. A World Bank report claims that over 30 million of the country's 60 million live in absolute poverty and that the situation has worsened during the past three decades. Among ASEAN nations, the Philippines has the highest level of poverty and the lowest calorie supply per capita. Furthermore, real wages have steadily dropped since 1960 and almost 60% of the population is either under- or unemployed. It is painfully obvious to even the most casual traveler that little of the urban economic recovery has filtered down to the impoverished *barrios*. These dismal statistics are especially discouraging since the Philippines lies within one of the most economically dynamic regions in the world. The country was once, in fact, the shining star of Southeast Asia, boasting the region's highest growth rates from 1950 to 1960. By 1980 it had fallen to dead last.

What went wrong? The World Bank reports that on a macroeconomic level, more than 50% of the gross national product is wasted in a hopeless attempt to reduce a staggering foreign debt of almost US$30 billion. On a micro-economic level are the factors of declining agricultural productivity, lack of crop diversity, and unequal ownership of basic assets. The country has long relied on a narrow base of commodity exports such as sugar, coconuts, minerals, and forest products. Even today, almost 70% of the population makes its living from agriculture, 10 million from sugar, and an estimated 20 million from coconuts. The collapse of world sugar prices and the fall in coconut productivity due to poor crop nutrition and an increasing number of senile trees have had a devastating effect on Filipino farmers. Unequal distribution of land and income is another problem. Studies show that moneyed mestizos of Spanish-Filipino or Chinese-Filipino blood make up less than 20% of the population but earn over 50% of the nation's total income. A Manila University study once claimed that most of the Filipino economy is controlled by a mere 60 mestizo families. And despite decades of land reform, land ownership patterns remain badly skewed. The Philippines has Asia's highest percentage of landless tenant farmers and the situation is getting worse; landless agriculturalists have grown from 10% in the '50s to an estimated 30-35% today. Land reform—by far the most controversial and emotional subject in the country—is getting another push under Ramos, but few experts believe agrarian reform will improve productivity or encourage the agricultural diversification that the country so desperately needs.

But the country's most pressing problem is the frightening population explosion. Filipinos have increased from 19 million in 1948 to over 60 million today. The population will soar past 100 million in another 25 years. This unchecked growth devastates the environment, threatens political stability, and keeps most Filipinos mired in absolute poverty. Simply no more land is left for population growth. Farmland population density is already higher than in Indonesia and nearly twice that of Thailand. Stopgap measures have been proposed by the World Bank to try to slow the annual rate of growth from the current 2.4-2.8% to 2% by the year 2000, but birth control and abortion are controversial subjects in the staunchly Catholic Philippines. The fact remains that unless strong action is quickly taken, all economic gains will simply be absorbed by the rapidly growing population.

FILIPINO CUSTOMS

Something of a false veneer lies over the people and culture of the Philippines. Things seem so familiar that many Western visitors are easily lulled into misguided complacency, thinking that what has been borrowed from the West has been absorbed into the inner core of Filipino society. This is a mistake. Filipino customs and beliefs are surprisingly different from Western values. The following might help avoid misunderstandings while traveling around the country.

Body Talk: Filipinos are masters at cleverly using their eyes, lips, and hands to convey a wide range of messages. Eyebrow talk is perhaps the most obvious. Raised eyebrows and a smile indicate a silent "hello" or "yes" to your question. Fixed, hard eye contact between males is an aggressive gesture best avoided. Ladies often purse their lips and nod their heads to indicate direction. The proper method to summon somebody is with a downward wave, not with a skyward wave and call. If the waiter doesn't respond, a soft *psssst* will do the trick.

Language: Filipinos place great emphasis on polite language and gentle conversation. They also desire to keep peace and please Western visitors. Since admitting ignorance to a question brings shame, most Filipinos instead answer "yes" or venture their best guesses. Be forewarned that the Filipino "yes" can mean "yes," "maybe," "no," "OK," or "I don't know," depending on the spirit in which it was given. Eu-

phemism is often used to maintain smooth interpersonal relations. Voice tone is always soft and gentle. Direct questions should be avoided. Before asking for directions, it would be polite to ask, "Excuse me, but may I ask you a question?" Filipinos, surprisingly, can also be blunt. Inquiries about your occupation, income, size of family, and how much you paid for your hotel room and camera are used to evaluate your social standing as well as just to make friendly conversation. No harm intended.

Nicknames: Most Filipinos have Spanish-sounding first and surnames. These Hispanic titles were only adopted in 1849 after a decree issued by the Spanish governor forced all Filipinos to take a Western surname for bureaucratic reasons. And yet, when you ask for somebody's name, it's just as likely to be a nickname such as Peachy, Ding Dong, Tingles, Pinky, Toytoy, or Ballsy. Filipinos love nicknames since they make people feel closer and add a degree of informality.

Hiya: Filipino values, often a marriage of Western values borrowed from Catholicism and Eastern values shared by other Southeast Asian peoples, are typified by *hiya,* the Tagalog term for "shame." Perhaps the most powerful glue of Filipino society, the desire to obey the rules of society and not rock the boat keeps most Filipinos from showing anger or displeasure. Western visitors should control their emotions and keep a sense of *hiya.*

THE PEOPLE

The Filipinos

And now for some more encouraging news. What separates the Philippines from the rest of Southeast Asia is the people—undisputedly the most charming, enthusiastic, and open in Asia. It might take years to make friends with a Chinese, but the Filipino becomes a close partner within minutes. Their hospitality is direct and honest, their smiles are warm and spontaneous. And, as you will soon notice on arrival in Manila, Filipinos are easy to relate to since most speak some English, attend Christian churches, and follow Western music and fashion trends as closely as anyone in the world.

Filipinos are a unified race of people racially related to Malaysians and Indonesians. To this

Malay stock has been added rich transfusions of Chinese, Indian, Spanish, and American blood, producing offspring such as Filipino-Spanish creoles and Filipino-Chinese mestizos. It's been a good marriage; racial tensions are rare. Filipinos are sometimes classified into 10 major cultural groups based on either language or religion. Eight of the nine groups are Christians who differ little except for their dialects. Filipinos also have their own peculiar set of strengths and weaknesses as described recently in a public report called the "Moral Recovery Program." It's an interesting list. Weaknesses were given as a lack of discipline, initiative, self-analysis, and self-reflection, plus extreme personalism, fatalism (*bahalana*), and the *kanya-kanya* (blame somebody else) syndrome. Their strengths were listed as their sensitivity to people's feelings, sense of humor and flexibility, strong family loy-

FILIPINO CUSTOMS

Amor Propio: Closely tied to the notion of "shame" is the Oriental notion of "face," or *amor propio*, literally "love of self." There are endless ways to lose face: arguing, being publically criticized, performing degrading labor, or not knowing the answer to a question. Preserving self-esteem is often why Filipinos just smile to your strange questions; that's better than admitting ignorance. Publicly criticizing or arguing with a Filipino should be avoided since this is a direct attack on his *amor propio*. Many Filipino males will fight for the preservation of their pride and *amor propio*.

Pakikisama: Filipinos strongly believe in sharing, camaraderie, and the ability to get along with others. Fitting in is more important than standing out. *Pakikisama* is also the reason why Filipinos spontaneously invite strangers in for dinner, quickly reach for the check in restaurants, and are willing to loan almost anything to anybody with little hope of recovery. It's also why they never publicly disagree with each other and think it's strange that Westerners travel alone. "Where is your companion?"—the constant inquiry to solo travelers—really means "What on earth did you do to deserve such an awful fate?"

Utan Na Loob: Reciprocal relationships and the need to repay debts of gratitude are other important components to Filipino society. Many relationships begin with a small gift, which must be repaid later with interest. The cycle escalates for a period of years or generations until a highly complex web of interdependencies has been created. Both Marcos and Aquino used *utan na loob* to create their political dynasties. Wealthy industrialists are often connected through this cycle. Western travelers who accept Filipino generosity also accept the principle of repayment.

Compadrazco: The Roman Catholic concept of standing as godfather to a child during baptism is another important element in Filipino life. This ritual creates powerful bonds of obligation not only between godfather and godchild but also between godfather and the child's parents. Since godfathers often provide financial support, jobs, and upward social mobility to their godchildren, parents will search out their wealthiest friend or relative to accept this religious obligation. Western visitors are sometimes invited to act as godfathers, but obligations should be carefully considered.

---

alties, and the ability to survive daily hardships. Whatever the truth of these findings, Filipinos certainly are a fascinating race of people.

The Chinese

Chinese and Filipino-Chinese mestizos form the single most influential racial group in the Philippines. It is hard to overstate their contributions to the history of the country. Chinese traders were active in the archipelago well before the arrival of Islam from Brunei and Christianity from Spain. Chinese merchants later dominated the immensely lucrative Spanish galleon trade, while Chinese craftsmen and artisans constructed most of Manila's churches, roads, and homes. Although periodically massacred or expelled by the Spanish, who feared their economic acumen, the Chinese have survived to gain almost complete control of the Filipino economy through hard work, intelligence, personal sacrifice, and the acceptance of extraordinarily thin profit margins. Many have married Filipino women. Their offspring, mixed-blood mestizos, now dominate the economy,

in place of the once-powerful Filipino-Spanish families. Today they are involved in virtually every major segment of the economy, from small *sari sari* stores to international mining and manufacturing consortiums.

However, not everything is fine in the Filipino-Chinese community. As elsewhere in Southeast Asia, there is the problem of Chinese assimilation into local society. While many Chinese have attempted to please the locals by adopting Filipino surnames and converting to Christianity, others continue to extol their cultural superiority by keeping their Chineseness through dress codes, private schools, newspapers, and other lifestyle choices. Interpreted by many as a rejection of Filipino culture, this nonconformity has nurtured strong anti-Sinitic feelings among less fortunate Filipinos. Some call them the Jews of Asia, an impolite but perhaps valid comparison based on Chinese socioreligious differences and economic successes in the face of government-sanctioned persecution and discrimination. It was, in fact, only in 1975 that Marcos

LANGUAGE

Over 70 dialects and 11 major languages are spoken throughout the Philippines. These include Tagalog, based on the Malay language and spoken by over 10 million residents of central Luzon, and the Cebuano language spoken by almost 20 million Visayans. Other languages include Ilocano spoken in northwest Luzon, Bicolano in southern Luzon, Pangasinese in northwestern Luzon, and Hiligaynon in Panay and eastern Negros. The national language is Pilipino, a variation of Tagalog, although English continues to serve as the lingua franca of the archipelago. This odd situation is a legacy of American rule, when foreign educators established their language as the medium of instruction in all public schools. Today, Pilipino is being promoted over English for reasons of national pride, but most Filipinos continue to speak a heady melange of English, Pilipino, a regional dialect, and Taglish, a bizarre mixture of Tagalog and American slang. The universality of English ensures that basic conversations are possible with almost everybody from college students to loin-clothed tribespeople.

Of course, peeling off a few phrases of Tagalog or Pilipino will help to establish your rapport and impress your hosts. It also helps save money. The language is complex in structure but easy to speak since most words are pronounced exactly as spelled. Important exceptions are consonants spoken with a Spanish inflection (Jose is pronounced as Ho-say), stretched out double consonants (ng is nang), double vowels pronounced as two syllables (Lake Taal is Lake Ta-al, maalam is ma-alam), and the interchangeability of F and P (as in Pilipino and Filipino). A few useful words and phrases:

Conversation

greetings	mabuhay
good morning	magandang umaga po
good evening	magandang gabi po
goodbye	paalam na po
please/thank you	paki/salamat po
you're welcome	wala pong anuman
yes/no	oo/hindi
How are you?	Kumusta po sila?
What is your name?	Anong pangalan mo?
How old are you?	Ilang taon ka na?
Where do you live?	Saan po kayo nakatira?
Where are you from?	Taga saan ka?
What is your job?	Anong tarbaho mo?
How much do you make?	Magkano ang iyong suweldo?
Are you married?	May asawa ka ba?
How many children?	Ilan ang anak mo?
You are beautiful!	Maganda ka!
I love you.	Mahal kita.
Where are you going?	Saan ka pupunta?
I am going to	upunta ako sa ...
no problem	walang problema
never mind	hindi bale

Bargaining

do you have ...?	meron ba kayong ...?
Where is a cheap hotel?	Saan may murang hotel?
How much is this?	Magkano ito?
too expensive!	masyadong mahal!
anything cheaper?	mayroon bang mas mura?
Where is my change?	Nasaan ang sukli ko?
It doesn't matter	Bahalana.

Numbers

1, 2, 3	isa, dalawa, tatlo
4, 5, 6	apat, lima, anim
7, 8, 9, 10	pito, walo, siyam, sampu
11, 12	labing isa, labing dalawa
20, 30	dalawampu, tatlumpu
40, 50	apatnapu, limampu
100, 1000	isang daan, isanglibo

Getting Around

How do I get to ...?	Paano ang pagpunta sa ...?
Where is the bus stop?	Saan ang hintayan ng bus?
Which bus is for Manila?	Aling bus ang papuntang Manila?
What town is this?	Anong bayan ito?
I want to go to Manila.	Gusto kong pumunta sa Manila.
I need ...	kailangan ko ng ...
bathroom	banyo
bus station	istasyon ng bus
police station	istasyon ng polise
village/town/city	barrio/bayan/lungsod
hill/mountain	burol/bundok

eased the naturalization criteria and made it possible for the Chinese to obtain Filipino citizenship. Despite this offer, it is estimated that today only 40% of the nation's 2.1 million Chinese have opted for naturalization.

Muslims

The Philippines' only large non-Christian Malay group is the Muslims who live throughout southern Mindanao and the Sulu Archipelago. Followers of Islam are divided into five major and five minor subgroups based on language and cultural background. All have resisted being assimilated into the Philippine nation, whether under Spanish, American, or Filipino control. The latest skirmish was the Muslim secessionist war, which engulfed Mindanao from 1973 to 1979. After claiming at least 50,000 lives and involving two-thirds of the Filipino army, an uneasy truce was arranged between the central government and the Moro National Liberation Front. Despite a large degree of self-rule, however, Muslims remain an unsatisfied group that resents the political and economic domination of the Christian majority.

Cultural Minorities

Perhaps the most colorful and fascinating groups in the Philippines are the designated cultural minorities who inhabit the mountainous interiors and rainforests of many Filipino islands. Most practice slash-and-burn or wet-rice cultivation and follow a syncretic religion which mixes elements of animism and Christianity. Although long considered by the Filipinos as dangerous and primitive, today they are respected for their ethnic diversity and encouraged to maintain their distinctive lifestyles. The most famous groups are the tribespeoples who live among the rice terraces of northern Luzon near Banaue, Bontoc, and Sagada. Most are now quite Westernized, preferring blue jeans to loincloths and aluminum roofs to thatched, but enough traditional culture and natural beauty remain to make this an outstanding travel destination. More authentic and less Westernized tribes are found in interior Mindoro, southern Mindanao, and Palawan. Problems of transportation and accessibility make these difficult journeys, although Lake Sebu in Mindanao has recently been attracting increasing numbers of determined travelers.

SUGGESTED READINGS

- ◆ Karnow, Stanley. *In Our Image: America's Empire in the Philippines.* New York: Random House, 1989. Having covered Asia for 30 years for *Time, Life,* and the *Washington Post,* the gifted author was in a special position to write this copiously detailed yet highly readable political history of the American experience in the Philippines. Karnow also authored *Vietnam: A History,* whose television companion won six Emmys, and a three-part documentary on the Philippines aired on PBS in 1989. Highly recommended.

- ◆ Manchester, William. *American Caesar.* New York: Little, Brown and Company, 1978. An absorbing biography of General Douglas MacArthur, one of America's last epic heroes.

- ◆ Roces, Alfredo and Grace Roces. *Culture Shock.* Singapore: Times Books International, 1985. This lively and highly amusing

guide to Filipino customs will prove indispensable to understanding the country and the people.

- ◆ Simons, Lewis M. *Worth Dying For.* New York: William Morrow, 1987. Simon dissects Aquino's rise and People's Power by analyzing the dynamics of Philippine society including the church, the military, business, and the political left. His sensitive vignettes of the common people give great life to what could have otherwise been another cliché about the forces of good and evil.

- ◆ Steinberg, David Joel. *The Philippines: A Singular and Plural Place.* Colorado: Westview Press, 1982. One of America's leading authorities on the Philippines packs a great deal of insight into this outstanding 150-page book. His chapters on Filipino society, the religious impulse, and the search for a useable past are a superb introduction to the country.

FESTIVALS

Few countries in Southeast Asia offer as many superb festivals as the Philippines. Each year, over 40,000 *barangays*—the smallest political divisions in the archipelago—sponsor fiestas to honor the local patron saints, commemorate historical events, or simply throw a party for friends and relatives. Fiestas are a time for renewal of friendships and communal homecomings, a chance to honor prominent citizens and crown beauty queens, to enjoy a weekend of music, or for religious piety, cockfights, lavish balls, and unparalleled hospitality. Most are small affairs centered in the village square, but others have grown into major events which merit national and even international attention. Whether small or large, all keep the Filipino calendar packed with an endless array of colorful and *enthusiastic* events. Though most festivals revolve around Christianity and therefore run the risk of becoming solemn, Filipinos eagerly add elements of pagan animism, Latin *machismo,* Hollywood glitz, *Star Wars* technology, sexuality, homespun humor, and natural gaiety to the religious pageantry. The results are a stunning riot of color and music with all the solemnity of Carnival in Rio. Attending a Filipino festival is often an unforgettable experience. Some of the more famous events are described below. Most are dated by the Western calendar and occur on fixed dates. The tourist office in Manila has the latest schedule.

January

Black Nazarene Procession: Manila's Quiapo district honors its centuries-old Black Nazarene image on 9 January with a mammoth *carroza* (gilded carriage) procession and nightly dramas. Filipinos believe that whosoever shoulders the carriage or touches the image will be cured of sickness and forgiven of all sins.

Mardi Gras: The Philippines' three most outrageous Mardi Gras festivals take place on the third weekend in the Visayas. None is actually a Mardi Gras, but all look, sound, and feel like their South American cousins. Taken from a pagan festival which commemorates the legendary barter of Panay between Negroid *atis* and seafaring Malays, the unforgettable spectacle occurs simultaneously in Kalibo (Panay Island) where it is called Ati Atihan, in Cebu City where it goes by Sinulog, and in Iloilo where it's called Dinagyang. Each honors the image of Santo Nino, the Infant Christ and patron saint

considered the most powerful of all Filipino miracle icons. A stately but moving religious procession is held on Friday evening. On the following day is a riotous parade of drummers, dancers, and thousands of Filipinos outlandishly dressed in animal skins, tribal spears, plastic plumage, bamboo plants, Spanish dresses, T'boli weavings, and NPA uniforms. Participants might be soot-stained Rambos, new-age zombies, African warriors, Cory clones, bar girls, or stoned astronauts. It's an unforgettable mixture of Carnival in Rio, Mardi Gras in New Orleans, and Halloween in San Francisco.

February

People Power Anniversary: On 22 February 1986, Defense Minister Enrile and General Ramos announced to a transfixed audience that Filipino forces stationed at Camp Aguinaldo had broken from the government of Ferdinand Marcos and thrown their support toward Cory Aquino. It was electrifying news. Moved by the tide of history and fearing the intervention of pro-Marcos forces, both Butz Aquino, brother of the slain senator, and Jaime Cardinal Sin, Catholic prelate for the Philippines, issued calls for people to congregate on EDSA, the ribbon of concrete that encircles Manila. Over the next few days, over a million Filipinos armed with little more than rosaries and flowers gathered to act as buffers between the rebel military and loyalist forces of Marcos. Today, the historic event is celebrated with day-long festivities where it all began in Quezon City on Epifanio De Los Santos Highway (EDSA).

March

Palm Sunday: The Sunday before Easter begins the week-long series of solemn processions, *canaculos* (a distinctly Filipino Passion play), *pabasas* (chanting of the gospels), *pasyons* (reading of the liturgies), and reenactments of the Last Supper.

Good Friday: Holy Week climaxes on Good Friday rather than Easter Sunday since Filipinos emphasize the penitence rather than the joy of Easter. This is the day that flagellants, bare to the waist and wearing a crown of leaves, atone for past sins by beating themselves bloody with glass-spiked leather whips. Even more electrifying are the crucifixions that take place in San Pedros, 50 km north of Manila, where several Filipinos allow themselves to be nailed to the cross, hoisted above the crowds, and hung crucified until they faint.

FESTIVALS

Easter: The final day of Holy Week is marked by *salubong*, a glittering procession of devotees who honor the reunion of Mary and Christ with prayers, chants, and waving masses of plaited palm fronds. Total darkness rules inside the church until midnight, when the priest lights the *paschal* candle.

Moriones Festival: Perhaps the most spectacular of all the week's rituals is the passion play held in Boac on Marinduque Island, 580 km south of Manila. From Ash Wednesday to Easter Sunday, hundreds of Morions dressed as Roman centurions wander the streets and reenact popular Biblical stories. The most popular legend surrounds Longinus, a Roman soldier whose eyesight was miraculously restored by a spilled drop of Christ's blood. After converting to Christianity, Longinus was arrested, tried, and executed by Pontius Pilate. This curious mixture of Christian history, animism, and local mythology has enough gore and passion to guarantee a spectacular weekend of entertainment.

April

Bataan Day: A parade of Filipino soldiers and American veterans honors those who fell at Corregidor and during the Bataan Death March. One of 11 national holidays celebrated in the Philippines. 9 April.

Jeepney King: Filipino folk art is celebrated with a jeepney beauty contest and crowning of a jeepney king. The contest was originally sponsored by an oil company but has been revived by the Department of Tourism.

Magellan's Landing: The historical event of 27 April, 1521 is faithfully reenacted on the beach at Mactan near Cebu. A fluvial procession of decorated *bancas* is followed by the planting of the cross and the baptism of tribal chieftain Humabon and his wife.

May

Santacruzan: May is a busy month for springtime festivals, but the most universal is the Santa Cruz de Mayo, a nine-day evening procession reenacting St. Helena's and Prince Constantine's search for the Santa Cruz ("True Cross of Christ"). Essentially a parade of Filipina beauties and their consorts, the basic cast of characters has been embellished with Methuselah, Negritos, Muslims, cherubs, and even the Queen of Sheba.

Pahiyas: San Isidro Labrador, patron saint of farmers, is honored throughout the country on 15 May with an afternoon procession past gaily decorated homes. Farmers provide a visual catalogue of their livelihood by transforming their homes into veritable hanging gardens, complete with chandeliers of vegetables, duck eggs, live fowl, rice cakes, cigarette boxes, and leaves colored with rice paste.

Olongapo Carnaval: Mardi Gras is celebrated with wild American-style abandon in the naval town of Olongapo.

June

Independence Day: On 12 June 1898, 97 Filipinos and one American signed an announcement that promised the Filipino people freedom from Spanish rule and national sovereignty. Fifty years later, Truman declared Philippine independence on 4 July 1946, but Filipinos prefer to celebrate the occasion on 12 June. Major festivities are held on the Luneta in Manila.

Pig Parade: 24 June is much less serious. This day honors St. John the Baptist with a bizarre Parada ng Lechon in Balayan, Batangas, south of Manila. This procession features dozens of freshly roasted and glazed pigs protected by raincoats to minimize baptism by beer, and barbed wire to discourage hungry spectators.

July

Pagoda Sa Wawa: Decorated *bancas* and a colorful Pagoda on the Water form a fluvial procession to honor the Holy Cross of Wawa. Held on the first Sunday in July in Bocaue, 27 km north of Manila.

Mountain Province Festivals: Cultural minorities in northern Luzon honor their gods and ancestors with movable feasts dated by animist calendars. The Grand Canao, now promoted as a major tourist attraction, brings together various indigenous cultures for a spectacular weekend of dancing, singing, and recitation of tribal epics. It's also celebrated in November or December as a fall harvest festival. Tourist information regarding many remote and/or tribal festivals should be double-checked before making a long journey.

August

Festival of the Performing Arts: The Department of Tourism and Cultural Center in Manila sponsor a month-long festival of the nation's top singers, dancers, and dramatists.

Davao Fruit Festival: The second-largest city in the Philippines celebrates the ripening of durians,

FESTIVALS

orchids, and other aromatics with agricultural exhibits and a Miss Durian competition.

Giants of Lucban: During the Lucban town fiesta on 19 August, residents proudly parade their leering collection of *gigantes* (five-meter giants) and *unanos* (dwarves) constructed from papier-mâché wrapped over bamboo frames. *Gigantes* also feature in January's Mardi Gras festivals.

September

Penafrancia Festival: The Virgin of Penafrancia, patron saint of Naga City, is honored on the third weekend of September with one of the most spectacular fluvial parades in the country. Even typhoons and a major bridge collapse in 1973 failed to discourage local devotees.

October

MassKara: Bacolod's charter-day celebration is one of the best fall festivals in the Philippines, conceived in 1980 to dramatize the Negrenses' happy spirit. Bacolenos by the thousands now make music and parade through the streets garbed in Mardi Gras-like costumes made of *nipa*, bamboo, cogon grass, and palm.

November

Day of the Dead: Filipinos celebrate their *Undas* or All Soul's Day at local graveyards with 24-hour vigils complete with votive candles, flowers, and blaring transistor radios.

December

Lantern Festival: Christmas is celebrated in the town of San Fernando, one hour north of Manila, with a spectacular display of native lanterns built of bamboo skeletons stretched with a translucent paper skin. Ranging in size from small stars to gigantic flatbed monsters, many have been ingeniously wired with hundreds of electric lights for dazzling and kaleidoscopic light shows.

Christmas: The Filipino Christmas season is reputedly the longest in the world, beginning with a series of predawn masses on 16 December and stretching to the Feast of the Three Kings on 6 January. Highlights include the Panunuluyan or Maytinis passion play as performed in Bulacan and Cavite and the Feast of the Three Kings celebrated with theater on Marinduque Island.

carnival in Cebu

PRACTICAL INFORMATION

GETTING THERE

Ninoy Aquino International Airport, 12 km from downtown Manila, is served by over 150 flights a week from all major Western and Asian cities. By air, Manila is 90 minutes from Hong Kong, two hours and 40 minutes from Bangkok, three hours from Singapore, seven hours from Sydney, 17 hours from San Francisco, and 19 hours from Europe. Visitors intending to spend most of the time in the Visayas can avoid Manila by inquiring about direct flights to Cebu. Travelers coming from Borneo or Indonesia should check on air connections from Kota Kinabalu to Zamboanga, and Manado to Davao.

All travelers are strongly advised to buy roundtrip tickets before arriving in Manila. Discount travel agencies in the Philippines are scarce and price competition between travel agents is minimal. Bucket shops in Tokyo, Hong Kong, Bangkok, and Singapore often beat Manila rates by 25-40% on both one-way and roundtrip tickets. American travelers will find the latest discount fares listed in the Sunday travel supplements of the *San Francisco Examiner, Los Angeles Times, New York Times,* and other large metropolitan newspapers. Discounted roundtrip fares from the U.S. west coast to Manila are currently US$725-900.

A handful of cruise ships such as Royal Viking Line and cargo/passenger freighters like American President and United States Lines include Manila as a port of call. The most useful sea route for travelers coming from the south would be a ship from Sabah to Zamboanga via the Sulu Archipelago. However, problems of piracy, Muslim insurgency, and kidnapping make this route both illegal and dangerous.

GETTING AROUND

By Air

Philippine Airlines (PAL) operates domestic flights to over 40 destinations throughout the country. Fares average under ten pesos per kilometer, making PAL internal flights among the lowest in the world. It is estimated that 60-70% of domestic routes are run below cost as a social obligation to far-flung communities.

PAL internal flights are made even cheaper by several discount programs. Night flights (1906-0400) are often discounted up to 30 percent. Students with a valid ISIC card are given 15% discounts. Seniors, groups, and members of the American military also receive discounts. All these discounts are seasonal and subject to cancellation.

Props are slightly cheaper than jets, and internal flights are even cheaper when you fly in the early morning or late at night. Because internal air travel is so cheap, domestic flights are often fully booked, especially during holidays and on weekends. You'll save time and money by booking all flights in advance. PAL's waiting-list system operates on a first-come, first-served basis, starting when the check-in counter opens or at midnight at larger airports. Several popular tourist destinations such as Boracay and Sicogon Island are served by small private airlines such as Pacific Air and Aeroflot.

By Boat

Touring the Philippines by boat is one of the pleasures of adventure travel in Southeast Asia. While conditions range from extremely basic to surprisingly luxurious, sea transport is always an excellent way to meet people and enjoy the romance of the open seas. Major sealines are served by luxury liners equipped with movie rooms, restaurants, and air-conditioned cabins. Less important routes have older and poorly maintained ships often purchased secondhand from Japan.

Most large shipping companies advertise their routes and schedules in the yellow pages. Current departures are listed in the newspapers and at the tourist office. Reservations are generally impossible to make over the phone. Tickets must be purchased in advance from travel agencies in larger cities or directly at the pier a few hours before departure. Arrive early for the best beds.

Sea travel is very slow but considerably cheaper than flying. Several classes are avail-

AIR ROUTES IN THE PHILIPPINES

© MOON PUBLICATIONS, INC.

able on most ships. Air-conditioned cabins for two, four, six, or eight persons come equipped with private bathrooms and catered dining. Often half of these private cabins are empty because most Filipinos can only afford to go third class. Cabins are about twice as expensive as third-class cots but only half the price of ordinary airfare. First-class air-conditioned dormitories cost 50% more than third class. Second class is rarely available.

By far the cheapest and most popular way to travel is on third-class cots spread across the deck or down below the water line. Deck passengers enjoy better air circulation but sometimes get wet during rainstorms. Be advised that third-class "deluxe" ensures a reserved bed, an absolute necessity unless you want to fight for floor space with "ordinary" passengers. Deck class is less than one-quarter the price of air travel. Interisland journeys over 12 hours usually include simple meals of rice and fish in third class and more elaborate meals in first and cabin classes. Bring along some extra food and drink to supplement the basic supplies available from the canteen.

Warning: Be extremely cautious about sea travel during bad weather and holidays. Filipino ships are often dangerously overloaded, poorly maintained, and lack life vests and lifeboats. Shipping disasters such as the 1987 sinking of the *Dona Paz*, in which over 3,000 passengers died, are on the rise. Much more dangerous than the large ships are smaller crafts and outriggers such as the MV *Jem,* which sank a few years ago en route from Looc to the resort island of Boracay. Never board an outrigger at night, during bad weather, or when it looks overloaded.

By Bus

Public buses connect most towns in the Philippines along a fairly good network of roads. Major routes are served by air-conditioned buses, while rural destinations are limited to minivans, overloaded jeepneys, and colorful rattletraps better suited for museums of indigenous psychedelia. Bus service is fast, frequent, and cheap but nowhere near as luxurious or dependable as in Thailand or Malaysia. Recommending specific buses is difficult since the Filipino bus industry is spread across dozens of companies that compete in a market neither dominated by a state monopoly nor by a handful of powerful transportation companies. The larger and more dependable bus companies in Luzon include Pantranco, Philtranco, and BLTB. Rather than stopping at every minor town, these buses make direct connections to their final destinations with a minimum of stops. Tickets with reserved seats can be purchased in advance from these companies. Otherwise, tickets are purchased directly at the terminal for the next available departure. Fares on rural buses are collected toward the end of the journey.

Other Transport

Jeepneys: Lavishly decorated with metallic reflectors, streamers, gyrating iron horses, pulsating lightbulbs, cheeky nameplates like "Virgin Busters," and Jesus statues that flash in rhythm with the music, jeepneys are obviously more than just the Filipino substitute for intra-city buses. They symbolize the clash of Asian sensibilities with Western consumerism, folk art with utilitarianism, and cold machinery with Filipino passion. More extravagant examples mix religious iconography and Western hedonism into something almost beyond description. Most Filipinos, of course, regard them simply as uncomfortable but convenient forms of public transportation found in nearly all towns throughout the archipelago. More information under "Manila."

Taxis: Taxis are only of importance in Manila and larger towns such as Cebu, Baguio, and Davao. Most are metered and rates are low—provided the meter is correctly calibrated. Unmarked vehicles and taxis with inoperable meters should not be taken unless you are absolutely sure of the correct fare and make a firm agreement with the driver in advance. Golden Taxi is considered to be Manila's most dependable and honest taxi company. They operate black cabs painted with gold-colored lettering.

TRAVEL FORMALITIES

Visas

Visitors to the Philippines may enter the country without a visa and stay for up to 21 days provided they hold an onward ticket. Visitors who arrive without a visa but would like to stay longer than the initial 21 days must obtain a visa waiver from the Commission on Immigration and Deportation on Magallanes Drive near the Gen-

SHIPPING ROUTES IN THE PHILIPPINES

PHILIPPINE SEA

LUZON

SOUTH CHINA SEA

MANILA

LUBANG   BATANGAS   LUCENA

PUERTO GALERA   SANTA CRUZ   VIRAC

CALAPAN   MINDORO   TABACO

PINAMALAYAN   GASAN   MARINDUQUE

ROXAS   ROMBLON   BULAN   MATNOG

ODIONGAN   MASBATE   ALLEN

SAN JOSE   MASBATE   CALBAYOG

MALAY   CATBALOGAN

KALIBO   ROXAS   SAMAR

PANAY   TACLOBAN

ILOILO   BACOLOD   CEBU   ORMOC

SAN CARLOS   CEBU CITY   LEYTE

TOLEDO   MAASIN

ARGAO   TALIBON   LILOAN

NEGROS   LOON   BOHOL   DAPA

SAMBOAN   UBAY   SURIGAO

DUMAGUETE   TAGBILARAN

SIQUIJOR   GUINSILBAN

TALISAYAN   BUTUAN

DIPOLOG   CAGAYAN DE ORO

OZAMIS   MINDANAO

PALAWAN

PUERTO PRINCESA

SULU SEA

COTABATO   DAVAO CITY

ZAMBOANGA

ISABELA   GENERAL SANTOS CITY

JOLO

TAWI TAWI   SULU ARCHIPELAGO

SIBITU

0   100 km

MALAYSIA
1. wheelin' and dealin'; 2. Penang fortuneteller (all photos this page by Carl Parkes)

MALAYSIA
1. Kuala Kangsar mosque; **2.** Kota Baru market (all photos this page by Carl Parkes)

PHILIPPINES DIPLOMATIC OFFICES

Australia	1 Moonah Place Yarralumla, Canberra	(026) 732535
Canada	130 Albert St. #606, Ottawa	(613) 233-1121
France	39 Avenue Georges Mandel, Paris 75016	704-6550
Germany	Argelanderstrasse 5300, Bonn	213071
Hong Kong	21F Regent Center, 88 Queen's Rd.	(01) 810-0770
Indonesia	6 Jalan Iman Bonjol, Jakarta	348917
Japan	11-24 Nampeidaimachi, Shibuya-ku, Tokyo	496-2731
Malaysia	1 Changkat Kia Peng, Kuala Lumpur	4832576
New Zealand	Boulcott St., Wellington	(202) 483-1414
Singapore	15 Scotts Rd. #505	373977
Thailand	760 Sukhumvit, Bangkok	391-0008
United Kingdom	9A Palace Green, London W8	(01) 937-1600
U.S.A.	1617 Massachusetts Ave., Washington, D.C. 20036	(202) 483-1414
	447 Sutter St., San Francisco, CA 94118	(415) 433-6666

eral Post Office in Manila. This waiver allows a stay of up to 59 days and costs P700. However, it is *strongly* advised that you obtain a visa in advance from a Filipino Embassy, since a visit to Manila's Immigration Department is something of a Kafkaesque experience.

Extensions beyond the 59-day limit can be obtained with proper application and payment of an Alien Head Tax, legal research fees, the fee for an Alien Certificate of Registration, and extension fees of P100 per month. Visitors who would like to stay longer than six months must secure a Certificate for Temporary Visitors which costs P400 plus P100 per month. Visitors who overstay their 59-day limit must pay an additional P500 fine on top of the P250 airport tax.

Tourist Information
The Department of Tourism (DOT) is the government agency responsible for tourism: general information, licensing of travel agents and tour operators, classifying hotels, and international promotion. The DOT maintains both overseas and domestic field offices with the head office located in the imposing Tourism Building on Agrifina Circle in Manila. An information center is also found at the Manila airport. Employees are extremely personable and anxious to help, but there is a perennial shortage of reliable and timely travel information. Wander the upper floors of the Tourism Building for an eye-opening look into the hellhole of Filipino bureaucracy. The situation in the regional field offices is even worse.

Maps
The patchwork arrangement of the Philippines makes a good map absolutely essential for all serious visitors. National maps provided by the Department of Tourism (DOT) are sketchy, although they do have a useful map of Manila and Makati. Best national map is the 1:1,000,000-scale *Republic of the Philippines Roadmap* published by the National Bookstore and sold in most bookstores in Manila. Highly recommended. The 1:1,500,000-scale APA-Insight map is also worthwhile though not as useful as the National Bookstore map. Detailed topographic maps of individual provinces can be purchased at the Bureau of Coast and Geodetic Survey office in Manila. These maps are very outdated but useful for navigation purposes. Neither the *Petron Map of the Philippines* nor the *Mobil Philippine Travel Map* are worth purchasing.

Currency
The unit of currency is the peso (Tagalog *piso*), symbolized by a capital P with two horizontal lines through the top. The peso, a floating currency divided into 100 centavos, in recent years

PHILIPPINES TOURIST OFFICES

OVERSEAS OFFICES

Australia	122 Castlereagh St., Sydney 2000	(02) 26756
Germany	Kaissestrasse 15, 6000 Frankfurt am Main	(069) 208-9395
Hong Kong	Regent Centre, 88 Queens Rd., Central	(05) 810-0770
Japan	11-24 Nampeidai Machi, Shibuya-ku, Tokyo	(03) 464-3630
Singapore	Philippine Embassy, 20 Nassim Road, Sing 1025	(022) 235-2184
United Kingdom	199 Piccadilly, London W1 V9 LE	(017) 734-6358
U.S.A.	3460 Wilshire Blvd. #1212, Los Angeles, CA 90010	(213) 487-4527
	447 Sutter St., San Francisco, CA 94108	(415) 956-4060
	556 Fifth Ave., New York, NY 10036	(212) 575-7915

REGIONAL OFFICES

Baguio	Tourism Bldg., Gov. Pack Road, Baguio, Luzon	(74) 3415
Cagayan de Oro	Sports Complex, Cagayan de Oro, Mindanao	(8822) 3340
Cebu City	Fort San Pedro, Cebu City, Cebu	(32) 91503
Davao	Apo View Hotel, Camus St., Davao City, Mindanao	(82) 74866
Iloilo	General Luna St., Iloilo City, Panay	(33) 78701
La Union	Cresta Del Mar Beach Resort, Bauang, Luzon	(27) 2411
Legaspi	Penaranda Park, Legaspi City, Luzon	(66) 4492
Manila	Tourism Building, Rizal Park, Manila	(2) 599-031
Tacloban	Senator Enage St., Tacloban City, Leyte	(69) 321-2048
Zamboanga	Lantaka Hotel, Zamboanga, Mindanao	(62) 3931

has fluctuated between 22 and 26 per dollar. Further devaluation is expected.

Exchange facilities are available at banks, major hotels, authorized exchange dealers, and money changers. All offer varying exchange rates, the worst at facilities in luxury hotels and the best from the money changers on Mabini Street in Manila. Banks are somewhere in the middle.

The Filipino exchange system is full of perils. Rates are unregulated and vary widely from dealer to dealer. It's important to shop around and compare rates before changing large amounts of currency. Remember that cash is king in the Philippines. American currency guarantees the highest rates, especially larger bills such as $50s and $100s. Smaller bills such as $20s are often discounted 5-10% below the highest rate.

Traveler's checks can be problematical. They can be cashed at major banks and American Express offices, but only at 5-10% below cash rates. Besides being a time-consuming ordeal, cashing a traveler's check in the provinces can be difficult, if not impossible. Passports and purchase receipts are required to cash traveler's checks.

Rates are highest at the Philippine National Bank and the Philippine Commercial and Industrial Bank. Better rates and no lines at Shoemart Department Stores in Manila. To get the highest possible rate and avoid ordeals at the bank, bring US$100 bills with you and do most of your business with the money changers in Manila. Currency declaration on arrival is unnecessary. Pesos can be reexchanged for dollars at the airport but an official receipt may be required.

Warning: Never attempt to change money on the street. Manila has dozens of street money changers who with the use of accomplices and phony policemen prey on unsuspecting travelers. It is virtually impossible for street vendors to legitimately offer a higher rate than licensed money changers. Remember: all street changers are professional con artists.

Telephone

The Philippine telephone network is operated by the Philippine Long Distance Telephone Company (PLDT) and community telephone systems in the provinces.

Local Calls: Domestic calls can be made from public pay phones and private businesses for two pesos. Domestic long-distance calls can be made by dialing 0 and then the area code. Dial 109 for operator-assisted domestic long distance. A few of the more useful area codes are listed in the "Philippines Area Codes" chart.

International Calls: Overseas calls and faxes can be made to the Philippines by dialing the international access code (011), then the country code for the Philippines (63), then the city code, followed by the local phone number. For example, to call a hotel in Manila from the U.S., dial 011-63-2 and then the local hotel number.

Rates from the Philippines are set in U.S. dollars by the government. A three-minute station-to-station call during the daytime to the U.S. costs US$9 plus US$3 for each additional minute. You can save money by making a quick call and having your friend return the call station-to-station.

Tours

Dozens of tour operators are located in Manila, though the most outstanding tours are offered by a Swiss-run group headquartered in Makati. Among the completely unique packages are a

PHILIPPINES AREA CODES

Manila	(2)
Bacolod	(34)
Baguio	(74)
Cebu City	(32)
Davao	(82)
Iloilo	(33)
Tarlac	(452)
Zamboanga	(62)

INTERNATIONAL CLOCK FOR THE PHILIPPINES

San Francisco	-14
New York	-11
London	-7
Paris	-6
Sydney	+3

one-week Air Safari around the archipelago to such far-flung destinations as Camiguin Island and Busuanga, a 21-day Prime Adventure that visits the T'boli of Mindanao and the sea gypsies of Tawi Tawi, and an exciting Discovery Cruise in the northern Palawan region. Expensive, but certainly the best possible organized tours in the country. Blue Horizons, tel. (2) 876071, fax (2) 815-4825, Manila Peninsula Hotel, Makati, Manila.

CAUTIONS

While most Filipinos are completely trustworthy and sincere about their interests in foreign visitors, a small percentage of the population are professional con artists who make their living by defrauding Western tourists. Caution must be exercised at all times. The good news is that fraud and theft in the Philippines are almost exclusively nonviolent encounters where the racketeer uses his wit and charm rather than weapons or physical threats. The bad news is that con artists are as thick as fleas in certain areas, such as Manila's Ermita District, Baguio, and many of the popular beach resorts. You *must* be careful about everybody who approaches you—no matter their appearance or the believability of their story. Thieves come in all shapes and sizes: kids hanging out on the street corner, matronly housewives, clean-cut students, lovely ladies, and elderly gentlemen dressed in three-piece suits.

My favorite story is of a German attorney who met two middle-aged ladies at Sunday church services in Manila. They offered a tour of the city and lunch followed by an afternoon film in a darkened theater. One of the women went for Cokes, which the German later recalled as tasting slightly strange. Three hours later he awoke from his drug stupor stripped of his watch, camera, traveler's checks, and other valuables. A few of the more common tricks are listed below.

The Come On

"Do you remember me . . . ?" should be an instant tip-off that you're being set up for fraud. The con artist usually claims that he met you at airport customs or immigration, drove your taxi, or knows a common friend. If you actually respond to such a ridiculous line, you're well on your way to being drugged, mugged, or invited in for a friendly game of cards.

Money Changers

As pointed out above under "Currency," all money changers working the streets are professional con artists who pass counterfeit bills and shortchange unsuspecting Westerners.

Pickpockets

Razor-blade artists work their trade on crowded buses and jeepneys. Child street vendors often distract their victims by waving their merchandise in front of the victim's face while another grabs the bag. Avoid people hiding their hands under newspapers and keep your valuables pressed closely against your stomach while in crowds.

Knock-out Drugs

Invitations for coffee or beer should in most cases be declined. Friendly strangers who offer free drinks may also be offering complimentary servings of Ativan, a potent drug that quickly leaves the victim helplessly dazed or completely unconscious. *Beware:* knock-out drugs are *extremely* common in the Philippines.

Card Games

One of the most popular cons involves a friendly game of cards. It begins when a well-dressed Filipino approaches a tourist and claims his cousin is a card dealer in the local casino. He then promises that great sums of money can be earned with the cooperation of a willing foreigner. To set the stage, a game is arranged at his house using a phony bankroll. After being taught the signals and winning a dozen straight games, the tourist feels very confident about the arrangement. Suddenly, a wealthy Chinese gambler arrives for a casual afternoon game. The game goes well with the provided bankroll

---

MOVIES FILMED IN THE PHILIPPINES

Apocalypse Now: The helicopter scenes in Francis Ford Coppola's masterpiece were filmed at Balera Bay, while the climactic explosion of Kurtz's Cambodian temple was staged on the riverbanks near Pagsanhan Falls. Tribal dance scenes were performed by the Ifugaos of Banaue. Coppola's ex-wife subsequently wrote an intriguing book about their problems with typhoons and clashing personalities.

Platoon: Most of this Academy Award-winning film was filmed in the Philippines.

The Year of Living Dangerously: One of the best films about contemporary politics in the region was filmed in the Philippines after Indonesian authorities refused to allow the Australian director to complete the film on location.

Born On The Fourth Of July: Ron Kovic's autobiographical novel was largely filmed in the northern Philippine province of Ilocos Norte. While there, director Oliver Stone and star Tom Cruise stayed in the Fort Ilocandia Resort Hotel, built by the Marcoses to house guests for their 1983 wedding of daughter Irene. Stone summed it up: "I have been all over the Far East, and the Philippines has the most natural wonders. The people give their hearts to you; it's like being in the old pirate country in the Carribean."

---

until the stakes grow alarmingly large and the tourist is forced to use his personal funds to cover the pot. This, of course, is the final hand where all those carefully rehearsed signals fail.

Other Cons

Be sure to retrieve *all* your luggage from the trunk of your taxi. Better yet, carry your gear with you in the rear seat. Inspect your room very carefully for trap doors in the closets and unlocked windows. Never leave valuables unattended in your hotel room. Valuables should instead be checked in hotel safes or in safe-deposit boxes at large banks for a nominal fee. Avoid dark alleys or rough sections of town after dark.

Drugs

The Philippines is neither a major producer nor a conduit for the hard drugs that plague other Southeast Asian countries. Marijuana is commonplace and cocaine is produced in small quantities, but the newest and most dangerous drug is *shabu,* a super-powerful methamphetamine that sends users on a racing, eight-hour-long high before the ensuing crash and depression. Though relatively cheap at US$25-50 a gram, *shabu* is also one of the most addictive and deadly drugs in the world. Stay clear.

LUZON

MANILA

Metro Manila, a conurbation of four cities and 13 municipalities, is not only the hub of Filipino politics and national economics, it also sets the pace in entertainment, culture, communications, and religion. From its humble beginnings on the banks of the Pasig River, today's city of nine million residents has spread haphazardly across 636 square kilometers from Manila Bay toward the Pacific Ocean. Like most other Asian cities, Manila is actually a maze of villages tied together with highways, shopping centers, neon signs, and urban sprawl.

It's a world of startling contrasts: international hotels that charge a daily rate in excess of the annual income of most Filipinos; miles of slums where people survive without electricity or running water; elegant suburbs where the Filipino elite live behind protective walls; smoking garbage pits where thousands survive by recycling the waste of others; exclusive nightclubs where jet-setters sip properly chilled champagne and discuss the latest fashions; burned-out hotels that face one of the world's most romantic harbors. Manila is alive and pulsating, confusing and exciting, one of Asia's most perplexing destinations.

Though the city boasts some of Asia's best nightlife and a handful of worthwhile sights, Manila lacks exotic charm and historical flavor because of its near complete destruction at the end of WW II. The following attractions can be quickly toured on foot and by public transport before heading off to the mountains and beaches.

The city is divided into several distinct neighborhoods. Hotels, restaurants, and most nightlife are located in the tourist sections of Ermita and Malate, just south of Rizal Park where the main tourist office is situated. Intramuros, the old historic quarter north of Rizal Park, can be reached on foot, but public transport is necessary to reach

more distant destinations. Malacañang Palace is undoubtedly the best sight in Manila, but Rizal Park, the Chinese cemetery, and the financial center of Makati are also worth visiting.

ATTRACTIONS

Ermita And Malate

Once a Muslim fishing village and later a wealthy residential neighborhood for leading Tagalog families, Ermita and Malate are the heart of Manila's tourist belt. A handful of large colonial-style homes still stand, but most have given way to hotels, antique shops, and bars set along M.H. del Pilar and Mabini streets.

Malate Church: A convenient spot to begin your walking tour is at this highly ornate church constructed in 1773 to replace the original Augustinian structure. The austere interior makes a strong contrast with the romantic facade of Spanish-Muslim balusters and Mexican baroque columns. Sunday services are open to the public. Rajah Sulayman Park just opposite has several good seafood restaurants, *calesa* drivers, and a statue of the Muslim sultan who ruled Manila prior to the Spanish era.

Mabini Street: Many of Manila's better antique shops are located along this chaotic street filled with money changers, hustlers, inexpensive pensions, touts who "remember you from immigration," and quality restaurants. Shopping for Filipino handicrafts is best at the sprawling flea market called Pistang Pilipino, an excellent place to get a general overview of what's available throughout the Philippines. Shell collectors will enjoy a visit to Carfel Seashell Museum at 1786 Mabini. The Manila Zoo and the Metropolitan Museum, with its changing exhibits and a money display, are south of Malate. Adriatico

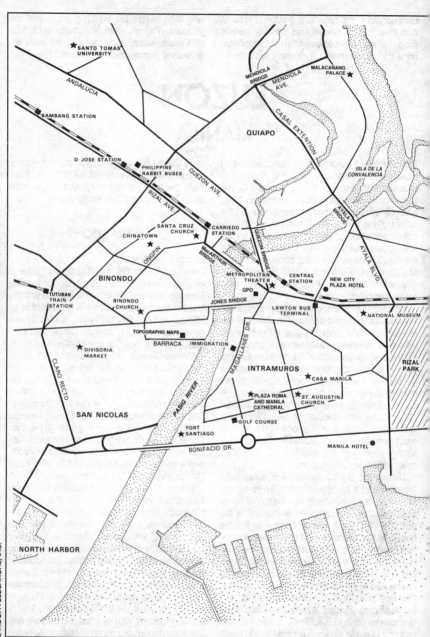

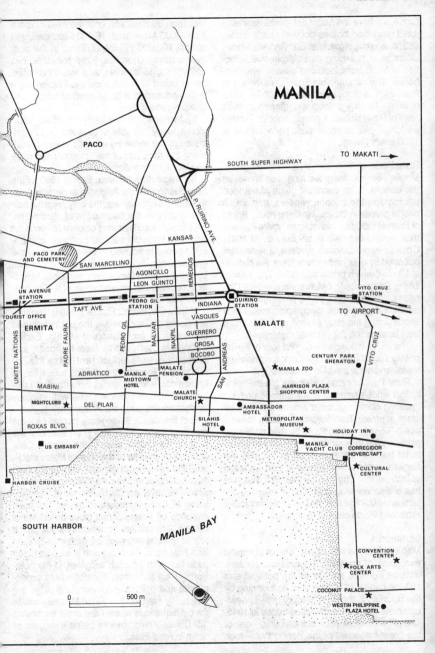

MANILA

TO MAKATI →

SOUTH SUPER HIGHWAY

PACO

P. BURINO AVE.

KANSAS

PACO PARK
AND CEMETERY

SAN MARCELINO

AGONCILLO

REMEDIOS

LEON GUINTO

VITO CRUZ
STATION

UN AVENUE
STATION

TAFT AVE.

PEDRO GIL
STATION

INDIANA

QUIRINO
STATION

TO AIRPORT →

TOURIST OFFICE

PADRE FAURA

PEDRO GIL

MALVAR

NAKPIL

VASQUES

MALATE

VITO CRUZ

ERMITA

GUERRERO

UNITED NATIONS

OROSA

BOCOBO

CENTURY PARK
SHERATON

MABINI

ADRIATICO

Manila
Midtown
Hotel

Malate
Pension

SAN ANDREAS

★ MANILA ZOO

NIGHTCLUBS ★

DEL PILAR

MALATE
CHURCH ★

HARRISON PLAZA
SHOPPING CENTER

ROXAS BLVD.

AMBASSADOR
HOTEL

SILAHIS
HOTEL

METROPOLITAN
MUSEUM ★

HOLIDAY INN

US EMBASSY

MANILA
YACHT CLUB

CORREGIDOR
HOVERCRAFT

★ CULTURAL
CENTER

HARBOR CRUISE

SOUTH HARBOR

MANILA BAY

CONVENTION
CENTER

★ FOLK ARTS
CENTER

COCONUT PALACE ★

WESTIN PHILIPPINE
PLAZA HOTEL

0   500 m

Circle is where the smart set drinks espresso amid gentrified homes converted into cafes, bistros, and gay nightclubs. San Andreas Market offers an outstanding albeit expensive selection of fresh fruits including durians and guabanos. The romantic old Spanish cemetery of Paco Park, a block from UN and Taft Avenues, is where famous patriots are interred in three rows of burial niches. A popular spot for Sunday weddings, plus chamber music performances at 1800 every Friday.

Rizal Park

Manila's 58-hectare green lung, also known as the Luneta, is an excellent place to wander, photograph the balloon vendors, and watch people parade in the early-evening hours. Points of interest include a planetarium where free cultural events are held every Sunday at 1645, Chinese and Japanese gardens, a restaurant operated by deaf and mute waiters, the National Library, which briefly starred in *The Year of Living Dangerously, balut* vendors, elderly Chinese practicing tai chi, young prostitutes of both genders, and a giant topographic map which floods during the rainy season and dries into a dust bowl during the summer months.

The tourist office on the ground floor of the imposing Tourist Building offers maps, sightseeing ideas, and other travel information.

Rizal Park is named after the great Filipino patriot whose remains are enshrined under a towering obelisk guarded around the clock by stern sentries. Translations of Rizal's famous poem "Mi Ultimo Adios" can be read on bronze plaques near the monument, though you'll need to be fluent in either Spanish or Tagalog. An English version can be read at Fort Santiago in Intramuros. The nearby National Museum has a disappointing collection of religious objects and botanical specimens but an impressive room on Filipino cultural minorities.

Intramuros

Manila's famous walled city, one of the finest examples of medieval fortress architecture outside Europe, served as the political and cultural capital of Manila from its founding by the Spanish in the 16th century until its near-complete destruction by Allied forces in 1945. The physical elimination of Intramuros—one of the great tragedies of the Pacific War—took

less than 30 days and cost the lives of more than 1,000 Americans, 16,000 Japanese, and almost 100,000 Filipino civilians. In the end, over a dozen churches, three convents, two cathedrals, 13 chapels, and two universities constructed in a rich Hispano-Filipino style were reduced to a great heap of rubble and creeping vegetation.

Sadly neglected and badly run-down, Intramuros today has little of exceptional interest, although the following attractions and a walk along the ramparts of the reconstructed walls can be recommended.

St. Augustine Church: Built in 1599 as the headquarters for the Augustinian order in Asia, this stone seminary was the only religious edifice to survive the destruction of Intramuros. An extensive collection of colonial religious art including valuable *santos, carrozas,* and antique books is housed in the museum on the ground floor. Across the street is Bario San Luis, the Muralla Restaurant, and Casa Maynila, an outstanding reproduction of a 19th-century Filipino mansion.

Manila Cathedral: Farther along is the modern home of Cardinal Sin, the outspoken and controversial archbishop of Manila. Earlier cathedrals destroyed by fires, typhoons, and earthquakes were replaced in 1958 by this Romanesque-Byzantine building, noted for its bronze doors, which depict the cathedral's history and stained-glass windows with religious symbolism unique to the Philippines.

Fort Santiago: Strategically located near the mouth of the muddy Pasig River is one of the best historical attractions in the country. Constructed on the site of the original Malay stockade, the century-old garrison served Spanish and Japanese forces as a diabolical prison in which the lower dungeons flooded at high tide, killing all those incarcerated below. The main entrance off Aduna Street faces an attractive plaza where soldiers sometimes parade past a row of antique automobiles rusting in Bastion San Francisco. Farther north a reconstructed gate, rich with Spanish insignias, is the noteworthy Raja Sulayman Theater, where experimental and politically controversial plays are frequently staged. The Rizal Museum inside the old barracks is where Rizal wrote his moving "Mi Ultimo Adios" before being executed at dawn in Rizal Park.

North Of The Pasig River

Quiapo: Manila is a city cut in half by the Pasig River. South of the river are the walled city of Intramuros, the tourist enclaves of Ermita and Malate, and the financial district of Makati. North is the heart of old Manila, a world of crowded alleys, Chinese temples, mosques, stinking canals, chaotic markets, *calesas*, slums, and churches. Religious life revolves around the Quiapo Church and its Shrine of the Black Nazarene, one of the most famous religious images in the country. Try to visit on Friday evenings when the faithful gather to request miracles from the life-size reclining figure. The long and hot 20-minute walk from the church to Malacañang Palace passes a gold-domed mosque, an outdoor brass market, and beautiful old buildings overlooking the muddy Pasig.

Malacañang Palace: This is not only the best attraction in Manila, it's one of the most fascinating spots in all of Southeast Asia. Since its construction in 1802, Malacañang has served as a country home for Spanish aristocracy, American generals, and, most significantly, Marcos and Imelda. When they fled the country in 1986, they took with them much of the national treasury but left behind the remnants of a reign of extraordinary self-delusion, indulgence, and vulgarity. A visit to Malacañang is an unforgettable glimpse into the lives of one of the strangest ruling couples in the world.

The tour begins in the ornate public rooms, passes through the Marcoses' separate bedrooms complete with magical pyramids and medical equipment, and finishes with a descent into Imelda's basement storeroom where her butterfly gowns, gifts, and 3,000 pairs of shoes are displayed. Don't miss the disco pumps with illuminated and rechargeable heels!

Public tours on Thursdays and Fridays 0900-1100 cost P20; private guided tours on Mondays and Tuesdays 0900-1100 and 1300-1500 cost P250; it's free but crowded on Saturdays. Opening hours and fees should be double-checked with the tourist office before heading out to Malacañang.

Chinatown: Straddling Quiapo and Tondo is Binondo, a modern crowded commercial center which serves as home for many of Manila's Philippine-born Chinese. The settlement dates from 1594 when the Chinese merchants were burned out of the Parian district and relocated north of the Pasig. The neighborhood lost most of its colonial charm after it was rebuilt in a modern style following the destruction of WW II, but a wander down the main street of Ongpin will turn up some interesting restaurants, temples, godowns, mah-jongg parlors, acupuncture clinics, and Chinese pharmacists.

Tondo: North of Chinatown is a densely populated slum with wooden shanties, Mother Teresa's Sisters of Charity on Tayuman Street, and Smokey Mountain, where hundreds of families make their livings salvaging refuse from an immense trash heap.

Chinese Cemetery: Manila's most unusual attraction is the eccentric 54-hectare cemetery located near the junction of Rizal and Aurora avenues. Behind the yellow exterior walls embedded with over 10,000 burial niches for the poor are hundreds of massive mausoleums complete with furniture, air-conditioned kitchens, and tiled bathrooms. These two-story memorials serve both to honor the deceased and to prove the economic success of the Chinese community. Take a jeepney marked Monumento or Caloocan City, or the Metro Rail to R. Papa Station.

Other Attractions

Cultural Center of the Philippines: Designed by Filipino architect Leandro Locsin, this magnificent collection of ultramodern buildings comprises some of the best contemporary architecture in Southeast Asia. The CCP houses a Cultural Center designed in classical opera-house tradition with curving staircases and glass chandeliers, a vast Folk Arts Theater where beauty pageants and cultural performances are staged, the Parthenon-like Manila Film Center, now closed due to structural problems, the Museum of Philippine Culture, the Coconut Palace, constructed in 1981 for the visit of Pope John Paul II, and the stunning Philippine Plaza Hotel. Jeepneys shuttle around the perimeter. To the intense embarrassment of local officials, this reclamation area is also home to a sizable population of squatters.

Makati: Approximately 10 km southeast of Ermita, this planned community of international banks, air-conditioned shopping centers, embassies, expensive restaurants, five-star

ERMITA AND MALATE

MANILA BAY

ERMITA

MALATE

ROXAS BOULEVARD
ALHAMBRA
KALAW
UNITED NATIONS
UN AVENUE STATION
GUERRERO
DEL PILAR
FLORES
BOCOBO
OROSA
TAFT AVENUE
ARQUIZA
MABINI
PADRE FAURA
SANTA MONICA
SALAS
ADRIATICO
SOLDADO
PEDRO GIL
PEDRO GIL STATION
MALVAR
OROSA
NAKPIL
LEON GUINTO
AGONCILLO
SAN MARCELINO
DEL PILAR
REMEDIOS
BOCOBO
SAN ANDRES
TAFT AVENUE
MABINI
ADRIATICO
QUIRINO STATION
QUIRINO AVENUE
CAROLINA

0   200 m

© MOON PUBLICATIONS INC

ERMITA AND MALATE

★ ATTRACTIONS
1. Rizal Park
2. National Library
3. Dept. of Tourism (DOT)
43. Paco Park
97. San Andreas Market
102. Manila Zoo

● ACCOMMODATIONS
6. Mabini Mansions
10. Manila Pavilion Hotel
    and Casino Filipino
14. Swagman Hotel
18. Southern Cross Hotel
22. Soriente Hotel
26. Pension Filipinas
27. La Corona Hotel
30. Diamond Inn
31. Aurelio Hotel
32. Iseya Hotel
34. Royal Palm Hotel
38. Midtown Inn
41. Tower Hotel
42. Casa Dalco I
46. Manila Tourist Inn
47. Mabini Pension
50. Park Hotel
53. Sundowner Hotel
    Kangaroo Club
55. La Soledad Pension
57. Ermita Tourist Inn,
    shipping agent
58. Santos Pension
59. White House Pension
60. Manila Midtown Hotel
61. Youth Hostel
62. Chateau de Bay Hotel
65. Las Palmas Hotel
68. Rothman Hotel
72. Rich and Famous Pension
73. New Olga Casa Pension

74. Olga Casa Pension
75. Pension Natividad
76. Adriatico Pension
77. Pearl Garden Hotel
78. Howard's Pension
    and Hot Pot
79. Malate Pension
80. Victoria Mansion
89. Casa Dalco II
92. Circle Pension,
    Penguin Cafe
94. Silahis Hotel
95. Euro-Nippon Mansions
96. Carolina Pension
98. Eden's Pension
101. MacArthur Hotel

■ RESTAURANTS
4. Slouch Hat
   Pub & Restaurant
5. Pizza Hut
8. Hong Kong Restaurant
9. McDonald's
16. Jumbo Garden Restaurant
25. Barrio Fiesta Restaurant
28. Shakey's Pizza
33. Guernica's Restaurant
35. Kaymayan Restaurant
49. Palai Dawn Restaurant
52. Rosie's Diner
66. Zamboanga Restaurant
67. La Taverna Restaurant
69. Green House Middle
    Eastern Restaurant
70. Dragon Express
    Teahouse
84. Moviola Bistro
85. Guernica's Restaurant
86. The Blue Cafe
87. Wok Inn Too
90. Bistro Remedios

91. Wok Inn
93. Cafe Adriatico
103. Aristocrat Restaurant
104. Tia Marias
105. Erieze International
     Steakhouse

■ NIGHTLIFE
23. Birdwatchers Bar
40. New Bangkok Bar
48. Firehouse Bar
64. Pistang Pilipino
81. Hobbit House
83. Hard Rock Cafe
100. My Father's Moustache

■ SERVICES AND SHOPPING
7. Singapore Airlines
11. InterBank
12. U.S. Embassy
13. Japan Airlines
17. Global Dive Shop
15. Korean Airlines
19. Alemar's Bookstore
18. Telex office
20. American Express
21. Philippines National
    Police (PNP)
24. Northwest Airlines
29. The Bookmark
36. Solidaridad Bookstore
39. Tesoro's Handicrafts
44. Ermita Post Office
45. Cathay Pacific
51. General Hospital
54. Philippine Airlines
56. Bobby's Laundry
63. Sarkies Buses
71. PLDT Long Distance
85. Carfel Seashells

hotels, and ritzy nightclubs is the most modern and wealthy suburb in the Philippines. Highlights include the Ayala Museum with its superb collection of ethnic art and historical dioramas, Makati Commercial Center, and the American Cemetery, which holds the remains of over 17,000 American and Allied troops who perished during WW II.

ACCOMMODATIONS

Budget
Budget accommodations under US$10 nightly are grouped together in the tourist belt of Ermita and Malate. Dorms for about P100 are available at the Malate Pension, Congress Fam-

ERMITA AND MALATE ACCOMMODATIONS

(prices in pesos unless otherwise indicated)

HOTEL	SINGLE	DOUBLE	ADDRESS	PHONE (2)
LUXURY				
Ambassador	US$70-100	US$80-140	2021 Mabini	506011
La Corona	US$70-80	US$80-90	1166 del Pilar	502631
Manila Pavilion	US$120	US$160	Orosa	522-2911
Manila Midtown	US$100-140	US$120-180	Pedro Gil	573911
Silahis	US$80-100	US$90-120	1990 RoxasBlvd.	521-0004
MODERATE				
Aurelio	US$34-40	US$34-40	Guerrero	509061
City Garden	US$30-35	US$35-40	1158 Mabini	521-8841
Las Palmas	US$30-35	US$32-40	1616 Mabini	506661
Manila Tourist Inn	US$25-35	US$25-35	487 Santa Monica	597772
Rothman	US$25-35	US$30-35	1633 Adriatico	521-9260
Soriente	US$25-35	US$25-35	1123 Bocobo	599106
Sundowner	US$40-50	US$45-60	1430 Mabini	521-2751
Swagman	US$32-40	US$32-40	411A Flores	599881
APARTELS				
Dakota Mansions	800-1000	800-1200	555 Malvar	521-0701
Euro-Nippon Mansion	700-800	800-1000	2090 Roxas	521-3921
Mabini Mansions	800-1000	800-1000	1011 Mabini	521-4776
Pearl Garden	600-800	600-800	1700 Adriatico	575911
San Carlos	500-700	600-800	777 San Carlos	590981
Southern Cross Inn	650-750	700-800	476 United Nations	581-6883

ily Pension, the Youth Hostel, and Manila International Youth Hostel. Rooms under P250 can be found, but they are usually cramped, dirty, and noisy. You must spend about P300 to find a decent room with fan and common bath. Comfortable rooms with a/c and private bath start at P300 but most average about P350-500. Some of these are excellent value.

Prices vary widely depending on several factors: single or double, fan or a/c, common or private bath, floor (lower floors are cheaper), and size of the room. Most inexpensive hotels will rent single rooms with large beds to couples for no extra charge. Tax and service charges are added only to the more expensive hotels.

Inexpensive hotels come in several styles. One-star hotels in the US$10-20 range generally face Manila Bay along Roxas Boulevard. These simple hotels are plentiful but are often run-down and subject to extended brownouts. Avoid any hotel that looks like a fire hazard. When in doubt, ask for a room on the ground floor for a quick exit. Pensions are large old houses converted into rabbit warrens of private rooms, dorms, common baths, storage bins, and dining facilities. Pensions are usually the best choice for budget travelers since they are friendly and cheaper than hotels. Mansions and apartels are small apartments with kitchen facilities that cater to long-term visitors. Motels are short-time lodges which cater to the drive-in love trade.

As with other major cities in Southeast Asia, the best deals are often filled by noontime. Visitors arriving in the late afternoon must often

ERMITA AND MALATE ACCOMMODATIONS

(prices in pesos unless otherwise indicated)

HOTEL	SINGLE	DOUBLE	ADDRESS	PHONE (2)
PENSIONS				
Carolina	180-400	220-600	2116 Carolina	522-3961
Casa Dalco I	220-280	250-420	1318 Agoncillo	598522
Casa Dalco II	320-460	320-460	1910 Mabini	508855
Casa Pension	140-180	160-240	1602 Leon Guinto	592387
Circle	250-300	350-400	602 Remedios	522-2920
Diamond Inn	250-300	250-300	1219 Del Pilar	593167
Eden's Tourist Inn	300-400	350-600	2158 Carolina	522-2389
Ermita Tourist Inn	450-550	500-700	1549 Mabini	521-8770
JC	180-250	180-250	1250 Bacobo	578485
La Soledad	120-160	150-300	1529 Mabini	500706
Howard's	140-180	140-180	1726 Adriatico	521-4845
Mabini	200-240	240-400	1337 Mabini	594853
Malate	260-400	280-750	1771 Adriatico	585-4898
Olga Casa	160-200	180-240	1674 Mabini	587647
Pension Filipinas	180-340	240-600	572 Arkansas	521-1496
Rich and Famous	160-200	180-320	1655 Leon Guinto	521-1488
Santos	180-240	200-300	1540 Mabini	595628
Travel Fast	500-600	600-750	599 Arkansas	569-0170
White House	180-250	220-520	465 Pedro Gil	522-1535
Yasmin	339	400-480	453 Arquiza	505134
Youth Hostel	85-100	105-140	4227 Tomar Claudio	832-0680

overnight in a dump or a more expensive hotel before moving to a pension the following morning. Taxi fare from the airport to the Ermita hotel district is P40. A good starting spot is Malate Pension on Adriatico Street. Though filled daily by noontime, it's a convenient place to have a quick bite before beginning your hotel search. A few of the larger, cleaner, and more popular places are listed below.

Malate Pension: Manila's largest and most popular pension has a coffee shop with American and Filipino dishes, French food in the Chateau, a TV room, a useful information board, harried but patient employees, newspaper vendors outside the gate, sports on the tube, and rooms in all price ranges. This travelers' scene will appeal to some but turn off others. A waiting list begins each morning around 0900. Bar girls are not allowed inside the rooms. 1771 Adriatico, tel. (2) 585-4898, fax (2) 596671; P80 fan-

cooled dorm, P100 a/c dorm; private rooms P260-400 fan, P600-750 a/c.

White House: A pleasant and clean pension located within earshot of the nightclubs on Del Pilar. One of the slightly more expensive but measurably better spots in Ermita. 465 Pedro Gil, tel. (2) 522-1535, P180-320 fan, P380-520 a/c.

Casa Dalco II: A beautiful and very clean 10-room pension conveniently located near shopping, sunsets, and nightlife. Filled daily by early afternoon. 1910 Mabini, tel. (2) 508855, P420-560 a/c.

Casa Dalco I: This lovely home with large rooms, high ceilings, and a peaceful yard is recommended despite being somewhat distant from Ermita. Well worth the walk from Ermita. 1318 Agoncillo, tel. (2) 598522, P220-280 fan, P300-420 a/c.

Pension Natividad: Receives good reviews from travelers and is fairly new, clean, and safe.

1690 del Pilar, tel. (2) 521-0524, P120-180 fan, P200-300 a/c.

Pension Filipina: One of the few pensions in Manila with charm and character. Rooms are large and well furnished with comfortable beds, but they are somewhat overpriced. 572 Arkansas, tel. (2) 521-1488, P180-340 fan, P440-600 a/c.

Carolina Pension: An American-owned pension with 21 clean rooms and courtyard dining. Tucked away on a quiet low-traffic street. Many of Manila's best pensions are located here in Malate, slightly removed from the tourist shops and rowdy nightclubs on Del Pilar. 2116 Carolina, tel. (2) 522-3961, P180-300 fan, P400-600 a/c private bath.

Eden's Tourist Inn: Another simple but clean pension on a quiet street near the Malate Catholic School. Twenty rooms and restaurant with "Deutche and Philippinishe Kuche." 2158 Carolina, tel. (2) 522-2389, P300-350 fan double, P500-600 a/c double.

Rich and Famous Pension: Fan-cooled rooms are clean but small, while a/c rooms are large and cheap. East of Taft Avenue near the universities; a 10-minute walk from Ermita. 1655 Leon Guinto, tel. (2) 522-1225, P160-320. A decent place although nobody rich or famous has ever stayed here.

Other Pensions: Manila's Tourist Office currently lists over 50 pensions in the Ermita-Malate area, so finding a room shouldn't be much problem. Most are inexpensive but only adequate for short stays. The following are above average. All have fan-cooled rooms for P200-250 and a/c from P350. Santos Pension on Mabini is popular with Peace Corps volunteers, who receive a discount. Olga Casa Pension on the same street has large rooms with wide beds. Another old favorite is Congress Family Pension on Del Pilar, with fan-cooled rooms and a dormitory. Dumps to avoid include the dirty and decrepit Youth Hostel and the following pensions: New Olga Casa, Traveler's, Manda, Lucky, and New Park Lodge.

Moderate

Swagman Hotel: This small Australian hotel, which caters to bachelors on holiday, offers good vibes and ice-cold beer plus friendly, helpful personnel. Swagman's other resort hotels are located at Playa Blanca Beach Resort in Ilocos Norte, and at Pacific Island Dive Resort in southern Luzon. Swagman is an excellent choice for middle-priced travelers. Further information by mail. 411 Flores, tel. (2) 599881, US$32-40.

Hotel Soriente: A modern, clean, 35-room hotel on a quiet side street. All rooms are a/c with private baths and, like most other mid-priced to luxury hotels, subject to an additional 12% government tax and a 10% service charge. Rates are negotiable during the rainy summer months. 1123 Bocobo-Flores, tel. (2) 599106, US$25-30.

Mabini Street Hotels: Over a dozen middle-priced hotels are strung along Mabini Street. Most charge US$25-45 for a/c rooms with private bath. Addresses, phone numbers, and prices are listed on the hotel chart. Popular spots include the Royal Palm at 1227 Mabini, Tower Hotel at 1313, Sundowner at 1430, Las Palmas at 1616, and the MacArthur at 2120.

Apartments: Visitors staying for longer periods should consider renting an apartment, a mansion, or an apartel. Most include large bedrooms, separate living and dining spaces, refrigerators, kitchenettes, TV, and phone. Discounts of 25-35% are granted for stays of one month. For example, Euro-Nippon Mansion on Roxas Boulevard charges P700-1000 daily but only P9000 monthly. Electricity is separate and based on meter readings. Security deposits should be used for the last month's rent.

Luxury

Manila's luxury hotels provide superb accommodations at some of the lowest prices in the region. Their long period of low occupancy and bargain-basement deals ended a few years ago, but rack rates remain much lower than in similar facilities in other Southeast Asian capitals. It's a sign of confidence that some hotels are now cautiously expanding and renovating their long-neglected properties. Another delightful surprise is the quality of hotel staffs, whose warmth and hospitality enliven any visit to Manila. The city has 13 five-star, six four-star, and 15 three-star hotels in all possible price ranges and locations. The following are recommended for their nostalgic appeals, sunset views, or convenient locations.

Manila Hotel: Charm and historic character are the draws at one the oldest and grandest hotels in the Far East. The breathtaking lobby inside this national landmark is worth a visit even if you can't afford the tariff. Rizal Park, tel. (2) 470011, fax (2) 471124, US$200-280.

Philippine Plaza: Sunsets are best from Manila's only luxury hotel perched directly on the edge of the bay. Managed by the Westin group, this 675-room property recently spent over US$10 million on room and lobby renovations. Recreational facilities include a lagoon-shaped swimming pool with a waterslide for the kids and island bar for the adults, a 24-hour health club, and tennis courts. CCP Complex on Roxas Boulevard, tel. (2) 832-3485, fax (2) 832-3485, US$160-240.

Manila Midtown Hotel: This luxurious hotel is ideal for visitors who would like to stay in a five-star hotel within easy walking distance of the tourist shops and nightclubs. The a/c lobby is a popular place for good coffee while reading local newspapers and the *Asian Wall Street Journal.* Pedro Gil at Adriatico, tel. (2) 573911, fax (2) 522-2629, US$100-180.

RESTAURANTS

Filipino

Being an international capital, Manila's food scene runs the gamut from Spanish paella and Indonesian rojak to Japanese tempura and American hamburgers. However, native Filipino cuisine should also be tried. Authentic Filipino dishes—mildly seasoned mixtures of pork, chicken, fish, and vegetables accompanied by rice and sauces—are unlike other foods in Southeast Asia. Reactions vary widely. Adventurous types enjoy the earthy taste sensations and freshness of the ingredients; others dislike the heavy sauces and overall blandness. Native restaurants throughout Manila and the rest of the country come in several styles. Less expensive ones are often *turo turo* (point point) style, which lets you point to whatever looks best, a convenient way to select something without blindly ordering off the menu. These are plentiful along Del Pilar and Mabini streets. Also worth searching for are *kamayan* restaurants, which serve Filipino fare on banana leafs without the use of silverware. It's hand to mouth in these places! While more expensive than *turo turo* cafes, the food and atmosphere are generally much better, plus many

also include a Filipino dance revue or fashion show with your meal. A few of the more popular Ermita restaurants:

Kamayan: The nature and style of Filipino speciality restaurants forever changed about 15 years ago when the first Kamayan restaurant opened in Manila. Food is eaten with the hands, which are washed in the earthenware water containers that line the wall. Try sizzling milkfish, shelled prawns, and chicken *binakol* charbroiled in a bamboo tube. 523 Padre Faura. Expensive.

Barrio Fiesta: The country's largest chain of restaurants specializing in native Filipino cuisine is famous for its *kare kare, inihaw na bangus,* and crispy *pata.* 110 Bocobo Street. Moderate.

Aristocrat: Filipino seafood and international specialities served in a large, informal restaurant. Try *alimango* (crabs wrapped in banana leaves), chicken honey, and *maliputo,* a locally raised freshwater fish. Open 24 hours. San Andreas at Roxas Boulevard. Moderate.

Buffets: Luncheon buffets at five-star hotels are one of Manila's best bargains. Although largely a Western smorgasbord, a selection of native dishes will also be included. Prices range from P200 at the Midtown, Silahis, and Manila Pavilion to P200-400 at the Sheraton, Hyatt, and Manila hotels.

Western And Chinese

Hula Hut: Rosie's Diner on the corner and the Hula Hut behind the Blue Hawaii serve great burgers, steaks, and daily specials from an extensive menu. Plus cute waitresses wrapped in Hawaiian costumes! 1427 Del Pilar. Inexpensive.

Iseya Hotel: Escape the belching jeepneys and street hustlers by riding the elevator to this patio restaurant on the sixth floor of the Iseya. Tasty Australian fare, inexpensive beer, and daily specials served around the clock by managers Phil and Laurie. Del Pilar and Padre Faura. Moderate.

Shakey's: The pizza is overpriced and lousy, but the place is air-conditioned and comfortable. Rock bands entertain in the evening at the Mabini branch. Rock 'n' roll in a pizzeria? Only in the Philippines! Mabini at Arquiza streets. Moderate.

Au Bon Vivant: Manila's most popular choice for *bourgeoisie cuisine Française* is tucked away in a narrow alley between Plaza Ferguson and UN Avenue. Nora Daza and her two daughters

FOOD AND DRINK

Filipino food is an intriguing blend of Malaysian, Chinese, Spanish, and—most importantly—American cuisines. You'll quickly discover—perhaps to your dismay—that hamburgers, hot dogs, and omelettes are popular throughout the country. You'll also discover that Filipino attempts at Western food have been less than successful. Rather than sticking with poorly prepared Western food, try native dishes such as *adobo* and *kare kare* served in the smaller cafes, or street food such as *lugaw* and steamed corn. Filipino food has great range but admittedly isn't popular with everybody. Critics have charged that native dishes often lack the complexity and refinement of other Southeast Asian cuisines and that sauces tend to be heavy or greasy and unimaginative. On the other hand, many dishes compensate with a freshness and simplicity that accentuate the natural flavors.

Eating in the Philippines is very inexpensive, though travelers can economize further by patronizing *turo turo* (point point) restaurants and the inexpensive street stalls. Also worth seeking out are *kamayan* restaurants, which serve native dishes on banana leaves without the use of silverware. Ordering in most restaurants is easy since menus are printed in English and service personnel speak some English. Note that many dishes are described simply by their method of cooking: any item stewed in vinegar and garlic is called *adobo*, sour soups are *sinigang*, food sautéed with tomatoes is *pangat*, food cooked in blood is *dinuguan*, and anything raw is *kilawin*. The Philippines also has one of Asia's largest selections of tropical fruits. Be sure to try a *guabano*!

Popular Filipino Dishes

adobo: a distinctive stew made from pork or chicken marinated in vinegar, garlic, soy sauce, and sugar. One of the most popular dishes in the country.

afritada: beef served Spanish style in a rich tomato sauce with olives, green peas, chopped potatoes, and slivered green peppers

asado: meat marinated in *kalamansi* juice and soy sauce, then fried and served with marinade and cubed potatoes, tomatoes, and onions

aso: dog. Popular in northern Luzon among the hilltribes.

baboy: pork

balut: fertilized but unhatched duck eggs incubated 17 days, then boiled and eaten. One of the more bizarre delicacies in the world. Filipinos believe that *baluts* ensure virility and fertility plus have aphrodisiac qualities. Novices should ask for the more mature *balut sa puti*. The proper technique is to pick the top off the shell, suck out the juice, shell completely, add vinegar and salt, and pop the crunchy fellow into your mouth. Several beers make this easier.

bangus: bony but delicious milkfish. Bred locally in fishponds.

bibingka: sweet rice cakes with coconut milk and white cheese

buko: young green coconut

calamares: squid

carne: beef

chicharon: fried pork rinds. Look for the expensive but superb rinds heavily cut with pork meat.

crispy pata: pigs' feet and forelegs fried golden brown, served with soy sauce, garlic, and *kalamansi* juice. Although most Westerners find this dish much too fatty, the crispy skin and accompanying sauce are delicious.

dinuguan: pork and intestines stewed in a rich, dark blood sauce. A mild but surprisingly tasty dish.

ginatan: anything cooked in coconut milk

gulay: vegetables

halo halo: a colorful dessert of shaved ice, colored sweets, white beans, corn, cubed fruits, and evaporated milk

hito: catfish

inihaw: Anything broiled over a charcoal fire is called *inihaw* or *ihaw*.

kare kare: beef, oxtail, or pig knuckles served in a spicy peanut sauce with rice and vegetables

kilawin: raw fish marinated in *kalamansi* juice, vinegar, and onions

lapu-lapu: rock bass

adobong pusit: cuttlefish soup with coconut milk and vinegar

lechon: roast suckling pig served with thick liver sauce. A traditional fiesta specialty.

lumpia: Filipino egg rolls

maise: steamed corn

mami: noodle soup with chicken, beef, or fish

manok: chicken

pancit: noodles prepared in several styles. Canton is egg noodles with meat and vegetables,

FOOD AND DRINK

guisado and *malabon* are thin rice noodles, *molo* is Chinese dumplings fried with garlic and meats.

pochero: beef and spicy sausage mixed with vegetables

pusit: cuttlefish

shrimp *rebosado:* baked shrimp

siopao: Chinese pork buns

sinigang: sour and delicious soup flavored with tamarind, lemon, and *calamansi*. This Filipino bouillabaisse is made from any kind of meat, fish, or shellfish, with tomatoes, radishes, and *kangkong* leaves added for flavor.

suman: long fingers of sweet rice wrapped in coconut leaves

tabala: raw oysters marinated in *calamansi* and garlic

tahong: steamed or baked mussels

tapa: a simple breakfast dish of dried beef and onions

Drinks

Filipino beer is among the finest and cheapest in the East, costing less than ten pesos per bottle. Longtime leader San Miguel is now being challenged by several new brews such as the lighter Carlsberg and less expensive Manila beer. Five-year-old Tanduay rum and locally produced gins and vodkas are all first-class spirits. Prices are ridiculously cheap at P20-30 per liter. Filipino wines, on the other hand, are disgustingly sweet and completely unappealing. Fortunately for the wine drinker, good-quality California wines are available at reasonable prices from duty-free shops in Manila.

Residents outside the larger towns often drink homebrews such as *tuba* and *tapey* rather than the more expensive beers or liquors. Both have an alcoholic content of only 12-18 proof but pack a deadly wallop with effects similar to tequila's. *Tuba* is made by extracting the sap from either *nipa* palms or the tops of young coconut palms. When drunk immediately after gathering, the yellow liquid is slightly sweet and palatable. Overnight fermenting turns the gentle firewater into something bitter and much more potent. Experts claim they can judge the hours of fermentation by the color alone. *Lambanog* is boiled *tuba* distilled in the true Kentucky moonshine manner. *Tapey* is an alcoholic beverage made from rice or corn popular with the hilltribes of northern Luzon. *Basi*, a homemade wine from Ilocos Norte, is made from crushed sugarcane juice compounded with barks and berries.

---

offer an outstanding fixed lunch for about P200. A la carte is more expensive. Reservations are recommended. 1133 Guerrera. Expensive.

La Taverna: Antipasto, osso bucco with saffron risotto, and homemade gnocchi are specialities in the big red building. 1602 Adriatico. Expensive.

Remidios Circle Bistros: Manila's trendy neighborhood for espressos, art talk, and nouvelle cuisine is centered around Rotary Circle in Malate. All of the following cafes are somewhat expensive but a refreshing change from pizzas and yet another pot of *adobo*. Prego Restaurant beneath the Paper Moon Disco is big on Italian pastas and veal dishes. Both Moviola and Cafe Adriatico are pricey but have relaxed atmospheres. Espresso is potent at the funky Penguin Cafe Gallery beneath the Circle Pension. Bistro Remedios offers first-class Filipino dishes including *dinengdeng* from Ilocos, *pancit molo* from Iloilo, and *kamansing*

bukid from Pampangna. Patio Guernica serves Spanish specialties like *paella, lengua,* and *callos*. Names, cuisines, and clientele change by the month.

Remedios Ave.: Just west of Remedios Circle, try the Wok Inn for great Chinese food, Erieze International Steak House for beef, and Tia Maria's for Mexican dishes.

ENTERTAINMENT

Cultural Shows

Cultural Center of the Philippines: Manila's impressive CCP is the center for Filipino cultural activities including new theater, dance, and music. Reasonably priced performances by both local and international groups can be seen in several theaters. Upcoming events are displayed on the signboard on Roxas Boulevard across from the Holiday Inn.

Metropolitan Theater: Resident companies of this graceful old art-deco theater include the Manila Symphony, the Dance Theater, the Metropolitan Chorus, and the Experimental Theater Group. Schedules are published in newspapers and the local publication *What's On*.

Fort Santiago: For over two decades the experimental PETA theater group has offered controversial plays about Filipino society and political change inside the walls of the old Spanish fort. PETA's leftist but thought-provoking plays have brought them not only fame but criticism from governments in Singapore and Malaysia, who somehow feel threatened by their revolutionary messages.

Rizal Park: Free performances are given in an open-air auditorium by Filipino artists each Sunday evening starting at 1645.

Paco Park: Open-air theater with concerts held at 1800 every Friday. Great atmosphere.

Dinner Shows

Pistang Pilipino: Manila's nightlife is undoubtedly the hottest in Asia. Whether you're a bachelor searching for companionship or a family with kids in tow, one of the best places to start is at Pistang Pilipino, an Ermita flea market which sponsors twice-nightly dance revues at 2000 and 2130. The dazzling show includes tribal dances, Muslim *kulintang* orchestras, Spanish-era maids twirling parasols, Carmen Miranda look-alikes, and the popular *tinikling* bamboo dance in which fat tourists are invited to make fools of themselves. The early show is free; the 2130 revue costs P100. Highly recommended. Del Pilar at Pedro Gil.

Restaurant Shows: Many of the better restaurants in Ermita and Makati put on nightly dinner shows for their guests. Dinner plus show runs P350-600. Current favorites include Zamboanga and Palais Daan on Adriatico Street in Ermita, and Josephine's in Malate. Sulo Restaurant in Makati has another popular show.

Hotel Shows: Dance shows at leading hotels are more expensive but also more elaborate and professional. The Manila Hotel is home to the Bayanihan Dancers, the internationally famous company that frequently tours the world's capitals. The Philippine Plaza also has an outstanding show. Show plus dinner costs P500-750; reservations are recommended.

Spanish flair at Pistang Pilipino

Folk, Spanish, And Discos

Hobbit House: Manila's nightlife includes more than dinner shows and cultural revues. The Hobbit House, one of the most popular small nightclubs in town, features Mexican food and live folk music by some of the country's top performers, such as Freddy Aguilar. Food and drinks are served by dwarf waiters. P70 cover after 2030. 1801 Mabini at Remedios.

My Father's Moustache: Another small nightclub with folk musicians. P50 cover. 2144 Del Pilar near Quirino.

Guernica's: Spanish guitar and regional dishes like *gambas* and *calamares* served in a peaceful restaurant in operation over 30 years. 1325 Del Pilar. More Spanish music at El Comedor on Adriatico.

Remedios Circle Clubs: Trendy and chic bistros include the Hard Rock across from Malate Pension and the overpriced Moviola. Cover charges sometimes include unlimited drinks.

Stargazer Disco: Manila's most famous high-society hangout is on the top floor of the Silahis Hotel. Cover is P100 on weekends; P80 weekdays. Fusion, *pinoy* jazz, and Charlie Parker imitators are featured in many of the other five-star hotels. Many of the groups are phenomenal. 1990 Roxas Boulevard.

Makati Clubs: Upscale entertainment is plentiful on Makati Avenue between Imelda and Buendia avenues. Current hot spots are the Rhythm and Booze Jazz Bistro, the Billboard for disco video, and Fuddrucker's Cafe. A nice change from the sleaze of Ermita.

Girlie Bars

Manila's nightclubs, bars, and strip joints are sandwiched along Del Pilar and Mabini in the heart of the tourist district. Although most of the clientele are foreign males searching for more than a cold beer, you'll also see wide-eyed students from nearby universities and curious European couples taking in what might possibly be the hottest nightlife east of the Suez. The range is enomous. Some establishments are just friendly watering holes for beer and darts, while others are fronts for many of the 15,000 women who work as prostitutes or "hospitality" girls in the 10-block Ermita red-light district. It's a scene straight from Dante's *Inferno*: garish neon, packed sidewalks, weaving jeepneys, loitering policemen, streetwalkers, transvestites and gays, kids selling steamed corn and cigarettes, barkers pulling confused visitors into darkened bars blasting the lastest rap music, plus miles of flesh and fantasy. It's Berlin in the '30s, Havana in the '50s, and, now, Manila in the '90s.

In 1993, the mayor of Manila closed down many of the raunchier bars, but the wealthier and more upscale nightclubs are still open for business.

An economical way to tour the war zone is during happy hours 1800-2000, when beers are half price and front row seats are still vacant. Clubs owned and operated by Westerners, such as the Firehouse and the Australian Club, are far more luxurious than the locally owned cafes. All feature go-go dancers in bikinis who advertise their charms under flashing disco lights. The ritual is fairly standard. After finding a chair and ordering a drink, the customer can choose to be left alone or accept the invitation of a lady and buy her a lady's drink, which usually consists of little more than colored water. Girls usually speak English, enjoy anybody with a sense of humor, and are much less mercenary than their counterparts in other Asian capitals. After a brief conversation about the customer's country of origin and hotel (to gauge his wealth), the girl can be taken from the bar by payment of a P150-250 bar fine which varies according to the prestige of the club, beauty of the lady, and time of night. Further services are negotiable. Precautions against disease should be taken. A few of the better clubs:

Firehouse: Manila's most famous go-go bar has built its reputation on beautiful women, great music, and friendly management. It's easy to understand why it was named one of the world's top 100 bars by *Newsweek!* Arrive early for a seat. Del Pilar at Santa Monica. Nearby clubs such as Dirty Harry's, the Pit Stop, and New Bangkok also burn nightly from 1800 to 0500.

Australian Club: Petite Filipinas dressed in Aussie outfits might seem strange but perhaps not odder than other bars where they are costumed as English schoolgirls, Thai dancers, or American cowpokes. Entertaining shows with choreographed dance routines are given nightly at 0900. Del Pilar near Salas.

Blackout: A cozy little club with cold beer, foreign magazines and newspapers, and afternoon videos of the latest sporting events. Expats, retired American servicemen, and foreign news correspondants do their schmoozing in the front room. 475 Padre Faura.

Kangaroo Club: A low-key Aussie nightclub, bar, and coffee shop with reliable information on hotels, entertainment, and travel throughout the Philippines. The A$20 membership fee also includes money-exchange services, baggage storage, help with visa extentions, and advice on organized tours and diving expeditions. Quite a deal. Sundowner Hotel, 1430 Mabini.

Other Entertainment

Cockfights: Boisterous bird fights are held every Sunday afternoon in several cockpits around Manila. Whether you came to gamble or just to observe, it's one of the most entertaining spectacles in the country. The highly prized birds are fitted with sharpened blades and displayed to the highly emotional crowd before bets are verbally placed with the *calador*. Watch closely—his constant patter and elaborate system of hand signals are quite amazing. The Pasay Cockpit on Dolores Street is the closest venue.

Sunset Cruise: A relaxing and inexpensive tour of Manila Bay can be made on the MV *Carina,* which leaves from the Rizal Park Pier about one hour before sunset. Highly recommended.

SHOPPING

Handicrafts are the best buys in the Philippines. This is *not* the place to buy electronics or other imported goods, but rather woodcarvings, shell items, rattanware, and tribal art. Manila has a great selection but, as elsewhere in Southeast Asia, prices will be much lower in the area of origin. For example, woodcarvings, guitars, and brassware are cheapest in Baguio, Cebu, and Mindanao, so save your major purchases for provincial markets. Bargaining is *de rigueur* except in large department stores. Always ask for the "best price" before making your first counter offer. Note that Filipino merchants do not discount prices as sharply as in Indonesia, although you should be able to save 20-30% on most purchases. Duty-free shopping for alcohol, cigarettes, and personal items can be done at duty-free shops at the Manila airport, Makati Commercial Center, and many five-star hotels. A few of the better hunting grounds:

Ermita: Manila's main shopping area for tourists has just about everything possible—from finely carved *santos* to gaudy pop paintings on black velvet. Pistang Pilipino, a vast open-air flea market comprised of almost 100 individual merchants, is an excellent place to get an overview of what's available throughout the country. Then walk north up Mabini Street to tour several quality handicraft and curio stores. The 1400 block has several worthwhile stores such as Terry's, Likha, and Via and Antica. T'boli Arts and Crafts at 1362 Mabini is stocked with a fascinating range of beaded necklaces, belts, clothing, and utilitarian items woven from T'boli *nalak*. Tesoro's across the street at 1325 Mabini is one of Manila's largest handicraft emporiums. Mandaya weavings from Mindanao can be purchased from Godilla in the nearby Dabaw Etnika Weaving Center. Continue walking north and turn left on Cortada, a potholed alley running between Mabini and Del Pilar. Here you'll find several Muslim brassware merchants. Henry

Beyer's Tribal Arts in the Padre Faura Mall, corner of Padre Faura and Del Pilar, specializes in Ifugao crafts from northern Luzon. Finally, Casa Maria Mall at the corner of Padre Faura and Roxas Boulevard has several cramped but well-stocked antique and handicraft stores.

Intramuros: Many of the better antique and handicrafts stores in Manila are located in Makati and the walled city of Intramuros. El Amanecer at 744 Calle de Palario (General Luna Street) sports three floors of Philippine arts and crafts, including Silahis for weavings, Bob Lane's Chang Rong Gallery for antique basketry, and Galeria de las Islas for paintings and Filipiniana books. The Barrio San Luis complex on the same street has a half-dozen emporiums, including Santamaria Arts for pottery and Capricci for antique jewelry. Casa Manila opposite San Augustin is also worth touring.

TRAVEL FORMALITIES

Tourist Information
The Department of Tourism (DOT) head office (tel. 502384) in the monstrous edifice in Rizal Park has a limited supply of printed information but plenty of knowledgeable employees. Licensed guides can be hired in room 201. Open daily 0800-1800.

Student Travel Australia and Ystaphil (tel. 832-0680) are located at 4227 Tomas Claudio Street in Paranaque, off Roxas Boulevard beside the Excelsior Hotel.

Manila also has two Aussie-owned clubs which provide travel information and tour services to their members. Both the Kangaroo Club in the Sundowner Hotel and the Swagman at the corner of Mabini and Flores sell air tickets, arrange visa extensions, and operate private resorts geared toward male visitors.

Maps And Literature
The free map of Manila, Makati, and Intramuros provided by the Tourist Office is excellent, although greater detail is provided in the *City Map of Manila* published and distributed by National Bookstore. Detailed topographic maps and nautical guides can be purchased at the Bureau of Coast and Geodetic Survey on Baracca Street in San Nicolas. Various publications are given away at hotels and nightclubs

in Ermita such as the touristy *What's On in Manila* for nightclub acts and the outstanding *Expat,* which provides a steady stream of relevant news, gossip, and honest restaurant reviews. Also look for the colorful and very helpful *Survival Map of Manila.*

Bookstores

Ermita has several small but well-stocked bookstores for literature on the Philippines and other travel destinations. Solidaridad Books, a friendly shop on Padre Faura at Adriatico owned by Philippine novelist Francisco Sionil Jose, specializes in revolutionary political literature. Alemar's on UN Avenue is worth checking, although National Bookstore in Makati has a much wider selection of Filipiniana books. Publications on local arts and crafts are available from the Ayala Museum in Makati and at Philippine Village near the airport.

Visas

Anyone planning to stay in the Philippines more than 21 days should obtain a visa *before* arrival. Extensions can be made at the Department of Immigration on Magallanes Drive in Intramuros near the General Post Office but it's quite a time-consuming hassle. The best strategy is to let someone else—such as the Boomerang Club, or one of the previously mentioned Aussie travel services—take care of this formality. Permit extensions can also be made in Angeles City and Cebu. Foreign embassies are located in Makati. Hours vary but most are open 0800-1200.

Communications

Mail: Registered letters, telegrams, and parcels can be mailed from the General Post Office near the river in Intramuros. Poste restante operates from a separate counter. The GPO is open daily 0800-1700 except Sundays 0800-1200. Ordinary mail can be sent from the Ermita post office at 1335 Mabini and the office in Rizal Park across from the Manila Hotel. Stamps are sold in nearby shops.

Telephone: International phone calls can be made from PLDT offices in the JC building at 1655 Taft in Malate and the Ramon Cojuangco building on Legaspi Street in Makati. Operator-assisted three-minute calls to Europe and America cost US$15 for the first three minutes. Local calls are made from shops and restaurants. Domestic long-distance area codes are: Angeles (455), Bacolod (34), Baguio (74), Cebu City (32), Davao (82), Iloilo (33), Manila (2), Tarlac (452), and Zamboanga (62).

Electricity: 220 volts in rural areas and either 110 or 220 volts in most cities. Portable radios burn out if the voltage isn't set correctly!

Media: Manila has about 20 morning dailies controlled by wealthy families who use them as forums for their political interests. The *Manila Bulletin* has the largest classified section and some balanced reporting. Other political dailies with gossip, sensationalism, and anti-foreign diatribes include the *Malaya,* the *Daily Inquirer,* and the *Chronicle.* Popular weekly publications include the highly recommended *Expat* mentioned above and the leftist political magazine *Midweek.*

Cinema: Movies are a great bargain in the Philippines. For just a few pesos you can disappear into an ice-cold theater and enjoy first-run American films. Recommended local films produced in recent years include Lino Brocka's *Bayan Ko* and *Manila in the Claws of Darkness,* Ishmael Bernal's graphic *Manila by Night,* and the acclaimed *Perfumed Nightmare* by Kidlat Tahimik. These, of course, are rarely seen since local audiences prefer soap operas and violence, plus films starring Kris Aquino, daughter of the former president.

Other Services

Most independent but licensed money changers are located on Mabini Street. Traveler's checks can also be cashed at the Equitable Bank on UN Avenue. Shoemart Department Store in Harrison Plaza also cashes traveler's checks at good rates, plus no lines.

Discount travel agencies are almost unknown in the Philippines—budget travelers should purchase roundtrip tickets before arriving in the country or expect to pay full fare for onward travel. Modest discounts off IATA rates are sometimes offered by STA, mentioned above, and Adam's Express Travel at 494 Flores Street in Ermita.

Alex Orbito of the Philippine Healer's Circle is Manila's leading authority on the controversial subject of Filipino faith healing. Further information about his Baguio tours and Manila demonstrations can be picked up from his office in the Manila Midtown Hotel.

BUS COMPANIES IN MANILA

Sarkies: A private company with luxury coaches and comfortable minivans. Departures to Baguio at 0700 on Friday, Saturday, and Sunday. To Banaue at 0700 daily. To Legaspi at 0800 and 1900 daily. Prices are about 30% higher than for ordinary bus companies, but the location in Ermita is very convenient. Del Pilar just opposite Pistang Pilipino, tel. 508959.

Philippine Rabbit (Santa Cruz): Frequent buses to Angeles and Baguio. 819 Oroquieta off Rizal Avenue in Santa Cruz, tel. 711-5811. Take a jeepney on Mabini marked Monumento or Metrorail to D Jose Station.

Philippine Rabbit (Caloocan): Buses to Angeles, San Fernando, and Vigan. Rizal Avenue Extension at 2nd Avenue, tel. 343488. Take Monumento jeepney or Metrorail to R Papa Station.

Victory Liner (Caloocan): Buses to Olongapo. 713 Rizal Avenue Extension in Caloocan near the Bonifacio Monument, tel. 361-1506. Take Monumento jeepney or Metrorail to North Terminal.

Victory Liner (Pasay City): Buses to Olangapo, Angeles, and Baguio. EDSA, Pasay City, just east of Taft Avenue, tel. 833-0293. Take Metrorail to EDSA Station and walk east.

Pantranco North: Buses to Baguio, Lingayen, and Hundred Islands. Buses to Banaue depart daily at 0730. 325 Quezon Avenue in Quezon City, tel. 997091. Take jeepney on Taft Avenue marked Project 8 or Fairview.

Lawton Terminal: A half-dozen small companies operate buses to nearby towns, such as Calamba, Los Banos, and Batangas (for Mindoro). Intramuros opposite City Hall. Take any jeepney on Mabini.

BLTB: Buses to Santa Cruz (for Pagsanjan Falls), Tagaytay, Nasugbu, and Batangas every 30 minutes. EDSA in Pasay City, tel. 833-5501. Take Metrorail to EDSA Station and walk east.

Philtranco: Formerly called Pantranco South. Recommended for long-distance buses south to Legaspi, Samar, and Leyte. It's even possible (though suicidal) to take a direct 44-hour bus to Davao City in southern Mindanao! EDSA in Pasay City, tel. 833-5061. Take Metrorail to EDSA Station.

Dangwa Tranco: Buses to Baguio and Banaue daily at 0730. Located at Cubao in Quezon City.

TRANSPORTATION

Airport Arrival

Manila International Airport is 12 km from city center. After immigration and customs you can pick up tourist information at the DOT counter and change money at the bank office. Rates are good; ask for small change for the cab drivers. Don't get freaked out by the enormous crowd of Filipinos waiting for friends and relatives. DMTC buses (yellow) going to Ermita wait at the foot of the airport driveway, but most people take a taxi to avoid delays and the possibility of getting lost.

All taxis in Manila are metered and the correct fare to any hotel in Ermita is P50-70. Before leaving, confirm with the driver that the meter is working properly and tell him you know the correct fare. Many drivers will try to renegotiate the fare as they roar down Roxas Boulevard, or illegally attempt to collect individual fares from each passenger. Ignore independent operators. Baggage should be carried inside the cab or at least carefully watched while it's being loaded in the trunk. Budget travelers unsure of their hotel should go directly to Malate Pension to begin their hotel search.

Getting Around

Taxis: Metered taxis in Manila are about the cheapest in Southeast Asia when operating properly with well-calibrated meters. Fares average about P8 per kilometer. There are some problems, however. Cab drivers waiting at the

SHIPPING COMPANIES IN MANILA

LINE	PIER	PHONE
Aboitiz	4	276332
Carlos Gothong	10	213611
Escano	16	217680
Negros	8	816-3481
Sulpicio	12	201781
Sweet	6	201791
Asuncion	2	711-0590
William	14	219821

SHIPS FROM MANILA

DESTINATION		FROM	LINE	DEPARTURES	HOURS
Bohol	Tagbilaran	Manila	William	Tues. 1900	32
Cebu	Cebu City	Manila	Sweet	Thurs. 0900, Sun. 1200	24
	Cebu City	Manila	Sulpicio	Sun. 1000, Tues. 1000	21
	Cebu City	Manila	William	Wed. 2000, Sun. 0800	20
Leyte	Tacloban	Manila	William	Fri. 0900, Mon. 1300	24
Masbate	Masbate	Manila	Sulpicio	Fri. 1000	19
Mindanao	Cagayan	Manila	Negros	Fri. 1400	40
	Davao	Manila	William	Thurs. 1900	58
	Davao	Manila	Sweet	Tues. 1400	59
	Zamboanga	Manila	William	Thurs. 2200	36
	Zamboanga	Manila	Sweet	Tues. 1400	34
Mindoro	San Jose	Manila	William	Mon. 0100	16
Negros	Bacolod	Manila	Negros	Tues. 1000	22
	Dumaguete	Manila	William	Thurs. 1200	30
Palawan	P. Princesa	Manila	William	Fri. 2200	24
Palawan	P. Princesa	Manila	Sulpicio	Thurs. 2000	36
Panay	Iloilo	Manila	Negros	Fri. 1400, Tues. 1500	24
	Malay	Manila	William	Fri. 1900	15
Samar	Catbalogan	Manila	William	Mon. 1200	22

airport and near tourist hotels often claim their meters are broken and then attempt to negotiate flat fees. Always confirm that the meter is operating before getting into any cab. Never take a cab with a broken meter. Royal Class taxis (white and blue), are considered honest, as well as EMP cabs with white bodies and yellow stripes.

Jeepneys: The secret to getting around Manila by public transport is to recognize a few important place-names. Signs above the driver and on the side refer to either a major suburb such as Cubao or Quiapo, an important landmark such as Monumento, or a major street such as Ayala in Makati.

Jeepneys going south along Del Pilar or Taft Avenues are marked either Libertad, Baclaran, Vito Cruz, or Pasay. These are useful for reaching the Cultural Center, the Philippine Village, and the zoo.

Jeepneys going north along Mabini or Taft are marked Quiapo, Santa Cruz, Divisoria, Blumentritt, or Monumento. All northbound jeepneys pass the Lawton bus terminal and GPO before passing over the Pasig River to Quiapo and Chinatown. Fare is P2 for shorter distances.

Front seats are the most highly prized since you can actually see where you are going. Drivers stop on demand when you hiss, rap on the roof, or call out *para* or *bayad*. Blasting disco music was mercifully banned in jeepneys a few years ago but the flashing Christs and cheeky slogans carry on.

Buses: Buses also display their destinations on the front and sides. Most buses follow a circular route from Taft Avenue in Ermita out to Makati, up EDSA highway into Quezon City, then south to Quiapo before returning to Ermita. Also vice-versa. Crowds and heat make public buses something of an ordeal. Manila, however, also has deluxe air-conditioned Love Buses, which cost only P10 and are usually half filled. An inexpensive and comfortable way to reach Makati from Ermita is on a Love Bus marked Ayala going south along Del Pilar.

Light Rail Transit: Manila's Metrorail or LRT is a fast and comfortable way to reach

Baclaran in south Manila, for the Philtranco and Victory Liner bus terminals, and to go north to Victory Liner and Philippine Rabbit bus terminals. The LRT also reaches Quiapo and the Chinese Cemetery. When time is important, take the LRT.

Car Rentals: Both international and local car-rental companies operate in the Philippines. International companies often charge both daily and mileage rates, but Filipino companies usually grant unlimited mileage for a small surcharge. National Car Rental in Makati charges P600 daily and P3500 weekly for Mitsubishi Colts. Motorcycles can be rented from Einstein's Books in Ermita.

Leaving Manila

By Air: Philippine Airlines's main office (tel. 889182) in the PAL building on Legaspi Street in Makati is as perpetually crowded as its branch office (tel. 586652 international flights, 509193 domestic) on Roxas Boulevard in Ermita. Watch out for pickpockets in both offices. PAL offices inside the Manila Hotel (tel. 494010) and the Intercontinental in Makati (tel. 893654) are much less crowded. PAL tickets and waiting-list status can be reconfirmed 24 hours by calling 832-3166.

Taxi fare from Ermita to Manila International Airport is P50-70; to the domestic airport is P40-60. Airport departure tax for international flights is P250.

AROUND MANILA

While the most popular destinations on Luzon are the Banaue rice terraces and the mountain towns of Bontoc and Sagada, several places of interest are close enough to Manila to be visited on shorter excursions. Travel agents in Ermita organize tours, but independent travelers will have little trouble reaching the following attractions by bus.

The five provinces south of Manila—Cavite, Laguna, Batangas, Rizal, and Quezon—are now united in an ambitious economic plan called Calabarzon, an international effort planned by a Japanese agency in cooperation with Filipino industries. The tourism sector includes two new national parks, an amazing amount of development near Lake Taal, and overdue improvements to beach and scuba-diving facilities in Cavite and Batangas provinces.

Routes

Corregidor, the famous organ at Las Pinas, and the Sarao jeepney factory are half-day visits, while the provinces south of Manila are best experienced on longer journeys.

A popular three- to five-day tour begins with a visit to Las Pinas Church and the nearby Sarao jeepney factory before continuing down to Tagaytay and Lake Taal. Accommodations are available on the volcanic ridge at Tagaytay and down at Talisay at the lakeside. Alternatively, after enjoying the views for a few hours and possibly descending down to lake level, local transport can be taken down to the beaches near Anilao or over to San Pablo, where a youth hostel overlooks beautiful Sampaloc Lake.

Beaches south of Manila—West Cavite, Nasugbu, and Anilao—are average, but they're convenient for visitors with only a few extra days in the country, plus the diving is considered quite good.

Within striking distance of San Pablo are the expensive private resort of Hidden Valley and an excellent museum at Villa Escudero. Hidden Valley is overrated, but the museum and park at Villa Escudero are highly recommended. Buses continue northeast to Pagsanjan for budget accommodations and river rides early the following morning.

Travelers with more time might spend a night at one of the hot-spring resorts between Los Banos and Calamba before trekking up Mt. Makiling. The return to Manila by bus takes about two hours. Otherwise, backtrack to Batangas City and take a boat across to Mindoro Island.

CORREGIDOR ISLAND

Guarding the entrance to Manila Bay is the tadpole-shaped "Rock" where American and Filipino forces made their final stand against the Japanese forces in 1942. After five months of constant bombing, the May 1942 surrender was followed by the infamous Bataan Death March, in which over 10,000 POWs died from beatings and executions.

Corregidor today is an eerie place of destroyed bunkers, mile-long barracks, and rusting batteries being swallowed by jungle vegetation. Visitors can wander through a museum with photographs of prewar Corregidor, see a Pacific memorial to those who died in the struggle, and walk around Malinta Tunnel where Douglas MacArthur, President Quezon, and General Wainwright once survived the intense shelling. During the day children sell machine-gun bullets to tourists, while metal dealers illegally dismantle the six-inch guns for scrap during the night.

Accommodations
Choices include the 31-room Corregidor Inn and the Corregidor Youth Hostel. Obtain reservations from the Philippine Department of Tourism.

Transportation
Corregidor tours are rather expensive and schedules change with the seasons. The tourist office can help with current details.

As of this writing, escorted trips cost P1000, last five hours, and leave daily at 0730 and 1300 from the boat dock near the Manila Hotel. Hovercraft service is occasionally available from the Cultural Center Complex.

LAS PINAS ORGAN

The world's only bamboo organ can be seen in the San Jose parish church in Las Pinas. Constructed by Father Diego Cera in 1817-22, the organ fell into disuse for almost a century until 1973 when Hans Gerd Klais, a German organ specialist, had it rebuilt in Bonn. Today the famous 3.5-ton Balik organ and its 832 bamboo and 130 metal pipes can be heard during Sunday services and sometimes during the day 0900-1100 and 1400-1600. Organ music tapes are sold in the gift shop.

Transportation
To reach Las Pinas, 12 km south of Rizal Park, take any bus on Taft Ave. marked "Zapote" or "Cavite" and ask the driver to drop you near the church. Public buses continue south past the Sarao jeepney factory and to Lake Taal.

SARAO JEEPNEY FACTORY

Three km south of Las Pinas in the town of Zapote is the Sarao Motors jeepney factory, where decorative bodies are mounted on Japanese frames for Manila's wild wagons. The operation began in 1953 when Leonardo Sarao saw the potential for converting American jeeps left behind after WW II into public-transportation vehicles. Sarao stretched the jeep chassis so that 10 people could be packed inside and then added the colorful paint job that somehow typifies what is most exuberant about the Filipino lifestyle. Today, the factory and its 450 employees crank out about 1,500 jeepneys per year, each costing about US$8000.

Tourists are welcome to wander around and watch the workmen; closed Sundays.

BEACHES NEAR MANILA

Beaches in Cavite and Batangas provinces just south of Manila don't rank with those of Cebu or Borocay but are convenient for short-term visitors without the time to visit more distant areas. Facilities are well developed and run the gamut from inexpensive chalets to luxurious resorts.

Resorts are located in three areas: expensive spots near Maragondon on the west coast of Cavite Province, family bungalows for weekenders near Nasugbu in western Batangas, and dive resorts popular with Westerners around Anilao in southern Batangas.

West Cavite Resorts
Beaches south of Cavite town are nothing spectacular and are almost entirely taken up with expensive resorts and private marinas. Reservations can be made through travel agents in Manila.

Puerto Azul Beach Resort: Puerto Azul is a five-star resort with several restaurants, a swimming pool, an 18-hole golf course, and 350 rooms overlooking Manila Bay. The palatial Marcos retreat with its great views of Corregidor is now open to the public. Ternate, Cavite, tel. (2) 574731, US$65-140.

Marabella Marina: An extravagant white-elephant condominium complex constructed by Ferdinand and Imelda—geared strictly toward wealthy Filipinos and Westerners. Ternate, Cavite, tel. (2) 732-1051, US$80-150.

Nasugbu Resorts

Better beaches and less expensive accommodations are available in western Batangas near the towns of Nasugbu and Matabungkay. Take a BLTB bus from Pasay City and a jeepney from Lian.

Maya Maya Reef Club: A private club with scuba diving, windsurfing, sailing, fishing, and tennis. Reservations must be made in Manila. Nasugbu, tel. (2) 810-6685, fax (2) 815-9288, P1000-1500.

White Sands Beach Resort: Another popular resort with good sand and decent diving is on a cove four km north of Nasugbu. Day visitors are charged an entrance fee. Nasugbu, tel. (2) 833-5608, P250-480.

Fortune Island: Until recent years the exclusive abode of marine turtles, Fortune Island was recently developed by owner Tony Leviste into a Mediterranean-style resort complete with swimming pool, dive facilities, and, believe it or not, fluted columns that resemble those of the Parthenon. Boats leave from Nasugbu but reservations must be made in Manila through the Fortune Island Resort Club.

Matubungkay Resorts

Less expensive spots popular with weekenders are concentrated on the beach just south of Nasugbu. Matubungkay's two-km beach is almost completely lined with cottages on the nearest adequate beach to Manila.

Swiss House Hotel: An average place with simple restaurant and clean rooms with fan. Matubungkay, no phone, P200-350.

Sea View Lodge: A Swiss-operated seaside bungalow whose reasonable rates don't rise dramatically on weekends. Matubungkay, no phone, P200-450.

Matubungkay Beach Resort: The top-end choice with restaurant, swimming pool, and tennis courts. Matubungkay, tel. (2) 817-6723, US$40-70.

Anilao Resorts

Scuba divers short on time should head directly to Anilao near Batangas City, the country's best bet for quick underwater adventure. Spread along the brown-sand beach are a half-dozen resorts with moderately priced accommodation in tents or cabins, restaurants, equipment rentals for those with NAUI or PADI cards, and organized dives to offshore islands. Dive shops in Manila can help with reservations. Take a BLTB bus from Pasay City and transfer in Batangas City.

Anilao Beach Resort: Operations popular with Westerners include Anilao Seasport, Dive 7000, Dive South Marina, and this less expensive resort just outside of town. Anilao, tel. (2) 834-1641, P300-450.

Aqua Tropical Resort: The region's best dive resort is four km south of Anilao. Facilities include a pool, a restaurant, and dive equipment. Their Manila office is in the Manila Midtown Hotel on Pedro Gil. Bagalangit, tel. (2) 587908, fax (2) 818-9720, P600-1200.

TAGAYTAY

Perched on a ridge 686 meters above sea level, Tagaytay City (City?), a sprawling collection of homes and shops, offers a spectacular vista over one of the world's most scenic volcanos. Today, the views, the lake, and the volcano form one of Luzon's most popular tourist destinations.

Tagaytay is also exploding into a tourism center that will soon rival anything else in the country. Upcoming developments include the expansion of the Taal Vista Lodge from 27 to over 750 rooms, plus a casino, a new 400-room Hyatt Hotel, hundreds of luxurious condominiums, and perhaps a cable-car ride from the ridge down to the shores of Lake Taal.

Palace In The Sky

Tagaytay's big draws are the views over Lake Taal and the fresh air, though a visit to the Palace in the Sky is well worth the effort.

Palace in the Sky: One of the more remarkable sights near Tagaytay is this magnificently situated, partially completed, and never-occupied home of ex-dictator Ferdinand Marcos. The rather amazing history of this ill-fated project is related on a signpost erected near the front entrance. The Palace briefly made newspaper headlines in May '89 when a helicopter used in filming a Chuck Norris movie crashed into a nearby ravine, killing four people. Early mornings guarantee unlimited views from Manila to Batangas and Corregidor.

Marcos's Palace in the Sky is located up a winding road five km east of Taal Vista Lodge. It's too far to walk, but jeepneys can be chartered from the Tagaytay road junction for P30.

Accommodations

Tagaytay is exploding with new hotels and guesthouses, so expect this short list to be dated by the time you arrive.

Taal Vista Lodge: Until the opening of the Hyatt, Tagaytay's leading hotel remains the best place for views, photographs, and lunch. Prior to renovation the hotel was a lousy place to stay, with overpriced and smelly rooms, but improvements are expected by late 1993. Cultural shows are given on weekends. Tagaytay, Manila, tel. (2) 810-2016, US$40-80.

Villa Adelaida: A less expensive hotel with pool and restaurant is several kilometers east of the Taal Vista Lodge in a suburb named Foggy Heights. Barangay Sungay, tel. (2) 876031, P550-800.

Private Homes: The market across the road from the Taal Vista Lodge can help with accommodations in private homes, but they also suffer from a rip-off-the-tourist mentality. The lack of reasonably priced accommodation forces many budget travelers back to Manila by nightfall or on to San Pablo, Pagsanjan, or nearby beach resorts.

Transportation

Tagaytay is 60 km south of Manila and can be reached in 90 minutes by BLTB bus from Pasay City. Look for a bus marked "Nasugbu."

TALISAY AND LAKE TAAL

Taal is not only one of the Philippines's most active volcanoes but also one of the deadliest in Southeast Asia. An explosion in 1911 killed over 1,300 people while another eruption in 1965 destroyed several villages and killed hundreds more. An eruption in 1992 forced the evacuation of thousands from the interior islands to more secure locations at Talisay and Tagaytay.

The present topography is somewhat complicated, but Taal itself is an enormous caldera filled by a vast lake in which sits Volcano Island

and its two cones: an extinct one on the northwest filled with cold water heavy with sulfuric acid, and an active cone on the southwest which occasionally belches forth sulfuric fumes and spits out ash. The principal town on the north shore is Talisay.

Volcano Tours

Volcano Island can be visited by hiring a *banca* and guide in Talisay on the north shore or San Nicolas on the southwest. Rates and all services must be firmly negotiated in advance, but figure on about P250-300 for boat, gasoline, and guide services. It's a common tactic of many boatmen to demand additional money for gasoline once you're in the middle of the lake.

Accommodations

Accommodations in Talisay include several simple resorts along the lake and Rosalina's Pension, at the intersection of the descending and lakeside roads. Rosalina charges P50-100 and can help with boat rentals and guides.

Transportation

Lake Taal can be reached from several directions, but the easiest route is by minitruck down from the road junction on Tagaytay Ridge, a steep and extremely winding journey. What a ride! Lake Taal can also be reached by bus from Pagsanjan via Los Banos, Calamba, and Tanauan.

SAN PABLO

This small town, famous for its seven crater lakes formed eons ago by volcanic activity, also serves as a convenient base for visiting the nearby attractions of Hidden Valley and Villa Escudero.

Attractions

Sampaloc Lake, directly behind City Hall, is the most accessible body of water in the vicinity. An early-evening stroll along the circular road will uncover floating fishpens surrounded by narrow bamboo rafts used by the fishermen, fields of cultivated water hyacinths, and the Kamayan Dagat Restaurant, which serves Chinese dishes and fish specialties made of tilapia raised in the nearby pens. Filipinos relaxing in outdoor cafes are happy to share shots of the local brew and chat with visitors.

San Pablo's other six lakes, all located outside of town, are difficult to reach without private transportation.

Accommodations

San Pablo has several inexpensive hotels in town, but it makes sense to stay near the lake and enjoy the views.

Sampaloc Lake Youth Hostel: San Pablo's best value is this clean and friendly hostel in a quiet residential neighborhood overlooking the lake. From the church, walk down Schetelig St. and turn left at the YH sign. Efarca Village, tel. 4448, P70-120.

Transportation

San Pablo is 87 km from Manila and can be reached in two hours with any BLTB, Philtranco, or Superlines bus marked Lucena, Daet, Naga, or Legaspi. From Pagsanjan, take a jeepney to Santa Cruz followed by another to San Pablo.

VICINITY OF SAN PABLO

Hidden Valley Springs

This 44-hectare private resort four km north of Alaminos offers picnic tables, hot springs dammed into artificial swimming pools, a small waterfall, and concrete paths leading through jungle thick with the massively buttressed trunks of huge dipterocarps.

Hidden Valley is a pleasant but touristy place, certainly not worth the stiff P600 admission fee.

Villa Escudero

One of the finest collections of arts and crafts in the Philippines can be seen in the superb museum at Villa Escudero, a private coconut plantation south of San Pablo. The late Don Arsenio Escudero was an incurable collector of almost everything: stuffed birds, silver spoons, coins, tanks and cannons, Filipino costumes, and magical amulets that stop bullets. On a more serious side, his large museum also displays a wide range of religious artifacts such as priceless *santos,* silver altars from well-known churches, and lovely Chinese celadons. After touring the museum, you can take a leisurely ride on a *carabao* cart and do a few laps in the icy swim-

ming pool. Bring your swimsuit. Admission on weekdays is P100.

Accommodations: Escudero cottages cost P500-800, depending on facilities.

Transportation: Villa Escudero is ten km south of San Pablo. Take a jeepney from San Pablo to the park entrance and walk one km through the coconut groves.

San Pablo To Pagsanjan

Between San Pablo and the falls at Pagsanjan are several worthwhile sights.

Nagcarlan: Fifteen km east of San Pablo is an old town with unusual residential architecture, a fine church dating from 1752, and a circular cemetery much like Manila's Paco Cemetery. Worth a quick stop.

Majayjay: The historic and largely untouched town of Majayjay a few kilometers south of the main road from Sambat is dominated by a monumental three-story church built between 1711 and 1730. Having survived all subsequent earthquakes, it remains the oldest religious structure in the country and an outstanding example of Philippine colonial baroque architecture.

Bridge of Whims: Also visit the Puenta del Capricho ("Bridge of Whims") five km from Majayjay. Constructed in the 1850s by a parish priest using forced labor, this huge stone bridge was partially destroyed in the film *Apocalypse Now.*

PAGSANJAN

Shooting the rapids on the Bumbungan River near Pagsanjan (pronounced Pak-SAN-han) is one of the most popular adventures near Manila. *Bancas,* which are pushed, pulled, and paddled by any of Pagsanjan's 1,200 licensed *banceros,* can be hired at local hotels or at the upriver Pagsanjan Falls Lodge. Fees are set by the government at P150 per passenger or P300 for solo riders. Boatmen expect a tip of P50-100; ignore pushy *banceros* who plead for larger tips by bragging about the generosity of other customers.

The journey begins in dugouts towed by motorized *bancas* which noisily roar through the canyon walls hung with curtains of mosses, lianas, orchids, and begonias, past wispy waterfalls and chattering monkeys armed with coconuts. A local tourist office now stands on the site of the Indochinese temple constructed for and then dramatically destroyed in Coppola's 1975-76 *Apocalypse Now*. Other scenes filmed along the riverbanks have appeared in *Platoon* and several of Chuck Norris's war sagas, and the infamous helicopter accident that killed Vic Morrow and three children during the filming of *The Twilight Zone* occured here. Vietnamese village film sets, complete with watchtowers and red flags, seem to have become permanent fixtures up here.

Eventually, the motorized *bancas* disconnect and the remaining 14 rapids are hurdled up to 30-meter Magdapio Falls, which thunders into an icy pool. For a few additional pesos, you can get yourself drenched on a raft guided along fixed wires. Bring a plastic bag for your camera.

The descending trip is exciting but not as amazing as the upriver pull. The entire journey takes about three hours. The only way to avoid tour groups who flood the river by late morning is to spend a night in Pagsanjan and do an early-morning river run. Whatever you do, avoid weekends, when the river resembles Disneyland.

Accommodations

Most budget accommodations are on Garcia St. alongside the river.

Willy Flores's Place: A longtime favorite operated by postman Willy, his wife Pacita, and their boatman son, Noli, all of whom can ad-vise on nearby hiking, swimming, dancing, and weekend cockfights. Also on the same street, but somewhat more expensive, is Pagsanjan Village Hotel and Riverside Bungalows. 821 Garcia St., no phone, P50-120.

Pagsanjan Youth Hostel: A peaceful but somewhat difficult place to find. Walk across the river, turn right, and look for the AYH sign. 237 General Luna St., tel. 2124, P60-100.

Camino Real Hotel: Best choice in the mid-priced range is this modest but very clean hotel on the main street near the bridge. 39 Rizal St., tel. 2086, P150-350.

Pagsanjan Falls Lodge: An upscale yet poorly maintained lodge popular with European pedophiles and Filipinos on group tours from Manila. The pool, however, is a relaxing place to hang out in the evening and enjoy views over the river. Maulawin, tel. 645-1215, P350-500.

Transportation

Buses to Santa Cruz leave from the Lawton bus terminal near City Hall. BLTB in Pasay City also serves Santa Cruz. Jeepneys continue from Santa Cruz to Pagsanjan. Ignore the tricycle drivers and watch your belongings as this is a *very* popular route for professional pickpockets and bag slashers.

From Pagsanjan, you can return to Manila via Santa Cruz or go directly to San Pablo, Lake Taal, Tagaytay, or Batangas for Mindoro, or head south toward Legaspi.

NORTHERN LUZON

Northern Luzon's varied topography, cultural minorities, beaches, and amazing rice terraces have made it one of the country's most popular destinations. Several weeks would be necessary to explore the more remote regions, but a quick loop through the central Mountain Province can be completed in seven to 14 days with public transportation.

A recommended counterclockwise loop visits the Banaue rice terraces and the lovely mountain town of Sagada before passing through Baguio on the return to Manila. This covers the highlights of northern Luzon, although those with more time might detour to the beaches on the west coast. Another bit of advice: contrary to tourist office promotions and the generally held belief of many Filipinos, Sagada and Banaue are far more pleasant and intriguing destinations than the congested city of Baguio.

ANGELES CITY

Clark Air Force Base, once the largest American military installation outside the U.S., is located 82 km north of Manila on the highway to Baguio. Prior to the eruption of Mt. Pinatubo, the U.S. operated the 9,000-man base, but it was abandoned in 1991 after being destroyed by the volcano.

Despite the enormous amount of volcanic ash which swirls around the streets, Angeles continues to be a classic study of the influence of a foreign military base on the local population, not to mention that it's some sort of surrealistic cowboy town.

Attractions

Parasitically surrounding the fences of the abandoned air base are dozens of surviving bars, nightclubs, strip joints, clip joints, restaurants, used-car dealers, souvenir shops, a casino, and short-term hotels that once served the recreational needs of servicemen.

It is expected that the 1993 campaign by the mayor of Manila to close many of the brothels on M.H. del Pilar Ave. will force much of the flesh trade north to Angeles City and nearby Olangapo.

Caution: Angeles is the con captial of the Philippines. Check your valuables at the front desk, ignore all touts, don't play cards, never get in empty jeepneys, and avoid *all* tricycle drivers—they extort huge sums from unsuspecting tourists.

Nightclubs

Nightclubs are concentrated along Fields Ave. and up Plaridel Ave. opposite the deserted air base. Surprisingly, professional live cabaret shows are still performed nightly at the "World Famous" Nipa Hut off MacArthur Highway.

Shopping

Angeles also has a great selection of shops selling Filipino handicrafts, wicker furniture, shellwork, and oddities such as dead, stuffed, boxing frogs.

This town is strictly for the weird and the brave; a place only Hunter S. Thompson could love.

Accommodations

Angeles's medium-quality hotels generally charge US$15-30 for air-conditioned rooms with private baths and TVs.

New Liberty Inn: Inexpensive option on Coching Alley off MacArthur Hwy. where rundown fan-cooled rooms cost P150-400. The old backpackers' favorite.

Flamingo Hotel: Just across MacArthur but with clean rooms. P150-250 fan, P250-350 a/c.

Swagman Narra Hotel: This spot hidden away on Orosa Street caters to Aussie bachelors on holiday. Facilities include a swimming pool, soccer matches on the tube, and an open-air bar filled with friendly escorts. US$18-35.

Kangaroo Clarkton Hotel: Located on Plaridel Ave. near Clarkview Gate. Similar facilities to the Swagman. US$18-35.

Transportation

Philippine Rabbit buses from Rizal Ave. in Manila stop in downtown Angeles a few kilometers from the hotels and nightclubs. Jeepneys shuttle from the bus terminal to the hotels on MacArthur Highway.

Direct air-conditioned coaches from the Swagman Club in Ermita to the Swagman Narra Hotel in Angeles are somewhat more expensive than Rabbit buses, but *much* more convenient; there's no obligation to stay at a Swagman hotel.

Buses back to Manila, up to Baguio, and over to Olongapo can be picked up where MacArthur Hwy. intersects the road to the Dau Expressway, just beyond McDonald's and the old tourist office on your left.

OLONGAPO

Perhaps without exaggeration, Olongapo once claimed to be the entertainment capital of the Philippines. Lined along the main thoroughfare of Magsaysay Dr. were dozens of clubs featuring the widest possible selections of live musical entertainment—country and western, heavy metal, new wave, ska, reggae, and rap. Some of the best music in Asia.

Prior to the Americans leaving the 5,000-man naval base of Subic Bay in late 1992, the best clubs were flashy California Jam with contemporary rock under great staging, Radio City for some of Manila's top bands, and cavernous Sierra Club for heavy-metal favorites.

It is now much quieter, but until the last club closes, anyone who enjoys great rock 'n' roll should consider the trip to Olongapo.

Also, Olongapo holds an annual Mardi Gras celebration on Fat Tuesday.

Accommodations
Obviously, rooms have been plentiful since the closure of Subic Naval Base.

Bayview Hotel: The budget traveler's favorite is located two blocks down Rizal Ave. from the Victory bus terminal. P80-150. (Try the *lugaw* soup at the church entrance just opposite.)

Moderate Hotels: Several hotels in the US$10-20 price range still survive on Rizal and Magsaysay avenues.

Transportation
Victory Liner serves Olongapo from Manila and Angeles.

BANAUE

The manmade rice terraces at Banaue have been called the Eighth Wonder of the World. Although rice-terrace culture is practiced throughout all of Southeast Asia, those near Banaue are incomparable in terms of magnitude and daring. Anthropologists and archaeologists believe they were constructed by the ancestors of the Ifugaos over 2,000 years ago. Today they soar from the valley depths to the mountain peaks almost a mile above, forming vast amphitheaters cleverly irrigated by manmade waterfalls that gently cascade down the terrace walls. Laid end to end the terrace walls would stretch around the world; the total amount of stone used exceeds that in the pyramids of Egypt. Aside from the spectacular topography, Banaue offers superb hiking, handicrafts, and Ifugao villages largely untouched by Westernization.

Attractions
Banaue: Banaue town is an unimaginative square surrounded by handicraft shops, cafes, inexpensive pensions, and the burned-out remains of the trade center. The market on Saturday morning is worth attending, although only the elderly continue to wear traditional clothing. A brief but informative history of the area is posted on the historical marker near the main road. Traveler's checks can be cashed at the Banaue Savings and Credit Coop, Banaue Hotel, and the Traveller's Inn, but rates are better at the PNB in Bontoc. Ifugao dance shows are given on Sunday evenings only during the high season at the Banaue Hotel.

Banaue Rice Terraces: The finest panoramic views of the terraces are from the viewpoint located four km up the Banaue-Bontoc road. Hike up the road or wander through the terraces via Bocus village. Banaue is most spectacular in the fall after the rains, when the ricefields are a brilliant green. Hiking during the summer months is difficult because of heavy rains and thick mud. Guides are only necessary for hikes beyond Batad. Prices should be agreed upon in advance.

Bocus and Matanglag: This half-day hike passes through the woodcarving and weaving village of Bocus before arriving in Matanglag, a bronzesmith center where fertility pendants are cast using the lost-wax method.

Tam An and Poitan: This short trek beginning just behind the Banaue Hotel includes the touristy weaving village of Tam An and Poitan, where several traditional Ifugao houses with *cogon* roofs still stand.

Batad: Batad's magnificent amphitheater of rice terraces, 12 km east of Banaue, is one of the highlights of the region.

Jeepneys can be chartered to the drop-off point for P200 one-way or P450 roundtrip for those who intend to return the same day. Hikers are met at the cafes overlooking Batad by either Francis, who figured in *Apocalypse Now,* Peter Gatic, or Vincente. Their P150 fee includes guide services, food, and accommodations such as Simon's Viewpoint Inn, Rita's, or Mount View Inn. Guides are unnecessary for visiting Batad and making short hikes. Rooms are also available at Foreigner's Inn down in Batad or with Delia Rybach in Cambulo.

It's a two-hour hike from Batad to Cambulo and five additional hours from Cambulo to Banaue. Further treks from Batad include a three-day hike to Talboc, Maggor, Patyay, and Cambulo. With proper supplies such as raingear, food, water, flashlight, and a guide you can also hike from Cambulo to Banaue via Pula and the Banaue viewpoint.

Tours can also be arranged through Delfins Trekking in the Patina Cafe.

Accommodations

Banaue has almost a dozen small hotels and pensions in the P40-100 price range and an up-scale hotel operated by the Philippine Tourism Authority.

Budget Guesthouses: Pensions at the top of the hill, such as Val Greg Hotel, Wonder Lodge, and Stairway Lodge, are slightly more expensive than those at the bottom such as the Brookside and the popular Traveller's Inn. Few of these places take advantage of the potential views but all are perfectly adequate for a night or two.

Banaue Youth Hostel: The hostel adjacent to the Banaue Hotel now costs P120 for non-members, but the place is very clean and you can use the swimming pool.

Banaue View Inn: An excellent choice for a few additional pesos is the clean and friendly lodge about 100 meters up the road toward

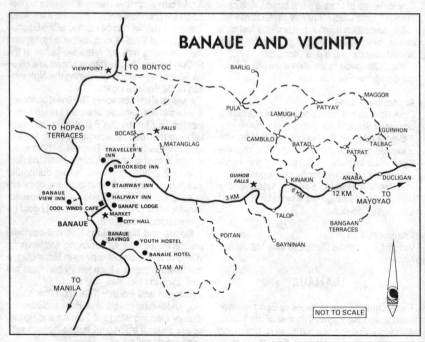

BANAUE AND VICINITY

VIEWPOINT ★   TO BONTOC

BARLIG

TO HOPAO
TERRACES

PULA

LAMUGH   PATYAY

MAGGOR

BOCAS   ★ FALLS
        MATANGLAG

CAMBULO   BATAD

GUINHON

TALBAC

TRAVELLER'S
INN

BROOKSIDE INN

STAIRWAY INN

GUIHOB
FALLS ★

PATPAT

BANAUE
VIEW INN

HALFWAY INN

COOL WINDS CAFE   SANAFE LODGE
            ★ MARKET

BANAUE   ■ CITY HALL

3 KM

KINAKIN   ANABA   DUCLIGAN

6 KM   12 KM   TO
            MAYOYAO

TALOP

BANGAAN
TERRACES

BANAUE
SAVINGS   YOUTH HOSTEL

BANAUE HOTEL

POITAN

BAYNINAN

TO
MANILA

TAM AN

NOT TO SCALE

PHILIPPINES
1. green Chocolate Hills; 2. Boracay sunset (all photos this page by Carl Parkes)

PHILIPPINES
1. parade pause; **2.** Kalibo calypso (all photos this page by Carl Parkes)

Bontoc. Rooms here start at P100 per person with common bath and P250 with private bath.

Banaue Hotel: Top-end choice is this rebuilt hotel, which largely caters to group tours and upscale travelers. Rooms cost from P1400, but 40% discounts are given during the low season from June to December.

Transportation

Banaue is 348 km from Manila, 44 km from Bontoc, and 220 km from Baguio.

Manila: The most convenient way to reach Banaue from Manila is on the Sarkies bus, which leaves daily at 0730 from their office in Ermita. Direct Pantranco buses leave from their Quezon City terminal daily at 0730. Alternatively, take a Pantranco or Dangwa bus to Solano (toward Cagayan Valley) and then the 1430 connection to Banaue.

Sarkies minibuses from Banaue back to Manila leave daily at 0930 from the market and at 1000 from the Banaue Hotel.

Bontoc: Buses to Bontoc leave from the market daily at 0500. If you miss that early departure, a bus passes the historical marker by the main road around 1100. The ride is magnificent.

Baguio: Buses to Banaue depart daily 0600-0700 from the Baguio bus terminal and take about eight hours via the less scenic southern route through San Jose and Bayombong.

A better option is the early-morning bus from Baguio to Bontoc, which snakes along the almost unbelievable Halsema mountain highway, one of the more spectacular roads in Southeast Asia. Direct connections from Baguio to Banaue are possible, though nearly all travelers take a connecting bus from Bontoc up to Sagada.

BONTOC

Though the provincial capital of Mountain Province is an important junction for travelers passing from Banaue to Baguio, the town itself has little aesthetic appeal. A few attractions are worth visiting, plus traveler's checks can be cashed at good rates from the Philippine National Bank north of the town square.

A word of caution about Bontoc. Despite the modern facade of concrete shops and corrugated roofs, you should remember that Bontoc is a very conservative town. Do not take photographs of the people without first asking permission. Bathing in the river at sunset is a pleasant experience, but you must remain well covered to avoid serious problems.

Bontoc is also a town in a remarkable state of transition: old women dressed in traditional costume with snake-bone ornaments in their hair make a startling contrast to young kids with cheeky T-shirts and thumping ghetto blasters. It is painfully obvious in Bontoc that Igorot tribal culture is quickly coming to an end.

Attractions

Bontoc Museum: This small but well-presented museum adjacent to the Roman Catholic church provides a useful overview of the arts and crafts of the three major tribes of the Cordillera: Ifugao, Bontoc, and Kalinga. Backyard displays include an authentic *ato* where elders assembled and a claustrophobic *ulog* where young unmarried girls once resided. Neither custom continues today. The tiny Kalinga handicraft shop just below the museum sells both genuine antiques and modern reproductions.

Masferre Photo Studio: While the Bontoc market is disappointingly sterile, be sure to pick up a few of the poignant black-and-white photographs of the mountain people sold at Eduardo Masferre's studio on the main road.

Weaving and Singing: Also of interest is the student weaving room in the All Saint's Elementary School a block south of the Chico River Inn. Sunday church services at St. Vincent's Church are a rare opportunity to hear the Bontocs sing.

Attractions Near Bontoc

Malincong Rice Terraces: The region's finest terraces are located directly behind the enormous hill that looms over Bontoc. A near-vertical hiking trail is plainly visible from town (the trail begins a few blocks beyond the PNB), but an easier strategy is to take the 0700 jeepney to Mainit, where you can soak in the hot springs before hiking back to Bontoc via Malincong. Guides and jeeps can be hired at Pines Kitchenette.

Kalinga Province: The road going northeast from Bontoc passes directly through the ancestral homeland of the Kalingas, former headhunters who have traditionally resisted all forms

BONTOC

of outside interference. A controversial plan to flood the Chico River Valley a decade ago for a monstrous hydroelectric dam worsened relations between the Kalingas and Manila and dramatically increased local popularity of the communist NPA. Law and order are in short supply up here. Anyone venturing into Kalinga should ask about security problems and leave all valuables back in Bontoc. Determined travelers might spend a night in Bugnay or Tinglayan, from where guides can be hired for treks to interior villages. Note that the famous Tucucan Bridge washed away a few years ago and has been replaced with a more functional concrete structure.

Accommodations
The isolation of Bontoc has limited accommodations to a few simple inns and one slightly better hotel.

Happy Home Inn: Bontoc's best budget choice is the rudimentary inn just opposite the Dangwa bus terminal. The water supply is sporadic, but owner David Yawan is most helpful with directions and advice.

Other Budget Inns: Mountain Inn and Chico River Inn are also inexpensive, though the owners aren't as helpful as David at Happy Home.

Pine's Kitchenette and Inn: Bontoc's top-end choice has a fairly good restaurant and clean rooms with common bath from P100.

Transportation
Bontoc is 44 km from Banaue, 143 km from Baguio, and 18 km down the hill from Sagada. Most travelers only overnight in Bontoc en route to Sagada, though the town makes a convenient base from which to explore the surrounding countryside.

Public transportation in spots like Bontoc is subject to delays, cancellations, and early departures depending on the whims of the driver and the capacity of the vehicle. In other words, buses and jeepneys arrive at irregular hours and leave whenever packed to capacity.

Sagada: With those caveats in mind, Skyland buses to Sagada leave daily at 0900 and 1500. Jeepneys to Sagada leave in the morning around 0800 and in the early afternoon around 1300.

Banaue: Dangwa buses to Banaue depart once daily around 0800. A jeepney from Baguio en route to Banaue passes through Bontoc sometime between noon and 1400.

Baguio: Dangwa buses to Baguio leave hourly 0600-0900 and take a full day to reach Baguio. Seats on the left provide the best views.

Kalinga: Jeepneys from Manila to Bugnay and the Kalinga region pass through Bontoc between 1300 and 1400.

SAGADA

Situated 18 km from and 600 meters above Bontoc, this small village hides itself amid spectacular limestone pinnacles and tall pines that sway in the cool mountain air. One of the most beautiful landscapes in the country, Sagada is also famous for its Igorot burial caves, vast subterranean caverns filled with limestone drippings and black rivers, crashing waterfalls, impressive rice terraces, colorful tribal weavings, and almost endless possibilities for hiking and mountain climbing. It's also a great place just to relax in the brilliant sunshine. Besides all this, Sagada offers some of the finest accommodations and food in the country. Small wonder that it has become a favorite destination for world travelers.

Attractions

Maps and further information on Sagada's sights can be picked up at Masferre's Guesthouse and other local pensions. Few of the following attractions are marked but most can be found by asking the locals for directions. Guides are also plentiful and jeeps can be hired for longer journeys. A rough map is included in this book but corrections would be highly appreciated. Traveler's checks can be exchanged at the Rural Bank of Sagada.

St. Mary's Church and Echo Valley: Episcopalian missionaries arrived in Sagada in 1904 to convert the locals and construct this oversized church. Beyond the church and graveyard on Mt. Calvary is a beautiful and mysterious limestone canyon with caves and hanging coffins. Fifteen minutes southeast from the center of Sagada.

Sagada Weavers: One of the few places in the Philippines to watch backstrap-loom weavers

slowly create colorful blankets, shawls, skirts, shoulder bags, and wallets. Prices are very reasonable. Weavings are also sold at the Sagada Cooperative. Nearby Masferre Studios sells old b/w photos. Fifteen minutes east.

Matangkib Cave and Underground River: Follow the cement path between the big boulders to a narrow limestone valley with hanging coffins near an underground river. As with many of the caves near Sagada, a guide and proper equipment are necessary for proper exploration. Twenty minutes east.

Bokong Falls: Take the trail between the houses beyond Sagada Weaving and follow the river. The larger falls one km beyond Little Bokong Falls have better swimming. Forty minutes north.

Ambasing Hanging Coffins: Local tribespeople have traditionally interred their dead in coffins hung high in remote caves to prevent the cadavers from being consumed by wild animals. The coffins beyond Ambasing (take the left fork) are easy to reach but a respectful attitude should be kept in all Igorot graveyards. Thirty minutes south.

Sumaging Big Cave: Look for the concrete steps to the left. Guides are necessary to explore the Kings Palace, the Dance Hall, and the Swimming Pool inside this vast subterranean world. Mr. Jacinto at the hospital has been leading amateur spelunkers for over 40 years. Guides and groups often gather at 0900 at the Shamrock. **Warning:** caving here is very dangerous because of vertical plunges and rocks covered with slippery bat scat. No coffins. Forty minutes south.

Farther South: Longer hikes beyond Sumaging pass Balangagand Cave (left at the waiting shed) before reaching Suyo and Ankileng in about three hours. Villages beyond Suyo include Data; Bagnen, with bathing streams and good views over the valley; and the pottery villages of Bila, Bauko, and Maggor.

West of Sagada: The road west of Sagada leads to a viewpoint in 30 minutes, Lake Danum in about one hour, the *carabao* trail up to Mt. Sipitan in two hours, Agawa Falls in three hours, and the stone agricultural calendar at Gueday in about four hours. A full day of hiking.

North of Sagada: Sagada's most spectacular waterfall is located three hours north at Fedilisan, a 30-minute hike down from Bangaan.

SAGADA

NOT TO SCALE

© MOON PUBLICATIONS, INC.

Bring your swimsuit for the icy pools. A downstream suspension bridge leads to a higher falls with more pools. The distinctively rocky Tanulon and Baang Rice Terraces, situated near the Amlusong River, are also accessible from the Sagada-Bangaan road. Jeeps can be taken from Sagada, although it's a wonderful all-day hike starting from Masferre Photo Studios.

East of Sagada: Walk down the road toward Bontoc, turn left at the village, and hike down through Kilong to the Tetepan Pools and Hanging Bridge across the Amlusong River. From Tetepan return to the road, hike north along the river to the Baang Rice Terraces, or continue across the river to Mainit, Guinaang, Malincong rice terraces, and eventually, Bontoc.

Accommodations

Places to stay in Sagada are superb value: recently constructed and still quite clean, crisp linens, wonderful views from the windows, candlelight dinners, fireplaces, buckets of hot water, freshly baked breads, and friendly management. Most charge P40-80 per person.

Masferre's Guesthouse: For over a decade Julia welcomed visitors with her singing, wholesome cooking, and advice on sightseeing. Julia's has now been renamed Masferre's, but it remains a cozy place with great views. A useful

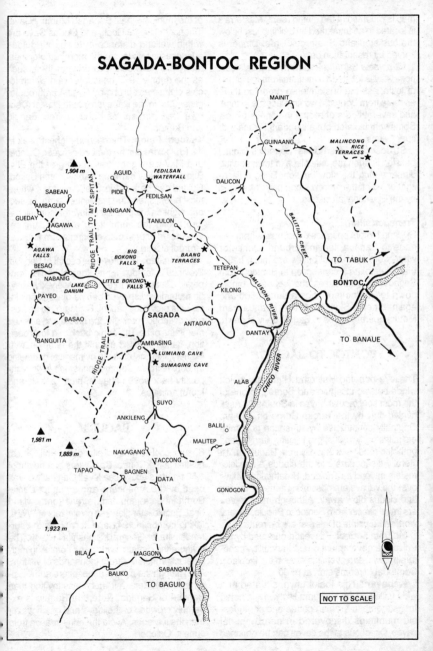

SAGADA-BONTOC REGION

NOT TO SCALE

map is mounted in the dining room. Masferre's is located in an unmarked tin building just below the bus stop and Shamrock Cafe. Dinner is served by reservation only.

Mapiyaaw Sagada Pension: Sagada's best homestay is located 15 minutes from the center of town; ask the bus driver to drop you there en route from Bontoc. Two fireplaces, a lounge, and several floors of rooms in various prices. Somewhat isolated but a wonderful place with super vibes.

St. Joseph's Resthouse: Sagada's original pension is often the only place in town serving dinner during the slow season. Bring a flashlight or fall off the narrow stone path. Managed by the Episcopalian sisters.

Transportation

Skyland Motors operates direct buses from Banaue to Sagada, leaving around sunrise or whenever filled. Direct buses are much better than attempting a connection in Bontoc. From Sagada, Skyland buses and jeepneys rumble down to Bontoc mornings around 0600 and again at noon. Skyland, Dangwa, and Lizard Motors operate buses to Baguio daily at dawn.

BONTOC TO BAGUIO

The eye-popping Halsema Highway, which winds between Baguio and Bontoc, is one of the most spectacular drives in Southeast Asia, rivaled only by the Taroko Gorge on Taiwan. Originally constructed by American gold miners in the early 1900s, this twisting, turning, and potholed road rises steadily from Baguio until it literally disappears into the clouds a few kilometers beyond La Trinidad. Breathtaking views over the valleys are possible whenever the fog and clouds blow away. Although most travelers travel directly from Bontoc to Baguio, several worthwhile points of interest are en route.

Mt. Data Lodge: This resort operated by the Philippine government offers tranquility, panoramic views, and evenings around the fireplace. Comfortable rooms start at P500.

Kabayan: This Ibaloi town, situated in a wide valley off the Halsema Highway, is noted for its aromatic Arabian coffee and centuries-old mummies discovered in nearby burial caves. Directions to the caves can be obtained

at the municipal hall. Banagao Mummy Cave, Tinongchol Burial Rock, and Opdas Cave are within walking distance of town, but guides are necessary to locate the more remote ones. Many are now locked to prevent theft, such as the daring 1977 helicopter raid which locals claim was sprung by foreign anthropologists. Stay in the Kabayan Youth Hostel. Dangwa Transport serves Kabayan from Baguio and Bontoc.

Mount Pulog: The second-highest peak in the Philippines can be climbed between October and May via a good trail starting at the Ellet Bridge, midway between Kabayan and Bokod. Guides can be hired in Ellet *barangay*, where most hikers spend the first night. Camp the second night on the plateau below the summit before hiking the summit for a frigid sunrise. Weather is unpredictable; bring warm and waterproof clothing.

La Trinidad: The provincial capital of Benguet Province is famous for its vegetables, its temperate climate, and three well-preserved Kabayan mummies displayed behind glass cases inside the provincial capitol. Estimated to be possibly over 500 years old, the naked and smoked mummies of La Trinidad crouch in a fetal position, hands pressed against the temples, with leathery skin crisscrossed by magical geometric tattoos. Narda's Cottage Industries sells high-quality handwoven shawls, plus baskets and Igorot antiques.

BAGUIO

Baguio, cool summer capital of the Philippines, nestles in the Central Cordilleras at a height of 1,524 meters above sea level. Originally developed by the Americans and architect Daniel Burnham as a mountain retreat from lowland heat, Baguio later played a pivotal role in WW II, taking bombs in 1941 and serving as the surrender site for General Yamashita in 1945. The invigorating climate, parks, and sprawling marketplace annually attract thousands of visitors, even though the big-city atmosphere and Westernized flavor make it *much* less inviting than Banaue or Sagada. Note that Baguio is extremely crowded on holidays and much wetter than the lowlands. Avoid the rainy season from June to October.

CENTRAL BAGUIO ACCOMMODATIONS

(prices in pesos unless otherwise indicated)

HOTEL	SINGLE	DOUBLE	ADDRESS	PHONE (2)
LUXURY				
Baguio Park	900-1000	100-1200	Harrison at Claudio	5626
Mt. Crest	800-1000	1000-1100	Urbano at Legarda	3324
MODERATE				
Ambassador	400-500	500-700	25 and 39 Abanao	2746
Baguio Holiday	500-600	600-750	10 Legarda	6679
Baguio Royal Inn	300-400	400-500	104 Magsaysay	5610
Belfranlt	500-600	700-900	Gen. Luna Road	5012
Burnham	400-500	600-700	21 Calderon	2331
Kisad Pension	350-450	500-600	Kisad	3507
Mount Peak Hotel	500-600	600-750	Abanao	3341
New Plaza	300-500	600-800	27 Abanao	4038
Swagman Attic	380-450	500-700	90 Abanao	5139
BUDGET				
Baden Powell House	280-380	350-540	26 Gov. Pack Road	5836
Baguio First	150	200	38 Bonifacio	2144
Baguio Garden Inn	140	200-250	5 Lapu Lapu	6398
Baguio Goodwill	200-300	300-400	58 Session	6634
Bayanihan	150	250-300	Otek at Chanum	4296
Benguet Pine Pension	280	350-600	82 Chanum Rd.	7325
Diamond Lodging	100-150	150-200	Gen. Luna Road	2339
Everlasting Pension	300	400-500	58 Magsaysay	3138
Highlander Lodge	100	150-200	Gen. Luna	7086
Leisure Lodge	180-250	250-350	143 Magsaysay	2524
Mido Lodging	150-200	200-400	Session	2575
Mountainside Lodge	100	150-200	173 Magsaysay	6483
Orange Country	120-160	120-160	27 Abanao	6775
Patria de Baguio	200	300-400	181 Session	4963
Rosebowl Lodging	220	250-350	Harrison	4213
Siesta Inn	250	350-450	Gov. Pack Road	7066
Silvertone Inn	180	250-350	Perfecto	3950
YMCA	80-100 (dorm)		Post Office Loop	4766

Attractions

Tourist Office and Museum: A useful map showing the sights outside the city center can be picked up at the tourist office on Governor Pack Road. The outstanding collection of tribal artifacts inside the adjacent Mountain Province Museum includes costumes, baskets, and rice-harvesting tools. An excellent place to learn about hilltribe culture. Open daily 0900-1200 and 1330-1700.

City Market: Baguio's bewildering public market overflows with a wide variety of temperate

CENTRAL BAGUIO

TO BONTOC, SAGADA, BANAUE

1
2
3
4
5 6

ST. LOUIS UNIVERSITY

BAGUIO MARKET

10

GENERAL LUNA RD.

MAGSAYSAY AVE.

12
13
14

MABINI

ST. LOUIS SILVERSMITHS

BAGUIO CATHEDRAL

17
18
19
22
20 21
65 23
27

SESSION RD.

29
24 25 26
28

30 31 33

GOVERNOR PACK RD.

KAYANG

39

41

34 35
36
37
38

CHUGAM

45
46
48
47 49
50
51
52

40

HARRISON

42 32

ASSUMPTION

53

ABANAO

54
55

56

59

57
58

LAKE DR.

67

44

BURNHAM PARK

66

LAKE DR.

60

61

62

KISAD RD.

64

TO MANILA

KENNON RD.

BAGUIO HOSPITAL

63

LEGARDA RD.

MARCOI HWY.

NOT TO SCALE

CENTRAL BAGUIO

● ACCOMMODATIONS
1. Baguio First Hotel
3. Baguio Garden Inn Hotel
4. Mountainside Lodge,
   Leisure Lodge
10. Highlander Lodge
12. Diamond Lodging,
    Villa Rosa,
    Belfranlt Hotel
13. Everlasting Pension
14. Silvertone Inn
19. Mido Lodging
22. New Plaza Hotel
26. Patria de Baguio
27. YMCA
29. Baguio
    Goodwill Lodging
34. Siesta Inn
36. Baden Powell
    House
40. Rosebowl Lodging
41. Burnham Hotel
43. Baguio Park Hotel
46. Mt. Peak Hotel
49. Ambassador Hotel
51. Orange
    Country Hotel

53. Bayanihan Hotel
55. Swagman Attic Hotel
61. Benguet Pine Pension
62. Mt. Crest Hotel
63. Baguio Holiday Hotel
64. Kisad Pension

■ RESTAURANTS AND NIGHTCLUBS
18. Cozy Nook
    Restaurant
21. Caprici Bar
23. Fireplace Pub
24. Bread of Life Bakery
30. Shakey's
31. Sizzling Plate
33. Barrio Fiesta
42. Harrison Country Den
45. Pier 66 Nightclub
47. Peek-a-boo Club
48. 168 Folkhouse
50. Country Disco
54. Sombrero Bar
58. Cafe by the Ruins
60. Spirit Nightclub
65. McDonald's

■ SHOPPING
16. St. Louise Silversmiths
25. Philippine Treasures
39. Maharlika Shopping Center
56. Banaue Handicrafts
59. Banaue Native Arts

■ TRANSPORTATION AND SERVICES
2. Philippine Rabbit buses
5. Jeepneys to La Trinidad
6. Dangwa Buses to Bontoc,
   Sagada, Banaue
17. Jeepneys to
    Camp John Hay,
    Wright Park,
    Hyatt, Mines View Park
20. Bank
28. Post Office
32. Philippines Airlines
35. Victory Liner Buses
37. Dagupan Buses
38. Pantranco Buses
44. Tourist Office
52. Marcitas Liner Buses
57. City Hall
66. Orchidarium

fruits and vegetables packed into narrow aisles named Broccoli Alley, Tomato Lane, etc. Stalls along Magsaysay Avenue and the adjacent Marhalika Shopping Complex peddle ethnic arts such as snake-bone headdresses and wooden *bulols,* but prices are much lower in Sagada and Banaue. Photographs are best in the open-air street markets to the rear.

Baguio Cathedral: Constructed in the '30s and modeled on a church in Saigon, Baguio's most famous landmark overlooks the city and Mt. Santo Thomas, highest peak in Benguet Province.

St. Louis Silver Shop: Exquisite and reasonably priced silverwork is meticulously crafted here by the students of St. Louis University.

Easter School Weaving: Conventional lowland looms and backstrap models favored by the mountain people produce some of the country's most famous weavings in this shop managed by the Episcopalian missionaries. Located

outside town. Take a jeepney marked Guisad from Kayang Street near City Hall.

Camp John Hays: Facilities at this former rest-and-recreation center for the American Air Force include a movie theater, tennis courts, a golf course, a swimming pool, a formal restaurant, and a cozy bar overlooking the 19th tee. The camp was returned to the Philippine government on 1 July 1991 and is now run by the Department of Tourism. Take a jeepney from Session Road.

Faith Healers: Baguio is a center for psychic magicians who barehandedly remove tumors without scars from trusting patients. Among the eight healers listed by the tourist office is Ramon Jun Labo, the owner of Nagoya Inn on Naguillian Road. Photographers are welcome for a small fee.

Accommodations
On 16 July 1990, Baguio was struck by a 7.7-Richter-scale earthquake, which toppled 30

buildings, killed over 500 residents, and buried much of the steep and beloved Kennon Road. Among the most spectacular disasters were the destructions of the Hyatt Terraces Hotel and many of the budget hostels near the bus terminal. Many of the surviving hotels have been closed until funds are raised for reconstruction.

Dorms: Dorm rooms from P80 are available at Patria de Baguio on Session Rd., the funky YMCA near the post office, and the Benguet Pine Pension described below.

Around the Bus Station: Baguio's inexpensive hotels near the bus terminal are convenient for early-morning departures, but most are run-down and only acceptable for an overnight crash. Avoid the noisy rooms facing the main streets. Traveller's Lodge, Emerald Inn, and Happiness Lodge were closed after the quake, but several low-end hotels survive on Lapu Lapu Street and along General Luna Road. As with all hotels in Baguio, rates are doubled and tripled during Christmas and Easter holidays.

Baguio Garden Inn: Cheap and fairly clean rooms are found at this hotel near the Philippine Rabbit bus terminal. Lapu Lapu St., tel. 442-6398, P140-250.

Benguet Pine Pension: South of Burnham Park is a lovely old home with a converted family room used as a communal dorm and private rooms in the rear. A new addition with conference room and restaurant was opened in 1992. 82 Chanum Rd., tel. 442-7325, P80 dorm, P280-600 private room.

Baden Powell House: Inexpensive hotels in better condition are near the top of Session Road. This clean and comfortable hotel is convenient for Victory, Dagupan, and Pantranco buses. 26 Governor Pack Road, tel. 442-5836, P100 dorm, P280-540 private room.

Swagman Attic Hotel: An Aussie-owned hotel with reasonably priced a/c rooms, billiards, and a relaxing restaurant. In the heart of Baguio's modest nightlife. 90 Abano St., tel. 442-5139, P380-700.

Restaurants

Session Road: Most of Baguio's restaurants are located along Session Road. Filipino food is served at Barrio Fiesta, Sizzling Plate, and Tahanang Pilipino. Familiar Western dishes are dished out at Shakey's, Jughead, and Baguio Chicken House. The Mandarin on Assumption Road is a popular Chinese cafe with well-prepared Cantonese dishes.

Bread of Life Bakery: This clean and comfortable cafe serves fresh breads, daily specials, and "bottomless" cups of native coffee. Prices are somewhat high but it's a great place to relax after shopping and sightseeing.

Cafe by the Ruins: Located on Chuntug Street across from Baguio City Hall and owned by an anthropologist, two journalists, and a visual artist, this eclectic restaurant features such unusual entrees as fish roe pâté, Ifugao chicken stewed with salted pork, and river eel harvested from rice terraces. Try their homemade *tapuey* (rice wine)—tasty but *very* potent.

Nightlife

Folk Clubs: Baguio's nightlife is evenly divided between cozy pubs that cater to university students and raunchy nightclubs filled with bar girls and blasting stereos. Both the Cozy Nook Restaurant and Fireplace Pub on Assumption feature popular folk musicians. Cafe by the Ruins mentioned above has installed an improvised bamboo stage for poetry readings, traditional dance, folk singers, and impromptu theater performances. Ask for tribal songs from the Cordilleras.

Abanao Street: Most of Baguio's low- to medium-quality nightclubs are located along Abanao Street near City Hall. Drinks are cheapest and music loudest at Pier 66, 168 Folkhouse, Peek-a-boo Club, and the Country Disco. Much better is Spirit, a beautiful nightclub in a converted mansion situated a few blocks from Abanao Street. The modest cover charge includes the first cocktail.

Go-go Bars: Baguio's low-end bars and strip joints are crammed together at the bottom of town near the Philippine Rabbit terminal. All are raunchy to the extreme.

Transportation

Baguio is 250 km north of Manila and 143 km south of Bontoc.

Air: PAL flies once daily during the dry season from Manila to Loakan, about 12 km from downtown Baguio. Flights during the rainy season are diverted to La Union airport, about one hour away from Baguio. PAL's office (tel. 442-2734) is in the Padilla Building on Harrison Road.

Bus: Baguio is a six-hour bus ride from Manila. Sarkies Tours and other private operators in Ermita are the most convenient options, but hourly buses also depart from the Philippine Rabbit, Victory Liner, Dangwa Tranco, and Pantranco North terminals. Victory Liner has the most frequent departures.

Dangwa Tranco has four buses daily to Bontoc between 0600 and 1000, one daily bus to Banaue at 0630, and a daily service to Kabayan at 1000. Time Transit on Magsaysay Ave. serves Vigan six times daily between 0600 and 1800. Marcitas Liner buses leave hourly for the San Fernando beaches in La Union.

HUNDRED ISLANDS

Scattered off the coast near the town of Lucap are dozens of coral islets bizarrely eroded into formations resembling giant toadstools and dome-shaped spaceships. Numerous legends are attached to the islands: tears of a lovelorn giant, mermaids once lived here, etc. Top draws are underwater caves, marinelife, and small sandy beaches tucked away on several of the islands—although none compare with those in the Visayas. Snorkeling, unfortunately, is mediocre since the waters are often murky and most of the coral beds have been badly damaged by dynamite fishing.

Six-man *bancas* from the park office at the Lucap pier charge about P300 for a full-day tour. Most go directly to Quezon Island, where the boatman waits while you sunbathe and snorkel before touring the other islands on the return to Lucap. Camping is allowed on Children's Island. Diving equipment can be rented from shops in Lucap.

After touring the islands, you might go west to Bolinao, a small unspoiled town associated with unexplained phenomena and tales of strange light. Attractions here include a museum displaying Chinese pottery and a fortresslike church with rare wooden *santos* and heavy doors carved in Spanish-Mexican style. Beaches out here are long, clean, and almost completely deserted. *Bancas* can be hired for skin diving off Santiago and Silaqui islands.

The A & E Garden Inn in Bolinao has rooms and huts under a spreading tamarind tree from P200. Also try Celeste Beach Resort for P200 in Bolinao.

Accommodations

Hotel rates in Lucap vary sharply according to the season and day of the week; bargaining works well Monday-Thursday. Lucap's two cheapest places are the R & E (Relax and Enjoy) and Kilometer One Youth Hostel situated one km back from the beach. Both have rooms from P80. Back in town, the Lucap Hotel and Gloria's Cottages are slightly more expensive. Best choice is Maxime By The Sea, with rooms overlooking the islands from P250. Alaminos has a pair of hotels but there's little reason to stay here.

Buses to Alaminos leave from Manila's Pantranco North bus terminal. Tricycles cost a few pesos out to Lucap.

DAGUPAN

This city of bridges and waterways, three km inland on the shallow Dagupan River, is a minor port and the market center for the province's produce. Best of the nearby beaches include Lingayan Beach (15 km west), Blue Beach (three km away near Banuan), and White Beach (15 km north at San Fabian). Dagupan is chiefly a transit spot en route to the beaches up north. Travelers coming from Hundred Islands must change buses here.

Accommodations

Villa Milagrosa Youth Hostel: Budget travelers usually stay in this hostel in the Marama Building. 26 Zamora St., tel. 4658, P80-140.

Lucky Lodge: An inexpensive lodge operated by Jimmy Din is found in the center of town. 12 Del Pilar St., tel. 3452, P50-80.

Victoria Hotel: Better rooms are in this two-star hotel on Dagupan's main street. Fernandez Ave., tel. 2081, P220-340.

SAN FABIAN

San Fabian, a small coastal town with strong faith-healing connections, was the home of the great healer Eleuterior Terte, who died in 1979. Japanese troops landed at nearby White Beach in 1941.

Accommodations

Residenz Patty Mejia: The family that runs the Center Beach Resort also accepts guests in its home near the market, three minutes by tricycle from the beach. Market Rd., P40-60.

Nibaliw West (Center) Beach: The main beach near San Fabian has a half-dozen resorts geared primarily to Manila residents on weekend escapes from the city. Choices include Center Beach Resort operated by the Mejia family, Holiday Village Resort, English-managed Breman's Resthouse, and Lazy A Beach Resort. All charge P120-380 depending on facilities.

Sierra Vista Beach Resort: Class-A spot with swimming pool, bar, and Windsurfer rentals. Nibaliw West Beach, tel. 7668, US$35-45 for a/c cottages.

BEACHES NORTH OF BAUANG

The beaches between Bauang and San Fernando to the north are considered some of the better choices in northern Luzon. Although cleaner beaches abound elsewhere in the Philippines, the convenient location near Manila and Baguio accounts for their popularity.

The region's association with former tourism ministers and ties with Marcos have brought a great deal of upscale development, including expensive resorts, good roads, and several memorials to the fallen president.

ACCOMMODATIONS NORTH OF BAUANG

Hideaway Beach Resort	P150-400
Jac Corpuz Cottages	P100-150
Chateau Inn	P150-220
China Sea Beach Resort	P450-600
Cabana Beach Resort	P550-650
Bali Hai Resort	P450-600
Coconut Grove Resort	P550-700
Cresta del Mar	P700-900
Sunset Bay Swiss Resort	P500-650
Blue Lagoon	US$22-35
Ocean Deep Resort	P200-350
Acupulco Beach Resort	P650-900
Miramonte Resort	P500-750

Accommodations

Over 20 beach resorts are located between Bauang and San Fernando. Most raise their prices sharply on weekends and often charge nonguests an entrance fee for the use of their picnic shelters. A small but useful tourist office is in the Cresta del Mar Hotel near Paringao, midway between Bauang and San Fernando.

SAN FERNANDO

San Fernando is the provincial capital and commercial center of La Union Province. Travelers coming up from Hundred Islands and en route to Baguio will probably need to spend the night.

Attractions

Museo de La Union: The small museum adjacent to the capitol complex focuses on local culture and archaeological findings.

Chinese Pagoda: The Friendship Pagoda on Zigzag Rd. offers good views over the "Town of Seven Hills."

Poro Point: On a somewhat different note, San Fernando's red-light district is near the former American military base and transmitting station at Poro Point.

Accommodations

Most visitors stay at one of the beach resorts just south of San Fernando near the town of Poro, but several acceptable hotels are on Rizal and Quezon streets.

Casa Blanca Hotel: Comfortable rooms in an old house about two blocks up from the bay. Rizal St., tel. (41) 3132, P80-200.

Plaza Hotel: San Fernando's leading hotel is located just down from the provincial capitol and on the road to Manila. Quezon Avenue, tel. (41) 2996, P260-650.

Transportation

San Fernando is 261 km north of Manila and 60 km west of Baguio. Philippine Rabbit and Times Transit buses take about six hours from Manila. Travelers coming from Hundred Islands must change buses in Dagupan. Marcitas Liner buses to Baguio depart opposite the Casa Blanca Hotel at the intersection of Rizal and Ortega streets.

VIGAN

Vigan, the capital of Ilocos Sur Province, was founded in 1572 by the grandson of Legaspi, who constructed the city in a style similar to that of Intramuros. Mercifully spared the destruction of WW II, Vigan remains a museum city with some of the best-preserved examples of Spanish colonial architecture in the Philippines.

The town and coastline to the north are also rich in Spanish domestic architecture and massive baroque churches constructed in a distinctive "earthquake" motif. One shouldn't, however, expect the great architecture of Avila or Burgos, since the Spaniards in the Philippines never achieved the degree of excellence they reached in their homeland. Nevertheless, Vigan and its nearby beaches and mountains make Ilocos Sur an eminently worthwhile destination.

Attractions

The Colonial Quarter: Modernization has arrived to some degree, but a leisurely walk through the old section still reveals cobblestone alleys, a baroque cathedral guarded by Chinese *fu* dogs, clip-clopping *calesas,* and mestizo mansions erected in the 18th century by wealthy Chinese traders.

Ayala Museum: The former residence of Jose Burgos now displays Burgos memorabilia, period rooms, a fine collection of Ilocano and Tingguian artifacts, and a 14-painting series depicting events of the Basi Revolt.

National Museum: A small but interesting museum with Spanish-era artifacts and memorials to Ferdinand Marcos, favorite son of Ilocos Sur Province.

Accommodations

Overnighting in Vigan is recommended, since the town best reveals its soul in the early-morning hours.

Grandpa's Inn: The backpackers' favorite is eight blocks east of the Philippine Rabbit bus terminal at the intersection of Bonifacio and Quirino streets. 1 Bonifacio St., tel. 722-2118, P100 dorm, P160-280 private rooms.

Cordillera Inn: A colonial-style inn recommended by several travelers is three blocks east of the Philippine Rabbit terminal. 29 Mena Crisologo St., tel. 722-2526, P180-280 fan, P320-680 a/c.

Transportation

Vigan is 407 km north of Manila and 196 km northwest of Baguio. Direct bus service is available from Manila, though most travelers stop at Hundred Islands or the beaches near Bauang before reaching Vigan. Buses from the plaza in San Fernando take about two hours to Vigan.

Buses to Manila, Baguio, and points north leave from the Philippine Rabbit terminal on General Luna St. and from the Times Transit terminal on Quezon Avenue.

NORTHERN COASTLINE

Magsingal

Colonial Spanish churches and deserted beaches are plentiful in Ilocos Sur and Ilocos Norte provinces. Bus service is dependable; inexpensive hotels are found in most of the larger towns.

The cream-and-white church in Magsingal, 13 km north of Vigan, is fitted with ornate baroque *retablos* carved of *molave* wood without nails. Note the incongruous pair of pregnant mermaids amid the religious imagery.

The nearby Museum of Ilocano Heritage and private museum of Mr. Angel Cortes are also worth visiting.

Badoc

Badoc's small but massively buttressed blue-and-cream church houses a statue of the Virgin Mary which locals claim washed ashore from China seven centuries ago. The reconstructed home of Juan Luna, an important 19th-century Filipino painter, is now a museum containing memorabilia, antique furniture, and reproductions of his paintings.

Paoay

The Philippines' most famous "earthquake" church stands in this prosperous town, situated four km west of Batac. Designed and constructed by Filipinos in 1704, it's a remarkable piece of architecture that mixes both Asian and Western styles: massive flying buttresses and crenellations influenced by the Majapajit culture of Indonesia, exterior staircases that lead nowhere, cantilevered facades carved with Chinese emblems of coral and limestone, a separate three-story watchtower used as a lookout by the Katipuneros during the Philippine Revolution. Like most other Ilocano religious architecture, the Paoay church is characterized by thick walls heavily buttressed to resist earthquake damage (hence the terminology), finials shaped like urns or pyramids, and Augustinian markings such as a transfixed heart and tasseled hats. The overall effect is one of simplicity and strength, one of the triumphs of Filipino architecture.

Laoag City

The provincial capital of Ilocos Norte Province, 486 km from Manila, is a convenient base for exploring the nearby churches and beaches.

Attractions: Attractions in town include the Sinking Belltower constructed four centuries ago by Augustinian fathers and the Italian Renaissance-style cathedral with urn-motif columns, *capiz* windows, and exterior staircases. The Marcoses donated the chandeliers. Also visit the Laoag Museum inside the old *tabacalera* and watch for rare *tarantillas*, six-passenger horse-drawn carriages that hark back to a less hurried time. Maps and other information can be picked up at the Department of Tourism office on Rizal Street.

Accommodations: The Texicano Hotel on the same street has clean singles from P100. Swagman Playa Blanca Resort in Curriamao, 25 km south of Laoag, has luxurious rooms facing a decent beach for P450-800. Facilities include Windsurfers, Hobie Cats, and other watersports equipment.

Laoag's delightfully named restaurants are the Magic Bunny Cafe and the Hot Stuff Food House! Also try the Peppermint Bakershop.

Sarrat

The former home of Ferdinand Marcos, eight km west of Laoag, is a small town radically transformed by the power and wealth of the deposed president. Sarrat features a Marcos Museum, a church where his daughter Irene was married in 1983 (5,000 guests, food for 100,000, estimated cost US$10 million), an air-

port large enough to handle jumbo jets, and the magnificently deserted 126-room Fort Ilocandia Hotel . . . another of his famous white elephants. The hotel was used by Tom Cruise and Oliver Stone during the 1989 filming of *Born On The Fourth Of July.*

Dingras, 16 km southeast of Laoag, boasts a massive ruined church whose imposing facade and roofless walls are both atmospheric and photogenic.

The sleepy town of Batac—the ancestral home of the Marcos family—is where Josefa Marcos (Ferdinand's mother) is displayed in an open casket. The upstairs Marcos Museum holds dozens of phony war medals, genealogical trees, vintage campaign literature, and 23 life-size Marcos mannequins.

Bacarra

The famous belltower and thickly reinforced church of Bacarra stand one km off the main highway, eight km north of Laoag. Inside the massive square belfry is a dome which collapsed during an earthquake in 1930, still poised in the same position. Great views from the top. Bacarra is also known for its ancient 17-string wooden harps carved by local craftsman and played during town fiestas.

Cape Bojeador

A one-km hike from the highway up to the Cape Bojeador Lighthouse is rewarded by spectacular views over the crashing ocean and nearby farmlands. Visitors are often directed along the narrow circular staircase by the friendly lighthouse keepers.

Pagudpud

The spectacular drive north from Laoag—the so-called "Riviera of the North"—passes magnificent coastline, deserted beaches, coves, corals, and pounding surf. The region's finest expanse of pure white sand is at Saud Beach, five km east of Pagudpud.

Accommodations are available at the Villa del Mar or at the mayor's guesthouse two km beyond Villa del Mar. Permission must be obtained in advance from the mayor in town.

SOUTHERN LUZON

The Bicol region of southern Luzon, formed by four contiguous provinces and the islands of Catanduanes and Masbate, is known for its smoking volcanos, hot springs, boiling lakes, caves, deserted beaches, *abaca* crafts, violent typhoons which devastate the region with depressing regularity, and spicy food typified by the small chili pepper dubbed the "Bicol Express."

Sightseeing Highlights

Bicolandia's greatest attraction is the perfectly symmetrical Mt. Mayon near Legaspi, but travelers with extra time and a sense of *bahala na* might also explore the beaches near Daet, soak in the hot springs at Tiwi, or do a side trip to Catanduanes or Masbate. Rizal Beach is also recommended, while Naga City's Penafrancia Festival held in September is considered one of the best in the Philippines.

Bicol also offers some excellent climbs. Mountaineers can challenge themselves on Mt. Isarog 15 km east of Naga, Mt. Iriga farther south, or the still-active and dangerous Mt. Mayon. Mount Bulusan near the southern tip is another possible trek.

Transportation

Bus service along the main highway from Manila to Legaspi is straightforward. Sarkies Tours in Ermita has daily nonstop buses to Legaspi departing at 0800 and 1900. Travelers who would like to stop en route or save a few pesos can use ordinary Philtranco buses, which leave hourly from the terminal on EDSA in Pasay City. Philtranco also has fast and comfortable direct a/c buses to Legaspi nightly at 1900.

Buses and jeepneys to outlying attractions around Bicol can be picked up in most towns. JB and Philtranco buses continue south from Legaspi down to Matnog, from where ferries cross in the mornings to Samar.

DAET

This provincial capital (pronounced diet), 350 km south of Manila, is the access point for several attractive beach and island resorts operated by Australian tour companies.

Attractions

The best mainland beach near Daet is at Bagasbas, five km from town. Another natural draw is Libmanan Caves, a complex of 19 caves dripping with stalactites and stalagmites one km off the highway between Sipocot and Naga City.

Accommodations

Most travelers only pass through Daet en route to San Miguel Bay or the Australian resort on Apuao Grande Island.

Karilagan Hotel: A clean and popular hotel in the center of Daet. 22 Moreno St., tel. 2265, P60-100 fan, P150-220 a/c.

Apuao Grande Island Resort: An Australian-managed resort with clean and comfortable *nipa* bungalows facing a dazzling beach, a restaurant, a bar, and endless water sports such as windsurfing, Hobie Cat sailing, and jet-skiing. The island is reached from the town of Mercedes, but most visitors make reservations and transportation arrangements through Swagman Resorts in Ermita. Sarkies Tours also sells package tours to Apuao Grande. Other resorts are planned for Canimo and Caringo islands.

SAN MIGUEL BAY

Independent travelers can cross San Miguel Bay by taking an early-morning jeepney from the Karilagan Hotel in Daet to Mercedes, from where a *banca* leaves at 1000 for Takal on the opposite side of the bay. Simple accommodations are available in Takal from a German/Filipina couple who collect books on Filipiniana.

Boats continue from nearby Siruma down to Bagacay near Naga City. Further information on San Miguel Bay and other attractions near Daet can be picked up in the Karilagan Hotel.

NAGA

Naga, a busy commercial enclave in the shadow of Mt. Isarog, is chiefly known for its fluvial Penafrancia Festival, held in late September. The town is also the region's principal cultural, religious, and educational center.

Attractions

Religious Icons: Sights around town include the black Nazarene inside the Spanish-Romanesque Naga Cathedral and the highly venerated Virgin image inside the modern Penafrancia shrine across the river. Sculpted in Salamanca, Spain, and shipped from Macau in the 17th century, this miraculous image holds immense significance for the people of Bicolandia. Almost as well-known are the bridges, which have collapsed twice during the fluvial processions.

Franciscan Church: Located in Milaor, five km south of Naga, this historic structure has been graciously spared the gaudy restoration of other Naga churches.

Mt. Isarog: The impressive volcanic cone, 15 km east of Naga, can be reached by jeepney from Abella St. to the *barrio* of Carolina, followed by a five-km hike past the luxurious Penafrancia Resort to the icy 12-meter falls at Malabasay. Mount Isarog can be climbed in two days from Hiwakloy *barangay* between Ocampo and Tiganon on the east side of the volcano. Ask the *barangay* captain to assign a guide.

Accommodations

Hotels in Naga are a few blocks south of the Philtranco terminal.

Naga City Guest House: A simple but adequate hotel for an overnight. Burgos St., tel. 2503, P80-120 fan, P160-200 a/c.

Aristocrat Hotel: Naga's best hotel has a popular restaurant and disco and can provide information on nearby attractions. Elias Angeles St., tel. 5230, P90-180 fan, P200-380 a/c.

Transportation

PAL's daily flight from Manila takes one hour. Philtranco buses take nine hours from Manila, two hours from Daet, and two hours from Legaspi. Sarkies buses leave from Angeles Street south of the library. Southbound buses can also be found on the main road to Legaspi just outside town.

IRIGA AND LAKE BUHI

Iriga, a small town hidden in the shadow of Mt. Iriga (also known as Mt. Isarog or Asog), serves as the connection point for visits to Lake Buhi and perhaps a climb up Mt. Iriga.

Iriga itself is a pleasant town with friendly people and a few good sights, including informative displays on local Negritos in the Ibalon Hotel and views from Calvary Hill to the rear.

Mt. Iriga

Mount Iriga can be climbed from Buhi via Esplana's Plantation or from the north side. Take a jeepney north toward Naga, turn right at San Pedro, and follow the road two km to the trailhead. Hotel owner and attorney Jose Reyes occasionally organizes visits to Negrito settlements on the slopes of Mt. Iriga.

Lake Buhi

Formed after the violent explosion of the mountain in 1641, this volcanic lake was once filled with microscopic freshwater fish called *sinarapan* or *tabios,* the world's smallest freshwater commercial fish, until indiscriminate harvesting and the introduction of predatory species largely eliminated it. Survivors can be seen in the aquarium at Buhi Municipal Hall and at the Peace Corps fish farm one km outside town.

Buhi is still quite beautiful and well worth the 17-km, 30-minute jeepney ride from Alfelor St. in Iriga. Boat charters are expensive, but reasonably priced ferries occasionally cross the lake to Bye Bye and Twin Falls. Budget accommodations are available in a lakeside pension.

Accommodations

Most of the Iriga's inexpensive hotels are near the railway station and about 100 meters from where buses stop.

Bayanihan Hotel: A good, clean hotel near the railway station. Jeepneys to Lake Buhi leave from this hotel. Governor Felix Alfelor St., tel. 556, P80-100 fan, P160-200 a/c.

Ibalon Hotel: Irigan's top-end hotel is worth visiting if only to see the Bicol Folkloric Museum, which contains carvings and curiosities connected with the Ibalon myth. The hotel is somewhat expensive but worth the price. San Francisco St., tel. 352, P300-420. Ask about their dormitory.

LEGASPI AND VICINITY

Albay's provincial capital lies in the shadows of Mt. Mayon, perhaps the world's most perfectly formed volcanic cone. No matter how many

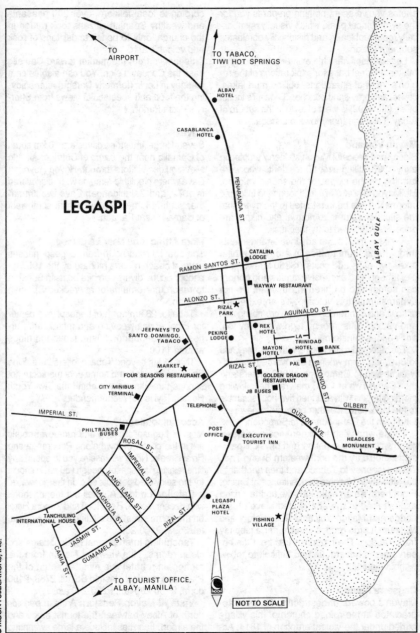

LEGASPI

TO AIRPORT

TO TABACO, TIWI HOT SPRINGS

ALBAY HOTEL

CASABLANCA HOTEL

PENARANDA ST.

ALBAY GULF

CATALINA LODGE

RAMON SANTOS ST.

WAYWAY RESTAURANT

ALONZO ST.

RIZAL PARK

AGUINALDO ST.

JEEPNEYS TO SANTO DOMINGO, TABACO

PEKING LODGE

REX HOTEL

LA TRINIDAD HOTEL

BANK

MAYON HOTEL

MARKET

FOUR SEASONS RESTAURANT

RIZAL ST.

PAL

CITY MINIBUS TERMINAL

GOLDEN DRAGON RESTAURANT

JB BUSES

ELIZONDO ST.

IMPERIAL ST.

TELEPHONE

GILBERT

PHILTRANCO BUSES

ROSAL ST.

POST OFFICE

EXECUTIVE TOURIST INN

QUEZON AVE.

HEADLESS MONUMENT

IMPERIAL ST.

ILANG ILANG ST.

MAGNOLIA ST.

TANCHULING INTERNATIONAL HOUSE

JASMIN ST.

RIZAL ST.

LEGASPI PLAZA HOTEL

CAMIA ST.

GUMAMELA ST.

FISHING VILLAGE

TO TOURIST OFFICE, ALBAY, MANILA

NOT TO SCALE

© MOON PUBLICATIONS, INC.

photos you've seen, nothing prepares you for the symmetrical peak, which visually, symbolically, geographically, and historically dominates southern Luzon.

Legaspi itself has little of interest, although it makes an ideal base for explorations of the region's thermal attractions, boiling mud lakes, caves, and gray-sand beaches. Legaspi's tourist office (tel. 4492) is west of town in the suburb of Albay. Take a jeepney toward Daraga.

Mayon Volcano
Sleepy and peaceful Mayon suddenly erupted in early 1993, killing over 60 residents who were farming on the slopes of the scenic volcano. Mt. Mayon is now off-limits, though the following information has been retained in the event that the situation returns to normal and hikers are once again allowed to try their luck.

All hikers must make advance arrangements through the tourist office in Albay. The hike takes two days and costs US$50 for two people, though less expensive guides and porters can sometimes be hired in Buyuhan. Do not underestimate this volcano: It's an extremely difficult and dangerous climb up crumbling ash and vertical cliffs through high winds, icy fog, and sudden rainstorms.

The standard route begins with a jeepney ride to Buyuhan, from where a dry riverbed gradually climbs up to Camp One at 800 meters and then Camp Two at 1,463 meters. The following morning begins with a rugged five-hour scramble to the top where, weather permitting, views extend from the Catanduanes to Sorsogon.

Those who wish to experience a midlevel climb without the expense and physical hardships should try the northwestern Buang Trail. Take a jeepney to Tabaco and then another to the Mt. Mayon National Park entrance at Buang. From here, it's an eight-km hike up the zigzag asphalt road to the abandoned Mayon Vista Lodge and Mayon Volcanic Observatory and Museum. Large groups can charter a jeepney from Tabaco. The mountain trail from the observatory is hazardous and difficult to follow without a guide.

Cagsawa Ruins
Mayon's powers of destruction are best appreciated at the ruined church of this village buried under the violent eruption of 1814. According to local folklore, over 200 peasants and wealthy Spanish citizens took refuge in the church, only to perish under tons of rock and volcanic ash.

Jeepneys from the market toward Camalig pass the Cagsawa sign. You can also catch a jeepney in Locin (formerly Daraga) after enjoying the food and spectacular views from Sherry's Pizza Parlor.

Caves
Several large limestone caves are 10 km south of Camalig near the *barrio* of Cotmon. Alfredo Nieva guides visitors through Hoyop Hoyopan Cave where Neolithic remains were discovered in 1972, and Calabidongan Cave two km farther south. More caves are 10 km southwest of Camalig near Pariaan.

More Attractions Near Legaspi
The coastal road north from Legaspi passes several beach resorts hit hard by the 1987 typhoon. Scuba divers can hire boats in Buhatan to reach the remains of a wrecked Spanish galleon.

Tabaco, 28 km north of Legaspi, is a center for Bicol *abaca* weaving and metalcraft. Ferries to Catanduanes Island leave mornings around 1100.

Tiwi, 11 km beyond Tabaco, offers the striking Sinimbahan ruins and some very mediocre hot springs three km north behind the Tiwi Youth Hostel. Tiwi is not recommended.

Accommodations
Most of Legaspi's cheap and run-down hotels are in the center of town along Penaranda and Rizal streets. None will inspire you to spend any time relaxing in Legaspi, though you really should try the spicy fried peanuts sold on the sidewalks.

Catalina Lodge: A small but friendly hotel with decent rooms. Rex Hotel and Xandra Hotel on the same street are similar. 96 Penaranda, tel. 3593, P100-250.

Tanchuling International House: Large and clean rooms, plus views of Mayon from the rooftop, in a hotel five minutes south of the Philtranco terminal. Jasmin St., tel. 2788, P100 dorm, P150-200 fan, P280-240 a/c.

Vista Al Mayon Pension: A clean *pension* north of Albay between the tourist office and the airport. Facilities include a large swimming

*Mayon and
Cagsawa ruins*

pool, lawns, and attractive rooms overlooking Mt. Mayon. Take a jeepney from the market to Albay and walk north across the river. Washington Dr., tel. 4811, P150-250.

Mayon Hotel: Clean and comfortable spot run by a friendly Chinese family. Recommended. Penaranda St., P150-200 fan, P250-350 a/c.

Legaspi Plaza Hotel: The best midpriced hotel in town offers live music nightly in its curiously named Aura Music Lounge. Lapu Lapu St., tel. 3344, P200-240 fan, P480-600 a/c.

La Trinidad Hotel: Legaspi's best hotel is centrally located and equipped with a swimming pool, a cinema, restaurants, and a shopping arcade. Rizal St., tel. 2951, P500-650.

Transportation

Legaspi is 545 km south of Manila.

Manila: Buses to Manila and points south leave daily at 0800 and 1900 from the Philtranco terminal west of the market. Manila is also served by J.B. Liner off Rizal, Sunshine Tours in the La Trinidad Hotel, and Sarkies in the Legaspi Plaza Hotel.

Local Transport: Jeepneys to Tabaco and Tiwi leave north of the public market. Minibuses and jeepneys to Albay, Casagwa, and Camalig leave west of the market.

To Samar: Travelers heading south to Samar must take a late-night or early-morning bus or jeepney to Matnog, since ferry service ends around 1300. Allow about four hours to Matnog,

including time-consuming changes in Sorsogon and Irosin.

Buses from Manila pass through Legaspi around 0300 or 0400 but are often filled with sleeping passengers. Philtranco offers direct buses from Legaspi to Catbalogan and Tacbalogan on a space-available basis, a useful service that saves time and hassle.

BULUSAN LAKE AND VOLCANO

Although rarely visited by Westerners, the landscape and natural foliage around Bulusan Volcano National Park are some of the loveliest in southern Luzon. Recent volcanic eruptions (the last was in 1988) have blessed the province with fertile soil blanketed with dazzling flora: thick rainforests, endless coconut groves, and spectacular tropical flowers. The region has been nicknamed the "Switzerland of the Philippines," an overstatement with an element of truth.

Volcano Climb

A very popular climb is the six-km hike from the town of Bulusan on the coast up to the crater lake and nearby Masacrot Hot Springs. Double-peaked Bulusan Volcano can also be climbed in shorter time starting from Barangay San Roque on the Irosin-Bulusan road.

Another set of hot springs, San Mateo, north of Irosin near the Bulusan Volcano Observatory, offers warm waters, rainforest hikes, and inexpensive dormitory rooms.

Visitors with cars can also follow the narrow road, midway between Bulusan and Irosin, which winds up to a mysterious crater lake, though the point of a visit should be a hike through the thick rainforests.

Rizal Beach

Rizal Beach, on the east coast near the town of Gubat, offers a fine combination of white sand, clean waters, and reasonably priced accommodations at the aptly named Rizal Beach Resort Hotel. Expats in Manila seem to love this place, though the sand doesn't compare with that of other spots in the Visayas.

MATNOG

Matnog is the departure point for ferries across to Samar. Boats leave in the mornings from 0900 to 1300, so an early departure is essential from Legaspi.

You might also be able to hitch a ride on one of the luxury buses coming down from Manila, but only on a space-available basis.

Accommodations

One inexpensive lodge is located in Matnog, though it's best to spend the night in Legaspi or at Rizal Beach and arrive in time to catch an early-morning boat to Samar.

ISLANDS TO THE SOUTH

The southern islands of the Philippines—the Visayas, Mindanao, and Palawan—comprise a necklace dripping with crystalline beaches, soaring volcanos, brilliant green coconut plantations, and some of the finest coral reefs in Southeast Asia. Most of the islands are tightly packed together in the Visayan group between Luzon and the sprawling island of Mindanao. Palawan, shaped like a shark pointing toward Borneo, offers travelers a chance to get somewhat off the beaten track on one of the more isolated islands in the archipelago.

ISLAND BY ISLAND

Bohol

Sandwiched between Cebu and Leyte is one of the most attractive islands in the Visayas. Although missed by many travelers who rush directly to Cebu, Bohol is especially rich in colonial architecture and beautiful beaches on nearby Panglao Island. The island's key attractions are the eerie geological formations called the Chocolate Hills, which figured in Eric Von Daniken's *Chariots of the Gods*.

Boracay

This small island just north of Panay has deservedly become the premier beach destination in the Philippines. Once a forgotten island known only to independent travelers, Boracay today is well developed with bungalows in all price ranges, simple restaurants, and low-key nightclubs facing one of the world's most dazzling beaches. It is also an intelligently planned resort, having avoided the pitfalls of other islands. Sunsets are superb, plus the people are warm and friendly.

Camiguin

Travelers who dislike crowds and commercialization should visit this idyllic little island situated off the north coast of Mindanao. Camiguin's isolated location and good (but not great) beaches have made it a favored destination by backpackers discouraged by the popularity of Mindoro and Boracay.

Cebu

The Visayan hub for politics, commerce, and transportation offers several good beaches and a handful of historical attractions in the capital city of Cebu. Restaurants, nightlife, and shopping are second only to Manila. The remainder of the island is a mixed bag. Typhoons have damaged the once-brilliant coral beds on the west coast, but the relatively protected beaches on the southeastern coastline are still in good condition. Beaches on Mactan Island near Cebu City are mediocre and only recommended for tourists on tight schedules.

Leyte

Noted for its historical ties to General MacArthur and WW II, Leyte chiefly serves as a transit point for overlanders traveling from Samar to Cebu. The island's handful of natural attractions such as national parks, waterfalls, and offshore islands can be reached with public transportation from Ormoc and the principal town of Tacloban.

Marinduque

Boac's Moriones Festival is one of the country's most famous religious pageants and the island's chief claim to fame. Aside from the frenzy of Holy Week, Marinduque is a relaxing place to linger, even though the beaches are relatively unimpressive by Philippines standards. A powerful typhoon in 1987 practically leveled the island.

Mindanao

The second largest island in the Philippines is a world of mindblowing contrasts: modern cities only hours from animist cultures, Christian fundamentalists and traditional Muslims, capitalist warlords battling with communist insurgents, a feudal but progressive land with all the strengths and weaknesses of Filipino society. Mindanao is also richly blessed with natural wonders such as the country's highest mountains, thick rainforests, swampy lowlands, and isolated beaches rarely visited by Westerners. It's also home to dozens of distinct tribes whose traditional lifestyles remain much less affected than those of northern Luzon. Highlights include the T'boli tribal area at Lake Sebu, a climb to the summit of Mt. Apo, and the beautiful islands around Surigao. Davao and Zamboanga serve as important transit points, although neither has any strong attractions or aesthetic appeal. Mindanao is also, unfortunately, an island troubled by Muslim resistance groups and heavy NPA activity near Cotabato and the Sulu Islands. Otherwise, Mindanao is relatively safe.

Mindoro

A trip to the country's seventh-largest island is synonymous with a sojourn at Puerto Galera, a beach resort five hours distant from Manila. Situated on an outstandingly beautiful harbor beneath soaring green mountains, it's a vision of paradise partially marred with hastily built cottages, an inadequate waste-disposal system, and other signs of an overcrowded tourist slum. And yet, a journey to Mindoro is still recommended for the relatively undeveloped beaches to the west and the virtually untouched interior and southern beaches. Mindoro is also an important connection on the overland/oversea route from Manila to Boracay.

Negros

The sugar island of the Philippines is worth visiting to learn about the highly charged political situation and, on a more traditional note, to ride the antique sugar trains near the capital city of Bacolod.

Palawan

The final frontier for the Philippines presents the determined traveler with some of the finest beaches, diving, and natural wonders in the country. Transportation is rugged, but inexpensive hotels and restaurants are plentiful. Key attractions include world-class beaches and diving at El Nido, topographic curiosities such as the underground caves near Port Barton, and the anthropological discoveries at Tabon. Allow as much time as possible but avoid Palawan during the rainy season. This is an island where days turn to weeks, weeks to months.

Panay

Shaped somewhat like a triangular kite fluttering between Negros and Mindoro, Panay's chief draws are the outstanding churches in Iloilo and the January festivals which celebrate the original pact between the indigenous *atis* and the *datus* from Borneo. Most travelers rush directly from Negros to Boracay or vice-versa, but those with extra time should explore the southern beaches and perhaps visit the expensive but beautiful private island of Sicogon.

Romblon

These three small islands are mainly visited by travelers going from southern Mindoro to Boracay.

Samar

The third-largest island in the Philippines serves as a stepping stone between Luzon and the Visayas. The western coastal route is perfectly safe, but you should inquire carefully before traveling through the interior, since deep poverty has led to widespread NPA control.

ROUTES AROUND THE VISAYAS

Visitors short on time should take advantage of inexpensive PAL domestic flights and travel directly to the island or beach of their choice. Those with more time and enough patience to deal with irregular boat departures can tour the Visayas on the following circuit. Boat connections between most islands are inexpensive and frequent—except from Boracay to Mindoro where the backlog of travelers and haphazard shipping schedules often causes long delays. Allow a minimum of one month to complete the following route and longer if you plan to explore the national parks or really unwind on the beaches. The Visayan loop can be completed in either a clockwise or a counterclockwise direction, but the clockwise route is perhaps a better choice since it saves Boracay and Mindoro for the final stretches. Palawan and Mindanao could be side trips from the Visayas or separate destinations starting from Manila.

Manila To Samar

Transportation is straightforward from Manila to Legaspi, but somewhat problematical from Matnog at the southern end of Luzon to Samar on Leyte, since ferry service ends around noon. An early start from Legaspi is necessary to avoid getting stranded in Matnog.

Samar To Cebu
Both air-conditioned and ordinary buses wind along the scenic road that skirts the west coast of Samar to Tacloban in Leyte. A relaxing option is the daily ship from Catbalogan to Tacloban. Ships depart daily from Ormoc to Cebu. Boat service from Maasin to Bohol is so undependable that most travelers go directly from Leyte to Cebu and then backtrack to Bohol.

Cebu To Boracay
Cebu City to Bacolod can be completed in a single day with an early start. Alternatively, you could sail from southern Cebu across to Dumaguete and then continue around the sugar island by bus. Bacolod is a good place to pause if transportation bogs down. Ships sail each morning from Bacolod to Iloilo on Panay, from where buses continue north to Kalibo. Outriggers constantly dart from Caticlan, two hours north of Kalibo, over to Boracay. Iloilo to Boracay can be done in a single day of steady travel. direct flights from Cebu to Kalibo are useful for those anxious to reach Boracay.

Boracay To Mindoro
Because of high winds and rough waters, this is often the stretch that fouls an otherwise trouble-free journey. Direct outriggers occasionally leave from Boracay to southern Mindoro, but most travelers sail north to Tablas before continuing west to Mindoro. This crossing should only be attempted on clear days. Alternatives when the weather looks bad are flying from Kalibo to Manila or backtracking to Iloilo. Palawan can be reached by boats from San Jose de Buenavista on southwestern Panay.

Mindoro To Manila
Several small boats leave in the mornings from Puerto Galera to Batangas on Luzon. Buses connect from Batangas to Manila.

BOHOL

Bohol, a relatively small island resting in the center of the Visayan archipelago, has much to offer in terms of history and natural attractions. The island was first visited in 1563 by Magellan's crew, which fled Cebu after the death of its leader. In 1565 Legaspi brought the island under Spanish rule by sealing a historic blood compact with a native chieftain named Datu Sikatuna. Major rebellions against Spanish rule broke out in 1622 and 1744, followed by a revolt against American occupation in 1901.

Bohol today is a sleepy place with great beaches and scuba diving, the famous geological formations nicknamed the Chocolate Hills, and some of the finest Spanish colonial church architecture in the Philippines.

Most travelers reach Bohol by air or sea from Cebu City and proceed immediately across to Panglao Island to enjoy the beaches and scuba diving. Buses from Tagbilaran reach the Chocolate Hills in the center of the island and continue around the island through towns dominated by magnificent Spanish churches.

Scuba Diving
Bohol deserves its praise as one of the finest diving spots in the Visayas. Org .nized dives to Balicasag Island, a 22-hectare island situated four km off Panglao, can be arranged through Jacques Trotin at the Bistro De Paris on Torralda Street in Tagbilaran. Other dive operators include the upscale Bohol Beach Club on Panglao and Thunder Dive Shop located immediately across the Tagbilaran-Panglao bridge. Two dives plus equipment rental cost US$35-45 depending on the number of participants. Skin-diving equipment can be rented from most bungalows. Other popular dive areas include Pamilican Island near Baclayon and Cabilao Island off Looc.

TRANSPORTATION

From Cebu
Tagbilaran is accessible twice daily by plane or boat from Cebu City. The Sweet Lines boat that departs Cebu at noon daily from Pier 2 arrives in Tagbilaran around 1630. To reach Panglao Island the same day, take a fast tricycle for P5 to the Tagbilaran market and catch the final bus at 1700. Three-man tricycles from Tagbilaran to Alona Beach cost P200-250. Ships also connect Cebu City with Tubigon and Talibon.

Getting Around

Ceres Liner buses from the main road in Tagbilaran leave hourly for all Bohol destinations, including the Chocolate Hills at Carmen. It's a long but pleasant walk from the turnoff to the lodge. Additional service to Carmen is provided by St. Jude jalopies departing from the rear of the public marketplace. Jeepneys from Tagbilaran to Alona Beach on Panglao leave four times daily until 1700. Also note Tagbilaran's tricycles, which have been cheerfully emblazoned with religious slogans.

Leaving

PAL flies twice daily from Bohol to Cebu City. Sweet Line ferries leave Tagbilaran nightly at 2300 and arrive in Cebu about five hours later. Tickets should be purchased in advance before 1700 on the day of departure from their office on Garcia Avenue. Trans Asia Shipping departs once daily in the morning for Cebu. Schedules change frequently.

A third alternative is a Ceres Liner bus, leaving twice daily and using a private ferry service from Loon to Argao. Seats can be booked in advance from Ceres's office, located four blocks down Garcia Avenue at Visarra Street. Small ferries leave Tubigon for Cebu several times daily. Boat connections to other destinations are shown at the end of the Bohol section.

TAGBILARAN

The provincial capital, principal port, and commercial center of Bohol is simply a stepping-stone to nearby beaches, churches, and other attractions. There is little reason to stay here unless you find yourself stranded between Cebu and Panglao.

Attractions

Best sight in town must be the tricycles emblazoned with humorous religious slogans, plus the old fire truck in the local station. All other attractions are outside town.

Baclayon Church: Constructed in 1595 by Jesuit missionaries, the Baclayon church, seven km east of town, is the oldest stone church in the Philippines. Although run-down and often closed, the painted ceilings, intricately carved altar, and small museum of religious relics can be toured by request. A small boy will direct you to the side door.

Tontonon Falls: Swimming is possible in the stream but not underneath the 10-meter falls at the hydroelectric station beyond Loboc.

Punta Cruz Watchtower: The ancient fortress near Maribujoc west of Tagbilaran once served as the island's stronghold against Muslim pirates.

Tarsiers: Bohol is also known for its tarsiers, miniature primates with large gogglelike eyes and long tufted nonprehensile tails. Related to lemurs and considered the smallest monkeys in the world, they are said to be so gentle that they cry themselves to death in captivity.

Accommodations

Most of the hotels are grouped together near the city center, though few travelers stay in Tagbilaran unless they miss the last jeepney out to Panglao.

Travelers Inn: Easy to find, fairly clean, and cheap. Garcia Ave., P100-160 fan, P250-350 a/c.

Vista Lodge: Similar to the Travelers Inn but in a somewhat quieter location. Lesage St., tel. 3072, P80-100 fan, P200-250 a/c.

LTS Lodge: Probably the best budget- to middle-priced choice in town. Try the tasty sweet-and-sour *lapu lapu* in the nearby Horizon Restaurant or the pizza in the Garden Cafe near the church. Garcia Ave., tel. 3310, P100-200 fan, P320-450 a/c.

Hotel La Roca: Tagbilaran's top-end choice offers a swimming pool, buffet dinners, and a/c rooms in all price ranges. Graham Ave., tel. 3179, US$15-25.

PANGLAO ISLAND

Bohol's finest beaches—and some of the best sand in this section of the Visayas—are on the southeastern coast of Panglao Island, where a wonderful combination of dazzling sand, swaying palms, warm waters, and colorful corals have made the island one of the premier beach destinations in the central Visayas.

All this beauty has not been lost on Manila's tourism officials (DOT, PVCC, PTA), who in 1992 announced a 20-year blueprint for tourism, in cooperation with the United Nations Development Program and the private sector. The main targets are ecotourism on Palawan, the relatively untouched island of Panglao, and Samal, another tropical island near Davao. While most of DOT's grand pronouncements ultimately change with new tourism directors, this ambitious plan makes it almost inevitable that Panglao will become a major beach-resort destination by the year 2000.

Panglao has a half-dozen beaches in various states of development. Alona Beach on the southwestern corner is a narrow but very popular stretch of sand. Just over the rocky headlands to the east is an immense stretch of dazzling sand that is simply called Bohol Beach. On the northwest corner are several more lovely beaches including Doljo Beach, Palm Island Beach about one km east of Doljo, and Momo Beach another kilometer farther east.

Attractions

Panglao has a few other points besides its beautiful beaches and comfortable accommodations. Swimming is possible but not especially alluring inside the bat-infested cave at Hinagdanan near Bingag. The nearby cathedral at Dauis displays notable ceiling murals and an unusual freshwater well on the steps of the main altar. The five-km walk from Alona Beach to Panglao town passes some beautiful wooden homes filled with tropical flowers and very friendly people.

Alona Beach

Alona Beach (more properly called Tawala Bay) is the most popular spot on the island, though it's also a small beach now almost completely developed with bungalows and midpriced hotels.

Accommodations: Nipa lodges include Alonaville, which charges P100-250 per cottage, Playa Blanca from P250 with two meals, Bohol Diver's Lodge from P200-350 with private bath, Hoyohoy Beach Resort from P300, and the upscale Alona Kew, where rooms start at P350. Top-end choice is the newish Crystal Coast Resort with swimming pool, dive facilities, and a/c rooms facing the water for US$18-45. Contact the Hotel La Roca in Tagbilaran. All resorts have cafes or restaurants.

Scuba: Scuba dives can be arranged through the aptly named Bohol Diver's Lodge, which also rents Windsurfers and skin-diving equipment, and from the Swiss diver who runs Atlantis Explorers. Three dives including gear rental cost

about P800. Note that snorkeling is possible at Alona but much better on the southwest coast at Cervera Shoal and adjacent islands.

Two top-notch dive centers on Alona Beach are Seaquest Scuba, run by a European, and Six Sea Divers, operated by a Filipino marine biologist. Both offer PADI certification programs.

Bohol Beach

A few kilometers north of Alona Beach is an amazing stretch of pure white sand with only one hotel, the expensive and often deserted Bohol Beach Club. Facilities include a swimming pool, a spa, tennis courts, water-sports facilities, and 40 individual bungalows for US$40-80.

The magnificent beach will probably remain sadly abandoned and lifeless until small-scale Filipino entrepreneurs are allowed to construct some less expensive huts for less affluent travelers.

North Coast Beaches

Three very attractive and uncrowded beaches are located on the northwestern corner of Panglao.

Doljo Beach: Good sand and shallow waters, plus access to several nearby islands, though accommodations on Panglao's westernmost beach are still limited to a few simple nipa huts.

Palm Island Beach: One km east of Doljo, but within the same general bay, is another stunning stretch of crystalline sand where the Palm Island Beach Resort charges P200-300 for rooms with fan and bath. Contact the Cliff Top Hotel in Tagbilaran.

Momo Beach: One km east of Palm Island Beach is another fine spot where the Gie Garden Hotel in Tagbilaran rents cottages to groups.

Transportation

Jeepneys from the Tagbilaran market leave four times daily until 1700. Late arrivals in Tagbilaran will probably need to overnight, although tricycles can be chartered at any time for the uncomfortable 22-km ride.

Jeepneys marked "Panglao" go to Panglao town near Doljo Beach and do not connect directly with Alona Beach. Jeepneys marked "Panglao-Tauala" follow the southern coastline and stop in Alona before continuing on to Panglao town.

Believe it or not, an airport is planned for Panglao Island.

SHIPS FROM BOHOL

DESTINATION	FROM	LINE	DEPARTURES	HOURS
Cebu	Cebu City	Tagbilaran	Sweet	2300	5
	Cebu City	Tagbilaran	TransAsia	2300	5
	Cebu City	Tagbilaran	Ceres Bus	0900, 1300	4
	Cebu City	Tubigon	Ceres Bus	0900, 1100, 1300, 2400	3
	Cebu City	Talibon	Ceres Bus	0900	4
Leyte	Maasin	Ubay	Ceres Bus	once daily	4
	Bato	Jagna	Ceres Bus	once daily	4
Luzon	Manila	Tagbilaran	William	Wed. 1300	36
Mindanao	Cagayan	Tagbilaran	TransAsia	Tues., Fri. 1900	6
	Cagayan	Jagna	TransAsia	Thurs., Sat. 1900	8
	Ozamis	Tagbilaran	William	Sat. 2400	7
	Plaridel	Tagbilaran	Sweet	once weekly	7
Negros	Dumaguete	Tagbilaran	William	Wed. 0100, Sat. 1200	3
Siquijor	Larena	Tagbilaran	William	3 times weekly	4

CHOCOLATE HILLS

Bohol's most famous draws are the hundreds of perfectly cone-shaped mounds located 55 km northeast of Tagbilaran and 10 km before the town of Carmen. These mysterious and otherworldly hillocks were either formed by prehistoric, submarine volcanic eruptions followed by sea erosion or, more romantically, they are the teardrops of a grief-stricken giant. Eric Von Daniken, in his book *Chariots of the Gods,* theorized that they were formed by extraterrestrials, a somewhat believable notion on a full moon night or weirdly misty morning.

Accommodations

The Chocolate Hills Resort, magnificently situated on top of a giant chocolate kiss, charges P50 for dorm beds and P150-380 for private cottages.

Transportation

Both Ceres Liner buses and St. Joseph wrecks serve Carmen. Look for the Coca-Cola sign. St. Joseph buses pass every two hours. For a great experience, arrive at the junction after sunset, hike in the darkness to the resort, and wake early for one of the world's most surreal sunrises.

JAO ISLAND

Jao (pronounced how) Island is an isolated and relaxing little island situated off the northeast coast of Bohol. Beaches are nonexistent and most of the coral beds have been destroyed by typhoons, but there's an air of tranquility and fine walks are possible through native villages famous for their *nipa* weavings.

Accommodations

Laguna Escondido Resort and Yacht Haven, managed by a crusty old German-Canadian sailor who entertains his guests with tales of Pacific crossings, charges P100-180 for a private cottage. Food here is much better than the average Filipino fare.

Transportation

Talibon can be reached by buses from Tagbilaran and the Chocolate Hills or by two boats leaving daily at 0900 from Pier 3 in Cebu City. Charter *bancas* from Talibon cost P100; regular *bancas* operated by Heinz cost P40. Ceres Liner buses back to Cebu leave Talibon daily at 0900. Jao Island is a place for quiet conversation and long books.

BORACAY

Once an isolated island known only to back-packers and world travelers, Boracay today is deservedly the most popular beach resort in the Philippines. The reasons are obvious: sand as fine and white as talcum powder, dazzling aquamarine waters, soaring coconut trees that hang over the beaches like in a scene from *South Pacific,* a harsh but inviting interior rich with strange vegetation and lonely coves, epic sunsets, plus some of the finest accommodations in the country. In a stroke of pure genius, the citizens of Boracay have resisted large-scale development, thereby preventing the environmental disaster which has ruined Sabang Beach on Mindoro. A 1993 master plan will soon bring fresh water from a new dam on Panay, a waste-water-treatment plant, and garbage-collection services to the immensely popular island.

It's also refreshing to see most tourist dollars going directly into the pockets of local Filipino entrepreneurs rather than international hotel corporations. The people are another great draw: they've remained warm, friendly, and much less mercenary than their counterparts elsewhere in Southeast Asia.

TRANSPORTATION

From Manila By Air

There are literally dozens of slow ways to reach Boracay but only one fast way: fly. PAL flies twice daily to Kalibo for about P1000-1200. Buses from Kalibo take two hours to Caticlan from where pumpboats shuttle constantly across the narrow straits to White Sand Beach. *Warning:* A serious bottleneck exists between Manila and Boracay. PAL flights from Kalibo are always filled several weeks in advance. To avoid getting stranded in Boracay (not half bad), you must make roundtrip reservations well in advance. Travelers on tight schedules should have their travel agents make these reservations before leaving home or contact a travel agent in Manila.

Alternatives to the Kalibo flight include flying to Iloilo and taking the 0930 Ceres bus direct to Caticlan or a Nandwani minibus to Kalibo. PAL also flies daily to Tablas on Romblon (the island north of Boracay), from where ferries shuttle down to Boracay from Sante Fe. Alternatively, both Aerolift and Pacific Air have direct flights from Manila and Cebu to the small landing strip at Caticlan for P2200.

From Cebu By Air

PAL flies four times weekly from Cebu City to Kalibo for P650.

Getting There By Sea

Several shipping companies sail from Manila to ports near Boracay. William Lines has weekly service to San Viray, a small port three km west of Caticlan. Aboitiz serves Dumaguit near Kalibo, as do William and Gothong. William also sails from Puerto Princesa on Palawan to Caticlan. It has been reported that this ship is a real nightmare, with giant rats, clogged toilets, etc.; cabin class is advised. Gothong serves Kalibo from Cebu City. Travelers on Mindoro can take a jeepney south to Mansali Beach near Roxas, from where boats leave twice weekly for Looc and Caticlan. See "Mindoro" for more information. Do not attempt this crossing at night or in foul weather.

Leaving

PAL and shipping tickets can be purchased in advance from several agents on Boracay. Ceres buses leave Caticlan for Kalibo daily at 0700 and 1200. The Boracay Shuttle leaves Caticlan at 0715 to catch the 1010 flight from Kalibo. The PAL flight from Kalibo to Manila should be booked well in advance, or you can try the *very* long waiting list. The weekly William Line ship from San Viray to Manila and Palawan can be booked from their office in San Viray. MV *Herlyn* and MV *Ibigen* go from Caticlan to Roxas on Mindoro. Small and dangerous outriggers cross from Boracay to Tablas, from where PAL flies daily at 1030 to Manila.

ATTRACTIONS AND ACTIVITIES

Boracay's most popular activity is lazing on the beach and taking an occasional dip in the turquoise water. It's a hard life in the tropics!

BORACAY

VAPAK BEACH

ILIG ILIGAN BEACH

BUNYUGAN BEACH

CLUB PANOLY HOTEL

LAPU LAPU BEACH

PUNTA BUNGA BEACH

PINAUNGAN

SIBUYAN SEA

DINIWID BEACH

FRIDAY'S
COSTA BLANCA
TYROL
PEARL OF THE PACIFIC
BEACHCOMBER
MISTRAL WINDSURFERS
GALAXY
RED COCONUT
BASURA BAR
MANGO RAY
SUMMER PLACE
TIROL
LORENZO'S
TITAY'S
SULU
TRAVELLER'S BAR
BARRACUDA
SAND BAR
SALLY CASIMERO'S
CHEZ DE PARIS

BALABAG
BULABOG

MANGAYAD VILLAGE

TOLOBHAN

MALABONOT

ANGOL
BANTUD

MANOC MANOC
YACHT CLUB

CAGBAN BEACH

TABLAS STRAIT

TO KALIBO

CATICLAN

AIRPORT

MALAY
SAN VIRAY
PANAY

0   1 km

MOON

© MOON PUBLICATIONS, INC.

Water sports are plentiful. Windsurfers can be rented by the hour or day from Richie's Mistral School or less expensively from the F2 Windsurfing Center. Hobie Cats and sailboats are also available. Scuba diving is mediocre near Boracay but fairly good farther afield at Sibay and Maniquin islands. Organized dives, equipment rentals, and certification courses are arranged through several dive shops. Mango Ray Restaurant sponsors weekly five-hour boat tours around the island. Cockfights are held Sunday afternoons in the Balabag cockpit.

Boracay also offers some fascinating topography and bizarre flora. Trails north from the main beach lead to pristine but *puka*-less Yapak Beach on the north coast. Other trails head east to Yapak Bat Cave, Ilig Iligan Beach, where a small museum displays shells and old costumes, and isolated Lapu Lapu Beach. Also visit the long, windy, and very mysterious beach 15 minutes east of White Sand Beach inhabited only by herds of wild pigs and a few hardy fishermen living in well-protected homes. Then walk south along a meandering trail past eerie lakes filled with dead trees, abandoned fishponds, and Negritos' simple huts. Buy a shell and children will point the way.

PRACTICALITIES

Boracay is a well-developed resort island with most necessary facilities. What you won't find are the nonessentials such as telephones, clocks, fax machines, an airport, air-conditioned taxis, and tour buses. The small but helpful tourist office in Mangayad near the Vienna Restaurant is very helpful. Traveler's checks can be changed through independent vendors, but rates are very poor except at Allied Bank in Magayad. Bring plenty of pesos in small bills.

A post office, a supply store, and a health clinic are located in Balabag. Both Aerolift Air Services at Lorenzo Beach Resort and Pacific Airways in Balabag fly daily between Manila and Caticlan (20 minutes from Boracay) for P2200. Advance reservations are necessary. Also try the PAL office next to Allied Bank in Balabag. Books in all languages are bought, sold, and traded at Jackson's Library behind the upscale Red Coconut Restaurant and at Cafe Espresso on the beach near Balabag.

Accommodations

Boracay's nipa huts, bungalows, and luxurious resorts dotting White Beach on the west coast are among the finest in Asia—clean, comfortable, and well priced. In 1982 the government wisely decreed that all huts must be at least 30 meters from the high-tide mark and constructed entirely of native materials. Inexpensive bungalows average P150-200 during the low season from June through October and P250-300 during the high months from November to June. Each is furnished with a large double bed and a private terrace overlooking an attractive garden. Most provide complimentary morning tea and snacks for breakfast . . . shades of Kuta Beach!

There's little reason to make any specific recommendation, since nearly every place on Boracay is great. A good strategy is to ask the boatman to drop you somewhere in the center of the beach (near Galaxy or Red Coconut Restaurant) to begin your bungalow search. Most of the inexpensive and middle-priced places are located here or slightly back from the beach.

Top-end resorts are concentrated at the north end, where the finest sand and clearest waters are also found. Superluxurious resorts such as Club Panoly on Punta Bunga (rooms from US$150) are now appearing on the more remote beaches.

Restaurants And Entertainment

Boracay has everything from simple Filipino cafes serving excellent *adobos* to fancy French restaurants with thick bouillabaisse and imported wines. Among the more exclusive places is the Red Coconut Restaurant for paella and Chinese specialties. Most bungalows have attached cafes specializing in fresh seafoods and Western breakfasts. Inexpensive seaside cafes, such as the friendly stall owned by the fabulous Miss Sally Casimero, are tucked away at the southern end of the beach. Bring a flashlight or you might tumble off the dirt path!

Boracay's nightlife runs the gamut from simple beachside folk houses to rowdy discos blasting out the latest tunes. Bazura Bar is a classy singles bar largely deserted before midnight, or try Sandcastles Disco on the southern end of the beach. Barracuda Bar and Galaxy Restaurant are best for Filipino folk singers, with their golden voices and long black hair. Great recorded reggae and samba rhythms are found at the Beachcomber to the north. Titay's Restaurant does a somewhat entertaining cultural show. Last but not least are the Boracay sunsets, which are always spectacular.

CAMIGUIN ISLAND

Camiguin is a picturesque volcanic island situated off the north coast of Mindanao favored by travelers searching for an alternative to Boracay. Although the beaches are rocky and less inviting than those found elsewhere in the Philippines, the island compensates with magnificent natural scenery, soaring volcanos, tiny offshore islets with good coral, hot and cold soda-water springs, crashing waterfalls, and friendly people who greet you with "Hi Friend" rather than the usual "Hey Joe." Accommodations are cheap and plentiful.

Transportation
Camiguin can be quickly reached with Air Link International Airways from Cebu City or with Tamula Shipping, which sails direct on Thursdays. A slower alternative is with one of several ships which depart evenings from Cebu for Cagayan de Oro on Mindanao. Buses take two hours to Balingoan, from where ferries shuttle across to Binone on Camiguin. Jeepneys continue to the provincial capital of Mambajao.

Also, direct ferries leave Cagayan de Oro four times weekly at 0800.

MAMBAJAO

The provincial capital of Camiguin is the island's main accommodation center and a good base for exploring the nearby beaches and waterfalls. The small tourist information center in the municipal hall across from the church has information on skin diving and climbing Hibok Volcano. The PNB cashes traveler's checks. Attractions in town include some old Spanish homes, Tia's antique collection, and the NACIDA Handicraft Center, which sells locally made baskets. Mambajao cleverly derives its name from *mamhaw* (let's eat breakfast) and *bajao* (leftover boiled rice)!

Accommodations
Inexpensive pensions are located in town and on the beaches a few kilometers west. Tia's Pension adjacent to the town hall and Camiguin Traveller's Lodge across from the market have singles for P80-220. The latter rents bikes and offers tips on sightseeing. Tia also manages some beachside cottages a few minutes outside town. Mambajao surprisingly has a pair of discos with hospitality girls. Across from Tia's Cottages are Shoreline Cottages for P200-250.

More accommodations are situated in small *barrios* west of Mambajao. First stop is at Turtles Nest Cottages in Kugita, three km west of town. Agoho, four km west of Kugita, has several fine places, including Swiss-owned Jasmin by the Sea, Morning Glory Beach Resort, Caves Beach Resort with tennis courts and surfboard rentals, and Camiguin Seaside Beach Resort. All have simple rooms from P150 and private cottages from P200. Turtles Nest rents diving equipment and arranges dive trips to White Island, the lava flows of Old Camiguin Volcano, and Hikdop Reef near Magting.

ATTRACTIONS NEAR MAMBAJAO

Katibawasan Falls
Beautiful 50-meter waterfalls plunge into an icy pool surrounded by lush vegetation and wild monkeys five km south of Mambajao. Take a *motorella* to Pandan and follow the trail.

Ardent Hot Springs
Visit this natural stone pool with 40-degree waters in the early morning, late at night, or on rainy days. Three km south of Kugita.

Hibok Hibok Volcano
In 1951 Camiguin's most active volcano erupted without warning, belching hot gases and absorbing so much oxygen that over 2,000 people instantly died from asphyxiation. Now dormant, 1,600-meter Hibok Hibok can easily be climbed in a single day during the dry season from November to May. Guides should be hired in Mambajao or at the COMVOL Station atop Payahan

Hill four km from town. Visitors to the volcanic observatory are welcome to watch the seismographic instruments and read old newspaper clippings about the '51 explosion.

CLOCKWISE AROUND THE ISLAND

Camiguin's 65-km road can be circumnavigated with a combination of bus, jeepney, and tricycles called *motorellas*. An alternative for groups is to charter a private jeepney for sightseeing; the local term is *pakyaw*. Motorcycles and bicycles can be hired from guesthouses and private individuals.

The standard clockwise route begins with an early-morning bus or jeepney from Mambajao towards Binone and Catarman. Touring the remainder of the island from Catarman to Mambajao requires a tricycle ride to Bonbon, a long but scenic walk to Naasag, and a final tricycle ride back to Mambajao. Get an early start and allow a full day for sightseeing.

Inexpensive accommodations are found on the east coast in Magting, Mahinog, and Binone.

Magting
Padilla's Cottages has inexpensive rooms and comfortable cottages overlooking the pebbly beach. Seven km from Mambajao.

Mahinog
Facing a rocky beach and Magsaysay Island (also known as Mantigue Island) is the Western-style Mychellin Beach Resort, where clean rooms with private baths cost P50-75 single and P80-150 double. Mychellin rents motorcycles and diving gear and can arrange boat trips across to Mantigue. Good value. Three km south of Mahinog.

Binone
Overlooking Taguines Lagoon, an artificial lake two km south of Camiguin's main port town, is very pleasant and inexpensive Lagoon Travel Lodge. Their restaurant serves fresh fish raised in private ponds.

Guinsiliban
Behind the elementary school is a 300-year-old watchtower used by the Spanish as a lookout against Moro pirates. Ferries to Cagayan de Oro depart from Guinsiliban at 0800 on Wed. and Fri., and at 1500 on Sat. and Sunday.

Cantarman
Camiguin's second-largest town was established by the Spanish in 1871 after the eruption of Mt. Vulcan Daan (Old Camiguin Volcano) destroyed their settlement at Bonbon. The region's chief draws are the Santo Nino Springs and the nearby 25-meter Tuwasan Falls. A circular route to both attractions begins 500 meters north of Cantarman.

Bonbon
Signs of volcanic destruction are plentiful just north of Bonbon: San Roque Church constructed by the Augustinians in the early 17th century and now largely buried from the eruption, a submerged graveyard only visible at extreme low tide, black lava falling into the ocean. Tricycles connect Cantarman and Bonbon but you'll need to walk the remaining five km to Naasag.

Tangub Hot Springs
Dozens of volcanic springs form bathing pools whose temperatures are regulated by the rising and falling of the ocean tides. Thus, the water's cool at high tide, too hot at low tide, and agreeably warm at mid-tide. A delightful place! Snorkeling is excellent near the lava flows.

CEBU

Residents of Cebu like to boast about their province and city: oldest university, church, and street in the country; more cathedrals and historical attractions than anywhere else; best beaches and the finest climate; coral reefs and aquamarine waters that rank among the tops in the country; freshest beer and rum (San Miguel and Tanduay are located here); most beautiful women; sweetest mangoes and creamiest *guabanos.*

Shaped somewhat like a giant snake that evenly divides the Visayas in half, Cebu is also an economic miracle that disproves the notion that prosperity never reaches the underdeveloped hinterlands. Credit for growth rates which have recently far outstripped those in Manila goes to Chinese-Filipino entrepreneurs, who comprise less than 15% of the population but, as elsewhere throughout Asia, almost completely dominate the local economy. Major challenges face "Lito" Osmena—one of the country's most successful and popular governors—but more than anywhere else in the Philippines, Cebu radiates a sense of hope and belief in a brighter future.

Scuba Diving

Cebu is the center for diving throughout the Visayan archipelago. Dive resorts with compressors, divemasters, and fully equipped boats are located throughout the island, but those on Mactan near Cebu City are the most convenient. Diving at Mactan includes the coral reefs surrounding the Olangos and the double-barriers reef at Caubian Island. Accommodations are rather expensive at Mactan.

Cebu's second-largest dive site is at Moalboal on the southwestern coastline. Though shoreline corals were wiped out several years ago by a powerful typhoon, excellent reefs remain around the Pescadores and the luxurious Japanese-owned resort island of Badian. Moalboal has inexpensive accommodations.

Other diving is possible at the upscale Club Pacific Beach Resort in Sogod north of Cebu City, and farther north on Bantayan and Gato islands.

One of Cebu's least-known dive areas is at Manureva Beach on the southeastern coastline near Lilo, perhaps the next upcoming beach destination on Cebu. Dives can be organized in Manila or directly with dive shops and top-end hotels in Cebu.

TRANSPORTATION

From Manila By Air

Cebu is the transportation hub of the Philippines. PAL has daily service from Manila and most other islands. International travelers should inquire about direct charters from America, Europe, Hong Kong, and Japan. This avoids having to mess with Manila—a good idea for visitors going directly to the beaches or dive resorts in the Visayas. City center can be reached from the airport on hourly shuttle buses or taxis, which cost P70 including the bridge toll.

Getting There By Ship

Cebu is served from Tagbilaran and Tubigon on Bohol; Ormoc, Maasin, and Tacloban on Leyte; San Carlos and San Jose near Dumaguete on Negros, and almost a dozen ports on Mindanao. Most useful are the twice-daily connections from Bohol, the daily 2200 Aboitiz boat from Ormoc, and the twice-daily ferry from San Carlos on Negros.

Leaving By Bus

Buses to Negros, Bohol, and southern Cebu destinations such as Moalboal and Argao leave Cebu City from the southern bus terminal on Rizal Avenue. Special direct services include the a/c Ceres Liner buses to Bacolod daily at 0600, Ceres Liner buses to Tagbilaran at 0800 and 1400, and ABC buses to Dumaguete at noon. Bus touts will direct you, but try to get on a bus that looks almost filled and ready to leave. Otherwise it's a long wait in the sweltering heat. Sunshine buses to Bacolod leave daily from the Rajah Hotel. Buses to northern Cebu leave from the northern bus terminal at Cuenco and Maxilom streets, and from the closer Rough Rider terminal at Cuenco and Padilla.

Leaving By Ship

Ships leave Cebu City from piers 3 and 4, within walking distance of city center. Tickets can be

SHIPS FROM CEBU

DESTINATION	FROM	LINE	DEPARTURES	HOURS
Bohol	Tagbilaran	Cebu City	Sweet	1200 daily	4
	Tagbilaran	Cebu City	TransAsia	1930 daily	4
	Loon	Argao	Kanloan	1100, 1400	2
	Tubigon	Cebu City	Anco	0600, 1200, 2200	3
	Talibon	Cebu City	Charisse	2100	4
Camiguin	Binone	Cebu City	Tamula	once weekly	8
Leyte	Maasin	Cebu City	TransAsia	2 times weekly at 2100	6
	Maasin	Cebu City	G & P	2 times weekly at 2100	6
	Ormoc	Cebu City	Aboitiz	Mon. at 2100	6
	Ormoc	Cebu City	Sulpicio	2200	6
	Tacloban	Cebu City	Sulpicio	Tues. at 1600	12
	Tacloban	Cebu City	W. Samar	Mon., Wed., Fri. at 1700	12
	Tacloban	Cebu City	K & T	Tues., Thurs., Sat. at 1800	12
Luzon	Manila	Cebu City	various	daily at 1000 and 1900	22
Mindanao	Butuan	Cebu City	various	daily at 1900	12
	Cagayan	Cebu City	various	daily at 1900	12
	Davao	Cebu City	Sulpicio	Mon. at 1400	24
	Dipolog	Cebu City	various	daily at 2100	9
	Iligan	Cebu City	various	daily at 1900 and 2100	12
	Ozamis	Cebu City	Gothong	Mon. at 1800	12
	Surigao	Cebu City	Sweet	Mon., Wed., Fri. at 1900	14
	Zamboanga	Cebu City	G & P	Mon. and Fri. at 1900	24
Negros	Bacolod	Cebu City	Negros	Fri. at 1200	12
	Dumaguete	Cebu City	G & P	daily at 2100	8
	Tampi	Talisay	Ferry	several times daily	1
	San Carlos	Toldeo	Ferry	daily at 0900 and 1600	2
Palawan	P.P.	Cebu City	check with William, Aboitiz		
Panay	Iloilo	Cebu City	William	Fri. at 2200	15
	New Wash.	Cebu City	Gothong	Fri. at 2000	20
	Roxas	Cebu City	Gothong	Wed. at 1200	18
Samar	Catbalogan	Cebu City	W. Samar	Mon., Wed., Fri. at 1600	14

purchased directly at the pier or from agents on Colon Street. Most ships leave in the evening and arrive the following morning, but schedules should be double-checked with the tourist office or at the wharf. The most useful routes are the noon ship from Cebu to Bohol, evening ships to Leyte, and the twice-daily ferry from Toledo to San Carlos on Negros. Travelers can overland to Bacolod in a single day with an early start. Boracay can be quickly reached by weekly ship to New Washington. See the chart, "Ships from Cebu," above.

CEBU CITY

The oldest and second-largest city in the Philippines is a friendly place without the overpowering pace and urban headaches of Manila. Cebu offers some historical landmarks connected with the Spanish era, good restaurants, a wide range of accommodations, and nightlife second only to that of Manila. More importantly, Cebu is a convenient base from which to explore the beaches and islands in the Visayas. The city is divided

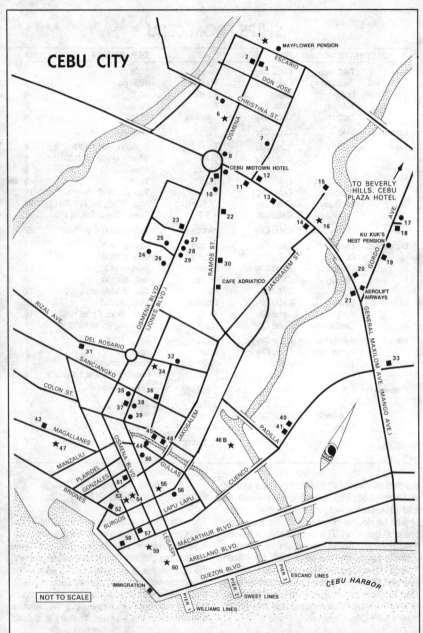

CEBU CITY

NOT TO SCALE

CEBU HARBOR

© MOON PUBLICATIONS, INC.

CEBU CITY

★ **ATTRACTIONS**
1. Capitol
6. Rizal Museum
16. Iglesia Ni Cristo Church
34. University of
    San Carlos Museum
46B. Casa Gorodo Museum
47. Carbon Market
53. Magellan's Cross
54. Basilica of
    Santo Niño Church
55. Cebu Cathedral
59. Independence Square
60. Fort San Pedro

● **ACCOMMODATIONS**
4. Jasmin Pension
7. Gali Pension
8. Park Place Hotel
10. Kan Irag Hotel
17. Magellan Hotel
18. St. Moritz Hotel
24. Royal Pension
25. Charter House
26. Frankfurter Hof
    Pension

27. Town and Country Hotel
28. Arbel's Pension
29. YMCA
32. Elicon Pension
35. Tagalog Hotel
38. Hotel de Mercedes
39. Cathay Century
44. Hope Pension
48. Skyview Hotel
50. Ruftan Pension
56. Patria de Cebu Pension

■ **RESTAURANTS**
   AND NIGHTCLUBS
2. Fast-food Stalls
3. Boulevard Restaurant
11. Kentucky Bar,
    The Club
13. Vienna Coffee House
14. Shakey's
15. Chika An Restaurant
18. St. Moritz Bar
21. Lighthouse Restaurant
22. Charlie's Jazz Club
23. Singuba Restaurant
36. Our Place

37. Pete's Kitchen
42. Stardust Bar
45. Gaw Restaurant
    and Nightclub
46. Gaisano Cafeteria
58. Eddie's Log Cabin

■ **TRANSPORTATION**
8. Airport buses
20. PAL
30. International Airlines
31. Southern Bus Terminal
33. Northern Bus Terminal
40. Rough Rider Buses
51. PAL

■ **SERVICES**
   AND SHOPPING
9. Robinson's
   Shopping Center
12. National Books
19. U.S. Consulate
41. Post Office
52. City Hall and PNB
57. Cebu Handicrafts Center
60. Tourist Office

between the older and somewhat congested downtown section near Colon Street and the newer uptown neighborhood around Fuenta or Osmena circles.

Attractions

Fort San Pedro: Cebu's Department of Tourism is located inside one of the oldest forts in the Philippines. The triangular bastion, founded by Legaspi in 1565, served for several centuries as a lookout for Muslim marauders and later as a garrison for Cebuano rebels captured during Spanish occupation. Later reincarnations included an American military camp, a city zoo, and a private nightclub.

Magellan's Cross: Cebu's most important historical landmark stands inside an unimposing kiosk near the city cathedral. Some say the *tindalo* wood case protects the original cross raised in 1521 by Magellan to commemorate the archipelago's first encounter with Christianity. Finely painted frescoes on the ceiling relate

the conversion of Rajah Humabon, his queen, and their 800 followers.

Basilica of Santo Niño: A small chapel in the rear of the oldest church in the Philippines houses the 30-cm image of Santo Niño de Cebu or Infant Jesus, one of the most powerful and revered icons in the Philippines. The adjacent basilica displays a rich collection of religious art and artifacts.

University of San Carlos Museum: Highlights of this small but worthwhile museum include a pair of mounted Philippine eagles and amazing giant crabs that climb coconut trees. Founded by the Jesuits in 1595, U.S.C. is now operated by the Societes Divini Verdi, a German Catholic order once popular in Southeast Asia.

Casa Gorodo Museum: The restored residence of Cebu's first Filipino bishop offers a rare glimpse into the lifestyle of a wealthy 19th-century trader. Difficult to find but highly recommended for its timeless atmosphere.

Beverly Hills Taoist Temple: Situated six km from downtown in the wealthy Chinese suburb of Beverly Hills stands a gaudy red-and-green temple dedicated to the teachings of philosopher Lao Tzu. Mystics predict the future and pick lottery numbers on Wednesdays and Sundays. Take a taxi or jeepney marked Lahug. Wealthy homes further remind you of Los Angeles and not the Philippines.

Practicalities

Information: The tourist office (tel. 91503) in San Pedro Fort is much more helpful than other DOT offices. Traveler's checks can be cashed at banks or with the money changers outside the post office and around Independence Square. The post office is located in the old Triton Hotel; take a Mabolo jeepney from downtown. Maps are sold at the National Bookstore on Maxilom Avenue. Note that several streets have been renamed: Mango is now Maxilom, Jones is Osmena, South Expressway is Rizal.

Transportation: PAL has an uptown office on Maxilom Avenue and a downtown center on Osmena. Other international airlines and travel agents are located near the Magellan Hotel and on Ramos Street. Buses to the airport leave hourly from Osmena Boulevard near Robinsons.

Taxis cost P10 around town, P20 to the pier, and P750 to the airport. Motorcycles can be rented from Locabike near the Magellan Hotel.

Buses to Negros, Bohol, Panay, and southern Cebu leave from the southern bus terminal on Rizal Avenue. Buses to northern Cebu leave from the northern bus terminal on Cuenco Avenue and from the Rough Rider terminal near the post office.

Budget Accommodations

Ruftan Pension: Cebu's most popular travelers' center has paper-thin walls but rooms are clean and the restaurant is a good place to meet other backpackers. Managers Fina and Jose offer advice and give discounts to Peace Corps volunteers. Legaspi near Manalili, tel. 79138, P150-350.

Surigao Pension: This clean, comfortable, and modern pension has a good restaurant overlooking downtown Cebu. Perhaps the best-value pension in the area. Ask for Cora. Sanciangko at the corner of Junquera, tel. 97857, is P120-180 with fan, P220-300 a/c single or double.

Royal Pension: Located somewhat off the beaten track in a friendly neighborhood, this quiet, clean, and very cheap pension is a good alternative to grungy downtown hotels. 165 Urgello, tel. 93890, P100-150.

Jasmin Pension: Upper Cebu is convenient for shopping, dining, and nightlife near Fuenta Circle. The Jasmin and nearby Loreta Pension (once voted the cleanest pension in Cebu) are good choices. Maria Christina near Osmena Boulevard, tel. 54559, P100-180 fan, P250-400 a/c.

Kukuk's Nest Pension: German-run guesthouse set in an old Bebuano home. Friendly atmosphere, great restaurant, excellent travel information. 157 Gorodo Ave., tel. 312310, P300-450.

Moderate To Luxury Accommodations

Town and Country (Townhouse): Beyond the depressing lobby are large rooms in all price ranges. Cheapest rooms on the fourth floor; discounts for longer stays. Good reports. Jones Avenue, tel. 78190, P100-180 fan, P280-360 a/c.

Tagalog Hotel: Attractive lobby with something of an old-time atmosphere. Recently refurbished and conveniently located in the heart of downtown Cebu. Sanciangko Street, tel. 72531, P180-250 fan, P280-500 a/c.

Hotel de Mercedes: A popular downtown hotel with reasonably priced rooms. Pelaez Street, tel. 97631, US$30-60.

Montebello Hotel: Spanish atmosphere, swimming pool, and attractive gardens within striking distance of downtown Cebu. Gorodo Avenue, tel. 313681, US$40-80.

Cebu Plaza Hotel: Cebu's only five-star hotel has a breathtaking view, although it's poorly located about eight km out of town. Lahug subdivision, tel. 311231, US$120-200.

Restaurants

Eddie's Log Cabin: Cebu's attachment to foreign expats is best experienced in this Western tavern owned by the American Cherokee contractor who made his fortune developing Beverly Hills . . . Cebu, not Los Angeles. Great sizzling steaks, salads, and homemade pies. Briones Street near Plaza Independenzia. Moderate.

Our Place: Go-go girls downstairs but great burgers, fries, and video films upstairs. Friendly and inexpensive.

CEBU CITY ACCOMMODATIONS

(prices in pesos unless otherwise indicated)

HOTEL	SINGLE	DOUBLE	ADDRESS	PHONE (32)
LUXURY				
Cebu Midtown Hotel	US$75-90	US$90-200	Fuente Osmena	219711
Cebu Plaza	US$120	US$140-200	Lahug subdivision	311231
Hotel de Mercedes	US$30-40	US$40-60	Pelaez St.	97631
Kan Irag	US$30-45	US$40-60	Ramos	211151
Magellan	US$60-90	US$80-120	Gorodo Avenue	74614
Montebello Villa	US$40-60	US$50-80	Banild subdivision	313681
Park Place Hotel	US$50-60	US$60-75	Fuente Osmena	211311
St. Moritz	US$50-60	US$60-80	Gorodo Avenue	61240
Sundowner Centerpoint Hotel	US$40-45	US$45-55	Plaridel St.	2118
BUDGET				
Arbel's Pension	80-120	100-150	57 Osmena Boulevard	62393
Cathay Century	300-350	350-430	Pelaez St.	97621
Elicon Pension	150-280	180-400	Junquera St.	73653
Frankfurter Hof	180-250	220-300	Osmena Boulevard	
Gali Pension	180-300	200-400	Juana Osmena St.	53698
Hope Pension	180-280	200-450	Manalili St	93371
Jasmine Pension	100-300	200-400	Garcia St.	54559
Jovel pension	250-300	300-350	24 Uytengsu Rd.	92990
Kukuk's Nest Pension	300-350	350-450	157 Gordo Ave.	312310
Mayflower Pension	250-300	350-400	Capitol Site	53687
McSherry Pension	280-350	400-500	Pelaez St.	52749
Patria de Cebu	50-80	100-150	Burgos St.	72084
Royal Pension	100-120	120-150	165 Urgello	93890
Ruftan Pension	180-250	200-350	Legaspi	79138
Tagalog Hotel	250-400	300-500	Sanciangko St.	72531
Town and Country	100-400	240-500	Osmena Boulevard	78190
YMCA	100-200	150-400	61 Osmena Boulevard	90125

Gaisano Cafeteria: Modern and clean downtown restaurant with tasty Filipino specialties. Nearby Pete's Kitchen is also recommended. Both are inexpensive.

Robinson's Shopping Center: This modern complex near Fuenta Circle has three clean and comfortable restaurants, Sizzling Plate on the ground floor, Maxim's Coffee Shop on the second, and the luxurious Lotus Garden for Chinese specialties on the fourth. Good places to cool off from the searing heat. Moderate.

Kentucky Bar: Perhaps the most popular joint in Cebu for expats to eat, drink, and raise hell till the early-morning hours. Pool table, country music, and cold beer. Mango Avenue east of Fuenta Circle.

Charlie's: Jazz club and restaurant with delicious *calamansi* and mango daiquiris. 171 Ramos Street. Somewhat expensive unless you go during happy hour 1700-1900.

Vienna Coffee House: Lousy cappuccino and pricey cakes but well stocked with current newspapers and German publications such as *Der Spiegel.* Mango Avenue. Moderate.

Pistahan Restaurant: Fresh seafood. 329 Gorodo Avenue. Moderate.

Cafe Adriatico: Upscale and trendy cafe in an old Cebuano home; excellent coffee and cozy atmosphere. Ramos Street. Moderate.

Nightlife

Entertainment in Cebu is divided between the low-end bars downtown and the classier places uptown along Osmena Boulevard and Maxilom Avenue.

Live Music: Charlie's Jazz Club on Ramos Street offers some of the best music in town, plus delicious daiquiris in a Casablanca atmosphere. The Boulevard on upper Osmena Boulevard and Shakey's on Maxilom Avenue are popular rock 'n' roll clubs. Raunchy and very loud bands blast away at Gaw Central Square on Colon Street. Hot Gossip Disco in Robinson's Shopping Center is Cebu's upscale nightclub.

Go-go Bars: St. Moritz, Cebu's hottest girlie bar, is located near the Magellan Hotel. The Club on Mango Avenue is basic but friendly and inexpensive. Our Place is rough but the best place in downtown Cebu. The Stardust on Magallanes is a wild taxi hall and cabaret which has been entertaining Filipino males for several generations. Only for the brave.

MACTAN ISLAND

One of the easiest excursions from Cebu City is across the bridge to Mactan Island, where the beaches are unspectacular but the diving and the handicraft industries are worthwhile diversions.

Attractions

Lapu Lapu Memorial: A huge stone on the northern coast at Punta Engano marks the spot where Magellan was killed by Lapu Lapu, the tribal chieftain now honored as the first Filipino to repulse foreign aggression.

Lapu Lapu Town: The Heidelberg (tel. 885569) and Silangan (tel. 88462) hotels are near the airport and convenient for early departures. Both have a/c rooms with private baths from P250.

Guitars: Visitors are welcome to tour the guitar factories in Maribago. Export-quality guitars cost P2000-3000.

Scuba Diving: Diving is best at Danajon Bank off northern Bohol and nearby Santa Rosa (Olango) Island, which costs P250-400 to reach by *banca.* An upscale resort geared to Japanese tourists recently opened on Santa Rosa Island. Dives are organized from all the first-class resorts on Mactan.

Accommodations At Buyong Beach

Most of Mactan's upscale resorts and moderately priced bungalows are set along this rocky and grayish strip of sand near the town of Maribago. Day visitors are often charged an admission fee to use the private beaches, though this can be credited against food or drink purchases.

Buyong Bungalows: Several low-priced bungalows remain at Buyong despite the construction onslaught which threatens to turn the strip into a Cebuano Miami Beach. Buyong Beach, tel. 81567, P250-500.

Hadsan Beach Resort: A 50-room resort just south of Maribago town offers a swimming pool, a cafe, and "12-hour room service." Nearby Club Kon Tiki (tel. 400310) is similar. Buyong Beach, tel. 70247, US$35-80.

Maribago Blue Waters Resort: Upscale choices on Mactan include the venerable Costabella Beach Hotel and Tambuli Resort, plus newer additions such as Pacific Cebu Resort, which caters to the Japanese market, and the 450-room Shangri-La Mactan, which opened in early 1993 on Punta Engano Beach. The Maribago Blue Waters has 22 guest rooms and eight bungalows on a decent stretch of white sand. Maribago, tel. 83347, fax 83934, US$95-180.

Accommodations At Marigondon Beach

Budget travelers often prefer the better sand and quieter environment a few kilometers south of Buyong Beach near the town of Marigondon. Boats can be hired for diving near Olango Island.

Parker's Beach Inn: A simple place overlooking the narrow beach with small but clean rooms. Marigondon, no phone, P150-250.

Hawaiian Village: Another simple place with both bungalows to the rear and private cottages directly facing the water. Marigondon, no phone. P150-250.

Transportation

Lapu Lapu on Mactan can be reached by taxi or "Opon Opon" jeepney from Manalili St. in Cebu City. Tricycles from Lapu Lapu to the beach cost P20-30.

ARGAO

Argao, 66 km south of Cebu City, is an old town with high limestone walls around its plaza and other remnants of the Spanish era. The eroding black-sand beach and the lack of coral reefs are disappointing, though somewhat balanced by watching Filipino fishermen pull in their early-morning catch. Better sand is found south near the village of Dalaguete. This, however, is a very relaxing place to spend a few days.

Accommodations

Most of Argao's accommodations are located in town, with an upscale resort ten km south at Dalaguete.

Rey and Carola's Bamboo Paradise: Argao's most popular homestay is two km south of town. Carola Rubia is a friendly German lady married to a Filipino musician and former policeman named Rey. Check the batik in the bedrooms and giant lobsters on the wall! Argao, tel. 271, P250-350.

Other Budget Accommodations: Another good choice is Angelita's, in town behind the church, where clean and modern rooms go for P300, and the simple but adequate Four Brothers Pension at the bus stop, which costs P80.

Argao Beach Club: A first-class resort, 10 km south of Argao, with 77 a/c rooms fronting a beautiful beach of pure white sand brought in by dump trucks. Reservations and transportation can be arranged from the Cebu Plaza Hotel. Casay, Dalaguete, tel. 314365, US$60-85.

Transportation

ABC buses depart hourly from the southern bus terminal in Cebu City. The 0800 bus departure connects the ferry from Argao across to Loon on Bohol.

SOGOD

Sogod, a small town 60 km north of Cebu City, is known for its white-sand beaches, caves, a church dating from 1832, and excellent diving at Capitancillo Reef and Nunez Shoal off Calanggaman Islet.

Accommodations

Club Pacific: Northern Cebu's finest beach resort is seven km north of Sogod. Activities include scuba diving, windsurfing, tennis, and cultural shows in the Magellan Restaurant. Transfers from Cebu City can be arranged by calling their office, or take a Rough Rider bus to Bingoy from the Elicon Hotel. Bingoy, tel. 79147, US$80-120.

BANTAYAN ISLAND

Bantayan Island, off the northwestern tip of Cebu, offers excellent diving and some of the most spectacular beaches in the region, especially along the southern coastline between Santa Fe and Maricaban. The island's superb combination of sun, sand, and sea will probably make it a major destination in the coming years.

Accommodations

Basic hotels are located in Bantayan, the island's largest town, in Santa Fe, the third largest, and at several beaches near Santa Fe.

Santa Fe Beach Resort: A large and well-developed resort with a cafe, Windsurfers, outrigger rentals, and boat charters to nearby islands and coral reefs. The resort is in Talisay, a few kilometers north of Santa Fe pier. Santa Fe, Cebu tel. 211339 or 82548, P300-400 fan, P900-1500 a/c doubles.

Kota Beach Resort: Another popular resort, one km south of Santa Fe and three km from the new airport, where the sand and waters are absolutely dazzling. Santa Fe, Cebu, tel. 75101, fax 53748, US$15-25 fan, US$36-45 a/c.

Admiral Lodging: Basic accommodation in the town of Bantayan. The Arriola family can advise on inexpensive accommodations on Bantayan. 21-23 Rizal Ave., tel. 215692, P80-300 fan, P450-500 a/c.

Transportation

Bantayan Island is 138 km northwest of Cebu City and 24 km from Hagnaya port near San Remigio.

Air: Pacific Air flies daily from Cebu City to the Santa Fe Airport.

Bus and Boat: To reach Bantayan in a single day, take either the 0600 a/c or 0500 ordinary bus from the North Bus Terminal in Cebu City to Hagnaya wharf, from where a regular public ferry departs daily at 0930 and reaches Bantayan in one hour. Late arrivals can take the night ferry, which leaves around 2130.

Ferries back to the mainland depart Santa Fe at 0600 and 0700 and connect with buses leaving at 0715 and 1300.

To Negros: Public ferries also shuttle from Bantayan across to Cadiz on Negros, a convenient route which avoids some backtracking.

SANTANDAR

Cebu's longest white-sand beach is at the southern tip of Cebu near the village of Liloan, two km south of Santandar. The beach is fairly attractive, offshore diving is good, and scuba excursions can be arranged to Sumilon and Apo islands.

Accommodations

Manureva Beach Resort: Jean Pierre Franck's isolated but lovely resort has a dive center, motorcycle rentals, and sailboards, and organizes big game-fishing expeditions. Santandar, tel. 16001, US$12-24 fan, US$25-50 a/c. Pierre cooks great French meals. Ask him about his postcard business.

Transportation

Santandar can be reached in a few hours with hourly ABC bus from the Southern Bus Terminal in Cebu City. It's a spectacular ride on a recently repaved highway.

MOALBOAL

Panagsama Beach, situated at the edge of a rocky promontory some 90 km southwest of Cebu and five km from Moalboal, remains a popular travelers' destination despite the tragic destruction of its beaches and offshore coral gardens by Typhoon Nitong in 1984. Locals say the tides were at their very lowest when the 280-km/h winds virtually sandblasted the once-famous coral beds into oblivion. The remaining beaches are rocky and unpleasant except for a narrow strip of sand just north of the expensive Moalboal Reef Club.

The scruffy town also suffers from a lack of planning, barking dogs, and hustling schoolchildren, although the underwater buttresses and coral-studded reefs around Pescador Island remain popular with scuba divers. Saavedra Dive Center charges US$25 per dive including equipment or US$200 for a five-day PADI-certification program. Other dive centers include Ocean Safari, run by Nelson Abenido; Visaya Divers; and Philippine Dive and Tour.

Accommodations And Transportation

Rooms and private cottages average P100-250 depending on facilities. Pacita's Bungalows to the left of the Coke sign is a popular place despite the lack of sand and sad shape of the huts. Norma's, Nanita's, Calypso, Cora's, and Pacifico Cottages are similarly priced.

Moalboal's two best lodging options are Sumisid Dive Lodge, which costs US$10-25, and the Moalboal Reef Club for US$25-50. Both include full board.

Moalboal can be reached in three hours by ABC bus from Cebu's southern bus terminal. Philippine Eagle goes direct at noon. Buses terminate in Moalboal, from where tricycles cost P10-15 out to Panagsama Beach.

SOUTH OF MOALBOAL

Badian Island Resort

Tremendous coral reefs untouched by dynamite fishing are situated near the only deluxe resort in western Cebu. Facilities include a swimming pool, a restaurant, and equipment for water sports. Badian, Cebu, tel. 61306, US$120-200.

Kawasan Falls

Two lovely waterfalls with natural swimming pools and simple huts for overnighters are located west of Matutinao. Alight at the Matutinao bridge and hike 30 minutes west through the beautiful river canyon. Matutinao also has a simple restaurant and hotel.

Transport To Dumaguete

Good alternatives to the standard ferry from Toledo on Cebu to San Carlos on Negros are the hourly boats from San Sebastian and Bato to Tampi near Dumaguete. Run to the jeepney or you'll be stranded.

LEYTE

Though visited only by overlanders passing from Luzon to Cebu, the island of Leyte has played a key role in Filipino history. In 1521 Magellan formed a blood compact with a local chieftain and subsequently held the first Christian Mass in Southeast Asia. Leyte was also the site of MacArthur's triumphant return at the end of WW II.

More recently, Tolosa—a small town slightly south of Tacloban—received international attention and a great deal of economic gain for being the birthplace of Imelda "Shoe Princess" Marcos. Aside from these historical sidelights, Leyte has a handful of beautiful but rarely visited national parks and some isolated islands perfect for the visitor who wants to get off the beaten track.

Transportation

Traveling across Leyte is rather straightforward. Travelers can reach Tacloban from Legaspi in a single nonstop day, provided they catch the morning ferry from Matnog on Luzon to Allen on Samar. Tacloban to Ormoc takes two hours by bus. Most travelers then catch a boat from Ormoc to Cebu City. Other departure options include flying with PAL, daily boats from Tacloban to Surigao in northeastern Mindanao, the twice-weekly ferry from Maasin to Surigao, and sporadic ferries from Maasin to Ubay on Bohol. See the chart, "Ships from Leyte," below. Schedules should be checked with the tourist office in Tacloban.

TACLOBAN

Leyte is an island both physically and psychologically divided by the central mountain range. The capital city of the eastern seaboard is home to the Waray people, who speak a local dialect and survive by raising coconuts. Ormoc, the economic and cultural center of western Leyte, is populated by Cebuanos who speak Cebuano, raise sugar, and regard Cebu City as their spiritual homeland. Tacloban itself is a medium-size deep-water port with a lively market but a limited number of sights.

Attractions In Town

The tourist office in the Children's Park at the north end of town has maps and other useful information.

Walking Tours: Their walking tour passes the Provincial Capitol, whose murals recall Magellan and MacArthur, the Price Mansion, where MacArthur once lived, and the anthropological museum in the Divine World University.

Heritage Museum: Top draw, however, is the Santo Nino Shrine and Heritage Museum on Calle Real two km south of downtown. On the site where the young and hungry Imelda once lived, the former first lady constructed a monument to her extravagance, self-importance, and appalling bad taste. The interior sports a baby Jesus surrounded by disco lights, a framed image of the Madonna done with pearls splashed across crimson velvet, and guest rooms for her friends instead of side altars. This audacious monument proves that Imelda not only matched but exceeded her husband's attempts to recast their personal histories in a more favorable light.

Attractions Outside Of Town

Tacloban's other draws are located outside of town.

Red Beach: The MacArthur monument at Red Beach, seven km south of Tacloban just before the town of Palo, can be reached on jeepneys leaving from the harbor stand. Like MacArthur, the images are larger than life.

Sohoton Park: Tacloban's other big attraction is actually located across the Leyte Gulf in Samar, although access is easiest from Tacloban. Sohoton National Park offers tropical jungle, waterfalls, and deep caves best explored during low tides. Take a jeepney from the harbor to Basey where forestry officials can help hire boats and guides to explore the park. A day visit is too rushed; plan on spending the night inside the park with the rangers.

Tolosa: Imelda fans might also visit Tolosa, 24 km south, where the Olot presidential beach resort was completely stripped after the fall of Marcos. Olot today is in ruins; the swimming

SHIPS FROM LEYTE

DESTINATION	FROM	LINE	DEPARTURES	HOURS
Bohol	Jagna	Bato	pumpboat	1000 daily?	4
	Jagna	Maasin	Escano	3 times weekly	4
Cebu	Cebu City	Maasin	G & P	Mon., Wed., Fri. at 2300	5
	Cebu City	Ormoc	Aboitiz	daily at 2200	5
	Cebu City	Ormoc	Aboitiz	Sat., Tues. at 1000	5
	Cebu City	Tacloban	various	nightly 1800-2000	12
Luzon	Manila	Ormoc	Aboitiz	Sat. at 2200	32
	Manila	Tacloban	William	Sat. at 1700	26
Mindanao	Surigao	Maasin	various	3 times weekly 0600	4
	Surigao	Liloan	various	daily at 0600	4
Samar	Catbalogan	Tacloban	W. Samar	3 times weekly	5

pool is now home to frogs and mosquitos rather than the rich and powerful.

Accommodations
Most of Tacloban's inexpensive hotels in the P50-150 range are along Romualdez St. a few blocks from the bus and jeepney stop.

San Juanico Travel Lodge: None of the low-end choices in Tacloban are very clean, but for an overnight crash try this spot in the center of town. 104 Justic Romualdez St., tel. 321-3221, P60-100.

Leyte State College House: A clean and comfortable student-run hostel, about five blocks south of Romualdez at the corner of Paterno and Santa Cruz streets. All rooms are a/c. 1 Paterno St., tel. 321-3175, P120-200.

Tacloban Village Inn: One of the few decent hotels in Tacloban after the 1992 closure of the upscale Leyte Park Hotel. Facilities include a "disco pad, adequate parking space," and a "Love Taxi." Veteranos St., tel. 321-2926, P180-300 a/c.

Information
Traveler's checks can be cashed at the PNB on Romualdez Street. PAL offices are located at the airport and in the Hotel Village Inn on Imelda Avenue. Buses and jeepneys to destinations on Leyte leave from the terminal between the market and the harbor. Philtranco, Ceres Liner, and Bachelor Express bus terminals are on Real Street.

BILIRAN ISLAND

Formerly called Panamo, 495-square-km Biliran Island can be reached on a direct bus from Tacloban to Naval, the main town. Naval has a few simple pensions such as the LM—or try the popular Agta Beach Resort three km north of Almeria. Boats leave Naval daily for Gigantan and Maripipi islands for secluded beaches and great snorkeling. Both islands have simple accommodations.

Other adventures near Caibiran on the east coast include bathing in sulfur springs at Mainit, the clear waterfalls at Tumalistis, and trekking to the summit of 1,178-meter Biliran Volcano. Guides can be hired from the mayor.

ORMOC

Ormoc, the main port and commercial center for western Leyte, chiefly serves as the departure point for ships to Cebu and as a base for exploring the nearby national parks.

Attractions
Attractions include the wharf and the market, the remains of an old bridge near City Hall, the Zaldibar Museum, a Japanese peace memorial, and Pura Beach, 12 km distant.

Farther afield is Tungonan Hot Springs, with a swimming pool and thermogeyser projects, and

Leyte National Park, with its sunken volcanic lake said to be the haunt of giant eels. Hikers might enjoy the 50-km Leyte Nature Trail, which begins near Ormoc.

Accommodations

Most of Ormoc's hotels are within walking distance of the bus terminal and the shipping port.

Eddie's Inn: Simple but clean rooms in a small hotel about four blocks from the bus terminal. Rizal St., tel. 2499, P60-100.

Pongos Hotel: A somewhat more expensive but cleaner choice down near the wharf.

Bonifacio St., tel. 2482, P80-120 fan, P150-220 a/c.

Don Felipe Hotel: Ormoc's top-end choice is also near the wharf. The hotel is divided into an inexpensive annex and the main building with more expensive rooms. Bonifacio St., tel. 2460, P60-100 fan, P150-420 a/c.

Transportation

PAL flies twice weekly from Ormoc to Cebu City. Ships to Cebu City depart nightly around 2200 and take about six hours.

MINDANAO

The second largest island in the Philippines is considered by many Filipinos to be the Wild South—a mysterious and exotic land of high mountains and impenetrable rainforest peopled by intransigent Muslims and pagan hilltribes. In reality, Mindanao is three-quarters Christian and largely developed with towns, roads, and other signs of urban progress. Its role as a meeting ground for Christians and Muslims has brought problems of political assimilation, but the island is also replete with natural wonders, diverse cultures, and dozens of minorities who remain less modernized than those in northern Luzon.

Highlights on Mindanao include the beautiful offshore islands near Surigao and a climb to the summit of Mt. Apo near Davao. Visitors interested in Muslim lifestyles will enjoy Marawi in the province of Lanao del Sur, while those intrigued by cultural minorities should visit Lake Sebu, one of the prettiest and least visited regions in the country. Davao and Zamboanga are nondescript cities with few sights, though both serve as gateways to more exotic destinations.

Most of Mindanao is relatively safe for Western visitors, but problems are a possibility in those areas controlled by the NPA or militant Muslim groups. Travelers should check with local tourist officials or embassies before traveling through the Lake Lanao region and the Sulu Archipelago.

TRANSPORTATION

Getting There
PAL serves major cities in Mindanao from both Manila and Cebu. Visitors who are short on time but would like to see a specific region such as Lake Sebu, Marawi, or Sulu should take advantage of PAL's low prices and fly directly to the nearest airport.

Several north-coast ports are served by shipping lines from Visayan cities such as Cebu, Tacloban, and Dumaguete. Cebu City has the most shipping connections, though the ferries from southern Leyte are convenient for travelers coming down from Luzon. Another good option is a ship from Dumaguete on Negros.

Getting Around
Buses that link the main cities rarely travel at night, making early-morning departures a necessity for longer journeys. Express buses with nonstop or five-stop signs are the quickest and well worth a few extra pesos.

A complete loop begins with the ferry from Maasin or Liloan in southern Leyte to Surigao in northern Mindanao, followed by a fast bus down to Davao. Buses continue west to General Santos City and Koronadel, from where jeepneys bounce the rough road to Lake Sebu. Then it's north to Marawi and west through Pagadian to Zamboanga. This very long journey can be shortened with flights between larger towns.

SURIGAO

Situated on a hook-shaped peninsula at the northeastern corner of Mindanao, Surigao mainly serves as a transit point for travelers coming down from Luzon and as the launching point for visits to the beautiful group of islands just off the mainland. The focal point is the plaza; a small tourist office is located on the second floor of City Hall.

Ferries from Leyte dock at the small harbor at the northern edge of town. Philtranco buses to Davao and Manila leave from the terminal on Gemina Street.

Accommodations
Budget accommodations include the Garcia Hotel a block beyond the plaza and the Flourish Lodge on Borromeo Street toward the main pier. Both have fan-cooled rooms from P100 and a/c rooms from P250. Top-end choice is the Tavern Hotel on Borromeo, where fan-cooled rooms go from P150 and a/c rooms from P300.

Attractions East Of Surigao
Surigao's top draw is the group of islands scattered to the east. Facilities are limited and few Westerners make it here, but those who do claim the islands are among the most beautiful in the region.

Boats to Dapa on Siargao Island leave in the early morning from the pier at the southern end of Borromeo Street. Jeepneys continue 14 km to the town of General Luna, where accommodations are found in beachside nipa huts. The 0700 jeepney back to Dapa connects with the 1100 boat to Surigao.

General Luna also serves as gateway to several small islands such as Guyam, Dako, and La Janoza. Snorkeling is reportedly as superb near Suyangan.

DAVAO CITY

Davao City, a modern commercial center located in south Mindanao, has three claims to fame: it's the Philippines' third most populous city after Manila and Cebu, its gerrymandered boundaries give it a greater land area than any other city in the country, and it's home to the nation's sweetest durians. Davao is also known for the Alsa Masa ("Masses Arise") defense movement, which has successfully battled the local NPA forces. Although unremarkable by most standards, Davao lacks the congestion of Zamboanga, plus it exudes a refreshing atmosphere of growth and success.

Attractions

Sights around town include the largest Buddhist temple on Mindanao, handicraft shops with outstanding Mandaya weavings, and the small museum and Dabaw Etnika handicraft shop at the Davao Insular Hotel.

Don't miss the wonderful durian monument erected by the Durian Appreciation Society in Magsaysay Park near the wharf. Durian season runs from March to June; otherwise try the candy or dried preserves sold at the Madrazo Fruit Center.

The tourist office in the Apo View Hotel has maps and more information on nearby beaches and islands, plus will advise on treks to Mt. Apo and visits to banana and abaca plantations. Extend visas at the Immigration Office in the Antwel Building near Magsaysay Park.

Samal Island

Across the straits and due east of Davao is an immense island of blazing sand and aquamarine waters which, until recently, remained quite un-

spoiled. However, in 1992 Samal was targeted as a major destination by the Department of Tourism and it now seems that large-scale development is only a few years away.

The once-famed Aguinaldo Pearl Farm on nearby Malipano Island closed several years ago in favor of an upscale resort, though scuba divers continue to explore the pair of WW II ships that lies in the nearby waters. Samal's best beach is Paradise Island Beach on the west-central coast near the towns of Kaputian and Tigala. The island also offers an aquarium, a marine zoo, and caves used for local burials.

Accommodations: Samal currently has about a dozen small resorts, which typically consist of thatched cottages set under swaying palms. Most have basic bungalows with common bath for P100-250 and private chalets from P300. Current choices near the town of Caliclic include Paradise Island Beach Resort, Coral Reef Resort, Samal Beach Park, Palm Hill Beach Resort, and Costa Marina.

The most extravagant choice is the Pearl Farm Beach Resort (tel. 62749), owned and operated by Margie Floirendo, a local beauty who swept the Miss Universe beauty contest a decade ago. The resort has 30 a/c bungalows elevated over the clear waters and priced from US$60 per night.

Transportation: Boats to Samal Island depart from several piers, including the Santa Ana Wharf north of town and the Davao Insular Hotel pier, and take about 45 minutes. Schedules are somewhat erratic, but the tourist office can help with current details.

Davao City Accommodations

Budget hotels are located downtown on San Pedro, Pelayo, and Pichon streets.

El Gusto Family Lodge: The travelers' favorite is clean, reasonably quiet, and centrally located near the Davao River. 51 Pichon (Magallanes) St., tel. 63832, P60-120 fan, P150-250 a/c.

Le Mirage Family Lodge: Another inexpensive yet decent place in the center of town. San Pedro St., tel. 63811, P60-120.

Royal House: A slightly better choice is behind the Maguindanao Hotel. 34 Claro Recto St., tel. 73630, P100-140 fan, P200-350 a/c.

Apo View Hotel: Aside from this centrally located choice, most of Davao's upscale hotels are some distance from city center. Facilities here include a swimming pool, a restaurant, and a tourist office on the ground floor. Camus St., tel. 74861, P800-1000.

Transportation

Davao's airport is located in Lanang about 12 km from city proper. Take a taxi for P60 or walk to the highway and hail a jeepney marked Panobo.

Shipping offices are located at the Santa Ana wharf about three km north of downtown. Ships leave daily to Zamboanga and twice weekly to Manila.

Philtranco, Ceres Liner, and Bachelor Express buses leave from the Ecoland Terminal across the bridge toward the dismal and over-priced nightclubs on MacArthur Highway.

MOUNT APO NATIONAL PARK

Mt. Apo, situated 40 km southwest of Davao, is at 2,954 meters the highest mountain in the Philippines. It's also a naturalist's wonderland. Winding trails to the summit pass by lakes, waterfalls, hot springs, and steam vents emitting sulfuric gases. Fauna slowly changes from virgin rainforest thick with giant mahoganies to windswept grasses that survive above the timberline. Wildlife ranges from the endangered Philippine eagle to tiny falconets and endemic species such as the Apo mynah.

The four- to five-day climb can be started from either Digos, Kidapawan, or New Israel near Bulatukan. The Davao Tourist Office will help with recommended gear, guides, and routes. Guides and porters can also be hired directly at less cost in Kidapawan and New Israel. A popular option is to hike from Kidapawan or New Israel (said to be an easier route) and then descend to Digos. Hiking season is from March to May.

Another attraction on the slopes of Mt. Apo is the Philippine Eagle Camp, a captive breeding station where visitors can see the magnificent birds at close range. Run by an American naturalist named Ron Krupa, the camp is located near Baracatan about 14 km off the main Davao-Digos highway. The camp also has good hiking. Recent troubles over a proposed geothermal plant have limited tourism. Check with the DOT before making the trip.

LAKE SEBU

Sebu, a picturesque lake surrounded by verdant green foothills in the heartland of South Cotabato, is perhaps the finest place in the Philippines to see what's left of the nation's cultural minorities. Beyond that, it's a wonderful region for hiking and relaxation in the clear, crisp mountain air. Highly recommended.

Inhabiting the Tiraray Highlands bounded by Surallah, Kiamba, and Polomok are some 200,000 T'boli people whose women are famed for their skills in *abaca* weaving, intricate brasswork belts, and ornamental combs.

Guides can be hired to explore the foothills and possibly visit the more distant tribes of Manobos and Mansakas. Some say the Tasaday are a four-day hike due west, but others claim it's a 30-minute motorcycle ride.

Don't miss the Saturday market: a photographer's dream.

Davao durian monument

Accommodations

Few visitors make the journey to Sebu, but those who do often stay much longer than anticipated.

Santa Cruz Mission: Accommodations are available about 15 minutes from the lake in a beautiful lodge constructed in traditional style by the Santa Cruz Mission. The older lodge down the road helps with the overflow. Rooms cost P50.

Baay Village Inn: Right on the lakeside is another spot where the hotel owner and "Honorable Vice Mayor," Bao Baay, can help with boat rentals and offer advice on trekking, caves, waterfalls, and forest resorts. Rooms cost P50.

Lakeview Lodge: Another good lakeside choice. P50-80.

Hillside View Park & Tourist Lodge: The latest in a series of additions at the lake. Clean and comfortable. P50-80.

Transportation

Lake Sebu is in the Alah Valley, south of Koronadel and the nearby village of Surallah. Public buses from Davao reach General Santos City and Koronadel, from where jeepneys continue down to Surallah and then up to the lake. The last jeepney leaves around 1500.

MARAWI AND LAKE LANAO

Marawi is an Islamic city set on the shores of the second largest lake in the Philippines. The temperate climate, attractive landscape, and Muslim culture make this a worthwhile stop, although political problems have held tourism to a minimum. Visitors should inquire carefully before traveling through the region.

Attractions

Sights around town include a boat tour of Lake Lanao, and the Aga Khan Museum of Islamic Arts and King Faisal Mosque on the campus of Mindanao State University (MSU). Politan Market near the lake is liveliest on Sundays and Thursdays. Antique royal houses of ruling Maranao families still stand in Dayawan.

Accommodations

Accommodations in Marawi are limited to the Marawi Resort Hotel on the MSU campus. The tourist office is also found here. Rooms and cottages cost US$12-20.

ILIGAN

Iligan is an important transportation center and gateway to the Muslim areas of Marawi and Lake Lanao.

Attractions

The city is known for its Sinulog festival, held in September, and a half-dozen waterfalls, including Maria Christina about nine km south of town. Take a jeepney marked Linamon to Agus Bridge and hike 30 minutes. A walk to the observation platform is worthwhile, though the falls have been largely ruined by an immense hydroelectric plant. The fish market and Muslim stores near the harbor are picturesque.

Accommodations

Randy's Lodge, City Lodge, and the popular Maxim Inn on Quezon Avenue have basic rooms from P60. More expensive places include the Iligan Village Hotel with single a/c rooms from P220, and the Maria Christina Hotel in the same price range.

Transportation

Ships arrive at the north end of town. Buses and jeepneys leave from the terminal on Roxas Avenue at the south end.

CAGAYAN DE ORO

The provincial capital and commercial center of Misamis Oriental is mainly a transit point for visitors heading to Camiguin or south toward Marawi.

Sights around town include the Maranao and Bukidnon artifacts at Xavier University and views across the river from the Bishop's Palace.

Outside town are the Huluga Caves, where ancient Chinese shards were unearthed, Macahambus Cave, where Filipino revolutionaries defeated American forces in 1900, and the Del Monte pineapple plantation for guided tours. A city tourist office is located behind City Hall on Victoria Street; the main tourist office is in the Sports Complex on Velez Avenue.

Accommodations

The Sampaguita Hotel on Borja Street has clean rooms with fan from P150 and a/c rooms from P280. The New Golden Star a block toward the river is slightly cheaper. Perlas Hotel on General Capistrano is also clean and fairly inexpensive. Those who need to make an early bus connection can try the Castle or New Asia Lodging House near the bus station. Top choice is the VIP Hotel, where rooms start at P600.

Transportation

Cagayan's terminal is located outside town in Lapasan District. Take a jeepney marked Lapasan from Cogon market. Jeepneys also go Velez Avenue to the pier for shipping offices. Ferries to Camiguin depart at 0800 four times weekly from the main pier.

DIPOLOG AND DAPITAN

Dipolog sometimes serves as an arrival point for travelers coming down from Cebu.

Attractions

The town's only draw is nearby Dapitan, where Filipino patriot Jose Rizal was exiled from 1892 to 1896 after his satirical and nationalistic novels offended Spanish officials. Deported to this isolated town in an attempt to kill his revolutionary fervor, Rizal was soon captivated by the people, tranquility, and simple beauty of the region. It's still a lovely place with its old St. James Church and Iberian plaza surrounded by raintrees. Residents have honored their favorite son with a small museum and tree-lined lanes named after his novels, poems, and Irish wife.

Accommodations

Small hotels are located in both Dipolog and Dapitan, though most visitors head directly to Dakak.

Ranillo's Pension House: Clean rooms and friendly management in Dipolog. Bonifacio St., tel. 3030, P60-120 fan, P180-240 a/c.

Dakak Park and Beach Resort: Northern Mindanao finally arrived on the international tourist circuit with the 1992 opening of this private resort north of Dapitan. Dakak features a 750-meter white-sand beach, 100 a/c cottages, tennis courts, a swimming pool, dinner cruises,

skin-diving facilities, and a host of entertainers brought down from Manila. Dakak Bay, Manila tel. 721-8164, Manila fax 722-2463, Cebu tel. 73586, Cebu fax 212378, US$75-150.

ZAMBOANGA

Southeast Asia is blessed with a handful of place-names so evocative that most tourist offices would kill for them: Mandalay, Borneo, Bandung, and Zamboanga. These destinations sometimes live up to their reputations, which isn't the case with Zamboanga, a hot and congested city filled with ugly concrete buildings, movie posters, tawdry nightclubs, and narrow streets crowded with blasting motorcycles.

Apparently, few travel writers actually come down here to do their research. Recent articles have described the city as "the garden of the Philippines" . . . "a provincial town where the pace of life is slow and unhurried" . . . "the heart of the intriguing exotica of Muslim-land." Hardly. Less than a third of the population are Muslims and signs of Islam barely extend beyond the fishing slum of Rio Hondo. Colorful *vintas,* primitive sailing crafts which once served as the symbols of exotic Zamboanga, have largely disappeared from local waters. The main reason to visit Zamboanga is to travel down through the Sulu Archipelago, which, despite reassurances given by local tourism officials, is a risky adventure.

Attractions

While it's not a dream vacation, Zamboanga does offer a handful of worthwhile sights.

Wharf: First stop should be the open-air market near the wharf, where enormous fish are weighed, cleaned, and hauled into pickup trucks. Durians of enormous size cost only P20 during the hot summer months.

Lunch: A friendly and helpful tourist office is inside the Lantaka Hotel, whose outdoor veranda is a great place for cocktails at sunset. Smugglers sell their goods legally in the claustrophobic barracks across from the hotel, but selections are ordinary and prices high.

Fort Pilar: A nicely restored old Spanish fort which has been incongruously capped with a highly revered shrine dedicated to Our Lady of the Pilar.

SHIPS FROM MINDANAO

DESTINATION	FROM		LINE	DEPARTURES	HOURS
Basilan	Isabela	Zamboanga	Basilan	3 times daily	2
Bohol	Tagbilaran	Cagayan	various	3 times weekly	6
	Jagna	Cagayan	TransAsia	Sun. and Tues. at noon	8
Camiguin	Binone	Balingoan	Tamula	5 times daily	2
Cebu	Cebu City	Butuan	various	once daily	12
	Cebu City	Cagayan	TransAsia	daily at 1900	12
	Cebu City	Iligan	Gothong	3 times weekly	12
	Cebu City	Surigao	various	daily at 1900	12
	Cebu City	Zamboanga	G & P	3 times weekly	24
Leyte	Liloan	Surigao	various	daily at noon	4
Luzon	Manila	Cagayan	William	Thurs. at 2300	30
	Manila	Zamboanga	various	daily	36
Panay	Iloilo	Cagayan	Negros	Sun. at 1600	15
Sulu	Jolo	Zamboanga	SKT	daily at 1900	9

Rio Hondo: Beyond the military checkpoint and aluminum mosque—one of the most photographed scenes in the south—stands the Muslim fishing community of Rio Hondo. People are friendly and it's perfectly safe to wander around this government-constructed housing project . . . but watch out for gaps in the planking!

Outside Town: Beyond Zamboanga are Santa Cruz Island, Pasonanca Park with a sequestered hotel, a few Badjao fishing villages, and penal farms where inmates sell their woodcarvings.

Accommodations

Hotels in Zambo are often run-down or noisy from street traffic.

Atilano's Pension House: A good escape from the noise, on a small alley just off the former Pasonanca Road. Major Jaldon St., tel. 4225, P80-150 fan, P180-240 a/c. Recommended.

First Lodge: Simple but very adequate rooms at bargain rates. Lim Ave., tel. 4231, P50-80.

Paradise Pension: Bridging the middle gap is this newish spot with clean rooms and friendly management. Barcelona St., tel. 3005, P380-420 a/c with private bath.

Lantaka Hotel: Zamboanga's only semiluxury hotel has a swimming pool and a tourist office and is right on the waterfront. Valderroza St., tel. 3931, US$28-40.

Transportation

PAL flies daily to Zamboanga from Manila, Cebu, and several towns on Mindanao. Boat departures are shown on the chart. Tricycles from the bus terminal or airport, four km outside town, to any hotel cost P15-20.

SULU ARCHIPELAGO

The string of islands that stretches from Zamboanga down to Borneo is home to dozens of Muslim groups who have resisted foreign control since the arrival of the Spanish. Sulu is rarely visited by Westerners since it lies almost completely off the beaten track. It's pure virgin country—something that can't be said of most of Southeast Asia. But there have been problems. In 1984 a German and an American were kidnapped and held for a full year before being released. In 1986 a Swiss tourist was abducted on Santa Cruz Island near Zamboanga and held for almost three months. Muslim groups such the Moro National Liberation Front (MNLF) and the Moro Islamic Liberation Front (MILF) seem to grab hostages solely for ransom, rather than for political revenge as with the NPA. Anyone traveling in the region should check carefully with tourism officials and embassies regarding the current political situation. You'll get all sorts of opinions. Everybody in Manila will tell you it's extremely dangerous, but then few people in Manila have ever been this far south. Tourist officials in Zamboanga claim that most areas are now relatively safe if you stick to the larger towns, stay indoors after dark, and travel only with large groups. Despite these hassles and risks, most visitors to this region seem to feel that the rewards far outweigh the problems.

Basilan

The island closest to Zamboanga is home to several Muslim groups, such as the Samal, the Tausug, the Badjao, and the Yakan, a peaceful and industrious minority who make up about one-third of the total population. A relatively safe place, Basilan is best visited for the Sunday market in Lamitan or during the Yakan Harvest Festival in November.

Ferries depart Zamboanga five times daily for Isabela, where you can stay at the Basilan Hotel or at other pensions near the market. The tourist office in the capital building can help arrange tours of nearby rubber and coffee plantations. Tourist literature claims "There you can see the Mayor himself for detailed facts"; perhaps worth a try.

Isabela's main draws are the beautiful beaches on nearby Malamaui Island and Lamitan's colorful Sunday market. Stay with Norbert and Rebecca Russ, a German-Yakan couple who live in Limook. Or try Basilan Hotel in Isabela, where rooms cost P150-200. It's best to return to Zamboanga before continuing south toward Jolo.

Jolo

The largest town in the archipelago, Jolo (pronounced Holo) is a convenient base for exploring the nearby islands, beaches, and isolated fishing villages.

Ships sail and PAL flies daily from Zamboanga. Sights include the wharf market for smuggled goods, a small ethnological museum at the university, and the NACIDA handicrafts shop.

Accommodations include the Helen Lodge and the Rinci Hotel. Outside town you must rely on local hospitality. Good beaches are located at Quezon and Maubuh at Lambayong.

Tawi Tawi

The southernmost province in the Philippines is mainly visited by travelers hoping to reach Sabah. Although it's technically illegal and often a risky adventure, authorities sometimes let foreigners with return tickets to Manila and permits obtained in Bongao continue south to Sempora on Borneo.

PAL flies daily from Zamboanga to Bongao, largest town and provincial capital of Tawi Tawi.

Do the market, visit the ethnological museum at MSU, check the views from the Capitol Building, feed the monkeys on Mt. Bongao, and snorkel at offshore islands.

Both the Southern Hotel and Lyn's Cottages have cheap rooms.

Sitangkai, just 40 km from Borneo, is dubbed the Filipino Venice for its crowded canals that substitute for roads. Yusof Abdulganih's pension is cheap, plus he'll advise on hiring *bancas* for local touring and reaching the Turtle Islands near Borneo.

MINDORO

A visit to Mindoro is almost synonymous with a sojourn at Puerto Galera, the closest good beach near Manila. The remainder of Mindoro is largely unexplored, though the breathtaking mountains, thick jungles, remote beaches, and cultural minorities offer endless possibilities for adventurous travelers.

Mindoro also serves as a transit point for visitors going to Boracay. The most popular route is by boat from Roxas in southeastern Mindoro and across to Tablas Island, from where *bancas* continue down to Boracay. Although a tiring and sometimes dangerous journey, this allows you to enjoy the beaches at both Puerto Galera and Boracay with a minimum of backtracking.

Scuba Diving

Mindoro's easy accessibility and well-preserved marine environment have made it one of the top dive locations in the Philippines. Among the highlights are the coral gardens situated off Long Beach; the famous shark cave near Escarceo Point; and the wrecks of a Japanese ship near the Boulders, a Spanish galleon near Verde Island, and another Spanish wreck in the Manila Channel (only discovered in 1983). Puerto Galera is also the launching point for dives to renowned Apo Reef, a 30-square-km reef off the west coast of Mindoro. Professional dive shops which can help with equipment rentals, boats, guides, and PADI certification include Capt'n Greggs on Sabang Beach, El Galleon on Small La Laguna Beach, and Reef Raiders in Ermita and on Big La Laguna Beach.

Transportation

Ferries leave daily around noon from Batangas to Puerto Galera. The easiest way to make the connection is on private a/c buses leaving at 0900 from the Sundowner Hotel in Manila. The cost is P340 and arrival time in Puerto is about 1400. A half-price alternative is the 0800-0830 bus from Lawton terminal or Pasay terminal direct to the ferry dock in Batangas.

Jeepneys waiting in Puerto Galera go in two directions: east to the busy beaches at Sabang and La Laguna or west to the relatively peaceful beach of White Sand. Sabang is best for scuba divers and party animals searching for bars and discos. White Sand is best for long walks, sunsets, and quiet evenings in simple restaurants.

PUERTO GALERA

Six hours south of Manila is this famous travelers' scene and tourist haunt set along a stunning harbor speckled with superb beaches and secluded coves. The magnificent wall of mountains that rises from the ocean and towers over the bay adds a wonderful sense of mystery and grandeur to the scene. One of the most stunning landscapes in Southeast Asia, parts of Puerto Galera are also crowded, noisy, polluted, and packed out with boozing tourists and bar girls. Fortunately, the beaches west of town are relatively undeveloped and still worth visiting. Hopefully the tragedy of Sabang will serve as a warning to other upcoming beach resorts in Asia: don't destroy yourself in the mad chase for the tourist dollar.

Puerto Galera Town

The beautiful harbor at Puerto Galera has evolved from a 10th-century entrepôt of Chinese junks and Indian *prahus* to ferries and *bancas* filled with travelers, tourists, and curious Filipinos. Accommodations are plentiful in town but there's little reason to stay here unless you plan on catching an early-morning ferry back to Batangas. It's best to immediately take a jeepney east to Sabang or west to White Beach.

Quality hotels west of the pier include the Villa Margarita White House, with rooms from P200, and the more expensive El Canonero; both are clean and comfortable and offer great views over the harbor.

Simple hotels in town charge about P100 per room. Best picks are Melxa's Greenhill Nipa Huts on Cobarrubias near the water, Malou's Hilltop Inn around the corner, Cristine's Place on the windy beach, and cozy Montiel's Nipa Huts a few blocks south. The Outrigger Hotel on the beach beyond the market charges P200.

Puerto Galera also has a small post office, a health clinic, and a bank that changes traveler's checks.

PUERTO GALERA

© MOON PUBLICATIONS, INC.

Near Puerto Gallera Town

The following accommodations are 10-20 minutes by foot or *banca* from the pier.

Boquete Island: Guesthouses include Cathy's Inn on the east coast with tennis, Windsurfers, and cottages from P100-400, and Coral Aquaria on the south coast with decent cottages and facilities in the same price range.

Encenada Beach: Ten minutes by jeepney east of town lies a small but lovely bay with two rather upscale spots. Encenada Beach Resort has a popular 24-hour bar, a dive shop, and 25 rooms which cost P500-800. Contact Iseya Hotel at 1241 Del Pilar in Ermita.

German-owned Tanawin Lodge is a better choice, with swimming pool, excellent restaurant, friendly management, and luxurious chalets US$25-50. Contact Afro-Asian Tours (tel. 521-8167) on Orosa St. in Ermita.

Coco Beach: A private beach dominated by the Coco Beach Resort, with swimming pool, tennis court, and large chalets from US$30.

Sabang Beach

Once an idyllic beach reached only by chartered *banca*, Sabang and nearby La Laguna beaches are now the "Little Ermitas" of Puerto Galera. Big La Laguna beaches around the corner are somewhat quieter and have better sand, plus the scuba diving is said to be the best on the island. All three beaches are packed with huts charging P150-500 during the wet summer months and P250-1000 from November to May.

Coco Beach

A pleasant resort that caters to upscale tourists. Bungalow plus transportation costs P600-1000.

White Beach

Though this stretch of sand lacks the fine curves of the above beaches, White Beach (also called San Isidro Beach) is much quieter and more relaxed. Diving is poor and the water is rough but the sand is good and the sunsets great.

Most of the small bungalows tucked away under the coconut trees have been constructed with little imagination, but some are clean and pleasant. Rates are slightly cheaper than at Sabang.

More bungalows are located farther west on Talipanan Beach. Best choices include the Talipanan Beach Nipa Huts, Talisay Cottages, and Mountain Cottages. The Ayala family keeps a private residence here.

SHIPS FROM MINDORO

DESTINATION	FROM	LINE	DEPARTURES	HOURS
Boracay	Beach	Roxas	Avenza	2 times weekly	6
Lubang	Tilic	Sablayan	William	Sat. at 2400	7
Luzon	Batangas	Calapan	various	5 times daily	2
	Batangas	Puerto	ferry	0730, 1300	2
	Manila	Sabalayan	William	Sat. at 2400	15
	Manila	San Jose	William	Wed. at 1900	16
	Marinduque	Gasan	Pinamalayan	various, once weekly	3
Panay	Malay	San Jose	William	Sat. at 1700	19
	Buruanga	San Jose	Jem	weekly	10
Tablas	Carmen	Bongabong	ferry	Sun., Wed., Fri. at 2100	6
	Looc	San Jose	Jem	Mon. and Thurs. at 1000	4
	Odiongan	San Jose	Herlyn	Sun. and Fri. at 1000	4

CALAPAN

The capital of Mindoro Oriental has little to offer the visitor except for ferry connections to Batangas several times daily. An alternative route to Puerto Galera from Manila for those who miss the noon ferry from Batangas is an afternoon ferry to Calapan and jeepney to Puerto Galera. Calapan is also known for its spring Sandugan Festival, which recreates the original encounter between Chinese traders and Mangyan tribespeople.

Accommodations

The Traveler's Lodge and Eric Hotel have cheap rooms, while the Riceland Inn is more upscale.

ROXAS CITY

Roxas is an important connection for travelers going down to Boracay. Accommodations are available in town, but most travelers prefer to stay on the beach at Catalina's Resort near town or at Melco Beach Inn one km north. Both places organize outriggers to Boracay.

Getting To Boracay

A wide variety of boats reach Boracay but only large and safe vessels should be taken. Do not take small outriggers or attempt the crossing during rough weather or after nightfall, since the Tablas Straits are extremely dangerous.

Some boats go directly to Boracay while others go via Tablas or Panay. In most cases, you'll need to overnight in both Roxas and the interim island before continuing to Boracay.

The William Line MV *San Jose* sails weekly for Malay on Panay, from where buses and outriggers go to Boracay. The MB *Jem* sank a few years ago but the MB *Herlyn* leaves three times weekly for Looc or Odiongan on Tablas, or Buruanga on the northwest tip of Panay. Another option is the weekly MV *Avenza* direct from Roxas to Boracay. Boat departures can be checked at Melco's and Catalina Beach Resort.

NEGROS

Shaped like a boot in the heart of the Visayan archipelago, this elongated island serves as an important stepping-stone for travelers island-hopping between Boracay and Cebu.

Negros is a friendly island with some historical sights, a soaring volcano for mountaineers, and wonderful old steam trains that draw rail enthusiasts from all over the world.

The island is made even more fascinating by the intricate web of political and economic forces that sweep across the land. As the undisputed center of the Filipino sugar industry, Negros has been riding a dangerous roller coaster since the late 19th century. While prices were high during the 1960s and '70s, thousands of migrant workers flooded northern Negros to cut the cane and earn a good living. Everybody seemed to prosper: field workers had plenty to eat, a handful of Chinese-mestizo hacienda owners became fabulously wealthy, and Bacolod was known as the city with the nation's highest number of Mercedes limousines.

But the devastating collapse of sugar prices in the early '80s led to social and economic turmoil, widespread poverty, and malnutrition reminiscent of an African famine. It also brought calls for land reform, the rise of militant Catholic priests who openly supported the demands of the communists, and the emergence of private militias organized by wealthy landowners to protect their financial interests. To the intense embarrassment of local officials, Negros became center stage for television crews and foreign politicians who dubbed it the "Ethiopia of the Philippines." The beleaguered island also became a leading prop in the morality play against Ferdinand Marcos.

Today it's a better scene here in "Sugarlandia." A surge in domestic sugar prices from under six cents per pound to almost 20 cents has reopened some of the closed mills and brought back a sense of hope to the Negrenese people. Bacolod is positively humming with good vibes and a feeling of prosperity. Crop diversification—a policy long advocated by both domestic and foreign consultants—has helped smooth out some of the destructive fluctuations. Through all this, the Negrenese have kept their enthusiasm for life and acceptance of *bahala na* . . . what will be, will be.

TRANSPORTATION

Air
PAL flies daily from Manila and Cebu City to Bacolod and Dumaguete.

From Cebu
The easiest way to reach Bacolod from Cebu is by direct a/c buses which depart Cebu City each morning from the central bus terminal. Otherwise, take a bus to Toledo City and then a ferry to San Carlos on Negros at 0900 and 1600. Boats return from San Carlos to Toledo daily at 0530 and 1300. Travelers in Moalboal might take the ferry from San Sebastian to San Jose or Tampi near Dumaguete before continuing around the island to Bacolod.

From Panay
Negros Navigation boats leave Iloilo for Bacolod daily at 0700 and 1500. Departures at the same times from Bacolod.

BACOLOD

Bacolod is a comparatively affluent city with a thriving commercial center, friendly people, and level sidewalks thanks to the 1981 visit of the pope. It's also the site of the famous Mass-Kara Festival, an October Mardi Gras bash that ranks as one of the liveliest events in the Philippines.

Buses from Cebu arrive at the northern bus terminal, from where jeepneys marked Libertad continue to city center. Taxis cost P30 from the harbor and P20 from the northern bus terminal. The tourist office is located a few blocks beyond the square on San Juan Street.

Attractions
Bacolod makes a good base for exploring the nearby sugar mills and national parks. Sights around town are limited to the century-old San

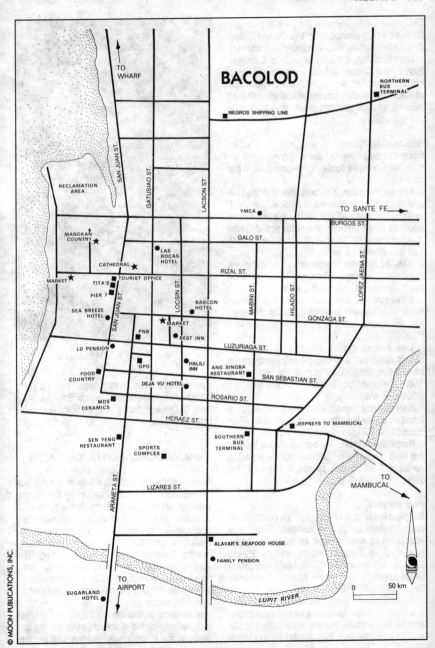

BACOLOD

TO WHARF

NORTHERN BUS TERMINAL

NEGROS SHIPPING LINE

SAN JUAN ST.

GATUSIAO ST.

LACSON ST.

RECLAMATION AREA

YMCA

TO SANTE FE

BURGOS ST.

MANOKAN COUNTRY ★

GALO ST.

LAS ROCAS HOTEL

CATHEDRAL ★

RIZAL ST.

MARKET ★

TITA'S

TOURIST OFFICE

PIER 7

LOCSIN ST.

MABINI ST.

HILADO ST.

LOPEZ JAENA ST.

SEA BREEZE HOTEL

BASCON HOTEL

GONZAGA ST.

★ MARKET

PNB

BEST INN

LD PENSION

LUZURIAGA ST.

GPO

HALILI INN

ANG SINGBA RESTAURANT

SAN SEBASTIAN ST.

FOOD COUNTRY

DEJA VU HOTEL

ROSARIO ST.

MDS CERAMICS

HERAEZ ST.

JEEPNEYS TO MAMBUCAL

SEN YENG RESTAURANT

SPORTS COMPLEX

SOUTHERN BUS TERMINAL

TO MAMBUCAL

ARANETA ST.

LIZARES ST.

TO AIRPORT

ALAVAR'S SEAFOOD HOUSE

FAMILY PENSION

SUGARLAND HOTEL

LUPIT RIVER

0   50 km

© MOON PUBLICATIONS, INC.

Sebastian Cathedral near the park and ceramics firms which produce some of the finest blue-and-white pottery in the country. Another important landmark is the Santa Clara or Barangay San Virgen Chapel outside town, known for its collage mural of almost 100,000 shells. Most of Bacolod's stately ancestral homes with their famous antique collections are also located in the suburbs.

Accommodations

Bacolod has plenty of hotels, but the inexpensive pensions are some of the grungiest in the country.

Family Pension: The best choice in the low-end market is this favorite of Peace Corps volunteers and international travelers a few blocks south of town. Look for the neon sign marked "Cactus Pub." 123 Lascon St., tel. 81211, P120-160 fan, P180-220 a/c.

YMCA: Another inexpensive choice is the run-down and largely deserted YMCA outside town. Burgos St., tel. 26919, P80-120.

Best Inn: An adequate spot but very noisy since it's in an alley overlooking the central market. Bonifacio St., tel. 23312, P80-120 fan, P180-220 a/c.

Las Rocas Hotel: Centrally located but rooms are small and overpriced. Renovations have been "scheduled" since my first visit in 1987! Gatuslao St., tel. 27011, P120-200 fan, P300-380 a/c.

Sea Breeze Hotel: An old but well-located hotel overlooking the reclamation area. San Juna St., tel. 24571, P500-650 a/c.

Sugarland Hotel: The best in town is located out near the airport. Facilities include a pool, a restaurant, and a roof garden. Araneta St., tel. 22460, P520-740 a/c.

Restaurants

Bacolod is famous for the gigantic collection of chicken stalls located in Manokan Country, a vast open-air amphitheater located in the reclamation area. Established in 1969 by a local butcher known as Mr. Slim, Manokan today feeds almost 5,000 people a day! For a friendly time, ask for Burt at Aida's stall.

Food Country across from the tourist office is a small German restaurant owned by Jochann and his Filipina wife. Sunset dinners are popular at Tita's Restaurant and Jumbo Food Center

Iron Dinosaurs at Victoria Mills

overlooking the reclamation area. The Sen Yeng Chinese restaurant on Araneta Street serves tasty Cantonese dishes besides being Bacolod's hottest disco.

MAMBUCAL AND MT. KANLAON

Nestled at the base of Mt. Kanlaon is a modest hill resort originally constructed by the Americans as an escape from the lowland heat of Bacolod. Mambucal is somewhat neglected and run-down, though the seven waterfalls, trails through thick forest, and views from the nearby Salesian Lodge are outstanding. The sprawling lodge overlooks a greenish boat pond. Rooms from P100 and individual cottages from P150. Take a jeepney from Libertad Street in Bacolod.

Mambucal is also the starting point for hikes to 2,465-meter Mt. Kanlaon, seventh highest peak in the Philippines. Guides and porters

SHIPS FROM NEGROS

DESTINATION	FROM	LINE	DEPARTURES	HOURS
Bohol	Tagbilaran	Dumaguete	William	Sat. at 1400	3
Cebu	Cebu City	Bacolod	various	3 times weekly	16
	Cebu City	Dumaguete	various	daily	8
	Toledo	San Carlos	ferry	0530 and 1300	2
	Talisay	Tampi	ferry	hourly until 1500	1
Luzon	Manila	Bacolod	Negros	3 times weekly	19
	Manila	Dumaguete	William	2 times weekly at 0800	24
Mindanao	Dipolog	Dumaguete	William	daily at 0800	4
Panay	Iloilo	Bacolod	Negros	daily at 0700 and 1500	3
Siquijor	Larena	Dumaguete	ferry	daily at 1400	3

can be hired from the tourist office in Bacolod or directly in Mambucal. Allow two or three days during the dry hiking season from March to May.

The quickest approach is from Masulog west of Kanlaon City, but it's much more scenic to take the longer trail from Mambucal. This well-marked route leads to a nature center and campsite in Margaha Valley, from where you approach the summit the following morning. Kanlaon is capped by two craters, a dormant cone sometimes used as a protected campsite and an active crater hissing with sulfuric vents.

IRON DINOSAURS

Perhaps the most intriguing sights on the island of Negros are the antique steam trains which haul sugarcane on the plantations near Bacolod. Originally manufactured in America, Germany, and England shortly after the turn of the century, these extremely rare "Iron Dinosaurs" now attract a steady stream of railway enthusiasts who come to photograph and ride the trains during the cutting season from September to May. Some mills use the steam locomotives for mainline work; others restrict them to shunting around the mill yard. Stationmasters can arrange rides. Visitors with limited time should wait for hourly arrivals in the main yard or check the nearby repair sheds.

Victoria Mills

The world's largest integrated sugar mill and refinery offers more than just old trains. Just as fascinating is a guided tour of the mill, a look at the Filipino company town, and the St. Joseph Chapel where an angry, psychedelic Christ glares down on the huddled masses. Victoria's 400 km of track are worked by modern diesels and about a dozen steams, including German Henschels dating from 1924-30, a Baldwin, and a '24 Bagnall imported from the Fanling railhead in Hong Kong. Visitors are welcome to walk down the tracks and inspect the repair yard. Buses from Bacolod reach the main intersection, from where jeepneys continue to the mill compound.

Hawaiian Mills

Midway between Bacolod and Victoria Mills, and two km north of Silay, stands another outstanding mill, which unlike Victoria uses diesels for shunting and steams on the main lines. This means you'll see more old engines here than at Victoria. Obtain a pass and walk directly through the sugar mill to the repair yard. Apart from a single '29 Henschel, all trains are Baldwins dated 1916-1928.

La Carlotta Mills

Most of the remaining steams from the closed Ma Ao Mill have been transferred to La Carlotta Mills, 50 km south of Bacolod. La Carlotta has 10 Baldwins, a Porter dating from 1912, and two '21 Alcos. Most engines are either dead or in poor condition. Hard-core train freaks might also visit the train remnants in the bright yellow livery at Ma Ao and ride the world's last working Shay at the Lopez Sugar Mill.

DUMAGUETE CITY

The provincial capital of Negros Oriental is a small town almost completely dominated by Silliman University, a Protestant school founded 1901 in a peculiar design somewhat reminiscent of 19th-century southern U.S. architecture. Today it has over 20,000 students and dozens of American professors.

Attractions
Top draw is the Silliman Anthropological Museum for artifacts, ethnic weavings, and sorcery instruments from Siquijor Island. Also of interest is a walk along the waterfront and the old Spanish watchtower on Al Fonseo Street across from the central park. Outside town there's a lookout point at the aptly named Camp Look Out and mediocre beaches both north and south. Dumaguete also serves as the jumping-off point to the outstanding dive sites of Siquijor Island. Coral reefs at Apo Island are best reached from Zamboanguita at the southern end of Negros. Note that the university has closed its nature reserve on Sumilon Island.

Accommodations And Restaurants
Cheap places in Dumaguete are rather grotty dives for students. Fortunately, the clean and comfortable Alumni House on campus near the museum rents rooms to tourists on a space-available basis. Fan rooms with soft beds, high ceilings, and private baths cost P60/100; a/c rooms cost P160/220. A good alternative in the same price range is Opena's Hotel, on Katada Street a block north of the Alumni House. Rooms here cost P140-200 fan and P250-350 a/c. Also try Al Mar Hotel on Rizal Ave. for P100-150.

Beach resorts outside town include the South Seas, three km north, and the El Oriente, two km south on Mangnao Beach. Both have rooms from P380.

Recommended restaurants range from the clean Chin Lung, which serves Chinese meals near the waterfront, and the nearby North Pole, one block north where Rizal Avenue intersects San Jose Street.

SIQUIJOR ISLAND

Twenty km offshore from the southeast tip of Negros lies Siquijor, the smallest province in the Philippines. Filipinos associate the island with images of voodoo and bizarre rituals, but there are also some sandy beaches, good snorkeling, and an undeveloped rural environment. Dive companies stop here since the island is blessed with coral reefs largely undamaged by dynamite fishing.

The main port of Larena has a tourist cottage uphill from the pier plus a fine beach at Sanduyan, five km north of town. Casa del Playa cottages on the beach cost P300-400. Other good beaches include Salaydoong near Maria, Paliton near San Juan, and Candanay near the town of Siquijor. The island is best reached by boat from Dumaguete.

PALAWAN

Situated not far off the northwest tip of Borneo, Palawan is an isolated and mountainous island covered with tropical rainforests inhabited by primitive tribes and some of the last remaining wildlife in the Philippines. Although many places of interest exist on the main island, the star attraction is undoubtedly El Nido on the northeast coast. Here, cataclysmic geological upheavals have left Bacuit Bay studded with a remarkable collection of limestone pinnacles and dazzling white beaches—scuba diving here is considered about the best in Southeast Asia. Other natural attractions include the underground rivers and deserted beaches at Port Barton. While Palawan has its drawbacks, such as terrible roads and limited accommodations, these are more than compensated for by the unspoiled beauty of the land and sea.

However, this island is also being ruthlessly plundered by the logging practices of the very rich and the slash-and-burn farming techniques of the very poor. The rate of devastation is shocking. Some consultants say that within 20 years the island could lose more than 60% of its forest cover. A German study claims that old growth will be completely gone in less than a decade. Much of this destruction results from the concessions of a politically influential timber tycoon who controls the logging industry on Palawan. The reasons are obvious: commercial loggers are the largest single source of money for political campaigns despite the 1992 halt to unapproved logging. Destructive fishing practices are another problem on Palawan. As elsewhere in the archipelago, Filipino fishermen often kill fish by squirting cyanide at them, a process that also destroys the coral reefs.

This environmental saga, on a smaller scale, resembles the horror show in Brazil. Petitions are gathered and the Roman Catholic Church joins the anti-logging movement. Environmentalists force through an anti-logging bill that few believe will stop the logging consortiums. Reprisals then follow. Two priests who campaigned against logging in Mindanao are killed. A reporter for the *Far Eastern Economic Review* receives death threats, and the island's leading timber tycoon files a US$1.2-million libel suit against the magazine. The political will to stop the rape of the forests seems to be rising in Manila, but unless logging is banned it seems likely that much of Palawan will become a tropical moonscape within the next generation.

Scuba Diving

The vast potential of scuba diving in the Philippines is best at the coral beds and offshore islands around Palawan. It is said that the underwater shelf surrounding the island contains almost 60% of the archipelago's coral reefs. Most divers head directly for El Nido, where dive shops can arrange equipment rentals, dive boats, and certification courses for beginners. Prices are reasonable. For example, Willie and Nora Amann at Bacuit Divers charge US$300 for a one-week course which includes two days of theory and six dives. Dives can also be arranged in Puerto Princesa with Norman Songco at Island Divers on Rizal Street. Other dive areas include the islands north of Busuanga Island, west of Linpacan Island, Cuyo, Tubbataha Reef, and coral beds south of Puerto Princesa. Snorkeling is also great; be sure to bring a mask and snorkel.

TRANSPORTATION

By Air

PAL flies daily from Manila and twice weekly from Cebu. Pacific Airways has expensive but direct flights from Manila to the Villa Librada airstrip near El Nido. Transportation is then provided to the Japanese-owned Ten Knots resort on Miniloc Island. Aerolift flies daily to El Nido for P2800.

By Ship

William Line and Asuncion Shipping sail weekly from Manila to Puerto Princesa, a three-day journey which costs P400-550. William also sails weekly from the towns of Malay and Iloilo on Panay.

Getting Around

Transportation on Palawan is still rough since the all-weather road from Puerto Princesa to El Nido remains on the drawing boards. At present, travelers can take a four-hour bus ride from Puerto Princesa at 0700 and 0900 to Roxas and then a one-hour jeepney to Port Barton. From here, either charter a six-man *banca* roundtrip to El Nido for P2000-4000 or return to Roxas and continue north with a combination of jeepneys and *bancas*.

The jeepney from Roxas to Taytay takes five hours. From Taytay to Umbacadero it's a short jeepney ride followed by a boat to El Nido for about P1200 per 10-man boatload. Stops en route include Liminancong and the privately owned island of Pangolusian. The return to Puerto Princesa is cheaper since the boatmen often need additional passengers.

PUERTO PRINCESA

Most visits to Palawan begin in Puerto Princesa, a large town set along magnificent Honda Bay. The tourist office has a desk at the airport, another in city hall, and a third in the Emerald Plaza Hotel. Be sure to change plenty of money for further travels.

Scuba dives at Honda Bay can be arranged with Island Divers across from the Badjao Hotel. Guides to Batak and Tagbanua settlements in the mountains can also be hired here. Buses and jeepneys leave from the terminal on Malvar Street. Sailing schedules change frequently and should be checked with the tourist office or William Line on Rizal Avenue and Palawan Shipping on Demangga Street. Motorcycles can be hired at Ensomo Studio.

Warning: Malaria is still very widespread on Palawan. All visitors should take malaria pills and keep covered during the rainy season.

Attractions

Sights around town are limited to the colorful market and a twin-spired cathedral. Tribal handicrafts can be purchased at Macawili Ethnic Shop near the market and at Karla's on Rizal Avenue.

Twenty-three km south of town is the Iwahig Penal Colony, a prison without bars where some 4,000 inmates farm, fish, and earn pocket money selling handicrafts to visitors. Within the 37,000-hectare settlement are several rivers with swimming pools, sulfur springs, and a butterfly habitat.

Also visit the Vietnamese refugee camp where a bakery produces excellent breads and croissants. Both camps, however, are now largely deserted and perhaps not worth the effort.

Accommodations

Over 20 guesthouses and hotels are located in Puerto Princesa.

Duchess Pension: The best spot in town is operated by the inimitable Joe and Cecille Concepcion, who provide timely information on local travel, tips on scuba diving and cross-island trekking, and other tidbits impossible to include in this abbreviated guide. Highly recommended. 107 Valencia St., tel. 2873, P80-250.

Abordo's Pension: Another good spot in the same price range, near the waterfront. Sand Oval St., tel. 2206, P60-140.

Yayen's Pension: A budget place, south of the airport, with a popular branch on a beautiful Honda Bay island. Manalo St., tel. 2261, P60-140 fan, P220-280 a/c.

Badjao Inn: Good, clean rooms in the mid-priced range. 182 Rizal Ave., tel. 2761, P200-260 fan, P340-440 a/c.

Asia World Hotel: Puerto Princesa's best has a swimming pool, a restaurant, and, of course, the most popular disco in town. National Rd., tel. 2022, P800-1200.

TABON CAVES

Southern Palawan's most important draw is the Tabon Caves, where fossilized remains of neolithic man were discovered in the early 1960s. Tabon is reached from Quezon, a five-hour bus ride from Puerto Princesa. Guides can be hired from the national museum in Quezon, though the caves will probably only interest visitors with a serious interest in anthropology.

More alluring are the nearby islands and beaches. The most accessible beach is the Tabon Village Resort on Tabon Beach, five km north of town, where attractive cottages cost P200. Also of interest are the offshore islands of Tamlagun and Palm, where a pair of Westerners have set some *nipa* huts.

HONDA BAY

Outstanding diving in shallow waters can be enjoyed among the small archipelago of glistening islands 10 km north of Puerto Princesa, near the gateway town of Tagburos.

Take a jeepney from the market toward Lourdes Harbor, alight at the Caltex tank, and walk toward the water. Day tours are organized by most guesthouses and hotels in Puerto Princesa. *Bancas* can be hired around the islands for about P450 daily or arranged in advance from Island Divers in Puerto Princesa.

Accommodations

Several islands now have bungalows with cafes and dive facilities.

Yayen's Bungalows: Yayen, of Yayen's Pension in Puerto Princesa, maintains several cottages on a private island in Honda Bay. Rooms cost P80-250 depending on the condition.

Starfish Island Resort: Isabel Gallardo runs a small operation with a half-dozen four-man bungalows in the P200-400 price range. Dive facilities and courses, including PADI certification and rescue, are provided by Island Divers. Food is unimaginative and expensive, so bring supplies from town and have the caretaker cook for you.

Meara Marina Resort: Another private resort operated by a pair of Austrians. Rooms cost P350-600.

NAGTABON BEACH

West of Honda Bay, on the opposite coastline of Palawan, lies another lovely stretch of sand facing two craggy islands, curiously nicknamed Hen and Chicken, perhaps after their contours. Here, the sand is pure and the waters are dazzling. Side trips can be arranged south to the Underground River and Tabon Cave.

Accommodations

Nagtabon's easy proximity to Puerto Princesa has brought several new resorts in recent years, including these two which represent good value.

Georg's Place: Georg Bauer and his Filipina wife, Lozy, operate a fine place surrounded by Bermuda lawns, swaying palms, and a semi-

circular cove of pure-white sand. Simple but comfortable cottages cost P150-300.

Zeny's Place: Another decent spot with *nipa* huts and a cafe facing the beach. Rooms cost P100-280.

Transportation

Nagtabon is 30 km northwest of Puerto Princesa in Barangay Bacungan. Jeepneys depart at 1000 from Puerto Princesa and cost about P100 to Nagtabon. Some jeepneys end in Maranat, from where you must hike one hour down to the beach.

THE UNDERGROUND RIVER

Another of Palawan's famous natural attractions is the Underground River in St. Paul National Park. Considered the longest underground river in the world, the vast cavern can be navigated by boat for almost half of its eight-km length.

But, like El Nido, it's a difficult and expensive destination. Approaches can be made from Puerto Princesa via Baheli, or from Port Barton. From Puerto Princesa the most common route is by jeepney to Baheli and then boat charter to the cave for P600. Alternatively, take a jeepney to Cabayugan and hike three hours to the ranger station east of Sabang.

The superbly situated ranger station is a great place to spend a few days. The Underground River can also be approached from Port Barton with outriggers for about P800. The tourist office has information, or ask other travelers in Puerto Princesa. Stay at St. Paul National Park for P50-80.

SAN RAFAEL AND TANABAG

San Rafael, a small town two km south of Tanabag, is a good stop for outstanding coral diving and mountain treks to Batak homelands.

Accommodations

Duchess Beachside Cottages: Joe and Cecille Concepcion of Puerto Princesa operate nine cottages facing a brownish beach and directly below Taraw Caves, which can be reached without a guide. The Underground River can be hiked to in about three days. Two-person cottages cost P120-180.

ROXAS AND PANDAN ISLAND

Roxas is a small fishing village fronted by several offshore islands.

Accommodations

Roxas: Bungalows in town include Gordon's, Gemalain's Inn operated by Mr. Rodriguez, and Rover's Luncheonette, which, sensibly enough, doubles as a cafe. Rooms here cost P50-80.

Pandan Island: Coco Loco Island Resort is an Italian-operated resort with sailboats, snorkeling, diving, sailboards, and 30 cottages priced at P150-220.

PORT BARTON

A fairly good beach and outstanding snorkeling at Port Barton have deservedly made it one of the more popular destinations on Palawan. Hikers can wander the lovely beaches to the south and trek to the inland waterfall to the north. Outriggers can be chartered to snorkel the coral beds surrounding Albagin and Exotica islands, while larger boats can be hired to the Underground Caves and up to El Nido at fixed rates maintained by a local trade union.

San Vicente, 20 km north of Port Barton, has another great beach just across the peninsula.

Accommodations

Port Barton has over a half-dozen modest resorts which charge P60-100 for basic *nipa* huts and P150-250 for better bungalows with private baths.

Port Barton: Beachside choices include Elsa's Beach House, El Bosero Inn, Paradiso Beach Resort, Shangri La Beach Resort, and Swissipilli Cottages.

Capsalay Island: Slightly north of Port Barton is a dazzling island with a set of cottages called Manta Ray Resort. Managed by Paola Sani and Tizianna, Manta Ray offers great vibes and some of the best Italian cuisine east of Venice. Contact Manta Ray Resort at 66 Valencia St., Puerto Princesa, tel. 2609, US$60-75.

EL NIDO

Talcum-powder beaches fringed with coconut palms, vast coral reefs teeming with an astonishing variety of fish, and spectacular limestone mountains soaring vertically from clear turquoise waters have made El Nido one of the most visually stunning destinations in the Philippines. The area's extremely remote location makes it both expensive and time-consuming to reach, a double-edged sword that also helps preserve the fragile environment.

Highlights include the beaches on Inabuyatan Island and coral reefs surrounding Tapituan and Matinloc islands. Dives and certification programs can be arranged with Willie and Nora at Bacuit Dive Shop. El Nido is a place where days turn to weeks and weeks into months.

Accommodations In Town

El Nido, the picturesque village nestled at the base of sheer limestone cliffs, serves as the main backpackers' center and launching point for dive trips throughout the Bacuit Archipelago. Accommodations are available at almost a dozen homestays. Note that El Nido lacks a bank, so bring plenty of pesos or greenback dollars.

Austria Guesthouse: Prospero Austria opened his lovely homestay in 1985 when backpackers began drifting into the region and has since maintained one of the most popular spots in northern Palawan. The homestay is about 100 meters from the wharf. Rooms cost P40-80.

Other Homestays: Mr. Ellis Lim in the green house near the water tower has rooms in the same price range, as does Manuel and Susan Jenato's across from the dive shop and Judge Paloma's next to the jetty.

Slightly more expensive are the newer guesthouses such as Lally Beach Cottage and Bay View Inn, where rooms with private baths cost P60-120.

Island Accommodations

Resorts within Bacuit Bay tend to be elegant but very expensive because of higher construction costs and supply problems with water and energy. As of this writing only two islands have been developed, though permits have been granted for another half-dozen island resorts near El Nido.

Pangalusian Island Resort: Some 15 km southwest of El Nido lies a dazzling island where a Scotsman named Jack Gordon has opened a small resort and cafe with dive facilities. A cottage with full board costs US$45-60 per day.

SHIPS FROM PALAWAN

DESTINATION	FROM	LINE	DEPARTURES	HOURS
Luzon	Manila	P. Princesa	William	Sun. at 1400	28
	Manila	P. Princesa	William	Wed. at 2200 (via Malay)	36
	Manila	P. Princesa	Asuncion	Tues. at 0800	32
Panay	Iloilo	P. Princesa	Palawan	Sat. at 2030	18
	Malay	P. Princesa	William	Wed. at 2200	18

El Nido Resort: One of the most exclusive resorts in the country and among Asia's most stunning natural destinations is this exclusive hideaway on Miniloc Island, 10 km southwest of El Nido. Contact Hotel Nikko, Edsa Highway, Manila, tel. 818-2623, fax 818-4127, US$180-300.

Transportation

El Nido is in northwestern Palawan, some 180 km from Puerto Princesa and 320 km southwest of Manila. The poor condition of the roads makes it necessary to either fly or take a boat for a portion of the journey.

Air: Ten Knots Air (tel. 812-0671) flies daily from Manila to El Nido for US$180 roundtrip. PAL flies daily to Puerto Princesa, from where Pacific Air Charter (Manila tel. 832-2731) operates commuter flights to El Nido, Coron, and Roxas. Aerolift flies four times weekly from Manila to Puerto Princesa.

Ship: Several shipping lines serve various destinations on Palawan from Manila and the Visayas. Palawan Shipping Line sails twice monthly from Manila via Panay, Sulpicio sails weekly from Manila, while Ascuncion Shipping has three ships to Palawan with intriguing stops in the northern islands of Cuyo, Culion, and Lubang.

Land: Several Puerto Royale buses depart the Puerto Princesa market daily from 0500 to 0700 and reach Roxas about five hours later. Jeepneys continue from Roxas north to Tabuan, from where outriggers sail up to El Nido via Liminangcong. Boatmen charge about P1000 for a 10-man outrigger; P100 per person. It's a spectacular journey.

PANAY

This triangular-shaped island is famous for its fine old Spanish churches, resort islands of Boracay and Sicogon, and highly charged Mardi Gras festivals held in January. Celebrating the original pact made between Muslim *datus* from Borneo and Panay Negritos, the festivals take place in all four provincial capitals. Kalibo's Ati Atihan is the most renowned and impressive, but Dinagyang in Iloilo, Harlaran in Roxas, and Binirayan in San Jose de Buenavista are just as lively and much less commercialized—like attending Carnival in Bahia rather than Rio.

Panay is also known for its friendly people, the Ilonggos, who welcome visitors with *hapit anay* (come in) and speak a languorous and seductive dialect which rises sharply at the end to make statements sound like questions.

TRANSPORTATION

By Air

PAL flies daily from Manila to Kalibo, Roxas City, and Iloilo City. The most popular connection is to Kalibo, from where buses and *bancas* reach Boracay in about three hours. If Manila-Kalibo is fully booked, fly to Roxas and continue by bus. Return tickets should be booked well in advance and reconfirmed upon arrival in Kalibo.

By Ship

Cheaper but slower options include the ships that serve various ports on Panay. The most convenient lines for reaching Boracay are

William to Malay and Gothong to New Washington, two small ports on the northern coast of Panay. Also, a weekly ship sails from Cebu City to Roxas and from Palawan to San Jose de Buenavista. Ferries from Bacolod to Iloilo leave twice daily at 0700 and 1500. Connections are also possible between Boracay and Mindoro. See Boracay for more information.

Getting Around

Ceres Liner operates a comfortable fleet of buses on Panay. Buses from Iloilo to Roxas take about four hours, plus another three hours to Kalibo. Ceres departs Iloilo at 0400 and 0930 direct to Boracay. If you oversleep, try the Nandwani Transport minibuses to Kalibo, which leave at 1030 and 1530 one block north of the main bus terminal. With an early start you'll be on the beach by late afternoon.

ILOILO

Iloilo, one of the more attractive towns in the Visayas, makes a good base for exploring the nearby churches, beaches, and islands. The curious name was given to the original settlement by Spanish conquistadors as an abbreviation for the original name of Ilong Ilong.

Attractions

The tourist office is at the far end of General Luna St. near the Sarabia Manor Hotel.

Iloilo Museum: Panay's rich cultural heritage is best seen in the Museo de Iloilo on Bonifacio Street. The small but worthwhile collection ranges from anthropological artifacts and jewelry excavated from pre-Spanish burial sites to British knockoffs, WW II memorabilia, and some outstanding *santos,* including a magnificent reclining Jesus.

Around Town: Downtown Iloilo is an odd mixture of ungainly shophouses covered with grit and attractive wooden architecture dating from the 1920s and '30s; Iloilo was apparently once a very prosperous town. Steaming native coffee and local weavings are sold in the colorful central market.

Accommodations

Most of the better pensions and hotels are a few blocks north of city center.

Family Pension House: A clean place but with very small and dark rooms. However, try their treehouse cafe for breakfast and nighttime entertainment. General Luna St., tel. 72047, P90-140 fan, P180-260 a/c.

Eros Pension House: Larger and brighter rooms in a quieter location one block east of Family Pension. General Luna St., tel. 76183, P90-120 fan, P160-200 a/c.

D'House Pension: A creaky old house with large rooms, high ceilings, and loads of atmosphere. 127 Quezon St., tel. 72805, P80-140 fan.

River Queen Hotel: The hotel near the museum looks touristy, but rooms are large and fairly clean. Bonifacio Dr., tel. 79997, P160-200 fan, P260-320 a/c.

Amigo Terrace Hotel: Iloilo's top-end choice offers beautiful a/c rooms, a swimming pool, and an excellent restaurant—a splurge guaranteed to revive your sagging spirits. Iznart St., tel. 74811, P440-580.

Transportation

Ships from Bacolod dock in the muddy estuary a few blocks from city center. Take a Molo-bound jeepney or walk 30 minutes.

Buses to Roxas, Kalibo, and Caticlan leave from the intersection of Mabini and Ledesma streets. Luxury Ceres buses leave from two blocks south on Rizal Avenue.

Ferries to various places on Guimaras Island leave from several different locations along the wharf. Boats to Bacolod leave daily at 0700 and 1500. All other boats to Manila and Mindanao leave from the main wharf near Fort San Pedro.

VICINITY OF ILOILO

Jaro

The suburbs of Iloilo are rich with historic Spanish architecture and romantic Antillean houses. Jaro, an elite residential center three km south of Iloilo, is known for its Gothic-style cathedral and hand-embroidered *pina* and *jusi* fabrics. Streets fanning from the plaza are lined with the mansions of wealthy sugar barons and Hispano-Filipino elite.

Molo

Even more impressive is the outstanding church in Molo, a wealthy Chinese quarter three km west of Iloilo. Constructed in the 1870s of coral rock,

PHILIPPINES
1. Tiboli portrait; 2. Sinulog smile; 3. Banaue terraces (all photos this page by Carl Parkes)

1

2

SINGAPORE
1. Malay wedding; **2.** Mandarin moment; **3.** ballerina beauty (all photos this page by Carl Parkes)

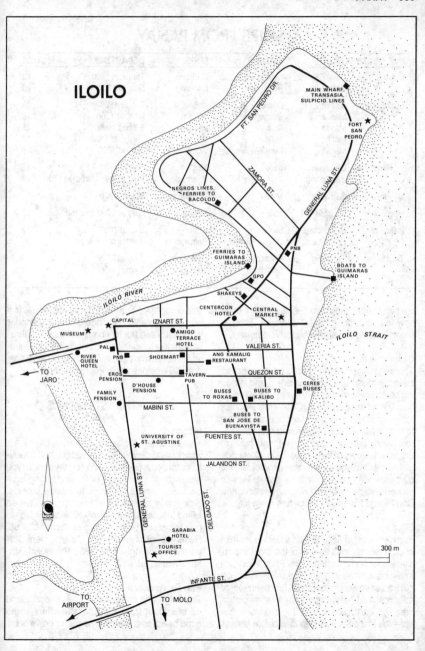

ILOILO

MAIN WHARF, TRANSASIA, SULPICIO LINES

FORT SAN PEDRO

FT. SAN PEDRO DR.

ZAMORA ST.

GENERAL LUNA ST.

NEGROS LINES, FERRIES TO BACOLOD

PNB

BOATS TO GUIMARAS ISLAND

FERRIES TO GUIMARAS ISLAND

GPO

SHAKEYS

CENTERCON HOTEL

CENTRAL MARKET

ILOILO RIVER

CAPITAL

IZNART ST.

ILOILO STRAIT

MUSEUM

AMIGO TERRACE HOTEL

VALERIA ST.

PAL

RIVER QUEEN HOTEL

PNB

SHOEMART

ANG KAMALIG RESTAURANT

TO JARO

EROS PENSION

QUEZON ST.

D'HOUSE PENSION

TAVERN PUB

CERES BUSES

FAMILY PENSION

BUSES TO ROXAS

BUSES TO KALIBO

MABINI ST.

BUSES TO SAN JOSE DE BUENAVISTA

UNIVERSITY OF ST. AGUSTINE

FUENTES ST.

JALANDON ST.

GENERAL LUNA ST.

DELGADO ST.

SARABIA HOTEL

TOURIST OFFICE

0   300 m

TO AIRPORT

INFANTE ST.

TO MOLO

SHIPS FROM PANAY

DESTINATION	FROM	LINE	DEPARTURES	HOURS
Cebu	Cebu City	New Washington	Gothong	Thurs. at 1200	22
	Cebu City	Roxas	Gothong	Sun. at 1800	20
Luzon	Manila	Dumaguete	Aboitiz	Sat. at 1500	16
	Manila	Dumaguete	William	Mon. at 1200	16
	Manila	Iloilo	various	5 times weekly	25
	Manila	Malay	William	Thurs. at 1600	16
	Manila	New Washington	Gothong	Sun. at 1200	16
Mindanao	Cagayan	Iloilo	Negros	Sat. at 1700	15
	Zamboanga	Iloilo	Sulpicio	Sun. at 2200, Wed. at 1700	18
Mindoro	San Jose	Malay	William	Sat. at 0700	
Negros	Bacolod	Iloilo	Negros	daily at 0700 and 1500	2
Palawan	P. Princesa	Malay	William	Sat. at 1000	17
	P. Princesa	SJ Buenavista	Palawan	2 times monthly	30
Tablas	Santa Fe	Boracay	pumpboat	daily at 0600	3
	Looc	Caticlan	outrigger	3 times weekly	3

the twin towers and Gothic Renaissance exterior now form a striking Panay landmark. Antiques are sold at several stores and private homes.

Guimaras Island

The large island south of Iloilo offers beaches, caves, waterfalls, springs, villages, and intriguing spiritual encounters. Ferries to Jordan depart hourly from the post office. Climb Holy Mountain for good views and then continue by jeepney to the Bayani Resort near Buenavista for a narrow sandy beach, a pool, hiking, and *nipa* cottages with views of Iloilo from P800. Other possible stays include the private island of Isla Naburot, owned by Alice Saldana, and a German-owned beach resort on Nagarao Island near San Isidro. The tourist office has more info.

Miagao

Forty km west of Iloilo stands a unique fortress-church which ranks as one of the most impressive works of architecture in the Philippines. Originally completed in 1797, the massive honey-colored sandstone monument has been repeatedly restored following damage by revolution, fire, and earthquake. Note the dissimilar towers—the first priest-foreman died before his work was completed. The superbly carved facade is a wild impressionistic collage of St. Christopher with Jesus and tropical botanical motifs: palms, papaya trees, scalloped arches, and fruiting guava trees. Reminds you of Gaudi's animistic cathedral in Barcelona or St. Paul's in Macau.

NORTHEAST ISLANDS

Sicogon

This beautiful 11-square-km private island is a wonderland of white-sand beaches and beautiful coral beds. Besides lazing on the beach, you can enjoy the swimming pool, windsurfing, scuba diving, and excursions to nearby islands. Sicogon is, unfortunately, a privately owned island that caters exclusively to visitors willing to pay the steep tariff. Cottages start at US$50. Reservations from Sicogon Development Corporation, Chemphil Bldg., 851 Pasay Rd., Makati, Manila, tel. 817-1160.

Pan De Azucar

This large and completely undeveloped island off the coast from San Dionisio offers some good beaches and small villages for brave backpackers. No accommodations except with the locals. Pumpboats leave from San Dionisio.

ROXAS

Aside from the Harlaran Festival held in October, Roxas is simply a transit point between Iloilo and Boracay.

Accommodations
The Beehive Inn on Roxas Avenue has rooms from P100. The River Lodge on Lapu Lapu is cheaper. A pleasant alternative is Marc's Beach Resort on Baybay Beach four km west of town, where rooms cost P150-200. Facilities include volleyball, tennis, and a disco.

KALIBO

Most visitors come for the annual Ati Atihan festival—Kalibo is otherwise just another transit town. Jeepneys shuttle from the airport into town where buses connect to Boracay. Be sure to reconfirm your return flight before leaving the airport.

Accommodations
Hotels in Kalibo with rooms under P50 include the High Chapparal Pension and LM Lodge a few blocks south of the bus and jeepney terminals. The Glowmoon Hotel has fancooled rooms for P120-200 and a/c rooms from P250.

SAMAR

The second largest island in the Visayas mainly serves as a stepping-stone between Luzon and Leyte. Its outstanding attraction, Sohoton National Park, is most easily reached from Tacloban on Leyte.

Samar is also known for it violent history and high level of communist control. Its bloodiest episode took place during the Philippine-American War in 1901 when an American general named Jake Smith turned Samar into a "howling wilderness" by slaughtering all male inhabitants over 10 years old in the village of Balanginga. Smith was court-martialed.

In recent years, the Communist Party of the Philippines has capitalized on the island's backwardness, isolation, and extreme poverty to where they now control much of the mountainous interior and remote east coast. Tourists, however, are left alone, and there's nothing to fear traveling along the west coast from Allen to Leyte.

Transportation
Ferries cross at least twice a day between Matnog and Allen. The most convenient connection is on direct Philtranco buses from Legaspi to Catbalogan and Tacloban. As these buses are often filled with passengers coming down from Manila, independent travelers should get an early start to connect with the ferry from Matnog. It's a spectacular ride through vast coconut plantations along the coast from Allen to

Catbalogan. Buses continue to Tacloban but a relaxing alternative is the large ship which sails from Catbalogan to Tacloban. Travel time from Allen to Tacloban is seven hours with direct Philtranco bus.

ALLEN

The port town for ferries from Luzon has several inexpensive pensions for later arrivals who miss the last ferry. A good alternative is the Spice of Life Resthouse on Buenos Aires Beach four km south.

Attractions
Most travelers head direct to Catbalogan on the southern road, though the north coast has a few attractions. Boats to Tinau and Biri islands leave from San Jose. Beyond the provincial capital of Catarman are the isolated offshore islands of Laoang, with its beautiful Onay Beach, and Batag with an important lighthouse offering panoramic views over the San Bernardino Straits. Simple hotels are located in Geratag near San Jose and Catarman.

CATBALOGAN

Another sleepy little town with little of interest except for transportation connections and the bank up the hill near the capitol building.

SHIPS FROM SAMAR

DESTINATION	FROM	LINE	DEPARTURES	HOURS
Cebu	Cebu City	Calbayog	Palacio	3 times weekly	12
	Cebu City	Catbalogan	W. Samar	2 times weekly	12
Leyte	Tacloban	Catbalogan	Sweet	3 times weekly	5
Luzon	Manila	Calbayog	Sulpicio	Wed. at 1000	16
	Manila	Catbalogan	William	Wed. at 1900	22
	Matnog	Allen	ferries	2 times daily before 1300	2

Accommodations

Most of the hotels are scattered around the bus stops in the north end. The Fortune Hotel on Del Rosario costs P60-100 for acceptable fan rooms. Kikay's, two blocks south on Curry Avenue, is another choice in the same price range.

Transportation

Western Samar Shipping sails to Tacloban every other day around noontime. Ask down at the wharf. It's a beautiful cruise past Buad and Daram islands in the scenic San Juanico Straits.

Journeys, like artists, are born and not made.
A thousand differing circumstances contribute to them,
few of them willed or determined by the will—
whatever we may think.

—Lawrence Durrell,
Bitter Lemons

Traveling is not just seeing the new;
it is also leaving behind.
Not just opening doors;
also closing them behind you, never to return.
But the place you have left forever,
is always there for you to see whenever you shut your eye.
And the cities you see most clearly at night,
are the cities you have left,
and will never see again.

—Jan Myrdal,
The Silk Road

I sought trains; I found passengers.

—Paul Theroux,
The Great Railway Bazaar

SINGAPORE

Every trip we take deposits us at the same forking of the paths: it can be a shortcut to alienation—removed from our home and distanced from our immediate surroundings, we can afford to be contemptuous of both; or it can be a voyage into renewal, as, leaving our selves and posts at home, and traveling light, we recover our innocence abroad.

—Pico Iyer,
Video Night in Kathmandu

The first condition of right thought is right sensation—the first condition of understanding a foreign country is to smell it . . . .

—T.S. Eliot

Life is short; live it up.

—Nikita Krushchev

INTRODUCTION

The Malay Chronicles relate that the Prince of Palembang, who claimed direct descent from Alexandar the Great, landed at this Srivijayan trading post in the 13th century and encountered a strange animal, "very swift and beautiful, body bright red, head jet black, breast of white, and larger than a he-goat." Although it was most likely a wild tiger, the Prince called it a lion, and Temasek the "Sea Town" became Singa Pura the "Lion City." Another story explains that this Sanskrit name actually derives from a sect of Bhairava Buddhism dominant at the 14th-century Majapahit courts whose Javanese priests adopted the lion motif as their religious symbol. Other 14th-century towns such as Singosari in East Java and Singaraja on North Bali used the term and it's possible that Singapore was the third of Southeast Asia's Lion Cities.

From its humble beginnings as a distended backwater of pirates and traders, this Chinese city-state of almost three million inhabitants has grown into one of the great success stories of Southeast Asia. Blessed with few natural resources except for its strategic location and a hard-working population, this futuristic metropolis enjoys the highest standard of living in Asia after Japan. With few slums, minimal unemployment, and little crime, Singapore excels as a post-industrial urban miracle that graciously

lacks such exotica as colorful slums, the *mañana* syndrome, 10-year-old shoeshine boys, and rampant bribery . . . all the romantic anachronisms that make Southeast Asia so fascinating to visit but so hellish to inhabit.

It is also quite possibly the most downright beautiful modern metropolis in the world. While many Asian cities are ugly, chaotic nightmares of faceless ferroconcrete boxes and hopeless traffic jams, Singapore is so clean and green that it richly deserves its self-proclaimed title of Garden City. Although the soaring skyscrapers and air-conditioned shopping centers bear little resemblance to the romantic port of Conrad or Kipling—and some visitors are disappointed with the concrete canyons and Instant Asia mentality—those who prefer safety and cleanliness with a touch of the Orient will find Singapore a refreshing change from the hardships of other Southeast Asian countries.

THE PHYSICAL SETTING

Singapore is a diamond-shaped island of 618 square km just across the causeway from Malaysia and one degree north of the equator. To the south is Java and to the west Sumatra, perhaps visible on a clear day. The main island and

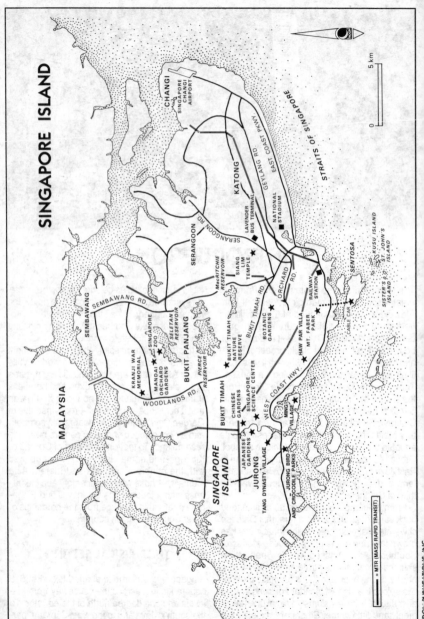

SINGAPORE'S CLIMATE

	Jan.	Feb.	March	April	May	June	July	Aug.	Sept.	Oct.	Nov.	Dec.
Avg. Maximum C	30°	31°	31°	31°	32°	31°	31°	31°	31°	31°	31°	31°
Avg. Maximum F	86°	88°	88°	88°	90°	88°	88°	88°	88°	88°	88°	88°
Rainy Days	17	11	14	15	15	13	13	14	14	16	18	19

some 54 smaller islets have an undramatic topography with two-thirds of the land lying less than 15 meters above sea level. The highest elevations are nothing more than foothills. Although Singapore has no important mineral or oil deposits and the soil is of poor quality, its deepwater anchorage and natural harbor on the Straits of Malacca have helped make it the region's leading shipping and commercial center.

Singapore is also a predominately urbanized country with little remaining wildlife or untended flora. Most of the tropical foliage that once covered the island has been completely cleared, although about 5% of the land remains forested and carefully preserved in the Bukit Timah Nature Reserve. You won't find untamed jungles or wild tigers, but you will find some of Asia's finest flora and fauna in its amazing parks and gardens. For example, over 2,000 varieties of orchids grow in the Mandai Orchid Gardens. Singapore Botanic Gardens, considered second in Asia only to Bogor's famous park, boasts one of the finest collections of tropical palms in the world. Best of all, the nearby Singapore Zoological Gardens has been designed in a sympathetic open-style architecture that won't make you pity the animals. Finally, the Jurong Bird Park boasts a gigantic five-acre walk-in flight aviary with thousands of brilliantly colored birds. Here in Singapore, flora and fauna have made their peace with the urban jungle.

HISTORY

Singapore's geographical location should have made for a long and important history, but prior to the development of the city by the British in the 19th century it was little more than a sleepy backwater ignored by both local and distant powers. Early records indicate that its thick mangrove swamps once served as refuge for ma-

rauding pirates and dumping ground for the remains of their victims. Colonists from Palembang in Sumatra arrived in 1287 and established a small fishing village later known as Singa Pura. Marco Polo possibly stopped here in 1284 on his voyage from China to Italy. At various times this isolated seaport was controlled by the Sumatran empire of Srivijaya and the Cholas from South India before being destroyed in 1376 by the Majapahit empire of East Java.

Singapore's modern history dates from 1819, when Sir Thomas Raffles of the East India Company stepped ashore to establish his great commercial emporium. Explorer, entrepreneur, politician, naturalist, historian, and visionary, Raffles ranks as one of the most important figures in modern Southeast Asia history. Originally he searched for a new trading post for the British, who had left the Indonesian archipelago after a territorial tradeoff with the Dutch. Neither Malacca nor Penang was proving too successful and Raffles was anxious to establish a free port which could control the sea route through the Malaccan Straits. Recognizing the geographic superiority of Singapore over Penang, Raffles claimed the island and founded the city after a little political maneuvering with the local sultans. His policy of free trade and strong British discipline was greeted enthusiastically by the Chinese and Muslim merchants. Singapore rapidly eclipsed other British ports and was soon designated capital of the Straits Settlements. During his nine months in Singapore, Raffles proved his humanity by abolishing slavery and gambling but also his racist notions by creating a city plan that carefully segregated the Chinese, Malays, and Indians into separate communities.

But disaster soon struck the great colonialist. Within a few years his children would be dead from tropical diseases and a fire would tragically destroy his invaluable records. Raffles was ordered back to England to face a lawsuit brought by his ingracious employer, the East India Company, who somehow considered him derelict in his duties. It was a terrible end for one of Britain's greatest visionaries, who, despite his impressive contributions to the British Empire, died in London a poor and despondent man at the age of forty-five.

Singapore continued to prosper as Chinese merchants planted pepper and gambier and then harvested a fortune. British acquisition of Hong Kong in 1842 and the opening of the Suez Canal in 1869 also fueled the growth of the city. Singapore came of age at the dawn of the automobile era when a British botanist, affectionately known as "Mad Ridley," persuaded Malayan coffee growers to try cultivating and processing a strange elastic product known as rubber. It was a raging success. By the early 20th century, Singapore, once an island of tigers and pirates, had become the region's leading economic power.

Singapore hummed along until February 1942 when it fell to the invading Japanese forces. More than just a massive fiasco with both tragic and comic overtones, the fall of Singapore heralded the end of British imperial influence in the Far East. Confident of their military superiority, the British had made Singapore their center of Asian naval power. Two powerful battleships were stationed in her harbor and massive 15-inch guns were installed on Sentosa Island pointing south. Both proved flawed. On 8 December the Japanese began their military offensive by destroying the American fleet at Pearl Harbor and invading Hong Kong and the Philippines. Forces were simultaneously landed in southern Thailand and northern Malaya near Kota Baru. British confidence in their "impregnable fortress" crumbled two days later when Japanese torpedo bombers sank both the *Repulse* and the *Prince of Wales* off Kuantan in the South China Sea. The Japanese commandeered bicycles, peddled down the Malay Peninsula, and easily took Singapore. It was a disaster, not only the largest capitulation in British history, but also a mammoth bluff by Japanese forces short on supplies and outnumbered almost three to one by British troops.

Three years of horror ensued. An estimated 25,000-50,000 Chinese were marched to the beaches and executed or tortured to death by the Japanese Kempeitai for being too Western.

Almost 30,000 Allied POWs were held in Changi Prison, an ordeal described by author James Clavell in his novel *King Rat,* and then marched to Thailand where thousands died constructing the bridge over the River Kwai. The carnage was complete. By the time the Japanese surrendered to Lord Mountbatten in 1945, it is said that over 100,000 civilians had perished from starvation, torture, or execution at the hands of their Japanese liberators.

Yet Singapore had mixed reactions after the surrender of Japan. While everyone was relieved that the occupation was over, few now believed that the British were either invincible or infallible. When Britain offered to dissolve the Straits Settlements it raised a very thorny question: should Singapore and Malaysia be united in a single country? Census figures indicated that Chinese would outnumber Malays in the new nation. Fearing both economic and racial domination by the Chinese, Malaysian leaders soon formed political parties that opposed the merger. Sympathizing with their plight, the British merged Malacca, Penang, and nine Malay states into the Federation of Malaya. Singapore was made a separate Crown Colony, a compromise that left Singapore for the Chinese and Malaya for the Malays.

In 1955 a young Cambridge-educated attorney named Lee Kuan Yew and a small group of lawyers, journalists, and teachers organized the People's Action Party (PAP). Their rallying cry was *"Merdeka"* (Independence) and "Merger with Malaya." In a daring move calculated to attract Chinese-speaking immigrants generally ignored by conventional political parties, Lee made peace with the Communists and allowed his grass-roots party to be almost entirely dominated by leftists. His strong anti-colonial and pro-labor line proved very popular with the proletariat classes. His determination to create an independent state whose citizens would owe loyalty to the nation rather than separate communal groups brought him a respectable showing in the 1955 election and a complete mandate in 1959. Lee then consolidated his power, ended his marriage of convenience with the Communists, and forged ahead with the political entity that has ruled Singapore since 1961.

Fearing that his young country could not survive without the natural resources of Malaya, Lee insisted on a united Singapore-Malaya na-

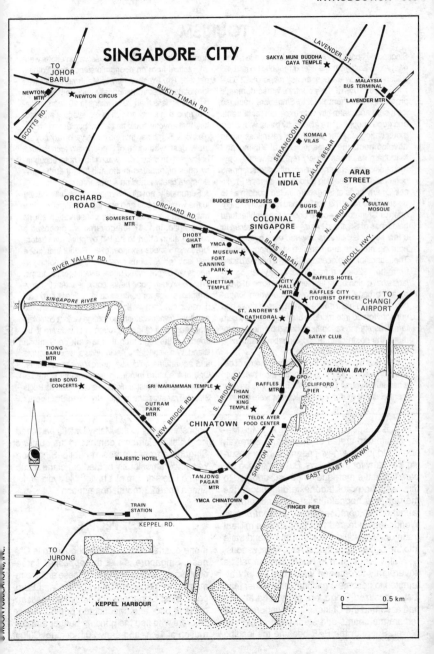

SINGAPORE CITY

TO JOHOR BARU

SAKYA MUNI BUDDHA GAYA TEMPLE ★

LAVENDER ST.

MALAYSIA BUS TERMINAL

LAVENDER MTR

NEWTON MTR

★ NEWTON CIRCUS

BUKIT TIMAH RD.

SCOTTS RD.

KOMALA VILAS •

LITTLE INDIA

SERANGOON RD.

JALAN BESAR

ARAB STREET

ORCHARD ROAD

ORCHARD RD.

BUDGET GUESTHOUSES •

COLONIAL SINGAPORE

BUGIS MTR

N. BRIDGE RD.

SULTAN MOSQUE ★

SOMERSET MTR

DHOBY GHAT MTR

YMCA •

BRAS BASAH RD.

NICOLL HWY

MUSEUM ★
FORT CANNING PARK ★

RIVER VALLEY RD.

★ CHETTIAR TEMPLE

RAFFLES HOTEL ■

SINGAPORE RIVER

CITY HALL MTR

RAFFLES CITY (TOURIST OFFICE) ★

TO CHANGI AIRPORT

★ ST. ANDREW'S CATHEDRAL

TIONG BARU MTR

SATAY CLUB ■

MARINA BAY

★ BIRD SONG CONCERTS

SRI MARIAMMAN TEMPLE ★

S. BRIDGE RD.

RAFFLES MTR

GPO ■

CLIFFORD PIER

OUTRAM PARK MTR

THIAN HOK KING TEMPLE ★

NEW BRIDGE RD.

CHINATOWN

TELOK AYER FOOD CENTER ■

SHENTON WAY

MAJESTIC HOTEL •

EAST COAST PARKWAY

TANJONG PAGAR MTR

TRAIN STATION

YMCA CHINATOWN

FINGER PIER

TO JURONG

KEPPEL RD.

KEPPEL HARBOUR

0   0.5 km

TOURISM

Singapore is one of the most popular stops in Southeast Asia. Last year the island republic hosted 4.5 million visitors, who spent an estimated US$2.5 billion, about 10% of the country's gross domestic product. Westerners flock to Singapore because it's a safe and clean city with excellent restaurants and good shopping. It's also a city beset with enormous changes. After decades of relentless urban development, the romantic city of Kipling and Maugham has been largely replaced with anonymous skyscrapers and air-conditioned shopping centers. As one leading guidebook states, "Physically, many parts of Singapore are so modern as to persuade you that the city has had no history." Singapore's Chinatown—once one of the architectural goldmines of Southeast Asia—has been reduced to a few neglected streets towered over by faceless housing projects and massive shopping centers. Thousands of irreplaceable Chinese homes dating from the 1920s and traditional Malay fishing villages have also been leveled in the name of progress. Perhaps the final blow came when Singapore's famous night markets were closed down and vendors forced into modern but faceless food centers. Despite the rationales offered by the government, the destruction of old Singapore remains a tragic and irreversible mistake.

Little was done during the spectacular orgy of destruction aside from the pleas of the local press and a handful of young Chinese architects. The government claimed that the old structures were unfit for human habitation and that preservation efforts were impractical from an economic standpoint. Nothing helped. The Preservation of Monuments Act was formulated to save historically important buildings but it listed less than 20 buildings in 20 years, a dismal record in a city so rich in extravagant architecture that anyone could find 20 monuments on a single block. Some say that the preservation agency actually destroyed more of Singapore's architectural heritage than it saved. It wasn't until hotel occupancy rates plummeted in the mid-'80s that the government finally acted on a preservation plan.

Fortunately, not all of Singapore has fallen victim to the wrecking ball and enough of Raffles' original town plan survives to make conservation efforts worthwhile. In 1987 the government proposed a conservation effort to be led by private investors lured with various tax incentives. Rather than just a few isolated religious structures, entire neighborhoods will be preserved under a variety of programs. While obviously good news, some fear that the government's urge for control and cleanliness may produce the dull and plastic look of an Asian Disneyland and hotel owners catering to foreign visitors complain that nearly half of the improvement funds are to be spent on the high-tech theme park on Sentosa Island. While special to Asian visitors, wax museums and aquariums hold little interest for Westerners. One of the more intriguing experiments is the revival of the transvestite nightlife area known as Bugis Street. Transvestites in squeaky-clean Singapore?

tion. This merger became feasible after the Malay-dominated states of Sabah and Sarawak agreed to join the new nation, thereby ensuring a plurality for the Malays. But it was soon apparent that the marriage of '63 was doomed to failure. Sukarno of Indonesia denounced the merger as a neocolonialist plot and formally launched his confused policy of *konfrontasi*. World leaders feared that Singapore's militant trade unions would transform the island state into the Cuba of Southeast Asia. Most seriously, Malay leadership in Kuala Lumpur felt its sovereignty threatened when Lee's party attempted to become a national force rather than just a localized Singapore party. The Malays had assumed the Chinese in Singapore would remain merchants and steer clear of political power. But after the PAP became the leading opposition party to the Malay UMNO party, radical Muslim elements demanded the ouster of Singapore from the new republic. Singapore was unceremoniously booted out of the republic and Lee's dream of a united Malaysia ended after a short 23-month honeymoon.

THE PEOPLE

If one-quarter of the world's population is Chinese, Singapore is just the opposite. Three-quarters of the population is Chinese and the remaining one-quarter Malay, Indian, and European. Most Singaporean Chinese are descendents of poor and uneducated South Chinese laborers who fled the grinding hunger and corruption of 19th- and early 20th-century China.

Arriving as indentured laborers obligated to work off their passage, most would quickly join a clan house, a type of mutual-assistance society which helped people from a similar district or who shared a common last name. Others fell into the secret societies which ran the gambling emporiums, opium dens, and brothels. Also imported were their beliefs in ancestor worship and the religious doctrines of Buddhism, Taoism, and Confucianism.

Hailing from all regions of China, Singaporeans today differ between themselves physically, linguistically, culturally, and by choice of profession. Hokkiens from Southern Fukien province, who comprise 40% of the population (the largest Chinese group in Singapore), are the country's most economically successful ethnic group. Displaying a touch of chauvinism, Hokkiens regard themselves as the republic's best group. Teochews from the Swatow region in Kwangtung form 20% of the population. Many Teochews have chosen to be fishermen. Cantonese from Hong Kong, who make up 17% of the population, gravitate toward professions in the arts, crafts, and restaurant industries. Hakkas and Hainanese, who form some 10% of the population, tend to work as manual laborers.

Peranakans (Straits Chinese) are one of the most intriguing groups in Singapore. This distinct social group came into being after mainland Chinese government prohibitions against the emigration of females forced many of the early Chinese settlers to intermarry with local Malay women. Speaking a Malay-Chinese patois, Peranakan men (Babas) and women (Nonyas) developed a rich and elegant subculture which tastefully combined Chinese, Malay, and English customs. Ladies, for example, wore Malay dresses but held their hair with Chinese hairpins. Men dressed in Chinese fashions but took up such nontraditional activities as cricket, polo, and high tea. Peranakans were smart, hardworking, and politically sophisticated. They became commercially successful by adopting British business customs and acting as compradores between British administrators and China-born immigrants. After amassing great wealth, Peranakans fled the ghettos of Chinatown to wealthy suburbs of baroque homes and broad boulevards. Peranakans eventually melded into mainstream society, and today, as a separate group with a distinctive culture, have large-

nonconformists not welcome

ly disappeared from modern Singapore. But you'll still find Peranakan food stalls, Nonya wedding ceremonies, and museum displays of Peranakan culture during your visit to Singapore.

You'll also notice some curious signs around town urging people to Speak More Mandarin or Be More Courteous. It's all part of Singapore's famous social campaigns, which cover everything from cleanliness and courtesy to drugs and eugenics. Good examples are the social-engineering efforts of the Singapore government. It seems that Singapore's Chinese are failing to breed in sufficient numbers. Over the last two decades the fertility rate has dropped from three to less than 1.5 children per family, far below the net reproduction rate. All this is bad news for a nation with an acute labor shortage and which needs an increasing population for economic growth. Also disturbing to government planners are the reproduction rates of various other racial groups: Malays at 2.05, Indians at 1.89. Reasons for the perennial decline in fertility and lopsided patterns of procreation include increasing wealth (rich nations breed slower than poor nations), increasing education (more education means fewer children), and a Singapore phenomenon called hypergamy, the tendency for local women to want only richer and more educated husbands. The result is that over 30% of Singapore's female college grads remain unmarried and childless into their thirties. To get the juices flowing and assure quality in a hoped-for baby boom, the government has passed legislation which favors the highly educated over the less educated and instituted matchmaking services for lonely hearts. Efforts are often clumsy or silly but the policies of reproduction are serious business here in Singapore.

FESTIVALS

There are few countries in the world where you can see so many festivals from so many cultures in so small an area. Encouraged as expressions of cultural diversity, the variety can be astounding: fire walking and self-mutilation in honor of Hindu gods, trance dances and medium seances for Taoist spirits, dancing lions and Chinese opera for the ghosts of departed ancestors, *pencak silat* and *main gasing* during Malay holidays. Chinese festivals, which include both private family affairs and public street celebrations, dominate the calendar. Malay festivals revolve around Muslim holidays and are generally closed to outsiders. Certainly the most spectacular of all Singaporean festivals are those celebrated by the Indian community. Visitors are welcome at all public festivals.

Festival Dating
Because nature has provided the world with two obvious time markers—the sun and the moon—festivals can be based on either solar or lunar calendars. Westerners use the familiar solar-based Gregorian calendar of 12 months

CHINESE FESTIVALS BY THE LUNAR CALENDAR

Moon 1	Chinese New Year	Day 1
	Birthday of the God of Wealth	Days 2 and 3
	Lantern Festival	Day 15
Moon 2	Birthday of Hung Shing Kung	Day 13
	Birthday of Kuan Yin	Day 19
Moon 3	Ching Ming Festival	Spring Solstice
	Birthday of Tin Hau	Day 23
Moon 4	Birthday of Buddha	Day 8
	Birthday of Tam Kung	Day 8
Moon 5	Dragon Boat Festival	Day 5
Moon 6	Birthday of Hau Wong	Day 6
	Enlightenment of Kuan Yin	Day 19
Moon 7	Festival for the Hungry Ghosts	Day 15
Moon 8	Mid-autumn or Moon Festival	Day 15
	Birthday of the Monkey God	Day 16
	Birthday of Confucius	Day 27
Moon 9	Chung Yeung	Day 9
	Death of Kuan Yin	Day 19
Moon 10	Birthday of Tat Moh	Day 5
Moon 11	Chung Yeung	Winter Solstice
Moon 12	Kitchen God Festival	Day 24

and 365 days while Chinese use a lunar-based calendar of 13 moons with 28 days. The disparity between these two systems makes exact dating of Chinese festivals difficult. To complicate matters further, the Chinese use a solar calendar for solstice-oriented festivals such as Ching Ming and Chung Yeung. Adjustments are made by adding a lunar month once every three solar years.

The "Chinese Festivals by the Lunar Calendar" chart includes the major festivals celebrated by all three ethnic groups in Singapore. The five major Chinese festivals celebrated in both Singapore and Hong Kong (Chinese New Year, Ching Ming, Dragon Boat, Mooncake, and Chung Yeung Festival) are described here and summarized in the Hong Kong chapter. Chinese festivals unique to Hong Kong are described under Hong Kong. Dates can be checked with the local tourist office.

FESTIVALS

January

Ponggal: A Hindu harvest festival celebrated by Tamils in both temples and homes. Colorful greeting cards and presents are exchanged. Enormous pots of boiled rice and vegetarian delicacies are consumed at temples. Check Perumal Temple on Serangoon Road.

International Kite Festival: Malay moon kites, Thai fighting kites, and Chinese dragon kites are judged for beauty and aerial height.

Thaipusam: An Indian festival of human endurance and self-sacrifice, considered among the most spectacular in all of Southeast Asia. Entranced devotees at the Perumal Temple prove their devotion to Subramaniam by shoving metal skewers through the skin of their forehead, cheeks, and tongues. Other instruments are jammed through the body and hung with fruits. The ritual culminates when a massive spiked cage (*kavadi*) is lowered onto the shoulders to pierce the chest and back with sharp metal spikes. Devotees then carry the burden in a three-km procession to the Chettiar Temple on Tank Road.

February

Chinese New Year: The most important social, moral, and personal festival of the year. A time for spiritual renewal, family reunions, and social harmony. The old are honored with mandarin oranges while the young receive red envelopes filled with lucky money called *hong bao* in Singapore and *lai see* in Hong Kong. All debts are settled and salaried workers receive year-end bonuses. Miniature peach trees symbolizing good luck are exchanged. Everybody calls out "*gung hay fah choi*," or "good luck making money." Clothes are purchased, houses cleaned, and calligraphers paint messages of good luck on red banners. A special salad of raw fish and 20 vegetables is prepared. The image of the Kitchen God (a deity who reports everybody's activities to the Jade Emperor) is courted with special candies, sweet wine, hell money, and dabs of sticky opium to seal the lips against speaking evil. After the bribe, he's taken outside and burned. Images of the Door Gods and the God of Wealth are replaced. The weeks' activities are climaxed with a dragon parade.

Lantern Festival (Yuen Siu): Chinese New Year ends with displays of brightly painted lanterns hung in windows and doorways. Ancestral halls are filled with finely crafted lanterns while auctions raise thousands for charities.

Chingay Processio: Chinese New Year also ends with a mad and crazy parade of stiltwalkers, snapping lions, bejeweled Indian dancers, cute pom-pom girls, Malay wedding couples, and armies of roller skaters. Volunteers carry giant flags over three stories high. One of the best parades in Singapore.

March

Birthday of Kuan Yin: One of the most popular figures in Chinese mythology, the Buddhist Goddess of Mercy is honored on her birthday in the second moon, date of enlightenment in the sixth, and date of death in the ninth.

Monkey God's Birthday: The Monkey God is a celebrated and beloved rascal who made himself indestructible and acquired miraculous powers after sneaking into heaven and stealing the Peaches of Immortality. During the temple ceremony in his honor, Taoist priests enter a trance to allow his spirit to enter their bodies. The medium then jumps around, scratches his armpit, howls, slashes himself with sharp knives, and scrawls magical symbols on scraps of paper. Frenzied efforts are made to grab these papers since some consider them winning lottery numbers. Chinese opera and puppet plays are performed in the courtyard. The Monkey God is honored twice yearly at the temples on Eng Hoon and Cummings streets.

April

Ching Ming: This important Chinese festival pays homage to departed ancestors. Families visit ancestral graves to perform traditional rites, clean weedy tombstones, repaint the inscriptions, and burn incense sticks and red candles. After the formalities, this "clear and bright" occasion often assumes the air of a lively party with blaring music, food, and games. Ching Ming is held on spring equinox and best seen—but never photographed—in the cemeteries along Upper Thomson and Lornie Road.

Songkran: Both a Buddhist religious holiday and a wet and wild water festival where absolutely everybody is drenched by water balloons, fire hoses, and buckets of colored water. On a more sedate note, this is the occasion when the sun enters the first month of the Buddhist New Year. Rites are performed in the Buddhist temple on Jalan Bukit Merah and at the Saptha Puchaniyaram Temple on Holland Road. Wrap your camera in plastic and don't forget your water pistol.

FESTIVALS (continued)

May

Birthday of Tin Hau: This popular festival honors the Sea Goddess, who walks on water, calms the seas, and ensures a bountiful catch. According to popular legend, Miss Tin was a 10th-century historical figure who lived on a small island near Hong Kong. During a terrible storm at sea, she miraculously saved her two brothers but lost her life while attempting to rescue her father. After centuries of veneration she was officially canonized by the Chinese court and promoted by royal edict to Queen of Heaven in the 17th century. Today she is honored by the local fishermen in both Singapore and Hong Kong, who decorate their boats for a seaborne parade.

Birthday of the Third Prince: This festival honors the miracle-working child-god who rides on the wheels of wind and fire. Entranced temple mediums slash themselves with swords and use blood from their tongues to write magical charms. A street procession of stiltwalkers, dragon dancers, and Chinese musicians follows. Check Leng Hyam Twoi Temple on Clarke Street at North Boat Quay.

Tam Kung Festival: Honors the second patron saint of the boat people. Celebrated in both Hong Kong and Singapore.

Vesak Day: Commemorates the birth, death, and enlightenment of Buddha. Devotees visit Buddhist temples to burn candles and offer donations. Best experienced at Temple of 1000 Lights on Race Course Road.

June

Dragon Boat Festival: Commemorates the tragic death of Wat Yuen, a 3rd-century government official who drowned himself to protest the injustice and corruption of Manchurian government. In symbolic recreation of the event, a colorful regatta of elegantly decorated boats races off the shore of the East Coast Parkway. Dragon boats are brought to life during a temple ceremony called "opening the light" in which each eye is painted with blood from a brown chicken. Sexes compete separately: *yang*-powered dragon boats are raced by the men while the women race *yin*-fueled Phoenix Dragons.

Ramadan: Muslim holy month during which neither food nor water may pass the devotee's lips in daylight hours. Mosques are filled with worshippers who fulfill their religious obligations. Sultan Mosque is surrounded by food stalls selling *halal* specialties.

July

Hari Raya Puasa: The end of Ramadan fast is marked by elaborate thanksgiving feasts in Muslim homes. Kampong Glam is the center for Singapore activities.

Enlightenment of Kuan Yin: Although the Buddhist Goddess of Mercy was originally a male deity from Tibetan Mahayana Buddhism, she miraculously changed gender when adopted by the Chinese. This immensely popular figure is honored three times yearly.

August

National Day: Singapore's Independence Day on 9 August is celebrated with a parade of school floats, military bands, and masses of flag wavers. Tickets to the event are available from the tourist office.

Festival of the Hungry Ghosts: A one-month celebration somewhat similar to Halloween. Chinese believe that the Gates of Hell are opened once a year to release restless and hungry spirits who died without proper funeral preparations. Ignored and troublesome, these disgruntled spirits must be placated with offerings of money, feasts, and free entertainment from Chinese opera and puppet shows. Life-sized paper models of *shiu yi* are burned in the streets before Taai Si Wong—the mythological figure who watches and records the whole event and then reports back to the Jade Emperor—is thrown on the bonfire, signaling the completion of earthly duties. This spectacular festival is an excellent time to witness Chinese street opera.

Market Festival: An extension of the Festival of the Hungry Ghosts. Local merchants offer food and free Chinese opera at temporary *matshed* constructions.

September

Navarathri Festival: This Hindu festival honors the consorts of the triumvirate of Brahma, Vishnu, and Shiva. The first three days are devoted to Durga (Shiva's mistress), the next three to Lakshmi (Goddess of Wealth and consort of Vishnu), and the last three to Saraswati (Goddess of Music and lover of Brahma). Classical Indian dance is performed nightly at the Chettiar Temple on Tank Road. A grand procession with a silver horse is held on the final day.

Mooncake Festival: Commemorates a 14th-century revolution during which Chinese patriots passed revolutionary messages hidden inside special cakes

FESTIVALS

and lanterns were used to signal the beginning of the revolution. Singapore shops sell heavy and bitter cakes (*yuet bang*) stuffed with sweet lotus seeds and eggs. The Mooncake Festival has other names: Moon and Lantern Festival in Singapore, Mid-autumn and Harvest Festival in Hong Kong.

October
Thimithi Festival: Hindu firewalking festival held at the Sri Mariamman Temple in Chinatown. A huge pit filled with fiery embers is sprinted across by devotees. Hot, crowded, and as fascinating as India herself.

Festival of the Emperor Gods: Honors the nine powerful Chinese gods whose possessed images are carried through the streets. Mediums enter trances in the temples. Another excellent opportunity to enjoy Chinese street opera. Celebrated on the ninth day of the ninth moon, a doubly auspicious date since Chinese astrologers consider nine the

male principle in Chinese cosmology. Best seen at the Chinese temples on Upper Serangoon Road and at Lorong Tai Seng.

Chung Yeung: Festival of Autumn Remembrance. Chinese honor their departed ancestors twice yearly: in the spring with Ching Ming and in the fall with Chung Yeung.

Birthday of Confucius: The famous sage and teacher is honored with ceremonies in local temples and at Confucius societies.

Death of Kuan Yin: The Buddhist Goddess of Mercy is honored once again.

November
Deepavali: This Hindu festival celebrates Rama's victory over the demon King Ravana and the return of Lakshmi to the earth. Thousands of tiny oil lamps make Deepavali one of the most enchanting of all Hindu festivals.

PRACTICAL INFORMATION

TRANSPORTATION

Airport Arrival
Except for travelers arriving overland from Malaysia, most visitors land at Changi Airport, located about 20 km east of city center. Considered among the most efficient and ultramodern airports in the world, Changi divides itself into Terminals I and II, connected by the Changi Skytrain in one minute. Most planes continue to land at Terminal I, though Terminal II will become more important in the next decade.

The Arrival Hall is on the first floor of Terminal I. First stop will be immigration and customs, followed by facilities such as baggage claim, left-luggage, two post offices, international telephone services, and a half-dozen restaurants and fast-food emporiums. The tourist counter has maps, festival information, and useful magazines like *Singapore Visitor* and *Guide to Singapore*. Money-exchange rates are fair, so change some traveler's checks and ask for coins if you intend to take the bus into town. The airport even has showers (S$5), a health spa and fitness center (S$15), and 56

hotel rooms which charge S$35-45 for up to six hours!

Room availability can be checked at the Singapore Hotel Association counter, though they can't help with dormitories or super-budget hotels. Red phones can be used to double-check on vacancies—a good idea since many dorms fill up by early afternoon.

Departure information is found at the end of this chapter.

Airport To Town
Visitors can reach most hotels in about 20 minutes by bus or taxi.

Taxis: Taxi stands are located just outside the Arrival Hall. Taxis cost S$12-18 to luxury hotels on Orchard Rd. and a few dollars less to hotels in central Singapore. Permitted surcharges (not shown on the meter) include S$3 for service from the airport and a 50% surcharge from midnight to 0600.

Buses: Singapore has a great bus service. Buses leave every 15 minutes from the bus terminal located in the basement; follow the signs. Budget travelers should take bus 390, which stops at the National Museum, a few blocks

DIPLOMATIC MISSIONS IN SINGAPORE

ASIAN

Brunei	7A Tanglin	474-3393
Burma	15 St. Martin	235-8704
India	31 Grange	737-6777
Indonesia	7 Chatsworth	737-7422
Japan	16 Nassim	235-8855
Malaysia	301 Jervois	235-0111
Philippines	20 Nassim	737-3977
Thailand	370 Orchard	737-2644

WESTERN

Australia	25 Napier	737-9311
Britain	Tanglin	473-9333
Canada	80 Anson	225-6363
France	5 Gallop	466-4866
Germany	545 Orchard	737-1355
New Zealand	13 Nassim	235-9966
U.S.A.	30 Hill	338-0251

east of the inexpensive guesthouses located on Bencoolen Street. Visitors going to the more expensive hotels should stay on the bus, which continues north up Orchard Road.

Train And Bus Arrival

Train: Singapore's train terminal is located west of downtown near Chinatown and Keppel Harbor. Taxis from the train station to Orchard Rd. cost S$8-10. Budget dorms on Bencoolen St. can be reached with bus 20 to Beach Rd. or bus 146 toward Serangoon Road. The Chinatown Guesthouse is a good option for late-night arrivals.

Bus: Visitors arriving by bus from Malaysia must get off at the Singapore border to have their passports stamped. Immigration is strict and it's best to be well dressed. After immigration, visitors can hop back on any available bus for the remainder of the journey into Singapore.

Buses from Malaysia terminate at the Masmara Bus Company Terminal (tel. 732-6555) at the junction of Lavender and Kallang Bahru, opposite the Kallang Bahru shopping complex and on the eastern edge of Little India. Bencoolen St. dorms are 30-45 minutes west on foot but it's a great walk through Little India. Visitors coming by bus from Malaysia and bound for Orchard Rd. hotels should ask the driver to drop them at Newton Circus.

The MTR station nearest to Masmara Bus Terminal is at Lavender, some 20 minutes away by foot.

Getting Around

Foot: Singapore is compact and most neighborhoods are best reached and explored on foot. Public transportation is only necessary to reach destinations outside the city center or for cross-town journeys.

Taxis: Taxis in Singapore are metered and honest. Basic rates are reasonable, though surcharges for airport pick-up, baggage, travel in the restricted city center, and late-night travel can add up. Empty cabs have blue lights. Downtown, taxis can only be hailed at designated taxi stands.

Buses: Buses are a great way to get around Singapore. Intercity fares are 50 cents to S$1 depending on the distance. Routes are listed in the Singapore Bus Guide available from local bookstores. Buses range from red-and-gray SBS buses to one-man operations which require exact change. Explorer Bus Tickets allow you to board any Singapore or Trans-Island Bus and then break your journey as often as you wish; a convenient way to explore the island without a pocket of change.

MRT: Singapore's S$5 billion 67-km Mass Transit System has two main lines. The north-south line runs from Yishun to Marina Bay and the east-west line connects Pasir Ris near the airport to Boon Lay beyond Jurong. Trains operate 0600-2400 and fares range from 50 cents to S$1.80.

Trishaws: A handful of the old rickshaws that have always congregated in the early evening near the Raffles and across from the National Museum still survives to serve the tourist trade. Daytime rides might be nerve-wracking, but late-night rides through Chinatown and Little India are worthwhile. Prices are negotiable, but figure on S$10-15 per hour. Trishaw drivers know the underside of Singapore.

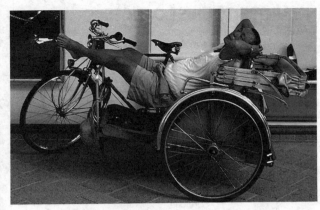

asleep at the wheel

TRAVEL FORMALITIES

Visas
Visas are not required for stays up to 90 days for Americans and citizens of most European countries. A 14-day permit is granted on arrival. Extensions may be obtained at the Immigration Department (tel. 532-2877) at 95 South Bridge Road.

Tourist Information
The Singapore Tourist Promotion Board (STPB) at Raffles City, 250 North Bridge Road, tel. 339-6622, is open Monday-Saturday 0800-1700. Ask about upcoming performances of Chinese street opera. The Singapore National Library has a room on Southeast Asian studies.

Maps
The free map from the tourist office is adequate for general orientation but anyone who needs more detail should purchase the Clyde Surveys map of Singapore. The *Secret Map of Singapore* will prove invaluable for walking tours of Chinatown, Little India, and the Arab Quarter. Food addicts should also purchase the excellent *Secret Food Map of Singapore,* which recommends specific dishes at specific restaurants.

Currency
The Singapore dollar (S$) is divided into 100 cents. Exchange rates currently range S$1.60-1.80 per U.S. dollar. Malaysian currency will only be accepted at an inferior rate. Traveler's checks can be changed in banks, hotels, and money changers on Orchard Road.

Post Offices
Letters and packages can be mailed from the General Post Office on Fullerton Road and from branch offices in Raffles City and on Orchard Road. Offices are open daily 0800-1800 except Sundays. The computerized Poste Restante at the GPO wins *Southeast Asia Handbook's* Award for Best Poste Restante in Asia. To win Best GPO they must add a packing service similar to that of the Bangkok GPO.

Telephones
International phone calls, telegrams, and telexes can be made 24 hours daily from the GPO. Rates are low compared to most Asian countries. Other phone centers are located at 15 Hill Street and the Telecom Building at 35 Robinson Road. International calls to Singapore (from America, Europe, etc.) can be made by dialing 011 (International Access Code), 65 (Country Code for Singapore), followed by the local phone number. Some useful numbers:

Directory Assistance	103
International Calls	104
Tourist Office	330-0431
Airport	542-5680
Taxi	452-5555
Immigration	532-2877
Police	999
Fire, Ambulance	995

SINGAPORE TOURIST OFFICES

Australia	60 Margaret St., Suite 1604, Sydney 2000	(02) 241-3771
	55 St. George's Terrace, Perth, W.A. 6001	(09) 325-8578
Canada	175 Bloor St. #1112, Toronto, Ontario M4W 3R8	(416) 323-9139
France	2 Place du Palais Royal, 75004 Paris	4297-1616
Germany	Poststrasse 2-4, D-6000, Frankfurt Am Main	069-231456
Japan	Yamato Seimei Bldg., Chiyoda-ku, Tokyo 100	(03) 593-3388
New Zealand	143 Nelson St. Box 3981, Auckland	(09) 358-2575
United Kingdom	126-130 Regent St., London W1R5FE	(071) 437-0033
U.S.A.	333 North Michigan Ave. #818, Chicago, IL 60601	(312) 220-0099
	590 Fifth Ave., 12th Floor, New York, NY 10036	(212) 302-4861
	8484 Wilshire Blvd. #510, Beverly Hills, CA 90211	(213) 852-1901

International Clock

San Francisco	-16
New York	-13
London	-8
Paris	-7
Rome	-7
Sydney	+3

Services

Water is safe to drink. Electric voltage is 230-250 volts AC at 50 cycles. Tipping is unnecessary, since most restaurants and hotels add a mandatory 10% service charge. Medical services are available from the Singapore General (222-3322) Hospital on Outram Road. Get low-cost immunization shots from the Health Center at 280 Tanjung Pagar Road.

SUGGESTED READING

◆ *Singapore*. Singapore: APA, 1980. Outstanding photographs and smooth text. Good background on history, culture, and sights.

◆ Barber, Noel. *The Singapore Story*. London: Fontana, 1966. History of Singapore from Raffles to Lee. Barber has written several other historical surveys of Singapore including *Sinister Twilight* and *The War of the Running Dogs*.

◆ Beamish and Ferguson. *A History of Singapore Architecture*. Singapore: Graham Brash, 1985. A tighlty written history of Singapore's colonial, ethnic, and modern architecture.

◆ Bloodworth, Dennis. *The Tiger and the Trojan*. Singapore: Times Books, 1986. The chief Far East correspondent for *The Observer* details the rise of Lee Kuan Yew.

◆ Clavell, James. *King Rat*. Fictional but evocative account of Clavell's internment at Changi Prison during WW II.

◆ Collins, Maurice. *Raffles*. Singapore: Graham Brash, 1966. Detailed history of the founder of Singapore.

◆ Gretchen and Lloyd. *Pastel Portraits*. Singapore: Singapore Coordinating Committee, 1984. Lloyd's superb photography makes this an excellent souvenir book.

◆ Siddique, Sharon. *Singapore's Little India*. Singapore: Institute of Southeast Asian Studies, 1982. Historical and cultural reconstruction of Singapore's Serangoon Road area with architectural renderings and personal interviews.

ATTRACTIONS

While modern Singapore may at first more closely resemble a tropical Manhattan than an Oriental oasis, a closer look uncovers a good deal of history that still remains between the concrete towers. Landmark buildings—especially those of religious character—have been preserved, while some sections of the older neighborhoods have been spared the wrecking ball. In the late 1980s an ambitious preservation plan was launched to save some of the old buildings and help revitalize the tourist trade.

The modern layout of Singapore is essentially the city plan of Raffles. During his visit in 1822, Raffles discovered his young settlement had grown into a jumble of disorderly shacks and streets. Raffles ordered planning committees to divide the town into distinct neighborhoods based on commercial and racial guidelines. Government buildings and churches were placed around the *padang,* commerce and boat quays near the mouth of the river, *godowns* farther upriver. To ensure racial harmony, Raffles gave the land south of the river to the Chinese, who subdivided their neighborhood into enclaves for each dialect group. Hokkien merchants took the land along the coast, Teochew food merchants settled near the river, Cantonese and Hakka took residence in the narrow lanes and alleys between the coast and river. Indians were given High Street but later moved out to Serangoon Road. Muslims settled in the *kampong* around Arab Street near the Sultan Mosque. The prime land along Beach Road and the central Esplanade was claimed by the British. Raffles's plan also included five-foot covered walkways to "ensure regularity and conformity."

Cultural assimilation and urban resettlement have somewhat blurred the lines, but to a surprising degree Singapore still retains these ethnic divisions. The juxtaposition of these cultures and their neighborhoods remains Singapore's greatest attraction. The following section is divided into convenient walking tours through Colonial Singapore, Chinatown, Little India, and the Muslim Quarter.

COLONIAL SINGAPORE

Raffles reserved the prized land on the waterfront and east of the river for the British. Around the large recreational square originally known as the Esplanade, British architects constructed government buildings, hotels, sports clubs, and churches in the then-popular Palladian style of architecture. Many of the early buildings were designed by architect George Coleman, a 31-year-old Irishman who had consulted with Raffles on the 1822-23 Town Plan. As Town Surveyor, Coleman successfully combined Palladian styles with tropical modifications such as shady verandas and louvered windows. Some of his finest architecture, such as the Armenian Church, the Caldwell House, and the Maxwell House, still stands. Coleman's house was unfortunately demolished in 1969 for the Peninsula Hotel and Shopping Center.

Singapore's other great architect was Alfred John Bidwell, an Englishman who had previously worked on the Saracenic-style Government Secretariat in Kuala Lumpur. Bidwell's neo-Renaissance buildings include the main wing of the Raffles Hotel, the Goodwood Hotel, the Stamford House, St. Joseph's Church, the Singapore Cricket Club, and the Victoria Theater and Memorial Hall. Together, Coleman and Bidwell created the finest colonial architecture in the East.

The following walking tour begins from Orchard Road and proceeds south toward the waterfront. Allow a full day or start from the National Museum and see the highlights in a few hours.

Botanic Gardens

Considered second in Asia only to the Bogor Gardens on Java. Visitors can tour the Herbarium, the experimental Orchid Garden, and the plantation where "Mad Ridley" began his experiments with the rubber tree. Ridley's discovery of a way to tap rubber without killing the tree eventually revolutionized the economies of Singapore and Malaysia.

Emerald Hill

This remarkable series of 150 prewar homes and shophouses was Singapore's first effort to preserve its endangered architecture. Also known as terrace or Malacca houses, these Chinese-baroque/Palladian residences were constructed between 1918 and 1930 by Peranakan Chinese who fused neoclassical European designs with Chinese features such as raised floors, gabled walls, and pier bases. Exteriors were painted in pastel shades inspired by the soft hues of Peranakan porcelains. Note the plaster motifs sculpted to resemble the embroidery of the *nonya sarong kebaya* and the intricately carved *pintu pagar* (fence door) that allowed ventilation but ensured privacy. Interiors were furnished with vintage clocks, teak furniture, and ancestral altars. Most buildings are closed to the public except for the Peranakan Museum, which provides a good if somewhat expensive look at traditional furnishings. Also visit the Peranakan exhibit in the National Museum.

Tan Yeok Nee Mansion

This classically styled Chinese house was constructed in 1885 by a wealthy Teochew merchant who made his fortune growing gambier and pepper. The building, with its massive granite pillars imported from China, was badly damaged by the Japanese Army during the war but later restored by the Salvation Army. Listed as a national monument in 1974, Tan's home is open to the public on weekdays. While not as impressive as Penang's Cheong Fat Tze Mansion, it remains Singapore's only example of this rare architectural style.

Chettiar Hindu Temple

This extravagant temple is dedicated to the Hindu god Subramaniam, son of Shiva and protector of celestial devas. The highly refined architecture reflects the wealth and refined taste of the Chettiars, a successful caste of moneylenders from South India. Balancing the wildly painted 23-meter *gopuram* (entrance) packed with

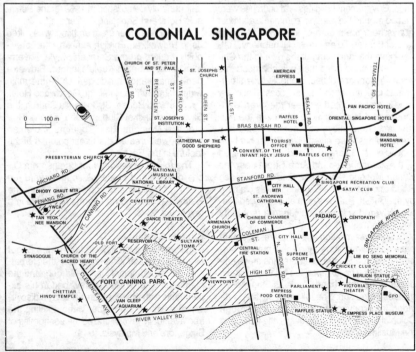

COLONIAL SINGAPORE

*art lovers
at the museum*

gods and goddesses is a massive wooden door carved with 72 lotus flowers. Though the interior is somewhat cold and impersonal, don't miss the extravagant drainage spouts and ceiling of etched glasswork which filters the falling light. Best visited during *puja* (prayer) hours in the early morning or sunset hours.

Fort Canning Park

Once known as Bukit Larangan ("Forbidden Hill") by Malays who believed it haunted by ghosts of ancient Singa Pura. Some say the hill was once covered with Malay palaces and royal courts, though excavations haven't uncovered any evidence. From the Chettiar Temple, follow the path up to the remains of the old fort, constructed in 1861 by the British. Only the gate remains after demolition in 1907 made way for the reservoir. Down below you'll find the *kermat* (holy tomb) of Sultan Iskandar Shah, last ruler of ancient Singa Pura. Elderly Malays often stand guard. Evocative cemetery plaques are mounted in walls at the bottom of the hill. Coleman is here, and Raffles himself requested to be buried here so that his bones "would mix with the ashes of Malayan kings."

Presbyterian Church

This small but elegant church constructed in 1877 is noted for its balanced facade of mixed architectural styles, including a Serlian motif flanked by square porticos and double Ionic columns. Revived by Palladio, this Romanesque treatment was enthusiastically adopted by amateur architects throughout the British Empire. Note the smaller but identical arrangement above and below the baroque scrollwork curling up from the entablature. Further details on the historical plaque.

National Museum

Originally opened as the Raffles Museum in 1887, Singapore's National Museum is both a good museum with a well-displayed collection of historical and ethnological artifacts and an excellent example of British colonial architecture. Of special note is the painted silver dome, so difficult to erect that it is said it literally drove the contractor mad. The History of Singapore Gallery has 20 historical dioramas. Audiovisual shows are given in the small auditorium. Don't miss the Straits Chinese Gallery and its superb collection of Peranakan fabrics, costumes, furniture, and a bridal chamber with an ornamented Chinese wedding bed. Upstairs are Chinese puppets, the famous 387-piece Haw Par Jade Collection (considered one of the finest in Southeast Asia), and the Trade Ceramics Gallery with its educational descriptions. Downstairs in the rear (easy to miss) you'll find a cramped gallery packed with Southeast Asian artifacts. Open daily except Mondays 0900-1700; admission S$1; tours daily at 1100.

St. Joseph's Institution

This outstanding Roman Classical building was constructed in 1867 by Brother Lothaire, a

French Catholic priest who worked at the school. Another French priest-architect, Father Nain, added the gracious curved wings at the turn of the century. Don't miss the surrealistic exterior green piping on the northwest corner! The government intends to move the National Art Gallery here.

Cathedral Of The Good Shepherd

Designed by amateur architect Denis McSwiney and constructed 1843-1846, this classical cathedral has a basilican ground plan and six porticoed entrances derived from Coleman's Palladian themes. Later additions included the tower, the spire, and three bays.

Convent Of The Infant Holy Jesus

This fine 19th-century French Gothic Revival convent was designed in 1890 by Father Nain, a Catholic priest who had also worked on St. Joseph's Institution. Note the Gothic flying buttresses, pointed arches, moody passageways, and peaceful cloisterlike gardens.

Armenian Church

The church of St. Gregory the Illuminator, Singapore's oldest ecclesiastical structure, was constructed in 1835 for the colony's 5,000 Armenians, who fled warfare between the Russians and the Turks. Considered the finest work of Coleman, who borrowed heavily from James Gibbs's *Book of Architecture* and his St. Martin in the Fields. Although the Armenian community was prosperous and influential in early Singapore, 20th-century emigration has left but a handful of Armenians to attend Sunday services. Just opposite are the photogenic Chinese Chamber of Commerce and the Central Fire Station.

Raffles Hotel

No visit to Singapore is complete without a stop at the splendid hotel that is "quite possibly more famous than Singapore itself." The Raffles was constructed in a French Renaissance style by the Sarkies brothers, three shrewd Armenians who also ran the Strand in Rangoon and the E&O in Penang. Early guests included Joseph Conrad and Rudyard Kipling, who wrote, ". . . Raffles Hotel, where the food is excellent as the rooms are bad. Let the traveller take note. Feed at Raffles and sleep at the Hotel de l'Eu-

rope." Tigran Sarkies wisely edited the verse to "Feed at the Raffles, where the food is excellent," omitting the part about the rooms. To compete with the luxurious Hotel de l'Europe, the Sarkies later conducted a massive renovation under the direction of architect Alfred John Bidwell. The hotel is also known for its tiger story and the creation of the Singapore Sling, a revolting combination of gin, cherry herring, Cointreau, Benedictine, pineapple, lime juice, and Angostura bitters. Later additions in the '60s and '70s failed to preserve architectural themes and the hotel was poorly marketed as Instant Nostalgia in Instant Asia. The hotel has recently been renovated to a more original style.

Raffles City

Inside this skyscraper you'll find the Singapore Tourist Promotion Board, Singapore Airlines, a bank with exchange facilities, a post office, and a well-stocked bookstore on the second floor. The cocktail lounge on the top floor has a S$10 minimum but your photos are guaranteed to be spectacular.

St. Andrew's Cathedral

This English Gothic Anglican church was designed by Coleman but rebuilt in 1853 by an amateur architect named MacPherson. Costs were minimal since as superintendent of convicts MacPherson had a steady source of cheap labor. Inside the soaring interior are stained-glass windows and plaster walls covered with Madras *chunam* made from egg white, shell lime, and sugar. The original church bell, donated by the daughter of Paul Revere, is now kept in the National Museum. Marble and brass memorial plaques are embedded in the walls and floors.

The Padang

Raffles in 1819 saw little more than thick mangrove swamps and a patch of green nicknamed Raffles Plain or the Esplanade. Today the Padang (Malay for central lawn) is surrounded by government buildings, churches, and private sports clubs. At one end lies the Singapore Cricket Club, constructed in 1877 as the city's all-white sports club. On the other end is the Singapore Recreation Club, constructed in 1882 for Eurasians. The nearby Satay Club is famous for its evening barbecues.

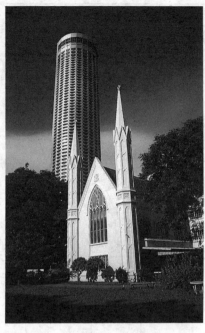

the future and the past

the symmetry and acts as a city landmark. A bronze statue of Raffles stands in front.

The adjacent Empress Place has been converted into a museum showcasing historical and cultural relics from the People's Republic of China. Parliament House to the rear marks the spot where Raffles first landed and met the Malay sultan who vacated his residence for the British. A copy of the Raffles statue stands on the riverbank.

Financial District
Across the iron girders of Cavenagh Bridge you'll find the gray-faced General Post Office, designed by Keyes and Dowdeswell as the final expression of classical architecture. Clifford Pier is where boats depart for harbor and island cruises. Change Alley, Singapore's original mall, has been leveled. An excellent place for lunch is the octagonal Telok Ayer Food Market, a delightful example of Victorian whimsy constructed in 1894 from cast-iron ribbing imported from England.

CHINATOWN

When Raffles landed in Singapore, he discovered a small Chinese business community firmly established along the banks of the Singapore River. Raffles assigned separate streets to each Chinese group: Hokkiens from Fukien settled along Amoy Street, Teochews from Swatow and Cantonese from Hong Kong in other areas. Clubs and clan associations (*kongsi*) aided those who shared common family names or hailed from the same regions. Others joined secret societies (*tongs*) which controlled the loan sharking, gambling, prostitution, and drug trade. Although outlawed by the British government, these societies remained influential until the Japanese occupation put an end to their power.

Chinatown thrived until the '50s, when young Singaporeans began fleeing the crowded tenement houses for modern housing complexes in the suburbs. Only the elderly or poor remained behind. Rent control kept living expenses low, but refurbishing became so expensive that properties were routinely neglected and fell into serious disrepair. Considered an unsalvageable anachronism by the '70s, Chinatown seemed doomed to destruction until an economic slowdown forced the government to come up with an

City Hall And Supreme Court
To the north stands the 1926 neoclassical City Hall, where during WW II the British surrendered to the Japanese. Three years later the Japanese presented their swords to Mountbatten. The equally imposing Supreme Court was built in 1937 on the site of the now-demolished Hotel de l'Europe.

The Colonial Heart
As noted earlier, Raffles himself dictated that the government buildings should be located on the north side of the Singapore River. Today these imperial buildings in Palladian, Gothic, Victorian, neo-Renaissance, and neoclassical styles form the political and historical heart of modern Singapore. Focal points include the Victoria Theater and Memorial Hall, which serves as home for the Singapore Symphony. Designed by architect Bidwell in 1905, this hybrid of classical and Renaissance elements is capped by an elegant clocktower, which strengthens

CHINATOWN

FORT CANNING PARK ★

HIGH ST.

★ PADANG

NEW OTANI HOTEL ●

COLEMAN BRIDGE

ELGIN BRIDGE

PARLIAMENT ★

VICTORIA THEATER ★

EMPRESS PLACE MUSEUM ★

FOOD CENTER ■

RIVERSIDE GALLERIA ■

BOAT QUAY RD.

RAFFLES STATUE ★

SINGAPORE RIVER

ELLENBOROUGH MARKET ■

CARPENTER ST.

UPPER CIRCULAR RD.

HONG KONG ST.

BAN SENG RESTAURANT ■

N. CANAL RD.

RAFFLES PLACE MTR ■

TAN SI CHONG TEMPLE ★

MELAKA MOSQUE ★

THONG CHAI MEDICAL INSTITUTION ★

HONG LIM PARK

PICKERING ST.

OVERSEAS CHINESE BANK ★

WAK HAI CHENG BIO TEMPLE ★

PHILLIP RD.

MARKET ST.

HAVELOCK RD.

FURAMA HOTEL ●

S. BRIDGE RD.

HOKIEN ST.

NANKIN ST.

CHIN CHEW ST.

CHINA ST.

FUK TAK CHI TEMPLE ★

CHURCH ST.

PEOPLES PARK SHOPPING ■

CROSS ST.

GREAT SOUTHERN HOTEL ●

TEOCHEW RESTAURANTS ■

MOSQUE ST.

JAMAE MOSQUE ★

PAGODA ST.

PEOPLE'S PARK COMPLEX ■

SRI MARIAMMAN HINDU TEMPLE ★

OLD CHINATOWN ★

YICK SANG RESTAURANT ★

IMAGE CARVERS ★

TELOK AYER FOOD CENTER ■

AMOY ST.

NAGORE DURGA MOSQUE ★

THIAN HOK KENG TEMPLE ★

JAYAKARTA RESTAURANT ■

PEARLS HILL

PEARLS HILL RD.

CHINATOWN SHOPPING ■

PAPER EFFIGIES ★

CLUB ST.

MEDIUM HOUSES

AL ABRAR MOSQUE ★

INN OF THE 6th HAPPINESS ●

MAXWELL FOOD CENTER

TIAN CHOR KENG TEMPLE

TELOK AYER ST.

AMOY FOOD CENTER ★

CECIL ST.

ROBINSON ST.

NEW BRIDGE RD.

JINRICKSHAW BLDG. ★

HUA TUO GUAN CAFE ●

MAXWELL RD.

METHODIST CHURCH ★

KRETA AYER RD.

NEIL RD.

DUXTON RD.

DUXTON HOTEL ●

TANJONG PAGAR RD.

MURRAY ST. RESTAURANTS ◆

AIR VIEW HOTEL ●

RESTORED SHOPHOUSES ★

NEW ASIA HOTEL ●

TANJONG PAGAR MTR ■

OUTRAM PARK MTR ■

PEARL CENTER ■

CHINATOWN GUESTHOUSE ●

AMARA HOTEL ●

0   200 m

© MOON PUBLICATIONS, INC.

ambitious preservation plan. The following walking tour begins at the Elgin Bridge and makes a clockwise circle through the better sections.

Wak Hai Cheng Bio Temple

Mornings are the best time to visit Chinatown. Begin your tour with a Malay breakfast in the Empress Food Center before crossing Elgin Bridge and walking down Boat Quay Road. The juxtaposition of old *godowns* and soaring skyscrapers forms one of Singapore's great sights. Turn right at the modern Overseas Chinese Banking Center to the Temple of the Calm Ocean on Phillip Street. Built in 1855 by Teochew Chinese fishermen for the Goddess of the Sea, this temple once bordered the waterfront before land reclamation pushed back the sea. Note the intricate roof carvings and finely carved interior ceiling beams.

Fuk Tak Chi Temple

This small but fascinating Shenist temple was built by Hakka and Cantonese immigrants who dedicated it to Toa Peh Kong, Chinese God of Wealth and Protector of the Poor. His image is depicted in mourner's sackcloth or as a bearded Hokkien sailor. Much of the temple's interest comes from its links with Taoism, the mystical and magical folk religion of the poor. Inside you'll find papier-mâché horses, magical figures used in trance ceremonies, and an altar filled with strange religious icons.

Nagore Durga Mosque

Though sadly neglected, this lime-green mosque built in 1830 by Tamil Muslims displays a curious marriage of disparate architectural styles: fluted Corinthian columns, half-moon fans, a pieced Islamic balustrade, Chinese towers, and Islamic minarets being attacked by tropical plantlife. Farther on you'll pass the modest Al Abrar Mosque constructed in 1855 by *chulias* Muslims from South India.

Thian Hok Keng Temple

Singapore's oldest Chinese temple is also the most spectacular in the city. Constructed in 1841 by the Hokkiens and dedicated to the Goddess of the Sea, the Temple of Heavenly Happiness is also a treasure trove of Chinese craftsmanship. Of special note are the door guardians, elaborate roof brackets which support the roof, and intricately carved granite pillars imported from China. All were carefully integrated into a spatial arrangement to balance the forces of *yin* and *yang*. Beyond the 19th-century courtyard stands the principal temple with images of Tin Hau and other gods whose mouths have been sealed with tobacco tar (formerly opium). Smaller pavilions to the rear are filled with ancestor tablets and images of Kuan Yin.

Amoy And Club Streets

Black flags stenciled in gold with mystical trigrams indicate the homes of Chinese mediums who communicate via seances with departed ancestors and wandering ghosts. Walk slowly around China, Chin Chew, Nanking and Hokkien streets . . . one of the most authentic sections left in old Chinatown. Return to Club Street (named for the trade guilds once located here) to watch idol carvers kept busy carving miniature gods and goddesses. Then walk up Club to the inclined terrain of Ann Siang Hill and South Bridge Road.

Sago, Tanjong Pagar, and Neil Roads

Sago Road was once a busy brothel district named after the factories that extracted starch from the trunk of the sago palm. Before being torn down a decade ago for redevelopment, Sago was where elderly Chinese came to die in Death Houses. Today it's just an empty lot most likely haunted by ghosts waiting for the return of prospective developers. A few surviving funeral stores on Sago still make paper reproductions of cars, houses, and yachts to be burned at funerals. Walk south to the Maxwell Food Center and the V-shaped Jinrickshaw Building wedged at the intersection. Designed in 1913 by Swan and MacLaren, this strategically placed building acts as a strong anchor between the older shophouses of Chinatown and the restored terrace homes on Tanjong Pagar and Neil roads. This is the largest block of Straits Chinese shophouses in Singapore.

Chinatown Center

The intersection of Trengganu and Smith streets is the heart of old Chinatown. Before street merchants were relocated in 1973 into faceless shopping complexes, this neighborhood dazzled the visitor with its vegetable stalls, roving food hawkers, and itinerant vendors selling everything from live snakes to counterfeit Rolexes. Although largely destroyed by urban redevelopment, it's still an active and colorful neighborhood with dozens of fascinating shops. Smith Street is best for Chinese teas, porcelain, beaded slippers, jade, bonsai trees, incense dolls, dried lizards, medicines, and haircuts. Temple Street merchants deal in paper effigies, *tai chi* shoes, and soy sauce. Look for the Chinese medical hall. Pagoda Street, once filled with opium dens and the center for Singapore's slave trade, is now lined with tailor shops. Mosque Street is famous for Teochew restaurants and old tea houses little changed from the '20s. Try the duck soup with salted vegetables, black chicken soup, Teochew *muay,* roast pig, and sweet yam paste.

Sri Mariamman Hindu Temple

Sri Mariamman was first constructed from *attap* and timber but expanded in 1842 by an Indian merchant named Naraina Pillai. Dedicated to the Mother Goddess Devi, this temple shows the three principal elements of Dravidian architecture: an interior shrine (*vimanam*) covered by a decorated dome, an assembly hall (*madapam*) used for prayers, and an entrance tower (*gopuram*) covered with brightly painted gods and goddesses. Prayer services are announced by wailing Indian clarinets, crashing cymbals, and the frenzied beating of drums. The nearby Jamae Mosque was built in 1835 by Muslim *chulias.*

Thong Chai Medical Institution

Named after the Cantonese theaters that once lined the road, Wayang Street features an extremely rare medical clinic constructed in traditional Chinese style. Cloud-shaped gables and glazed green tiles cap what is now an antique store. Several old warehouses (*godowns*) still stand along North Boat Quay Road.

LITTLE INDIA

Serangoon Road is Singapore's "Little India." Originally brought here as indentured workers to clear the jungles and drain the swamps, the 200,000 Indians of Singapore now influence the country far beyond their modest numbers. Most are from the south but others include Coromandel Muslims (*chulias*), Malabar Muslims (*kakaks*), North Indians (*Bengalis*), Malayali from Kerala, Sikhs from the Punjab, and Orang Bombays from Gujarat. Like the Chinese, they also grouped together according to religion, state of origin, and choice of occupation. Tamils settled along Serangoon Road and moved into white-collar occupations. Sikhs, Sindhis, and Gujaratis took High Street and found work as textile merchants, tailors, and policemen. Intermarriage between Indian Muslims and Malays produced a class called the Jawi Peranakans. The most powerful and highly visible caste is that of the Chettiars, wealthy moneylenders from Madras who have financed many of the city's most elaborate temples.

Singapore's Little India is an outstanding place to experience the exotic sights, sounds, and smells of India. The heart lies in the small alleys near at the western end of Serangoon Road. Streets farther east have been redeveloped and lost much of their charm, though the outstanding architecture on Jalan Besar and Petain Road is worth visiting.

Hindu god in Little India

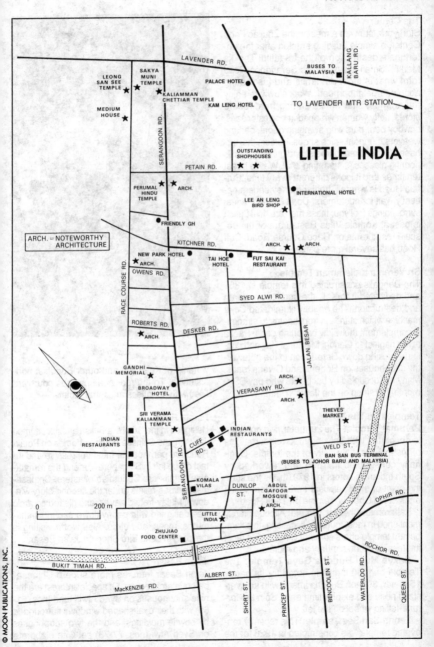

The Center

Start your tour with a meal in the Zhujiao Food Center, a simple building erected after the unfortunate destruction of the beautiful Thekka Market. Small alleys across Serangoon Road form what is most authentic and fascinating about the neighborhood. Walk slowly to enjoy the aromas, sitar music drifting from record stores, hefty women wrapped in polyester saris, cowboy beer bars with swinging doors, garland weavers, pungent spice shops, goldsmiths, turbaned Sikhs, street barbers, and grinning Tamils pouring glasses of steaming *chai*. Walk a street ten times and it looks different every time. Buffalo Road is where Chettiar moneylenders patiently wait for customers. Don't let the modest surroundings fool you; these men are rich! Lunch is best at Komala Vilas Restaurant or the upscale restaurants on Race Course Road. Cuff Road has several more cafes.

Sri Verama Kaliamman Temple

The Bengalis constructed this temple in 1881 and dedicated it to Kali, the goddess of death and destruction. The brightly illuminated Coke machine which stands in front seems to strangely complement the wildly cavorting gods. Pause at the neglected Gandhi Memorial Hall and continue walking down Serangoon to the noteworthy shophouses on Roberts and Owens roads. Many are occupied by bachelors who pay S$10 monthly to sleep on the floors in shifts.

Temples To The East

Perumal Temple: The 20-meter *raja gopuram* is decorated with polychromed reincarnations of Vishnu, the main deity of the temple. Originally constructed in 1855 and reworked by South Indian sculptors in 1970, this is the starting point of the Thaipusam procession, which ends at the Chettiar Temple on Tank Road.

Kaliamman Chettiar Temple: Although rarely mentioned in most tourist publications, this flamboyant temple offers some of Singapore's most impressive Hindu statuary and murals.

Sakya Muni Buddha Gaya Temple: The Temple of 1000 Lights is noted for its gaudy 15-meter, 300-ton Buddha image with an oversized nose and elephantine ears. Spin the fortune-telling wheel on the left.

Leong San See Temple: This recently renovated temple was constructed in 1926 for the

Muslim tailor

worship of Kuan Yin and other Buddhist bodhisattvas. To the rear is a spacious courtyard filled with countless ancestral tablets.

Petain Road

Designed in the '30s by a British architect named Jackson, the Chinese-baroque homes on Petain Road are perhaps the most impressive and intact group left in Singapore Among the remarkable details are Corinthian pilasters, Chinese-inspired bas-reliefs under the second-story windows, Malay-fretted eaves, and glazed ceramic tiles designed with peony flowers, chrysanthemums, roses, and birds. Also worth visiting is the Lee An Leng Bird Shop on Jalan Besar.

Jalan Besar

Jalan Besar features more superb Chinese-baroque architecture. Of special interest are the nine shophouses on Syed Alwi Road (nos. 61-69) with their oval-shaped windows surrounded by bowtie moldings, and the two shophouses on Syed Alwi (nos. 77-78) set with elaborate window architraves and European tiles. Another highlight is the flamboyant pair at the junction of Jalan Besar and Veerasamy Road. These three-story wonders are enduring reminders of Singapore's rich architectural heritage. The Garut Road "Thieves" Market has more motorcycle parts and shrink-wrapped radios than thieves. Final stop is the Abdul Gafoor Mosque, which fuses Islamic arches with Roman columns. The dilapidated remains of the original mosque stand on Mayo Street.

ARAB STREET AND THE MUSLIM QUARTER

Sultan Mosque

Between Bencoolen and Arab streets you might visit the Kwan Yin Temple and try a durian at the colorful fruit market on Queen Street. The medium temple on Johore Road displays Taoist trance daggers and magical images whose mouths have been sealed with tobacco. Top draw in Singapore's Muslim quarter is the Sultan

Mosque, a Saracenic building designed in 1924 by Swan and MacLaren with onion-shaped domes, four-corner minarets, pointed trefoils, and cinquefoil arches over the balconies. Modestly dressed tourists may enter the mosque via the rear entrance on Muscat Street. Inexpensive cafes on North Bridge Road serve tasty *murtabaks* and *biryanis*.

Back Streets And The Sultan's Palace

North Bridge Road passes herbalists, perfume shops, and Islamic supply stores to Sultan Road. Turn right and walk past Alsagoff Arab School to Hajjah Fatimah Mosque, which was designed by a British architect in 1846 for a wealthy Malaccan-born lady. Pahang Street has traditional stonecutters and blacksmiths. Istana Kampong Glam, at the end of the alley, is the former palace of the sultan. Constructed around 1836 and influenced by architect Coleman, this modest house is scheduled for renovation and possible conversion into a Malay cultural complex. To the left is an impressive bungalow once occupied by Malay royalty.

Arab Street

Bussorah and Kandahar streets are excellent streets to wander and purchase prayer rugs, Korans, and ginger drinks called *sarabat*. Shops on Arab Street are packed with imported batiks, Indonesian brasswork, fragrant basketware, exotic perfumes, jewelry, traditional medicines, and *barang haji*—everything required for a pilgrimage to Mecca. A fine change from the airconditioned shopping centers of Orchard Road.

ATTRACTIONS OUTSIDE THE CITY

Singapore Zoo

The best zoo in Asia. Over 2,000 animals including rare and endangered species live in this open-air zoo situated by the Seletar Reservoir. Unlike most Asian zoos, this one uses natural barriers instead of iron bars and impersonal cages. Animals include Sumatran orangutans, Thai elephants, Malaysian tigers, and small Komodo dragons. Arrive by 0900 for breakfast with the orangutans. Animal shows throughout the day. Open daily 0830-1800; admission S$6. The adjacent Mandai Orchid Gar-

ARAB STREET
(KAMPONG GLAM)

FATIMAH MOSQUE
SULTAN RD.
MALABAR MOSQUE
ARAB SCHOOL
STONECUTTERS
SULTANS PALACE
ROCHOR CANAL RD.
SABAR MENANTI CAFE
PLAZA HOTEL
SULTAN MOSQUE
BASKETS
ARAB RESTAURANTS
ARAB ST.
ARAB SHOPS
GOLDEN LANDMARK HOTEL
BAN SAN BUS TERMINAL (BUSES TO JOHOR BARU)
MEDIUM TEMPLE
OPHIR RD.
N. BRIDGE RD.
VICTORIA ST.
MOSQUE
BEACH RD.
FRUIT MARKET
QUEEN ST.
ROCHOR RD.
ROCHOR CENTER
FATTY'S RESTAURANT
BUGIS MTR
BUGIS NIGHT MARKET
WATERLOO ST.
BENCOOLEN ST.
KWAN YIN TEMPLE
0   100 m

© MOON PUBLICATIONS, INC.

views over the Padang

dens are easily visited. Take bus 171 from Bukit Timah or Queen roads.

Jurong Bird Park
This 20-hectare park, one of Singapore's best attractions, boasts the world's largest collection of Southeast Asian birds inside a gigantic aviary, and the Nocturnal House which cleverly uses modern technology to turn day into night. Bird shows at 1030 and 1500. Arrive before 0900 for buffet breakfast in the songbird terrace, but avoid the weekends, when it's jammed with Singaporeans. Open daily 0900 to 1800; admission S$6. Take a bus to Jurong Interchange and transfer to bus 250, or MRT to Boon Lay, then take buses 251, 253, or 255 from the interchange.

Haw Par Villa
Tiger Balm Gardens has recently been redeveloped and expanded into a multimillion-dollar Chinese mythological theme park with lasers, robotronics, an artisans village, boat rides through the world of Chinese spirits, and a hologram-studded journey with the Monkey God. Designed by the same people responsible for Knott's Berry Farm and Lotte Theme Park in Seoul. Open daily 0800-2000; admission S$16. Take the MRT to Buona Vista, then bus 200 to Pasir Panjang Road.

Jurong Crocodile Park
Over 2,500 crocodiles including 25 distinct species are found in the natural junglelike settings of Singapore's newest wildlife attraction. Feeding at 1100; wrestling at 1300. Open daily 0900-1730; admission S$5.

Bukit Timah Nature Reserve
This 71-hectare section of tropical forest offers hiking paths up to Singapore's highest peak at 162 meters. The six-lane Bukit Timah Expressway was destructively cut through the forest in 1986 despite objections from the Nature Reserves Board. Open daily; free admission.

Sentosa Island
A multimillion-dollar leisure and recreation resort with an artificial swimming lagoon, wax displays, a butterfly park, two beaches, a golf course, a roller-skating rink, musical fountains, a maritime museum, and an underwater world with see-through tunnels. Recent additions include Asian Village, Rasa Sentors Resort Hotel (S$200-450), and the Sentosa Riverboat. Open daily 0800-2200; admission S$5-9. Ferries and cable cars cross from the World Trade Center.

Southern Islands
Both Eastwind (tel. 533-3432) and Water Tours (tel. 533-9811) do bay cruises past various islands from Clifford Pier. Day sails cost S$25; twilight cruises cost S$40. Too expensive? Regular ferries (tel. 321-2792) for just S$6 depart from the World Trade Center to St. John's and Kusu islands at 1000 and 1330.

2

SINGAPORE
1. emperor of China; **2.** Singapore skyline; **3.** little India (all photos this page by Carl Parkes)

THAILAND
1. Khon dancers; 2. hilltribe portrait (all photos this page by Carl Parkes)

Chinese And Japanese Gardens

The 14-hectare Chinese Gardens in Jurong are decorated with miniature temples, pagodas, arched bridges, and lakes surrounded by wispy willows. The adjacent Japanese Gardens are the largest outside Japan. Open daily 0900-1800; admission S$3. Take the MRT to Chinese Garden Terminal.

Bird Singing

Sunday morning bird-singing concerts are held behind the Palace Hotel on Jalan Besar and at the junction of Tiong Bahru and Seng Poh roads.

Tang Dynasty Village

Singapore's largest and newest theme park attempts to re-create the most famous era in China's history—the 7th-century peak of the Tang Dynasty centered in the ancient capital city of Xian—with architectural reproductions of the Imperial Palace, housing estates, and an underground chamber filled with more than 1,000 replicas of Xian's famed terra-cotta warriors. Tang Dynasty village is located in Jurong and is open daily 0900-2000. Admission is S$15-20. Take the MRT to Chinese Garden Terminal and walk south.

PRACTICALITIES

BUDGET HOTELS

The accompanying maps and hotel charts show the locations and published rates of most guesthouses and hotels in Singapore. Central Singapore, near the National Museum and Bencoolen St., has a good supply of cheap hotels, plus it's within easy walking distance of sights and facilities such as the tourist office and the post office. Central Singapore, however, is best suited for those more interested in sightseeing than shopping, since Orchard Rd. shopping centers are about 20 minutes away. A handful of inexpensive dorms are also found in Chinatown and near Orchard Road.

Bus 390 from the airport first passes Raffles City and the tourist office before stopping near the National Museum and the YMCA. Travelers can easily walk a few blocks to the guesthouses and inexpensive Chinese hotels located on or near Bencoolen Street.

Taxis from the airport cost S$12-14. From the train station take buses 10, 97, 100, 125, or 880. From Finger Pier take buses 125, 146, or 175 from Anson to Selegie roads.

Central Singapore

Bencoolen Street dorm beds cost S$6-8 in a large room with six or more beds and S$7-9 in a room holding four beds. Most dormitory operations also have individual rooms for S$20-25. Dorms are usually hot, crowded, and poorly maintained but are also friendly, cheap, and useful places to meet other travelers and exchange travel information.

Moving slightly upscale are a handful of old Chinese hotels which have so far escaped the wrecking ball. These relics will most appeal to couples on a budget who need privacy and don't enjoy the congested atmosphere of dorms.

173 Bencoolen Street: The Hong Guan Building, Singapore's most famous crash pad, has dorms and inexpensive private rooms on all seven floors. The building itself is somewhat tricky to find since it isn't signposted (dorms in Singapore are technically illegal), but someone lounging out front will direct you through the driveway to the elevator in the rear.

Goh's Homestay on the sixth floor is a favorite, though the party atmosphere and general mayhem may not appeal to everyone. On a more personal note, this is where I met Bill Dalton in 1979 and eventually went on to write this beast you are hauling around Southeast Asia. 173 Bencoolen, 6th Floor, tel. 339-6561, S$7-9 dorm, S$20-25 private rooms.

Why Not Homestay 1: The crowded conditions in the Hong Guan Building have brought a second wave of guesthouses, including a pair of Why Nots in central Singapore. This branch has been running full steam for several years and receives good reports from travelers. 127 Bencoolen St., tel. 338-0162, S$8-10 dorms, S$20-25 rooms.

Why Not Homestay 2: Spotless rooms, a small kitchen for cooking, and friendly management make this another good choice. Re-

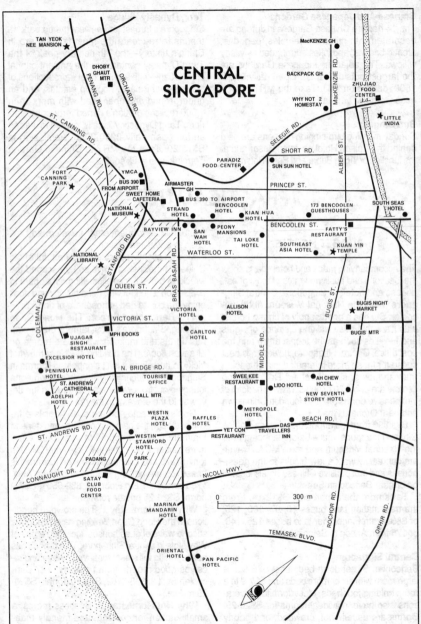

CENTRAL SINGAPORE

TAN YEOK NEE MANSION ★

DHOBY GHAUT MTR

PENANG RD.

ORCHARD RD.

FT. CANNING RD.

MacKENZIE GH

BACKPACK GH

WHY NOT 2 HOMESTAY

MacKENZIE RD.

ZHUJIAO FOOD CENTER

ALBERT ST.

★ LITTLE INDIA

SELEGIE RD.

SHORT RD.

PARADIZ FOOD CENTER

SUN SUN HOTEL

PRINCEP ST.

FORT CANNING PARK ★

YMCA

BUS 390 FROM AIRPORT

AIRMASTER GH

SWEET HOME CAFETERIA

BUS 390 TO AIRPORT

BENCOOLEN HOTEL

KIAN HUA HOTEL

173 BENCOOLEN GUESTHOUSES

SOUTH SEAS HOTEL

NATIONAL MUSEUM ★

STRAND HOTEL

BAYVIEW INN

SAN WAH HOTEL

PEONY MANSIONS

TAI LOKE HOTEL

BENCOOLEN ST.

FATTY'S RESTAURANT

SOUTHEAST ASIA HOTEL

KUAN YIN TEMPLE ★

STANFORD RD.

NATIONAL LIBRARY ★

BRAS BASAH RD.

WATERLOO ST.

QUEEN ST.

COLEMAN RD.

VICTORIA ST.

VICTORIA HOTEL

ALLISON HOTEL

BUGIS NIGHT MARKET ★

BUGIS ST.

BUGIS MTR

MIDDLE RD.

UJAGAR SINGH RESTAURANT

MPH BOOKS

CARLTON HOTEL

EXCELSIOR HOTEL

PENINSULA HOTEL

N. BRIDGE RD.

ST. ANDREWS CATHEDRAL ★

ADELPHI HOTEL

TOURIST OFFICE

CITY HALL MTR

SWEE KEE RESTAURANT

LIDO HOTEL

AH CHEW HOTEL

NEW SEVENTH STOREY HOTEL

BEACH RD.

WESTIN PLAZA HOTEL

RAFFLES HOTEL

METROPOLE HOTEL

YET CON RESTAURANT

DAS TRAVELLERS INN

ST. ANDREWS RD.

WESTIN STAMFORD HOTEL

PADANG

PARK

CONNAUGHT DR.

NICOLL HWY.

ROCHOR RD.

SATAY CLUB FOOD CENTER

0   300 m

MARINA MANDARIN HOTEL

TEMASEK BLVD.

OPHIR RD.

ORIENTAL HOTEL

PAN PACIFIC HOTEL

© MOON PUBLICATIONS, INC.

BUSES FROM BENCOOLEN STREET

DESTINATION	BUS
Airport	390 from Bras Basah Road
Arab Street	Walking distance
Botanic Gardens	106
Chinatown	81, 83, 101, 103, 134, or 166
Clifford Pier	97, 125, 131, 161, or 172
Crocodile Farm	81, 83, 97, or 111 from Selegie Road
GPO	97, 125, 131, 146, 163, 172, or 175
Jurong Bird Park	198 to Jurong Interchange, then buses 251, 253, or 255
Malaysia	Lavender Street Terminus, Ban San Street Terminus, bus 170 from Queen St.
Ming Village	198 to Jurong Interchange, then bus 245 to Pandan Road
Newton Food Circus	170, 171 from Rochor Centre
Orchard Road	64, 65, 106, or 111
Railway Station	97, 125, 146, or 163
Siong Lim Temple	146 from Selegie Road
Sentosa Island	97, 125, 146, or 163 to World Trade Center
Temple of 1000 Lights	81 or 83 from Middle Road
Haw Par Villa	97
Zoo/Orchid Gardens	171 from Orchard Road YMCA

ception is on the second floor. 189 Selegie, 2nd Floor, tel. 338-6095, S$8-10 dorm, S$25-40 private rooms.

Mackenzie Guesthouse: Although somewhat distant from central Singapore, many consider this the friendliest dorm in town. Features include free breakfast and coffee, lounges, and kitchen facilities. Best of all, the helpful owner seems genuinely concerned about his guests. 114A Mackenzie, tel. 334-4980, S$6-8 dorm, S$20-25 room with fan, S$35-40 a/c room.

Backpack Guesthouse: Guesthouses and dorms on Mackenzie Rd. are generally cleaner, quieter, and slightly cheaper than those on Bencoolen. Backpack is another popular alternative to the Hong Guan Building. 15 Mackenzie Rd., tel. 334-9820, S$6-8 dorm, S$25-35 rooms.

Das Travellers Inn: This longtime favorite moved from Little India several years ago and will probably move again in the future but is presently located about 100 meters east of the Raffles Hotel. Rooms are only average but there's a good supply of information on travel down to Indonesia or north to Thailand. Like most other dorms in Singapore, the place has complimentary breakfast (until noon), tea, and coffee. Take bus 390 from the airport to Raffles City. Reception is on the fourth floor. 87 Beach Rd., tel. 338-7460, S$6-10 dorm, S$20-40 rooms.

San Wah Hotel: Bencoolen Street's old-style Chinese hotels are cheap but somewhat rundown and will probably be razed in the next few years. Prices have risen in recent years in line with most hotels in Singapore, and bargaining is recommended. The San Wah is overpriced but has some old-world atmosphere (that's good and bad) and is slightly cleaner than the others such as the Tiong Hoa, Tai Loke, and Kian Hua hotels. 36 Bencoolen, tel. 336-2428, S$40-55.

Chinatown

Chinatown Guesthouse: Johnny's place has dorms, private rooms, and kitchen facilities in an unusual Chinatown location well removed from

BUSES FROM ORCHARD ROAD

DESTINATION	BUS
Airport	390
Arab Street	7 to Victoria Street, then walk to Arab Street
Bukit Timah Reserve	171, 173, 182 to Bukit Timah Shopping Center
Chinatown	124, 143, 167, 174, 182, or 190
Clifford Pier	CBD 1 or TIBS 850
Crocodile Farm	111 outside Orchard Parade Hotel
Japanese Gardens	198 to Corporation Road, then 154
Jurong Bird Park	198 to Jurong Bus Interchange, then 251, 253, or 255
Little India	64, 65, 92, 106, or 111
Ming Village	143 to Teban Gardens, then 245 to Pandan Road
Railway Station	167
Raffles City	1, 7, 14, or 16
Sentosa Island	65, 143, or 167 to World Trade Center
Mythological Park	143
Zoo/Orchid Gardens	171

the standard backpackers' trail. The guesthouse is near a public swimming pool, above a 24-hour Indian cafe, and close to the Outram Park MRT station. From the train station, take buses 84, 145, or 167 to Kreta Ayer Rd. and look for the Konica sign. Bus arrivals from Malaysia should take the MRT to Outram Park. 325 D New Bridge Rd., 5th Floor, tel. 220-0671, S$8 dorm, S$22-30 rooms.

MODERATE HOTELS

Central Singapore

The single biggest problem with accommodations in Singapore is the yawning gap between the budget guesthouses near Bencoolen St. and the very expensive hotels scattered around the city. The ongoing shortage of hotel rooms has allowed even the simplest of hotels to increase rates to unreasonable levels and tight government control over new construction leaves little hope for price relief in the near future. As with Bangkok and Hong Kong, you're left with little choice between a crowded dormitory and some international wonder that caters almost exclusively to wealthy tourists. Almost certainly the best bargains are the YMCAs, fol-

lowed by a few hotels located on the outskirts of the tourist districts.

YMCA International House: Centrally located between the shopping centers of Orchard Rd. and the historical attractions in central Singapore, this is probably the best low-priced hotel in Singapore, if you don't mind the groups of teenagers charging around. All rooms have a/c, private baths, and color TV. Additional facilities include a budget-priced restaurant, a rooftop swimming pool, a billiards room, and a health club. Excellent value; advance reservations are strongly recommended. 1 Orchard Rd., tel. 337-3444, fax 337-3140, S$20 dorm, S$75-85 a/c single, S$85-95 a/c double.

YWCA Hostel: Both married couples and single women are welcome at this hostel, a good-value spot in a great location midway between the Orchard Rd. shops and attractions in colonial Singapore and Chinatown. 6/8 Fort Canning Rd., tel. 336-3150, fax 737-2804, S$15 dorm (women only), S$45-50 a/c single, S$50-60 a/c double.

Bencoolen Hotel: A basic but reasonably clean hotel with a/c rooms, private baths, and the rooftop Bartizan restaurant. This and the adjacent Strand Hotel are two of the better low-end hotels in Singapore, though neither can be

CENTRAL SINGAPORE ACCOMMODATIONS

HOTEL	SINGLE	DOUBLE	ADDRESS	PHONE (2)
LUXURY	S$	S$		
Excelsior	180-200	200-250	5 Coleman	338-7733
Marina Mandarin	340-380	400-460	6 Raffles	338-3388
Oriental	340-380	380-460	6 Raffles	338-0066
Pan Pacific	320-360	320-360	6 Raffles	336-8111
Peninsula	180-220	200-260	3 Coleman	337-2200
Raffles	650-800	650-800	113 Beach	337-8041
Allson	200-240	220-260	101 Victoria	336-0811
Westin Plaza	280-320	300-380	2 Stamford	338-8585
Westin Stamford	250-300	280-350	2 Stamford	338-8585
MODERATE				
Bayview Inn	140-160	160-200	30 Bencoolen	337-2882
Bencoolen	90-120	100-140	47 Bencoolen	336-0822
Carlton	300-340	320-360	76 Bras Basah	338-8333
Golden Landmark	150-180	160-200	390 Victoria	297-2828
Metropole	80-100	100-120	41 Seah	336-3611
Mayfair	65-80	85-100	Armenian	337-5405
New Seventh Storey	60-80	70-90	Rochor	337-0251
South East Asia	60-75	60-75	190 Waterloo	338-2394
Strand	100-120	100-120	25 Bencoolen	338-1866
YMCA	75-85	85-95	1 Orchard	337-3444

BUDGET

HOTEL	SINGLE	DOUBLE	DORM	ADDRESS	PHONE
Backpack Guesthouse	25-35	25-35	6-8	15 Mackenzie	334-9820
Das Travellers Inn	20-30	25-40	6-10	87 Beach, Fl. 4	338-7460
Goh's Homestay	20	25	7-9	173 Bencoolen, Fl. 6	339-6561
Hawaii Guesthouse	20	25	6-8	173 Bencoolen, Fl. 2	338-4817
Kian Hua	30-40	40-50		81 Bencoolen	338-3492
Peony Mansions	20	25	6-8	52 Bencoolen, Fl. 5	
Philip Choo's	20	25	7-9	173 Bencoolen, Fl. 3	
San Wah	40-50	55-65		36 Bencoolen	336-2428
Mackenzie Guesthouse	20	25	6-8	114A Mackenzie	334-4980
South Seas	35-45	50-60		Bencoolen	
Tai Loke	30-35	35-45		161 Middle	337-6209
Why Not Homestay 1	28-35	35-40	8-10	127 Bencoolen	338-0162

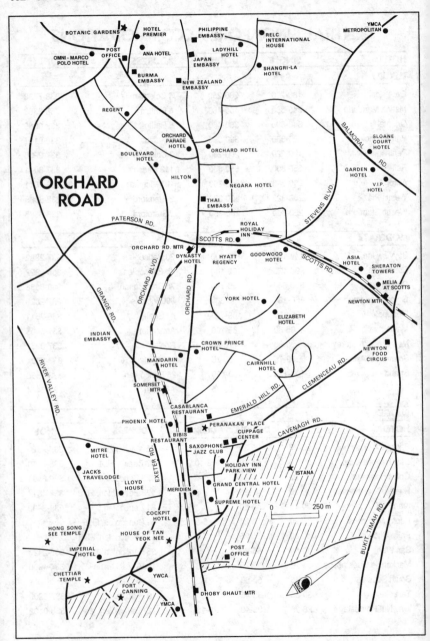

considered any type of bargain. 47 Bencoolen, tel. 336-0822, fax 336-4384, S$85-130.

Metropole Hotel: One of the better midrange hotels is this newish nine-story high-rise well situated behind the Raffles Hotel and within walking distance of most Singaporean attractions. 41 Seah St., tel. 336-3611, fax 339-3610, S$80-120.

Orchard Road

Queen's Hotel: Less expensive hotels in the Orchard Road neighborhood are tucked away on smaller roads. Queen's is small and somewhat run-down but it has a swimming pool, a nightclub, and a health club. 24 Mt. Elizabeth, tel. 737-6088, S$70-90.

Jack's Travelodge: One of the newer low-end hotels near Orchard is a good choice for economical travelers who don't mind being a 10- to 15-minute walk from the shops. All rooms are a/c with attached bath and TV. Residents can use the adjoining AA swimming pool. 336 River Valley, tel. 732-9222, S$70-95.

Hotel Premier: Off the beaten track but prices are reasonable. Staffed by students from the adjacent Singapore Hotel Training and Educational Center. Inexpensive fixed dinners are served in the school restaurant. Facilities include a/c rooms with attached baths, private balconies, and a small swimming pool. Nassim Hill, tel. 733-9811, S$140-160.

Chinatown

Chinatown YMCA: More formally called the Metropolitan YMCA International Centre, this older but less expensive property is located near the train station and Finger Pier. Convenient for late-night train arrivals. 70 Palmer Rd., tel. 222-4666, S$25-35 a/c common bath, S$40-45 a/c private bath.

Majestic Hotel: Located on the fringe of Chinatown and near the Outram MRT station, the Majestic is one of the last Old World hotels in Singapore. The hotel is quiet, clean, and far removed from tourist enclaves; very good value in the moderate category. 31-37 Bukit Pasoh Rd., tel. 222-3377, fax 223-0907, S$40-60.

Station Hotel: As the name suggests, this hotel is located in the railway station near Finger Pier. The location isn't very good but the hotel, once again, might be useful for late train arrivals and early-morning departures. Keppel Rd., tel. 222-1551, S$50-60.

LUXURY HOTELS

Central Singapore

Raffles: Since 1881 this famous colonial hotel has hosted royalty, film stars, and famous writers. All rooms are suites with a/c, private bath, color TV, and minibar. Restaurants include the Tudor-style Elizabethan Grill and three-storied Tiffin Room, both as famous as the hotel itself. 113 Beach Road, tel. 337-1886, fax 339-7650.

Westin Stamford and Westin Plaza: The amazing 73-story Raffles City complex, which towers over downtown Singapore, is home to the Singapore Tourist Office, Singapore Airlines, a post office, and a well-stocked bookstore on the second floor. The south side is taken up by the Westin Plaza, popular with upmarket business travelers, and the 73-story Westin Stamford, which caters to business groups and conventioneers. The Compass Rose cocktail lounge at the very top wins the *Southeast Asia Handbook* Award for Most Outrageous View in Singapore. Westin Plaza: 2 Stamford, tel. 338-8585, fax 338-2862, S$320-400. Westin Stamford: 2 Stamford, tel. 228-8585, fax 337-1554, S$280-360.

Chinatown

Aside from the standard collection of cookie-cutter luxury hotels, a pair of unusual boutiques are located in the renovated shophouses near the Tanjong Pagar historical district.

Duxton Hotel: Located in the heart of the rehabilitated Tanjong Pagar district, the Duxton features 50 high-ceilinged rooms decorated with colonial-era furnishings. Features include a French restaurant, complimentary English breakfast, and an elaborate tea daily on the veranda. A refreshing change from most of Singapore's faceless hotels. 83 Duxton Rd., tel. 227-7678, S$150-220.

Inn of the Sixth Happiness: Another restored gem with 48 rooms composed of traditional wood-beamed ceilings, shuttered windows, embroidered silk bedspreads, ceiling fans, and turn-of-the-century decor. The Inn also has an Italian restaurant and a Chinese cafe specializing in Cantonese cuisine. Highly recommended. 33 Erskine Rd., tel. 223-3266, S$140-220.

ORCHARD ROAD ACCOMMODATIONS

HOTEL	SINGLE	DOUBLE	ADDRESS	PHONE (2)
LUXURY				
Boulevard	250-280	280-320	200 Orchard	737-2911
Crown Prince	200-220	200-220	270 Orchard	732-1111
Dynasty	220-260	240-280	320 Orchard	734-9900
Goodwood	400-520	460-650	22 Scotts	737-7411
Hilton	280-320	320-380	581 Orchard	737-2233
Hyatt Regency	380-420	420-500	10-12 Scotts	733-1188
Imperial	260-300	320-360	1 Jalan Rumbia	737-1666
Le Meridien	300-340	340-380	100 Orchard	733-8855
Mandarin	340-400	380-460	333 Orchard	737-4411
Orchard Parade	280-320	300-360	1 Tanglin	737-1133
Omni Marco Polo	250-280	300-360	247 Tanglin	474-7141
Orchard	180-220	200-280	442 Orchard	734-7766
Park View Holiday Inn	210-240	240-270	11 Cavenagh	733-8333
Regent	340-380	360-420	1 Cuscaden	733-8888
Royal Holiday Inn	300-340	320-360	25 Scotts	737-7966
Shangri-La	420-600	500-680	22 Orange Grove	737-3644
ANA	400-460	400-460	16 Nassim Hill	732-1222
Sheraton Towers	400-460	400-460	43 Scotts	737-6888
York	260-300	300-340	21 Mt. Elizabeth	737-0511
MODERATE				
Asia	140-160	180-200	37 Scotts	737-8388
Cairnhill	180-200	200-220	19 Cairnhill Circle	734-6626
Cockpit	160-180	240-280	6/7 Oxley Rise	737-9111
Melia at Scotts	260-300	400-440	45 Scotts	732-5885
Garden	160-200	180-220	14 Balmoral	235-3344
Grand Central	140-160	160-180	Cavenagh	737-9944
Ladyhill	160-180	180-200	1 Ladyhill	737-2111
Negara	240-260	260-280	15 Claymore	737-0811
Phoenix	200-240	240-280	Somerset	737-8666
Premier	140-160	140-160	Nassim Hill	733-9811
RELC International	140-160	140-160	Orange Grove	737-9044
Supreme	100-120	120-140	15 Kramat	737-8333
BUDGET				
Jack's Travelodge	70-95	70-95	336 River Valley	732-9222
Sloane Court	100-120	140-160	Balmoral	235-2311
YWCA	45-60	50-70	6-8 Fort Canning	336-3150
YMCA	75-85	85-95	1 Orchard	337-3444

Orchard Road

Most of Singapore's first-class hotels are located in the tourist belt/shopping district of Orchard Road. Though far removed from Chinatown and Little India, it's a beautiful area of trees, parks, and modernistic architecture. All the big names are here—Hyatt, Holiday Inn, Sheraton—but older properties at lower rates can be found a few blocks off the main drag. Taxis from the airport cost S$14-18, or take a bus from the airport basement.

Goodwood Hotel: Perhaps the most romantic hotel in Singapore. Designed by Swan and MacLaren, who rebuilt the old Teutonia Club in a German style with large semicircular gables and octagonal towers. A memorable stay, especially in the S$3000 Brunei Suite. 22 Scotts Rd., tel. 737-7411, fax 732-8558, S$400-650.

Shangri-La: Consistently voted one of the world's top hotels. Located on 12 acres in a quiet residential neighborhood. 22 Orange Grove, tel. 737-3644, fax 733-7220, S$420-680.

Le Meridien: French style and Oriental service in a cantilevered nine-story hotel managed by Air France. The swimming pool and location are terrific. 100 Orchard, tel. 733-8855, fax 732-7886, S$300-380.

RESTAURANTS

Time to eat *lah*. Singaporeans' love of food is more than just a passing fancy—it's an obsession that inspires both enthusiasm and reverence. Singapore's reputation as the food capital of Asia must be credited to to its multiracial society, which cooks up everything from Peking duck and Penang *laksa* to Indian curries and Malaysian *mee*. Selection is beguilingly diverse, colorfully served, and gives gastronomically curious travelers the chance to try a wide variety of intriguing and inexpensive local specialties.

Despite all this, it *is* possible (even easy) to have a mediocre meal in Singapore. A quick look at *Dining Out In Singapore* and *Singapore 101 Meals* (both distributed by the tourist office) will help point you in the right direction. Gourmands should purchase the brilliant *Secret Food Map of Singapore*, which wisely suggests specific dishes at each restaurant. Also useful is *The Food Paper,* a monthly tabloid edited and written by food critic Violet Oon. Suggested

dishes are also mentioned below. Most importantly, patronize those restaurants packed with locals and select dishes which seem popular. Remember that atmosphere often has little to do with the food. An air-conditioned restaurant is certainly more comfortable than a hawkers' center, but many Singaporeans find their best meals in hawker stalls. Just watch the Mercedes pull up!

The following restaurants were chosen for personality, atmosphere, and good food at reasonable prices. Suggestions for the next edition of this book are appreciated. Please include a map with exact location, sample prices, and recommended dishes.

Central Singapore

Fatty's: Fatty, a jovial chef dressed in his ever-present T-shirt, once ruled as the King of Albert Street. After the government forced all street vendors to move to modern food centers, Fatty took his reputation, cooking skills, and personality to Albert Complex where he still packs 'em in. Albert Street near Bencoolen. Cantonese. Inexpensive.

Kwan Yin Vegetarian Restaurant: It's amazing what can be done with bean curd. Located in the Southeast Asia Hotel near the Kuan Yin Temple on Waterloo Road. Cantonese. Inexpensive.

Bugis Street: Singapore's favorite late-night food spot and gathering point for transvestites has been revived under the latest tourist plan. Prices from the street vendors are somewhat high but the lively scene is worth checking out. Victoria and Queen streets near Rochor Road and Cheng Yan Place.

Swee Kee: Singapore's most famous spot for Hainanese chicken rice with homemade chili sauce. 51 Middle Road. Inexpensive.

Yet Con Chicken Rice: As the name implies, the specialty is chicken rice, though locals also rave about the Hainanese-style roast pork (*babi panggang*) with sweet black sauce and pickled vegetables, and steamboat fondue cooked at the table. 25 Purvis Street. Inexpensive.

Great Shanghai: Specialties include fresh seafood, drunken prawns, and chicken baked in a clay pot. Mayfair Hotel on Armenian Street. Shanghainese. Moderate.

Ujagar Singh: One of the less expensive North Indian restaurants in Singapore. Sikh specialties from mutton brain marsala and mutton kebabs to mutton leg curry and salted *lassis*. Nicely situated in a prewar coffee shop on Saint Gregory Place off Hill Street. Inexpensive.

Rendezvous: Singapore's oldest *nasi padang* restaurant has lost some of its old-world atmosphere to modernization but the lunch buffet is still good. Raffles City Shopping Center. Indonesian. Inexpensive.

Tiffin Room: A Raffles Hotel restaurant famous for its timeless atmosphere and colonial tiffin curry, an Indian lunch served with a variety of sambals. Indian and Continental. Expensive.

Orchard Road

Peranakan Place: Several restaurants with unique ambience have been constructed inside this famous cluster of restored terrace houses. Recommended spots include the Plaza, a popular place for beer between shopping trips, and Bibi's Nonya Restaurant, for inexpensive lunches in a beautiful setting. Their nightly Baba Wedding shows are dazzling if somewhat expensive. Trendiest of all is Casablanca Bar and Restaurant, a foreign-owned spot popular with expats. Aziza's Restaurant serves expensive but authentic Nonya cuisine.

Goodwood Hotel: Extravagant buffets in one of Singapore's most attractive hotels. Expensive.

Mandarin Hotel: The Belvedere Restaurant serves top-notch luncheon buffets with unlimited oysters and salmon. The adjacent Chatterbox is known for Hainanese chicken rice. Great views from the top floor. Expensive.

Cairn Court: A slightly off-the-beaten-track restaurant with modestly priced buffet lunches. Famous for their hand-pulled noodle specialties. Cairnhill Hotel. Szechwan.

Silver Spoon: Coffee shop decor but the *laksa* is superb. Supreme House on Penang Road. Moderate.

McDonald's: Only mentioned because it claims to hold the world's record for most Big Macs served on opening day, 45,000. Good place to watch trendy young Singaporeans in their shades and miniskirts. Singapore might only be 239 square miles in area but it boasts 25 McDonald's, 30 Kentucky Fried Chickens, 15 Burger Kings, and a dozen Shakey's—a fast-food density of nearly one outlet for every two square miles.

Chinatown

Mosque Street: The half-dozen restaurants just off New Bridge Road serve roast suckling pig, black chicken soup, and other Teochew specialties. Chiu Wah Lin is the most popular but the others are less crowded. Enjoy a cup of tea in the old-style Tai Tong Hoi Kee Tea House just opposite. Teochew. Inexpensive to moderate.

Murray Street: Singapore's Food Alley in the narrow alley just off Maxwell Road is somewhat similar to Hong Kong's famous lane in Causeway Bay. Restaurants are upscale, polished, and known for their imaginative dishes and unusual regional specialties. Try Hokkien noodles at Ben Hiang, Teochew chicken at Tai Seng, Indonesian *padang* at Kartini, Indian *tandoori* at Moti Mahal, or Hakka meat-stuffed beancurd at Moi Kong Hakka. Popular at lunchtime but practically deserted at night. Expensive.

Ban Seng: Situated in the traditional Teochew District, old-time favorite Ban Seng's specialties include fried crayfish with soya beans, steamed carp with sour plums, stuffed sea cucumber, and a dessert of mashed yams (*oh nee*). 79 New Bridge Road. Inexpensive.

Ellenborough Market: Some of the best Teochew food stalls are located on the third level of this unassuming block where stallholders display specialties on plates and can help with specific recommendations. Also, dessert out on glutinous balls (*ah balling*). New Bridge and Teochew Street. Inexpensive.

Hua Tuo Guan: Chinese have long believed that psychic *yin* and *yang* can be balanced through herbal foods—especially soups—cooked with medicinal herbs. Hua Tuo Guan serves herbal teas, iced plum juices, and medicinal desserts in a renovated shophouse marked by huge brass and copper urns. 22 Tanjong Pagar Road. Inexpensive.

Kingsland: The innovative dishes created at Kingsland—one of Singapore's most popular vegetarian restaurants—range from mock beef satay and mock smoked duck to mock sourfish and authentic yams sautéed with red mushrooms. People's Park Complex #03-43. Inexpensive.

Happy Realm Vegetarian Cafe: Buddhist nuns, robed monks, and backpackers from Chinatown Guesthouse often visit this cafe known for its vegetarian creations such as Robe of

Honor, curried vegetables, and emerald fresh soup. Pearl Centre #03-16. Inexpensive.

Flying Dutchman: Resembling some sort of Dutch ship landlocked amid renovated Chinese shophouses, this cozy two-level restaurant provides a welcome escape from an endless succession of generic food stalls and artificial shopping-mall cafes. The Dutchman serves both continental fare and Dutch specialties such as Dutch pea soup and deep-fried meatballs (*bitterballen*). Duxton Hill Road. Moderate.

Pagi Sore Nasi Padang: As the name implies, this simple coffee shop located in the historic Tanjong Pagar District specializes in Indonesian dishes such as fishhead curry, grilled chicken (*ayam panggang*), and grilled fish (*ikan panggang*). 20 Duxton Road. Inexpensive.

Apollo Hotel: The Luna Coffee Shop has a famous, long-running Nonya luncheon buffet. Moderate.

Little India

Komala Vilas: Singapore's most famous vegetarian cafe offers a downstairs section for light meals and an air-conditioned upstairs room for overheated tourists. This 40-year-old restaurant now serves its endless buffets on aluminum plates rather than banana leaves. Utensils are offered, but Indian food always tastes best when eaten by hand. 76 Serangoon Road. Inexpensive.

Banana Leaf Apollo: This long-running favorite is known for its highly spiced fishhead curry. Waiters will tone down the fiery concoction on request. Also located nearby are another half-dozen Indian restaurants in the low-to-middle price range. 56 Race Course Road. Moderate.

Fut Sai Kai Vegetarian Cafe: Vegetarian chefs in Singapore are often judged by how closely their dishes resemble meat, from pseudo beef creations to sour fish curries. This particular restaurant is known for its vegetarian chop suey (*sai kai song sop*), sweet-and-sour beancurd (*kum chin tao foo*), and sugarcane flowers with black moss and mushrooms. 143 Kitchener Road. Inexpensive.

Arab Street (Kampong Glam)

North Bridge Road: Just opposite the Sultan Mosque in Kampong Glam are three cheap Muslim-Indian restaurants which date from the mid-1930s, Singapore's oldest Indian cafes. Or-

dinary food, but the timeless atmosphere is memorable. The Jubilee serves "High Class Muslim Meals" in its colorful upstairs dining section. The adjacent Islamic and Zam Zam restaurants are known for mutton curries and chicken *biryanis*. 791 North Bridge Road. Inexpensive.

Sabar Menanti: Inside the quaint corner coffee shop called Nam Mui you'll find day laborers and local office workers chowing down on lunchtime Malay specialties such as barbecued fish (*ikan bakar*), beef in coconut sauce (*rendang*), and curried chicken (*ayam opor*). Arrive early before the pots run dry. 62 Kancahar Street. Inexpensive.

HAWKER FOOD STALLS

Whether you're a world traveler or a two-week tourist, hawker centers are the best places to eat in Singapore. Named after the mobile food carts which once roamed the streets, hawker centers offer great food at rock-bottom prices. There are a few ground rules. Diners can sit anywhere and are not obligated to patronize any particular stall. Just claim your table, order soup from one stall, drinks from another, and desserts from a third. Ordering is easy since most stalls specialize in a limited number of dishes clearly labeled in English. Tablesharing is the rule. Pay when you're served. Most stalls serve Chinese food, but Indian, Malay, Indonesian, and Nonya dishes are also popular. One caution: hawkers are extremely competitive and can sometimes get pushy about finding customers. Don't be talked into anything; take your time before selecting.

Central Singapore

Sweet Home Cafeteria: A small collection of breezy food stalls located in a lovely, tranquil park near the National Museum. Pricey but great atmosphere. Travelers staying in the Bencoolen dorms will find this and the Paradiz Food Center very convenient.

Paradiz Food Center: A clean and modern food center with wide selections of Chinese, Indian, and Malay stalls. One of the less expensive hawker centers in town. Selegie Road near Bencoolen.

Satay Club: This attractive collection of open-air Malay food stalls serves up Indian and Chi-

CHINESE MENU

bak kut teh: pork soup highly seasoned with garlic and chilies

bee hoon: rice vermicelli often used in *laksa*

bird's-nest soup: thick soup made from boiled swiftlet nests and barley sugar. An expensive delicacy; more than just regurgitated bird saliva.

carrot cake: giant white radishes steamed and fried in egg, garlic, and chili

char kway teow: fried noodles and clams in a black bean sauce

char siew fan: barbecued pork with rice and sliced cucumber

chicken rice: boiled chicken served over rice steamed in chicken stock. The popular Hainanese version is served with chili-ginger sauce.

chwe chia pow: translucent pork buns filled with prawns, beans, and turnips

claypot rice: baked rice served with Chinese sausages, salted fish, diced chicken, vegetables, and duck

congee: rice porridge

foo yong hai: crab-meat omelette

hokkien mee: thick yellow noodles and vermicelli fried with prawns and pork in a rich sauce

kway teow: flat white rice noodles, also called *hors fun*

mee: spaghetti-like yellow noodles made from wheat flour

mee pok: flat noodles made with wheat and egg, often dusted with flour

mee suah: long noodles kept in dried form

mi fun: rice vermicelli

moi: porridge

or luak: oyster omelette

or chian: oyster omelette

popiah: spring rolls filled with meats, sweet black paste, and vegetables

pow: steamed pasty buns filled with pork in a sweet sauce, chicken sautéed in garlic, sweet red bean paste, or sweet lotus seed

rojak: salad of bean sprouts, pineapple, white turnip, and fried bean cake tossed in a peanut and shrimp paste; the Chinese version of *gado gado*

shark's-fin soup: thick and expensive glutinous soup made from boiled shark fins

steamboat: Chinese fondue. Thinly sliced meats and vegetables are cooked individually at the table in a clear broth. Called Mongolian hot pot in Hong Kong.

swee kow: prawn dumpling soup

tahu pok: stuffed and barbecued bean cakes served with shrimp paste

tung hoon: transparent noodles made from mung beans

yong tau foo: Hakka eggplant and bean curd stuffed with fish paste and minced meat, served in a thick stock

---

nese, but it's Malay *satay* that makes it so famous. It's great fun to watch the muscular Malay guys furiously fan those fires! Near the waterfront on Queen Elizabeth Walk within walking distance of the Raffles. Open only at night. Highly recommended.

Empress Place: An undistinguished building but a handy place for a Malay breakfast of *nasi lemak* before touring Chinatown. On the riverfront just east of Chinatown.

Orchard Road

Newton Circus: This attractive, clean, and convenient food center is justifiably popular with tourists and locals alike. Despite cavils from natives that it's expensive and only for tourists, it's worth the trip for the excellent seafoods and fun atmosphere. Newton Circus is Singapore's late-night spot, packed until the wee hours with trendy nightclubbers. A five-minute cab ride or a 20-minute walk from Orchard Road. A word of caution: merchants are pushy and will overcharge the unwary if they think they can get away with it.

Cuppage Center: Known for its Indian food stalls, Cuppage is crowded at lunchtime with office workers but less hectic in the evening. Located on the second floor of an office complex on Cuppage Road just behind the Centrepoint Shopping Complex. Somewhat cheaper than Newton Circus.

Chinatown

Telok Ayer Food Center: One of Singapore's most memorable eating places is located inside the wrought-iron Victorian pavilion near the waterfront. Packed with frantic office workers at lunchtime but relaxed in the afternoons.

Chinatown Food Centers: Chinatown has two grubby food centers popular with locals and brave visitors. To the rear of People's Park Shopping Center on New Bridge Road is a sad collection of stalls whose saving grace is Toh Kee, a no-nonsense Cantonese joint in operation since 1922. Food stalls inside the Chinatown Shopping Complex serve strange dishes such as fried snake, roast bear claw, and rice porridge with entrails.

DISHES TO TRY

Chinese Food

Singapore restaurants and food stalls serve dishes from southern China (Cantonese, Hokkien, Teochew, Hainan, Hakka), northern China (Beijing and Shanghai), and western China (Szechwan and Hunan). Selection can be somewhat confusing but it's best to organize a large group and go banquet style. Ordering, however, should *not* be by individual selection, since this often results in a boring collection of sweet-and-sours or expensive combinations of shark's-fin soups and fried bear's claws. Instead, let the person most familiar with Chinese food or the restaurant take charge and order for the entire group.

Chinese meals often begin with a cold meat dish, followed by seafood, beef or pork, vegetable, chicken, and finally a soup to cleanse the palate. A well-balanced meal should have the five basic taste sensations of sweet, bitter, salty, spicy, and acidic. Cool yin dishes such as fruit and vegetables should balance spicy yang dishes like meats and hot soups. The following dishes are worth trying.

Beijing: Peking cuisine, the labor-intensive royal cooking of northern China, is quite distinct from southern dishes. Dishes are mildly spiced and often served whole without being diced into bite-sized pieces. Mutton and goat are more popular than pork. Perhaps the most famous dish of the north is Peking duck. First basted with syrup, the bird is then slowly roasted over charcoal while the skin turns a crisp golden brown. In better restaurants the waiter will carve the duck at your table and carefully remove the highly prized skin from the meat. The

skin is then rolled in wafer-thin pancakes and eaten with plum sauce, onions, and cucumbers in a manner somewhat akin to a Mexican taco. The meat is returned to the kitchen to be sauteed in a brown sauce with bean sprouts and later served as duck soup. Some restaurants charge extra for the soup.

Cantonese: The old cliché that the world has only three great cuisines—Chinese, French, and Italian—fails to consider the amazing regional varieties of China. Equally revealing is the Chinese proverb which states that one should ideally be born in Soochow (renowned for beautiful women), dress in Hangchow (best silks), die in Liuchow (best coffin wood), and eat in Guangchow (Canton). Cantonese food is characterized by quick stir-frying in light peanut oil and the modest use of seasonings and delicate sauces to bring out the natural flavors. Stir-frys are often flavored with black beans, oyster sauce, and soy sauces. Freshness and crispness are emphasized. Most Westerners are quite familiar with Cantonese dishes such as sweet and sours, *won ton* soups, spring rolls, and *dim sum* since most Chinese restaurants in the West are owned and operated by Cantonese. Be forewarned that Cantonese food can also be bland, heavy, over-sweet, and smothered under unimaginative sauces made from sugar and thickened starch. Pick your dishes carefully.

Dim Sum: Cantonese hors d'oeuvres are called *dim sum*, a term which literally means "touching the heart." This breakfast-buffet encompasses a wide variety of steamed and fried Chinese appetizers which are wheeled around the restaurant on carts by young girls who traditionally sing rhymes extolling the virtues of the food. These "little hearts" can be fried cakes, miniature pork ribs, fatty chicken feet, or sweet rolls and dumplings stuffed with prawns, pork, and spiced chicken. Simply point at the dishes which look best. Plates are left piled on the table to be counted later to calculate the bill. *Dim sum* is served continually from early morning until mid-afternoon, but it's best to arrive early to enjoy the widest possible selection.

Hokkien: Although most Singaporeans can trace their ancestry to Fuzhou, the capital of Hokkien (Fujian) province, this heavy and simple food has never been very popular here. The one big hit is Hokkien fried *mee* (noodles), considered by many the national dish of Singapore. Other popular Hokkien dishes include pork buns, stewed pork in black bean sauce, and Hokkien spring rolls.

Teochew: The Teochew (Chaozhou or Chiu Chow in Hong Kong) people come from southeastern Guangdong province near Canton (Guangdong). Dominating the hawker industry, they are sometimes called the Sicilians of China because of their fiery temperament and love of hearty food. Seasonings are minimal. Famous dishes include thick shark's-fin soup and lighter dishes such as braised goose and suckling pig served with piquant dipping sauces. Other specialties include *or luak, char kway teow, moi,* and steamboat, a Teochew original now popular with everyone. Meals often begin with a thimbleful of "Iron Buddha" tea, a powerful and astringently bitter concoction that aids digestion and keeps you awake all night.

Hainan: The food from the large island off the coast of southern China includes broiled pork chops, braised steaks, and roast pig with sweet sauces. Although some say the food is unimaginative and overly Westernized, Hainanese chicken rice (*kai fan*) and steamboat are two of Singapore's most popular dishes. Serving this Chinese dish similar to Swiss fondue, the waiter delivers a pot of bubbling broth and an assortment of raw meats, fishes, and vegetables which are dipped briefly in the cauldron before being eaten with chilies and soy sauces. Mongolian barbecue is a variation in which a hot griddle rather than a pot of boiling liquid is used to cook the meats.

Hakka: Basic to the extreme, the food of the hard-working hill people from the western edge of Kwangtung province is chiefly known for its frugal use of animal parts such as pig brains, tripe, and bone stock. Among their most popular dishes are salt-baked chickens, salted cabbage, and *niang do fu* (stuffed bean curd).

Shanghai: Similar to Peking but somewhat sweeter and oilier, Shanghainese cuisine is distinguished by elaborate methods of preparation such as prawn seasoning, crab eggs for cooking fat, and pork stocks. Seafood dishes include braised eel sauté and smoked yellow fish. Shanghainese hairy crabs are all the rage during the autumn months but the most famous dish is "drunken chicken," a whole chicken stuffed with mushrooms, wrapped in lotus leaves, sealed in a clay mudpack, and then slowly baked in a wine sauce for eight hours. The clay pot and a hammer are then presented to the host who whacks away until the vessel cracks open and releases its fragrant aromas. Also try drunken prawns (live shrimps dropped into boiling wine).

Szechwan: The secondmost popular cuisine in Singapore (after Cantonese), this fiery cuisine from the cold mountains of western China might remind you of Padang or Thai food with its prodigious amounts of garlic, chili peppers, and blazing sauces. Not all dishes are hot; some are sweet, sour, or bitter. Try chicken fried with dried chilies, bean curd with minced pork, and sweet-and-sour soups. Another great dish is smoked duck which has been marinated in a mixture of wine, chilies, and orange peel for 24 hours before being smoked over camphor wood chips. Delicious! Other recommended dishes include chili bean paste in wine, eggplant sauteed in garlic sauce, spicy smoked ham, pigeon in bamboo cup, and stewed mutton.

Hunan: Chairman Mao (from Hunan) once said that all the world's greatest revolutionaries come from chili-loving areas. Hunan food is a blazing cuisine which brings fire to the mouth and tears to the eyes. Specialties include air-cured meats, thinly sliced sweet hams, steamed breads, and dark soy sauces which distinguish Hunan from Szechwan dishes.

Indian Food

Where's the best Indian food in Asia? After six months of travel in India, I would agree with those who say that Indian food is best in Singapore. The secret is fresher produce, higher-quality meats, cleaner cooking oils, and the considerable cooking skills of Singapore's Tamil, Punjabi, and Bengali chefs. All place special importance on the complex curries made from spices (cumin, cardamom, coriander, garlic, chili, fennel, etc.) added to a slowly simmering mixture of yellow onions, ripe tomatoes, and heavy yogurt. Curries can be either mild or blazing hot, but rather than running for the water fountain, it's better to eat a few mouthfuls of rice since *nasi* washes away the offending chili oils more effectively than water. Dishes are accompanied by vegetarian side dishes such as *dal* and mango condiments called *chutneys.* Best of all are the freshly baked breads such

INDIAN MENU

biryani: steamed yellow rice with chicken and saffron

chapati: flat unleavened bread made from wholemeal flour

fishhead curry: red snapper in a fiery curry gravy; Singapore's most famous Indian dish

kambing: thick mutton soup served with French bread

kway teow goreng: Indian-style fried noodles

murtabak: fried bread filled with minced mutton and egg and served with a small side dish of curry sauce. Watching the *murtabak* man is half the fun of ordering this delicious bread.

papadum: deep-fried lentil bread usually dipped in curry sauces

paratha: flaky Indian bread fried in oil and served with curry sauce

rojak: fried prawns, potatoes, and bean curd served with sweet curry sauce

roti: bread

as unleavened *chapatis,* light-as-air *puris,* and crispy *papadums.* Top choice is *paratha,* the tasty Singapore classic which provides a good show during preparation. The *paratha* man first works a handful of dough into a thin film almost a meter wide, folds it over into a multi-layered pastry, and then flaps it on the hot-oiled griddle. When eaten straight with a side of curry sauce this delicious bread is *paratha kosong;* filled with minced meat, onion, and egg it becomes a *murtabak.*

South Indian Food: Distinct from northern dishes, south Indian food is a spicy cuisine which uses coconut milks rather than mild yogurts, breads made from rice rather than wheat, and vegetarian ingredients rather than the meat dishes employed by northern chefs. Restaurant styles also differ. Northern Indian restaurants are often expensive joints with elaborate furnishings and tuxedoed waiters. Southern Indian restaurants are mostly inexpensive vegetarian cafes where meals are served on banana leaves rather than china, an authentic touch that drives health authorities mad. Banana-leaf dining is great theater. First, a waiter flaps down the waxy leaf and a pile of steaming rice. Another ladles up mounds of curries, *dals,* and *chutneys.* Food is eaten barehanded to improve

the taste . . . especially with those rivers of curry running down your forearm! One secret to successful feeding is to pinch the rice with the tips of your fingers and then quickly scoop it to the mouth. When all else fails, put your face closer to the leaf. Washbasins in the corner are used for cleaning up. South Indian classics include the somewhat pricey fishhead curry and less expensive specialties like *marsala dosa, keema, vindaloo,* and vegetarian dishes made with okra and *brinjal.*

North Indian Food: North Indian food tends to be milder, smoother, and employ a more subtle use of spices than South Indian dishes. Northern cooks prefer *ghee* (clarified butter) over the heavier oils favored in the south. Mogul cuisine is typified by the *tandoori* in which chicken or meat shish kebabs are marinated and then slowly baked in a clay oven *(tandoor).* Local Indian chefs have also created dishes unique to Singapore such as *kambing,* a rich mutton soup served with chunks of French bread, and *rojak,* an Indian salad of fried prawns, cuttlefish, and vegetables with a sweetish yet spicy sauce. Also try Indian *mee goreng,* thick yellow noodles fried with mutton, bean curd, and peas in a tomato sauce.

Malay Food

Centuries worth of migration between Indonesia and the Malay Peninsula has given Singapore a cuisine which combines the best of both cultures. Malay dishes are often highly spiced with the prodigious use of cloves, chilies, lemon grass, coriander, shallots, prawn paste, tamarind, scented roots, and aromatic grasses. Dishes are generally cooked in the morning and served at room temperature throughout the day. Visitors unaccustomed to three-alarm meals will be happy to learn that Malay dishes are made smoother and milder with the use of heavy coconut creams and rich peanut sauces. The result? *Some of the best food in Singapore!* After Chinese food becomes bland and Indian food repetitive, Malay food will surprise and delight you with its uniqueness. The standard dish is *satay,* which unlike the Indonesian version is marinated in spices *before* barbecuing. Malay soups such as *laksa* and *soto ayam* are delicious broths thickened with liberal amounts of coconut cream. *Nasi lemak,* a smorgasbord breakfast of tasty hors d'oeuvres and rice cooked in coconut milk, is an exciting if somewhat unusual way to begin your day. Malay vegetarian dishes win over even the most dedicated of carnivores. Also try Indonesian-derived recipes such as *gado gado, nasi padang, rendang,* and Malay originals like *tahu goreng, ikan assam,* and *mee goreng.* Malay food is addicting.

The biggest roadblock to becoming a Malay food fanatic is finding it. Because of its complexity and Malay disinclination to be entrepreneurial, Malay food remains largely limited to home cooking and a few food stalls in Singapore's hawker centers. Don't expect a big sign announcing "Malay Food Sold Here." Stalls are often managed by friendly housewives who are great cooks but lack Chinese marketing skills. When you finally find the solitary stall, wedged between the 12th Hainanese Chicken Rice and 17th *mee goreng* stall, it's *closed.*

Nonya Or Peranakan Food

If Malay food is the best in Singapore, then Nonya or Peranakan food is the most unique. Peranakans are the offspring of mainland Chinese males (Babas) and their Straits-born Chinese-Malay wives (Nonyas). Peranakan dishes combine Chinese ingredients such as mushrooms and oyster sauces with Malay spices such as peanuts, coconut creams, and preserved soybeans. The resulting Chinese-Malay cuisine is unique but, like Malay food, difficult to find. Fortunately, a recent revival of Nonya cooking has made dishes like *laksa lemak, mee siam,* and *poh piah* easier to find. Hawker stalls which once served Malay food now sell trendy Nonya specialties.

A MALAY MENU

ayam goreng: Malay fried chicken

gado gado: vegetable salad covered with a peanut and coconut sauce. Served with prawn crackers. A favorite dish of both Malays and Indonesians.

ikan bilis: fried and crunchy anchovies. Served with *nasi lemak.*

ikan sadin: canned sardines in tomato sauce

kari ayam: curry chicken

kerang: fried cockles

lontong: vegetables and rice cakes covered with coconut gravy. One of Singapore's classic dishes. Superb.

mee rebus: Malay noodle soup in a rich and spicy sauce

nasi goreng: fried rice

nasi lemak: Malaysian breakfast. Combination plate of coconut rice, *ikan bilis,* peanuts, and sautéed vegetables. Probably an acquired taste but addictive once you become accustomed to it.

nasi padang: Sumatran style of buffet dining. A dozen individual dishes are brought to your table and laid out for your selection. You pay only for those that you eat. Most Singaporeans just point out a dish in the front window.

rendang: Indonesian-style curry served with beef or chicken. Very spicy.

sambal: fiery chili sauce liberally used in Malay cooking

satay: skewers of chicken, beef, or lamb grilled over charcoal and served with peanut sauce

sayor: Malay for vegetables

soto ayam: spiced chicken soup with vegetables and potatoes

sotong: cuttlefish

tahu goreng: deep-fried bean curd covered with pungent peanut sauce

tahu lemak: bean curd cooked in coconut-milk curry

telor goreng: fried eggs

udang sambal: prawns fried in a sambal hot sauce

NIGHTLIFE

Hotel Shows

Unless you are fortunate enough to be in Singapore during a public festival, the only opportunities to watch traditional dance are the packaged cultural shows sponsored by local hotels. Typical performances include Chinese lion and fan dancers, Indian *bharat natyam,* the Malaysian martial art *bersilat,* and a Malaysian wedding demonstration. Hotel shows are contrived but nevertheless provide an introduction to regional dance forms. Shows cost S$35-45 with dinner, less for show alone. Current venues are listed in *Singapore Visitor.*

Raffles Hotel: Two shows are now being held in the renovated grand dame of Singapore.

NONYA OR PERANAKAN MENU

kueh pie tee: vegetarian won tons

laksa: noodle soup highly spiced with coconut, chilies, and aromatic spices. A classic dish of Singapore.

mee siam: rice vermicelli fried with chili and prawns. Served in a sweet-sour thin gravy.

Peranakan kueh: Nonya sweet rice cakes flavored with coconut and palm sugar

poh piah: vegetarian rice cakes

The most popular is the 45-minute multimedia review, "Raffles Revisited," which relates the history of Singapore via the legends of the Raffles Hotel. Daily at 1100, 1300, and 1400, S$5. "The Life and Times of Singapore" is a brief but colorful recap of the three major cultures which comprise modern Singapore: Chinese, Malay, and Indian. Daily at noon, S$10. Raffles Hotel, Seah Street Entrance, tel. 331-1732.

Mandarin Hotel: "ASEAN Night" features dance and music of Singapore, Malaysia, Thailand, the Philippines, and Indonesia, performed poolside at 1900 nightly except Mondays. Mandarin Hotel, 333 Orchard Rd., tel. 737-4411, S$25 show only, S$45 with dinner.

Hyatt Regency: Poolside "Malam Singapura" showcases the dance and music of Malaysia. Nightly except Sundays at 1900. 10-12 Scotts Rd., S$25 à la carte, S$45 with dinner.

Cockpit Hotel: The latest contender for the tourist buck, "Singapore Sling Show" presents a nightly cultural show in the Cockpit's Merlion Ballroom. 6/7 Oxley Rise, tel. 737-9111, 1900 dinner and 2000 show, S$38 show with buffet.

"Instant Asia": The old show from the now defunct Rasa Singapura Food Fair, and later the Raffles Hotel, moved several years ago to a new location several kilometers from central Singapore. The 1800 dinner is followed by a 45-minute cultural review. Singa Inn Seafood Restaurant, 920 East Coast Rd., tel. 345-1111, free with dinner.

Bibi's Restaurant: This finely restored restaurant in Peranakan Place presents nightly shows of local comics, Singapore amateur theater, or re-creations of a Baba Nonya wedding. 180 Orchard Rd., tel. 732-6966, S$32-45 with Peranakan dinner.

Other Cultural Events

Singapore is neither a cultural capital nor a cultural wasteland, due to the efforts of the Singaporean government.

Western Classical Music: During the symphony season, the Singapore Symphony conducts weekend concerts in the Victoria Concert Hall at Empress Place. Upcoming programs are listed in the local press, in *Singapore Visitor,* and at the tourist office. Victoria Concert Hall, tel. 339-6120, S$10-45.

Chinese Classical Music: The complexity and seemingly cacophonous mixture of ill-related sounds often discourages Western listeners from Chinese music, though with some listening many of the classics are quite tuneful and melodic. Most performances are sponsored by the Singapore Broadcasting Corporation, tel. 256-0401, ext. 2732.

Chinese Opera: Glittering costumes, elaborate makeup, and Technicolor stage displays make Chinese opera one of the most spectacular of all Asian theater arts. Open-air performances of Chinese *wayang* are most common during festivals such as the Festival of Hungry Ghosts and Birthday of the Third Prince, but smaller performances occur on a weekly basis. Since all Chinese street operas require city permits, locations and times can be confirmed at the Singapore Tourist Office.

Nightclubs, Pubs, And Discos

Singapore's less formal nightlife revolves around cocktail lounges, English pubs, hostess clubs, Chinese cabarets, and discos. Dress standards are high and most clubs refuse admittance to

DRINKS AND DESSERTS

bubor chacha: dessert made from sweet potato and tapioca boiled in coconut milk. Served either hot or cold.

bubor hitan: black glutinous rice covered with hot coconut milk

chendol: iced coconut milk and palm-sugar syrup

goreng pisang: banana fritters

ice kachang: shaved-ice dessert served with syrup, evaporated milk, and jellies

tahu chui: soybean milk

Instant Asia review

improperly dressed visitors, so leave the blue jeans, T-shirts, and tennis shoes in your hotel.

Warning: Except for a handful of simple pubs and sidewalk cafes, nightlife in Singapore can be very expensive. Before running up the tab, carefully check cover charges, prices for drinks and appetizers, and if you happen to be a solo male, surcharges for female conversation. Fortunately, some clubs have rolled back prices and instituted no-cover and all-you-can-drink specials as listed in the useful *Guide to Singapore*.

Saxophone Jazz Club: Live jazz performances nightly at the tiny bar next to Cuppage Center just off Orchard Road. The Sax is a great place to hang out and mix with local expatriates, plus it's cover-free and offers happy-hour prices daily 1800-2000. 23 Cuppage Terrace, tel. 235-8385. Highly recommended.

The Yard: Located in a converted Chinese shophouse in trendy Holland Village, this English pub features ales, darts, and an open-air courtyard to the rear. Other nearby pubs and/or wine bars worth checking out include **Beefeaters** at 417 River Valley Rd. and **Palms Wine Bar** down the street. 294 River Valley Rd., tel. 733-9594.

Paddles: Just across the river from Empress Place, Paddles is a comfortable little spot in which to booze away a hot afternoon. 66 Boat Quay Rd., tel. 535-2607.

Tanglin Shopping Center: Several decent pubs and nightclubs are located in the shopping complex just off Orchard Road. Anywhere Nightclub features Tania, the resident band that has entertained locals for over a decade, while California Jam is a hard-rock joint with blasting music played by rather tame DJs. 19 Tanglin Road.

Flag and Whistle English Pub: Renovated Tanjong Pagar historic district features several newish pubs such as this Chinese yuppie hangout known for its steak and kidney pies, ploughman's lunches, and happy hours all day on Sundays. 10 Duxton Hill Rd., tel. 223-1126.

Elvis' Place: The King himself recently descended from a spaceship and was sighted inside this lavender club located in the trendy Tanjong Pagar District. Owners Koh and Jerry Wee claim to possess every recording of Elvis. 1 Duxton Hill Rd., tel. 227-8543.

Zouk: Inside these three adjoining and converted *godowns* you'll find cafes, pubs, restaurants, a cozy wine bar with jazz music that evokes a North African ambience, and an adjacent disco that claims to be the largest in Singapore. 17-21 Jiak Kim St., tel. 738-2988.

Orchard Towers: One-stop shopping for live bands and discos here. Celebrities Nightclub in the basement features live rock bands from Singapore, the Philippines, and occasionally the States. Caesar's on the second floor is a Romanesque place with live bands, DJs, and toga-clad waitresses. Top Ten on the fourth floor is a converted cinema, which explains the high ceilings, terraced seating, and echoing acoustics. All charge covers of S$15 weekdays and S$25 weekends. Orchard Towers, 400 Orchard Road.

Somerset Bar: An expensive jazz club with top-notch American and European jazz artists. Westin Plaza Hotel, 2 Stamford Plaza, tel. 338-8585.

Red-light Districts

Singapore for the bachelor can't compare with Bangkok or Manila but sleaze discreetly survives on Kampong Kapor Road between Desker and Rowell streets, Flanders off Petain, and the alley off Ophir south of Queen. Singapore's largest red-light district is in Geylang, about five km east of downtown.

SHOPPING

Shopping in Singapore's air-conditioned malls is hardly an exotic experience but it's a comfortable way to pick up electronics and camera supplies. Prices are low since Singapore is a duty-free port, but rock-bottom prices have largely disappeared because of inflation, soaring rents and wages, and the increasing strength of the Singapore dollar. The bottom line: prices are competitive with Hong Kong but not necessarily cheaper than in America. The best source of accurate information on shops and their specialties is *The Secret Map of Singapore*.

Shopping Tips

Compare Prices: All possible purchases should be priced at home *before* going to Singapore. Try local discount houses or call 47th Street Photo (800-221-7774). Ballpark estimates of prices in Singapore can be checked before departure with the Singapore Tourist Promotion Board. The STPB also suggests you shop around, since prices vary sharply even on "fixed-price" items. Department store price tags help indicate general ranges.

Bargaining: Despite suggestions to the contrary, bargaining is *de rigueur* throughout much of Singapore. Ask for 30-50% off jewelry, 20-30% on other items, and 10-20% in fixed-price stores. Remember the basic rule of bargaining: discounts are only given to those who *ask*.

Methods of Payment: Traveler's checks should be converted into Singapore dollars before shopping, since checks are only accepted

at poor exchange rates. Credit cards are highly recommended for large purchases to provide protection against fakes, misrepresentation, poor workmanship, product switching, and so on. Besides providing an inexpensive form of insurance, credit cards also offer interest-free loans until due date.

Other Guidelines: Avoid touts and beware of super-low prices on brand-name goods unless you are searching for an imitation. Always insist on a receipt and a worldwide warranty. National guarantees of workmanship or authenticity are useless after you've returned home. Check serial numbers on all electronics to make sure they match the warranty. Never accept photocopied warranties.

The STPB: Merchants who display gold Merlions have promised to sell their goods at reasonable prices, issue receipts, and display tags which list prices and discounts. Unethical practices should be reported to the Singapore Tourist Promotion Board.

What To Buy

Electronics: Asian dumping practices and the purchasing power of American chains have made electronics cheaper in New York than in Singapore. Prices, however, are lower than elsewhere in Southeast Asia, so stock up on film, lenses, and other accessories.

Clothing: Prices for top-quality fashions from reputable shows are comparable to the States. Tailor-made suits are much cheaper in Bangkok because of sharply lower wages. Beware of seconds, rejects, and overruns.

Handicrafts and Antiques: Singapore offers Southeast Asia's widest selection of Asian antiques and handicrafts. Most can generally be taken out of the country without special licenses or permits. Prices are lower than in the States but higher than in the countries of origin. For example, Balinese woodcarvings that cost US$20 in Bali can cost US$60-80 in Singapore. Selection and quality are also better in country of origin.

Where To Shop

Orchard Road: Singapore's Golden Mile is nonstop department stores, air-conditioned shopping complexes, and upscale boutiques. Prices in most stores are fixed, but bargaining continues in smaller stores. Orchard Road is more expensive than elsewhere because of higher rents.

Central Singapore: Shopping centers in central Singapore should theoretically offer lower prices because of lower rents. Determined shoppers can peruse the shops in Albert Complex, Rochor Centre, and Bras Basah Complex.

Chinatown: People's Park Shopping Complex and People's Park Center offer some of the lowest electronics prices in town. Perhaps, but be prepared to bargain aggressively or be fleeced by unscrupulous shopkeepers. Comparison shopping is a *must*.

Little India: Serangoon Road and the nearby alleys offer the most colorful shopping experience in Singapore. The perfect place for bangles, baubles, and psychedelic posters of Shiva.

Arab Street: An old-fashioned shopping district brimming with Indonesian batiks, silks, Muslim laces, Filipino handbags, silver filigree, *jamu*, and religious paraphernalia from Korans and prayer rugs to *haji* caps. Walking-shopping tours start at Arab and Beach streets near the wonderful basket shops.

LEAVING SINGAPORE

Airport

Singapore is a good place to find cheap airline tickets. Try STA (tel. 734-5681) in the Orchard Parade Hotel, Airmaster Travel (tel. 338-3942) at 36 B Prinsep Street, and adjacent Airpower Travel (tel. 337-1392) at 36 C Prinsep Street.

Others advertise in the *Straits Times,* but be cautious about friendly strangers with great deals—swindles have been reported. Note that fares between Singapore and Malaysia are the same dollar figure in both currencies. This means that identical tickets are about 30% cheaper when purchased in Malaysia.

Taxis to the airport from Orchard Road cost S$15-18 including the S$3 airport toll. Budget travelers on Bencoolen can take bus 390 to the airport from Bras Basah Road. Departure tax is S$5 to Malaysia and S$12 otherwise.

To Malaysia

Bus: Buses for Malaysia depart from the Lavender Bus Terminal (tel. 293-5915) at Lavender and Kallang Bahru and, more conveniently, from the Ban San Bus Terminal at the corner of Queen and Arab streets, near the Bugis MRT terminal. However, service is most frequent from the Lavender Street terminus. From Victoria Street take buses 122, 133, 145, or 147, or take the MRT to the Lavender station, then take another bus north or walk for about 30 minutes.

Johor Baru can be reached by taxi or bus 170 from Rochor Road, Rochor Canal Road, or Bukit Timah Road. Buses continue from the Johor Baru bus terminal to all destinations in Malaysia.

Taxi: Share taxis are a fast and convenient way to reach Malaysia. Fares are about 50% higher than for ordinary buses. Taxis leave from the Ban San terminal at Queen and Arab streets, or contact Malaysia Taxi Service (tel. 298-3831) at 290 Jalan Besar or Kuala Lumpur Taxi (tel. 223-1889) at 191 New Bridge Road.

Train: Current schedules are shown in the transportation chart, though the tourist office and Singapore Railway Station on Keppel Road (tel. 222-5165) have exact departure times and prices. The train station can be reached from Orchard Road with bus CBD 1. From Bencoolen Street take buses 97, 125, 146, or 163.

Ship: The cruise ship *Muhibah* sails from Singapore to Kuantan (east coast of peninsular Malaysia), Kuching (Sarawak), and Kota Kinabalu (Sabah) before returning to Singapore. The ship has a swimming pool, a gymnasium, a restaurant, and car facilities. Contact Searo Feri Agencies (tel. 225-9938) in the Jit Pob Building at 19 Keppel Road, or Mansfield Travel (tel. 737-9688) behind the Ocean Building on Collier Quay.

To Thailand

Travelers in a great hurry may want to skip Malaysia and head directly to Thailand by air, train, or bus.

Air: Budget travel agents in Singapore currently charge about S$185-220 one-way to Bangkok or S$350-400 roundtrip. Hat Yai and Phuket in southern Thailand are reached via Penang, a highly recommended stop if you only have time for one destination in Malaysia.

Train: Malaysia has two train lines but the line that connects to Thailand runs from Singapore through Kuala Lumpur, Butterworth, Alor Star, and the border crossing at Padang Besar before reaching Hat Yai the following day. Exact departures and fares can be confirmed at the

LEAVING SINGAPORE

BUS SERVICE TO MALAYSIA

DESTINATION	HOURS	FARE (S$)	DEPARTURES
Johor Baru	30 min.	1.50	Every 10 minutes
Malacca	5	11	Hourly 0800-1600
Kuala Lumpur	9	17	0900, 2100
Ipoh	12	25	1830
Penang	14	31	1830
Mersing	4	11	0900, 1000, 2000
Kuantan	8	16	0900, 1000, 2000
Kota Baru	14	30	0730

TRAIN SERVICES TO MALAYSIA AND THAILAND

DESTINATION	TYPE	HOURS	1ST,	2ND,	3RD	DEPARTURES
Kuala Lumpur	Express	6				0700, 1500
	Normal	9	60	28	14	0745, 0830, 1625, 2000
Penang	a/c	14			50	0700
	Non-a/c	14			40	0700
Bangkok	Express	23		106	42	2000

FERRY SERVICES TO BATAM AND TANJUNG PINANG

DESTINATION	COMPANY	FARE (S$)	DEPARTURES
Batam	Yang, Indo Falcon	20	hourly 0800-1800
Batam	Dino, Neptune Orient	20	hourly 0800-1800
Tanjung Pinang	Inasco	65	1000, 1430
Tanjung Pinang	Dino	60	0930, 1500

tourist office or by calling the Singapore Railway Station at 222-5165.

The International Express is fast but expensive due to supplemental charges and somewhat inconvenient since it requires an overnight stop in Butterworth. Undoubtedly the most luxurious and expensive option is the new Orient Express, which runs weekly between Singapore and Bangkok.

Bus: Thailand is, in my opinion, far too distant for bus travel unless you are impoverished and desperate to reach the Land of Smiles in record time without breaking the bank. The main bus departure point to Thailand is at the Golden Mile Complex, 5001 Beach Rd., near the Lavender MRT terminal. Numerous travel agents at the complex charge S$25-30 to Hat Yai and S$55-65 to Bangkok.

To Indonesia

Air travel is the quickest and most convenient method to reach Indonesia, though a sea/air journey through the Riau Archipelago saves some money (US$25-40) and provides a look at the outlying islands.

Air: Several airlines fly from Singapore to Jakarta, Bali, and various towns in Sumatra such as Medan, Padang, Palembang, and Pekanbaru. Discounted one-way airfare to Jakarta is currently around S$180-220, while roundtrip is about S$250-280. Bali costs S$420-460 one-way or S$640-680 with stops in Jakarta and Yogyakarta. Budget tickets are sold at STA, Airmaster Travel, and Airpower Travel.

Sea and Air: Direct sea connections from Singapore to Indonesia do not exist, but indirect passage with a combination of boat and air is possible via Batam and Bintam, two Indonesian islands which comprise the Riau Archipelago immediately south from Singapore. Although the journey is somewhat time-consuming, it's less expensive and certainly more interesting than a direct flight from Singapore. Figure on a full day of travel and savings over direct air connections of US$25-50.

More information can be found under "Riau Archipelago" and "Pekanbaru" in the Indonesia chapter.

Step one is a high-speed ferry from Finger Pier or the World Trade Centre in Singapore to the island of Batam, an upscale resort island popular with Singaporeans. Over 20 daily departures from 0730 to 1800 are provided by Yang Passenger Ferry Service (tel. 223-9902), Dino Shipping (tel. 221-4916), Indo Falcon Shipping (tel. 220-3251), Neptune Orient Lines (tel. 278-9000), and Inasco Enterprises (tel. 224-9797). Fares are S$16-20 one-way and S$25-30 roundtrip. Reservations are necessary only on weekends.

Garuda and/or Merpati fly daily from Batam international airport to Jakarta (about US$110), Padang, Pekanbaru, Palembang, Balikpapan, and Pontianak.

A second ferry continues to Bintam (principal town is Tanjung Pinang), from where Merpati flies to similar destinations, though service is less frequent than from Batam.

Alternatively, several shipping companies provide direct passage from Singapore to Tanjung Pinang on Bintam Island. Dino Shipping departs at 1000 and 1500, takes about four hours, and costs S$50 one-way and S$80 return. Passengers proceed through customs and immigration and, unless advance arrangements were made with a travel agent in Singapore, usually spend a night in Tanjung Pinang.

Onward travel from Tanjung Pinang is best done by air, though a few hardy souls might consider a sea connection. Adventurous travelers seeking a Conradian experience can take medium-sized boats from Tanjung Pinang to Pekanbaru in Sumatra, a 15- to 24-hour banana-boat experience that costs US$12-18 depending on class. Buses continue from Pekanbaru to Bukittinggi and then up to Lake Toba. Reports vary wildly on the trip; some travelers love the journey while others find it monotonous but tolerable.

Another option is the twice-monthly Pelni ship KM *Lawit* to either North Sumatra (near Medan) or Jakarta. The *Lawit* is a luxurious German-built ship with seven first-class cabins, 10 second-class cabins, and covered deck class for 866 passengers. Total fare is S$120-240 depending on class.

Note: Travelers intending to catch a Pelni boat should arrive in Tanjung Pinang on the correct day or expect to be stranded while waiting for air passage.

I have always had a fanatic belief that travel enriched individual lives, increased the community's prosperity, raised a nation's living standards, opened political barriers, and most important, functioned as the most effective eye-opener between different cultures. We in the travel business are a lucky lot to be in such a useful, joyful, and peaceful endeavor
　　　　　　　　—Eugene Fodor, *Condé Nast Traveler*

People generally think of travel in terms of displacement in space, but a long journey exists simultaneously in space, in time, and in the social hierachy . . . Travel can hardly ever fail to wreak a transformation of some sort, great or small, and for better or for worse, in the situation of the traveller.

　　　　　　　　—Claude Lévi-Strauss, *Tristes Tropiques*

Do not be amazed by the true dragon.
　　　　　　　　—Dogen Zenji, *Fukanzazenji*

THAILAND

In traveling: a man must carry knowledge with him, if he would bring home knowledge.

—James Boswell,
Life of Samuel Johnson

There are only three things which make life worth living: to be writing a tolerably good book, to be in a dinner party for six, and to be traveling south with someone whom your conscience permits you to love.

—Cyril Connolly,
A Romantic Friendship

A good holiday is one spent among people whose notions of time are vaguer than yours.

—J.B. Priestley

INTRODUCTION

For most Westerners, Thailand's image as an Eastern paradise perhaps derives from *The King And I* and sobriquets bestowed by creative copywriters—Land of Smiles, Land of the Free, The Most Exotic Country in Asia. While the hyperbole is somewhat excessive, Thailand unquestionably deserves its accolade as one of the world's premier vacation destinations. Annual tourist arrivals have exploded in the last decade from under one million to over six million for excellent reasons: superb archaeological sites, glittering temples, lively nightlife, outstanding shopping, superlative culture, exuberant festivals, and culinary treasures to delight even the most demanding gourmet. Thailand is also blessed with an incredibly varied range of natural attractions: expansive national parks, fertile plains, remote jungles, pristine beaches washed by turquoise waters, and tropical islands bathed in endless sunshine.

All this is perfectly complemented by the Thai people, who have graciously preserved the traditions of a unique culture while embracing the conveniences of modern living. Perhaps because of their religion and belief in *chai yen* (cool heart) and *sanuk* (life is a pleasure!), Thais display an extraordinary sense of serenity, courtesy, humor, and well-being. More than anything else, it is the people that make Thailand such a wonderful place to visit.

HISTORY

Thailand's earliest recorded inhabitants were Buddhist Mons who formed the loosely knit Dvaravati kingdom in the Chao Praya basin from the 6th to 11th centuries. From the 8th to 12th centuries, Hindu Khmers expanded westward from Kampuchea and absorbed the Mons into their powerful empire. Mons today have largely disappeared in Thailand, although a sizable Mon community still exists in Myanmar. The Thai (Tai) people arrived later; two theories speculate as to their origins. Most believe they migrated from southern China during the 11th and 12th centuries and settled among the Khmers and Mons already residing in the central plains. Others argue that Neolithic cave settlements near Kanchanaburi and recent discoveries of a 6,000-year-old Bronze culture at Ban Chiang prove that the Thais preceded the Mons and Khmers.

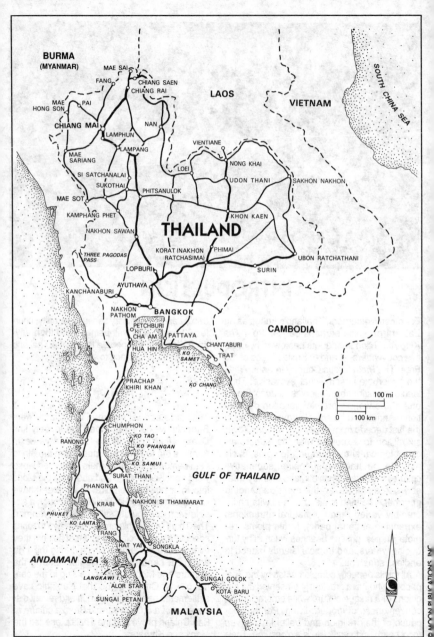

SIGHTSEEING HIGHLIGHTS

Bangkok

Thailand's rich and kaleidoscopic tapestry of tourist attractions is enough to keep most visitors busy for months, though a single region could be explored well in a month. Visitors generally arrive by air at Bangkok, a chaotic and unnerving metropolis of immense traffic jams and modern highrises. Appalled by the problems, many travelers make the mistake of pausing only long enough to buy a plane ticket and then moving out as quickly as possible. While Bangkok is certainly an urban planner's nightmare, it is also home to dozens of dazzling Buddhist temples, outstanding restaurants, superb shopping, and one of the liveliest nightlife scenes in the world. You will also be surprised at the vitality and friendliness of many of its eight million residents . . . if you survive the heat and congestion.

Vicinity Of Bangkok

It may sound implausible, but enough historical monuments, beaches, and natural wonders are located within a 200-km radius of Bangkok to keep most visitors busy for weeks, if not months.

Pattaya: Thailand's eastern seaboard boasts several highly developed beach resorts, of which Pattaya is the most famous. One of the largest beach resorts in Asia, this low-powered Riviera of the East annually attracts over a million pleasure-seekers for its breathtaking range of water sports, restaurants, and legendary nightlife. Lively, chaotic, exciting, polluted, highly commercialized, and tacky, Pattaya in the past catered almost exclusively to military personnel or single businessmen who filled the bars and nightclubs. Today the resort appeals primarily to families, with attractions such as zoos, botanical gardens, and water parks for the kiddies. Although the beaches are inferior to those of Phuket or Samui, the proximity to Bangkok makes it convenient for visitors with limited time.

Ko Samet: To escape the high-rise development of Pattaya, many travelers continue eastward to this *kris*-shaped island south of Rayong. The beaches here are fairly good (though they can't compare with those in the deep south), and facilities are limited to simple bungalows and small restaurants that shut down at sunset. The remote, peaceful, and quiet alternative to Pattaya.

Nakhon Pathom: Often visited on a day-trip from Bangkok or as a brief stop en route to Kanchanaburi, this small town one hour west of Bangkok is home to the world's tallest Buddhist monument.

Damnern Saduak: Thailand's most authentic floating market, two hours south of Bangkok, is much less commercialized than the artificial floating bazaar in Bangkok. Take a tour or see it yourself with an early start.

Kanchanaburi: This beautiful and relaxing region, three hours east of Bangkok, offers inexpensive floating guesthouses, refreshing waterfalls, hiking, and cool caves filled with Buddhas. Highly recommended for history buffs (the Bridge over the River Kwai is located here), nature lovers, and anyone annoyed with Bangkok's traffic jams.

Ayuthaya: For over 400 years the riverine-island town of Ayuthaya, two hours north of Bangkok, served as the second royal capital of Thailand. Though largely destroyed by the Burmese in 1767, many of the restored architectural ruins provide eloquent testimony to the splendor of Thailand's most powerful empire. Ayuthaya and Sukothai are Thailand's largest and most impressive archaeological sites.

Lopburi: Although nothing special, Lopburi offers some modest Khmer ruins and an old summer capital for Ayuthayan kings and makes a convenient stopover en route to the Northeast.

Khao Yai National Park: Thailand's most popular park, four hours northeast of Bangkok, boasts a dozen hiking trails, refreshing waterfalls, and protected wildlife such as elephants and hornbills. Another popular stop en route to the Khmer monuments of the Northeast.

Central Thailand

Sukothai: In 1238 the Thai people proclaimed their independence from Khmer suzerainty and founded Sukothai, the first truly independent Thai capital. For over a century Sukothai ruled the region and created a Golden Age of Thai Arts that left behind a treasure trove of outstanding temples, stupas, and elegant Buddhas. Most of the ruins have been restored and surrounded by manicured gardens and refreshing pools. A brief visit to *both* Ayuthaya and Sukothai is highly recommended for visitors interested in Thai architecture or history.

Si Satchanalai and Kampang Phet: Satellite towns of Sukothai with architecture dating from the 13th and 14th centuries. Both can be visited as side trips from Sukothai.

SIGHTSEEING HIGHLIGHTS

Northern Thailand

Chiang Mai: With its wealth of cultural and historical attractions, superb shopping, great food, friendly people, and delightful weather, Chiang Mai deservedly ranks as one of Thailand's leading tourist destinations. Unlike many Asian cities, which have lost their charm and character from unmanageable growth, this city of one million residents has graciously preserved many of its lovely teak homes and tree-shaded roads. Chiang Mai also serves as a convenient base for trekking into the countryside, touring the infamous Golden Triangle area, and visiting the historic towns of Lamphun and Lampang.

Hilltribes: Living in the remote highlands near the Thai-Burma-Laos borders are shifting agriculturalists who cling to ancient lifestyles despite encroaching Westernization and assimilation efforts by the Thai government. An organized trek of five to 10 days is a unique and memorable experience.

Mae Hong Son: The Shangri-La atmosphere of this small village near the Burmese border attracts travelers who want to get slightly off the beaten track.

Golden Triangle: For over 20 years a steady stream of travelers has bused from Chiang Mai to Thaton, floated down the Kok River to Chiang Rai, and then continued up to Chiang Saen—the real heart of the Golden Triangle. Today, opium production has largely shifted to Laos and Burma, and tour buses are more common than drug warlords—don't expect a Wild West atmosphere.

Northeastern Thailand

The sprawling plateau bordered by Laos and Cambodia is Thailand's forgotten destination. Known locally as the Issan, the dry and rugged northeast is home to a boisterous people with a distinctive culture, a handful of impressive Khmer temples, and several worthwhile national parks. Otherwise, there is little of great interest—save this region for last.

Korat: Nakon Ratchasima is an undistinguished city which serves as the gateway to the Khmer temples and national parks of the northeast.

Khmer Monuments: Once under the suzerainty of the Khmers, the northeast today offers several impressive stone castles erected by the Cambodians to honor their gods and kings. Two of the most impressive are at Pimai and Phanom Rung near Korat, a convenient launching base for visitors with limited time.

Ban Chiang: This important archaeological site, where the world's first Bronze Age civilization flourished some 6,000 years ago, is primarily of interest to archaeologists.

Surin: Visitors from around the world arrive each November to attend the enormously popular Elephant Round-Up of Surin.

Ubon Ratchathani: Famous for its Candle Festival, which marks the beginning of Buddhist Lent. Festivals are a major attraction in the northeast.

Phu Kradung National Park: A forested plateau situated between 1,200 and 1,500 meters; mysterious, moody, and icy cold at nights.

Southern Thailand

The tropical beaches of southern Thailand are, together with those of the Philippines, the finest in Southeast Asia. All are in various stages of development and appeal to different classes of travelers.

Hua Hin: The first major beach resort south of Bangkok appeals to European families seeking a middle-priced sun-and-fun destination without the tawdriness of Pattaya. Safe, clean, and easy to reach.

Ko Samui: This Penang-sized island, with its superb beaches and lovely coconut palms, was first opened in the 1970s by hippie travelers who quietly whispered about the tranquil, virgin hideaway. By the mid-1980s, commercial developers were constructing international-standard hotels, restaurants, nightclubs, and a small airport to receive daily flights from Bangkok. Despite these disturbing trends, much of Ko Samui remains a destination of great beauty and tranquility.

Phuket: Blessed with magnificent coves and powdery white beaches, Phuket has developed into Southeast Asia's largest and most popular seaside resort—the Waikiki of the East. Although much more commercialized than Ko Samui, the island offers the upscale visitor an outstanding array of luxurious hotels, superb restaurants, water sports, and nightclubs that go full tilt until sunrise. A wild place for those with enough money to keep the game going. Travelers torn between choosing lively Phuket or idyllic Ko Samui should visit both.

Ko Phi Phi: This exquisite little island located midway between Phuket and Krabi is the first of an archipelago that stretches all the way to Malaysia. Ko Phi Phi is stunning, small, and packed to capacity during the winter tourist season. Travelers are already discovering the more remote, untouched islands to the south.

BANGKOK'S CLIMATE

	Jan.	Feb.	March	April	May	June	July	Aug.	Sept.	Oct.	Nov.	Dec.
Avg. Maximum C	32°	32°	34°	35°	34°	33°	32°	32°	32°	31°	31°	31°
Avg. Maximum F	90°	90°	94°	95°	94°	92°	90°	90°	90°	88°	88°	88°
Rainy Days	2	1	3	4	18	19	19	19	17	14	4	1

Sukothai Period, 1220-1378

The brief but brilliant kingdom of Sukothai marks the true beginning of the Thai nation and remains to this day a source of great pride. While Sukothai's preeminence lasted less than 200 years, it gave rise to uniquely personified forms of architecture, sculpture, and even political structure. Under the leadership of King Ramkamheng (1278-1318), revered today as the father of Thailand, Sukothai fused Khmer and Mon traditions into a dynamic kingdom that ruled Southeast Asia from Laos to Malaysia. Military power and economic prosperity allowed the development of highly refined artistic achievements, including the world-renowned Sawankalok celadon and Buddha styles of great creativity and sensitivity. Ramkamheng's successors were less ambitious; by the late 14th century Sukothai had become a vassal state of upsurgent Ayuthaya.

Ayuthaya Period, 1378-1767

Sukothai's gradual decline was followed by the rise of Ayuthaya. Within a century of its founding by an ambitious Tai prince from U Thong, this riverine capital had become a major military power and the grandest city in Southeast Asia. Western visitors who arrived during the 16th and 17th centuries described Ayuthaya as a splendid metropolis with a population larger than London's. Among the *farangs* (foreigners) was Constantine Phaulkon, a Greek adventurer who rose to great power in the court of King Narai. After he attempted but failed to convert the king to Christianity, a palace rebellion broke out in which Phaulkon was executed and all Westerners expelled. It was during this period of self-imposed isolation that Ayuthaya created its own golden age of arts and architecture. This came to an end after the Burmese became jealous of their wealth and mounted a series of military campaigns against the city. In 1763 the Burmese attacked, and after two years of resistance they had slaughtered most of the population and burned the city to the ground. Not only did they destroy the artistic and literary heritage of Ayuthaya, they also pulled down many of the magnificent Buddhist temples and reliquaries—an act of horror which still profoundly shocks the Thais.

Bangkok Period, 1767-Present

The destruction of Ayuthaya was a devastating setback. But with typical Thai resilience, an ambitious half-Chinese soldier named Taksin rallied the nation and established a new capital in Thonburi, a sleepy fishing village just across the river from modern Bangkok. Within 10 years Taksin drove the Burmese from Thailand and expanded Siamese sovereignty from Chiang Mai to the deep south. As the son of a Chinese tax collector, Taksin repopulated the country with Teochew Chinese trade merchants, whose taxes provided significant revenue for the fledgling state. But the strain of long years of warfare took its toll, and Taksin apparently went insane with delusions of grandeur and paranoia. After imagining himself an incarnate Buddha, Taksin was executed in the manner prescribed for royalty: placed in a velvet sack and beaten to death with a sandalwood club.

Word of the coup d'etat eventually reached General Chakri, a popular Thai military leader on expedition in Cambodia. Chakri was called back to Thonburi and crowned King Rama I, first ruler of the dynasty which continues to the present day. Fearful of attack by Burmese forces, Rama I transferred his capital across the river to present-day Bangkok and attempted to re-create the former magnificence of Ayuthaya with the construction of royal temples and palaces. The city continued to be called Bangkok by Western mapmakers, but Rama I renamed it a multisyllabled Sanskrit moniker abbreviated as Krung Thep

SUGGESTED ITINERARIES IN THAILAND

DESTINATION	1 MONTH	2 MONTHS	3 MONTHS
Bangkok	1 week	1 week	2 weeks
Chiang Mai	7 days	3 weeks	3 weeks
Sukothai/Ayuthaya	1 day	3 days	4 days
Kanchanaburi	4 days	1 week	10 days
East Coast	2 days	4 days	1 week
Northeast	—	4 days	2 weeks
Ko Samui	1 week	1 week	10 days
Phuket	—	3 days	4 days

("City of Angels"). Rama II (1809-1824), an outstanding poet, is chiefly remembered as the author of the Thai Ramayana. The British defeat of the Burmese during the reign of Rama III (1824-1851) allowed the Thais to expand their national boundaries to Malaysia, Laos, and Vietnam.

The King And I

Thailand's modern phase begins with King Mongkut (Rama V, 1851-1868), better known to the Western world as the autocratic despot in *The King and I*. Mongkut was actually an enlightened ruler whose imaginative diplomacy kept Thailand free from the European colonial expansionism that swallowed Burma, Malaysia, and French Indochina. During his 25 years of monkhood prior to being crowned Rama V, Mongkut learned a dozen languages, studied astronomy and modern history, and, perhaps most importantly, established the Thammayut sect of Buddhism which purified the religion and made it less vulnerable to Western ideology. His search for knowledge convinced him that Thailand's only hope for political independence lay through European-style reforms such as those proposed by his English governess, Anna Leonowens, who eventually penned her fanciful memoirs, *The English Governess at the Siamese Court*. Anna was apparently an unhappy and homesick widow who plagiarized old books on Burma and stitched it all together in her book, which portrayed Mongkut as Rousseau's Noble Savage and Anna as the prim Victorian Christian who single-handedly modernizes the backward nation. Anna's gruesome tales of eastern harem life supported her after

she left Bangkok (and certainly made a great deal of money for Yul Brynner), but no race of people enjoy having foreigners laugh at one of their great men—both the book and film have been banned in Thailand. Still, several years ago the present queen took an entourage of 45 people to see Yul Brynner star in the New York stage production!

King Chulalongkorn, 1868-1910

Mongkut's son, Chulalongkorn, continued Mongkut's policies of transforming Thailand from a medieval kingdom into a modern and progressive nation. Chulalongkorn outlawed slavery, developed educational opportunities, and balanced the territorial ambitions of the British and French with modest concessions to both countries. During his 42-year reign—second longest in the country's history—Chulalongkorn completely reorganized its administrative system and abandoned several ancient royal customs including ceremonial prostration. He nevertheless clung to some autocratic customs such as polygamy on a grand scale, keeping a grand total of 92 wives who bore him some 77 children. Chulalongkorn also continued to appoint men of royal descent to high administrative posts, a practice which offended the European-educated elite. Despite his reluctance to grant full democratic rights to his people, his long list of achievements has made him the most honored of all past kings.

Modern Times

Chulalongkorn's bold reforms also created a new bourgeois intelligentsia unhappy with its lack of power within the royalist government. The pressure cooker finally blew in 1932 when a bloodless coup d'etat instigated by French-educated Thai intellectuals supported by the military toppled the absolute monarchy. A constitutional government headed by an army general was formed and Siam was renamed Thailand. The Thai government declared war on the Western allies in 1941 after the Japanese invaded, a face-saving formality which allowed them to recover territories lost to the French and British. With the defeat of the Japanese, a group of Free Thai politicians seized power and placed King Rama VII on the throne. This experiment with democracy ended when the young king was mysteriously murdered in his bed and a military dictatorship seized power. Except for a three-year hiatus of democratic rule in the mid-1970s, Thailand has since been ruled by an alliance of military and civilian politicians.

GOVERNMENT

Thailand is a constitutional monarchy with a bicameral legislature consisting of a Senate appointed by the king and a National Assembly elected by the people. The National Assembly is composed primarily of the liberal-leaning Chart Thai, Social Action, and Democrat parties, three political groups who often form coalitions to work with the military. Both chambers elect a prime minister who chooses a cabinet of 20 ministers. Thailand's leading political figure of the early 1980s was smiling Prem Tinsulanonda, a handsome enigma who confounded the critics by holding the job of prime minister for almost eight years—an amazing accomplishment when you consider that Thailand since 1932 has suffered through a dozen coups and 13 constitutions. Nineteen eighty-eight proved to be a watershed in Thai politics after public pressure for an elected leader brought the arrival of Chatichai Choonhavan, a business-minded politician who favors democracy over military rule. Chatichai fell from power in 1992 during a military coup in which dozens of citizens were murdered near Democracy Monument in Bangkok.

Thailand today appears to be moving toward a compromise government of military influence but civilian control. The emerging hierarchy seems to be comprised of freely elected democratic leaders who work with ex-military leaders, the government bureaucracy, and powerful Chinese businessmen who control the economy.

The Monarchy

Another stabilizing factor is the overwhelming prestige of the royal family. Although the monarchy was shorn of its powers half a century ago, the Thais continue to view their king as a near-divine being who carries the real force of governmental power. The present ruler, Bhumipol Adulyadej, was born in 1927 in Cambridge, Massachusetts, where his father was studying medicine at Harvard University. Adulyadej received his education in Switzerland before claiming the throne as Rama IX in 1950. Not only amiable and intelligent, he is also a gifted painter and a talented jazz saxophonist who has led all-star jam sessions with such luminaries as bandleader Les Brown and singer Patti Page! His jazz compositions include "Hungry Man's Blues" (can you imagine Queen Elizabeth writing a jazz ballad?) and the three-movement "Manora Ballet," previewed in Vienna during a royal visit. Despite an automobile accident which took an eye, his deft handling of a sailboat won him the gold medal at an international yachting competition. In what is now the longest reign of any Thai king, Bhumipol has earned immense popularity as the working monarch who guides and unifies the nation as head of state and protector of national traditions. Based on Thailand's laws of succession, Crown Prince Maha Vajiralongkorn, the king's only son, will succeed his father to the throne, although his sister, Princess Maha Chakri Sirindorn, enjoys great popularity among the Thai people. Portraits of the king, queen, and royal family are seen everywhere in Thailand. All foreign visitors are expected to behave respectfully toward the royal family, an acceptable caveat since there is little doubt that the Thai monarchy has *earned* this honor.

THE PEOPLE

The Thais

Thailand is one of the most racially homogeneous countries in Southeast Asia: about 82% of the country's 60 million inhabitants are Thai. This

LANGUAGE

Far too many travel books have called Thai an impossible language. The truth is that the vocabulary and syntax are not difficult to grasp. With a few weeks of diligent practice and a basic dictionary almost anyone can communicate the essentials. And like everywhere else, even a few rudimentary phrases will help make friends and save money.

Thai is a monosyllabic and tonal language with 44 consonants, 24 vowels, and five tones. Script is written from left to right without separation between words. There are no prefixes or suffixes, genders, articles, plurals, or verb conjugations. If this makes Thai appear to be a simple language, consider the following.

Thai is a tonal language in which each word can be pronounced with five different tones: low, middle, high, rising, or falling. Each tone completely changes the meaning of the word. *Suay* with a rising tone means "wonderful" but with a falling tone means "bad fortune." Obviously, most Thai words should be double-checked with a native speaker for correct pronunciation.

The transliteration of Thai script into Romanized script is an inexact science and there is no accepted standardization of spelling. Each word can be spelled several different ways—such as the avenue in Bangkok variously rendered as Rajadamnern, Ratchadamnoen, and Rajdamnoen. A town south of Bangkok can be spelled either Petchburi, Petchaburi, or Phetchaburi. The simplest possible spelling has been used in this book, but it's no more consistent or correct than anybody else's.

Thai has several unique sounds that cannot properly be expressed with Roman letters. For example, there are sounds midway between D and T and others midway between B and P. Fortunately, Thai pronunciation is much more logical and consistent than English. Pity the poor Thai student studying English when confronted with cough, rough, though, thought, and through!

Common Expressions

Mai pen rai: Roughly translates to "never mind" or "it doesn't matter," suggesting a state of mind similar to the Buddhist philosophy of disregarding the unimportant events of life since what happens is inevitable and it doesn't help to get uptight. This rather happy-go-lucky attitude is an essential element of the Thai spirit, although it sometimes irritates the rigid Westerner. Learning to say *mai pen rai* in the event of a delayed train or lost luggage will help keep your sanity while on the road!

Sanuk: "Pleasure" or "fun." Thais believe life is meaningless without fun! Everything is judged as either pleasurable or not pleasurable. Food, drink, sex, sports, festivals, and fairs are all great fun. Even a poorly paid job is acceptable if pleasurable. *Tuk tuk* drivers roar around corners on two wheels for the sake of *sanuk.*

Pai Tio: To wander aimlessly, hang out, or just waste time. Going *pai tio* is definitely *sanuk.* Strolling aimlessly on a warm evening is the ultimate in *pai tio.* When a Thai asks you where you are going, just

Mongoloid race largely speaks a common language, shares a unified script, and follows the same Buddhist faith. As a racially tolerant people they have assimilated large numbers of Mons, Khmers, Chinese, and other smaller groups to a degree which precludes any typical Thai physiognomy or physique. Thais generally speak one of four dialects which are mutually intelligible with some degree of difficulty. Central Thai, the official dialect of government and business, has come to dominate over the northern dialect spoken in Chiang Mai and the northeastern dialect laced with Khmer loanwords. A southern dialect is spoken near the Malay border.

Thais on the whole are a delightful race of people who believe life is to be enjoyed so long as no one impinges on another's rights. Many

decline to be fanatical about productivity or deadlines. Foreign visitors are often perplexed with their stubborn resistance to the Westerner's fast-paced, ulcer-prone life. This attitude is epitomized by the phrase *mai pen rai* (never mind).

Thais have personal first names such as Porn ("Blessings"), Boon ("Good Deeds"), Sri or Siri ("Glory"), Som ("Fulfillment"), and Arun ("Dawn"). Since Thais are normally addressed by their first names rather than their family names, don't be surprised if they call you "Mr. John" or "Miss Judy." The prefix *khun* is the ubiquitous title which substitutes for Mr. or Mrs. Affectionate nicknames such as Frog, Rat, Pig, Fat, or Shrimp are more popular than first names!

Perhaps because of their Buddhist upbringings, Thais detest any form of conflict and will go

LANGUAGE

respond with a friendly *pai tio*. Here are some other useful words and expressions:

Conversation

hello (used by males)	*sawadee krap*
hello (used by females)	*sawadee ka*
please/thank you	*kaw roo nah/krap kun*
excuse me	*kaw toot*
yes/no	*mi/mai*
How are you?	*Sabai dee rue?*
fine	*sabai dee*
What is your name?	*Khun cheu arai?*
My name is —.	*Phom cheu —.*
Where do you live?	*Yoo tee nai?*
Do you understand?	*Khao jai mai?*
I don't understand.	*Mai khao jai.*
I cannot speak Thai.	*Phut Thai mai dai.*
never mind	*mai pen rai*

Getting Around

where is —?	*— yoo tee nai?*
when?	*meua rai?*
today	*Wan nee*
tomorrow	*meua wan nee*
how many kilometers?	*gi kilo pai?*
bus station	*sathan rod meh*
train stations	*athan rod tai*
police	*sathan tamruat*
gas station	*pam namman*
embassy/post office	*sathan toot/prai sani*

restaurant/hospital	*raan ahan/rong payaban*
airport/market	*sanam bin/talaat*
telephone/bathroom	*tora sap/hang nam*
hotel	*rongrem*
city/district/town	*nakhon/amphoe/muang*
village/street/lane	*ban/thanan/soi*
bridge/river/canal	*saphan/mae nam/klong*
island/beach/bay	*ko/hat/ao*
mountain/hill	*doi/khao*

Bargaining

Do you have —?	*— mi mai?*
How much?	*Thao rai? (ki baht?)*
Too expensive!	*Fang pai!*
You must be joking!	*Kun pot len!*
something cheaper?	*me tuk gwa ti mai?*
Do you have a cheaper room?	*Me hawng tuk gwa ti mai?*
Ten baht okay?	*Sip baht dai mai?*
Okay, I'll take it.	*Toklang*

Numbers

1, 2, 3	*nung, song, sam*
4, 5, 6	*si, ha, hok*
7, 8, 9, 10	*chet, pat, kow, sip*
11, 12	*sip-et, sip-song*
20, 25	*yi-sip, yi-sip-ha*
30, 40	*sam-sip, si-sip*
100, 1000	*nung roi, nung pan*

to great pains to avoid confrontation and preserve harmony. This attitude—*jai yen* (cool heart)—is strongly favored over *jai rohn* (hot heart). One form of violence you *must* avoid is face-to-face criticism. Unlike Westerners, who criticize friends without ruining relationships, Thais see criticism as highly personal attacks which often lead to grave consequences. To make friends and enjoy yourself in Thailand, keep a *jai yen*.

Thais are also a race of people obsessed with social ranking. Correct social conduct only happens after superior-inferior roles have been determined through direct questions such as "How much do you earn?" and "How old are you?" Westerners should consider such inquiries as friendliness or a form of flattery rather than an invasion of privacy. Social ranking is

also reflected in the Thai language, including dozens of ways to say "I" depending on the speaker's social status. The top of the structure is fairly obvious: the king, his family, and the Buddhist priesthood. Below that are the variables of age, social connections, lineal descent, earnings, and education.

The Chinese

Thailand's largest and most important minority group are the Chinese. Early immigrants included the Hokkiens, who arrived during the late 18th century (Rattankosin Period) to serve as compradores and tax collectors for the Thai royalty, and the near-destitute Teochews, who became the leading merchants in early Bangkok. Later arrivals included thousands of economic refugees fleeing massive crop failures and wide-

CONTEMPORARY BUDDHISM IN THAILAND

Modern Buddhism is divided into the Theravada school adopted in Sri Lanka, Thailand, and Burma, and the Mahayana version favored in China and Japan. Thais further subdivide Theravada into the less-rigorous Mahanikaya order, the majority cult, and the stricter Thammayut order followed by less than 10% of the population. Thailand's Buddhist *sangha* is currently headed by Somdej Pra Yana-sangworm, the same monk who supervised the young King Bhumipol during his 15-day residency at Wat Bowornives in Bangkok. As one of the most powerful individuals in the country, Somdej faces several thorny challenges: the declining interest in Buddhism among the young, the corrupting influence of *phi* propitiation (see below), and widespread decadence within the Buddhist *sangha*. Today in Thailand, it's not uncommon for monks to predict lottery outcomes, practice faith healing, distribute phallic symbols, sell magical charms, and charge hefty fees for ceremonial services. The country's monastic image was further damaged after it was revealed that several monasteries were selling bogus royal decorations.

Rebellion against conventional Buddhism is symbolized by Pra Bodhirak, an unorthodox but immensely popular and charismatic rebel who preaches his iconoclastic viewpoints from the Santi Asoke (Peace, No Sorrow) headquarters on the eastern outskirts of Bangkok. Defrocked and under heavy legal pressures from the government, Bodhirak insists that Thai Buddhism has been badly corrupted by the decadent practices and superstitious beliefs mentioned above. His message of nonmaterialism and religious purity has hit home: popularity has soared and even the current governor of Bangkok supports Bodhirak's platforms of religious reform.

Spirit Propitiation

Buddhism might be Thailand's dominant faith but it has never completely replaced older religious traditions such as Hinduism and spiritualism. Hindu ceremonies still play an important role in Thai society, largely because ceremonies for life passages such as births, deaths, and marriages were never prescribed by the Buddha. Brahmanic astrologers also prepare the national calendar and preside over annual rice-planting ceremonies.

But more important are the powers of astrology, the occult, and wandering supernatural spirits called *phi,* homeless and unhappy apparitions who can

young monks in Sukothai

cause great harm to the living unless appeased with frequent offerings. *Phi* are propitiated (not worshipped) for dozens of reasons: they are asked to influence the future, to grant wishes, to guarantee the success of a financial venture, to help one pass a school exam, to restore health to a sick family member, or to help a worshipper win the weekly lottery. Believed to exist in all shapes and sizes, some *phi* enjoy a permanent existence unbounded by the law of karma while others are reincarnations of dead human beings who have returned to haunt the living. People who died violently or whose funeral rites were improperly performed are especially dangerous, since witches can force them to consume the internal organs of the living. Others can make you remove your clothes in public! Although these practices are not in accordance with the teachings of the Buddha (karma teaches individual responsibility; spirit propitiation places responsibility on outside forces), *phi* homage doesn't necessarily conflict with the reverence that Thais feel for Buddhist philosophy. The average Thai is a Buddhist who was mar-

CONTEMPORARY BUDDHISM IN THAILAND

ried according to Hindu rituals but makes frequent offerings to placate animist spirits.

Spirit Houses

One of the most powerful forms of *phi* are the guardian spirits called *chao phi*, of which the guardian spirit of the house (*chao thi* or *pra phum* in Khmer) is the most important. Thais believe that every plot of land harbors a spirit who must be provided with a small doll-like house. This curious spirit home, located on the exterior lawn where no shadow will ever fall, is furnished with a replica of the residing spirit holding a double-edged sword and a big book which lists deeds of the occupants. Other figurines include slaves, elephants, and sensuous dancing girls . . . to keep the ghost happy! After proper installation by a Brahman priest at the auspicious place and time, human occupants continue to make daily offerings of flowers, joss sticks, and food to placate the touchy spirit.

Thais also honor eight other household spirits including one troublesome fellow who resides in the door threshold. That's why it is proper behavior to step *over* rather than *on* the threshold. In recent years it has become popular to erect extremely elaborate shrines dedicated to the four-faced Hindu god, Lord Brahma. Thailand's most famous Brahmanic image is displayed at the Hyatt Grand Erawan Hotel shrine in Bangkok, although in the strictest sense this is not a spirit house, but in a category all its own.

Monkhood

To gain heavenly merit, improve their karma through correct living, and bring honor to their parents, many young Thai men elect to become monks for periods from a few days to several months. Initiates take vows of poverty and are allowed few possessions: three yellow robes, an alms bowl, and a strainer to filter any living creature from the water. Final daily meals are eaten before noon, while the remainder of the day is spent meditating and studying Buddhist scriptures. Although instructed to remain unemotional and detached about worldly concerns, many are surprisingly friendly to Westerners and quite anxious to practice their English. The Golden Mount in Bangkok is an excellent place to meet the monks.

---

spread starvation in 20th-century China. As elsewhere in Southeast Asia, Chinese immigrants worked hard, educated their children, and today completely dominate the trade and finance sectors of the local economy. It has been estimated that 60% of Thailand's largest companies are controlled by Sino-Thais (Thai nationals of Chinese descent), and almost 100% of Thai banks are controlled by a handful of extremely wealthy Sino-Thai families.

But unlike in other countries in Southeast Asia, the massive concentration of wealth in Chinese hands has not brought widespread racial conflicts or discriminatory legislation. Thailand's racial harmony is perhaps the result of widespread intermarriage. According to legend, King Mongkut (himself of Chinese lineage) encouraged Chinese immigration and intermarriage with Thai women, social intercourse which he hoped would give future generations the traditional Chinese qualities of industry and thrift. As a result, it is now difficult if not impossible to distinguish ethnic Thais from Sino-Thais; perhaps 50% of Bangkok's population is ethnically Chinese. Sino-Thais have taken on Thai sur-

names and speak Thai rather than Chinese. Consequently, the Thai government has rarely been motivated to pass discriminatory laws but has let the Chinese help build the economic miracle of modern Thailand.

Other Peoples

Nearly one million Malay Muslims live in the southern provinces bordering Malaysia. Many are fishermen or rubber tappers who sometimes view public education as an attack on their cultural autonomy. Muslim separatist movements such as the United Pattani Freedom Movement have largely been suppressed by the Thai government.

Inhabiting the hills near Chiang Mai are some half-million seminomadic tribespeople who migrated down from southern China over the last few centuries. The 20 distinct tribes range from sophisticated groups like the Meos to primitive peoples like the Phi Tong Luang. All were relatively isolated from the outside world until commercialized trekking and government assimilation programs began in the 1970s. More information under "Chiang Mai."

BUDDHISM

Theravada Buddhism, the state religion of Thailand, is practiced by 90% of the population. Buddhism began in southern Nepal with the teachings of its founder, Siddhartha Gautama (563-483 B.C.), a wealthy aristocrat who rejected his princely upbringing after four alarming encounters with an aged man, a sick man, a corpse, and finally an ascetic. Shocked and disillusioned, Siddhartha renounced his royal life and began a 45-year quest for truth. After self-mortification and temptation failed, he solved the riddle of existence while meditating beneath the sacred Bo tree at Bodgaya, India. The Buddha then set in motion the Wheel of Life and organized his *sangha* (monastic community) comprised of *bhikkus* (monks). These pilgrims codified existing Buddhist doctrine and dialogues onto palm leaf to form a three-part compendium of works called the Tripitaka ("Three Baskets of Wisdom").

Buddha's great achievement was to reform a calcifying Hinduism by reinterpreting traditional Hindu doctrines such as karma, reincarnation, and nirvana into a dynamic movement which promised salvation through personal effort rather than Brahmanic magic. He envisioned a middle path lying between the extremes of ascetic self-denial and worldly self-indulgence as the most practical way to achieve freedom from the endless cycle of death and rebirth.

After his death, some 500 disciples gathered to recite his teachings and form the Theravada branch of Buddhism to help maintain the purity of original traditions. The early Christian era saw the rise of Mahayana Buddhism, a school which promised a tangible paradise through the worship of supernatural intermediaries called bodhisattvas. Buddhism spread rapidly throughout India and was carried to Southeast Asia by the missionaries of Indian King Asoka (272-232 B.C.). The final irony is that Buddhism, as a major force, eventually died out in the country of its origin.

PRACTICAL INFORMATION

GETTING THERE

Air

Thailand is served by over 50 international airlines from major world capitals and cities in Southeast Asia. Most visitors arrive at Bangkok's Don Muang International Airport (see "Bangkok" for arrival information and further transportation arrangements), although flights are also available to Phuket and Hat Yai from Malaysia. The Penang-to-Phuket flight is highly recommended since it's reasonably priced and saves a full day of land travel. Travelers with limited time should purchase a roundtrip ticket from their home country and buy any additional tickets in Thailand. Package tours of two or three weeks often include discounted hotels and internal flights to popular destinations such as Chiang Mai or Phuket. Travelers with more time should purchase one-way tickets to Bangkok and make all future travel arrangements in Thailand, an option which adds flexibility and saves money since Bangkok travel agents sell some of the world's cheapest airline tickets.

From the U.S.: Thai International, Korean Air, Pan Am, Northwest, and China Air all offer super-APEX flights to Bangkok for US$900-110 from U.S. West Coast cities. Discounted flights for US$750-850 are available from agencies which advertise in major metropolitan newspapers. Because flights are often fully booked and discounted seats sell quickly, it's very important to book at least two months before your intended departure date. Budget agencies are described in the main Introduction.

From England: Thai International, British Airways, Philippine Airlines, and Qantas offer direct flights from London to Bangkok. If you don't mind time-consuming plane changes, cheaper fares are available from Kuwait Airlines, Gulf Air, and Royal Jordanian. Budget tickets are available from Trailfinders (tel. 01-603-1515), Hann Overland (tel. 01-834-7367), and other agencies listed in *Time Out* and *TNT* magazines.

From Australia: One-way economy tickets from Sydney and Melbourne cost A$1100 and A$950 from Perth and Cairns. Advance-purchase one-way tickets cost only A$600-700 from Sydney when purchased at least 21 days in advance. Cheap-flight specialists include Student Travel Australia (see the main Introduction for addresses and phone numbers), Travel Specialists (tel. 267-9122), and Sydney Flight Centre (tel. 221-2666).

Train

The International Express (IE) departs Singapore every morning and arrives in Kuala Lumpur by nightfall. Visitors may overnight in the Malaysian capital or continue north by night train to Butterworth, the terminus for Penang. The IE departs Butterworth the following day around 1300, crosses the Thai border, and arrives in Hat Yai about three hours later. The IE departs Hat Yai at 1700 and arrives in Bangkok early the following morning. Schedules change frequently and should be double-checked with the stationmasters in Singapore or Malaysia. The IE is limited to first and second class and somewhat expensive because of supplemental charges for a/c, superior classes, and sleeping berths. While the International Express from Singapore to Bangkok has romantic appeal and is probably the most luxurious train in Southeast Asia, it's a long and exhausting journey best experienced in shorter segments.

Ordinary trains no longer run between Malaysia and Thailand. Diesels from Butterworth terminate at the border town of Padang Besar. Travelers can walk across to Thailand and wait for public transport. This transfer is very time-consuming; most travelers prefer buses or shared taxis. More details under "Penang" and "Kota Baru."

Bus

Crossing the Thai border by public bus can be tricky. Most buses on the west coast of Peninsular Malaysia terminate at Changlun, a small and isolated Malaysian town some 20 km from the border. From Changlun, you must attempt to hitchhike the distance to Sadao in southern Thailand—not an easy task. Private buses are much easier. Buses direct from Penang to Hat Yai, Ko Samui, and Phuket can be booked through travel agents in Penang. Public transport on the east coast is fairly straightforward. Ordinary buses from Kota Baru terminate at the Thai border, a one-km walk along the train tracks from Sungai Golok in Thailand. Both trains and public buses leave Sungai Golok for Hat Yai and Bangkok. Immigration can be

fairly lax at this border; be sure to get your passport stamped.

Taxi

Crossing the border by public bus or ordinary train can be a haphazard and time-consuming ordeal. Most independent travelers prefer private buses direct to their Thai destinations or share taxis, which are fast, comfortable, and well priced. This also avoids getting stranded at the border waiting for a bus or a train. These lumbering old Mercedes or Chevys can be found in Penang at the waterfront taxi stand and in Georgetown downstairs from the bus terminal. Budget hotels in Penang can arrange pick-up directly from your hotel. Share taxis can also be chartered in Kota Baru.

Sea

Looking for something unusual? Longtailed boats depart several times daily from Kuala Perlis in Malaysia for Satul in southern Thailand, a useful service for visitors coming from Langkawi. Be sure to have your passport stamped by immigration officials in Satul. Buses continue up to Hat Yai and points north. Asia Voyages Pansea (described below) also sails from Sumatra and Penang to Phuket. Private services from Langkawi to Phuket are also available on a bimonthly basis.

GETTING AROUND

Air

Domestic flights are provided by Thai International, which merged with Thai Airways several years ago. The consolidation greatly benefits international travelers, who can now purchase all necessary tickets in one package, thus ensuring a worry-free trip with guaranteed connections and seats. Major destinations are served by Airbuses and Boeing 737s, while smaller towns are reached with Shorts 330 aircraft. Internal flights are fairly expensive when compared to rail travel, but highly recommended on those routes not served by train or luxury buses. For example, the flight from Chiang Mai to Mae Hong Song takes only 30 minutes and costs 310B while the bone-crushing bus ride takes a full 12 hours and costs 120B. Bangkok Airways, Thailand's only domestic airline, flies six times daily from Bangkok to Ko Samui and several times daily between Samui, Phuket, and Hat Yai.

FESTIVALS

Most Thai festivals are connected with either Buddhism, the annual cycle of rice planting, or commemorations honoring past kings. Religious festivals are movable feasts dated by the Thai lunar calendar; state holidays follow the Western calendar. Exact dates should be checked with the Tourist Authority of Thailand (TAT). Current listings are also given in the *Bangkok Post*.

January
Don Chedi Memorial Fair: The decisive battle of King Naresuan and the Burmese is re-enacted each year on 24-30 January. Don Chedi is west of Bangkok near Kanchanaburi.

Pra Nakhon Khiri Fair: Petchburi, a small town south of Bangkok, sponsors a light and sound presentation that illuminates its outstanding monuments.

February
Maha Puja: Buddha's revelations to his 1,250 disciples at Bodgaya are marked with merit-making ceremonies such as releasing of caged birds, burning of incense, and a lovely procession of flickering candles around the temple. Held on the full moon of the third lunar month.

Pra That Phanom Chedi Fair: This important festival held in Nakhon Phanom (northeastern Thailand) honors a holy relic of the Buddha.

Chiang Mai Flower Festival: This popular fair features a beauty pageant, a floral float parade, and cultural entertainment. Visitors should be prepared for enormous crowds.

Red Cross Fair: This commercialized, crowded, and somewhat disappointing festival in Bangkok offers nightly dance performances, music, and exciting *takraw* competition.

March
Pra Buddha Baht: Buddhist devotees gather at the shrine of the holy footprint near Saraburi for religious rites and a bazaar.

Thao Suranari Fair: This festival honors the national heroine who rallied local people to repel invaders from Vientiane. A homage-paying ceremony and victory procession are held at her memorial in Korat (Nakhon Ratchasima), northeastern Thailand.

April
Pattaya Festival: Thailand's major beach resort hosts a weeklong festival of beauty queens, floral floats, fireworks, cultural dancing, kite flying, and motorcar races. One of the biggest festivals in Thailand.

Chakri Day: This national holiday, held on 6 April to commemorate the reign of Rama I (founder of the Chakri dynasty), is the only day of the year when Bangkok's Pantheon at Wat Pra Keo is opened to the public.

Songkran Festival: Thailand's New Year is celebrated nationwide as the sun moves into Aries. Buddha images are purified with holy water, young people honor their parents by pouring perfumed water over their hands, and traditional sand pagodas are built in the temples. Fun-loving Thais have cleverly turned this religious ritual into a wild and crazy water-throwing festival during which everyone is smeared with white powder and drenched with buckets of ice-cold water. Unsuspecting tourists are a prime target—leave the camera at your hotel!

Pra Pradang Songkran Festival: The Mon community in Samut Prakan south of Bangkok sponsors a Mon festival with parades, Mon beauty queens, and continual deluges of water throwing. Organized tours of this unusual festival can be booked through the Siam Society in Bangkok.

May
Coronation Day: King Bhumibol's coronation is celebrated on 5 May with a private ceremony in the royal chapel.

Royal Ploughing Ceremony: This elaborate Hindu ritual marks the beginning of the rice-planting season. A richly decorated plough is pulled by garlanded Brahman across the Sanam Luang in Bangkok, while Brahman priests solemnly plant sacred rice seeds and predict the success of the coming harvest.

Visaka Puja: This most sacred of all Buddhist holidays commemorates the birth, death, and enlightenment of Buddha. Merit-making ceremonies are identical to the Maha Puja.

Rocket Festival: People of the dry northeast hold this festival to ensure plentiful rains. Bamboo rockets are launched into the sky before the night's activities of music, dancing, and drinking. Held on the second weekend in May throughout the Issan. The town

FESTIVALS

of Yasothon hosts the most famous of all rocket festivals, complete with beauty queens and an elaborate parade.

July
Asalha Puja: Commemorates Buddha's first sermon to his five disciples and marks the beginning of the annual three-month rains retreat. During this Khao Phansa (Buddhist Lent), many young Thai males temporarily enter the Buddhist priesthood. Held on the full moon of the eighth lunar month.

Candle Festival: Ubon Ratchathani celebrates the beginning of Buddhist Lent with a gigantic procession of floats carrying huge candles designed to burn for its duration.

August
Longan Fair: Lamphun celebrates the popular fruit with a Miss Longan Beauty Contest, agricultural displays, and a small parade.

Queen's Birthday: Municipal buildings are illuminated with colored lights during this national holiday held 12 August.

September
Phuket Vegetarian Festival: Islanders of Chinese ancestry follow a strict vegetarian diet for nine days. The festival begins with a parade of white-clothed devotees who walk across fire and drive spears through their cheeks—the Chinese version of Hindu Thaipusam.

October
Tod Kathin: The end of Buddhist Lent and the rainy season is celebrated with elaborate boat races in Nan, Surat Thani, Nakhon Phanom, and Samut Prakan. Highlighted by a procession of royal barges down the Chao Praya to Wat Arun, where the king presents new robes to the monks.

Wax Candle Festival: The end of the Buddhist rains retreat is celebrated in Sakhon Nakhon with a parade of beautifully embellished beeswax floats in the form of miniature Buddhist temples.

Chonburi Buffalo Races: Local farmers sponsor races and a beauty contest for decorated buffalo.

Chulalongkorn Day: Thailand's beloved king is honored with a national holiday on 23 October. Wreaths are laid at his equestrian statue in Bangkok's Royal Plaza.

Pra Chedi Klang Nam Festival: The riverside *chedi* in Samut Prakan, some 30 km south of Bangkok, hosts a popular festival with colorful processions and boat races.

November
Loy Kratong: Thailand's most famous and charming festival honors both the Buddha and ancient water spirits. Banana-leaf boats, each carrying a single candle, are floated in the rivers and lakes—a wonderful and delicate sight. Loy Kratong is celebrated in both Sukothai and Chiang Mai, although Sukothai is a better venue because of the smaller crowds. It's sometimes possible to see both festivals since Sukothai's is often held the previous night.

Golden Mount Fair: Bangkok's most spectacular temple fair features folk drama, barkers, freak shows, countless food stalls, and a lovely candlelight procession around the temple.

Ayuthaya Boat Races: An international event that attracts both local and foreign crews.

Deepavali: The Hindu Festival of Lights is celebrated at a small ornate Indian temple on Silom Road in Bangkok. Religious zealots perform amazing feats of self-mutilation.

Surin Elephant Roundup: Over 100 elephants engage in staged hunts, comical rodeo and elephant polo, and a tug-of-war between a lone elephant and 100 men. Visitors can ride the pachyderms around town. Held in Surin on the third Saturday in November.

Pra Pathom Fair: Folk dramas, beauty pageants, and a parade take place in Nakhon Pathom at Pra Pathom Chedi, world's tallest Buddhist monument.

River Kwai Bridge Week: A nightly *son et lumière* relates the grim history of this world-famous bridge. Visitors can ride WW II-vintage steam engines across the bridge.

December
King's Birthday: Bhumibol's birthday on 5 December is celebrated with a grand parade and city-wide decorations of flags, portraits of the king, and brilliantly colored lights.

Tourism Festival: The Tourist Authority of Thailand promotes the nation's number-one industry with dance performances, regional cultural shows, and a fireworks display in Bangkok.

Train

Trains are the best form of transportation in Thailand. Not only are they comfortable, punctual, and inexpensive, they're much safer than buses and an excellent way to meet people. The drawbacks? Trains are slow, they don't go everywhere (but you'd be amazed the places they do go!), and they're often fully booked during holidays. Trains from Bangkok to Chiang Mai in the north or to Hat Yai in the south should be booked well in advance.

Types and Classes: Thai trains come in four types. Diesel railcars and ordinary trains stop at every single town and are very, very slow—avoid these except on short journeys. Rapid trains are almost twice as fast as ordinary trains and have a modest 20B supplemental charge. Express trains have a 30B supplemental charge and are slightly faster than the rapid trains. Trains are also divided into three classes. Third class is the cheapest but the seats are hard and sleeping facilities are limited to floorspace, usually littered with peanuts, durian shells, and grandmothers. However, third class is quite adequate on all but the longest journeys. Second class offers padded seats and more legroom, costs double the price of third class (about the same price as an a/c bus), and can be reserved with sleeping berths. First class's comfortable reclining seats are double the price of second class. Put this all together and the fastest/ cheapest train ticket is third class on a rapid train. Best choice for overnight travel is second class with a lower sleeping berth.

Charges: Supplementary charges are placed on all trains except for diesels and ordinary services. Rapid trains are 20B extra; express costs 30B more, 2nd class a/c is an extra 50B. Sleeping berths also carry supplemental charges. Second class, non-a/c is 70B in the upper and 100B in the lower berth. Second class a/c is 170B lower and 200B upper berth. Take the lower berth; it avoids the noisy overhead fan. First class with a/c is 250B double cabin and 350B single cabin. To compute the final cost, you must know the type of train (ordinary, rapid, express), the class (first, second, third), and whether you want a/c or a sleeping berth.

Timetables: Train schedules, available free of charge from the Rail Travel Aids counter in Bangkok's Hualampong Station, are among the most important pieces of travel information in

THAILAND AIR ROUTES

Thailand. Purple brochures list condensed timetables for the southern train line; blue brochures list the north, northeastern, and eastern lines. Other information on exact fares, refunds, breaks in journeys, ticket alterations, and validity of return tickets is also described. Complete timetables for each trunk line are sold at the same counter.

Thailand Rail Pass: Blue 20-day rail passes which cost 1500B include unlimited second- and third-class travel; supplemental charges not included. Red passes cost 3000B; all supplemental charges are included.

Bus

Bus transport in Thailand is fast, clean, and reasonably comfortable on shorter journeys. Most

THAILAND TRAIN ROUTES

CHIANG MAI

LAMPANG

NONG KHAI

KHON KAEN

PHITSANULOK

NAKHON SAWAN

UBON RATCHATHANI

LOPBURI

KORAT (NAKHON RATCHASIMA)

NAM TOK

AYUTHAYA

NAKHON PATHOM

BANGKOK

ARANYAPRATHET

KO SAMUI

NAKHON SI THAMMARAT

PHUKET

HAT YAI

KOTA BARU

GEORGETOWN

MALAYSIA

NOT TO SCALE

usually 30-70% more expensive than government buses, but complimentary meals and transportation from your hotel to their bus terminal is often included. Finding the correct bus is straightforward, since somebody will nearly always materialize to show the way; gum salesmen expect you to purchase a pack in exchange for directions!

Buses are convenient but there are some drawbacks. Coaches constructed for Thai body sizes are ridiculously cramped for long-legged Westerners. There are also safety concerns. Far too many drivers behave like suicidal maniacs hell-bent on destruction. Sensible precautions include never sitting in the front row or riding with drivers who plaster Rambo photographs all over the front window. More problems, especially on luxury buses in the deep south, are armed robberies and confidence artists who use knockout drugs. Thai police videotape passengers to discourage robbery but, like your mother once told you: *never accept food or drink from strangers.* The following notice is posted in the Bangkok TAT office:

WARNING BEWARE

When travelling to the South or North, do not accept foods, drinks, or sweets from strangers no matter how friendly they may appear. You might be drugged even after hours of friendly travelling. Don't be fooled!

TOURIST POLICE

---

buses provide reclining airline-style seats and video movies (porn and kung fu are popular), plus smiling hostesses who crank up the air-conditioning and serve icy drinks. Seats are often reserved—a great relief from the disorganized condition of most Asian buses. Both a/c and non-a/c buses are available on major routes. Cheapest are the ordinary coaches operated by the government bus company called Bor Kor Sor (also called Baw Kaw Saw). Departures are usually from city terminals located on the outskirts of town. Air-conditioned buses operated by independent companies are

Car Rental

Thailand is an outstanding country to tour with rented transport. Contrary to popular belief, traffic is moderate and manageable throughout the country, with the exception of Bangkok. Highways are in good condition and most directional signs are labeled in English. Familiar agencies such as Avis and Hertz maintain offices in the larger towns. Less expensive rentals are available from local agencies, but carefully check the car's condition before handing over your money. Many offer reduced monthly rates which include insurance and unlimited mileage. Split by four people, this can be an economical and flexible way to tour Thailand. An International

Driver's License is required and insurance is mandatory. Cars are often stopped by policemen, who collect exorbitant gratuities from unlicensed drivers for temporary driving permits.

Motorcycle Rental

Bikes can be rented in Chiang Mai, Chiang Rai, Mae Hong Son, Sukothai, Ayuthaya, Kanchanaburi, Ko Samui, and Phuket. Motorcycles are unavailable in Bangkok, but long-term rentals of larger bikes are possible in Pattaya. Rates start at 150B for motorscooters and climb sharply for larger bikes. In most cases, a 100cc motorscooter is completely adequate for local touring. Experienced motorcyclists should have few difficulties with the traffic, though Thailand is no place for beginning cyclists; far too many Westerners have ended their vacations in the hospitals of Ko Samui and Phuket. No matter how experienced you are you should drive defensively, never operate a motorcycle while high, and always wear a helmet, long pants, a long shirt, and hard shoes to prevent injury on minor spills.

Cruises And Yachts

Both luxury ships and private yachts sail the warm seas around Thailand. Seatran Travel (tel. 251-8467 in Bangkok; tel. 211809 in Phuket) in the Metro Trade Center on New Petchaburi Road in Bangkok operates two luxurious ocean liners from Phuket. Excursions on the older *Seatran Queen* include East Of Phuket (three days, US$175-300), Similan Archipelago (four days, US$200-325), and Hat Yai To Phuket (three days, US$200-325). Excursions on the more luxurious *Seatran Princess* include Phuket-Similan-Ranong (four days, US$225-300), Phuket-Ko Phi Phi-Tarutao Marine Park (four days, US$250-375), and Phuket-Sumatra-Penang (six days, US$700-800).

Private yachts for cruising, scuba diving, and big-game fishing can be arranged from Asia Voyages Pansea offices located in Bangkok (tel. 235-4100), Phuket (tel. 216137), Hong Kong (tel. 521-1314), Singapore (tel. 732-7222), Paris (tel. 432-61035), Brussels (tel. 217-9898), and London (tel. 491-1547). Yachts in Thailand and throughout Southeast Asia can also be chartered from Ocean Voyages, 1709 Bridgeway, Sausalito, California, 94965 (tel. 415-332-4681). A third possibility is to contact Dave

Owen at South East Asia Yacht Charter, 89-71 Thaweewong Road, Phuket (tel. 076-321292).

SCUBA DIVING

Thailand's soaring popularity with Western visitors is partially due to adventure-travel possibilities ranging from trekking in the Golden Triangle to diving the aquamarine waters of the Andaman Sea and the Gulf of Thailand. Experienced divers can explore underwater wrecks and coral canyons, while beginners can obtain PADI and NAUI certification from dozens of accredited dive schools. Thailand's two principal dive locations are at Pattaya near Bangkok and in the vicinity of Phuket, where dive conditions at nearby Similan, Surin, and Taratao islands rival the best in the world. Dives can be easily arranged directly in Bangkok, Pattaya, and Phuket, or in advance from Sea and Sea Travel (tel. 415-434-3400) in San Francisco, Tropical Adventures (tel. 800-247-3483) in Seattle, and from any worldwide office of Asia Voyages Pansea.

TRAVEL FORMALITIES

Visas

All visitors to Thailand must have valid passports. Those who intend to stay less than 15 days and have proof of onward passage may enter the country without visas. Extensions are *not* allowed. It has been reported that visitors who overstay are fined approximately 100B per day at the airport. Foreign nationals intending to stay longer than 15 days must obtain visas in advance from a Thai diplomatic mission. One-month nonextendable transit visas cost US$5. A 90-day nonimmigrant visa for business purposes costs US$15 and requires a valid reason for the extended stay. Employment is forbidden unless a work permit is obtained. Nonimmigrant visas approved for business or working purposes are valid for 90 days. Every alien who stays in Thailand over 90 days in a calendar year must obtain a tax-clearance certificate, which involves a 20,000B bank guarantee or a guarantee given by a land-owning Thai citizen. The second type of guarantee is often given by the tax officers themselves as a means of supplementing their incomes.

VISA OPTIONS

No Visa . . . . 15 days
Transit Visa . . . . 30 days
Tourist Visa . . . . 60 days
Non-Immigrant Visa . . . . 90 days

The most popular option is the 60-day tourist visa, which costs US$10 and can be extended once for 30 days at the discretion of Thai immigration. Second extensions are occasionally granted to neat, clean, and polite visitors. Applications for extensions should be made two to three days in advance at the Immigration Division on Soi Suan Plu off Sathorn Road in Bangkok, tel. 286-9176. Visas can also be extended at regional offices located throughout the country.

Multiple-entry Visas
The visas described above permit only one entry. Visitors intending to make several entries and exits from Thailand—and who want to avoid time-consuming delays at immigration in Bangkok—should obtain multiple-entry visas in advance. The four-month double-entry tourist visa costs US$20, twice the cost of a single-entry visa. A long-term visitor might purchase a two-entry nonimmigrant visa, which allows six months in Thailand with one quick visit to a neighboring country. Travelers going to Burma without multiple-entry visas should pick up re-entry visas for 300B each at the Immigration Division on Soi Suan Plu in Bangkok. All visas must be used within 90 days of issue. Visas can be quickly and easily obtained in most capital cities in Southeast Asia. Thai consulates are also located in Penang and Kota Baru.

Tourist Information
The Tourist Authority of Thailand (TAT) is courteous, efficient, and sincerely interested in helping you have the best possible time in the country. TAT offices, located in major towns throughout the country, are well supplied with accurate travel and hotel information. Ask for the schedule of upcoming festivals and events; useful for planning your vacation. Colorful brochures can be requested from overseas TAT offices listed below. Bangkok's main TAT office is located on Rajadamnern Avenue.

Maps
APA Map of Thailand: This outstanding map can be purchased at bookstores throughout the country. Maps published by Shell and Esso are poor.

Latest Tours Guide to Bangkok and Thailand: Lists major bus routes in Bangkok—an absolute necessity for bus riders in Bangkok.

THAI DIPLOMATIC MISSIONS

Australia	111 Empire Circuit, Canberra, 2600	731149
	Exchange Bldg., 12th floor, 56 Pitt St., Sydney	
	464 Saint Kilda Rd., Melbourne	
Canada	85 Range Rd., #704, Ottawa, Ontario K1N8J6	(613) 237-0476
	250 University Ave., 7th floor, Toronto 110	
	1155 Dorchester Blvd., #1005, Montreal 102	
	700 W. George St., 26th floor, Vancouver	
France	8 rue Greuze, Paris 75116	4704-3222
England	30 Queens Gate, London SW7 5JB	(01) 589-2834
Germany	Ubierstrasse 65, 5300 Bonn 2	(0228) 3550-6568
New Zealand	2 Cook St., Box 17-226, Wellington	735358
U.S.A.	2300 Kalorma Rd., Washington, D.C. 20008	(202) 667-1446
	801 N. Labrae Ave., Los Angeles, CA 90010	(213) 937-1894
	53 Park Place #505, New York, NY 10007	(212) 732-8166

INTERNATIONAL CLOCK FOR THAILAND

San Francisco	-15
New York	-12
London	-7
Paris	-6
Sydney	+3

Market Map of Bangkok and *Map of Chiang Mai:* Both of these immensely useful and highly recommended maps are the personalized creations of artist Nancy Chandler, a longtime resident who offers her trustworthy advice on public markets, restaurants, and tourist attractions.

United States Geological Survey Maps: Topographic maps produced by the U.S. Government are available in Chiang Mai bookstores. Although somewhat useful for independent trekkers, superior locally produced maps are now coming on the market.

Association of Siamese Architects Maps: These four stylish maps (Bangkok, Grand Palace, Canals of Thonburi, Ayuthaya) are well drawn but useless except for the guide to Thonburi temples.

Currency

Thailand's basic unit of currency, the *baht* (B), is pegged to a basket of currencies heavily weighted toward the dollar. Currently the exchange rate is approximately 27 *baht* to the dollar. Rates fluctuate little against the dollar but swing widely against European currencies depending on dollar-European currency rates of exchange. Each *baht* is divided into 100 *stang.* Coins come in 25-*stang,* 50-*stang,* one-*baht,* two-*baht,* and five-*baht* denominations. Only the one- and five-*baht* pieces are in common circulation. Thai coinage is confusing to Westerners since it's labeled only in Thai script and identical coins have been minted in different sizes. For example, the five-*baht* coin has progressively shrunk from a monstrous nickel-and-copper heavyweight down to the size of an American quarter. There is no currency black market. Traveler's checks can be cashed at banks throughout Thailand—even the smallest towns have foreign-exchange services. Surprisingly, Thai banks rather than independent money changers offer the best rates. Foreign banks sometimes charge a 12B service charge; take your business to Thai banks only.

International Telephone

Thailand has one of the best phone systems in Southeast Asia. Connections are clean and crisp. International calls can be made directly by dialing 001, country code, area code, and local number. Calls can also be made from central telephone offices located in most larger towns. Minimum charge is for three minutes. Station-to-station calls cost about US$10 per three minutes, the cheapest in Asia except for Singapore and Hong Kong.

ETIQUETTE AND CUSTOMS

Thais are an extremely tolerant and forgiving race of people blessed with a gentle religion and an easygoing approach to life. And yet, visitors would do well to observe proper social customs to avoid embarrassment and misunderstandings.

Royalty: Thais hold their Royal Family in great reverence. All visitors are expected to show respect to all royal images, including national anthems preceding movies and royal portraits on Thai currency. While many Thais will cheerfully criticize their national and local governments, Thai royalty is never openly criticized. Friends come fast when you praise the king and wear an amulet of his lovely wife!

Buddha Images: Thais are a deeply religious people who consider all Buddhist images extremely sacred—no matter their age or condition. Sacrilegious acts are punishable by imprisonment . . . even when committed by foreign visitors. Several years ago a group of tourists posed for photographs on top a Buddha image in Sukothai. The developing lab in Bangkok turned the negatives over to a Bangkok newspaper, which published the offending photographs on the front page. Public outrage was so strong that the foreigners were arrested and put in jail. More recently *Sports Illustrated* was refused permission to use religious shrines as backdrops for its 1988 swimsuit issue, and a *Vogue* model was arrested the following year for posing beside a religious monument in Phuket.

THAI TOURIST OFFICES

OVERSEAS

Australia	56 Pitt St., 12/F, Sydney 2000	(02) 277549
England	49 Albemarle St., London WIX3FE	(01) 499-7670
France	90 Champs Élysées, Paris 75008	4562-8656
Germany	58 Bethmannstrasse, D-6000, Frankfurt	(069) 295704
Hong Kong	Fairmont House #401, Central	868-0732
Japan	Hibiya Mitsui Bldg., Yurakucho, Tokyo	(03) 580-6776
Malaysia	206 Jalan Ampang, Kuala Lumpur	248-0958
Singapore	370 Orchard Rd.	235-7901
U.S.A.	5 World Trade Center, #2449, New York, NY 10048	(212) 432-0433
	3400 Wilshire Blvd., #1101, Los Angeles, CA 90010	(213) 382-2353

DOMESTIC

Bangkok	4 Rajadamnern Nok Ave., 10100	(662) 282-1143
Chiang Mai	135 Chiang Mai-Lamphian Rd., 50000	(053) 248604
Hat Yai	Soi 2, Niphat Uthit 3 Rd., 90110	(074) 243747
Kanchanaburi	Saengshuto Rd., 71000	(034) 511200
Korat	2102 Mittraphab Rd., 30000	(044) 243427
Pattaya	382 Chai Hat Rd., 20260	(038) 428750
Phitsanulok	209 Boromtriloknart Rd., 65000	(055) 252742
Phuket	73 Phuket Rd., 83000	(076) 212213
Surat Thani	5 Talat Mai Rd., 84000	(077) 282828

Temple Dress Codes: All Buddhist temples in Thailand have very strict dress codes, similar to Christian churches in the West. *Shorts are not acceptable attire in Buddhist temples—men should wear long pants and clean short-sleeved shirts.* Women are best covered in either pants or long skirts, and shoulders should not be exposed. Leather sandals are better than shoes since footwear must be constantly removed. Rubber flip-flops are considered proper only in the bathroom, not in religious shrines. Buddhist temples are extremely sacred places; please dress appropriately.

Monks: Buddhist monks must also be treated with respect. Monks cannot touch or be touched by females, or accept anything from the hand of a woman. Rear seats in buses are reserved for monks; other passengers should vacate these seats when necessary. Never stand over a seated monk since they should always remain at the highest elevations.

Social Customs

Modest Dress: *Shorts are considered improper and low-class attire in Thailand,* only acceptable for schoolchildren, street beggars, and common laborers . . . not wealthy tourists! Shorts and bathing suits are fine at beach resorts, but no matter how hot the weather, long pants and dresses should be worn in urban environments. Public displays of affection and beach nudity are also offensive.

Emotions: Face is very important in Thailand. Candor and emotional honesty—qualities highly prized in Western society—are considered embarrassing and counterproductive in the East. Never lose your temper or raise your voice no matter how frustrating or desperate the situation. Only patience, humor, and *chai yen* (cool heart) bring results in Thailand.

Personal Space: Thai anatomy has its own special considerations. Thais believe that the head—the most sacred part of the body—is inhabited by the *kwan,* the spiritual force of life.

MOVIES FILMED IN THAILAND

Man With the Golden Gun: Chase scenes in this James Bond flick were filmed in Phangnga Bay near Phuket. One towering limestone pinnacle has been renamed James Bond Rock, a standard attraction on every tour of the bay.

Deer Hunter: Many of the exciting river scenes (falling from the helicopter, held captive in submerged bamboo cages) were filmed along the River Kwai just west of Kanchanaburi. Bar scenes were shot inside the Mississippi Queen on Patpong Road in Bangkok.

Good Morning Vietnam: Robin Williams wakes up the troops in this 1987 film. The Minh Ngoc Bar was actually a little food store converted into a GI bar complete with American flags and jukebox. Bangkok's notorious Patpong Road served as Saigon's Tu Do Street, complete with fiberglass replicas of the old blue-and-yellow Renault taxis.

Killing Fields: Hua Hin's Railway Hotel served as Phnom Penh's leading hotel. Some of the beach scenes were filmed at Bang Tao Bay on Phuket. Spaulding Gray's monologue *Swimming to Cambodia* provides humorous commentary on the filming.

Casualties Of War: Much of the 1990 hit starring Michael Fox and Sean Penn, and directed by Brian De Palma, was filmed in Thailand.

Never pat a Thai on the head even in the friendliest of circumstances. Standing over someone—especially someone older, wiser, or more enlightened than yourself—is also considered rude behavior since it implies social superiority. As a sign of courtesy, lower your head as you pass a group of people. When in doubt, watch the Thais.

Conversely, the foot is considered the lowest and dirtiest part of the body. The worst possible insult to a Thai is to point your unholy foot at his sacred head. Keep your feet under control; fold them underneath when sitting down, don't point them toward another person, and never place them on a coffee table.

A Graceful Welcome: Thailand's traditional form of greeting is the *wai,* a lovely prayerlike gesture accompanied with a little head nodding. Social status is indicated by the height of your *wai* and the depth of your bow: inferiors initiate the *wai,* while superiors return the *wai* with just a smile. Under no circumstances should you *wai* waitresses, children, or clerks—this only makes you look ridiculous! Save your respect for royalty, monks, and immigration officials.

CAUTIONS

Theft

Theft in Thailand is usually by stealth rather than by force, and armed robbery is rare except in isolated situations. The biggest problem is razor-blade artists on public buses in Bangkok; carry your bag directly in front of you and be extra alert whenever somebody presses against you. Keeping them in hotel safes is the best way to protect valuables, but you should be cautious about dishonest hotel employees who steal cash or surreptitiously use credit cards. American Express reports that Thailand has the highest ratio of fraudulent-to-legitimate card use of all its markets, second highest in monetary value only to that of the United States. Hotel fraud is a major problem in Chiang Mai guesthouses, where dishonest hotel clerks sometimes remove credit cards from stored luggage and run up large bills with the cooperation of unscrupulous merchants. Credit cards should be sealed to discourage unauthorized charges, and a complete receipt of stored goods including the serial numbers of traveler's checks should be obtained.

Knockout drugs are another serious problem. Large numbers of Western visitors are robbed each year by sleeping drugs administered by professional con artists who often spend hours (even days!) gaining their confidence. Never accept food or drinks from a stranger. Also be wary of strangers who offer tours of the city or private boat cruises in Bangkok.

AIDS

Love and lust in Thailand have taken an ugly turn since authorities first detected AIDS in 1984. According to a government survey released in 1992, Thailand had almost 400,000 HIV-positive cases—most of them drug addicts—while 76 people had developed AIDS-Related Complex. The World Health Organization reckons that 25,000 people in Thailand are now infected with the virus. Most of those have not yet developed symptoms and continue to engage in gay and heterosexual prostitution, unwittingly infecting their customers. Largely controlled by the triumvirate of brothel owners, police, and politicians with financial interests, Thailand's roaring sex-for-money trade will probably continue growing into the 1990s. And so will AIDS. Sexually active Westerners and Thais alike would obviously do well to exercise caution.

Drugs

Thailand also suffers from a soaring drug problem. Local law-enforcement officials make little distinction between grass and heroin.

Penalties are harsh: over 700 foreigners are now incarcerated in the Bangkok and Chiang Mai prisons on drug charges—not pleasant places to spend 10 years of your life. Raids conducted at popular travelers' hotels in Bangkok and Chiang Mai often involve drugs planted by overzealous police officers. Arrested, booked, and fingerprinted, the frightened Westerner spends a night in jail before posting a US$2000 bail and passport as collateral. Even the smallest quantities bring mandatory jail sentences; life imprisonment is common for sizable seizures. The obvious message with drugs in Thailand is *don't*.

SUGGESTED READING

Some advance reading will go a long way toward understanding Thailand and the Thai people. Most of the following are best read before you leave, though *Mai Pen Rai, Culture Shock, Thai Ways,* and *Guide to Thailand* (four highly recommended books) are available in Bangkok.

♦ Blofel, John. *Bangkok, The Great Cities.* New York: Time-Life, 1973. Good local insight into both the upside and the downside of this vibrant metropolis.

♦ Clarac, Achille. *Guide to Thailand.* Malaysia: Oxford University Press, 1981. The most comprehensive traveler's guide to the arts and architecture of Thailand. Rudimentary practicalities, but highly recommended for historical background and cultural coverage.

♦ Cooper, Robert, and Nanthapa Cooper. *Culture Shock.* Singapore: Times Books International, 1982. A humorous paperback which succinctly explains the Thai people, their customs, and hidden rules for correct social etiquette. A delightful book filled with great insight and charm, especially the discussion on Thai smiles.

♦ Geo, Veran. *50 Trips through Siam's Canals.* Bangkok: Duang Kamol, 1979. A

fascinating but outdated guide to the confusing labyrinth of rivers and canals that stretch across southern Thailand. Included are over 30 maps, Thai prices, and brief descriptions of the temples.

♦ Hollinger, Carol. *Mai Pen Rai.* Boston: Houghton Mifflin, 1965. The story of an American housewife and her humorous introduction to life in Bangkok. One of the warmest books you will ever read. Highly recommended.

♦ Hoskin, John. *Guide to Chiang Mai and Northern Thailand.* Hong Kong: Hong Kong Publishing, 1984. Detailed and up-to-date information on the attractions of northern Thailand. Oriented toward visitors with rental cars.

♦ Lewis, Paul, and Elaine Lewis. *Peoples of the Golden Triangle.* London: Thames and Hudson, 1984. Paul and Elaine have worked as missionaries among the tribals of northern Thailand since 1947. This lavishly illustrated book is the best available guide to these intriguing peoples.

♦ Segaller, Denis. *Thai Ways.* Bangkok,: Allied Newspapers, 1984. A collection of short essays on Thai ceremonies, festivals, customs, and beliefs. This and his sequel *More*

SUGGESTED READING

Thai Ways are great books to read while traveling in the country.

♦ Van Beek, Steve, and Luca Invernizzi Tettoni. *Arts of Thailand*. Hong Kong: Travel Publishing Asia Limited, 1985. The best introductory guidebook to Thai arts in print. Great photos!

♦ Warren, William, and R. Ian Lloyd. *Bangkok's Waterways*. Bangkok: Asia Books, 1989. Dependable and well-researched advice on self-guided boat tours on the Chao Praya River and its *klongs*.

♦ Warren, William, and Luca Tettoni. *Legendary Thailand*. Hong Kong: Travel Publishing Asia Limited, 1986. Outstanding photographs and a clean text; a good introduction to the land and people.

BANGKOK AND VICINITY
BANGKOK

Thailand's sprawling, dynamic, and frustrating capital offers more variety, sights, and wonders than any other destination in Asia. Far too many visitors, hearing of the horrendous traffic jams and searing pollution, stop only long enough to glimpse a few temples and pick up cheap air tickets before departing for more idyllic environs. To some degree this is understandable. Packed into the sweltering plains of the lower Chao Praya are some 10 million residents, 80% of the country's automobiles, and most of the nation's commercial headquarters—a city strangled by uncontrolled development. Without any semblance of a city center or urban planning, traffic grinds to a standstill during rush hours and dissolves into a swamp after summer monsoons. Worse yet is the monotonous sprawl of Chinese shophouses and faceless concrete towers that more closely resemble a Western labyrinth than anything remotely Eastern. It's an unnerving place.

To appreciate the charms and fascinations of Bangkok you must focus instead on the positive: dozens of magnificent temples that form one of Asia's great spectacles, countless restaurants with superb yet inexpensive food, legendary nightlife to satisfy all possible tastes, excellent shopping, and some of the friendliest people in the world. Nobody enjoys the heat, humidity, or traffic jams, but with patience and a sense of *mai pen rai,* Bangkok will cast an irresistible spell.

HISTORY

Unless a Thai is condescending to foreign ignorance, he will never call his capital city Bangkok ("City of Wild Plums") but rather will refer to it as Krung Thep, "City of Angels." Krung Thep actually begins the string of honorariums that comprises the official name, a mammoth tongue twister which, according to Guinness, forms the longest place name in the world.

Bangkok sprung from a small village or *bang* filled with wild olive and plum trees called *kok.* At first little more than a trading suburb to Thonburi ("Money Town"), Bangkok rose to prominence after Burmese forces destroyed Ayuthaya in 1767 and General Taksin moved his armies south. Taksin soon went insane (claiming to be the final Buddha) and was dispatched to Buddhist nirvana in time-honored fashion—a sharp blow to the back of the neck.

Rama I, Taksin's chief military commander, was recalled from Cambodia to found the dynasty which rules to the present day. Fearing further Burmese attacks, Rama I moved the city across the river and relocated the Chinese merchants south to Sampeng, today's Chinatown. Bangkok was formally established on 21 April 1782, with the consecration of the city's foundation pillar at Lak Muang. Rama I constructed his capital to rival once-glorious Ayuthaya: palaces were erected with brick salvaged from Ayuthaya, temples were filled with Ayuthayan Buddhas, and concentric canals were dug to emulate the watery kingdom. The city was then renamed Krung Thep, a title rather ignominiously ignored by Western cartographers, who continued to call it Bangkok.

ATTRACTIONS

Admission Fees

The Grand Palace/Wat Pra Keo Complex will probably be your first experience with the notorious two-tier fee system for selected temples, museums, and historical sites in Thailand. In late 1985 the Fine Arts Department began charging foreigners significantly higher admission fees than Thais. For example, entrance to the Grand Palace is 100B for foreigners but free for Thais. Although rarely noticed by tourists (lower entrance fees for locals are posted only in Thai script), this double standard has proven contentious for Western travelers, who resent

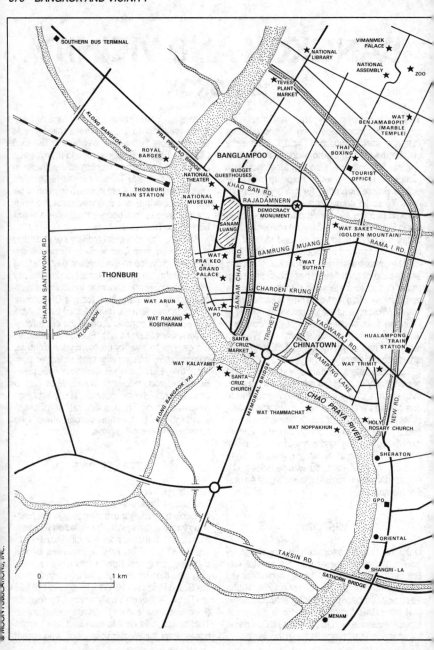

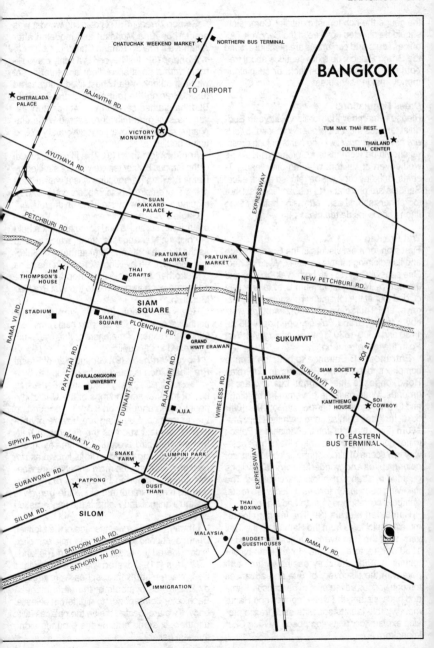

the gouge-the-rich-tourist mentality. Complaints should be directed upstairs at the Bangkok TAT office. Touts and con artists are plentiful around the Grand Palace; be extra cautious about free boat rides, invitations to lunch, or suspicious money-making schemes.

Dress Regulations

Please remember that foreign visitors to Buddhist temples must be properly dressed. *Shorts are never appropriate.* Long pants or long dresses should be worn instead. Women should be well covered. Visitors wearing dirty jeans, T-shirts, or halter tops will be refused admittance. Sandals are preferable to rubber slippers. Photographers should ask permission before taking flash photos inside temples.

Wat Pra Keo

First stop for most visitors is the Grand Palace and its adjoining temple complex, Wat Pra Keo. One sensible plan to see both Wat Pra Keo and the nearby National Museum is to take a free guided tour at the museum (Tuesdays, Wednesdays, and Thursdays at 0930), and then walk down to the Grand Palace, open daily 0830-1130 and 1300-1530. Time permitting, visit Wat Po in the late afternoon.

Entrance (1): Entrance to both the temple complex and the Grand Palace is on Na Pralan Road opposite the Sanam Luang parade grounds. Walk past the government buildings and turn left down the narrow corridor. The 100B ticket includes admission to both the **Coin Museum (2)** on the right and the Vimanmek Palace in northern Bangkok. Through the narrow gateway is a scene of almost unbelievable brilliance: golden spires and wonderfully ornate pavilions guarded by strange mythological creatures. The following description follows a clockwise route; numbers correspond to map and legend.

Ramakien Murals (3): The interior cloister murals depict tales from the Ramakien, the Thai version of the Ramayana. Originally painted in 1850 and restored for the Rattankosin bicentennial in 1982, the story begins by the north gate with the discovery of Sita and advances through various adventures of her consort Rama and his assistant, the white monkey god Hanuman. Marble tablets opposite each fresco provide explanatory texts composed by King Chulalongkorn.

Golden *Chedi* (4): This dazzling wonder was erected by King Mongkut and modeled after Ayuthaya's Pra Sri Ratana Chedi.

***Mondop* (5):** Just beyond is a richly carved library with a solid-silver floor and interior set with a mother-of-pearl chest filled with sacred texts. Gracing the four corners are exquisite Buddha statues carved in a 14th-century Javanese style and miniature sacred white elephants, symbols of royal power. Normally closed to the public.

Angkor Wat Model (6): This miniature model of the famous Khmer temple was constructed by Rama IV when Kampuchea was a vassal state of the Thai empire. Photographers can get an intriguing aerial view by standing on the railing.

Gabled *Viharn* (7): The Pra Viharn Yot, decorated with ceramics and porcelain, once held the historic Manangasila stone, which served as the throne for King Ramkamheng of Sukothai. Discovered by King Mongkut in the ruins of Sukothai during his monkhood, the stone has since been transferred to the Wat Pra Keo Museum.

Royal Mausoleum (8): The Pra Naga in the northwest corner of the complex holds urns containing the ashes of members of the royal family. Closed to the public.

Royal Pantheon (9): Ground plan of Prasat Pra Thepbidon is a Greek cross capped by a yellow *prang*. Standing inside are life-size statues of the first seven kings of the Chakri dynasty. Open annually on 6 April. Surrounding this magnificent building are bizarre mythological animals such as the *kinaree,* a half-human, half-bird creature of Hima ayan origins, and glaring guardian lions known as *norasinghs*. Flanking the main entrance are slender *chedis* supported by a frieze of mythical *garuda* birds—important since the *garuda* is Vishnu's animal and Rama is the reincarnation of Vishnu.

Library (10): The west facade of the Montien Dharma, second library of the temple complex, is considered the finest of its kind in Thailand.

***Prangs* (11):** Covered with glazed ceramic tiles, these eight Khmer spires were erected by Rama I as symbols of the eight planets. Each color corresponds to a different celestial body. Two are located inside the palace walls; another six stand outside the grounds along the east gallery.

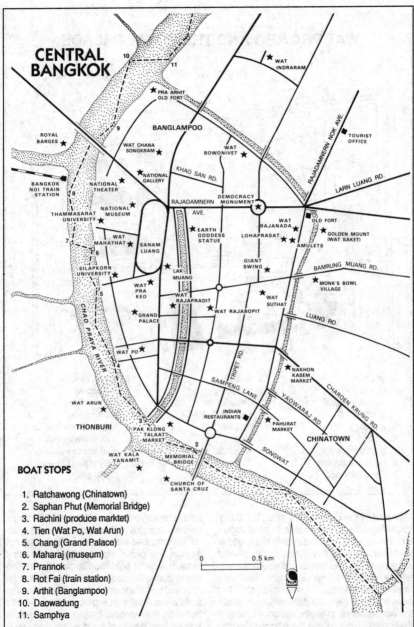

CENTRAL BANGKOK

10
11

★ WAT INDRARAM

★ PRA ARHIT OLD FORT

BANGLAMPOO

ROYAL BARGES ★

9

★ WAT CHANA SONGKRAM

★ WAT BOWONIVET

TOURIST OFFICE ■

KHAO SAN RD.

RAJADAMNERN NOK AVE.

LARN LUANG RD.

BANGKOK NOI TRAIN STATION

8

★ NATIONAL THEATER

★ NATIONAL GALLERY

RAJADAMNERN AVE.

DEMOCRACY MONUMENT ★

OLD FORT ■

THAMMASARAT UNIVERSITY

★ NATIONAL MUSEUM

EARTH GODDESS STATUE

WAT RAJANADA ★

★ GOLDEN MOUNT (WAT SAKET)

7
6

★ WAT MAHATHAT

SANAM LUANG

LOHAPRASAT ★

AMULETS

SILAPKORN UNIVERSITY ★

LAK MUANG

GIANT SWING

BAMRUNG MUANG RD.

5

★ WAT PRA KEO

★ WAT RAJAPRADIT

★ WAT RAJABOPIT

WAT SUTHAT ★

★ MONK'S BOWL VILLAGE

★ GRAND PALACE

LUANG RD.

WAT PO ★

4

CHAO PRAYA RIVER

TRIPET RD.

★ NAKHON KASEM MARKET

WAT ARUN ★

SAMPENG LANE

YAOWARAJ RD.

CHAROEN KRUNG RD.

3

THONBURI

PAK KLONG TALAAT MARKET

INDIAN RESTAURANTS ■

★ PAHURAT MARKET

CHINATOWN

BOAT STOPS

WAT KALA YANAMIT ★

2

MEMORIAL BRIDGE

SONGWAT

★ CHURCH OF SANTA CRUZ

1. Ratchawong (Chinatown)
2. Saphan Phut (Memorial Bridge)
3. Rachini (produce marktet)
4. Tien (Wat Po, Wat Arun)
5. Chang (Grand Palace)
6. Maharaj (museum)
7. Prannok
8. Rot Fai (train station)
9. Arthit (Banglampoo)
10. Daowadung
11. Samphya

0   0.5 km

MOON

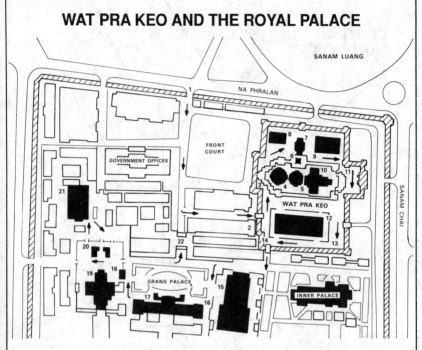

WAT PRA KEO AND THE ROYAL PALACE

© MOON PUBLICATIONS, INC.

1. entrance
2. coin museum
3. *Ramakien* murals
4. golden *chedi*
5. *mondop*
6. model of Angkor Wat
7. gabled *viharn*
8. Royal Mausoleum
9. Royal Pantheon
10. library
11. *prangs*
12. Chapel of the
    Emerald Buddha
13. belltower
14. *yaks*
15. Amarinda
    Audience Hall
16. Royal Collection
    of Weapons
17. Grand Palace
    Audience Hall
18. Amporn Pimok Pavilion
19. Dusit Audience Hall
20. courtyard doorways
21. Wat Pra Keo Museum
22. double gates

Chapel of the Emerald Buddha (12): Bangkok's Royal Temple is Thailand's most important and sacred *wat*. Constructed at the end of the 18th century by King Rama I, this splendid example of Thai aesthetics and religious architecture houses the Emerald Buddha, Thailand's most venerated image. So small and distant that it can hardly be seen, the jade image symbolizes the independence, strength, and good fortune of the country. Thais believe this religious talisman holds the magical power of the king, who thrice annually changes the holy garments from a golden tunic studded with diamonds during the hot season to a gilded monk's robe for the rainy season. A solid gold robe is placed over the image during the cool season. Shoes must be removed and photography is prohibited. Interior walls are painted with superb frescoes. Murals between the window frames depict *Jataka* scenes from the life of Buddha; the universe is portrayed in Buddhist astrological representation on the back wall behind the altar. The wall fronting the altar (above the entrance) relates the temptation and victory of Buddha over Mara. Guarding the entrance are two mythical bronze lions, masterpieces of Khmer art. Also note the unusually ornate boundary stones and towering manlike creatures called *yaks* **(14),** sharp-fanged mythological creatures dressed in Thai costumes and wielding huge clubs. An elaborate **Belltower (13)** stands in the opposite corner. *Kinarees* and *garudas* brandishing *nagas* complete the amazing scene.

Grand Palace

Bangkok's former royal palace, an intriguing blend of Italian Renaissance architecture and classical Thai roofing, was begun in 1783 by King Rama I and improved upon by subsequent rulers. If Wat Pra Keo evokes the Orient, then the Grand Palace will remind you of Europe.

Amarinda Audience Hall (15): Originally the private residence of Rama I and Hall of Justice, Vinchai Hall today serves as a royal venue for coronations and ceremonial state events. An antique boat-shaped throne on which early kings received homage stands behind; the present king uses the frontal Western throne.

Grand Palace Audience Hall (17): Eccentric, half-Western, and half-Oriental, the Chakri Maha Prasat was constructed in 1882 by King Chulalongkorn to commemorate the centenary of the Chakri Dynasty. Designed by a British architect, this Italian Renaissance palace was incongruously superimposed with a Thai *prasat* roof at the king's request—a strangely successful fusion of disparate styles. The Grand Palace served as the royal residence until King Ananda was shot in bed under mysterious circumstances in 1946. His brother, the current King Rama IX, subsequently moved out to the more spacious Chitralada Palace. Visitors are allowed inside the state reception room decorated with European furnishings and the **Royal Collection of Weapons (16).** Left of the museum is a gateway leading to the Inner Palace, once the residence of the king's children and concubines. Closed to the public.

Amporn Pimok Pavilion (18): At one time, Rama IV would alight from his elevated palanquin, present himself to the crowd below, enter this delicate little pavilion, remove his ceremonial hat and gown, and then proceed into the throne hall. So quintessentially Thai is the architecture that Rama V reproduced it at his Bang Pa In summer retreat, and a replica was exhibited at the World's Fair in Brussels.

Dusit Audience Hall (19): Mounted on a marble platform in the shape of a Latin cross, this magnificent building is widely considered Thailand's finest example of royal architecture. Once used for outdoor receptions, today the building serves for ceremonial lying-in-states of deceased kings. Note the interior paintings, throne built by King Mongkut, four guardian figures donated by wealthy Chinese businessmen, and **Courtyard Doorways (20)** painted with colorful sentries.

Wat Pra Keo Museum (21): Features inside this fine little museum include a scale model of the Royal Palace-and-Wat Pra Keo complex—useful to sort out the confusing labyrinths. Javanese Buddhas and the famous Manangasila Throne are displayed upstairs. Best of all (this is important), it's air-conditioned! Exit through the **Double Gates (22).**

Lak Muang

Across the road from the Grand Palace stands a newly renovated marble pavilion housing a *lingam*-shaped monument covered with gold leaf and adorned with flowers. This foundation stone, from which all distances in Thailand are measured, was placed here by King Rama I to provide a home for the unseen landlord-spirits of the city. Thais believe these magical spirits possess the power to grant wishes, win lotteries, guarantee healthy children, and protect the fate of the city. Thai classical-dance performances sponsored in the rear pavilion by satisfied supplicants include Ramakien routines, the most popular version being an Eastern *Swan Lake* called the *Manora*. Early morning and late afternoon are the busiest and best times to watch the dancing; extra busy two or three days before a lottery.

National Museum

This museum, the largest and most comprehensive in Southeast Asia, serves as an excellent introduction to the arts of Thailand—it should not be missed. Collections are open daily except Mondays and Fridays 0900-1200 and 1300-1600. Detailed information is provided in

NATIONAL MUSEUM TOURS

Thai Art and Culture . . . . Tuesday
Buddhism . . . . Wednesday
Pre-Thai. . . . . Tuesday, Thursday
Thai Pottery . . . . 1st, 2nd Tuesday
Buddhasawan Chapel . . . . . . 3rd Tuesday

the *Guide to The National Museum Bangkok* sold at the front desk. To quickly sort through the artifacts, which range from Neolithic discoveries of Ban Chiang to contemporary Bangkok pieces, museum volunteers conduct free guided tours starting at 0930 from the ticket desk. *These tours are highly recommended.* English, French, German, Japanese, and Spanish tours are also given. Call 224-1333 for further information. English-language tours are listed in the "National Museum Tours" chart.

Wat Mahathat

The "Temple of the Great Relic" serves as one of Thailand's great centers of Buddhist learning and national headquarters for the Mahanikaya sect practiced by over 90% of the Buddhist population. Vipassana ("Insight") meditation techniques are a specialty of the amazingly friendly head abbot; visitors can obtain further information from the office in Section five. Weekends are an excellent time to visit a lively outdoor market which runs right through the temple grounds. A small *soi* (alley) through the back entrance crosses Maharat Road and opens into the temple's most famous sight: a plaza filled with shops selling Buddhist amulets, freshly cast Buddha images, and monk accessories such as begging bowls and orange robes.

Sports At The Sanam Luang

Although this huge public ground in front of the Grand Palace is used for royal cremations and the annual ploughing ceremony, you'll more likely come across traditional Thai sports such as kite flying and *takraw.*

Thailand is perhaps the only country in the world where a children's sport has developed into a form of combat. Kite fighting began after an Ayuthayan governor quelled a local rebellion by flying massive kites over the besieged city and using jars of explosives to bomb it into submis-

sion. Less-violent competitions, such as the coveted King's Cup in April, are held today between two different types of kites with gender-inspired characteristics. Male kites (*chulas*) are sturdy three-meter star-shaped fighting vessels fixed with bamboo barbs on reinforced strings. Female kites (*pakpao*), on the other hand, are diminutive one-meter kites set with long tails and loops of string. The male kite attempts to snag the female and drag her into his territory, while the female uses her superior speed and maneuverability to avoid the male and force him to the ground.

Takraw, one of Thailand's most popular sports, comes in several versions. Circle *takraw* involves bouncing a light ball made of braided rattan, the object being to keep the ball in motion as long as possible without using the hands. Points are awarded for employing the least accessible body parts such as knees, hips, and shoulders. Basket-*takraw* players attempt to kick the rattan ball through a ring elevated 6-10 meters above the ground. Net *takraw*—unquestionably the most exciting version—is played almost exactly like volleyball but without hands. Overhead serves and foot spikes in this variation require an amazing degree of dexterity and acrobatic skill!

Though formally banned by the Thai government, pairs of male Siamese fighting fish (*Betta splendens regan*) still do combat in the side streets for the benefit of gamblers. Captured in swamps and raised in freshwater tanks, when placed in common tanks these pugnacious fish transform themselves into vividly colored fighting creatures complete with quivering gills and flashing tails. Also popular is insect fighting, which pitches enormous horned male beetles against each other for the charms of a female attendant. The battle ends when the weaker beetle dies on its back.

Earth Goddess Statue

Just opposite the Royal Hotel stands a small white pavilion and a female image that illustrates one of the most beloved tales of Buddhist folklore. According to legend, Buddha in the throes of meditation was repeatedly tempted by the evil goddess Mara and her sensual dancing ladies. So impressed was Torani with his courage, compassion, and moral willpower that she wrung her long hair, setting loose a tidal wave that swept away Mara and her evil armies.

TEMPLE ARCHITECTURE

Thailand has over 30,000 Buddhist temples, which share, to a large degree, common types of structures. The following descriptions will help sort through the dazzling yet bewildering buildings found throughout the country.

The *Wat*

The entire religious complex is known as a *wat*. This term does not properly translate to "temple," since temple implies a singular place dedicated to the worship of a god, while *wats* are multiple buildings dedicated to the veneration—not worship—of the Buddha. *Wats* serve as religious institutions, schools, community meeting halls, hospitals, entertainment venues, and homes for the aged and abandoned. Some even serve as drug-rehabilitation centers.

Wat titles often explain much about their history and function. Some are named after the kings who constructed them, such as Ayuthaya's Wat Pra Ram, named for King Ramatibodhi. Others use the word Rat, Raja, or Racha to indicate that Thai royalty either constructed or restored the building. Others are named for their Buddha images, such as Wat Pra Keo in Bangkok, which holds the Keo or Emerald Buddha. Pra (also spelled Phra)—the term that often precedes important Buddha images—means "honorable." Thailand's most important *wats* are called Wat Mahathat, a term that indicates they hold a great (*maha*) relic (*that*) of the Buddha. Wat Mahathats are found in Bangkok, Chiang Rai, Sukothai, Ayuthaya, Phitsanulok, Petchburi, Nakhon Si Thammarat, Yasothon, and Chai Nat.

Bot

Bots, the most important and sacred structure in the religious compound, are assembly halls where monks meet to perform ceremonies and ordinations, meditate, give sermons to lay people, and recite the *patimokkha* (disciplinary rules) every fortnight.

The Exterior: Ground plans vary from quadrilateral *cellas* with single doors to elaborate cruciform designs with multiple entrances. All are identified by *bai sema,* eight boundary stones which define the consecrated ground and help ward off evil spirits. *Bai semas* are often protected by small tabernacles richly decorated with spires and runic symbols. *Bot* window shutters and doors are often carved and decorated with gold leaf and mirrored tiles or engraved with mother-of-pearl designs. But the most arresting sights are the multitiered roofs covered with brilliant glazed tiles. Roof extremities end with *chofas,* graceful curls that represent *nagas* or mythological *garudas.* Wriggling down the edges of the bargeboards are more *nagas,* which act as heavenly staircases between earthly existence and Buddhist nirvana. Some of the best artwork is found in the triangular pediments: images of Vishnu riding his Garuda or Indra riding elephant-headed Erawan.

The Interior: Stunning interior murals often follow identical arrangements. Paintings behind the primary Buddha image depict scenes from the Traiphum, the Buddhist cosmological order of heaven, earth, and hell. Have a close look at the punishments of the damned—they might remind you of Hieronymus Bosch's painting of Dante's *Inferno* (devils dancing around, people being speared or boiled alive, etc.). Less interesting side walls are decorated with incidents from the life or earlier incarnations of the Buddha. The most spectacular murals, always located on the front wall above the main entrance, depict the Buddha's enlightenment or

chedi

TEMPLE ARCHITECTURE

his temptation by Mara. Shoes must be removed before entering all *bots* in Thailand.

Viharn

Secondary assembly halls where laymen pay homage to the principal Buddha image. *Viharns* are architecturally identical to *bots* except for the lack of consecrated boundary stones. Larger *viharns* are surrounded by magnificently decorated cloisters filled with rows of gilded Buddha images.

Chedi

Chedi is the Thai term for the Indian stupa. In ancient times, these dome-shaped monuments held relics of the Buddha such as pieces of bone or hairs. Later prototypes were erected over the remains of kings or saints, and today anybody with sufficient *baht* can have one constructed for his or her ashes. *Chedis* consist of a three-tiered base representing heaven, hell, and earth, and a bulbous stupa placed on top. The small pavilion (*harmika*) near the summit symbolizes the Buddha's seat of meditation. Above this is a multitiered and highly stylized umbrella ringed with moldings representing the 33 Buddhist heavens. Pinnacles are often capped with crystals and

religious prasat

precious jewels. The world's largest *chedi* is located in Nakhon Pathom, one hour west of Bangkok.

Prang

These towering spires, some of the most distinctive and exciting monumental structures in Thailand, trace their architectural heritage back to the corner towers of Cambodian temples. Although these phallic-shaped structures are set on a square base like the *chedi*, many have achieved a more elegant and slender outline than Kampuchean prototypes. Lower tiers are often ringed by a frieze of demons who appear to be—depending on your perspective—either dancing or supporting the tower. Summits are typically crowned by the Hindu thunderbolt, symbol of Shiva and religious holdover from ancient traditions. Thailand's most famous *prang* is Wat Arun, just across the river from the Grand Palace.

prang

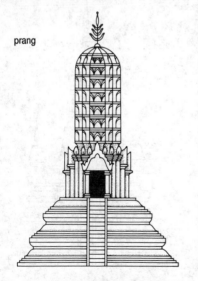

Mondop

These are square, pyramidal-roofed structures that enshrine highly venerated objects such as palm-leaf Tripitakas (Buddhist bibles) or footprints of the Buddha. Thailand's most famous example is the *mondop* of the Temple of the Buddha's Footprint at Saraburi.

Prasat

These elegant little buildings have ground plans in the form of Greek Crosses. *Prasats* may serve either religious or royal functions. Those designed for

TEMPLE ARCHITECTURE

secular or royal purposes are capped with familiar multiple rooflines; religious *prasats* are crowned with *prangs*. Thailand's most famous *prasat* is located at Bang Pa In, one hour north of Bangkok.

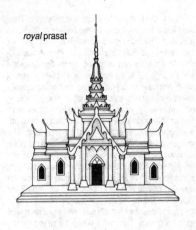

royal prasat

Other Structures

Sala: Open-walled structures used by pilgrims to escape the heat and by monks as casual dining rooms. *Salas* also serve as overnight shelters for pilgrims during temple festivals.

Ho Rakang: Bell or drum towers that summon monks to services and meals.

Ho Trai: Elevated, graceful libraries that house Buddhist canonical texts. *Ho trai* are built on stilts to prevent rats and white ants from devouring the precious manuscripts.

Kuti: Monk's quarters. Often the simplest yet most attractive buildings in the *wat* complex. Older *kutis* are frequently on the verge of collapse; those in Petchburi are most evocative.

Kanbarien Hall: Used for religious instruction.

Wat Po

Bangkok's oldest and largest temple complex was founded in the 16th century and radically remodeled two centuries later by Rama II into an open-air university for his Thai subjects. Crammed into the courtyards are a bewildering number of chapels, rock gardens, bizarre statuary (Chinese guards wearing European top hats), educational tablets, belltowers, and dozens of small *chedis;* student guides can be hired. Highlights include an artificial mound covered with figurines of holy men in contorted positions of meditation and massage; the main chapel, considered a masterpiece of Thai religious architecture; and surrounding cloisters displaying almost 400 Ayuthayan-style Buddhas. Certainly the most famous sight is the gigantic 46-meter Reclining Buddha housed under a claustrophobic shed in the western courtyard. Thailand's largest reclining Buddha is difficult to appreciate in such tight settings, but note the intricate mother-of-pearl designs on the footsoles, which depict the 108 signs of the true Lord Buddha.

More intriguing perhaps is the College of Traditional Medicine in the eastern courtyard. This royal-sponsored mini-university of massage, herbal medicine, and Chinese acupuncture offers inexpensive, traditional Thai rubs: 80B for 30 minutes, 120B for one hour. Thirty hours of professional instruction spread over 10 or 15 days costs 3000B.

Wat Arun

This monumental 86-meter Khmer-style *prang,* one of the largest religious monuments in the country, towers above the Chao Praya to form Bangkok's most impressive and famous landmark. Better known as the Temple of the Dawn, Wat Arun symbolically represents the Buddhist universe, with its trident-capped central tower indicating Mount Meru, and the four smaller towers depicting the four worldly oceans. Reflective beauty comes from thousands of multiglazed Chinese porcelains embedded into the structure by Buddhist devotees. Take a ferry from the Tha Tien Pier behind Wat Po.

Also situated in Thonburi is the enormous **Wat Kalayanamit,** whose imposing dimensions are dictated by the huge Buddha image it enshrines, and the **Royal Barges Museum,** which houses more than 50 restored longboats.

Wat Rajapradit

Constructed in 1864 by King Mongkut to complete the holy triumvirate of Ayuthayan temples,

ICONOGRAPHY OF THE BUDDHA IMAGE

Visitors to the National Museum and temples of Thailand are often confused by the variety of Buddhas they find. The following description will help sort out the basic symbolism and describe the delicate balancing act between religious symbolism and the artist's urge to create new forms. First-time visitors often consider Buddhist images monotonous lookalikes created with little imagination or originality, a not unfair judgment since Buddhist sculptors have traditionally been copyists who depicted Buddha images exactly as described in Pali religious texts. The image's comprehensible and undisturbing symbolism is conveyed in dozens of ways: feet must be engraved with 108 auspicious signs; toes and fingers should be of equal length; hands should resemble the opening of lotus buds; arms should extend all the way to the knees; the magical spot between the eyes and protuberance from the forehead must represent enlightenment. Creativity was also stifled by the sculptor's desire to exactly reproduce earlier images that had demonstrated magical powers. According to legend, an authorized Buddha image carved during Sakyamuni's lifetime absorbed his magical potency; sculptors believed that exact likenesses of the original would share these magical powers and provide the pious with supernatural protection.

Despite these religious straitjackets, Thai artists successfully created a half-dozen unique styles that stand today as some of Asia's most refined art. Important characteristics that typify Dvaravati (6th-11th centuries), Khmer (11th-14th centuries), Northern (10th-16th centuries), Sukhothai (13th-15th centuries), Ayuthaya (1350-1767), and Bangkok styles (1767-present) are described in the Introduction.

Mudras Of The Buddha

Buddhist images throughout Thailand share common body positions (seated, standing, walking, and

calling the earth to witness

reclining) and hand gestures (*mudras*) that symbolically represent important events in the life of Buddha. Standing images depict Sakyamuni taming evil forces and bestowing blessings. Walking figures illustrate the Buddha returning to earth after preaching to his mother and deities in heaven. Reclining images embody the Buddha at the exact moment of nirvana—not sleeping as visitors often assume! Sitting Buddhas relate various stories: meditating, witnessing divinity, or setting in motion the wheel of the law. Understanding the following *mudras* will prove invaluable when examining Buddha images throughout Southeast Asia.

Calling the Earth to Witness *Mudra:* Seated in either a full- or half-lotus position, the Buddha reaches forward to touch the ground with his right hand, an immensely popular *mudra* that symbolizes the Buddha's victory over the demons of Mara and testifies to his enlightenment.

Dispelling Fear *Mudra:* One or both hands are held at shoulder level with the palms turned out-

reclining

ICONOGRAPHY OF THE BUDDHA IMAGE

meditation

Dispensing Favors *Mudra:* Almost identical to the position of Dispelling Fear except that the palm is completely exposed, open, and empty, this *mudra* symbolizes the Buddha's vows of assistance and gifts of truth.

Turning the Wheel of the Law *Mudra:* Both hands are held before the chest with the thumb and forefinger of the right hand forming a circle. Representing the position that set in motion the wheel of the Buddhist law, this indestructible wheel also symbolizes karma, samsara, and the reality of nirvana.

ward. Used with both walking and standing Buddhas, this *mudra* evolved from a legend in which the Buddha raised his hand to subdue a rampaging elephant intent on his destruction. Also called the triumph over evil or giving of protection *mudra.*

Meditation *Mudra:* With one hand resting on the other and both legs crossed in a lotus position, this classic attitude represents the final meditation and enlightenment under the bodhi tree. Eyes are closed and breath is held to concentrate on the truth.

Adoration *Mudra:* Generally performed by bodhisattvas or lesser angels giving homage to the Buddha, this hand gesture is formed by joining both hands together vertically at the level of the breast—exactly like the Buddhist *wai.*

turning the wheel of law

dispelling fear

this picturesque *wat* is noted for its interior murals with clear views of Bangkok during the 1860s and Khmer *prangs* superbly carved with images of four-faced Brahma.

Wat Rajabopit
Constructed in 1863 by King Chulalongkorn just as Western influence arrived in Thailand, this architectural curiosity features unusual relief carvings of impassive European soldiers, a tall *chedi* encasing a Buddha seated on a Khmer-style *naga,* and a royal cemetery filled with tombs styled after Indian *chedis* and miniature Gothic cathedrals. Chapel exteriors display familiar Thai rooflines and mother-of-pearl inlays, but the interior will shock you with its uncompromising Italian-Gothic decorations.

Wat Suthat
Constructed in the second quarter of the 19th century, this rarely visited complex is chiefly known for its huge bronze 15th-century Sukothai Buddha located in the *viharn* and exquisite frescoes which adorn the walls of the *bot.* These fabulous murals—considered among the finest in Thailand—were painted during the reign of Rama II with flat tints and primitive perspectives which predate Western influences. Note the delightful choice of subject matter and special brush techniques used to distinguish original artwork from restorations.

Giant Swing
Opposite Wat Suthat tower a pair of red teak pillars once used for the Brahmanic "Ceremony of the Swing." Before being banned in 1932, teams of young Hindu priests would swing a full arch of 180 degrees and try to snatch a bag of gold coins between their teeth. Some bit the gold, others bit the dust.

Wat Rajanada And The Amulet Market
Wat Rajanada is chiefly noted for its popular amulet market at the far left end of the courtyard. Buddhist amulets make great gifts and, unlike Buddha images, may be legally taken out of the country without official permits.

Lohaprasat
To the rear of Wat Rajanada stands a curious pink building which resembles, more than anything else, an ornate wedding cake festooned with 37 candle-spires. Lohaprasat was designed to resemble ancient temples in Sri Lanka and India which, according to legend, served as mansions for the Buddha and his disciples. Earlier prototypes have long since disappeared, leaving Bangkok's structure the world's only surviving example of this unique style.

Golden Mountain
One of the few places from which to peer (smog permitting) over sprawling Bangkok is high atop the 78-meter artificial mountain just outside the ancient capital walls. Modeled after a similar hill in Ayuthaya and once used as a dumping ground for victims of plague, the hilltop is surmounted by a modest *chedi* which enshrines Buddha relics donated by the Nepalese government. Visitors climbing the 318 steps are often approached by young monks anxious to practice their English and older, cynical monks more interested in rock music than nirvana. Wat Saket, at the foot of the mount, sponsors Bangkok's liveliest temple festival each November.

Wat Bowonivet
Somewhat off the familiar tourist route, Wat Bowonivet is the immensely prestigious retreat where Prince Mongkut (of *The King and I* fame) founded the Thammayut sect of Thai Buddhism and served as chief abbot during a portion of his 27-year monkhood. Wat Bowonivet is perhaps the most popular temple in Bangkok for meditation instruction; ask at the international section. Of special merit inside the otherwise undistinguished *bot* are a bronze Sukothai Buddha, considered one of the finest of the period, and walls blanketed with extraordinary murals. Far removed from the traditional concept of Thai art, these dark and mysterious frescoes are the highly personalized work of a Thai artist named Kru Ing Khong who revolutionized classic Thai artwork with his original use of three-dimensional perspective, moody shading, and fascinating use of Western subjects: Englishmen at the horse races, American ships arriving with missionaries, Colonial buildings, and Dutch windmills.

Chinatown
Raucous and seething Chinatown is your best bet if you're looking for the old East in Bangkok.

MAGICAL MEDALLIONS

Thais believe protection against malevolent spirits, reckless *phis,* and black magic can be guaranteed with amulets, small talismanic icons worn around the neck or waist. Extraordinarily powerful amulets derive their magic from having been blessed by Buddhist monks or issued by powerful organizations such as the military or the monarchy. For example, those produced by the king and distributed to policemen have acquired considerable renown for their protective powers. Votive tablets found buried inside the relic chambers of ancient stupas are also deemed extra powerful. Amulet collection is big business here in Thailand; over a dozen publications are devoted exclusively to their histories and personal accounts of their powers.

Each profession favors a certain style: taxi drivers wear amulets to protect against accidents, thieves to protect against the police; American soldiers during the Vietnam War became fascinated with their miraculous powers. Color is also important: white amulets arouse feelings of love, green protects against ghosts and wild animals, yellow promotes successful business deals, red offers protection against criminals. But black is the most powerful color—it provides *complete* invincibility. Among the more bizarre amulets are those fashioned after the phallus (*palad khik*) and realistically carved from rare woods, ivory, or horn. Related to Hindu lingam worship, *palad khik* are attached to cords and worn around the waist. A great way for Westerners to make friends and influence people is to proudly wear an amulet of the king or queen.

Wat Trimit: The "Temple of the Golden Buddha" and its three-meter golden image have a story as fabulous as their reputation. Covered with stucco to disguise its value from Burmese invaders, this Sukothai-style Buddha lay neglected until its transfer in 1953 to a neighboring temple. The statue fell from the crane, the plaster cracked, and workmen discovered the wondrous image inside—five tons of solid gold. Open daily; no admission charge.

Yaowaraj Road: Walk slowly to appreciate the spectacle: dazzling gold stores with mirrored interiors and richly carved wooden chairs, traditional calligraphers working on the sidewalk, herbal stores with displays of antler horn and strange roots, restaurants, and neon signs flashing Chinese characters—sensory overload to rival anything in Asia.

Sampeng Lane: Much too narrow for cars, this canvas-roofed lane is crammed with shopkeepers, gold stores, clothing merchants, prewar architecture, and porters hauling heavy loads. Once known as the Green Light area from the lanterns which illuminated the brothels and opium dens, this *highly recommended* alley epitomizes what is most alluring about Chinatown. Be sure to visit the century-old gold shop at the corner of Mangkon Street.

Chakrapet Road Indian Restaurants: To the left are several inexpensive restaurants such as the Royal India and Cha Cha with excellent *marsala dosas* and sweets wrapped in silver foil. Good food in earthy surroundings.

Pahurat Indian Market: Sampeng Lane terminates at the old cloth market where Sikh and Chinese merchants peddle Indian saris, Malaysian batiks, and Thai silks from enormous open-air tables.

Nakhon Kasem Market: Once Bangkok's antique center, most of the dealers have since moved to shopping centers near the tourist centers. A few dusty stores hold on, surrounded by hardware shops and copper merchants.

Wat Benjamabopit

Designed by the half-brother of King Chulalongkorn and erected at the turn of the century, the "Marble Temple" is considered one of the great sights of Bangkok. Chiefly known for its superb harmony and pleasing symmetry, it also offers an outstanding collection of 52 Buddha statues, both originals and quality reproductions. Each has been carefully labeled as to the country of origin and period; better than art school! Note the "Starving Buddha" cast from an original in Lahore and the outstanding Dvaravati images protected against theft by iron grills.

Vimanmek Palace

Designed by a German architect named Sandreczki and once the residence of Rama V, this well-restored palace now serves as a private museum displaying a rich collection of royal regalia. Inside the world's largest golden teak structure is the eclectic assemblage of King Chulalongkorn, including period furniture, the country's first shower, and a photograph of Thomas Edison signed "to the King and Queen of Siam." Open daily except Sundays 0930-1630; included in the admission fee to the Grand Palace and Wat Pra Keo.

Jim Thompson's House
Jim Thompson was the legendary American architect-entrepreneur who settled in Thailand after WW II and almost singlehandedly revived the moribund silk industry. No trace was found of Thompson after he disappeared in 1967 while hiking near Cameron Highlands. Jim's maze of seven Thai-style teak houses has since been converted into a small private museum filled with his priceless collection of Asian antiques, pottery, and curiosities. A small gift shop sells fine reproductions of Vessantara Jataka and Brahma Jati horoscopes. Open daily except Sundays 0900-1600; admission is an unreasonable 130B.

Visitors seriously interested in Thai arts might also visit the private collection at the Prasat Museum located in the Bangkok suburb of Hua Mak. Phone 253-9772 for more information.

Phallic Shrine
Dedicated to Chao Tuptim (Pomegranate), a Thai female spirit, this tangled mini-jungle shrine has become somewhat notorious in the foreign press for its hundreds of stylized and realistic phalluses contributed by childbearing devotees. Considered a combination fertility-prosperity shrine since the lingam symbolizes both regeneration and good fortune. Bangkok's strangest shrine is located on the grounds of the Hilton at the end of Soi Som Si next to Klong Saen.

Siam Society
Thailand's premier research group publishes the scholarly *Journal of the Siam Society,* restores deteriorating murals, and maintains a 10,000-volume library of rare and valuable editions. Of special interest to foreign visitors is the Society Travel Club (tel. 258-3491), which sponsors professionally led excursions to important temples, archaeological digs, and noteworthy festivals—some of the best available in Thailand. On the grounds is the Kamthieng House, a restored century-old residence noted for its ethnological artifacts and teak lintels which hold ancestral spirits and guarantee the virility of

the inhabitants. Located on Soi 21 just off Sukumvit Road. Open daily except Sundays and Mondays 0900-1200 and 1300-1700; admission 30B.

Suan Pakkard Palace
The royal residence of Princess Chumbhot, one of Thailand's leading art collectors, offers an eclectic range of Thai artifacts from Ban Chiang pottery to Khmer sculpture. Disassembled and brought down from Chiang Mai, the complex of traditional Thai homes also includes the 450-year-old Lacquer Palace transferred from Ayuthaya. The semiprivate gardens which surround the home provide a welcome relief from the dirt and noise of Bangkok. Open daily except Sunday 0900-1600; admission 100B.

Snake Farm
King cobras, green pit vipers, and banded kraits are milked daily at 1100 and 1400 (weekends at 1100 only) inside Thailand's Pasteur Institute. The extracted venom forms the basis for snakebite serum. Cholera, smallpox, typhoid inoculations, and rabies treatments are also available. Open daily 0830-1600; admission 50B.

Erawan Shrine
Thailand's devotion to animist spirits and Hindu deities is best appreciated in the famous shrine on the grounds of the Grand Hyatt Erawan. The memorial was erected after hotel construction halted from a series of seemingly random disasters: the marble for the lobby disappeared at sea, workmen died under mysterious circumstances, and cost overruns threatened to crush the hotel project. After spirit doctors summoned for advice informed the hotel owners that they must erect a shrine to Brahma, the mishaps ended and word of the miracle spread throughout Thailand. Today, it's a continual circus of devotees, incense, flowers, images of the elephant god Erawan (the three-headed mount of Brahma), plus free performances of Thai dance—a crazy and magical place.

Bangkok Floating Market
Thonburi's floating market epitomizes what is most crass and callous in the tourist trade. Once an authentic and colorful scene, the market completely died out in the '60s as modernization forced boat vendors to leave town and move

into modern shopping centers. Threatened with the loss of revenue, tour operators came up with a rather awful solution: hire a few Thai ladies to paddle around and *pretend* to be shopping. Disneyland feels genuine when compared to this outrage, perhaps the most contrived rip-off in the East.

Damnern Saduak Floating Market

Much less touristy than Bangkok's tawdry affair is the Damnern Saduak *klong* market, 109 km southwest of Bangkok. Between 0600 and 0900 dozens of vendors conduct business from their sampans filled with fruits, vegetables, and noodles. The TAT encourages visitors to visit this market rather than the Bangkok fraud; they provide maps and transportation information. Arrive early to beat the tour groups! Public buses leave from the Southern Bus Terminal every 20 minutes from 0600 and take two hours. From the Damnern Saduak Bus Station, either walk along the canal or take a taxi boat for 10B to the Kui Floating Market. Tom Kem Market is just around the corner. Khun Pithak Floating Market is farther south. Boats may be hired to tour all three markets for 300B. To see the markets at daybreak, spend the night in Damnern Saduak at the small Chinese hotel. Damnern Saduak can also be approached from Nakhon Pathom on bus 78, and from Kanchanaburi by bus 461 to Bang Piar intersection, then minibus or bus 78.

Do-it-yourself Canal Tours

Bangkok's waterways offer exceptional sightseeing opportunities and reveal what is most attractive about the city. Canal enthusiasts should purchase *50 Trips Through Siam's Canals* by George Veran or the recently published *Bangkok's Waterways* by William Warren. The *Thonburi Canal* map by the Association of Architects is also useful. Chartered longtail boats from the landing stages at Tha Saphan Phut (*tha* translates to pier) and Tha Tien are somewhat expensive at 150-200B per hour. Less pricey and much more authentic are the ordinary longtail river taxis which race up and down all the smaller canals, picking up and dropping off passengers until they finally turn around and return to their starting points. Prices average about 5B in each direction or 10B roundtrip. These boats leave regularly from Tha Saphan Phut, Tha Tien, and Tha Maharaj. Boatmen rarely speak English,

---

ROMAN-ROBOT FANTASIES

From Hong Kong to Singapore, economic success has dramatically transformed Asian skylines from low-rise colonial to high-tech Houston. But Bangkok's boom has unleashed a wave of innovative architecture unrivaled anywhere else in the region. Refusing to clone Western prototypes, the architects of Bangkok have invented some amazing fantasies: corporate headquarters that resemble Roman palaces, condo complexes that fuse art-deco facades with Thai rooflines, fast-food emporiums buried inside rocket ships, Mediterranean stucco homes, Bavarian half-timbered cottages—Hollywood holograms in the City of Angels.

This new and exciting movement is led by an iconoclastic architect named Sumet Jumsai and an innovative design firm called Plan Architect. Sumet's Bank of Asia Robot building near Silom Road—a humorous mixture of an external skeleton fitted with giant nuts and bolts—illustrates the marriage of high-tech themes with cartoon consciousness. The postmodern McDonald's on Ploenchit Road combines gleaming glass walls with Roman columns. Suburban developments include English castles complete with moats and the new headquarters for the *Nation* newspaper, an 11-story sculpture inspired by the whimsical designs of cubist painter Georges Braque. Bangkok is now more than just Thai temples and nocturnal delights, it's home to some of the most creative modern architecture in the world.

---

but it's almost impossible to get lost. Just sit down, smile, and enjoy the ride. All of the following tours can be made with ordinary boats. **Warning:** beware of slick professionals who offer free guided tours and then blackmail you for a 1000B gasoline fare in the middle of the river. Never get into a longtail boat alone.

Chao Praya Express Boat: One of the cheapest, easiest, and most relaxing water journeys in Bangkok is on the public boat which shuttles up and down the Chao Praya River daily from 0600 to 1800. Sights along the central section include the Grand Palace, Wat Arun, and several other impressive *wats* on the Thonburi side. The boat continues 18 km north to Nonthaburi and makes 35 stops on both sides of the river; visitors can alight and return at any point. Gov-

Bangkok silhouette

ernment-controlled rates vary from three to nine *baht* depending on the distance.

Budget All-day River Trip: Each Saturday and Sunday at 0800 a sleek boat leaves from the Maharaj Pier behind Thammasarat University, stops briefly at the Thai Folk Arts and Crafts Center, and reaches the Royal Summer Palace at Bang Pa In shortly before noon. The return journey visits the fascinating Wat Pailom Stork Sanctuary before arriving back in Bangkok around sunset. Inexpensive and enjoyable, but only recommended for visitors with sufficient time. Don't you wish somebody would unplug that obnoxious loudspeaker?

To Klong Mon: Longtails leave every 30 minutes between 0630 and 1800 from Bangkok's Tha Tien Pier behind Wat Po. The trip passes temples, orchid farms, and young boys leaping into the murky waters. Fare is 5B in each direction.

To Klong Bang Waek: Longtails leave every 15 minutes from the Tha Rachini landing stage and scream down Klong Bangkok Yai before turning left into Klong Bang Waek. Travelers can either remain on the boat for the roundtrip or hop off to explore Thonburi temples. Rachini Pier is also a good place to charter eight-man longtails at 150-200B per hour.

To Klong Tan: This unusual journey originates under the New Petchburi Road bridge (near the Pratunam Market) and passes through beautiful residential neighborhoods until it intersects Klong Tan. Then it's left to Bangkapi for lunch or right down Klong Tan to Sukothai Road Bridge at Soi 73. Buses return back to the center of town.

ATTRACTIONS NEAR BANGKOK

Ancient City

Muang Boran, 33 km south of Bangkok, is a 200-acre outdoor park and architectural museum filled with full-sized and reduced-scale replicas of Thailand's 65 most important monuments and temples. The entire park is enormous, somewhat neglected, rarely visited, and murderously hot in the summer. Ancient City can be visited on a Muang Boran group tour (tel. 222-8145) or by bus from the eastern bus terminal to Samut Prakan, where minibuses continue to Ancient City and the Crocodile Farm. Over 30,000 crocodiles lounge around murky swimming pools inside the world's largest reptile farm. Wrestling matches are staged hourly; daily feedings at 1700. The beasts are then skinned and sold to Chinese restaurants that specialize in exotic meats. Also included in the admission price is a small zoo with oddities such as smoking chimpanzees and dancing elephants. Touristy and weird. Located six km before Ancient City. Open daily 0800-1800; admission 100B.

Rose Garden

This upscale resort, 32 km west of Bangkok on the road to Nakhon Pathom, features landscaped gardens, a modern hotel, a lake, restaurants, a swimming pool, an 18-hole golf course, and replica of a Thai village. Open daily 0800-1800; the 150B admission fee includes a cultural show at 1500. Often included with group tours of the Damnern Saduak Floating Market, Nakhon Pathom, and the nearby Samphran Crocodile Park. Buses leave from the southern bus terminal in Thonburi.

Safari World
Asia's largest wildlife park opened several years ago in a Bangkok suburb at Kilometer 9 on Ramintra Road. Attractions include a wildlife section toured by free coaches, a Bird Park with walk-in aviary, restaurants, and an amusement park. Open daily 1000-1800; admission 100B.

ACCOMMODATIONS

Bangkok in many ways resembles Los Angeles—an urban nightmare spread across vast flatlands without a recognizable city center. For quick orientation, think of the city as individual neighborhoods with distinct personalities, hotel price ranges, and styles of restaurants and nightclubs. The old royal city along the banks of the Chao Praya holds most of the temples and sightseeing attractions. Banglampoo, near the old city, and the area surrounding the Malaysia hotel cater to budget travelers. Silom Road and Siam Square are the upscale tourist districts lined with luxurious accommodations and fine restaurants. Sukumvit is a middle-priced neighborhood of good-value hotels, restaurants, shopping, and lively nightlife.

Hotel prices and occupancy levels in Bangkok have followed a wild roller-coaster ride of boom-and-bust cycles since the early 1980s. The country's incredible surge in tourism after 1987 (Visit Thailand Year) forced prices at top hotels above 3000B (US$120) and kept occupancy levels hovering around 85-95%. This, in turn, brought a huge expansion in recent years. Over 20 major hotel projects have been announced and many of the major international hotels are planning new wings and extensions. The estimated 12,000 additional rooms which will be in place by 1995 will dramatically ease prices and make it much easier to find a room during the high season from November to March. Also helping is the astonishing increase in the num-ber of condominiums—many are now being converted into high-rise hotels. In the meantime, advance reservations are essential.

Prices cited in the hotel charts are published rack rates, subject to negotiation during periods of low occupancy and the slow season from March to November. Most rooms, except for budget guesthouses, carry an additional 10% service charge and 11% government tax.

Banglampoo—Budget
Bangkok's headquarters for backpackers and budget travelers is centered around this friendly little neighborhood just a few blocks from the temples and museums in the royal city. Most guesthouses, restaurants, and travel agencies are located on Khao San Road, a term synonymous with Banglampoo. Some guidebooks have complained that Banglampoo isn't very Thai, but it's much more authentic than other tourist areas in Bangkok! From the airport, take ordinary bus 59, a/c bus 3AC, taxi for 150-200B, or minibus for 100B.

At last count, Banglampoo had over 60 guesthouses, which charge about 40B for dorms, 60-100B for singles, and 120-300B for doubles. The most obvious drawbacks are the extraordinarily small rooms, problems of theft, and the terrible noise from the motorcycles which race around late at night. For a good night's sleep, it's important to find a clean and comfortable room tucked away on a side street rather than directly on Khao San Road. Most guesthouses fill by early afternoon; do your room search in the early morning when travelers depart for the airport and bus stations. Most Banglampoo guesthouses are identical in cleanliness and size, but a handful of superior choices are shown on the "Banglampoo" map and described here.

Buddy Guesthouse: Midway down Khao San Rd., Buddy Guesthouse is a good place to begin your room search. Though the rooms are perpetually filled, you can drop your bags and enjoy a quick meal in the comfortable cafe in the rear. A less-packed restaurant is upstairs. Buddy Guesthouse, like most other guesthouses in Banglampoo, has a variety of rooms from basic cubicles to small a/c rooms with private bath. 137 Khao San Rd., tel. (02) 282-4351, 60-250B.

Hello Guesthouse: A 30-room guesthouse with a popular streetside cafe. 63 Khao San Rd., tel. (02) 281-8579, 60-150B fan, 180-250B a/c.

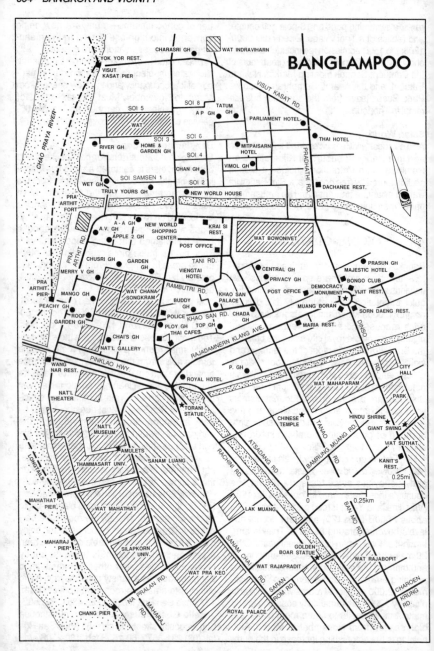

BANGLAMPOO

Ploy Guesthouse: A big place with very large rooms with private bath. Entrance is around the corner from Khao San Road. The second-floor lobby includes a small cafe and the coldest soft drinks in Bangkok. Recommended. 2 Khao San Rd., tel. (02) 282-1025, 60-200B.

Chart Guesthouse: An easy-to-find 20-room guesthouse with a great cafe. All rooms have fans; no a/c. 61 Khao San Rd., tel. (02) 281-0803, 60-140B.

C.H. Guesthouse: Big and popular place with 27 rooms and a packed video cafe on the ground floor. Recommended. 216 Khao San Rd., tel. (02) 282-2023, 60-150B fan, 200-220B a/c.

Lek Guesthouse: One of the original guesthouses in Banglampoo. Always filled, but worth checking with Mr. Lek Saranukul. 125 Khao San Rd., tel. (02) 281-2775, 80-140B.

Central Guesthouse: Both Central and Privacy guesthouses to the east of Tanao Rd. are quiet and somewhat run-down but exude a homey Thai feeling. Alleys branching off Khao San have several more peaceful guesthouses. 69 Tanao Rd., tel. (02) 282-7028, 60-120B.

Apple 2 Guesthouse: For a slightly Felliniesque experience, walk past the grazing cows and horses of Wat Chana Songkram (an animal refuge in the middle of Bangkok!) to the alleys and guesthouses which surround the temple. Apple 2 is a long-running favorite located in a quiet back alley. The big rambling teak house with songbirds and upstairs rooms is also called "Mama's." 11 Trok Kai Chae, tel. (02) 281-1219, 70-120B.

Peachy Guesthouse: Slightly more expensive than Khao San cubicles, but the rooms are clean, spacious, and furnished with writing tables and standing closets. Air-conditioned rooms are available. Perpetually filled, but sign the waiting list. Avoid rooms facing Pra Arthit Rd. or adjacent to the TV room. 10 Pra Arthit, tel. (02) 281-6471, 100-160B.

Merry V Guesthouse: One of the best guesthouses behind Wat Chana Songkram has clean rooms and a very comfortable restaurant. 35 Soi Chana Songkram, tel. (02) 282-9267, 60-160B.

Truly Yours Guesthouse: Some of Banglampoo's quietest guesthouses are located across the bridge north of Khao San Road. All provide an opportunity to experience Thai homestays in a traditional neighborhood. Samsen 1 Rd. has Truly Yours and Villa guesthouses,

RAJADAMNERN AVENUE BUSES

3AC, 59	Airport
12AC.	New Petchburi
39AC.	Northern Bus Terminal
45	Rama IV
15, 121	Silom
7AC	Southern Bus Terminal
2, 11AC . . .	Sukumvit, Eastern Bus Terminal

while Samsen 3 Rd. has the River, Clean and Calm, and Home and Garden guesthouses. Worth the walk. All charge 60-120B.

Tavee Guesthouse: To really escape the travelers' scene in Banglampoo, walk north up Chakrabongse Rd. and turn left on Sri Ayuthaya Rd. at the National Library. Near the river are three idyllic guesthouses including the Shanti, Sawatdee, and Tavee. The latter is at 83 Sri Ayuthaya Rd., tel. (02) 282-5349, 60-120B.

Banglampoo—Moderate
Khao San Palace Hotel: The dark and small rooms, probably the cheapest a/c rooms in Bangkok, come equipped with private baths, warm water, and horizontal mirrors geared to short-time business. 139 Khao San Rd., tel. (02) 282-0578, 280-340B fan, 360-420B a/c.

Nith Charoen Hotel: Another good midpriced hotel located in the heart of Banglampoo. Comfortable lounge with a useful bulletin board. 183 Khao San Rd., tel. (02) 281-9872, 300-340B fan, 420-460B a/c.

A-A Guesthouse: One of Banglampoo's best-value guesthouses has five floors of rooms ranging from common-bath cheapies on the fourth and fifth floors to private-bath a/c rooms on the lower floors. Quietly tucked away in a small alley. 84 Pra Sumeru Rd., tel. (02) 282-9631, 120-160B common bath, 200-240 private bath with fan, 300-380B private bath with a/c. Highly recommended.

New World House: A large, modern apartment complex with luxury features at a bargain price. All rooms are air-conditioned, with private bath, telephone, laundry service, and views over Banglampoo. Recommended for anyone who intends to stay a week or longer. Located just across the river. 2 Samsen Rd., tel. (02)

281-5596, 300-350B daily, 1800-2000B weekly, 7000-8000B monthly.

Banglampoo—Luxury

Royal Hotel: This well-priced hotel is within easy walking distance of Bangkok's attractions—an excellent place in a great location. Reservations can be made from the hotel counter at the airport. Budget travelers and overheated travel writers often spend their mornings in the a/c coffee shop reading the *Bangkok Post.* 2 Rajadamnern, tel. (02) 222-9111, fax (02) 224-2083, 1400-1800B.

Viengtai Hotel: Banglampoo's longtime favorite has sharply raised prices and failed to make any improvements; not recommended. 42 Tanao, tel. (02) 282-8672, fax (02) 281-8153, 1200-1500B s or d.

Malaysia Hotel Area—Budget

Surrounding the Malaysia Hotel are about 20 budget guesthouses which comprise Bangkok's once-great traveler's center. Most backpackers have deserted the area for Banglampoo, though the neighborhood remains popular with first-time visitors. Soi Ngam Duphli is a short taxi ride from the nightlife areas of Patpong and Sukumvit but very distant from the temples in old Bangkok. From the airport take a/c bus 4AC, taxi from the highway for 150-200B, or the direct minibus for 100B.

Freddy's #2 Guesthouse: A clean and friendly guesthouse recommended by many travelers. Freddy runs two other guesthouses in the neighborhood, though #2 is the best of the lot. Soi Si Bamphen, 60-80B s, 100-120B d.

Madam Guesthouse: The area's quietest guesthouses are located in a back alley and cul-de-sac off Soi Si Bamphen. All can be recommended for their solitude rather than for their cleanliness. Madam is a cozy if rustic homestay known for its friendly proprietor. Ramshackle rooms in the old house go from 60B.

Lee #3 Guesthouse: Adjacent to Madam Guesthouse and far removed from the horrendous traffic that blasts along Soi Si Samphen is another old house converted into a backpackers' crash pad. A popular place to nod out in the sunshine. Rooms cost 60B.

Honey Guesthouse: The latest addition to the guesthouse scene is this modern, clean, and comfortable 35-room building just down from the Malaysia Hotel. Rooms are available with common or private bath, with fan or a/c. Hefty discounts are given for monthly residents. The adjacent Greco-Roman style Diana Inn is also recommended. 35 Soi Ngam Duphli, tel. (02) 286-3460, 120-160B inside rooms, 180-200 with balcony.

Malaysia Hotel Area—Moderate

Midpriced hotels in this neighborhood have sadly declined in recent years, but the nearby YMCA and King's Mansion are excellent values. These two hotels are located midway between the Malaysia Hotel and Silom Road and described below under "Silom Road—Moderate."

Malaysia Hotel: A decade ago, the legendary Malaysia was the favored gathering place for budget travelers, who enjoyed the low rates, a/c rooms, swimming pool, and 24-hour room service. A large and very famous noticeboard offered tips on visas, crash pads, and how to see the world on a shoestring. Today, the noticeboard is gone, the coffee shop doubles as a video arcade, and the "Day Off Pub—Paradise for Everyone" features freelance prostitutes and nightly girlie shows. Rates have sharply risen. Standard a/c rooms which cost 120B in 1980 now run over 500B, without any improvement in facilities. The Malaysia may be cheap by Bangkok standards, but it suffers from rude service, indifferent management, and a lack of basic maintenance. 54 Soi Ngam Duphli, tel. (02) 286-3582, 520-800B.

Privacy Hotel: If the scene at the Malaysia turns you off, try this less expensive but very run-down alternative. 31 Soi Ngam Duphli, tel. (02) 286-2339, 220-360B.

Boston Inn: Once the best-value hotel in the neighborhood, the Boston Inn now seems about to collapse into a heap of concrete. Perhaps a Thai experiment: how long can a hotel survive without even the most rudimentary maintenance? The noticeboard has sadly declined into nothingness, the once-popular travel agency has fled, and the a/c rooms have been closed down. Whew! Soi Si Bamphen, tel. (02) 286-1680, 120-180.

Silom Road—Moderate

Once a luxurious residential neighborhood for wealthy merchants, the Silom-Surawong area has since grown into Bangkok's premier finan-

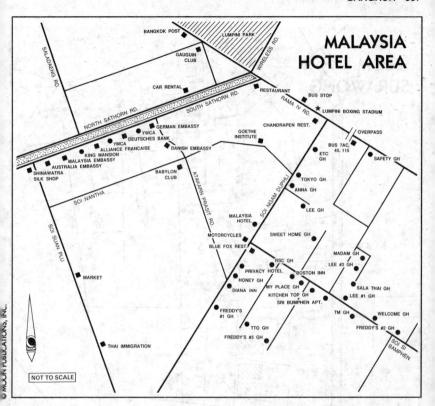

MALAYSIA HOTEL AREA

NOT TO SCALE

cial and commercial district. Some of the city's finest luxury hotels—the Oriental, the Shangri-La, and the Sheraton Royal Orchid—are located here. The area also offers leading department stores, antique and jewelry shops, and the sleazy nightlife that thrives along notorious Patpong Road. Silom is exciting and vibrant but also noisy and crowded with high-rises. An inner-city experience.

Naaz Guesthouse: Indians patronize several of the small and very inexpensive guesthouses on New Rd. near the GPO. Conditions are extremely rough, but if you want a cheap crash pad and don't mind the Calcutta atmosphere, then the Naaz might be adequate. Other similar spots are around the corner on Soi Puttaosod and to the rear on Nares Road. Several good Indian restaurants are nearby. 1159 New Rd., tel. (02) 235-9718, 100-150B.

Madras Lodge: Better hotels which cater to the Indian community are on alleys off Silom Road. Madras Lodge and Cafe is a newish three-story hotel about 200 meters down Vaithi Lane, two blocks east of the Hindu temple. An exceptionally quiet location. Silom Rd. Trok 13, tel. (02) 235-6761, 180-300B fan, 400-600B a/c.

Bangkok Christian Guesthouse: Clean, safe, and comfortable but probably too straitlaced for most visitors: geared to "Christian travelers visiting the work of the Church in Thailand." On the other hand, it's blessed with a pleasant garden and a homelike atmosphere; a quiet refuge within easy walking distance of Silom and Patpong. 123 Sala Daeng, Soi 2, tel. (02) 233-6303, 400-500B fan, 600-800B a/c.

Swan Hotel: This inexpensive little hotel is ideally located within walking distance of the GPO, inexpensive Indian restaurants, and river

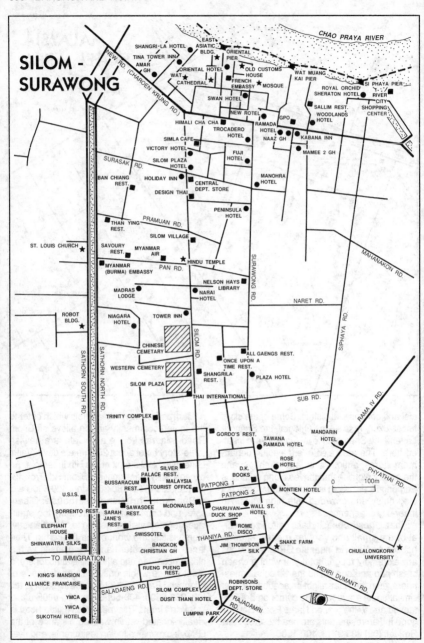

RAMA IV ROAD BUSES

5	Siam Square, Banglampoo
115	Silom, General Post Office
7AC.	Train Station, Royal Palace

taxis behind the Oriental. All rooms include private bath and telephone, plus there's a small pool and an adequate coffee shop. The Swan needs some obvious improvement, but it remains excellent value for budget travelers. Reservations are accepted for a/c rooms only, and flight number and arrival time are required. Credit cards and traveler's checks are not accepted. 31 Soi Charoen Krung (former Customs House Lane), tel. (02) 234-8594, 400-550B fan, 650-800B a/c.

Kabana Inn: Opposite the GPO and river taxis, the Kabana is another Indian-operated hotel with relatively clean rooms at bargain rates. All rooms are a/c with telephone and hot showers. 114 New Rd., tel. (02) 233-4652, 1200-1500B.

King's Mansion: Though constantly filled with long-term residents, this aging property is one of the better bargains in the Silom Rd. area. King's Mansion is located near many embassies and Thai Immigration, and only 10 minutes from Silom and Patpong. Air-conditioned rooms with private bath cost under 5000B per month. 31 South Sathorn Rd., tel. (02) 286-0940, 400-450B fan, 500-600B a/c, 650-750B a/c with refrigerator and TV.

YMCA Collins House: This modern, spotless, and comfortable hotel is one of the better hotel bargains in Bangkok. All rooms are a/c with private bath and mini refrigerator. There's also a pool and a health club. Reservations require one night's deposit. 27 South Sathorn, tel. (02) 287-1900, fax (02) 287-1996, 1100-1600B.

YWCA: The McFarland wing is less luxurious but also less expensive than the newer YMCA Collins House. Unfortunately, the swimming pool is perpetually filled with screaming kids. 13 South Sathorn, tel. (02) 286-1936, 500-700B.

New Hotel: A new hotel with modern a/c rooms furnished with color TVs, small refrigerators, and telephones. American breakfast is included. A fine little place with friendly management. 1216 New Rd., tel. (02) 233-1406, fax (02) 237-1102, 800-1200B.

Swissotel: Formerly the Swiss Guesthouse under the direction of Andy Ponnaz, this recently renovated and reconstructed Swiss-managed hotel has 57 air-conditioned rooms with all the amenities. Good location, with swimming pool and restaurant. 3 Convent Rd., tel. (02) 233-5345, fax (02) 236-9425, 3200-3800B.

Silom Road Accommodations—Luxury

Luxury hotels are the strong suit of this neighborhood. First choices are the fabulous hotels which face the Chao Praya River. Several new properties are now being constructed across the river in Thonburi.

Oriental Hotel: Since it first opened in 1876, this award-winning hotel on the banks of the Chao Praya has remained the undisputed grande dame of Bangkok. Even if you can't afford to stay, have a look at the Writers' Bar, try the Siamese buffet lunch, or enjoy an evening cocktail on the terrace. Some of the old charm has given way to modernization, but the Oriental remains among the best hotels in the world. 48 Oriental Ave., tel. (02) 236-0400, fax (02) 236-1939, 5200-6800B. Or try the Oriental Suite at 45,000B per night!

Shangri-La Hotel: This US$100 million hotel boasts 650 beautiful rooms facing the river and overlooking a stunning swimming pool. Facilities include a health club, a business center, and a spectacular glass-enclosed lobby with seven-meter-high windows. Many consider the Shangri-La more impressive than the Oriental. 89 Soi Wat Suan Plu, tel. (02) 236-7777, fax (02) 236-8579, 4400-5800B.

Royal Orchid Sheraton Hotel: This new hotel upriver from the Oriental has 700 rooms with uninterrupted views of the river. The adjacent River City Shopping Complex features two floors devoted to antiques. 2 Captain Bus Lane, tel. (02) 234-5599, fax (02) 236-8320, 4600-5500B.

The Sukothai: Thailand's first capital serves as the inspiration for one of the newer luxury hotels in the Silom District. A good location away from the traffic and surrounded by greenery. 13 South Sathorn Rd., tel. (02) 287-0222, fax (02) 287-4980, 4400-5800B.

SIAM SQUARE

SRI AYUTHAYA RD.

FLORIDA HOTEL

SIAM CITY HOTEL

★ SUAN PAKKARD PALACE

PHYATHAI RD.

PETCHBURI RD.

MAKKASAN RD.

MAKKASAN TRAIN STATION

EXPRESSWAY

BAIYOKE TOWER

INDRA HOTEL

FIRST HOTEL

SAVOY INN

INDONESIAN EMBASSY

PRATUNAM MARKET

RAJAPRAROB RD.

BANGKOK PALACE HOTEL

ASIA HOTEL

PANTIP PLAZA

PETCHBURI RD.

JIM THOMPSON'S HOUSE
BED & BREAKFAST GH

A-ONE INN
RENO HOTEL
PRANEE BLDG.
MUANGPHOL LODGING
KRIT THAI MANSION

SIAM CENTRE

WORLD TRADE CENTER

ANOMA PAVILION HOTEL

CHITLOM RD.

HILTON HOTEL

SIAM INTERCONTINENTAL HOTEL

ZEN CENTRAL

NARAYANA PHAND

MOON SHADOW

MERIDIEN HOTEL

TOKYU DEPT. STORE

NOVOTEL HOTEL

SIAM SQUARE

RAMA 1 RD.

ERAWAN SHRINE ★

CENTRAL DEPT. STORE

SWISS EMBASSY

BRITISH COUNCIL

SEE FAH REST.

COCA GARDEN NOODLES

GRAND HYATT ERAWAN

AMARIN PLAZA

PLOENCHIT RD.

BRITISH EMBASSY

DUTY FREE

PENINSULA PLAZA

VINOTHEK

IMPERIAL HOTEL

HENRI DUNANT RD.

REGENT HOTEL

ROYAL BANGKOK SPORTS CLUB

RAJADAMRI RD.

ISRAEL EMBASSY

SPANISH EMBASSY

DIETHELM TRAVEL

VIETNAM EMBASSY

NEW ZEALAND EMBASSY

AMERICAN EMBASSY

CHULALONGKORN UNIVERSITY

WHOLE EARTH REST.

LANG SUAN RD.

SOI TONSIN

WIRELESS RD.

RUAM RUDI RD.

A.U.A.

NEIL'S TAVERN

MOON

0   0.25mi
0   0.25km

BROWN SUGAR NIGHTCLUB

OLD WEST SALOON

SOI SARASIN

LUMPINI PARK

© MOON PUBLICATIONS, INC.

Siam Square—Budget To Moderate
This centrally located neighborhood, named after the Siam Square Shopping Center on Rama I, is the city's premier shopping district and home to several of Bangkok's most exclusive hotels. The 62-story World Trade Center and several new hotels have brought fresh energy to this otherwise neglected neighborhood. All of the inexpensive hostels and hotels are situated opposite the National Stadium on Rama I Road.

National Scout Hostel: Few Westerners stay here, but inexpensive dorms are located on the fourth floor. Rama I Road adjacent to the National Stadium, dorms cost 40B; men only.

The Bed and Breakfast Guesthouse: A small and absolutely spotless guesthouse. All rooms are a/c with hot showers and telephone. Continental breakfast is included. Recommended. 36/42 Soi Kasemsan 1, Rama I Rd., tel. (02) 215-3004, fax (02) 215-2493, 400-550B.

A-One Inn: Another new and very clean guesthouse with friendly management and quiet location down Soi Kasemsan 1. All rooms are a/c with private bath and telephone. Very safe since "my husband is the police man and stay at A-One along the time." Excellent value. 25/13 Soi Kasemsan 1, Rama I Rd., tel. (02) 215-3029, fax (02) 216-4771, 450-600B.

Muangphol Lodging Department: Somewhat ragged but recommended if the Bed and Breakfast or A-One Inn is filled. All rooms are air-conditioned. 931 Rama I, tel. (02) 215-3056, 450-550B.

Pranee Building: An older hotel operated by a motorcycle collector; check his fine collection of Triumphs. Inexpensive monthly rentals. 931/12 Soi Kasemsan 1, tel. (02) 280-3181, 350B small room with cold shower, 450B large room with hot shower.

Krit Thai Mansion: This clean and modern hotel is entered through the lobby restaurant and coffee shop. Easy to find since it faces Rama I Road. 931 Rama I, tel. (02) 215-3042, 900-1200B.

Siam Square—Luxury
Like Silom Road, this neighborhood excels in the expensive category. The following hotels are surrounded by immense grounds, a refreshing change from properties hemmed in by concrete towers and noisy construction zones.

Regent Hotel: Formerly known as the Bangkok Peninsula, this stately structure overlooking the Royal Bangkok Sports Club is considered one of the city's finest hotels. The afternoon high-tea ritual is worth experiencing. 155 Rajadamri Rd., tel. (02) 251-6127, fax (02) 253-9195, 4400-5500B.

Siam Intercontinental Hotel: Built on 26 acres of tropical gardens next to the Srapatum Palace, this oasis of tranquility is far removed from the noise and grime of the city. Included in the tariff is a sensational array of sports facilities such as a mini-golf course and a jogging trail. Rama I, tel. (02) 253-0355, fax (02) 253-2275, 4600-5800B.

Grand Hyatt Erawan: The venerable lady has been completely reconstructed in an amazing pseudo-Roman style; another first-class architectural monument for modern Bangkok. 494 Rajadamri Rd., tel. (02) 254-1234, fax (02) 253-5856, 4000-8500B.

Hilton International Hotel: Tucked away on the nine-acre Nai Lert Park and surrounded by gardens and bougainvilleas, Bangkok's Hilton is another tropical oasis in the middle of the noisy, polluted city. Popular with business travelers. 2 Wireless Rd., tel. (02) 253-0123, fax (02) 253-6509, 4400-7000B.

Sukumvit—Budget
Thailand's longest road (it stretches all the way to Cambodia!) is quickly becoming the tourist center of Bangkok. The neighborhood is very distant from Bangkok's temples, but it's less hectic than Silom Road and the middle-priced hotels which line the road from Soi 1 to Soi 63 are exceptionally good value. Sukumvit also offers great sidewalk shopping between Soi 3 and Soi 11, dozens of outstanding and modestly priced restaurants, English pubs, great bookstores, countless shoe merchants and tailor shops, discount travel agencies, and a nightlife scene second only to Patpong's.

Hotels are available in all price ranges from budget guesthouses to luxurious high-rises, but the neighborhood's claims to fame are the middle-priced lodgings for 600-1000B. Yet even the hotels under 600B are often equipped with a/c rooms and small swimming pools. Middle-range hotels generally include comfortable a/c rooms, swimming pools, travel services, taxis at the front doors, and fine restaurants. Deluxe hotels above 1000B are starting to appear, though it will be years before the neighborhood can compete with the five-star wonders on Silom Road and around Siam Square.

Golden Gate Hotel: Simple, clean, modern hotel with a/c rooms, TV, massage parlor, and 24-hour coffee shop. Soi 2, tel. 251-5354, 350-500B.

Sookswasdi: An older but very quiet motel with large rooms equipped with kitchen facilities. Somewhat rustic but fairly clean; popular with long-term visitors. Located on a back alley off Soi 11, tel. 253-3425, 250-350B single or double.

Miami Hotel: An old hotel with dozens of decent rooms overlooking the courtyard swimming pool. Fan rooms are very basic, but all a/c rooms include TV, private bath, and maid service. One of the most popular cheapies on Sukumvit Road. Reservations can be made from the hotel counter at the Bangkok airport. Soi 13, tel. (02) 253-0369, fax (02) 253-1266, 200-250 fan, 550-650 a/c.

Crown Hotel: Another old hotel constructed for the American GI trade in the 1960s. Very funky, but the small pool provides a refreshing dip in the hot afternoon. All rooms are a/c; a longtime favorite with many visitors. Soi 29, tel. (02) 258-4438, 450-650B.

Uncle Rey's Guesthouse: A clean but cramped high-rise with small, fully furnished a/c rooms with private bath and hot showers. Tucked away in an alley opposite the Nana Hotel. No pool, no yard. Soi 4, tel. (02) 252-5565, 400-550B.

Happy Inn: A small and very simple hotel with clean rooms and a good location near the nightlife and shopping centers. Soi 4, tel. (02) 252-6508, 500-600B.

Atlanta Hotel: An old travelers' favorite that hangs on with a minimum of maintenance. The dreary lobby is compensated for with fairly clean rooms, a cheery little cafe, and a surprisingly good pool in the backyard. Proprietor Dr. Charles Henn, son of the German immigrant who founded the Atlanta in 1952, is now renovating the property with attention to the increasingly rare '50s decor. The cheapest hotel in the Sukumvit neighborhood. Soi 2, tel. (02) 252-1650, 150-250B fan with common bath, 200-300B fan with private bath, 400-500B a/c with private bath.

Sukumvit—Moderate

Mermaid's Rest: Beautiful, small, Scandinavian-run guesthouse with fan and a/c rooms, outdoor barbecue with European buffet, and small swimming pool around a pleasant garden. Highly recommended. Soi 8, tel. (02) 253-2400, fax (02) 253-3648, 350-400B fan, 600-700B a/c, 700-900B a/c in the new wing.

White Inn: A beautiful and unique lodge decorated in an olde English-Tudor style with a/c rooms, swimming pool, and sun terrace. Highly recommended. Soi 4, tel. (02) 252-7090, 650-900B.

Dynasty Inn: Fine little place with comfy cocktail lounge, CNN on the cable TV, and very clean a/c rooms. Excellent location just opposite the Nana Hotel; often filled by noontime. Soi 4, tel. (02) 250-1397, fax (02) 252-9930, 800-900B.

Nana Hotel: A big hotel with all the standard facilities such as nightclubs and restaurants. Recently refurbished a/c rooms include private bath, TV, and refrigerator. The Nana is conveniently located within easy walking distance of the nightlife and shopping districts; one of the better middle-priced spreads on Sukumvit. Recommended for visitors who want a big hotel at a decent price. Soi 4, tel. (02) 252-0121, 850-1000B.

Golden Gate Hotel: A basic but clean hotel with a/c rooms, TV, massage parlor, and 24-hour coffee shop. Soi 2, tel. (02) 251-5354, 800-900B.

Maxim's Inn: Sukumvit in recent years has added a dozen small hotels in the *sois* near the Ambassador Hotel, especially between Sois 9 and 13. All are clean and comfortable, but Maxim's is more luxurious and has a better location at the end of a short alley. If filled, check the adjacent World Inn; same price range. Soi 9, tel. (02) 252-9911, fax (02) 253-5329, 900-1200B.

President Inn: Several new, small inns are in the short alleys near Soi 11. Most were constructed in the early 1990s, so the rooms and lobbies remain in good condition. Choices include the President Inn, the Business Inn, the Bangkok Inn (German management), the Comfort Inn, and the Swiss Park Inn. All charge 800-1200B for clean a/c rooms furnished with color TV, telephone, and mini refrigerator. Soi 11, tel. (02) 255-4230, fax (02) 255-4235, 800B-1200B.

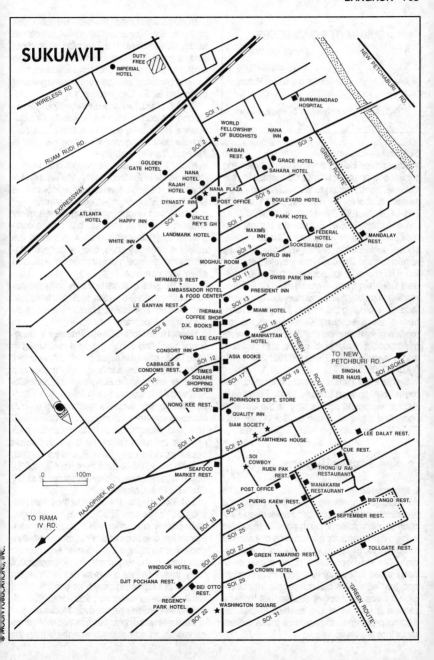

SUKUMVIT ROAD BUSES

1AC	Chinatown, Wat Po
2	Banglampoo
8AC	Siam Square, Grand Palace
11AC	Banglampoo, National Museum
13AC	Northern Bus Terminal, Airport

Sukumvit—Luxury

Ambassador Hotel: An enormous hotel and convention complex with 1,000 rooms, 14 restaurants, health center, tennis courts, and jumbo swimming pool (easily crashed). Soi 11, tel. (02) 251-0404, fax (02) 253-4123, 2600-3800B.

Landmark Hotel: Sukumvit's largest and most luxurious hotel. Superb location near shops, restaurants, and nightclubs. Carefully aimed toward the business traveler, each of the 415 rooms is equipped with a computerized videotext that provides airline schedules, stock-market data, and important business contacts . . . including the names and phone numbers of top executives. Other pluses include rooftop restaurants on the 31st floor, a swimming pool, a health club, convention facilities, and a friendly staff. Soi 6, tel. (02) 254-0404, 3800-5000B.

Swiss Park Hotel: A centrally located 108-room hotel opened in early 1991. Features a rooftop swimming pool, a cafe on the Seventh floor, and a business center. Soi 11, tel. (02) 254-0228, fax (02) 254-0378, 3000-3600B.

RESTAURANTS

Banglampoo

Al-fresco dining along Khao San Road is a pleasant way to meet other travelers and exchange information, though none of the cafes will win any awards for great cuisine or elaborate atmosphere. Banglampoo's other problem, besides the mediocre food, is the presence of noisy video cafes that ruin good conversation and turn otherwise colorful people into boob-tube junkies. A pleasant escape, but hardly a reason to visit Asia! The solution to this disturbing problem is to patronize those restaurants that are video-free.

Buddy Cafe: One of the more elegant cafes on Khao San Rd. is tucked away behind the Buddy Guesthouse. The Thai food is bland but safe, a good introduction for first-time visitors fearful of chilies. The upstairs restaurant provides a pleasant escape from the mayhem of Khao San Road. Inexpensive.

Thai Cafes: Several unpretentious cafes around the corner from Khao San on Chakrabongse Rd. offer a good selection of unusual dishes. Best in the morning when the food is freshest. Very inexpensive.

Night Food Stalls: Authentic Thai food is found nightly in the food stalls at the west end of Khao San Rd. and a few blocks north toward the New World Shopping Center. Inexpensive.

New World Shopping Center: Nearly every shopping center in Thailand has a food complex on its top floor. Prices are rock bottom, the quality is generally good, and the service is instantaneous since most are self-service food stalls. Inexpensive.

Krai Si: Small, clean, and very chilly restaurant with Japanese sushi, sashimi, tempura, and Western specialties. Look for the sidewalk sushi man. Moderate.

Royal Hotel Coffee Shop: Travelers in Banglampoo will find this the closest restaurant in which to escape the searing heat. An excellent place to relax in the morning, enjoy a good cup of coffee, and read the *Bangkok Post*. Moderate.

Wang Nar: Located underneath the Thonburi Bridge, this riverside restaurant is an outstanding spot for authentic, reasonably priced Thai food. Patrons can sit outdoors on the deck or inside the a/c restaurant to the rear. Sample prices: chicken curry 50-80B, catfish 60-80B, *ring ring* fish 70B, urgent beef pork liver 60B. Super atmosphere. Highly recommended. 17 Chao Fa Road. Moderate.

Yok Yor: Also on the banks of the Chao Praya, Yok Yor serves Thai, Chinese, and Japanese dishes in a rather wild atmosphere: waitresses are dressed in sailor outfits and passengers disembarking from the river taxi saunter right through the restaurant! Try *hoh mok,* duck curry, and *noi na* ice cream for dessert. Yok Yor is on Wisut Kaset Rd., down from the National Bank, a very pleasant 30-minute walk through back alleys which skirt the river. Moderate.

Maria Restaurant: Rajadamnern Avenue serves as an administrative center during the day, as restaurant row in the evening. Scattered along the broad avenue are a half-dozen moderately priced restaurants popular with Thai civil servants and businesspeople. Maria's is a large a/c place with both Chinese and Thai specialties. Rajadamnern Avenue. Moderate.

Kanit's: Both French specialties and Italian pizzas are served in very elegant surroundings. Considered the best European restaurant in this section of town. Owned by a friendly Thai lady and her German husband. 68 Ti Thong Rd., near the Giant Swing and Wat Suthat. Moderate to expensive.

Malaysia Hotel Area

Blue Fox: A crazy scene of slightly bent Thais and travelers escaping the searing heat. Good Western food but the Thai dishes are bland and monotonous. Inexpensive.

Food Stalls: A large collection of tasty, authentic, and inexpensive Thai food stalls is located just across Rama IV near the Lumpini Boxing Stadium. Point to a neighbor's dish or look inside the pots. Great atmosphere. Inexpensive.

Silom Road

Serious gourmets should purchase the *Bangkok Restaurant Guide* published by Asia Books. Although somewhat dated (the first and final edition was published in 1988), the maps and descriptions of dishes are immensely helpful.

Patpong Restaurants: Almost a dozen excellent restaurants are on Patpong Road. Expatriates gather on Sunday evenings in the English pub at Bobby's Arms for a round of draft and Dixieland music. Trattoria d'Roberto is known for its Italian specialties such as veal dishes and chocolate desserts. The Australian Club is a comfortable a/c lounge with imported beers from Down Under, plus helpful literature on local nightlife spots. Dating from the days of the Vietnam War, the venerable Thai Room remains an expat/Peace Corps hangout that serves Thai-Mex and Italian specialties. Most Patpong restaurants are open until midnight. Moderate.

Charuvan Duck Shop: Around the corner from Patpong is an old travelers' favorite with, what else, duck specialties over rice and inexpensive curries. An a/c room is behind the open-air cafe. 70 Silom Road. Inexpensive.

Himali Cha Cha: The long-running Himali Cha Cha, located up a small alley off New Rd.,

near the GPO, is known for its tasty curries, *kormas,* fruit-flavored *lassis,* tandoori-baked breads, and North Indian specialties served in an informal setting. Cha Cha, owner and head chef at Himali's, was once Nehru's private chef. 1229 New Rd., tel. (02) 235-1569. Moderate.

Simla Cafe: The less expensive Simla Cafe, off Silom Rd. in a small alley behind the Victory Hotel, is another popular choice for Indian and Pakistani dishes. 382 Soi Tat Mai, tel. (02) 234-6225. Inexpensive.

Budget Indian Cafes: Cheap open-air Muslim cafes on New Rd. serve delicious *murtabaks* and *parathas,* but noxious fumes blowing in from the road could kill you. A filling lunch or dinner costs under 50B per person. Indian street vendors sometimes gather opposite the Narai Hotel near the small Hindu temple. The Chandni, on the second floor at 422 Surawong Rd. next to the Manohra Hotel, has great food served under a video screen blasting out wild Hindu films. Madras Cafe in the Madras Lodge is also recommended for its authentic atmosphere and South Indian specialties. Perhaps the best choice for excellent Indian and Malay food at rock-bottom prices is the Sallim Restaurant, adjacent to the Woodlands Hotel near the GPO. Inexpensive.

Robinson's Department Store: For a quick bite at bargain prices, try the Dairy Queen on the main floor. A well-stocked grocery store is located downstairs. Silom Center, Silom at Rama IV roads. Inexpensive.

Bussaracum: Restaurants found in luxury hotels generally cater to the foreign palate and temper the degree of garlic and chilies used in their dishes. For something more authentic, try this elegant dining establishment for pungent dishes whose recipes stem from the royal palace. 35 Soi Phipat 2, tel. (02) 235-5160. Bussaracum 2, a newer and more modern extension, is wedged inside the Trinity Complex. 425 Soi Phipat 2, tel. (02) 234-2600. Very expensive.

Than Ying: Many of the finest restaurants in the Silom neighborhood are tucked away in the neighborhood alleys between Silom and Sathorn Tai roads. Than Ying is an old favorite known for its authentic royal-style Thai cuisine. 10 Soi Pramuan. Expensive.

Rueng Pueng: Traditional Thai dishes from all regions of the country plus outstanding sal-

FOOD AND DRINK

Whether enjoyed in a first-class restaurant or from a simple streetside stall, the cuisine of Thailand is unquestionably one of the great culinary treats of the East. Thai food—a hot and spicy spectrum of exotic flavors—takes its roots from the best of neighboring countries: smooth coconut creams from Malaysia, rich peanut sauces from Indonesia, fiery curries from India, sweet-and-sour sauces from China. Thai cuisine derives its essential character from local ingredients such as coconut milk, lemon grass, tamarind, ginger, coriander, basil, and peanuts blended together with the ubiquitous and intimidating chili. Adorning nearly all dishes to some degree, Thai chilies vary in pungency in inverse proportion to their size. The tiny ones called *prik kee noo* (ratshit peppers) are treated with respect even by the Thais. On the other hand, the large green and yellow *Capsicum annum* are noticeably less aggressive. To survive the heat, remember that even the hottest of chilies lose much of their fierce flavor when safely cocooned in a mouthful of rice. When in doubt, do as the Thais do—eat more rice.

Ordering a meal outside a tourist venue can, at times, be difficult, since few restaurants offer English-scripted menus or have English-speaking waiters. The best solution is to indicate a dish being served to other Thai patrons, or wander in the kitchen, peer in the pots, and point to whatever looks promising. Westerners who find chopsticks the major challenge of Eastern dining will happily note that Thais—being an immensely practical people—eat with forks and spoons, the spoon being the main implement rather than the fork. Tables are generally set with a variety of condiments: fermented fish sauce made from anchovies or shrimp paste called *nam pla,* a hot, pungent sauce known as *nam prik,* and a vinegar-green chili extract called *nam som.* Tamarind sauces and cucumbers fried in coconut oil are other popular accompaniments.

The perfect complement to a Thai dinner is an ice-cold bottle of either Singha or Kloster, light, smooth, and tasty beers brewed according to German recipes. Two spirits to approach with extreme caution are Mekong and Kwang Tong, 70-proof molasses-based spirits that pack an abnormal, almost psychotropic wallop—the tequila of Thailand. Moonshine whiskey is popular since distillers can easily undercut by five times the price of heavily taxed legal whiskey. It's said that only two households in each village don't make moonshine: the government's excise office and the Buddhist *wat.*

A THAI MENU

Meat, Chicken, And Fish
gai: chicken
mu: pork
nua: beef
pet: duck
kung: prawns
pla: fish

Cooking Methods, Condiments, And Sauces
pat: fried
yang: barbecued or roasted
nam pla: fish sauce
nam prik: red spicy sauce
nam som: vinegar with chili sauce
nam buay wan: sweet plum sauce
nam yam hai: oyster sauce
nam king: ginger sauce
nam preo wan: sweet-and-sour sauce

Soups
tom kha kai: a rich chicken-and-coconut-milk soup flavored with lemon grass, lime leaves, galangal, and shallots. Thailand's greatest soup is served throughout the country.
tom yam: a hot-and-sour broth prepared with lemon grass, lime leaves, and chili. Called *tom yam kung* with shrimp and *tom yam kai* with chicken. Almost as good as *tom kha kai.*
kow tom: thick rice soup
kow tom pla: thick rice soup served with fish
kow tom mu: thick rice soup served with pork
kow tom kung: thick rice soup served with prawns
kang chut: a mild flavored soup with vegetables and pork
kang liang: a spicy soup with shrimp, vegetables, basil, and pepper

Rice Dishes
kow pat: fried rice
kow pat kai: fried rice with chicken
kow pat mu: fried rice with pork
kow pat kung: fried rice with shrimp
kow na: steamed rice
kow na kai: steamed rice with sliced chicken
kow na pet: steamed rice with roast duck

FOOD AND DRINK

Noodle Dishes
kuay teow: wide rice noodles
kuay teow ratna: rice noodles in a meat gravy
kuay teow hang: rice noodles with meat and
vegetable served without the meat gravy
kuay teow pat thai: rice noodles fried Thai style
bah mee: wide yellow wheat and egg noodles
bah mee ratna: wheat noodles in meat gravy
bah mee hang: wheat noodles with meat and
vegetable served without the meat gravy

Curry Dishes
kang pet: spicy curry made from sweet coconut
milk flavored with lemon grass, chilies, and
shrimp paste. Served with either pork, chicken,
beef, fish, or prawns. Perhaps the most popular
dish in Thailand.
kang matsaman: a milder version of Muslim curry
laced with beef, potato, onion, coconut milk, and
peanut
kang wan: Green curry thickened with coconut milk,
eggplant, sweet basil, and lime leaves. Be careful with this one.
kang kari: Yellow curry with tumeric; a mild version
of an Indian curry
kang baa: Thailand's hottest curry—for veteran fire-
eaters only

Salads
yam: salad
yam nua: beef salad with mint, basil, spring onion,
garlic, and chili
yam het: mushroom salad
yam mamuang: green mango salad
yam tang kwa: cucumber salad
yam hoi: cockle salad

Drinks
nam plao: plain water
nam tom: boiled water
nam cha: tea
nam manao: iced lime juice
nam som khan: fresh orange juice
nom: milk
coffee ron: hot coffee with milk
coffee yen: iced coffee with milk
o liang: iced black coffee with sugar
Mekong: Thai whiskey distilled from grains and
molasses
sang som: rum liquor made from sugarcane
lao kao: rice liquor, locally produced

Sidewalk Snacks And Desserts
satay: barbecued skewers of meat served with
peanut sauce and cucumbers in vinegar and
sugar
sang kaya: custard made from coconut milk, sugar,
and eggs
chow kway: black-grass pudding shredded and
mixed with a sugar syrup over ice
boh bok: green-grass drink made from crushed
vines and sugar water. Bitter.
roti sai mai: small flat pancakes with strands of
green or pink spun sugar wrapped inside
kanom buang: miniature tacos. Made from batter
poured on a hot griddle and then folded over and
filled with shredded coconut, egg yolk, and green
onions.
tong krob: golden yellow balls made from egg yolks
and rice flour, then dusted with sugar
kao glab pat maw: thin crepe filled with fried shrimp,
pork, peanuts, sugar, coconut, and even fish
sauce. Delicious.

ads are served in a converted Thai house, a common sight in Bangkok these days. 37 Soi 2, Saladeng Rd., down from the Christian Guesthouse. Expensive.

Once Upon A Time: A wonderful romantic restaurant with outdoor dining under little twinkling lights. Nicely located in a quiet back alley, but within walking distance of most hotels. Decho Rd., Soi 1. Moderate to expensive.

All Gaengs: Unlike most Thai restaurants, All Gaengs has been stylishly decorated with art-deco touches and a shiny baby grand piano. Along with the jazz, enjoy shrimp curry,

yam dishes, and *nuea daed dio,* a beef dish served with a spicy dipping sauce. Surawong Road. Moderate.

Siam Square
Many of the best restaurants in this neighborhood are located in luxury hotels or the a/c shopping centers of Siam Square, Siam Center, and Peninsula Plaza.

Tokyu Food Centre: Shopping centers are your best bets for quick, inexpensive Thai and Western dishes. Tokyu Department Store, at the intersection of Rama I and Phyathai roads, features a roomy, a/c, sixth-floor dining emporium with dozens of great food stalls.

Coca Garden Noodles: A colossal, noisy restaurant packed with Chinese families and groups of hungry teenagers. Serves a wide variety of inexpensive noodle dishes, along with chicken, fish, and seafood specialties. 461 Henri Dunant Rd. at the southeast corner of Siam Square Shopping Center, tel. (02) 251-6337. Moderate.

Blue Moon and Moon Shadow: In the short alley adjacent to the Meridien Hotel are two small cafe-clubs modeled after American Western saloons. The Blue Moon bar features some of the best jazz and R&B combos in Thailand, while the downstairs Western cafe specializes in seafood entrees. Try the *pla krai* in green chili curry. 145 Gaysorn Rd., tel. (02) 253-7552. Moderate.

Old West Saloon: A mini nightlife and restaurant scene has sprung up in recent years along Soi Sarasin, south of Siam Shopping Center near Lumpini Park. Old West, one of the oldest Western clubs in Bangkok, features Thai-cowboy grub and live country music behind the swinging saloon doors. 231 Soi Sarasin, tel. (02) 252-9510. Inexpensive.

Siam Intercontinental: This hotel's all-you-can-eat luncheon buffet is one of Bangkok's least expensive splurges. The Indra Regent also has a moderate-priced buffet. Diners must be well attired; no shorts or sandals.

Whole Earth Restaurant: Outstanding if slightly expensive vegetarian and Thai specialties accompanied by classical guitar or folk music. 933 Soi Languan, Ploenchit Road. Moderate.

Amarin Plaza: Upscale Japanese and Thai restaurants are on the lower floor. Note the wild Greco-Roman-Thai architecture of the adjacent McDonald's.

Sukumvit

Ambassador Food Center: Over 50 fast-food stalls serve up Thai, Japanese, and Western dishes at reasonable prices. This is a great place to look at and learn about Thai dishes and begin your food crawl in the Sukumvit neighborhood. Most dishes cost under 30B, and you pay by coupon. The streetside Bangkapi Terrace is a good place to escape the midday heat and enjoy a very cheap luncheon buffet. Soi 11. Inexpensive.

streetside delights

Cabbages and Condoms: Owned and operated by Mechai Viravaudya, "Condom King" and former director of the national birth-control center (next door), this curiously named place offers excellent food in a/c comfort plus some truly strange items at the front desk . . . condom keychains and T-shirts you won't find back home! Highly recommended. Soi 12, tel. (02) 252-7349. Moderate.

Yong Lee Restaurant: A very funky cafe popular with budget travelers and local *farangs* who rave about the Thai and Chinese specialties. Soi 15. Inexpensive.

Thong Lee Restaurant: A very popular and simple shophouse with good food at low prices. Try the *muu phad kapi* (spicy pork in shrimp paste) and the *yam hed sot* (fiery mushroom salad). Soi 20. Inexpensive.

Night Food Stalls: Some of the best food in Bangkok is found in the food stalls along Sukumvit Road. Many of the dishes are pre-cooked and displayed in covered pots. Also try *som tam,* a spicy salad made from shredded raw papaya and palm sugar, fried chicken with sticky rice, and *pad thai,* sautéed bean sprouts with chicken and peanuts. Delicious! Food stalls are near the Grace Hotel, the infamously seedy Thermae Coffee Shop, both ends of Soi Cowboy, Washington Square nightlife center, and on Sukumvit at Soi 38. Wonderful food and a great way to mix with the locals.

Lemongrass Restaurant: Embellished with antiques in both the interior dining room and exterior courtyard, Lemongrass offers atmosphere and regional dishes from all parts of Thailand. Try the hot fish curry, barbecued chicken, *larb pla duk yang* (smoked catfish in northeastern style), and *nam takrai,* a cool and sweetish drink brewed from lemongrass. Soi 24 near the Calypso Cabaret, tel. (02) 258-8637. Moderate.

Seafood Market Restaurant: This *very* expensive seafood restaurant is worth a look even if the prices cause heart failure. Don't miss the enormous Phuket lobsters and giant prawns. Soi 16 at Soi Asoke, tel. (02) 258-0218. Expensive.

Soi 23 Restaurants: Almost a dozen popular restaurants are down Soi 23, a few blocks off Sukumvit Road. Ruen Pak is an excellent-value cafe located in a renovated wooden house. Best bets include Thong U Rai with live music, Cue for French cuisine, Le Dalat Vietnamese restaurant, Wanakarm Restaurant with traditional dishes in a/c dining rooms, Pueng Kaew's experimental Thai-Western dishes, September for art-deco 1930s atmosphere, Bistango steak house, and Black Scene with live jazz. An excellent place to wander and snack in the late evening.

Bankeo Ruenkwan: This old and partially renovated house serves up top-quality seafood in a/c comfort. Soi 12, tel. (02) 251-8229. Expensive.

Djit Pochana: One of the most successful restaurant chains in Thailand has three outlets in Bangkok that serve authentic Thai dishes without compromise to Western palates. Try their excellent-value luncheon buffet. Soi 20, tel. (02) 258-1605. Moderate.

Robinson's Department Store: Cheap eats are available in this pricey emporium from McDonald's on the main floor and a downstairs Food Court with several self-service cafes that serve Thai and Japanese dishes. Sukumvit Soi 19.

Green Route Restaurants: Many of Bangkok's finest restaurants are on the so-called Green Route, a street which runs between Sois 39 and 63, midway between Sukumvit and New Petchburi roads. Try Gourmet Gallery at Soi 49, the Library at Soi 49, Laicram at Soi 49, or Piman on Soi 49. All provide expensive but elegant dining experiences.

Soi 55 Restaurants: Another concentration of fine restaurants is on Soi 55 (Soi Thonglor) between Sukumvit and the Green Route. Favorites include the Art House in a lovely country house, funky Barley House with nightly jazz, L'Hexagone French restaurant, simple Sanuk Nuek, and an English pub called the Witch's Tavern.

Tum Nak Thai: According to the *Guinness Book of World Records,* Tum Nak Thai is the world's largest restaurant: 10 acres of land, a capacity of 3,000 seats, over 100 professional chefs, and 1,000 servers decked out in national costumes. Some waiters use roller skates to speed up service! A classical dance show is given nightly at 2000. Take a taxi from your hotel. 131 Ratchadapisek Rd., tel. (02) 277-8833. Moderate.

CULTURAL ENTERTAINMENT

Free Thai Dance

Lak Muang Shrine: Amateurish but authentic *likay* is sponsored around the clock by various donors; have a quick look after touring the Grand Palace.

Erawan Hotel Shrine: The famous pillar in the courtyard of the Grand Hyatt Erawan is among the more intriguing scenes in Bangkok. No matter the hour, a steady stream of devotees arrives to offer flowers, wooden elephants, and hire the somewhat unenthusiastic dancers. Most active in the early evening and just before the weekly lottery.

Center of Traditional Performing Arts: Outstanding performances of Thai dance, drama, and traditional music are given each Friday at 1700 on the fourth floor of the Bangkok Bank, Parn Fah Branch, just off Rajadamnern in the Banglampoo district. The room is dull but the performances are quite good—so good, in fact, that shows are always packed; arrive an hour early or expect to stand in the back. Upcoming performances are listed on the noticeboard in the TAT office.

THAI PERFORMING ARTS

Khon

The glory of Thai classic theater is the *khon,* a stunning spectacle of warriors, demons, and monkeys who perform acrobatics and highly stylized movements while wrapped in brilliant costumes. *Khon* has its roots in court-sponsored ballets which thrived under royal patronage until the military revolution of 1932 ended Thailand's absolute monarchy. Accompanied by the surrealistic sounds of the Thai *pipat* orchestra, the *khon* typically takes its storyline from either the Javanese Inao legend or the Indian Ramayana, called the Ramakien ("Glory of Rama") in Thailand. Actors and actresses never speak but rather mime narration provided by professional troubadours and choruses. Originally a masked drama, modern *khon* has unmasked heroes and celestial beings, though demons and monkeys continue to wear bizarre head coverings. *Khon* is also an endangered artform, the only remaining venue in Thailand being Bangkok's National Theater. Performances are sponsored several times yearly—an superb theatrical experience not to be missed.

Lakhon

While *khon* is male-oriented and relies on virtuosity in strength and muscular exertion, the courtly *lakhon* impresses its audience with feminine grace and elegant fluidity. *Lakhon* presents episodes from the Ramakien, Manora folktales of southern Thailand, and Lakhon Jatri, itinerant folk dances used to exorcise evil spirits. Lakhon is traditionally accompanied by a chorus and lead singers instead of *khon*-style recitation, though these distinctions are no longer strictly followed. The costumes of elaborately embroidered cloth and glittering ornaments surpass the brilliance of even the *khon.* Unlike the *khon,* actresses are unencumbered by masks, allowing them to combine singing and dialogue with their dance postures. Highly refined body gestures display a complex encyclopedia of movements, while emotion is conveyed by the demure dartings of the eyes and highly stylized, very specific movements of the hands. The dance itself lacks the dramatic leaps and whirling pirouettes of Western ballet—the feet are kept firmly planted on the stage—but a great deal of dramatic tension and sensuality are achieved by the movement of the upper torso. *Khon* and *lakhon* are often combined into grand shows for the benefit of both visitors and Thais.

Thai dancers

Likay

If *khon* and *lakhon* are classical art, then *likay* is slapstick comedy performed for the masses. The obvious lack of deep artistic talent is made up for with unabashed exuberance and a strong sense of earthiness. As a form of people's theater performed at most provincial fairs, *likay* relies heavily on predictable plots, outrageous double entendres, and lowball comedy. Performers interact directly with the audience, which responds with raucous laughter at their political sarcasms and sexual innuendo. Costumes worn by the untalented but enthusiastic actors run from gaudy jewelry to heavy makeup. It is ironic that television, the universal destroyer of traditional theater, has helped keep *likay* alive with daily performances of soap-opera sophistication.

Thai Puppetry

A third type of court drama is the *nang,* or shadow play, which enjoyed great popularity during the reign of King Mongkut. Thai puppetry is occasionally performed in three versions at dinner dance shows.

THAI PERFORMING ARTS

Nang Yai: This form of puppetry uses larger than life-sized leather puppets painted with vegetable dyes for daytime performances and left translucent for nighttime shows. Oxhide figures are manipulated in front of the screen by puppeteers and illuminated by candles that cast eerie colored shadows. Examples of this vanished art are displayed in the *wayang* room of the National Museum.

Nang Talung: This variation, closely related to the *wayang kulit* of Indonesia, uses smaller and more maneuverable puppets. Still popular in southern Thailand where performances are occasionally given during temple festivals.

Hun Krabok: This version, a vanished art, uses rod puppets similar to Chinese stick puppets. Puppets are still created by the famous Thai painter, Chakrabhand Posayahrit.

Popular Dance

Fawn Lep: Ladies from the north of Thailand perform classical movements while wearing long artificial fingernails.

Ram Wong: A slow and graceful dance that cleverly fuses traditional *lakhon* hand movements with Western dance steps. Performed at most informal gatherings and *very* popular after a few shots of Mekong whiskey! Westerners who try the *ram wong* always appear incredibly clumsy, although their comical efforts are appreciated by the gracious Thais.

Sword Fighting—*Krabi Krabong*

Originally devised by warriors to practice combat techniques, sword fighting is only performed today in conjunction with a dinner-dance show. A complete cycle begins with sharpened swords and then moves through combat with poles, knives, and finally hand-to-hand combat. Real swords give the fighters deadly potential in this skillful and exciting sport.

Traditional Music

Backing up the *khon, lakhon,* and *likay* is the music of the *pipat,* Thailand's strange but captivating orchestra. Most Westerners find the surrealistic flavor of Thai music difficult to appreciate, as it seems to lack harmony or melody. Traditional Thai music is based on a five-tone diatonic scale with neither major nor minor keys—more closely related to medieval Christian music or the abstract compositions of Ravel than conventional Western compositions. Similar to Javanese and Balinese *gamelan,* the Thai percussive orchestra is composed of five to 15 instruments such as drums, xylophones, gongs, metallophones, woodwinds, strings, and flutes. Musical passages indicate specific actions and emotions (marching, weeping, anger) that are immediately recognized by the dancers. Thai music is abstract, highly syncopated, and emotionally charged, but delightfully moving with repeated hearings.

National Theater

Thai classical dance performances are given at the National Theater's outdoor stage at irregular intervals between November and May. Sunday afternoons are the most likely times to find performances. Check the *Bangkok Post* or the noticeboard at the TAT office, or just walk by and see if a crowd is gathering. Shows are free but it helps to bring a blanket and claim a spot in the early afternoon. Full-length *khon* performances are given several times yearly by the Fine Arts Department inside the theater, an expensive but unforgettable spectacle.

Dinner/Dance Shows

First-time visitors who wish to sample an overview of Thai dance can attend performances in almost a dozen a/c Thai restaurants. Brief demonstrations of *khon, lakhon,* and *likay* folk dancing, Thai martial arts, puppetry, and sword-fighting follow a northern Thai *khon toke*-style dinner. Prices range from 250B to 500B; transportation is often included. Performance times and prices can be double-checked by calling the restaurant or inquiring with the TAT. Some find these highly abbreviated performances artificial and unsatisfying, but the glittering costumes and elegant dance styles are most impressive.

Baan Thai: Like most Thai restaurants with dance performances, Baan Thai recreates a traditional Thai house with polished teakwood floors, elegant furnishings, and tropical gardens. Nightly shows from 1900. 7 Sukumvit Soi 32, tel. 258-5403.

Piman: One of Bangkok's more elegant and expensive shows takes place inside this beautiful reproduction of a Sukothai-era house. Admission 500B. 46 Sukumvit Soi 49, tel. 258-7866.

Chao Praya Restaurant: Travelers staying in the guesthouses of Banglampoo often attend the cultural show across the Pinklau Bridge in Thonburi. Packages sold by travel agents include transportation, dinner, show, and possibly a cocktail in the adjacent Paradise Music Hall.

Hotel Shows: Dance performances are also given in the Sukothai Restaurant of the Dusit Thani Hotel and in the Sala Thai on the rooftop of the Indra Regent.

Oriental Hotel Photo Show: Photographers will enjoy the Kodak Siam Show given at poolside every Sunday and Thursday between 1100 and 1200; admission 100B.

Thai Kick Boxing

Thai boxing is the street fighter's dream of Western boxing mixed with karate and a bit of *tae kwon do*. Barefoot pugilists prior to WW II wrapped their hands in hemp mixed with ground glass and the fight went on for as long as anyone could stand . . . or had any blood left. Today the boxers wear lightly padded gloves and a few rules have been introduced to control the carnage. An interesting ritual takes place before the match begins. Wailing music from a small orchestra of Java pipe, two drums, and cymbal sets the mood. Often fixed with colored cords and protective amulets, the two contestants enter the ring, kneel and pray to the spirits for victory, and then begin a surrealistic slow-motion dance designed to show off their talents while emulating their teachers' movements. Spectators make their bets as the boxers pound and kick each other with ever-increasing frenzy. The drama is heightened by the cacophonous musical accompaniment. At the end of five three-minute rounds or the merciful intervention of the referee, the fight ends and a winner is declared. This spectacle is best watched from ringside rather than with the rabble up in the circular gallery.

Thai kick boxing can be experienced at the Lumpini Stadium on Rama IV Road (near the Malaysia Hotel) every Tuesday, Friday, and Saturday at 1800 and at 1330 on Saturdays. Superior boxers meet at Rajadamnern Stadium (near the TAT office) every Monday, Wednesday, and Thursday at 1800, and on Sundays at 1700 and 2000. Admission is 50-200B. Thai boxing goes center stage on TV every Sunday afternoon.

NIGHTCLUBS AND BARS

Bangkok's nightlife is perhaps the most notorious in the world. Bars, brothels, live sex shows, massage parlors, gay nightclubs, roving transvestites, sex cabarets, all-night coffee shops, child prostitutes, and barber shops that provide more than just haircuts—the range of sexual services is simply amazing. Bangkok alone has an estimated 500,000 prostitutes, and it's said that almost one-third of all visitors to Thailand come for sex. Despite AIDS, local opposition, and the conservative moral attitudes of the Thai people (the vast majority are incredibly puritanical), Thailand's roaring sex industry seems destined to remain a major attraction well into the 1990s.

Patpong

Bangkok's most notorious red-light district is located on Patpong 1 and 2 between Silom and Surawong roads. Once owned by the Patpong family and made popular by American soldiers on leave from Vietnam, this infamous collection of go-go bars, cocktail lounges, live shows, street vendors, pushy touts, and pre-teen hustlers forms a scene straight from Dante's *Inferno*. Less intense bars are located in the Sukumvit district at Washington Square, inside the Nana Entertainment Complex, and along Soi Cowboy, a small lane between Soi 21 and 23. During the day Patpong is almost deserted except for a pair of excellent bookstores and several cozy pubs which screen the latest videos in a/c comfort. Between 1800 and 2000 the bars spring to life with smaller crowds and happy-hour prices—an excellent time to look around without draining your wallet. From 2000 until around 0100, some 30-50 go-go bars and live-show nightclubs operate at full tilt, packed with both overseas visitors and Thais who generally accept rather than condemn the sex trade. Single males, Western females, and even families are welcome to enter a club, watch a show, and perhaps attempt a conversation with the surprisingly friendly ladies. Moral questions aside, the whole scene is much less depressing or intimidating than red-light areas in the West!

Girls may be taken from the bars by paying a bar fine of 200-300B, though this charge can be avoided by meeting the girl out front after closing hours. Services for the night run 300-800B depending on the popularity of the girl and how wealthy she considers her client. Most girls cannot be trusted; valuables should be checked in the hotel safe and female visitors should sign in at the hotel register.

Among the better clubs are King's Castle, Queen's Castle, and the Mississippi Club, where scenes from *The Deer Hunter* were filmed. Patpong also served as Saigon's Tu Do Street for Robin Williams's *Good Morning Vietnam*. On Sundays, the Napoleon Lounge has a music fest of straight-ahead mainstream jazz performed by both Western and Thai artists. The most irritating sidelights to Patpong are the hordes of overly aggressive barkers who accost Westerners with offers of private shows featuring young girls whose special talents are explicitly listed on calling cards. Very few visitors enjoy these shows, but if you must, be sure to establish the total cover charge and price for drinks *before* going upstairs for the show—misunderstandings are common. Massage parlors and "barber" shops are also found in Patpong, while the gay clubs on Patpong 3 feature transvestites (*gatoeis*) in hilarious follies revues.

Sukumvit

Soi Cowboy: Bangkok's second most active bar area is located off Sukumvit Road between Sois 21 and 23. The area gets its name from a black American nicknamed "Cowboy" who owned one of the first bars on the street. Soi Cowboy is a refreshing change from the hype and hustle of Patpong, more relaxed and low-key with less pressure to spend or buy the girls drinks. Crowds tend to be smaller and made up of locals rather than tourists. The girls expect less money since they lack the sophistication and aggressiveness of the Patpong ladies. Drinks run around 40B; buyout fees 50-100B. Also set with terrific food stalls and friendly British pubs, Soi Cowboy is the slow and sleazy counterpoint to the flash and glitter of Patpong.

Nana Plaza: Bangkok's newest and liveliest go-go-bar scene features three floors of clubs, cafes, and rock 'n' roll cabarets with outstanding sound systems. Woodstock and Asian Intrigue are the current favorites.

Washington Square: Another low-key nightlife scene is located on Sukumvit Road between Sois 22 and 24. The mixture of bars, restaurants, food stalls, and cinemas has a somewhat American atmosphere with names like the Texxan Restaurant and Ex-Pats Retreat. Darts, snooker, videos, and Sunday afternoon barbecues are the main attractions rather than go-go girls and sex shows.

Grace Hotel: Thailand's sleaziest sex scene takes place inside the 24-hour coffee shop located on the ground floor of the Grace Hotel. Like some sort of Oriental bazaar, the noisy dive is always jammed with freelancers too wild or independent to be employed by any self-respecting bar or nightclub. Four jukeboxes at the four corners play four different tunes simultaneously . . . just too weird. Although the clientele is now mainly Arabs, the decadent atmosphere of the "Amazing Grease" is worth investigating in the early-morning hours after the Patpong clubs have closed.

Massage Parlors: Countless massage parlors, Turkish baths, and steam baths are found throughout Bangkok. Large numbers have cropped up in the last few years on lower Sukumvit and along New Petchburi Road, north of Sukumvit. Filled with numbered ladies patiently waiting in viewing rooms, these giant pleasure palaces are absolutely guaranteed to infuriate Western women. All sorts of services are available.

Discos

Discotheques in Bangkok are absolutely astounding, rivaled in the East only by the clubs of Manila. Cover charges run 60-100B during the week, 120-200B on weekends; a complimentary drink or two (or three) is usually included.

Rome Club: A relatively small but exceedingly hot videotheque frequented by fashionably dressed gays, trendy art-club types, and *gatoeis* who hang out in the upstairs annex until the midnight transvestite revue. Rome Club is conveniently located in the gay nightlife district of Patpong 3.

Freakout: Trendy young Thais favor the heterosexual discos and pubs on both sides of Silom Plaza. Dining tables in the plaza provide good people-watching, while adjacent discos such as Virgin and Freakout Supertheque pack in the young crowds. Silom Plaza on Silom Rd., near Thai International Airlines.

LIVE THAI ROCK 'N' ROLL

Unlike in Manila, most of the clubs in Bangkok feature recorded music rather than live entertainment. The scene, however, has improved with the arrival of *dontree pher cheevit*, a fresh musical force that breaks away from the traditional love themes to raise issues of social injustice. Early efforts at political consciousness by a group named Caravan proved too radical for public airing, but Carabao in the late '80s caused a major sensation with their song "Made in Thailand." The hit both ridiculed Thai obsession with foreign-made goods and inadvertently promoted the government's Buy-Thai program! Other Carabao songs have described the plight of Bangkok's prostitutes and poor rural farmers. Instead of simply plagiarizing Western pop melodies to back up Thai lyrics, Carabao has successfully fused American country rock with traditional Thai music. Remember the 1986 disco hit "One Night in Bangkok"? Banned in Thailand.

NASA Spacedrome: Bangkok's flashiest disco is a multimillion-dollar dance emporium that packs in over 2,000 sweating bodies every weekend. At midnight, a spaceship descends to the floor amid smoke, flashing lights, and the theme song from *2001: A Space Odyssey*. For sheer spectacle, nothing else compares in Thailand. Ramkamheng Rd., 100 meters north of New Petchburi Rd. in the Bangkapi neighborhood.

The Palace: Perhaps the trendiest of all Bangkok discos, the Palace is frequented by young Thais who hail from the country's wealthiest families. 379 Vipavadee Rangsit Hwy., on the road to the airport.

Paradise Music Hall: Another gigantic dance emporium with the standard amenities of flashing lights, laser videos, and booming disco music. Arun Amarin Rd. in Thonburi, just across the bridge from Banglampoo; a good choice for travelers staying on Khao San Road.

Bars

Bangkok has few bars in the traditional sense, largely because any ordinary restaurant, including the smallest streetside noodle shop, can legally sell beer and other spirits. However, a new breed of nightery has emerged in the early 1990s that caters to foreigners and English-speaking Thais who appreciate tavern ambience.

Soi Sarasin: A very welcome addition to Bangkok's night scene is the collection of intimate nightclubs and cozy restaurants located on Soi Sarasin, just off Rajadamnern Rd. and immediately north of Lumpini Park. Modeled after European bistros with clean decor and sidewalk tables, these clubs appeal to young Westerners and professional Thais rather than the go-go crowd. Best bets include the Brown Sugar, with good jazz, and the Old West Saloon, which re-creates an American Wild West atmosphere.

Soi Lang Suan: Around the corner from Soi Sarasin is another street with a good selection of pubs favored by expats and yuppie Thais. Among the most popular are Round Midnight for jazzophiles and the trendy European-run Vinothek with its extensive wine cellar.

Soi Gaysorn: In the short alley adjacent to the Meridien Hotel (Siam Square area) are two small cafe-clubs modeled after American Western saloons. The Blue Moon bar features some of the best jazz and R&B combos in Thailand, while the downstairs western-style Moon Shadow Cafe specializes in seafood entrees.

Sukumvit Soi 33: Cozy clubs curiously named after European painters are tucked away in a quiet *soi* off Sukumvit Road. All offer happy-hour drink specials and are popular with Western expatriates who live nearby. Try the Vincent Van Gogh or Renoir Club.

SHOPPING

Bangkok enjoys a well-deserved reputation as the Shopping Capital of Asia. Popular products include Thai silks, gemstones, tailor-made suits and dresses, inexpensive shoes, bronzeware, and traditional handicrafts. Imported items such as electronics, watches, cameras, and film are much cheaper in the duty-free ports of Hong Kong or Singapore. Prices are fairly uniform across town, but selection varies between neighborhoods: Chinatown is best for gold chains, Silom Road for silks and antiques, Sukumvit for leather goods and tailors, Siam Square for high fashion and cheap clothing, Banglampoo for handicrafts and tribal artifacts.

Anyone seriously interested in shopping should purchase Nancy Chandler's outstanding *Market Map of Bangkok*.

Local Markets

Weekend Market: Among the more fascinating shopping experiences are the simple markets packed with foods, flowers, clothing, and more exotic items. The granddaddy of all Thai flea markets is Chatuchak's monstrous affair out near the airport on Paholyothin Road. Take a bus and watch for the large carnival tent on the left. Open weekends 0900-1800.

Pratunam Market: A sprawling rabbit warren of clothing shops, hygienic food stalls, vegetable wholesalers, and shoe merchants is located at the intersection of Petchburi and Rajaprarop roads. Open 24 hours; perhaps the single best place in Bangkok to shop for inexpensive clothing. Don't get lost!

Banglampoo Market: Conveniently located near the budget guesthouses on Khao San Road; check the alleys packed with inexpensive clothing and the main floor bargains in the New World Department Store. An inexpensive self-serve cafeteria is on top.

Pak Klong Market: Bangkok's most colorful and smelly vegetable and fruit market hangs over the riverbanks near the Memorial Bridge.

Teves Flower Market: A permanent sidewalk market with plants and (occasionally) flowers flanks a canal one km north of Banglampoo.

Thieves' Market: Touted in many tourist books as an antique shopping district, though the only antiques and thieves are the shopkeepers.

Shopping Tips

Bargaining: Absolutely necessary except in the large department stores. It's challenging and fun—*if* you keep your sense of humor. Haggle with a smile; let the shopkeeper laugh at your ridiculous offer while smiling back at his absurd asking price. Bargaining is a game, not a life-or-death struggle. Expect a discount of 20-30%, not the 50% discount given in some tourist centers such as Bali. As elsewhere in Asia, knowing a few numbers and key phrases will send prices plunging.

Refunds, Receipts, and Guarantees: As a general rule, goods once purchased cannot be exchanged or returned. Deposits are also non-refundable. Carefully examine all merchandise

---

BANGKOK PHONE NUMBERS

Tourist Office	282-1143
Tourist Police	221-6209
Tourist Assistance	281-0372
Immigration	286-9176
Airport	523-6201
Train Station	223-7010
Eastern Bus Terminal	391-2504
Northern Bus Terminal	279-4484
Southern Bus Terminal	411-0511
General Post Office	233-1050
Phone Information	13
International Calls	100

---

since receipts and guarantees issued by local retailers are of dubious value after you have returned home.

Touts: Touts are paid commissions for rounding up customers. All expenses, including taxi rides and lunches, are added to your bill. Avoid them.

Fakes: Thailand also enjoys a reputation as the Counterfeit Capital of Asia. Most fakes, such as Lacoste shirts and Cartier watches, are advertised and sold as fakes. More dangerous to your pocketbook are colored glass being peddled as rubies and newly manufactured Buddhas sold as genuine antiques. Experts at Bangkok's National Museum estimate that 90% of the items sold at the city's antique stores are counterfeit! Unless you are an expert or prepared to gamble large sums of money, a sound policy is to shun expensive antiques and simply purchase reproductions.

PRACTICALITIES

Tourist Information

The Tourist Authority of Thailand (TAT) at 4 Rajadamnern Avenue near the Democracy Monument is well organized and very helpful, but only if you request specific information. Their bulletin board lists upcoming festivals, dance performances, and warnings about safety and rip-offs. Useful publications available from major hotels and the TAT include *Bangkok This Week*, the *Sightseeing and Shopping Map of Bangkok*,

Thaiways, Pattaya, and *Where.* The publications department across the hall sells large-scale highway maps and souvenir slides. All TAT offices in the country are open Monday-Saturday 0830-1630. Bus passengers should also pick up *Latest Tour's Guide to Bangkok and Thailand* or *Latest Edition Bangkok Thailand* for current routings. Complaints about unfair business practices can be directed to the Tourist Assistance Center located next door to the TAT office; open daily 0800-2400.

Bookstores
Bangkok's bookstores are among the finest in Southeast Asia. Best selections are found at Asia Books on Sukumvit Soi 15, D.K. Book House in Siam Square, and Bookseller on Patpong Road. Asia Books in the Galerie Lafayette on Rajadamri Avenue has an exceptional collection of books on Asian art. Used books are sold at Chalermnit Books on Ploenchit near the Grand Hyatt Erawan and in the small bookstore on Soi 24 near the Impala Hotel. The National Library and Chulalongkorn University Library are open to the public, as is the AUA Library on Rajadamri. The Siam Society library on Sukumvit Soi 21 is open to members only.

Visas
Bangkok is a popular place to pick up visas for onward travel. Most embassies accept visa applications from 1000 to 1200 only, and they will often require your passport overnight. Nepalese visas are issued on the spot but must be used within 30 days. Philippine visas should be obtained before arriving to avoid the byzantine procedures at Manila's immigration department. Indonesian entry permits are now granted on arrival, making visas unnecessary for most visitors. The Indian Embassy is a disorganized mess with hordes of impatient people getting their first tastes of Indian bureaucracy. Embassies are spread out all over town and extremely time-consuming to reach. It's *much* easier to let a travel agency obtain your visa.

Communications
Telephone: International telephone calls can be made 24 hours a day, seven days a week from the telecommunications annex next to the General Post Office. Calls to North America and Europe cost about US$10 for the first three minutes. Local phone calls cost 1B at red phones and 3B from private phones in stores and restaurants. Thai area codes are listed in the Thailand Introduction. Telegrams can be wired from local post offices.

Mail: The General Post Office on New Road is open 0800-2000 Monday-Friday and 0800-1300 on weekends and holidays. The GPO also offers a wrapping service for parcels . . . don't you wish all GPOs in Asia had this? Their poste restante isn't quite as organized as Singapore's, but at least they appear to be keeping track of all those letters.

Newspapers: Thailand's two major English-language papers, the *Bangkok Post* and the *Nation,* are an invaluable source of information on events, festivals, local gossip, international events, and sports back home. The *Bangkok Post* wins my vote for best English-language newspaper in Southeast Asia.

Travel Agents
Bangkok has a wide choice of travel agencies dealing everything from nightclub tours to jungle safaris. Local sightseeing tours can be arranged through most agencies, but major destinations are best purchased from Diethelm Travel (tel. 252-4041) at 544 Ploenchit Road, World Travel (tel. 233-5900) at 1053 Charoen Krung Road, and Sea Tour (tel. 251-4862) in the Siam Center on Rama I Road.

Discount travel agencies located near the guesthouses on Khao San Road and the Malaysia Hotel are excellent sources for cheap flights, visas, discount bus and train travel, and counterfeit student cards. Recommended bucket shops in Banglampoo include Ronny's Tours and Overland Travel, an honest, courteous, and well-organized outfit. Student Travel Australia adjacent to the Viengtai Hotel is honest and dependable but crowded, slow, and more expensive than other agencies. The STA office (tel. 233-2582) in the Silom district at 33 Surawong Road is faster and less hectic. Be very cautious with travel agencies near the Malaysia Hotel. J Travel has been the subject of complaints for dishonest sales practices for over 15 years, and yet they remain in business. Where Travel on Ngam Dupli Road appears reputable, but don't be lulled into complacency by a large office or a well-established location. Take precautions! Never hand over your money until you have carefully examined your ticket for price, expiration dates, and endorsements. It also helps to check the airline's reservation list before parting with your money.

Other Services

Medical: Excellent medical facilities and English-speaking doctors are available in the Bangkok Christian Hospital at 124 Silom Rd. (near Patpong) and the Bangkok Nursing Home on Convent Road.

Language Instruction: The American University (AUA) at 170 Rajadamri Rd. offers comprehensive group lessons, sells language tapes, has a cheap cafeteria, and operates a public library filled with Western books and magazines. Private language instructors also advertise in the *Bangkok Post.*

Educational Tours: Bangkok's Siam Society sponsors bimonthly group tours to important historical and archaeological sites in Thailand. Led by experts in their fields, these outstanding and reasonably priced tours are highly recommended for all visitors. Also check the Fine Arts Department at Bangkok University and the bulletin board in the National Museum. Unique, free, and personalized tours of Bangkok temples, plus overnight visits to nearby villagers, can be arranged through the Volunteer Guide Group, Box 24-1013, Ramkamheng Rd., Bangkok 10241.

Buddhist Meditation: Increasing numbers of travelers are investigating Buddhism and *vipassana* (insight) meditation during their visits to Thailand. The International Buddhist Meditation Centre (Dhamma Vicaya Hall) in the rear of Wat Mahathat provides information on retreats and weekly lectures on Thai Buddhism and its significance to Thai culture. Upcoming English-language lectures are listed in the *Bangkok Post.* Call (02) 511-0439 or (02) 511-3549 for more information.

Another source is the World Fellowship of Buddhists, where English-language meditation classes for Western visitors are held on the first Sunday of every month 1400-1730. Sukumvit Rd. between Soi 1 and Soi 3.

A useful bookstore is located across from Wat Bowonivet, though meditation instruction is no longer offered at this *wat.*

For excellent up-to-date descriptions of all meditation temples in Thailand, read *A Guide to Buddhist Monasteries and Meditation Centres in Thailand* by Moon author Bill Weir. The authoritative tome is available from the World Fellowship of Buddhists on Sukumvit Rd., Asia Books, Dharma Seed in Massachusetts, and Insight Meditation West (P.O. Box 909, Woodacre, CA 94973). Insight Meditation West (tel. 415-488-0170) is America's best resourse for retreats, books, and other information on *vipassana* meditation.

TRANSPORTATION

Airport Arrival

Bangkok's Don Muang International Airport, 25 km north of the city, is a busy, modern place with a post office, left-luggage facilities, international phones, and several restaurants including an inexpensive dining area on the top floor. After immigration and custom formalities, exchange some money at the currency booth (good rates), then visit the tourist information center for maps and magazines. Hotel reservations at better hotels in Bangkok, Pattaya, Chiang Mai, and Phuket can be made at the Thai Hotel Association booth in the arrival lounge. The adjacent Airport Hotel has rooms from 1800B plus free transportation into the city.

Bangkok's hotels are 30-90 minutes from city center depending on traffic. Minibus and limousine tickets are sold from a special counter in the arrival section. Minibuses are reasonably priced and take you directly to your hotel. Airport taxis waiting out front are somewhat more expensive than ordinary taxis flagged down on the highway, 50 meters out the front door. Do not take gangster taxis with black license plates. Ordinary non-a/c buses—crowded and slow but very cheap—can be flagged down on the highway. Air-conditioned buses listed below are less frequent but much more comfortable; expect a wait of 15 to 30 minutes.

Getting Around Bangkok

Bangkok is a hot, bewildering metropolis without any recognizable city center—a place where only the certified insane attempt to walk any great distance. Aside from roaming the neighborhood near your hotel, a taxi, *tuk tuk,* or bus will be necessary. The good news is that public transportation is very cheap; the bad news is

TRANSPORT FROM THE AIRPORT TO BANGKOK

TRANSPORT	DEPARTURE & DESTINATION	FARE (B)	LAST SERVICE
Limousine	Tickets from airport counter	300	Midnight
Taxi	From airport departure lounge	200	All night
Taxi	From highway out front	150-180	All night
Minibus	From airport counter direct to any hotel	120	2100
Bus 3AC	Banglampoo	10	2000
Bus 4AC	Siam Square, Silom, Malaysia Hotel	10-15	1900
Bus 10AC	Thonburi, Southern Bus Terminal	10	2000
Bus 13AC	Siam Square, Sukumvit	10-15	2000
Bus 29AC	Siam Square, Train Station	10	2200
Bus 29	Siam Square, Train Station	10	2200
Bus 59	Banglampoo	2	2200

that traffic in Bangkok is among the world's worst. Avoid rush hours (0800-1000 and 1500-1800), when the entire city comes to a complete standstill.

Taxis: Air-conditioned taxis are plentiful but, incredibly enough, unmetered. All fares must be negotiated in advance. Medium-length journeys (e.g. Sukumvit to Silom) should cost 50-80B, while longer trips (outer Sukumvit to the Grand Palace) average 80-120B. Never pay more than 150B to go *anywhere,* and ignore those absurd fares (often double or triple) posted in the luxury hotels. So much for the old saw about asking hotel employees for correct taxi prices!

Tuk Tuks: Affectionately named after their obnoxious sounds, motorized *samlors* are noisy three-wheelers that race around at terrifying speeds, take corners on two wheels, and scream through seemingly impossible gaps. *Tuk tuks,* the cheapest form of private transportation in Bangkok, cost 30-50% less than taxis but you must bargain hard and settle all fares in advance. Since few drivers speak any English or understand a map, be sure to have your destination written down in Thai or know how to pronounce it properly. If you can't speak Thai, raise a few fingers: two for 20B, three for 30. Smile and grin during price negotiation. If the driver won't come down to a reasonable price then do the taxi ballet . . . walk away shaking your head until he pulls up and waves you inside. Then hold on to your seat.

Ordinary Buses: Non-a/c buses are unbelievably crowded, but they cover a very comprehensive network and cost only two *baht.* The oddly named *Latest Tour's Guide to Bangkok & Thailand* shows most bus routes. Signs at bus stands also help. Service is sporadic (especially in the evening), so write down several different bus numbers unless you care to wait a long, long time. *Beware of thieves using razor blades,* especially on crowded buses.

Air-conditioned Buses: Air-conditioned buses are *much* more comfortable than ordinary buses, plus you have a reasonably good chance of finding a seat. Air-conditioned buses cost 5-15B depending on the distance; destinations are listed in English on the exterior of the bus. Service ends nightly at 2000.

River Boats: The Chao Praya Express Boat is hands-down the *best* way to get around Bangkok. These open-air boats are fast, cheap, exciting, and a refreshing escape from the horrors of land transportation. Boats operate daily from 0600 to 1800 and charge 3-10B depending on the distance—especially useful between Banglampoo and the GPO. Two other types of boats work the river: short and stubby ferries which shuttle across the river and longtailed boats (*hang yao*) that race up and down the smaller canals.

Leaving Bangkok By Bus

Provinces throughout Thailand can easily be reached with public and private buses. Bangkok has three public bus terminals which serve different sections of the country. Each station has different departments for ordinary and air-con-

A/C BUS SERVICE FROM BANGKOK

DESTINATION	TERMINAL	KM	HRS	FARE (B)	DEPARTURES
Ayuthaya	Northern	74	1½	35	every 10 minutes
Ban Phe (Samet)	Eastern	223	3	80	0700, 0800, 0900, 1600
Bang Pa In	Northern	63	1	30	every 20 minutes
Chiang Mai	Northern	713	9	280	0900-1000 (4 x), 2000-2145 (8 x)
Chiang Rai	Northern	844	13	300	1930, 1945, 1950, 2000
Hat Yai	Southern	1031	14	380	every 15 minutes 1730-2015
Hua Hin	Southern	201	3	90	hourly
Kanchanaburi	Southern	129	2	60	hourly
Kampang Phet	Northern	358	5	150	1200, 2230
Korat	Northern	256	4	100	every 15 minutes
Krabi	Southern	867	14	300	1900, 2000
Lampang	Northern	668	8	220	0930, 1100, 2030, 2130, 2200
Lopburi	Northern	153	3	80	every 20 minutes
Nakhon Pathom	Southern	56	1	30	every 30 minutes
Pattaya	Eastern	132	2	60	every 40 minutes
Petchburi	Southern	135	2	60	hourly
Phitsanulok	Northern	498	5	90	hourly
Phuket	Southern	891	14	300	0800, 1830, 1900, 1930, 2000, 2030
Rayong	Eastern	182	3	80	hourly
Sukothai	Northern	440	5	160	1040, 2220, 2240
Samui Island	Southern	779	16	290	2000
Surat Thani	Southern	668	12	230	2020, 2040
Surin	Northern	451	6	170	1100, 2130, 2200, 2210
Tak	Northern	420	5	150	1300, 2210, 2230
Trat	Eastern	315	7	120	hourly 0600-1000, 2000-2400

ditioned buses. All are well organized and have English-language signs over most ticket windows. Departures are frequent for most destinations throughout Thailand; the most difficult task is reaching the terminal!

Northern/Northeastern Bus Terminal: Destinations in the north and northeast are served by two sprawling adjacent terminals on Paholyothin Rd., on the highway toward the airport near Chatuchak Market. Take any bus going toward the airport and look for the modern complex on the right side of the highway. The Northern Terminal is divided into two wings. The first section on the right is for air-conditioned coaches (tel. 02/279-4484), the second for ordinary buses (tel. 02/279-6222).

Southern Bus Terminal: All buses to southern Thailand depart from the new terminal on Nakhon Chaisri Rd. in Thonburi. Tickets are sold from the windows near the main road. Call (02) 435-1200 or (02) 435-1199 (a/c) and (02) 434-5557 (ordinary) for further information.

Eastern Bus Terminal: The Eastern Bus Terminal on Sukumvit Rd. near Soi 63 serves east-coast resorts such as Pattaya, Rayong, Ko Samet, and Ko Chang. Take any bus going down Sukumvit and watch for the small terminal on the right. Call 391-9829 or 392-9227 for information on a/c services, and 392-2391 for regular buses.

Private Buses: In addition to these three government terminals, a dozen-plus small, independent bus companies operate from private terminals located throughout the city. Private buses are 30-50% more expensive than government buses, but complimentary meals and hotel pick-up are often provided, an important consideration in Bangkok. Private buses can be booked through travel agents, but compare prices carefully as they vary enormously.

By Train: Bangkok has two train stations. Hualampong Station handles trains to the north and northeast and *most* services to the south. The Thonburi or Bangkok Noi station handles some trains to the south. Travelers going south must carefully check on the correct station. Trains from Bangkok should be booked well in advance, especially for popular destinations such as Chiang Mai, Surat Thani (junction for Ko Samui), and Hat Yai. Time and hassles can be avoided by making seat reservations from a travel agent. Tickets are also sold directly at Hualampong Station in the Advance Booking Office to the *right* of the entrance; people in the long lines to the left are purchasing same-day tickets. Be sure to pick up condensed timetables—extraordinarily useful pieces of paper.

By Air: Taxis to the airport cost 150B and take 30-90 minutes depending on traffic. Departure tax is 20B for domestic and 150B for international flights.

AROUND BANGKOK

SRI RACHA

The next place of interest on the Sukumvit Hwy. is the busy fishing village of Sri Racha, best known as the production center for a pungent-sweet fish sauce called *nam prik si racha*. Sri Racha is a tidy little place which has won awards as the cleanest town in the kingdom. Facilities include several banks which exchange traveler's checks, a postal center, and an immigration office.

Attractions
Temples: Surasak 2 Singha Rd. has the small Wat Sri Maha Racha on the north side and a larger Chinese temple in a back alley to the south. The market is worth a wander, as are the stilted houses flanking the nearby pier.

Ko Loi: For a quick ride, ask the *samlor* driver to take you to the famous island linked to the mainland by a 1.5-km bridge. The temple features a *chedi*, a *viharn,* and a lifelike wax statue of a monk known for his miraculous healing powers. In 1959 the monk disappeared for good (allegedly with all the donations), but superstitious Thais continue to visit his shrine. The causeway is flanked with colorful fishing boats laden with arrow-shaped fish traps constructed from *nipa* palm. Fare is 10B each direction.

Accommodations
Few visitors spend the night in Sri Racha, though several inexpensive hotels are along the waterfront and on the roads which connect the highway with the seashore. All have breezy open-air restaurants where you can enjoy the local seafood specialties.

Samchai Hotel: On the rickety pier across from Surasak 1 Rd., the Samchai has simple fan-cooled rooms from 120B and air-conditioned rooms from 250B. 3 Chomchonpon Rd., tel. (038) 311134.

Siri Wattana Hotel: Another seaside hotel with rooms with bath for 80-120B, plus views over the ocean. 35 Chomchonpon Rd., tel. (038) 311307.

Grand Bungalows: Better rooms are found in the hotel on the southern pier. 9 Chomchonpon Rd., tel. (038) 312537, 400-1000B.

Restaurants
Seafood Restaurants: Lining the seafront are several seafood restaurants serving local specialties such as sautéed oysters and shellfish. Another popular restaurant is at the end of the pier past the stilted houses. Few have English-language menus or list prices, so check carefully before ordering.

Central Market: The most economical spot for meals is the market near the clock tower and opposite city hall.

WEIRD WHEELS

The most amazing sidelight to Sri Racha is the presence of its bizarre but strangely elegant *samlors,* three-wheeled motorbike-rickshaws elongated to outrageous lengths and fitted with huge car or smaller motorcycle engines. Their days are numbered since new licenses are no longer issued.

Home & Garden Restaurant: On Jermjonpol Rd. near the Sukumvit Hwy. is a more luxurious if less atmosphic restaurant.

Transportation

Buses from Bangkok's Eastern Bus Terminal take about 90 minutes to reach Sri Racha, from where you can walk or hire a *samlor* down to the waterfront and departure pier for Ko Si Chang. Buses from Sri Racha to Bangkok and Pattaya can be hailed on the highway or taken on Chomchonpon Rd. just past the Srivichai Hotel.

KO SI CHANG

Ko Si Chang, about 12 km off the coast from Sri Racha, once served as Thailand's custom port and was among the country's most popular weekend destinations. Today it's a sleepy place chiefly visited for the decaying palace of King Chulalongkorn and its highly revered Chinese temple.

Attractions

Ko Si Chang's two principal sights can be seen as you approach on the boat ride from Sri Racha: a Chinese temple standing prominently to the right and the ruins of the old royal palace to the left. Si Chang is very compact and both places are within walking distance from the arrival pier. Alternatively, hire a *samlor* for a three-hour tour.

Chinese Temple: It's a hot climb up to San Chao Por Khao Yai, but you're rewarded with outstanding marbled floors inside the shrine, a cool natural grotto with Buddha images, plus a Buddha's footprint and excellent views from the 268-meter summit.

Chulalongkorn's Summer Palace: The ruins of King Rama V's old summer retreat are one km left of town at the end of a roadway too narrow for cars. Construction began in 1889 after Rama's physician recommended Si Chang as a place for rest and recuperation for his royal consort and her son. Among the early buildings were the two-story Wattana Palace, the octagonal-shaped Phongsri on a nearby hill, and the Aphirom, with front and rear porches. A well was dug to supply water, a lighthouse erected to provide safe passage for

ships, and 26 roads were constructed to link the scattered residences.

The surviving foundations, crumbling staircases, beautiful flowering trees, and eerie reservoir blanketed with dead leaves form a pleasant if somewhat unspectacular sight. The Bell Rock near the top of the hill rings nicely when struck with a stick. It's hard to locate: look for the Thai script with yellow paint. The Asdangnimitr Temple, farther up the hill, once served as the king's meditation chambers but is now locked to protect Rama's portrait and a Buddha image cursed with large ungainly ears.

Accommodations

The solitary fishing village on Ko Si Chang has three simple guesthouses to the left of the pier. Two of them, signposted in Thai script only, have small rooms from 100B. The English-signposted Tiewpai Guesthouse has private rooms for 120B, a dormitory for 40B, and a/c rooms for 250B.

Transportation

Ko Si Chang can be reached with small fishing boats which depart hourly from the Sri Racha pier on Soi 14, between the seafood restaurants. The shuttle sputters past Russian oceanliners, a large naval station, and cargo ships before docking at the island's nondescript Chinese fishing village. The last boat back to Sri Racha departs at 1500.

PATTAYA

Once a "sleepy fishing village" popular with harried Bangkokians and American GIs on R&R, Pattaya has since mushroomed into a major beach resort covered with high-rise hotels, roaring discos, fine restaurants, throbbing go-go bars, and lively transvestite clubs that comprise Thailand's original sex capital. Today, this low-powered Riviera of Southeast Asia is undergoing an image crisis as it transforms itself from a bachelor's paradise to a sophisticated retreat catering to middle-aged couples and families. Although it's still fashionable to condemn Pattaya as superficial, overbuilt, unplanned, congested, polluted, tawdry, and having nothing to do with the *real* Thailand (all true), most of the three million annual visitors

WONG AMAT BEACH

WONG AMAT

PATTAYA

MINI SIAM ★

TO BANGKOK

A C BUS TO BANGKOK

N. PATTAYA RD.

CITY HALL

SUNSHINE GARDEN

SUKUMVIT HWY.

RESORT HOTEL

ORCHID LODGE

PALM GARDEN

TIFFANY'S SHOW

REGENT

COTTAGE

CABANA

NORTH PATTAYA

SOI 1

ROYAL CRUISE

SOI 2

COUNTRY

SOI 3

WEEKENDER

ALCAZAR SHOW

ROYAL NIGHT BUNGALOW

SOI 4

SOI 5

GRAND SOLE

BEACH RD.

PATTAYA PALACE

SOI 6

NOVOTEL

SUMMER PLACE

PATTAYA 2 RD.

TO SIAM COUNTRY CLUB, RACE CIRCUIT, ELEPHANT VILLAGE

MERLIN PATTAYA

NIGHT MARKET

MONTIEN

CENTRAL PATTAYA RD.

BUS TO RAYONG

SOI 7

BUSES TO NORTH & NORTHEAST

SOI 8

IMMIGRATION

TOURIST OFFICE

OCEAN VIEW

SOI 9

CAESAR'S PALACE

CHEAP HOTELS

SIAM BAYVIEW

SOI 10

HONEY INN

SOI 11

SOI 12

DIANA INN

SOI 13 LEK

SOI YAMATO

SOUTH PATTAYA

POST OFFICE

ROYAL GARDEN

GUESTHOUSES

PALM VILLA

BUS TO BANGKOK

P.K. VILLA

RUEN THAI REST.

DONGTAN BEACH

ROYAL WING

GRACE DISCO

MARINE BAR

ROYAL PALACE

SIMON CABARET

SOI 14

PLAZA

ROYAL CLIFF

SEAFOOD REST.

SOI 15

SOI DIAMOND

S. PATTAYA RD.

SIAM BAYSHORE

BEER BARS

CK

BEVERLY PLAZA

YACHT CLUB

★ VIEW POINT

DREAM VILLA

MIDTOWN

ASIA

★ BIG BUDDHA

JOMTIEN BAYVIEW

THEP PRASIT RD.

PATTAYA WATER PARK

CONDOTEL

ROYAL JOMTIEN RESORT

TO KO SAMET, RAYONG, CHANTABURI, TRAT

MERMAID'S BEACH RESORT

GUESTHOUSES

CASA JOMTIEN

JOMTIEN BEACH

SWAN BEACH RESORT

BUS TO BANGKOK

SIGMA RESORT

moon

NOT TO SCALE

seem to come away satisfied with its wide range of hedonistic offerings.

Attractions

Named after the southwestern monsoon wind that sweeps the east coast during the summer months, Pattaya is a beach resort dedicated to the pursuit of pleasure and love of *sanuk*. The range of activities is nothing short of amazing— sunbathing, parasailing, skin diving, golf, game fishing, zoos, night markets, and the world-famous nightlife. Pattaya divides itself into North Pattaya (deluxe hotels, fine restaurants, low-key nightlife), South Pattaya (moderate hotels and restaurants, notorious nightlife), and Jomtien Beach (family resort hotels and water sports).

Beaches: Pattaya's biggest disappointments are the narrow and brownish beach—vastly inferior to the crystalline shores of Phuket or Samui—and the polluted waters, which were recently declared a "hazardous zone" by a government-sponsored study on environmental pollution. For better sand and a sense of privacy, try an offshore island or Wong Amat Beach in North Pattaya.

Water Sports: Pattaya has eight scuba-diving shops, including the Seafari Sports Center in the Royal Garden Resort and the Scuba Professionals in the Dusit Resort Hotel. Basic courses start from 2000B per day. Visitors undeterred by the pollution can rent windsurfers (150-200B hourly), waterscooters (250B hourly), parasailers (250B for 10 minutes), Lasers (300-400B hourly), and Hobie Cats (500-600B hourly). All rates are subject to bargaining and higher on weekends. Check fuel supplies and condition of equipment, and never sign papers which promise liability. Fleecing ignorant tourists is big business in Pattaya.

Fishing Trips: Big-game fishing can be arranged at Jenny's Bar on Beach Road, Phar Lap Restaurant in North Pattaya, and Dieter Floeth at Deutsches Haus on Beach Road.

Elephant Shows: Pachyderms haul logs and play soccer at the elephant *kraal* located about five km from town.

Big Buddhas: Fine views over Pattaya can be enjoyed from two modern Buddhas in South Pattaya.

Outer Islands: Islands near Pattaya offer better sand and diving than the mainland beaches. Converted fishing trawlers leave from South Pattaya piers, opposite Soi 14, and adjacent to Tangkae Restaurant, daily at 0830 and cost 40-50B roundtrip. Travel agents arrange glass-bottom boat trips for 200-250B. Prices vary depending on quality of meals, diving equipment, and number of islands visited. Tours usually include Ko Rin or Ko Pai before stopping at Ko Larn (Coral Island), a highly developed resort fixed with several upscale hotels, pricey restaurants, a golf course, and dive shops. Pack food and drinks if you're counting *baht*.

Nong Nooch Village: A 600-acre tourist resort with landscaped gardens, a mini-zoo, and cultural shows daily at 1000 and 1500. Tickets from travel agents cost 250-300B and include transportation.

Mini Siam: Over 80 miniature reproductions of Siamese temples and palaces are located on Sukumvit Road; admission 200B.

Pattaya Water Park: An enormous beachfront park with waterslides, swimming pools, and restaurants—perfect for families. Located between Pattaya and Jomtien Beach; admission 50B adults, 30B children. Bungalows cost 800-1000B on weekdays, 1000-1400B weekends.

Bira Circuit: A 2.4-km racetrack with international events and a race school managed by Pacemakers AG, a European-based company involved in the racing tire business. Rentals include go-carts, Formula 3 models, and Ford 2000s.

Accommodations

Some 266 hotels are estimated to be operating in and around Pattaya. Further construction of a reported 55 condominium blocks and 10 new hotels will boost Pattaya's estimated 18,000 rooms to over 25,000 by 1995.

Hotels are grouped together in several areas. Wong Amat Beach in the far north offers several luxurious hotels tucked away in a semirural setting on the best beach in the area. North Pattaya has a good selection of moderate to luxury hotels while those in central Pattaya are conveniently located near the markets. South Pattaya hotels are inexpensive and noisy but popular with single males. Pattaya's cheapest hotels (100-150B) are located on Pattaya 2 Road just opposite Soi 11—basic concrete cubicles only adequate for short stays. To the south are luxury hotels such as the Royal Cliff and facilities along Jomtien Beach, a family area lined with moderately priced hotels. Tariffs vary according to day and season. Weekdays are cheaper; rates are cut about 40% during the slow season from May to October. Bargain hard.

Budget Accommodations
Contrary to popular belief, Pattaya has a good selection of fan-cooled rooms in the 200-250B price range and a/c rooms in the 300-400B range. Most are basic cubicles but come equipped with adequate furniture and private baths and are perfectly acceptable for short stays. Pattaya's cheapest hotels are on Soi Post Office, Soi Yamato, and Pattaya 2 Rd. opposite Soi 11.

   Soi Post Office: Post Office Alley has several good travel agencies, the well-stocked D.K. Books, and almost a dozen small hotels with decent fan-cooled rooms for 200-250B and a/c rooms for just 300-350B. Best bets include Sureena, Thips Guesthouse, Post Stuben Guest Haus, French-owned Riviera Beach Hotel, Swedish favorite Hasse Erickson, and Malibu at the end of the road.

   Soi Yamato: Named after a Japanese restaurant on the left, this alley has eight hotels in the 200-350B price range, such as Porn Guesthouse, German-operated Eiger Bar, Norwegian Hotel Norge, Texxan Inn, owned by a retired USAF officer, upscale Meridian Hotel, and other cheapies such as PS, Siam, and Nipa guesthouses.

   Pattaya 2 Road Guesthouses: Ten inexpensive hotels are located back on Pattaya 2 Rd. just opposite Soi 11. Small rooms with fans cost 150-200B and 200-250B with air-conditioning.

   Sea & Sun Inn: Overlooking the beach is a small but clean hotel with fan rooms from 300B and a/c rooms from 400B. Good location and friendly management. 325 South Pattaya Rd., tel. (038) 422945.

   Diana Inn: Simple rooms and a good pool make this a popular spot for budget travelers who want basic frills at low cost. Pattaya 2 Rd., Soi 11, tel. (038) 429675, 350-600B.

   Palm Villa: Pattaya's best budget hotel has all a/c rooms and an attractive swimming pool and is within easy walking distance of the bars. Pattaya 2 Rd., Soi 13, tel. (038) 429099, 400-600B.

   Royal Night Bungalows: An old and slightly seedy hotel centrally located on a quiet alley.

The Motel 6 of Pattaya. Soi 5, tel. (038) 428038, 400-600B.

Moderate Accommodations
Most Pattaya hotels priced in the 600-1000B price range include air-conditioned rooms with private bath, a restaurant, and a small swimming pool. Some charge an additional 20% for tax and service.

   Honey Inn: A clean, quiet, and well-located hotel with a spacious swimming pool and discounts for long-term visitors. 529 Soi 10 Pattaya 2 Rd., tel. (038) 421543, fax (038) 421946, 550-700B standard, 700-800B deluxe doubles.

   P.K. Villa: Superbly located right on the beach, Pattaya's largest villa has a good pool, a breezy restaurant, and a friendly atmosphere. 595 Beach Rd., South Pattaya, tel. (038) 428462, fax (038) 429777, 500-800B low season, 600-900B high season.

   Lek House: A new hotel with a large swimming pool, a billiards hall, and a rooftop terrace. All rooms furnished with TV, refrigerator, and hot showers. Pattaya 2 Rd. and Soi 13, tel. (038) 425550, 800-1000B.

   Caesar's Palace Hotel: Las Vegas comes to Pattaya in this pseudo-Romanesque 200-room hotel. The compound includes a large pool and tennis courts. Pattaya 2 Rd. Soi 10, tel. (038) 428607, fax (038) 422140, 900-1200B.

Luxury Accommodations
Luxury hotels are concentrated in North Pattaya and on Jomtien Beach to the south.

   Royal Wing-Cliff Hotel: Pattaya's most expensive and exclusive hotel offers 86 executive suites in its Royal Wing, private butlers, a beautiful pool, and elevators down to the private beach. Cliff Rd., tel. (038) 421421, fax (038) 428511, 4500-8000B.

   Dusit Resort Hotel: Situated on 15 acres of lovely gardens with great views, two swimming pools, three tennis courts, sauna, billiards, and a health club. Best hotel in North Pattaya. 240 Pattaya Beach Rd., tel. (038) 425611, fax (038) 428239, 2600-4500B.

   Wong Amat: Far from the maddening crowd, this low-rise bungalow is nicely set on Pattaya's best beach. Popular with discriminating Europeans; highly recommended. Wong Amat Beach, tel. (038) 418118, 1500-2000B s, 1600-2200B d.

Jomtien Beach

Mermaid's Beach Resort: European escape with 100 well-designed rooms, private dive boats, and swimming pool just 100 meters from the sandy beach. Jomtien Beach, tel. (038) 231907, fax (038) 231908, 850-1400B double.

Ambassador Jomtien: Thailand's largest hotel has international restaurants, an amoeba-shaped swimming pool, and 5,000 rooms with views over the Gulf of Thailand. Monstrous in conception. Jomtien Beach, tel. (038) 231501, 1200-3000B.

Restaurants

Pattaya's dining choices include everything from Arabic and French to Scottish and Japanese—a place where Thai food is an endangered species.

Food Fair: Seafood restaurants at the south end of Beach Road let you personally select your entree, cooking styles, and accompanying sauce, but it's advisable to avoid touts and to double-check cooking charges *before* ordering. Expensive to outrageous.

Soi Diamond Street Stalls: Good cheap alfresco dining.

Central Pattaya Road: Several popular restaurants with low prices and wide selections are located just east of Pattaya 2 Road. The marketplace is also worth investigating.

Dolk Riks: Indonesian dishes and Thai specialties are prepared by an Indonesian-born food critic and artist in Nakorn Center, north Pattaya. Expensive.

Wee Andy's: A Scottish cafe chiefly known for its misspelled menu of "flied lice, sirloin stakes," and "gurrys." 19 Beach Road. Moderate.

Sri Esarn: Authentic northeastern Thai dishes. Pattaya Middle Road. Moderate.

Nightlife

South Pattaya between Soi 13 and Soi 16 is a nonstop barrage of heady go-go bars, seedy nightclubs, high-tech discos, and outrageous live shows that cater to every possible sexual persuasion. No matter how you feel about flesh for sale, it's an amazing experience to wander down Pattaya Beach Road past mud wrestlers, Thai kick boxers, open-air cinemas, touts, transvestite clubs, and whatever new gimmick sweeps the night scene. A good place to start is on Soi Diamond, a small and totally crazy lane

transvestite follies

opposite the huge Grace Disco. Lively ladies working the street drag reluctant customers up to the bar stools and push them into the better bars such as Caligula (live shows), Blackout (better furnishings), Firehouse (not as good as Manila's), and Limmatquai (inexpensive drinks). Despite all the sex and sin, Pattaya nightlife is light-hearted and good-natured, lacking the depressing pathos of Western red-light districts.

Transvestite Shows: South Pattaya's best entertainment options are the hilarious transvestite shows that take place nightly in the Simon Cabaret (50-100B) and the monstrous Marine Bar that caters to "girls, guys, and in-betweens." If you haven't noticed by now, transvestites *(gatoeis)* are plentiful here in Pattaya. Since most Westerners have a difficult time distinguishing between girls and *gatoeis,* proceed with caution unless you seek a wild war story. Professional shows are given at Tiffany's and Alcazar Cabaret, which bills itself as having the largest transvestite troupe on Earth! Both are located in North Pattaya and cost 200-250B.

Discos: Disco Duck in the Pattaya Resort Hotel on Central Pattaya Road is your best bet.

Information

The TAT office on the beach has maps, hotel lists, and free magazines such as *Explore Pattaya* and *What's On,* two great sources for shopping and nightlife venues. The *Pattaya City Map* produced by the local Rotary Club is also recommended. Visas may be extended at Thai immigration on Soi 8. International phone calls can be made 24 hours daily from the exchange service at the corner of South Pattaya and Pattaya 2 roads—and from Simon Cabaret! Pattaya Police urge visitors not to carry too much money around, never to accept drinks or food from strangers, to keep off motorcycles unless experienced, and to check prices before buying *anything.*

Getting Around

Compact Pattaya is served by *songtaos* which cruise the main roads and, within the city limits, charge a flat fee of five *baht. Songtaos* to Jomtien Beach cost about 40B. An excellent way to avoid the obnoxious drivers is with a rented motorcycle; just remember to point out any damage to the bike *before* taking off. Larger bikes are available, but be careful—frightening numbers of tourists end their vacations on the streets of Pattaya.

Transportation

From Bangkok: Air-conditioned buses from Bangkok's Eastern Bus Terminal depart every 30 minutes between 0630 and 2100, cost 60B, and terminate at the poorly located station on North Pattaya Road. Flag down a public *dongtao* for just 5B. Private a/c buses from major Bangkok hotels cost 120B. Buses depart from the Bangkok airport at 0900, 1200, and 1900; tickets are sold at the Thai Limousine desk.

Leaving Pattaya: Blue and silver a/c buses depart for Bangkok's Eastern Bus Terminal every 30 minutes from the station on North Pattaya Road. Air-conditioned buses run on the hour direct to Bangkok's Northern Bus Terminal; there are frequent direct connections to Chiang Mai. Other services are provided by Diamond

Coaches from Nipa Lodge and Erawan buses from the Siam Bayview. Buses to the airport leave hourly between 0700 and 1700 from the Regent Marina Hotel. Orange public buses to Rayong and Ko Samet can be hailed on the main highway.

KO SAMET

This hot and dry island lying 6 1/2 km offshore is blessed with fine white beaches and clear blue waters sandwiched between craggy headlands. Thais know Samet as the island where Sunthorn Phu, Thailand's greatest poet, based his most famous work, *Pra Apaimanee.*

Ko Samet's great appeal is its easy accessibility to Bangkok and the complete lack of commercialization: the ax-shaped island was declared a national park in 1981 to prevent overdevelopment. As a result the island is blessedly free of high-rises, discos, traffic jams, prostitutes, and other distractions. The downside is that most bungalows are overpriced and lack water. Restaurants serve disappointing food and the piles of trash that blow around are downright depressing.

Though the squeaky sand is about the finest in Thailand and the beautifully shaped coves are inviting, Samet sorely needs some attention before it will begin to approach the comfort and attractiveness of Ko Samui or Phuket.

Accommodations

Samet's eastern seaboard is partitioned into a series of beaches and coves filled with bungalows of varying quality. Those on the northern beaches are the most developed; those to the south are generally primitive bamboo huts, badly overpriced at 80-150B per person. Prices rise sharply during the winter and on weekends, when Thai teenagers, hippies, gays, and folk musicians pack the island. Camping is legal and free anywhere on the island—bring a tent and improve your lifestyle. Better bungalows in the 250-800B range are described below.

Hat Sai Kao: "Diamond Sand," Ko Samet's longest and most impressive beach, is popular with families with children and tourists down from Pattaya. Located 10 minutes by foot from Na Dan ferry landing, Sai Kao Beach offers over a dozen moderately priced bungalows with

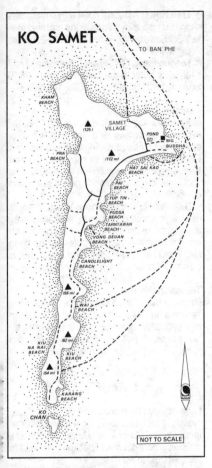

KO SAMET

TO BAN PHE

KHAM BEACH

(125 I)

SAMET VILLAGE

POND

BIG BUDDHA

PRA BEACH

(112 m)

HAT SAI KAO BEACH

PAI BEACH

TUP TIN BEACH

PUDSA BEACH

TARNTAWAN BEACH

VONG DEUAN BEACH

CANDLELIGHT BEACH

(56 m)

WAI BEACH

(62 m)

KIU NA NAI BEACH

KIU BEACH

(54 m)

KARANG BEACH

KO CHANG

NOT TO SCALE

fice with poste-restante facilities. Popular guest-houses include Naga's Bungalows for freshly baked goods and a sprawling library of yellowing paperbacks, Samed Villa with a good restaurant with bamboo furniture, noisy Sea Breeze Bungalows, Ao Pai Huts with over 70 rooms priced 100-600B, and lovely Nop's Restaurant with blinking lights, Buddhas, Balinese music, and lovely views. A great place to dine.

Tup Tin and Pudsa Beaches: Two small bays with several sets of bungalows are located over the craggy headlands. Tup Tin Bungalows is a very popular place on a good beach blessed with hanging palms. Recommended.

From Tup Tin Bungalows, the road veers right to cross the island and dead-end at Ao Pra, where a pair of bungalows stands on Samet's only readily accessible west-coast beach. Excellent sunsets.

Tarntawan Beach: "Sunflower Beach" is dominated by Tarntawan Bungalows, with huts for 100-600B. Tarntawan Beach manages to retain a hippie atmosphere compared to Diamond and Wong Duan beaches.

Vong Deuan Beach: Ko Samet's second-most-popular beach (after Hat Sai Kao) is on a beautifully arched bay bisected by a rickety pier. This is actually a yuppie destination filled with tourists from Pattaya and Europeans on package holidays. Sea Horse Travel, in the middle of the beach, changes traveler's checks, has a mobile telephone, and sells tickets to Ko Chang and Bangkok. Swiss-managed Delfimarin Diwa Diving Center arranges scuba dives to nearby coral beds and shipwrecks and longer multi-day journeys to islands near Ko Chang.

Vong Deuan can be reached directly from the Ban Phe pier, but you'll need to inquire about the correct boat. Boats back to Ban Phe depart daily at 1130, 1530, and 1830. The beach has five midpriced-to-expensive bungalows. Tents can be rented from the shop at the north end of the beach from a beautiful lady named Pia.

Popular accommodations include Malibu Garden Resort for 400-750B, simple and cheap Sea Horse, the relatively luxurious Vong Deuan Resort with standard bungalows from 600B and sea-view chalets from 900B, and Vong Deuan Villa with a miniature golf course, billiards tables, and rooms for 600-2500B. The restaurant has good food with great views from the terrace. Tel. (01) 321-0789.

restaurants and water-sports facilities that face the broad beach. As with nearly all places on Ko Samet, most bungalow operations have old huts constructed a decade ago and new bungalows erected just last month. All charge 150-300B for simple huts with common bath and 300-600B for individual bungalows with fan and private bath. Try Seaview (100-250B), Toy and VK Vila (150-300B), Diamond (150-500B), Ploy Talay and White Sand (200-500B), and Sai Kaew Villa (300-800B).

Pai Beach: Pai Beach (also called Phai Beach) is a small cove with several bungalows, travel offices such as Citizen Travel, and a small post of-

Candlelight Beach: This long and rocky beach has two sets of primitive bungalows that offer an escape from the commercialism of other beaches.

Wai Beach: A fairly nice beach dominated by the upscale Samet Ville Resort. Fan-cooled rooms cost 600B per person and include three meals, drinks, and the boat ride from Ban Phe.

Kiu Beach: Ko Samet's most attractive beach is clean, quiet, and graced with a beautiful row of swaying palm trees. Enjoy sunsets from the western beach and from the hillside viewpoint. Kiu Coral Beach Bungalows charges 80-500B in better chalets. Ao Kiu is a very long walk from Hat Sai Kao Beach, but well worth the trouble if you're looking for peace and solitude.

Transportation

Air-conditioned buses leave every two hours for Ban Phe from the Eastern Bus Terminal in Bangkok and hourly to Rayong, from where minibuses continue for Ban Phe. Boats to Ko Samet leave regularly from the Ban Phe pier. Be careful climbing onto these converted fishing boats—mishaps are common. Why don't they build some ladders? Some boats go to Samet Village; others go directly to Hat Sai or Vong Deuan Beach. Unless you enjoy long and dusty hikes, take a boat direct to one of the latter beaches. Minibuses return from Ban Phe back to Rayong until sunset. Don't believe taxi driver scare stories, "Last bus already go."

TRAT

Trat, 312 km from Bangkok, remained almost completely off the tourist trail until the discovery of Ko Chang in the early 1990s. Trat now chiefly serves as a transit point for visitors heading to Ko Chang and other islands in the southeast. Trat is an ordinary town with an extraordinary future; you can almost feel the heady air of prosperity.

Accommodations

Max & Tick's Guesthouse: The backpackers' center in Trat is a clean and friendly place with current information on Ko Chang and other nearby islands. Check the bulletin board. Look for the sign, D.C. Guesthouse. 58-60 Sukumvit Rd., tel. (039) 511449, 60-120B.

Trad Hotel: A decent hotel with small coffee shop is up the alley opposite the morning market. Soi Sam, tel. (039) 511091, 140-250B fan, 240-750B a/c.

Tanguenseng (TNS) Hotel: A clean and relatively new hotel in the center of town. 66-77 Sukumvit Rd., tel. (039) 511028, 100-200B.

Restaurants

Modern Market: The new market on Sukumvit Rd. is the best place for cheap eats in a clean environment, plus shopping for basic supplies. Check the impressive fish market in the rear. Inexpensive food stalls are on the ground floor. Top Star Cafe on the third floor is a semiluxurious option.

Golf Pub & Coffee Shop: Western decor, records mounted on the walls, live music in the evening, and a good selection of Thai and Western dishes make this a popular *farang* hangout. The Thai owner once lived in the States. Sukumvit Rd. past the cinema. Inexpensive.

Transportation

Ordinary buses from Bangkok's Eastern Bus Terminal on Sukumvit Rd. depart in the mornings until 0900, cost 65B, and take about eight hours to reach Trat. Air-conditioned buses cost 120B, but do the journey in six hours.

LAEM NGOP

Laem Ngop, 17 km south of Trat, is the departure point for boats to Ko Chang and other remote islands. Most of the activity is centered at the pier, where dozens of backpackers wait for the next boat to Ko Chang.

Accommodations

Laem Ngop has several small guesthouses that cater to backpackers and travelers who miss the last boat to Ko Chang in the late afternoon.

Laem Ngop Guesthouse: Laem Ngop's best guesthouse is 200 meters up the highway away from the pier. The owner can help with diving excursions, sportfishing, and extended cruises. 46 Moo 1, tel. (039) 512634, 40-60B.

Other Guesthouses: Overflow from Daniel's place is handled by Chut Kaew Guesthouse and Laem Ngop Inn farther up on the right side of the road. Both have rooms for 100-150B.

Transportation

Travel agencies on Khao San Rd. in Bangkok have small minibuses direct to Laem Ngop. Services are provided by both Sea Horse and S.T. Travel. Minibuses are convenient, but the air-conditioning rarely works and they travel at frightening speeds. Both services will attempt to put you on private boats that take you to remote beaches where you are a captive audience. Skip this scam and take another boat to the beach of your choice.

Public buses from Bangkok's Eastern Bus Terminal to Trat are both safer and more comfortable for the full-day journey. Minibuses from the main road in Trat continue 17 km south to Laem Ngop and charge just 10B per passenger.

Ordinary and a/c buses depart throughout the day for Pattaya and Bangkok. The Sea Horse minibus departs daily for Bangkok at 1145.

KO CHANG

Ko Chang ("Elephant Island") is, after Phuket, Thailand's second-largest island, some 30 km in length and eight km broad at its widest point. Covered with dense jungle and bisected by a steep wall of mountains, Chang remained almost completely untouched until the early 1990s.

By 1992 the island had achieved fame as Thailand's next major resort destination. Local authorities jumped on the tourism bandwagon. The Thai government constructed a large pier on the east side of Ko Chang and then blasted a concrete road which now encircles most of the island. Ko Chang today resembles the early stages of Ko Samui: a tropical island firmly mesmerized by the promise of mass tourism.

Despite all the construction and development, Ko Chang remains one of the most beautiful islands in Thailand. Most accommodations still are simple bamboo bungalows rather than concrete hotels filled with package tourists, and a majority of Chang's 5,000 residents still make their living from fishing rather than tourism. Discos, nightly videos, noisy motorcycles, and beer bars are still several years away. Ko Chang is a wonderfully refreshing change from the hustle of Samui and Phuket. The time to visit Ko Chang is *now*.

East Coast Attractions

Most visitors are content to simply relax on one of the west-coast beaches. Ko Chang, however, is a spectacular island blessed with thick tropical jungle, small waterfalls, and narrow trails which follow the deep interior valleys.

Dan Mai: The only sizable village on the east coast has a small market, a fishing pier, and a surprisingly large villa owned by the local mayor. Mayom Pier, four km to the south, is an important embarkation point. The largest town on Ko Chang is Salak Pet, a somnolent fishing village located in a protected cove on the south coast.

Visitor Center: Local authorities have erected a small visitor center near Mayom Waterfall on the east coast. Adjacent concrete bungalows with private bathrooms cost 300-500B per night and can be hired from local park officials.

Mayom Waterfall: A few kilometers south of Dan Mai is a six-level waterfall and swimming pond 500 meters off the primitive road. Tham Mayom Huts, about 50 meters north, has five simple bungalows priced from 100B.

Don Keo Waterfall: An unmarked path just north of the broken wooden bridge leads through rubber plantations to these modest falls.

Beaches: The east coast of Ko Chang is rarely visited because of its brownish sand and mangrove swamps. One exception is the lovely Saithong Bungalows, with 24 basic and 10 almost-luxurious huts with private bath. Peaceful and relaxing.

West Coast Beaches

Ko Chang's best beaches are all on the west coast. Most accommodations are simple bamboo bungalows with mattresses on the floor and illuminated by oil lamps. Restaurants are funky places with good food but rudimentary service; you'll probably be ignored to the point of starvation until you approach the front counter.

Construction of new bungalows is going on at a furious pace as professionals from Bangkok arrive to milk the tourist boom, so expect major changes from the following descriptions. In general, you should take a ferry to the beach of your choice and then wander around to inspect a few places. Most bungalows are filled during the high season from October to March, but tents can be rented while waiting for vacancies. Ko Chang is, technically speaking, a national park where camping is legal anywhere.

White Sand Beach: Hat Sai Khao, the longest and most popular beach on Ko Chang, is the original escape on the island. The concrete road which skirts the back side of the beach goes south to Klong Prao Beach and cuts through the mountains at the northern end to Klong Son Beach. Alternatively, a narrow trail heads north over the ridgetop and brings you to Klong Son in one hour. White Sand Beach is a good place to enjoy the sand and meet other travelers.

Over a dozen bungalows are spread along the beach. All charge 60-100B for bamboo huts with mattresses on the floor and common bathrooms located back toward the road. Bungalows are almost identical, but restaurants vary from primitive to almost sophisticated. Popular choices include White Sand Beach Resort near the trailhead, Boom Dam and Cookie Bungalows slightly to the south, Sabbai Bungalows with a pleasant semicircular restaurant, better huts at Honey Resort, and Sun Sai Bungalow Resort at the extreme south.

Klong Prao Beach: The road from White Sand Beach veers inland and skirts the rocky cape at Chai Chet until it approaches the coastline near Klong Prao River. Klong Prao Beach is a long and relatively undeveloped beach with huge tracts of property covered with little more than coconut groves and wild vegetation. Some great hikes can be made east into the mountains which bisect the island. The path to Klong Prao Waterfall is two km south from Coconut Beach Bungalows.

Accommodations are widely scattered along Klong Prao Beach, making bungalow-hopping a difficult proposition. Starting from the north end, Coconut Beach Bungalows features 12 extremely beautiful bamboo huts for 60-160B set under swaying palm trees, a romantic spot recommended for couples. Ko Chang Resort features a/c A-frames with hot showers for 1500-2500B.

The road continues south past the path to Klong Prao Waterfall and across the Klong Prao River to PSS Bungalows, beautifully situated on a sandy tip facing the broad mouth of the river. Farther south is Magic Bungalows, one of the best-value places on Klong Prao Beach.

Kai Bae Beach: The last major beach on the west coast has a narrow strip of sand crowded with over a dozen bungalows, including Coral Bungalows on the rocky promontory, Nang Nuan 2, Kae Bae and Kae Bae Beach Bungalows, recommended Porn Guesthouse, and finally Nang Nuan 1.

Bang Bao Beach: A beautiful bay and private pier are on the primary beach on the south coast of Ko Chang. Most of the beach is dominated by Bang Bao Resort and Sunset Bungalows.

Long Beach: Perhaps the most spectacular beach and finest waters on Ko Chang are near the southeastern tip. The original bungalows mysteriously burned down several years ago, but new operations will probably be running by the time you arrive.

North Coast Beaches

Klong Son, an almost completely untouched fishing village in a well-protected harbor on the north coast, has several inexpensive bungalows, a small mosque, a supply shop, and several seafood restaurants on a rickety fishing pier. Motorcycle taxis reach Klong Son from Saithong Guesthouse, or you can hike one hour over the mountains from White Sand Beach.

Transportation

Fishing trawlers converted into ferryboats leave from Laem Ngop daily from 0900 to late afternoon. Prices are fixed and it's best to purchase tickets directly from the boat owner rather than the middleman who operates a counter at the pier.

Boats from Ko Chang back to Laem Ngop leave twice in the mornings around 0830 and 1100. Exact departures are posted at most guesthouses. Completion of the concrete road around the island will dramatically change the transportation scene.

WEST OF BANGKOK

NAKHON PATHOM

Your first glimpse of the massive *chedi* at Nakhon Pathom is staggering. Soaring over 125 meters into the hot blue skies, this is the most sacred Buddhist monument in Thailand and the world's largest *chedi*, surpassing even the gilded wonder in Yangon. Although the dome-shaped reliquary lacks the staggering detail of Yangon's Shwedagon, its fairyland of auxiliary *bots*, *ubosots*, Buddha images, and curious substructures makes for a fascinating afternoon of exploration. For best impact, approach the *chedi* from the north side facing the train station.

Accommodations
Although usually just a stopover en route to Kanchanaburi, good hotels in all price ranges are available.

NAKHON PATHOM *CHEDI*

NUN'S HOUSES

ORIGINAL CHEDI REPLICA

SEATED BUDDHA

NAKHON SI THAMMASART REPLICA

HOLY TREES

MEDITATION CHAMBERS

MINIATURE MOUNTAIN

DVARAVATI SEATED BUDDHA

SOUTH VIHARN

CHINESE TEMPLE

EAST VIHARN

WEST VIHARN

SALA

BUDDHA STATUES

CHEDI

NOT TO SCALE

MINIATURE MOUNTAIN

MUSEUM

BELL CHAPELS

PUBLIC HALL

VIHARA PRA RUNG ROCHANARIT

TEMPLE OFFICES

CHAOPO PRASATONG

GRAND STAIRCASES

PRAKAN PAKKLOD

CEREMONIAL HALLS

© MOON PUBLICATIONS, INC.

Budget: Inexpensive lodgings include: Mit Phaisal at 120 Phayapan Rd., tel. 242422, 120-160B; Siam Hotel at 2 Rajadamnern, tel. 241754, 140-300B; Muang Thong at 1 Rajwithi, tel. 242618, 100-200B.

Mit Thaworn: Two cheap hotels are near the train station. The Mit Thaworn (Mittaowan) and adjacent Mit Phaisal (Mitphaisan or Mitfaisal) have rooms acceptable for a short stay. Both are up a short alley off the busy street market. 305 Rot Fai Rd., tel. (034) 243115, 100-160B.

Nakorn Inn: Best upscale choice in town is the Nakorn Inn off the main road. This hotel has a coffee shop, a convention room, and 70 a/c rooms. 55 Rajwithi Rd., tel. (034) 251152, fax (034) 254998, 500-800B.

Transportation
Buses leave from Bangkok's Southern Bus Terminal and take an hour. To return to Bangkok, take bus 81 from the north side of the *chedi*, next to the canal. For Kanchanaburi, take bus 81 from the southeast corner of the pagoda. Trains from Thonburi and the south also stop here.

KANCHANABURI

Kanchanaburi is known for the bridge made famous by Pierre Boulle's celebrated novel of WW II, *The Bridge Over the River Kwai,* and the subsequent Academy Award-winning motion picture directed by David Lean in which William Holden and Alec Guinness whistled a very popular musical score. The rather ordinary bridge is nothing special, but Kanchi's relaxed atmosphere and nearby waterfalls, caves, and river trips make this one of *the* most enjoyable destinations in Thailand. Travelers intending to stay just a day or two often extend their visits to a week or more.

War Museum
Before going out to the bridge, be sure to visit the JEATH Museum, its name an acronym for the primary nations (Japan, England, America/Australia, Thailand, Holland) that participated in local action. Modeled after POW camps of the period, the simple bamboo structure contains war memorabilia, photographs, personal recollections, and graphic descriptions of tortures committed by the Japanese. More than just a museum, it's an immensely moving memorial to the 16,000 Allied POWs plus 50,000-100,000 Malay, Chinese, and Indians who died from lack of medical attention, starvation, and torture during construction of the 400-km Death Railway. The best way to tour the remaining sights is with a bicycle rented from the restaurant just across the street. Most guesthouses also rent bikes.

The Bridge
The world-famous bridge, five km from the center of town, was constructed in just over 12 months by some 60,000 Allied prisoners from Singapore and another 250,000 slave laborers from Japanese-occupied countries. Although an estimated 50,000-100,000 lives were sacrificed, the project was not a success; the bridge was only used *once* before British bombers from Sri Lanka destroyed the fourth, fifth, and sixth spans on 13 February 1945. The Japanese replaced the missing girders with two square beams, ironically stamped, Made in Japan. Be careful walking across the bridge and keep an eye out for slow-moving trains. The outdoor Train Museum just opposite displays a steam engine and an ingenious Japanese supply truck that operated on both road and rails. The Japanese War Memorial to the south is dedicated to those who "died through illness during the course of the construction"—a pleasant-enough euphemism. The bridge is too far to walk; hire a bike or motorcycle or take a minibus from Chao Kunen Road.

Kanchanaburi War Cemetery
With its neatly arranged tombstones and poignant messages, this final resting place for 6,982 Allied war prisoners forms one of the most moving tableaux in Southeast Asia. A private foundation in London keeps the cemetery supplied with fresh flowers and supports the Thai gardeners who maintain the lovely grounds. The adjacent Chinese Cemetery is a study in contrasts; pauper tombs hidden away against the walls, tombstones of the wealthy elevated like Chinese pagodas.

Vicinity Of Kanchanaburi
Kao Poon Cave: Limestone caves near Kanchanaburi often serve as Buddhist temples filled with Buddhist and Saivite images illuminated

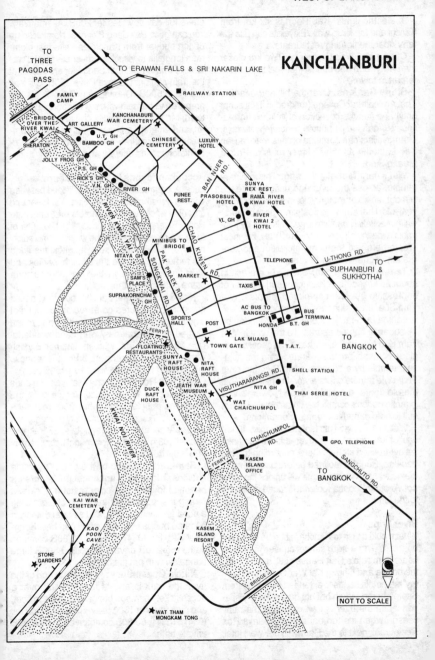

KANCHANBURI

NOT TO SCALE

with electric lights. Kao Poon is six km from Kanchi and too far to walk. Bicyclists can use the ferry near the floating restaurants.

Chung Kai War Cemetery: Two km closer than Kao Poon and almost identical to its counterpart in town.

Stone Gardens: Over the hill and near the Thai Agricultural College (marked in Thai script only) is a curious collection of volcanic formations surrounded by poured concrete walkways. Motorcyclists can continue on this road to Ban Keo Museum and the Khmer ruins at Prasat Muang Sing.

Wat Tham Mongkam Tong: This ordinary temple, across the river and difficult to reach without a bike or motorcycle, is known for a 70-year-old Thai nun who floats in a pool of water while meditating *and* whistling. This neat trick attracts a steady stream of devout Thais, but most Westerners find the commercialism and zoo-like atmosphere rather tawdry.

Temples on the Hill: Situated on a hilltop about 20 km south of Kanchanaburi is a pair of impressive but half-completed temples. Wat Tam Sua, the Chinese-style pagoda to the left, is fronted by a fat, jolly Buddha surrounded by 18 superbly carved figures. To the right is Wat Tam Kao Noi, which, perhaps in a show of religious competition, is separated from the adjacent temple by a concrete wall. This attractive Thai-style temple offers a worship hall with cool marble floors, a mound-shaped tower, and a gigantic Buddha complete with automated treadmill to help expedite monetary donations!

Wat Pra Dong: This isolated temple, 40 km east of Kanchanaburi, is revered for its immense yellow-frocked stone, where, according to Thai tradition, Buddha reclined before ascending to the heavens. A young monk will unlock the main *bot*. Another Buddha footprint is found on the hill to the left.

River Trips

What would a visit to Kanchanaburi be without a boat trip? Three-hour sunset cruises in longtail boats from Nita's Raft House cost 100B to visit the bridge and Chung Kai War Cemetery. Luxury raft hotels sponsor extended river trips from September to March but not during the dry season when the river is low, or during the rainy season when it's too dangerous. Sunya Rex Restaurant, next to the Rama River Kwai Hotel,

offers full-day voyages for 200B. Alternatively, you can go to Pak Sang Pier near Namtok some 60 km upriver from Kanchi and hire fast eight-man longtails to visit the upriver caves and waterfalls. Prices from Pak Sang Pier are posted at the train station: to Lawa Cave 300B, Sai Yok Yai Falls 500B, Daowadung Cave 700B. Be prepared to bargain with the boatman. Back in town, Mr. Pirom Angkudie, civil servant, historian, and amateur archaeologist, can be recommended for his three-hour sunset tours of nearby historical and cultural attractions.

Accommodations In Kanchanaburi

Local accommodations can be divided between floating guesthouses on the Kwai Yai River and a variety of conventional hotels on Sangchuto Road. River-based guesthouses in the center of town are pleasant during the week but incredibly noisy on weekends when Bangkokians flood the region. To escape the all-night parties and blasting disco boats, try the guesthouses north of the park toward the bridge.

Nita Guest House: Kanchi's best land-based guesthouse features quiet rooms, communal dining facilities, and a comfortable living room. Owned and operated by warm and wonderful Nita Mrigalakshana, who speaks her English with a broad Texas accent. 3 Visuthararangsi, tel. (034) 511130, 50-80B s, 100-150B d.

Nita Raft House: Several floating crash pads are located along the banks near the city park. Nita's is a popular choice, but store your valuables at her guesthouse for safety reasons. Ask for Supachai and Miss Seangthip. 27 Pakprak Rd., tel. (034) 514521, communal floor space is 40B, 80B doubles.

Sam's Place: One of the better riverside choices in central Kanchanaburi features a beautiful foyer and a cozy restaurant (with a *farang* menu), wooden reclining chairs facing a pond filled with ducks, and several detached bamboo bungalows with small porches. Songkwai Rd., tel. (034) 513971, 60-80B common bath, 150-200B private bath, 250-300B large bungalow with private bath.

Nitaya Guesthouse: At the north end of the riverside park is an old favorite with over a dozen rickety bamboo bungalows, a disco boat, and river tours at 1300 daily. Songkwai Rd., tel. (034) 513341, 60-80B common bath, 150-180B private bath.

Farang River life

River Guesthouse: Several new guesthouses have recently opened on Soi 2 to the north of central Kanchanaburi. All are somewhat distant from the discos and fairly quiet. River GH is a simple place run by Mr. Ek, who also sponsors boat tours. 42 Rongheeboi Rd. Soi 2, tel. (034) 512491, 50-100B.

P.S. Guesthouse: Excellent views and a cozy restaurant make this a good choice. 54 Rongheeboi Rd. Soi 2, tel. (034) 513039, 50-80B common, 120-150B private bath.

Jolly Frog Guesthouse: The largest guesthouse in Kanchanaburi has over 50 rooms facing a central courtyard filled with palms and grass. Features include motorcycle rentals, a spacious circular dining hall, German management, and minibuses to Bangkok daily at 1100 and 1430. 28 Maenamwae Rd., tel. (034) 514579, 50-80B common, 120-150B private bath.

U.T. Guesthouse: A genuine homestay in a light blue, modern, two-story house about 100 meters back from the river. Peaceful, friendly, and cozy. 275 River Kwai Rd., tel. (034) 513539, 60B per person.

Bamboo Guesthouse: The most idyllic guesthouse in Kanchanaburi is at the end of a dirt road about 300 meters before the bridge. Big lawn with a small pond; often filled but otherwise highly recommended. Call first to check on vacancies. 3-5 Soi Vietnam, tel. (034) 512532, 60-120B bamboo bungalows, 250-500B upstairs rooms in a red brick building.

V.L. Guesthouse: The only other land-based budget guesthouse worth recommending (besides Nita's) is this modern place opposite the River Kwai Hotel. Rooms are very clean, well furnished, and include a private bath; an excellent deal for anyone who dislikes riverside accommodation. 18/11 Sangchuto Rd., tel. (034) 513546, 120-160B fan, 250-300B a/c.

Duck Raft House: For better facilities in the 550-650B price range (s or d), check the offices of this floating hotel near Nita Raft House.

Kasem Island Resort: Kanchanaburi's first upscale raft hotel features seven bamboo cottages and 20 houseboats with private baths, patios overlooking the river, and an excellent floating restaurant. Facilities are only adequate but managers are making improvements. Head office is at Chukadon Wharf, 27 Chaichumpol Rd., tel. (034) 511603, Bangkok reservation tel. (02) 391-6672, fax (02) 391-5085, 650-750B.

River Kwai Family Camp: This land-based resort seven km north of town offers horseback riding (250B per hour), canoe rentals (100B), and two-day wildlife safaris organized by Mrs. Lee Rhodes. Popular with expatriate families from Bangkok. Box 2, tel. (034) 512733, 450-700B.

Rama River Kwai Hotel: Kanchi's oldest upscale hotel is popular with businessmen, tour groups, and Japanese visitors. All rooms are a/c and come with private bath, TV, and video, but why stay here when you can float on a raft? 284 Sangchuto, tel. (034) 511269, 600-1000B.

Sheraton River Kwai: A joint Thai/American property opened recently near the famous bridge. Facilities include two pools, tennis courts, and five restaurants. Tambon Ta Makam, tel. (034) 234-5599, fax (034) 236-8320, 2200-3600B.

River Kwai Raft Resorts

Kanchanaburi province currently has over 50 registered raft hotels located on the upper reaches of the Kwai Yai (near Namtok and Sai Yok Falls), at Sri Nakharim Lake, and on Krung Kravia Lake near the Myanmar border. The daily per-person charge of 450-600B often includes three meals and boat transportation. Some are quite simple and operate without electricity; others have swimming pools and a/c rooms with hot water. Those most popular with Westerners are the River Kwai Village Hotel, River Kwai Raft, River Kwai Farm, and River Kwai Jungle Raft (Floatel Raft House)—all located on the Kwai Noi River. Travel agents in Bangkok can make reservations and help with transportation. Advance reservations are unnecessary except on weekends. The Kanchi tourist office and travel agents near the bus stop can also help.

Restaurants

Krua Thien Tong and Ruen Ploy: Kanchanaburi's best restaurants are the half-dozen floating cafes tied up at the south end of fitness park. Arrive for the sunset and try deep-fried freshwater catfish or frog legs fried in garlic.

Pae Karn: Another floating restaurant known for its *log tong* and country-style Thai dishes such as *tom yam pla* made with giant river carp. Unfortunately, the highly prized *pla yi sok* fish (Julien carp, the fish used for those terrific street signs), favored for its fatty and succulent meat, has been hunted nearly to extinction. Other species now substitute.

Cheap Eats: Cheap meals are found at the outdoor food stalls on Sangchuto Road near the bus terminal. Sunya Rex is a favorite travelers' hangout, as is the lively Cowboy Club located between the bus station and the river.

Getting There

Buses to Kanchanaburi leave every 30 minutes from the Southern Bus Terminal in Bangkok and take three hours. Trains for Kanchi leave three times daily from Thonburi Station.

TRANSPORTATION AROUND KANCHANABURI

DESTINATION	BUS	HRS.
Bangkok	81	3
Nakhon Pathom	81	1½
Nam Tok	8203	1
Sai Yok Falls	8203	2
Three Pagodas	8203	6
Ratchaburi	461	2
Suphanburi	411	2½
Bophloi	325	1½
Erawan Falls	8170	2

Whirlwind tours are also possible. A special train leaves Bangkok's Hualampong Station weekends at 0615, stops at the *chedi* in Nakhon Pathom for 40 minutes (from 0735 to 0815), pauses for 30 minutes at the Kanchi bridge (0930 to 1000), and takes a three-hour lunch break at Nam Tok (1130 to 1430), enough time to visit the nearby waterfall or go down to the river for a quick look. On the return trip, it stops for 45 minutes at the war cemetery (1605 to 1650) before arriving back in Bangkok at 1930. Whew! Advanced booking is recommended.

Getting Around

Bicycling is the perfect way to get around Kanchi. Ratty old bikes can be rented from most guesthouses and just opposite the War Museum. Motorcycles cost 150B per day at the Honda dealer. Experienced cyclists will find this an excellent way to explore the countryside and visit remote temples and caves. A slow but romantic alternative is the funky third-class train which leaves Kanchanaburi daily at 0600 and 1030 and arrives in Namtok two hours later. Visit the river or a nearby waterfall before catching the 1520 train back to Kanchanaburi. See the "Transportation Around Kanchanaburi" chart for buses from the Kanchanaburi bus terminal.

Leaving Kanchi

Ordinary Bus 81 for Bangkok and Nakhon Pathom departs from the main bus terminal while a/c buses leave from the office on Sangchuto

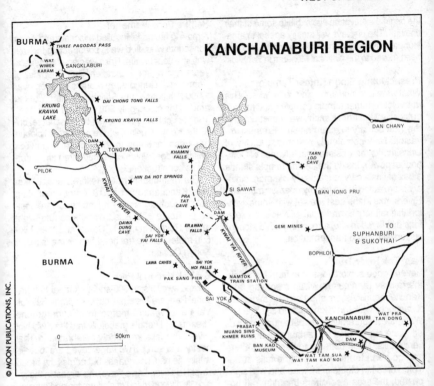

KANCHANABURI REGION

Road. To Ayuthaya, take Bus 419 to Suphanburi (two to three hours), then yellow Bus 703 to Ayuthaya (45 minutes). To Sukothai, take Bus 487 to Nakhon Sawan (four hours), then Bus 99 to Sukothai (three hours). To the floating market at Damnern Saduak, take Bus 461 to Bang Phya intersection, walk down the road, then take Bus 78 or the minibus to the last stop in Damnern. The market is 1.2 km south. Alternatively, take Bus 81 to Nakhon Pathom and then Bus 78 to Damnern Saduak.

KANCHANABURI REGION

The waterfalls, limestone mountains, caves, and other natural wonders around Kanchanaburi comprise one of the loveliest regions in Thailand. An excellent place to relax and enjoy the area's great natural appeal is on a raft house, though most sights can be visited on day-trips

from Kanchanaburi. Topography is somewhat confusing. There are actually two River Kwais in the province: Kwai Yai (Big Kwai), which flows from Sri Nakarin Lake, and Kwai Noi (Little Kwai), which starts at Krung Kravia Lake near the Burma border. Both merge near Kanchanaburi into the Mae Klong River, which flows into the Gulf of Thailand. Attractions and raft hotels situated along the Kwai Noi can be reached on bus 8203, but private transportation is necessary to reach the somewhat isolated Ban Kao Museum and Prasat Muang Sing Ruins. Accommodations are available on both rivers and at Tongpapum, Sangklaburi, and Three Pagodas Pass.

Ban Kao Museum

One fortunate outcome of the railway's construction was the discovery by a Dutch prisoner of some important Neolithic artifacts in 1943. A Thai-Danish archaeological team continued the excavations in 1961, and today a small museum near the original excavation site exhibits some of their findings. The displays will mostly appeal to amateur paleontologists since the major artifacts have been moved to the National Museum in Bangkok.

Prasat Muang Singh Khmer Temple

What were Cambodians doing so far west? This marvelous Khmer temple complex and military outpost, 45 km from Kanchi, was constructed in the 12th century to guard against Burmese invasion. Now completely restored, the City of Lions marks the westernmost advance of Cambodian power. Inside the central temple stands a pair of finely carved statues, while more statuary is protected in the nearby open-air museum. Riverbanks to the east are set with some comfortable rafthouses and a pair of Neolithic skeletons displayed *in situ;* a recommended stop for visitors with hired transportation.

Nam Tok River Trip

Several good explorations start from Nam Tok, the railway terminus for visitors coming from Kanchanaburi. Visitors short on time might hire a *samlor* or walk three km north to Sai Yok Noi Waterfall, an unremarkable, perpetually crowded place surrounded by restaurants and souvenir stalls. Much better is to flag down a bus and go north to the more pristine falls at Sai Yok. Three km off the main road and well signposted, the area also offers beautiful raft hotels floating underneath the Golden Gate-like hanging bridge. But the best option is to hire a tricycle from the train station for 5B and go downhill to Pak Sang Pier. From here, eight-man longtail boats can be hired for upriver journeys. Boat prices, listed at the train station and above (under "Getting Around"), are prohibitively expensive except for larger groups. A recommended six-hour journey stops at Lawa Caves, biggest caves in the region, and Sai Yok Yai Falls, where the famous Russian-roulette scenes from *The Deer Hunter* were filmed. This tour costs about 1000B per boatload—not bad for five or six people. Better yet, spend the night at the River Kwai Village Hotel or the Floatel Raft House, two beautiful raft hotels which charge 600B for lodgings, boat ride, and three meals. Travel agents will make arrangements from Bangkok or Kanchanaburi. Last train departs Nam Tok for Kanchi at 1530. Public buses ply the highway until nightfall.

Hellfire Pass Memorial

A moving memorial to Allied prisoners and Asian conscripts who died while constructing the railway line near Hellfire Pass was erected several years ago by the Australian-Thai Chamber of Commerce. During three months of labor, over 1,000 Australian and British prisoners worked around the clock; only 300 survived the ordeal. The park consists of a series of trails that reaches the Konyu Cutting, where a memorial plaque has been fastened to the rock, and Hin Tok trestle bridge, which collapsed three times during its construction.

The memorial is near Hellfire Pass, 80 km from Kanchanaburi and 18 km north of Nam Tok. English signs marking the turnoff are posted on Route 323. Bus travelers should alight at the Royal Thai Army Camp and then hike 500 meters to the trailhead, which leads to the Konyu Cutting.

Sai Yok National Park

Tucked away inside 500-square-km Sai Yok National Park are the small but very pretty Sai Yok Yai Falls, which emerge from underground streams and tumble gracefully into the Kwai Noi River. The falls are widely celebrated in Thai poetry and song. Two large caves are located within the park boundaries but across the broad Kwai Noi River. Lawa Cave, the largest in the region, is a wonderland of stalagmites and dripping stalactites. Dawa Dung Cave is northwest of Sai Yok on the west bank of the Kwai Noi River.

The park entrance is about 38 km north of Nam Tok, but the falls and river are hidden three km off the main road. Bus travelers should get off at the national park sign and then flag down a passing car or face a long and dusty walk. Motorcycle taxis may be available. Within sight of the curious bridge are several beautiful raft hotels where bamboo bungalows cost 450-600B.

Tongpapum

The first major town between Kanchanaburi and Three Pagodas Pass is Tongpapum, a cowboy village of twisted, rutted streets, ragged children, and hand-pump gasoline stations. Tongpapum lies at the southern edge of the vast Krung Kravia Lake created by the Khao Lam Dam, a major hydroelectric source for Bangkok and central Thailand.

Tongpapum Accommodations

A few hotels are located on the main road which runs off the highway.

Som Chai Nuk Bungalows: Friendly place with decent fan-cooled rooms with private bath from 100B, a/c from 200B.

Si Thong Pha Phum Bungalows: Another place, farther down the main road, has 28 fan and a/c rooms in the same price range.

S. Bunyong Bungalows: Another similar choice at the end of the street.

Kao Laem Raft Resort: Several upscale raft hotels are on nearby Krung Kravia Lake, including this popular retreat. Lake Rd., Bangkok tel. (02) 277-0599, 400-600B

Thongphaphum Valley and Ban Rimdoi: Two other lake resorts. Lake Rd., tel. (034) 513218, 600-800B.

Sangklaburi

Sangklaburi is an old Mon town inhabited by an ethnic mix of Mon, Karen, Burmese, and Thai. The main attraction is an old Mon temple called Wat Wang Vivangkaram, three km southwest of town toward the reservoir, and a newer stupa, Chedi Luang Paw Utama, modeled after the Mahabodhi shrine in Bodgaya, India. Another good trip is to 36-tiered Takhian Thong Falls and to Kroen Tho Falls just across the Burmese border. Note that there are no banks in Sangklaburi; change enough money in Kanchanaburi.

Sangklaburi Accommodations

P Guesthouse: Travelers usually stay at this guesthouse, 900 meters north of the bus stop on the edge of Songkalia Lake. Proprietor Darunee Yenjai can help arrange treks to nearby Mon villages, a Thai town submerged by the dam, and the longest handmade wooden bridge in Thailand, which leads to an old Mon village. He also rents motorbikes. Rooms cost 60-150B.

Songkalia River Huts: Several raft hotels are outside town, including this spot two km north of town toward Wat Mon, where the Songkalia River empties into the lake. Lake Rd., Bangkok reservations tel. (02) 427-1583, 300-500B.

Runtee Palace: Another option, 15 minutes by boat from the Saphan Runtee pier. Bangkok tel. (02) 314-2656, 1000-1400B including boat ride and meals.

Sangklaburi Transportation

Sangklaburi is 220 km from Kanchanaburi. Bus 8203 departs Kanchanaburi daily at 0645, 0900, 1045, 1315, and takes about five hours to reach Sangklaburi. Motorcyclists should allow a full day with stops at Ban Kao Museum, Muang Sing Khmer ruins, Nam Tok, and a brief swim at Sai Yok Yai Falls. Gasoline stations are located in Nam Tok, Tongpapum, and Sangklaburi.

Three Pagodas Pass

The border crossing into Burma at Three Pagodas Pass is named after a trio of historic cone-shaped *chedis* known as Pra Chedi Sam Ong. Centuries ago this was the spot from where marauding Burmese armies marched into Thailand on their traditional invasions. Today the small trading post at the pass is the scene of political struggles between the Burmese government, the Mon National Liberation Army (MNLA), the Karen National Union (KNU), and the All Burma Students Democratic Front (ABSDF), which has set up an opposition government to fight the regime of Ne Win.

Three Pagodas Pass remains in a constant state of flux. During the mid-1980s it thrived as a prosperous trading town dominated by the Karens, who collected a five-percent tax on all goods smuggled across the border. After the political disruptions in 1988, the Burmese government renewed its military offensive against the Karens and Mons by attacking Three Pagodas Pass and burning the shantytown to the ground. The village has since revived itself but remains a staging ground for military and political struggle.

Locals can point out the few sights around town: the three whitewashed pagodas, the site of the old station that marked the end of the Death Railway, and the track itself, which according to Thai archaeologists follows a route that dates back to the earliest human settlement in the region.

Westerners are occasionally allowed to cross the border and visit the adjacent Burmese village where handicrafts, cheroots, and silver jewelry are sold in the local market. Conditions change with the season and should be double-checked with other travelers and the TAT office in Kanchanaburi.

Three Pagodas Pass Accommodations
Most travelers visit Three Pagodas Pass on day-trips from Sangklaburi. **Three Pagodas Pass Resort** is the only choice at the border. Pass Rd., tel. (034) 511079, Bangkok reservations tel. (02) 412-4159, 300-450B.

Three Pagodas Pass Transportation
Three Pagodas Pass is 241 km from Kanchanaburi and 22 km from Sangklaburi along a rough road passable only during the dry season from October to June. The road turns off Route 323 about four km before Sangklaburi. Minitrucks to the border leave Sangklaburi each morning and return in the late afternoon.

Erawan Falls
Kanchanaburi's finest waterfalls, 60 km from town, can be easily reached by public bus. The series of 15 falls is most impressive and less crowded at higher elevations. Keep climbing! Like all falls in Southeast Asia, Erawan is best during the rainy season or immediately afterwards from September to November. Bring a bathing suit and take the 0800 bus to beat the crowds. Sri Nakarin Lake has fishing, luxurious raft hotels, and weekend boat tours aboard the *J.R. Queen* from the Khao Laem Dam. Both blue and star sapphires are mined north of Bophloi.

NORTH OF BANGKOK

BANG PA IN

This strange collection of palaces and pavilions in Thai, Italian, Victorian, and Chinese architectural styles once served as summer retreat for Thai kings. Highlights include a delicate water pavilion replicated for international expositions, an elaborate pavilion modeled after a Chinese royal palace, and a six-sided Gothic-style tower. The white marble memorial across the small bridge honors Chulalongkorn's first queen, who tragically drowned in full view of her entourage. At the time of the 1881 incident, royal law demanded death for any commoner who dared touch royalty. The law was changed soon afterwards. A fun cable car whizzes across the river to Thailand's only European-styled Buddhist temple. Bang Pa In is more odd than amazing, but it's an easy stopover between Bangkok and Ayuthaya, 20 km north. Visitors with limited time should spend their time fully exploring Ayuthaya. Buses leave from Ayuthaya and Bangkok's Northern Bus Terminal.

AYUTHAYA AND VICINITY

Ayuthaya, 72 km north of Bangkok, served as Thailand's second capital for over four centuries. The city's scattered ruins, colossal Buddhas, decaying *chedis,* and multitude of soaring *wats* restored by the Fine Arts Department provide eloquent testimony to the splendor of this medieval metropolis. Recently declared a national historic park, Ayuthaya has been successfully developed into one of the country's major tourist attractions—a must-see for all visitors to Thailand. Though Ayuthaya is often a day-trip from Bangkok, it really takes two days of leisurely wandering to properly appreciate the sense of history evoked by the far-flung ruins. Travelers who enjoy romantic ruins or have an interest in Thai history should allow two full days *each* to Ayuthaya and Sukothai.

History
Ayuthaya was founded in 1378 by Ramatibodhi, an ambitious Thai prince from U-Thong who transferred his capital south to escape a small-pox plague. Ramatibodhi soon invited Sri Lankan monks here to reinforce Theravada Buddhism and maintain religious purity. Ayuthayan kings, however, were not the benevolent and understanding Buddhist monarchs of Sukothai, but rather paternal Khmer-influenced kings who hid themselves behind walls of ritual, taboo, and sorcery. As reincarnations of Shiva, they became focal points for political and religious cults which, in turn, sharply defined all levels of society. If Sukothai was the kingdom of love, Ayuthaya was the kingdom of war. Armies were raised, campaigns launched, and by the end of the 14th century Ayuthaya controlled Southeast Asia from Malacca to Angkor. Manpower was ensured by national military con-

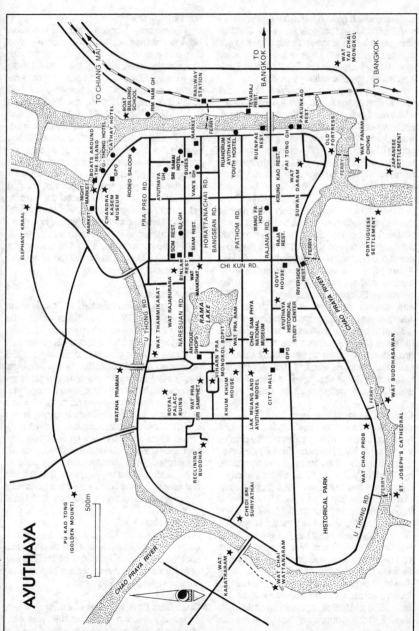

AYUTHAYA

scription, which gave Ayuthaya the strength to resist, expand, and conquer Burmese, Cambodian, and Muslim empires. Ayuthaya fell to the Burmese in the 16th century but was quickly restored by Naresuan the Great, one of Thailand's most revered military heroes.

Ayuthaya was also an important commercial center. First on the scene were the Portuguese, who traded guns and ammo for rice and gems. Emissaries dispatched in 1685 by Louis XIV were dazzled by the city's opulence; they reported it larger and grander than contemporary London or Paris. Among the foreigners, King Narai (1657-1688) welcomed a colorful Greek adventurer, Constantine Phaulkon, who stirred up local resentment by preaching Christianity to the Buddhist monarch. When word spread that a dying Narai was close to conversion, xenophobic Thai nobles seized the throne and had the Greek executed. All Westerners were expelled and Ayuthaya entered into its own Golden Age of Arts—an amazing period of vibrant art, literature, and education. But in early 1763, an enormous Burmese army overran Chiang Mai and massed for a final assault on Ayuthaya. After two years of siege, the city capitulated and most of the citizens were marched off to Burma for slave labor. Ayuthaya was burned to the ground—tremendous art treasures, museums, countless temples, priceless libraries, and historical archives all destroyed—an act of horror which still profoundly shocks the Thais.

Chandra Kasem Museum

King Thammaraja constructed this 17th-century palace for his son, who subsequently claimed the throne as King Naresuan. Partially destroyed by the Burmese, the palace was reconstructed by King Mongkut and later converted into one of Ayuthaya's two museums. The Chantura Mukh Pavilion immediately on your left features an impressive standing Buddha flanked by a pair of wooden images and a finely detailed royal bed. Behind this pavilion stands the Piman Rajaja Pavilion, filled with rare Thai shadow puppets and dozens of Ayuthaya and Sukothai images. Outside to the rear is the startling Pisai Salak Tower, constructed by Narai to follow the moon's eclipses. Chandra Kasem is open daily from 0900 to 1600 except Mondays and Tuesdays. Exit the grounds and walk past the Hud Ra Market.

Wat Rajaburana

King Boromaraja II constructed this temple in 1424 to commemorate his two brothers who died on elephantback fighting for the throne; Boromaraja wisely skipped the battle. Inside the Khmer-style *prang,* a secret crypt once guarded dozens of 15th-century murals, 200 Lopburi bronzes of Khmer-Bayon style, 300 rare U-Thong Buddhas, 100,000 votive tablets, and a fabulous treasure trove of priceless gold objects. Thailand's equivalent of the Tutankhamen treasure lay untouched until 1957 when scavengers stumbled on the buried crypt. Much of the booty vanished into international art markets before the government stepped in, stopped the treasure hunters, and placed the remainder in the Ayuthaya National Museum. A fascinating story, although the temple has been badly restored with shiny concrete *garudas.* Wat Rajaburana costs 20B for Westerners; it's free after 1630. Almost everything of interest can be seen from the street.

Wat Mahathat

King Boromaraja constructed his "Temple of the Great Relic" in 1374 to honor his dream about a Buddha relic. Many valuable artifacts, including a tiny gold casket said to contain Boromaraja's holy relics, were discovered during a 1956 restoration project conducted by the Fine Arts Department. Except for the miniature gold casket, now displayed in the Ayuthaya National Museum, most of the treasures have been moved to Bangkok. Although the temple largely lies in ruins, the monumental floorplans and wildly directed pillars are impressive for what they suggest. One classic sight (in the southeast corner) is a dismembered Buddha head firmly grasped in the clutches of the banyan roots. Take a photo and return 10 years later—it will have grown to a higher level. Admission is 20B; free after 1630.

Wat Pra Ram

Ramesuan, second king of Ayuthaya, constructed this beautiful temple in 1369 as the burial spot for his father, King Ramatibodhi. The elegant Khmer-style *prang* casts a beautiful reflection in the placid lily ponds.

Chao Sam Phya National Museum

Thailand's second best museum was constructed in 1959 from sale proceeds of the Wat

1980

1990

Rajaburana votive tablets. The main floor holds dozens of statues, votives, lacquer cabinets, decorated palm-leaf manuscripts, and priceless objects discovered inside the left shoulder of the Pra Mongkol Bopit Buddha. All major art styles are represented—Dvaravati, Lopburi, U-Thong, Sukothai; Ayuthayan kings were apparently avid collectors of early Thai art. Second floor, eastern room, contains dazzling gold objects unearthed from Wat Rajaburana in 1956. The western room holds the previously described Buddha relic from Wat Mahathat. Look carefully: it's one-third the size of a rice grain and protected by five bronze stupas inserted one inside the other. A building to the rear is filled with artifacts not native to Ayuthaya. Both museums are open daily except Mondays and Tuesdays from 0900 to 1600.

Lak Muang, Ayuthaya Model, Khum Khum House

Ayuthaya's modern city pillar is nothing special but the interior scale model will help with your orientation. The Khum Khum House, con-

structed in 1894 as the city jail, is an outstanding example of traditional Thai architecture. The Fine Arts Department is located here.

Viharn Pra Mongkol Bopit

Thailand's largest Buddha image is crammed into this modern, claustrophobic temple. After the original structure was destroyed in 1767, the immense statue sat outdoors until the present building was erected in 1951. Perhaps the black statue with its mysterious mother-of-pearl eyes should have been left alone—an image of this size and power needs a great deal of *room*. Restaurants across the parking lot serve spicy soups and cold drinks.

Wat Pra Sri Samphet, Royal Palace

Wat Pra Sri Samphet, a famous trio of 15th-century Sri Lankan-style *chedis*, once the royal temple within the walls of the palace, enshrines the ashes of three Ayuthayan kings. Their perfect symmetry has made them one of the most photographed scenes in Ayuthaya; the very essence of Middle Kingdom architecture.

pre-restoration Wattanaram

Unfortunately, insensitive restoration projects and repeated whitewashings have tragically obliterated all architectural detail. Admission is 20B, but the *prangs* can be easily seen from the road. To the north are the ruins of the old Royal Palace destroyed by the Burmese. Nothing remains except for a few scattered foundations.

Watana Praman

This tremendous *bot,* originally constructed in 1503 as a royal monastery and completely rebuilt in 1987, is one of the most impressive temples in Ayuthaya—a must-see for all visitors. The combination of striking architecture and pleasant country surroundings makes Watana Praman a refreshing change from monuments controlled by the Fine Arts Department. Inside the first temple (note the rambling history on the noticeboard) stands a fabulous gold-leaf, six-meter Ayuthaya-style Buddha surrounded by painted pillars, highly polished floors, and roofs carved with concentric lotus buds. A truly magnificent room! The small eastern chapel guards a Dvaravati-style Buddha seated in the Western style with splayed feet, considered one of the masterpieces of Mon Buddhist art. Free admission.

Reclining Buddha

This smiling Buddha image, heavily restored in 1956, is perhaps the most attractive reclining image in Thailand. Cows occasionally graze in front of the yellow-robed image once covered by a wooden *viharn.* Cokes at the refreshment stand are expensive!

Wat Chai Wattanaram

This magnificent and completely unrestored temple complex is absolute proof that heavy-handed restoration projects often ruin historical monuments. Overgrown with weeds, Buddha torsos being swallowed by creeping vines, cows grazing next to the leaning *prangs* . . . everything desirable about mysterious temples of the East. Wat Chai Wattanaram was constructed in 1630 by King Prasat Tong. Fantastic at sunset. *Stop Press:* Sources claim that the notorious Fine Arts Department has started restoration. Dear God, say it isn't so.

North Of Ayuthaya

The following attractions can only be reached with hired *tuk tuk* or *samlor.*

Pu Kao Tong (Golden Mount): To commemorate the 2,500th anniversary of Buddha's birth in 1956, this large temple almost five km outside the city walls was capped with a $2^1/2$-kg solid-gold orb. Somebody immediately stole it, but views from the top of the 80-meter *chedi* are still outstanding. Pu Kao Tong was originally constructed by the Burmese to commemorate their conquest of Ayuthaya in 1569 but subsequently remodeled in Thai style.

Elephant Kraal: Wild elephants were once battle trained inside this teak stockade. Old-fashioned elephant roundups were re-created here in 1891 for Czar Nicholas II and in 1962 for Danish royalty.

South Of Ayuthaya

The following sights are all situated near the south tributary of the Chao Praya River. Those on the opposite side can be reached with local ferries. U Thong Road can be toured by bike or minitrucks that circulate along the road.

St. Joseph's Cathedral: A classical 17th-century Catholic church constructed by Monsignor de Beryte during the reign of King Narai.

Wat Buddhasawan: Ramatibodhi lived here during construction of his new capital. The general layout is derived from Angkor Wat. A large central *prang* represents Buddhist Mt. Meru; the six smaller *prangs* signify the outer heavens; the mangy dogs represent nothing.

Portuguese and Japanese Settlements: King Narai encouraged foreign traders to set up residential centers south of Ayuthaya. Most were burned by the Burmese and little remains except for memorial plaques.

Wat Panom Chong: Home to the Thailand's largest single-cast bronze Buddha, a 14th-century 20-meter image donated by a Chinese emperor whose daughter had married a local Thai prince. Archaeologists believe the statue is 25 years older than Ayuthaya itself. Surrounding the exterior courtyard are dozens of stucco-covered Buddhas. Sightseeing boats from the nearby landing stage charge 200B to circumnavigate Ayuthaya.

Wat Yai Chai Mongkol: King Naresuan constructed this temple to commemorate his victory over the Burmese in 1592 and his slaying of the crown prince in a dramatic elephant duel. Encircling the massive *chedi* are some 135 Buddhas and a reclining image with Naresuan's personal spirit house.

Wat Suwan Daram

This rarely visited temple is one of the most attractive and fascinating in Ayuthaya. The curving, concave foundation of the boat-shaped exterior illustrates mankind's voyage toward nirvana. Elaborate doors and interior murals, usually shown by young monks anxious to practice their English, rank among the best in Thailand. Unlike most other temples in Ayuthaya, this one still serves as an active monastery. A wonderful little gem.

Accommodations

Several new guesthouses have opened in recent years to provide cheap accommodations for backpackers.

Ayuthaya Guesthouse: Formerly known as B.J. Guesthouse, Ayuthaya's original homestay is 50 meters up a small alley running north from Naresuan Road. Great atmosphere plus bicycles for rent. 76/2 Chao Prom Rd., tel. (035) 251468, 50-80B.

B.J. Guesthouse: The most popular guesthouse in Ayuthaya has 20 rooms in a cinderblock building about 10 minutes west of the market. Banjong, the lady owner, is a good cook and can help with travel tips. 19/29 Naresuan Rd., tel. (035) 251512, 60-80B.

Ruandrum Ayuthaya Youth Hostel: Perhaps the most beautiful lodging in Ayuthaya is located in a series of teak houses overlooking the river. The central wing was built by an Ayuthayan aristocrat in the traditional central Thai *panya* style. The owner, Praphan Sukarechit (Kimjeng), has renovated the adjacent homes and refurbished all the rooms with antiques and curiosities. 48 U-Thong Rd., tel. (035) 244509, 200-300B. The dormitory will cost around 100B per person.

Pai Tong Guesthouse: A floating hotel on a reconstructed barge. Rooms are small and the atmosphere is strange, but two good restaurants are located nearby. U-Thong Rd., 60-100B.

Sri Samai Hotel: Ayuthaya's central hotel was once a clean and comfortable place with a fairly decent restaurant. Standards, unfortunately, have dropped, and the hotel can no longer be recommended for any reasons aside from its convenient location near the marketplace. 12 Chao Prom Rd., tel. (035) 245228, 300-400B fan, 400-500B a/c.

Wang Fa Hotel: Although this hotel serves the short-time trade for locals, the clean and modern rooms make this the best budget hotel in Ayuthaya—better than the Sri Samai or the U-Thong. All rooms have large beds with adequate furniture and private bath. 1/8 Rajana Rd., tel. (035) 241353, 150-200B fan, 250-300B a/c. Three-hour room rentals cost 100B.

U-Thong Hotel: A rudimentary hotel for those who want traditional facilities at moderate cost. The U-Thong has rather dirty rooms with fan and common bath and a few a/c rooms with private bath. Avoid rooms facing the street. The nearby Cathay Hotel is similar in quality and price. 86 U-Thong Rd., tel. (035) 251505, 120-300B.

U-Thong Inn: Two km east of central Ayuthaya and rather isolated, this is the only semiluxurious hotel in town. 210 Mu 5, Rajana Rd., tel. (035) 242236, fax (035) 242235, 800-1200B a/c.

Restaurants

Most travelers dine in their guesthouse or at the market, though several good restaurants are along the river and near the monuments on Chi Kun Road.

Night Market: The old night market has been relocated from downtown to a new location on the river across from the Chandra Kasem Museum. A small selection of food stalls complements the hawkers' emporiums. A comfortable place to spend an evening.

Pakunkao Floating Restaurant: The better of Ayuthaya's two floating restaurants is hardly spectacular, but the atmosphere is relaxed and the food is tasty. U-Thong Road. Moderate.

Krung Kao Restaurant: A small, modern, and air-conditioned spot with Thai specialties and an English-language menu. Try the pepper steak or chicken sautéed with garlic. On Rajana Rd. near the bridge. Budget.

Youth Hostel: Kimjeng's wife operates a well-appointed restaurant furnished with antiques and knickknacks. The menu includes both Thai and Western dishes. 48 U-Thong Road. Moderate.

Binlar Restaurant: A large, open-air nightclub with rock music and Thai cabaret singers. Good food at reasonable prices, a popular hangout in the evenings. Naresuan Road. Budget to moderate.

Raja Restaurant: Dine outdoors surrounded by ponds filled with water lilies. Great atmosphere in a very quiet location. Rajana Road. Moderate.

Getting There

Buses leave every half-hour from Bangkok's Northern Bus Terminal and take one hour. Stay on the bus until it arrives in the center of town; get off at the bridge and you are fed to mercenary taxi drivers. Trains leave Bangkok ten times daily. From the station, stroll to the river and ferry across the river. Public boats no longer operate between Ayuthaya and Bangkok or Bang Pa In. From Bangkok, one-day luxury excursions to Ayuthaya and Bang Pa In organized by the Oriental Hotel leave daily at 0800 and cost 800B with lunch. Minibuses from Ayuthaya to Bang Pa In leave from Naresuan Road. Buses to Sukothai leave at 1020, 1235, and 1500. Trains go north five times daily.

Getting Around

Most visitors attempt to see Ayuthaya on a single day-trip from Bangkok—a serious mistake. Ayuthaya is a sprawling place with dozens of great temples. Forget about walking; rent either a bicycle, a motorcycle, a longtail boat, or a minitruck. Bicycles are highly recommended. B.J. Guesthouse rents bikes for 30B and motorcycles for 120B daily. Six-man longtail boats chartered from the landing stage near the U-Thong Hotel cost 150-200B for the standard three-hour circular tour. Minitrucks cost 150-200B for an afternoon tour, which should include the Golden Mount, Wat Chai Wattanaram, St. Joseph's Cathedral, and Wat Panom Chong. Central temples can be reached by foot. Temples on the opposite riverbanks can be reached with small ferries for one *baht.* Local *tuk tuks* and minitrucks cost 10B for any distance. Ayuthaya, with over 1,100 registered three-wheelers, claims title as *tuk tuk* capital of Thailand.

LOPBURI

Lopburi is a pleasant and friendly little town with enough historic architecture to merit an overnight stop en route to Sukothai or Khao Yai. All major attractions are centrally located within the old town; hurried visitors can visit them on a three-hour walking tour. Hotels are within easy walking distance of the train station, but Lopburi's main bus terminal is located in the new town, about three km east of the old historic center. Minibuses shuttle west to the old town.

History

One of Thailand's oldest and most historic cities, Lopburi has served as home to Neolithic settlers, an independent Dvaravati kingdom called Lavo (6th-10th centuries), and finally a Khmer military outpost (10th-13th centuries). It was during the third period that Cambodian architectural and artistic patterns fused with traditional Mon styles to produce the famous Lopburi style—one of Thailand's most important and distinctive regional art movements. The city rode the roller coaster of Thai history, its importance declining in the 13th century with the weakening of Angkor power but rising in the 17th with the ascension of King Narai (1657-1688). During Narai's rule, Lopburi served as Ayuthaya's alternative capital after the Gulf of Siam was blockaded by Dutch ships. It was a time of intrigue, scandal, and strong personalities. King Narai, himself an extraordinary leader, employed French architects sent by King Louis XIV to design his military forts in Ayuthaya, Bangkok, and Nonthaburi, and his summer capital at Lopburi. Westerner adventurers such as the Greek Constantine Phaulkon arrived seek-

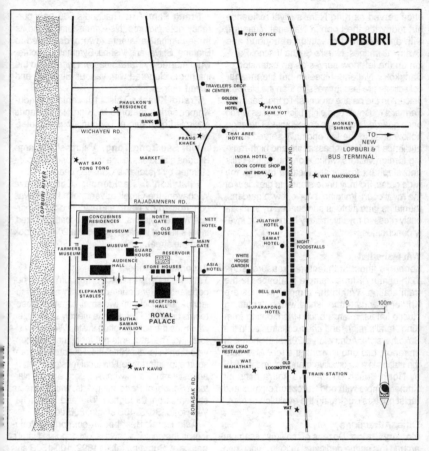

ing their fortunes. With little education or diplomatic background, this rambling seaman and ex-gunrunner dazzled the king with his remarkable linguistic skills (he spoke both ordinary and royal Thai), unwavering sense of loyalty, and legendary trading acumen: in three years, Phaulkon earned Narai's royal treasury an enormous amount of revenue by out-trading even the Moors. Phaulkon was rewarded with the prime ministership and two magnificent residences in Ayuthaya and Lopburi, where according to legend he annually spent 14,000 crowns on wine alone! But Phaulkon failed in his delicate balancing act between the Thai court and French interests. Alarmed at Phaul-

kon's power and the conversion attempts of Jesuit priests, palace ministers seized the throne in 1688 and ordered Phaulkon tortured, gutted, and beheaded.

Royal Palace

Buildings inside the enormous enclosure were constructed by Narai, King Rama III, or King Mongkut in the 1860s. A beautiful old house stands immediately to the right of the main eastern gateway. To the left are remnants of a water reservoir and storage houses, while straight ahead through the crenellated walls are the inner courtyard and several noteworthy buildings. The Chantom Pisan Pavilion on the right once served as King Narai's royal residence but today it's the Lopburi National Museum, with an indifferent collection of Lopburi and Dvaravati images. Narai's Suttha Vinchai Pavilion on the left now serves as an extension of Bangkok's National Museum but the meager collections are less impressive than the statuary placed on the palace grounds. To the rear are a Farmer's Museum and eight bijou houses which once guarded the king's concubines. The eerie hollow shell to the left originally served as an audience hall for ambassadors and high-ranking foreign visitors, while more audience halls and elephant *kraals* are located through the wide gates. To truly understand the grandeur of the royal court, imagine it laid out with gardens, fountains, and statues surrounded by sumptuously dressed royalty, military leaders, and lovely concubines.

Wat Mahathat

Lopburi's finest architectural treasure is the 12th-century Khmer temple just opposite the train station. Within the temple grounds are Khmer *prangs* embellished with outstanding stucco lintels, a large brick *viharn* dating from King Narai's reign, and *chedi* constructed in the Sukothai style. Admission is 20B at the northern entrance; this one is worth the fee. Also near the station is a locomotive manufactured in 1919 by North British Locomotive and a decrepit Khmer temple with odd European statues and racist posters illustrating the evolution of man.

Other Attractions

Monkey Shrine: Dozens of monkeys scamper around this shrine dedicated to Kala, Hindu god of time and death. Behind the old Khmer shrine is a modern temple with a highly revered four-armed Buddhist image. The upper level has dozens of monkeys lazing in banyan trees. Hold on to your camera.

Wat Nakonkosa: Bangkok's Fine Arts Department is currently restoring this 12th-century pile of brick and rubble.

Prang Sam Yot: Thailand's 500-*baht* currency note pictures this Khmer temple and its three distinctive laterite towers, dedicated to Brahma, Shiva, and Vishnu. Symmetry is somewhat marred by Narai's eastern *viharn* and the interior is cluttered with various Buddhist and Hindu images.

Prang Khaek: This 11th-century Hindu-Khmer shrine restored by King Narai stands encircled by traffic at Lopburi's busiest intersection.

Wat Sao Tong Tong: A surprisingly large Buddha statue sits inside this *wat* originally constructed by Narai as a Christian chapel.

Phaulkon's Residence: Chao Praya Wichayen, the Greek adventurer's home, was constructed by Narai as residence for important Western visitors. Although recently restored, there's little of interest here. Save 20B and look from the street.

Accommodations

Traveler's Drop In Center: Lopburi's small but popular travelers' center is actually an English-language school with two small communal bedrooms upstairs. Richard, the friendly Thai citizen who runs the school, often invites Western visitors and Thai students out for dinner and conversation in local nightclubs. Richard is a great source for information on local music, vegetarian restaurants, the swimming pool, and the Nartasin School of Performing Arts, which attracts students from throughout Thailand. 34 Wichayen Road, Soi 3, 40B single, 80B double.

Asia Hotel: Best bet for comfortable lodgings in the center of town is just opposite Narai's palace. 1 Surasak, tel. 411892, 100-150B single, 150-250B double.

Suparapong Hotel: Several inexpensive hotels are strung along Naprakan Road just opposite the train station. Rooms at the Suparapong, the Thai Sawat, the Julathip, and the Indra start from 80B single and 120B double. Nearby Bell Bar is a popular spot to spend an evening.

CENTRAL THAILAND

PHITSANULOK

Central Thailand's largest commercial center is also one of the country's oldest and most historic cities. Straddling the Nan River some 400 km north of Bangkok, Phitsanulok served as an important trading post of the Sukothai empire and as a provincial capital of the Ayuthaya empire. While most visitors enjoy the genuine Thai atmosphere and complete lack of tourists, few are impressed with the concrete shophouses put up after the disastrous 1959 fire that leveled the wooden town. The town's saving graces are magnificent Wat Mahathat and the extraordinarily friendly people.

Central Thailand's transportation hub can be reached by air, train, or buses from Bangkok's Northern Terminal. Buses terminate at either the downtown train station or the main bus terminal northwest of town. Minibuses shuttle to city center.

Attractions

Phitsanulok's major spectacle is the Jinaraj Buddha inside Wat Mahathat, one of the few Ayuthayan-period temples to survive the catastrophic fire. Regarded as one of Thailand's most beautiful and sacred images, the highly polished late-Sukothai bronze has been reproduced for Bangkok's Marble Temple and the Thai temple at Bodgaya. Fine interior murals and elaborate mother-of-pearl inlays are also worth noting; a small museum stands to the left.

Nearby Wat Rajaburana and its partially reconstructed Ayuthayan-period *chedi* boasts an interior nothing short of spectacular. Several Khmer ruins are under restoration 10 km south.

Information on other nearby temples and monasteries is available from the regional TAT office, tel. 252742, at 209 Boromtrailokanat Road in the Surasi Trade Center, two blocks south of the clock tower.

Accommodations

Two good guesthouses have opened in the last few years, and several low-end hotels are located near the train station.

Youth Hostel: Phitsanulok's official youth hostel is somewhat isolated but otherwise an excellent place to stay. The owner, Sapachai Pitaksakorn, worked in Bangkok as a computer programmer before returning to his hometown and opening the hostel in 1990. The hostel is two km south of the train station, one km from the airport, and four km from the bus terminal. A *samlor* should cost 10B from the train station or airport, 25B from the bus terminal. Bus 3 goes from the bus terminal to the hostel. From the train station, take bus 4 south down Ekathotrot Rd., then left on Ramesaun Rd., then right on Sanambin Road. 38 Sanambin Rd., tel. (055) 242060, 50B dorm, 100-200B.

Number 4 Guesthouse: Several years ago the schoolteachers from Sukothai opened this small guesthouse in the north part of town. The lovely teakwood home has a courtyard patio which faces a street made rather noisy from the cars and nearby train line. The guesthouse is located on the left side of Ekathotrot Rd., about two km north of the big traffic circle. Bus 4 from the city bus terminal near the train station goes up Ekathotrot Rd. and passes the poorly marked guesthouse. Bus travelers coming from Sukothai should get off after the bridge but before the traffic circle and take a *songtao* going up Ekathotrot Road. Rooms cost 60-120B.

Sombat Hotel: Inexpensive hotels in the 80-150B range are near the train station on Sairuthai and Phayalithai roads. All are conveniently located in the center of town, but none are clean or very quiet. The Sombat Hotel is probably the best of a somewhat dismal lot. Overflow is handled by the nearby Unachak, Hoh Fa, and Asia hotels. 4 Sairuthai Rd., tel. (055) 258179, 70-160B.

Rajapruk Hotel: The best luxury choice in town has 110 a/c rooms, a Thai-Chinese restau-

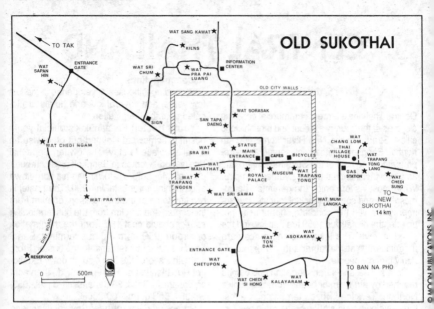

Old Sukothai

rant, a nightclub, car rentals, and a swimming pool. The owner's wife is an American, and English is spoken by some of the staff. The main drawback is the poor location outside town center, across the train tracks.

Restaurants

Phitsanulok has a wide selection of restaurants, from a/c dining in upscale hotels to alfresco meals down by the river.

Floating Restaurants: Several popular floating restaurants are tied up just south of the bridge. Than Tip has been recommended as the best, followed by Yardfan Floating Restaurant and then the Songkwae Houseboat. The boats wait for a full house, then serve meals as they slowly sail up and down the Nan River. No food or drink minimum. Puttabucha Road. Moderate.

Hern Fa Restaurants: Perhaps more fun than the floating restaurants are the hilarious food vendors who set up their portable shops each evening on the banks of the Nan River. A brilliant display of cooking and acrobatics is included with every order. First, the cook fires up the wok and sautées a mixture of vegetables and meats. A waiter then climbs to the top of a nearby truck and attempts to catch the mixture flung skyward

by the chef. Misses are fairly common, but the best moment is when a drunken Westerner agrees to take the role of waiter and catch the flying morning glory. Inexpensive.

Night Market: Over a dozen good food stalls are on the riverbanks just south of the Hern Fa restaurants. Inexpensive.

Top Land Arcade: A welcome relief from the daytime heat is provided in the a/c restaurant on the top floor of Phitsanulok's largest shopping center. Boromatrailokanat Road. Inexpensive.

SUKOTHAI

Thailand's original capital and birthplace of the Thai nation is one of the preeminent archaeological sites in Southeast Asia. Situated 450 km north of Bangkok where the northern mountains intersect the central plains, Sukothai is to Thailand what Angkor is to Cambodia, Borobudur is to Indonesia, and Pagan is to Burma. Spread out over the 70-square-km National Historic Park are dozens of magnificently restored temples, palaces, Khmer *prangs,* gigantic Buddha images set with enigmatic smiles, and a fine museum which safeguards the grandeur of ancient

Sukothai. The town also offers several good guesthouses, friendly little cafes, and opportunities to become acquainted with the local Thais. Sukothai is also a convenient base for exploring the nearby ruins of Sri Satchanalai and Kampang Phet. Sukothai is the best stop between Bangkok and Chiang Mai—don't miss it.

History

The most brilliant empire in Thai history, Sukothai was founded in 1238 by two rebellious Thai princes who liberated themselves from Khmer domination by establishing Thailand's first independent kingdom. Preaching a philosophy of political cooperation rather than military might, early kings of Sukothai ("Dawn of Happiness") successfully united many of the small principalities between Laos and Malaysia to form a nation which never fell under foreign domination. Under the enlightened leadership of King Ramkamheng (1278-1318), Sukothai enjoyed its Golden Age of political, cultural, and religious freedoms as proclaimed by a famous tablet that recorded "Sukothai is good. There is fish in the water, rice in the fields, and the king does not levy tax on his subjects. The faces of the people shine bright." Ramkamheng was not only a clever warrior, but also a brilliant scholar who devised the modern Thai alphabet from Mon and South Indian scripts, introduced a free-trade economic system, promoted Theravada Buddhism as taught by Sri Lankan monks from Nakhon Si Thammarat, and personally dispensed justice from his Manangasila throne. During his remarkable rule, citizens could ring a bell mounted outside the royal palace and ask the king to pass judgment on their problems. Sukothai prospered through a succession of six kings but was abandoned in 1378 after losing a power struggle with rising Ayuthaya.

Orientation

Sukothai is divided into two sections. The unattractive new town has the hotels, restaurants, and transportation facilities. Old Sukothai with the museum and ruins is 14 km west. Minibuses to the old city leave across the bridge about 200 meters on the right side, just beyond the police station. Old Sukothai ruins have been divided into five zones lettered A through E, with zones A, B, and D each charging a 20B admission fee. Sukothai's ruins are widely scattered;

THE ARTS OF SUKOTHAI

Sukothai during the reign of Ramkamheng blossomed into a grand city of palaces, temples, monasteries, and wooden homes protected behind imposing earthen walls. Unlike Ayuthaya, which was destroyed by the Burmese, much of Sukothai's great architecture and art still stands in good condition.

Architecture: Sukothai's superb range of religious and secular buildings—from Khmer *prangs* covered with terrifying *nagas* to Sinhalese *chedis* capped with distinctive lotus-bud towers—has been restored with varying results by UNESCO and the Fine Arts Department. Some have retained their original flavor and still show ancient craftsmanship; others have been insensitively restored with heavy-handed techniques.

Sculpture: Sukothai's crowning artistic achievement was sculpture, most notably the sensual, otherworldly walking Buddha. Often cast of bronze using the *cire perdu* (lost-wax) method, the typical walking Buddha image is elongated with a flowing, androgynous body and hand raised in the attitude of calming fears and giving reassurance. The other arm hangs rhythmically and follows the sensual curve of the torso, while the head is shaped like a lotus bud capped by the flame of enlightenment. Perhaps the most intriguing feature is the enigmatic smile, which somehow reflects a state of deep inward contentment and spirituality. The total effect is one of marvelous power and sensitivity; rarely has any religious image so successfully conveyed the unspeakable faith of the creator.

Stucco: A combination of lime, sand, and sugarcane juice was used to create Buddha images and the exquisite moldings that decorated many of Sukothai's finest architectural monuments. Since stucco hardens in just a few hours, the artists were forced to work quickly but with great care.

Paintings: All paintings in Sukothai have been destroyed by the elements or stolen by art collectors, except for a handful of ornamental designs and stone engravings. Thai painting came of age during the Rattanakosin or Bangkok period.

Ceramics: Great quantities of high-quality ceramics were produced in nearby Sawankalok. See "Sri Satchanalai."

hire a *tuk tuk* at 30-50B per hour, a five-passenger taxi for 500B for a full day, or a bicycle for 20B from the stores just opposite the museum. Visitors on foot are limited to central ruins inside zone A. Determined bicyclists who don't mind working up a sweat can reach all major monuments in a single day, including those to the far west and south. Bullock-cart tours sponsored by the International Friendship Center begin just outside the northern gate of the historical park. All ruins are described on English-language signboards and are now safe to visit.

Please remember that all Buddhist images—no matter their age or condition—are considered sacred objects to the Thais. Visitors should be properly dressed and never touch or climb on any image. This is no joke! Several years ago, a few Westerners—dressed only in shorts—posed for photographs on the shoulders of a Buddha. A national scandal erupted after the Bangkok photo lab turned the negatives over to a local newspaper, which then printed them on the front page. The Westerners were thrown in jail.

Ramkamheng National Museum
Located inside the old city walls and just before the entrance gate to zone A, Sukothai's museum offers an outstanding introduction to the arts and crafts of historic Sukothai. Inside the spacious building are Khmer statues, Sukothai Buddhas, Sawankalok ceramics, and other archaeological artifacts. Facing the front entrance stands a bronze walking Buddha, considered the finest example of its kind in the country. Ground floor highlights include a model of the ancient city (useful for orientation) and a replica of the four-sided pillar inscribed with Thailand's first written script. The original, now displayed in the Bangkok Museum, was discovered by King Rama IV while on pilgrimage during his period of monkhood. Dozens of superb statues are exhibited upstairs. Sculpture on the exterior grounds includes a rare phallic shrine of Khmer origins. Open daily except Mondays and Tuesdays 0900-1200 and 1300-1600.

Central Sukothai (Zone A)
Statue of King Ramkamheng: Sukothai's great ruler sits on a replica of the historic Manangasila throne, discovered a century ago and now kept in Bangkok's Grand Palace Museum. The stone slab is charged with enough magic and mystical potency to make it an object of reverence to many Thais. Visitors can summon the ghost of Ramkamheng by ringing the bell on the right!

Wat Mahathat: Sukothai's principal monastery and royal temple once contained 185 *chedis,* a dozen *viharns,* and a central *bot* gilded with stucco surrounded by reflective moats. Most structures have collapsed and wooden buildings have been destroyed by fire or insects, but large Buddhas and fine stucco remain intact. The best friezes are those of disciples walking in ritual procession around the base of the main *chedi* and the southern *chedi's* demons, elephants, and lion-riding angels. Excellent views over the compound can be enjoyed from the summit of the largest *chedi.*

Royal Palace: Ramkamheng's great palace is marked only by its foundations.

Wat Sri Sawai: This well-preserved Khmer sanctuary, surrounded by two concentric enclosures and a deep moat, was originally constructed by the Khmers prior to the founding of Sukothai. Some original *nagas* and *garudas* still cling to the pediments, but much of the stucco exterior has been poorly restored with rough concrete. Many wish the ruins had been left untouched except for necessary support work.

Wat Trapang Ngoen: This well-placed *chedi,* on a small island in the center of Silver Lake, is the focal point for Sukothai's Loy Kratong Festival.

Wat Sra Sri: Simplicity of design and elegance of location make this one of Sukothai's most attractive temples. The central tower, with its bell-shaped dome, square base, and tapering spire, is typical of the Sinhalese style adapted by Sukothai's Theravadan architects.

North Of The City (Zone B)
Wat Pra Pai Luang: This unrestored 12th-century "Temple of the Great Wind," about one km north of Wat Mahathat, was originally constructed by the Khmers as a Hindu sanctuary in the center of their military stronghold. Triumphant Thais later converted it to a Buddhist monastery second in religious importance only to Wat Mahathat. Two of the original three Khmer *prangs* have collapsed and the remaining tower was pillaged in the '50s for its valuable collection of Hindu and Buddhist images.

Pottery Kilns: Archaeologists have uncovered several large kilns that once produced the most famous celadons in all of Southeast Asia. An informative display on these enormous walk-in kilns can be seen in the Sukothai Museum.

Wat Sri Chum: Sukothai's most impressive Buddha, a monumental 15-meter image seated in the subduing Mara pose, is a must-see for all visitors to the city. It's a lively scene as Thai pilgrims arrive to pray, make offerings, and burn incense in front of the enormous and superbly modeled hand. A narrow and claustrophobic passageway leads to the roof past slate slabs engraved with Jataka scenes. Illuminated only by small windows, these unusual carvings are easily missed in the dark corridor. No guardrail lines the roof; be careful up here. Note that the sign designating the temple turnoff is marked in Thai script only.

West Of The City (Zone C)

Wat Sapan Hin: The 12-meter standing Buddha overlooking the scattered ruins of Sukothai seems to bless the entire region. Good views are guaranteed visitors who survive the hot climb up the jumble of stone slabs. The brick-paved floor of the adjoining *chedi* has been raided by temple robbers—a depressing but familiar sight at many remote and unprotected temples.

Wat Chedi Ngam: The dirt road winds past several more temples before turning left and returning to the city. This round Sinhalese-style *chedi* has also been vandalized by thieves who burrowed a deep hole in the backside. Afterwards, enjoy a swim in the reservoir farther down the road.

South Of The City (Zone D)

Wat Chetupon: Entrance to the southern monuments is made through the admissions gate near this temple. Wat Chetupon is chiefly known for its pair of 10-meter stucco Buddhas; the walking image is considered one of the finest in Thailand. Crumbling but still in original condition (as of this writing), adjacent images are now surrounded by scaffolding.

Wat Chedi Si Hong: Decorating the base of this *chedi* currently under restoration are stucco elephants and *garudas* molded with great imagination. The dirt track continues past several small temples before intersecting the road north to the city.

East Of The City (Zone E)

Wat Trapang Tong: This *chedi,* surrounded by a symmetrical pool called the Golden Lake, contains a footprint of the Buddha honored each year during Loy Kratong.

Wat Trapang Tong Lang: A panel on the southern side shows the descent of Buddha to earth surrounded by angels and bodhisattvas. Sukothai's most famous stucco relief has tragically deteriorated and lost much of its artistic appeal. A reproduction is displayed in the museum.

Wat Chang Lom: This circular Sinhalese-design *chedi,* supported by a ring of 36 sculpted and ruined elephants, can be reached by walking through the grounds of the Thai Village House.

Wat Chedi Sung: Considered the finest *chedi* of the Sukothai period. Easily visible from Wat Trapang Tong Lang.

Accommodations

Most guesthouses and hotels are in new Sukothai, a nondescript town of concrete shophouses and streets too wide for the traffic. The great news is that Sukothai's rising popularity has brought almost a dozen new guesthouses and cafes that cater to budget travelers. All charge 60-100B for single rooms and 80-120B for doubles.

Number 4 Guesthouse: Started by four local schoolteachers (hence the name), this lovely teakwood home is clean, quiet, and immensely popular with budget travelers. Rooms downstairs are somewhat noisy because the plywood walls don't reach the ceiling, but terrific private rooms are located upstairs. 170 Tanee Rd., tel. (055) 611315, 40B dorm, 60-100B private rooms.

Yupa Guesthouse: Sukothai's original guesthouse is in a private home on a small road west of town. The home was constructed by Yupa Mekapai for his family of five children and is now operated by Yupa and his wife. Yupa has an open-air restaurant, laundry facilities, motorcycles and bikes for rent, plus lovely balcony views over the river and city. 44 Pravet Nakorn Rd., tel. (055) 612578, 40B dorm, 60-120B private rooms.

Sky House: Though somewhat distant from downtown, Wattana's place is actually a modern townhouse converted into backpackers' quarters after the units failed to sell. Each room has a private bathroom and everyone gets a free bike. The Sky office near the bus terminal provides free transportation. 58 Bypass Rd., tel. (055) 612237, 40B dorm, 60-120B fan, 150-200B a/c with private bath.

O2 Guesthouse: Opened in 1989, O2 Guesthouse is a genuine homestay operated by a Thai history teacher and a Thai cooking instructor. The 12-room teakwood home sits in a lovely compound of old residences inhabited by the extended family of aunts, uncles, and grandchildren. 26/4 Rajuthit Rd., tel. (055) 612982, 60-100B.

Somprasong Guesthouse: Another new guesthouse has opened across the river near the Yupa Guesthouse. Somprasong features shiny wooden floors, a large porch on the second floor, rooms separated by short walls and chicken wire, free bicycles, and motorcycles for hire. Once again, this is a traditional homestay where you'll become friends with the family. 32 Pravet Nakorn Rd., tel. (055) 611709, 50-100B.

Chinawat Hotel: The best budget-to-moderate hotel in Sukothai is well located in the center of town near the bus terminals and restaurants. Chinawat serves as Sukothai's information center, with a wide range of maps, brochures, and travel tips on buses and nearby attractions. The hotel has 40 rooms with private baths, a money-exchange service, overseas-calls facilities, laundry, organized tours, and a popular restaurant which serves both Thai and Chinese dishes at reasonable cost. 1 Nakorn Kasem Rd., tel. (055) 611385, 80-120B fan, 160-220B a/c.

River View: A somewhat luxurious hotel on the banks of the Yom River with clean rooms, private baths, a patio restaurant, and lobby with TV. Pricier than other moderate hotels, but a big improvement in comfort and cleanliness. All rooms come with a/c and private bath. 92 Nakorn Kasem Rd., tel. (055) 611656, fax (055) 613373, 250-350B.

Northern Palace Hotel: The old Kit Mongkol has been completely renovated and renamed. New facilities include a swimming pool, a snooker parlor, and a coffee shop which doubles as a nightclub for evening entertainment. All rooms are a/c with private bath. 43 Singhawat Rd., tel. (055) 611193, 650-900B.

Vitoon Guesthouse: Just opposite the entrance to Sukothai Historical Park are several rudimentary guesthouses with basic cubicles and bicycle rentals.

Thai Village House: Sukothai's old cultural center operates souvenir shops and a small zoo with peacocks and black bears. Wooden bungalows decorated in traditional Thai style are equipped with fan or a/c rooms with private or common baths. Beautiful teakwood dorms are also available at low cost. Located one km before old Sukothai on the right side of the road. 214 Charotvithiwong, tel. (055) 611049, 50B dorm, 350-600B private rooms.

Pailyn Sukothai Hotel: Sukothai entered the high-end market in early 1992 with the opening of the monstrous 238-room Pailyn Hotel about four km before the entrance to the Sukothai Historical Park. The Pailyn has several restaurants, a swimming pool, a disco, a fitness center, conference facilities, and shuttle services to the ruins and new Sukothai. Charotvithiwong Rd., tel. (055) 612893, Bangkok reservations (02) 215-7110, 1200-2500B.

Restaurants

All of the hotels in Sukothai have restaurants, but smaller cafes offer a unique culinary and aesthetic experience.

Night Market: Cheap eats are plentiful at the market which sets up nightly in the alley near Win Tours and the Rainbow Cafe. Popular dishes include *pad thai, gawetio thai nam* (noodle soup with peanuts and greens), *yam nom tok* (spicy beef), and *kanom jinn* (Thai spaghetti). Other choices include mussel omelettes, thick rice soups, ice *kachang,* and *won ton* dishes.

Take-away Food Stalls: Across the street from the night market are several foodcarts that serve food to go wrapped in plastic bags. Simply point to the more appealing dishes and say *ha baht.* A grand total of 25 *baht* will guarantee a delicious and filling meal that you can consume back at your guesthouse. Take-away dishes are often more tasty and varied than stir-fried food from the night market.

Rainbow Cafe: Next to the bus station is a popular open-air restaurant with European fare, Thai noodles, and terrific ice cream. Rainbow is owned by the Chinawat Hotel and has an upstairs a/c dining room.

Dream Cafes: Sukothai's most eclectic restaurants are the brainchildren of Ms. Chaba Suwatmaykin, who has outfitted her cafes with

an amazing collection of memorabilia such as old telephone sets, bottles, and ancient gramophones. The small outlet across from Win Tours is an intimate coffee shop with a sign that reads: "The best coffee is as black as devil, hot as hell, pure as a fairy, fragrant as love."

Dream Cafe 2 at 861 Singhawat Rd. has a menu with over 200 items. Try *kao tang naa tang* (fried rice with pork and rambutan), *muu kam wan kanaa sop* (grilled pork with honey and vegetables), or *laab* (spicy northeastern-style minced pork).

Transportation

Buses leave from Chiang Mai's main terminal and Bangkok's Northern Bus Terminal 10 times daily. The nearest train terminus is at Phitsanulok, 60 km from Sukothai. Buses leave Phitsanulok for Sukothai from the Soon Bus Terminal northeast of town. Win Tours has three a/c buses daily for Bangkok and Chiang Mai. Ordinary buses operated by Bor Kor Sor (the government transportation company) leave eight times daily for Bangkok and six times daily for Chiang Mai. Buses to Sri Satchanalai and Sawankalok leave across the street from the Chinnawat Hotel. Buses to Tak leave four blocks up the main street. Buses to old Sukothai leave from the dirt yard 200 meters across the bridge. Don't get suckered into an expensive *tuk tuk* or taxi ride.

SRI SATCHANALAI

The evocative ruins of old Sri Satchanalai rest 56 km north of Sukothai between Sawankalok and the new town of Sri Satchanalai. Once a provincial capital and twin city for the Sukothai empire, Sri Satchanalai eventually fell to Burmese attack and was absorbed into the Ayuthayan empire. Although less extensive than the ruins at Sukothai, the superb setting, absence of tourists, and lonely sense of the past makes Sri Sat (the local term) a most memorable place.

Buses leave opposite the Chinnawat Hotel and take an hour to reach the ruins, 18 km beyond Sawankalok. New Sri Satchanalai is 12 km further. Chinnawat Hotel sponsors a six-hour tour for 160B to the Old City, Ko Noi Kiln, and weaving factories at Hat Sieo. Most visitors return to Sukothai before nightfall, but simple hotels are found in both Sawankalok and New Sri Satchanalai.

Attractions

Three areas interest visitors: the Old Town with the ruins, Wat Mahathat to the south, and pottery kilns to the north. The local office of the Fine Arts Department contains a relief model of the city.

Wat Chang Lom: Supported by 39 crumbling and headless stucco elephants, this Sinhalese-style *chedi* was constructed in 1285 by King Ramkamheng and possibly modeled after Wat Mahathat at Nakhon Si Thammarat. The walls of the *chedi* base are set with rows of niches containing 19 rare stucco Buddhas, while the site is enclosed by a beautiful laterite brick wall distinguished by terraced shoulders, ornamental pilasters, and niches penetrated by four gates.

Wat Chedi Chet Teo: Seven rows of lotus-bud *chedis* around the main structure replicate important shrines from neighboring monasteries. Formerly the burial grounds of Sukothai princes, the monument's large central *chedi* was modeled after Sukothai's Wat Mahathat.

Wat Kao Panom Pleung: Satchanalai's hilltop "Temple of the Mountain of Fire" shows Lanna influence and offers fine views across the hazy valley. Another ruined *chedi* caps the loftier hill to the rear.

Wat Nang Phya: Near the southern wall stands a 15th-century *viharn* famed for excellent stucco floral moldings which imitate Ayuthayan woodcarvings.

Wat Kok Sing Karam: Slit windows of Khmer design and original stucco characterize this ancient sanctuary one km south of old Sri Satchanalai. Follow the path along the river. Farther south and set back from the river is another large Khmer tower with finely carved Buddhas.

Wat Sri Ratana Mahathat: No visit to Sri Satchanalai would be complete without a stop at this remarkable temple. Situated on a promontory in the bend of the Yom River, this Ayuthayan-style *prang* was erected in the 15th century over an important Khmer sanctuary and embellished with outstanding stucco reliefs and superb walking Buddha images cast in various styles. From here, walk to the main highway and flag down a bus to Sukothai.

Pottery Kilns: Sri Satchanalai potters during the 14th and 15th centuries produced the finest glazed ceramics in Southeast Asia. Pottery aficionados can wander around dozens of ruined but systematically excavated kilns which once produced world-famous Sawankalok stoneware, celadon, and decorated vases with distinctive blue-gray glaze. Although it was once believed that Ramkamheng brought potters from China, recent research indicates that much of the technology was developed locally. The kilns are five km up a riverside path from the central ruins.

Accommodations

Most visitors return to Sukothai before nightfall, but simple hotels are found in Sawankalok and the new town of Si Satchanalai and near the ruins.

Wang Yom Resort: About 300 meters south of the park entrance is an upscale development that features a beautiful restaurant, a handicraft village, and comfortable bungalows set in landscaped lawns and tropical gardens. Wang Yom (tel. 055-642244) has 20 a/c cottages for 1200B and 15 simple country huts for 400B. The adjacent Kang Sak Restaurant caters to tour groups.

Sawankalok: Simple hotels in Sawankalok, 20 km south of the ruins, include the Muang Inn on Kasamrat Rd. and the Sri Sawan Hotel on Thesaban Damri Road. Both have fan-cooled rooms from 130B and a/c rooms from 220B.

Si Satchanalai: The new town of Si Satchanalai is 12 km north of the ruins. Kruchang Hotel, 300 meters north of the Bangkok Bank, has rooms with bath from 120B.

KAMPANG PHET

Kampang Phet is an old garrison town on the banks of the Ping River some 85 km from Sukothai. Established in 1347 by King Li Thai, the small town served as a regional capital for the Sukothai empire until 1378, when the final sovereign surrendered to Ayuthaya.

Modern Kampang Phet is a completely ordinary place, but inside the trapezoid walls of the old northern city are several intriguing *wats* in various states of repair and restoration, a worthwhile National Museum organized by the Fine Arts Department, and other *chedi* and sculpture of great historical significance. The museum provides quick historical background and general orientation to the widely scattered monuments; day-trippers can store bags here. Wat Pra Sri Iriyabot and Wat Chang Rob—Kampang Phet's three best monuments—are outside the crenellated ramparts to the northwest. Many of the outlying *wats* and Buddhist monasteries predate even Sukothai but were heavily restored during Ayuthayan occupation. Taken together, Kampang Phet serves as the third most important historical and archaeological site in central Thailand.

Accommodations

Kamphang Phet has an inexpensive Chinese hotel near the bridge and several midpriced hotels in the new section of town, about four km from the bus terminal. Minibuses from the bus terminal go across the river and down Ratchadamnoen Rd. to the hotels and the information center.

Nittaya Prapa Hotel: The cheapest hotel in town is adjacent to the southwestern corner of the roundabout near the bridge and old town. Nittaya Prapa lacks an English sign and can be difficult to find but is conveniently located near the central ruins and national museum. 49 Thesa 1 Rd., tel. (055) 711381, 60-100B.

Korchokchai: Another one in the budget category, rooms here run 100-200B s or d. Ratchadamnoen Soi 6, tel. 711531.

Ratchadamnoen Hotel: Like most other hotels in Kamphang Phet, the Ratchadamnoen is an older property with both fan and a/c rooms in a variety of price ranges. Hotel owners assume that all Western travelers are rich and want an expensive a/c room rather than a cheaper fan-cooled room. 114 Ratchadamnoen Rd., tel. (055) 711029, 100-150B fan, 220-280B a/c.

Phet Hotel: The best hotel in town has 235 a/c rooms, a coffee shop, a small swimming pool, and the Princess nightclub. 99 Vichit Rd. Soi 3, tel. (055) 711283, Bangkok reservations (02) 215-2920, 350-600B.

Transportation

Kamphang Phet is 85 km southwest of Sukothai. Most visitors take a bus from Sukothai and spend a single night before continuing northwest to Tak and Mae Sot. The bus terminal is inconveniently located three km from town on the west side of the river. Travelers coming from Sukothai might get off the bus at the ruins and continue into town with a *samlor* or public minibuses.

TAK

Tak is a provincial capital 423 km north of Bangkok on the east bank of the Ping River. The town is at the intersection of Hwy. 1, which connects Bangkok with Chiang Mai, and the Pan-Asian Hwy., which in a more perfect world would link Singapore with Istanbul.

Tak is rarely visited by Western tourists, though the town has some outstanding teakwood architecture and is known throughout Thailand as the birthplace of King Taksin. The town also serves as a useful base for excursions to the hilltribe center and waterfalls of Lansang National Park (19 km west), the traditional riverine settlement of Ban Tak (23 km north), and water sports at Bhumibol Dam (65 km north), the largest artificial lake in Southeast Asia.

Attractions
Wooden Architecture: With an abundance of teak, Tak has traditionally permitted residents to construct their homes and businesses from the valuable wood. Despite recent destruction, Tak still boasts several streets and neighborhoods blessed with old teakwood structures carved and assembled with great skill. Both Mahathai Bamroong and Taksin roads have fine examples, especially in the northern stretches near Thai Air and Wat Bot Mani Sibunruang. An amazing collection of teak homes is in the small alleys just south of the town park.

Another location known for traditional teakwood homes is the small village of Ban Tak, 23 km north of Tak on the banks of the Ping River.

King Taksin Shrine: Across the road from Wat Sibunruang is a small modern chapel dedicated to the early Chakri king who hailed from Tak. A celebration in his honor is held in Tak each year in early January.

Accommodations
Tak Hotel: A popular choice for budget travelers with 29 fan-cooled rooms. 18 Mahathai Bamroong Rd., tel. (055) 511234, 100-150B.

Mae Ping Hotel: Down the road is a slightly larger hotel with somewhat cheaper rooms.

231 Mahathai Bamroong Rd., tel. (055) 511807, 80-120B.

Sanguan Thai Hotel: Near the central market and shopping district. 619 Taksin Rd., tel. (055) 511265, 100-180B.

Viang Tak 1 Hotel: Top-end choices are the two branches of the Viang Tak. The original branch has 100 a/c rooms in an older neighborhood. 25 Mahathai Bamroong Rd., tel. (055) 511910, 500-800B.

Viang Tak 2 Hotel: The best hotel in Tak is on the main drag near the river. Facilities include a comfortable restaurant, a small nightclub, and a dining veranda overlooking the river. Chompol Rd., tel. (055) 512686, fax (02) 235-5138, Bangkok reservations (02) 233-2690, 500-800B.

Transportation
Most visitors reach Tak by bus from Sukothai or Kamphang Phet. The bus terminal is northeast of town across ultrabroad Highway 1. *Songtaos* shuttle into town. Air-conditioned buses to Bangkok can be booked from the private bus office off Mahathai Bamroong Rd. just north of the Viang Tak 1 Hotel.

MAE SOT AND VICINITY

Mae Sot is one of the most intriguing towns in the region and a great place to experience Thailand off the beaten track. Initial impressions are that Mae Sot has little of real interest aside from some dusty Burmese architecture, food, and customs which have spilled over the border. A closer look, however, reveals a complex society composed of Burmese, Thais, Chinese, and tribal minorities such as Karen and Hmong. Mae Sot also benefits from its isolated location and almost complete absence of Western tourists.

The opening of the road from Mae Sot north to Mae Sariang now presents a unique way to reach Chiang Mai from central Thailand. The journey is long and rough but covers some beautiful countryside rarely seen by Western travelers. From Mae Sariang, buses continue to Mae Hong Song, Pai, and finally Chiang Mai.

Attractions
Temples: *Wats* and monasteries in Mae Sot reflect Burmese influence brought across the

nearby border. Wat Chumphon Khiri, the largest *chedi* in town and visible from the morning market, is covered by brass brickwork and surrounded by 20 smaller plaster *chedis*. Adjacent to Wat Mae Sot Luang are a small *chedi* and a reclining Buddha completely covered with shiny brass plates.

Markets: Two of the chief attractions in Mae Sot are the morning market, which occurs in the narrow alleys near the Porn Thep Hotel, and the central market on the southern road. Both are filled with a gaggle of Thai, Burmese, Chinese, and Muslim traders who compete with the gem vendors operating from nearby shops. A very colorful cattle market is held one km from Mae Sot at Poe Thong every Wed. and Sun. morning.

Burmese Border: Five km west of Mae Sot is one of the three direct highway links between Thailand and Burma, the other two being Hwy. 106 north of Chiang Mai and north of Chiang Rai at Mae Sai. The trading post is commercialized and overrun with tourist shops, but visitors can gaze across the narrow Moi River to watch local merchants conduct the carefully regulated trade between Myawaddy and Rim Moi. Minibuses to the border crossing leave from Prasat Vithi Rd., one block west of the Siam Hotel.

Attractions Near Mae Sot: The following attractions are somewhat difficult to visit except on an organized tour or with a rented motorcycle. **Wat Wattanaram** is a Burmese temple with a large alabaster Buddha three km west of Mae Sot on the road to the border. **Wat Prathat Doi Din Kui,** 12 km northwest of town, is a forest monastery with a hanging rock shrine similar to the monument in Kyaiktiyo, Burma. North of Mae Sot, near the village of Mae Ramat, is Wat Don Keo with Pra Hin Oon, a small Buddha carved from a large block of marble.

South of Mae Sot

Highway 1090 goes south from Mae Sot toward a series of border towns and natural attractions such as waterfalls and national parks. Transportation has recently improved with the completion of a new road from Pob Rab to Umphang via Ban Rom Klao. *Songtaos* to Umphang depart in the early morning behind the Porn Thep Hotel.

Some 25 km south of Mae Sot is the small town of Waley, where Thais, Burmese, and Karens conduct smuggling operations between the Burmese town of Phalu and the Thai border. *Songtaos* to Waley depart from the mosque and behind the Porn Thep Hotel in Mae Sot.

Some of the last remaining stands of teakwood forest are in Umphang Forest, 150 km south of Mae Sot. Highway 1090, which reaches Umphang, passes several natural attractions. Tararak Waterfalls, 27 km south of Mae Sot, and Pra Charoen Waterfalls, 37 km south, are lovely cascades best visited during the rainy season from June to December. Midway to Umphang is the village of Ban Rom Klao 4, whose population consists mostly of Hmong and Karen hilltribes. Accommodations in Umphang include the Um Phang Huts for 200B and bungalows on the Mae Klong.

Accommodations

Mae Sot Guesthouse: Backpackers generally stay in this lovely teakwood house west of town in a quiet residential neighborhood. The owners can help with free maps and information on trekking in nearby provinces. 736 Indrakiri Rd., 40B dorm, 60-90B.

Mae Sot House: Maesot Travel Centre operates a small guesthouse on the highway just outside town. 14/21 Asia Hwy., tel. (055) 531409, 40-60B.

First Hotel: An old favorite opposite the former bus terminal. Rooms are large and clean with private bath. Keys are provided on small piston rods. 444 Indrakiri Rd., tel. (055) 531233, 140-180B fan, 220-300B a/c.

Siam Hotel: The most popular midpriced hotel in Mae Sot has a shopping center, a cafe, and an outlet for SP Tours. 185 Prasat Vithi Rd., tel. (055) 531376, 120-180B fan, 220-350B a/c.

Mae Sod Hill Hotel: A luxury hotel complete with swimming pool, two tennis courts, coffee shop, and disco. Each a/c room includes TV, refrigerator, and telephone. 100 Asia Hwy., tel. (055) 532601, fax (055) 532608, Bangkok reservations (02) 541-1234, 900-1200B.

Transportation

Mae Sot can be reached by bus from Sukothai, Tak, Bangkok, or Chiang Mai. Thai Airways flies four times weekly from Chiang Mai and Phitsanulok.

Leaving Mae Sot is problematical since buses leave from several different locations. Tickets can be purchased and timetables checked at the

Siam and First hotels. Government buses to Bangkok depart three times nightly between 2000 and 2100 from the office on Indrakiri Road. Sukothai Tours opposite the First Hotel has buses to Tak every 30 minutes and service to Phitsanulok at 0930. Tranjit Tours in the First Hotel also goes to Bangkok. Tavorn Frame Tours in the Siam Hotel has buses to most destinations including Tak, Phitsanulok, and Bangkok. The Mae Sot Guesthouse can help with details.

MAE SOT TO MAE SARIANG

One of the most adventurous journeys in Thailand is along the winding road which leads north from Mae Sot to Mae Sariang. This route provides a unique way to reach the far north since it avoids backtracking to Tak or Phitsanulok. The road skirts the banks of the Moi River, a geographical oddity which flows north through the Dawna Range until it intersects the Salween, which in turn continues south though the Burmese Shan states.

Accommodations
Several guesthouses and resorts have recently opened on the highway between Mae Sot and Mae Sariang. Tan Song Yang, a rather prosperous village some 83 km north of Mae Sot, has three guesthouses. Chao Doi House, one of the most remote but memorable lodges in central Thailand, is on a mountaintop some 15 km east of Mae Salit. Ask the bus or *songtao* driver to drop you at the police box near Mae Salit, then hitch a ride up the mountain. Chao Doi House has been highly recommended by several travelers. Mon Krating Resort, an upscale resort on a hilltop east of Mae Salit and 135 km north of Mae Sot, is for group tours.

Transportation
Highway 1085 is now fully paved, though direct bus service from Mae Sot to Mae Sariang is still under development. As of this writing, the journey can only be completed with a series of buses and *songtaos* which cover limited segments of the highway. *Songtaos* depart in the early morning from Mae Sot and terminate at the small village of Mae Salit, slightly north of Tha Song Yang. Travelers often spend the first night at Chao Doi House (see above).

From Mae Salit to Ban Tha Song Yang (not to be confused with Tha Song Yang) a chartered *songtao* will probably be necessary and cost about 100B per person. Public buses and *songtaos* from Ban Tha Song Yang to Mae Sariang cost an additional 50B. Travelers have reportedly done the entire journey in a single day, but it's a long and very tough haul.

NORTHERN THAILAND

Northern Thailand's cool mountainous landscapes, friendly people, unique arts and architecture, dazzling handicrafts, unsurpassed ethnological variety, and superb shopping make it one of the highlights for any visitor to Thailand. While the region has lost some of its innocence to commercialization and modern developments, much of it remains a pristine destination still rich with distinctive customs and cultures. Best of all, the pace of life has stayed delightfully measured and people continue to exude the warmth and hospitality that first popularized the north.

ROUTES

Chiang Mai can be reached directly from Bangkok by air, train, or bus, but stopovers in Ayuthaya and Sukothai are highly recommended for visitors interested in history and archaeology. Travelers in Kanchanaburi can avoid backtracking to Bangkok by busing directly to Ayuthaya via Suphan Buri. Dozens of routes are possible from Chiang Mai. Tribal trekking into the neighboring hills has become somewhat commercialized in recent years, but most travelers who undertake a five- to seven-day adventure still seem satisfied with their experiences. Mae Hong Son, a western frontier town with mountainous scenery and Burmese temples, attracts travelers who enjoy venturing slightly off the beaten track and want to trek a more remote, untouched region. An exhausting but rewarding bus journey loops through Mae Sariang and Mae Hong Son before returning to Chiang Mai via Pai. Lampang and Lamphun are two outstanding side trips from Chiang Mai.

Then it's off to the infamous Golden Triangle! The standard journey begins with a four-hour bus ride to Thaton, where longtail boats load up passengers and depart at 1300 for an exciting but deafening five-hour downriver trip to Chiang Rai. Before returning to Chiang Mai, a few days can be spent visiting the villages, hilltribes, and historic ruins of the Golden Triangle. Then it's back to Bangkok or a detour through the northeast via Phitsanulok. Depending on the current political situation, an intriguing option is to visit Laos and run the Mekong River from Luang Prabang to Vientiane. Shades of 1968!

CHIANG MAI

Chiang Mai, principal city of the north, is the favorite destination for many travelers to Thailand. Situated on the banks of the River Ping and surrounded by green hills and lazing rivers, this thriving city is blessed with a mellow flavor and a cool, dry climate—the perfect remedy to the sweltering cities of the south. It's a world apart. With its unique forms of architecture, dance, music, food, and festivals, Chiang Mai has always been a region both physically and emotionally separated from the remainder of Thailand. The people not only consider themselves superior to their cousins in Bangkok, they also happily agree with the national consensus that their fair-skinned ladies are the most beautiful in the country.

While Chiang Mai provides a refreshing change from the ordeals of Bangkok, travelers expecting a charming little village of wooden houses and rural lanes are in for a rude surprise. Commercial development and the rise of mass tourism have brought not only comfortable hotels and quality restaurants, but also concrete high-rises and traffic jams in even the smallest of *sois*. Nevertheless, Chiang Mai still retains enough traditional charm and warmth to make it one of Southeast Asia's most enjoyable destinations.

CHIANG MAI

TO CHIANG RAI

HIGHWAY 1019

SUPERHIGHWAY

TO BORSANG & SAN KAMPHANG

TO BANGKOK

POY LUANG HOTEL

CHIANG MAI BUS ARCADE (BANGKOK, CHIANG RAI, MAE HONG SON, ETC.)

HIGHWAY 1006

TRAIN STATION

McCORMICK HOSPITAL

G.P.O.

MENGRAI KILNS

BIG TREE

GYMKHANA CLUB

AMERICAN BAPTIST MISSION

BUSES TO BORSANG & SAN KAMPANG

BOXING STADIUM

THAI TRIBAL CRAFTS

INDIAN CONSULATE

RIVERSIDE REST.

BUSES TO BUS PHUN

TAT

TO LAMPHUN

HIGHWAY 106

PING RIVER

MENGRAI BRIDGE

SUPERHIGHWAY

CHARON PRATET RD.

EMPRESS HOTEL

RIM PING HOTEL

NANG NUAL RESTAURANT

LANNA HOSPITAL

WAT CHAI SRI PHUM

WAT PA PAO

DARETS GH

TAPAE GATE

NIGHT MARKET

TO FANG & THATON

WAT KU TAO

WAT CHIANG MAN

CHANG PUAK GATE

MOON MUANG RD.

BUSES TO DOI INTHANON

CHIANG MAI GATE

NATIONAL THEATER

HIGHWAY 107

CHANG PUAK BUS TERMINAL (FANG, THATON)

THAI AIRWAYS

JAIL

WAT CHEDI LUANG

WAT MENGRAI

SILVER SHOPS

OLD CHIANG MAI CULTURAL CENTER

LIBRARY BUSES TO DOI SUTHEP

FANTASTIC ROOM

WAT PRA PONG

WAT PRA SINGH

WAT PUAK HONG

SUAN PRUNG GATE

HIGHWAY 108

BANYEN ANTIQUES

SUAN DOK GATE

YMCA

RINCOME HOTEL

MARBLE PUB

CHIANG MAI ORCHID HOTEL

HENNESY NIGHTCLUB

THE PUB

WAT SUAN DOK

500m

0

CHIANG MAI NATIONAL MUSEUM

WAT CHET YOT

HUAI KEO RD.

IMMIGRATION

TO HOT, DOI INATHON, HANG DONG & MAE HONG SON

SUTHEP RD.

AIRPORT

TO DOI SUTHEP, PALACE

ZOO

CHIANG MAI UNIVERSITY

TRIBAL RESEARCH CENTER

WAT UMONG

© MOON PUBLICATIONS, INC.

HISTORY

Chiang Mai's original inhabitants were not Thais but Lawas, members of a primitive tribe forced from the fertile valley by Mons, who established a thriving empire at Haripunchai (present-day Lamphun). Medieval Chiang Mai was founded in 1292 by King Mengrai, a Thai-Laotian prince from Chiang Saen who had previously founded Chiang Rai in 1261 and conquered Haripunchai in 1281. After discovering his military headquarters poorly situated and subject to floods, Mengrai began searching for a new Lannathai capital. According to legend, the present-day site was chosen after his entourage spotted three lucky omens—two white barking deer, two white sambar deer, and a white mouse. With the aid of 90,000 workers, construction began on a royal city, a regal palace, and Buddhist temples protected by earthenwork walls and 10-meter moats. Mengrai ruled for 21 years before being struck by lightning at the intersection of Rajadamnern and Pra Poklao Road; an unlucky spot now marked by a modest spirit temple dedicated to the ambitious king.

Some 17 Thai monarchs ruled the Lannathai Kingdom of northern Thailand during the next 240 years. Chiang Mai enjoyed its own Golden Age during the mid-15th century reign of King Tilokaraja, a beloved ruler who organized the Eighth Buddhist World Council in 1477 and constructed many of the present-day temples. But warfare between Chiang Mai and the Burmese undermined the kingdom's vitality; in 1556 the kingdom fell to the Burmese, who ruled until 1774. Most Burmese architecture in Chiang Mai dates from this period. It wasn't until 1775 that King Taksin, founder of Bangkok and defender of Thai sovereignty, drove the Burmese from the war-torn city and moved the remaining population south to Lamphun. Taksin's successor, King Rama I, appointed a governor-prince who revived Chiang Mai's hereditary line of rulers; they presided over the semiautonomous state until 1938.

ATTRACTIONS

Chiang Mai's temples range stylistically from early Mon and Sukothai prototypes to Ayuthayan and Burmese-style monuments. North-ern architects characteristically favored large multilayered roofs that swoop down lower than those of Bangkok temples and muted exterior colors that typically employ less of the brazen reds, yellows, and blues found on southern temples. Northern architecture is also noted for flamboyant decoration and woodcarving such as filigree umbrellas and long-necked lions which reflect its two centuries of Burmese occupation. Some of the following temples stand in original condition while many others have been heavily restored in unrepresentative styles. Older temples have largely disappeared except for their crumbling *chedis*, which often predate by several centuries the primary *bot* and *viharn*.

The following walking tour describes temples on Tapae Road, followed by those inside and outside the old city walls. Chiang Mai has 80 registered temples and over 1,000 in the province, but the best monuments for rushed visitors are Wat Pra Sing, Wat Chedi Luang, Wat Chiang Man, Wat Chet Yot, and Wat Suan Dok.

Tapae Road Temples

Four temples of varying architectural interest are on Tapae Rd. between the shopping district and Tapae Gate.

Wat Saen Fang: Approached up an undulating *naga*-flanked lane that parallels new construction and crumbling old walls, Wat Saen Fang features a Burmese-style *chedi* decorated with corner cannons and whitewashed *singha* lions, a Burmese-style building used as a monks' residence, and a brightly painted *viharn* fronted by modernistic, abstract *nagas*.

Wat Bupparam: Three interior *viharns* illustrate the past, present, and future of Thai religious architecture. To the left is a soaring, garish, and ostentatious monument to bad taste that displays every gimmick used in modern Thai architecture: gaudy colors, ferroconcrete instead of wood, slapdash workmanship on the window eaves and pillared supports, and strange mythological animals that resemble Disney worm-dragons rather than traditional Thai creatures. Other buildings make better impressions, especially the tiny, three-centuries-old wooden *viharn* to the right. Exquisitely decorated with stucco on wood and modeled with superb proportions, the ancient structure features unusual horizontal windows set with old wooden pegs and a mysterious interior filled with dozens of Buddha images.

Wat Mataram: The Burmese-style *viharn* is distinguished by an entrance doorway beautifully carved with the Buddha preaching to the animals, and small tinkling bells which dangle from roof *nagas*. Don't get killed crossing Tapae Rd. to the next temple.

Wat Chettawan: This sanctuary attains great charm from its secluded location and broad lawns that support a family of hens and roosters. Note the moral sayings tagged to the trees: "If everything is gotten dreamily, it will go away dreamily too."

The adjacent **Croissant Cafe** is an excellent spot for coffee, conversation, and, what else, croissants.

Wat Chedi Luang

Named after the massive but partially ruined *chedi* behind the modern *viharn*, this famous monument was erected in 1401 by animist King Sam Feng Ken, allowed to fall into ruin, then restored by Sam Feng Ken's son King Tiloka, who raised the monument to 90 meters. An earthquake in 1546 partially destroyed the *chedi*, although the well-preserved foundations still give a strong impression of its architectural magnitude. Some claim the triple-roofed *viharn* once held the famous Emerald Buddha, brought from Lamphun by Tiloka in 1468 and later moved to Bangkok via Luang Prabang. Today it displays 32 Jataka panels and a bronze standing Buddha cast in 1441. *Nagas* flanking the staircase are considered some of the finest in Thailand. Located in the idyllic courtyard is a remarkably large gum tree, the city's Lak Muang shrine, and the adjacent Wat Pan Tao, which features a well-carved *viharn* and monks' quarters.

Wat Mengrai

Some say the 4.5-meter bronze Buddha inside this rather ordinary temple is a life-size model of King Mengrai himself. As noted above, the gigantic but luckless king was killed by lightning just a few blocks away.

Wat Chiang Man

Wat Chiang Man was constructed by King Mengrai in 1296, but all of the present structures, aside from the ancient *chedi* in the rear, are reconstructions which date from the 19th and 20th centuries.

Central *Viharn:* Directly through the entrance gates stands an older *viharn* with an elaborate gable richly carved with images of Erawan, the three-headed elephant which is now the symbol of royal patronage.

Modern *Viharn:* The building to the right is chiefly known for its pair of sacred images protected behind glass doors and two iron gates. To the left is the Crystal Buddha, Pra Setang Khamani, an image miraculously endowed with rainmaking powers and the centerpiece for the annual Songkran Festival. The Marble Buddha on the right, Pra Sila, is an Indian bas-relief image carved in the Pala style of the 8th century. Both are highly venerated and considered the most powerful images in northern Thailand.

Bot: To the left of the central *viharn* is a small modern chapel and an old *bot* surrounded by flowering plants and a brilliant green lawn. The 19th-century Lanna-style *bot* contains a fine collection of Lanna and U-Thong bronzes, plus an undeciphered stone slab carved in ancient hieroglyphics.

Library: Between the old *bot* and the rearside *chedi* stands an elevated *ho trai* (library), considered a masterpiece of woodcarving and lacquer decoration despite a recent repainting in gaudy colors.

Chedi: Behind the modern *viharn* towers one of the more interesting buildings in the complex, a 15th-century square *chedi* supported on the backs of 15 life-size stucco elephants. The use of elephant buttresses reflects Sri Lankan influences filtered through the Thai empires at Sukothai and Kamphang Phet.

Wat Pra Singh

Wat Pra Singh ("Monastery of the Lion Lord") was founded in the 14th century to house the ashes of King Kham Fu and serve as the principal religious center of the Lanna kingdom. The complex is composed of several buildings of varying architectural and artistic merit that form the most famous *wat* in Chiang Mai.

Central Viharn: A modern yet stately *viharn* constructed in 1925 but restored several years ago.

Library: A registered historical monument, the *ho trai* of Wat Pra Singh features outstanding stucco devas and scrollwork around the concrete foundation which supports the delicate wooden building. The divinities were inspired by those of Wat Chet Yot, while the upper structure of teak paneling has been lacquered in red with gilt trim.

Bot: Directly behind the central *viharn* stands a Lanna-style *bot* constructed entirely of wood with an impressive entrance of stucco and gold leaf.

Chedi: To the rear of the *bot* stands a circular stupa erected in the 14th century to house the ashes of King Kham Fu. According to architectural traditions borrowed from Sri Lanka, the bulbous reliquary is mounted on sacred elephants constructed from brick and plaster.

Viharn Laikam: The most famous and beautiful structure at Wat Pra Singh—and among the most elegant structures in all of northern Thailand—is the small chapel in the southwest corner of the *wat* compound. Viharn Laikam was built in 1811 in Lanna-style architecture before the influences of Bangkok began to dominate the north.

The exterior is a remarkable mélange of fine proportions and delicate woodcarvings in the window frames and ancient doorways. Interior murals, though dimly lit, remain the best preserved in Chiang Mai and provide a glimpse of the religious and civil traditions of 19th-century Siam.

More significant than the murals is the central Buddha image, the mysterious and ultrapowerful Pra Buddha Singh. Cast in northern Thailand during the late 15th century, exact copies of the highly venerated image are also enshrined in Wat Buddhaisawan in Bangkok and Wat Mahathat in Nakhon Si Thammarat.

Chiang Mai National Museum

Tribal costumes and a small collection of Buddha images are housed in this well-maintained but rather unimpressive museum. Kilns which once fired the famous Thai celadons have been reconstructed on the front courtyard. Open Wednesday-Sunday 0900-1200 and 1300-1600.

Wat Chet Yot

From both historical and architectural standpoints, this temple, also known as the Seven Spires Monastery, is considered the most important in Chiang Mai. Founded by King Tiloka in 1455 and modeled after the Bodgaya monu-

ment where Buddha attained enlightenment, Wat Chet Yot served as a monastery and center of Lanna Thai Buddhism for several centuries. In 1457, Tiloka convened the Eighth Buddhist Council here to commemorate the 2,000th anniversary of the Buddhist era. Subsequent kings covered the temple with a profusion of gold ornamentation, tragically stripped by the Burmese in 1556. Mounted on the walls of the small but beautiful seven-spired Mon-Burmese *bot* are 12 stucco figures of seated divinities framed by standing figures. As unified ensembles, they form the finest stucco figures in Thailand.

Wat Umong

Most of this forest *wat,* located five km outside of town, has disappeared, except for ruined *chedis* and meditation grottoes dating back to 1265. A large map at the entrance describes the layout and bizarre highlights like the Spiritual Mural Painting Hall and Herb's Garden. Scattered around the grounds are trees thoughtfully tagged with amusing admonitions, fragments of Buddhist statuary, and old-style meditation huts built without the use of nails.

Wat Suan Dok

This monumental but completely ordinary temple is chiefly known for its beautiful Chiang Saen-style bronze Buddha cast in 1504. Most of the temple's architectural value was lost during restoration, although it remains important to the local Thais during the annual Songkran Festival. A royal graveyard is located nearby.

Other Attractions

Tribal Research Center: Chiang Mai University's small museum and research library provides an excellent introduction to the various hilltribes. Located in building 15 at the far end of campus; pick up a map from the rector's office. Open Monday-Friday 0830-1200 and 1300-1700.

Chiang Mai Zoo: Thailand's largest zoo, with an arboretum and an enormous open-air bird sanctuary, was founded by a Westerner who donated hundreds of endangered animals to the local government. Open daily 0800-1700. Fresh milk, yogurt, and cheese are sold across the street at the Thai-German dairy stall.

Old Chiang Mai Cultural Center: Handicrafts are hawked during the day from replicas of hilltribe dwellings; northern Thai-style *khan* *tok* banquets and hilltribe dancing are presented each evening. (See "Nightlife," below.) Laddaland, another hilltribe theme park with morning dance demonstrations, is disappointing.

Chiang Mai Jail: Foreigners doing time on drug charges enjoy visits from travelers who bring food, magazines, and good cheer. Rajwithi Road.

Bicycle Rides: A relaxing bicycle ride through older sections of Chiang Mai is *highly* recommended. An excellent neighborhood to tour is across the Ping River near the American Baptist Mission. Popular with missionary groups, foreign medical associations, and Western expats, it's a beautiful enclave of narrow alleys, elaborate teakwood homes, and old commercial buildings surrounded by gardens and landscaped lawns. Then ride south down Highway 106 (the old Chiang Mai-Lamphun Road) to the Gymkhana Club, Mengrai Kilns, and the big tree festooned with offering scarves and miniature shrines. Continue south another kilometer, cross the Mengrai Bridge, and ride north along Charon Pratet Road past the Sacred Heart Cathedral and the former British Consulate back to town. Skip this tour and you've missed the *real* Chiang Mai.

Attractions West Of Chiang Mai
Wat Phratat: One of northern Thailand's top attractions is the pair of golden 16th-century stupas which overlooks Chiang Mai from the summit of Doi Suthep. According to legend, the shrine was erected in 1383 after a wandering white elephant carrying a sacred Buddha relic stopped here, trumpeted three times, and promptly died—an auspicious sign by Thai standards. In 1935, Lamphun abbot Sri Vinchai announced the construction of the winding road up to the 1,000-meter summit and, with the help of thousands of volunteers, completed the project in just six amazing months. The stupa is approached up a monumental, heart-pounding, 290-step staircase flanked by tremendous mythical *nagas* which symbolize man's progress from earth into nirvana. The present temples are rather ordinary, but on clear days views over the misty valley are absolutely spectacular. Doi Suthep is 20 km west of Chiang Mai. Minibuses leave from the Chang Puak gate (north gate) and cost 35B up and 25B down. Bring warm clothing.

Royal Palace: Pu Ping Palace, official winter residence of the royal family, is generally closed to the public, but the beautiful gardens of roses, orchids, and bougainvillea are open weekends and holidays from 0830 to 1630. Five km beyond and a short minibus ride from Wat Doi Suthep.

Hmong (Meo) Hilltribe Village: Northern Thailand's saddest and most commercialized hilltribe village is three km up a rough dirt road beyond the palace. Here, costumed Meo villagers pose for photographs, sell poor-quality handicrafts to busloads of bewildered visitors, and actually charge money to let tourists watch them smoke opium!

Attractions East Of Chiang Mai
Borsang Village: Thailand's famous umbrella village is located nine km east of town, just beyond the handicraft shops, remaining monkeypod trees, cool streams, and small villages constructed of teak. Borsang is a touristy but nevertheless pleasant place to photograph umbrellas drying in the sun and watch the lovely ladies deftly paint the satin, cotton, and paper parasols. Red-and-white minibuses leave from Charon Muang near Bumrung Raj road. Bicyclists should allow plenty of time for shopping in the countless handicraft shops.

San Kampang: Northern Thailand's silk and cotton-weaving village is where, in a show of pure concentration, young girls weave cloth on primitive handlooms while ignoring the tourists. Weavers in the large Shinawatra workshop are paid about 100B for their daily 10 meters. Worth a journey for visitors interested in traditional weavings or Thai silk. Four km beyond Borsang. Same minibuses as above.

Attractions South Of Chiang Mai
Muangkung: Ten kilometers south of Chiang Mai is a small pottery village which produces red pots from natural irons and black pots from charcoal. Minibuses leave from the Chiang Mai Gate.

Hang Dong: Craftsmen in this town produce both bamboo baskets and woodcarvings from old tree stumps and paddy mortars. Thirteen km south of town. Same minibus as above.

Chom Tong: This small junction town is chiefly known for Wat Pra Tat Sri Chom Tong, a beautiful Burmese-style temple on the left side of the main road. Constructed between 1451 and 1516, this well-maintained temple features a central facade and gilded gables carved with remarkable skill. Fifty-eight km from town.

Doi Inthanon National Park: Often hidden behind a swirling mass of fog and rain, Thailand's highest mountain (2,565 meters) offers beautiful scenery, evergreen montane forests, dwarf rhododendron groves, rare birdlife, and impressive waterfalls: 20-meter Mae Klang Falls located 10 km from the park turnoff, Wachiratan Falls 20 km from Chom Tong, and Sri Phum Falls at Kilometer 31. Other stops along the winding 47-km road include a Meo village and experimental farm where hilltribes raise alternative crops, several Karen villages, and the summit grave of Chiang Mai's final king. Bring warm clothing and rain gear. Since regular transportation is sporadic, you must go on motorbike or charter a pickup in Chom Tong for 500-600B. Hitching is possible on weekends from the turnoff, one km before Chom Tong.

ACCOMMODATIONS

Budget Accommodations

Chiang Mai's 100-plus guesthouses comprise one of the finest accommodation scenes in all of Asia. Guesthouses, ideally, are teak houses owned and operated by local families with fewer than a dozen rooms that face a courtyard filled with flowers, books, and lounge chairs. A perfect guesthouse is also a source of trekking services, bike rentals, and advice on sightseeing, restaurants, and shopping. Genuine guesthouses—a marvelous experience for everyone no matter their age or wealth—have become so popular that many of Chiang Mai's conventional hotels are now calling themselves "guesthouses."

Guesthouses and hotels are located in four areas of town. Those on the east bank of the Ping River are comfortable and quiet, but a bicycle (often provided free) is necessary to get around. Between the Ping River and Moon Muang Rd. are midpriced guesthouses and hotels ideally located within walking distance of the night market and shopping centers. Inside the old city walls is the largest concentration of guesthouses, especially in the northeast corner. West of town, in the direction of Doi Suthep, are the upscale hotels, which are quiet and luxurious but far removed from the temples and restaurants.

Guesthouse prices are fairly uniform throughout Chiang Mai. Low-end choices charge 60-120B for simple rooms with fan and common bath or 100-220B with fan and private bath. The emerging trend appears to be better guesthouses with a/c rooms and private bathrooms in the 250-400B range, described under "Moderate Accommodations." Standards of comfort and cleanliness are similar, but those guesthouses which appear to offer superior ambience have been briefly described below.

The question of which guesthouse to recommend is a difficult one: ask a dozen travelers and you'll get a dozen different selections. The best tactic is to take a minibus from the main bus terminal, or hire a tricycle from the train station, to the general neighborhood and make a walking inspection. Guesthouse touts at the bus and train stations are fairly reliable sources of information. Other travelers throughout Thailand are often happy to make personal recommendations, and these will often prove your best choice.

Daret's Guesthouse: The backpackers' center in Chiang Mai has a popular outdoor cafe with good food and dozens of rooms with fan and private baths. Daret's also rents motorcycles and sells treks. 4 Chaiyapoon Rd., tel. (053) 235440, 80-150B fan.

Moon Muang Golden Court: A new three-story hotel with patio restaurant, travel services, and 30 rooms in various price ranges. Clean and well located near the center of town. 95 Moon Muang Rd., tel. (053) 212779, 140-220B fan, 250-300B a/c.

Rendezvous Guesthouse: Another new hotel on a quiet back street with large rooms, common hot showers, and giant TV in the garden courtyard. Rajadamnern Rd. Soi 5, tel. (053) 248737, 100-150B fan.

Ampawan House: Just across from the Rendezvous is another new place that is modern, clean, and very quiet due to its alley location. Rajadamnern Rd. Soi 5, tel. (053) 210584, 100-150B fan.

Pata Guesthouse: An old wooden house with rustic charm and tree-covered courtyard. Rooms are small and somewhat dark, but adequate. Moon Muang Rd. Soi 6, tel. (053) 213625, 60-100B fan.

Moonshine House: A modern hotel just opposite Wat Chiang Man with clean rooms and

CENTRAL CHIANG MAI

★ Wat Ku Tao

HIGHWAY 107

■ Bus Terminal North to Fang, Thaton

■ Minibuses to Doi Suthep

★ Wat Chiang Yuen

★ Wat Pa Pao

■ Chiang Puak Gate

Honey Chicken

■ Khum Kaew Palace Khantoke Rest.

■ Thai Airways

Wang Keo Rd.

★ Wat Chiang Man

★ Wat Duan Chang

Rajwithi Rd.

Rajapranikai Rd.

★ Wat Duang Di

Rajadamnern Rd.

● La Villa Pension

★ Wat Pan Tao

★ Wat Chedi Luang

Rajamanka Rd.

★ Wat Mengrai

● Anodard GH
● Nat GH

Moon Muang Rd.

Chaiyapoon Rd.

★ Wat Chettawan

★ Tapae Gate

★ Wat Mataram

D.K. Books

Aaron Rai Restaurant

Loi Kroa Rd.

■ Garden Restaurants

■ Blue Moon Nightclub

Pra Poklao Rd.

■ Buses South to Hot. Chong Thom

Chiang Mai Gate

● Silver Shops

Wua Lai Rd.

Sri Don Chai Rd.

■ Suriwong Books

★ National Theater

■ Your Place Bar

★ Wat Chiang Man

Chiang Mai President Hotel

Chiang Mai Restaurant

Chiang Moi Rd.

★ Wat Sri Phum

U.S. Consulate

City Offices

Tai Wang Rd.

Chiang Moi Rd.

Market

★ Wat Saen Fang

Post

Telephone

Tapae Rd.

★ Wat Bupparam

● Mosque

Chiang Inn

● Galare GH

Porn Ping Hotel

Night Market

● River View Diamond Hotel

Novotel Suriwongse Hotel

Le Chalet Rest.

● Lanna Thai GH

Dusit Inn

Ansuran Night Market

■ Bang Keo Restaurant

Chiang Mai Plaza Hotel

Whole Earth Restaurant

● Ban Kaew GH

● Alliance Francaise

Chiang Klan Rd.

● Season Shopping Center

Empress Hotel

Lanna Palace Hotel

Charon Pratet Rd.

★ Wat Chai Monkol

TAT

● Chiang Mai GH

● Chumpol GH

Chiang Mai Tea House

Bus to Lamphun

Charonraj Rd.

HIGHWAY 1009

● Mee GH

● Bain Garden

Colonial Heritage Restaurant

■ The Gallery Restaurant

Riverside Cafe

Ping River

New Lamduon Faham Rest.

Hollanda GH

Highway 106

Family House

● Pun Pun GH

Wang GH

Je T'aime GH

River Restaurant

0   300m

© MOON PUBICATIONS, INC.

tasty meals prepared by Duan, wife of the English owner. A very friendly place. 212 Rajaphanikai Rd., 80-150B fan.

Racha Guesthouse: Racha and the adjacent Supreme Guesthouse are modern, clean places with good-value rooms. Both are off the beaten track and popular with long-term visitors. Moon Muang Rd. Soi 9, tel. (053) 210625, 80-120B fan.

Rose Guesthouse: Popular spot with beer garden decorated with hanging parasols, cane chairs, and other attempts at atmosphere. Services include motorcycle rentals, overseas phone calls, and trekking services. Good value. 87 Rajamanka Rd., tel. (053) 276574, 80-150B fan with common bath.

Moderate Accommodations

Most of the newer guesthouses which have recently opened in Chiang Mai are charging 150-250B for a clean room with fan and private bath, and 250-500B for an a/c room. While somewhat more expensive than the budget guesthouses listed above, the improved cleanliness and touch of luxury make these an outstanding value.

Gap's Antique House: One of Chiang Mai's finest guesthouses offers antique decor with modern amenities, plus a memorable cafe filled with artworks and teakwood carvings. Rajadamnern Rd. Soi 4, tel. (053) 213140, 250-500B a/c.

Fang Guesthouse: Beautiful four-story hotel with small garden, open-air dining room, and outstanding rooms with private bath. Highly recommended. 46 Kampangdin Rd. Soi 1, tel. (053) 282940, 200B fan, 300-400B a/c.

Top North Guest House: Not really a guesthouse, but a modern, clean, good-value hotel with reasonably priced a/c rooms and less expensive fan rooms. Located on a quiet back street in the old city. Top North even has a swimming pool! 15 Moon Muang Rd. Soi 2, tel. (053) 278900, fax (053) 278485, 150-250B fan, 300-500B a/c.

Baan Kaew Guesthouse: Tucked away in an alley just south of Alliance Française is this beautiful and quiet guesthouse with spacious gardens and a comfortable restaurant. A real escape from the hustle and bustle. 142 Charoen Prathet Rd., tel. (053) 271606, 300-350B fan, 400-500B a/c.

Pension La Villa: The somewhat isolated location is compensated by the lovely teakwood house and elevated dining room with some of the best Italian food in Chiang Mai. Italian management. 145 Rajadamnern Rd., tel. (053) 215403, 200-250B fan, 250-300B a/c.

Living House: Another modern and very clean guesthouse in a convenient location near Tapae Gate. Friendly manager and a small restaurant. Tapae Rd. Soi 5, tel. (053) 275370, 200-250B fan, 250-300B a/c.

Lai Thai Guesthouse: A very large 90-room guesthouse which faces the old city and ancient moat. Rooms are clean and the restaurant is a popular hangout for both backpackers and tourists. Highly recommended. 111 Kotchasan Rd., tel. (053) 271725, fax (053) 272724, 300-350B fan, 400-500B a/c.

YMCA: The Chiang Mai Y has a swimming pool, a restaurant, convention facilities, and over 200 clean and comfortable rooms. Unfortunately, it's outside of city center and isolated from the shops and the night market. 11 Mengrai Rasmi Rd., tel. (053) 221819, fax (053) 215523, 80-200B a/c dorm, 300-600B a/c rooms with private bath.

Riverside Guesthouses

All of the guesthouses which hug the west bank of the Ping River offer either fan or a/c rooms with private baths, comfortable restaurants, and delightful views over the river. As with all other guesthouses and hotels in Chiang Mai, vacancies are scarce during the busy season from Nov. to March and advance reservations are strongly recommended. Reservations by fax are much better than phone calls or relying on the Thai mail system.

River View Lodge: The River View Lodge is nicely decorated with Thai furnishings and traditional woodcarvings and has a wonderful little restaurant. The helpful and courteous owner speaks flawless English. An excellent upscale addition to the Ping River guesthouses. 25 Charoen Prathet Rd., tel. (053) 271109, fax (053) 279019, 1000-1800B.

Galare Guesthouse: A modern Thai-style guesthouse with both fan and a/c rooms with private baths. None of the rooms offer river views, but Galare remains a good choice in a great location. 7 Charoen Prathet Rd., tel. (053) 293885, 400-450B fan, 500-700B a/c.

Luxury Accommodations

Upscale hotels in Chiang Mai are conveniently located downtown near the night market or away from town toward Doi Suthep. Rates quoted in the accompanying hotel chart are high-season prices in effect from Nov. to March. Discounts of 30-50% are offered during the hot summer months from March to June and during the rainy season from July to November. All hotels charge an additional 11% government tax and a 10% service charge.

Novotel Suriwongse: In the center of town near the night market and restaurants are several luxurious hotels with all the standard amenities. The Suriwongse is comanaged by a French hotel chain and caters to group tours and business travelers. 110 Changklan Rd., tel. (053) 270051, Bangkok reservations tel. (053) 251-9883, fax (053) 270064, 1800-2500B.

Chiang Mai Orchid: Chiang Mai's original four-star hotel has maintained a good reputation despite the opening of newer and more luxurious properties. The principal drawback is the location outside town. 100 Huay Kaeo Rd., tel. (053) 222099, Bangkok reservations (02) 233-8261, fax (053) 221625, 2800-3500B.

Empress Hotel: Chiang Mai's first luxury hotel with convention center opened in 1991 just south of city center. The 17-story landmark features various function rooms, restaurants, and the most exclusive disco in town. 199 Changklan Rd., tel. (053) 278000, fax (053) 272467, 1600-2800B.

RESTAURANTS

Chiang Mai offers a wide range of dining experiences, from northern Thai dishes to European and Asian specialties. Prices are very low, and dining environments run the gamut from simple street stalls to elaborate teakwood homes and riverside cafes and nightclubs.

Daret's Restaurant: Chiang Mai's most popular travelers' hangout serves fairly good food plus outstanding fruit shakes and smoothies in a friendly atmosphere. Daret's is also a great place to meet other travelers and swap information. Chaiyapoon Road. Inexpensive.

JJ Restaurant: A modern, clean, a/c cafe with bakery, espresso, ice cream, and Thai and American dishes. Great spot for breakfast and the *Bangkok Post.* Montri Hotel. Moon Muang Road. Inexpensive.

Croissant Cafe: Walking tours of Chiang Mai might start with breakfast at either JJ Restaurant, Times Square, or this small a/c cafe near the Tapae Rd. temples. Not much atmosphere but decent food and a good escape from the traffic and noise. 318 Tapae Road. Inexpensive.

Times Square Roof Garden: Great views and thick coffee can be enjoyed from the rooftop cafe near Tapae Gate. Enter through the dark lobby of the Times Square Guesthouse and climb the back steps to the roof. Best at breakfast. Tapae Rd. Soi 6. Inexpensive.

AUM Veggie Cafe: Among the excellent dishes are vegetarian spring rolls, tofu specialties, and meatless entrees drawn from the traditions of the north and northeast. Great food at rock-bottom prices served by followers of the Indian guru, Satya Sai Baba. Moon Muang Rd. just south of Rajadamnern. Inexpensive.

Thai German Dairy: Excellent Western dishes such as muesli, homemade yogurt and breads, porridge, and pizza. Dairy products are fresh and safe to eat. Moon Muang Rd. Soi 2. Inexpensive.

Aaron Rai: Some of the city's best northern Thai dishes are served in this simple cafe near Tapae Gate. An English-language menu is available. Native specialties include *gang hang ley* (pork curry), *nam prik* (spicy salsa), and *kao neow* (sticky rice). Be sure to try the unlisted regional favorite, *laab,* a dish of diced pork mixed with chilies, basil, and sautéed onions. Other selections include *tabong* (fried bamboo shoots) and *sai owa* (sausage stuffed with pork and herbs). Brave souls can feast on *jing kung* (roasted crickets) and other exotic specialties. 45 Kotchasan Road. Inexpensive.

Bierstube: Ask a local where to dine and the answer will often be this cozy restaurant in the center of Chiang Mai. Though the German and American dishes are popular, Bierstube cooks some of the best Thai dishes in town. Friendly management and waitresses. 33 Moon Muang Road. Moderate.

The Pub: Superb English and French meals served in a homey place considered one of the most genial gathering spots in town. The Pub is decorated in English fashion with darts, old beer signs, a collection of cigarette packs, and a roaring fireplace in the winter months. Outside town but worth the *tuk tuk* ride. Highly recommended. Huay Kaeo Rd. near the Rincome Hotel. Moderate.

Whole Earth Restaurant: Thai, vegetarian, and Pakistani dishes served in a beautiful Thai building surrounded by lovely gardens. Nightly entertainment at 1900 ranges from Indian sitar to Thai folk guitar. No shoes in this very elegant restaurant. 88 Sri Donchai Road. Moderate.

Bankao Restaurant: Upscale and memorable, the teakwood "Old House" near the Ansuran night market is a romantic spot with loads of atmosphere. Sit upstairs for piano music, photographs of the royal family, and decent entrees priced from 70 to 100 *baht*. Bankao is touristy but not badly overpriced. Ansuran Road. Moderate to expensive.

Chalet: French dishes served in a genuine old northern teak mansion. Chef John Evalet operates one of Asia's most famous French restaurants on the banks of the Ping River. 71 Charoen Prathet Road. Expensive.

The Hill Restaurant: Somewhat reminiscent of a Tom Sawyer house, the Hill is a weird multilevel treehouse situated in a small forest. Food is only average but the atmosphere is unique and prices are low. 122 Suan San Sai Road. Inexpensive.

Markets

Chiang Mai has one major night market and several small spots popular with Thais and budget travelers.

Ansuran Night Market: Chiang Mai's most lively and authentic dining experience is the food market which operates nightly on Ansuran Rd. between Chang Klan and Charoen Prathet roads, just around the corner from the night bazaar. Dozens of stalls prepare a wide range of inexpensive dishes. Try rich mussel omelets from the sidewalk showman, steamed crabs large enough for two people, and grilled fish served with choice of sauces. Other possibilities include honey chicken roasted over an open fire, fried noodles with shrimp and bean sprouts, and the spectacle of "flying morning glory." English-language menus are often available, though the point-at-the-pot method of ordering is more direct. Ansuran Road. Inexpensive.

Thor Loong Market: Budget travelers staying in the guesthouses near Tapae Gate often frequent the street stalls and cafes of Thor Loong. Chaiyapoon Road. Inexpensive.

Restaurants
East Of The Ping River

Some of the best restaurants are across the river in the old neighborhood once favored by foreign missionaries and diplomats.

Riverside Cafe: Probably the most popular *farang* hangout in Chiang Mai offers relaxed dining on its Thai entrees, then stay for the live music which ranges from light folk to heavy rock. 9 Charoenraj Road. Moderate.

Gallery Restaurant: This outstanding place combines an art gallery with a beautiful garden in a renovated Chinese shophouse. Superb atmosphere with pleasant views across the river. Highly recommended. 25 Charoenraj Road. Moderate.

Bain Garden: In the compound of the old Bombay-Burma teak consortium is a simple cafe with low-priced meals. Not fancy, but it offers a refreshing garden atmosphere across from an imposing mansion owned by a Chinese jade merchant (not Khun Sa). 2 Wat Gate Rd. Soi 1. Inexpensive.

Colonial Heritage: An old mansion converted into an upscale restaurant with a spacious backyard dining area. A memorable place for northern Thai specialties. 8 Wat Gate Rd. Soi 1. Moderate.

Dinner Dance Shows

Chiang Mai's classic dining experience is *khantoke,* a traditional northern buffet accompanied by a brief demonstration of Thai dance. It's completely touristy but also fun, reasonably priced, and one of the few opportunities in Thailand to see traditional dance. *Khantokes* cost 200-300B and reservations should be made in advance. Photographers can request a spot in the front row, center stage. A typical *khantoke* dinner includes:

Kao neo: glutinous rice pinched into bite-size pieces and dipped into a variety of sweet and spicy sauces;

sai oua: spicy Chiang Mai sausage roasted over a fire fueled with coconut husks;

naem: pickled pork sausage;

nam prik ong: minced pork cooked with chilies and shrimp paste;

gang hang lay: Burmese curried pork mixed with tamarind or *kathorn;*

larb: a northeastern dish of minced meat mixed with fresh mint leaves.

Old Chiang Mai Cultural Center: Since 1971, the complex south of downtown has been presenting meals and dance shows in its teakwood compound. After a very mild but unlimited meal, northern Thai dances are presented in the dining room, followed by hilltribe and folk dances in the adjacent amphitheater. Be sure to try a hand-rolled cigar filled with locally grown tobacco. 185 Wulai Road. 300B.

Khum Kaew Palace: A large teakwood residence near Thai Airways also presents *khantoke* meals and traditional dance. Rajaphanikai Road. 250B.

Diamond Hotel: The most convenient location for *khantoke* is the teakwood mansion behind the Diamond Hotel and near the banks of the Ping River. Unlike the Old Chiang Mai Center, this is an intimate spot where everyone is guaranteed a close look at the dancers. Diamond Hotel. 350B.

NIGHTLIFE

Nightlife in Chiang Mai is a subdued affair limited to a few nightclubs and restaurants with live music.

Night Bazaar: Chiang Mai's best nightlife activity is wandering around the night bazaar on Changklan Road. Several small beer bars are located in the basement of the central emporium. More rewarding are the free dance shows given nightly from 2100 to 1200 in the rear of the Vieng Ping Market.

Riverside Cafe: The hippest spot in town offers entertainment from folk guitar to country-and-western and heavy rock. The Riverside is uncomfortably packed with *farangs,* but it's the best place to meet and mix with local expatriates. 9 Charoenraj Road.

Chiang Mai Tea House: Also on the east side of the Ping River, this cozy joint is the low-key alternative to the brash Riverside. Jazz and folk rock are popular here. 27 Chiang Mai-Lamphun Road.

Marble Bar: Cozy and high-class with intimate jazz combos in a refined atmosphere, just above a marble store. 100 Huay Kaeo Rd., just past the Chiang Mai Orchid Hotel.

The Pub: Second only to the Riverside in popularity, this English inn has a warm atmosphere plus jazz or folk musicians. Huay Kaeo Rd. near the Rincome Hotel.

Fantastic Room: Daeng Fantastic, Thailand's most famous jazz musician, headlines in this small club along with visiting musicians and friends. Open from 1800 to 2400. Arrug Rd. below the Chiang Roy Hotel.

Hennesy Nightclub: An old-fashioned taxi-dance hall patronized almost exclusively by Thai males who pay small sums to dance with young girls dressed in Thai cheerleader outfits. A very strange place. Muang Mai Hotel on Huay Kaeo Road.

Traditional Massage: Thai curative techniques (without sex) are practiced and taught in various places in Chiang Mai. The Petngarm Hatwait behind the Diamond Hotel has traditional ("Ancient") massage from 200B per hour. Ancient massage is also given at the Blue Moon Nightclub on Moon Muang Rd. and at the Chiangmai Sauna Club on Chotana Road. The best deal is at the Rinkaew Complex (old Chiang Mai Hospital) across from the Old Cultural Center, where an hour of professional massage from the talented instructors costs only 100B. The Northern Blind School near Suan Dok Gate also offers authentic but low-priced Thai massage from blind masseuses.

PRACTICALITIES

Tourist Information
The very helpful tourist office (tel. 235334) on the Chiang Mai-Lamphun Road has free maps, magazines, and lists of bus and train departures, hotels, guesthouses, and licensed trekking agencies. Open daily 0900-1630. The Tourist Police are also located here.

Mail
Chiang Mai's main post office, on Charon Muang Road near the train station, is open Monday-Friday 0900-1700 and Saturday until noon.

International Telephone
Phone calls can be made from the main GPO, the branch on Praisani Road, the airport, and until midnight from the international telephone service at 44 Sri Dornchai Road.

Immigration
Visas can be extended at Thai Immigration (tel. 213510) near the airport. India, Japan,

and the U.S. maintain consular posts in Chiang Mai.

Books and Maps

Chiang Mai's best bookstore is Suriwong Books on Sri Don Chai Road. Hudson Enterprises on Tapae Road and the bookstore near the Tapae Gate occasionally have large-scale USGS topographical maps. The a/c reading room inside the United States Information Service (USIS) on Rajadamnern Road stocks current magazines and newspapers. David's Traveler Library in the Saithum Guesthouse off Moon Muang Road is a good source of trekking information, while Nancy Chandler's *Map of Chiang Mai* is absolutely indispensable for information on restaurants, local transportation, and important place-names in Thai script—*highly recommended!*

Other

Obtain medical services from McCormick Hospital, tel. 241107. Transcendental meditation classes are given at the Whole Earth Restaurant, Wat Ram Poeng near Wat U Mong, and the Buddha Dhamma Center near Laddaland. Runners can join the Hash House Harriers (tel. 211550) at the Pub. English-language schools sometimes hire native English speakers but at very low pay.

Warning

Penalties for the use or possession of drugs are extremely severe in Thailand. Tricycle drivers sell the dope and turn you in for the reward. Guesthouses are periodically raided by the police and those who can't immediately settle their fines go directly to jail. Chiang Mai is a town with heavy drug penalties.

TRANSPORTATION

Getting There

Bus: Air-conditioned public coaches depart from Bangkok's Northern Bus Terminal three times daily 0900-1000 and eight times daily 2000-2145, cost 250B, and take 10-12 hours. Non-a/c buses depart hourly and cost 150B. Most buses stop at Chiang Mai's Arcade Bus Terminal out-

side town, from where yellow minibuses 3 and 4 continue to hotels and guesthouses. Alternatively, several private bus companies in Bangkok offer similar service at comparable prices. Book these through travel agents; hotel pick-up is usually provided. Buses are fast and cheap but also cramped, cold, and hair-raising. Valium from local pharmacies will help.

Train: Except for air services, second-class coach with sleeper is the fastest and most comfortable way to reach Chiang Mai. Express trains depart Bangkok's Hualampong Station nightly at 1800, 1940, and 0640, take 13 hours, and cost 440B in second class with lower sleeping berth. Rapid trains depart at 1500 and 2200 and take 15 hours. Ordinary trains leave throughout the day. Advance reservations are recommended. Tricycles from the station cost 10B to any guesthouse.

By Air: Thai International's five daily flights to Chiang Mai take one hour and cost 1400B. Taxis from the airport to most hotels cost 50B. Dragon Air flies once weekly from Hong Kong direct to Chiang Mai.

Getting Around

Chiang Mai is a compact town and all sights in the central section are within walking distance. To explore the more far-flung destinations, a rented bicycle or motorcycle is recommended. Bikes cost 20-25B and motorcycles 100-150B daily from guesthouses and shops near Daret's Restaurant on Moon Muang Road. Check the condition carefully and drive safely! Tricycles cost 5-10B for most short trips. Local yellow minibuses numbered 1-4 and described on Nancy Chandler's map ply four routes around town.

Leaving Chiang Mai

Public buses for most destinations in Chiang Mai Province leave from the Chang Puak Bus Terminal north of the city. Minibuses to Doi Suthep leave from Chang Puak Gate. Minibuses to points south leave near the southern Chiang Mai Gate. Buses to more distant destinations such as Chiang Rai, Mae Hong Son, Sukothai, and Bangkok leave from the Chiang Mai Arcade Bus Terminal northeast of town.

HILLTRIBE TREKKING

One of Thailand's most memorable experiences is visiting and living briefly among the semino-madic hilltribe people of northern Thailand. Most of these agriculturalists migrated here from Laos and southern China via Burma over the last century. Today, despite the inroads of West-ernization and government programs to en-courage their assimilation into mainstream Thai society, these groups have to a surprising de-gree maintained their distinct languages, ani-mist customs, patterns of dress, and strong sense of ethno-consciousness.

Although these packaged adventures are called "treks," they more closely resemble long walks than some Nepalese marathon. Treks generally last three to seven days and involve several hours of daily hiking over foothills, wad-ing across streams, and tramping under bam-boo forests before spending the evening in a local village. After a late-afternoon arrival at the village, visitors are welcome to politely wander around, watch the women weave or pound rice, play with the kids, and take a few discreet pho-tos. Western comforts are rare: accommoda-tions are limited to wooden floors in the head-man's house, bathrooms are in the distant bush-es, and bathing takes place in nearby streams. Dinner is often a simple meal of sticky rice, boiled vegetables, and hot tea. After the plates are cleared, dozens of villagers, children, curi-ous teenagers, and shy young girls fill the lodge for an awkward but fascinating conversation conducted through your interpreter-guide. You can ask about their customs and beliefs, but be prepared to explain yours and perhaps sing a song! Opium is offered after the villagers wander back to their houses and all the children have been put to bed.

Where To Go
Golden Triangle: Hilltribe villages are scat-tered over most of northern Thailand but the first trekking, some 20 years ago, was in the Golden Triangle area north of the Kok River. Although the hill people continue to live and dress in traditional manner, some of the more accessible villages have been overtrekked and have become sadly commercialized. This is,

however, one of the only areas to visit Akhas and the easiest place to do some self-guided trekking without the use of a guide. Pick up *The Mae Kok River* map from Suriwong Books in Chiang Mai and then take the bus up to Thaton. Self-guided treks can start here or halfway down the river. Another good spot to start is Mae Sa-long, a small Kuomintang village northwest of Chiang Rai. Guesthouses in Chiang Dao, Fang, Thaton, Chiang Rai, Chiang Saen, and Mae Salong can help with details.

North of Chiang Mai: The region around Chiang Dao and Wiang Papao, midway be-tween Chiang Mai and Fang, was the next area opened to explorers. Treks typically begin with a three-hour jeep ride to a drop-off point on the Chiang Mai-Fang highway, then half a day of hiking to reach the first village. Trekking groups occasionally pass each other and the villagers are now quite accustomed to Westerners.

Mae Hong Son: The early '80s saw the focus shift west of Chiang Mai toward the isolated town of Mae Hong Son, the newest and least com-mercialized trekking area in Thailand. Trekking agencies are located in Chiang Mai, Mae Hong Son, Pai, Soppong, and Mae Sariang.

Trekking Tips
Research: Paul and Elaine Lewis's *Peoples of the Golden Triangle* is the best of recently pub-lished books. Other useful books include the Time-Life publication of Frederic Grunfeld's *Wayfarers of the Thai Forest,* which details Akha lifestyles, and *Highlanders of Thailand,* which provides a comprehensive collection of well-edited essays, including a chapter on the ef-fects of tourism. These books are difficult to find in Chiang Mai and should be read in advance. *People of the Hills* by Preecha Chaturabhand is somewhat trashy (sex lives of the Akhas) but available locally and small enough to be car-ried on the trek. A few hours browsing in the Tribal Research Center at Chiang Mai University will also help.

When to Go: Winter months (late October to early February) are the ideal time to enjoy the cool nights and warm days without the threat of rain; also the best season to find poppies in

PEOPLES OF THE HILLS

Inhabiting the hills of northern Thailand are thousands of hilltribe peoples who struggle to maintain their traditional lifestyles against poverty, overpopulation, and the pressures of encroaching civilization. Most of these semi-nomadic tribes are of Tibetan-Burmese or Tibetan-Chinese origin, having migrated across the border from southern China via Burma less than 100 years ago. Today they wander from camp to camp employing slash-and-burn (swidden) farming techniques to cultivate rice, vegetables, and their most famous crop: opium. Swidden agriculture typically begins in January, when secondary or tertiary forests are cut down and left to dry before being burned in March or April. Rice is planted in the fertilizer ash after the monsoon rains break in June. Rice stalks are cut four months later with small hand sickles, then threshed and winnowed to remove the chaff. Opium and maize are planted in October and harvested during a 10-week period from December to January. Although one of the world's oldest agricultural techniques, slash-and-burn farming is extremely destructive since it depletes the soil of important nutrients and leaves the fields abandoned to useless shrub such as *lalang*. It also perpetuates tribal migrations, making it impossible to divide the region into neatly defined ethnic districts.

Thailand's hilltribes are sometimes described as peaceful people living in idyllic harmony with nature—something of a forgotten Shangri-La—but nothing could be further from the truth. Most are extremely poor and live in dirty wooden shacks without running water, adequate sanitation, medical facilities, or educational opportunities for their children. Illiteracy, disease, opium addiction, and deforestation are other problems. Uncontrolled erosion and soil depletion have reduced crop yields, while land, once plentiful and rich, has become scarce from tribal overpopulation and the arrival of land-hungry lowlanders. Royal aid projects provide help and discourage opium production in favor of alternative cash crops, but tribal political power remains minimal since tribespeople are stateless wanderers, not Thai citizens. The Thai government recognizes six major groups of hilltribes, subdivided into dozens of subtribes with distinct language, religious beliefs, customs, costumes, and historical backgrounds. The following descriptions include those tribes most likely to be encountered by trekkers. The Western tribal designation is given first, followed by the local Thai terminology.

Akha (Ekaw)

Population: 27,000
Origin: Yunnan, China
Location: Golden Triangle

Considered among the poorest and least sophisticated of all hilltribes, the Akhas are also among the most dazzling in costume. Women's dress typically includes a long-sleeved jacket and a short skirt woven from homespun cotton dyed dark blue with indigo. The crowning glory is the Akha headdress, an elaborate pile of cloth stretched over a bamboo frame festooned with bird's feathers, iridescent wings of beetles, silk tassels, dog fur, squirrel's tails, and Indian silver rupees. Leggings are worn to protect against brambles and thorns. The shy and retiring Akhas construct their villages at high elevations to escape neighbors and provide privacy for opium cultivation. Primitive wooden figures flanking the village entrance gates are carved with prominent sex organs to ensure fertility and ward off evil spirits. Don't touch these talisman gates or the bamboo spirit houses scattered throughout the village. Most villages have giant swings used during festivals, and courting grounds where young people meet to find mates. Homes are enormous structures divided into separate sleeping quarters for males and

Akha

PEOPLES OF THE HILLS

females. Like most tribespeoples, Akhas are animists who believe that the spirits of nature, departed ancestors, and graveyard-dwelling malevolent ghosts must be appeased with frequent animal sacrifice. Despite efforts to preserve their traditional lifestyle, Akhas face the challenges of poverty, political impoverishment, deforestation, overpopulation, and discrimination from other tribespeople, who consider them the bottom of the social order.

Hmong (Meo)
Population: 65,000
Origin: Laos
Locations: Chiang Mai, Laotian border

The Hmong, called Meo by the Thais, are a fiercely independent people who fled Chinese persecution over the last century for the relative peace of northern Thailand. Today the second largest tribal group in Thailand, the Hmong have become the country's leading opium producers by establishing their villages on mountain tops—higher elevations are considered best for opium cultivation. Thai Hmong are subdivided into White and Blue, color distinctions that refer to costume hues rather than linguistic or cultural differences. Despite their isolation, Hmongs are not shy or rare; you will see them in Chiang Mai's night market selling exquisite needlework and

Karen

chunky silver jewelry. Traditional female costume includes a short jacket of Chinese design, circular silver neck rings, and a thickly pleated dress handwoven from cannabis fiber. Their striking and voluminous hairstyle is made by collecting old hair and braiding it together into a bun. Young people enjoy sexual freedom and premarital sex is the rule rather than the exception. Courting begins during the New Year festivals when teenagers meet and make arrangements to rendezvous again during rice-planting season. Early sexual sprees end when the prospective husband makes a monetary offering of five silver ingots to the girl's parents.

Karen (Yang, Kariang)
Population: 275,000
Origin: Burma
Location: Thai-Burma border

Thailand's largest hilltribe is the only group not heavily engaged in opium cultivation. Settlements are so numerous that most trekking groups pass through at least one of several subdivisions. Karens are divided into the Sgaw, who live near Mae Hong Son, and the Pwo to the south of Mae Sariang. Smaller Burmese groups include the Kayahs (Karenni or Red Karens) in Kayah State (just across the border from Mae Hong Son) and the Pao who live in southern Shan state. Karens are a peaceful, honest,

Hmong

PEOPLES OF THE HILLS

Lahu

and hardworking people who use sound methods of swidden agriculture to save topsoil and minimize cogon growth. Their women are superb weavers whose multicolored skirts, blouses, and wedding garments have become prized collectors' items. Female dress often denotes marital status: young girls wear white cotton shifts while married women wear colored sarongs and overblouses. Multiple strands of beads are popular, but most women shun the heavy silver jewelry favored by other tribal groups. Males are often covered with elaborate tattoos that permanently satisfy ancestral spirits and eliminate expensive spirit ceremonies. Religious beliefs run the gamut from animism and Buddhism to visionary millennial movements that prophesy a future, messianic king. Karen Christians call him the final Christ, Buddhists call him the fifth and final incarnation.

Lahu (Musser)
Population: 45,000
Origin: Southwestern China

Locations: Chiang Dao, Fang, Golden Triangle
Lahus are one of the most assimilated of all northern tribes. Most belong to the Black (Lahu Na) or Red (Lahu Nyi) linguistic groups while a minority speak two dialects of the Yellow (Lahu Leh and Shi). Older Lahus, who haven't yet adopted modern costume,

dress in black robes richly embroidered with red zigzagged stitching and silver ornaments. Children often wear Chinese beanies sprouting red puff balls. Like most tribals, Lahus are animists who believe their village priests can exorcise evil spirits with black magic and heal the sick with sacred amulets. And like the Karens, they anticipate a messianic movement lead by Guisha, the supreme Lahu God who created the heavens. Their most famous postwar messiah was Maw Naw, the Gibbon God who failed in his attempts to restore true Lahu religion and lead his people back into Burma. Ceremonial life revolves around the lively New Year festival in which, after dancing, top spinning, and other games, males court females by blowing gourd signals and poking them with sticks through the slats of the bamboo floor. Special pavilions are available for marriage proposals and lovemaking.

Lisu (Lisa)
Population: 20,000
Origin: Burma

Locations: Chiang Dao, Fang, Mae Hong Son
Thailand's premier opium cultivators and the most culturally advanced of all hilltribes are an outgoing, friendly, and economically successful group of people. While most hilltribe villages are poor and dirty,

Lisu

PEOPLES OF THE HILLS

Lisu villages are often clean and prosperous, loaded with sewing machines, radios, motorcycles, and perhaps a Datsun truck. Terrific salespeople, they enjoy setting up stalls and selling their handicrafts in Chiang Mai's night market. Their enthusiasm and determination to outshine every other tribal group are reflected in their beautiful and extremely stylish clothing. Females typically wear brilliant blue skirts topped with electric red blouses and rakish turbans festooned with long strands of multicolored yarn. This dazzling costume is complemented by a cascade of silver buttons and long dangling ornaments that hang over the chest. Lisu religion revolves around the familiar animist spirits, but also weretigers and vampires that might take possession of a person. Lisus are also noted for their complicated marriage rituals and hedonistic New Year festival of endless dancing, drinking, and religious rituals.

Mien (Yao)
Population: 35,000
Origin: Southern China
Location: Chiang Rai Province

Mien are a hard-working and materially advanced people whose Chinese characteristics have made them the cultural sophisticates of Thai tribals. Called Yao by the Thai, the Mien originated in southern China as a non-Han group before migrating into Thailand via Laos between 1910 and 1950. Most have dutifully kept their Chinese cultural links such as Chinese script and Taoist religion. Sacred scrolls

Mien

that function as portable icons (similar to Tibetan *tankas*) are their great artistic creations. When unrolled and hung up, these Taoist tapestries change ordinary rooms into temporary temples. Tragically, most have been sold to Bangkok antique merchants by impoverished Mien. Yao women wear large black turbans, distinctive red boas around their necks, and loose-fitting pants embroidered with stunning pastiches of triangle, tie-dye, and snowflake designs.

---

full bloom. The rainy months (June to September) can be difficult if not impossible.

Group or Self-guided Tour?: Organized treks are best because of language difficulties, security problems, and the possibility of getting lost on the winding trails.

Selecting the Trekking Agency: Chiang Mai's 40 registered trekking agencies meet together monthly to make reports to the police department, set agreements on rates, and discuss problems. Neither the TAT nor the Tribal Research Center makes specific recommendations on trekking agencies, but everyone agrees that the most important factors are the qualifications of the guide. Meet with him to determine his age, maturity, trekking experience,

knowledge of tribal customs and local dialects, and sensitivity to the hilltribes.

Trek Details: Make a firm agreement on all services the trekking company will provide. How many days will the trek last? Since it takes at least two days to reach the relatively untouched villages, a trek of five to seven days will prove much more rewarding than shorter treks. How big will the group be? Groups of more than six people are large and unwieldy and should be avoided. What areas will be visited? Everybody promises the "newest untrekked area," but exactly how many other trekking groups will be in the region with yours? Crossing tracks with another group is to be expected, but it should still be held to a minimum. What hilltribes will be visited? Ideally you should visit three or four distinct groups rather than just five Karen groups in five days. What about the price? Rates set by the Chiang Mai Trekking Guide Association average 800-1000B for a five-day trek, but special trips with elephant rides and river rafting are much more expensive. What else is included? Lodging, food, and transportation are normally factored with the package price, but check on exclusions. Rucksacks and sleeping bags for cooler winter months may also be provided.

Behavior: Experts emphasize the importance of remembering that hill people are human beings with customs, values, and emotions just as valid as those of the tourist. Visitors should act politely and observe local customs. Your guide can advise on local taboos such as avoiding villages marked with bamboo crosses or touching the fertility symbols which guard some villages. Modesty should always be observed. Revealing halter tops on the ladies and nude bathing in the local streams are definitely taboo.

Before unpacking the camera, establish some kind of rapport with the villagers. Most tribespeople allow photos when taken discreetly, but it's best to ask permission. Rather than handing out sweets, cigarettes, cheap trinkets, or money for photos, offer food, Band-Aids, disinfectants, soap, toothpaste, and other necessities.

Warning: Should the trekking company or guesthouse offer to keep your valuables, both parties should prepare a complete list of valuables and issue an itemized receipt. Some travelers report that stored valuables, such as traveler's checks or camera equipment, have disappeared during their trek. Even worse, trekkers' credit cards have been surreptitiously used to purchase goods in Bangkok with the cooperation of agreeable shopkeepers—a theft undetected until your Visa bill arrives back home. To prevent this type of fraud (more common than robbery during the trek), make a detailed report and leave all valuables in a locked bag for which you have the only key.

VICINITY OF CHIANG MAI

LAMPHUN

Thailand's oldest town makes a fine day outing from Chiang Mai. According to Siamese chronicles, the ancient 7th-century city was founded by a wandering hermit named Suthep who invited Lopburi's Mon princess Chama Devi to reign as the city's first queen. During the next six centuries, Lamphun (then known as Haripunchai) served as capital for an independent Mon kingdom until it fell to King Mengrai's Lanna Thai kingdom in 1281 and was occupied by the Burmese in 1556. Most of the present attractions date from the early 16th century except for one amazing temple which dates from the Mon (Dvaravati) period.

Lamphun is 26 km south of Chiang Mai and can be reached by green buses which leave every 30 minutes from Lamphun Road near Nawarat Bridge. Visitors with extra time might stop en route at the McKean Leper Rehabilitation Institute, four km off the main road and open Monday-Friday 0800-1700, and the basket-weaving village of Saraphi. Mr. Tu in the Thai Airways information office near the bus stop has information on local silk factories and excursions down the Ping River.

Attractions

Lamphun Museum: A small but worthy collection of Lanna Thai art is displayed inside this branch of the National Museum just opposite Wat Haripunchai. Open Wednesday-Sunday 0900-1200 and 1300-1600.

Wat Prathat Haripunchai: Lamphun's royal monastery, on the left side of the main street, was founded in 897 by a Mon king to enshrine a sacred Buddha relic. Of the dozen-plus beautiful buildings, two of the best are the 50-meter Chiang Saen-style *chedi* covered in copper plates and a 19th-century Lanna-style library elevated above the ground to protect against termites. Many of the buildings owe their Burmese flavor to 20th-century reconstructions.

Wat Kukut: Also known as Wat Chama Devi, this intriguing *chedi* is a must-see for all visitors to Lamphun. The taller of the two *chedis* dates from 1218; it's perhaps the finest example of Dvaravati architecture left in Thailand. By constructing this pyramidal *chedi* with five diminishing tiers graced with 15 diminishing Buddhas, Mon architects created both a monument of great artistic merit and a clever optical illusion. Located one km up the small street next to the museum.

Accommodations

Most visitors see Lamphun on a day-trip from Chiang Mai, though a few Thai hotels are scattered around town.

Lamphun Hotel: Simple rooms with common or private baths are available in the yellow building four shops down from the corner. Also called the Notanon Hotel. 51 Inthayong Rd., tel. (053) 511176, 60-100B.

Tu's Guesthouse: Mr. Tu, a local character who hangs out near the bus stop, rents rooms in his home and offers tours to local silk factories and down the Ping River. Ask for him in the shops near the National Museum.

Sawat Ari Hotel: Another hotel marked only with a Thai sign, near Wat Kukut. Chamdevi Rd., 60-100B.

Suan Kaeo Bungalows: More luxurious digs are six km outside town on the road to Lampang. Highway 11, Km 6, 120-200B.

LAMPANG AND VICINITY

Lampang, 100 km southeast of Chiang Mai on the arterial highway between Bangkok and the north, was once a sleepy town known for its temples and nostalgic horse-drawn carriages. Today it's a busy commercial center of 50,000 residents with some of the finest Burmese-style temples in Thailand.

Lampang is a very long day-trip from Chiang Mai or an excellent one-day stopover between Chiang Rai and points south. Buses from Chiang Mai take three hours and leave from the Arcade Terminal and the bus stop on Charonraj Road just across the Ping River. Maps to the following hotels and attractions can be obtained at the Lampang tourist office at the eastern end of Thakrownoi Road, a 15-minute tricycle ride east from the bus or train terminals.

Attractions

Wat Chedi Sao: Located across the Wang River and outside the city limits, this rather unimpressive temple is saved by its peaceful location among the rice paddies. The tourist map shows it as temple number one.

Wat Pra Keo Don Tao: Although located in the middle of a disorienting neighborhood and difficult to find, this Burmese shrine with its massive *chedi*, well-carved Burmese-style chapel, small museum, and Thai-style temple is worth seeking out.

Wat Pra Fang: Central Lampang has three magnificent temples that rank among the finest Burmese structures in the country. Wat Pra Fang, just opposite the Thai Airways office, features a delicate *chedi* surrounded by seven small chapels filled with alabaster Buddhas that represent the seven days of the week.

Wat Sri Chum: Excellent woodcarving and inlaid colored glass make Sri Chum one of Lampang's great sights.

Wat Sri Rong Muang: Lampang's most awesome Burmese sanctuary dazzles the visitor with its glittering multicolored exterior of carved wood and corrugated iron, superb interior woodcarving, and vast collection of sacred images donated by wealthy patrons.

Budget Accommodations

Lampang has about 20 hotels in all price ranges. Most are in the downtown district on Boonyawat and Robiwang roads.

Sri Sanga Hotel: Just east of the Lampang Hotel is a small hotel with inexpensive fan-cooled rooms and better a/c rooms. 213 Boonyawat Rd., tel. (054) 217070, 60-100B fan, 180-220B a/c.

Tip Inn: A small guesthouse with tiny rooms near the river and Riverside Cafe. Riverside Rd., 60-100B.

Thai Guesthouse: Nobody speaks English, but the Thai Guesthouse has several teakwood cabins and a communal longhouse in a wonderful location overlooking the Wang River. Pongsanuk Rd., 80-150B.

Asia Lampang Hotel: Centrally located, the remodeled Asia Lampang has conference facilities, a "Sweety" Room, and the Kumluang Restaurant with "Thai, Chinese and Uropean food by the professional cookers." 229 Boonyawat Rd., tel. (054) 217844, 250-330B a/c rooms.

Tipchang Hotel: Lampang's largest hotel features a nightclub, a 24-hour coffee shop, a swimming pool, and an eighth-floor restaurant that overlooks the river and adjacent nine-hole golf course. 54 Takranoi Rd., tel. (054) 218078, 300-450B.

Lampang River Lodge: Sixty beautiful Thai-style bungalows are six km south of town on the banks of the Wang River. All rooms are a/c with private bath and riverside verandas. 300 Moo 1 Tambol Chompoo, 1200-1800B, tel. (054) 215072, Chiang Mai reservations tel. (053) 215072.

Attractions Near Lampang

Wat Prathat Lampang Luang: One of northern Thailand's finest monuments is the 11th-century walled temple located 20 km southwest of Lampang. The massive complex includes a pair of modern Chinese temples, sagging *bodhi* trees supported by pilgrim posts, dozens of Buddha images including an effigy carved from jade, six *viharns* with outstanding facades, and a monumental 45-meter *chedi*.

Minibuses from Lampang reach Koh Ka, a small town four km off the main road. From Koh Ka, take a motorcycle taxi or walk three km to the monastery.

Elephant School: Thailand's official elephant training camp is located between Chiang Mai and Lampang. Here in a beautiful wooded basin, mahouts train young pachyderms each morning 0700-1100, except on Buddhist holidays and during the hot season from March to June. This is the real thing—not a tourist performance! Take an organized tour from Chiang Mai.

Pha Thai Caves: Some 339 steps lead up to this 400-meter cave filled with limestone formations, stalagmites, and Buddha images illuminated by a string of electric lights. Entrance is 800 meters off highway H1 just past kilometer stone 665, 66 km north of Lampang. Buses can be flagged down in Ban Pang La.

MAE SARIANG

This small town, midway between Chiang Mai and Mae Hong Son, serves as a good base for treks and river adventures down the Yuam and Salween rivers, which separate Thailand from Burma. Progress has arrived slowly to the region, a blessing for the town, which has retained many of its fine old wooden buildings and simple temples constructed in Burmese-Shan style.

Attractions

Temples: A quick stroll around compact Mae Sariang turns up a few temples of fairly recent vintage. Wat Jong Sung (Wat Uttayarom), a modest temple which dates from 1896, fronts the more impressive Wat Sri Boonruang, which was constructed by Burmese craftsmen in 1930 in the typical architectural style of the borderlands. Wat Chong Kham down near the bridge is another example of Burmese monastic architecture with multitiered roofs, wooden latticework, and the inevitable corrugated-tin roof.

River Excursions: The main reason to visit Mae Sariang is to enjoy a boat ride down the Salween or Yuam rivers. Excursions can be organized at the Riverside Guesthouse and from Lek in the Sweet Pub. River journeys are best undertaken from December to March, just after the end of the rainy season. The Salween River journey begins with a jeep ride from Mae Sariang across the Danwa Range to Mae Sam Lap, a small village 46 km southwest of Mae Sariang on the banks of the Salween. Accommodations in the Riverside Huts chalets include verandas which overlook the Salween. Boat trips are also possible south from Mae Sam Lap down to the junction of the Salween and Yuam rivers and the small village of Mae Leh Ta.

Accommodations

Mae Sariang has a handful of simple guesthouses and hotels that cater to the steady trickle of Western tourists.

Riverside Guesthouse: Best choice in town is the lovely guesthouse overlooking the Yuam River. The breezy restaurant is a great place to relax after a long bus ride. 85/1 Lang Panit Rd., tel. (053) 681188, 60-350B.

Kamolsorn Hotel: A new and modern three-story hotel with big fan-cooled rooms and private baths. Very clean and comfortable. A much better deal than the Mitaree. Wai Seuksa Rd., 200B.

Transportation

Mae Sariang is 200 km southwest of Chiang Mai and 165 km from Mae Hong Son. Buses leave the Arcade Bus Terminal in Chiang Mai every two hours and take four or five hours to reach Mae Sariang. The same service is offered from the bus terminal in Mae Hong Son.

Songtaos from Mae Sariang to Tak are sporadic and subject to delays. One *songtao* departs in the early morning for Mae Sam Lap. Another leaves for Tak down Hwy. 1085, but service usually terminates in the town of Sop Ngao or Tha Song Yang, 90 km south of Mae Sariang. The road is now fully paved, but government regulations still prevent direct service between Mae Sariang and Tak. More details under "Mae Sot."

MAE HONG SON

Tucked away close to the Burmese border and hemmed in by the mountains surrounding the Pai River Valley, this small and somnambulant town is rapidly developing into one of Thailand's more popular off-the-beaten-track destinations. Before the tortuous 369-km road from Chiang Mai was completed in 1965, the town served as a convenient dumping ground for disgraced bureaucrats, who nicknamed it the Siberia of Thailand. Today it can be reached by air in 30 minutes and is promoted as Thailand's Shangri-La—complete with lost valleys, tribal trekking, caves, rivers, and waterfalls. While not the mystical vision described in tourist literature, the attractive scenery and sense of remoteness make it a welcome change from the more touristy destinations in Thailand. Mae Hong Son now has several hotels, almost a dozen guesthouses, a post office with phone services, several banks that cash traveler's checks, trekking agencies, a handicraft center, and motorcycle-rental shops.

Attractions

Doi Kong Mu: Not everybody enjoys the noisy and unattractive town of Mae Hong Son, but there's enough of interest to make it worth a few days. Top draw is the 424-meter peak at the north end of town, which offers great views and a modest *chedi* constructed by Governor Singnatraja in 1874, the same year Mae Hong Son was declared an official Thai settlement.

Wat Hua Wiang: Several modest temples constructed in Burmese style with corrugated roofs arranged in diminishing tiers are located in the center of town. This particular temple, wedged between the morning market and the bus station, holds a highly venerated brass Buddha cast in Burma and subsequently hauled over the mountains. The adjacent market is occasionally visited by hilltribe ladies dressed in traditional garb.

Wats Chong Kam and Chong Klang: Picturesquely located on the banks of placid Jongkum Lake are two Burmese-style *chedis* which provide outstanding photographs in the misty morning hours. The latter temple contains a famous collection of 35 wooden figures (*tukatas*) inspired by the Buddhist Vessantara Jataka. Shown by request only.

Trekking: Mae Hong Son Province is 50% Shan (Thai Yai), 2% Thai, and 48% hilltribe people including Karens, Lawas, Lahus, Lisus, and Meos. Villages near Mae Hong Son are now well trekked but less deluged than those near Chiang Mai. Further treks can be arranged to the dangerous border town of Mae Aw and to a small village where several Paduang women now reside. Crossing the Burmese border on the Pai River to visit Karenni army camps is possible but illegal and dangerous. Treks cost 200-250B per day and can be arranged through guesthouses and trekking agencies such as Don Enterprises on the main road, and from Rin, Thomas, and Lanna Tours.

Budget Accommodations

Mae Hong Son's soaring popularity has brought dozens of guesthouses, several middle-priced hotels with a/c rooms, and five luxury hotels and countryside resorts. New facilities are being added each month. Simple rooms with fan, mattress, and common bath cost 40-60B s and 60-80B d, but the trend seems to be better rooms in the 100-200B price range.

Sang Tong Huts: Great views over ricefields and banana plantations make this somewhat remote guesthouse one of the best in Mae Hong Son. Sang Tong offers individual *nipa* huts plus a comfortable sitting room and a small library. Pracha Uthit Rd., 100-200B.

Golden Huts: Adjacent to Sang Tong is a series of individual *nipa* huts clinging to the hillside amid trees, ferns, and winding walkways. Huts with hot showers cost extra. Traditional Thai massage and medicinal steam baths are available in the adjacent watchtower. Pracha Uthit Rd., 100-150B.

Mae Hong Son Guesthouse: Also about 15 minutes from town is another popular guesthouse with small huts and nine wooden rooms. A good place to escape the crowds, though a bicycle will be needed for local transportation. Pracha Uthit Rd., 50-100B.

Garden Guesthouse: Back in town is a quiet spot with solid, dark rooms covered with teak paneling and a great reception area. Khunlum Prathat Rd., 140-180B.

Sabanga Guesthouse: Centrally located and placed nicely back from the street, Sabanga has a small garden and an elevated patio in front of the rooms with common baths. Udom Chowne Rd., 100-120B.

Jungle King Guesthouse: Offers five excellent teak rooms with mosquito nets and mattresses on the floor. Friendly management plus new bicycle rentals and trekking information. Pradit Jongkam Rd., 40-60B.

Chong Kham Lake Guesthouses: Several small places surround the wonderful lake and fitness park in the center of town. Baitong Guesthouse is a rudimentary collection of bamboo huts on the verge of collapse, while Rose and Chong Kham guesthouses are somewhat better spots with views over the lake. Rim Nong Guesthouse is on the southern edge. 50-100B.

Pen Porn Guesthouse: Clean and modern spot up the hill and away from the noise. All wood-decor rooms come with fan, private bath, and hot showers. Doi Kong Mu Rd., 150-200B low season, 200-250B high season.

Hotels

Tara Mae Hong Son Hotel: Mae Hong Son came of age with the opening of this 104-room four-star hotel operated by the Imperial group of hotels. Facilities include a convention center, a swimming pool, and several restaurants. Highway 108, Bangkok tel. (02) 254-0023, 2000-2500B.

Holiday Inn: The latest addition to the hotel scene is south of town on the road to Mae Sariang. 114/5 Khumlun Prathat Rd., tel. (053) 612108, fax (053) 611524, Bangkok reservations (02) 254-2614, 2400-2800B.

Resorts

Several luxury resorts which cater to Thai weekenders and upscale Western travelers are south of town.

Mae Hong Son Resort: Six km south on the banks of the Pai River, Mae Hong Son Resort has 30 comfortable bungalows surrounded by manicured lawns, camping facilities, and a good restaurant. 24 Ban Huai Duea, tel. (053) 235344, Chiang Mai tel. (053) 236269, 1000-1200B fan, 1400-1800B a/c.

Rim Nam Glang Doi Resort: Four km south of town is another luxury resort with bungalows, campsites, and a dormitory for budget travelers. Ban Huai Duea, tel. (053) 611298, 1000-1500B.

Getting There

Buses leave Chiang Mai's Arcade Terminal six times daily and take 10-12 grueling hours to reach Mae Hong Son via the southern route. An overnight pause in Mae Sariang is a good way to break the ordeal. Public buses along the northern route through Pai are somewhat quicker. The most comfortable options are the three daily air flights which take 30 minutes and cost 380B. Tickets are heavily booked, so it's best to confirm reservations immediately upon arrival in Mae Hong Son, or play it safe and purchase a roundtrip ticket. A popular compromise is to fly to Mae Hong Son but return by bus.

MAE HONG SON TO PAI

Pha Sua Waterfall

Attractions located off the main road can only be reached with rented motorcycle or chartered minitruck. Turn left at Km 17 shortly before Huia Pha and continue past Mok Cham Pae and Huai Khan to these modest bathing falls, located 11 km off the main road. Visitors with hired transport can continue north to the Pang Tong Royal Palace, several hilltribe villages, and the smuggling towns of Napapak and Mae Aw, controlled by renegade forces of the Kuomintang—a dangerous region best avoided during the opium-smuggling season from January to May.

Fish Cave

Domesticated carp are fed papaya in a rock pool 17 km north of Mae Hong Son. A one-km dry cave is situated across the road and south 100 meters. Huai Pha is the last town for 50 km.

Huay Hea

A Thai signpost 56 km from Mae Hong Son marks the road north to the Black Lahu village of Ban Jabo and Huay Hea, 16 km from the junction and just one km from Myanmar. Stay at the Lahu Guesthouse, managed by the village schoolteacher.

Soppong

Accommodations in Soppong, the main village between Mae Hong Son and Pai, include Dim, J, and the aptly named So-Cheap Guesthouse. Since there is little reason to stay here, most travelers continue six km north through the Lahu village of Vanaluang and the Shan village of Ban Tun to the popular Cave Lodge Bungalows, operated by Australian John Spies and his Thai wife. John has authored several articles about trekking and spelunking and is an invaluable information source on the region's 10 limestone caves. Most visitors start with a huge river tunnel called Tham Lot (*tham* means cave in Thai) filled with stalactites, a deep interior river, and recently discovered prehistoric coffins. The 8.3-km Nam Lang Cave, 20 km downstream, is reputedly one of the longest in Southeast Asia.

PAI

Pai is one of the most beautiful destinations in Thailand. Situated in a broad valley surrounded by mountains and rivers, the idyllic landscape and easygoing pace of life remind you of Chiang Mai several decades ago. This is the kind of place where days lead into weeks and weeks into . . . you get the idea.

Attractions

Wat Mae Yen: A 30-minute walk east of town past a Shan village is the "Temple on the Hill," under the patronage of a community of vegetarian monks and situated at the top of a 350-step staircase.

Waterfalls: Pai has several waterfalls best visited during or shortly after the monsoon season. The most popular is Morpang Falls, seven km west of town on the road past the hospital. Another small series of falls is east of town toward Wat Mae Yen.

Pong Rone Hot Springs: Eleven km southeast of town are several minor hot springs fed by bamboo pipes and located adjacent to a small stream. Hardly spectacular, but a welcome soak after a long and dusty bike ride.

Trekking: Pai is one of the most popular trekking areas in northern Thailand. Most treks head north and make overnight stops in Shan, Black Lahu, and Lisu villages before rafting down the Pai River. An elephant camp is also on the banks of the Pai River. The easiest way to avoid crowds is to skip any trek that includes a river trip or an elephant ride. You have been warned.

River Trips: The Pai River and a tributary of the Ping near Doi Inthanon National Park are northern Thailand's most popular river-and-trekking destinations. Short day-trips down the Pai River begin north of town near the elephant camp. A longer multi-day journey to Mae Hong Son starts at Ban Muang Pang, 26 km south of Pai, and continues downstream to Pang Mu, eight km north of Mae Hong Son.

Guesthouses

The dusty town of Pai has over a dozen modest guesthouses. Most are on the main road but the best places are found along the river and on the outskirts of town.

Charlie's Guesthouse: Conveniently near the bus stop, Charlie's is a clean and comfortable place with friendly management. Rungsiyanon Road. Ordinary rooms cost 40-80B. Special rooms include Sweet Rooms II and III at 160-250B.

Big Guesthouse: Also on the main road is another clean guesthouse with a small cafe over a pond. Rungsiyanon Road. 50-100B.

Nunya's Guesthouse: A two-story hotel with rooms tucked away in the back courtyard. 84 Rungsiyanon Rd., 50-140B.

Pai River Lodge: River Lodge has a dozen bamboo huts arranged in a semicircle around the central dining area. Run-down but a good location facing the Pai River. Huts cost 40-60B.

Shan Guesthouse: Perhaps the best guesthouse in Pai is the series of individual wooden huts at the south end of town near some beautiful ricefields. Shan's is run, logically enough, by a Shan who once worked the oilfields in Saudi Arabia and his Aussie co-owner who printed up business cards which read: "You can check out any time you like . . . but you can never leave." A good slogan for a town like Pai. Rungsiyanon Rd., 60-100B.

Transportation

Buses from the Arcade Bus Terminal in Chiang Mai depart at 0700, 0830, 1100, and 1400 and take about four hours to cover the 134 km to

Pai. Minitrucks from Mae Hong Son to Pai also take four hours and leave several times daily between 0700 and 1300. The road from Mae Hong Son is incredibly rugged and winding but has spectacular views over some of the most isolated regions of Thailand.

Buses from Pai to Chiang Mai depart hourly from 0630 to 1430. An a/c bus departs once daily around 1130. Passengers should arrive early and grab the first available seats. Minitrucks to Soppong and Mae Hong Son depart every two hours between 0700 and 1430.

GOLDEN TRIANGLE AREA

Thailand's infamous Golden Triangle—properly located on the Mekong where Burma, Laos, and Thailand intersect—is the mysterious and untamed land where powerful opium warlords, remnants of Chiang Kai-Shek's Kuomintang army, and communist insurgency groups once fought for control of Southeast Asia's immensely lucrative opium traffic. The Triangle's Wild West image attracts large numbers of curious travelers who come searching for caravans of mules hauling tons of high-grade opium. The reality is somewhat different. Smuggling continues to some degree, but visitors should also prepare themselves for modern towns, lines of tour buses, and a countryside completely in touch with the 20th century. Don't be discouraged by the commercialization—the varied scenery and sense of remoteness still make the Triangle an enjoyable destination.

CHIANG MAI TO THATON

Most travelers take the 0740 or 0830 bus from Chiang Mai directly to Thaton to catch the 1300 longtail boat ride down to Chiang Rai—the most popular river journey in northern Thailand. Visitors with more time might make the following stops or day-trips from Chiang Mai.

Mae Sa Valley
This beautiful valley, 30 minutes north of Chiang Mai, features (in order from the turnoff at Mae Rim) fishing ponds; orchid farms; Mae Sa Resort; a small private museum with Ban Chang potteries; Rose Garden; Mae Sa Waterfall, popular with Thai families; an elephant camp; Erawan Resort, with hilltribe dancing daily at 1100 and 1400; and countless resorts with bamboo cottages and neatly trimmed gardens. The elephant camp gives daily pachyderm shows at 0900 with rides afterwards for 250B. Upscale accommodations in thatched-roof bungalows are available at a dozen resorts, including the Mae Sa Valley Resort, where individual lodges cost from 500B. The Mae Sa road continues circling counterclockwise until it reconnects with Highway 108 near Hang Dong, an excellent day-trip for motorcyclists. Organized tours of the valley can be arranged in Chiang Mai. Buses to Mae Rim leave from Chang Puak Bus Terminal. From Mae Rim, either walk, hitchhike, or wait for an infrequent minibus.

Elephant Training Camp
This privately owned elephant camp 56 km north of Chiang Mai sponsors daily shows at 0930 for 50B. Elephant rides through the jungle cost 100B with bargaining. Touristy but fun.

Chiang Dao Caves
Five km west of Chiang Dao is a cave that extends deep into the heart of Thailand's third-highest peak. Meditating Buddhas have been placed inside the illuminated front cave, but guides with torches must be hired to explore farther inside the 10-km cave. A highly venerated Buddhist monk lives in a cave two km distant.

Fang
Once an outlaw post controlled by armed mercenaries and opium warlords, this modern little town 151 km north of Chiang Mai is now firmly under the supervision of the Thai military. Trekking to nearby Shan and Chinese villages can be arranged at the Metta Wattana, Sri Chukit, and Wiang Fang guesthouses, though most local tribals now dress in Western clothes. Crocodile Dundee Guesthouse, one km south of town, is a superb place. Highly recommended!

THATON AND KOK RIVER

Thaton, a picturesque town on the banks of the Kok River, chiefly serves as a launching point for downriver trips to Chiang Rai. An imposing white Buddha, who seems to be contemplating the steady stream of Western travelers, dominates the town. Hike up for excellent views over the valley. Self-guided treks to nearby villages are easy but less than pristine since this region has been trekked for over 20 years. Robberies are commonplace; be careful. Cheap guesthous-

es include the highly recommended Thips Travelers House upriver from the bridge, the quiet Chan Kasem 2 across the river, and the Siam Kok adjacent to the boat launch.

Longtail boats leave Thaton at 1300, cost 160B, and take four hours down the Kok River to Chiang Rai. Brief stops are made at Mae Salak for police registration and photos of the hanging bridge and at the Highland Forestry Development Project for cold drinks. Early stages of the journey are relatively uncommercialized, but lower sections toward Chiang Rai are plagued with refreshment stalls, souvenir

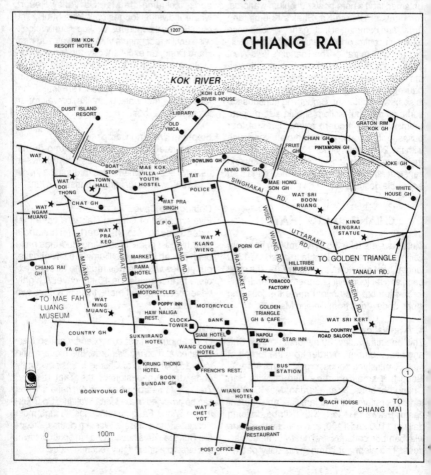

shops, TV antennas, and tacky signs announcing Lahu Village. Longtail boat rides are exciting and provide a glimpse of the countryside, but not everyone is thrilled with the speed, noise, and cramped quarters. Bamboo houseboats, constructed per order in Thaton, are excellent alternatives. Six-man bamboo rafts with cabin and primitive lavatories cost 2500B per boat and take three relaxing days to Chiang Mai . . . if they aren't capsized on the rocks. Trekking is another alternative. Prospective hikers should consult the *Mae Kok River Map* by Joseph S. rather than the sketchy and too-large-scale U.S. topographic maps. Joseph advises "Only Tourists Destroy Tourism." Hikes can be made from a dozen different drop-off points such as Ban Mai and Mae Salak, but bring along food, appropriate clothes, small change, gifts, and a sense of caution. Robberies are common; leave your valuables in Chiang Mai.

CHIANG RAI

Chiang Rai is a peaceful and easygoing town without the hustle—or the great sights—of Chiang Mai. Despite the lack of any major attractions, tourism is on a sharp rise, as indicated by the new tourist office and the amazing hotel developments being laid on the bewildered little town. The city was founded in 1262 by King Mengrai as the nation's first independent kingdom, but the fickle king later moved his forces south to Lamphun and finally Chiang Mai. Each year in February the city sponsors a week of traditional northern culture during the colorful Wai Samae Fah Luang Festival.

Attractions

Chiang Rai's modest monuments include Wat Pra Keo, where Bangkok's Emerald Buddha was discovered in 1436, and a reproduction of the sacred Chiang Mai Buddha inside Wat Pra Sing. Wat Chet Yot was copied from the seven-spired monument of the same name in Chiang Mai. Also worth checking out are the panoramic views from City Hall and the fat, jolly Buddha who sits in the Wat Klang Wieng courtyard. Believe it or not, this is the fifth and final Buddha! Chiang Rai is also a good base for exploring the Golden Triangle and initiating river journeys down the Kok River to the mighty Mekong. Self-guided trekking is easiest from Mae Salong, 67 km northwest of Chiang Rai.

Budget Guesthouses

Chiang Rai has exploded with dozens of new guesthouses in recent years. Operators are always on hand to greet boat arrivals from Thaton and bus customers from Chiang Mai.

Chat Guesthouse: Several years ago the old Chat moved to a much nicer location in a small alley near the boat landing. Chat has a cozy cafe, laundry services, and information on trekking. Trairat Rd. Soi 1, tel. (053) 711481, 50-150B.

Koh Loy River House: A new place on the river behind the old YMCA, with spacious grounds and a pleasant restaurant overlooking a tributary of the Kok River. All rooms are large and clean and include private baths with hot showers. 485 Tanam Rd., tel. (053) 715084, 120-240B. Very good value.

Pintamorn Guesthouse: Operated by some Germans and a Hawaiian named Bob Watson, Pintamorn compensates for its isolated location with clean rooms, good food, and some of the best motorcycles in Chiang Rai. 199/1 Mu 21 Soi Wat Sriboonruang, tel. (053) 714161, 60-120B with private bath.

Ya House: The old Lek Guesthouse is a funky, cramped, but popular place with communal rooms and five bamboo bungalows in the rear courtyard. 163/1 Banphaprakan Rd., tel. (053) 713368, 40-80B.

Fruit Guesthouse: Tucked away in a quiet residential neighborhood and overlooking a small creek, Fruit offers good vibes and a great escape from the hustle of Chiang Rai. A tricycle from the pier costs 10B. 91/2 Kohloy Rd., 60-100B.

Moderate Accommodations

Chiang Rai has several midpriced hotels that bridge the gap between budget guesthouses and the luxury hotels.

Boon Bundan Guesthouse: The best deal in town has 36 new rooms centrally situated near the bus station and clock tower. All rooms are clean and modern and include private baths with hot showers. Boon Bundan also has a fine restaurant, a pool, trekking services, and rental motorcycles. 1005/13 Chet Yod Rd., tel. (053) 717040, fax (053) 712914, 150-250B fan, 350-400B a/c.

Rach House: A small but very clean hotel tucked away in a back alley away from the noise of Chiang Rai. All rooms are a/c with private baths and hot showers. Good value, and not a *farang* in sight. 90/2 Sanpanard Rd., tel. (053) 715969, 300-400B.

Golden Triangle Guesthouse: Right in the heart of Chiang Rai is this small hotel that blends modern amenities with traditional touches such as thatched walls, teakwood furniture, and Thai paintings. 590 Paholyothin Rd., tel. (053) 711339, fax (053) 713963, 700-900B.

Luxury Accommodations

Wiang Inn: Top choice in the center of town is the three-star Wiang Inn Hotel with swimming pool, several restaurants, disco, and traditional massage parlor. Well located near the bus station and night market. 893 Paholyothin Rd., tel. (053) 711543, fax (053) 711877, 1400-1800B.

Wang Come Hotel: A big hotel with all the standard amenities including a circular pool, a lively coffee shop, and convention facilities. 896 Pemawiphata Rd., tel. (053) 711800, fax (053) 712973, 1500-2000B.

Dusit Island Resort: The splashiest addition to Chiang Rai's expanding tourist scene has been erected on a large delta island in the Mae Kok River. 1129 Kraisorasit Rd., tel. (053) 715777, fax (053) 715801, Bangkok reservations (02) 238-4790, 3200-3800B riverview rooms.

Restaurants

Most of the restaurants in town are in the alleys near the Wang Come Hotel.

Night Market: Though it pales in comparison to the grand affair in Chiang Mai, a small but lively night market with food stalls operates on Trairat and Tanari roads near the Wang Come Hotel.

Cheap Cafe: The corner cafe just east of the clock tower has great dishes for just 20B, plus a friendly manager who cooks, serves, and collects the money. Clock Tower Circle. Inexpensive.

Bierstube: Karl Leinz from Mainz runs a small cafe that serves Thai dishes prepared by his wife and German specialties from sauerkraut to *weisswurst*. A popular spot for local expatriates. Karl also runs a trekking agency and has motorcycles for rent. 897 Paholyothin Road. Moderate.

French's: Big buffalo steaks and cold beer are served in this cozy cafe on restaurant row. Chet Yot Road. Moderate.

Baitong Cafe: Australians Ken Jones and Ray Sawyer operate the popular restaurant just opposite the Wang Come Hotel. 869 Pemawipat Road. Moderate.

Napoli Pizza: Best Italian dishes and pizzas in Chiang Rai are served in the expatriate favorite just up from the night market. 595 Paholyothin Road. Moderate.

Getting There

Buses from Chiang Mai's Arcade Bus Terminal take either the direct three-hour route on the new highway or the old five-hour route via Lampang. Check carefully. Green buses leave every 30 minutes from the Nawarat Bridge terminal.

MAE SALONG (SANTIKHIRI)

Mae Salong is a precariously situated Chinese village populated by descendants of the Kuomintang Nationalist Army (93rd Regiment), who fled China after their defeat and the Communist takeover in 1949. Initially welcomed by the Thai government as protective forces against Chinese and warlord aggression, they soon took up opium cultivation and smuggling. Drug warlord Khun Sa made his base in the region at Ban Hin Taek (now Ban Thoed Thai) until the early 1980s, when he was routed by the Thai military. Soon afterward, the Thai government officially renamed the Kuomintang village Santikhiri, a pleasant term which means "Mountain of Peace."

Mae Salong today is a sleepy—and often cold—place where Mandarin is still spoken by the older residents and homes remain guarded by ancient protective talismans.

Attractions

Mausoleum: The most striking landmark in Mae Salong is the mausoleum of General Duan Xi Wen, the former chief of staff of China's 93rd Regiment who led 2,000 Chinese Kuomintang soldiers and their families into Thailand.

Morning Market: A lively hilltribe market is held at the west end of town past the school in the mornings between 0500 and 0800.

THE OPIUM TRAIL

In Homer's *Odyssey,* Helen of Troy mixes a potion "to quiet all pain and strife, and bring forgetfulness of every ill." Thomas De Quincey, author of *Confessions of an English Opium Eater,* tells how he experienced music like perfume and ecstasies of divine enjoyment, living a hundred years in one night. Southeast Asia is the world's largest source of illicit opium, producing an estimated 1,000-2,000 tons annually from Burma, Laos, and northern Thailand. The opium trail begins in the early spring as farmers scour the countryside looking for highly alkaline soils best suited for cultivation. Some say the sweeter taste of limestone soil can actually be recognized by the discriminating palate! Fields are cleared of standing trees by a spectacular burnoff, and planting begins in September after the tree ash has dissolved into natural fertilizers. The soil is chopped, turned, and strewn with select poppy seeds. By January, bright red and white flowers appear, blossom, and then drop away to reveal an egg-shaped bulb filled with resinous opium. The bulb is scored (like a Vermont maple or Malay rubber tree) with a three-bladed knife, and the milky sap then rises to the surface before turning into brownish-black droplets. Tribeswomen return the following morning to scrape the bulb and deposit the residue into a cup hanging around their necks. The sticky gum is then packed into banana leaves, tied into bundles, and sold to Chinese middlemen who refine it to morphine or heroin and export it to Western countries. The upward spiral of its value is amazing: one kilo of raw opium worth only US$200 in Burma brings US$250,000 as heroin in the west.

Road to Thaton: A wonderful dirt road winds past the school and the morning market and continues 48 km down to Thaton on the banks of the Kok River.

Trekking: Mae Salong is an excellent place to begin self-guided treks to nearby hilltribe villages. Rough but adequate maps of the region can be picked up from Rainbow, Mae Salong, and Shin Shane guesthouses.

Accommodations

Mae Salong Guesthouse: Up the hill and on the left is a small guesthouse (tel. 053-712962) with trekking information, a fading but useful map posted on the wall, and horseback tours to nearby villages. Rooms cost 80-120B with hot showers outside the compound.

Shin Shane Guesthouse: Another barebones guesthouse just off the main road in an old wooden Chinese home. 50-80B.

Rainbow Guesthouse: A rudimentary spot with views from the cafe and a solitary room with three beds. 40-60B.

Mae Salong Villa: Two km down the road is a medium-quality place with an elevated restaurant and comfortable rooms equipped with hot showers. Highway 1234, tel. (053) 713444, 400-600B.

Mae Salong Resort: The best hotel in town is wonderfully located up a steep road with views over the entire valley. Popular with visiting Chinese and Thais. Mae Chan, tel. (053) 713400, fax (053) 714047, 400-600B.

Transportation

Mae Salong lies 36 km west of Pha Sang (Basang or Pasang) on top of Doi Mae Salong, 1,418 meters above sea level. From Chiang Rai, hire a motorcycle or take the green bus to Pha Sang, three km beyond Mae Chan, from where minibuses continue up the winding road to Mae Salong. Minitrucks from Pha Sang run from 0800 to 1700 and cost 40B up, 30B down.

CHIANG SAEN

The once-powerful city of Chiang Saen is one of Thailand's oldest and most historic towns. Founded in the 10th century by Thai commanders as the first independent principality in northern Thailand, Chiang Saen was later destroyed by Khmer forces but re-established by King Mengrai in 1259. It was then abandoned in favor of Chiang Mai but revived in the 14th century by Mengrai's grandson, a devout Buddhist who constructed most of the existing *stupas* and *chedis.* Today, over 100 monuments in varying states of collapse and restoration bear witness to the city's turbulent history. None compare with those in Sukothai or Ayuthaya, but the sleepy atmosphere and outstanding location make Chiang Saen a fine spot to relax for a few days.

The Golden Triangle loop is best done counterclockwise (Chiang Rai-Chiang Saen-Mae Sai-Mae Chan-Chiang Rai) to allow sufficient time in Chiang Saen. Minibuses to Sop Ruak leave from the Sala Thai Restaurant. Boat journeys on the Mekong are another possibility; ask at guesthouses.

Attractions

Chiang Saen offers a great little museum and several restored temples that bear witness to the city's turbulent history. None compare with those in Sukothai or Ayuthaya, but they are worth a quick look to help pass the day.

Chiang Saen National Museum: This museum, on the main road near the old west gate, provides an excellent introduction to the handicrafts, carvings, and splendid Buddhas of the Chiang Saen Period, considered among the most beautiful in Thailand.

Wat Chedi Luang: Behind the museum towers an immense 58-meter octagonal *chedi* (spelled Wat Jadeeloung on the sign) perhaps constructed in 1331 by King Saen Phu but reconstructed in 1551 shortly before the Burmese seized Chiang Saen.

Wat Pasak: Beyond the reconstructed walls of ancient Chiang Saen lies the city's oldest surviving *chedi*, constructed in 1295 and a testament to the importance of the valley before the rise of Chiang Mai and the Lanna kingdom.

Wat Prathat Chom Kitti: Two km northwest of town, on a hill with good views over the Mekong River, Wat Prathat Chom Kitti and the small ruined *chedi* of Wat Chom Chang are old monuments which scholars believe also predate the founding of Chiang Saen.

Tobacco Kilns: The rich soil and climatic conditions of Chiang Saen have long made the region a principal source of Virginia tobacco and temperate vegetables such as cabbages and tomatoes. Some of the most interesting sights near Chiang Saen are the tobacco kilns northwest of town on the road to the Golden Triangle. Visitors are welcome to wander through the yards and inspect the smoking kilns kept fired with prodigious amounts of coal.

Wat Prathat Pha Ngao: One of the most awesome and mysterious Buddha images in Thailand is displayed inside a temple 4.2 km east of Chiang Saen on the road to Chiang Khong, an amazing image that has rarely been mentioned in travel literature on Thailand.

Accommodations

Chiang Saen offers several basic but relaxing guesthouses on the banks of the Mekong River. Mid-level guesthouses are now appearing as the focus slowly shifts from budget to better-quality digs.

Lanna Guesthouse: One of the most popular spots in Chiang Saen appears rudimentary at first glance, but the funky surroundings seem absolutely perfect in such a laid-back town. A friendly and fun place to idle away a few days. 39 Rimkhong Rd., 40-100B.

Chiang Saen Guesthouse: Not much atmosphere, though the rooms are fairly clean and manager Chan Chai is friendly. Good central location. 45 Rimkhong Rd., 40-100B.

Siam Guesthouse: An old and run-down dive with three bungalows crammed together. 294 Rimkhong Rd., 60-80B.

Gin Guesthouse: Two km west of town is a wonderful place with A-frame chalets facing grassy lawns and an inner orchard filled with lychee and mango trees. 60-350B.

Transportation

Buses from Chiang Rai to Chiang Saen take about an hour and pass through countryside where villagers still harvest rice without the use of machinery. Chiang Saen can also be reached by minitrucks from Mae Sai. *Songtao* service to the Golden Triangle is sporadic and not as reliable as a rented motorcycle or bicycle. Minitrucks to Chiang Khong leave in the mornings from the market along the river.

SOP RUAK

Thailand's notorious Golden Triangle is centered at Sop Ruak, a haphazard collection of teetering guesthouses, simple restaurants, and souvenir stalls on the banks of the Mekong River. The actual intersection of Thailand, Laos, and Burma is conveniently framed by a modern signpost—worth a photo for friends back home. Although the mysterious scenery encourages fantasies about drug smugglers and opium warlords, modern Sop Ruak is more popular with tour groups than armed terrorists.

Wat Pu Kao, up a winding dirt road to the rear, boasts an impressive outdoor Buddha and excellent views over the river.

Inexpensive but extremely rudimentary accommodations are available at Fung Kong, BUA, Sea Wan, and Golden Triangle adjacent to the memorial. Golden Lodge has more luxurious rooms, but no matter where you stay, beware of drug setups and police raids! Cantilevered restaurants in the one-horse town serve riverfish, soups, Cokes, and prodigious amounts of Mekong. Sop Ruak is nine km from Chiang Saen and can be reached by rented bicycle or minitruck from the Sala Thai Restaurant. From Mae Sai, charter a minitruck.

MAE SAI

Mae Sai, 891 km from Bangkok, is the northernmost town in Thailand and the final stop before crossing the Mae Sai River into Burma. Mae Sai claims a mysterious location, but it's hardly more than a nondescript town of concrete shophouses, video stores, souvenir shops, and Chinese restaurants with little appeal except for the bridge to Burma and views from Wat Doi Wao.

Attractions

The Bridge: The border crossing into Burma (the sign says "MAYANMA") is where Thai citizens arrive searching for Chinese goods, sweet orange wine, and Burmese cheroots, while Burmese from Tha Khi Lek and Kengtung (100 km north) cross the bridge for shaving blades, pens, and Western medicines—a strange collision of cultures. Westerners can now cross the bridge, obtain a Burmese visa in Tha Khi Lek, and continue by truck or jeep to Kengtung—one of the newest travel destinations in Southeast Asia. More details in the Burma chapter.

Wat Prathat Doi Wao: A long flight of over 200 steps and a *naga*-flanked balustrade lead up a small hill with views of white pagodas, a Chinese cemetery, and the tin roofs of Tha Khi Lek inside Burma.

Guesthouses

Most visitors spend a few hours at the bridge and perhaps climb the hill for views, then head east to Sop Ruak or the idyllic town of Chiang Saen. If you decide to stay, Mae Sai has several well-placed guesthouses down near the river and a handful of better hotels on the main road.

Mae Sai Guesthouse: The best place to escape the concrete drabness of Mae Sai and relax in a riverside setting is the series of bungalows about one km west of the bridge. A *samlor* costs about 15 *baht*. 688 Wiang Pakam Rd., tel. (053) 732021, 50-200B.

Mae Sai Plaza Guesthouse: A decent place much closer to town but with less atmosphere than the Mae Sai Guesthouse. Some 100 bungalows hang precariously from the cliff which rises sharply from the left side of the road. 386 Sairomjoi Rd., tel. (053) 732230, 80-250B.

Chad Guesthouse: The second-best place in Mae Sai is a favorite of motorcyclists, who can obtain good maps and helpful advice from the Thai-Shan family of owner Khun Chad. Located in a quiet neighborhood about two km southwest of the bridge. Recommended. Soi Wangpan, 50-120B.

Top North Hotel: A 32-room hotel just 100 meters from the bridge. Convenient to reach and popular with mid-level travelers. 306 Paholyothin Rd., tel. (053) 731955, 200-250B fan, 350-450B a/c.

Transportation

Buses to Mae Sai leave every 15 minutes from Chiang Rai and take about 90 minutes. Both buses and minitrucks reach Mae Sai from Chiang Saen and Sop Ruak. Siam First Tours on the main road has nightly a/c buses direct to Bangkok.

THE REMOTE NORTH

CHIANG KHONG

Most travelers return to Chiang Rai from Chiang Saen, but motorcyclists and those intrigued with the more remote destinations in northern Thailand can continue east to the small town of Chiang Khong, located on the banks of the Mekong River and directly opposite the Laotian town of Ban Houei Sai. The chief interest in Chiang Khong is simply watching the river flow from a cafe or the lawn of the Mae Khong Resort.

Accommodations
Ban Tam Mi La Guesthouse: Best choice in town is the small Thai-style guesthouse on the main road near Wat Kao. The owners can help with sightseeing excursions to nearby waterfalls, caves, tribal villages, and the historical sights at Doi Patang. 8/4 Sai Klang Rd., 40-80B.

Mae Khong Resort: Great views and a comfortable cafe make this resort a popular, if somewhat expensive, alternative to the Ban Tam Mi La. Sai Klang Rd., 160-350B.

Transportation
Chiang Khong is about 75 km east of Chiang Saen. Minitrucks leave in the morning from the riverside market in Chiang Saen.

PHAYAO

Phayao is a medium-sized town on Hwy. 1 midway between Lampang and Chiang Rai. Though rarely visited by Westerners, Phayao has several worthwhile temples and a magnificent location on the edge of Phayao Lake.

Attractions
Wat Sikhom Kham: The principal temple in Phayao and among the most significant sanctuaries in northern Thailand, Wat Sikhom Kham is highly regarded by scholars for its 400-year-old Buddha image housed inside the central viharn. Outside and on the grounds to the north is another of those bizarre collections of stucco statues so popular in modern Thailand.

Modern Temple: Don't miss the exquisite murals which grace the modern viharn back by the lake. The viharn itself is a masterpiece of architectural design, blessed with great symmetry and a wonderful location on the edge of the lake. Inside the dazzling viharn are some of the finest modern murals in all of Thailand, designed and painted under the supervision of an extremely talented artist named Angkarn Kalyanaponsga.

Accommodations
Chalermsak Hotel: The cheapest place in town is directly across from the minibus station and very close to the bus terminal. 915 Phahonyothin Rd., tel. (054) 431063, 70-120B fan.

Tharn Thong Hotel: Phayao's largest hotel has 96 rooms with fans or a/c. 55 Donsanam Rd., tel. (054) 431772, 180-220B fan with private bath, 280-360B a/c.

PHRAE

Phrae is a modern provincial capital made prosperous from coal mining and the logging industry. The city once served as a Burmese outpost during their occupation of Thailand and today is known for its temples, which uniquely combine Burmese and Laotian styles.

Attractions
Wat Chom Sawan: The Burmese heritage of Phrae is demonstrated by this Shan-style temple constructed some 80 years ago outside the old city walls.

Wat Sra Bo Kaew: Another Burmese-style temple with a Shan chedi and richly decorated altars inside the modern viharn.

Wat Prabat Ming: Near the center of town, Wat Prabat Ming Muang Vora Viharn features a modern viharn and an 18th-century bot constructed in the Laotian style with sloping columns and a slate-covered roof.

Wat Luang: Chief interest here are the Burmese-style chedi and decorated wooden beams inside the central viharn.

Ban Prathup Teakwood House: Certainly the most curious sight in Phrae is the old teakwood home in Ban Prathup (also called Ban Sao Roi Tan), about one km west of town. Constructed from an almost unbelievable amount of precious wood, the opulent home and private museum is a testament to the breathtaking beauty of teakwood and man's insatiable lust for the precious commodity.

Wat Prathat Choe Hae: Phrae's most famous temple is eight km west of town, about one km beyond the village of Padang, at the top of a teak-clad hill cut by two stairways flanked by Burmese lions and guardian *nagas*. The right-hand stairway leads to a small shrine which houses the highly revered Buddha image of Pra Chao Tan Chai, widely believed to have the power to grant wishes and cure sterility.

Muang Phi (Ghost City): Eighteen km from Phrae, off Hwy. 101 on a side road just before Km 143, is an eerie natural wonder created by soil and wind erosion: surrealistic chimneys, magic mushrooms, or asteroid dwellings . . . depending on your perspective.

Accommodations

Number 4 Guesthouse: Several years ago, the four schoolteachers from Sukothai opened a branch guesthouse in a teakwood home tucked away in a quiet residential neighborhood. They also have motorcycles for rent and can help with visits to Mrabi ("Yellow Leaf") tribal villages. 22 Soi 1 Yantara Kitkosol Rd., 40-80B.

Charoen Road Hotels: The Sri Wattana, Ho Fa, and Thep Wiman hotels all have basic rooms at basic prices. 153 Charoen Muang Rd., tel. (054) 511047, 80-120B.

Nakhorn Phrae Hotel: Western travelers who need a better hotel with standard amenities stay at the Nakhorn Phrae just opposite Thai Airways. The hotel offers tourist information, maps, and guided tours from the *samlor* drivers who hang out at the front door. 69 Rajadamnern Rd., tel. (054) 521901, 220-280B a/c rooms with private bath.

Maeyom Palace Hotel: Phrae's newest and most luxurious hotel is just west of the bus terminal. 181 Yantara Kikosol Rd., tel. (054) 522906, fax (054) 522904, 1100-1600B.

Transportation

Ordinary buses from the Arcade Bus Terminal in Chiang Mai depart for Phrae daily at 0800, 1100, 1500, and 1700. Air-conditioned buses depart at 1000 and 2200. Each service takes about four hours. Train commuters should alight at Den Chai, from where minitrucks shuttle continuously up to Phrae.

NAN

Situated in the most remote region of northern Thailand, Nan ranks high among travelers, who regard it as similar to Chiang Mai of three decades ago. The landscape combines the mountain vistas of Chiang Mai with the bucolic charms of the lazy, brown river which slowly winds to the east.

Attractions

Nan National Museum: An excellent starting point for an exploration of Nan is the centrally located museum, recently opened in a palace (Ho Kham) constructed in 1903 by Prince Phalida.

Wat Chang Kham Vora Viharn: Across from the museum stands a temple and *chedi* constructed in 1547 with elephant buttresses around the perimeter.

Wat Phumin: The finest architectural piece in Nan dates from 1603, with extensive restorations in 1867 and 1991. The temple is chiefly noted for its outstanding murals, which provide a historical study of local society some 100 years ago.

Wat Suan Tan: Highlights include a 40-meter *prang* with a spire of Khmer design and a 15th-century *viharn* which enshrines an important Buddha image named Pra Chao Thong Tip.

Mrabi Hill Tribe: Phrae and Nan both serve as launching points for excursions to the Mrabi tribes, called Phi Thong Luang by the Thais and nicknamed the Spirits of the Yellow Leaves from the color of their temporary leaf huts. The Mrabi are elusive nomadic hunters whose very existence remained mythical until their discovery by a jungle expedition several decades ago.

Accommodations

Kiwi Guesthouse: Nan's first guesthouse is operated by a Kiwi named Peter who provides trekking information, bicycle and motorcycle rentals, and tips on nearby waterfalls and border excursions. Mahawong Rd., tel. (054) 710658, 40-80B.

Sukasem Hotel: A simple Thai hotel conveniently near the bus terminal and across from the night market. 119 Anathat Wararicharad Rd., tel. (054) 710141, 100-160B.

Devaraj Hotel: Nan's best hotel offers large, clean rooms with hot showers, a popular cafe with cabaret singers in the evening, and tourist information. 466 Sumon Devaraj Rd., tel. (054) 710094, 200-250B fan, 200-600B a/c.

Transportation

Nan is 668 km north of Bangkok and 318 km southeast of Chiang Mai. Thai Airways flies once daily from Chiang Mai (400B) and Phitsanulok (425B) via Phrae. Ordinary buses depart from Chiang Mai at 0800, 1100, 1500, and 1700, and take eight hours along the old route via Lampang and Phrae. Air-conditioned buses leave at 1000 and 2200. Buses from Chiang Rai depart at 0930 and take four hours to cover the 270 kilometers.

The nearest train terminus to Nan is at Den Chai, 20 km south of Phrae. Minitrucks and buses from the Den Chai train station head north to Phrae and Nan.

NORTHEASTERN THAILAND

Known as the Issan, northeastern Thailand is a vast and arid limestone plateau bounded by the Mekong River to the north and small mountains to the south and west. An unfortunate combination of sandy soil and overpopulation has brought droughts, floods, poverty, and political discontent to the region. The government has responded with new roads and a concerted effort to sell the area as a tourist destination. The relative lack of historical or cultural attractions and the large distances between points of interest makes this a tough job, though the Issan is unquestionably the most authentic and untouched region in the country. Top draws include dozens of colorful festivals and a rich collection of restored Khmer temples which, taken together, form the finest spectrum of Cambodian architecture in the world. Naturalists will enjoy trekking around Phu Kradung National Park or simply gazing across the Mekong River from Nong Khai. The opening of Laos has dramatically increased tourism—at least on the route from Bangkok to Nong Khai—plus the near-complete absence of Western visitors carries strong appeal to those travelers who enjoy getting off the beaten track and want to find the "real" Thailand.

ROUTES

Several routes are possible depending on your interests and time. Visitors keen on Khmer architecture but with a limited schedule should use Korat as a base for short side trips to the nearby monuments. Visitors with 10-14 days can complete a western loop through Korat, Khon Kaen, Udon Thani, Nong Khai, Chiang Khon, Loei, and Phu Kradung National Park before exiting west to Phitsanulok. This abbreviated loop covers a few Khmer temples and provides a quick look at the Issan. Travelers with over three weeks can circumnavigate the entire region through Korat, Khon Kaen, Udon

Thani, Sakhon Nakhon, That Phanom, Ubon Ratchathani, and Surin.

KHAO YAI NATIONAL PARK

Thailand's most popular national park, south of Pak Chom and 200 km northeast of Bangkok, is a world of rich and diverse flora, from evergreen and rainforest to *lalang* and rolling hills of tropical grasslands. A small visitor center a few kilometers north of the closed Khao Yai Motorlodge offers some haphazard but informative displays on local wildlife and hiking trails.

Attractions
Waterfalls: Hiking trails starting from the visitor center lead to several waterfalls and limestone caves. Most are difficult to find and best reached with private vehicles or tours organized by the park or a private company such as Jungle Adventures in Pak Chom.

Hiking Trails: A guide distributed at the headquarters describes 12 hiking trails originally made by wild elephants. Trails near the visitor center are in good condition, but distant trails are often buried under wild vegetation and difficult to follow.

Wildlife: Wildlife inside the 2,168-square-km park, such as wild elephants and birds such as hornbills, are extremely shy and rarely seen. Best bets are "Night Shining" truck drives organized by the motor lodge.

Tours
Park Tours: Day tours sponsored by park rangers to various waterfalls and viewpoints leave daily around 0900 and 1300 from the visitor center.

Jungle Adventures: As of this writing, only one private company organizes comprehensive tours for Westerners. Jungle Adventures (tel. 044-312877) at 752/11 Kongvaksin Rd. Soi 3 in Pak Chom sponsors 36-hour tours to various spots inside the park such as Buddhist caves, bat caves, three waterfalls, viewpoints, and a rainforest jungle, and offers a night safari. Tours cost 700B including breakfast, guide services, and guesthouse accommodations in Pak Chom. Call first to verify if they are still in business.

Accommodations

Juldis Khao Yai Resort: A private corporation operates an expensive set of luxurious chalets fixed with facilities such as tennis courts and a swimming pool and offers animal-spotting tours. 54 Mu 4 Dhanarat Rd., Bangkok tel. (02) 255-4960, fax (02) 255-2460, 1500-2000B.

Jungle Adventures Guesthouse: The small private tour operator in Pak Chom operates a small guesthouse in an alley due south of the stoplight. 752/11 Kongvaksin Rd. Soi 3, Pak Chom, tel. (044) 312877, 60-150B.

Getting There

Khao Yai is 200 km northeast of Bangkok on the road to Nakhon Ratchasima. Buses from Bangkok's Northern Bus Terminal to Pak Chom take three or four hours on the Friendship Highway, constructed during the Vietnam War by the Americans. Note the changes: the Khao Yai region has gone from untamed wilderness to condo/golf course hell in just 10 years.

The turnoff to Khao Yai is five km before Pak Chom. Since only limited bus service is available from Pak Chom, independent travelers should ask the bus driver to stop at the small Khao Yai signpost on the right side of the road and then wait for a minitruck or hitchhike up to the park.

KORAT (NAKHON RATCHASIMA)

Korat, officially called Nakhon Ratchasima, is the region's largest city and gateway to the northeast. The modern town has little charm, but it's an ideal base from which to explore the nearby Khmer ruins and rest up after a long bus or train ride from Bangkok. Korat was established during the reign of King Narai, but its heyday was during the early '70s when it served as a major base for U.S. forces assigned to the Vietnamese conflict. Massage parlors, racy nightclubs, and Turkish baths are the most telling legacies.

The TAT office is inconveniently located on Mukmontri Road at the extreme west end of town, three km west of the train station. Take any local bus going in that direction. Buses from Bangkok's Northern Bus Terminal take three hours; trains from Hualampong Station take five. Bangkok Airways serves Korat three times daily with 35-minute flights. Buses from Korat to Pimai, Khao Yai National Park, Surin, and all other northeastern towns leave from the terminal on Atsadat Road. Korat made international news in August 1993 when the Royal Plaza Hotel suddenly collapsed, killing almost 90 people.

Attractions

Khunying Mo Statue: Modern Korat spreads around a statue honoring Thao Suranari, the national heroine who in 1826 convinced Korat ladies to seduce and then murder invading Laotian soldiers. Complete with a strange but once-fashionable haircut, her highly revered image is a constant source of veneration; stages for itinerant musicians and local dancers are nearby.

Korat Museum: A small branch of the National Museum which displays Khmer artifacts and prehistoric earthenware is located in the compound of Wat Suthachanda.

Nightclubs: Korat's most dubious attractions are the enormous nightclubs and massage parlors left over from the Vietnam War era.

Pakthongchai: Thailand's best-quality silk is produced in the silk-weaving village of Pakthongchai, some 30 km south of Korat.

Budget Accommodations

Korat Doctor's Guesthouse: Dr. Sunan's hostel is Korat's first spot geared for backpackers rather than tourists. The good doctor of Bangkok and his sister Sue operate one of the friendliest places in the northeast, providing information on tours to nearby Khmer monuments, motorcycle rentals, laundry service, and transportation schedules. 78 Sueb Siri Rd. Soi 4, tel. (044) 255846, 50-120B.

Siri Hotel: Korat's most memorable hotel/pub is constantly filled with budget travelers, Vietnam vets, foreign-service employees, and American GIs doing temporary duty at the nearby Thai airbase. The downstairs VFW restaurant has great Western food, sizzling T-bone steaks, and ice-cold beer—the best place to hang out and throw darts in Korat. 167 Poklang, tel. (044) 242831, 80-250B.

Moderate Accommodations

Korat Hotel: Popular with group tours, this old hotel features a nightclub and a massage parlor that roar on weekends. 191 Atsadang, tel. (044) 242260, 200-250B fan, 300-450B a/c.

Klang Plaza Hotel: Tourism came of age in Korat with the 1992 opening of several new deluxe hotels including the Klang Plaza, the Sheraton, and Dusit Inn. Klang Plaza has the best location of the three, being only a few blocks from city center. Chomsurang Rd., tel. (044) 254998, 1600-2400B.

Restaurants

Night Market: Food stalls are plentiful in the night market on Manat Rd. just north of the Chomsurang Hotel and in the day market just west of the Thao Suranari Statue. Try the fresh fruit shakes and point-and-order food stalls.

VFW Cafe: Certainly the most curious restaurant in the northeast is the small, crowded cafe on the ground floor of the Siri Hotel. As the name implies, the cafe serves as headquarters for the Veterans of Foreign Wars (VFW) and is the gathering point for dozens of American veterans who served in the Vietnam conflict and then retired here in Korat. The a/c cafe resembles an American truck stop and serves good burgers, beer, and T-bone steaks in three sizes. Recommended for a flashback to the sixties. Inexpensive.

Transportation

Korat is 256 km northeast of Bangkok. Thai Airway flies four times weekly from Bangkok for 650B. Ordinary and a/c buses from the Northern Bus Terminal in Bangkok leave every 15 minutes and take four hours to reach Korat. Thirteen trains a day depart from Hualampong Train Station in Bangkok. Most convenient are the rapid trains at 0615 and 0650, express at 0820, and ordinary diesels at 0910, 1105, 1145, and 2225.

Korat has an ordinary bus terminal in Burin Lane near the First Hotel and Erawan Hospital, and an a/c bus terminal on the Friendship Hwy. (Mittrapap Road) about 500 meters north of town. The ordinary terminal has buses to nearby sights such as Ban Don Kwian and Phimai, plus major towns in the northeast such as Udon Thai and Nong Khai. Bus Terminal II on Friendship Hwy. serves all major towns in the northeast.

KHON KAEN

Khon Kaen, 449 km from Bangkok and strategically located at the intersection of Friendship Hwy. and National Rd. 12, is an important cross-

---

FESTIVALS OF THE NORTHEAST

Northeast festivals are some of the most colorful, authentic, and lively in the country. A perfect visit would include at least one of the following events. The Bangkok TAT has a complete list with exact dates.

Yasothon Rocket Festival: Issan Thais fire homemade rockets into the clouds during the dry season to bring rain and ensure a bountiful harvest. The Yasothon Festival, Thailand's most spectacular pyrotechnic display, begins on Saturday morning with a parade of enormous rockets elaborately decorated with *nagas,* traditional Thai orchestras, and lovely *serong* dancers. Rockets are launched on Sunday; duds are dumped in mudholes. Second weekend of May.

Ubon Candle Festival: The commencement of Thai rains retreat for young monks (*phansa*) is celebrated in Ubon Ratchathani by over 4,000 participants who haul enormous wax candles carved with *garudas,* elephants, and heroes from Thai mythology. A Miss Candlelight pageant is also held. Late June or early July.

Sakhon Nakhon Wax Temple Festival: Large and elaborate beeswax temples are paraded to honor ancestors and the Buddha. Full moon of the 11th lunar month, often mid-October.

Nakhon Phanom Boat Races: Rainy season ends with dozens of boats, shaped like mythological *nagas,* furiously paddled by teams of 40 men and women. Pimai sponsors races on a smaller scale.

Surin Elephant Round-up: One of the most popular and highly promoted festivals in Thailand. The big day starts with an elephant round-up using lassos and a well-trained female as bait and continues with elephant races, dances, a tug-of-war between one elephant and 70 men (guess who wins), and hilarious elephant soccer matches. Festivities end with a colorful procession of pachyderms and mahouts dressed in 17th-century costume. Tours organized by Bangkok travel agents should be booked well in advance. Third weekend in November.

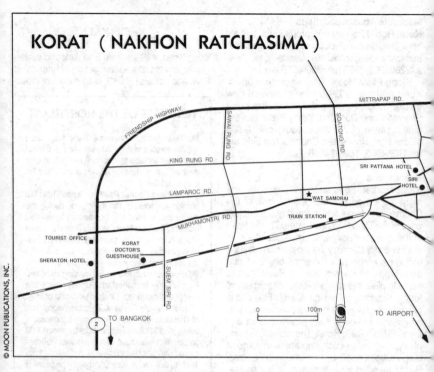

KORAT (NAKHON RATCHASIMA)

MITTRAPAP RD.

FRIENDSHIP HIGHWAY

SAWAI RUNG RD.

SOATONG RD.

KING RUNG RD.

SRI PATTANA HOTEL

SIRI HOTEL

LAMPAROC RD.

★ WAT SAMORAI

MUKHAMONTRI RD.

TRAIN STATION

TOURIST OFFICE

KORAT DOCTOR'S GUESTHOUSE

SHERATON HOTEL

SUEM SIRI RD.

2 TO BANGKOK

0   100m

TO AIRPORT

© MOON PUBLICATIONS, INC.

roads and gateway for visitors arriving from Korat, Phitsanulok, and northern Thailand.

A TAT office opened several years ago in the municipal offices in the north section of Khon Kaen. The December Silk and Friendship Festival features silk displays, cultural performances, and the crowning of Miss Silk.

Attractions

Khon Kaen National Museum: The leading attraction in Khon Kaen offers a small but high-quality collection of arts, with special emphasis on the Dvaravati Period and Ban Chiang artifacts. The museum is open Tues.-Sun. 0900-1700.

Khon Kaen Silk: The finest silk in Thailand is produced near Korat, in Chaiyaphum, and in Chonnabot, a small *mut mee* silk-weaving village 56 km southwest of Khon Kaen. Several shops in town offer silks and handicrafts, but the best selection is found at the Prathamakant Handicraft Center (tel. 043/224736, fax 043/

224080) at 79 Ruenrom Rd., just one block east of the train station.

Accommodations

All accommodations are within walking distance or a short *songtao* ride from the bus station. Train passengers can take the yellow minitruck which shuttles into town.

Sansumran Hotel: Behind the funky green wooden exterior is a popular and conveniently located hotel with rooms arranged left and right off the central corridor. 55-59 Klang Muang Rd., tel. (043) 239611, 80-120B.

Suksawad Hotel: Another old wooden place with rooms in various price ranges. Suksawad is well located in a quiet alley, and the managers seem friendly if somewhat disorganized. 2 Klang Muang Rd., no phone, 60-120B.

Roma Hotel: The old favorite has been renovated and improved with a new lobby, elevators, and reconditioned rooms. Good value for middle-priced travelers. 50 Klang Muang

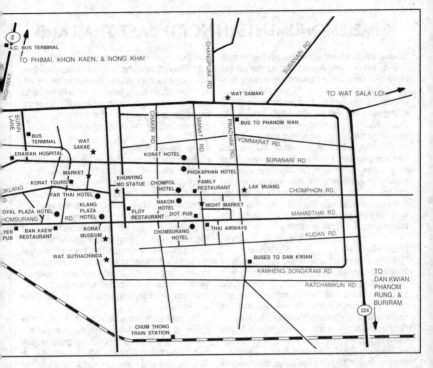

Rd., tel. (043) 236276, 140-200B fan, 280-380B a/c.

Phu Inn: Tucked away in a small alley near the central market is a cozy, clean, and modern hotel with coffee shop, business services, and 98 a/c rooms. 26-34 Sathid Juthithum Rd., tel. (043) 243174, 500-750B.

Kosa Rama Hotel: Of the three big hotels in Khon Kaen—the Kosa Rama, the Kaen Inn, and the Khon Kaen—the Kosa is probably in the best shape, with a decent coffee shop, a popular disco, a postage-stamp swimming pool, and acceptable furnishings in the a/c rooms. 250 Srichan Rd., tel. (043) 225014, 650-750B.

Transportation

Khon Kaen is 449 km northeast of Bangkok, 190 km north of Korat, and 115 km south of Udon Thani. Thai Airways flies three times daily from Bangkok for 1300B and three times weekly from Chiang Mai for 1400B. Five trains leave daily from Bangkok and take seven hours by express or eight hours on rapid train. Trains depart Korat at 0600, 0823, 1145, 1226, and 1515. Buses leave hourly from the ordinary bus terminal in Korat and take about three hours to reach Khon Kaen.

UDON THANI

This busy commercial center, 560 km northeast of Bangkok, served as home to thousands of American servicemen until 1975 when the base was closed and returned to the Thai government. A legacy of sorts continues, with Western military advisers and diplomatic personnel still stationed here and the massage parlors and nightclubs now popular with Thai businessmen. Tourist information can be picked up at the Charoen Hotel, the Bangkok Bank, the Governor's Office, and the small tourist office just opposite the bus terminal. Udon's train station is two km away; take a trishaw.

KHMER MONUMENTS IN NORTHEAST THAILAND

Southeast Asia's finest Khmer *prasats* (castles) still open to Westerners lie scattered across the dry plains near Korat. Once a powerful empire that controlled Southeast Asia from Angkor to Burma, the Khmers erected dozens of magnificent temples and military fortresses from the 10th to 13th centuries. Although the Hindu-Buddhist monarchy fell to foreign invaders in 1431, their expansive monuments still bear witness to their artistic vision and primeval sense of grandeur. Pimai is an easy day-trip from Korat, but the remainder of the following monuments are widely scattered and difficult to reach without an organized tour. Bangkok's Siam Society and National Museum occasionally sponsor group excursions; day tours can be arranged in Korat through travel agents and first-class hotels.

Prasat Hin Pimai

Thailand's most accessible and best-preserved *prasat hin* (stone castle) is located 46 km north of Korat. Dating from the end of the 11th century, the sandstone complex of Pimai is contemporary with and may have been modeled after Angkor Wat. The complex was magnificently restored by Bernard Groslier, the former director of restoration at Angkor who wisely insisted that stucco work be left in original condition. Bravo! Entrance is through a southern gateway flanked by stone-barred windows—one of the more distinctive features of Khmer architecture. The cruciform central sanctuary with its carved doorways and Ramayana lintels is considered one of Thailand's finest examples of Khmer stonework. As with other prototypes, the central *prang* symbolizes Mount Meru (holy mountain and heavenly city of Brahma), while the seven major levels and 33 lesser tiers of the *prangs* represent the levels of perfection necessary for nirvana. Pimai's perfect symmetry and wealth of sculptural detail make it a must-see for all visitors to the northeast.

The open-air Pimai Museum at the north end of town safeguards many of the more valuable and well-carved lintels. A gigantic banyan tree (*Ficus benjamini*) spreads its branches one km northeast of town. Buses leave Korat hourly. The Pimai Hotel south of the ruins has fan-cooled rooms from 100B.

Prasat Panom Wan

Set in an evocative and tranquil setting 20 km north of Korat, this small but attractive Khmer temple can be visited in conjunction with Pimai. Originally built as a Hindu temple, the 10th-century *panom* (hill) sanctuary follows the standard layout of a courtyard dominated by a central *prang* surrounded by four smaller towers. Direct buses leave from Wat Samakkhi in Korat, or take a Korat-bound bus from Pimai; ask the bus driver to let you off at Ban Long Thong, and then walk or hitch the remaining six kilometers.

Prasat Panom Rung

Perhaps the most striking and complete Khmer temple in Thailand is this 12th-century hilltop monument located 84 km east of Korat. Like most *prasats,* Panom Rung was originally dedicated to Shiva but later converted to Buddhist use after Mahayanism was adopted by Jayavarman VII. Staircases leading up the temple are flanked by ruined *nagas* which, like Chiang Mai's *wat* on Doi Suthep, symbolically transport the visitor from the realm of the earth to the world of the gods. The magnificent location atop a volcanic mountain offers splendid views south to the Cambodian border and traces of the Khmer highway that once connected Angkor with Pimai.

The completion of the 38-million *baht* restoration project in 1988 culminated with the return of the valuable Narai Banthomsin lintel. Apparently stolen by art collectors in the early '60s, spirited away to America, and sold to the Chicago Art Institute, the stone crosspiece was subsequently spotted by an archaeologist who contacted the Thai government. A trade was negotiated for an artifact of equal artistic merit; the lintel now surmounts the main eastern entrance. The remainder of Panom Rung boasts a great deal of remarkably clear and delicate stonework. From Korat, take a bus east to Nang Rong, minibus to Ban Taepek, and then walk or hitch the remaining seven kilometers. All tours include this temple.

Prasat Muang Tam

Although older and less well preserved than Panom Rung, this 10th-century fortress also offers outstanding carvings and intriguing architectural symbolism. Clusters of *nagas* ring the inner ponds (the primordial oceans of Hindu-Buddhist cosmology), while window mullions and delicately carved lintels relate themes from Hindu mythology. Restoration, partially funded by the German government, will be completed by 1994. Prasat Muang Tam is five km southeast of Panom Rung. From Prakon Chai, take

KHMER MONUMENTS IN NORTHEAST THAILAND

a bus southwest and hitchhike eight km from the signpost. Tours from Korat often include this temple.

Prasat Hin Ban Pluang

As with other major Khmer monuments in the Issan, this small but beautiful 11th-century Khmer temple was constructed on the royal road that once connected Angkor with Pimai. Located 30 km south of Surin and four km south of a small town called Prasat.

Prasat Kao Pra Viharn

One of the most spectacular but inaccessible jewels of Khmer architecture appears ready to welcome visitors after a span of nearly three decades. In 1962 the World Court ruled that the famous *prasat* was in Cambodian territory despite the main entrance being located on Thai soil. The disputed ownership and political problems held tourism to a trickle until 1990, when Khao Pra Viharn was finally cleared of land-mines and wire fences and reopened to the public. Constructed between the 11th and 13th centuries, the temple is laid out in a series of courts and *gopura* on a spur of the Dongrek mountain range. Hindu myths are depicted in the rich craftsmanship of the stairways, lintels, and pediments situated on three levels connected by paved stone avenues. Travel agents in Korat can help arrange transportation.

Attractions

Udon Thani: The city's few sights are limited to a popular Weekend Market which runs in the *very* early morning hours and Wat Muchimawat opposite the Technical College.

Ban Chiang: Udon's top draws are the ar-chaeological excavations, pottery, and Bronze-Age artifacts discovered at Ban Chiang, 58 km east of Udon Thani. Among the world's oldest, these important findings have prompted many scholars to rethink Southeast Asian history and challenge the traditional notion that civilization began in the Middle East or China. A small and meager museum open Wednesday-Sunday only displays the *in situ* diggings. Direct buses leave from Udon's terminal; or take any bus east, change at the Ban Chiang turnoff near Nong Han, and continue the remaining five km by trishaw.

Erawan Caves: The stalactite caves of Tham Erawan, 50 km west of Udon, are filled with Buddha images illuminated by electric lights. Take a bus and look for the Tham Erawan sign.

Accommodations

Sri Sawat Hotel: Budget travelers usually stay in this small hotel just up from the clock tower. 123 Prachak Rd., tel. (042) 221560, 60-120B.

Pracha Pakdee Hotel: Across the street is a clean and modern hotel with good-value rooms. 156 Prachak Rd., tel. (042) 221804, 140-160B fan, 240-260B a/c.

Queen Hotel: An older joint that gets the overflow from the Sri Sawat and Pracha Pak-dee. 6 Udon Dusadi Rd., tel. (042) 221451, 100-140B fan, 200-220 a/c.

Charoen Hotel: Tour groups en route to Ban Chiang usually stay at the Charoen, considered the best in town. 549 Pho Sri Rd., tel. (042) 221331, fax (042) 246126, 400-500B in the old wing, 650-750B in the new wing.

NONG KHAI

Nong Khai rates as the most popular destination in the northeast. Superbly located at the terminus of the Friendship Hwy. on the banks of the Mekong River, the small and rather sleepy town is chiefly known as an important link with Laos and the national capital, Vientiane. A highly recommended journey west from Nong Khai to Chiang Khan passes through great landscapes, a culturally diverse environment, and charming towns almost completely unaffected by tourism.

Attractions In Town

The River: A new bridge completed in 1994 with the help of the Australian and Lao governments will probably phase out the boat crossing in Nong Khai, but the riverbank trailhead is still a popular spot at which to enjoy a meal from the cantilevered restaurant.

Wat Po Chai: Tucked away in a back alley east of the bus terminal, Wat Po Chai houses a highly venerated solid-gold statue called Luang

Pho Phra Sai, cast in Laos and brought here from Vientiane by General Chakri.

Wat Khaek: Certainly the most bizarre and memorable temple in northeastern Thailand is the strange Hindu-Buddhist wonderland of Wat Khaek (also called Wat Phuttama Makasamakhom), located four km east of town at the end of a dusty side road, a few hundred meters beyond St. Paul School. Look for the sign marked "Sala Kaeoku."

Attractions Outside Town

Wat Bang Puan: Eighteen km southwest of Nong Khai is a modern Laotian-style *chedi* built by a ruler from Vientiane and reconstructed in 1978 by the Fine Arts Department. Wat Ban is unimpressive aside from several Buddhas displayed under open tin roofs and a small museum filled with wooden figurines. Wat Bang Puan can be reached with a *songtao* to Ban Nong Hong Song and a second minitruck west to the compound.

Wat Prathat Buakok: Far more interesting than Wat Bang Puan is this Laotian stupa and historical park 55 km southwest of Nong Khai.

Ban Phu Historical Park: A dirt road shortly before Wat Buakok leads two km uphill to one of the most curious geological sights in Thailand. An information center at the park entrance shows hiking trails through the bizarre rock formations named after Buddhist legends and ancient folk tales. English-speaking guides are usually on hand. The historical park is 13 km from the town of Ban Phu, which can be reached by *songtao* from either Nong Khai or Si Chiang Mai. A chartered *songtao* will be necessary from Ban Phu, or a chartered *samlor* from Ban Tu.

Across To Laos

Although crossings to Laos are permitted for Thai citizens at Nakhon Phanom, That Phanom, and Mukdahan, the only legal entranceway for Westerners in this region is at Nong Khai. Visas should be obtained whenever possible in advance from the Laotian Embassy in Bangkok. Guesthouses and travel agencies in Nong Khai can sometimes help with border formalities, but entrance regulations change with the seasons. Currently, independent travelers are required to join a group tour, which guarantees a visa and access to the capital city of Vientiane. Travel beyond Vientiane requires additional permits

for each supplemental destination. The best strategy is to first check with travel agencies and guesthouses in Bangkok, especially around Khao San Road.

Accommodations

Mut Mee Guesthouse: Probably the most popular guesthouse in town, Mut Mee is favored for its beautiful outdoor restaurant overlooking the Mekong, excellent meals, and reliable information provided by the management. 1111 Kaeworawut Rd., no phone, 80-150B.

Sawasdee Guesthouse: Nong Khai's newest and cleanest guesthouse provides 16 rooms in a convenient location near the center of town. 402 Meechai Rd., tel. (042) 412502, 80-120B fan, 250-350B a/c.

Nong Khai Grand Hotel: Nong Khai tourism came of age in 1993 with the opening of several luxury hotels that anticipate the 1995 completion of the bridge to Laos. Highway 212, 1600-2400B.

Transportation

Nong Khai is 615 km northeast of Bangkok, 356 km north of Korat, 51 km north of Udon Thani, and 20 km southeast of Vientiane. Trains from Bangkok depart daily at 0615, 1900, and 2030, and take 10-12 hours. Sleepers are available on the 2030 service. Ordinary and a/c buses depart hourly from 0530 to 0800 and 2000 to 2130 from the Northern Bus Terminal in Bangkok.

SI CHIANG MAI

Si Chiang Mai is a thriving commercial center 58 km west of Nong Khai and just across the river from Vientiane. Most of the population are Lao and Vietnamese citizens who fled here after the Communist takeover of Laos and today remain stateless people without passports or land-ownership rights.

Attractions

Top draws include a roaring business in the production of spring-roll wrappers and Wat Aranyabanpot, about 10 km west of town. Temple fans may also want to visit Wat Hin Mak Peng, west of Si Chiang Mai and 30 km before Sang Khom, a peaceful forest monastery known for its rigorous precepts followed by a large community of monks and *mae chis.*

Accommodations

Tim Guesthouse: Several years ago a Swiss citizen named Jean-Daniel Schranz opened a small guesthouse on the riverfront road between Sois 16 and 17. Rimkhong Rd. Soi 16, tel. (042) 451072, 40-120B.

SANG KHOM

The atmosphere improves considerably in the small town of Sang Khom, 63 km west of Nong Khai. Populated by Thais rather than the Laos and Vietnamese, Sang Khom is a useful base from which to visit the region's waterfalls, temples, and caves.

Accommodations

Five guesthouses are on the riverbanks in Sang Khom. All have simple bungalows priced from 40 to 80 baht.

River Huts: First on the right is the deserted yet friendly Sunflower Guesthouse, followed closely by the River Huts, which offers boat trips down the Mekong, bicycle rentals, rough maps, and "lice removal—one *baht* each." Rimkhong Rd., 40-60B.

DD Guesthouse: Probably the best in town, DD features a useful wall map, herbal saunas for 25B, and expert Issan dinners prepared by Mr. Pong. Seven bungalows, but only two face the river. 190 Rimkhong Rd., tel. (042) 412415, 60-80B.

TXK Guesthouse: Sang Khom's original guesthouse has the distinct advantage of being somewhat removed from the other places, which are badly crammed together. TXK is widely known for its excellent communal meals prepared by Mr. Root. Rimkhong Rd., 40-80B.

PAK CHOM

The Lao village of Pak Chom is the prettiest and most laid-back town between Nong Khai and Chiang Khan. Travelers seeking to discover what is most authentic and charming about rural Issan will enjoy a few days gazing at the river and wandering around the surrounding countryside. A wonderful, almost completely untouched destination.

Accommodations

Maekhong Guesthouse: The best place in town has a dozen bamboo bungalows at the end of a dirt trail at the north end of Pak Chom. The locale and atmosphere of the Maekhong will remind you of the Golden Triangle before the arrival of mass tourism. Walk west of town until you reach the small signpost on the right. 40-80B.

Chumpee Guesthouse: The only alternative to the Maekhong is the rather dismal collection of bamboo huts thoughtlessly crammed together near the river two blocks east of the main intersection. 50-80B.

CHIANG KHAN

Chiang Khan is a fairly large town on the banks of the Mekong River. Almost entirely constructed of teakwood homes now covered with a fine patina of red dust, Chiang Khan guarantees a refreshing change from Thai towns created from concrete and cinderblock.

Attractions

River Trips: Guesthouses in Chiang Khan arrange upriver boat trips through sublime scenery to Menam Heuang and the point where the Mekong turns north into Laos.

Kaeng Khut Ku: A large set of rapids and a scenic overlook are located five km east of Chiang Khan at the end of a very long side road. Kaeng Khut Ku can be reached from Chiang Khan by *songtao, tuk tuk,* rented bicycle, or boats chartered from local guesthouses.

Accommodations

Nong Sam Guesthouse: Previously called the Tamarind Guesthouse, the friendliest place in Chiang Khan is operated by a Brit named Rob, his Thai wife Noi, and their two children (Nong and Sam) who look Thai but have the frantic energy levels of Western kids. Chai Khong Rd. Soi 12, no phone, 60-100B.

Nong Ball Guesthouse: Previously called the Nong Sam Guesthouse, Nong Ball is a large and comfortable place that runs a close second to Nong Sam. Chai Khong Rd. Soi 16, no phone, 60-100B.

Transportation

Chiang Khan is 50 km north of Loei and about 160 km west of Nong Khai.

Buses from Nong Khai to Chiang Khan and all other towns on the Mekong leave from the street just beyond the Suzuki dealership. Direct service to Chiang Khan takes about five hours but is available only in the early morning.

LOEI AND VICINITY

Midway between the north and the northeast on the western edge of the Issan plateau, the provincial capital of Loei is an important transit spot for visitors arriving from northern Thailand and a useful base for visiting Phu Kradung National Park.

Attractions

The region's principal sights are the three national parks outside town.

Phu Kradung National Park: This outstanding park, on a sloping plateau 82 km south of Loei, is a high-elevation retreat set with pine trees, tall grasses, six waterfalls, dozens of hiking trails, and fields of springtime azaleas and rhododendrons. The park closes from July through October when monsoon rains reduce the trails to muddy quagmires. The trail begins at the base of the mountain at Ban Si Than, where the Park Service operates an information center with maps, a restaurant, and bungalows. The total distance of about nine km takes four or five hours.

Park headquarters at the summit has a small shop with basic provisions, another restaurant with hot meals, bungalows, tent sites, and maps which describe the 50 kilometers of trails. Visitors should bring warm clothes, extra food, flashlights, candles, and insect repellent. Accommodations include 16 10-man bungalows that cost 500-1500B. Tents cost 50B per night. Bedding and blankets can be hired.

Reservations can be made in Bangkok with the National Park Division of the Forestry Department (tel. 02-271-3737) or with the Forestry Department in Loei (tel. 042-800776) on the main highway inside the provincial offices.

Phu Luang National Park: An 848-square-km wildlife reserve controlled by the Forestry Department to help protect the remaining wildlife.

Accommodations are similar to Phu Kradung's, with group bungalows from 500B and tents on-site for 50B. Reservations can be made at the provincial offices in Loei. Bring food, drink, warm clothes, a flashlight, and candles.

Phu Luang is 26 km south of Loei down Hwy. 201 and then 15 km west from Wang Saphung. Although somewhat closer than Phu Kradung, Phu Luang is more difficult to visit because of its inaccessibility and lack of organized transportation. The easiest option is a tour arranged by the Forestry Department at the Loei Provincial Office.

Tha Li: Another lovely town somewhat similar to Pak Chom is eight km south of the Heuang River in a remote valley about 50 km west of Chiang Khan and 45 km north of Loei.

Dan Sai: About 86 km west of Loei is the small town of Dan Sai, an important junction point chiefly known among the Thais for its strange ghostly procession called Pi Ta Khon ("Dance of the Ghosts").

Lom Sak: Lom Sak is a small town in a fertile valley between the Phang Hoei Mountains to the east and the southern extension of the Luang Prabang Range to the west. Lom Sak is a major transit point for visitors traveling between Phitsanulok and Loei and Khon Kaen.

Accommodations

Muang Loei Guesthouse: Budget travelers usually stay in the guesthouse two blocks east of the bus terminal. Services include bicycle and motorcycle rentals and organized tours to the nearby national parks. Ruamchai Rd., tel. (042) 812302, 50-90B.

Phu Luang Hotel: A good middle-quality hotel with big rooms, private baths, and acceptable cafe. 55 Charoenraj Rd., tel. (042) 811570, fax (042) 812558, 150-200B fan, 250-300B a/c.

Udom Thai Hotel: Loei's most popular hotel is similar to the Phu Luang and King hotels but has perhaps the better location in the center of town. 112 Charoenraj Rd., tel. (042) 811763, 150-200B fan, 250-300B a/c.

Transportation

Loei is 520 km northeast of Bangkok, 344 km north of Korat, and 269 km east of Phitsanulok. Buses leave eight times daily from the Northern Bus Terminal in Bangkok. Loei can also be reached by bus from Phitsanulok via Lom Sak.

THE FAR NORTHEAST

BUNG KHAN AND VICINITY

Highway 212 leaves Nong Khai and continues 135 km east to the small town of Bung Khan, on the Mekong River just opposite the Laotian village of Muang Paksan.

Attractions

Phu Wua Wildlife Park: A small nature park on Phu Wua Mountain, 45 km southeast of town, features several waterfalls, crumbling cliffs, and a small forest *wat*.

Wat Phu Tauk: Formally known as Wat Chedi Kiri Viharn, Wat Phu Tauk (or Phu Tok) is one of the most sacred forest temples in the northeast. It is also among the most spectacular in location, being on a sandstone mountain which soars vertically from the flat dry plains. The complex is 47 km southeast of Bung Khan. Take a bus or minitruck south from Bung Khan 25 km down to Ban Siwilai, from where *songtaos* continue 22 km east on the dirt road to the temple. Visitors can spend the night.

Accommodations

The Santisuk, Somanmit, and Neramit hotels on Prasatchai Rd. in Bung Khan have fan-cooled rooms for 60-100B.

SAKHON NAKHON

Sakhon Nakhon is a provincial center 647 km from Bangkok, on the edge of 32-square-km Nong Han Lake, Thailand's largest natural lake.

Attractions

Wat Chong Chum: Sakhon Nakhon's major religious monument features a modern white-washed Laotian *chedi* that encases a 10th-century Khmer *prang*.

Wat Pa Suthawat: A small temple and modern museum opposite the provincial hall displays the paraphernalia and wax figure of Achaan Man, the fierce meditation master whose intensity is reflected in his lifelike image.

Wat Pa Udom Somphon: Buddhist pilgrims visit this temple to honor and view the religious emblems of Achaan Fan, a *vipassana* master whose life-size wax image is displayed inside the central *viharn*. The temple is three km outside of town.

Phu Phan National Park: Seventeen km southwest of town on Hwy. 213, this 645-square-km nature preserve offers hiking trails, three waterfalls, and forest cover over a vast expanse of remote mountains.

Accommodations

All of the following hotels are within a few blocks of the bus terminal on Raj Pattana Road.

Sirimit Hotel: Two blocks east of the bus terminal. Yuwa Pattana Rd., tel. (042) 711416, 60-100B.

Dusit Hotel: A large hotel on the same road. 1782 Yuwa Pattana Rd., tel. (042) 711198 120-160B fan, 220-280B a/c.

Imperial Hotel: Sakhon Nakhon's best hotel. 1892 Sukkasem Rd., tel. (042) 711119, 200-350B.

Transportation

Sakhon Nakhon is 145 km southeast of Bung Khan, 117 km west of Nakhon Phanom, and 155 km east of Udon Thani. Direct buses are available from Ubon Ratchathani, Nakhon Phanom, That Phanom, Kalasin, Korat, and Bangkok.

NAKHON PHANOM

Nakhon Phanom is set along the banks of the Mekong River, across from the small Laotian town of Muang Ta Kaek (Muang Khammouan). Attractions in town include the modern murals inside Wat Sri Thep—and simply gazing across the river into Laos.

Accommodations

River Inn Hotel: Probably the best budget hotel in town and the only decent place on the river features a terrace restaurant with good food and views into Laos. 137 Sunthon Wichit Rd., tel. (042) 511305, 80-150B.

First Hotel: A good alternative to the River Inn is provided by the large hotel across from the clock tower and close to the river and the immigration office. 370 Si Thep Rd., tel. (042) 511253, 80-120B fan, 220-250B a/c.

THAT PHANOM

That Phanom, a small town on the banks of the Mekong River midway between Nakhon Phanom and Mukdahan, is a major pilgrimage site and home to the most sacred religious monument in the northeast.

Attractions
Wat Prathat That Phanom: Highly venerated by both Thai and Laotian citizens, the Laotian-style *chedi* of That Phanom forms the talismanic symbol of the Issan people and a source of magical power for the residents of Laos. Disaster struck in 1975 when the principal tower collapsed after heavy rains, but local authorities have since reconstructed the monument.

Renu Phanom: Renu Phanom is a small village renowned for the weaving of cottons, silk fabrics, and a rare version of Thai *ikat*. The turnoff to Renu Phanom is 12 km north of That Phanom and 44 km south of Nakhon Phanom.

Accommodations
Niyana Guesthouse: Lovely and vivacious Niyana operates a popular guesthouse with kitchen facilities, a garden, and information on boat trips for travelers. 73 Weteshawrachon Rd., no phone, 50-100B.

Hotels: Chai Von Hotel at Phanom Phanarak Rd. has 20 fan-cooled rooms for 70-120B. Saeng Thong Hotel, on the same street but after a right turn through the archway, has similar facilities at identical prices.

Transportation
That Phanom is 52 km south of Nakhon Phanom and 225 km north of Ubon Ratchathani. Buses and *songtaos* from the intersection near the Nakhon Phanom Hotel in Nakhon Phanom take about 90 minutes to reach the *chedi* in That Phanom. Buses from the terminal in Ubon Ratchathani to Nakhon Pathom pass through That Phanom.

YASOTHON

Yasothon is rarely visited except during the Rocket Festival held in mid-May to celebrate the end of the dry season and ensure heavy rains throughout the region. Book rooms well in advance or join one of the many tours organized by travel agencies in Bangkok.

Accommodations
Yasothon has six small hotels in the center of town on Chang Sanit and Uthai Ramrit roads. Surawet Wattana Hotel (tel. 045-711690) at 128 Chang Sanit Rd. has 30 fan-cooled rooms that cost 80-120B. On the same street you'll find other hotels in the same price range, such as Suk Niran (tel. 045-711196), Serm Siri, and Phan Pricha. Yot Nakhon Hotel (tel. 045-711122) at 141 Uthai Ramrit Rd. is the largest in town and the only place with a/c rooms.

UBON RATCHATHANI

Ubon Ratchathani—often called simply Ubon—is a major destination being positioned as the international gateway to Laos, Cambodia, and Vietnam. Ubon is a major economic center with an international airport, industrial estates, a new university, and major hotels earmarked for both business and leisure visitors. The TAT office (tel. 045-243770) at 264 Kuan Thani Rd. has maps and sponsors weekend tours to the sights near the Mekong River.

Attractions
National Museum: A good overview of the historical development of the lower Issan and a broad selection of Khmer and Thai artifacts are displayed in the 19th-century building once used as the office of the provincial governor.

Wat Supatnaram: Dedicated to the Thammayut sect of Buddhism, Wat Supatnaram on the Moon (Mun) River reflects the complex interaction of religious traditions in Southeast Asia.

Wat Tung Sri Muang: Constructed during the reign (1824-51) of King Rama III, this *wat* is renowned for its Tripitaka library elevated in the middle of a small pond, ancient *mondop*, and erotic wall murals.

Wat Ba Na Muang: Four km northeast of town on the road past the airport, the latest addition to the *wat* scene is this exotic creation covered with dark red glazed tiles and fronted by an eccentric royal barge filled with dozens of red-tiled boatmen.

Wat Nong Pa Pong: This temple served as the residence of a meditation master named Achaan Cha, a disciple of the famous Achaan Man (1870-1949), who is credited as the inspiration for over 40 forest monasteries located throughout the Issan. Achaan Cha died in 1992 after a long illness. Wat Nong Pa Pong can be reached by *songtao* or bus from Ubon, 15 km northwest.

Wat Pa Nanachat: Westerners interested in Buddhism and *vipassana* meditation are advised to visit the forest monastery across the road from Wat Nong Pa Pong. This is a Western-oriented temple with a Canadian abbot, a Japanese vice-abbot, and several dozen European and American monks who speak English. Laypeople are welcome to stay as guests and conduct brief studies of Buddhism and insight meditation.

Accommodations
Ubon has over 20 hotels that charge 80-150B for fan-cooled rooms and 220-350B for a/c rooms with private baths.

Tokyo Hotel: A clean and popular hotel in the center of town two blocks north of the park. 178 Upparat Rd., tel. (045) 241739, 90-140B fan, 220-250B a/c.

Racha Hotel: Somewhat north of city center is a low-priced hotel with both fan and a/c rooms. 149 Chaiyangkun Rd., tel. (045) 254155, 80-140B fan, 220-250B a/c.

Ratchathani Hotel: A very large hotel nicely situated in the center of town across from the tourist office and the National Museum. Probably the best midpriced place in Ubon. 229 Kuan Thani Rd., tel. (045) 254599, 150-200B fan with private bath, 260-340B a/c.

Transportation
Ubon is 629 km northeast of Bangkok and 370 km east of Korat. Thai Airways flies once daily from Bangkok. Ubon is connected by rail with Bangkok via Korat, Buriram, and Surin. Seven trains leave Bangkok daily. An express train with sleepers departs at 2100 and arrives in Ubon the next morning at 0705. Rapid trains without sleepers leave at 0650, 1845, and 2245. Rapid trains leave Korat at 1136 and 2356. The train station is five km southwest of town in the suburb of Warin Chamrun. Take a taxi, *tuk tuk,* or bus.

Buses leave every 15 minutes from the Northern Bus Terminal in Bangkok and take 12 hours to reach Ubon. Air-conditioned buses leave Bangkok from 1900 to 2130. The Ubon Bus Terminal is on Chaiyangkun Rd. about four km north of city center. Take public bus 2 or a *songtao* for 20 *baht*. An a/c bus terminal is on Palo Rungrit Rd., two blocks north of the TAT office.

SURIN AND VICINITY

Most visitors associate Surin with its famed Elephant Fair, held on the third weekend in November. Though the festival is certainly the highlight, Surin is well located near several Khmer temples and serves as a base for visits to an elephant camp, basketry and silk-weaving villages, and, with special permission, a Cambodian refugee camp.

Attractions
Elephant Fair: Perhaps the most internationally famous festival in Thailand, Surin's annual weeklong Elephant Fair is something like the Super Bowl but without the bowl, beer, or football. Tours with transportation and accommodations can be booked through the TAT and several tour operators in Bangkok.

Tha Klang Elephant Village: City ordinances prohibit Surin citizens from keeping elephants as house pets, so most elephants live in Tha Klang, 58 km north of Surin. Overnight homestays can be arranged by Mr. Pirom at Pirom Guesthouse in Surin.

Silk-weaving Villages: Two villages which specialize in traditional silk production and weaving are within 20 km of Surin. Khawao Sinarin, north of Surin on Hwy. 214, and Ban Chanron, east of town on Hwy. 2077, both produce and sell hand-woven silks.

Prasat Sikhoraphum: Thirty km east of Surin near the town of Sikhoraphum is an 11th-century Khmer *prasat* recently restored by the Fine Arts Department. Note the Shiva lintel over the central *prang*.

Prasat Pluang: Twenty km south of Surin near the silk-weaving town of Ban Pluang is another restored *prasat,* constructed in the late 11th century during the reign of King Suriyavoraman I.

Prasat Ta Muen And Muen Tom: Two clusters of recently opened Khmer ruins are exactly on the Thai-Cambodian border, some 55 km due south of Surin and quite close to the ruins at Muang Tam and Phanom Rung. Both ruins are inaccessible by public transportation but can be reached with a private car hired in Surin or Buriram.

Prasat Phanom Rung And Muang Tam: Prasat Phanom Rung is widely considered the most impressive Khmer monument in Thailand. Muang Tam is about nine km southeast of Phanom Rung. Both monuments can be visited on day excursions from Surin or Buriram.

Accommodations

Pirom Guesthouse: The backpackers' hotel scene in Surin improved dramatically several years ago with the opening of this guesthouse, two blocks west of the market and 500 meters from the bus terminal and train station. Mr. Pirom has converted his six-room teakwood house into a very cozy place with the best travel information in the province. 272 Krung Sri Rd., no phone, 60-100B.

Memorial Hotel: A clean and inexpensive hotel well located in the center of town near the temples and restaurants. 186 Lak Muang Rd., tel. (045) 511288, 160-240B fan, 260-340B a/c.

Tarin Hotel: Top hotel in town is the Tarin, a few blocks south of city center. 60 Sirirat Rd., tel. (045) 514281, fax (045) 511580, 800-1200B.

Transportation

Surin is 457 km northeast of Bangkok and 198 km east of Korat. Surin is connected by rail with Bangkok via Korat and Buriram. Seven trains leave Bangkok daily. Buses leave every 15 minutes from the Northern Bus Terminal in Bangkok and take 10 hours to reach Surin.

BURIRAM

Although Buriram lacks any great attractions within the city boundaries, the town can serve as a base for exploring the numerous Khmer monuments located south along the Cambodian border. Archaeologists have identified over 50 *prasats* in Buriram Province, of which almost a dozen have been restored by the Fine Arts Department.

Accommodations

Chai Charoen Hotel: Just opposite the train station is an acceptable spot for an overnight crash. 114 Niwat Rd., tel. (044) 611640, 80-150B.

Thai Hotel: Somewhat better rooms about three blocks from the train station. 38 Romburi Rd., tel. (044) 611112, 120-180B fan, 280-380B a/c.

Buriram Plaza Hotel: The latest and greatest hotel is in the center of town. Buriram-Surin Rd., tel. (044) 411123, 650-900B.

SOUTHERN THAILAND

The long and narrow peninsula of southern Thailand offers a dazzling array of thick jungles, rugged mountains, limestone pinnacles and emerald-blue bays, fishermen and sea gypsies, graceful temples, coral reefs, colorful marinelife, and some of the most spectacular beaches in Southeast Asia. Landscapes, religions, languages, and even the people change as you travel deeper into the south: rice paddies give way to rubber plantations, Muslim mosques outnumber Buddhist temples, even the beaches seem to change . . . they get better!

Southern Thailand's two most popular destinations are the tropical islands of Phuket and Ko Samui. Both have distinct personalities which appeal to slightly different types of travelers. Phuket, the more developed of the two, offers a stunning combination of superb beaches, upscale hotels, outstanding seafood restaurants, sports activities from parasailing to scuba diving, and raunchy nightlife rivaled only by Bangkok's or Pattaya's. Most of the island is highly commercialized but a few beaches are still pristine . . . at least for the moment. Ko Samui is a relatively simple and absolutely beautiful island on the east side of the peninsula. Though rapidly approaching saturation point, the atmosphere remains much less frantic than on Phuket. In fact, deserted beaches in southern Thailand have become much harder to find, but with nearly 2,000 km of coastline and hundreds of untouched islands, a few gems still await discovery.

ROUTES

Most visitors head directly to Phuket or Samui from Bangkok, but travelers intrigued with Thai architecture and painting should visit Petchburi for a recommended four-hour walking tour, described below. Those who prefer a more leisurely approach can also try the family-oriented beach resorts of Hua Hin or Cha Am. One possible route is an early-morning bus to Petchburi for the walking tour, then afternoon bus to Hua Hin. Visitors with limited time can reach Phuket and Samui directly by air. Bangkok Airways flies twice daily between Samui and Phuket. Four rapid and three express trains leave Bangkok daily for Surat Thani, the launching point for ferries over to Samui. Phuket is off the rail line. Advance reservations from Bangkok's Hualampong Station or a travel agent are strongly recommended on all trains going south. Regular and a/c buses leave frequently from Bangkok's Southern Bus Terminal, while private buses can be booked through travel agents.

PETCHBURI

Petchburi (also spelled Phetchburi, Petchaburi, Phetburi, and Petburi!), 126 km south of Bangkok, is a charming town with a half-dozen outstanding temples. All can be easily visited on the four-hour walking tour described below. Much of the city's superb art and architecture reflect its long and rich history. Founded as a Mon city which traded with Europe during the Middle Ages, Petchburi fell to the Khmers in the 12th century, to Sukothai a century later, and to Ayuthaya in 1350. The town is a treasure house of historical artifacts from nearly all possible eras: Mon sculpture unearthed within the ancient city walls; a small but intriguing Khmer temple in a quiet neighborhood; monastery walls gilded with Thailand's finest Ayuthaya-period murals; Wat Mahathat's 19th-century *prang* soaring into the sky; a hilltop palace of neoclassical inspiration. It's difficult to understand why Petchburi has been dropped from many of the recent guides to Thailand and Southeast Asia!

Attractions
Wat Yai Suwannaram: Petchburi's artistic fame is chiefly due to the murals here and at Wat Ko Keo Sutharam. Thai murals typically date from the fall of Ayuthaya in 1767 until about 1910, when royal patronage ended. Those in Ayuthaya were almost completely destroyed by the Burmese; only Petchburi murals survive to illustrate early Thai painting. Among the best are the 17th-century worshipping divinities in the small *bot* of Wat Yai Suwannaram. Most are

PETCHBURI

NOT TO SCALE

© MOON PUBLICATIONS, INC.

chipping and desperately need attention, although the interior door murals are still in good condition. The adjacent wooden *sala,* supported by wooden pillars, is one of Thailand's few surviving examples of this genre.

Wat Borom: This small but attractive temple back toward the railway tracks shows finely plastered roses around the windows and a whitewashed exterior slowly fading into psychedelic patterns.

Wat Trai Lok: A typical monk's quarters complete with TV antennas, sleeping dogs, and a pet monkey in the tree.

Wat Kampang Lang: Three Khmer towers are the oldest structures in Petchburi. Original stucco can still be seen on the back side of the central *prang.* The adjoining *wat* is a wildlife refuge for wild turkeys, roosters, and other unidentifiable birds.

Wat Pra Song: Two unique and rather strange belltowers face the primary *bot.* Al-

though in danger of falling down, the wonderful old monks' quarters to the right are more appealing than the modern replacements to the rear of the courtyard.

Wat Ko Keo Sutharam: Don't miss Petchburi's most famous temple! Some of Thailand's finest, best-preserved, and oldest murals, dated by inscription to 1734, are guarded inside the small *bot.* Side walls of dramatic triangles show scenes from the life of the Buddha and comical figures of Arab merchants, a Jesuit wearing the robes of a Buddhist monk, and other big-nosed *farangs.* Facing the Buddha is a wall of Buddhist cosmology (this scene is usually *behind* the Buddha image), while the posterior wall shows Buddha's victory over the temptations of Mara. Just below Buddha is Torani, the Earth Goddess so impressed by Buddha's willpower that she washed away Mara's evil armies by wringing water from her hair. The superb execution, careful attention to detail, and high degree of originality make these murals among the great achievements of Thai art. Wat Ko Keo Sutharam is located back down a side alley and somewhat difficult to find. Look for the small blue plastic signs. Ask a monk to unlock the door and watch carefully—it's a strange kind of lock.

Wat Mahathat: The enormous white *prang* of Wat Mahathat (Monastery of the Great Relic) dominates tiny Petchburi like a giant rocketship resting on a launch pad. Climb the late-Ayuthayan style *prang* for views over the town. Outside the temple enclosure near the east entrance is a *bot* with impressive Buddha images and patches of remaining murals.

Khao Wang Palace: A steep and ungraded path leads up the hill past fat monkeys to a neoclassical palace constructed in the 19th century by King Mongkut. Outstanding views from the observation platform. Wat Kao Bandait, another beautiful temple with historical significance, is three km west of town at Bandait hill. Of Petchburi's dozen caves filled with Buddhas, stalactites, and *chedis,* the most famous is Khao Luang, two km north of town.

Accommodations

The Chom Klao Hotel on Pongsuriya Road has simple rooms from 60B, but most people stay at the clean Khao Wang Hotel on Rajavithi Road, where modern fan-cooled rooms with private bath cost 100B; a/c rooms from 200B. Day-trippers can store their bags at the train station or in the small office at the bus station. Petchburi, however, is a very pleasant town and a good place to learn something about Thai history, art, and contemporary Thai life.

HUA HIN

Hua Hin, 170 km south of Bangkok on the sunrise side of the gulf, is a mellow, middle-class Thai beach resort favored by families and travelers seeking peace and quiet. The beach is unspectacular and the modern town undistinguished, but the beautiful bay and the picturesque backdrop of green hills make this a fine place to relax for a few days. Early risers can watch fishermen set sail, then walk six km south to a pair of limestone hills for excellent views from the nearby Krilas cliffs. During the day there's little to do but relax, read a book,

wander around the beach, and perhaps visit the quaint building next to the train station which once served as the private waiting room for Thai royalty. Nightlife revolves around seafood dinners and drinks at simple open-air cafes. Popular restaurants are found near the guesthouses on Naretdamri alley, at the fishing piers, and at the night market. One of the area's major attractions is Sam Roi Yot National Park 35 km south, a wonderland of limestone caves, strangely disfigured mountains, and secluded beaches. Tours can be arranged at the travel agency opposite the tourist office, or you can hire a motorcycle at 200B per day from the nearby shop. More information on trekking, local transportation, and train departures is available from the helpful tourist office.

Accommodations

Hua Hin's dozen-plus guesthouses are tucked away in the alleys one block back from the beach. Rooms during the low season and midweek start from 100B, while weekend, holiday, and high-season rates (Oct.-March) are 200-350B.

Beach Road Guesthouses: Sriosrapusin, Europa, and Sunee guesthouses have simple fan-cooled rooms for 150-250B. Cheaper rooms are found in the private homes down the alley at the S.M., M.P., and Pattana Thai-Dutch guesthouses. M.P. Guesthouse features a useful noticeboard and a cozy veranda.

One block north is another narrow alley with several inexpensive guesthouses such as Crocodile, Phuen, and Ban Pak; most charge 100-150B.

Thai Tae Guesthouse: A newer place in a quiet location slightly back from the street. 6 Damnern Kasem Rd., tel. (032) 511906, 150-250B fan, 350-450B a/c.

All Nations Guesthouse: Aussie-run guesthouse with clean rooms and ice-cold beer. 10 Decharnchit Rd., 150-250B.

Subhamitra Hotel: An older six-story hotel with a small pool and clean, large rooms. Away from the action, but a good-value choice. Amnuayasin Rd., tel. (032) 511208, 200-300B fan, 400-500B a/c.

Chat Chai: Another reasonably priced guesthouse, Chat has rooms for 120-250B s and d. 59 Petchkasem Rd., tel. (032) 511034.

Jed Pee Nong Hotel: Very popular spot with small swimming pool and great outdoor cafe.

HUA HIN

4

KLAI KANGWON ROYAL PALACE

TO BANGKOK

PETCHKASEM RD.

NABKEHAS RD.

NAREB DAMRI RD.

GULF OF THAILAND

CHOMSIN RD.

KIWI RESTAURANT

PANACHAI HOTEL

CHAT CHAI HOTEL

SEAFOOD RESTAURANTS

ALL NATIONS GH

DECHARNCHIT RD.

BUS TERMINAL

NIGHT MARKET

POOLSUK RD.

SEA BREEZE HOTEL

HUA HIN GOLF COURSE

SIRI PETCHKASEM HOTEL

A C BUS STOP

RESTAURANTS

MOD HOTEL

SUBHAMITRA HOTEL

BUS STOP

CROCODILE GH

FRESH INN

AMNUAYASIN RD.

LA PROVENCE RESTAURANT

BAN PAK GH

WAT HUA HIN

SUNEE GH

EUROPA GH

MELIA HUA HIN

DAMNERN VITHI RD.

PATTANA THAI - DUTCH GH

ROYAL TRAIN STATION

M.P. GH

BAN BOOSARIN

S.M. GH

K DANG'S GH

CITY BEACH HOTEL

SIRIN HOTEL

RESTAURANTS

DAMNERN KASEM RD.

THAI TAE GH

MARKET

TRAIN STATION

GOLF INN HOTEL

TOURIST OFFICE

GPO

JED PEE NONG HOTEL

GEE GH

SOFITEL CENTRAL HOTEL

TO SURAT THANI & KO SAMUI

4

PATCHARA HOTEL

BAAN SOMBOON HOTEL

0   100m

13/7 Damnern Kasem Rd., tel. (032) 512381, 450-550B.

Sirin Hotel: An attractive and spotlessly clean cantilevered hotel centrally located near the beach and restaurants. Very luxurious. Damnern Kasem Rd., tel. (032) 511150, 950-1200B.

Sofitel Central Hotel: Hua Hin's most famous hotel is the grand old dame constructed in 1921 by Prince Purachtra. Formerly known as the Railway Hotel, the European-style hotel has been completely renovated and redecorated by a French hotel firm. Damnern Kasem Rd., tel. (032) 512021, fax (032) 511014, Bangkok reservations (02) 233-0974, U.S. reservations (800) 221-4542, 3400-6500B.

Royal Garden Resort: Hua Hin's other luxury choice, about two km south of town, is a stunning crescent-shaped, low-rise complex with a pool, tennis courts, and a sports center outfitted with catamarans, Lasers, and sailboards. 107 Petchkasem Rd., tel. (032) 511881, fax (032) 512422, Bangkok reservations (02) 251-8659, 3200-5400B.

PRACHUAP KHIRI KHAN

One of the more delightful and untouristy towns in the northern third of southern Thailand is the unassuming village of Prachuap Khiri Khan, situated on a magnificently arched bay flanked by towering limestone peaks. Prachuap Khiri Khan ("Town Among Mountains") lacks historical monuments, and the beach inside the city limits is disappointing, but the genuine Thai feel and nearby geological attractions make it an excellent stop for visitors with extra time.

Attractions

Khao Chong Krachok: Looming over the northern end of the bay is a limestone buttress called Mirror Tunnel Mountain after an illuminated arch which appears to reflect the sky. Visitors can climb the stairway to enjoy the panoramic views over the bay.

Ao Noi Beach: Fairly clean and white beaches are located both north and south of town. Ao Noi, six km north and reached by mini-trucks heading up Chai Thale Rd., has several small spots such as Ao Noi Beach Bungalows, where a Thai-German couple rents rooms from 450B.

Accommodations

Yutichai Hotel: The first hotel near the train station has decent rooms in a convenient location. 35 Kong Kiat Rd., tel. (032) 611055, 80-140B.

Inthira Hotel: Directly across from the night market is a popular spot with inexpensive rooms. No English sign, but look for the car in the lobby. Phitak Chat Rd., no phone, 60-100B.

Thetsaban Mirror Mountain Bungalows: Facing the bay in the north end of town is a collection of seaside bungalows owned and operated by the city. Suseuk Rd., tel. (032) 611150, 150B double rooms, 400B individual bungalows.

Had Thong Hotel: The newest hotel in Prachuap features a small swimming pool, a comfortable cafe, and well-furnished a/c rooms. 7 Suseuk Rd., tel. (032) 611960, fax (032) 611003, 600-750B.

Transportation

Prachuap Khiri Khan is 252 km south of Bangkok and 82 km south of Hua Hin. Trains from Bangkok's Hualampong Station leave nine times daily from 0900 to 2155. Buses leave regularly from Bangkok's Southern Bus Terminal and from the bus station on Sasong Rd. in Hua Hin.

CHUMPHON

Almost 500 km south of Bangkok and situated on the Kra Isthmus, Chumphon is an extremely drab provincial capital. Chumphon offers little of interest to most visitors, aside from the several fine beaches on the eastern perimeter and scuba diving considered among the finest in Thailand. It also serves as a departure point for boats to Ko Tao, an option which saves heading down to Surat Thani. Chumphon Travel Service (tel. 077-501880) at 66 Thatapao Rd. can help with transportation, hotel reservations, and boats to Ko Tao.

Accommodations

Sri Taifa Hotel: The travelers' favorite is a Chinese hotel with a decent restaurant, balcony views, and 20 fan-cooled rooms. 74 Saladaeng Rd., tel. (077) 511063, 80-160B.

Srivena Hotel: Another budget choice in the center of town. Saladaeng Rd., no phone, 60-90B.

Jansom Chumphon Hotel: The best hotel in town opened in 1991 just down from the large Ocean Shopping Center. Facilities include a restaurant on the lobby floor, a massage parlor, and the Town Disco. 188/65 Saladaeng Rd., tel. (077) 502502, fax (077) 502503, 750-1000B.

WAT SUAN MOK

Wat Suan Mokkhablarama—the Garden of Liberation—is a forest monastery near Chaiya dedicated to the study of *dhamma* and *vipassana* meditation. Today, Wat Suan Mok is the most popular temple in Thailand for Westerners to study Buddhism and traditional forms of Thai meditation.

Both novice and experienced practitioners of *vipassana* are invited to join other Westerners during the 10-day meditation retreats held on the first day of each month. Instruction is provided in English. The daily program includes a 0400 wake-up and meditation session, breakfast, morning lectures on Buddhism, chores around the international center, lunch, private study, afternoon tea, an evening lecture, and a soak in the mineral baths.

Accommodations

The basic fee of 600-800B includes dormitory accommodations, vegetarian meals, and all instruction. Visitors are expected to follow local guidelines such as modest dress and periods of silence.

Transportation

Wat Suan Mok is on Highway 41, about 50 km north of Surat Thani and four km south of the junction to Chaiya. Buses from the main bus terminal in Surat Thani take about 50 minutes to reach the temple entrance. Taxis can be hired from the train station at Phun Phin. Buses and *songtaos* also connect central Chaiya with Suan Mok.

SURAT THANI

Located on the southeastern coast of southern Thailand 644 km from Bangkok, the prosperous port of Surat Thani chiefly serves as a launching point for ferries to Ko Samui, Thailand's third-largest island and one of Southeast Asia's leading tourist destinations.

The Surat Thani TAT office (tel. 077-281828) is inconveniently located at 5 Talad Mai Rd. in the east end of town. An excellent resource for exploring Surat Thani Province and the nearby islands is the *Map of Koh Samui, Koh Tao & Koh Phangan* published by Prannock Witthaya Publications.

Budget Accommodations

Most visitors head directly to Ko Samui, but late arrivals may need to overnight near the train station in Phun Phin or in downtown Surat Thani.

Lipa & Kasem 2 Guesthouses: Adjacent to the bus terminal are several small guesthouses acceptable for an overnight crash. Both have cafes and travel agencies with tickets to Ko Samui, Phuket, and Krabi. 80-140B.

Thai Thani Hotel: Also next to the bus terminal is this sprawling old hotel with amazing wooden furniture on the ground floor and reception facilities on the third floor. 442 Talad Mai Rd., tel. (077) 272977, 160-200B fan, 260-300B a/c.

Bandon Hotel: A very clean hotel entered through a Chinese coffee shop. Recommended. 168 Na Muang Rd., tel. (077) 272167, 100-180B.

Wang Tai Hotel: The best hotel in Surat is inconveniently located south of town near the tourist office but offers a swimming pool, a cabaret nightclub, and a restaurant overlooking the Tapi River. 1 Talad Mai Rd., tel. (077) 273410, fax (077) 281007, 550-650B.

Accommodations In Phun Phin

The train station for Surat Thani is 14 km west in the town of Phun Phin. Except for the very late trains, all arrivals are met by buses which connect directly with the boats to Ko Samui. Late-night arrivals can take a taxi into Surat Thani or stay at one of the guesthouses opposite the train station. Among the choices with rooms from 100B are Tai Fah, Sri Thani, and Kaew Fah guesthouses.

Transportation

Surat Thani is 644 km south of Bangkok and two hours by boat from Ko Samui.

Train: Trains depart nine times daily 0900-2155 from Hualampong Station in Bangkok. The 1630 and 1920 overnight trains with sleepers are recommended, since they arrive in the early morning and allow plenty of time to catch a boat to Ko Samui. Reservations are strongly recommended. The State Railways also sells combination tickets to Ko Samui which include all necessary train, bus, and boat connections.

Trains for Surat Thani terminate 14 km west in Phun Phin. Buses wait for passengers and then connect directly with Ko Samui. Advance reservations for trains departing from Phun Phin can be made at travel agencies on Ko Samui and in Surat Thani at Panipat Tours near the bus terminal.

Bus: Air-conditioned and ordinary buses depart from the Southern Bus Terminal in Thonburi daily 0700-0830 and 1900-2100, arriving in Surat Thani 11 hours later. Private bus companies in Bangkok offer VIP coaches with fewer seats and extra leg room. Most sell all-inclusive packages which include boat transportation to Ko Samui.

Boats To Ko Samui

Boat tickets to Ko Samui can be purchased at **Samui Tours** on Talad Mai Rd. and from slightly pricier **Songserm** agents near the waterfront on Na Muang Road. Boats depart daily

0730-1600 from either Don Sak Pier, 50 km east of Surat, or Khanom, 60 km east. A slow overnight boat departs at midnight from the pier in Surat Thani.

Tickets to Ko Phangan are sold at the office near the pier. The head office of Songserm Travel (tel. 077-272928) at 295 Talad Mai Rd. also sells tickets to Ko Samui and Ko Phangan.

KO SAMUI

Thailand's third largest island, 247 square km, lies in the warm seas of the gulf some 560 km south of Bangkok. With its long beaches of dazzling white sand, aquamarine waters, and sleepy lagoons fringed with palm trees, this tropical retreat has justifiably become one of Southeast Asia's premier beach resorts.

The island was opened up two decades ago by shoestring world travelers who trickled in to construct their simple thatched huts on the deserted beaches. The island's reputation soon attracted Thai and foreign developers who replaced the bamboo huts with middle-priced bungalows and luxury hotels geared strictly for well-heeled tourists. The island is now a major tourist destination with some 500,000 visitors a year and over 240 hotels and bungalows currently lining the beaches.

For better or for worse, Samui is now caught somewhere in the middle between being a backpacker's paradise and an upscale resort with all the glitz, glamour, and problems that plague Pattaya and Phuket. The island's remote location once held overbuilding and commercialization to a tolerable level, but this happy state of affairs ended with the opening of an airport in 1989.

Samui is best visited from January until the monsoons begin in September. Torrential rains often lash the island from October until late December; try Phuket. Accommodations are fully booked during July, August, and Christmas holidays.

ATTRACTIONS

Samui's claims to fame are sandy beaches, clear waters, and a thriving coconut industry, which provides the main occupation of most of Samui's 35,000 residents. At times it seems the entire island is yanking down coconuts with long swaying sticks or burning huge piles of coconut shells! Watch for trained *ling gang* monkeys which deftly climb the palm trees, spin the coconut until it falls to the ground, and then return for their reward. Nearly every part of the coconut is used: flesh for eating, milk for cooking, and fiber for thatching and bed stuffing.

Around The Island
Samui is about 70 km in circumference and can be easily toured in a single day. The following sights are described in counterclockwise order starting from Chaweng Beach. Samui's splendid scenery is best seen by rented car or motorcycle—but first, a word of caution: Motorcycle touring is deceptively dangerous. Far too many Westerners are killing or badly crippling themselves on the two-lane highway that circles the island. Please drive slowly, stay sober, and wear long pants, shoes, and a shirt to prevent sunburn and protect against minor scrapes.

North Coast
Begin your tour with a motorcycle ride along the dirt road which hugs the coast to the magnificent dry-docked fishing boats at Chong Mon Bay—a highly recommended route through fabulous scenery. Samui's famous 12-meter Big Buddha statue, surrounded by meditation huts elevated on stilts, is a few kilometers west. The Boput Beach intersection is marked with a bewildering collection of identical Buddhas neatly arranged before a small temple.

Naton
Ko Samui's main commercial center and primary arrival/departure point is an unappealing hodgepodge of overpriced hotels, restaurants, travel agencies, souvenir shops, banks, and other necessary services such as immigration and police.

West Coast
Hin Lad Waterfalls and bathing pools, two km south of Naton, can be reached with a half-hour hike up a narrow pathway through thick jungle. Motorcyclists might *try* to follow the unmarked

road east from Ban Saket to the top of the mountain. Other west coast bays such as Ta Ling Ngam and Leaen Hin Khom have little of interest aside from their peace and solitude.

South Coast

Na Muang Waterfall and bathing pools (nothing special) lie at the end of a narrow road through durian plantations. Laem Sor Pagoda forms a picturesque setting against the blue waters.

East Coast

Chaweng and Lamai—Ko Samui's two largest and most popular beaches—are located on the east coast. A large and humorously mislabeled sign—"Wonderfull Rock"—shows the way to phallic-shaped formations. Lamai town preserves a small cultural hall filled with old lanterns, gramophones, and agricultural implements used in the coconut industry. Locals sponsor lively buffalo fights during major festivals several times yearly.

Ang Thong Marine National Park

This archipelago of 40 islands west of Ko Samui can only be visited by organized tour. Bring equipment for the outstanding diving, and allow time to climb Uttihayan Hill and swim in the blue lagoon. Accommodations at park headquarters include tents and bungalows.

ACCOMMODATIONS

Ko Samui has a half-dozen beaches in various stages of development and with distinct personalities. Chaweng Beach and Lamai Beach on the east coast are the most popular for good reasons: best sand, longest uninterrupted terrain, and ideal climate. North-coast beaches such as Bophut and Menam are quieter and less expensive, but the sand isn't as white or as plentiful. Robinson Crusoe types might check the isolated bungalows on the west and south coasts.

Each beach appeals to different types of travelers, depending on their finances and desired ambience. One possible plan of action is to spend your first few days on Chaweng or Lamai, then move to a more isolated beach if you crave solitude and want to escape the beer gardens, discos, and pick-up bars.

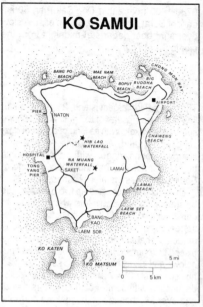

Ko Samui beaches offer all ranges of accommodations, from cheap shacks under 100B to luxurious hotels with landscaped gardens and swimming pools. Basic wooden huts with electricity, mosquito nets, and common bath charge 60-150B. Most of these original hippie huts have been torn down and replaced with better bungalows with tiled rooms, verandas, private baths, and comfortable mattresses. These cost 300-600B during the slow season, and generally double in the high summer months and Christmas holidays. Many of these middle-priced bungalows represent extraordinary value when you consider the comfort level and fabulous beach just a few steps away. Air-conditioned bungalows with fancy restaurants and manicured gardens cost 800-1500B, while luxury hotels over 2000B per night are now commonplace on most beaches.

Nathon

Few travelers stay in Nathon except to catch an early morning boat back to Surat Thani. However, most of the island's services are located here.

Services: Banks in Nathon are open daily 0800-1600, with outside exchange facilities open until 2200. The Post and Telecommunications office (tel. 077-421013) at the northern end of the waterfront road handles mail, post restante, faxes, telegrams, and money transfers. The GPO is open Mon.-Fri. 0830-1630 and weekends 0830-1200. The Overseas Call Office upstairs from the post office is open Mon.-Fri. 0700-2200, and weekends 0830-1200. Phone calls can also be made from larger hotels throughout the island and from metered phones in local markets and pharmacies. The cheapest place is the office in Nathon.

Tourist visas can be extended for an additional 30 days at the immigration office on the north end of town. Bangkok Airways (tel. 077-421196) on Beach Rd. distributes a timetable for flights to Bangkok (six times daily) and Phuket (once daily at 1230).

Travel Agents: Songserm Travel Center (tel. 077-421228) on the beachfront road is the largest outlet in town for boats to Surat Thani and Ko Phangan. World Travel Service (tel. 077-421475) is another major tour operator that can book transportation, confirm airline tickets, and book rooms at Samui hotels if you arrive without reservations. Phantip Travel (tel. 077-272230) sells car-ferry tickets to Surat Thani.

Town Guesthouse: Two small and inexpensive guesthouses are in the alley one block back from the pier. 140-180B.

Chao Ko Bungalows: North of town past the post office is a quiet operation with 20 comfortable if somewhat expensive bungalows. North Nathon, tel. (077) 421214, 300-600B.

Seaside Palace Hotel: The best place in town is overpriced but conveniently near the pier and restaurants. 152 Beach Rd., tel. (077) 421079, 300-350B fan, 400-600B a/c.

Chaweng Beach

The six-km curving beach at Chaweng is divided into three sections: Chaweng Noi (Little Chaweng, to the south), Chaweng Yai (Big Chaweng, in the center), and North Chaweng Yai (Big Chaweng, to the north). The minitruck from Nathon takes the southern turnoff to the beach near First Bungalows and continues north up the beachside road until it terminates at Samui Cabana. Tell the driver which hotel to stop at or expect to be dropped at the northern end. Charlies is a centrally located guesthouse with over 100 low-priced rooms; a good place to start your bungalow search.

Thawee, Maeo, and Chaweng Noi Bungalows: Three sets of cheap bungalows wedged at the southern end of the beach. All are friendly places popular with budget travelers for over a decade. 50-250B.

Fair House: A very popular midlevel spot on squeaky-clean sand. Like most other bungalows at Chaweng, Fair House has older huts in the bargain category and more expensive chalets added in the last few years. 4/3 Chaweng Beach, tel. (077) 421373, 450-1200B.

White House and the Village: The White House and two nearby properties—the Village and Princess Village (see below)—are the best midpriced places on Chaweng Beach. The White House and the Village are identically priced; the Village is a newer and better choice. Chaweng Beach, Box 25, tel. (077) 421382, 1200-1800B.

Munchies Resort: A longtime favorite whose name harks back to the days of mushroom omelettes and magic brownies, which are no longer available in their cozy restaurant. 17 Chaweng Beach, tel. (077) 421374, 300-600B fan, 1000-1500B a/c chalets.

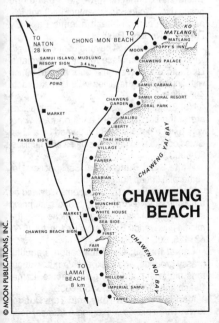

coconut collectors

Samui Pansea Resort: A stunning set of bungalows connected with wooden walkways and surrounded by tropical foliage. Tons of charm; a much better choice than the expensive hotels to the north. 38/2 Moo 3 Chaweng Beach, tel. (077) 421384, fax (077) 421385, 2200-3800B.

Princess Village: A rare chance to sleep in traditional teak houses from Ayuthaya, restored and elevated over lily ponds. This unique creation of Thai architect Patcharee Smith has great character. Chaweng Beach, Box 25, tel. and fax (077) 421382, 2400-3600B.

Charlies Bungalows: The largest travelers' center on Ko Samui now has three extremely popular branches with over 100 low-priced bungalows. Still owned and operated by the famous Teera, also known as Mama. Chaweng Beach, no phone, 100-250B.

JR Bungalows: Beautiful shady courtyard, palms, and ferns make this an excellent low-priced choice. 90/1 Chaweng Beach, tel. (077) 421401, fax (077) 421402, 250-550B.

Lucky Mother: Very popular and well-priced bungalows facing a beautiful sandy courtyard and swaying palms. Highly recommended. 80-300B.

The Island: High-quality rooms at very low prices. Recommended. Box 52, tel. (077) 421288, fax (077) 421178, 300-600B.

JR Palace: Wild architecture and creative interior decorations distinguish this well-priced set of bungalows. 300-600B.

K John Bungalows: Unusual octagonal bungalows, pet monkey, and friendly management. Recommended. 150-250B.

Family Bungalows: Very good value for budget travelers. 50-150B.

Marine Bungalows: Another inexpensive place with decent bungalows. As at most other Chaweng spots, videos are shown nightly in their breezy restaurant. 150-300B.

Lamai Beach

Ko Samui's second-most-popular beach has been developed in a rather haphazard manner with little thought to traffic patterns or hotel aesthetics. The beach is long and beautiful, and a visit can be made to the fishing village at the north end, but bungalows in the central region are packed closely together and the nightlife is turning toward noisy discos and bar girls—a bad sign.

Dozens of bungalows crowd the center, but those isolated on the hills to the east are quieter and more relaxing. Unlike Chaweng Beach, Lamai still has a good supply of inexpensive bungalows in the 80-150B range. Budget travelers should check the western end of the beach (Noi, White Sand, Samui Pearl) and just east of the central beach (Marine Park, My Friend, New Huts, Tapi).

Rocky Chalet: Just beyond Lamai is a popular and very clean place run by two Germans, Linn and Erwin Werrena, on a private beach with scuba-diving facilities. 438 Lamai Beach, 400-900B.

Noi Bungalows: Many of the cheaper places are at the south end of Lamai on narrow but very private beaches. Noi is owned by a Thai-Swiss couple who cater to singles and families. 80-300B.

White Sand Bungalows: Backpackers' favorite with cheap huts. 50-80B.

Casanova Resort: Huge rooms elevated on a hillside, a lovely restaurant, and a stunning swimming pool make this a good choice in the middle price range. 124 Lamai Beach, tel. (077) 421425, 800-1000B.

Lamai Inn 99: Central location, beautiful grassy grounds, and inexpensive huts without fans make this another good choice. Lamai Beach, tel. (077) 421427, 150-600B.

Marine Park, New Huts, and Tapi Bungalows: Three places with aging A-frames, good music, and the feel of Lamai a decade ago. Nearby My Friend and No Name bungalows are also cheap and very popular. Recommended for budget travelers. 80-120B.

Bay View Villa: A stunning restaurant and an idyllic location make the Bay View one of the finest places away from central Lamai. Highly recommended. North Lamai Beach, tel. (077) 272222, 200-300B.

Blue Lagoon: Upscale hotel complex with inexpensive small bungalows, a/c suites, and an attractive pool. North Lamai Beach, tel. (077) 421178, 400-2400B.

Chong Mon Beach

Ko Samui's prettiest bay is a graceful crescent with excellent sand and offshore islands with deserted beaches. Chong Mon was considered well off the beaten track until the 1990 opening of the immense Imperial Chong Mon Resort, which creatively utilized the old fishing boats which once lined the bay. Chong Mon now has regular minitruck service from Nathon and Chaweng Beach.

Sun Sand Resort: A superb arrangement of 33 individual bungalows, a breezy restaurant, and stunning views over Chong Mon Bay have made this resort a popular choice with European group tours. Highly recommended. Chong Mon Beach, tel. (077) 421024, fax (077) 421322, 950-1200B.

P.S. Villa: The spotless bungalows, spacious lawns, and bamboo restaurant make this the best bargain on the beach. Chong Mon Beach, tel. (077) 286956, 200-400B.

Choeng Mon Bungalows: Three classes of bungalows which increase in price the closer to the beach. Chong Mon Beach, no phone, 200-400B.

Imperial Tongsai Bay: A super-exclusive Mediterranean-style hotel with 24 hotel rooms and 48 individual a/c cottages overlooking a private beach just north of Chong Mon Bay. One of the most spectacular resorts in the world. Ban Plailaem, Bophut, tel. (077) 421451, fax (077) 421462, 4800-8000B.

Big Buddha Beach

Ao Bang Rak—more commonly called Big Buddha after the nearby image—offers almost a dozen inexpensive to moderate bungalows on an arching beach which is narrow and brownish but generally deserted. Bungalows are clean and comfortable, though beach conditions and noise from highway traffic here make Bophut and Mae Nam beaches more idyllic locations.

Boats to Ko Phangan depart near the Buddha daily at 1530 and return from Had Rin on Ko Phangan at 0930.

Farn Bay Resort: An expensive hotel with Thai dance shows on weekends. But, as their brochure claims, "No more hustle-bustles, no more pollution, no more rat-race." Big Buddha Beach, tel. (077) 273920, 1000-1600B.

Nara Lodge: An American-operated hotel with renovated rooms, pool, and ambience popular with families. Box 9, tel. (077) 421364, 950-1500B.

Big Buddha Bungalows: Large new wooden bungalows and friendly management make this one of the best bargains on the beach. Recommended. Big Buddha Beach, no phone, 200-500B.

Bophut Beach

Travelers who want to escape the congestion of Chaweng or Lamai will find Bophut an acceptable alternative. The narrow and coarse beach isn't as impressive as Chaweng or Lamai, but many visitors consider the friendly people and sense of isolation adequate compensation. Bophut also has wonderful sunsets.

Cafes here once served the most potent magic-mushroom soups on the island, but the banning of psychedelics in 1989 forced the trade over to Ko Phangan and Ko Tao.

Bophut is a convenient departure point for Ko Phangan. The *Hadrin Queen* departs daily at 0900 and 1300 for Had Rin Beach on the southeast corner of the island.

Smile House: At the edge of town is a very clean place with small fan-cooled bungalows and pricier a/c chalets, plus a wonderful pool surrounded by palms. Bophut Beach, tel. (077) 421361, 350-1250B.

Ziggy Stardust: Beautiful Lanna-style bungalows, a lovely garden, and a popular restaurant make Ziggy's a great choice for midlevel travelers. Bophut Beach, no phone, 450-1250B.

Peace Bungalows: A longtime favorite located away from town on a quieter stretch of sand. Low-end bungalows are dismal, but those in the 250-400B range are clean and comfortable. Bophut Beach, tel. and fax (077) 421357, 150-600B.

World Bungalows: One of the most popular and reasonably priced places at Bophut features a small swimming pool, lush gardens, and a luxurious restaurant facing the deserted beach. Bophut Beach, tel. and fax (077) 421355, 150-250B small bungalows, 550-650B large bungalows, 900-1000B a/c chalets.

Mae Nam Beach

Mae Nam is an isolated and relatively undeveloped beach midway between Nathon and Chaweng Beach. Over a dozen inexpensive to midlevel bungalows on this beach are signposted on the main highway. Beaches are narrow, but the solitude and remote location are quite appealing.

Laem Sai and Mae Nam Villa: Both of these inexpensive and very popular guesthouses are at the end of the cape which forms the extreme southern end of Ao Mae Nam (Mae Nam Bay). Mae Nam Beach, no phones, 80-250B.

Rainbow: Good-value bungalows constructed with brick and wood. Bophut Beach, 60-200B.

Moon Huts: Attractive bamboo bungalows, an elevated restaurant with views, and a brilliant stretch of sand make well-named Moon a good choice. Recommended. 67/2 Mae Nam Beach, no phone, 200-250B.

Lolita Bungalows: Lolita boasts an excellent beach with stunning palms, easy access to the town of Ban Mae Nam, and decent bungalows in all possible price ranges. Mae Nam Beach, no phone, 100-700B.

Mae Nam Resort: Beautiful bungalows, comfortable restaurant, and grassy landscapes make this the best midpriced resort at Mae Nam Beach. Highly recommended. Mae Nam Beach, tel. (077) 272222, 200-500B.

Shangrila: Inexpensive bungalows, new restaurant, and safe swimming make Shangrila popular with families. Mae Nam Beach, no phone, 80-200B.

Coco Palms Village: Escape the crowds at the west end of the beach. Coco Palms is a friendly place with great meals prepared by a Western chef. Good value, plus dazzling aquamarine waters. Mae Nam Beach, no phone, 400-600B.

South Coast Beaches

The following bungalows and hotels are described from west to east, starting with Emerald Bay and ending at the town of Ban Hua Thanon.

Sea Gull and Pearl Bay Bungalows: Emerald Bay (Pungka Beach) is a stunning destination tucked away at the southwest corner of Ko Samui. The road terminates at several wonderful spots on a sandy beach flanked by striking limestone mountains. Both hotels above have rooms for 80-300B.

River Garden Bungalows: A great place with friendly managers, a good beach, and a small river with wading fisherwomen. Recommended. Bang Kao Bay, 100-150B.

Samui Orchid Resort: A fabulous resort hidden away on a 25-acre coconut plantation. Features two large swimming pools, a luxurious restaurant, and small but well-appointed bungalows on a deserted beach. Ban Harn Beach, tel. (077) 421079, 650-1400B.

Cozy Bungalows: Inexpensive huts set on grassy grounds under swaying palms. Within walking distance of an interesting fishing village. Recommended. Ban Harn Beach, 150-250B.

TRANSPORTATION

Getting There

Ko Samui is 644 km south of Bangkok and 84 km northeast of Surat Thani. Travel agents in Bangkok sell package tickets which include all necessary transfers and boat connections. Although tours are the easiest way to reach Ko Samui, independent travelers will have few problems reaching the island on their own. Ko Samui is a major tourist destination, and transportation touts are always there to greet you, take your hand, guide you to the appropriate connection, show you to your seat, collect your money, and deliver you to Samui. No need to worry about confusing place-names or variable schedules—someone is *always* there to point the way. Don't you just love Thailand?

Air: Bangkok Airways (tel. 02-255-8964 in Bangkok) at 144 Sukumvit Rd. flies from Bangkok to Ko Samui six times daily and once daily from Phuket.

Train: The State Railway has rapid trains with sleepers from Bangkok to Surat Thani (Phun Phin Station) at 1730, 1830, and 1920. All arrive early enough to catch the 0730 boat to Ko Samui. Overnight trains with sleepers are comfortable and very popular; advance reservations are *absolutely* necessary. The State Railways also sells package tickets direct to Samui.

Bus: Four ordinary and a/c buses depart from the Southern Bus Terminal in Thonburi nightly between 1900 and 2030. Buses arrive the next morning in Surat Thani, from where minibuses continue to the ferries to Ko Samui.

Ferry: Several different types of boats go from Surat Thani to Ko Samui. Express boats leave from Tha Thong pier, six km east of Surat Thani, and arrive at Nathon three hours later. Minitrucks continue to the beaches. Car and passenger ferries depart from Don Sak pier, one hour east of Surat, and terminate three hours later at Thong Yang jetty, about four km south of Nathon. Finally, a slow boat leaves from the harbor in Surat Thani nightly at midnight.

Samui Tours and Songserm Travel in Surat Thani are the principal operators, with different departures during the day. Buses depart from the Samui Tours office on Talad Mai Rd. in Surat Thani daily at 0650, 0830, 1030, 1230, and 1530. Buses depart daily at 0730, 1130, and 1400 from the Songserm head office and from a stop near the harbor.

Leaving Ko Samui

Express ferries leave Nathon daily at 0730, 1200, 1330, and 1530. Exact departure times are listed at travel agencies near the pier. Night ferries leave around 2300 and arrive in Surat the following morning. Travel agents on Ko Samui sell direct tickets to Bangkok, Phuket, Krabi, Hat Yai, Penang, and even Singapore. Air-conditioned buses from Nathon are about twice as expensive as public non-a/c buses from the Surat terminal. Night departures are also offered.

Ordinary buses from the Surat Thani bus terminal to Bangkok take about 10 hours and depart five times daily from 0700 to 1230, and every half hour from 1700 to 2100. Buses for Phuket take seven hours and depart eight times daily from 0530 to 1300. Buses to Hat Yai take five hours and leave at 0830 and 1130.

Train service from Surat Thani can be tricky since advance booking is necessary to reserve a seat. Tickets can be purchased from small travel agents at the beaches and from larger agencies such as Songserm Travel in Nathon.

KO PHANGAN AND KO TAO

KO PHANGAN

Phangan Island, 20 km north of Ko Samui, is a wild and primitive place with isolated beaches, tropical jungles, and arching coves accessible only by long hikes or chartered boats. For those searching for the Samui of a decade ago, Ko Phangan seems a return to the mid-1970s, with its colonies of gypsyish travelers bedecked with amulets and beads, more concerned with blazing sunsets and local herb than raucous nightclubs and air-conditioned resorts. During the day there's little to do but relax on the beach and perhaps rent a motorcycle to visit some of the local waterfalls. Nightlife remains limited to a few video shows. Ten-day meditation retreats are directed by Buddhist monks at Wat Khao Tam.

The best sand is found on the southern and eastern sides of Ko Phangan. Beaches to the north and west are narrow and spotted with mangrove swamps, but they offer coral beds and the best sunsets on the island.

Thong Sala

Thong Sala is the main port and commercial center of Ko Phangan. No one stays in Thong Sala, but all necessary services are near the pier and the main street along the beach, including a bank which changes money at fair rates and several travel agencies which sell tickets to Surat Thani, Ko Samui, and Ko Tao. A post office and an overseas phone office are just south of the pier on the first paved street. Several shops rent motorcycles at 150-250B per day.

Transportation

Thong Sala and other beaches on Ko Phangan can be reached by boat from Surat Thani, Nathon, Bophut, and Big Buddha Beach.

From Surat Thani: Phangan Ferry Company (tel. 077-286461) boats depart from Surat Thani daily at 0720 and arrive at Thong Sala at 1100. Tickets are sold at their office at 10 Chon Kasem Rd. just across from the pier. Songserm Travel also serves Ko Phangan via

Ko Samui. A night ferry departs at 2300 and arrives at dawn at Thong Sala. Boats return twice daily to Ko Samui from Thong Sala and Had Rin Beach.

From Nathon: Songserm Travel boats depart daily at 1000 and 1530 from Nathon and arrive in Thong Sala about one hour later. Tickets can be purchased at the Songserm Travel office near the pier.

From Bophut Beach: The *Hadrin Queen* departs daily at 0930 and 1530 from the small pier in the town of Bophut and takes about 45 minutes to Had Rin Beach. This is the most convenient option for travelers staying at Chaweng and beaches on the north coast of Samui.

From Big Buddha Beach: A fishing boat to Had Rin Beach departs from the east end of Big Buddha Beach daily at 1530.

South Coast Beaches

Thong Sala Beach: Also called Ao Bang Charu, Thong Sala Beach has mediocre sand but is a convenient place for early boats to Ko Tao or back to Ko Samui. Like all of Ko Phangan's beaches, Thong Sala has a continuous string of wooden bungalows in the 50-250B price range. Charm Beach Resort is a typical example, with primitive shacks from 50B and deluxe chalets with toilet, shower, and fan from 200B. Chokana Resort is similar.

Ban Tai Beach: The beach starts to improve about two km east of Thong Sala, near the small villages of Ban Tai and Ban Khai. Just east of town are several inexpensive bungalows such as Birdsville, SP Resort, Pink's, Triangle Lodge, Liberty, and Mac Bay Resort with rooms for 50-150B.

Ban Khai Beach: Ban Khai is the last town before the road ends at the rocky headlands. Beaches here are narrow but very quiet, clean, and dotted with impressive granite boulders. Sabai, Baan Kai Bay Huts, Phangan Lodge, Lee Garden, Free Love, Copa, Pan Beach, Rainbow, Golden Beach, and Boom's all have bungalows for 50-150B. Better chalets for 150-250B are available at Lee Garden, Green Peace, Golden Beach, Sun Sea Resort, and Thong Yang.

Had Rin Beach West: Had Rin West and East were the first beaches to open up on Ko Phangan some 10 years ago. Both have excellent sand and aquamarine waters but suffer from overdevelopment and piles of trash which wash up on the shore. Bungalows at the end of the rocky coastline are now being torn down for more expensive places.

Star, Bird, Sun Beach, Sandy, Seaside, Rainbow, Coral, Palm Beach, Neptune's, Black and White, and Friendly House have huts for 50-150B.

East Coast Beaches

Had Rin Beach East: The eastern side of the craggy peninsula features white powder sand, arched in a curving cove flanked by rocky cliffs. Scuba diving is fairly good, and the surf gets high during the stormy months from October to February. Boats from Mae Nam and Big Buddha beaches on Ko Samui head directly to Had Rin East. The beach can also be reached with longtails from Thong Sala, Ban Tai, and Ban Khai.

Over a dozen bungalows occupy virtually every square centimeter of the original and most popular beach on Ko Phangan. Bungalows from south to north include Tai Chi Chuan, Paradise, Sea Garden, Haad Rin, Tommy's, Palita, Seaview, Mountain Sea, and Serenity Hill.

Yang Beach: Six km north of Had Rin and about midway up the east coast is a lovely little cove with coconut palms and sparkling sand. Sea Hill Hat Yang Bay Resort has several bungalows for 50-120B.

Sadet Beach: Had Sadet and nearby Had Thong Reng are now receiving some visitors who arrive by longtail from Had Rin or public minitruck from Thong Sala. The road from Thong Sala ends a few kilometers beyond Ban Thong Nang, making the beach a long hike or a treacherous motorcycle ride. Bungalows include Pra Thip, Ka Wao, and several places aptly called No Name Bungalows.

Ta Pan Beach: Thong Ta Pan Bay is formed by two small bays, Ta Pan Noi to the north and Ta Pan Yai on the south. Ban Thong Ta Pan can be reached by truck from Thong Sala. Bungalows near the village on Ta Pan Yai Beach include Pen's, Pingjun Resort, and Chanchit Dreamland. Ta Pan Noi Beach has Thong Ta Pan Resort at the northern end and Panviman Resort (tel. 077-272570) in the south.

North Coast Beaches

Bottle Beach (Khuat Beach): The far northeastern corner of Ko Phangan offers an immaculate and isolated beach with squeaky white sands and excellent swimming in the protected cove. Bottle Beach—the perfect place to *really* escape civilization—can be reached by longtail boats from Chalok Lam or Had Rin beaches. Sea Love, Bottle Beach, and O.D. bungalows at the northern end have wooden shacks for 50-100B.

Chaloklum Bay: The north-shore fishing village of Chaloklum (Chalok Lam) faces a curving bay ringed with emerald-green mountains. Beaches near the town are brownish but improve sharply to the east, especially at Khom Beach. Trucks take about 90 minutes from Thong Sala. Thai Life, Fanta, and Chalok Lam Resort near the town have acceptable bungalows for 50-80B. Wattana Resort at the west end of the bay has over a dozen huts in various price ranges.

West Coast Beaches

Mae Hat Beach: Similar to the situation on Ko Samui, beaches on the west coast tend to be brown and coarse but compensate with coral beds and blazing sunsets. Mae Hat Bungalows and Mae Hat Villa are on the beach path to the north. Both have huts for 50-100B. Better operations on the southern side include Mae Hat Bay Resort and Island View Cabanas. Both have older huts for 50-100B and newer chalets with private bath and fan for 150-250B.

Yao Beach: Bungalows on the small cove include Sandy Bay, Ibiza, Had Yao, Blue Coral Beach, Phong Sak, and Dream Hill Bungalows.

Chao Phao Beach: The beach at Chao Phao is somewhat brownish and dotted with mangrove trees, but coral beds and spectacular sunsets make this a popular alternative to Had Rin Beach. Bungalows for 50-100B include Bovy Resort in the south, Seetanu, and Sea Flower.

Si Thanu Beach: The circular cove of Si Thanu is near the small fishing town of Si Thanu. Beachside bungalows include Loy Fah at the southern end of the cape, Ladda Guesthouse near the town, and Sea View and Laemson on the northern stretches.

Wok Tum Bay: Bungalows at the southern end include the O.K., Kiat, Darin, and Tuk.

Pla Laem Beach: The four-km road north of Thong Sala passes some decent beaches almost continuously lined with inexpensive bungalows and better spots with private bath and fans. A track behind the main road leads up to Mountain View Resort and Bungtham Bungalows. Beachside bungalows include Beach, Cookies, Sea Scene, and Darin.

Nai Wong Beach: The rocky beach just north of Thong Sala is a convenient location for travelers taking early morning boats to Ko Samui and Ko Tao. Phangan Bungalows has basic huts and more luxurious chalets with private baths. Charn and Siriphun are low-end favorites, while Tranquil Resort at the north end has a popular restaurant and bungalows in all price ranges. All bungalows are within walking distance of the Thong Sala pier.

KO TAO

Tiny Ko Tao is 38 km north of Ko Phangan and 58 km from Ko Samui. Named after its peculiar shape, which resembles a kidney bean or an abstract turtle shell, Ko Tao measures just seven km long and three km wide, for a total area of 21 square km. The population of 750 is occupied with coconuts, fishing, and bungalow operations, which attract a steady trickle of world travelers. The island is chiefly known for its outstanding coral beds off nearby Ko Hang Tao and Ko Nang Yuan and a half-dozen beaches with fairly good sand and crystal-clear waters.

All of the beaches now offer bungalows that charge 40-80B for rooms with common baths and more expensive operations with private bath and fans.

Ban Mae Hat

Ban Mae Hat is the principal town and arrival point for all boats from Surat Thani, Ko Samui, Ko Phangan, and Chumphon. The town has several cafes, dive shops that organize trips to Nang Yuan Island, and travel agents who sell boat tickets to Chumphon and points south. Exchanging money on Ko Tao can be costly, so bring plenty of small bills.

Accommodations on the northern beach include Nuan Nang, Dam, and Khao Bungalows. All have small huts for 40-60B and larger rooms for 80-120B.

West Coast Beaches

Sai Ree Beach: North of Ban Mae Hat is Laem Choporo Cape, followed by a long stretch of sand called Sai Ree Beach and the fishing village of Ban Hat Sai Ree. Accommodations include Sai Ree and O Chai Cottages near Ban Hat Sai Ree. The trail continues north to Sun Lodge, Mahana Bay, and C.F. Bungalows just opposite Ko Nang Yuan.

Sai Nuan and Sai Nual Beaches: Hikers can follow the seaside trail south to a pair of small coves with several inexpensive bungalows: Neptune, Somat, and Cha bungalows on Sai Nuan, quickly followed by Sai Thong, Sabai, and Char Huts over the cape.

South Coast Beaches

Chalok Ban Kao Bay: Bungalows west of town include Laem Klong, Tarporn, Laem Tap, and Sunset on Chun Chua Beach. South of town are K. See, Koh Tao Cottages with superior bungalows at higher prices, Tato Lagoon, and Freedom Bungalows.

Thianok and Sai Daeng Beaches: Thianok (Thien Ok) has Niyom Huts and Rocky Resort, while Sai Daeng has Kiat and Bai Sai Daeng bungalows. All cost 50-100B.

East Coast Beaches

All of the following beaches can only be reached on foot or on longtails leaving from Ban Mae Hat and Chalok Ban Kao. Every possible cove now has simple bungalows which charge 50-80B, plus big discounts for travelers staying several weeks.

Luk Beach: Ao Luk Resort sits on a small beach reached by trail from Chalok Ban Kao.

Tanot Beach: Tanot Bay and Diamond bungalows have huts for 50-80B on the 100-meter beach.

Mao Beach: Three km east of Ban Mae Hat are several small coves for the determined escapist. Laem Thian, about 900 meters south of Mao, has one set of bungalows.

Hin Wong Beach: Four km northeast of Ban Hat Sai is a curving bay with a very narrow beach. Sahat Huts cost from 30B.

Ma Muang Beach: The northern tip of Ko Tao has Mango Bay Resort with wooden bungalows from 30B.

Ko Nang Yuan

Some of the finest diving in the region is found on three interconnected islands off the northwest corner of Ko Tao. Dive companies on Ko

Samui arrange three-day dive packages for about 5000B, including all equipment, transportation, and lodging. Rooms at Nang Yuan Bungalows cost 80-100B.

Transportation

Ko Tao is midway between Ko Samui and the mainland town of Chumphon. As of this writing there are no direct boat services from Surat Thani.

From Ko Samui: Subject to seasonal weather patterns, Songserm has an express boat to Ko Tao daily at 0900 from Nathon pier. Slower boats are available from Ko Tao Tours.

From Ko Phangan: Songserm Travel and Ko Tao Tours have boats to Ko Tao from Thong Sala. Services are subject to cancellation during the rainy season from October to January.

From Chumphon: Back-door services are available from Chumphon, an option which saves traveling down to Surat Thani or Ko Samui. Schedules change frequently and should be checked with Chumphon Travel Service (tel. 077-501880) at 66 Thatapao Rd. just north of the bus station and Thatapao Hotel. Fishing boats currently depart from Chumphon harbor at midnight on Mon., Tues., Thurs., and Friday.

PHUKET

The island of Phuket—Southeast Asia's most popular beach resort—is located in the sparkling green Andaman Sea 885 km south of Bangkok. Like all other successful beaches in Asia, Phuket was discovered by backpackers searching for an escapist holiday of simple huts, local food, and cheap grass. Facilities were limited or nonexistent; early arrivals slept on the sand or lived with locals. The scene was so idyllic that William Duncan wrote in his 1976 guide that "for a few years more, Phuket may be allowed to sleep undisturbed, for this island province is not yet ready to cater to the needs of foreign tourists. There are no first-class hotels or restaurants . . ." But word of the tropical paradise spread among world travelers, and soon a steady trickle of curious visitors tiptoed down to Phuket, hoping to beat the rush and inevitable commercialization.

In the remarkably short span of just one decade, the island has transformed itself from hippie paradise to yuppie nirvana. Present-day Phuket will disappoint travelers who dislike commercial development and find perverse pleasure in running down resorts once they become popular. Yet Phuket remains an outstanding holiday destination. First, few islands in the world can boast of so many excellent beaches in so small an area. Comparisons between Phuket and Ko Samui are almost inevitable, but I'd say that Phuket's half-dozen beaches are just as beautiful as, and certainly more plentiful than, the handful on Ko Samui. Secondly, Phuket's enormous size has allowed the beaches to absorb a great deal of development without being completely overwhelmed. Areas such as Patong have suffered badly from cheap hotels and noisy bars, but other regions have generally been spared the tourist-ghetto fate of Pattaya and Puerto Galera. Besides all this, Phuket offers outstanding scuba diving, a national park, several waterfalls, tin mines, pearl farms, Buddhist temples, villages of sea gypsies, deserted beaches where turtles come to lay their eggs, and bizarre limestone formations used in the filming of *The Man with the Golden Gun.*

ATTRACTIONS

Visitors to Phuket generally spend the first few days relaxing on the beach and working on their tans, but to discover the beauty of the island you should rent a motorcycle or car and visit the remoter regions. The following attractions are described in clockwise fashion starting from Patong Beach.

Ban Thalang: About 50 meters south of the central intersection stands 200-year-old Wat Pra Na Sang and its modern counterpart on the left. Exterior doors of the modern *bot* feature well-carved guardians on the right, while the older structure features *bai sema* that resemble giant pawns from a monstrous chess set.

Wat Pra Thong: One of the most bizarre Buddha images in Thailand lies half-buried in the middle of an otherwise ordinary temple about one km north of Thalang.

Khao Prapa Tao National Park: Four km east of Thalang is one of the most spectacular scenes

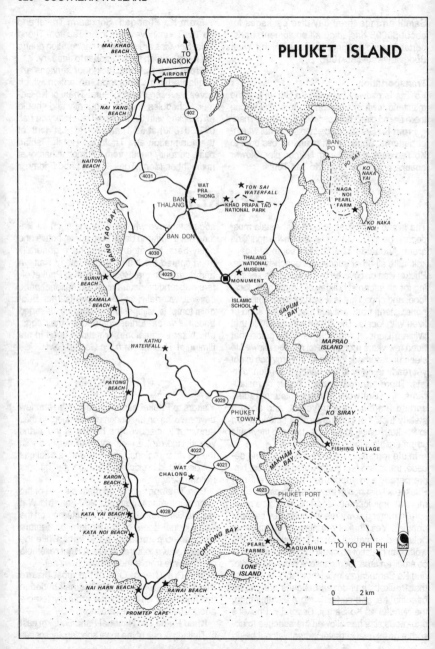

PHUKET ISLAND

MAI KHAO BEACH

TO BANGKOK

AIRPORT

NAI YANG BEACH

402

4027

NAITON BEACH

4031

WAT PRA THONG

BAN THALANG

TON SAI WATERFALL

KHAO PRAPA TAO NATIONAL PARK

BAN PO

PO BAI

KO NAKA YAI

NAGA NOI PEARL FARM

KO NAKA NOI

BANG TAO BAY

BAN DON

4030

4025

THALANG NATIONAL MUSEUM

MONUMENT

SURIN BEACH

KAMALA BEACH

ISLAMIC SCHOOL

SAPUM BAY

MAPRAO ISLAND

KATHU WATERFALL

PATONG BEACH

4029

PHUKET TOWN

KO SIRAY

4022

4021

MAKHAM BAY

FISHING VILLAGE

WAT CHALONG

4023

PHUKET PORT

KARON BEACH

KATA YAI BEACH

4028

CHALONG BAY

TO KO PHI PHI

KATA NOI BEACH

PEARL FARMS

AQUARIUM

LONE ISLAND

NAI HARN BEACH

RAWAI BEACH

PROMTEP CAPE

0   2 km

on Phuket: an awesome park which provides a rare opportunity to experience the splendor of an endangered rainforest. This might be your *only* chance to see a rainforest; don't miss it.

Pearl Farm: Ao Po is the departure point for visits to Naga Island Pearl Farm on Naka Noi Island. Phuket travel agents can arrange tours to the farm that provide insight into the considerable skills of pearl cultivation.

Thalang National Museum: This museum, 100 meters east of the Heroines Monument, is a new attraction with displays on local history, industry, the environment, and a highly prized 9th-century Vishnu image discovered near Takua Pa. Open Tues.-Sat. 0900-1630.

Ko Siray: Ko Siray is an extremely disappointing fishing village consisting of dusty roads, rough tin huts, and kids yelling "ten *baht,* ten *baht"*—an experience best avoided.

Panwa Cape: Phuket's Marine Biology Research Center and Aquarium on the south coast contains displays of tropical sealife and fishing devices. On the grounds of the Cape Panwa Sheraton Resort stands a classic Sino-Portuguese mansion filled with a quality collection of antique furniture and art objects.

Wat Chalong: The largest and most sacred temple of the 29 monasteries on Phuket.

Seashell Museum: An impressive collection of shells is exhibited in the modern, blue-tiled building on Hwy. 4021 just north of Rawai Beach.

Rawai Beach and Tristan Jones: West of the fishing village is the small boat which crossed the Kra Isthmus in 1987 with a crew of disabled sailors, including a blind German and a one-legged Englishman named Tristan Jones.

Promtep Cape: Promtep Cape and the viewpoint at the south end of Kata Noi Beach are the best spots on Phuket for spectacular sunsets.

PHUKET TOWN

The capital of Thailand's only island province has great shopping, dependable communication facilities, and delightful examples of Indo-Portuguese mansions constructed by Chinese barons who found their fortunes in tin and rubber rather than tourism. Though not as impressive as Penang's Malaccan-style terrace houses, they add charm and atmosphere to an otherwise ordinary city. The Provincial Town Hall

might look familiar—it served as the French Embassy in the film *The Killing Fields.* Phuket Tourist Office (tel. 212213) has maps and information on upcoming festivals, discounts at newly opened hotels, and schedules for weekend Thai boxing. Open daily 0800-1600. Thai immigration on Phuket Road south of town can extend visas. Phuket town also has a post office on Montri Road and 24-hour telephone services around the corner.

Accommodations

Few visitors stay in Phuket town unless they arrive late or need to catch an early bus.

On On Hotel: Established in 1929, the historic On On is the best choice for budget travelers and a popular spot at which to hang out and wait for evening buses. 19 Phangnga Rd., tel. (076) 211154, 80-180B fan, 220-350B a/c.

Wasana Guesthouse: The only other budget spot worth mentioning is just past the market. A clean place with friendly managers. 159 Ranong Rd., tel. (076) 211754, 200-300B.

Thavorn Hotel: A convenient midlevel hotel in the center of town near shops and restaurants. Facilities include a coffee shop, a lounge, and a swimming pool. All rooms are a/c. 74 Rasada Rd., tel. (076) 211333, 350-550B.

Metropole: A first-class hotel with over 400 rooms, convention facilities, and a massive lobby overloaded with marble. Centrally located. 1 Soi Surin, Montri Rd., tel. (076) 215050, fax (076) 215990, 1800-2800B.

Phuket Merlin: The finest hotel in Phuket town is just north of downtown. 158/1 Yaowaraj Rd., tel. (076) 212866, 1800-2800B.

THE BEACHES

Phuket's major beach resorts are all located on the western coast of the island. Each differs from the other in natural setting and degree of development, but all offer superb sand, warm waters, and endless sports activities. Most hotels charge 400-800B for clean, modern rooms, and up to 2000B in super-luxurious resorts with all possible amenities. Contrary to popular belief, simple bungalows under 150B are still available at many beaches. An easy way to locate a hotel is to tell your minitruck driver which beach you want and what price range you can afford.

Phuket's hotels use a double-pricing system. Rates are highest during the high season (November-May), when Europeans flood the island, but discounted 30-50% during the rainy season (May-October), when tropical storms lash the west coast. Rainy-season refugees should flee east to the drier island of Ko Samui. Luxury hotels add a 10% service charge, an 11% government room tax, and an 8.25% food and beverage tax. Phuket's most popular beaches are, in order, Patong, Karon, Kata, and Nai Harn. The following beaches are described in clockwise order starting from the north.

Nai Yang Beach
National Park Bungalows: Accommodations from park headquarters (tel. 076-212901) include campsites from 60B, bungalows off the beach for 200-300B, and beachside chalets for 500-800B.

Pearl Village: Located on the edge of the national park, Pearl Village is probably the most isolated and quietest hotel on the west coast of Phuket. Nai Yang Beach Box 93, tel. (076) 311338, fax (076) 311304, 3000-3800B.

Nai Ton Beach
Looking for an immaculate yet absolutely deserted beach? Nai Ton fits the bill. The only drawback is the complete lack of formal accommodations, except for several private residences that rent rooms to visitors. Check at the cafe at the end of the beach or with the owner of the blue-and-white cafe in the middle.

Bang Tao Bay
Bang Tao Lagoon Bungalows: Travelers wanting to escape the crowds but not break the bank are well served by this small operation near the fishing village at the south end of the bay. Recommended. 72/3 Moo 3 Tambon Cheang Talay, Amphur Talang, tel. (076) 391396, 350-650B.

Dusit Laguna Resort: Thailand's leading hotel chain offers 240 luxurious rooms, two swimming pools, tennis courts, water sports, and other amenities such as matching private lagoons facing a deserted beach. 390 Srisoontorn Rd., Tambon Cheong Talay, Amphur Talang, tel. (076) 311320, fax (076) 311174, 4500-6800B.

Surin Beach
Pansea Hotel: An upscale property owned and operated by one of the most prestigious hotel chains in Thailand. Pansea Beach, tel. (076) 311249, fax (076) 311252, 4000-6000B.

Amanpuri Resort: Few resorts in Asia can compare with the almost legendary Amanpuri—a place for the privileged few with prices to stop your heart: high-season rates *start* at 9000B! Pansea Beach, tel. (076) 311394, fax (076) 311100, 9000-18,000B.

Kamala Beach
Budget Bungalows: Several inexpensive bungalows and cafes are tucked away on the north end of the beach and down the path on Laem Sing Beach. Villagers in town also rent rooms at negotiable rates.

Phuket Kamala Resort: Situated on the central bay is a midpriced resort with swimming pool and dive facilities. 74/8 Moo 3 Kamala Beach, tel. (076) 212901, 1800-2400B.

Patong Beach
This crowded yet beautiful four-km-long beach is the island's liveliest and most popular, the Pattaya of Phuket. Although it's fashionable to condemn Patong as overdeveloped, raunchy, polluted, expensive, and the worst example of unplanned madness (all true), the beach is outstanding and daytime activities run the gamut from sailboarding and snorkeling to parasailing and sunbathing. Your impression will largely depend on what you expect from Phuket: Patong is a place for parties and good times, not solitude and contemplation!

Soi San Sabai: Although budget travelers avoid Patong and generally head to Karon-Kata, over a dozen bungalows still survive with rooms for 250-400B. The best hunting ground is on Soi San Sabai, the eastern extension of Bangla Rd. in the central beach area. Soi San Sabai is a good location since it's within walking distance of the beach and Soi Bangla nightclubs but somewhat removed from the general mayhem.

Best bets include Summer Breeze Pension with a/c rooms from 500B, Suksan Mansion with fan rooms from 300B and a/c rooms from 400B, and Duck Tonight and Charlies Tonight at 250-350B for fan-cooled rooms.

Bangla Road: Soi Bangla is the heart of the beast—a nonstop string of honky-tonk bars, wild nightclubs, pick-up joints, raging discos, and low-life restaurants. Hence, bungalows are noisy, but easy to find after consuming a

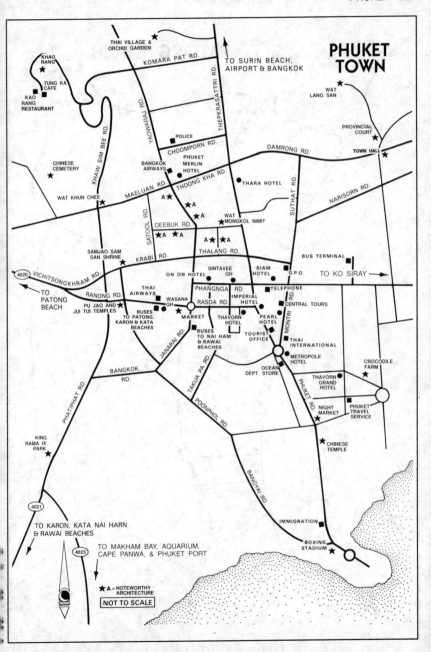

PATONG BEACH

TO KAMALA BAY, SURIN BEACH & BANG TAO BEACH

TO PHUKET TOWN

PRA BARAMI RD.

TEMPLE

THAVEWONG RD.

RACHAUTIT RD.

SAINAMYEN RD.

HOSPITAL

HIDE AWAY BAR

200 YEAR RD.

FOODSTALLS

POST OFFICE

GOLDEN LAND SHOPPING

SONG ROI PI RD.

HOSPITAL

GERMAN BAKERY

SIMON CABARET

TO KARON & KATA BEACHES

0   200m

MOON PUBLICATIONS © MOON

PATONG BEACH

1. Thavorn Bay
2. Nerntong Resort
3. Patong Lodge
4. Diamond Cliff
5. Panorama Beach
6. Best Gh
7. Similan
8. A.A. Villa
9. Sunset Mansion
10. Eden
11. P.S. 2
12. Patong Penthouse
13. Swiss Mansion
14. Shamrock
15. Berliner GH
16. Beau Rivage
17. Patong Seaview
18. Patong Grand Condotel
19. Odin's GH
20. Star
21. Ladda Apts.
22. Patong Bayshore
23. Club Andaman
24. Casuarina
25. Jeep 2
26. William Swiss
27. Phuket Cabana

28. Thara Patong
29. Nipha
30. Vises
31. New Tum
32. Royal Crown
33. Asia Guesthouse
34. Royal Paradise Hotel
35. K.S.R.
36. Patong Bay
37. Patong Beach Bungalow
38. Patong Bay Garden
39. Patong Villa
40. Islet Mansion
41. Safari Beach
42. Sandy House
43. Swiss Garden
44. Jeep 1
45. Valentine & Nordic
46. Neptuna
47. K
48. C & N
49. P.S.
50. Expat
51. Suksan Mansion
52. Super Mansion
53. Jagerstube
54. Summer Breeze

55. Duck Tonight
56. Ban Sukothai
57. Tropica
58. Patong Inn
59. Patong Beach
60. Palace
61. Patong Resort
62. Patong Ko
63. Banthai Beach
64. Club Oasis
65. Happy Home
66. Paradise Hotel
67. Holiday Inn
68. Patong Merlin
69. Holiday Resort
70. Thamdee
71. Seagull Cottages
72. Swiss, Bay View, Patong, & K.V.
73. Coconut Village
74. Holiday
75. Duang Chit
76. Coconut Cottages
77. Coconut Village
78. Coral Beach
79. Patong Hill
80. Le Meridian

case of Singha. Swiss Garden, Jeep 1 (tel. 076-321264), Valentine (tel. 076-321260), and Nordic Bungalows cost 250-350B fan and double for a/c.

Rachautit Road: Several inexpensive hotels are north of Bangla Road. Expat Hotel (tel. 076-321300) is quiet but has somewhat overpriced a/c rooms from 800B facing a small pool. P.S. and C & N bungalows cost 300-400B. Farther north are Jeep 2 (tel. 076-321100), Star (tel. 076-321517), Scandinavian-run Odin's Guesthouse, and the spotless Ladda Apartments with rooms from 350B.

Lower Thavewong Road: A half-dozen small, inexpensive hotels are tucked away at the south end of the beach road, variously spelled Thavewong, Thawiwong, Taweewong, and Taveewong! Swiss Hotel (tel. 076-321008) costs 1500-1800B, Bay View House 1000-1200B, Patong Bed & Breakfast 800-1000B, and K.V. House (tel. 076-212236) 800-1000B.

On the Beach: Several midpriced hotels are right on the beach. Sandy House (tel. 076-321458) lacks beach views but has cheap a/c rooms for 700-900B. Islet Mansion (tel. 076-321404) has rooms without views from 700B, and seaside vistas for 1000-1200B.

Patong Beach Hotel: A gorgeous pool, outstanding views from the top floors, and spacious rooms make this deluxe hotel one of the better bargains at Patong. Bananas Disco is also recommended. 94 Patong Beach, tel. (076) 321301, fax (076) 321541, 1500-2400B.

K Hotel: Beautiful gardens, a small pool, and efficient German management make this another good choice; popular with European group tours. Rachautit Rd., tel. (076) 321124, 800-1400B.

Neptuna Hotel: A lovely French-owned hotel with sculpted gardens, an intimate French cafe, and a small but acceptable pool. Recommended. 82/49 Rachautit Rd., tel. and fax (076) 321188, 1400-1800B.

KARON AND KATA BEACHES

TO PATONG BEACH

KARON BEACH

KARON - KATA

KATA YAI BEACH

KATA NOI BEACH

HOSPITAL

CLUB 44

BAR BEER

EASY RIDER BAR

POST OFFICE

4028

TO PHUKET TOWN →

TO NAI HARN BEACH & PROMTHEP CAFE

0   500m

© MOON PUBLICATIONS, INC.

KARON AND KATA BEACHES

1. Karon On Sea
2. Kampong Karon
3. Karon Viewpoint
4. Lume & Yai
5. Phuket Ocean Resort
6. Coco Cabana
7. Dream Huts
8. Phuket Golden Sand
9. Karon Hotel
10. Karon Guesthouses
11. Crystal Beach Hotel
12. Karon Bungalow
13. Much My Friend Guesthouse
14. South Seah Resort
15. Karon Villa
16. Royal Wing
17. Sand Resort
18. Karon Sea View
19. Phuket Arcadia
20. Thavorn Palm Beach Hotel
21. Karon Inn
22. Karon Village
23. Green Valley Bungalows

24. Holdiay Village
25. Sandy Inn
26. Brazil
27. Jor Guesthouse
28. Phuket Island View
29. Krayoon Bungalow
30. Ruam Thep Inn
31. Karon Beach Hotel
32. Marina Cottages
33. Kata Villa
34. Kata Tropicana
35. Garden Resort
36. Happy Huts
37. Fantasy Hill
38. Kampong Kata
39. Hallo Guesthouse
40. Kata On Sea
41. Peach Hill Hotel
42. Lam Sai Village
43. Rose Inn
44. Dome
45. Inter House
46. Kock Chang
47. Bougainvillea

48. Club Med
49. Sawasdee Guesthouse
50. Kata Sanuk Village
51. Kata Beach Resort
52. Kata Plaza
53. Sea Bees
54. Bell Guesthouse
55. P&T Katat House
56. Hayashi
57. Friendship Guesthouse
58. Sea Wind
59. Chao Kheun
60. Boat House
61. Cool Breeze Bungalow
62. Kata Delight
63. Pop Cottages
64. Chins, Sweet Home, Mr. At Guesthouse
65. Kata Thani
66. Island Bungalow
67. Kata Noi Riviera
68. Mansion
69. Kata Noi Club
70. Chew Bungalows

condemn Patong as overdeveloped, raunchy, polluted, expensive, and the worst example of unplanned madness (all true), the beach is outstanding and daytime activities run the gamut from sailboarding and snorkeling to parasailing and sunbathing. Your impression will largely depend on what you expect from Phuket: Patong is a place for parties and good times, not solitude and contemplation!

Soi San Sabai: Although budget travelers avoid Patong and generally head to Karon-Kata, over a dozen bungalows still survive with rooms for 250-400B. The best hunting ground is on Soi San Sabai, the eastern extension of Bangla Rd. in the central beach area. Soi San Sabai is a good location since it's within walking distance of the beach and Soi Bangla nightclubs but somewhat removed from the general mayhem.

Best bets include Summer Breeze Pension with a/c rooms from 500B, Suksan Mansion with fan rooms from 300B and a/c rooms from 400B, and Duck Tonight and Charlies Tonight at 250-350B for fan-cooled rooms.

Bangla Road: Soi Bangla is the heart of the beast—a nonstop string of honky-tonk bars, wild nightclubs, pick-up joints, raging discos, and low-life restaurants. Hence, bungalows are noisy, but easy to find after consuming a case of Singha. Swiss Garden, Jeep 1 (tel. 076-321264), Valentine (tel. 076-321260), and Nordic Bungalows cost 250-350B fan and double for a/c.

Rachautit Road: Several inexpensive hotels are north of Bangla Road. Expat Hotel (tel. 076-321300) is quiet but has somewhat overpriced a/c rooms from 800B facing a small pool. P.S. and C & N bungalows cost 300-400B. Farther north are Jeep 2 (tel. 076-321100), Star (tel. 076-321517), Scandinavian-run Odin's Guesthouse, and the spotless Ladda Apartments with rooms from 350B.

Lower Thavewong Road: A half-dozen small, inexpensive hotels are tucked away at the south end of the beach road, variously spelled Thavewong, Thawiwong, Taweewong, and Taveewong! Swiss Hotel (tel. 076-321008) costs 1500-1800B, Bay View House 1000-1200B, Patong Bed & Breakfast 800-1000B,

Karon Beach. Manager Eric Conger runs one of the better-value places. Recommended. 33/76 Patak Rd., 300-400B.

Karon Guesthouse: Spotless rooms and friendly management make this another good-value place in north Karon. Rooms with fan and private bath cost 250-350B depending on length of stay.

Crystal Beach Hotel: A large, modern hotel with restaurant, travel facilities, and well-priced rooms. 36-10 Patak Rd., tel. (076) 381580, 350-700B.

Thavorn Palm Beach Hotel: Four swimming pools, five restaurants, luxurious rooms, and enormous grounds (just try to find the reception desk!) make this the best upscale choice on Karon Beach. 128/10 Moo 3 Karon Beach, tel. (076) 381034, fax (076) 381555, 3400-6000B.

Kata Beach

Kata's two beaches—Kata Yai in the north and Kata Noi to the south—once served as Phuket's main hippie area until Club Med opened its facilities in 1978. Now, both have been largely blanketed with upscale hotels and expensive restaurants. Kata Yai is almost completely dominated by Club Med, though public access is provided by a beachside road. Kata Noi is a cozy cove with good sand and plenty of inexpensive bungalows.

Contrary to popular folklore, over a dozen bungalows and small hotels on Kata Beach have rooms for 300-500B. Most are on Kata Noi Beach near the expensive hotels, or at the south end of Kata Yai near Kata Plaza.

North Kata Yai Beach: Several small spots near the clubs and Easy Rider Bar have acceptable if sometimes noisy rooms. Hallo Guesthouse (tel. 076-381631) is a modern high-rise with clean fan and a/c rooms for 350-700B. Good value. Nearby Rose Inn, Dome Bungalows, Kata On Sea, and Inter House are nothing special but have cheap rooms from 300B. Sawasdee Guesthouse (tel. 076-381905) is another choice with clean and modern well-priced a/c rooms for 350-600B.

South Kata Yai Beach: Several inexpensive places are near Kata Plaza. Best choice is Kata Sanuk Village (tel. 076-381476), with a small pool, a comfortable restaurant decorated with European porcelains, and decent bungalows for 600-700B. Friendship, Sea Bees, and Bell

Guesthouse have rooms for 300-600B. Long-time favorite Bell offers older *nipa* huts for just 150-200B.

Kata Noi Beach: Hippiedom survives in several bungalows wedged back from the big hotels that dominate the beach. Cool Breeze on the hill behind Kata Inn has four bungalows for 100B, three at 200B, and eight for 500B. Chin's above the Western Inn Restaurant and nearby Sweet Home Bungalows costs 200-300B. Chew Bungalows are run-down but situated on a great stretch of beach far removed from the hordes of tourists. Rooms cost just 200-300B.

Peach Hill Hotel: A clean and modern hotel with a Chinese restaurant, a snooker hall, and 40 a/c rooms. Centrally located on Kata-Karon Beach. 113/16 Patak Rd., tel. (076) 381603, fax (076) 212807, 600-800B including breakfast.

Kata Noi Riviera: Several good-value hotels are at the south end of Kata Noi, including the Riviera just opposite the deserted beach. 3/21 Moo 2 Karon Beach, tel. (076) 381726, 300-700B.

Nai Harn Beach

Phuket's most picturesque lagoon is backed by sweeping hills studded with coconut palms and exotic scrub. Once the haunt of hippies and backpackers, Nai Harn hit the big times with the 1985 opening of the extravagant Phuket Yacht Club. The entire valley is now under massive development and most of the natural lagoons have been converted into condo complexes with private waterways.

Budget Accommodations: Most of the cheap huts have disappeared, except for a small collection of rudimentary bungalows just below the Phuket Yacht Club. Grandpa's and Coconut Huts cost 150-250B. Ao San Bungalows, located through the driveway of the Phuket Yacht Club, is a fine place tucked away on a private cove with old huts from 250B. Sunset Bungalows on the opposite side of the cove has both *nipa* huts and concrete cubicles for 200-500B.

Phuket Yacht Club: One of the most exclusive hotels on Phuket Island dominates the northern end of Nai Harn Bay. Facilities include a small swimming pool, a fitness club, and five dining venues under Swiss supervision. Nai Harn Beach, tel. (076) 381156, fax (076) 381164, 5000-9000B.

Rawai Beach

Beaches south and east were the original destinations for international tourists. Unfortunately, the region has suffered from past offshore tin mining, and the once-pristine beaches now tend to be muddy, unappealing, and lacking the natural splendor of Patong and Karon beaches.

Budget Accommodations: Rawai Garden Resort has several large and lovely bungalows overlooking ponds and surrounded by coconut trees. Room rates vary by the season—and how wealthy you appear—but probably run 250-350B.

Rawai Plaza Bungalows (tel. 076-381346) opened in 1990 with new, but unimpressive, bungalows for 300-500B. Porn Mae Bungalows (tel. 076-381300) has six decrepit *nipa* huts from 100B, and newer concrete rooms for 250-500B. Rawai Resort (tel. 076-381302) appears deserted, but the grounds are spacious and the bamboo bungalows are a good value at just 150-300B.

TRANSPORTATION

Getting There

Air: Phuket is a direct air flight from Bangkok, Hat Yai, Surat Thani, Penang, and Ko Samui. Travelers coming from Penang should take advantage of the inexpensive flight, which avoids a full day of overland travel. Limousines from the airport to the town of Phuket cost 50B; taxis are 150B per carload.

Bus: Direct a/c buses from Bangkok, Ko Samui, Hat Yai, and Penang can be arranged through travel agents. Ordinary buses leave every 15 minutes 1800-2200 from Bangkok's Southern Bus Terminal in Thonburi. Night buses are fast and cheap but tiring because of wild driving and freezing a/c. Knockout drugs are commonplace; *never accept food or drinks from strangers in Thailand.* Buses terminate at the main bus stop in Phuket town, a few blocks east of the tourist office.

Getting Around

Privately operated minibuses from Phuket town to Patong, Kata, and Karon beaches cost 10-30B depending on your bargaining abilities. Drivers generally collect commissions from hotels and guesthouses. Less-expensive public minibuses to the same beaches leave from the local bus station on Ranong Road beyond the public market. Go here if private charters ask outrageous prices. Minibuses to Rawai and Nai Harn beaches leave from Bangkok and Ranong roads. *Tuk tuks* and minibuses within Phuket town cost 5B. Taxis are unmetered and expensive, but cars and motorcycles can be rented in town and at most beaches—a great way to get around and avoid the hassles of public transportation.

VICINITY OF PHUKET

Phangnga Bay

The surrealistic and unforgettable limestone mountains in Phangnga Bay costarred with James Bond (if you consider Roger Moore the *real* James Bond) in *The Man with the Golden Gun.* A typical excursion glides through mangrove swamps, countless limestone outcroppings, and caves with prehistoric rock paintings, and stops briefly at Ko Panyi, a commercialized Muslim sea-gypsy village constructed entirely on stilts. Nearby Khao Ping Gan (Leaning Mountain) is James's famous cliff. Boat tours last four to six hours, cost 350-400B per person from Phuket agents, and leave in the mornings 0800-1000 from the port of Tha Don, 10 km from Phangnga town.

Independent travelers can cut costs dramatically by joining an organized party directly at the launching point. First, take an early-morning bus from Phuket town to Phangnga (93 km), then minibus to the boat dock at Tha Don. Early-morning bus arrivals between 0600 and 0800 are often met by Sayan Tamtopol, who has been leading excellent tours for almost 10 years. The 200B price includes the boat tour, a seafood dinner, and a memorable night in a Muslim fishing village. An early start from Phuket is essential, but a better strategy is to spend a night in Phangnga and hook up with Sayan the following morning. Otherwise, 10-man longtail boats chartered directly from the boatmen cost 300-400B with bargaining.

Phangnga town is supplied with several small and inexpensive hotels on the main street, such as Ruk Phangnga and Ratanapong near the bus stop. Phangnga Bay Resort in Tha Don has a swimming pool, a restaurant, and a/c rooms from 660B.

Surin Islands National Park

Four hours from the west coast of southern Thailand lie the five islands which comprise Ko Surin National Park. Blessed with shallow-sea corals, a hypnotizing undersea world, and pristine beaches, Ko Surin has recently opened to tourism—as shown by the estimated 20,000 visitors who reached the islands last year. The Surin archipelago is home to some 3,000 sea nomads or Chao Lay ("People of the Sea"), who prefer to call themselves *mokens.*

Surin National Park is comprised of two large islands—Ko Surin Nua and Ko Surin Tai—and several other islets inhabited by the Chao Lay. Scuba diving is said to be best in the coral reefs between the two large islands.

Accommodations: The National Park Service operates several bungalows and campsites on the southwest side of Ko Surin Nua, the northern island which is home to a small community of Chao Lay. Six-man bungalows cost 600-1000B and two-man tents cost 60-100B.

Transportation: The Surin Islands are midway between Phuket and Ranong, about 60 km west of Khuraburi. Weekend boat tours from December to April are organized by the Jamsom Thara Hotel in Ranong and large tour operators in Phuket such as Songserm and Asia Voyages. Package tours cost 1000-1500B for day visits, including transportation and meals, 2000-2500B for a two-day, one-night excursion, and 3000-3500B for three days and two nights.

Similan Islands National Park

The nine islands of the Similan archipelago are widely regarded by underwater experts as among the finest dive destinations in Southeast Asia. Reaching the Similans and exploring the stunning corals and beaches is time-consuming and expensive, but worth the effort for serious divers and determined beach enthusiasts.

The Similans, 95 km northwest of Phuket and 65 km east of the closest mainland town of Thap Lamu, can only be visited during the dry season from November to April.

Accommodations: Bungalows on Ko Miang cost 450-1000B, depending on the size of the cabin and the number of people. Independent travelers are allowed to share the cabins on a space-available basis. The Park Service also maintains 40 two-man tents which cost 150B per night. Similan and Bhangu islands also have campsites.

Transportation from Phuket: Dozens of tour operators on Phuket Island organize both day-trips and five-day excursions. Songserm Travel (tel. 076-214472, fax 076-214301) charges about US$100 for a one-day tour which leaves Phuket hotels at 0630 and returns at 2000. Five-day tours with transfers, accommodations, and meals cost US$600-700, with an additional US$20 daily charge for scuba equipment.

Transportation from Thap Lamu: Cheaper options are fishing boats and private charters departing from Thap Lamu, about 40 km south of Takua Pa or 109 km north of Phuket. It's best to contact the bungalows north of Thap Lamu near Khao Lak National Park, such as Khao Lak Resort, Khao Sok Bungalows, or Poseidon Bungalows.

THE DEEP SOUTH

KO PHI PHI

Phi Phi's almost indescribable combination of powdery white sands, brilliant blue waters, soaring limestone cliffs, and colorful corals makes it one of the most beautiful islands in all of Asia. Ko Phi Phi (spelled Pee Pee and Pi Pi in other guidebooks) is now deluged with over a quarter-million annual visitors who completely pack every square centimeter of land and sand. Despite the almost unbelievable ecological devastation, many visitors still regard the island as a wonderful place to laze in the sun, snorkel around the coral beds, and perhaps enjoy spectacular views from the limestone peak behind the small village.

Attractions

The primary island of Phi Phi Don is an hour-glass-shaped islet with narrow crescent bays wedged between soaring limestone mountains. To appreciate the beauty of the island, take the path from the back side of Tonsai village to the mountain **viewpoint** where a thatched hut restaurant sells expensive soft drinks.

Boat Tour: For most visitors, the highlight of Ko Phi Phi is an all-day boat tour from Tonsai Beach to coral beds including a one-hour stop at stunning Bamboo Island and a jaunt around Phi Phi Ley, an uninhabited island whose pristine beauty surpasses even that of Phi Phi Don. All tours feature stops at amazing Maya Bay for skin diving, fiordlike Lo Samah Bay, and an hour-long visit to famous Viking Cave, an immense cathedral named after cave pictographs which vaguely resemble ancient Viking ships.

Budget Accommodations

Bungalows and resorts are located on Lo Dalam Bay (200 meters north of the boat dock), throughout the interior (follow the path to the right of the dock), Tonsai Beach (both directions from the dock), and along Long Beach (20-minute walk east from the pier). Cheap rooms on Phi Phi are almost extinct.

Lo Dalam Bay: Gift Bungalows has rudimentary huts for 100-150B, though the place is usually full and the owners are impossible to

find. Nearby Chong Khao has similar digs for 150-250B. Charlie's Resort (tel. 02-224-2786) is a low-priced, acceptable-quality complex with rooms for 400-800B. The overflow is handled by adjacent Krabi Pee Pee Resort (tel. 075-611484), with 60 rooms for 300-600B.

Interior Bungalows: Probably the best mid-level place on the island is a cantilevered hillside complex called P.P. Viewpoint Resort (tel. 075-612193), where individual bungalows connected by rickety wooden walkways cost 650-900B. Great place. Another excellent choice is Rimna Villa (tel. 076-212901), with well-spaced clean bungalows for 500-800B overlooking a small valley. Nearby Gipsy Village (radio tel. 01-723-0674) has 30 new bungalows in perfectly straight lines. 250-400B.

Tonsai Beach: Phi Phi Don Resort has small bamboo bungalows back from the water for 150-200B and large concrete cubicles facing the water for 350-500B. Pee Pee Andaman Resort (tel. 01-213-0691) is a large operation with over 100 huts in all price ranges. Their primeval shacks cost 100-150B, good-value huts with private bath are 200-250B, and better beachside chalets with private bath cost 400-500B. Pee Pee Andaman has some good-value bungalows for 400-600B.

Long Beach: Farther east on Had Yao (Long Beach) are Funnyland, Viking Village, and Long Beach Bungalows with bamboo huts and wooden A-frames for 200-450B, plus newer rooms at twice the price.

P.P. Paradise Pearl is an old favorite with over 100 bungalows priced 350-800B.

Transportation

Ko Phi Phi is 40 km southeast of Phuket and 42 km southwest of Krabi. The island is served by an amazing variety of boats from both Phuket and Krabi. Daily boat service runs during the dry season from October to June, with limited crossings during the monsoons from July to October.

From Phuket: Songserm has 10 boats that cost 200-250B each way, take two hours, and depart several times daily from Phuket harbor at Ao Makham. Travel agents on Phuket sell tickets which include transportation to Phuket pier.

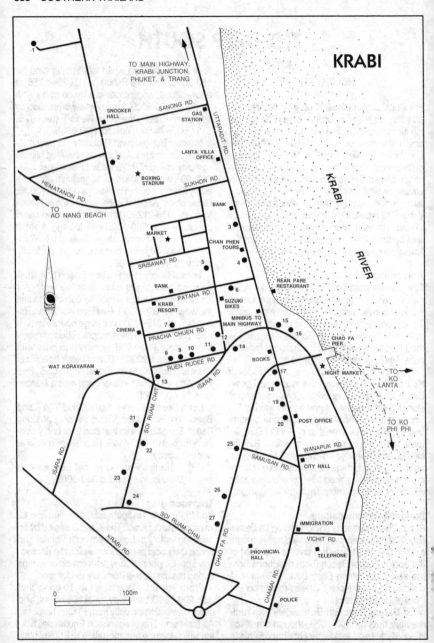

KRABI

TO MAIN HIGHWAY,
KRABI JUNCTION,
PHUKET, & TRANG

SNOOKER
HALL

SANONG RD.

GAS
STATION

UTTARADIT RD.

KRABI

RIVER

LANTA VILLA
OFFICE

2

BOXING
STADIUM

SUKHON RD.

HEMATANON RD.

TO
AO NANG BEACH

BANK

MARKET

3

CHAN PHEN
TOURS

4

SRISAWAT RD.

5

BANK

PATANA RD.

6

REAN PARE
RESTAURANT

KRABI
RESORT

SUZUKI
BIKES

CINEMA

7

PRACHA CHUEN RD.

MINIBUS TO
MAIN HIGHWAY

15

16

CHAO FA
PIER

8   9   10   11

12

14

WAT KORAVARAM

RUEN RUDEE RD.

BOOKS

NIGHT MARKET

TO
KO
LANTA

13

ISARA RD.

17

SOI RUAM CHIT

18

19

TO KO
PHI PHI

21

20

POST OFFICE

22

25

SAMUSAN RD.

WANAPUK RD.

CITY HALL

23

ISARA RD.

24

26

SOI RUAM CHAI

27

KRABI RD.

CHAO FA RD.

IMMIGRATION

VICHIT RD.

PROVINCIAL
HALL

TELEPHONE

CHAMAI RD.

POLICE

0   100m

KRABI

1. Rong's Guesthouse
2. Ban Sib Guesthouse
3. Vieng Thong Hotel
4. Jungle Guesthouse
5. B&B Guesthouse
6. New Hotel
7. K.P.B. Guesthouse
8. Coconut Guesthouse
9. Walker Guesthouse
10. K.L. Guesthouse
11. Mark and May Guesthouse
12. Pine Guesthouse
13. Seaside Guesthouse
14. Krabi Thai Hotel
15. L.R.K. Guesthouse
16. Thammachat Guesthouse
17. Songserm
18. Sea Tours Guesthouse
19. Kanaab Maw Guesthouse
20. Cha Guesthouse
21. Ruamjid Guesthouse
22. Lek Guesthouse
23. New Best Guesthouse
24. Sunshine Guesthouse
25. Friendly Guesthouse
26. Chao Fa Valley Resort
27. R.R. Mansion

From Krabi: Transportation from Krabi includes over a dozen daily departures on anything from fishing boats to sleek cruisers. Krabi guesthouses sell tickets, or you can wander down to the pier and take the next available boat.

KRABI

Krabi Province is one of the most geologically interesting and scenically stunning landscapes in Thailand. Krabi town is a pleasant place but has little to offer except for a good selection of guesthouses and transportation connections to nearby destinations such as Ko Phi Phi, Pranang Cape, and Ko Lanta.

Attractions

Wat Tham Sua: Tiger Cave Monastery, seven km east of Krabi, is a decade-old meditation retreat set in a natural amphitheater of caves and gigantic trees. Thailand's most important forest *wat* welcomes Western visitors. From Krabi, take a minitruck to the junction at Talat Kao, then any bus heading south to the turnoff to the monastery. The monastery is two kilometers up the road.

Reclining Buddha: Most of the attractions are well off the main highway and best reached with rental motorcycle. Bring along the *Guide Map of Krabi* published by V. Hongsombud—an absolute necessity. A colorful concrete Buddha lies serenely under a pair of limestone peaks on Hwy. 4034.

Shell Cemetery: Su San Noi is a famous shoreline collection of fossilized seashells at Laem Pho, 19 km west of Krabi. Although a rare geological phenomenon, Su San Noi actually resembles a slab of parking lot that fell into the ocean; unimpressive and hardly worth the effort.

Accommodations

The best guesthouses are on the new street of Ruen Rudee, or outside town in quieter locales.

Walker Pub & Guesthouse: "A Place for all Nations" is a clean and modern joint with authentic beds (not mattresses on the floor) and a popular cafe with country-and-western music. 34-36 Ruen Rudee Rd., tel. (075) 612756, 100-150B.

Seaside Guesthouse: A new, clean, and quiet spot. 105/5 Maharaj Rd., tel. (075) 612351, 100-150B fan, 250-300B a/c.

K.L. Guesthouse: Another good choice with 43 rooms tucked between their a/c cafe and the liquor store. 28 Ruen Rudee Rd., tel. (075) 612511, 100-250B.

K.R. Mansion: Slightly outside town is a very comfortable guesthouse with fully furnished rooms, spotless bathrooms, and a popular cafe. A recommended escape from downtown Krabi. 52/1 Chao Fah Rd., tel. (075) 612545, fax (075) 612762, 120-200B.

Rong's Guesthouse: Krabi's most peaceful guesthouse has great views and a comfortable restaurant about one km northwest of town. Another idyllic alternative to Krabi town. 17 Maharaj Rd., no phone, 100-150B.

Krabi Thai Hotel: Krabi's best has less expensive rooms in the old building and more luxurious choices in the newer wing. 7 Isara Rd., tel. (075) 611122, fax (075) 612556, 250-350B fan, 500-800B a/c.

Transportation

Krabi is 815 km south of Bangkok, 176 km east of Phuket, 211 km southwest of Surat Thani, and 282 km north of Hat Yai.

Boat: By far the most interesting approach to Krabi is by sea from Phuket via Ko Phi Phi. Boats depart 0700-1100 from Phuket and take about three hours to Ko Phi Phi. Boats continue from Ko Phi Phi to Krabi at 0900 and 1300. A better option is direct boat from Ko Phi Phi to Ao Pranang (Pranang Cape), the premier beach destination near Krabi.

Bus: Most buses from Bangkok, Phuket, Surat Thani, Ko Samui, Trang, and Hat Yai drop passengers in Talat Kao (Krabi junction), a small town five km north of Krabi. Minitrucks continue south to town for five *baht*.

AO NANG BEACH

Geographical terminology is somewhat confusing around Krabi. Ao Nang Beach, 17 km northwest of Krabi, is a disappointing stretch of sand that caters mostly to group tourists shuttled here by uninformed travel agents. Hat Nopharat Thara is a somewhat better beach to the north. Pranang Cape—also called Ao Phra Nang (Pranang Beach) or Laem Phra Nang (Pranang Cape)—is one of the most stunning destinations in Thailand and the focal point for informed visitors.

Longtail boats to Pranang Beach leave on demand from the waiting shed in the middle of the beach. Ao Nang is best considered an overnight stop en route to Pranang Beach.

Accommodations

Bungalows are springing up weekly to serve the ever-increasing crowds. Minitrucks from Krabi pause at the Bank of Siam and the boat launch to Pranang Beach, then continue west past the bungalows facing the beach. The best spots appear to be P.S. Cottages (directly on the beach), Coconut Garden with simple huts arranged around a landscaped courtyard, and semiluxurious Krabi Resort for upscale visitors.

Transportation

Ao Nang can be reached from Krabi in 40 minutes with minitrucks leaving from Uttaradit Rd. near Chan Phen Tours.

PRANANG CAPE

Pranang Cape is comparable only to the wonders of Ko Phi Phi: an amazing landscape of soaring limestone mountains, aquamarine waters, and squeaky white sand in an outlying corner of paradise. The special grandeur of Pranang comes from the limestone cliffs encrusted with vegetation that resembles an instant designer garden, and pinnacles leeched by rains into phantasmagoric shapes not unlike embryonic dollops of dripped wax. Pranang Beach is composed of silken sand so white it almost hurts your eyes. Few places in Thailand offer such a stunning combination of water, sand, and land.

Compared to Phuket or Ko Samui, Pranang is still somewhat off the beaten track, but the pace of change has accelerated in recent years, and it seems inevitable that serious damage will be done unless government officials stem the uncontrolled development. Bungalows are now packed together and occupy almost every square centimeter of available land, while discos blast away until dawn. Pranang—like Ko Phi Phi—is a very small place that has quickly become overwhelmed without any signs of government intervention.

Attractions

Princess Cave: A large cave at the south end of Pranang Beach derives its name from a mythical sea goddess who gave birth to her earthly lover.

Princess Lagoon: Spectacular views and unforgettable photographs are possible by climbing the steep trail up the limestone peak behind Princess Cave. Ropes help with the treacherous trail.

Diamond Cave: Up the hill behind Diamond Cave Bungalows is a large cave with a short walkway and dripping stalactites.

Ko Poda and Chicken Island: Islands east of Pranang Beach provide excellent diving and simple accommodations on deserted beaches. Day-trips and overnight stays can be arranged through most bungalows.

Accommodations

Pranang Cape is divided into three beaches with distinct price classes. Pranang Beach at the south end has the most expensive digs, Railey West is midpriced, while Railey East is the last refuge of cheap bungalows under 100B. Bungalows are filled to capacity during the high season from November to March, when visitors must sometimes camp out under the coconut trees while waiting for a vacancy.

Railey Beach East: Also called Nam Mao Beach, Railey East has Sunrise Bungalows with semiluxurious chalets for 300-500B, Queen Bungalows for 150-250B, Diamond Cave Bungalows for 60-120B, and Hillside Bungalows for just 50-100B.

Pranang Beach: The south end of the cape offers the finest sand, the best swimming, yachts bobbing in the blue lagoon, and a pair of mid-priced resorts: Pranang Bay Village (Krabi tel. 075-611944) for 250-500B and Phra Nang Place (Krabi tel. 075-612172) with elevated bungalows for 300-650B.

Railey Beach West (Lailei Beach): The longest and most popular beach, with a half-dozen bungalow operations and private homes at the northern edge. Sunset Bungalows at the western end cost 350-600B, Railey Bay and Starlight Bungalows offer ordinary bungalows for 200-350B, while Sand & Sea has average rooms for 150-300B.

Transportation
Pranang Cape is 15 km northwest of Krabi and can only be reached by longtail boat from Krabi or Ao Nang Beach. Don't confuse Ao Nang with Pranang; if you are on a beach with a road, you haven't reached the latter.

Boats from Krabi take about 45 minutes. Ask to be dropped on Railey Beach West, not the first stop at Pranang Beach. Boats from Ao Nang take about 15 minutes.

KO LANTA

The search for an undiscovered paradise is quickly pushing travelers south from Krabi toward the Malaysian border and dozens of islands near Trang and Satun. Ko Lanta today has over a dozen bungalows stretched along the west coast, from the northern village of Ban Sala Dan down to Ban Sangka U at the southern tip.

Ko Lanta has a few drawbacks, such as its isolated location that demands long travel, inconsistent sand, murderously hot weather or summer monsoons, a lack of organized trans-portation, and a lack of imaginatively constructed bungalows. And although the island also lacks the stunning topography and pristine beaches of Ko Phi Phi and Pranang Cape, visitors searching to escape the crowds and willing to endure some transportation hassles will probably enjoy their discovery.

Accommodations
Ban Sala Dan: The largest village on Ko Lanta is where most boats from Krabi and Ko Phi Phi terminate. Ban Sala Dan is a typical Thai fishing village, with several cafes, travel agencies, and motorcycle rentals.

Kor Kwang Beach: Deer Neck Cabanas and Kar Kwang Beach Bungalows are west of town on the rocky promontory called Laem Kor Kwang.

Klong Dao Beach: Almost a dozen bungalows are in northwestern Ko Lanta, including Lanta Villa, Lanta Charlie Bungalows, Sea House, and attractive Lanta Garden Bungalows. All cost 50-250B.

Palm Beach: South of Klong Dao is a beautiful four-km beach with excellent pure-white sand and small surf in the winter months. Mr. Bat at Lanta Palm Beach Bungalows rents simple but decent bamboo huts for 50-150B. Let's hope future hotel owners are blessed with some sense of aesthetics.

Klong Khong Beach: Nine km south of Ban Sala Dan is a small beach with limited sand but plenty of offshore corals for diving and an excellent grove of swaying palms. Marina Huts, just south of the small village of Ban Klong Khong, is a beautifully situated guesthouse with about 30 A-frame bamboo huts for 50-120B, plus a tent campsite on grassy lawns. Recommended.

Klong Nin Beach: Klong Nin is a five-km-long, perfectly straight, and absolutely deserted beach with a handful of fishing boats pulled up over tons of white sand. Great potential here. Lanta Andaman Bungalows is an ugly dive without views of the beach. Lanta Paradise Island offers about 40 bungalows priced 80-250B. Huts, unfortunately, are unimaginatively packed together in rows four deep, and the restaurant is nothing short of tacky.

Kan Tiang Beach: Eighteen km south of Ban Sala Dan is the final series of coves and deserted beaches. Sun Sea Bungalows on Had Kan Tiang offers bamboo huts for 50-120B.

Transportation

Ko Lanta Yai is 100 km southeast of Krabi, 77 km northwest of Trang, and 12 km from the mainland pier at Ban Bo Muang. The most convenient way to reach Lanta is by direct boat from Krabi or Ko Phi Phi. Travel agents sell tickets and can advise on the latest schedules.

TRANG

Trang is the gateway to one of the newest tourist regions in Thailand. The town itself is reasonably clean and within a day's journey of 20 waterfalls within national parks, limestone caves filled with Buddhist images, wildlife sanctuaries, broad and deserted beaches on the western coastline, and a half-dozen small islands with pure-white beaches and outstanding diving. Great potential here.

Attractions

Kachong National Park: Almost a dozen waterfalls are 20 km east of Trang on Hwy. 4125, which runs south from Hwy. 4. Kachong National Park has limited wildlife but plenty of birds, a wildlife museum, beds in shared bungalows for 100B, and the Blue Trail, which leads up to the primary falls. The falls are best visited during or immediately after the rainy season.

Pak Meng Beach: Pak Meng is a small fishing village 38 km from Trang. The modest beach has a few small cafes, an offshore limestone peak called Ko Meng, and the fishing pier, from where boats depart in the mornings for Ko Hai and Ko Kradan.

Chang Lang Beach: Hat Chao Mai National Park headquarters is on a long and deserted stretch of sand called Chang Lang, 47 km from Trang. Bungalows here cost 600B, or use a tent site on the front lawn.

Chao Mai Beach: Hat Chao Mai (Hat Yao) is probably the most attractive and popular mainland beach near Trang. Several Thai entrepreneurs have recently opened simple bungalows on Chai Mai, such as Mr. Wong's and Sinchai's Chao Mai Resort, owned and operated by a friendly guy who once served in Vietnam with the Thai army. Longhouses cost from 100B.

Chao Mai can be reached by shared taxi from Bangkok Bank in Trang to the port town of Kantang, followed by a ferry ride across the inlet, from where minitrucks leave around 1100. Late arrivals can hire a motorcycle taxi for about 60B.

Ko Hai: Tour operators in Trang can help with transportation and escorted tours to the nearby islands. Ko Hai features sandy beaches, crystal-clear waters, and excellent diving on the west coast. Bungalow choices include Koh Hai Village for 250-1000B, Koh Hai Villa for 150-300B, and Koh Ngai Resort for 400-1400B. Reservations and transportation can be arranged by their travel representatives in Trang.

Ko Muk: Ko Muk ("Pig Island"), the second-largest island in Chao Mai National Park, is considered the premier dive site of the archipelago. Accommodations are provided at Koh Mook Resort, where modern individual bungalows cost 150-200B with common bath and 200-300B with private facilities.

Ko Kradan: Kradan, a teardrop-shaped formation south of Ko Muk and Ko Hai, is another lovely island administered by the Parks Department. Ko Kradan Resort has tents for 150B, old bungalows from 500B, and newer chalets from 800B.

Ko Libong: Trang's largest island has three Islamic fishing villages accessed by regular ferries from Kantang. Accommodations include homestays at Shosin Guesthouse in the middle fishing village, camping, and inexpensive shelters operated by the Botanical Department at Juhoi Cape Wildlife Sanctuary at the eastern tip. Take a longtail from Sinchai on Chao Mai Beach.

Ko Sukorn: Ko Sukorn is the final island near Trang. Accommodations at Black Pearl Bay Resort (Bangkok tel. 02-279-8317) cost 150-500B. Photos and further information can be picked up at the Koh Teng Hotel in Trang.

Accommodations

Koh Teng Hotel: Trang's backpackers' center offers a very useful bulletin board with maps and bus schedules, photos of nearby beach resorts, and a notebook with firsthand tips on current travel conditions throughout Trang Province. Rooms are spacious and clean, and the manager is extremely helpful. 77-9 Rama VI Rd., tel. (075) 218622, 120-180B.

Queen Hotel: A good-value hotel near several decent restaurants and nightclubs. Visetkun Rd., tel. (075) 218119, 160-180B fan, 160-300B a/c.

Thumrin Hotel: Trang's only luxurious hotel features a comfortable cafe, convention facilities, and a limited amount of tourist information from the front desk. Thumrin Square, tel. (075) 211011, fax (075) 218057, 600-1200B.

Transportation

Trang is 870 km south of Bangkok, 136 km south of Krabi, and 163 km northwest of Hat Yai.

Rapid train no. 41 departs from Bangkok's Hualampong Station at 1830 and takes 16 hours to Trang. The train back departs at 1400. Air-conditioned buses from Bangkok's Southern Bus Terminal take about 14 hours to Trang. Direct bus service is also available from Krabi, Satun, and Hat Yai.

Motorcycles are a handy way to quickly tour the region. Bikes can be rented from the Koh Teng Hotel, from freelance operators who hang out in the market, and from a fellow named Prechai at the Pak Meng bus stop.

KO TARUTAO NATIONAL PARK

The 61-island archipelago of Tarutao comprises one of the final frontiers in Thailand untouched by mass tourism. The remote location at the extreme southwestern corner of Thailand—only five km from the Malaysian island of Langkawi—has served to maintain the pristine nature of Tarutao, which remains a wild and relatively untouched destination blessed with stunning beaches, tranquil bays, and a seemingly endless number of deserted islands. Go now and avoid the rush.

The Islands

Ko Bulon Lae: This small island is reached from Pakbara. Pansand Resort on the beach facing the mainland offers campsites and private bungalows for 150-600B.

Tarutao Island: Ko Tarutao is the largest and closest island to the mainland port of Pakbara. Boats from Pakbara land at Pante Malacca Bay on the north coast, where park rangers rent bungalows and tents, maintain a visitor center with displays on local ecology, and raise endangered hawksbill turtles. Visitors can hire longtails or walk south at low tide to Ao San, eight km south of Pante, where campsites are located near a small fishing settlement. Visitors

can also camp on Tala Wao Bay or stay in primitive longhouses for about 50B. Tala Wao is a four-hour hike from Pante Bay.

Ko Adang: Adang Island, 43 km west of Tarutao and about 80 km from Pakbara, is the archipelago's third-largest island. Laem Son at the south end of Ko Adang has a national-park office with bungalows for 600B and campsites from 60B.

Ko Lipe: South of Ko Adang lies a four-square-km islet, the archipelago's only populated island aside from Tarutao. Visitors can camp at the park office or rent a bungalow from the local sea gypsies. The island can be reached by longtail from Ko Adang.

Ko Rawi: The second-largest island in the Tarutao archipelago is uninhabited, aside from visiting fishermen.

Accommodations

The National Park Service operates bungalows and campsites on several islands. Four-man concrete bungalows cost 600B, deluxe 10-man bungalows cost 800B, and campsites cost 60B. Bungalows and campsites are at Pante Malacca Bay on the north side of Tarutao Island, at Laem Son at the south end of Ko Adang, and on the east side of Ko Lipe. Backpackers can camp at almost any beach. Reservations can be made at national park headquarters in Bangkok (tel. 02-579-4842) or at the Pakbara office (tel. 074-711383) near the pier.

Transportation

Tarutao Island is 28 km from Pakbara, a mainland port 65 km north of Satun and 100 km south of Trang.

Buses south from Trang take two hours to Langu (La Ngu), from where minitrucks and motorcycle taxis continue west to Pakbara. Langu has a bank, so change enough money and bring along extra food and drink.

Direct connections from Krabi are provided by Leebi Travel on Isara Road. Pakbara can also be reached via Langu with public transportation from Satun and Hat Yai. Travel agents in Hat Yai arrange escorted tours on weekends which include transportation and accommodations. Alternatively, take a bus from Hat Yai toward Satun but get off in the dusty village of Chalung, from where *songtaos* continue north to Langu.

Boats to Tarutao depart daily from Pakbara at 1030 and 1400, but only during the tourist season from November to May. Tarutao National Park is *closed* during the May-Nov. monsoon season.

SATUN

Satun is a small town which chiefly serves as a departure point for sea travel south to Langkawi and Kuala Perlis in Malaysia. Travelers heading from Hat Yai to Tarutao National Park need not stop in Satun but can change buses in Chalung, an intersection town about 20 km north of Satun.

The Thai Immigration Office on Buriwanit Rd. near the canal might be the most important place in town. All travelers leaving Thailand by sea *must* obtain an exit stamp from this office. Immigration can also help with quickie Malaysia visas.

Accommodations
Satun Thani Hotel: While not the cheapest spot in town, this small hotel has a cozy a/c cafe, friendly management, and very clean rooms with private baths. 90 Satun Thani Rd., tel. (074) 711010, 120-180B fan, 220-260B a/c.

Oasis Guesthouse: Rudimentary digs with mattresses on the floor. Run by an ex-accountant who speaks decent English. Riverside Rd., no phone, 50-80B.

Wang Mai Hotel: Satun's only luxurious hotel has a coffee shop, a disco, and 108 a/c rooms. 43 Satun Thani Rd., tel. (074) 711607, 600-900B.

Transportation
Bus: Buses from Hat Yai leave from the bus terminal on the outskirts of town. Easier but somewhat more expensive options are share taxis which depart opposite the post office near the railway station.

Boat: Boats to Kuala Perlis in Malaysia take about 90 minutes and leave from two locations. Longtails depart several times daily from the city pier on Klong Bambang near the Rain Thong Hotel. Larger boats leave from Tammalang Pier in the estuary about 15 km south of Satun.

More useful than boat travel to Kuala Perlis is direct service to Langkawi Island, a well-developed Malaysian resort destination just 90 minutes south of Satun. Boats to Langkawi depart daily at 1600 from Tammalang pier and return

from Langkawi daily at 1300. Tickets cost 150B and can be purchased on the ship or from Charan Tours near the Thai Airways office.

HAT YAI

Hat Yai—the dynamic commercial center and transportation hub of southern Thailand—receives wildly divergent reviews from visitors. Many feel the city is monotonous and oversized and lacks any compelling reason for one to stay more than a few hours. Others enjoy the outstanding shopping, lively street markets, and heady nightlife, and don't mind that Hat Yai is a clean and well-ordered city rather than some romantic fishing village.

Travelers from Malaysia who have little interest in Hat Yai can proceed directly to Songkhla, Krabi, Phuket, or Ko Samui by changing buses, taking the next train, or waiting for a share taxi near the train station. Schedules can be quickly checked at the score of travel agents near the Cathay Hotel, three blocks east of the train station.

Thai Immigration is on Nasatani Rd. near the Utapao Bridge. The Malaysian Consulate is in Songkhla.

Attractions
Wat Hat Yai: Hat Yai's only temple of note features a 35-meter reclining Buddha inside a *viharn* on Petchkasem Rd., four km southwest of town toward the airport.

Southern Thai Culture Village: Cultural shows from 1600 to 1730 Wed.-Sun., and weekend dinner shows from 1900 to 2030. Tickets from travel agencies include roundtrip transportation from your hotel.

Bullfights: Thai-style bullfighting matches are held on the first Saturday of each month at the Hat Yai Bullfighting Arena, on Hwy. 4 near the airport.

Accommodations
Most of Hat Yai's 60-plus hotels are in the center of town along the three Niphat Uthit roads, also called Sai Nueng (Rd. 1), Sai Song (Rd. 2), and Sai Sam (Rd. 3). Train arrivals are within easy walking distance of most hotels. Buses from the Malaysia border usually stop at the main bus terminal outside town, from where minitrucks continue to city center. Bus arrivals

from Songkhla can walk or take any *songtao* heading south.

Cathay Guesthouse: Hat Yai's traveler center is a friendly and clean place with a popular cafe. The bulletin board and travelers' logs are gold mines of information on upcoming beaches, new guesthouses, and travel tips on visas and shopping. Overall, the best-value spot in Hat Yai. Arrive early to find a room. 93/1 Niphat Uthit 2 Rd., tel. (074) 243815, 60B dorm, 120-180B common bath, 180-220B private bath.

King's Hotel: An older hotel centrally located near the train station and popular Washington Nightclub. 126 Niphat Uthit 1 Rd., tel. (074) 243966, 180-250B fan, 250-340B a/c.

Tong Nam Hotel: Small and clean, the Tong Nam has a good fast-food cafe on the first floor, "Ancient Massage" in the lobby, and some of the cheapest a/c rooms in Hat Yai. 118-120 Niphat Uthit 3 Rd., tel. (074) 244023, 120-180B fan, 220-280B a/c.

Montien Hotel: Adjacent to the King's is a high-rise hotel with sparsely furnished but large and comfortable a/c rooms. 120 Niphat Uthit 1 Rd., tel. (074) 234386, fax (074) 230043, 340-600B.

Central Sukhontha Hotel: A small swimming pool, the Zodiac disco, and brightly decorated rooms make the Sukhontha a popular choice. Sanehanusorn Rd., tel. (074) 243999, fax (074) 243991, 500-650B.

Regency Hotel: Teakwood lobbies, a restaurant-cum-cabaret, and very large rooms make the Regency the best in town. 23 Pracha Thipat Rd., tel. (074) 234400, fax (074) 234515, 1000-1600B.

Restaurants

Food Stalls: A small but lively market sets up nightly in the northeast corner of central Hat Yai, on Suphansan Rangsan Road. Other food stalls are located on Sheuthit Rd., opposite the Oriental Hotel. Inexpensive.

Fueng Fah Restaurant: A small, clean a/c cafe with buffalo steaks and other Western specialties. Suphansan Rangsan Road. Moderate.

Osman's Restaurant: A small Malay cafe with regional specialties such as *soup daging, udang goreng, nasi etek,* and *telor bungkus.* A pleasant change from Thai fare. Niphat Uthit 2 Road. Inexpensive.

Muslim Cafes: Tasty Muslim and Indian dishes are prepared at three simple cafes at the south side of central Hat Yai. Aberdeen, Share-fa (Ruby's), and Mustafa 2 have English menus listing vegetable *korma,* mutton curry, and fish *marsala* served with fresh *chapatis.* An even *better* change from Thai fare. Niyomrat Road. Inexpensive.

Getting There

Air from within Thailand: Thai Airways International flies twice daily from Bangkok via Phuket, and weekly from Pattani and Narathiwat.

Air from Malaysia: Thai Airways and Malaysian Air fly once daily from Phuket and Kuala Lumpur. The Hat Yai airport, 12 km west of town, is served by inexpensive minitrucks and private limousines.

Train from Bangkok: Trains from Hualampong Station to Hat Yai depart at 1235 (rapid), 1400 (special express), 1515 (special express), and 1600 (rapid). The 1515 and 1600 departures are recommended, since they arrive at 0704 and 0850. Sleepers are available on all trains. Advance reservations from the Bangkok station or a travel agent are *strongly* recommended on all trains going south, especially on weekends and holidays.

Train from Malaysia: The International Express leaves Butterworth (the train terminus for Penang) daily at 1340, crosses the Thai border, and arrives in Hat Yai three hours later. The IE is limited to first and second class and somewhat expensive because of supplemental charges for a/c and superior classes. Reservations can be made from Penang travel agents.

Ordinary trains no longer connect Butterworth with Hat Yai but rather terminate at the Malaysian border town of Padang Besar. Walk across the border, have your passport stamped, and catch a bus to Hat Yai.

Taxi from Malaysia: Share taxis are an important travel component in southern Thailand since they are fast, comfortable, and relatively inexpensive—about the same price as an a/c bus. Share taxis leave 0600-1000 from the Butterworth station just across the channel from Penang. Share taxis from Kota Baru terminate at the border, from where you have your passport stamped and continue to Sungai Golok by rickshaw or *tuk tuk*.

Bus from Malaysia: Bus 29 from Kota Baru terminates in the Malaysian border town of Rantau Panjang, where you have your pass-

HAT YAI

Map labels:

TO BANGKOK

BUSES TO SONGKHLA

PETCHKASEM RD.

TO SONGKHLA

NIGHT FOODSTALLS

TO SONGKHLA

TO IMMIGRATION, WAT NAI YAI, AIRPORT, & PHUKET

SUPHANSAN RANGSAN RD.

FUENG FAH RESTAURANT

PETCHKASEM RD.

SOPHIA FABRICS

1

2

DUANG CHAN RD.

TAXIS

3

POST OFFICE

OCEAN DEPT. STORE

BIRD'S NEST RESTAURANT

5

PRACHA THIPAT RD.

4

NIPHAT UTHIT 2 RD.

10

D.K. BOOKS

SAENG CHAN RD.

6

ZODIAC DISCO

11

7

8

9

12

HOLLYWOOD DISCO

16

NIPHAT UTHIT 1 RD.

14

13

15

17

NASATANI RD.

RATAKAN RD.

THAMNOEN VITHI RD.

CAFE

MAE TIP RESTAURANT

DIM SUM CAFE

TRAIN STATION

19 20 O CHA RESTAURANT

21

25

24

FOODSTALLS

D.K. BOOKS

22

26

27

FOODSTALLS

18

23

OSMAN'S RESTAURANT MOTORCYCLES

SANEHANUSORN RD.

HAAD YAI DEPT. STORE

KIMPRADET RD.

MANASRUDE RD.

BANK

28

HILLMAN RESTAURANT

29

CHINESE TEMPLE

30

PREDAROM RD.

TECK NGEE RESTAURANT

KLONG TOEY

THAI AIR

31

SEAFOOD GARDEN

NIYOMRAT RD.

NAKORN NAI CAFE

32

NIPHAT UTHIT 3 RD.

RELAX PUB

MUSLIM CAFES

MAE TIP RESTAURANT

33

PADUNG PAKDEE RD.

ANRATANAKORN RD.

35

SOI 2

34

BIRD SHOP

TOURIST OFFICE

GAS

BEST CAFE

CAKE HOUSE

THAI NIGHTCLUBS

0   100m

36

37

SRIPOONAVART RD.

TO BUS TERMINAL & MALAYSIA

38

NOON

HAT YAI

1. Singapore Hotel
2. Inter Hotel
3. Asian Hotel
4. Regency Hotel
5. L.K. Hotel
6. Mandarin Hotel
7. Yong Dee Hotels
8. Park Hotel
9. Savoy Hotel
10. Central Sukhotha Hotel
11. Grand Plaza Hotel
12. Tong Nam Hotel
13. Metro Hotel
14. Laem Thong Hotel
15. Indra Hotel
16. Prince Hotel
17. Nora Hotel
18. Rajthanes Hotel
19. Lada Guesthouse
20. Louise Hotel
21. Cathay Hotel
22. Montien Hotel
23. King's Hotel
24. Sakoi Hotel
25. Kim Hua Hotel
26. Oriental Hotel
27. Rado Hotel
28. Pacific Hotel
29. New World Hotel
30. B.P. Grand Tower Hotel
31. Central Hotel
32. Sakura Hotel
33. Emperor Hotel
34. Scala Hotel
35. Kosit Hotel
36. Lee Gardens Hotel
37. Amarin Hotel
38. Florida Hotel

port stamped and continue to the Sungai Golok train or bus station by *tuk tuk* or trishaw.

Leaving Hat Yai
Train: Trains going north to Phattalung, Surat Thani, and Bangkok depart at 1534, 1617, 1814, and 1849. Sleepers are available on all trains. Trains going south to Sungai Golok on the Malaysian border near Kota Baru depart at 0452, 0605, 0810, 1035, and 1322. Trains to Padang Besar and Penang depart once daily at 0704.

Taxi: Hat Yai has several share-taxi stands that specialize in specific destinations. Taxis to Phattalung, Nakhon Si Thammarat, Trang, Narathiwat, and Sungai Golok leave near the night market.

Bus: The public bus terminal (tel. 074-232789) is in a remote spot in the southeast corner of Hat Yai. An easier if somewhat more expensive option is private service arranged through travel agents near the Cathay Hotel.

SONGKHLA

Songkhla is a deceptively sleepy beach resort picturesquely situated between the Gulf of Thailand and a saltwater sea called Thale Sap ("Inland Sea") or Songkhla Lake. Somewhat off the beaten track and overshadowed by the economic powerhouse of Hat Yai, Songkhla has largely escaped commercialism and blessedly remained a pleasant and charming town of Sino-Portuguese buildings, bobbing fishing boats, and beaches filled with Thai families rather than Western tourists.

Songkhla facilities include a post office, several banks, a Malaysian Consulate (tel. 074-311104) at 4 Sukum Rd., and a tax-clearance office near the golf course. The American Consulate closed in 1992.

Attractions
Songkhla National Museum: The regional history of Songkhla and the deep south can be traced in this 19th-century Sino-Portuguese mansion, constructed as a private residence for a wealthy Chinese merchant who later served as governor of Songkhla Province. Open Wed.-Sun. 0900-1600.

Old Town: A fairly interesting walk through the old town can be made in about an hour, starting at the museum and walking south along the waterfront.

Wat Machimawat: Wat Klang—the oldest and most important temple in Songkhla—features beautiful murals of 19th-century life in Songkhla and episodes from the Jatakas.

Samila Beach: The focal point of Songkhla is the eight-km stretch of sand dotted with seafood restaurants, a municipally owned hotel, and hardly any tourists, since Thais leave sunbathing to mad dogs and unenlightened backpackers.

Ko Yoh: Yoh Island is known for its seafood restaurants, traditional weavings, and the Institute of Southern Thai Studies with its newly opened Folklore Museum.

Khu Khut Bird Sanctuary: A large 520-square-km wildlife refuge, similar to Thale Noi near Phattalung, is 50 km north of Songkhla near the town of Sathing Phra. Accommodations and boat tours of the inland lake are available at park headquarters. Buses from Songkhla stop at Sathing Phra, from where motorcycles continue three km to park headquarters.

Accommodations
Holland House: Cozy spot near the clock tower in the center of town. 28 Ramvithi Rd., tel. (074) 322738, 130-250B.

Narai Hotel: The backpackers' favorite is somewhat isolated but compensates with travel tips, bicycle rentals, and decent rooms in the yellow building with a red-tiled roof. Recommended. 14 Chai Khao Rd., tel. (074) 311078, 90-150B.

Suksomboon 1 Hotel: Acceptable rooms in a small place near the clock tower. 40 Phetchkiri Rd., tel. (074) 311049, 140-220B fan, 280-320B a/c.

Samila Beach Hotel: Top-end choice with water-sports equipment rentals, a small pool, a golf course, and seaside rooms facing the bronze mermaid. 1 Rajadamnern Rd., tel. (074) 311310, fax (074) 322448, 800-1200B.

Transportation
Songkhla can be reached from Hat Yai in 30 minutes by green buses which depart on Petchkasem Rd. near the Hat Yai Plaza Theater. Share taxis leave from the President Hotel. Buses stop at the clock tower and then continue to a halt on Saiburi Rd. near Wat Chang. Thai Transportation Company in the Chok Dee Hotel sells a/c bus tickets to Bangkok.

PATTANI

Thailand changes dramatically south of Hat Yai. Suddenly, Islamic mosques outnumber Buddhist *wats*, Yawi (a Malay dialect influenced by Arabic) doubles with Thai as the lingua franca, and old men sport Muslim *haji* caps rather than Buddhist robes. The style of domestic architecture changes from Thai to Malay, while women living outside the urban areas wear lace veils or brightly colored clothing typical of Muslim housewives.

Farangs are extremely rare in the deep south, aside from a handful of travelers heading from Hat Yai down to Kota Baru in Malaysia. Visitors who need to overnight or have a strong interest in Thai-Malay culture will discover the most pleasant interlude to be the idyllic fishing village of Narathiwat. Pattani, Yala, and Sungai Golok are modern concrete towns with little of great interest except for their political backgrounds, mosques, and women dressed in traditional Muslim garb.

Accommodations
Riverside Hotels: Three wooden Chinese hotels are across from the police station and just down from the bridge. Thai Ann Hotel is entered through an old cafe, while Thai Wa is back behind a fairly modern restaurant. Sing Ah Hotel features a small cafe overlooking the river. All three are rough but survivable and have fan-cooled rooms for 80-120B.

Palace Hotel: This five-story hotel, the best deal in central Pattani, is set back in a quiet alley away from noisy Phipat Road. 38 Soi Preeda, tel. (073) 349171, 120-180B fan, 200-250B a/c.

YALA

Yala Province and its Betong district on the Malaysian border comprise the southernmost region of Thailand. Yala itself is a modern and clean commercial center fashioned around a gridiron layout of roads with city parks and lakes in the perimeter.

Attractions
Birds: Yala town is known for its ASEAN Bird Singing Contest held in March.

Wat Kuha Phimok: Believed to date from the Srivijaya era, the cave complex at Wat Kuha Phimok (also called Wat Na Tham) features a highly venerated reclining Buddha image considered by southern Thais equal in religious stature to Wat Boromothat in Nakhon Si Thammarat and Wat Chaiya in Surat Thani Province. Six km west of town on the road toward Hat Yai.

Accommodations

Budget Hotels: Several inexpensive Chinese hotels are near the train station and taxi stops. The Yuan Tong Hotel in the yellow-and-white wooden building, Aun Aun Hotel in the five-story gray concrete tower, and Kok Tai Hotel with green shutters have acceptable if somewhat dreary rooms for 80-140B.

Thep Vimarn Hotel: Slightly more expensive but a big leap in comfort are the clean rooms in the deserted hotel just beyond the imposing Yala Rama Hotel. 31-37 Sri Bumrung Rd., tel. (073) 212400, 100-150B fan, 250-300B a/c.

Transportation

Buses to Yala leave from the main bus terminal in Hat Yai and from the bus halt in the south end of Sungai Golok. Buses from Yala to Hat Yai leave from a small office on Sirirot Rd. a few blocks south of the central market. A private bus company across from the train station can help with a/c coaches to Phuket, Ko Samui, and Bangkok. Taxis from Yala to various destinations leave from several spots near the train station.

NARATHIWAT

This small and sleepy fishing village is the most pleasant stop between Hat Yai and Sungai Golok. The town itself lacks any great monuments or historical sites, but the undisturbed wooden architecture, deserted beaches, and laid-back atmosphere make it a wonderful spot to escape the more congested and touristy towns of southern Thailand.

Attractions

Walking Tour: A very agreeable three-hour walking tour can be made starting from the clock tower and heading north along the riverfront road toward the Muslim fishing village and cafes at Narathiwat Beach. You'll pass bird shops on the left, brightly painted *kolae* fishing boats at the north end, Narathiwat Mosque, and then, across the bridge, a typical Muslim fishing village where kids yell "Hello good morning," and several cafes with English-language menus.

Wat Khao Kong: Six km south of Narathiwat is a small hill called Khao Kong on which local Buddhists have constructed the largest seated Buddha in Thailand. Take any bus or minitruck heading south down Hwy. 42 toward Sungai Golok.

Accommodations

Narathiwat Hotel: The cheapest spot in town is the yellow wooden hotel marked with a small English sign. Rooms fronting the street are noisy and need renovation, but rooms facing the Bang Nara River are good value and worth requesting. 341 Phupa Pakdee Rd., tel. (073) 511063, 80-120B.

Bang Nara Hotel: Another budget spot similar to the Narathiwat but without the river-view rooms. Hok Huay Lai and Cathay hotels are in the same price range. 174 Phupa Pakdee Rd., tel. (073) 511036, 80-120B.

Yaowaraj Hotel: Narathiwat's second-largest hotel offers clean rooms with private bath at reasonable prices. 131 Pichit Bamrung Rd., tel. (073) 511148, fax (073) 511320, 120-180B fan, 220-280B a/c.

Tan Yong Hotel: Narathiwat's finest hotel features a snooker hall, Ladybird ancient massage, and a popular restaurant with live cabaret with young girls dressed as cheerleaders. 16/1 Sopa Prisai Rd., tel. (073) 511477, fax (073) 511834, 650-800B.

Transportation

Share taxis from Sungai Golok leave from the train station and take about one hour to Narathiwat. Taxis from Hat Yai depart on Niphat Uthit 2 Rd. near the Cathay Hotel. Buses leave every two hours from the halt in the south end of Sungai Golok. Buses from Hat Yai leave from the main bus terminal in the southeastern outskirts of town.

SUNGAI GOLOK

Sungai Golok (or Sungai Kolok) is the final town for visitors heading south from Thailand to the east coast of peninsular Malaysia. Aside from its immigration functions, the town serves as a short-time brothel for Malaysian males who pack the hotels, nightclubs, and massage parlors on weekends. Sungai Golok offers nothing for Western travelers except for a small but useful tourist office at the border.

Warning: The Thai border closes nightly sometime between 1700 and 2100, depending on the whim of immigration officials and border guards. Unless you care to spend a night in Sungai Golok—not a pleasant thought—arrive early enough to conduct border formalities and catch a share taxi down to Kota Baru.

Accommodations

The local tourist office claims that Sungai Golok has 44 hotels in all price categories. Most cost 120-160B fan, 220-450B a/c, or 350-600B in better hotels.

Budget Hotels: Travelers arriving late at night can quickly locate an inexpensive hotel on Charoenkhet Rd. or the parallel avenues to the west. Hotels on Charoenkhet Rd. with rooms for 100-150B include the Chiang Mai, the Pimarn, the Shanghai, the Asia with a tiled lobby and aquariums, and the Savoy with potted plants on the balcony. The very inexpensive Thaliang (Thai Lieng) has rudimentary rooms from 80B and a small coffee shop with caged songbirds.

Merlin Hotel: A very large and central hotel whose brochure shows photos of lovely girls taking soapy baths, cutting hair, and sitting in bedrooms dressed in blue party dresses. You get the idea. 40 Charoenkhet Rd., tel. (073) 611003, fax (073) 613325, 220-260B fan, 320-400B a/c.

Transportation

Buses from Hat Yai can be arranged through travel agents near the Cathay Hotel, though most services head southwest toward Penang and Kuala Lumpur. Ordinary buses leave from the Hat Yai bus terminal on the outskirts of town.

Bus: Buses generally arrive and depart from the train station in Sungai Golok, adjacent to the Valentine Hotel, or from the bus terminal on the south end of town near the cinema and An An Hotel. Ordinary buses to Bangkok leave throughout the day until 1630 from both locations.

Taxi: Share taxis are the fastest way to travel in the deep south. Share taxis from Hat Yai, Satun, Pattani, and Narathiwat stop at the train station in Sungai Golok, from where *tuk tuks* and pedicabs continue east to the Malaysian border.

Share taxis to all towns in the deep south leave from 0700 to 1600 from the Sungai Golok train station. Travelers arriving from Malaysia should proceed directly to the train station and find the next available taxi.

Train: Train arrivals in Sungai Golok are greeted by trishaw drivers who continue to the border. There is no direct train service between Sungai Golok and Kota Baru.

Getting To Malaysia

The border is about two km from the train station in Sungai Golok. Thai Immigration will check your visa expiration date and charge 100B per day for overstays beyond the allotted period.

Malaysian authorities across the Sungai Golok River grant free entry permits to most Western visitors on arrival. You then walk into the small Malaysian border town of Rantau Panjang. To the right is a small cafe where you can dine and wait for the next available share taxi to Kota Baru. The cafe manager and taxi drivers accept Thai *baht* at fair exchange rates.

The Westerner is drawn to the tradition of the Easterner, and almost covets his knowledge of suffering, but what attracts the Easterner to the West is exactly the opposite—his future, and his freedom from all hardship. After a while, each starts to become more like the other, and somewhat less like the person the other seeks. The New Yorker disappoints the locals by turning into a barefoot ascetic dressed in bangles and beads, while the Nepali peasant frustrates his foreign supplicants by turning out to be a traveling salesman in Levi's and Madonna T-shirt. Soon, neither is quite the person he was, or the one the other wanted. The upshot is confusion.

—Pico Iyer, *Video Night in Kathmandu*

One of the chief delights and benefits of travel is that one is perpetually meeting men of great abilities, of original mind, and rare acquirements, who will converse without reserve.

Disraeli, *Coningsby*

Etymologically a traveler is one who suffers travail, a word deriving in its turn from Latin tripalium, a torture instrument consisting of three stakes designed to rack the body.

—Paul Fussell, *Abroad*

THAILAND
1. Wat Pra Keo fantasy; **2.** Loy Kratong, Sukothai (all photos this page by Carl Parkes)

INDONESIA
1. Gunung Kawi ricefields; **2.** *legong* dancer; **3.** handmade brooms
(all photos this page by Carl Parkes)

INDONESIA

*Travel can be one of the most rewarding
forms of introspection.*

—Lawrence Durell,
Bitter Lemons

INTRODUCTION

Indonesia is a land of superlatives. Arching gracefully between Asia and Australia, this vast archipelago—some 13,000 islands inhabited by over 170 million people—offers overwhelming diversity, from magnificent volcanos plunging into icy blue lakes to pristine beaches and sparkling coral gardens. Indonesia is a primeval world of astonishing beauty and complexity, kaleidoscopic in culture, perhaps the richest historical and ethnographic destination in the world. This is a land as varied, complex, and colorful as any place on earth, a "Destination of Endless Diversity" with the power to overwhelm and delight everyone from the one-week visitor to Bali to the multi-entrance traveler en route to Irian Jaya.

THE PHYSICAL SETTING

The outer limits of this 6,400-km stretch of islands (*Dari Sabang ke Merauke,* or "From Sabang to Merauke") are as far from each other as California is from Bermuda or Perth is from Wellington. Indonesia has a total area of five million square km (about one million more than the United States) of which more than two million are land. Of the 10 largest islands in the world, Indonesia claims the better part of three (New Guinea, Borneo, and Sumatra); in addition

there are about 30 small archipelagoes, each containing literally thousands of islands. Of the 13,677 islands that make up its territory, some 6,000 are named and only 992 are permanently settled. A country of incredible and diverse beauty, there are mind-stupefying extremes: 5,000-meter-high snowcapped mountains of Irian Jaya, sweltering lowland swamps of eastern Sumatra, open eucalyptus savannahs of Timor, lush rainforests of West Java, with lava-spewing volcanos the whole length.

Most Indonesians live and die within sight of a volcano. This archipelago sprawls through a part of the western Pacific known as the Ring of Fire. Registering up to three earthquakes per day, this region is home to over 400 volcanos, 70-80 of which are still active. The islands are the site of the earth's two greatest volcanic cataclysms in history (Krakatoa and Tambora); each year there's an average of 10 major eruptions. All this volcanic activity not only destroys but also brings gigantic benefit by aiding growth and life. The whitish ash produced by an eruption, rich in minerals, reaches a wide area of surrounding land. Rivers carry ash even farther by way of irrigation canals to the crops. Thus Indonesia has some of the most fertile land on the planet. In places it's said you can shove a stick in the ground and it'll sprout leaves.

Climate

Indonesia straddles the equator, so the days are all the same length. This country has a typical equatorial climate with only two seasons: wet and hot. The wet lasts from November to March, and the hot from May to October. Rainfall fluctuates wildly depending on the season. Winter monsoons from the north bring short but drenching cloudbursts. Sometimes it rains so hard it's like falling into a swimming pool; with a roar the skies upend, spilling a solid wall of water on the earth below. Summer monsoons from the south bring hot winds and little rain. Rainfall also varies dramatically depending on the island. Locales east of Java have sharply defined dry seasons, the duration increasing

the closer the area is to Australia. In the far southeastern islands such as Timor and Roti, the dry season can last up to seven months. Sumatra and Kalimantan, lying closer to the equator and farther from Australia, have *no* dry seasons. In Indonesia it's always hot, but due to mountain breezes and elevation, there's roughly one degree of cooling for every 90-meters increase in elevation.

Fauna And Flora

Forty different species of mammals are scattered throughout the archipelago and there are 150 state-supervised game parks and nature reserves. Among its mammals are great apes such as the orangutan with its shaggy blazing-orange

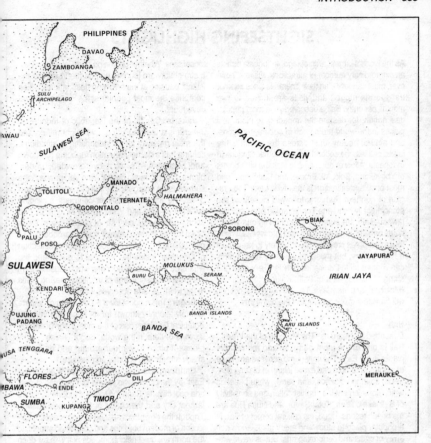

coat, deep-black wild cattle, 35-centimeter-high miniature deer, clouded leopards, mountain goats (*serow*), wild warthogs, the sun bear with a large white circle on its chest, and long-snouted tapirs that gallop like stallions tossing their heads and whinnying. The fauna of Irian Jaya (western New Guinea) resembles that of Australia: vividly colored birds of paradise, spiny anteaters, mouse-like flying possums, bandicoots. Reptiles include giant monitor lizards, the reticulated python (the world's longest snake, up to nine meters long), and deep croaking geckos.

Bird species number in the thousands: peacocks, pheasants, partridges, turkey-sized pigeons, jungle fowl that incubate their eggs in volcanic steam, black ibises flying in V-formations, and the hornbill of the Kalimantan jungle, which sounds like a puffing locomotive when it flies. Insect forms number in the hundreds of thousands: fabulously colored butterflies; aquatic cockroaches; praying mantises like bright green banana leaves; beetles in the shape of violins; submarine-diving grasshoppers; the world's most extraordinary moth, the atlas, whose wingspan measures 25 centimeters across; and spiders which catch and devour small birds in giant webs.

In Indonesia's seas are found the world's most expensive shell (the glory of the seas), crabs (*birgus*) that can clip down coconuts and open them on the ground, freshwater dolphins, and fish that climb mango trees looking for insects!

SIGHTSEEING HIGHLIGHTS

As the world's largest archipelago, Indonesia boasts an extraordinary number of attractions. Visitors, however, must carefully plan their itineraries since internal transport is rugged and visits are limited to two months per entry. Bali is deservedly the most popular destination, for despite the impact of tourism, few places in the world are so rich in culture, traditions, and natural beauty. Just across the straits is the island of Java, the second most visited destination in Indonesia. Allow enough time to visit the high points of Yogyakarta, Solo, Mt. Bromo, and Bandung. Third most popular destination is the idyllic Lake Toba region of northern Sumatra, followed closely by the ethnologically rich Tana Toraja region of central Sulawesi. Both are superbly relaxing regions where hours turn into days and days melt into weeks. These four major areas provide enough variety to keep most travelers busy, but those intrigued by remoteness can venture off to the islands of Nusa Tenggara (the string of islands east of Bali), Kalimantan, Maluku (Molucca), and Irian Jaya. The following descriptions will provide a quick overview of the highlights.

Bali

Described by Nehru as "The Morning of the World," Bali is one of the most beautiful and memorable places in the East. The very name conveys an image of magic—a remote and exotic island of blazing ricefields, soaring volcanos, and sandy white beaches which complement the sophistication and sensitivity of Balinese culture. Kuta, Sanur, and Nusa Dua are the beach resorts. Ubud, the cultural center of Bali, is a popular place to study and enjoy the island's rich array of crafts and performing arts. But as travel writers have been pointing out for generations, the arrival of Westerners has made an impact on the fragile island. Some areas have sadly degenerated into tourist traps and some Balinese have taken to mercantilism with a vengeance. So is Bali ruined? Absolutely not. Despite the wrenching changes, most of the island remains as peaceful and beautiful as when tourism discovered it in the 1930s.

Java

Indonesia's principal island is one of the richest, lushest, and most densely populated regions on the earth: the political, economic, and cultural center of Indonesia. As the genesis of powerful maritime and agricultural kingdoms, Java boasts most of the nation's best-preserved religious monuments and his-

torical sites. Whether beginning from Jakarta or Bali, a straightforward journey can be made across the island, pausing at the following destinations, which comprise the most popular stops on the Central Java route.

Jakarta: Capital of the Republic of Indonesia, Jakarta is a teeming city of over eight million and the main gateway for all Indonesian destinations. Jakarta has a dismal reputation for being run-down and hectic—Asia's most overcrowded, underplanned, and chaotic capital. And yet, beneath the surface is an energetic city full of interest and surprise. The chief drama is in its contrasts, a blinding collision of East and West where air-conditioned sports cars hurdle past street peddlers and sleek office towers throw shadows across cardboard hovels. Jakarta highlights include the superb collection of Orientalia inside the National Museum and the wharfside Makassar schooners, which together form the greatest assemblage of traditional sailing crafts in the East. Jakarta deserves a chance.

Bogor: This modest town 60 km south of Jakarta is internationally known for its huge and verdant Botanical Gardens, one of the most magnificent collections of flora in the world. Bogor is also a fairly pleasant place to wander around and enjoy the shady streets and colonial architecture.

Bandung: Once referred to as the "Paris of the East" by the Dutch, who valued its tree-lined streets and cool climate, Bandung today is Indonesia's third largest city and the center of Sundanese culture. Though the downtown section is a nondescript collection of modern buildings and congested streets, to the north are quiet neighborhoods rich with art-deco architecture dating from the 1930s. A walking tour is fully described in the text.

Yogyakarta: Java's foremost cultural center is a small and friendly town that offers dazzling performances of Ramayana theater, *gamelan* in the Sultan's Palace, *wayang golek, wayang kulit,* and crafts from outstanding batik and designer clothing to leather goods and pounded silver. Best of all, the town is relaxed and has immensely good vibes; the leading destination on Java.

Vicinity of Yogya: As well as being the cultural center of Javanese culture, Yogya is the gateway to some of Java's most spectacular monuments. Scattered around the countryside are the remains of ancient Buddhist and Hindu kingdoms, of which Borobudur and Prambanan are the most magnifi-

SIGHTSEEING HIGHLIGHTS

cent. Built in the 8th century on a hill overlooking green ricefields, Borobudur presents the world's largest and most complete collection of Buddhist relief sculpture. Prambanan is Indonesia's most famous Hindu temple complex. Farther afield is the eerie Dieng Plateau, where ancient Hindu shrines silently stand among the misty plains. All can be reached on public buses or seen on inexpensive day tours.

Solo: Sixty km east of Yogya is the sleepy town of Solo, Java's alternative city of culture. Solo has a pleasant small-town atmosphere and a few important sights, but it's best considered a place to relax and escape the tourism that dominates Yogya. In fact, so few tourists stop here that absolutely everybody seems thrilled to meet you!

Malang: Malang is a hilly city of parks, villas, broad boulevards, old Dutch homes, and some of the friendliest people in the archipelago. It's also a launching point to nearby East Javanese temples, hill resorts, and climbs up volcanos. Malang also symbolizes the rapid modernization of Indonesia; here in this remote and once-sleepy town you'll find air-conditioned shopping centers, one-hour photo shops, and video stores on almost every street corner.

Mt. Bromo: East Java's most spectacular sight is watching the sun rise from the volcanic rim of Gunung Bromo. Just as memorable, and certainly less crowded, is a hike across the sea of sand on the evening of a full moon.

Surabaya: Pity poor Surabaya. Indonesia's second largest city is considered by most travelers as hardly better than Jakarta—a hot, dirty, and noisy industrial hub on Java's swampy northern coast that suffers from all the typical ills of unplanned cities in Southeast Asia. But like Jakarta, Surabaya also deserves a second chance. Almost completely undisturbed since the '30s, Surabaya offers magnificent Dutch architecture, a wharf with dozens of impressive Makassar schooners, and beautiful little neighborhoods where people smile in amazement at the Western tourist. Beneath the heat, dirt, and noise is a city with more history and atmosphere than most places in Asia.

Sumatra

This gigantic island—fifth largest in the world—is economically and strategically the most important island in Indonesia. Called the "Africa of Southeast Asia," Sumatra's broad reach of steamy jungles,

swampy lowlands, clear rivers, spectacular waterfalls, crater lakes, and vast wildlife preserves makes it one of the world's great frontiers. Sumatra's two primary tourist destinations are Lake Toba in the north and Bukittinggi in the west.

Lake Toba: One of the world's largest crater lakes is also home to the Bataks, local tribespeople descended from Neolithic immigrants of 1,500 years ago. Lake Toba is remote and relaxing, a wonderful place to do nothing but read a good book and stare out at the glassy waters.

Bukittinggi: West Sumatra boasts some of the most exciting scenery you'll ever see: peaks looming over deep canyons, splendid sheltered valleys, great high plateaus, terraced ricefields, volcanic lakes. Most of the people are Minangkabau, a tribal group remarkable for its unique matrilineal society and magnificent style of domestic architecture. Bukittinggi is a small university town that serves as a good base for exploring the Minangkabau countryside. Nias Island and its megalithic ruins are also worth visiting.

Nusa Tenggara

The six major islands east of Bali that comprise Nusa Tenggara are home to dozens of ethnic groups, astounding natural wonders, smoking volcanos, superlative snorkeling, virgin game reserves, megalithic cultures, and the largest reptiles in the world. Nusa Tenggara (the "Southeastern Islands") is a fascinating but long and very difficult overland journey with erratic transportation across rugged roads. Most destinations can be quickly reached by air.

Lombok: Though it doesn't compare with its more famous neighbor (just 20 minutes by air from Bali), Lombok compensates with three beautiful islands off the northern coastline and the spectacular peak of Mt. Rinjani.

Komodo: Nusa Tenggara's chief attractions are the giant monitor lizards which live undisturbed on the island of Komodo. The sole survivors of carnivorous dinosaurs, *Varanus komodoensis* now draw thousands of travelers who endure four to five days of hard land travel from Bali.

Flores: Considered by many perhaps the most beautiful of all Indonesian islands, Flores has grandiose volcanos, multicolored lakes, stretches of savannah, and tropical deciduous forests. Some of the best skin diving in Southeast Asia lies off the northern coastline. Roads are horrendous, but flights go direct from Bali.

SIGHTSEEING HIGHLIGHTS

Sumba: Sumba is the source of the most handsome and highly prized *ikat* fabrics in Indonesia. Merpati flies daily from Bali.

Sulawesi

The world's most peculiarly shaped island is home to an amazing diversity of societies including the fiercely Islamic Bugis, the prosperous Christian Minahasans of the north, and the animist-Christian Torajans in the south-central region. This variety, along with some spectacular scuba diving and natural landscapes, has made Sulawesi the fourth most visited island in Indonesia, after Bali, Java, and Sumatra.

Tana Toraja: Aside from the Balinese, the richest cultural group in Indonesia is the Torajans of Sulawesi. Both Christian and animist, Torajan funerals are amazing ceremonies that can last for weeks and involve thousands of people depending on the status of the deceased. Torajans are also known for their textiles, burial caves, and remarkable domestic architecture with structures that resemble wooden ships riding an ocean of tropical foliage.

North Sulawesi: The northeastern arm of Sulawesi features prosperous towns, refreshing hot springs, friendly people, and some of the finest coral formations in the world.

Due to its extreme geographic fragmentation, Indonesia is richer in plant species than either the American or the African tropics. Its total number of flowering plant species is more than 35,000. To cite only a sample of Indonesia's floral wealth, there are 250 species of bamboo, 150 species of palm, and in the more fertile areas flowers are rampant—hibiscus, jasmine, allamanda, frangipani, bougainvillea, lotus lilies a half meter wide. Java alone has 5,000 plant species, and there are twice as many species of plants on Borneo as in all of Africa. The tall hardwood rainforest trees of Irian Jaya rival the giant sequoias of California; banyan trees planted outside the royal cities of Central Java are connected with authority and are populated by hordes of spirits; the corpse plant of Sumatra smells like putrefying animal flesh; the largest bloom in the world, the rafflesia (one meter wide), inhabits Sumatra; the luxurious vegetation of Borneo hosts the seductive colors of orchids, which glow in the perpetual twilight of the jungle.

HISTORY

When you read Indonesian history, you read world history. Indonesia is a subtle blending of every culture that ever invaded it—Chinese, Indian, Melanesian, Portuguese, Polynesian, Arabian, English, Dutch, and American. Indonesia's history is a story of wave after wave of migrations of peoples who either absorbed earlier arrivals, killed them off, or pushed them into less favorable regions such as deep forests, high mountains, or remote islands. This ongoing and unending process explains Indonesia's astounding ethnic diversity.

Indonesia's prehistory begins on Java, one of the earliest places in the world where man lived. In 1891 the fossil skull of an ape man (*Homo erectus*) was discovered at Trinil in Central Java. This erect near-man lived at a time when Europe was under ice, most of Indonesia was a part of Asia, and the Sunda Shelf was above water. He walked to Java, which was then a high mountainous island covered in wild jungle. This species of very early man ranged from Africa all the way to the glacial border of Europe and to China, some 500,000 years ago at the very beginning of the Pleistocene era. Negritos, a pygmy people who began to radiate through the islands some 30,000 years ago, were the first known human migrants into Indonesia. Genetic traces of these short, woolly haired, round-headed people are found in the jungles of East Sumatra, the uplands of the Lesser Sundas (Nusa Tenggara), and the remote highlands of Irian Jaya.

Anthropologists say the present-day Malay peoples of Indonesia came in two great waves, spreading through Sumatra, Borneo, Sulawesi, and Java. First came the so-called Proto-Malays (Caucasoid Malays), who possessed a neolithic-level culture. They are represented today by the Batak of Sumatra, the Toraja of Sulawesi, and the Dayak of Borneo. Next came the Deutero-Malays, who carried a more developed

Bronze Age civilization from Indochina. Deutero Malays are represented in all the ports and coasts of the Greater Sunda islands of Sumatra and Java. Today, generally speaking, the Proto-Malays occupy the agricultural interiors while the Deutero-Malays have settled the coastal regions.

Indian chroniclers wrote of Java as early as 600 B.C., and the ancient Hindu epic, the Ramayana, also gives mention of Indonesia. By the 2nd century A.D. Indian traders had arrived in Sulawesi, Sumatra, and Java. The stage was set for Hinduism. India, at the time of its colonializing efforts, was considered the pinnacle of civilization and at the apex of its cultural vigor. Local Indonesian rulers most likely invited the high-caste Brahmans to immigrate and work as a literate bureaucracy. Indian influences touched the ruling classes but ignored the rural people, who followed animism. Indonesians by the 4th century were using the South Indian Palava script to carve Mahayana Buddhist inscriptions. Sanskrit loan words found in the Indonesian language today indicate the specific contributions Indians made during their period of influence. Also introduced were legal practices as well as wet-rice cultivation, animal husbandry, glass, metaphysics, philosophy, and the Hindu concept of a divine ruler with unchecked powers.

Early Kingdoms

The Indonesian-Indian era reached its apogee in the 14th-century Javanese Majapahit Empire. Though the Golden Age of Indonesia thrived just over 100 years (1292-1398), Majapahit is remembered as Indonesia's greatest state because it established Indonesian unification and an Indonesian identity. The Majapahit Empire made a powerful and lasting impact on modern Indonesian culture as new and exciting native styles were fused with the traditions of India. The results can be seen everywhere. The *kraton* courts of Solo and Yogya remain strong enclaves of Hindu-Javanese Majapahit culture. The religion and culture of Bali, including the *gamelan* orchestra and the five-note scale, were inherited from India. Motifs and styles of old Hindu-Javanese culture permeate modern Indonesian art: all over Java you can see monumental gates constructed in Hindu style; Indian epic poems have been adapted into living Indonesian theater; Indian mythic heroes domi-

nate the plots; Indonesia's present state motto is a Sanskrit phrase; even the national emblem of Indonesia (the largest and most populous Muslim state in the world) is the mythical bird Garuda . . . the mount of the Hindu God Vishnu!

When Islamic traders arrived in the 15th and 16th centuries, they found all the great islands of Indonesia to be a complex of well-established Indianized kingdoms. The expansion of Muslim trade marked the beginning of the Islamic period in the archipelago. The capture of Malacca by the Portuguese in 1511 ousted Muslim merchants, scattering them all over insular Southeast Asia, taking their faith with them and spreading Islam even farther afield. Islam caught fire first in far northern Sumatra and then spread to Java, taking hold most solidly in those areas of Indonesia which had been least affected by the Hindu civilizations of the past. Hindu princes converted to Islam for reasons of trade, wealth, and power. The converted rulers adjusted to indigenous sentiments by permitting sultans to be worshipped as saints after death. Pre-Islamic signal towers became Muslim minarets; native Indonesian meeting halls were transformed into mosques. Demak was the first important Javanese city to turn Muslim (in 1477), followed by Cirebon (in 1480). In 1487, a coalition of Muslim princes attacked what was left of the Hindu Majapahit Empire. By the end of the 15th century 20 Muslim kingdoms ruled over the entire archipelago. Indonesia had become, and still remains, the largest Islamic nation in the world.

European Arrivals

The Portuguese were the first bearers of European civilization to Indonesia. Carrying *their* God with them to be embraced by the heathens, these vigorous and bold southern Europeans arrived in Indonesia a full 100 years before the Dutch but lasted only 150 years, until 1512. Portuguese involvement was largely commercial and did not involve territorial expansion. They set up fortified outposts in sheltered harbors to guard their trade routes and to offer respite and repair facilities for their fleets. Keeping the upper hand by virtue of their superior striking power, weaponry, and navigation techniques, the Portuguese were little more than pirates who acquired tribute and booty while exploiting whatever commodities they came upon: slaves, gold, textiles, spices. Portuguese influence ended in 1570 when they foolishly murdered the sultan of Ternate and the inhabitants threw them off the island.

Next in line were the British and the Dutch, who arrived for spices in the early 17th century. The two great maritime powers even kept outposts alongside each other in Banten, Macassar, Jakarta, and Ambon. Though treaties dictated a degree of cooperation, the underlying rivalry and enmity erupted at last on the island of Ambon in 1623 when the Dutch tortured and executed all the personnel of the English factory. The Ambon Massacre essentially ended English influence in Indonesia, aside from a brief reoccupation in 1811-1816 during the Napoleonic Wars. By the time Dutch traders reached the East Indies, they discovered they had a government, cities, monumental temples, irrigation systems, handicrafts, orchestras, shipping, art, literature, cannon fire, harems, and astrological systems. The Dutch began with a small trading company at Banten in 1596. When these ships returned to Holland with their valuable cargoes of spices, it touched off wild speculation and an explosion of speculative trading companies. Over 65 ships sailed to the East Indies from 1598 to 1605. To prevent rival Dutch companies from competing amongst themselves, a private stock company called the Vereenigde Oost-Indische (VOC) was chartered in 1602 to trade, make treaties, build forts, maintain troops, and operate courts of law in all the East Indies lands.

The Dutch did everything they could to isolate this closed insular world from all outside contact. Within 10 years of gaining their first foothold in Batavia in the early 17th century, they were sinking all foreign vessels they found in Indonesian waters. They opened strategic fortified factories and trading posts over the length of the archipelago. Internal Indonesian dynasties, continually feuding amongst themselves, were easy prey for the Dutch, who suddenly found themselves masters of huge amounts of unintended and unexpected territory. Using a combination of arms, treaties, treachery, and puppets, they increasingly took control of the internal affairs of Indonesian states. The Dutch institutionalized imperialism in the form of a huge bureaucracy of colonial civil servants who turned virtually all of Java into a vast state-owned labor camp run somewhat like an American slave plantation. Profits enabled the Dutch masters to build railways, pay off the national debt, and even start a war with Belgium. Indonesians were treated as third-class citizens, always a sure sign that revolution is on the way.

The Rise Of Nationalism

Intellectuals and aristocrats were the earliest revolutionaries against Dutch colonial rule. Diponegoro, the eldest son of a Javanese sultan, was the country's first nationalist leader, as well as being a masterful guerrilla tactician. In 1825, Diponegoro embarked on his holy war, a costly struggle of attrition and scorched-earth policy in which 15,000 Dutchmen and 250,000 Indonesians died. At one point the Dutch even considered pulling out of Java. Diponegoro was eventually lured into false negotiations, arrested, and sentenced to death. Today his face is on coins and street signs.

Nationalist organizations continued to protest the extreme dissatisfaction and impatience the Javanese masses had for the colonial regime. Everyone awaited a Ratu Adil, a Righteous Prince who would free them from their oppressors. An organization of middle-class traders started the Sarekat Islam (Muslim Society), which by 1917 had 800,000 members. Momentum was building. The final push began in 1926 when an ex-engineer named Sukarno established the PNI (Indonesian National Party). With his oratorical power and domineering, charismatic style, Sukarno soon emerged as Indonesia's most forceful political personality. The PNI demanded complete independence but sought this goal through Gandhi-style noncooperation. The Dutch responded with further ruthless exploitation of Indonesia's natural resources. A police state was imposed and political opportunists were thrown into jail.

The fall of Indonesia to the Japanese in 1940 had a shocking and sobering effect. Suddenly the Dutch didn't seem so powerful. The Indonesians were at first gratified that their Asian brothers had freed them by overthrowing the Dutch. But the Japanese soon showed themselves to be even more ruthless, fascist, and murderous than the Dutch had ever been. Indonesia suffered terribly; workers were made to bow to Japanese soldiers and wear identification tags; almost 300,000 were conscripted to work as slave laborers in the jungles of Burma and Malaysia; Indonesian women were forced into prostitution; the land was exploited of every possible resource: oil, rubber, rice, and iron were all shipped to Japan for the war machine.

Once the Japanese surrendered, bands of politically aligned young people (*laskar*) sprang up to fight the returning Dutch who embarked on ruthless "pacification" exercises, attacking cities and butchering hundreds. Outraged world opinion rallied behind the newly declared Republic. *Merdeka!* ("Freedom!") was on everybody's lips. The high drama ended on 27 December 1949 when the Dutch reluctantly transferred sovereignty to a free and independent Indonesia.

Modern Challenges

Sukarno was elected president of the new federal state and Indonesia was recognized by the United Nations. But it was a deeply troubled time for the new country. Politicians scrambled after power, cabinets fell every six months, and dissension erupted between the military, religious, left-wing, and conservative factions of the embryonic government. By 1955 there were 169 political parties fighting for only 257 seats. To end the national nightmare, Sukarno announced his policy of "Guided Democracy," which gave final authority to Jakarta and the ruling military clique. By the late '50s Sukarno had seized total power, press censorship was enforced, and politicians and intellectuals were jailed. Sukarno's mood darkened as his government left the U.N. and grew violently anti-Western and pro-communist. To prevent the creation of a Malaysian Federation in 1965, Sukarno launched his ill-advised campaign of confrontation. His once-brilliant leadership had broken into disparate political ideologies that borrowed from Marxism, nationalism, and Islam. Billions of dollars were squandered on colossal stadiums, conference halls, and Soviet-style statuary; inflation ran over 650% yearly; foreign debts threatened to sink the country. Indonesia had reached the breaking point.

On the night of 30 September 1965, six top generals and their aides were abducted and brutally murdered, allegedly by communists attempting a coup. What followed was one of the most massive retaliatory bloodbaths in modern world history. An unknown general named Suharto mobilized the army against the communist conspirators while Muslim youths burned the PKI (communist party) headquarters to the ground. Over the following months all of Java ran amok. An estimated 250,000 to 500,0000 people, including a disproportionate number of Chinese, were murdered by rampaging mobs. Communism was obliterated and a new order came to power. Although his implication in the plot was never made clear, Sukarno's power was systematically undermined by the new regime until his death in June 1970.

THE PEOPLE

Such an influx of peoples has flowed into Indonesia from China, Arabia, Polynesia, Southeast Asia, Indochina, and later from Portugal and Holland, that you can't say that Indonesians are one people. The country is in fact an ethnological gold mine, the variety of its human geography (336 ethnic groups) without parallel on earth. Welded together by a unifying lingua franca and intermarrying freely, Indonesia has all the Asian cultures, races, and religions; they worship Allah, Buddha, Shiva, and the Christian God—and in some places an amalgam of all four. Shades of skin vary from yellow to coal black. Each group strives to discover how all these differences can unite all Indonesians in beautiful harmony. The motto clasped in the talons of Garuda, the menacing eagle that is the state crest, is *Bhinneka Tunggal Ika* ("Unity in Diversity").

Being a collection of local archipelagic nations, many Indonesians identify themselves in local terms: Orang Toraja, Orang Sawu, Orang Mentawai, etc. This sense of local identity and strong connection to one's tribe has fostered an attitude of tolerance toward other cultures summed up in the Indonesian expression *"Lain desa, lain adat"* or "Other villages, other customs." And get along they must, as there are regional differences (between the devout matrilineal Minangkabau and the syncretic hierarchal Javanese); class conflicts (animist villager and orthodox Muslim landlord); racial minorities (Chinese, Eurasians, Indians, Negritos); religious minorities (Christians, Buddhists, Hindus); and local minorities (Kupang Buginese, Surabaya Madurese, Jakartan Ambonese). Indonesia is a society so complex that if it didn't already exist, nobody would ever dream of inventing it.

Many of Indonesia's ethnic pockets have remained isolated because of the archipelago's size, jungles, swamps, highlands, and complex customs. You can find ways of life which are 5,000 years apart—a journey through time. Cross sections of the people live in the Neolithic, Bronze, Middle, and Nuclear ages. Some Indonesians wear rings and rats' ribs in their noses; others read the *Asian Wall Street Journal* and breakdance. If they have mingled at all, it's taken place near the sea. Many of the mountain tribes have never recovered from past invasions or migrations, when they were scattered into the hills by conquerors who took over the richer valleys and coasts. The Kubu and Mamak tribes of Sumatra, the Punan of Kalimantan, and the Alfuro of Maluku are all descendants of the so-called Veddoids from central Asia who drifted into the archipelago over 10,000 years ago.

Indonesia has the fifth largest population in the world (about 173 million), which equals the combined population of all other Southeast Asian countries. Better health care, falling infant mortality (80 per thousand births in 1985), and longer life expectancy (averaging 56 years in 1985) are keeping more people alive. The population of Java (the size of California) alone has quadrupled this century to 91 million, well over a third of the population of the United States. The population of Jakarta is over eight million. The largest condom factory in Asia is found here, producing 130 million condoms a year.

Wherever you travel in Indonesia you'll hear the word *adat*. Meaning customary law, this is the word Indonesians utter when you ask them a question about a custom which they practice but don't know why or how it began. They just say, "It is *adat.*" Adat is Common Law, an unwritten and unspoken law which covers the actions and behavior of each inhabitant in every village and city *kampung* (neighborhood) in Indonesia. Evolving from a distant time when villages were largely self-governing, it dictates everything—what foods are eaten and when, ceremonies for and duties to the ill or the dead, ownership of land and irrigation systems, architecture of family houses and granaries, criminal and civil cases such as theft and rights of inheritance, relations between older and younger brothers and sisters, the order in which daughters will marry, whom they will marry, how they will marry, how guests are to be treated—everything, the total way of life.

LANGUAGE

Such is the diversity of tongues in Indonesia (250 speech forms, each with its own regional dialects) that often the inhabitants of the same island don't all speak the same native language. The tiny island of Alor alone hosts some 70 different dialects, and on Sulawesi 62 languages have been identified. Fortunately, one language, Bahasa Indonesia, is taught in all schools from the elementary grades. Though it's almost universally known as a second language, Bahasa Indonesia is the only cultural element that unifies the entire population. First used mainly as a political tool in 1927 with the cry "One Nation, One Country, One Language," it's the only language used in broadcasting, in official and popular publications, in advertisements, and on traffic signs. All the films shown in Indonesia are required by law to be dubbed in standardized, modern Indonesian. Most of the country's regional languages change forms and endings to show deference to the one addressed, but Bahasa Indonesia does not. Thus, Indonesian has been one of the main forces behind the democratization of all the different classes and races of the country.

If you're traveling in a foreign land it's impossible to understand the culture unless you have some knowledge of the language. Learning the language is the miracle drug that minimizes culture shock. Here are some tips. First learn the numbers, the time, and the calendar systems, the mastering of which will spare you much frustration and money. Avoid Indonesians who try to speak to you in English; they're your most formidable obstacle to learning their language. The only way to learn another language is to never speak your own. If you live with a non-English-speaking family, you'll be semifluent in a month. You have to learn it . . . to *survive!* Concentrate at first on just listening and speaking. It takes only a few weeks to learn the sound system properly, then you're on your way. You must hear Indonesian spoken and speak it every chance you get. Immerse yourself in it. Listen and constantly repeat words and phrases, impressing them on your memory. Only after you've learned the pronunciation should you take on the written language. Don't worry about making grammatical errors or common mistakes; this self-consciousness is a tremendous block to learning. You *have* to make mistakes to learn. "Perfect" Indonesian is also of little concern to Indonesians, who will always give you the benefit of the doubt. And you still get points for trying! Although at first you may not have a substantial vocabulary, try to use what words you *do* know skillfully. You'll be flabbergasted what you can say with a vocabulary of only 500 or so words. In one month of diligent work you'll be speaking the "market talk" or Pasar Melayu. This is all you'll need for bargaining, getting around, and relating to people. Cafes, bus stops, markets, kiosks, and offices are the best classrooms in the land. While waiting anywhere, start up a conversation. Educated Indonesians who delight in teaching you will make themselves known. They are very patient, repeating and writing words out, teaching you idioms, and breaking sentences down for you. If you move around and stay with the people, all you really need is a good dictionary. Never go anywhere without it and never stop asking questions. Listen to the radio. Translate songs, labels, posters, signs, banners, newspapers, tickets, handouts. Ask, ask, ask questions.

ARTS AND CRAFTS

With its giddy variety of insular environments, Indonesia is unique as a place where so many beautiful traditional crafts have been made for thousands of years. Superb craftsmanship and the longest traditions are best seen in the simplest crafts: the palm weaving of Bali, the flutemaking of the Torajans, the basketry of the Rotinese, the lizard motifs on Batak magic wands and houses, and infinite other examples of traditional domestic and cultic art. Indonesian arts and crafts lend themselves especially to attractive decorative items and furnishings for contemporary Western homes. Batik, queen of Indonesian artforms, can be fashioned into

upholstery, and the superb *ikat* textiles can make unique wall hangings.

Shopping in Indonesia is a real hit-or-miss treasure hunt; you must doggedly search every corner of a shop to find what you are looking for. Indonesians have different tastes, so look for that item which strikes your fancy. Many villages or city *kampung* specialize in their own crafts. If you want to know what crafts an area or city specializes in, just ask the locals what gifts they take to out-of-town relatives when they visit. This way, you find out what is cheap, unique, or rare about that place. If the plastic arts interest you, always head for ASRI (School of Fine Arts), art centers in the larger cities where painting, drawing, graphics, sculpture, and the decorative arts are taught.

The best buys are usually in the town or island where a particular craft is produced. There's a much wider selection and the artisans are often more agreeable to bargaining than city shopkeepers who pay higher overheads. This is not always the case, however, because even in remote areas you are regarded as a rich foreigner and peer pressure from other villagers could escalate prices. Crafts in shops are acquired either by middlemen who travel to crafts areas or from people in need of money who approach the shop with family heirlooms. You will often find shops selling similar goods located in a particular neighborhood or all in a row on a certain street or stretch of road. Locations of shops may be scattered and inconvenient, and hours of operation uncertain. Because of the helter-skelter location of shops and markets and Indonesia's wide cultural and geographic diversity, it's best to narrow your focus to a particular craft or artform, then design your itinerary. For example, if primitive art interests you, fly to Medan, Lake Toba, Rantepao, southern Maluku, and Irian Jaya. If it's batik you want, plan a route through Java that takes in the batik centers of Jakarta, Cirebon, Yogya, Solo, and Pekalongan. Or you can simply wander around Indonesia sampling all its different crafts. In general, shopping is the best in Bali and Yogyakarta.

PRACTICAL INFORMATION

GETTING TO INDONESIA

Indonesia can be entered by air through seven major gateways. Most travelers, though, still land at Jakarta, Bali, or Medan. Prices of flights into Indonesia change constantly. As soon as the "Official Airlines Guide" is published each month, it's already out of date. Check the latest and cheapest tickets in the Sunday travel section of major metropolitan newspapers. Then call STA, Council Travel, and other budget agencies for ballpark figures.

From America

Current fares from discount agencies and consolidators on the West Coast of North America average US$850-950 roundtrip and US$1000 roundtrip from New York. STA and Council Travel can advise on Pacific routings. See the main Introduction for addresses and phone numbers. Airlines serving Indonesia from the U.S. include United, TWA, Northwest, Quantas, JAL, and China Air. Most airlines have toll-free numbers for current fares, timetables, connections, etc. Call (800) 555-1212 for airline 800 numbers. Tickets purchased from airlines are generally full fare, although discounts are occasionally given.

Garuda flights from L.A. stop at the remote town of Biak, where the local natives patiently wait at the runway for the twice-weekly arrival. Consider flying one-way to Biak and continuing with local aircraft across the archipelago—the backdoor approach is an excellent alternative since you enter through the most spectacular parts of Indonesia—the outer islands. Other great ways to reach Indonesia include the South Pacific routing through Tahiti and Australia and the North Pacific routing through Japan, Hong Kong, and Southeast Asia. Details in the main Introduction.

From Europe

Most travelers make a stop in Bangkok or Singapore, although several airlines now offer direct flights to Jakarta or Bali. Trailfinders and STA sell budget tickets. Fares average £300-400 one-way to Jakarta or £600-750 roundtrip. Bali costs slightly less one-way but slightly more roundtrip. The weekly *Time Out* contains ads for many bargain airfares and discount travel agencies. Intriguing alternatives to a direct flight are inexpensive round-the-world tickets and one-way tickets to Australia or New Zealand with stops in India, Bangkok, or Hong Kong.

From Australia

Both Qantas and Garuda fly to Bali and Jakarta from Australia's main cities: Sydney, Melbourne, Darwin, Perth, and Port Hedland. Tickets are expensive and deep discounts such as those available in London and America are nonexistent. The best deals are APEX tickets, which must be reserved and paid for at least three weeks in advance, and seven- to 28-day excursion fares from travel agencies. Avoid high season from November to February.

Another cheap way to reach Indonesia is to join a group tour, which can cost even less than APEX fares. The cheapest and certainly the most intriguing approach is the twice-weekly Merpati flight from Darwin to Kupang (Timor) for A$225 one-way. The more expensive Darwin to Bali flight is also recommended since stops are permitted in Maumere, Ruteng, Labuhanbajo, Bima, and Ampenan—a sensible way to avoid the nightmare of land travel across Nusa Tenggara.

TOURIST OFFICES OVERSEAS

Australia	4 Blight St., Cape Court House, Sydney NSW 2000	232-6044
Europe	Wiesenhuettenstrasse 17, D-6000 Frankfurt/Main	(069) 233677
U.S.A.	3457 Wilshire Blvd., Los Angeles, CA 90010	(213) 387-2078

EXPLORATORY CRUISES

Sailing through the most remote reaches of Indonesia also seems to be gaining in popularity. Itineraries are designed to offer the widest collection of peoples, places, sights, and sounds, including a complex variety of primitive cultures almost completely untouched by the outside world.

Abercrombie & Kent: This well-known operator conducts dozens of land-based tours plus Indonesian voyages on its 96-passenger *Explorer*, purchased in 1992 from defunct Society Expeditions. 1520 Kensington Rd., Oak Brook, IL 60521, tel. (800) 323-7308.

Seaquest Cruises: Salen Lindblad, once known for its Indonesian tours aboard the 162-passenger *Frontier Spirit*, was acquired in 1992 by this Floridian cruise operator. The *Frontier Spirit* sails extremely unusual itineraries to isolated islands near Nusa Tenggara, Borneo, and Sumatra. 600 Corporate Dr. #410, Fort Lauderdale, FL 33334, tel. (800) 223-5688.

P & O: Indonesia's only luxury mini-cruiser, the MV *Island Explorer*, operates across the islands of the Lesser Sundas (Bali, Lombok, Sumbawa, Flores, Sawu, Sumba) for 10 months of the year and cruises Jakarta, Krakatau, Ujung Kulon, and south Sumatra during December and January. Standard twin cabin costs US$2300 for 10-day Bali to Kupang, and US$1800 for nine days from Jakarta. In America call Abercrombie and Kent at 1 (800) 323-7308.

Renaissance Cruises: Three super-luxury cruises: Singapore-Bali (20 days from US$7000), Nusa Tenggara (14 days from US$5000), Singapore-Hong Kong (22 days from US$7000). Call (800) 525-2450 for their brochure detailing their 25 worldwide itineraries.

Sea Trek: Travelers bored with luxury ships should check out Sea Trek. Beginning from Bali, their traditional tall-masted Bugis schooners sail across the Lesser Sundas and off to the Moluccas (Maluku) and Sulawesi. Rates average US$100-130 per day—the least expensive and most adventurous sailing in the archipelago. Passage can be booked through American adventure travel operators (try Adventure Center and Overseas Adventure Travel) or write to Sea Trek, Herengracht 21, 1016 BG Amsterdam, Holland.

From Singapore

The most popular approach to Indonesia is the daily flight from Singapore to Jakarta or Bali. One-way fares currently stand at US$100-150 to Jakarta and US$180-250 to Bali. Budget agencies advertise in the *Straits Times,* though the very cheapest deals are passed from traveler to traveler. Ask about the special UTA Singapore-U.S.A. ticket for US$800 with stops in Jakarta, Bali, Australia, New Zealand, and Tahiti; an incredible deal.

Direct sea connections from Singapore to Indonesia do not exist, but indirect passage is possible via Batam and the Indonesian island of Tanjung Pinang. You'll save some money but it can be a slow and frustrating experience filled with delays and cancellations. Step one is a ferry from Finger Pier to the Singaporean island of Batam. A second ferry continues to the Indonesian island of Tanjung Pinang, where passengers proceed through customs and immigration and usually spend a night. The MV *Lawit* leaves Tanjung Pinang twice monthly for either Jakarta *or* Belawan (near Medan in north Sumatra). This luxurious German-built ship has seven first-class cabins, 10 second-class cabins, and covered deck-class accommodations for 866 passengers. Total fare is S$120-240 depending on class. Allow three full days from Singapore. *Arrive in Tanjung Pinang on the correct day unless you don't mind waiting for up to two weeks for the next boat!*

You can also fly from Batam to Jakarta if you miss your connection. For reservations and further information in Singapore, contact STA (tel. 734-5681) in the Ming Court Hotel on Tanglin Road, German Asian Travels (tel. 533-5466) in the Straits Trading Building on Battery Road, Yang Shipping (tel. 223-9902), Dino Shipping (tel. 221-4916), or Inasco Shipping (tel. 224-0698).

An erratic and rugged cargo boat sails weekly from Tanjung Pinang to Pekanbaru in south Sumatra. The Conradesque journey sails up the Siak River for 36 hours to Pekanbaru for Rp30,000 deck class or Rp45,000 in the cabin. The experience has been both highly praised and strongly damned by travelers.

From Malaysia

The second most popular way to reach Indonesia from Southeast Asia is the US$80 daily flight

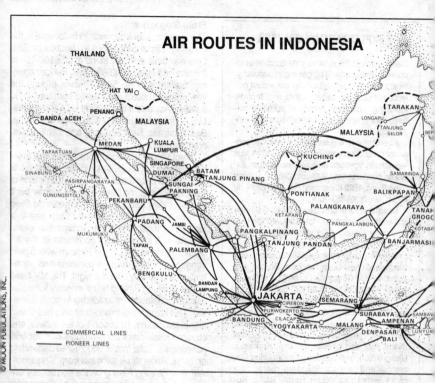

AIR ROUTES IN INDONESIA

COMMERCIAL LINES
PIONEER LINES

© MOON PUBLICATIONS, INC.

from Penang to Medan in northern Sumatra. Garuda also flies from Kuala Lumpur to several towns in Sumatra, including Medan, Padang, and Pekanbaru. A regular ferry sails from Penang twice weekly to Medan's port of Belawan. Tickets cost US$50 second class. Garuda and Merpati also fly between Kalimantan and the Malaysian states of Sabah and Sarawak.

GETTING AROUND INDONESIA

By Air

Surface transportation, as usual, is cheaper but means a lengthy land or sea passage. Given the limited two months you have in Indonesia, if you want to see the islands beyond Java, Sumatra, and Bali, flying is almost unavoidable. Prices are reasonable, flights are safe, and service is adequate. Always try to get a seat in front of the wings so you can enjoy some of In-

donesia's spectacular volcanic and marine scenery during your flight.

State-run Garuda Indonesia, the largest Indonesian airline, serves a limited number of domestic routes for international clients who need direct connections. They have essentially withdrawn from the domestic market. All other routes, as well as some border-crossing flights to Australia and eastern Malaysia, are now flown by Merpati using DC-9s, F-28s, Airbuses, and Fokkers. Other airlines such as Bouraq offer additional flights on a zany collection of aircraft including DC-3s, Vanguards, 707s, Viscounts, Skyvans, and Twin Otters. These alternative airlines concentrate in the low-traffic fringe areas not served by Garuda or Merpati. No matter the airline, always confirm flight availability and book a seat well in advance—especially important in the eastern islands where flights are less frequent and seats tend to fill up quickly. Airport departure tax is Rp2000-6000 for internal flights

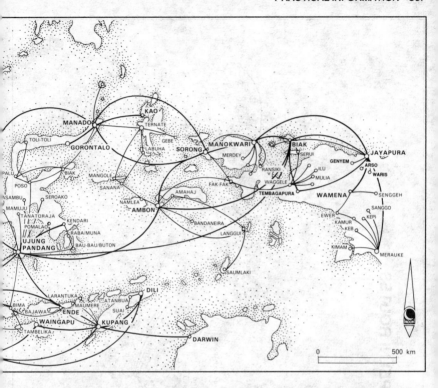

and Rp15,000 for external flights. Baggage allowances are from 10 kg on smaller planes such as the 16-passenger Fokker Friendship up to 20 kg on larger aircraft; excess baggage charge is about Rp5000 per kg (if they even bother to charge you). Airport luggage-storage facilities charge Rp2000-3000 per day.

By Sea

Sea transportation—in one form or another—is available to and from all the inhabited islands of Indonesia. The range of sailing craft is nothing short of fantastic: *prahu* which can sail virtually anywhere, Makassarese and Bugis schooners (*kapal layar*) hauling timber from Borneo to Jakarta, speedboats (*spetbot*) and bulky river ferries, outrigger canoes, luxury cruise ships hauling wealthy tourists and veteran travel writers. Frozen as they are in a 19th-century time warp, it's an unforgettable experience riding on Indonesian vessels.

Watch the PBS special "Ring of Fire" for inspiration! Check with a *syahbandar* (harbormaster) in any of the thousands of ports of Indonesia about the comings and goings of boats and their prices. Or ask around the harbor first to find a ship sailing where you want to head, then go to the shipping company office. This is when knowing Indonesian really pays off.

The most reliable oceangoing shipping company is state-owned Pelni, which has seven new German ships sailing from one end of the archipelago to the other (Banda Aceh to Sorong) on fixed schedules. Pelni ships are fast, sleek, modern, safe, and comfortable. All are completely air-conditioned (even deck class!) and designed to carry 1,000-1,500 passengers in four classes and *ekonomi*. Pelni gets to just about everywhere at two-week intervals. Fares are standardized and very reasonable; in fourth class you sleep in an eight-berth cabin with your own locker; in third class, there are six beds; in second

PELNI ROUTES

JAYAPURA

SORONG

TERNATE

AMBON

BAU/BAU

KUPANG

ENDE

WAINGAPU

BITUNG

TOLI-TOLI

PANTOLOAN

BIMA

TARAKAN

LEMBAR (LOMBOK)

UJUNG PANDANG

PADANGBAI (BALI)

BALIKPAPAN

SURABAYA

SEMARANG

PONTIANAK

KETAPANG

BANJARMASIN

T.G. PRIOK (JAKARTA)

MUNTOK

BENGKULU

500 km

0

MALAHAYATI (BANDA ACEH)

LHOKSEUMAWE

DUMAI

PADANG

SIBOLGA

BELAWAN (MEDAN)

© MOON PUBLICATIONS, INC.

PELNI SHIPS AND ROUTES

Kerinci—The ship for western Sumatra: Jakarta, Surabaya, Ujung Pandang (Sulawesi), Kalimantan, Jakarta, Padang (Sumatra), Sibolga (Sumatra), Jakarta.

Kambuna—Central Indonesia: Jakarta, Surabaya, Ujung Pandang, Kalimantan, Bitung (Sulawesi), Kalimantan, Lombok, Bali, Jakarta, Belawan (Sumatra), Jakarta.

Rinjani—The outer islands: Jakarta, Surabaya, Ujung Pandang, Bau Bau (southeastern Sulawesi), Ambon (Malukus), Sorong (Irian Jaya), Ambon, Bau Bau, Ujung Pandang, Surabaya, Jakarta, Belawan, Jakarta.

Umsini—The outer islands: Jakarta, Surabaya, Ujung Pandang, Bitung (northern Sulawesi), Ternate, Sorong, Jayapura (Irian Jaya), Sorong, Ternate, Bitung, Ujung Pandang, Surabaya, Jakarta.

Tidar—Central Indonesia: Surabaya, Ujung Pandang, Balikpapan (Kalimantan), Tarakan (Kalimantan), Ujung Pandang, Surabaya.

Lawit—The east coast of Sumatra: Jakarta, Muntok (eastern Sumatra), Kilang (eastern Sumatra), Dumai (eastern Sumatra), Belawan, Jakarta, Pontianak, Jakarta.

Kelimutu—The Nusa Tenggara route: Semarang, Banjarmasin (Kalimantan), Surabaya, Lombok, Ujung Pandang, Bima (Sumbawa), Ende (Flores), Dili (Timor), Kupang (Timor), Waingapu (Sumba), Ujung Pandang, Lombok, Surabaya.

class, four beds; and in first class, two beds. First-class fare includes TV, day and night videos, bathrooms with hot showers, comfortable beds, palatable meals. Economy-class bunks fit 50-60 people; you're assigned a numbered space on long, low, wooden platforms, each with its overhead baggage rack. A couple that wants to stay together should book either first or second class. Economy is adequate for shorter hauls but fourth class is preferable for longer journeys. Arrive at dockside at least three to four hours before sailing to secure a good bunk.

Train Travel

Indonesia has 7,891 km of track, all on Java, Madura, and Sumatra. Java's rail system, the most extensive in Indonesia, runs the whole length of the island, connecting the east coast with the ferry for Bali and the west coast with the ferry to Sumatra. In Sumatra, trains connect the port of Telukbetung with Palembang and Lubuklinggau in the south, while other tracks connect Padang with inland Lake Singkarak and the port of Belawan with Medan in the north.

Trains are heavily booked. It's often difficult to obtain tickets at the last minute. Double-check schedules. If you board a train without a reserved seat, you'll end up standing and swaying the whole way. Seat reservations at some stations and for some trains are available only one day in advance; in other cities tickets can be bought three days before departure; in yet other cities, only one hour before departure! In Jakarta, tickets can be bought only on the day of departure, so rise early, get in line, and expect to wait for as long as two to three hours. A roundtrip by train cannot be booked; return reservations must be made at the point of departure. To save the hassle of getting to a station and waiting in line, reservations may be made in advance through a travel agency for a small charge.

Local Transportation

The choice of native transport available will amaze you. Besides trains and taxis, which are the most convenient and the most expensive, there are *bemo, helicak, bajaj, becak,* and other contraptions used for short distances. The most important thing to understand about travel in Indonesia is the concept of *jam karet,* or "rubber time." Times of departure are stretched or contracted depending on the whim of the driver, pilot, or captain, and how full or empty the passenger seating is. So don't be in a hurry. No one else is! Avoid traveling during religious holidays such as Idul Fitri (the end of the Islamic fasting month), when millions of Indonesians hit the road to visit relatives. You must compete with them for transport and tourist facilities, and prices skyrocket.

Motorcycles provide a fast, convenient and inexpensive way to get around. Ride one with great caution, as serious motorcycle accidents on Indonesia's often congested, madcap roads are all too common. Indonesia is not the place to learn to ride a motorcycle. Bring warm clothes for highlands, where the temperature drops considerably. An International Driver's License endorsed for motorcycles is usually required before you can rent one. Without one, you'll need to get a special local license on Bali. Motorcycles can be rented on Bali and Lombok, in Yogyakarta and Surabaya, and at Lake Toba.

TRAVEL FORMALITIES

Visas

Indonesia offers a 60-day visa-free entry for most foreigners who enter the country through an approved gateway city or port. There are several important conditions. All visitors must possess a passport valid for at least six months after arrival. Two-month tourist passes cannot be extended. If you want to stay longer, the only option is to leave the country and return for another stamp. Thirdly, all visitors must possess a ticket out on arrival. This requirement can be satisfied by purchasing the least expensive ticket and then requesting a refund if unused. The

APPROVED GATEWAY CITIES

Java	Jakarta Airport
	Jakarta Seaport
	Surabaya Airport
	Surabaya Seaport
	Semarang Seaport
Bali	Ngurah Rai Airport
	Padangbai Seaport
	Benoa Seaport
Sumatra	Medan Airport
	Belawan Seaport
	Pekanbaru Airport
	Padang Airport
Riau	Tanjung Pinang Seaport
	Batam Airport
	Batam Seaport
Sulawesi	Manado Airport
	Manado Seaport
Kalimantan	Pontianak Airport
	Balikpapan Airport
Maluku	Ambon Airport
	Ambon Seaport
Timor	Kupang Airport
Irian Jaya	Biak Airport

IRON DINOSAURS

A decade ago Java was still the equivalent of a wildlife sanctuary for rare engines, with over 700 active steam locomotives made up of no less than 69 classes. Occasionally you can still see locos puffing out of the railyards in Madiun, and behemoths such as Mallets or Hartmanns, their smokestacks belching steam and soot, can also be seen hauling rolling stock up severe gradients in the vicinity of Bandung at Cibatu. A big draw for rail buffs is the open-air museum at Ambarawa in Central Java, where 22 steam locomotives have been let out to pasture. Charter groups can enjoy the thrill of a steam-hauled ride aboard a vintage Swiss-built cogwheel tank loco from Ambarawa to Bedono through scenic hilly terrain; book through the PJKA office on Jalan Thamrin in Semarang.

two cheapest and most convenient exit points are Medan-Penang (one-way ticket out is US$80) and Jakarta-Singapore (student fare is US$120-150).

Another important restriction is that only those visitors who enter and exit through *approved* gateway cities will be granted the two-month tourist pass. This includes all popular gateway cities, so very few travelers need to worry about this. Those travelers who intend to enter or exit through nonapproved gateway cities must obtain a one-month visa in advance from an Indonesian consulate. These can be extended 30 days by paying a landing tax of Rp50,000. Nonapproved cities to beware of include Jayapura (Irian Jaya) and Tarakan (Kalimantan). Approved gateway cities are listed below.

Other possible visas include a Business Visa and a Visitor's Visa for students or those with Indonesian sponsors. Special certificates from the police called *surat jalans* are sometimes necessary to explore the more remote areas of Indonesia, such as interior Irian Jaya. This letter must be presented on demand to army, police, immigration, or customs officials: a reassuring sign that you are being a fine, cooperative tourist.

Tourist Information

Indonesian tourist offices, both overseas and domestic, are very poorly stocked aside from a few colorful and relatively generic brochures.

INDONESIAN DIPLOMATIC MISSIONS OVERSEAS

Australia	8 Darwin Ave., Canberra ACT 2600	(062) 73-3222
Canada	287 Maclaren St., Ottawa, Ontario K2P0L9	(613) 236-7403
France	49 rue Cartambert, Paris 75116	503-0760
Germany	Bernkasteler Strasse 2, Bonn 5300	(0228) 328990
Japan	9 Higashi Gotanda, 5-Chome, Shingawa, Tokyo	441-4201
Netherlands	Tobias Asserlaan #8, Den Haag	(070) 469796
New Zealand	70 Glen Rd., Kelburn, Wellington	75895
Papua New Guinea	P.O. Box 7165, Baroko, Port Moresby	251-3116
United Kingdom	157 Edgeware Rd., London W22HR	(01) 499-7661
U.S.A.	2020 Massachusetts Ave., Washington, D.C. 20036	202-775-5200
	5 East 68th St., New York, NY 10021	(212) 879-0600
	3457 Wilshire Blvd., Los Angeles, CA 90010	(213) 383-5126
	1111 Columbus Ave., San Francisco, CA 94133	(415) 474-9571
	233 North Michigan Ave., Chicago, IL 60601	(312) 938-0101

Letters and personal visits even to the national headquarters in Jakarta are almost completely useless. Garuda and Natrabu Travel offices in Western countries are often much more helpful than tourist offices. Visiting the regional offices in places like Yogyakarta and Bandung is worthwhile, however, since you may come across an exceptionally knowledgeable employee who sincerely wants to help you discover what is most beautiful about his or her country.

The really valuable and up-to-date travel information you'll get from other travelers along the way—cheapest and friendliest *losmen,* where to eat and drink, best beaches, most beautiful walks, spectacular ruins, mystics, where to learn *kris* making. The many Indonesians you inevitably meet can tell you where *wayang,* dance, or folk dramas are happening, where to find the best crafts. This book will fill in the basics and give you enough maps to find your way around, but the sheer complexity of Indonesia prevents *Southeast Asia Handbook* from going into great detail. To really understand the mind-blowing diversity, rumors, dirt, and glory of Indonesia, buy Bill Dalton's *Indonesia Handbook.*

Maps
The best folded maps of Indonesia available are the APA Roadmaps: *Bali* (scale 1:180,000), *Sumatra* (1:1,500,000), *Java and West Nusa*

Tenggara (1:1,500,000), *Kalimantan* (1:1,500,000), etc. Costing US$6.95 each, these beautiful maps feature vivid eight-color printing, topographic features in realistic relief, and major city plans in close-up margin inserts. These maps can be found at better hotels in Indonesia, but it's best to bring them with you. Another high-quality folded map is *Hildebrand's Travel Map of Western Indonesia.* At US$5.95, this up-to-date map clearly presents the country's topography, roads, towns, and cities. Beware of local maps; village locations seem determined by throwing darts at the map.

Currency
The Indonesian monetary unit is called the *rupiah* (Rp). Study Indonesian currency and coins until you're familiar with all the denominations. Bills are all the same size but different colors. When changing large amounts, banks usually give you Rp10,000 notes, which could make it difficult to get your wallet or moneybelt shut! But changing even a Rp10,000 bill in the outlying provinces of Indonesia could prove troublesome. If heading for the outer islands, it's best to accept only Rp1000 and Rp5000 notes. In mid 1994 one U.S. dollar was worth 2,150 *rupiah.*

U.S.-dollar traveler's checks are most widely accepted, though it's also easy to cash other well-known currencies such as Australian dol-

TOUR OPERATORS

Indonesian companies are really starting to get into the adventure/special-interest travel market. The following are some major inbound operators whose services and reliability are top-notch.

Natrabu: Indonesia's second largest tour operator sponsors a wide variety of tours, including a 14-day Java-Bali overland expedition for US$1400, a nine-day Jakarta-Yogyakarta tour for US$850, a seven-day Sumatra trip for US$450, and a five-night Lake Toba tour for US$250. Other tours are offered to Sulawesi and Irian Jaya and across Nusa Tenggara. All packages include accommodations, meals, and guide services. Natrabu offices are located in most Indonesian cities. In America call (800) 628-7228; in California call (800) 654-6900.

Pacto: Pacto Tours is an Indonesian-based travel agency with offices in most Indonesian cities. Sobek (below) is their American representative. Tours are somewhat cheaper than Natrabu tours and geared toward Indonesians rather than Westerners.

Mountain Travel-Sobek: Offers rafting trips on the remote Alas River of northern Sumatra. Eight-day tours from Medan cost US$1100 for land only. Other tours include a 10-day Islands of Fire on Bali and Java for US$2400, including airfare from Los Angeles; a 10-day tour of Irian Jaya for US$1700 air inclusive; an eight-day Kalimantan river trip for US$1400. Call (800) 227-2384.

Vayatours: Indonesia's third-largest tour operator offers a wide variety of excursions from Bali to Irian Jaya. In America call (213) 487-1433 or (800) 999-8292 outside California.

Geo Expeditions: A 21-day expedition through Ujung Kulon Reserve (led by wildlife naturalist Emmy Hafild), a visit to Krakatau, orangutans on Kalimantan, and the dragons of Komodo make this an exceptionally exciting tour. US$3000 without air. Call Geo at (800) 351-5041 or (209) 532-0152 in California.

Wilderness Travel: Fifteen-day tours across Java and Bali from US$2000 plus air. Call (800) 368-2794 or (510) 548-0420 in California.

Adventure Center: One-stop source for adventure tours in Indonesia and throughout Southeast Asia. Call (800) 227-8747 or (800) 228-8747 inside California.

Overseas Adventure Travel: Large East Coast adventure wholesaler with unusual tours to Indonesia, Borneo, and New Guinea. Call (800) 221-0814.

Select Tours: Small California agency with unusual tours led by an expert in the folklore and mythology of the outer islands. 901 North Pacific Highway, Suite 212 B, Redondo Beach, CA 90278, tel. (800) 356-6680.

Bicycle Tours: Backroads Bicycle Tours (tel. 800-533-2573) bikes around Bali for 12 days, while Asian Pacific Adventures (tel. 213-935-3156) takes 17 days to bike Lake Toba.

Scuba Diving: Both See & Sea (tel. 415-434-3409) in San Francisco and Tropical Adventures (tel. 800-247-3483) in Seattle dive the crystal-clear waters of Indonesia. In Jakarta contact Jakarta Dive School (tel. 583051, ext. 9008) in the Hilton Hotel or Dive Indonesia (tel. 380107 ext. 76024) in the Borobudur Intercontinental Hotel. Both organize dives to the superb corals at Flores and off northern Sulawesi.

Danu Enterprises: Judy Slattum, author of a wonderful book entitled *Masks of Bali*, and her Balinese husband, Made Surya, sponsor several extremely unusual tours such as "Traditional Masks of West Java" and "The Healing Arts of Bali." Prices are reasonable and guides (Judy and Made) are first-rate. 313 McCormick Ave., Capitola, CA 95010, tel. (408) 476-0543.

Maluku Adventures: Mike Espinosa's tour company specializes in off-the-beaten-track destinations in the eastern provinces of the Moluccas and Irian Jaya, including dive trips near Ambon, treks across the Banda Islands, and horse excursions on Sumba. Wild stuff! 910 Cloud Ave., Menlo Park, CA 94025, tel. (415) 854-1321.

Art Trek: A small but creative company geared toward artists and art lovers. Trips are cosponsored by major museums and include instruction on watercolors, personal journals, and art history. P.O. Box 807, Bolinas, CA 94924, tel. (415) 868-1836.

Garuda Orient Holidays: The single largest wholesale-tour operator to Indonesia markets a series of packages to all possible destinations in the archipelago. Garuda covers not only the standard tourist routes to Bali and Central Java, but also adventure tours and river safaris as described in their 70-page catalog. 3457 Wilshire Blvd., Suite 207, Los Angeles, CA 90010, tel. (800) 247-8380, fax (213) 389-1568.

lars, Deutschmarks, Netherlands florin, French and Swiss francs. Bank Expor Impor Indonesia, Bank Negara Indonesia, and Bank Rakyat Indonesia have branches virtually the length and breadth of the country, from Aceh to Kupang. When exchanging large amounts, it's worth shopping around to get the best rate. Surprisingly, the highest rates are found in tourist towns such as Kuta, Yogya, and Rantepao. Avoid exchanging money at airports, train stations, and leading hotels. Indonesia has no black market.

Take enough money with you in the first place so you won't have to go through the hassle of having money wired, a service which costs up to US$15. Travelers who've been caught short have found that it may take several weeks to get money remitted by wire from Australia, North America, or Europe. Then there's the horror story of the Indonesian bank that kept the money wired to them for a month and invested it! If you're really stuck, a telex is a much faster way to transfer money than ordinary telegrams or moneygrams. Before you go, get your bank's telex number. A slower way is to wire home and ask for an international money order.

Indonesia's cheapest destinations are right along the travelers' trail, but watch out; you'll spend more here on fruit smoothies and batik underwear than you ever will in Irian Jaya. Ask for receipts for entrance fees to temples but don't raise a fuss since the "guards" are only trying to feed their families. Bribes are often necessary to expedite legal paperwork, get the last seat on the train, obtain a permit to visit a remote tribe, get out of jail. You know when it's coming: "The matter must be referred to another department. Come back next week."

Bargaining

Bargaining will teach you much about the real Indonesia. Always try to get the lowest price the seller will accept. The more Indonesians overcharge, the less interaction there is, the less respect there is, and the more impoverished the communication becomes. Bargain for everything: medicine in drugstores, hospitalization, immigration fees, entrance charges to museums or temple sites, no matter what type of establishment it is, even "fixed-price" shops. Bargaining should be good-humored, not infuriating, a game won by technique and strategy, not by anger or threats. This isn't a one-way process at all—Indonesians enjoy it. It's how most Indonesians relate with you. Before you go shopping, ask your hotel proprietor, houseboy, driver, or anyone who is uninvolved with the shop what the *correct* price for the item or service is. Indonesians themselves are always swapping price information as a way of keeping their costs down. Compare prices, learn about the quality, and then ask for the beginning price. Never make the first offer! Offer a quarter to half of the asking price. When you reach your highest price, don't budge. Instead, try "The Walk Away," as feigned disinterest makes for good deals. The real secret to successful bargaining is *never to appear to care*. This is absolutely necessary with *becak* drivers; just smile, shrug your shoulders, and walk slowly away with cocked ears. Often the driver will call you back, agreeing to your last bid. Never hover around, fondle, or show enthusiasm for your *true* interest. Instead, include the item with other articles you want, as if it's a second thought, "Oh, how much for this too?" Finally, remember that it's bad manners to continue to bargain after a deal has been struck, a service has been rendered, or an item has been bought.

SUGGESTED READINGS

More than any other destination in Southeast Asia, Indonesia is the country where advance reading will reap the greatest rewards. The country is far too rich, complex, and expansive to be covered adequately by any singular guidebook to Southeast Asia. This handbook covers the highlights in fairly good detail, but anyone venturing off to explore the outer islands should arm themselves with Bill Dalton's *Indonesia Handbook,* also published by that small but dedicated outfit in Chico, California. Dalton's masterpiece will always need some fine tuning, but the depth of background information and extraordinary writing style make it one of the remarkable achievements of contemporary travel literature.

♦ Blair, Lawrence. *Ring of Fire.* New York: Bantam Books, 1988. An extraordinary journey to the most remote corners of the archipelago. This book and the accompanying PBS film series stand as one of the great achievements of contemporary adventure travel. Highly recommended.

♦ Draine, Cathie. *Culture Shock.* Singapore: Times Books, 1986. Another in the outstanding series of handy guides to customs, social etiquette, and world views of the Indonesians. A useful travel companion.

♦ Kallen, Christian and Richard Bangs. *Islands of Fire, Islands of Spice.* San Francisco: Sierra Club Books, 1988. Travel adventure tightly interwoven with historical and cultural observations. Outstanding text marred by dreadful photography.

♦ Koch, Christopher. *The Year of Living Dangerously.* New York: Penguin, 1978. Peter Weir's evocative movie of love and loyalties in Jakarta, 1965, was based on this tightly penned novel.

♦ Lubis, Mochtar. *Twilight in Jakarta.* New York: Vanguard, 1964. Political corruption and the underbelly of Javanese society as viewed by Indonesia's most important modern writer. Mochtar's other works include *The Indonesian Dilemma,* which focuses on the shortcomings of the Indonesian personality, and *A Road With No End,* which established his literary reputation.

♦ McDonald, Hamish. *Suharto's Indonesia.* Australia: Fontana Books, 1980. The best introduction available to the complex world of Indonesian politics, with fascinating accounts of Suharto, corruption, the collapse of Pertamina, Timor, and the fate of Indonesia's political prisoners. Highly recommended.

♦ Holt, Claire. *Art in Indonesia.* Ithaca, New York: Cornell University Press, 1967. A modern classic written for the generalist rather than the academic.

♦ Oey, Eric. *Indonesia.* Singapore: APA Publications, 1986. Brilliant writing and superb photography make this a singular introduction to the archipelago. A vast improvement over the APA guides to Bali and Java.

♦ Stewart, Ian Charles. *Indonesians: Portraits from an Archipelago.* Singapore: Concept Media, 1983. A spellbinding photographic essay of 280 full-color portraits. Currently the finest photographic record of the peoples of modern Indonesia.

♦ Wallace, Alfred Russel. *Malay Archipelago.* Singapore: Graham Brash, 1983. A reprint of the 1869 classic, which, among countless observations, uncovered the orang-utan's love for durian. A brilliant, exhaustive, and valid study of natural phenomena as well as an exciting travelogue.

JAVA

When fossil remains of the erect ape *Pithecanthropus erectus* were found on Java in 1891, scientists surmised that Java was the original location of the Garden of Eden. The most famed of all of Indonesia's islands, Java is also one of the richest, lushest, most densely populated on earth and ranks among the loveliest regions anywhere. Deep purple and fiery volcanos tower majestically over a land of intense green plains, twisting mountain passes, cool hillside resorts, remote crater lakes, extraordinary Hindu temples, wild game parks, botanical gardens, serene beaches, dense rainforests, vast savannah, thick bamboo groves, stands of teak, and squalling, teeming cities. Java was the genesis of Indonesia's powerful maritime and agricultural kingdoms and contains the best-preserved and highest number of monuments, many completed centuries before Columbus discovered America. Java is both young and old, rich and poor. Many areas resemble India because of the congestion, the rice paddies, the explosive colors: "I see India everywhere, but I do not recognize it," said the great Bengali poet Tagore when he visited Java in 1927.

Though Java is the smallest of the Greater Sunda islands, it is inhabited by the bulk of Indonesia's population, over 120 million residents packed into only 7% of the country's land mass. With their light brown skin, straight black hair, high cheekbones, and slender builds, the Javanese originally belonged to the Oceanic branch of the Mongoloid race. But the Javanese "race" is actually a blending of every race that ever established itself on the island. Java's people belong to primarily four major cultural-lingual ethnic groups: the Sundanese of West Java (about 30 million), the Javanese of Central and East Java (about 80 million), the Tenggerese from the area in East Java around Mt. Bromo (300,000), and the Madurese inhabiting the long island of Madura near Surabaya in East Java. The largest group, the Javanese, are also, in terms of cultural and political influence, the most important.

Java is officially divided into the provinces of West, Central, and East Java, plus the special territories of Jakarta and Yogyakarta. Travelers generally follow a route from Jakarta through Bogor, Bandung, Yogyakarta, Solo, Mt. Bromo, and Surabaya to Bali. Central Java offers the greatest number of historical and cultural attractions. Visitors short on time often use Yogyakarta, the cradle of Javanese culture, as a base for exploring the temples and natural sights. West Java offers beach resorts for wealthy Jakartians and several cities worth brief explorations. Bandung's art-deco architecture and Bogor's famous Botanical Gardens are the top draws. The gateway city of Jakarta also warrants some time. East Java's top attraction is sunrise at Mt. Bromo, along with visits to Malang, the zoo in Surabaya, and nature reserves in the extreme east.

GETTING AROUND JAVA

By Train

Two parallel train lines run the island's whole length: a northern coastal line (Jakarta-Cirebon-Semarang-Surabaya-Banyuwangi) and a central line (Jakarta-Cirebon-Yogyakarta-Solo-Surabaya-Banyuwangi). Trains provide an outstanding way to tour Java. No point on the island is more than 80 km from a station. Trains, especially for the longer hauls, are far more comfortable than hot, tiresome, crowded, and dangerous buses. Stations are located in the center of town, unlike bus terminals, which are often several kilometers away. Departures are frequent (though not as frequent as for buses).

All classes and comfort zones are represented. Java's luxury-class trains such as the Bima and the Mutiara Utara have air-conditioned sleepers and dining cars. Seats can be reserved through travel agencies such as Carnation Travel on Jalan Menteng in Jakarta. The small service charge is well worth avoiding the long ticket lines at most train stations. Westerners can also avoid lines by appealing directly to the stationmaster. Express and ordinary trains come in three classes. Prices double from third to second class and again from second-class ordinary to second-class express. Second-class express is therefore four times the cost of third-class ordinary. While this may cost more, unreserved train and third-class trains should be avoided since most are badly overcrowded and unbearable in the hot weather. Student discounts are available on most trains.

By Bus

Buses on Java are frequent and comprehensive but slow, painful, nerve-wracking, and dangerous. The rule of thumb: trains are best for longer journeys, buses are OK for shorter hauls. Buses' biggest advantage over trains is that they leave much more frequently. There's no need to check a schedule. Just go to the bus terminal and get on the next departing bus. Like trains, buses come in different types and classes. Ordinary buses are plentiful but much less comfortable than *ekspres* or *bis malam* buses, which travel nonstop on all the major roads. *Bis malam* (night buses) depart in the late afternoon or early evening, traveling faster and cooler on less congested roads, but you sacrifice sightseeing for speed. Sleep, alas, is completely impossible as the drivers drive like madmen, weaving around wrecks, wandering cattle, and blind mountain passes. Sit in the back if you value your life. Unless you're in a big rush, it's preferable to take day buses and get a good night's sleep. Ticket collectors are honest but you should try to present correct fare rather than wait for change.

JAKARTA

Also known as Ibu Kota, the "Mother City," this teeming metropolis of 12 million is Indonesia's capital—the brain, treasury vault, and nerve center of the country. The world's ideas, technology, and fashions first touch Indonesia here. It's the literary center and headquarters for the mass media: a quarter of all of Indonesia's newspapers are printed here. The city has a

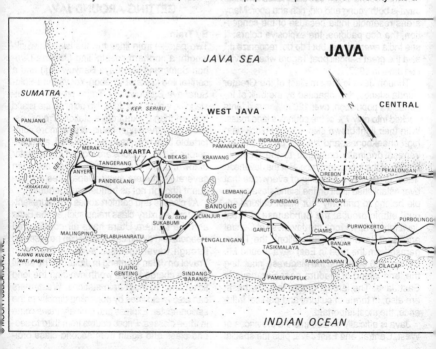

film industry, a modern theater academy, a prestigious university, and the oldest medical school and clubhouse in Southeast Asia. Jakarta is where all the big contracts are signed, the strings pulled, the rake-offs skimmed. Here live the most- and least-educated people of Indonesia. Eighty percent of all foreign investment comes through here, and most of the money stays here. Here are Indonesia's most expensive buildings and its murkiest slums—great rivers of steel, glass, and granite winding through endless expanses of one-story *kampongs*. At 650 square kilometers, Jakarta is almost three times the size of the entire island of Singapore, plus it's growing at a staggering rate. Programs aimed at the 21st century envision the evolution of a megalopolis called Jabotabek which will encompass more than 7,500 square kilometers, from Bogor in the south to Tanggerang in the west. The population is expected to reach 25 million by the year 2005. Jakarta is the present and the future of Indonesia.

Jakarta's history began in the early 1600s when Dutch traders established a fortified trading post in the small Javanese fishing village of Jayakarta. In 1619, they overcame the Bantenese rulers and burned the village to the ground. The Dutch then built a small garrison which withstood two assaults (1628 and 1629) by a mighty army of 80,000. Repelling subsequent attacks, the Dutch became more and more entrenched. Renaming the site Batavia for a medieval Germanic tribe that once occupied the lowlands of Holland and Belgium, they built a completely new city of intersecting canals, and houses with tiny windows and red-tiled roofs—a Little Holland in the Tropics. Batavia (pop. 32,000 in 1639) soon became the trade center for the Dutch East India Company, from where Dutch governors sent voyagers out to open new trading routes. Known as the "Pearl of the Orient," with massive agricultural wealth flowing through, Captain Cook called the port "the best marine yard in the world." With the proclamation of Indonesian independence in 1945, the name Jakarta—an abbreviation of its native name Jayakarta—was readopted.

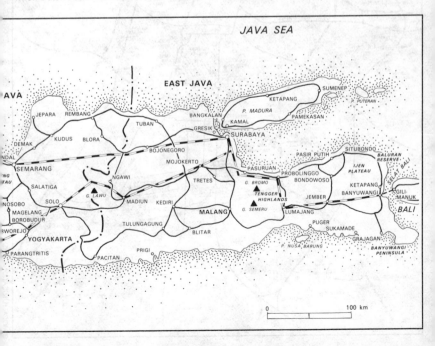

JAKARTA BAY

OLD SHIPS

JL. PLUIT SELATAN

PASAR IKAN

Maritime Museum

MARINA BOATS TO 1000 ISLANDS

HORIZON HOTEL

ANCOL AMUSEMENT PARK

JL. MARTINADATA

TO TANJUNG PRIOK HARBOR AREA (1 km)

JL. KOPI

DRAWBRIDGE

WAYANG MUSEUM

MUSEUM OF FINE ARTS

OLD BATAVIA (KOTA)

JAKARTA MUSEUM

KOTA TRAIN STATION

PORTUGUESE CHURCH

JAKARTA

CHINATOWN (GLODOK)

JL. GAJAM MADA

CHINESE TEMPLE

NIGHT WARUNGS

NIGHT WARUNGS

NATIONAL ARCHIVES BLDG.

TO KALIDERES BUS TERMINAL

JL. HASYIM ASHARI

JL. JUANDA

GPO

JL. MERDEKA

BHARATA THEATER

GROGOL BUS TERMINAL

UTARA

ISTIQLAL MOSQUE

PASAR SENEN TRAIN STATION

TO AIRPORT

JL. CARINGIN

MERDEKA SQUARE

GAMBIR TRAIN STATION

SENEN BUS TERMINAL

JL. SUPRAPTO

NATIONAL MUSEUM

JL. MERDEKA SELATAN

HYATT ARYUDATA

JL. PARMAN

ORCHID GARDEN

JL. KEBON SIRIH

TANAH ABANG TRAIN STATION

TOURIST INFORMATION

JL. JAKSA

BUDGET HOTELS

JL. HASYIM

TEXTILE MUSEUM

TANAH ABANG BUS TERMINAL

SARINAH DEPT. STORE

JL. SUMATRA

T.I.M.

GRAND HYATT

HOTEL INDONESIA

JL. BONJOL

PASAR SURABAYA ANTIQUES

PASAR BLORA

JL. DIPONEGORO

PROCLAMATION MEMORIAL

JL. SUBROTO

TO TAMAN MINI INDONESIA PARK

TAMAN RIA REMAJA

SRIMULAT THEATRE

TO KEBAYORAN

JL. RASUNA SAID

TO CILILITAN BUS TERMINAL

STADIUM

HILTON

TO ZOO

0   1 km

© MOON PUBLICATIONS, INC.

Jakarta today is the kind of city the uninitiated traveler has nightmares about. By day the city seems to hide itself. Walking is a grueling ordeal which provides little insight: Jakartians themselves get around in cars or buses, and roadside shops are being replaced by large air-conditioned plazas. Most travelers attempt to arrive, find a connecting flight or train to Bali or Yogyakarta, and leave the capital, if possible, within the same day. And yet the city has a great deal of interest. By using public transportation, you can quickly reach and tour the museums and Dutch colonial architecture located in Old Batavia. The National Museum is highly recommended. Forty km south of town is an amusement park which presents full-scale replicas of houses from the country's 27 provinces. Antique hunters will enjoy the roadside stalls at Jalan Surabaya while some of the older neighborhoods remain districts of banyans, bougainvillea, and Dutch *de Stijl* architecture. First stop should be the tourist office. Pick up a map, a list of current exhibitions and upcoming performances, and *Jakarta See for Yourself,* which describes buses to the main sights.

ATTRACTIONS

National Museum

Also called the Museum Pusat (Central Museum) or Gedung Gajah (for the bronze elephant outside the entrance), this museum contains the richest collection of Indonesiana in the world. Although poorly lit and almost completely devoid of English descriptions, you could spend days in the prehistory and ethnographic sections alone. The Hindu-Javanese antiquities exhibit rivals Leyden Museum's in Holland, while the ceramic collection is regarded as one of the largest and rarest collections outside China. Don't miss the tremendous relief map which graphically shows the volcanic spread of the archipelago. Other rooms are ethnological gold mines, though most of the 85,000 items haven't been dusted since the Dutch left. Ten minutes on foot from Jalan Jaksa. Open Tuesday-Thursday 0830-1400, Friday to 1100, Saturday to 1300, Sunday to 1500. The English tours given several times weekly at 0930 by spirited volunteers are *highly* recommended. *Gamelan* performances Sunday mornings at 0930. A tremendous museum; arrive when the doors open!

Merdeka Square

Independence Monuments: Monas, a Russian-built marble obelisk in the center of Merdeka Square, was built in 1961 during the Sukarno era to commemorate the struggle for independence from the Dutch. The gigantic phallic needle rises 137 meters and is topped with 35 kg of pure gold leaf to symbolize the flame of freedom. Wryly called "Sukarno's last erection," it provides an excellent orientation point and a knockout view from the observation room. Beneath the monument is a museum with dioramas relating Indonesia's history from prehistoric Java Man to the struggle for independence.

Merdeka Palace: Surrounding the one-square-kilometer Merdeka Square are several important buildings dating from the early 19th century. The presidential palace, though closed to the public, is lavishly appointed with Dutch colonial furniture, a neoclassic dining hall, and ceiling decorations resembling Ambonese lace. To the rear along Jalan Veteran stands Istana Negara, a palace originally constructed by wealthy Dutch traders.

National Mosque: Designed by a Christian Batak architect and commissioned by Sukarno (this city still very much wears his mark), the massive six-level Istiqlal Mosque, with its minarets and grandiose lines, is reputed to be the largest mosque in Southeast Asia and second largest in the world. Check your shoes and follow the guard past the giant drum to the central prayer hall supported by 12 columns representing the Javanese zodiac and five prayer levels representing the principles of *Pancasila* (the state philosophy). On Fridays, noontime services can be discreetly observed from the upper tiers.

Emmanuel Church: This unique classicist Dutch Protestant church was erected between 1834 and 1839 by architect J.H. Horst, who incorporated elements from Greek temples, Renaissance theaters, and the Roman arena in its circular construction. The whole interior is nicely bathed with an even, well-diffused light.

Old Batavia

Jakarta's best two attractions are the National Museum and the collection of Makassar schooners in Old Batavia. Also called Kota, this rela-

NATIONAL MUSEUM

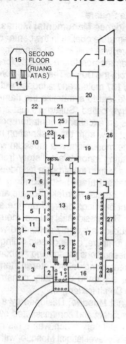

1. entrance hall
2. ticket windows
3. historical collection
4. exhibition room
5. numismatic collection

Library
6. lending service
7. reading room
8. administration of the library
9. librarian's office
10. book storage
11. book bindery

Archaeological Collection
12. rotunda
13. inner court (statuary)
14. treasure room (2nd floor)
15. bronze collection (2nd floor)
16. audio-visual room

Ethnographic Collection
17. Java and Sumatra
18. woodcarving
19. Bali, Kalimantan, and Sulawesi
20. Irian Barat, Maluku, and Nusa Tenggara
21. foreign ceramics
22. prehistory
23. manuscript collection
24. administrative offices
25. director
26. storage of archaeological objects
27. training center
28. bathrooms

© MOON PUBLICATIONS, INC.

tively small northern area was the waterfront swamp where the Dutch first settled and then remained for 330 years. The ships and all museums can be visited in one morning, but an early start is essential to avoid the afternoon heat. Take buses P1 or 70 from Jalan Thamrin to the Jakarta City Museum.

Dutch Bridge: Begin your walking tour at the sole remaining 17th-century drawbridge, which once marked the southwest corner of the old Dutch fort. Through the 18th century ships could sail under the drawbridge, and continue up the Ciliwung River past the Chartered Bank and Toko Merah building. Jakarta's best old architecture is on this street—so walk slowly!

Watch Tower: Gedung Syahbandar, the towerlike harbormaster's building, once served as a lighthouse and meteorological station equipped with all the high-tech instruments of the day. Chi-

nese inscriptions on the floor are weight standards. Now closed to the public. Have lunch at the nearby cafe or go hungry until you reach Chinatown.

Maritime Museum: Museum Bahari consists of two recently restored Dutch East India Company warehouses (1652) which formerly guarded mountains of coffee, tea, pepper, cloth, tin, and copper. Spice-trade memorabilia and maritime models fill the interior.

Pasar Ikan: Once a fascinating neighborhood of fish markets and old stores selling embalmed turtles, Jakarta's old seafaring center is now a rather ordinary commercial center of clothing and hardware stores.

Harbor: This 500-year-old harbor area remains one of the most important calls for sailing vessels from all over the archipelago. Row upon row of handmade shallow-draft oceangoing Makassar schooners form the world's greatest collection of traditional sailing craft. A scene straight from Conrad; don't miss it! Boatmen can be hired to tour the waterfront.

Wayang Museum: This two-story building has nine rooms containing priceless collections of puppets from all over the world, including family-planning puppets, Sumatran dolls used during the Indonesian resistance movement, Punch and Judy from England, and French marionettes donated by François Mitterand. *Wayang kulit* and *wayang golek* performances accompanied by *gamelan* Sunday mornings at 1000. Jakarta's second-best museum.

Jakarta City Museum: Once the City Hall of Batavia, this magnificent two-story building constructed in 1710 is one of the nation's finest examples of Dutch colonial architecture. Holds an amazingly rich collection of massive antique furniture and VOC memorabilia.

Museum of Fine Arts: Balai Seni Rupa houses a permanent exhibition of Indonesian paintings, from the Raden Saleh era up to contemporary times. The art is poorly lit and mediocre except for a self-portrait of a young painter in front of slums. Museum Keramik, a highly overrated and disappointing ceramics museum, shares the same building.

Portuguese Church: Gereja Sion, Jakarta's oldest standing house of worship, features a magnificent organ, a pulpit, and Dutch tombstones embedded in the northern wall. The most beautiful tomb is of Governor-General Zwaardecroon, who asked to be buried here so that he might "sleep amongst the common folk."

Glodok: Jakarta's Chinatown has quickly changed from a struggling *kampong* into a thriving commercial center blanketed with air-conditioned shopping centers and luxury hotels—a jarring intersection of old poverty and new wealth. Walk east, sticking to the canals and under bridges: here you'll see poverty as grinding as anywhere in Asia.

Other Attractions
Textile Museum: A permanent exhibition of cloths and weavings from all over Indonesia. Located in Tanah Abang 15 minutes on foot west of Sarinah Department Store.

Taman Mini Indonesia: A 120-hectare open-air cultural/amusement park, 12 km south of the city. Touristy, difficult to reach, exhausting to explore, but a window into the cultural and environmental complexity of Indonesia. Pavilions built in traditional style exhibit artifacts, customs, and lifestyles of the peoples of each of Indonesia's 27 provinces. Indonesians will proudly tell you that there will be no need to see the rest of Indonesia if you visit this park. Free traditional dance performances on Sunday mornings. Take buses P11, P16, 406, or 408 from Sarinah to the chaotic Cilitan Terminal and continue with double-decker bus 408.

ACCOMMODATIONS

Budget
Jakarta's inexpensive guesthouses and hostels are located around Jalan Jaksa, within easy walking distance of the tourist office, sightseeing attractions, and the Gambir Train Station. All fill up fast, so arrive early for the best rooms.

Noordwijk: Top choice is the secure and friendly Hostel Noordwijk (or Norbek), where you can practice your Dutch with the amiable owner. Norbek is small, cozy, and filled by noontime. Jalan Jaksa 14, tel. (02) 330392, US$6-10 fan, US$15-25 a/c.

Wisma Delima: Once the most famous hostel in Jakarta, the Delima has been sabotaged by its own success. Hasn't changed a bit in 10 years—bad lighting, stuffy, noisy, cramped. Jalan Jaksa 5, US$6-10.

Others on Jalan Jaksa: Nick's Corner Hostel has a pretentious facade, surly management, and grossly overpriced rooms cost US$30-45, but decent dorm beds are just US$4. A much better choice is Tator Hostel with fan rooms for US$7-14 and a/c rooms from US$15. Recommended.

Jalan Kebon Sirih Barat Dalam: Borneo Hostel 1 on this side street has rooms for US$7-12 but adjacent Borneo Hostel 2 is cleaner and more spacious. Hostel Bintang Kejora is similarly priced but blessed with surprisingly friendly managers. Also try Pondok Wisata 16 with an inexpensive dorm and rooms from US$6, Pondok Wisata Jaya with rooms for US$6-10, and Kebon Sirih Hostel in the same price range.

Jalan Kebon Sirih Timur: Bloemsteen ("Flower Stone"), Palm Hostel, and Kresna are all rather cramped but reasonably priced at just US$5-8.

Cipta Hotel: Best bet for mid-level travelers in the Jalan Jaksa neighborhood is this clean and

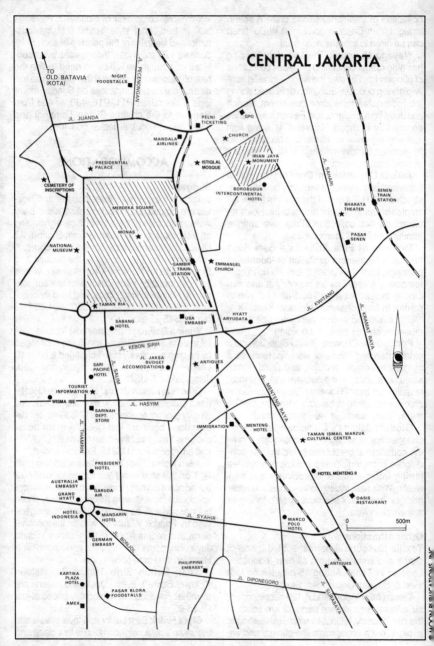

CENTRAL JAKARTA

TO OLD BATAVIA (KOTA)

NIGHT FOODSTALLS

JL. PECENONGAN

JL. JUANDA

PELNI TICKETING

GPO

MANDALA AIRLINES

CHURCH

ISTIQLAL MOSQUE

IRIAN JAYA MONUMENT

PRESIDENTIAL PALACE

CEMETERY OF INSCRIPTIONS

MERDEKA SQUARE

MONAS

BOROBUDUR INTERCONTINENTAL HOTEL

JL. SAHARI

SENEN TRAIN STATION

BHARATA THEATER

PASAR SENEN

NATIONAL MUSEUM

GAMBIR TRAIN STATION

EMMANUEL CHURCH

TAMAN RIA

JL. KWITANG

JL. KRAMAT RAYA

SABANG HOTEL

USA EMBASSY

HYATT ARYUDATA

JL. KEBON SIRIH

SARI PACIFIC HOTEL

JL. JAKSA BUDGET ACCOMODATIONS

ANTIQUES

JL. SALIM

TOURIST INFORMATION

WISMA ISE

JL. HASYIM

SARINAH DEPT. STORE

IMMIGRATION

MENTENG HOTEL

JL. MENTENG RAYA

TAMAN ISMAIL MARZUK CULTURAL CENTER

PRESIDENT HOTEL

HOTEL MENTENG II

AUSTRALIA EMBASSY

GRAND HYATT

GARUDA AIR

JL. THAMRIN

HOTEL INDONESIA

MANDARIN HOTEL

JL. SYAHIR

OASIS RESTAURANT

MARCO POLO HOTEL

0   500m

JL. BONJOL

GERMAN EMBASSY

PHILIPPINE EMBASSY

ANTIQUES

KARTIKA PLAZA HOTEL

PASAR BLORA FOODSTALLS

JL. DIPONEGORO

JL. SURABAYA

AMEX

MOON

JL. MENTENG RAYA

INDONESIA
1. Mas procession; 2. Lombok cattle traders (all photos this page by Carl Parkes)

INDONESIA
1. tall ships, Jakarta Harbor; **2.** getting around, Yogya style (all photos this page by Carl Parkes)

CENTRAL JAKARTA ACCOMMODATIONS

HOTEL	SINGLE	DOUBLE	ADDRESS	PHONE (021)
LUXURY				
Borobudur	US$250-400	US$300-450	Jl. Lapangan Banteng	370108
Grand Hyatt	US$300-450	US$300-450	Jl. Thamrin	390-1234
Indonesia	US$200-300	US$200-300	Jl. Thamrin	320008
Mandarin Oriental	US$275-350	US$300-495	Jl. Thamrin	321307
President	US$150-200	US$180-250	Jl. Thamrin 59	320508
Sari Pacific	US$200-250	US$250-350	Jl. Thamrin	323707
MODERATE				
Bali Intercontinental	US$22-35	US$25-40	Jl. Wahid Hasyim 116	334967
Kartika Plaza	US$55-80	US$55-80	Jl. Thamrin 10	321008
Marco Polo	US$50-70	US$60-80	Jl. Cik Ditiro 19	325409
Menteng	US$45-60	US$50-75	Jl. Gondangdia Lama	325208
Sabang Metropolitan	US$60-65	US$65-85	Jl. Agus Salim	354031

modern hotel, which offers 30% discounts at the front desk. Jl. Wahid Hasyim 53, tel. (021) 390-4701, fax (021) 326531, US$70-80.

Moderate

Jalan Jaksa: Jakarta's budget neighborhood also has several good middle-priced hotels for those who want air-conditioning and cleaner rooms. The three best choices are the Karya, the Djody, and the Djody 2. The Karya Hotel has fan rooms from US$15 and a variety of a/c rooms for US$25-35. Both Djody and Djody 2 have large, clean, if somewhat dark rooms with fan from US$10 and a/c rooms from US$18.

Sabang Hotel: Well located on Jalan Agus Alim, the Sabang gives more bang for your buck than most other international-style hotels. Jalan Agus Salim, tel. (021) 354031, US$40-70.

Luxury

Jakarta has recently gone through a mini-hotel boom, adding a Meridien, a Regent, and a second Hyatt, making a total of eight five-star properties. Rates from US$200, plus another 20% in government taxes.

Grand Hyatt: Located in the heart of Jakarta's business district, this 455-room hotel features a conference room, an extra-large swimming pool, and a three-story atrium overlooking the Welcome Monument (Hansel and Gretel). Jalan Thamrin, tel. (021) 390-1234, US$300-450.

Hilton: Jakarta's most highly regarded hotel

more closely resembles a self-contained village than any hotel in the traditional sense. An open-air bar in the gardens draws many of Jakarta's elite. In 1993, the Hilton opened the largest convention center in Indonesia. Jalan Gatot Subroto, tel. (021) 570-3600, fax (021) 583091, US$250-375.

Borobudur Intercontinental: This 1,172-room hotel, largest in Indonesia, is another city within a city with its massive landscaped gardens, seven restaurants, and large population of expatriates residing within the walls. Travel Indonesia and Dive Indonesia are located upstairs. Jalan Lapangan Banteng, tel. (021) 370108, fax (021) 386-9595, US$250-450.

Mandarin Oriental: Boasting the best location in Jakarta, the Mandarin features spacious rooms and sophisticated style. Jalan Thamrin, tel. (021) 321307, fax (021) 324-669, US$275-495.

RESTAURANTS

Western food in Jakarta is poorly prepared and overpriced but *warungs* and *warung* complexes (*puja seras*) serve tasty authentic fare at rock-bottom prices. No matter where your hotel is, you're never more than a few hundred meters from a delicious taste experience. Food stalls are clustered in several neighborhoods:

Jalan Agus Salim: Jakarta's restaurant row is conveniently located just one block from Jalan Jaksa. A nonstop lineup of Indonesian, Chinese, and Western restaurants, from Colonel Sanders and a Japanese bakery to the clean White House Restaurant, which serves Reagan burgers and Thatcher fried chicken! Streetside *sate* vendors set up their carts at the south end of the street.

Puja Sera 5: Another outstanding site for cheap meals and great selection is the collection of dozens of independent *warungs* inside the clean and lively warehouse on Jalan Kebon Sirih. Akin to the food markets of Singapore, this assembly of stalls serves up the entire spectrum of Indonesian dishes—from *nasi campur* to fiery *sambals*. More expensive than ordinary *warungs,* but it's well lit and clean, a great place to bring a large group for communal meals.

Other Choices: The Sarinah car park turns into a food market in the early evening hours. Another popular place to *warung* wander is Jalan Peconongan, north of Merdeka Square, where some 50 informal food stalls operate from twilight to midnight. Chinese food stalls and flash discos can be found farther north on Jalan Manga Besar. Not a tourist in sight.

ENTERTAINMENT

Performing Arts

The tourist office brochure titled *Jakarta Permanent Exhibitions and Regular Performances* includes a useful guide to theater and dance venues. Current listings are given in their monthly *Guide to Jakarta.*

Taman Ismail Marzuki: Jakarta's cultural center sponsors weekly performances of traditional theater, Islamic poetry readings, comedy competitions, photographic exhibitions, jazz dance, film festivals, and indigenous dramas. The showcase for the nation, this is where you will see Indonesia's finest performing-arts companies. A bilingual calendar is available (sometimes) from the tourist office.

Bharata Theater: Authentic *wayang orang* and *ketoprak* performances are given nightly at 2000 except Mondays and Thursdays in the hall on Jalan Kalilio. This is one of Indonesia's few remaining theaters that sponsor classical drama. Packed with Javanese—abundant local color: highly recommended.

Jakarta skyline

National Museum: *Wayang golek, wayang kulit* and *gamelan* performances are given Sunday mornings at 0930. A must-see for anyone passing through Jakarta on a Sunday.

Wayang Museum: Wonderful shadow puppet and wooden marionette theater Sundays at 1000.

Taman Mini Indonesia: Sunday morning performances are given 1000-1200 in the pavilions for West Java, Yogyakarta (*wayang kulit*), East Java, and West Sumatra. The park is incredibly crowded but worth visiting for the shows.

School of Folk Art: The Fine Arts Department at the National University of Indonesia occasionally features Cirebon-style *gamelan*, Sundanese traditional dancing, *suling* orchestras, and *wayang topeng, kulit,* and *golek* puppet theater.

Srimulat Theater: *Ludruk* comedy shows are given nightly in the complex in Taman Ria Remaja near the Hilton. Recent titles included "Salamat Datang Mr. Dracula," "Idola Casanova," and "Gadis, Gadis Sexy," to give you some idea of the audience. Shows are amateurish and poorly attended but you can get in free by walking through the Ria Jaya Restaurant.

Borobudur Hotel: Dance and music from various regions of Indonesia every Saturday at 1900. Dinner plus show costs only US$18.

Nightlife

Opinions about nightlife in Jakarta are divided between those who think it's a dull place and others who, perhaps expecting no-alcohol signs and veiled women, are surprised by the number of bars, nightclubs, discos, and massage parlors. Most of the city's nightlife revolves around the luxury hotels, but a fairly active scene has grown up on Jalan Wahid Hasyim near Jalan Jaksa. Prices are high but early-bird discounts are common before 2200. For example, Faces Disco has a Rp10,452 entrance fee but it's free before 1030, and Sunday nights are "White Nights," when Caucasians are admitted free. The nearby Parrots is a four-story restaurant and discoteque which caters to all ages; Rp8362 for first drink. The venerable Jaya Pub, behind the Jaya Building across from Sarinah, is a pleasant piano bar where artists, writers, musicians, and filmmakers hang out. Minimal cover charge.

Other nightlife is somewhat distant from the hostels on Jalan Jaksa. Ancol is a large and overrated amusement park in north Jakarta. A rowdy time can be had at the George & Dragon Pub on a side road off Jalan Thamrin between Hotel Kartika and Hotel Indonesia. Jakarta's transsexuals and female impersonators (*banci*) hang out in the Pasar Blora area past the sleazy nightclubs on Jalan Tanah Abung Timor. Jakarta's largest red-light district is in north Jakarta in Kramat Tunggak.

SHOPPING

Shopping in Jakarta is something of an ordeal because of the heat and traffic hassles, but a

JALAN JAKSA ACCOMMODATIONS

HOTEL	SINGLE	DOUBLE	ADDRESS	PHONE (021)
MODERATE				
Cipta Hotel	US$30-40	US$35-45	Jl. Wahid Hasyim 61	323334
Karya	US$15-25	US$15-35	Jalan Jaksa 32	320484
Wisma Indra	US$35-45	US$40-60	Wahid Hasyim 63	337432
BUDGET				
Bintang (Kejora)	US$5-6	US$5-8	Jl. Kebon Sirah 52	323878
Bloomsteen	US$6-12	US$6-12	Kebon Sirih 173	
Borneo	US$6-15	US$6-15	Kebon Sirih 35	320095
Djody 2 Hotel	US$12-24	US$12-24	Jl. Jaksa 35	346600
Djody Hotel	US$10-20	US$10-20	Jl. Jaksa 27	346600
Hotel Nick	US$6-15	US$8-20	Jl. Jaksa	
Noordwijk	US$6-15	US$8-25	Jl. Jaksa 14	330392
Tator Hostel	US$6-9	US$10-18	Jl. Jaksa 37	325124
Wisma Delima	US$6-9	US$6-12	Jl. Jaksa 5	

few shops and neighborhoods are worth exploring. First stop should be at the Sarinah Department Store on Jalan Thamrin. Like an Indonesian Macy's, it has everything from Borneo *perang* and coral jewelry to batik slippers and Batak woodcarvings. Don't miss the comprehensive array of batiks on the third floor, reasonably priced handicrafts on the fourth, and the well-stocked bookstore on the fifth. A good place for the newcomer to become acquainted with what's available, but at rather high, fixed prices.

Antique hunters usually head directly for Jalan Surabaya, where dozens of merchants sell a mixed bag of antiques, fakes, and hopeless discards. The small alley one block east of Jalan Jaksa (Jalan Kebon Sirih Timur Dalam) has several excellent antique shops, plus, of all things, an antique motorcycle dealer who specializes in Harleys! Shoppers should also check the 40-odd handicraft shops in the Hilton's Indonesian Bazaar.

PRACTICALITIES

Tourist Information
The Jakarta Visitor's Information Center on Jalan Wahid Hasyim has an excellent supply of maps and other information on Jakarta. This will be your best chance to find out about upcoming festivals in Indonesia. The free city map provided by the tourist office is comprehensive, but for extended sojourns you'll need either the Falk City Map or the Catra Buana Map of DKI Jakarta. The Directorate General of Tourism (Indonesia's national tourist organization) on Jalan Kramat Raya offers very little practical information.

Communications
International phone calls can be made around the clock in the Jakarta Theater Building opposite the Sarinah Department Store. Jakarta's General Post Office and poste restante is on Jalan Pasar Baru northeast of Merdeka Square. Open 0800-1600 Monday-Friday, 0800-1300 on Saturdays. From Sarinah take buses 10, 11, or 12.

Government Office Hours
All Indonesian immigration offices, tourist information centers, and museums are open 0800-1500 Monday-Thursday, 0800-1130 on Fridays, and 0800-1300 Saturdays. Rule of thumb: do all official business and sightseeing *early* in the day!

TRANSPORTATION

Airport Arrival
The Soekarno-Hatta International Airport 26 km west of city center is served by limousines (Rp30,000), taxis (Rp20,000), private hotel shuttles (Rp8000) and blue-and-white Damri mini-

buses (Rp4000) which leave every 30 minutes 0300-2200. Travelers going to the Jalan Jaksa area should get off at the Gambir Train Station and walk 15 minutes.

If you want to avoid Jakarta altogether, take the minibus to Jalan Thamrin, then a city bus to the Rambutan Bus Terminal (buses P11, P16, 406, or 408), where you can board a bus to Bogor, Bandung, or Yogyakarta.

Getting Around Jakarta

Indonesia's premier city—sprawling, bustling, congested—is a bitch to get around in: it's 25 km north to south, hot and muggy; the traffic is horrendous; streets maddeningly change names every two or three blocks; major thoroughfares are freeways without pedestrian overpasses. Hardly any non-Indonesian ever walks. The most comfortable method to tour Jakarta is in air-conditioned taxis. Drivers are honest and rates are incredibly low; Rp1000 for flagfall and only Rp600 for each additional kilometer.

Air-conditioned Blue Bird taxis with driver cost Rp15,000 per hour. Public buses are slow and crowded but adequate except during rush hour. Bag slashers are a major problem on ordinary buses; take the Patas buses (express buses marked P) instead. Most city destinations can be reached with buses from Jalan Thamrin near the Sarinah Department Store. Others leave from Gambir Train Station and from Jalan Kebon Sirih near Bank Duta. All of the buses listed in the "Buses Around Jakarta" chart leave from Jalan Thamrin unless otherwise noted.

Travel Agencies

The Pelni ticketing office (tel. 358398) on Jalan Pintu Air behind the National Mosque is open 0830-1200 and 1300-1400 Monday-Friday, Saturdays till noon. Discount travel agencies are listed below. Jakarta's two leading domestic tour operators are Pacto Tours on Jalan Cikini Raya and Vayatours next to Kaliman Travel. Both can set you up with bus tours to Bali and trekking expeditions in Sumatra.

Leaving Jakarta

Air: Air tickets are sold by a variety of airlines and travel agencies. Garuda has offices in the Wisma Nusantara building (tel. 334425) on Jalan Thamrin and in Hotel Borobudur (tel. 359901). Merpati (tel. 413608) and Bouraq (tel.

BUSES AROUND JAKARTA	
DESTINATION	**BUS**
Old Batavia	P1, P11, 70
Cilitan Bus Terminal	P11, P16, 406
Pulo Gadung Bus Terminal	59
Kalideres Bus Terminal	16
Kota Train Station	P1, P11, 70
Pasar Senen Bus/Train	10, 11, 12
GPO	10, 11, 12
Blok M, Kebayoran	P1
Taman Ismail Marzuki	34
Zoo (from Gambir)	87, 90
Tanjung Priok (Kebon Sirih)	P14

655194) are both on on Jalan Angkasa near the Kemayoram Airport.

Discounts are available from Carnation Travel (tel. 344027) on Jalan Menteng Raya, Indo Shangrila Travel (tel. 639-2831) on Jalan Gajah Mada, Kaliman Travel (tel. 330101) in the President Hotel, and Vayatours (tel. 336640) on Jalan Batu Tulis.

Indo Shangrila quotes the following one-way student fares: Singapore US$100, Bangkok US$220, Manila US$320, Hong Kong US$305, Los Angeles US$455, and Europe US$580. Normal fares are about 25% pricier. Special fares from Jakarta include Korean Air to Los Angeles with six North Pacific stops for under US$800; UTA to Los Angeles with five South Pacific stops for under US$700.

Minibuses leave Gambir Train Station for the airport every 30 minutes. Airport tax is Rp12,000 on international and Rp4000 on domestic flights. Duty-free cartons of Gudang Garam are sold at the airport!

To Singapore: Both Garuda and Merpati charge US$160-180 for direct flights to Jakarta. Pelni hasn't sailed direct from Jakarta to Singapore since the days of *konfrontasi* in the early '60s, but some options exist. First, fly Merpati or Garuda to Batam Island and then board the one-hour ferry to Singapore. Three of Pelni's new passenger ships sail biweekly to the north Sumatran city of Medan, from where you could explore Lake Toba then fly across to Penang.

By Train: Jakarta's five major stations have trains departing for all points on Java and Sumatra. Tickets can be purchased two hours before departure or in advance from Carnation Travel on Jalan Menteng Raya. Their modest service charge is well worth it! Trains for most Javanese cities (Bogor, Bandung, Yogyakarta, Surabaya) depart several times daily from Gambir Station, within walking distance of Jalan Jaksa. Trains for Sumatra leave twice daily from Tanah Abang Station. Most travelers prefer the faster buses from Jakarta's Kalideres Station.

By Bus: Jakarta also has several different bus terminals which serve different regions on Java and Sumatra. Buses to Bogor and Bandung depart from the Rambutan Terminal in south Jakarta. Take Patas bus P16 from Jl. Thamrin Buses to Sumatra depart from Kalideres Terminal in northwest Jakarta. Take bus 913 or bus 26 from Gambir train station. Buses to Yogyakarta, Solo, Semerang, Surabaya, and Bali leave from Pulo Gadung Terminal in east Jakarta. All buses are badly overcrowded. Much better are the private a/c buses which leave from express bus offices on Jalan Kebon Sirih. Private minibuses and share taxis also operate from the Jalan Jaksa area.

By Ship: All ships depart from the Tanjung Priok Harbor in northeast Jakarta, almost 20 km from city center. Schedules can be checked with the tourist office or at the Pelni ticketing office (tel. 358398) on Jalan Pintu Air behind the National Mosque. To reach the harbor, take buses P1 or 70 from Jalan Thamrin to Kota, then bus 64 or minibus M15 to the Pelni office or dock one. Transit visitors can use express bus P22 from the harbor to Kalideres Bus Terminal (for Sumatra).

WEST JAVA

Extending from Krakatau volcano in the west to Cirebon in the east, the province of West Java is a diverse and culturally rich region of beautiful mountains, deep-green tea plantations, rugged wildlife reserves, lush botanical gardens, fertile rice paddies, and beaches with magnificent coral formations.

Transportation is well developed. From Jakarta's Kalideres Station, buses leave regularly for the historic town of Banten, the port connection at Merak (to Sumatra), the beautiful beaches at Carita, and Labuan, access point for Ujung Kulon National Reserve.

Buses east to Bogor and Bandung leave from the Cilitan Terminal in south Jakarta. Trains depart from Gambir Station.

BANTEN

At one time an important trading center in Southeast Asia, Banten today is known for its historical remains of the once great Bantenese Islamic kingdom. Sights include a partially restored palace, a small museum which houses 200-year-old archaeological objects, and an Islamic school where you could run into hundreds of veiled schoolgirls all in white. Don't miss the impressive mosque outside town on the road to Serang. Banten is also the departure point for boat rides to Nusa Dua, an island bird sanctuary populated by herons, cormorants, and storks. If you're here for just the day, leave your pack at the police post.

Accommodations are available in Serang. From Jakarta's Kalideres Station, board a bus to Merak, but get off in Serang, from where minibuses continue to Banten.

MERAK

Ferries to Sumatra depart at 1100 and 2300 and take about five hours to reach Panjang. Buses to Merak depart hourly from the Kalideres Bus Terminal in Jakarta. Trains leave Jakarta at 0600 and 1600 from the Tanah Abang Train Station. Both trains connect with the ferry. Inexpensive *losmen* are near the train station.

CARITA BEACH

Just a few hours by bus from Jakarta lie some of the most attractive beaches in Java. From Anyer Beach in the north to Labuhan in the south—a stretch of almost 60 km—the Dutch-built road winds past sandy beaches and warm seas just perfect for swimming, snorkeling, fishing, and sailing. Anyer Beach is dominated by the distant form of Krakatau and an old iron lighthouse placed here in 1885 after the original was destroyed by the famous explosion.

Accommodations

Over 20 beach resorts and budget hotels are located south of the Anyer lighthouse in the direction of Carita Beach, a beautiful two-km-long, immaculate, white-sand beach situated within the protective enclosure of a U-shaped bay.

Carita Krakatau Beach Hotel: Of dozens of places to stay, the backpacker's favorite is this guesthouse operated by Dr. Axel Ridder, who provides boat charters to Krakatau and Ujung Kulon and offers current travel information in his breezy newsletter. Jl. Raya Labuan, tel. (0254) 21043, US$3-5 budget huts across the road, US$25-45 luxurious Badui-style bungalows on the beach.

Wira Carita: Clean and friendly resort with swimming pool, tennis court, and gardens. Jl. Raya Anyer, US$12-20.

Anyer Beach Resort: Spacious a/c bungalows plus a small pool. Jl. Raya Karang Bolong, tel. (021) 510503, US$35-45.

Mambruk Beach Resort: The finest hotel complex on the west coast. Facilities include a pool with sunken bar, several restaurants, and tour excursions. Jl. Raya Karang Bolong, tel. (021) 769-5367, US$55-140.

KRAKATAU VOLCANO

Over a century ago, in the early misty hours of 27 August 1883, the island of Rakata Besar disintegrated in the most violent explosion in recorded history. When the central mountain erupted, an enormous amount of rock was heaved out, and the island collapsed, allowing sea water to rush into the fiery crater. The resulting explosion was catastrophic. The volcano unleashed a series of titanic detonations with a force of 100,000 hydrogen bombs. Countless tons of rocks, dust, and pumice were hurled 27 km into the sky. Volcanic clouds circling the earth turned the sun blue and green, causing sensational sunsets for years. Volcanic debris landed on Madagascar on the other side of the Indian Ocean. The boom was heard in Brisbane, over 4,000 km away. Atmospheric waves circled the globe seven times. Tidal waves reached 30 meters high and raced across the seas at over 500

km/h, wiping out 163 villages along the coasts of western Java and southern Sumatra and rocking vessels as far away as the English Channel. The chain of explosions all but destroyed Rakata Besar, leveling its original crater and digging a submarine cavity 300 meters below sea level. Almost 40,000 people died. Afterwards, all remained calm until 1927 when a thick plume of steam roared from the sea bed, giving birth to Anak Krakatau ("Son of Krakatau"), which has since risen 150 meters above the sea.

Day-trips to Krakatau can be arranged in Labuhan, Carita, or Pasauran. Though Pasauran is geographically the closest to Krakatau, it's easier to arrange boat transport from Labuhan or Carita. Krakatau is in most cases a one-day roundtrip. Rent a good boat; don't take any chances. Rates vary from US$50-100 for six-man boats to US$80-150 for 10-man boats. Tours arranged by Pacto and Natrabu in Jakarta often include a Badui village and Ujung Kulon Wildlife Reserve. The ideal season is April to September. But no matter what time you go, the volcano is always in a different mood. Surrounding waters could be 60 degrees centigrade, hot ash blackens your face, the roar is deafening, charcoal smoke clouds the sky. If you're there during an active phase, see flaming boulders the size of basketballs tossed out like pebbles.

UJUNG KULON RESERVE

This completely untamed wilderness lies on the far west tip of Java, connected to the rest of the island by a narrow boggy isthmus. Two separate national parks here total more than 420 square km, one located on the Ujung Kulon Peninsula and the other on the island of Panaitan across a narrow strait. Opened by the Dutch in 1921 as a refuge for the threatened Javan rhinoceros, the establishment of this last large area of lowland forest on Java has since been credited with saving a number of rare life forms from extinction. Observation towers have been erected, and unspoiled beaches with beautiful coral formations lie off the south and west sides. Permits are available from the friendly PPA forestry officers in Labuhan, who also help with accommodations and boat charters. Jakartan travel agents sell four-day tours of Ujung Kulon

BOGOR

JL. MARTADINATA

WISMA MIRAH

JL. A. YANI

JL. SUDIRMAN

■ WARUNGS

WISMA KARUNIA

WISMA TELADAN

ELSANA HOTEL

■ MERDEKA BEMO STATION

PENG. DAMAI

JL. PENGADILAN

R.R.I. (WAYANG KULITI)

■ WAYANG GOLEK SHOP

SEMPUR KENCANA GUESTHOUSE

BOGOR INN

HOTEL PANGRANGO

ABU'S PENSION

JL. MAYOR OKING

JL. PERMAS

JL. SARTIKA

TRAIN STATION

JL. IR. JUANDA

JL. GUNUNG GEDE

SALAK HOTEL

■ WARUNGS

JL. P. MUSLIHAT

WISMA PERMATA

JL. KANTOR BATU

ORCHID HOUSE

BOTANICAL GARDENS

PRESIDENTIAL PALACE ★

TEA HOUSE

JL. PELEDANG

TOURIST OFFICE ★

GPO

FIRMAN PENSIONE ●

PURI BALI LOSMEN

JL. IR. JUANDA

JL. PAJAJARAN

0   150m

BOTANICAL GARDENS ENTRANCE ★

ZOOLOGICAL MUSEUM ★

PHPA ■

BUS TERMINAL ■

GONG FACTORY ★ ★

JL. EMPANG

JL. KENCANA

© MOON PUBLICATIONS, INC.

from US$100 including accommodations in a guesthouse on P. Peucang, a photo safari with guide, all meals, and two nights at relaxing Carita Beach. Tours from Labuhan could cost half as much.

BOGOR

Founded over 500 years ago, Bogor is built around a huge, verdant botanical garden, one of the most magnificent in the world and one of Indonesia's major tourist attractions. It's a pleasant but somewhat busy town of pretty Dutch villas, tropical foliage, and the sweetest *murtabaks* in Indonesia.

Botanical Gardens
This incredible 87-hectare estate is one of the leading botanical institutions in the world, as well as an important scientific research center. The gardens have been here for over 170 years; Bogor has risen up around them. Behind the towering walls you'll discover hundreds of species of trees, an herbarium with 5,620 plant species, a cultivated park of paths, pools, glades, shrubs, lawns, open-air cactus gardens, great twisting foot-thick overhead vines, enormous waterlilies, with a river bubbling through it all. About 13,000 specimens of native plants have been collected not only from all over the Malay Archipelago but from many other tropical regions as well. The Orchid House is permanently closed but the Zoological Museum displays birds, gigantic Japanese crabs, and the last (now stuffed) rhino from Tasikmalaya. Bogor's Botanical Gardens are a spectacular experience sadly marred by tremendous piles of trash and litter. Open daily 0800-1600.

Other Attractions
Presidential Palace: Formerly the Dutch governor's mansion, today this is a ceremonial government hall with graceful colonnaded frontage, a domed and mansard roof, and spotted deer roaming undulating lawns under big shady trees. Inside the mansion are sumptuously appointed rooms, lavish reception chambers, and Sukarno's infamous collection of erotic art. The palace drew international press attention several years ago when talks were held here between rival Cambodian factions. Closed to the general public, but group tours can be arranged from Safariyah Tours on Jalan Sudirman. Individuals can sometimes join prebooked tours on a last-minute basis.

Walking Tour: Much of Java's charm is best enjoyed in the traditional Dutch neighborhoods, which stand apart from the congested and unpleasant business centers. Begin the following walking tour at the entrance gate to the Presidential Palace. Walk east, turn left down the steps into the small neighborhood of Lebak Kantin, and ask someone to direct you toward the residence of Dase Spartacus, a partially blind carver of outstanding and reasonably priced *wayang* puppets. Return to the palace gate and walk north up Jalan Sudirman, exploring the red-tiled neighborhoods down the valley on the right. Popular *warungs* are found at the intersection of Jalan Sudirman and Jalan Yani. Return to city center through the eastern neighborhoods.

Accommodations
Bogor has finally established itself on the traveler's map with the arrival of several good *losmen* and homestays in the quiet neighborhoods.

Abu's Pension: The best place is Abu's Pension, where owner-and-famous-personality Abu Bakkar rents clean dorms and beautiful rooms overlooking the river. Great meals in a friendly atmosphere. Abu also acts as a local tour guide and can help with minibuses to almost everywhere. Whatever you do, avoid the dismal and depressing Losmen Dumai farther down the street. Jl. Mayor Oking 15, tel. (0251) 322893, US$5-15.

Puri Bali Losmen: Another excellent choice is the small and cozy Puri Bali Losmen around the corner from the tourist office. I Made Taman, the Balinese owner (and former director of the Botanical Gardens), and his two sons are gracious and lively hosts who seem quite selective about who gets to stay. Jalan Paledang 50, tel. 317498, US$5-10.

Firman Pensione: Adjacent to the popular Puri Bali Losmen is a modern, friendly homestay whose senior owner is something of a chess pro; call him *jablud* if he wins. They also operate side trips to nearby volcanos and hot springs. The favorite of backpackers. 48 Jl. Paledang, tel. (0251) 323246, US$5-12.

Wisma Karunia: North of the Botanical Gardens are several middle-priced guesthouses

BOGOR BOTANICAL GARDENS

JL. JEN. SUDIRMAN

GATE

BHINNEKA GARDEN & HOLY *BANYAN* TREE

MEDICINAL PLANTS

JL. G. GEDE

ORCHID HOUSE

PALACE GROUNDS

JL MUSLIHAT

PALACE WALL

ASTRID AVE.

2nd CANARIUM AVE.

SULAWESI

CLIMBERS

OIL PALMS

TEA HOUSE

DUTCH CEMETERY

1st CANARIUM AVE.

WATER LILIES

BAMBOOS

LAKE

AUSTRALIA

TOURIST OFFICE

PALMS

FOUNTAIN

PALMS

JL. PALEDAN

RATTAN

TROPICAL RAINFOREST

WATER PLANTS

FERNS

WILD CORNER

CACTUS

SHRUBS

JL. RAYA PAJAJARAN

INSCRIBED STONE

S. GILIWUNG

PHPA

JL. SURYA KENCANA

JL. EMPANG

1. National Biological Institute (central office)	4. Presidential Palace
2. Bibliotheca Bogoriensis	5. Teysmann Memorial
3. Herbarium Bogoriensis	6. Olivia Raffles Memorial
	7. nursery
	8. entrance

9. office
10. Treub Laboratory
11. Museum Zoologieum Bogoriense

with large, clean, and comfortable rooms in quiet neighborhoods. Karunia and nearby Wisma Teladan are pleasant escapes, popular with Dutch travelers. 34 Jl. Sempur, tel. (0251) 323411, US$8-15.

Ramayana Guesthouse: Also clean with Balinese touches and plenty of services: guides, taxis to Bandung, organized treks. Good location and friendly managers. Jl. Juanda, tel. (0251) 320364, US$10-25.

BOGOR ACCOMMODATIONS

HOTEL	SINGLE	DOUBLE	ADDRESS	PHONE (0251)
MODERATE				
Bogor Inn	US$15-20	US$20-30	Jl. Kumbang 12	328134
Hotel Pangrango	US$20-40	US$25-50	Pangrango 23	328670
Salak	US$20-35	US$25-40	I.H. Juanda	22091
Wisma Karunia	US$8-12	US$10-15	Sempur Kaler	23411
Wisma Mirah	US$12-18	US$15-20	Martadinata	23520
Wisma Permata	US$20-30	US$35-45	Jl. Raya Pajajaran 35	323402
Wisma Teladan	US$8-12	US$10-15	Sawojajar	25327
BUDGET				
Abu's Pension	US$5-10	US$6-15	Mayor Oking 15	322893
Firman Pensione	US$5-10	US$6-12	Jl. Paledang 48	323246
Puri Bali Losmen	US$5-10	US$6-10	Paledang 50	317498

Mirah Sartika Hotel: Tucked away in a small alley, Bogor's newest hotel offers spotless rooms plus perfect silence. Jl. Dewi Sartika 6, tel. (0251) 312343, fax (0251) 315188, US$30-55.

Salak Hotel: This venerable Dutch-era hotel is currently under restoration and, if additional investors can be found, will someday be Bogor's largest and most exclusive hotel. Looks hopeless at the moment.

Bogor Inn: Pleasant hotel with friendly management and small pool. Breakfast is included with both the fan-cooled and a/c rooms. 12 Jl. Kumbang, tel. (0251) 328134, US$20-50.

Hotel Pangrango: The best hotel in Bogor features a pool and spotless a/c rooms with private bath and TV. 23 Jl. Pangrango, tel. (0251) 328670, US$20-50.

Restaurants And Nightlife

Bogor's liveliest food scenes are the streetside food stalls and rudimentary *warungs* on Jalan Veteran just across the river. *Murtabaks* can be light, heavy, appetizers, main courses, or *manis*—the sweetest experience of your life.

Wayang golek is performed Saturday nights at 2100 at the RRI national radio building in the Sempur suburb. Traditional Sundanese performing arts can be arranged with Mrs. Asikin at the dance and music school on Jalan Binimarga.

PUNCAK PASS

Some of West Java's loveliest scenery and most impressive volcanos lie between Bogor and Bandung, in a region known as the Puncak or "summit."

Attractions

Cisarua: Activities in the region near Cisarua include a new African-style Safari Park, where lions and tigers graze in open spaces, and the Gunung Mas tea estate, which welcomes visitors daily 0900-1700.

Cipanas: Several kilometers beyond Cipanas is the Kebon Raya Cibodas—a high-altitude branch of the Bogor Botanic Gardens—blessed with virgin jungle, some 5,000 specimens of plants, and a trail which leads to the summits of Mt. Gede and Mt. Pangrango. PHPA officials in the parking lot provide permits and route maps to hikers, who should dress warmly and allow six to eight hours to complete the exhilarating climb.

Accommodations

Simple hotels and luxury resorts are in Cisarua and Cipanas and directly at the summit of Puncak Pass. Avoid weekends, when escapees from the city flood the region.

By far, the finest place to stay in the region is in the town of Cibodas, just below the entrance to the botanical gardens—superb views over tea plantations, countless hikes, and day-long treks to Genung Gede and Pangrango. Take a bus from Bogor to the town of Cimacan, then another bus up the hill to Cibodas. Best accommodations include Freddy's Homestay, Wisma Jamur, Pondok Pemuda Cibodas, and Cibodas Guesthouse.

Freddy's Homestay: Small but clean; the favorite of most backpackers. Situated on the right side of the road down a narrow alley. US$3-10.

Wisma Jamur: The "Mushroom House" run by Miss Nina is another great choice for budget travelers. Guides will find you on arrival. US$6-14.

Kopo International Youth Hostel: Clean rooms, friendly management, and hearty breakfasts. Ask the bus driver to drop you at the Cisarua gas station. 557 Jl. Raya Puncak (Cisarua), tel. (0251) 4296, US$2-8.

Cibodas Botanical Gardens Guesthouse: A lovely lodge directly inside the gardens. Reservations can be made at the Bogor Botanical Gardens. US$5-10.

Pondok Pemuda Cibodas: Excellent location near the PHPA office in the town of Cibodas. Convenient for volcano trekking and visiting the nearby tea plantations. Jl. Raya Puncak, US$3-10.

Megamendung Permai: Upscale resort with huge swimming pool, popular with Jakartans on weekends. Cipayung, tel. (0251) 4871, US$25-45.

Puncak Pass Hotel: A colonial-era hotel located just below the pass. Good value. Jl. Raya Puncak, tel. (0255) 2503, US$25-55.

BANDUNG

Once known as the Paris of Java, Indonesia's third largest city makes a great stop between Jakarta and Yogyakarta. Bandung is a bustling center of Sundanese cultural life, the site of at least 50 universities and colleges, such prestigious institutions as the Nuclear Research Center and Indonesia's only aircraft industry, and one of the world's largest concentrations of Dutch art-deco architecture. The Dutch loved it here and constructed most of their colonial government offices not in the sweltering plains of Jakarta but in the cooler elevations of Bandung, one of the least-known and most underrated highland cities in Southeast Asia.

Bandung's great attraction isn't ancient Indonesian ruins or religious monuments, but the phenomenal collection of Dutch architecture constructed between the turn of the century and WW II. The Dutch hired some of their best and brightest architects to build what was intended to be their new capital of Indonesia. Schooled in the art-nouveau and art-deco movements then sweeping Europe, these young and innovative architects successfully adapted contemporary Western styles with Indonesian motifs to create in Bandung a unique tropical Indo-European style. The result is a remarkably rich collection of modern early-20th-century Dutch architecture. Best of all, Bandung's colonial architecture hasn't been destroyed, as in Jakarta which has torn down most of its most important and beautiful buildings. The city's architectural heritage is guarded and promoted by a coalition of local preservationists, architects, and academics who comprise the Society for Heritage Conservation. Thanks to their efforts, tourism has soared as Dutch travel companies include the city on their popular nostalgia tours.

Downtown Bandung

Downtown Bandung is the standard mess of desultory modern buildings and traffic jams. Ignore all this and explore the upper neighborhoods, which have largely retained their colonial charm, broad tree-lined streets, and idyllic pace of life. The following walking tour begins at the tourist office and moves north through beautiful neighborhoods to the old capitol and the Bandung Zoo.

Merdeka Building: An architectural tour of Bandung landmarks should begin with the Gedung Merdeka (Asia-Afrika Building), where two of Bandung's most famous Dutch architects, Wolf Schoemaker and A.F. Albers, combined their talents in the '30s to build what was originally a Dutch clubhouse. The building achieved fame in 1955 when Sukarno invited leaders of 29 developing nonaligned nations to an international solidarity conference. Interior displays and photographs relate the momentous occasion.

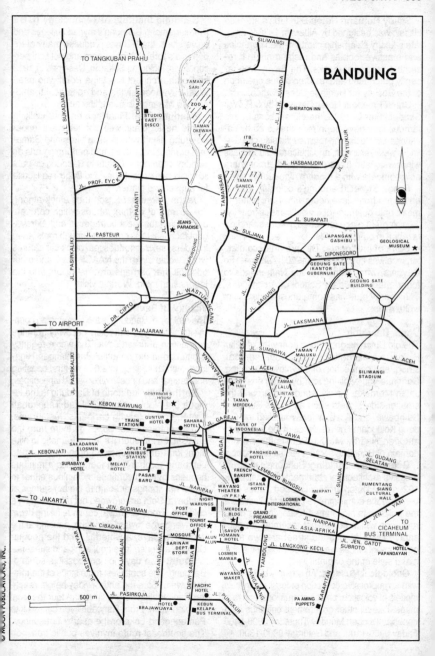

BANDUNG

Savoy Homann Hotel: Bandung's art-deco classic was designed by Albers in 1938 to emulate a luxury steamship complete with portholes and massive lobbies and restaurants that resemble vast open decks. The Savoy was recently purchased and restored by the chairman of the Society for Heritage Conservation.

Grand Preanger Hotel: Designed by C.P. Wolf Schoemaker in 1928, the old sections of this famous lady have been nicely restored by Javanese architects who retained the sleek parallel lines, wide verandas, and intricate leaded-glass windows. Palm trees and a deco atmosphere now compete with a modern nine-story tower.

Braga Street: Bandung's colonial heart is under fire from developers who want either to mall it or to gut many of the old classics from the '30s. A great place for coffee, pastries, and relaxation in outdoor cafes.

Bank of Indonesia: This pre-art-deco masterpiece was constructed in 1920 by architect Ed Cuypers, who returned to the Netherlands to found the Amsterdam School of Architecture. The nearby park has some unusual statues of white rhinos.

Upper Bandung

The old Dutch neighborhood northwest of Jalan Braga is a delightful escape from the heat, smog, and congestion of downtown Bandung. Continue your walking tour by going east from Jalan Merdeka, slowly wandering around the smaller side streets such as *jalans* Sumatra, Sumbawa, and Aceh, where you'll find the Gedung Kologdam, the residence of the army commander. Nearby Maluku Park is the cruising domain of Bandung's transvestites and *bancis*.

Gedung Sate Building: Bandung's most impressive architectural statement was built in the 1920s by a Dutch architect named James Gerber. Now the administrative center of West Java, the building is nicknamed "Sate" for the metal roof rods which somewhat resemble art-deco satay sticks! Across the street are two more government offices which closely follow the spirit and style of the original.

Geological Museum: An ordinary building but with an impressive collection of fossils, minerals, models of volcanos, photos of eruptions, and relief maps. Like all other government buildings in Indonesia, it's open Monday-Thursday 0900-1400, Friday 0900-1100, and Saturday 0900-1300.

Bandung Institute of Technology (ITB): Premier among Bandung's myriad colleges and universities, the ITB has produced many of Indonesia's foremost engineers and political personalities, including Sukarno. Designed in 1918 by Dutch architect Maclaine Pont, who used West Javanese styles and spectacular ship-prowed Minangkabau architecture.

Bandung Zoo: Final stop on your walking tour is the large and well-planned zoo in upper Bandung, filled with tropical birds and Sumatran orangutans. Martial and performing arts on Sunday afternoons. Return to Bandung on public minibuses or continue up to Dago Tea House for sunset and dinner.

Jeans Paradise: Kitsch runs amok among the dozens of clothing shops which compete by erecting the most outrageous and extravagant facades: taxis crashing through roofs, alien invaders, sexual goddesses, black caricatures which would make the NAACP howl, and other oddities that perhaps provide insight into the Indonesian mind. Worth a visit.

Vicinity Of Bandung

The real joy of Bandung is the surrounding countryside where you can really get away from the congestion of urban Java. The whole regency is situated in the beautiful Parahiangan Highlands, which soar up to 2,000 meters, boasting spectacular and unbelievably varied landscapes.

North: Thirty km north of Bandung is the famous but highly commercialized Tangkuban Crater, complete with car parks, restaurants, and an entrance fee. Buses go there from the train station although it's more dramatic to hike eight km from the Jayagiri dropoff. Return to Lembang (probably on foot unless a minibus happens by) and continue by minibus either to Ciater hot springs or south to the hot springs at Maribaya. Both are crowded but refreshing on a cold day. From Maribaya, continue hiking down the river gorge toward Bandung, pausing at the Japanese Cave, a waterfall, and the popular Dago Tea House for a cool drink and sunsets.

South: Two day-trips are possible south of Bandung. The southwest route stops at the market town of Soreang and Ciwidey before reaching Rancabali, where visitors can tour the local tea plantation. From Rancabali you can walk to Pantenggang Lake or the nearby hot springs. The southeast route involves public transport

BANDUNG ACCOMMODATIONS

HOTEL	SINGLE	DOUBLE	ADDRESS	PHONE (022)
LUXURY				
Grand Hotel Preanger	US$140-220	US$140-220	Asia Afrika 81	431631
Istana	US$50-80	US$60-100	Lembang 21	433025
Kumala Panghegar	US$50-70	US$60-80	Asia Africa 140	52142
Panghegar	US$75-100	US$80-120	Merdeka 2	57584
Savoy Homann	US$80-120	US$100-150	Asia Africa 12	432244
MODERATE				
Guntur	US$10-15	US$12-16	Otto Iskandar 20	50763
Melati	US$8-12	US$10-15	Kebonjati 24	50080
Sahara	US$5-10	US$8-15	Otto Iskandar 3	51684
BUDGET				
Sakadarna	US$3-6	US$4-8	Kebonjati 50	439897
Sakadarna Inter.	US$3-6	US$4-8	Kebonjati 34	420-2811
Surabaya	US$3-5	US$4-6	Kebonjati 71	436791

to Cileuleng, from where Mt. Papandayan can be hiked in a full day. Guides and jeeps might be necessary. Yoga at the tourist office can help.

Accommodations

The cheap hotel district is around the train station.

Yossie Homestay: Bandung's newest, cleanest, and most popular spot for backpackers is operated by friendly Yosep and his American wife. Rooms are immaculate, plus impromptu folk concerts happen nightly in the dining area. Ask about tours to nearby volcanoes, hot springs, silk weaving villages, and direct minibuses to Pagandaran. Jl. Kebon Jati 53, tel. (022) 420-5453, US$2 dorm, US$5-8 rooms.

Sakadarna International Travellers Homestay: Bandung's super-budget scene also includes this flagged, two-story *losmen* and the older, less spacious but identically named *losmen* on the same street. The owners run a restaurant with Sundanese specialities, sell puppets, and organize sightseeing trips and buses to other points in Java. Two minutes from the train station, eight minutes from downtown, a 20-minute walk from the central bus terminal. Jalan Kebonjati 34, tel. 420-2811, US$5-8.

Sakadarna Losmen: Great information source but perpetually noisy with kids and TV. A real homestay experience. Jalan Kebonjati 50, tel. (022) 439897, US$3-8.

Surabaya Hotel: Recently restored colonial hotel with huge rooms, comfortable (collapsing) furniture, dozing attendants, a seediness both repulsive and memorable. Jalan Kebonjati 71, tel. 436791, US$6-25.

Hotel Sahara: Somewhat dark but quieter and more private than the *losmen* on Jalan Kebonjati. Jalan Otto Iskandar 3, tel. (022) 51684, US$5-15.

Melati II Hotel: A new middle-priced hotel just opposite the Sakadarnas. Comfortable and clean; good enough for an overnight. Jalan Kebonjati 24, tel. (022) 50080, US$8-15.

Panghegar: Bandung's three finest hotels are the Savoy Homann and the Grand Preanger (two art-deco classics described above) and the Panghegar Hotel a few blocks north. While not a relic from the '30s, the Panghegar is modern and clean and features the city's best views from its skyview lounge. Jalan Merdeka 2, tel. (022) 57584, US$75-120.

Grand Hotel Preanger: Bandung's only five-star hotel features a renovated art deco wing

VICINITY OF BANDUNG

© MOON PUBLICATIONS, INC.

NOT TO SCALE

and 150 rooms in the new tower, plus pool and nightclub with rockin' Filipino bands. Jl. Asia Afrika 81, tel. (022) 431631, fax (022) 430034, US$140-220.

Restaurants
Start with the food stalls which set up nightly opposite the tourist office, and try *ikan mas, sayur asam, soto mas, papas* (chicken or fish wrapped in banana leaf), *karadok* and *lontak* (similar to *gado gado*), and other Sundanese and Madurese specialties. Two popular and inexpensive restaurants worth investigating are the Minang Jaya overlooking the central plaza and the self-service Galaya across from the Ku-

mala Preanger Hotel. Babakan Siliwangi in the extreme north is Bandung's most famous Sundanese restaurant.

Performing Arts
Although Bandung is often touted as the center of Sundanese culture, locating a dance or music performance is difficult to impossible; this isn't Yogyakarta, where a strong tourist industry helps keep traditional arts alive. Tourist-office recommendations and schedules for upcoming performances should be taken with a large grain of salt.

Sundanese Dance: Bandung's cultural heart beats around the Music Conservatory (Konservatori Karawitan) on Jalan Buah Batu.

tropical treasure

Both resident schools—the ASTI (academic, professional level) and the SMKI (high-school students)—occasionally stage performances of Sundanese dance and drama. Traditional Sundanese dance is also performed Wednesday evenings 2000-2200 in the restaurant of the Hotel Panghegar on Jalan Merdeka. One-drink minimum. Jaipongan dance is performed nightly in the Sanggar Langen Setra nightclub on Jalan Tegal Lega south of the Kebu Kelapa bus terminal. Don't waste your time on this sleazy, hokey, and sad spectacle.

Wayang Golek: Traditional wooden puppet plays are given Saturday nights at 2100 at the Yayasan Pusat Kebudayaan (YPK) Cultural Institute on Jalan Naripan. Funky but authentic. Also Fridays and Saturdays at 2000 at the Rumentang Siang Cultural Hall on Jalan Ahmad Yani in the Kusambi shopping district.

Angklung: Tour groups can arrange performances of Sundanese bamboo xylophone orchestras and *wayang golek* by calling Pak Ujo Studios at tel. 71714. Individuals can join the Wednesday afternoon shows on a space-available basis. *Angklung* rehearsals are held Sunday mornings in the Rumentang Siang Cultural hall.

Pencak Silat: Indonesian martial arts can be seen at the student academy on Gang Haji Yakub Mondays and Thursdays 1900-2100. *Pencak silat* is often staged at the zoo on Sunday mornings.

Ram Fights: Exciting contests in which champion rams ferociously butt heads can be seen Sunday mornings 0800-1200 in north Bandung near the town of Lendeng. Matches are local, low-level competitions tied in with breeders' efforts to upgrade the quality of their rams. As orthodox Muslims, the Sundanese are forbidden to gamble. Thus, almost unbelievably, no money changes hands at these contests; they are staged purely for the pleasure of the handlers and breeders! Locations change weekly; the tourist office can help.

Shopping

Bandung's two most acclaimed *wayang golek* carvers are Pa Aming on Jalan Karapitan near the river and Pa Roechiyat at 22 Jalan Pangarang south of the tourist office. Everybody knows what you want; somebody will point the way. Many of Bandung's best antique shops are located on Jalan Barga. Sin Sin Antiques at Jalan Barga 56 offers a wide selection of batik and Sundanese masks. Don't miss the discount-clothing emporiums in Jeans Paradise!

Transportation

Bandung's train station is centrally located near inexpensive *losmen* and within quick trishaw distance of the better hotels on Jalan Asia Afrika.

Bus passengers will be dropped at outlying terminals. Travelers coming from the west (Bogor or Jakarta) will arrive at the Kebu Kelapa bus terminal in south Bandung, about 20 minutes on foot from the train station. Trishaws can also be hired. Bus passengers coming from the east (Pagandaran or Yogyakarta) will be dropped at the *extremely* distant Cicaheum bus terminal on the eastern edge of Bandung. *Bemos* and buses heading west toward the center of town wind through darkened neighborhoods before finally arriving 45 minutes later at the Kebu Kelapa terminal. Don't panic, just stay on the bus.

Choices leaving Bandung include trains, buses from the two public bus terminals described above, or the private buses which leave from Jalan Kebonjai near the train station.

PAGANDARAN

This small fishing village midway between Bandung and Yogyakarta is one of the few beach resorts on the south coast of Java. There's a certain primitive beauty and sense of remoteness to the region. Hikes can be organized through the peninsular national park just south of the town. All of the original growth was destroyed by fire several decades ago, but guides such as Toha (with his ponytail and antique hiking boots) can point out the black and gray monkeys, *banteng* pasture, flying foxes, Japanese bunkers, caves, and an outstanding waterfall which plunges dramatically into the ocean. White Beach on the western coast offers fine sand and a small bathing pool with a degree of privacy.

Accommodations

Standards of cleanliness of the 50 or so losmen, hotels, and bungalows are rising all the time. Pagandaran is now firmly on the tourist trail and five-star hotels will soon be appearing on the once pristine beachfront.

Prices are also rising as organized groups of Europeans and Australians arrive to fill the hotels and resorts. Bare bones losmens under US$5 are still available, but most places now charge US$6-10 for fan-cooled rooms and US$12-20 for a/c rooms.

Budget Losmen: Much better than the decrepit and overpriced places listed below under Losmen Mini Dua are the small losmen in the small alleys in the center of town, away from the beach. Jaya, Budi, Damar Indah, Surya Indah, and the clean South Coast Huts all have decent rooms for US$5-10 and give hefty discounts for longer stays.

Bamboo Guesthouse: A great choice in a very quiet location just one block from the beach behind the Surya Beach Hotel. Jl. Baru, tel. (0265) 379419, US$4-6.

Delta Gecko Village Homestay: Special note must be made of this idyllic escape five km west of Pagandaran in a coconut grove, near the village of Cikembulan. Vegetarian restaurant, lamps at dinnertime, psychedelic bicycles, and small library all run by resident artist "Delta Agus" and his German-Australian wife Kristina. A remote place for contemplation and arts, not party animals or beach hounds. Cikembulan, no phone, US$5-15.

Adam's Homestay: Attractive rooms, small pub, and authentic cappuccino in a fine place run by a German lady and her colorful Indonesian husband and former world traveler. Jl. Pamugaran Bulak Laut, tel. (0265) 379164, US$12-25.

Sandaan Hotel: Good value choice with spotless rooms facing a small but attractive pool. Recommended. Jl. Pamugaran Bulak Laut, tel. (0265) 379165, US$12-15 fan, US$20-30 a/c.

Bulak Laut Bungalows: Pseudo-Bukkitingii cottages provide some atmosphere and welcome relief from the uncreative architecture that plagues most of Pagandaran. Jl. Pamugaran Bulak Laut, tel. (0265) 39171, US$10-15 fan.

Pantai Indah Barat Resort Hotel: Upscale hotel with swimming pool, tennis courts at their adjacent sister hotel on the east beach, and a/c rooms with TV and refrigerator. Good central location. Jl. Kidang Pananjung, tel. (0265) 379004, fax (0265) 379327, US$40-65.

Surya Beach Hotel: Best in town is this comfortable hotel with lovely pool, two restaurants, a/c rooms with TV and refrigerator, plus friendly staff. Jl. Pamugaran Bulak Laut, tel. (0265) 379428, fax (0265) 379289, US$40-65.

Pagandaran's dozen-plus *losmen* are clustered near the southern end of the road leading down from the bus terminal. Rates are higher on weekends and doubled during major holidays.

Losmen Mini Dua: Low-end choices include Mini I, Mini II, Laut Biru, the Ramamangun, and Losmen Mini Dua. All are simple homestays where you'll meet the entire family and the teenagers who hang out in town. Jl. Kalenbuhaya, US$2-5.

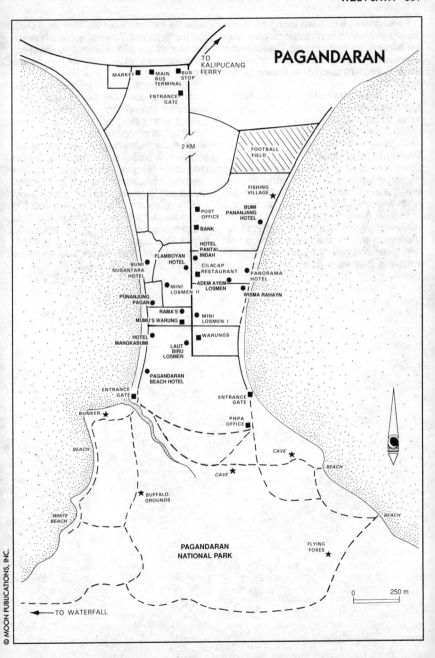

PAGANDARAN

Panorama Hotel: Hotels facing the beach are more expensive but in better condition than the *losmen* in the center of town. The Panorama offers rather bizarre Tyrolian-style accommodation at bargain rates. 187 Jl. Kidang Pananjung, US$6-15.

Bumi Nusantara Hotel: The best middle-quality hotel on the west coast is a worthy attempt at traditional architecture. Jl. Pantai Barat, US$8-14 fan, US$25-40 a/c.

Getting To Pagandaran

Direct minibuses are available from travelers' *losmen* in Bandung and Yogyakarta. Alternatively, take an ordinary bus to Banjar, 63 km north, and continue to Pagandaran by local bus or minibus. Arrivals at the Pagandaran bus terminal are greeted by a wild collection of aggressive *becak* drivers who grab luggage, yell, beg, plead, and generally scare the hell out of everyone. Stay calm. *Becaks* are necessary since the *losmen* are several kilometers south and too far to walk. The correct fare from the bus terminal to a *losmen* is Rp1000; the *becak* driver receives a hefty commission from the *losmen* operator.

Pagandaran can be reached in another more intriguing way. Each day around noon a slow boat sails the backwaters from Cilicap to Kalipucang, a small fishing port near Pagandaran. Travel agents in Yogyakarta sell minibus tickets which make the connection. The five- to six-hour journey passes endless mudflats, twisted mangroves, simple villages, and a modern prison which holds detainees from the 1965 revolution. The scenery improves at the western end. On arrival at the Kalipucang Pier, walk 200 meters across the bridge to the main road, from where buses continue into Pagandaran. Boats depart Kalipucang for Cilicap daily at 0700, 0900, and 1300. Only the 0700 departure will get you to Yogyakarta in one day.

YOGYAKARTA

One of the largest villages in the world, Yogyakarta (usually shortened to "Yogya"—pronounced "JOAG-jah") is Java's cultural and educational capital—Indonesia's Kyoto. For centuries a royal city and major trade center, Yogya today has the highest-ranking court in the country; it's a city of monuments, palaces, highly respected music and dance schools, brilliant choreographers, drama and poetry workshops, folk theater, *wayang* troupes . . . a superb destination for world travelers. It's also one of the best places to shop in Southeast Asia, boasting talented batik specialists, leather craftsmen, and some of the country's most successful modern artists. Within easy striking distance are some of Indonesia's finest monuments, including the world-famous ruins of Borobudur and Prambanan. Yogyakarta is also well served by an outstanding selection of budget *losmen,* comfortable hotels, and restaurants serving the regional specialties of Central Java. Small wonder that Yogya, with the possible exception of Bali, has become the leading attraction in all of Indonesia.

History

Yogya lies in the center of Java's "Realm of the Dead," a city surrounded by ancient ruins. A relatively new city, Yogya was founded in the middle of the 18th century after Dutch pressure split the Mataram Empire of Central Java into the twin kingdoms of Solo and Yogya. For the Javanese, Yogya has always been a symbol of nationalistic passion and resistance to alien rule. It was the stubborn center of guerrilla struggle against the Dutch and the first capital of the infant republic during the War of Independence. During the Dutch occupation, the sultan locked himself in his *kraton* and only negotiated with the Europeans from the top of his palace, looking down on them with all his people watching. Finally, in 1948 the Dutch launched an all-out attack on the city, dropping 900 paratroopers, heavy bombs, and rocket fire. Sultan Hamengkubuwono IX, one of Indonesia's most beloved and respected leaders, immediately declared his support for the rebels. When the Dutch finally abandoned their dreams of colonial reconquest, Yogya was designated a Special Territory, re-

sponsible to the central government in Jakarta and not the provincial head in Central Java.

Yogya today is ruled by Sultan Hamengkubuwono X (formerly Prince Mangkubumi), a 45-year-old businessman, lawyer, and head of the local chapter of the ruling Golkar Party. Contrary to popular opinion (which assumed the Mataram Dynasty's significance would fade with the death of Hamengkubuwono IX), the 1989 coronation of Prince Mangkubumi was according to tradition and surprisingly lavish. Offerings were presented to the Goddess of the Southern Seas, respects were paid at the royal tombs at Imogiri, and trips were made to the two volcanos, Merapi and Lawu. The current sultan enjoys the immense goodwill generated by his famous father, but much of his claims to divine rule will depend on whether he can marshal those still-powerful supernatural forces of Central Java.

ATTRACTIONS

Yogya is a compact town and almost everything can be reached on foot, although bicycling is a great alternative. An early start is imperative since all museums and palaces close by 1300. The following sights are described in a walking tour beginning from the tourist office on Jalan Malioboro.

Central Market

Perhaps the most colorful market in Indonesia. Sprawling out from under an immense shed are hundreds of stalls selling everything from macrame to mutton and mangoes. The narrow access road, clogged with overloaded *becaks* and tremendous piles of vegetables, is a photographer's dream, but you must be quick since Indonesians don't like being treated as foreigner's models. Best experienced at the crack of dawn.

Vredburg (Perjuangan) Museum

This beautiful Dutch fort was constructed directly across from the palace square to consolidate Dutch military advances in the archipelago. With its gun emplacements overlooking the

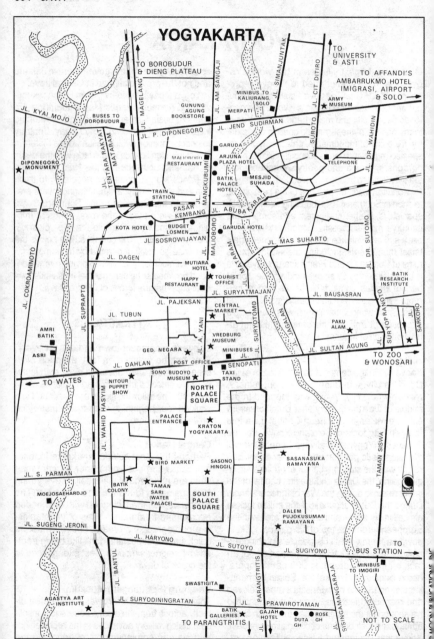

YOGYAKARTA

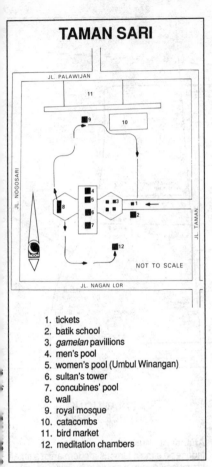

TAMAN SARI

JL. PALAWIJAN

11

10

9

JL. NOGOSARI

8

4
5
3
6
7

1

2

JL. TAMAN

MOON

12

NOT TO SCALE

JL. NAGAN LOR

1. tickets
2. batik school
3. *gamelan* pavillions
4. men's pool
5. women's pool (Umbul Winangan)
6. sultan's tower
7. concubines' pool
8. wall
9. royal mosque
10. catacombs
11. bird market
12. meditation chambers

main north gate, it stands today as a reminder of the uneasy relations between the Dutch occupiers and the Javanese sultanate. Now carefully restored, the interior relates recent Yogya history through a series of illuminated dioramas. Best of all, it's air-conditioned! Open Saturday and Sunday 0900-1400.

Sono Budoyo Museum

Yogyakarta's finest museum contains a first-rate collection of Javanese, Madurese, and Balinese arts and crafts; comprehensive exhibits of batik, Dongson drums from Timor, rare *wayang* puppets of long-nosed Dutch soldiers, a spe-cial room devoted to Bali, and complete *gamelans* from both Yogya and Cirebon. The building was designed by a Dutch architect who followed the traditional *kraton* (palace) arrangement of a *pendopo* (open Javanese pavilion) with narrow *pringgitan* (passageways) leading to the *dalem* (inner royal courtyards).

The Palace

Founded in 1757 by the first sultan of Yogyakarta, this open-air *kraton* features classical Javanese palace-court architecture at its finest. Facing the immense *alun alun* (open square) are several open pavilions used only for special ceremonies. An educational display of wall reliefs which depict Indonesian history (look for *kraton* construction, Diponegoro, and Sukarno) can be found by walking clockwise around the first palace, but the main palace entrance is located on the opposite, *western* side. The exterior Museum Kareta Kraton is filled only with an unimpressive collection of royal coaches. The main palace is open Sunday-Thursday 0900-1230, Friday and Saturday to 1100. Everyone must be well dressed; men should wear long pants, women must be very modest.

First Courtyard: Palace tours are conducted by gracious guides dressed in traditional court attire who have often spent their lives in the service of the sultan. First stop is the five *gamelan* orchestras, including the Nagawilaga, tuned to the *slendro* scale (five equal notes per octave), and Gunturmadau, tuned to *pelog* (seven unequal distances per octave). The tour continues past wedding *gamelans* and gilded palanquins through the central entrance into the main pavilion.

Central Courtyard: Buildings inside the main courtyard include the residence of the sultan's family (noted by the three yellow doors), breezy pavilions used for *gamelan* performances and tea ceremonies, and special areas where infidels once drank liquor. The Golden Pavilion, with its well-carved pillars and strong elements of color symbolism, is considered the most distinguished architectural feature of the *kraton*.

Third Courtyard: The Kesatrian Courtyard is dominated by the lovely pavilion in which *gamelan* and dance rehearsals are held Sunday mornings at 1030. Pavilions around the plaza display European-style art, royal regalia, interesting old photographs, and family-tree charts

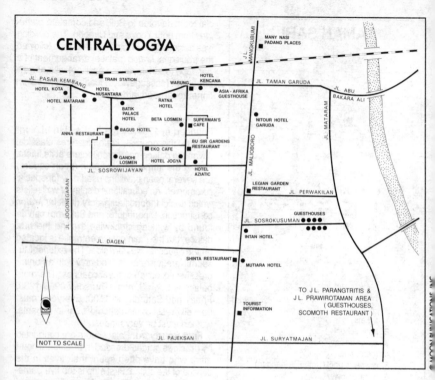

CENTRAL YOGYA

NOT TO SCALE

which show that sultans never worried about Indonesia's family-planning slogan, *dua anak cukup* ("two is enough").

Water Palace

Taman Sari is an old pleasure park built in feudal splendor between 1758 and 1765 for the sultan and his family. Like the Hanging Gardens of Babylon, Taman Sari once had lighted underwater corridors, cool subterranean mosques, meditation platforms in the middle of lily ponds, *gamelan* towers, and galleries for dancing, all in mock-Spanish architecture. Princesses bathed in flower-strewn pools, streams flowed above covered passageways, and boats drifted in man-made lakes. Today, most of the "Fragrant Gardens" are in ruins but enough remains to make a visit worthwhile. The accompanying map shows the highlights. An excellent bird market is located at the northern end but it's impossible to reach directly from Taman Sari.

ATTRACTIONS OUTSIDE YOGYA

Affandi Art Museum

Indonesia's most famous modern artist's small art museum is in a modern building on Jalan Adisucipto some eight km east of town. Although considered an expressionist with a style somewhat similar to Van Gogh's, his early works in the second gallery display his great talents for naturalism. Affandi died in May 1990 at the age of 83 after a long illness. The batik gallery of Sapto Hudoyo is nearby.

Kota Gede

Once the capital of the old Mataram Kingdom and older than Yogya itself, Kota Gede is now the center of Central Java's thriving silver industry. Visitors are welcome to wander around big workshops full of men and boys hammering on anvils, filing, polishing, heating, and soldering on strips of bright silver, using the simplest of hand-tools. Display rooms sell everything from steelworker's hard hats embossed with your name to silver replicas of Borobudur and Prambanan. Tom's Silver is the largest and the favorite of all tour groups. Kota Gede is six km southeast of Yogya. Take city bus 4 from Jalan Malioboro.

Imogiri

A cemetery for the royal houses of Yogya and Solo since the early kings of Mataram. Climb barefoot up the 346 warm stone steps, a great sun-dappled stairway like a ladder leaning up against the sky to the burial grounds on top. The mighty Sultan Agung was the first Javanese king to be interred here, in the mid-17th century. Since then, nearly every king—including the last sultan, who died in October 1988—has found his final resting place on this highly venerated hill. Imogiri lies 20 km southeast of Yogya, a 30-minute minibus ride from the main terminal. Interior tombs are usually closed, but guides will walk you around the exterior. Take a minibus from Jalan Menteri Superno at Taman Siswo.

Parangtritis Beach

The coast south of Yogya is a windy, wild, and barren region known for its haunted seas, crashing surf, and dangerous riptides. It is also said to be the home of Ratu Loro Kidul, the Sea Goddess who lives beneath the waves and is married not only to the founder of the Mataram Empire but also to the current sultan of Yogya. Like Neptune, her hair is green and full of shells and seaweed; she holds court over sea nymphs and creatures of the deep. Venerated and feared by the Javanese, Loro Kidul is summoned by a gong on the evening of the Muslim day of rest, when a bamboo tray of rice, bananas, jasmine flowers, cosmetics, and coconuts is offered to the eternally youthful goddess. Don't wear green; that's *her* color, and she has been known to yank people into the sea for the transgression. Parangtritis, obviously, isn't a beautiful beach resort with swaying palms, but some people enjoy the primitivism, wild flavor, and end-of-the-world atmosphere. Cheap *losmen* are plentiful. Take an hourly Jatayu Bus from the main bus terminal.

ACCOMMODATIONS

Budget

Yogyakarta is Java's *losmen* mecca, with dozens of small but clean and comfortable spots. Almost all are sandwiched in the streets and alleys (*gangs*) immediately south of the train station. Only those which appeared to be clean and friendly, with a degree of atmosphere, are mentioned below. Conditions change frequently; updates are appreciated!

The cheapest places under US$3 are located in the two alleys which run between Jalan Kembang and Jalan Sosrowijayan. First stop might be at a small cafe like Superman's or Bu Sir Gardens for a quick drink and a little networking. Super-budget *losmen* on Gang 1 include Lucy Losmen, Beta Losmen, and Hotel Joyga, but all are rather dark and cramped. Possibilities along Gang 2 include Bagus Hotel and Heru Jaya Losmen, plus the better-than-average Gandhi Losmen. Inspect a few, looking for security and ventilation—Yogya is a hot and muggy city.

Moving up a notch to around US$5-8, you'll find a much better selection of *losmen* and budget hotels. The best are located on Jalan Kembang across from the train station and on Jalan Sosrowijayan just a few steps down from Jalan Malioboro. Both the Indonesia Hotel and Hotel Aziatic on Jalan Sosrowijayan are good places for couples on tight budgets. Ask for a room on the top floor of the Indonesia. Clean and comfortable hotels on Jalan Kembang include the security-conscious Hotel Kota, the Ratna Hotel where rooms cost US$6-12, and the Asia-Afrika Guesthouse where fan-cooled rooms cost US$6-10. All are reasonably well kept and very good value.

Moderate Accommodations In Central Yogya

Yogya's accommodations really begin to excel in the US$20-35 price range. All of the following are located within easy walking distance of the train station.

Batik Palace Hotels: Directly opposite the station you'll find the luxurious Batik Palace Hotel, where fan-cooled rooms start at US$5 and a/c rooms go from US$26. Another branch of the Batik Palace is located a few blocks north of the train station on Jalan Mangkubumi.

CENTRAL YOGYAKARTA ACCOMMODATIONS

HOTEL	SINGLE	DOUBLE	ADDRESS	PHONE (0274)
LUXURY				
Garuda	US$90-120	US$110-160	Malioboro 72	66353
MODERATE				
Batik Palace	US$16-30	US$20-45	Kembang 29	2149
Mutiara	US$25-35	US$30-45	Malioboro 18	4531
New Mutiara	US$30-45	US$40-60	Malioboro	4530
Peti Mas	US$15-20	US$18-30	Dagen 39	61938
BUDGET				
Asia-Afrika	US$6-15	US$10-22	Kembang 25	4489
Aziatic	US$3-6	US$4-8	Sosrowijayan	
Gandhi	US$2-5	US$2-5	Gang 2	
Indonesia	US$3-6	US$3-6	Sosrowijayan	87659
Intan	US$4-8	US$5-10	Sosrokusuman	
Kota	US$5-12	US$8-15	Kembang 79	

Rooms up here cost US$28 single a/c and US$35 double a/c. This one has a swimming pool.

Peti Mas Guesthouse: The neighborhood's other good property in the same price range is the Peti Mas Guesthouse on Jalan Dagen, a couple of blocks south of the train station. Peti Mas consistently receives good reports from travelers who enjoy the small garden and pool. Jalan Dagen 39, tel. (0274) 61938, fax 71175, US$12-15 fan with common bath, US$20-25 a/c with private bath.

Moderate Accommodations
On Jalan Prawirotaman

Yogya's best-value hotels in the middle price range are located in a residential neighborhood about three km south of the train station. It's a beautiful and relaxing area far removed from the noise and grit of central Yogyakarta. *Becaks* from the train station to Jalan Prawirotaman cost about Rp2000. At last count, the neighborhood had 15 guesthouses. Economy rooms cost just US$5-8, standard rooms with fan average US$6-10, standard rooms with a/c cost US$12-18, deluxe a/c suites cost US$25-30. All properties have restaurants, cocktail lounges, and gardens, and several have swimming pools. The Garden Restaurant on the north side of the street is a beautiful alternative to hotel dining.

Rose Guesthouse: Top choice is the modern and clean hotel midway down the street on the right side. Tariff includes full breakfast, tea, snacks, and the use of their swimming pool, largest and nicest in the neighborhood. Jalan Prawirotaman 22, tel. (0274) 77991, US$5-10 fan, US$14-20 a/c.

Duta Guesthouse: Another clean and well-priced guesthouse with gardens and a small swimming pool. Jalan Prawirotaman 20, tel. (0274) 72064, fax 72064, US$10-15 with fan, from US$20 a/c.

Luxury

Garuda Hotel: Yogyakarta's most stylish and best-located hotel is the newly restored Garuda on Jalan Malioboro. Opened in 1911 and expanded with Indo-European wings in the '30s, this is one of the few luxury hotels in Indonesia with charm, character, and a sense of history. Jalan Malioboro 72, tel. (0274) 66353, fax (0274) 63074, US$140-340.

Ambarrukmo Palace Hotel: Yogya's largest hotel is popular with tour groups but it's inconveniently located on the outskirts of town en route to the airport. Jalan Adisucipto, tel. (0274) 88488, fax (0274) 63283, US$120-280.

RESTAURANTS

Yogya is a godsend for vegetarians: bean cakes, *rempeyek* (peanut cookies), vegetable soups, and the *makan asli* speciality called *gudeg,* a delicious mixture of jackfruit cooked in coconut milk with eggs, tofu, and beansprouts covered with a rich and spicy sauce. Also try *opor ayam,* slices of chicken simmered in coconut milk; and sumptuous *mbok berek* or *ayam goreng*—fried chicken that Colonel Sanders can't hold a candle to.

Travelers' cafes near the train station serve the standard road fare of guacamole pancakes, watery fruit smoothies, and other Kuta dishes. At Superman's, travelers sit sardined with other Westerners, listening to tired versions of old Stones and Cat Stevens hits. Better food and atmosphere are found at Bu Sir Garden Restaurant (try the *gado gado*) and Eko Cafe in the same alley. You can also escape the crowds and enjoy superior food at intimate Anna's on Gang 2. Mama's, the longtime favorite on Jalan Kembang, has lost its following in the last few years. Instead, spend your *rupiah* at the French Grill Lima around the corner from Hotel Aziatic.

Curiously, the finest food in the Sosro area is found at the two tiny food stalls located on Gang 1 at Jalan Kembang. The plates of unidentifiable foods are strange, cheap, and completely delicious—Yogya cuisine at its most authentic. Yogya's other great dining experience is latenight *ayam goreng* (fried chicken) served in a festive atmosphere on Jalan Malioboro every evening after 2000. Mats are unrolled and students play guitar: a great time is guaranteed for all.

Most of Yogya's cafes and restaurants are found along Jalan Malioboro. None are spectacular but at least you get to try the local dishes and enjoy the company of Indonesians. Closest to the *losmen* is the Legian Garden Restaurant, an upstairs eatery which specializes in both Western and Indonesian dishes. Helen's down the street has sadly degenerated into a self-service fast-food joint. The Mirah Restaurant in the lobby of the old Mutiara Hotel is classy,

comfortable, and reasonably priced with most dishes costing just Rp3000-6000. Across the street you'll find the popular Shinta Restaurant, and the Columbo, which specializes in unusual fruit drinks made from durian, sirzat, and *apel*.

PERFORMING ARTS

Yogyakarta is the performing-arts capital of Java and one of the two finest places in Indonesia to experience the cultural riches of the archipelago. Most of the shows are geared toward the tourist, although this in no way detracts from their excitement or authenticity. Tourist venues are often better funded and have more lavish props and costuming than authentic productions. You will not understand the words but the magical scenes will fascinate and hold your attention for several hours. The tourist office has a list of the latest venues and schedules.

Ramayana

Dalem Pujokuseman: Yogya's most extraordinary performances are held three times weekly in the open-air pavilion a block off Jalan Katamso. Arrive early for the best seats. Photographers can claim the mats at stageside. The Ramayana is performed in four segments over consecutive evenings. Shows begin with a short description by the *dalang,* followed by three introductory dances, usually a *topeng* or *golek* taken from the Mahabharta or Panji cycles. Before the main event, the dancers mentally prepare themselves with a few moments of quiet contemplation. Unlike the frantic movements of the Balinese, Javanese dance is a highly refined and hypnotic choreography which resembles a ballet in slow motion. Battle scenes are reserved for the climactic finish. Do not confuse this performance with the vastly inferior Sasanasuka Ramayana given at the THR.

Prambanan Ramayana: These de Mille-like spectacles take place in the newly constructed 1,011-seat amphitheater which overlooks the Loro Jonggrang temple complex at Prambanan. Performances are held on four successive full-moon nights each month from June to October. This six-episode contemporary *sendratari*-style ballet is based on traditional *wayang orang* dancing of classical Javanese theater. The plot is a modernized, dramatized version of the Indian epic poem, the Ramayana. The Prambanan temple panels are, in effect, re-enacted live. Taking part are an entire *gamelan* orchestra, scores of beautifully and grotesquely costumed dancers, singers, and musicians, with monkey armies, strutting menacing *rawana*, acrobatic miracles, giant kings on stilts, clashing battles, *real* fire. Tickets for admission and transportation can be purchased in advance from the tourist office, travel agencies, or any large hotel. One of the most spectacular theater productions in Indonesia.

Kraton: Court rehearsals of Javanese dance and *gamelan* can be observed in the royal palace on Sundays at 1030. *Gamelan* only on Mondays and Wednesdays at 1030.

Arjuna Plaza Hotel: Abbreviated versions of the Ramayana are performed in the French Grill Thursdays at 1900.

Sasanasuka: Amateurish and poorly attended shows performed by struggling students, transvestites, and last-minute fill-ins. Forget it.

Wayang
Nitour Show: Wooden puppet shows daily except Sunday at 1100 inside the studio at Jalan Dalhlan 71. Touristy but one of the few guaranteed spots to watch some *wayang golek*.

Agastya Art Institute: A training school for *dalangs* (puppetmasters). Visitors can watch lessons daily from 1500 to 1700. It's on Jalan Gedongkiwo over the RR tracks, about three km from the city in a small *kampong*.

RRI: Radio Republic Indonesia sponsors all-night shadow-puppet plays on the second Saturday of the month in the Sasono Hinggil just south of the *kraton*. A completely authentic experience.

Arjuna Plaza Hotel: Shadow plays for tourists every Tuesday at 1900.

SHOPPING

Yogyakarta is rivaled only by Bali for variety of arts and crafts. Top buys are batiks, leatherwork, and performing-arts tools such as *wayang kulit* and *wayang golek* puppets. Many of the fashion designers have married traditional materials with the latest designs to produce beautiful clothing at outstanding prices.

To get acquainted with the full range of crafts offered, visit first the government-sponsored Yogyakarta Crafts Center across from the Ambarrukmo Hotel and the chaotic Central Market on Jalan Malioboro. Then slowly walk up and down Jalan Malioboro, pausing at the half-dozen shops which specialize in Indonesian crafts. Best bets include the outstanding array of batiks in Terang Bulan (near the market), a handful of small antique stores opposite the Garuda Hotel near the RR tracks, musical instruments and Ramayana costumes in Toko Jawa (opposite the Mutiara Hotel), and Toko Setia for *wayang* puppets.

Batik
Yogya's most famous craft is batik. Outlets can be found throughout the city but a large concentration of shops is located south of the *kraton* near the water palace and on Jalan Prawirotaman near the middle-priced hotels. Some young entrepreneur will almost certainly want to show you around and receive a commission for his services. Although there is absolutely no need to use sales touts, they're worth employing if you enjoy their company and don't mind paying the fee.

Take your time; there's a great deal of mass-produced junk in Yogya. Batik produced with silkscreen printing methods or copper printing stamps called *cap tulis* should be very inexpensive. Hand-painted batik (*batik tulis*) will cost more, but even then, quality varies enormously. Some artists just draw the outline and have teams of girls fill in the intricate details . . . assembly-line fashion. Results are often the worst kinds of clichés: blazing Indonesian sunsets, doe-eyed Balinese dancers, psychedelic crashing beach scenes. Before spending any sizable amount of money, investigate the market and educate yourself. Terang Bulan, Yogya's batik supermarket on Jalan Malioboro, has a good selection in all price ranges. Then visit several private galleries such as Amri Batik west of the river and Kuswadji's near the *kraton*. Batik shops often come down 30% on the original asking price.

Yogyakarta is an excellent place to learn something about the complex art of batik. Dozens of schools here charge 5,000-20,000 *rupiah* weekly, including materials, to teach the history of batik; traditional designs; formulas for waxes; how to prepare and use both chemical and natural dyes; how to hold, use, and clean the *canting* (wax pen) and *jegul* (brush); how to apply wax in fine and thick lines, how to remove wax from cloth. Recommendations from other students are best, but the tourist office has an approved list. Before handing over your money, talk to the instructor and look at his work.

PRACTICALITIES

Tourist Information

The tourist office (tel. 3543) on Jalan Malioboro is one of the best in Indonesia. They can help with maps, calendars of upcoming festivals, schedules of performing arts, Prambanan shows, and recommendations on where to shop. Train and bus schedules are posted on bulletin boards. Open daily except Sundays 0800-2030.

Yogya's largest bookstore is Gunung Agung, at the corner of Jalan Mangkubumi and Jalan Diponegoro. Look for a copy of Michael Smithies's *Yogyakarta, Cultural Heart of Indonesia* or Jacques Dumarcay's *The Temples of Java,* two outstanding guidebooks published by Oxford in Asia.

Mail And Telephone

The post office is located inside the historic building on the corner of Jalan Senopati and Jalan Yani. All packages must be inspected by customs before mailing. The Pos Paket is in a side room; poste restante is just to the left of the main entrance. Phone calls can be made around the clock from the phone center on Yos Sudarso, about 15 minutes by *becak* from city center.

Travel Agencies

Travel agents around town can help with organized tours to Dieng Plateau, minibuses to Cilicap, and Ramayana plays at Prambanan. Several honest and dependable agents keep shop on Jalan Sosrowijayan near the Indonesia Hotel. Pacto Travel (tel. 2740) on Jalan Mangkubumi sells tours and traveler's checks and functions as the representative of American Express.

TRANSPORTATION

Arrival

Air: Yogya's airport is 10 km from town on the road to Solo. Taxis from the airport to city center cost about US$4. Buses and minibuses leave about 200 meters from the terminal entrance.

Train: Yogya's train station is nicely located right in the middle of town, within easy walking distance of the budget *losmen* and the Garuda Hotel on Jalan Malioboro. Train schedules are posted in the lobby.

Bus: Yogya's main bus terminal is inconveniently located about four km southeast of city center. It's not on the map but about three inches right! Most public buses going west on Jalan Veteran will reach Jalan Malioboro and the budget *losmen* near the train station. *Becaks* cost Rp2000 to city center. Private bus companies often drop you near the train station; eat at the Padang restaurant just opposite if you arrive before dawn.

Getting Around

Yogyakarta is a compact town and almost everything of interest is within walking distance. A great way to save time and get some exercise is on a bicycle rented from the restaurants and *losmen* near Jalan Sosrowijayan. Streets here are filled with friendly "hellos" and the jangle of bicycle bells. Motorcycles can be rented from several shops on Jalan Kembang. Traffic is light, roads are in good condition, and service stations are plentiful—there is absolutely no finer way to explore the countryside and monuments at Prambanan than on a motorcycle! Minibuses are no longer allowed within the city limits.

Becaks: Prices are extremely reasonable, costing around Rp600 per km or Rp1500 by the hour. There's no shortage of them, so if you don't get this rate or near it, just walk away and give your business to the competition. Many drivers approach you proposing Rp300-500 per hour, but their intention is to take you on a shopping tour. If you're interested, this is an excellent way to shop around, though you pay higher prices to cover their commissions.

Leaving Yogyakarta

Air: Tickets can be purchased from Garuda (tel. 4400) on Jalan Mangkubumi, Merpati (tel. 4272) on Jalan Sudirman, and local travel agents. Flights to Jakarta and Bali should be booked several days in advance. To reach the airport from city center, take any minibus going to Solo and get off in front of the terminal.

Train: Train travel is one of the small pleasures of any journey across Java. They're safe, quiet, restful, and allow you the time to meet Indonesians, always the highlight of any visit. A wide variety of trains leaves Yogyakarta every day, but it's best to avoid the slow and crowded third-class coaches. Departure timetables are posted in the train station. Purchase your ticket in advance or expect to stand.

Bus: Buses leave Yogyakarta from several different areas. The main public terminal is about four km southeast of town on the road to Kota Gede. Buses leave 0330-1900 every 10-15 minutes for all the towns on Java. Every public bus that runs down Jalan Malioboro goes to the main bus terminal. Buses also leave from private company headquarters located on Jalan Mangkubumi and Jalan Diponegoro, north of the train station. These long-distance buses usually leave 500-1930 and travel straight through the cool night. Sleep is difficult if not impossible; expect to spend the next day recovering in bed. Minibuses also leave from the travel agencies on Jalan Sosrowijayan in the heart of the tourist quarter. These are fast, convenient, and surprisingly comfortable ways to reach almost all tourist destinations in Central Java.

JAVANESE CULTURE

The *Kraton*

When the temple-city concept arrived from India, the *kraton* developed as the Indonesian counterpart. These walled fortified palaces of Javanese rulers became the centers of political power and culture. Containing several thousand people, each of these self-contained regent mini-cities was tied to a dynasty, and each new dynasty founded a new *kraton*. The most famous *kraton* of Java are in Yogya and Solo, Central Java. As in India, these fortresses incorporated all that the surrounding region would need in the way of commerce, art, and religion. They contained banks, baths, shops, temples, massage and meditation chambers, schools, workshops, scribes, concubine quarters—everything needed for both body and soul.

Religion

Agama Jawa (The Religion of Java) has evolved into an incredible blending of doctrines and practices. An estimated 148 religious sects exist on Java, mainly in East and Central Java. From its early years, Javanese Islam has been a merger of Sufism (Islamic mysticism), Hinduism, and native superstition. Today Islam is the professed religion of 90% of its inhabitants. But the Javanese differ widely in the intensity of their beliefs. Only five to 10 percent adhere to a relatively purist form of Islam (*santri*), some 30% to a syncretic and Javanized version of Islam, while most of the remaining consider themselves only nominal Muslims. The latter group is known as *abangan*, professed adherents of Islam, but whose practices and thinking are closest to the old Javanese mysticism, animism, and Indo-Javanese traditions. There are vast parts of Java, especially Central Java, that are still Hindu-Buddhist. The *wayang* theater is almost completely non-Islamic, its roots reaching deep into myths and sagas of ancient Javanese heroes. Javanese *pamong* (tutors), black magicians, mystic teachers, and *dukun* (healers), famous for their oracular powers, have often influenced powerful politicians.

Batik

Java produces the world's finest batik, an art of great antiquity. The word is derived from a Javanese word meaning fine point, though in everyday usage it means wax printing or wax-resist painting. Batik is traditionally used for clothing; even on formal occasions one may wear open-necked batik shirts, blouses (*kebaya*),

skirts (*saura*), or dresses. Formerly, batik fabrics were used mainly to make *sarong*, women's skirts, scarves, and men's headgear; cloth even had a strong cultic function. Nowadays batik is used in housecoats, long dresses, blouses, ties, belts, slippers, hats, umbrellas, sportjackets, as well as in interior decorating and fashion: wall and carpet designs, lampshades, tablecloths, napkins, bedspreads, shopping bags, briefcases, fans. Even school uniforms in Indonesia have subdued batik patterns in them.

Several sizes are available: *Kain panjang* length is three times its width; a *dodot* used for high court ceremonies is four times its width; the *sarong* is two times its width. Other forms include the *slendang*, a breast and shoulder cloth worn by women, and *kain kepala*, a head cloth worn by men.

Batik tulis is the most prized and expensive batik. Designs of *batik tulis* are usually drawn on fine cotton, linen, or, for those who can afford it, silk. Finely detailed designs are first drawn freehand with a pencil on the textile, then hot liquid wax, impervious to dye, is applied with a penlike instrument called a *canting*. The areas *not* to be colored are filled in with wax. The cloth is then passed through vats of dyes before the unwanted wax is removed, a process repeated four or more times until the overall pattern and effect are created.

Batik cap (pronounced "chop") uses copper stamps to impress the wax patterns onto the fabric—a faster and cheaper method. Made from strips of metal and wire meticulously soldered together, *caps* are themselves collectors' items and objects of great art. In use since 1840, this process is making batik more and more a mass-produced craft, though some *cap batik* is superior to *batik tulis* work.

Gamelan

Gamelan is the broad name for many varieties of xylophonic orchestras with bronze, wooden, or bamboo keys on wooden or bamboo bases or resting on tubular resonators. *Gamelan* is the most widespread type of orchestra in the archipelago, especially on Java and Bali. The most sophisticated of these orchestras is the Central Javanese *gamelan*, usually composed of about a dozen musicians and used as accompaniment in *wayang* and dance performances. In its complete modern form, a *gamelan* orchestra could comprise 70-80 instruments including solo vocalists (*pasinden*) and up to 15 choir (*gerongan*) members. An ethereal sound, from thin

JAVANESE CULTURE

tinkles to deep booming reverberations, is created when rows of small bronze kettle-shaped discs of varying sizes, with raised nipples, are hit with cudgel-like sticks. *Gamelan* music can't be compared with Western polyphonic music, but it's much looser, freer, more flighty and unpredictable—curiously melancholy, even disturbing.

Dance

Since the split of the Mataram Kingdom into the vassal states of Yogya and Solo in 1775, the art of court dancing has evolved differently in each of these central Javanese *kraton*. These cultural capitals have always been artistic rivals: Solo considers Yogyanese dancers too stiff and Yogya thinks Solonese dancers are too slack and casual. The differences between the two schools are still recognizable today, though unimportant.

The tradition of classical dancing was once looked upon as a sacred legacy by the courts. Dancers selected from the lower-class families of the *kraton* population could take part only in supporting roles in the royal plays. It wasn't until 1918 when the Krida Beksa Wirama Dance School was founded outside the walls of the Yogya *kraton* that Javanese dance was taught to the common Indonesian: the royal monopoly on dancing was at last broken.

In court dancing, the emphasis is on angular graceful poses and smooth subtle gestures. This type of dancing is far removed from Western theories of art and reflects the ultra-refinement of Javanese courts. Having evolved at a time of warring states, classical dancing is executed with all the deliberation of a slow march and the precision of a drill maneuver. Sometimes years of arduous muscular training is required to execute certain gestures such as arching the hand until the fingers touch the forearm (to imitate the opening of flower petals). Dancers are incredibly detached, yet their inaction and long periods of immobility are just as important as the action. All these pauses, silences, and motions arrested in space, with lowered eyes and meditative poses, make Javanese dance absolutely hypnotic to watch.

The Ramayana is the most widely seen performance, but also watch for the *serimpi*, the slow, graceful, and highly disciplined classical dance of Central Java—one of the oldest and most sacred Javanese court dances. Originating over 400 years ago, this dance is dedicated to the dreaded South Sea Goddess Nyai Loro Kidul, who was said to have appeared to the first ruler of the dynasty, Sultan Agung (1613-45), expressing her love for him by dancing and singing before him. Other dance forms include the *reyong,* a masked dance in which a great leering tiger's head is worn, and *kuda kepong,* East Java's famous horse-trance dance, in which entranced men ride bamboo-weave hobbyhorses to the mad rhythms of drums, gongs, and flutes.

Wayang

Named for a Javanese word meaning literally "shadow" or "ghost," *wayang* is a theatrical performance of living actors, three-dimensional puppets, or shadow images held before a screen lit from behind. The word can also refer to the puppets themselves. Most often the chants are in Kawi (Old Javanese), as archaic a language today as Shakespearean English. *Wayang* performances are staged when some transitional event occurs in a family's life: birthdays, weddings, important religious occasions, or as ritual entertainment during family feasts or *selamatan.* Coming of age (puberty), a circumcision, promotions in rank, even the building of a new swimming pool—all could be excuses for a show. While providing entertainment, the *wayang* media also teach the meaning and purpose as well as the contradictions and anomalies of modern life. The policies of the government are even explained in terms of *wayang* theater, not only by the puppet-masters but also in newspaper editorials and even in government statements.

Wayangs are led by the *dalang,* an immensely talented playwright, producer, principal narrator, conductor, and director of this shadow world. He's an expert in languages and highly skilled in the techniques of ventriloquism. Some *dalang* (or their wives) even carve their own puppets, maintaining a cast of up to 200 which are kept in a big wooden box (*katok*). He must be familiar with all levels of speech according to the *dramatis personae,* modulating his voice and employing up to nine tonal and pitch variations to suit each of the puppets' temperaments. The *dalang* has a highly developed dramatic sense, and if he has a good voice, his chants are beautiful and captivating to hear. He must also be intimately versed in history, including complex royal genealogies; music (melodies, modes, phrases, songs); recitation (both *gamelan*

JAVANESE CULTURE

and spoken); and eloquence (an extempore poet creating a warm or terrifying atmosphere); and he must possess a familiarity with metaphysics, spiritual knowledge, and perfection of the soul. Traveling from village to village and city to city, he has as many fans as a film star.

Wayang Kulit

A "shadow play" using two-dimensional puppets chiseled by hand out of buffalo or goat parchment, with the appearance of paper dolls but with arms that swivel. Shadow plays are surrealistic collisions of Hindu epic, Muslim folklore, slapstick humor, sexual innuendo, political guidance, and village gossip—Krishna meets Punch and Judy. Since a *wayang kulit* puppet is a stylized exaggeration of a human shape, it's really a shadow of a shadow. Many different styles exist. Palembang performs its own version, using its own dialect (a sort of Melayu slang), while in South Kalimantan another style called *wayang banjar* is in vogue. In Jakarta, *wayang kulit* is performed in the local Batawi dialects. But by far the most popular is the *wayang kulit* form practiced in Central and East Java and on Bali, where it has been developed as a spellbinding medium for storytelling.

Wayang Golek

Puppets in the round. Since *wayang golek* is the imitation by human actors of the movements of the shadow puppets, the three-dimensional *wayang golek* puppets imitate human beings imitating the shadow puppets. These puppets are much more like our Western ones, except that rods are used to manipulate them, not strings. No shadow or screen is used. The audience faces the *dalang* and watches realistic people in miniature. Different *gamelan* musical pitches set the mood. Generally performed in the daytime, *wayang golek* is less ceremonial, less magical, and more worldly than shadow puppetry.

Wayang Topeng

Masked theater that mimes the stories of the *wayang golek* in which men act like puppets. Sometimes the dancers themselves speak their roles, other times the *dalang* speaks for them with the actors just marching on and off stage. Although classical Javanese language (Kawi) is most often used, it's spoken in a less stylized form than in *wayang orang*. Troupes on Java consist of male dancers; female roles are taken by young boys before their voices change. Masks are often similar to the heads of *golek* puppets. Each region of Java and Bali features a different style of *topeng* masks, costuming, and dancing. The most active *topeng* centers are in East Java and on Bali. On stage the shiny beautiful masks with big mysterious eyes seem suspended in the air. An entire *wayang topeng* troupe consists of perhaps 20-25 people, and a set of *topeng* traditionally contains 40-80 pieces.

Wayang Orang

Called *wayang wong* in Javanese, these are abstract, symbolic dance plays, with or without masks, employing actor-dancers who dress up like *golek* puppets. Masks are usually only worn by actors playing animals: monkeys, birds, or monster roles (for example, the King of Demons in the Ramayana). A *dalang* may recite and chant, but the dialogue is most often spoken by live actors and actresses wearing shiny costumes of gold and black, and rich deep-colored batik silks. Because of its hilarious antics, *wayang orang* is more intelligible and more of a spectacle to Westerners than other *wayang* forms. But *wayang orang* is also by far the most expensive to stage. A boxful of leather or wooden puppets is much cheaper to maintain than a whole troupe of live actors who have to be fed, clothed, transported, and paid. Consequently, *wayang orang* is the rarest *wayang* form—a real privilege to see if you ever get the chance.

CENTRAL JAVA

PRAMBANAN

It took a staggering agricultural productivity to enable pompous feudal monarchs to erect temples to their own glorification. Thus the rich Prambanan Plain, 17 km northeast of Yogya on the road to Solo, has the most extensive Hindu temple ruins in all of Indonesia. Between the 8th and 10th centuries, Central Java was the island's wealthiest and most powerful region. South-central Java was controlled by the Hindu-influenced Mataram Kingdom, while the Buddhist Saliendra Dynasty controlled the north. Both kingdoms and religions apparently lived in peace. Lying today among villages and green ricefields with the sharp peak of Mt. Merapi in the background, most of these temple complexes were abandoned in the 13th century when the Hindu-Javanese kings moved from Central to East Java. Around 1600, all extant temples were toppled by an earthquake, then slowly buried by the eruptions of Mt. Merapi. In the 19th century their blocks were carried off to pave roads and build sugar mills, bridges, and railroads. The Dutch started restoration work in the late 1930s. The following temples or *candi* (pronounced CHON-di) were used mainly for royal ceremonies rather than religious rites.

To get there, take any minibus on Jalan Mataram going toward Solo. Prambanan is also within reasonable biking distance on a special biking lane. Motorcycles are terrific. Or round up a group and charter a taxi for the day; the ruins are widely scattered. Keep a sharp lookout for small signs posted by the archaeological service.

Prambanan Temple Complex

The largest temple complex on Java, Prambanan's central courtyard contains three large structures: a main temple dedicated to Shiva, flanked by those of Brahma (to the south) and Vishnu (to the north). Besides these, the complex originally contained 244 minor temples (*candi perwara*), all arranged in four rows. Only two of these have been restored. The two small *candi* at the side of the main terrace were probably the treasuries where the jewels and gold were kept. The tall, elegant central temple is both a wonder of restoration and a synthesis of northern and southern Indian architectural styles. But it is the lavish decorations, panels, motifs, and reliefs that tell the Ramayana stories that remain Prambanan's chief wonder—some of the most famous Hindu sculpture in the world. To follow the story, hire a guide and begin at the east stairway, slowly wandering past trees of heaven surrounded by animals, pots of money, half-women and half-bird creatures, armies of monkeys, noble heroes, beautiful heroines. The four-armed statue of Shiva in the center might remind you of the Jaggernat temple in Bubaneshwar, south of Calcutta.

Candi Sewu

Walk or ride your bicycle to the following temples, which are less crowded, less commercialized, and just as fascinating as the main temple complex. The "1,000 Temples" one km north of Prambanan is now largely in ruins but slowly being reconstructed from the ground up. It consists of a large but disassembled central temple (Candi Induk) surrounded by 28 smaller temples all carved with identical standing Vishnus (à la Kahjuraho) and another 240 smaller *perwara* shrines. To assist pilgrims in their meditations, the whole complex was built in the shape of a mandala, complete with fat demons (*dwarapala*) who guarded the gates.

Candi Plaosan

Attributed to a 9th-century Saliendra princess, Plaosan combines the functions of both Mahayana Buddhist temple and monastery. The rectangular central temple, restored in 1960, is cut with cells displaying the various incarnations of the Buddha: past, present, and future. The peaceful ricefields beyond lend dignity to the scene.

Kraton Ratu Boko

This hilltop collection of ruins can only be reached by motorcycle. Very little remains of King Boko's *kraton,* but there are grand views over luxuriant rolling green fields, bamboo groves, and the feathery palms of Prambanan

VICINITY OF
YOGYAKARTA

Plain. A pair of smaller and recently restored temples is found farther down the road.

Candi Kalasan

Kalasan is the oldest Mahayana Buddhist temple in Indonesia to which a date can be set: A.D. 778. Set in a small park just off the Yogya-Solo highway, Kalasan was once a royal mausoleum completely covered in multicolored shining stucco, unique niche decorations, and probably the most beautiful kala heads in Central Java. All of the Dhani Buddhas which once stood inside the exterior niches have been plundered, aside from a single figure on the south side. But note the outstanding kalas with their crowns of plants and companions of bodhisattvas. The exquisite but empty interior is bathed in light, flooding down from the sky.

Candi Sari

Situated in the middle of coconut and banana groves, the design of Candi Sari is woven together superbly, like a basket. The second floor once served as the priests' dormitory. The entire structure is a sculptor's feast of mythological kinnaris, blooming lotus buds, old men with finely carved waterspouts between their legs, and, most importantly, the 36 bodhisattvas dancing and playing instruments. A peaceful, wonderful place.

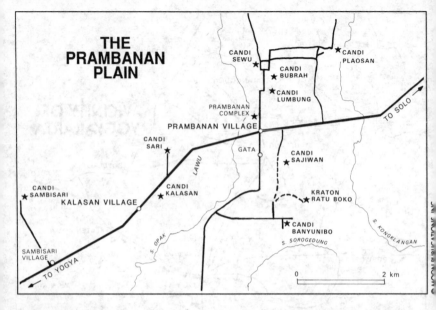

THE PRAMBANAN PLAIN

CANDI SEWU
CANDI PLAOSAN
CANDI BUBRAH
CANDI LUMBUNG
PRAMBANAN COMPLEX
PRAMBANAN VILLAGE
TO SOLO
CANDI SARI
GATA
CANDI SAJIWAN
CANDI SAMBISARI
KALASAN VILLAGE
CANDI KALASAN
LAWU
KRATON RATU BOKO
S. OPAK
SAMBISARI VILLAGE
TO YOGYA
CANDI BANYUNIBO
S. SOROGEDUNG
S. KONGKLANGAN
0   2 km

Candi Sambisari

This 9th-century Shiva temple was discovered in 1966 when a farmer broke the blade of his plow against a stone. Sambasari has been carefully restored and can be studied in a perfectly preserved state, unmarred by plunderers or the elements. Best features are the interior *lingam-yoni,* eight-armed Vishnus, and adjoining images of Agastya and Ganesha. Candi Sambisari, however, is less impressive than other temples and very difficult to find; go straight when the road veers right and continue up the dirt road through the split gate.

BOROBUDUR

This colossal, cosmic mountain is one of the most imposing creations of mankind—nothing else like it exists! Erected 200 years before the Notre Dame and Chartres cathedrals, it also predates the Buddhist temple of Angkor Wat in Kampuchea by three centuries. Built with more than two million cubic feet of stone, it's the world's largest stupa, and the largest ancient monument in the Southern Hemisphere. Borobudur is related to both the Indian monu-

ments of northwest India and the terraced sanctuaries of prehistoric Indonesian architecture. Although the structure has many characteristics of the Central Javanese style (A.D. 700-950), it has little else in common with other Buddhist temples in Southeast Asia. Persian, Babylonian, and Greek influences have also been incorporated into Borobudur's art and architecture. Planned by men with a profound knowledge of Buddhist philosophy, on it Buddha and Shiva are spiritually the same being.

Used for veneration, worship, and meditation, this giant monument was an achievement of the Vajrayana sect of the Tantric School of Buddhism, which found acceptance in Indonesia around A.D. 700. The feudal Saliendra princes—not elite savages but highly advanced technicians—erected it with peasant labor between 778 and 850. No one knows how this great structure was built at a time when modern engineering techniques were yet to be developed. No nation or group of men could possibly build it today. Thousands of laborers, slaves, carvers, sculptors, carriers, and expert supervisors worked for decades rolling logs, working ropes, levers, hammers, mallets, and chisels, using only their hands and arms. The monument took perhaps 10,000 men a century to build. Records indicate that the population of the countryside of Central Java was drastically reduced after the completion of Borobudur in the 9th century; it exhausted five generations. The Saliendras were finally overthrown by Hindus on Java in 856, and Borobudur was abandoned soon after completion. It might have started to collapse just when the sculptors were putting on the finishing touches; there's evidence of work initiated to reinforce the base, and some panels were found to have trace marks begun on them.

The monument was buried under a thousand years of volcanic eruptions and tropical growth until discovered by an English colonel during the British occupation of Indonesia in 1814. In 1855 Borobudur was cleared, and the long process of restoration began. The work was at last completed in 1983 at a cost of over US$25 million. President Suharto himself presided over the formal opening ceremony in March 1983.

Approached from the main entrance, Borobudur seems to be an unspectacular, almost impassive shape, like something carved out of solid rock. The structure was constructed to look like the holy Mt. Meru of India, the mythological model of the Buddhist universe. This unique building combines symbols of the circle (heaven), of the square (earth), and of the stupa into one coherent whole. The 10 terraces from the base to the main topmost stupa represent the individual stages toward perfection in a man's life. The pilgrim's walk (ignore the Indonesian tourists more interested in you than the carvings) takes you around the temple nine times before reaching the top. Visitors are symbolically swallowed by the *kala* monster upon entering, thus giving new spiritual life. The five-storied pyramid is subdivided vertically into three spheres of Buddhism, symbolizing religious microcosms: the base is the "world of passion" with reliefs illustrating worldly life and toil; the next four terraces depict Buddhas's life and the "world of formlessness." As you climb higher, the reliefs become more heavenly until man has eliminated desire, though still tied to the world of the senses.

Borobudur's crowning glory isn't the complex cosmology or its massive size; it's the phenomenal quality of the sculpture. There are 1,500 pictorial relief panels of Buddha's teach-

ings, plus 1,212 purely ornamental panels—one of the largest and most complete ensembles of Buddhist reliefs in existence, amounting to a virtual textbook of Mahayana Buddhist doctrine in stone. Once glistening with bright purple, crimson, green, blue, and yellow paint, over 8,235 square meters of stone surface are carved in high relief, telling scholars much about the material culture of 8th- and 9th-century Central Java. There are lessons on history, religion, art, morality, literature, clothing styles, family life, architecture, agriculture, shipping, fighting arts, dancing—the whole Buddhist cosmos. Sculptors trained in the best tradition of Indian classical temple building poured their abundant talents into the most delicate, intricate details. The distance through all the galleries to the summit is a walk of over five km, a labyrinth of narrow corridors. To read all the reliefs from the beginning of the story, go through the door on the east side. Take the time to think, dream, sit, and stare.

Also of interest are the nearby temples of Candi Pawon and Mendut, three km east of Borobudur. Mendut is a genuine 9th-century temple of worship, not a *candi* to the dead. Contemporary with Borobudur, the temple has extensive galleries and terraces, and a stupa on its pyramid-shaped roof. A very sophisticated knowledge of Buddhist and Shivaistic texts, Indian iconography, symbolism, and monumental architecture was crucial to build it.

Transportation

The single biggest problem with Borobudur is the gigantic crowds who flood the monument each morning by 0900. Borobudur is open daily 0700-1730. To enjoy it without the crowds you must arrive at the crack of dawn. Buses north to Muntilan, the jumping-off point for Borobudur, depart from Jalan Magelang in north Yogyakarta. You must change buses in Muntilan. Allow two hours by public bus. It's better to find an inexpensive tour that leaves Yogya by 0600 and allows you a minimum of four hours at the site. Tours which also include Dieng Plateau are rushed but acceptable when time is short.

Accommodations

The best way to beat the crowds is to overnight in a *losmen* on the road which approaches the monument. Losmen Citra Rasas, Losmen

Saraswati, and Villa Rosita, to the west of the complex, offer decent rooms for US$3-6. Best spot is the spotless and friendly Lotus Guesthouse about 500 meters up the road on the east side of the monument. Perfectly quiet, plus oil lamps—not electricity!

KALIURANG AND MT. MERAPI

Kaliurang is an old Dutch hill resort 26 km north of Yogya nestled on the southern slopes of Mt. Merapi. There's a strong European flavor to the township. It's also a superb place for outdoor activities, hiking, and swimming under icy waterfalls. Almost everybody comes up here to climb Mt. Merapi, but if the weather and horror stories about the climb change your mind, there's plenty of hiking to do for a few days: to the observatory on Mt. Plawangan, east to the dam, west to Tritis for the best volcano views, or the three-hour trek to Mt. Turgo, a recommended warm-up before the assault on Merapi.

Mt. Merapi is a seriously difficult hike. Its name means "Fire Mountain" for good reasons. Considered one of the most dangerous volcanos in the world, Merapi has repeatedly exploded, spewing forth lava and ash which devastate the land with disturbing regularity. Vulcanologists see frightening similarities to Mt. St. Helens and fear that the growing pressure dome on the Yogya side will soon explode, unleashing a pyroclastic flow which would consume everything in its path and kill thousands. With that cheerful thought in mind, Merapi can be climbed either from Kaliurang or from Selo on the north side. From Kaliurang, you must depart at midnight to make sunrise on top. Most hikers are satisfied to fork left above the treeline to see the crater rather than continuing two more hours up to the summit. It's vital to return to the treeline by 0900 or risk getting lost in the thick clouds. From Selo, it's four hours to the summit. Usually less cloudy but still a formidable climb with major risks.

Transportation And Accommodations

Minibuses leave Yogyakarta from Jalan Mataram and from the intersection of Jalan Sudirman and Sangaji (Terminal Terban).

Perhaps the best thing about Kaliurang is a homestay called Vogels, one of the most com-

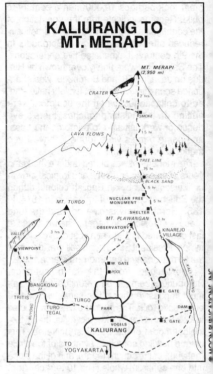

fortable and hospitable lodges in Indonesia. Vogel is an effusive Christian who generously dispenses advice and cautions about climbing the mountain, besides running a wonderful guesthouse. A great place to relax, read a book, do some hiking, and socialize with other travelers.

DIENG PLATEAU

The oldest temples of Java lie at 2,093 meters on this pear-shaped plateau, 130 km northwest of Yogyakarta. A religious center possibly since megalithic times and certainly from the beginning of the Java-Hindu era, this enchanting highland offers lovely mountain scenery, a bracing climate, fascinating volcanic fissures, endless hiking possibilities, and ancient Hindu temples named after the heroes of the *wayang*. Dieng was once a huge volcano which erupted. The remaining caldera, after thousands of years of

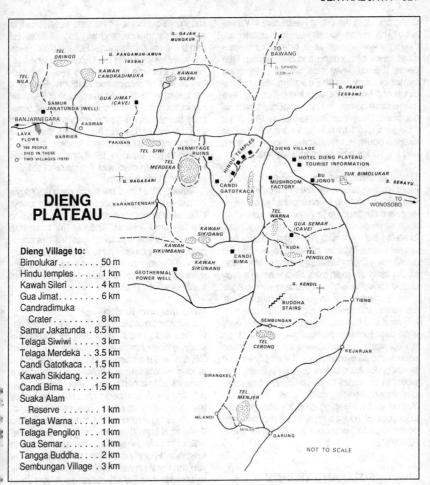

DIENG PLATEAU

Dieng Village to:
Bimolukar . . . . 50 m
Hindu temples . . . . . 1 km
Kawah Sileri . . . . . . 4 km
Gua Jimat . . . . 6 km
Candradimuka
  Crater . . . . 8 km
Samur Jakatunda . 8.5 km
Telaga Siwiwi . . . . . 3 km
Telaga Merdeka . . 3.5 km
Candi Gatotkaca . . 1.5 km
Kawah Sikidang. . . . 2 km
Candi Bima . . . . . 1.5 km
Suaka Alam
  Reserve . . . . 1 km
Telaga Warna . . . . . 1 km
Telaga Pengilon . . . 1 km
Gua Semar . . . . 1 km
Tangga Buddha. . . . 2 km
Sembungan Village . 3 km

weathering, has become a soggy plateau with dozens of geothermal spots where one can walk right up to the rims of boiling, smoking, odorous cauldrons. In June 1979, poisonous gases rose from underground passages and from several lakes, killing 150 villagers. Dieng is also extremely wet and cold; bring sweaters, jackets, and gloves.

Only eight of perhaps 200 original temples have been restored in the central valley. All were built by the Saliendras sometime in the 8th century and dedicated to Shiva as places of wor-

ship, not to glorify kings, as were the later Hindu-Buddhist monuments of Central Java. Candi Bima, 1.5 km south of Dieng Village, is unique in Indonesia: faces in its roof seem like spectators looking out of windows, reminiscent of its more sophisticated ancestors at Prambanan and Mendut. Named after members of the Pandava clan from the Mahabharta epic, none of the Dieng monuments are very large or particularly impressive, although the location is superb.

Best of all are the hikes though the valley. Maps are available from the tourist office in

Dieng and from the Dieng Restaurant in Wono-sobo. The energetic can walk to Sembungan, the highest village on Java, or explore the volcanic lakes of Sikidang and Sikumbang. Gua Semar (Semar Cave) is believed to be the exact center of Java and the dwelling place of the clown god Semar. Suharto himself comes here to meditate before making important political decisions! Other possibilities include Gua Jimat ("Death Cave") from which so much carbon dioxide pours out that animals can't survive, and the 13-km hike down to Bawang.

Transportation And Accommodations

From Yogya, take a minibus to Muntilan, visit Borobudur, return to Muntilan, change to Mage-lang, and continue up to Wonosobo. Late-afternoon minibuses climb up to Dieng, but it's better to spend the night with Agus and his wife (ex-lawyer turned "Master of *Nasi Goreng*") at his outstanding Dieng Restaurant and Losmen one block east of the main road. Somewhat of a Jerry Garcia lookalike and general *bon vivant,* Agus is the resident expert on nearby volcanos, hikes, and lakes; ask about his nightly slide show.

Buses and minibuses from Wonosobo slowly wind past tobacco plantations, rugged steep landscapes with clouds below the road, bamboo aqueducts, pale eucalyptus, TV antennas, and sleeping volcanos before arriving in Dieng. Adjacent to the small tourist office are two small *losmen* with freezing cold rooms—bring warm clothes and a sleeping bag. It's also possible to join one of Yogya's myriad tour groups which do day-trips to Borobudur and Dieng for under Rp10,000.

SOLO AND VICINITY

Solo, or Surakarta, is Java's oldest cultural center, the traditional, original capital of the Javanese kingdom—not Yogya. Once just a village in the middle of a forest, Solo became the seat of the Mataram Kingdom in the mid-18th century when the previous capital of Kartosuro (12 km west) was reduced to rubble during a war with the Dutch. An auspicious site near the Solo River was chosen by the sultan, who constructed his new palace in 1745. This dynasty lasted only 10 years, after which the realm was partitioned between Solo and Yogyakarta. The

sultan of Solo funneled his vast wealth into the arts: music, dance, and *wayang* all flowered under the royal patronage. But the Solo rulers mistakenly sided with the Dutch, and when Indonesia became a republic in 1950, the sultanate lost all recognized authority. Bad luck continued in 1985 when the palace of Pakubu-wono, the youngest of the royal houses, tragically burned down during restoration—a sign that the sultan had lost his *wahyu,* the mystic authority that all Javanese leaders are supposed to possess. In 1988, the 37-year-old Prince Jiwokusomo was proclaimed the 9th sultan of Mankunegara.

Although the city is often compared to Yogya because of its royal palaces and batik industry, cultural offerings and shopping opportunities are far more limited. And yet the town has enough of interest to keep most visitors occupied for a few days. The tourist office on Jalan Slamet Riyadi has maps and the staff can answer questions about upcoming festivals and transportation.

Mangunegaran Kraton

Actually not a *kraton* but a 200-year-old Javanese aristocrat's home built on a splendid scale, entirely from solid teak. Since the fire of '85, the lesser palace has taken pride of place among Solo's tourist attractions. The palace consists of two parts: the *pendopo* (reception hall) and the *dalem* (ceremonial halls) flanked by the royal living quarters. The giant *pendopo,* with its zany painted ceiling of Javanese Zodiac designs, is considered one of the finest examples of stately Javanese wood architecture in existence. Friendly and informative guides show you the royal regalia, such as golden chastity belts made for priests, *wayang golek* from Jawa Timur, and a superb collection of magical *kris* daggers. Open daily 0900-1400. Dress conservatively. This palace is far more interesting than the *kraton* in Yogyakarta.

Kasunanan Kraton

Before the fire of 1985, gaudy vulgarity was the dominant theme in the grand Solo Kraton. All the gold vessels, gilded furniture, mirrors, and flamboyant hangings seemed like stage props in the home of a colossal profiteer. One antique building which survived the fire is the multistoried minaret, Panggung Songgo Buwono, seen over

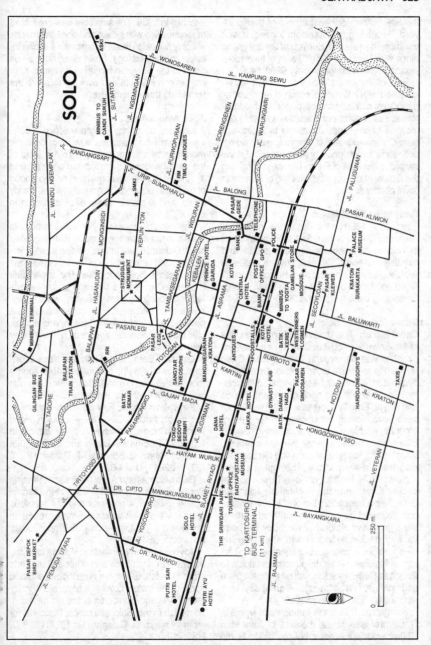

SOLO

JL. WONOSAREN
JL. KAMPUNG SEWU
ASKI
JL. SUTARTO
MINIBUS TO CANDI SUKUH
JL. NGEMINGAN
JL. PURWOPURAN
RM TIMLO ANTIQUES
JL. SORENGENEN
JL. WARUNGMIRI
JL. KANDANGSAPI
JL. URIP SUMOHARJO
JL. BALONG
JL. PALUGUNAN
JL. WINDU NGEMPLAK
SMKI
PASAR GEDE
PASAR KLIWON
JL. MONGINSIDI
JL. KEPUN TON
JL. WIDURAN
TELEPHONE
JL. HASANUDIN
STRUGGLE 45 MONUMENT
KEBALEN
PRINCE HOTEL
GARUDA
BANK
POLICE
PALACE MUSEUM
GAMELAN STORE
JL. TAMBANSEGARAN
KOTA
POST OFFICE GPO
MOSQUE
KRATON SURAKARTA
JL. ASRAMA
CENTRAL HOTEL
BANK
MINIBUS TO YOGYA
PASAR KLEWER
SECOYUDAN
JL. PASARLEGI
PASAR LEGI
ANTIQUES
FOODSTALLS
KOTA HOTEL
BATIK KERIS
WESTERNERS LOSMEN
JL. BALUWARTI
BALAPAN
RRI
TOTOGAN
SANGYAR THEOSOPHI
MANGUNEGARAN KRATON
O. KARTINI
SUBROTO
MINIBUS TERMINAL
BALAPAN TRAIN STATION
BATIK SEMAR
JL. GAJAH MADA
DYNASTY PUB
PASAR SINGOSAREN
JL. NOTOSU
JL. KRATON
TAXIS
GILINGAN BUS TERMINAL
JL. TAGORE
JL. PASARNONGKO
TOKOKO BEDOYO SERIMPI
JL. SUDIRMAN
DANA HOTEL
CAKRA HOTEL
BATIK DANAR HADI
JL. HONGGOWONGSO
HARDJONEGORO'S
JL. TIRTOYOSO
JL. HAYAM WURUK
RADYAPUSTAKA MUSEUM
JL. VETERAN
JL. DR. CIPTO
MANGKUNGSUMO
JL. SLAMET RIYADI
TOURIST OFFICE
JL. BAYANGKARA
PASAR DEPOK BIRD MARKET
JL. PEMUDA UTARA
JL. TOSODIPURO
SOLO HOTEL
THR SRIWIDARI PARK
TO KARTOSURO BUS TERMINAL (11 km)
JL. DR. MUWARDI
PUTRI SARI HOTEL
PUTRI AYU HOTEL
JL. RAJIMAN
250 m
0

the wall in the northeast corner of the courtyard. According to an ancient legend, it was used by the rajas of Surakarta as a trysting place with Nyai Loro Kidul. Tours of the reconstructed palace are given daily 0900-1400.

East of the *kraton* is Suaba Budaya Museum, filled with a lavish collection of regal pomp: a model of a *dalang* and his puppets, an odd international assortment of statues, valuable collections of old Hindu-Javanese bronzes, ancient Chinese porcelains, demonic gargoyle figureheads which once graced splendid royal barges, a diorama of Prince Diponegoro fighting the Dutch, and a superb collection of European royal coaches.

Radyapustaka Museum

Founded in 1890 by the Dutch, the Institute of Javanese Culture is the oldest such organization in Indonesia. The museum today is dark and exhibits are poorly labeled, but the exquisite *kris* daggers and classical Java-Hindu statues of Shiva and Durga on the porch are worth seeing. Open daily except Mondays 0900-1230.

Attractions Near Solo

Candi Sukuh: This Hindu temple on the slopes of Mt. Lawu was built in the 15th century just as Islam was penetrating coastal Java. Often referred to as Java's erotic temple, the terraced pyramid at Sukuh has been compared in architectural form with the ruins of ancient Mexico and Egypt. Equally impressive is the superb location overlooking the whole Javanese plain, an unforgettable spectacle of sweeping panoramas across the Solo valley, purple mountains, lakes, rolling foothills, shimmering terraced *sawah,* trees in every shade of lush greenery.

Sukuh is 36 km east of Solo. Take a double decker three km to the terminal on Jalan Sutarto, then a minibus 25 km east to Karangpandan, followed by a minibus eight km north to the signpost at Nglorok. Everybody will point the way. It takes an hour of hard, steep slogging on a surfaced road to get to the temple. Don't return to Nglorok; rather, hike two hours down to Grojagan Sewu waterfalls (left off the main path) and finish in Tawangmangu. A great day! Last minibus for Solo leaves at 1600.

Sangiran: This is the famous site where a Dutch professor found the skull of Java Man (*Pithecanthropus erectus,* but now called *Homo erectus*) in 1936. The small but well-organized museum, filled with fossils and bone fragments, will only appeal to those visitors with a strong interest in paleontology. From Solo, take a bus north to the Sangiran turnoff at Kalijambi (one km beyond Kalioso) and walk or hitchhike the remaining three kilometers.

Accommodations

A travelers' scene has finally developed in Solo, which many backpackers now favor over the more commercialized scene in Yogya. Most of the useful addresses are located on or around Jl. Ahmad Dahlan—a convenient neighborhood of old Dutch buildings, narrow alleyways, trendy cafes, and almost a dozen decent losmen in the US$3-8 price range.

The principal travelers' rendezvous point is the small but extremely popular **Warung Baru** on Jl. Dahlan. Great music, reliable travel information, and wonderful food from mountainous fruit salads to local specialties. The whole affair is presided over by a beautiful and vivacious lady appropriately named Sunny, whose generous heart and irresistible smile makes this a perfect place for breakfast, lunch, and dinner. Her bicycle tours receive rave reviews. Say hello from Carl!

Losmen Solo Homestay: Spacious courtyard, friendly help, and acceptable rooms (sometimes noisy) make this the most popular budget spot near Warung Baru. US$3-5.

Keprabon Hotel: Few travelers stay here, but this old place is a real rarity—a Dutch period hotel with art deco touches in the windows and furniture. Rooms are clean and face a quiet inner courtyard. Good value. Jl. Dahlan 12, tel. (0271) 32811, US$4-8.

Relax Homestay: A few blocks from Warung Baru, but an excellent alternative to the central scene. Spacious grounds and six fabulous rooms in the main building. Smaller rooms to the side are just that—*small.* Jl. Erapu Sedah, no phone, US$3-8.

Joyokusuman Homestay: Visitors studying Indonesian mysticism and other spiritual arts often stay in this remote guesthouse situated south of the kraton. Lovely grounds, pleasant atmosphere, and big rooms in the old mansion, home to a former Solonese prince. Discounts for monthly stays. Jl. Gajahan, tel. (0271) 32833, US$5-12.

SOLO ACCOMMODATIONS

HOTEL	SINGLE	DOUBLE	ADDRESS	PHONE (0271)
LUXURY				
Kusuma Sahid Prince	US$40-65	US$45-90	Sugiyopranoto 22	46356
MODERATE				
Cakra	US$25-35	US$30-45	Riyadi 201	45847
Mangkunegaran Palace	US$25-35	US$30-45	Pura Mangkunegaran	35683
Solo Inn	US$25-35	US$30-45	Riyadi 366	36075
BUDGET				
Central	US$3-6	US$4-8	Dahlan 32	42814
Dana	US$8-15	US$10-18	Riyadi 286	33891
Kota	US$4-6	US$6-8	Riyadi 123	32841
Putri Sari	US$4-6	US$6-8	Riyadi 382	46995
Westerners	US$3-5	US$4-6	Kidul 11	33106

Hotel Kota: Convenient location right in the center of town. Old but tidy; worth a look. Jl. Slamet Riyadi 123, tel. (0271) 32481, US$4-6 fan, US$12-18 a/c with color TV.

Westerners Losmen: Pak and Ibu Mawardi's Homestay is a friendly and clean spot where almost all travelers spend their time in Solo. Singing birds and bicycle rentals—an island of peace in the center of the city. Difficult to find and poorly marked; in the narrow alley down from the modern Singosaran market. Kemlayan Kidul II, tel. (0271) 33106, US$3-6.

Putri Sari Hotel: Simple, modern, and clean hotel on the western edge of town. Jalan Riyadi 382, tel. (0271) 46995, US$4-8.

Dana Hotel: A sprawling, somewhat decrepit hotel with a touch of old-world atmosphere. Great lobby. Jalan Riyadi 286, tel. (0271) 33891, US$8-18.

Kusuma Sahid Prince Hotel: Solo's finest hotel is situated on five acres of landscaped gardens near the Mangunegaran Palace. Beautiful pool and live *gamelan* in the lobby nightly from 1700. Jalan Sugiyopranoto 22, tel. (0271) 46356, fax 44788, US$95-235.

Restaurants

Jalan Teuku Umar Food stalls: Solo is a city with a distinctive local cuisine. Try *nasi liwet* (rice in a delicious coconut sauce), *nasi gudeg* (rice with jackfruit), *susu sugar* (fresh milk), *wedhang ronde* (ginger tea with peanut), and *serabi* (miniature pancakes). All can be inexpensively sampled in the terrific night food stalls just off Jalan Riyadi. Here, tents emblazoned with their specialties serve some of the best food in Indonesia to *becak* drivers, students, businessmen, Chinese laborers, and travelers.

Jalan Diponegoro: Solo's restaurant row has a half-dozen cafes which serve local dishes at fair prices. Malioboro looks the best.

Centrum Restaurant: This popular Chinese restaurant near Westerners Losmen serves tasty but somewhat expensive dishes. Try giant spring rolls and frog's legs fried in butter and garlic.

Performing Arts

Kraton Mangunegaran: Javanese dance rehearsals accompanied by *gamelan* are given on Wednesday mornings at 1000; *gamelan* only on Saturday mornings. The Javanese orchestra, originally from Demak and dating to 1778, has been given the honorific name Kyai Kanyut Mesem ("Drifting in Smiles"). Swallows dip and dive amongst the rafters as the *gamelan* plays, as if enraptured by the music.

Kasunan Kraton: Javanese dance rehearsals are given on Sundays at 1000 in the reconstructed Morokoto Hall.

Sriwidari Amusement Park: *Wayang orang* shows are given nightly, 2000-2300 except Fridays and Sundays, in the theater next to the tourist office. Simple to the extreme, but one of Indonesia's last venues for traditional Javanese drama.

ASKI: Solo's leading fine-arts conservatory occasionally sponsors student recitals. Check with the tourist office.

RRI: Solo's best *wayang kulit* and *wayang orang* can be experienced on irregular Saturday evenings at 2000 in the Radio Republic Indonesia building on Jalan Marconi near the train station.

Instruction

Solo is an important center for Javanese mysticism and white-magic meditation techniques called *sumarah*. Classes are given in the home of Ananda Suyono on Jalan Ronggowarsito 60, half a block east of Kraton Mangkunegaran. Also by Pak Swondo on Gang 1 Jalan Kratonan. Puppet instruction and monthly all-night performances can be seen in the home of Dalang Anom Suroto on Jalan Notodiningrotan behind the Hotel Cakra. Classes in Javanese performing arts are given at the SMKI (high-school level) and the STSI (university level) located north of Jalan Sahrir. The tourist office can help with referrals and exact locations.

Shopping

Batik: Solo is a batik-producing center of long standing; it's an artform that remains an important source of local revenue and pride. Solo-style batik designs with their somber classical colors of indigo, brown, and cream are noticeably more traditional than Yogya's. Many claim that Solo is a better place to buy than Yogya. Shops are located all over town; the tourist office has a list. Batik Semar, Dinar Hadi, and Batik Keris—three major producers of Solo-style batik—are all safe, reliable, and reasonable. You should also compare quality and prices inside Pasar Klewer, Indonesia's largest emporium of fabrics and batiks.

Handicrafts: Antique buffs should wander the confusing maze of stalls inside Pasar Triwindu, just east of Jalan Diponegoro. Hardjonegoro on Jalan Kratonan offers one of the largest *kris* collections in Java, but expect to pay anywhere from 100,000 to five million *rupiah! Gamelans* are tailor-made at the Bale Agung shop just north of the Kraton Kasusunan. A meager and disappointing collection of theatrical supplies and dancers' costumes is sold at Toko Bedoyo Serimpi.

Transportation

Solo's principal bus terminal is located three km north of downtown, about 1200Rp by *becak* to Westerners. Minibuses from the adjacent terminal are faster and less crowded than public buses. To reach Yogya, hail a westbound bus from the main bus terminal. Trains to Surabaya leave five times daily from the Balapan Station.

THE NORTHERN COAST

CIREBON

Like most of the northern coastline, Cirebon (pronounced chirry-BON) is not on the popular tourist routes of Java. It boasts no golden sandy beaches or trendy travelers' hotels or restaurants, but it's a clean, well-run town, and it's worth a diversion—especially for its rich variety of arts and crafts and historical attractions. Lying between the sea and the mountains, Cirebon's hot temperatures are often buffeted by cool mountain breezes. An ancient precolonial port town on the border of West and Central Java, Cirebon is the meeting point of the Sundanese and Javanese cultures; its local dialect is a blending of the two (the city's name derives from the Javanese *caruban,* or "mixture"). The sultanate here was split into two main houses, Kanoman and Kesepuhan, both of whose palaces are open to visitors, occasionally hosting court dances and *gamelan* recitals. The interiors and furnishings manifest a fantastic conglomeration of Sundanese, Javanese, Islamic, Chinese, and Dutch civilizations.

Kraton Kasepuhan

In 1478, Kraton Pakungwati surrendered to Sunan Gunung Jati. In that same year, the city of Cirebon proclaimed itself an Islamic principality and work began immediately on Kraton Kasepuhan. Over the centuries, the palace grew decrepit, but it was partially restored in 1928 by a Dutch archaeologist. Located in the southeast corner of the city, west of the *alun alun* and next to the graceful tiered-roof Mesjid Agung. Cirebon's most famous reliefs—cloud patterns (*mega mendung*) and rocks (*wadas*)—are seen on the whitewashed entrance. Domestic tourists come in the morning; by afternoon it's usually deserted because of the heat, so you might have the place to yourself. A comatose place very much smelling its age, the sultanate has long since been deposed and the sultan is now a banker.

Kraton Kanoman

Walk straight through the market, Pasar Kanoman, to this palace built by Pangeran Cakra-

buana in the 17th century. Woodcarvings on the main door of the hall symbolize the opening date (the Javanese date of 1510 translates to A.D. 1670). Kraton Kanoman has a restful courtyard of shady banyan trees and kids flying kites. Find the man with the key to the Gedung Pusaka ("Heirloom Building") inside the *kraton* compound to see the incredible coach, prize attraction of Kanoman. The three creatures depicted on this royal carriage are symbols of earthly and metaphysical powers: the *paksi* or great mythical *garuda* bird represents the realm of the air; the *naga* (snake bird) represents sea; and the *liman* or *gajah* represents land. All of them are combined in one Pegasus-like creation called the *paksi naga liman.* All of these fused symbols are considered by the Javanese the strongest creatures of their elements.

Taman Sunyaragi

A grotesque three-story, red-brick-and-concrete grotto, four km southwest of town on Jalan Sunyaragi. Taman Sunyaragi has gone through several transformations since its initial construction in 1703 during the reign of Pangeran Arya. Originally the resthouse of 14th-century royalty, Sunan Gunung Jati used it as a country palace for his Chinese bride, Ong Tien, who died just three years after arriving on Java. It is, in fact, still referred to locally as the Taman Sari ("Pleasure Gardens") of the Chinese Princess.

Cirebon Batik

Stylistic nuances and the bright accents of Cirebon batik—an art which is a composite of so many incoming cultures and religions—are found nowhere else on Java. Traditionally, the motifs most associated with Cirebon batik are Chinese in origin. Glorious mythological animals such as dragons, tigers, lions, and elephants, and of course "rocks and clouds" (likened to weather patterns), are executed in light to dark coloring. Sealife, so vital to the economic well-being of the city, is also frequently portrayed. Since the artists' guilds decreed that only men may work in batik, Cirebon became one of the few locales on Java where females did not draw and paint the cloth. This has infused the area's batik with bold, masculine designs, a minimum of busy detail, and large, dramatic portions of free space, quite distinct from the batik of other north-coastal or Central Java areas. View the zenith of this artform in Cirebon's *kraton* museums, though all the finest pieces have been sold and only small collections are left.

Around Pasar Pagi on Jalan Karanggetas, one of Cirebon's main streets, are numerous batik shops. Also check out the GKBI (Batik Cooperative) at Jalan Pekarungan 33, which sells a wider selection of Cirebon batik than any other outlet. Some of Cirebon's finest batik is made in Trusmi near the town of Weru, six km west of Cirebon. Although the batik is actually made here, it's not necessarily cheaper—you just have more of a selection. Back in town, family workshops such as Masina's proliferated during the 1920s and '30s, and their extraordinary hand-drawn technique is a throwback to that golden age.

Accommodations

Asia Hotel: A whole row of inexpensive *losmen* is found on Jl. Siliwangi right down from the train station. All are relatively clean and quiet, but most travelers stay at the Hotel Asia, about 15 minutes from the train station and down near the waterfront. Located in an old Dutch home, the whole building is something of a Cirebon antique all fixed up with old wooden furniture and whitewashed walls. 15 Jl. Kalibaru, tel. (0231) 22183, US$6-10.

Grand Hotel: A colonial relic with a multitude of large rooms in every price range, a restaurant with extensive menu, and a splendid veranda. 98 Jl. Siliwangi, tel. (0231) 25457, US$15-35.

Cirebon Plaza Hotel: Five minutes from the train station and the intercity bus terminal. 54 Jl. Kartini, tel. (0231) 22062, fax (0231) 24258, US$35-52.

Bentani Hotel: Fairly new hotel with pool, three restaurants, and decent rooms. Jl. Siliwangi 69, tel. (0231) 203246, fax (0231) 207527, US$55-75.

Park Hotel: Best in Cirebon with deluxe lobby, pool, and 91 a/c rooms; the favorite of expats working the nearby oil refineries. Jl. Siliwangi 107, tel. (0231) 205411, fax (0231) 205407, US$60-80.

PEKALONGAN

Pronounced "Pek-KAL-long-ahn," Pekalongan lies on the north coast 101 km west of Semarang on the road to Jakarta. Pekalongan has always been a fortress and trade city; visible to this day are the remains of a VOC fort built in 1753, later turned into a prison by the Dutch. On 7 October 1945, the Pekalongan residency became the first in Indonesia to free itself of Japanese rule.

Attractions

Pekalongan is worth a single day of exploration.

Batik: Pekalongan is chiefly famed for its distinctive batiks sold in a half dozen shops scattered around town. Most of the fabric appears mundane so expect a hard search for better quality product.

Old Dutch Quarter: Try the following half-day walking tour of the old Dutch and Chinese sections, a few blocks north of the main street. First, wander around the old Dutch quarter just across the Loji Bridge and enjoy the former Resident's Mansion, imposing Post Office, Dutch Reformed Church (1852), Kota Madya (former Dutch City Hall), Societeit Corcle (Dutch Clubhouse), and remains of the VOC Fort, now a prison.

Chinatown: Cross the bridge, turn right, and stop in the active Po An Thian Chinese Temple for a few moments, then continue south past a street lined with impressive old homes inhabited by Chinese merchants.

Pasar Banjarsari: A fascinating market filled with all the standard food products, plus batik merchants selling the less expensive stamped fabric. Then walk east to the small Arab Quarter and batik shops such as Jacky's, Toko Yen, and Tobal Batik Factory.

Accommodations

Few travelers pause here, but several acceptable *losmen* are near the train station.

Hotel Gaja Mada: The most cheery and personable option of the budget spots opposite the train station, 11A Jl. Gajah Mada, tel. (0285) 41185, US$3-6.

Hotel Istana: Pekalongan's top-end choice is also on Jl. Gajah Mada, some 200 meters west of the train station. 23 Jl. Gajah Mada, tel. (0285) 61581, US$10-24.

BATIK

Pekalongan's batik has made the city reknowned throughout Southeast Asia. Also known as Kota Batik ("Batik City"), Pekalongan is Indonesia's third leading production center (after Yogyakarta and Solo) for famed colorful hand-waxed, machine-printed batik using distinct motifs. First visit the Batik Museum on Jalan Pasar Ratu to understand how Pekalongan plays a leading role in the evolution of modern Indonesian batik. Note the exuberant use of bright, bold colors and naturalistic figures such as animals and flowers instead of the more traditional and muted motifs.

The town has numerous batik factories and shops; as in Yogya, peddlers with their bundles of batik approach you on the street, come up to restaurant tables, and hang around the hotel lobbies. The whole town is involved in batik. Wander through the streets and look through doorways. If you see bamboo drying racks it means the establishment is one of hundreds of batik factories in town. The nationwide co-operative GKBI on Jalan Salim 39 represents more than 500 local batik producers, selling original Pekalongan batik in various designs and qualities. Two of the region's finest batik factories are Batik Susilo in the nearby village of Wiradesa (known for its silk *kains* and *slendangs*) and Umar Hadi Batik in Buaran village in south Pekalongan. For really superb work, visit the Leonardo of batik, Pak Oey Tjoen, in Kedungwuni, nine km from Pekalongan. Unbelievably intricate designs, using eight or nine colors on one piece.

Prices vary considerably depending on method of production, quality, and point of sale. Mass-produced stamped *batik cap sarongs* cost only Rp8000-10,000, but hand-painted *batik tulis* costs anywhere from Rp20,000-100,000. Recognizable usually by red and blue birds and flowers on white or pink backgrounds, Pekalongan batik can also be some of the most *alus* ("refined") on the island; you could easily pay Rp250,000 for a fine piece.

SEMARANG

The administrative capital of Central Java is located on the north-central coast 120 km north of Yogyakarta. Quite unlike the gentle, age-mellowed *kraton* cities of Yogya and Solo, Semarang is a busy harbor city, a government, trading, and industrial center, as well as a major fishing port. The population is 1.2 million, of which 40% is Chinese. It's the only port open to large ships on this stretch of coast, and cruise ships often call here. Semarang is mainly used as a launching point to the hill resorts, temple complexes, and batik towns described below.

Attractions

The Semarang tourist office in the Wisma Pancasila building on the five-road town square (Simpang Lima) has maps and brochures. A quick walk around the city center will uncover some grand old buildings, including the Lawang Sewu ("1,000 Doors"), which formerly served as the headquarters of the Netherlands Indies Railway company, and the 18th-century Blenduk Church, a domed Protestant church once used as the Dutch state church. Despite the modernization of Semarang, peeling VOC warehouses still overlook the old harbor. Semarang's leading sight is Gedung Batu ("Stone Building") and Sam Poo Kong Temple, a great cave-temple complex about 30 minutes southwest of downtown. One of the largest and most honored Chinese temples in Indonesia, Gedung Batu houses the spirit of a Ming Dynasty Chinese admiral who landed on Java in 1406 with a fleet of 62 vessels and 27,000 sailors. Twice a month multitudes of pilgrims arrive at this rare double sanctuary, sacred to both Buddhists and Muslims.

Because of its large Chinese community, the city has been a center of *jamu* (traditional medicines and potions) production for hundreds of years: the factories of Cap Jago, Nonya Meneer, and Borobudur are all based here. Makam Pandan Arang (also called Makam Bergota) is an old cemetery and pilgrimage place once known as Pulau Tirang; silting over the years has created a hill in the middle of the city with nice views. Also visit Semarang's 400-hectare THR for comical chimpanzees, *wayang* and *ketoprak* dramas, as well as rock bands and exhibits of traditional arts.

Accommodations

Most of the inexpensive *losmen* are in the center of town, near the traffic circle and Johar Shopping Center.

Singapore Hotel: Right in the center of town and only a ten-minute walk from the Tawang Train Station. Clean and quiet with friendly managers; best budget spot in town. Jl. Imam Bonjol 12, tel. (024) 543757, US$5-8.

Hotel Rahayu: Popular mid-priced choice with clean rooms and good vibes. Jl. Imam Bonjol 35, tel. (024) 542532, US$7-9 fan, US$12-18 a/c.

Patra Jasa Hotel: Four-star hotel with swimming pool, bowling alley, and tennis courts in a quiet location in the hills above Semerang. Needs renovation, but friendly and unpretentious. Jl. Sisingamangaraja, tel. (024) 314441, fax (024) 314448, US$110-180.

Oewa-Asia Hotel: An old Dutch colonial hotel with small but quieter rooms in the rear and more expensive a/c rooms up front. Jl. Imam Bonjol, tel. (024) 23144, US$5-15.

Losmen Jaya: A big, breezy place. Rooms should be cheaper, but breakfast is included and the managers are friendly. 87 Jl. Haryono, tel. (024) 23604, US$4-8.

Graha Santika Hotel: Semarang's newest luxury hotel, with all possible amenities, is five blocks south of the train terminal, near the tourist office and Matahari Shopping Center. 116 Jl. Pandanaran, tel. (0231) 413115, fax (0231) 413113, US$85-150.

Transportation
Trains arrive at the Tawang Station, about three blocks north of the hotels on Jalan Pemuda and Bonjol. The Terboyo Bus Terminal is six km east of city center. Flag down a local bus heading west on the nearby highway. The main city conveyances are bright orange Daihatsus, which run like ants all over town.

VICINITY OF SEMARANG

Ambarawa
The train museum in this small mountain town some 40 km south of Semarang boasts about 25 steam engines constructed from 1891 to 1927 in Germany, Holland, and England. The only operating cog railway on Java can be experienced on the Railway Mountain Tour from Ambarawa to the villages of Jambu and Bedono, 15 km uphill. Ride in antique coaches, remodeled according to the original designs and hauled by a

1903 steam locomotive. The cogwheel is still running, its beautiful engine in prime shape. All working parts are original. The engineer starts burning fuel wood and coal in the locomotive around 0400 and by 0900 the engine is ready for the climb. In the middle of the climb the cogwheel stops and the passengers hop down, take pictures, rest, and have a picnic. To sign up for this special tourist attraction, inquire at the PJKA office on Jalan Thamrin in Semarang, or at the Municipality Tourist Office (Dinas Pariwisata) in Wisma Pancasila on Jalan Simpang Lima.

Gedung Songo
At a delightful elevation of around 900 meters, this archaeological park is probably the most beautiful temple location on Java. Constructed sometime in the 8th century, the modern name means "Nine Temples"—even though only seven are still standing. Though most of the shrines are dedicated to Shiva, one is set aside for Vishnu, a Hindu god rarely worshipped on Java. See Temple II with its well-preserved *kala-makara* relief on the portal; this site was chosen with great care for magnificent views that take in Ungaran (2,050 meters), Danau Rawapening, Merbabu (3,142 meters), and even hazy Merapi (2,914 meters). Walk the ancient pilgrims' trails; allow about one hour to visit all the sites.

Gedung Songo is about 15 km from Ambarawa and seven km from Bandungan on the southern slopes of Gunung Ungaran. Take a minibus from Bandungan or, better yet, walk from Bandungan through a region of vegetable patches, roses, and pine trees. Bandungan has several inexpensive *losmen*.

Kudus
The name Kudus has its origins in the founding of a mosque here in 1546 by Sunan Kudus, one of Java's *wali* (holy men). Though a staunch Islamic town (censuring looks if you wear shorts), some old Hindu customs prevail: cows may not be slaughtered within the city limits and schoolboys still spend a night at the shrine of Sunan Muria to improve their chances in exams. Sights include the ancient Al Manar Mosque which, by combining both Hindu and Islamic architecture, actually looks like a Javanese Hindu temple. To the rear is the elaborately carved and inlaid mausoleum of Sunan Kudus.

Kudus is the Indonesian clove center. Clove cigarettes were invented in the 1920s by an entrepreneur who claimed the smoke ameliorated his asthma. Indonesians now smoke over 36,000 tons of cloves a year, outstripping domestic supplies, as well as importing cloves from Madagascar and Zanzibar. Free tours are given at the factories of Noryorono, Seokun, Jambu Boh, and Chinese-owned Djarum, now the biggest clove factory in Indonesia, having made spectacular ground on Gudang Garam in recent years. Djarum's 17 factory buildings each produce a million hand-rolled *kretek* cigarettes per day. Five hundred people work in gigantic rolling sheds; some roll up to 5,000 a day. It's a scene from early-18th-century England, on the eve of the Industrial Revolution.

Jepara

Once the main port of the mighty 8th-century Hindu Mataram Empire, Jepara today is a scruffy country town noted only for its wood-carving industry. Except for the hinges, no nails, screws, or metal joinery are used. The wood comes from Blora and Cepu in East Java—teakwood mostly, but also mahogany, *kayu meranti,* and *sono* wood. Coming into town you start to see shops with bedstands, tables, chairs, couches, and cabinets piled high inside and out. Paid by the meter, men come in from the surrounding villages to carve in the shops. To see them in action, visit the nearby villages of Tahunan, Mantingan, and Blakang-gunung. Many shops are concentrated along Jl. Pemuda.

EAST JAVA

A heavily populated but undertouristed area of 30 million, East Java abounds with bursting cities, towns, and *kampongs* along roads which run through ceaselessly nurtured ricefields and mountain slopes patched with fruit, coffee, and tea plantations. East Java is to Central Java as Mississippi is to Virginia: deep, deep Java, considerably more rural and less touched by the West.

Regional history began in the 10th century with the rise of King Airlangga, who forged a unified nation before his death and the subsequent division of his fragile empire. The Kediri Dynasty (1049-1222) was followed by the murderous but artistically inclined Singosari Kingdom (1222-1292), which constructed dozens of beautiful and highly original temples near Malang. Kartanagara, last of the Singosari rulers, was succeeded by King Wijaya, who founded the Majapahit Empire (1294-1478), which ruled most of Java from its headquarters at Trowulan. The most powerful and famous of all early East Javanese kingdoms, Majapahit mastery declined after the death of Hayam Wuruk in 1349 and the arrival of Islamic power in the 15th century. East Java fell to the Mataram Empire of Central Java in the 17th century; most of the Hindu-Buddhist artisans, philosophers, and politicians fled to Bali.

Except for a brief stay in Surabaya and the sunrise hike on Mt. Bromo, travelers usually pass straight through on the Yogya-Bali stretch.

Although the province is well off the beaten tourist path, the area's far-flung attractions can provide some unusual side trips through magnificent countryside. East Java has seven towering volcanos and seven wilderness reserves, including Meru Betiri, probably the last habitat of the Java tiger. For batik lovers, virtually every textile center in East Java—Sidoharjo, Madura, Tulungagung, Trenggalak, and Tuban—uses its own motifs and styles.

SURABAYA

Its melodious name belies the true nature of this city—a hot and dirty industrial hub with broad, busy streets, red-tiled houses with neat little gardens, a six-lane boulevard, horrendous traffic jams, quiet cul-de-sacs, technical universities and religious schools, thriving nightclubs, 40 cinemas, bowling and billiards centers, four railway stations, at least 30,000 *becaks,* a splendid zoo, and multistory shopping complexes with speed lifts and freezing air-conditioning. But with a reputation hardly better than Jakarta's, few travelers spend more than a single night in the city.

Surabaya, however, is the last traditional Indonesian city in the archipelago, the final place to see old Dutch architecture on a large scale, timeless neighborhoods little changed from the

'30s, and Islamic enclaves where men in fezlike hats gather around minaret-topped mosques. This city exudes an extraordinarily strong atmosphere. The following one-day tour will give you a quick glimpse at Indonesia's second most important city.

Surabaya Harbor

The accompanying map is adequate for most visitors, but to really find the back streets you'll need the large-scale Sena map of Surabaya, available from the bookstores on Jalan Tunjungan. To begin your tour of old Surabaya, take bus 1 from Tunjungan Shopping Center to Surabaya Harbor, where you can check shipping schedules on the second floor and grab a dish of *gado gado* from the nearby *warungs*. *Becaks* cost Rp300 down Jalan Kalimas Baru to Position IV Gate, the entrance to the old Kalimas Harbor where some 50 tall-masted Bugis schooners continually load and unload timber from Kalimantan. Before approaching the guardhouse, hide your camera and promise "no photo"—the Indonesian Naval Yard is just opposite and paranoia runs high.

Ampel Mosque

Exit the harbor area and hire another *becak* for Rp300 to Mesjid Ampel, the large but unassuming mosque hidden up an alley filled with heady perfume shops, veiled women hawking dates, and emporiums of religious goods. Ampel Mosque was constructed by Sunan Ampel, one of the nine saints credited with bringing Islam to Indonesia; his tomb in the rear is generally closed to infidels. Visitors must be well dressed to walk through Surabaya's Arab Quarter.

Dutch Architecture

Unlike Jakarta, which has largely destroyed most of its old Dutch warehouses and government centers, Surabaya has retained a great deal of its old colonial atmosphere. From Ampel Mosque, walk south through the old casbah area to Jembatan Merah (Red Bridge), once the throbbing center of the Dutch commercial district, today a haunted ghostland of impressive Dutch warehouses and business emporiums. The interior of the GPO is most impressive.

Recross the bridge and continue on foot through Chinatown to the Old Dutch Cemetery. It's best to walk along the canal and avoid the major thoroughfares. This deserted and weedy cemetery is incredibly rich with memories; crumbling and rusting headstones tell history better than any guidebook. The adjacent neighborhood is a delightful cross-hatching of narrow alleys with original Dutch street signs and lovely Dutch homes displaying graceful art-deco glasswork. Many of Surabaya's wealthiest citizens live on the nearby streets of Ambengan, Kamboja, and Kemuning.

City Center

Grahadi: The former residence of the Dutch governor but now the official residence of East Java's governor. In front is another of Surabaya's atrocious heroic monuments that commemorate Indonesia's 1945 war for independence.

Joko Dolog Statue: The Singosari Dynasty "Fat Boy," a Buddhist stone statue 100 meters back from Jalan Pemuda (look for the green Garuda gate), depicts the great King Kartanagara seated on a pedestal inscribed 1289. The statue was transferred to this spot from its site near Malang by the Dutch about 300 years ago.

Majapahit Hotel: Known as the "Oranji Hotel" during Dutch times and the "Yamato Hotel" during the Japanese occupation, the Majapahit is where East Javanese independence from the Dutch was declared shortly after WW II. The ensuing Battle of Surabaya was a turning point in their five-year struggle.

Surabaya Zoo

One of the most complete, largest, and oldest zoos in all of Indonesia and probably the number-one attraction in Surabaya. The zoo boasts over 500 species of animals, including three large adult and six infant Komodo dragons which sleep peacefully in a large sandy pit. Open daily 0730-1700. North of the zoo on Jalan Taman Mayangkera is a small historical and archaeological museum which houses Mesolithic farming tools, stone statuary from the Majapahit period, Koranic manuscripts, ceremonial beds, *wayang,* photos of old Surabaya, a very good paper-money collection, and early 20th-century technology including a Daimler steam-driven motorcycle. English texts. Take Bemo V opposite the Garden Palace Hotel.

Accommodations

Surabaya would be much more tolerable if it had just a single good travelers' hostel. Unfor-

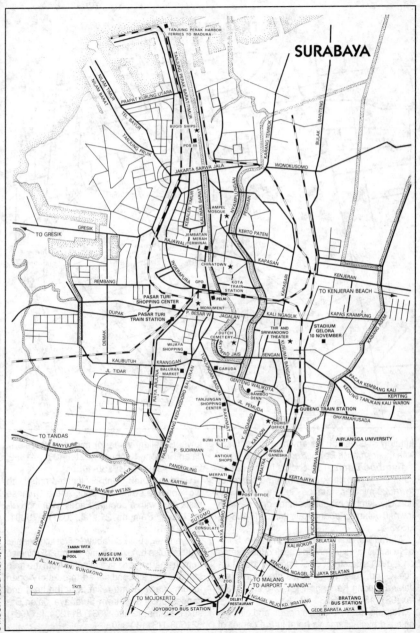

SURABAYA

CENTRAL SURABAYA

© MOON PUBLICATIONS, INC.

tunately, it doesn't have anything to compare with the *losmen* in Bali or Yogyakarta.

Bamboo Denn: Top choice in the cheap segment is this dank *losmen* in the center of town, 20 minutes from the Gubeng Train Station. Claustrophobic but about the only game in town. 6 Jalan Ketabang Kali, tel. (031) 40333, US$3-8.

Wisma Maharani: Best value in central Surabaya is this large, rambling guesthouse located on a quiet side street back from the tourist office. Good vibes; room prices are negotiable. Jalan Embong Kenongo 73, tel. (031) 44839, fax (031) 45435, US$30-40.

Remaja Hotel: Clean, modern, and air-conditioned businessman's hotel in the center of

town. Excellent value for mid-level travelers. Jalan Embong Kenongo 12, tel. (031) 41359, fax (031) 510009, US$30-40.

Garden Hotel: Centrally located hotel with a/c rooms, a swimming pool, and a Chinese restaurant with a popular Friday-evening buffet. Jalan Pemuda 21, tel. (031) 470001, US$100-180.

Hyatt Regency: Surabaya's first luxury hotel is 30 minutes by taxi from the airport, 15 minutes from the harbor, and five minutes from the train station. The air-conditioned three-story open atrium is a welcome relief from the heat and congestion of downtown Surabaya. Jalan Basuki Rakhmat 124, tel. (031) 511234, fax (031) 521508, US$180-360.

CENTRAL SURABAYA ACCOMMODATIONS

HOTEL	SINGLE	DOUBLE	ADDRESS	PHONE (031)
LUXURY				
Hyatt Regency	US$180-220	US$200-360	Basuki Rakhmat 124	511234
Garden Palace	US$130-160	US$150-180	Yos Sudarso 11	479250
Simpang	US$110-140	US$120-200	Pemuda 1	42151
MODERATE				
Elmi	US$70-90	US$80-120	Sudirman 42	471571
Garden	US$100-180	US$120-180	Pemuda 21	470001
Majapahit	US$50-80	US$60-100	Tanjungan 65	43351
Ramayana	US$40-60	US$55-80	Basuki Rakmat 67	46321
Remaja	US$15-30	US$20-40	Embong Kenongo 12	41359
BUDGET				
Bamboo Denn	US$3-6	US$4-8	Ketabang Kali 6	40333
Maharani	US$8-10	US$8-22	Embong Kenongo 73	44839
Wisma Ganesha	US$5-8	US$6-10	Jl. Taman Prapen	818705

Restaurants

For a city of its size, the food scene in Surabaya is disappointing: expensive and poorly prepared dishes served in noisy, desultory cafes. Perhaps the best venue for good value and pleasant surroundings is the Pasar Kayoon night market a few blocks from the Bamboo Denn. *Warungs* opposite the train station are hot and crowded and serve little worth recommending. To eat well in Surabaya, you'll need to spend some extra *rupiah*. The Friday-evening *ristafel* buffet in the Garden Hotel is a worthy splurge. Other places to escape the searing heat and eat in comfort include the Chez Rose for familiar Western dishes and Max's Restaurant a few blocks south. Both Tunjungan and Surabaya Delta shopping centers have countless fast-food joints like Colonel Sanders and Swensen's. Remember the travelers' axiom: sleep hard but eat well.

Entertainment

Sriwandowo Theater: Adjacent to the massive new shopping complex and down the alley from the THR (pronounced TAY-HAH-AIR) Amusement Park, you'll find a miserable tin shed where some of Indonesia's last *ketoprak* and *wayang orang* take place. Completely authentic performances of lowbrow Javanese comedy rich in sexual innuendo, heroic tales taken from the Ramayana, and live *gamelan*. Great entertainment.

Taman Budaya: Students at Surabaya's Performing Arts Center can be seen in the mornings rehearsing *negremo* and *gandrung* dances and practicing bamboo *kalintang* music, *ketoprak, janur* (young coconut-leaves arrangement), Chinese historical dramas, and old Javanese legends like *Aryopenangsang* and *Angreni Larung*. Student recitals are given weekly.

Siswo Bodoyo: The rather deserted theater just outside the zoo sponsors entertaining *ketoprak,* gaudy Javanese soap operas overacted by flaming transsexuals, fat spinsters, and comely young maidens in full Majapahit costumes.

Red Lights: The Jarak and Bangunrejo districts are world-renowned brothels, superb sociological studies in the dynamics of poverty-sharing. Take a W *bemo* from downtown Surabaya to Jarak, a huge honky-tonk Mexican border town in the Orient. In row upon row of gaudy little dollhouse shanties, 15,000 girls and women of all sizes, shapes, ages, races, and humors work and live. Tandes is another entertainment district. Take a *becak* through market and canal areas that never sleep.

Shopping

Good hunting along Jalan Tunungun. The second-floor batik showroom in the Sarinah department store sells "hand-drawn high and medium quality" *sarongs* from Rp25,000 and machine-stamped wraparounds for Rp8000-12,000. Surabaya is also known for its Chinese and Javanese tailors on Jalan Embong Malang ("Street of 1,000 Tailors"), who can cut you a pair of made-to-measure trousers in an hour or so for only Rp9000! A whole row of small antique and curio shops lies near the Bumi Hyatt on Jalan Basuki Rakhmat and along Jalan Urip Sumohardjo. On Jalan Raya Darmo are the Rokhim (no. 27) and the Whisnu (nos. 68-74). If you know what you're looking for and know how to bargain, you can still find some good buys. Both the Tunjungan and Surabaya Delta shopping centers have dozens of shops worth exploring.

Services

The Surabaya tourist office on Jalan Pemuda has basic literature and can answer questions about upcoming festivals, the bull races on Madura Island, dance performances at Padaan, and transportation to outlying attractions. There's a convenient post office near the Joko Dolog statue. The telephone office (Kantor Telepon) is on Jalan Diponegoro at the corner of Jalan Kapuas.

Transportation

Air: Surabaya's airport is 15 km south of the city, Rp8000 by taxi—or walk one km from the terminal for public buses. Taxis to the airport wait at the Gubeng Train Station.

Trains: Trains from Jakarta and Semarang arrive at the Pasar Turi Station. Trains from Yogyakarta, Solo, and Bali arrive at the Gubeng Station, within walking distance of most *losmen* and hotels. Trains leave from Gubeng Station two times daily to Bali, three times daily to Yogyakarta, and seven times daily to Malang. Remember: train travel is safer and less grueling than bus journeys.

Buses: Buses arrive at the Bungurasih (Purabaya) Terminal, some 10 km southwest of city center. Walk over to the main street and take a public *bemo* or bus 2 north to Jalan Pemuda. Get off when you see the big, modern Tunjungan shopping center on your left. Buses to towns on the north coast of Java depart from the Jembatan Merah Terminal. Several private

bus companies with direct services and reserved seats are located on Jalan Rakhmat just opposite the Ramayana Hotel.

Ship: Surabaya is an important departure point for Pelni ships to Sulawesi and Kalimantan. Schedules are posted on the second floor at the harbor and at the Pelni ticketing office (tel. 21694) on Jalan Pahlawan. Pelni is open daily except Sundays 0900-1600, Saturdays until 1300. Appeal directly to the ticketmaster, book your passage, and escape to Malang.

ATTRACTIONS NEAR SURABAYA

Mojokerto

Forty-two km southwest of Surabaya, the small town of Mojokerto is a convenient base for exploring the Majapahit ruins around Trowulan. Visit the local museum to see the magnificent sculptural group of Vishnu being carried on the back of Garuda, the centerpiece of a fascinating series of reliefs around the main room. Taken from the Belahan baths near Trawas and known as the Airlangga Statue, one theory holds that the 11th-century Vishnu figure is that of King Airlangga himself. Many other lifelike statues, relics, carved stoned reliefs showing daily scenes—and umpteen plaques with ancient writing on them—fill this museum. Afterwards, wander through the original quarter of town with its finely made old Dutch houses. Inexpensive *losmen* are situated near the bus terminal and in the center of town, three km distant.

Trowulan

This small agricultural community 12 km southwest of Mojokerto was once the capital of the mighty Majapahit Empire (1292-1389), which, under the ruthless and efficient Gajah Mada, controlled most of the islands of the archipelago in the 14th century. The arrival of Islam forced the Majapahits, the final Hindu kingdom in Indonesia, to flee east to Bali, taking with them their religion, culture, and artistic traditions.

Constructed entirely from brick with no stonework, granite, or sandstone, the temple remains of Trowulan lie scattered over a 15-square-km area. First visit the small but informative Museum Purbakala, renowned for its remarkable collection of terra-cotta figurines and small heads, toys, clay masks, bronze statues,

TROWULAN

CANDI BHRE KAHURIPAN

TO MOJOKERTO (15 km)

NOT TO SCALE

WARINGAN LAWANG (200 m FROM ROAD)

CANDI BERAHU

MAKAM PUTERI CEMPA

CANDI SITI INGGIL

KOLAM SEGARAN

MAKAM PANJANG

TO JOMBANG (15 km)

MUSEUM PURBAKALA

SANGGAR PEMELENGAN

CANDI BAJANG RATU

PENDOPO AGUNG

VILLAGE

SUMUR UPAS

TO MAKAM TROLOYO

CANDI TIKUS

From museum to:

C. Berahu	1 km
C. Siti Inggil	½ km
C. Tikus	4 km
C. Bajang Ratu	4 km
Sanggar Pemelengan	2 km
Kolam Segaran	1 km
Makam Pankamg	2 km
Waringan Lawang	1½ km
C. Bhre Kahuripan	6 km
Pendopo Agung	1½ km
Sumur Upas	1 km
Makam Troloyo	2 km

© MOON PUBLICATIONS, INC.

and much more. It's a museum of fragments, so you really have to use your imagination. A large tabletop map shows the locations of the nearby temples and tombs. Day visitors can leave their packs at the museum and either hire a *becak* (four hours for about Rp7000) or hike along the winding lanes. A sensible route is up to Candi Siti Inggil, back to Candi Berahu, then northeast down the highway to Waringan Lawang. From here walk on to Bajang Ratu; it's less than one km between Bajang Ratu and Candi Tikus. You might have to cut (carefully) across ricefields in your meanderings. To spend 15-20 minutes at each site will take six hours

walking. The walk down lanes of laughing children and people working *padi* is at least as satisfying as the temples themselves.

Buses from Surabaya's Bungurasih Station toward Jombang fly past the turnoff to Museum Purbakala; ask to get off at the main intersection and hire a *becak*. If coming from Jombang, go to Mojoagung first, then take a minibus to Trowulan.

Pandaan
Spectacular performances of the Ramayana are given twice monthly from May to October in the open-air Candra Wilwatikta amphitheater 45 km south of Surabaya. Held against the flawless cone of Mt. Penanggungan, this is Indonesia's most famous Ramayana production after the spectacle at Prambanan. Exact dates can be confirmed with the Surabaya tourist office.

MADURA ISLAND

One of Indonesia's undiscovered gems, this large, rugged island is blessed with numerous fine white-sand beaches, unpeopled countryside, inexpensive and uncrowded *losmen,* and unique cuisine. Here you can glimpse a bygone rural life, extinct in many other parts of Java. Although only 30 minutes from Surabaya by ferry, Madura is almost totally free of tourists; you could spend a week here and not see another Westerner.

Attractions
Sights on Madura include Air Mata, the island's oldest and most beautiful cemetery. Located on a hill in the northwest near Arasbaya, 11 km northeast of Bangkalan, Air Mata ("Water of the Eye") is a vast complex of very old graves, including that of Ratu Ibu (1546-1569), a descendant of Sunan Giri, the great East Javanese saint.

Accommodations
Inexpensive *losmen* are found in all the principal towns, though the best base for island explorations is Sumenep, an urbanized town with far more atmosphere than Pamekasan.

Losmen Wijaya I: Sumenep's budget spot, near the bus terminal and town square, is clean, friendly, and helpful. 1 Jl. Wahid Hasyim, tel. (0351) 21532, US$3-12.

RUNNING OF THE BULLS

Madura is chiefly famous for its bull races, which attract visitors from around the world, but it's also known for its small and dark women who walk with a sensual grace and are renowned all over Indonesia for a special style of movement during lovemaking called *goyang madura*.

As intriguing as that may sound, the island is mainly visited for its *kerapan sapi* bull races held during August and September. Like a scene out of *Ben Hur*, these thrilling, high-speed spectacles of sleek racing bulls take place on Sundays at Bangkalan's stadium, usually coinciding with the arrival of tourist cruise ships. Prior to the grand finale, traditional games, ceremonies, parades of decorated bulls, *gamelan* orchestras, and night bazaars fill the towns. The bulls are decorated with gilt and tinsel, leather bibs, flower-tasseled horn sheaths, silver-studded head harnesses, and bells that jangle from the high, enameled yokes that couple the two bulls of each team. The teams are paraded through the town under ceremonial parasols to the accompaniment of drums, gongs, flutes, and bells before the rostrums fill with wild spectators. The race is held on a grassy straightaway 120 meters long: 24 pairs of racing bulls are matched up, their ornaments stripped off, and the beasts lined up with their brightly dressed jockeys. Each is given a generous tote of *arak* from a bamboo tube, then *gamelan* music is played to excite the bulls. The three-man judging panel takes its place. Dead silence before the race begins. The bulls look heavy and awkward, but watch: The starter drops his flag and the teams lunge forward, the riders straddling skids slung between the yoked bulls, the rear of the skids dragging along the ground. Jockeys prod and flog the animals mercilessly with thorns and spiked rods. With snorting nostrils and mud flying, the bulls look determined to trample the crowd. They can cover 100 meters in nine seconds flat, faster than the world's human track record. Race dates can be checked at the tourist office in Surabaya.

Hotel Safari Jaya: Another inexpensive option in Sumenep, just five minutes from the town square by *becak*. 90 Jl. Trunojoyo, tel. (0351) 21989, US$3-12.

Hotel Garuda: A fairly clean old house with high ceilings and spacious rooms. The best bud-get option in Pamekasan, though you might also consider the Trunojoyo Hotel around the corner. 1 Jl. Masigit, tel. (0351) 81589, US$3-6.

Transportation

Ferries leave hourly from Tanjung Perak, Surabaya's port, across the narrow strait to the harbor town of Kamal. An alternative approach is from Panarukan, west of Situbondo; ferries leave daily at 1300 for Kalianget in eastern Madura, returning to Panarukan at 0700 the next day. Madura's transportation system is outstanding; minibuses travel to practically everywhere worth going to on the island.

MALANG

One of Java's most pleasant and attractive provincial towns is located in the mountains 90 km south of Surabaya. Established by the Dutch in the late 18th century as a coffee-growing center, Malang today is a bustling city of well-planned parks, sprawling markets, big villas, wide clean streets, one-hour photo shops, abundant trees, air-conditioned shopping centers, and old Dutch architecture—a resort city for overheated lowlanders and dynamic proof of Indonesia's amazing economic gains in the last decade. Although Malang can't compare culturally with a city like Yogya, its surrounding countryside boasts a half-dozen small but precise temples constructed by ancient East Javanese Hindu kingdoms and an easygoing atmosphere that provides a welcome relief from the exhausting journey across Java.

Attractions

Malang itself has little of importance aside from a few markets and people-watching. At Pasar Besar, in the old section below the town park, tobacco traders haggle and *becak* drivers doze in the morning sunshine. The night market on Jalan Brawijaya is mostly just a lineup of simple *warungs*. Best bet is to wander the town square at sunset, cracking hot peanuts and picking out handmade toys (*wayang kulit,* flutes, robot heads, wooden dragons) from the itinerant merchants. The calls of "Hallo!" and "Where are you going?" will drive you nuts, but as Bill Dalton points out in his *Indonesia Handbook,* "You can't get angry at 160 million Indonesians." Nearby

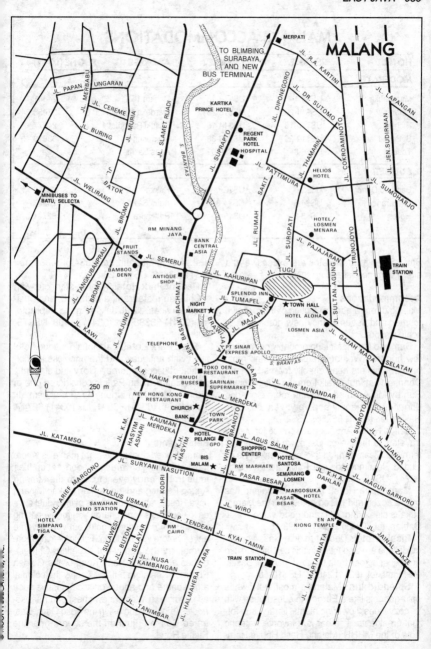

MALANG

MALANG ACCOMMODATIONS

HOTEL	SINGLE	DOUBLE	ADDRESS	PHONE (0341)
MODERATE				
Margosuka	US$8-14	US$10-18	Dahlan 15	24841
Pelangi	US$14-20	US$18-25	Merdeka Selatan	27456
Richie	US$10-16	US$14-18	Basuki Rachmat 1	24877
Splendid Inn	US$19-25	US$23-30	Majapahit 4	63618
Tosari	US$6-8	US$8-10	Agus Salim	
BUDGET				
Bamboo Denn	US$2	US$2	Hakim	66256
Semarang	US$4-6	US$4-6	Agus Salim	24317
Helios	US$5-8	US$5-8	Pattimura	62741

Batu, Selecta, and Tretes are expensive and highly commercialized hill resorts.

Accommodations

Malang offers a good selection of inexpensive *losmen* and several fancy new hotels for upscale visitors.

Bamboo Denn: Malang probably gets only a few hundred Westerners per year, and most budget travelers head directly for the Bamboo Denn, a 15-minute walk from the bus terminal. Run by Mr. Achmad, this one-room eight-bed dormitory is friendly and very, very quiet. Jl. Hakim, tel. (0341) 66256, US$2.

Helios Hotel: Another good choice for budget travelers is the Helios just down from the bus terminal. Clean, comfortable, and breakfast is included. Recommended. Jl. Pattimura, tel. (0341) 62741, US$5-15.

Margosuka Hotel: Downtown Malang has over a dozen mid-priced hotels, but the Margosuka is clean, modern, and good value. 15 Jl. Dahlan, tel. (0341) 24841, US$8-15.

Richie Hotel: Decent middle-class accommodations are also found in this centrally located hotel, just across from the town park. Jl. Basuki Rachmat, tel. (0341) 24877, US$10-18.

Splendid Inn: Malang's most worthwhile splurge feels like a European guesthouse with its cozy vibes, flowering plants, library, and formal breakfasts. The bar is a favorite watering hole of the MHHH (Malang Hash House Harri-ers). 4 Jl. Majapahit, tel. (0341) 66860, fax (0341) 63618, US$14-28

Regent Park Hotel: A three-star hotel with a Chinese restaurant, a nightclub, and business services. 12 Jl. Jaksa Agung Suprapto, tel. (0341) 63388, fax (0341) 61408, US$75-90.

Tugu Park Hotel: Fabulous boutique hotel filled with antiques and the priceless art collection of a local attorney. Cozy and elegantly understated, Tugu Park is considered one of the finest hotels in Indonesia. A real gem. Jl. Tugu 3, tel. (0341) 63891, fax (0341) 62747, US$80-110.

Restaurants

As mentioned above, the night market is where most of Malang's *warung* vendors set up their tents in the early evening. Both the Minang Agung Padang and the Rumah Makan Minang Jaya Restaurant bring dozens of individual dishes to your table (and charge you for everything you touch!) unless you point out your favorite entree before you sit down. For something more formal, try the pricey but excellent Chinese dishes at the New Hong Kong or the Golden Phoenix. Nostalgia buffs will enjoy the colonial atmosphere and anachronistic standbys such as *uitsmijter* (Dutch sandwiches) and *haagsehopjes* (mocha candies) in the Toko Oen ("Castrated Donkey") just off the square near the Richie Hotel.

Transportation

Buses and trains from Surabaya and Yogyakarta are plentiful, but for an unusual approach try taking buses through the mountain passes around Batu or hike down from Mt. Bromo. Leaving Malang, take the day train (best), a public bus from the main terminal, or a private night coach from the Permudi office adjacent to the Richie Hotel. Malang has three bus terminals: Arjosari for Bromo, Surabaya, and Bali; Gadang (five km south of town) for Blitar; Landung Sari for Batu, Selecta, Mojokerto, and Kediri.

TEMPLES NEAR MALANG

Malang is an excellent base for visiting the astonishingly rich Hindu ruins of East Java. A popular day-trip is from the Blimbing *bemo* station in north Malang to Candi Singosari, backtrack to Blimbing, another *bemo* east to Candi Jago at Tumpang, and another to Candi Kidal in Kidal. Finally, return to Malang via Tajinan.

East Javanese temples and bas-reliefs are distinct from those in Central Java. In Central Javanese art, mastery is shown in the handling and modifying of Hindu styles, but characteristic Indonesian elements are much more dominant in East Javanese ruins. The nationalistic Majapahit Kingdom, which lasted only the lifetime of Gajah Mada, introduced a Javanization of styles, a return to a flatter and highly stylized method of carving in which the figures resemble shadow puppets used in *wayang*. Bodies are sculpted delicately and seen from the front, while the head and feet are turned sideways; a sculptural technique perhaps borrowed from the ancient Egyptians. The temples themselves are more slender, with narrow bases, and on a less grandiose scale than those of Central Java. Many of the following have been completely disassembled and reconstructed by the Indonesian government.

Candi Singosari

Dating from the 13th century, this Shiva shrine is the most imposing monument left of the murderous Singosari Dynasty. It was built to honor King Kartanagara, the mad despot who mortified Kublai Khan's emissaries by cutting off their noses and tattooing "NO!" across their foreheads, an act which precipitated the launching of 1,000 Mongol troop ships against Java in 1293. Candi Singosari's unique feature is its base and central *cella* (inner sanctum), but overall this temple is rather ordinary for its lack of ornamentation. Most of the original statues now form the backbone of the world-famous Hindu-Javanese collection at the Leiden Museum in Holland, including the renowned Prajnaparamita image. Take a *bemo* to Blimbing or direct to the town of Singosari, 10 km north of Malang, and walk left 500 meters down Jalan Kartanagara. Twin Singosari demons glare at passersby another 200 meters up the country road. Time permitting, turn right and head northwest for six km until you reach Sumberawan village, where one of Indonesia's two sole surviving stupas is located (the other is Borobudur).

Candi Jago

Candi Jago, a memorial to Singosari King Vishnuvardhana, dates from 1268 and yet has distinct connections with the prehistoric monuments and terraced sanctuaries found in Java's mountains. Take a *bemo* to Tumpang, walk 100 meters up Jalan Wardhana, and look just beyond the mosque. To the right of the entrance are a pair of finely carved *kala* heads flanking an impressive six-armed image of Durga. The monument incorporates Buddhist sculptures, Krishna reliefs, Arjuna's fretful night in his hermitage, earthy scenes from everyday life, superb *wayang*-style reliefs of bulbous-nosed Semeru and Chinese pagodas, and some of the earliest and most grotesque *panakawan* carvings.

Candi Kidal

This small but lovely sanctuary is an architectural jewel, one of the most perfect examples of Singosari temple art. Hidden inside a papaya grove, the richly carved 13th-century *candi* has elaborate reliefs of medallions and *kala*-heads on the main body, while statues of Garuda guard its base. The entire temple was recently disassembled, each brick labeled, and then laboriously reconstructed from the ground up. Kidal is eight km southwest of Tumpang. *Bemos* out here are absolutely the most crowded vehicles I've ever ridden (except for rush-hour buses in Rangoon).

Panataran

Ten km north of Blitar and 80 km southwest of Malang, this is the largest and most imposing complex of ruins in East Java, and one of the largest temple sanctuaries in all of Indonesia. The Panataran temple group took 250 years to build, starting in about 1197, during the Singosari Dynasty. Three gradually rising walled courtyards are laid out on a long field; see dance-play platforms, terraces, shrines, and the same *gapura* gateways found in almost every village in East Java today. Temple reliefs show the transition from three-dimensional to two-dimensional representations: figures tend to take second place to the decorations. One of the most striking structures is the Naga Temple on the second terrace and the surrounding colossal carvings of protective coiled serpents carried by priests—a sight that would make any medieval thief shudder. The whole complex has been completely restored and is very well maintained. To get there, take a bus to Blitar and continue by *bemo* or minibus to Nglegok village, from where *dokars* go to Desa Panataran, two km farther northeast along the main road.

Hotel Sri Lestari: Most visitors to Blitar overnight in this clean and centrally located hotel, which also arranges quick transportation up to Panataran and the imposing tomb of President Sukarno. Great restaurant. Jl. Merdeka 173, tel. (0342) 81766, US$4-6 fan, US$20-32 a/c.

MOUNT BROMO

A convenient stop for travelers between Bali and Surabaya and the most popular of all of East Java's travel destinations, this active 2,392-meter-high volcano is enclosed by perpendicular walls and an awesome sea of sand. The tremendous caldera has three mountains within it—craters within one huge crater—the Bromo-Semeru Massif. From Bromo's peak are stunning views of active Gunung Semeru, Java's highest mountain. Although Bromo can still vent steam and ash, smoke profusely, and occasionally boom from the central crater, lava has not been ejected in historical times.

The Trek

No matter how much you've heard about it, you won't be prepared for this ethereal, unforgettable spectacle. Dry-season visitors (April-November) stand the best chance of seeing a bloodred sunrise; in the wet season, you might as well sleep late and stroll across the sand sea during the warmer part of the day. Dress warmly and be prepared for *hundreds* of tourists: Bromo is to Java as Yosemite is to California. The entire hike takes about five hours. The ascent to the Bromo crater from Cemoro Lawang takes about two hours by foot on a well-marked trail; just follow the yellow brick road. Guides and horses are unnecessary. Under clear skies sparkling with stars, with the wind whistling, follow the long line of trekkers across the sea of sand and climb the 250 steps to the narrow rim. It's possible to walk all the way around the rim in one hour, but it's precarious in places and very dusty, like fine flour. Travel light—this is a hard, cold, and dusty climb.

Transportation

Buses from Bali, Malang, and Surabaya's Purabaya Bus Station go to Probolinggo. Ask to be dropped at the Bromo turnoff, or the nearby Bayuangga bus terminal. Skip Probolinggo! Take a *bemo* immediately up to Ngadisari (three km below the rim) or spend the night in Probolinggo at the Hotel Bromo Permai II directly opposite the bus terminal. *Bemos* to Bromo first leave Probolinggo at 0400, but you'll never make sunrise on the crater. From Ngadisari, either walk up the very steep road, hire a horse, or hitch a ride with a vegetable truck up to rimside Cemoro Lawang. *Bemos* back to Surabaya and Malang leave Ngadisari daily at 0900 and 1100; buy tickets from Daftar Harga Travel Service.

Probolinggo Accommodations

Inexpensive hotels are down in Probolinggo, in Ngadisari (three km down from the crater rim), and at Cemoro Lawang, on the edge of the crater. It's best to stay in Cemoro Lawang, though this is usually determined by your arrival time in Probolinggo and the availability of transportation up the mountain.

Hotel Bromo Permai II: A very popular spot in the center of town which serves as the travelers' center and information source for Bromo and nearby regions. Late-night arrivals from Bali can crash in the lobby or drink thick, rich coffee in the Depot Siola beyond the mosque. 237 Jl. Sudirman, tel. (0335) 41256, US$3-8.

Ratna Hotel: Better-quality a/c rooms at very reasonable prices. 16 Jl. Sudirman, tel. (0335) 21597, US$10-15.

Mt. Bromo Accommodations

Ngadisari is the small town at the end of the line for all minibuses from Probolinggo. You can spend the night here, hike up to the rim in about an hour, or catch a ride on a jeep for about Rp1000. Ngadisari is rough, but homestays are plentiful and the local people are quite friendly.

Hotel Bromo Permai: Right on the rim with wonderful views, but rooms are small and overpriced. Fortunately, there's a decent cafe with hot meals, free maps, and a good crowd of travelers to meet in the evenings. Rooms can be booked in advance at the Bromo Permai in Probolinggo. Cemoro Lawang, US$2-3 dorm, US$6-12 private rooms.

Losmen Lava: A small and friendly homestay about 50 meters below the crater rim. Best backpackers choice near the volcano. Cemoro Lawang, tel. (0335) 23458, US$3-6.

Yoschi's Homestay: A clean and comfortable place, but far less scenic than the Bromo Permai. Check their logbook for trekking tips. Jl. Bromo-Ngadisari, tel. (0335) 23387, US$3-8.

Grand Bromo Hotel: Bromo has recently experienced a hotel boom as Indonesian operators rush to meet increased demand. This new upscale hotel is very distant from the crater but positively luxurious, with marble baths and an elegant restaurant. Jl. Bromo Ngadisari, US$45-80.

GUNUNG SEMERU

Also called Mahameru or "Great Mountain," Mt. Semeru is one of the world's most beautiful peaks and at 3,676 meters the highest mountain on Java. According to legend, all the other mountains of Java fell away from Semeru on its mythological journey from the Himalayas.

Still smoking and belching out hot ash and solidified chunks of lava, Semeru can be climbed in three long and exhausting days from either Bromo or Malang. The difficulty isn't with the climb but rather with the extreme cold and long walks from your last possible *bemo* stop. Bring food, companionship, a flashlight, and *very* warm clothing.

From Bromo, hike five hours across the sea of sand to Ranopani and register with the PPM. From Malang, take a *bemo* to Tumpang, Gu-

bugklakah, Ngadas, and finally Ranopani. It's then a four-hour walk along a soil path through bamboo and tall grasses to Ranu Kumbolo, where a deserted lakeside hut serves for overnighters. Time permitting, it's better to continue hiking four hours to a shelter marked Arcopodo. Depart the next morning at 0330 for the 0530 sunrise. From the summit, it's five hours to Ranu Kumbolo, four more to Ranopani, and eight more to Tumpang. Recovery takes several days.

EAST JAVA PARKS

Baluran National Park

A reserve since Dutch times, created as a national park only in 1980, Baluran is one of Indonesia's most accessible yet little-known game reserves. Baluran is unusual for Java in that it encompasses a mountainous area that gives way to open forests, scrubland, and white-sand beaches washed by the Bali Straits. Baluran has coastal marshes, open rolling savannah, swampy groves, crab-eating monkeys, and grasslands with huge wild oxen. For Java, the game-watching conditions are unique. This is Java's one bit of Africa.

The entrance to this 250-square-km reserve is at Batangan, just three km north of Wonorejo and 37 km from Banyuwangi. Report to the PPA guardpost and head 12 km down the all-weather road to park headquarters at Bekol. Accommodations are available at the Bekol Guesthouse and the Bama Guesthouse three km east on the beach. Wildlife is most abundant around the watering holes and salt licks in the early morning or sunset hours.

Ijen Plateau

This remote region offers savannah landscapes, ruggedly beautiful panoramas, cool weather, grand hiking, dormant volcanos, and a placid, bright crater lake. Tourists haven't made it up here yet and it's still quite primitive, but that's part of the appeal. Bring food, warm clothing, and rain-gear.

The Ijen crater, with its haunting turquoise-blue lake streaked with yellow sulfurous patterns, is a one-hour hike from the vulcanologist station at Ungkup Ungkup. Buses from Banyuwangi reach Licin, a six-hour hike from Ungkup Ungkup. *Bemos* from Bondowoso or Wonosari in the west terminate at Jampit, five hours from Ungkup Ungkup.

Meru Betiri Reserve

From a conservation point of view, this is one of the most important reserves on Java. Established in 1972, the 50,000-hectare Meru Betiri game park lies on Java's rugged southeast coast where thickly wooded hills rise steeply to an elevation of over 1,000 meters. Though best known as the last refuge of the Javan tiger, Meru Betiri is also of considerable botanical importance as one of the few remaining areas of relatively undisturbed primal montane forest on Java. It is the only known habitat of two of the island's endemic plant species, the *Rafflesia zollingeriana* and *Balanphora fungosa*. The reserve's two highest peaks, Mt. Betiri and Mt. Tajem, catch the rain and create a sort of rain pocket; this makes the reserve often wetter than surrounding areas and accounts for the unbelievably thick jungles. The reserve's steep, densely wooded hills also provide a final stronghold for the indigenous Javan tiger (*harimau macan jawa*), which inhabits the estate's hilly eastern boundary.

The fastest access to the reserve is from Glenmore, which is reachable by bus or *bemo* from Banyuwangi. A comfortable PPA resthouse provides food and lodging within the reserve.

Another resthouse, closer to the turtle nesting beach, is Wisma Sukamade, an elegant old Dutch plantation surrounded by dense jungles and a breathless expanse of coastline. Highly recommended.

Banyuwangi Reserve And Granjagan Surfing

Java's finest surf crashes down at Plengkung, 15 km east of Grajagan. Surfers claim that picture-perfect waves roll in every five minutes, average three to four meters, and can break for miles. Organized surfing ventures can be arranged through travel agents in Bali. Otherwise, take a bus from Banyuwangi to Granjagan and continue by fishing boat to Plengkung, where bamboo bungalows and simple *warungs* have been constructed on the beach. Bring food and drink from Bali.

BANYUWANGI

This is the jumping-off point for Bali. The ferry terminal is at Ketapang, eight km north. *Bemos* shuttle between the Banyuwangi public bus station and the ferry terminal. Being an important travel junction, Banyuwangi also has several private bus companies with terminals scattered around the city. Travelers who purchase direct bus or train tickets between Bali and Java will simply bypass Banyuwangi. Independent travelers who need detailed advice on regional attractions can visit the tourist office on Jalan Diponegoro for maps, information about the parks described above, or surfing conditions in Granjangan.

Accommodations

Over 30 *losmen* and hotels are found in this messy, noisy town. Pass straight through unless you want to visit one of the East Java national parks or simply enjoy Javanese cacophony at its finest.

Hotel Baru: The best spot for budget travelers has 42 spacious, airy rooms adjacent to their popular cafe. The owners also help with tips on nearby surfing beaches. 82 Jl. Pattimura, tel. (0333) 21369, US$3-8

Wisma Blambangan: Situated right on the town square with cleanish rooms in all price ranges. 4 Jl. Wahidin, tel. (0333) 21598, US$5-12.

Manyar Hotel: The best hotel in town is overpriced but conveniently located just one km south of the ferry terminal for Bali. Jl. Situbondo, tel. US$12-35.

BALI

When the first Dutch war yacht pulled into Bali in the late 16th century, the whole crew immediately jumped ship—it was heaven on earth. It took the captain two years to round up his men before he could set sail back to Holland. Bali was really put on the map back in the 1930s when several popular documentaries were made about this paradise-like island. Then the world knew, and Bali has remained a tourist colony for well-nigh 50 years now—an Isle of Capri of the Western Pacific.

This tiny tropical island just off the eastern coast of Java is both Indonesia's masterpiece and one of the world's greatest cultural jewels. Inhabited by almost three million residents, this 5,500-square-km island is a stunning vision of towering volcanos, beautiful beaches, and magnificent layers of sculpted ricefields. But it is Balinese culture that has entranced the world for centuries. Here, life and art are completely interwoven to an extent unheard of in the West. Every Balinese citizen, from the simplest peasant to the highest-caste noble, considers himself an artist whose birthright demands the continual creation of music, dance, and crafts to honor the gods and maintain the island's natural balance.

The island's physical beauty and artistic heritage attracts enormous numbers of tourists from all over the world. Although this sounds negative, the inevitable commercialization has, contrary to popular belief, brought a higher standard of living and served to revitalize and preserve traditional Balinese culture. Instead of discarding their past, the Balinese have adapted and even grown stronger in their basic faiths. Overcommercialized tourist ghettos such as Kuta and Sanur obviously have little to do with the "real" Bali, but authentic lifestyles remain alive and well in hundreds of villages which haven't changed in 50 years. Bali is still an island where you can get lost—you don't need directions; just head for the hills. Best of all, the highlights are still free: orange and gold tropical sunsets, an astoundingly rich culture, the dynamite smiles of the children, the sound of the palms, the talcum-powder beaches and coral dive sites.

INTRODUCTION

HISTORY

Historically speaking, Bali is a fossilized Java. After the Balinese escaped the control of the Sumatran Srivijaya Empire (7th-13th centuries), the island came under the control of various East Javanese kingdoms who introduced the same Hindu theologies and artistic models that dominated the Javanese courts. Balinese culture came of age in the 16th century when Islam began to move across the island of Java. To escape Islamic domination, most of the Hindu Majapahit aristocracy, court philosophers, priests, architects, artisans, painters, and craftsmen took refuge on Bali. The tiny island became the last remaining Hindu outpost in Southeast Asia, an important repository of traditional Majapahit religion and culture, and the final resting place for the old Indo-Javanese civilization.

Except for occasional incursions by the Dutch and English, Bali remained almost completely isolated until the tragic events of 1894. To avenge a massacre of Dutch soldiers by the Balinese, the Dutch government ordered an attack on the royal court of Mataram. Rather than surrender, the king and his entourage committed *puputan,* a form of ritualistic suicide in which the unarmed Balinese hurled themselves against the heavily fortified Dutch. The gruesome spectacle was repeated in Denpasar in 1906, and later at the royal courts at Gelgel and Klungkung. Bali was incorporated into the Dutch Empire, but only after all remaining lineal descendants of the Majapahit Empire had committed suicide or been killed by the Dutch.

Tourism began in the 1930s after several famous artists, photographers, and writers took residence in Bali. Walter Spies (formerly the bandmaster at the Yogyakarta court) and Dutch artist Rudolf Bonnet moved to Ubud, where they taught Western painting styles and techniques still evident in contemporary artwork. Other early visitors included Miguel Covarrubias (the Mexican ethnologist who wrote *The Island of Bali*), Mark Twain, German novelist Vicki Baum (*Tale of Bali*), and American anthropologist Margaret Mead, who made several films on Balinese dance and ritual. WW II was followed by the highly charged rule of Sukarno and the bloody 1965 Indonesian revolt against the communists. Bali had a terrible experience: an estimated 100,000 Balinese were murdered after rival political parties ran amok. Tragedy struck again in 1963 when the devastating eruption of Mt. Agung killed thousands.

THE LAND

Bali is like one big sculpture. Every earthen step is manicured and polished, every field and niche is carved by hand. Once a geographic extension of Java, Bali still resembles it, mountains and all, sharing much the same climate, flora, and fauna as its mother island. There are few flat areas; hills and mountains are everywhere. The surface of the island is marked by deep ravines, fast-flowing rivers, and a soaring volcanic chain, an extension of Java's central range. Terracing and irrigation practices are even more elaborate and sophisticated than on Java, with remarkable systems of aqueducts, small dams, underground canals, and water carried by tunnels through solid rock hillsides. There's alpine country with mountain streams, moss, prehistoric ferns, wildflowers, creepers, orchids, leeches, butterflies, birds, and screaming monkeys. The western tip is the unspoiled, uninhabited wilderness of Bali. Legend has it that Bali's first inhabitants had their origins here in a lost, invisible city.

PEOPLE AND SOCIETY

The three million inhabitants of Bali are primarily descendants of Malay races that migrated to the island thousands of years ago from the Asian mainland. Most Balinese speak both the national dialect and Balinese, a tricky language which is subdivided into familiar forms between friends, middle Balinese used in polite society, and high Balinese spoken between the higher castes. Ninety percent belong to the Sudra (workers) caste and name their first child Wayan, the second Made, the third Nyoman, and the fourth Ketut—repeating the name cycle with the fifth child! Higher castes include the Brahmans (priests and teachers), who add Ida Bagus before their name; Wesyas (warriors and administrators), who add I Gusti; and Ksatria (former royalty), who add Dewa. Caste rules today are generally ignored except at formal occasions.

Balinese life is an endless series of rituals and ceremonies that mark important moments in a person's life. Rituals begin with the child's first birthday at 210 days, followed by puberty rites for the girls, teeth-filing ceremonies for both sexes, marriage rituals, and finally, elaborate funerals. Rather than being considered senseless or burdensome, Balinese rituals help preserve community values, encourage artistic pageantry, and give the people a firm sense of self-worth and emotional security.

Village life also involves community service. Most of the important decisions are made according to the customary laws of *adat* by the *desa* (village) council of married adults. Meetings are often held in the *bale agung*, open-air pavilions located inside temple courtyards. Large *desas* are subdivided into cooperative groups called *banjars*, which help each other with home building, festivals, and cremations. Balinese farmers are also expected to join the village *subak*, a farmers' federation which distributes the water from the higher ricefields down to the lower levels. Balinese society derives much of its economic and spiritual success from these powerful social organizations.

RELIGION

Bali is the largest Hindu outpost in the world outside of India. Although Hinduism originated in India, on Bali it has developed along lines all its own. Indeed, the forms of Hinduism practiced in the two lands are as different as the forms of Christianity practiced by the Ethiopians and the Episcopalians. And the way the Balinese practice their island form of frontier Hinduism is still their greatest art.

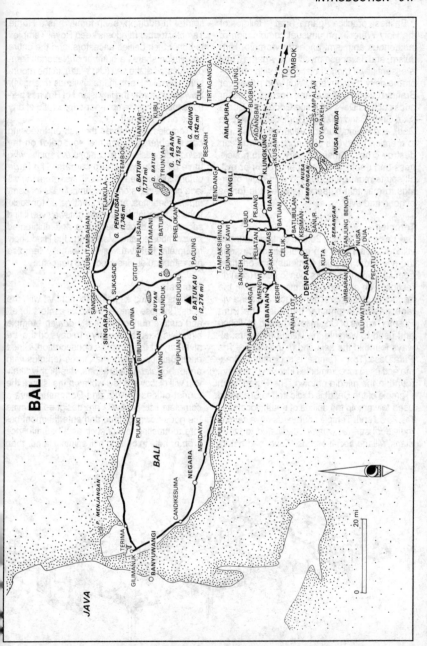

Balinese practice Agama Tirtal ("Religion of the Holy Water"), an unusual combination of indigenous animism, ancestor worship, Hinduism, and Javanese mysticism. Agama Tirtal is essentially a monotheistic faith with one supreme deity (Sanghyang Widi) who rules over Brahma, Vishnu, Shiva, and dozens of lesser gods such as Dewi Sri (Rice Goddess), Surya (Sun God), Candra (Moon God), Sakenon (Sea God), and Hyang Gunung (Mountain God)...not to mention hundreds of minor spirits who can destroy crops, cause insanity, or bring sickness and death! Whether benevolent or evil, all spirits must be appeased with daily offerings to maintain balance between the forces of good and evil.

Temples

Bali has an estimated 20,000 temples found in villages, seashores, on mountaintops, and in the ricefields. All *pura* (temples) are oriented from *kaja* (mountain) direction to *kelod* (sea) direction, with secondary shrines located in the *kangin* (sunrise) direction. Each Balinese village has three primary temples. The Pura Puseh (Temple of Origin) is dedicated to Vishnu and used to worship the village founders; always found in the *kaja* end of the village. The Pura Desa (Town Temple) is dedicated to Brahma and used for ceremonies involving the living; found in the middle of town. The Pura Dalem (Temple of the Dead) is dedicated to Shiva and used to worship the deities of death; located in the *kelod* end. Temple courtyards have several individual shrines (*merus*) dedicated to family clans, village social organizations, and nature

spirits. In addition, each family has a Home Temple, former rajadoms keep Royal Temples to honor their deified ancestors, and the entire population shares a number of National Temples located at the sea (Ulu Watu), in the mountains (Besakih), and in the lowlands (Mengwi). Now you see why the tiny island of Bali has perhaps the highest temple-per-capita ratio of any place on the planet!

Temples are entered through an imposing *candi bentar* (monumental split gate) on the *kelod* side, designed to confuse evil spirits, who have difficulty with sharp corners. The large outer courtyard features pavilions where the village *gamelan* is stored, assembly halls for community meetings, and frequently a pit for cockfighting. Through the second gateway you'll find sacred relics, temple heirlooms, and multiroofed *merus* modeled after Mahameru, the Hindu holy mountain. Festivals aside, Balinese temples are rather quiet, deserted, and peaceful.

Festivals

Besides serving as points for contact with the gods, Balinese temples serve as centers for art and culture during the yearly *odalan*—temple birthdays celebrated every 210 days on the anniversary of the temple's consecration. Since each Balinese village has three temples with annual *odalan* celebrations, it is highly likely you will discover a few while on the island; the tourist offices in Kuta and Denpasar have a complete list. Festivals are designed to invite the gods down for food and entertainment before requesting favors such as a bountiful rice crop or help in battling evil spirits. Rather than

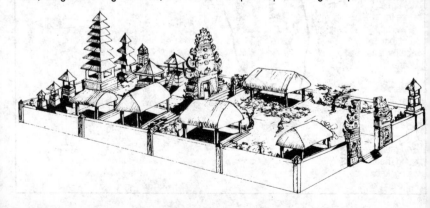

solemn occasions, festivals are lively social events with smiling kids, dancing grandmothers, gambling, myriad food stalls, chanting priests, *gamelan* music, and performances of *wayang*. Women bring enormous pyramids of rice cakes and flowers; offerings for evil spirits are placed on the ground, those for good spirits are stacked around the main altars. *Pemangku* (temple priests) chant in Sanskrit before the rice-cake towers and sacred images are carried to the ocean for a ceremonial bath and purification rites. At night, old women slowly dance the *pendet,* puppeteers perform *wayang,* and *pemangkus* enter into trances. *Odalans* end with the rising sun and final prayer as the villagers return to their homes—an excellent way to appreciate the religious devotion and zest for life that characterize the Balinese.

Funerals

Another event worth attending is a Balinese funeral—among the most spectacular sights on the island. Rather than sad and solemn affairs, Balinese funerals are joyous celebrations that liberate the soul from the body for the journey back to heaven. First, the corpse is cleaned and displayed in the house for friends and neighbors. Most are temporarily buried until an auspicious date arises and enough money has been raised for the ceremony. On the appointed day, the entire village constructs a gigantic tower, carves the coffin, and creates art for burning. En route to the Temple of the Dead, the procession spins the coffin to confuse the soul (so it won't return to the village and raise hell!) and then transfers the corpse to a funeral sarcophagus. The magnificent tower is set on fire before the ashes are carried to the sea. Tourists are welcome to watch and even photograph the event, but it's best to be well dressed (no shorts or halter tops) and remain unobtrusive and respectful of local traditions.

Proper Attire

Great importance is laid on proper dress when visiting temples and attending local festivals. The recommended attire for males includes *sarong, saput* (second smaller *sarong*), *slendang* (sash around waist), sleeved shirt, and *udung* (headdress). Ladies should be fitted in *sarong, kebaya* or sleeved shirt, and *selendang*. On no account should you *ever* visit a temple in shorts, halter tops, or anything that appears immodest—this is scandalous behavior that only serves to insult the Balinese.

TRANSPORTATION

Getting There

Air: Bali's Ngurah Rai International Airport is three km south of Kuta and 12 km south of Denpasar. Garuda operates flights to Bali from most major Indonesian cities, plus flights from Singapore, Bangkok, Manila, Hong Kong, Tokyo, Europe, and Los Angeles. Qantas serves Bali direct from Sydney, Melbourne, Perth, and Darwin. Travelers with limited time should purchase advance roundtrip tickets and check on group tours and voucher discounts. Other international airlines generally stop in Jakarta, where you must transfer to a connecting Garuda flight.

Airport arrival involves customs, a hotel booking counter (more expensive hotels only), a poorly stocked tourist-information counter, a money changer desk, and transportation touts. Taxi tickets are sold at the taxi counter, or walk out 200 meters to the *bemo* stand for a cheap ride to Kuta. Hooking up with a hotel tout isn't a bad idea.

Other: Direct buses from Surabaya and Yogyakarta reach both Denpasar and beach resorts. From Denpasar it's an easy *bemo* ride to Kuta but watch your bags: Bali is full of clever thieves. Trains also reach Bali from Java; reserved seats are strongly recommended. Ships reach Bali from Ujung Padang Surabaya, and Nusa Tenggara.

Getting Around

Bemos: These serve every possible place on Bali and provide the cheapest but most time-consuming way to get around. From Kuta, Sanur, and Nusa Dua, *bemos* reach Denpasar, from where other *bemos* leave for all destinations. Prices are negotiable; unsuspecting tourists are always overcharged: always check the correct fare with your *losmen* manager or tourist office before setting off. See the "*Bemos* on Bali" chart for sample prices. *Bemo* charters run about US$25 daily; an excellent way for a large group to tour the island. Most *bemos* stop running at sunset and are infested with thieves—be cautious.

Motorcycles and Jeeps: Despite safety concerns, motorcycles and jeeps are certainly the best way to explore the back roads and find festivals. Motorcycles cost about US$5 per day. Be sure to purchase insurance, inspect the bike before leaving, and exercise caution on the crowded and dangerous Balinese roads. This is *not* the place to learn how to ride—dozens of foreigners die each year on beautiful Bali. Riders without international licenses must obtain them in Denpasar.

TOURIST INFORMATION

Tourist Information
Tourist Offices: Tourist offices in Kuta and Denpasar can help with maps and schedules of upcoming festivals. Ubud's privately operated tourist office is exceptional. Most offices are open daily 0900-1600 except Fridays, when they close around noon.

Diplomatic Offices: Consulates in Denpasar include those of Australia (tel. 35092, fax 31990), France (tel. and fax 33555), Japan (tel. 31308), and Norway and Denmark (tel. 35098 and 33053, fax 34834 and 38013). Consulates in Sanur include those of Germany (tel. 88826), Italy (tel. 88996), Sweden (tel. 88408), and the U.S. (tel. 88478). Other consulates include the Netherlands' (tel. 51094) in Kuta and Switzerland's (tel. 51735) in Legian.

Immigration: The Indonesian Immigration Office on Jl. Puputan Raya, near the main post office in Denpasar, is open Mon.-Thurs. 0900-1400, Fri. and Sat. to 1100. Another office is located on the road to the airport.

Mail: Mail should be directed to the small post offices in Kuta or Ubud, rather than the inconvenient postal center in Denpasar.

Telephone: International phone calls can be made from most major hotels and the telecommunications office in Denpasar. Calls are very expensive. The area code for southern Bali is 0361, northern Bali 0362, and eastern Bali 0366. To dial Bali from America or Europe, dial 011 (the international access code), 62 (the country code for Indonesia), the area code *minus the zero* (361 in most cases), and finally the local number.

Weather: Bali is best visited during the dry season from April to October, although the mon-

BEMOS ON BALI	
Airport-Kuta	Rp600
Kuta-Denpasar	Rp600
Denpasar-Sanur	Rp700
Denpasar-Ubud	Rp1000
Denpasar-Klungkung	Rp2000
Denpasar-Singaraja	Rp350
Denpasar-Kintamani	Rp1500
Denpasar-Padangbai	Rp2500
Denpasar-Gianyar	Rp120
Denpasar-Amlapura	Rp2600
Denpasar-Bedugul	Rp180
Denpasar-Tampaksiring	Rp1600

soons from November to March are relatively light and usually only disrupt the afternoons. Bali is overrun with Australians during the Christmas holidays and with Europeans in July and August, when advance hotel reservations are strongly recommended.

Health: Minor medical problems can be handled at the General Hospital in Denpasar or at several private clinics in Sanur and Nusa Dua. Call your consulate or the Bali Hyatt (tel. 88271) for emergency evacuation or for serious medical problems.

Suggested Readings
Other recommended guidebooks include Bill Dalton's *Indonesia Handbook* and *Bali Handbook,* published by Moon Publications; *Bali and Lombok,* published by Lonely Planet; *Bali* from APA; and *Bali* from Cadogan. Hugh Mabbett's *The Balinese* is an outstanding guide, plus it's available on the island. Background reading includes the originals such as *Island of Bali* by Miguel Covarrubias, *Dance and Drama In Bali* by Walter Spies, and *Trance in Bali* by Jane Belo. All three classics offer tremendous insight into Balinese culture but should be read *before* you arrive.

SHOPPING

Shopping on Bali runs the gamut from outstanding paintings and woodcarvings to mass-produced junk churned out for indiscriminate

BALINESE PERFORMING ARTS

The world marvels at the complexity, refinement, and grace of Balinese art. Life and artistic creation are completely intertwined to the point where there are no words for "art" or "artist"—everyone is *expected* to be an artist. Dance and drama come in three general forms: *wali* (sacred performances) that serve as rites of exorcism, *bebali* (ceremonial performances), and *bali balihan* (simple amusement) sponsored in staging areas and accompanied by *gamelan* orchestras. Balinese dance—from the squatting "Indian" stances to the darting eyes and elaborate costuming—are derived from Indian origins, though modified by centuries of Javanese and Balinese refinements. Like everything else on the island, dance and drama fashions change as new fads are absorbed by dance troupes and *gamelans*.

Ramayana Ballet

Together with the epic war story of the Mahabharta, the romantic adventure of the Ramayana forms the basis for most local dance and drama. Complete Ramayanas were rarely performed until just a few years ago, when the Denpasar Conservatory of Art and Dance began popularizing full performances with elaborately costumed performers and *gamelan gong* orchestras. Today, abbreviated spectacles are given in the tourist venues; excellent introductions to the lovely and enchanting story.

Barong (Kris Dance)

The *barong* dance serves to exorcise evil spirits and ensure the triumph of the *barong* white magic over the witch Rangda's black magic—a powerful and sacred struggle between the powers of good and evil. Magical masks must be treated with great respect: carved by village masters, purified with prayer, stored in a special pavilion, covered with sacred cloth to contain the magic, and meditated upon by the actors who believe that the spirits of the gods inhabit the masks when worn. Extensive offerings are first made to protect the performers against evil spirits. Then the *barong*—a furry female lion-like creature manipulated by two men—enters the stage. Slowly, the fingernails of Rangda slide around the corner. Evil and horrible, she is the stuff of nightmares. The fight seems lost until a group of *kris*-armed men attempt to kill Rangda. The evil witch uses her hypnotic magic to force the men into a suicidal stabbing spectacle, but this is soon countered by the superior power of the *barong*. The men are

later revived from their trances by holy water sprinkled by the village priests.

Kechak (Monkey Dance)

Picture this: A moonlit night in front of the temple, burning torches encircle the 100 dark-skinned men who sit on the ground in concentric circles, arms waving and continuously chanting "chak-a-chak chak" in perfect synchronization while the Ramayana is performed by costumed actors in the center. This is the *kechak*—Bali's most famous dance. A powerful and mesmerizing male chorus represents Hanuman's monkey army, which aids Rama in his quest for Sita, his captured queen. The hypnotic chanting serves to drive off black spirits and ensure the triumph of good over evil. There is good reason why the *kechak* seems so Hollywood. In 1928, German artist Walter Spies and Baron Von Messon (a film director) collaborated with Kathryn Myerson (a Martha Graham choreographer) to create the *kechak*, an event filmed by Von Messon!

Legong Dance

Balinese dance connoisseurs consider this highly stylized dance between two divine maidens the epitome of Balinese femininity, coquettishness, and supreme dance technique. Reciting a 13th-century East Javanese fable, three women enter the stage: a female attendant (*condong*) and two beautiful young girls tightly wrapped in gold brocade with headdresses of frangipani flowers. After a short introductory dance by the *condong*, the young girls (chosen for their beauty, suppleness, and pre-menstrual purity) perform a tightly-choreographed duet of dramatic gestures, angular body movements, and dozens of special hand movements that help tell the story. The nose-to-nose love scene is especially moving! The *legong* is worth seeing a dozen times.

Sanghyang (Trance Dances)

Balinese dances are often performed by auto-hypnotized trance dancers who have allowed the spirits of gods (*sanghyang*) to descend from heaven and take control of their actions. Rather than a sign of insanity or senility, trance is regarded as a higher, but completely natural, state of consciousness, a conduit between the gods and mortals. Closely related to the more familiar *legong* is *sanghyang dedari*, a shamanistic trance dance performed by two young girls. Both stand on the shoulders of male dancers

BALINESE PERFORMING ARTS

and exactly mimic the movements of their partners. After collapsing on the ground, the girls are revived by priests. *Sanghyang jaran,* the hobbyhorse trance dance called the "fire dance" in the tourist brochures, features an auto-hypnotized man possessed by horse spirits who runs through bonfires of coconut husks, kicking up a real firestorm. It's good fun when he punts burning coconuts into the tourist seats!

Topeng (Masked Drama)
Topeng relates the deeds and adventures of local Balinese kings and warriors; a symbolic meeting ground for spiritual and worldly concerns. The finely carved masks link the wearer to a spiritual realm charged with magic potency. Talented performers make their masks breathe, sweat, and cry, but amateurs are disparagingly referred to as carpenters who do nothing but push around wood. The special bond (*taksu*) that develops between the actor and his mask can only be discovered with meditation, prayers, dreams, and deep trance. Full-masked kings and gods are unable to talk—it is the half-masked clowns who provide the ribald and hilarious dialogue. Acting as interpreters for their dignified masters, clowns satirize the self-importance of their masters, teach lessons to the children, and make fun of the tourists. Recent additions include a long-nosed, camera-laden, and bad-mannered tourist; he draws the biggest laughs.

Other Dances
Kebyar: A dramatic and strenuous male solo dance that portrays the stylized movements of the Bali-

nese warrior. *Kebyar* can be performed in either a standing or sitting position, as popularized by Mario, the legendary dance musician.

Baris: A male warrior dance performed by soldiers brandishing spears, lances, *kris* daggers, swords, and shields.

Janger: A group of a dozen seated men and women who juxtapose the graceful femininity of the girls against the dramatic gestures of the aggressive male warriors.

Oleg Tambulilingan: A tender love duet between a lovely maiden and her handsome suitor that depicts the courting ritual of two bumblebees.

Barong Landung: Usually performed on Serangan Island, this giant puppet dance is sung in Balinese with plenty of bawdy humor.

Arja and **Drama Gong:** Balinese soap operas filled with love, humor, misery, and slapstick melodrama.

Performance Venues
Balinese dance is presented in highly abbreviated versions at tourist venues, though the best performances take place during temple anniversaries (*odalan*) held every 210 days; tourist offices have weekly schedules. Don't dismiss the tourist shows as worthless or inauthentic—they often feature some of the best dancers and musicians, besides providing their communities with an important source of income. It's best to see both: tourist performances are good introductions, and temple festivals uncover the emotional realism often missing from tourist performances.

---

tourists. First, check the shops in Kuta and visit the villages that concentrate on one particular craft. Best of all, find the artisans' homes for top quality at lowest prices. Most shops are located on the road between Denpasar and Ubud.

Paintings
Prior to the arrival of European artists in the 1930s, Balinese artists painted their *iders-iders* (temple scrolls), *langse* (large rectangular paintings), and astrological calendars in the formalized *wayang* style developed hundreds of years earlier in East Java. The introduction by Spies and Bonnet of Rousseauistic themes of strange forests, technicolor vegetation, and scenes of or-

dinary Balinese life brought fresh creativity. Bali's art center is in Ubud, where dozens of artists maintain home studios. Ubud's museums serve as excellent introductions to contemporary styles. Traditional *wayang* paintings and astrological calendars are produced in Klungkung and near Kamasan, two km south of Klungkung. Excellent *wayang* paintings are displayed on the ceiling of the Kerta Gosa (Hall of Justice) in Klungkung.

Woodcarving
Mas—a small town just south of Ubud—is Bali's woodcarving center. Lower prices are found in Batuan and Pujung. Styles range from primi-

tive forms to wild abstractions carved in glossy ebony and teak.

Other Crafts

Stonecarving remains one of the few Balinese arts that still serves religion rather than tourism. Batubulan is Bali's stonecarving center. Inexpensive batik is plentiful in Kuta. Gianyar and Pujung are weaving villages. Tenganan still produces a limited amount of double-*ikat* fabric. Celuk is known for silver and gold filigree work.

SPORTS

Surfing

Surfers usually start at Kuta where five- to six-foot tubes are common on the reef one km offshore. Bali's best surf is found at Ulu Watu, in the extreme south corner of the island. Take a *bemo,* hike three km, and descend down the tricky concrete stairway. Other possibilities include Padang Padang Beach north of Ulu Watu, Sanur Beach during the windy winter months,

Canggu Beach north of Kuta, and Nusa Lembongan island just opposite Sanur. Surfing shops can help with details and arrange package surf trips to Java.

Scuba

Diving is rather disorganized, though excellent reports have been received about Pulau Menjangan Nature Reserve (northwest Bali) and Tulamben (northeast coast) where a well-preserved wreck of an American steamship lies in shallow waters. Dive shops are found in Kuta and Sanur.

Warnings

Bemo thieves working in groups operate on all the popular tourist routes. Keep your *losmen* room tightly locked and windows closed at night. Brazen thieves will slide long bamboo poles into your room, hook your pack, and help themselves. It's best to leave your valuables in safety boxes, or carry them with you at all times. Drugs are almost completely unavailable in Bali. Magic-mushroom omelettes, soups, and shakes are still sold, but prices are stiff and potency is low.

SOUTHERN BALI

Each of the three beach resorts of southern Bali—Kuta, Sanur, and Nusa Dua—offers a distinct personality that attracts its own breed of travelers. Kuta is the home for budget and moderate-rate visitors. Sanur is the original luxury area set with older but luxurious hotels on a quiet beach. Nusa Dua is Bali's most expensive and luxurious spot—a bold attempt by the Indonesian government to limit tourism to one region and protect the environment from destruction. The logic is correct; without strong planning, the annual deluge of over 700,000 tourists would devastate the island.

None of the following beach resorts have much to do with the "real" Bali, but their superb beaches, shopping, restaurants, and nightlife make them excellent places to begin your vacation. All can serve as bases for easy day-trips to the temples and handicraft villages. Visitors intrigued with local culture can overnight in Ubud and other small villages in the east and north.

KUTA AND LEGIAN BEACHES

Once sleepy Balinese fishing villages popular only with backpackers, the rollicking honky-tonk tourist villages of Kuta and Legian are now almost completely overrun with Aussie students on holiday, bleach-blond surfers, European jet-setters, local motorcycle punks, pimps, and armies of hawkers. Kuta is mad, crazy, and completely chaotic, but *never* boring; one of the hottest scenes in Asia. Despite the negative press, Kuta still offers a fine beach, wonderful sunsets, outstanding shopping, nonstop cut-rate hedonism, and hundreds of economically priced accommodations. It's fortunate that the cancer of Kuta is confined to this relatively small enclave, an arrangement of great benefit to the rest of the island. Despite its dramatic and chaotic growth, if you accept it for what it is, Kuta remains a fun place to spend a few days.

Legian Beach, three km north of Kuta, is slightly removed from the raging vortex. Start your visit in either place, but don't let local pleasures seduce you from discovering the rest of the island.

Budget Accommodations

Kuta and Legian now offer a total of around 5,000 hotel rooms, ranging from luxurious US$500-per-night presidential suites with private swimming pools to simple *losmen* which cost US$3-15 depending on facilities.

Rooms under US$5 are simple affairs with bare walls, double beds, and shared bathrooms, but often include a free breakfast of tea and bananas. Rooms for US$6-15 should be comfortably furnished, include a private bath, and be very clean. *Losmen* and bungalows near the beach are more expensive, while the least expensive and quietest *losmen* are located on the back alleys, not on the main roads. Prices are negotiable during the slower spring and fall months but rise sharply in August for the French invasion and around Christmas and Easter for the Aussie wave. Categorizing a *losmen* as "budget" or "moderately priced" is difficult, since most offer older rooms under US$5, more luxurious cottages in the US$6-15 range, and a/c chalets for US$15-35.

The nicest places are the smaller, family-run homestays located down the smaller lanes, rather than the impersonal large hotels along noisy and polluted Kuta Beach Road. Hotel touts at the airport and bus station in Denpasar often provide free transportation to their *losmen,* an easy way to get settled for the first night. The following morning you can hunt for a *losmen* which better fits your needs and budget. A few samples in alphabetical order:

Arena's Cottages	US$6-10
Ayu's Bungalows	US$6-12
Baleka Beach Inn	US$8-18
Blue Ocean	US$12-18
Bruna Beach Inn	US$14-30
Dewa Baratha	US$10-18
Kuta Suci	US$6-15
Made Beach Inn	US$5-8
Mama Beach Club	US$6-10
Puspa Beach Inn	US$4-8
Taman Meka	US$4-6
Yoga Pension	US$3-6
Yulia Beach Inn	US$3-20

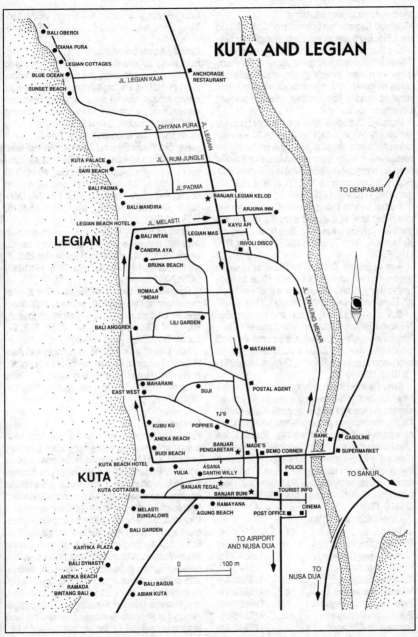

KUTA AND LEGIAN

BALI OBEROI
DIANA PURA
LEGIAN COTTAGES
BLUE OCEAN
SUNSET BEACH

JL. LEGIAN KAJA — **ANCHORAGE RESTAURANT**

JL. DHYANA PURA

JL. LEGIAN

KUTA PALACE — JL. RUM JUNGLE
SARI BEACH
BALI PADMA — JL. PADMA

TO DENPASAR

BALI MANDIRA

★ **BANJAR LEGIAN KELOD**

LEGIAN BEACH HOTEL — JL. MELASTI →

ARJUNA INN

KAYU API

LEGIAN

BALI INTAN
CANDRA AYA
BRUNA BEACH

LEGIAN MAS

RIVOLI DISCO

JL. TANJUNG MEKAR

ROMALA INDAH

BALI ANGGREK

LILI GARDEN

MATAHARI

MAHARANI
EAST WEST

SUJI

POSTAL AGENT

TJ'S

KUBU KU
ANEKA BEACH
BUDI BEACH

POPPIES

★ **BANJAR PENGABETAN**

MADE'S

BEMO CORNER

BANK

GASOLINE
SUPERMARKET

KUTA BEACH HOTEL

YULIA

ASANA SANTHI WILLY

POLICE

TO SANUR

KUTA

KUTA COTTAGES

★ **BANJAR TEGAL**
★ **BANJAR BUNI**

TOURIST INFO

MELASTI BUNGALOWS
BALI GARDEN

RAMAYANA
AGUNG BEACH

POST OFFICE

CINEMA

TO AIRPORT
AND NUSA DUA

KARTIKA PLAZA
BALI DYNASTY
ANTIKA BEACH
RAMADA
BINTANG BALI

BALI BAGUS
ABIAN KUTA

0   100 m

TO NUSA DUA

Moderate Accommodations

Kuta and Legian also boast dozens of hotels in the US$25-75 range, situated along Kuta Rd., along Kuta Beach Rd., and facing the ocean. These hotels represent great value, since many offer a/c rooms, private baths, and swimming pools at lower rates than the luxury hotels that now dominate the southern and northern beaches.

Poppies Cottages: Perhaps the most popular set of cottages in Kuta, Poppies has 24 well-designed chalets set in a beautiful garden. The restaurant is highly recommended. Perpetually filled, so make reservations well in advance. P.O. Box 378, Denpasar 80001, tel. (0361) 751059, fax (0361) 752364, US$65-80.

Aneka Beach Bungalows: A relatively new place just across the road from the beach. Attractive bunglows and swimming pool. Jl. Pantai Kuta, tel. (0361) 752892, fax (0361) 771777, US$45-80.

Asana Santhi Willy: Small hotel with clean rooms furnished with antiques. Real atmosphere and just two minutes from the beach. 18 Jl. Tegalwangi, tel. (0361) 751281, US$30-45.

Bali Mandira: This hotel, and nearby Bali Niksoma Beach Cottages, are somewhat isolated from Kuta and offer a welcome dose of peace and quiet. Facilities include tennis courts and water sports. Jl. Padma, Legian, tel. (0361) 751381, US$40-75.

Kuta Beach Hotel: A longtime favorite in the heart of Kuta and right on the beach. The hotel stands on the site of the original Kuta Beach Hotel, constructed as Kuta's first hotel in 1936 by a pair of wandering Americans. Robert Koke also introduced surfing to Bali (he once lived in Hawaii) and renamed the beach "Kuta" from the original Dutch spelling of "Koeta." The hotel is now managed by Natour. P.O. Box 393, Denpasar, tel. (0361) 751361, fax (0361) 751362, US$80-150.

Other midpriced hotels:

Bali Anggrek Inn	US$45-60
Garden View Cottages	US$40-55
Kuta Bungalows	US$45-60
Kuta Cottages	US$24-45
Melasti Bungalows	US$55-70
Palm Beach Cottages	US$50-80
Puri Rama Cottages	US$45-65
Ramayana Cottages	US$45-60
Sandi Phala	US$40-55
Yasa Samudra	US$25-45

Luxury Accommodations

Kuta and Legian's outer beaches are home to upscale hotels with every possible convenience, such as lobbies so large you get lost, open-air dining rooms, luxurious gardens, and evening *gamelan* performances around the swimming pool. Rates quoted below include the 17.5% government tax and service charges.

Kartika Plaza Beach Hotel: An Aerowisata-managed hotel (subsidiary of Garuda Airlines) set on a private beach with 82 bungalows, 305 guest rooms, five restaurants, two swimming pools, and sports facilities. P.O. Box 84, Denpasar, tel. (0361) 751067, fax (0361) 752475, US$140-260.

Santika Beach Hotel: A new complex with over 200 bungalows, three pools, tennis courts, family units, and convention facilities for 250. Jl. Kartika, tel. (0361) 751267, fax (0361) 751260, US$120-280.

Ramada Bintang Bali Resort: An almost overwhelming hotel complex with over 400 rooms and an enormous pool facing a private beach. P.O. Box 1068, Denpasar, tel. (0361) 753292, fax (0361) 753288, US$150-280.

Bali Oberoi: One of the finest hotels in Asia is tucked away at the northern end of Legian, between ricefields and the sea. Jl. Kayu Ayu, tel. (0361) 751061, fax (0361) 752791, US$180-460.

Restaurants

Kuta and Legian streets are packed with restaurants serving everything from Chinese seafood and Mexican tacos to Balinese steaks and fiery Padang dishes. Whether you choose a simple *warung* or a first-class retreat, the choices are excellent and reasonably priced. Breakfast at cozy Made's Warung is recommended for people-watching, music, vibes, cappuccino, and tasty Indonesian specialities. Dozens of seafood restaurants are found along the main road connecting Kuta and Legian. A popular option is to select your fish, sauce, and method of preparation. Three good choices in central Kuta include the Mini, Indah Sari, and Prawita Garden restaurants. Top yuppie hangout is Poppies Restaurant, where the food is almost as good as the atmosphere. An unusual way to finish the evening is sipping *tuak* (rice wine) with the Balinese in the *warungs* off Kuta Beach Road.

Practicalities

Kuta and Legian are self-contained communities with money changers, postal services, travel agents, motorcycle shops, one-hour photo labs, and whatever else you could possibly need. The tourist office on Jalan Airport distributes a surprisingly good collection of brochures and schedules. Mail can be directed either to the nearby post office or, better yet, to any of the private postal agents in Kuta and Legian. Garuda is in the Kuta Beach Hotel; Qantas is in Sanur's Bali Beach Hotel.

Transportation

Bemos to the Tegal *bemo* stop in Denpasar depart from "*bemo* corner" in the middle of town. Blue buses can be hailed on the main Kuta-Denpasar road. From Tegal, you must take a three-wheeler across town to the appropriate terminal. Kereneng Terminal is for buses and *bemos* to Ubud, Kintamani, Gianyar, Padangbai, Amlapura, and Tampaksiring. Ubung Terminal is for Singaraja, Gilimanuk, Bedugul. Fares are listed in the "*Bemos* on Bali" chart in the Bali Introduction.

SANUR BEACH

Bali's Waikiki is the quiet, safe, and more expensive alternative to Kuta and Legian. European and American tour groups come here to luxuriate in well-appointed hotels, attend poolside performances of *legong* and *wayang*, and feast on Balinese seafood—everything except walk on the beach! Sanur is a sleepy place where all the restaurants are hidden in hotel lobbies and nightlife fades away before midnight. On the other hand, the beach is broad and clean, swimming is safe, and sunrises over Nusa Penida are unforgettable.

Attractions

Sanur in the 1920s and '30s was the favored spot of Western artists such as Walter Spies and American anthropologist Margaret Mead. Most of the original residences have disap-

peared, except for the former home of Jean Le Mayeur, the Belgian impressionist painter who moved to Sanur in 1932 and stayed for 26 years. The house-turned-museum is shabby, smothered by the Bali Beach Hotel, and often closed; knock loudly, somebody will open the door.

Sanur water sports are superior to those in Kuta or Legian. Visitors can rent brightly painted outriggers to visit offshore islands, water-ski, tour the lagoon in glass-bottomed boats, snorkel over coral gardens, dive, spearfish, and windsurf. Culture, of the organized type, is equally plentiful. Public performances of Balinese dance are given nightly in all major hotels. Dinner plus show costs about US$20, but remember that many of Bali's finest dancers work the hotels in Sanur and Nusa Dua.

Moderate Accommodations

Sanur has little in the budget category but a good selection of middle-priced hotels in the US$25-50 range.

Rani Hotel: Cheap *losmen* (under US$10) are located on Jl. Segara near the American Consulate and the police station. West of the main road you'll find the Rani, Taman Sari, and Hotel Sanur Indah. All three *losmen* are old but fairly clean and cost under US$10. Jl. Segara, tel. (0361) 288578, US$6-10.

Tourist Beach Inn: An older *losmen* with clean and quiet rooms only 100 meters from the beach. Jl. Segara, tel. (0361) 288418, US$10-16.

Mars Hotel: Conditions are better and prices only somewhat higher at the Mars and Bali Continental hotels near the golf course. Rooms come with a/c, private baths, and hot water. 46 Jl. Hangtuah, tel. (0361) 288236, US$20-35.

Taman Agung Beach Inn: Not directly on the beach, but among the most pleasant *losmen* in Sanur. Breakfast is included. Both fan and a/c rooms are available. Jl. Tanjung Sari, tel. (0361) 288549, US$8-12 fan, US$15-22 a/c.

Luxury Accommodations

Sanur is a beach resort almost completely lined with first-class hotels and luxurious bungalows hidden beneath swaying palms.

Tanjung Sari Hotel: A small bungalow resort established in 1962 and still considered one of the coziest and most charming spots in

SANUR

TO DENPASAR

TO GIANYAR

JL. SANUR

ANANDA HOTEL

SANUR AGUNG HOTEL
SANUR VILLAGE HOTEL

ALIT'S BUNGALOWS

BALI CONTINENTAL

MARS HOTEL

DIWANG KARA HOTEL

LE MAYEUR MUSEUM

GOLF COURSE

BALI BEACH HOTEL

LENNY RESTAURANT

BALI BEACH COTTAGES

TAMAN SARI

RANI HOTEL

POLICE

TOURIST BEACH INN

JL. SEGARA

POST OFFICE

U.S. CONSULATE

SEGARA VILLAGE HOTEL

MARKET

SATAY HOUSE

BALI QUEEN HOTEL

BARUNA BEACH HOTEL

BALI MOON RESTAURANT

SINDHU BEACH HOTEL

IRAMA INN

LA TAVERNA BALI HOTEL

JL. TANJUNG SARI

GAZEBO BEACH HOTEL

BALI SANUR BUNGALOWS

JL. BAJA LETKOL NGURAH RAI

TANJUNG SARI BUNGALOWS

BUNGALOWS 2

SETIA TOURS

SANTRIAN 1 HOTEL
WERDHAPURA HOTEL

PACTO TOURS

SWAZTIKA RESTAURANT

LAGHAWA INN

RAMAYANA RESTAURANT

TAMAN AGUNG

VILLA BATUR

KULKUL RESTAURANT

BALI SANUR 2 HOTEL

0   0.5 km

BALI HYATT

LEGONG RESTAURANT

WISMA BAHARI

SANTRIAN 2 HOTEL

TO KUTA, AIRPORT

SEMAWANG BEACH INN

SANUR BEACH HOTEL

© MOON PUBLICATIONS INC

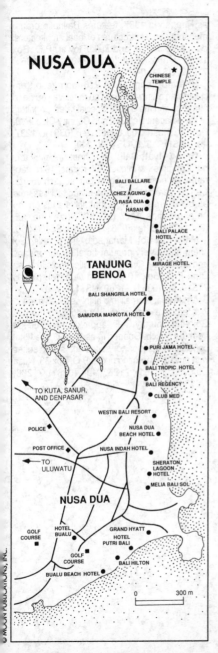

Sanur. This elegant retreat features 24 two-story native-style bungalows, all impeccably furnished with Indonesian antiques and set in an exotic tropical garden. Fabulous gardens, outstanding food, and genuine hospitality. Jl. Tanjung Sari, tel. (0361) 288441, fax (0361) 287930, US$100-280.

Sanur Beach Hotel: Operated by Garuda's Aerowisata group, the Sanur Beach has recently been completely renovated to compete with the finer hotels in Asia. All possible facilities, including a pool beyond belief. However, watch out for the prostitutes who work the adjacent Semawang Beach Inn. P.O. Box 279, Denpasar, tel. (0361) 288011, fax (0361) 287566, US$140-280.

Bali Beach Hotel: The granddaddy of Sanur is the immense Bali Beach Hotel, erected during the Sukarno era in the early 1960s. After Bali's tallest hotel structure was completed in 1965, *banjar* elders demanded and were granted an islandwide ordinance which stopped all new hotel construction higher than a palm tree. The rule has since been adopted all over the island, even in the exclusive resort of Nusa Dua. Despite the monolithic size, the Bali Beach features good service, 14 restaurants, an adjacent six-hole golf course popular with Japanese tourists, all possible water sports, offices for Garuda and Qantas, and nightly performances of Balinese dance around an immense swimming pool. No need to ever leave your hotel. Jl. Hang Tuah, tel. (0361) 288271, fax (0361) 287917, US$110-260.

NUSA DUA BEACH

Bali's most luxurious and exclusive hotels are located on Bukit Peninsula, at the southernmost extremity of the island. This full-scale, totally self-contained tourist enclave forms the centerpiece of the Indonesian government's master plan for regional tourism. Though completely isolated from the heartland of Bali, Nusa Dua is blessed with a superb beach and over a dozen four- and five-star hotels designed in traditional Balinese styles.

Bukit Peninsula Attractions
Several worthwhile sights are located around the desolate peninsula.

Uluwatu: Top draw is this small but superbly situated temple, considered one of the six most sacred on Bali. The structure is unimpressive but views are breathtaking, especially at sunset.

Surfing: Some of Indonesia's finest surfing beaches are near Uluwatu. Turn at the sign 200 meters before the parking lot and hike two km down to Sulubun Beach. Simple *warung* provide food and accommodation.

Benoa Harbor: Private yachts in need of fresh crew sometimes moor in Bali's principal harbor.

Serangan Island: Turtle Island is touristy but worth visiting during major festivals.

Accommodations

Nusa Dua now has all the major international chains in the southern portion of the peninsula, and a handful of locally owned and less expensive hotels in the northern stretches.

Most hotels offer complimentary transportation from the airport. Private taxis cost about US$6.

Rasa Dua: Hotels under US$15 are near the fishing village of Tanjung Benoa. Most are clean and comfortable and good value. Rasa Dua and other nearby homestays such as Hasan Homestay and Chez Agung are situated across the road from the beach. Jl. Pratama, Tanjung Benoa, tel. (0361) 71751, US$12-28.

Nusa Dua Beach Hotel: The region's first hotel, home to local and foreign dignitaries such as Reagan in 1987, features Balinese craftsmanship and all structures of local architecture: *puri, bale banjar,* and *kulkul* tower. P.O. Box 1028, Denpasar, tel. (0361) 71210, fax (0361) 71229, US$140-200.

Sheraton Lagoon: A 276-room resort enclosing an artificial lagoon so massive you need a map to find the beach. Special rates for golfers at the adjacent Bali Golf and Country Club. P.O. Box 77, Nusa Dua 80363, tel. (0361) 71237, fax (0361) 71326, US$200-340.

Grand Hyatt Bali: An almost unbelievable hotel complex with over 700 rooms, 10 restaurants, six swimming pools, a/c, squash courts, Camp Nusa for kids, scuba-diving facilities, and an old Balinese temple that still stands on the hotel grounds. P.O. Box 53, Nusa Dua, tel. (0361) 71188, fax (0361) 72038, US$200-380.

Melia Bali Sol: Managed by the Spanish Sol chain and a very popular hotel for Europeans and Japanese. One of the livelier spots in Nusa Dua. P.O. Box 1048, Nusa Dua, tel. (0361) 71510, fax (0361) 71360, US$180-240.

Amanusa: A small and highly exclusive resort located on a grassy knoll overlooking the Bali Golf and Country Club, approximately one km from the beach. Opened in early 1993, the hotel consists of 32 superior suites and seven suites with private swimming pools. P.O. Box 33, Nusa Dua, tel. (0361) 71267, fax (0361) 71266, US$360-840.

CENTRAL BALI

Bali's scenic wonders, architectural heritage, and artistic achievements are best experienced in the land located between Denpasar and the mountains. Central Bali is a region blessed with terraced ricefields carved exquisitely out of hills and valleys, densely settled villages surrounded by groves of coconut palms, and long stretches of sandy beaches almost completely unvisited by foreign travelers. Highlights can easily be seen on day-trips from the southern beach resorts, but those who wish to enjoy a more traditional side of Bali can easily steer clear of the tourist stomping grounds and spend a few days unwinding in a remote Balinese village. *Bemos* connect all the towns, but the finest approach is to simply walk from village to village, across the ricefields and through the forests.

Described below are all the major attractions, but be forewarned: all are badly overrun with super-aggressive salesmen who rank among the most obnoxious in Asia. Quite honestly, it is unnecessary to visit any of the following temples if you intensely dislike touts and beggars. To minimize the ordeal, never join a group tour (unless you want to serve as a moving target) but rather hire a motorcycle or jeep, get an early start, and bring along patience and humor. Most temples now collect fees for parking, entrance, and sash rental, a minor irritation that can be avoided by bringing along your own sash. Visitors wearing shorts or immodest halter tops are often denied entrance; arrive well dressed or expect to be turned away.

DENPASAR

Bali's largest city is a disaster: roaring motorcycles, smelly buses, unending congestion, and drab modern architecture. Denpasar is also the island's transportation center through which all *bemos* circulate, and the government hub for postal services, immigration, hospitals, and telecommunications. Conduct sightseeing and official business early; government offices and museums close in the early afternoon.

Attractions
Denpasar (Badung is the local name) has few charms aside from an excellent museum and some antique shops on the main road. First visit the Badung Tourist Office for maps and information on transportation and upcoming festivals. The Bali Museum off Puputan Square houses an outstanding collection of masks, puppets, and archaeological treasures from Neolithic implements to recent discoveries. Museum architecture incorporates three distinct styles of Balinese palaces: the main building resembles the Karangasem palaces of eastern Bali, the left structure is modeled after the northern Singaraja style, and on the right is a Tabanan prototype from western Bali. Adjacent Pura Jaganatha is a state temple dedicated to Sanghyang Widi, supreme god of Bali Hinduism.

Shoppers should pause briefly at the Sanggraha Handicraft Center in Tohpati on the outskirts of Denpasar en route to Batubulan. This government-run artists' cooperative sells quality merchandise at low, fixed prices; useful reference points for further shopping.

Denpasar's cultural offerings include student rehearsals and a spectacular yearly Bali Arts Festival held at the KOKAR Academy of Art. *Wayang kulit* and *legong* are performed weekly at the Pemecutan Palace Hotel.

Accommodations
Nobody stays in Denpasar, but if stranded near the Tegal *bemo* terminal, try the Taman Suci Hotel just across the street or the inexpensive Penginapan Tambora on Jalan Tambora.

Superior alternatives include the Dutch-built Bali Hotel near city center, where a/c rooms cost from US$30, and the Pemecutan Palace Hotel a few blocks north of the Tegal Terminal. Rooms here with fan cost only US$15-25.

Transportation
Denpasar has four *bemo* terminals that serve different parts of the island. All are connected by three-wheelers. Tegal serves Kuta, Legian, Sanur, and the airport. Kereneng serves all towns in central and eastern Bali including

DENPASAR

UBUNG BUS STATION
TO TABANAN
TO BLAHKIU
JL. MARUTI
JL. HOS T.JOKROAMINOTO
JL. SETIABUDI
JL. KARTINI
JL. YUDISTRA
JL. NANGKA
JL. PATIMURA
KOKAR ACADEMY OF ART
JL. SERUNI
JL. RATNA
KODAK OFFICE (FOR DRIVERS LICENSE)
BABI GULING GIANYAR
JL. SUPRATAM
TO GIANYAR AND UBUD
JL. VETERAN
ADI YASA
BELIMBING
JL. TERATAI
GARUDA AIRLINES
STADIUM
JL. N.A. KEDODONG
HOTEL AMI
MERPATI
WISMA TARUNA (YHA)
JL. G.K. SAHADEWA
JL. RAMBUTAN
JL. ANGSOKA
JL. D. PATJAR
JL. PALAWA
TO LEGIAN
JL. DR. WAHIDIN
BAJAI TO KERANENG
RESTAURANT ATOOM BARU
JL. ARJUNA
BANK NEGARA INDONESIA
BALI HOTEL
LOSMEN ELIM
JL. KEPUNDUNG
JL. MELATI
KAMBOJA
KERENENG BUS STATION
RESTAURANT HONG KONG
LOKITSARI SHOPPING CENTER TEGAL TRANSPORT
JL. GAJAHMADA
RESTAURANT SELERA
TELEPHONE OFFICE TELEGRAPH AND TELEX
JL. RIDJASA
G. SEMERU
KUMBASARI SHOPPING CENTER
PASAR BADUNG
BANK DAGANG NEGARA
JL. TERNATE
JL. UDAJANA
JL. KALIASEM
BADUNG TOURIST OFFICE
BALI MUSEUM
JL. HAYAMWURUK
ART CENTER KESIMON
G. MERPATI
G. BATUR
G. KAWI
G. TAMRIN
BERINGIN JAYA
JL. BELITON
JL. LET REGUG
TO SANUR
PEMECUTAN PALACE HOTEL
JL. HASANNUDIN
SUCI TERMINAL
JL. DEBES
JL. SUTJI
JL. KADJENG
TERMINAL TEGAL
M A SHOPPING CENTER
PROTESTANT CHURCH
JL. PUTRA
TWO BROTHERS LOSMEN
JL. G WILIS
JL. BUKTTUNGGAL
JL. MAJ JEND SUTOJO
JL. PITJA
RUMAH MAKAN AYAM TALIWANG
HOTEL DENPASAR
JL. DIPONEGORO
JL. M T HARYONO
JL. LIMA BESAR
JL. SUDIRMAN
JL. IMAM BONJOL
LIBI SHOPPING CENTER
TO AIRPORT AND KUTA BEACH
JL. YOS SUDARSO
DINAS PARIWISATA FOR BALI
GOVERNOR'S OFFICE
POST OFFICE
IMMIGRATION OFFICE
PAKET POS
HOTEL ARTA
BOURAQ AIRLINES
JL. NITI MANDALA
R.S.U. PUSAT AT SANGLAH
JL. NIAS
TO BENOA

0   250m

BOB RACE

legong *dancers*

Ubud, Klungkung, Padangbai, Amlapura, and Kintamani. Ubung in the far northwest corner serves the north and west of Bali including Gilimanuk, Sangeh, Mengwi, and Singaraja. Ubung is also the departure point for buses to Java.

NORTHWEST OF DENPASAR

Attractions in southwest Bali are generally visited on day-trips from Kuta and Denpasar. The westernmost sections beyond Tabanan are rarely seen, except from the window of a speeding bus. *Bemos* to Sangeh, Mengwi, and Tanah Lot leave from Denpasar's Ubung Terminal.

Sempidi, Lukluk, And Kapal
Sempidi features a trio of temples carved in the unrestrained styles of western Bali. Lukluk is known for its finely carved Pura Dalem. Kapal is a ceramic center which produces folksy, gaudy pottery articles as well as temple ornamentation and sacred motifs. Shops along the road display a bizarre collection of religious figures, heroes from pop culture, ceramic girl scouts emblazoned with hideous paint jobs, and other figures more closely related to Tijuana than Balinese sensibilities. While in Kapal, visit the Majapahit-period Pura Sada near the central marketplace. The 64 stone seats, similar to megalithic ancestral shrines, commemorate warriors who died in battle.

Tanah Lot
Evoking a misty Chinese painting, the small pagoda-like temple at Tanah Lot is but one of a series of splendid water temples which honor the guardian spirits of the sea. Situated off a black volcanic sand shore, Tanah Lot is one of the most photographed and sketched temples in Asia. The monument was constructed by a Javanese priest remembered for his successful efforts in strengthening the religious beliefs of the people. Ironically, anything even faintly resembling a spiritual atmosphere is dissipated by the 250 meters of souvenir stalls which clog the approach. At peak tourist hours (anytime after 1000 and at sunset), it's a mob scene where fees are extracted to park your motorcycle, hire a sash, take pictures, and enter the temple. Sunsets are the worst: arrive at the crack of dawn.

Mengwi
The quiet town of Mengwi once served as an important regional capital until 1891 when the dynasty was defeated and subjugated by the neighboring rival kingdoms of Badung (Denpasar) and Tabanan. Mengwi's superb Pura Taman Ayun is the second-largest state temple on the island. The original structure dates from 1634 but was restored and enlarged in 1937. Surrounded by a lily-clogged moat, Pura Taman Ayun is dedicated to the ancestors of the Mengwi Dynasty and features dozens of shrines capped by *meru* roofs which complement the tranquility of the sleepy grounds. The adjacent art center and restaurant are equally deserted except when tour buses arrive.

Sangeh
Built by the royal family of Mengwi in the 17th century, the holy monkey forest of Sangeh is dedicated to Vishnu as a place of quiet meditation. Today it functions as a *subak* temple where hundreds of wild and aggressive monkeys earn their keep by stealing glasses, cameras, and hats from tourists. Before entering the darkened walkway, secure all valuables

and carry a stick to fend off the beasts. Booty can sometimes be repurchased from Balinese touts who control the mischievous animals. Visitors foolish enough to arrive with a tour group will find Sangeh a rude place of pestering peddlers and begging children; otherwise, it's a quiet and serene nature reserve in the middle of an enchanted forest.

DENPASAR TO UBUD

The road from Denpasar to Ubud has evolved into a nonstop lineup of villages that specialize in particular crafts. Much is junk churned out for indiscriminate tourists, while some is high-quality art priced accordingly. From Denpasar, first visit the Sanggraha Craft Center for a general overview of crafts at fixed prices. Leave early enough to catch the outstanding *barong* performance at 0900 in Batubulan.

Batubulan

Renowned for its decorative stonecarving, Batubulan offers a handful of shops where child artisans chip away to liberate the heroes, gods, and demons from the silent blocks. Stone sculpture is seldom bought by tourists and therefore remains a nearly intact artform. The talent of its artisans can be seen on the gate of Batubulan's Pura Puseh, only 150 meters east of the main road. The outstanding gateway is mindful of South Indian gateways, though the sculptures aren't old but modern copies taken from library books borrowed from the Archaeological Service.

Batubulan's great attraction is the daily 0900 performance of the *barong*. Shows are given at several locations marked by parked tourist buses. While strictly geared to the tourist, all are professional and provide great photographic opportunities.

Celuk

Bali's silver- and goldsmithing centers are located at Kuta, Kamasan near Klungkung, and in Celuk, where generations of craftsmen have maintained their hereditary trade. Silver filigree work here is amazingly detailed with designs of vivid imagination. Prices soar when the tourist buses pull up between 1000 and 1130 but return to more sensible levels in the early afternoon.

Sukawati And Batuan

These large crafts villages 15 km from Denpasar specialize in both wind chimes and *wayang kulit* production. Puppet masters still practice their craft in Puri Sukawati. Shopping is best in the two-story Pasar Seni just opposite the marketplace. Batuan is a painting and weaving village where young painters continue to paint in traditional styles. Batuan is also famous for its dances; performances of *baris* and *topeng* are given daily at 0900.

Mas

Mas is the woodcarving center of Bali. While many of the shops now churn out mass-produced knockoffs for the international market, exquisite and pricey pieces are still produced by Balinese masters. For the best prices, comb the back lanes and allow enough time to bargain while sipping coconut milk. Ida Bagus Nyana, Ida Bagu Gelodog, and Ida Bagus Ambara are all well-known carvers of masks. Both Ida Bagus Anom and I Wayan Muka carve phantasmagoric masks used in traditional dramas. The site of Pura Taman Pule is believed to have been built on the original site chosen by Niaratha, a 15th-century Javanese immigrant credited with founding many of Bali's most sacred temples. Return to Sakah and continue east to Blahbatuh.

Blahbatuh

The remarkable Pura Gaduh features a massive head of the fearsome mythological giant, Kebo Iwo, a legendary strongman who served as the final minister of Bedulu prior to its conquest by the Majapahit Kingdom in 1343. It's said he carved with his fingernails many of the ancient stone monuments on Bali.

The nearby village of Bona is known for its basketry and nightly performances of *kechak*. Unfortunately, many of the companies have lost their touch and now present overpriced, disappointing shows.

Bukit Dharma

North of Blahbatuh near Kutri is the hill of Bukit Dharma, from where a steep path leads to the worn but arresting statue of King Airlangga's mother. Surrounded by flames, she is in the shape of the six-armed goddess of death Durga delivering the death blow atop a bull possessed by a demon; considered one of the most finely

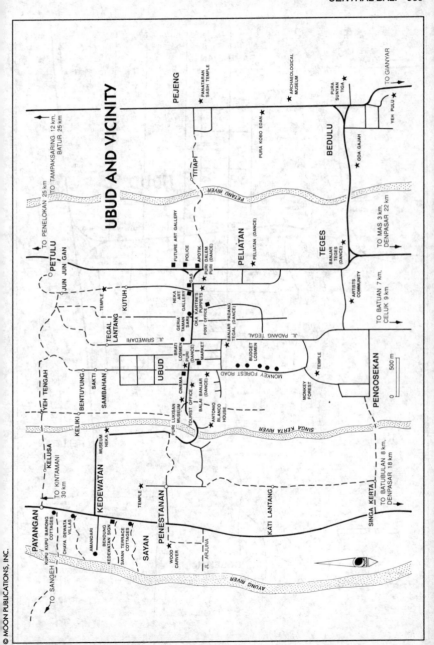

UBUD AND VICINITY

© MOON PUBLICATIONS, INC.

TO SAYAN

ULUN UBUD COTTAGES

★ MUSEUM NEKA

ANANDA COTTAGES

SAMBAHAN

JL. SUWATA

JL. SRIWEDARI

TO PENELOKAN

PURI BINGI NAMBE ★

ANOM'S DANCE SCHOOL

AGUNG PASTI'S ●

PURI MERTA SARI BUNGALOWS ●

UBUD

FUTURE ART GALLERY

TELEPHONE

BUNUNG MERTA BUNGALOWS

SITI BUNGALOWS

SUCI INN ●

HOTEL TJAMPUHAN

BEGGARS BUSH

PUGIG ●

PURI LUKISAN MUSEUM ★

HOTEL PURI SARASWATI

CINEMA

PURI SAREN HOTEL ★

BRATI ●

NEKA ART GALLERY ●

POLICE

BANK

HOTEL MENARA

TOURIST OFFICE ★

BALAI BANJAR (DANCE)

MARKET

OKA KARTINI'S ●

SADIA ●

SARI ●

★ ANTONIO BLANCO HOUSE

TO PENESTANAN

OKAWATI'S ● ●

BADRA ●

SHANA ●

TANTRI ●

PURI DALEM PURI (DANCE) ★

POST OFFICE

TIRTASARI PELIATAN (DANCE) ★

SURAWAN ●

SPORTS FIELD

★ BANJAR PADANG TEGAL (DANCE)

JL. SUGRIWA

JL. JNBAWAN

KARYAWAN ●

FROG POND INN ●

KARSA MAHA ●

MUDITA ●

MENDRA ●

KARSI ●

JAYA ●

WASRA'S ●

UBUD INN ●

MONKEY FOREST HIDEWAY ●

JL. HANOMAN

MONKEY FOREST ★

KUBUKU WINDCHIMES ★

DETRI INN ●

JATI ●

JL. COKGEDERAI

PELIATAN

MADRI ●

BALI BREEZE ●

★ COMMUNITY OF ARTISTS

BANJAR TEGES (DANCE) ★

TO GIANYAR

PENGOSEKAN

TO PENESTANAN AND SAYAN

TO MAS AND DENPASAR

TO BATUAN AND CELUK

OKA ●

0 — 500 m

© MOON PUBLICATIONS, INC.

wrought sculptures left from the early Pejeng Kingdom. Views of Sanur and eastern Bali can be enjoyed through the fields of coconut palms.

Gianyar

The small, bustling administrative center of Gianyar is known for its hand-woven and hand-dyed textiles produced by textile shops and factories scattered along the main road. The workers are too poor themselves to wear any of the *sarongs* they make—they wear cheap dresses instead. The old Gianyar Palace in the center of town is one of the few royal palaces that survived the Dutch invasion in the early 20th century. Closed to the public; visitors can peer in through the gates.

Sidan Pura Dalem

Gianyar is disappointing, but Pura Dalem near Sidan is perhaps Bali's finest Temple of the Dead. To the right of the extraordinary split-gate entrance stands a *kulkul* drum tower covered with reliefs of tormented sinners being punished by hungry dogs and devil giants. To the left is Pura Rajapati, capped by three electric lights! Beyond the gate in the right corner is the throne of witch-queen Rangda. Don't miss this temple.

UBUD

Ubud is the art and culture center of Bali, the place to get closer to the *real* Bali. Culturally speaking, Ubud is to Bali as Yogyakarta is to Java and Kyoto to Japan. Ubud lacks a tourist infrastructure; big hotels with nightclubs and golf courses are not here, though luxurious bungalows with comfortable amenities are springing up by the week. Your first impression on arrival will be negative. Central Ubud is a messy place plagued with belching *bemos*, an uninspiring modern market, and tacky souvenir shops. Don't be discouraged. Within five minutes of *bemo* corner you'll discover idyllic *losmen* perched precariously in the middle of verdant ricefields, splashing rivers filled with smiling children, and small villages where many of Bali's finest artists can teach you the secrets of batik, *gamelan*, *barong*, mask carving, painting, and the art of the *dalang*.

Ubud was popularized in the 1930s by Walter Spies and Rudolf Bonnet, two Western artists who moved here to study and then revolutionized contemporary Balinese art. At the time, traditional religious art had degenerated into highly formalized and rigid forms no longer in demand by the Balinese themselves. German artist Spies and Dutchman Bonnet demonstrated to the Balinese artists that painting could be free of set formulas, using real people in a natural environment rather than courtly models. They introduced the concept of the three dimensions, the imaginative use of strong colors, modern graphic elements, a wider range of subject matter, and provided the materials for the work. A new realism was born which soon developed into a sophisticated, naturalistic style. Ubud and neighboring communities today support hundreds of artisans who are constantly creating new styles of painting and sculpture.

Attractions

Ubud Museum: Puri Lukisan ("Palace of Paintings") includes a range of art spanning the years from the 1930s to the present, arranged in chronological order to demonstrate the evolution of contemporary styles. Set around beautiful gardens of fountains, statues, and pools, Puri Lukisan features exclusively Balinese art created by Kembang, Lempad, Medja, Gerudug, and a small room with examples of the gaudy Young Artists School. Unfortunately, the non-air-conditioned museum is poorly lit and neglected to the point of scandal.

Antonio Blanco House: Erotic sketches and the illustrated poetry of Ubud's mad Filipino-Catalan artist can be viewed inside his private residence in Campuan. Better than the gallery is the airy workspace where Antonio watches American soap operas on his satellite TV.

Museum Neka: Ubud's finest museum exhibits painters from all over Indonesia as well as foreign artists who have worked on Bali. The complex is divided into seven buildings arranged around distinct styles and artistic movements: Room 1 offers traditional Kamasan and Pengosekan artwork; Room 2 features 16 outstanding pieces by I Gusti Nyoman Lempadi; Room 3 is devoted to Affandi portraits, three dancers by Anton, and works by Azia; Room 4 specializes in foreign artists such as Spies, Bonnet, and Arie Smit; Room 5 boasts more work by Meier, Snel, Blanco, Friend, Covarrubias, and 15 outstanding works by W.G. Hofker, a Dutch artist who lived on Bali from 1938 to 1944; Room 6 serves as a pavilion-library. Neka is a superb art trip.

Artist Villages: Penestanan, a small village one km through the ricefields beyond Campuan, is where the Young Artists School developed in the mid-1950s under the influence of Arie Smit. Here, strong colors and bold modern designs are favored over the soft pastels of their predecessors; it's a style not beloved by everyone. Pengosekan, five km south of Ubud, is another famous artist village known for its classical traditions and production of more lucrative decorative arts. Homestays and study groups are found in both villages.

Monkey Forest: Monkey Forest Road curves around the perimeter of Ubud's leading tourist trap; wear a sash and feed the monkeys (hold onto your camera).

Walks Around Ubud

Ubud's finest experience isn't touring museums or temples, but rather a long day of meandering through the stunning ricefields, deep gorges, and swift flowing rivers. Suddenly, Bali becomes a magical place, far removed from the hype of hustle of the tourist traps.

Northern Ricefields: Ubud's best hikes are north through the fields to Petulu. Motorbikes can maneuver along the narrow paths, but it's more pleasant to allow four-six hours on foot. From *bemo* corner near the cinema, walk north through Sambahan, Sakti, and Bentuyung (end of the paved road) to the right fork toward Jun Jun Gan. Turn left at the intersection in Jun Jun Gan, pass the temple, and take the right fork to Petulu and the heron sanctuary. Rather than hiking down the main road, return to Jun Jun Gan and walk south past the small temple to Kutuh and the Neka Art Gallery in Ubud.

Monkey Forest Walk: Walk south down Monkey Forest Road, pause for coffee and music at Kubu Ku Windchimes, and continue south to Pengosekan and then west to Sing Kerta. Then it's north to Penestanan and back to Ubud; a wonderful tour of monkeys, windchimes, and artist villages.

Northwest to Sayan: Take the trail north under the viaduct (*before* the river) to Keliki and Yeh Tengah, then west to Kelusa and the main road at Payangan. Pause at Sayan Terrace

Cottages for coffee and explore the scenic Ayung River valley before returning to Ubud.

East to Pejeng: Hike east from the Apotik to the Petanu River, Titiapi, and Pejeng to tour the temples, the museum, Yeh Pulu, and Goa Gajah; an outstanding combination of scenery and history.

Budget Accommodations

Ubud has over 100 *losmen* that offer simple but clean rooms for US$4-10. Most have been constructed to resemble traditional Balinese family compounds and provide a welcome relief from the commercialism of Kuta and Sanur, while others are residences of painters and dancers who offer personal instruction on the performing arts. The Bina Wisata Tourist Office near the main crossroads can tell you about budget homestays operated by performing artists, upcoming festivals, dance performances, shuttles down to Kuta and Candidasa, and proper dress for temple touring.

The sheer range is almost staggering, though homestays are most plentiful down Monkey Forest Rd. and tucked away on the small lanes in all directions. Others, less touristy and much quieter, are found in the neighboring villages of Campuan, Penestanan, Peliatan, and Pengosekan.

After arriving in Ubud, it's best to inspect a few for the perfect combination of atmosphere and amenities. Travelers who wish to escape the schlock shops of Ubud should go directly to one of the smaller villages mentioned above or check those homestays well off Monkey Forest Road. Discounts are given for longer stays; expect to pay US$3-5 per day on a monthly basis. The following is only a small sampling of the possibilities.

Hotel Menara: Bungalows with rooms overlooking the ricefields. Learn *gamelan* and dance, and peruse their very complete arts library. Founded by Cokorda Mas, resident connoisseur who coestablished the Ubud Museum in the 1950s. Ubud Road (opposite the museum), US$5-10.

Puri Merta Sari Bungalows: Clean and comfortable surroundings in traditional Balinese architecture. Good breakfast and friendly management. 12 Jl. Suweto, US$5-10.

Agung Rai Pasti's: Some of the most memorable homestays in Ubud are those overlooking one of the many small streams which flow through the district. This favorite is small (five rooms) but worth the effort to locate up a small alley past Hans Snel's Bungalows. Jl. Kejeng, US$5-8.

Frog Pond Inn: Another dependable spot with friendly managers and good vibes. Monkey Forest Rd., US$4-10.

Masih Homestay: Beautiful rooms rented by Ibu Masih, who will teach you Balinese dance and talk all night about his art. Monkey Forest Rd., US$5-10.

Monkey Forest Hideaway: Spacious, airy rooms right over the forest, plus a small swimming pool where local children splash in the afternoons. Located at the bottom of the hill on the right-hand side just before the forest. Monkey Forest Rd., US$5-15.

Moderate Accommodations

Ubud also boasts dozens of semiluxurious bungalows for US$20-45, often constructed in the layout of a Brahman palace with individual *bale* converted to Western tastes with full bathrooms and front verandas. All offer large rooms with native furniture, modern bathrooms, and verandas with views of inner courtyards or across ricefields and rivers.

Gunung Merta Bungalows: A smaller homestay recommended by several travelers for the hospitality and insight provided by owner Ida Bagus Tilem. Peliatan, Ubud 80571, tel. (0361) 95463, US$20-30.

Hotel Puri Saren Agung: Cokorda Agung, descendant of Ubud's noble family, operates bungalows within his royal compound, decorated with handcarved furniture and Balinese antiques. Traditional dance performances are given weekly within the courtyard. Puri Saren is the oldest hotel in Ubud and dates from the Dutch era. P.O. Box 15, Ubud, tel. (0361) 28871, US$35-50.

Oka Kartini's: Oka's homestay features lovely bungalows surrounded by gardens and elaborately carved statuary. She also gives good prices on artwork, stores your luggage, and finds you a dance instructor. Excellent puppet shows given weekly. Oka's is opposite the big Neka Art Gallery in Padangtegal, US$25-40.

Hotel Puri Saraswati: Central location and good reputation have long made this one of Ubud's classic Balinese homestays. The former royal palace also features a pool and extensive gardens. On the main road adjacent to Ubud's Saraswati Temple. US$35-45.

Okawati's Homestay: One of the oldest, and therefore most legendary, homestays in Ubud offers quiet rooms overlooking verdant sawah and pool. The restaurant is still operated by Oka herself. Just off Monkey Forest Rd., tel. (0361) 95063, US$15-35.

Siti (Hans Snel) Bungalows: Now managed by his wife, Hans Snel's half-dozen bungalows and orchid gardens are another favorite with return visitors. P.O. Box 227, Denpasar, tel. (0361) 28690, US$35-45.

Cahaya Dewata: Ubud's best views are found in the bungalows overlooking the Ayung River in Kedewatan. Both Cahaya Dewata and nearby Kupu Kupu Barong Cottages (see below) are worth visiting for their cafes even if you can't afford the bungalows. Kedewatan, Ubud, tel. (0361) 35140, US$45-60.

Hotel Tjampuhan: Older but well-maintained bungalows in a spectacular location overlooking the Ubud River. Walter Spies stayed here in the 1930s. P.O. Box 15, Denpasar 80001, tel. (0361) 28704, fax (0361) 95155, US$50-75.

Taman Harun Cottages: One of the most famous woodcarving galleries on Bali also offers 17 private cottages with swimming pool, lotus gardens, restaurant, and a private temple complex which reflects the wealth of Nyana and his celebrated grandfather, Tantra. In the woodcarving village of Mas. P.O. Box 216, Denpasar 80001, tel. (0361) 88511, US$40-55.

Luxury Accommodations

Ubud's finest hotels are in Kedewatan, near the Ayung River and about four km northwest of Ubud.

Kupu Kupu Barong Cottages: Perched on the edge of a cliff where the valley plunges into the river, Kupu Kupu offers breathtaking views, a cozy restaurant, 22 cottages, and six terraced apartments. P.O. Box 7, Ubud 80571, tel. (0361) 95479, fax (0361) 95079, US$300-640.

Amandari: Brainchild of Australian architect Peter Muller and run by Amanresorts, this super-luxury development offers 28 detached suites surrounding a 30-meter-long saltwater pool. P.O. Box 33, Ubud 80571, tel. (0361) 71267, fax (0361) 71266, US$375-950.

Performing Arts

Ubud and its neighboring villages are major dance centers where a performance is held nearly every night of the week. Schedules are available from the Ubud tourist office and from touts selling tickets around the town's main crossroads. Seats are unreserved; it's best to arrive at least 45 minutes early for front-row views. Performances vary according to the quality of the *gamelan* and skill of the individual dancers who rotate throughout the week: see the *legong* a dozen times and you'll experience both ineptitude and brilliance.

For example, the *legong* at Balai Banjar (Sekehe Gong Sadha Budaya Ubud) is breathtaking, while the Tirtasari troupe in Peliatan does a poor *legong* but compensates with Bali's finest *gamelan*. See the stunning Mahabharta at Banjar Teges, but avoid the disastrous *kechak* in Bona. A brief schedule:

Puri Ubud	Monday	*legong*
	Friday	*barong*
Balai Banjar	Tuesday	*rajapala*
	Thursday	*gabor*
Banjar Tegal	Sunday	*kechak*
	Tuesday	*legong*
Banjar Teges	Tuesday	*mahabharta*
Peliatan	Friday	*legong*
Puri Dalam	Saturday	*legong*
Bona	Friday	*kechak*
Batubulan	Daily	*barong*
Kartini Hotel	Thursday	*wayang*

Practicalities

A unique, locally managed, nongovernmental tourist information center is located on the main road diagonally across from Puri Lukisan. It's staffed by helpful volunteers who post dance schedules and notices of ceremonies and work to preserve the fragile environment and culture of Ubud. The local post office in Padang Tegal accepts poste restante and offers *paket post* services for mailing parcels. International phone calls can be made from the nearby *kantor telpon*.

VICINITY OF UBUD

Bedulu

With over 40 old temples in the region near Bedulu and Pejeng, this area contains Bali's richest collection of antiquities, from the earliest

known kettledrums and clay stupas to relatively modern Shivaite sculptures and cut-rock Buddhist sanctuaries. Bedulu was once the seat of the old Balinese kingdom of Pejeng and the last indigenous dynasty to hold out against the mighty Majapahit Empire, which invaded Bali in 1343 and introduced Majapahit culture and institutions. After the fall of the Pejeng Dynasty, the Hinduization of Bali accelerated, culminating in the massive cultural migration to Bali of the Majapahit court around 1515.

Archaeological Museum: Two km north of Bedulu is Gedong Arca, a small museum with such pre-Hindu artifacts as megaliths, bone ornaments, and copperplate inscriptions.

Pura Kobo Edan: Across the road and up a dirt alley is the "Mad Buffalo Temple," home to a four-meter image of a dancing figure endowed with a remarkably realistic penis. Perhaps a Balinese version of the East Javanese Singosari magic temples, the conquering Bima figure seems inspired by both Shivaite and Tantric Buddhist cults, two religions which merged on Bali by the 14th century.

Pura Penataran Sasih: Chief shrine of the old Pejeng Kingdom, this temple boasts one of the most famous examples of Bronze Age art in Indonesia. The so-called "Moon of Pejeng" is considered a masterpiece of bronzesmithing, though its origins might be Indonesian, Kublai Khan, Chinese Ming, or the Dongson culture of

North Vietnam. The treasure is poorly located at the top of a towerlike shrine; bring binoculars.

Yeh Pulu

Lying between the Petanu and Pakerisan rivers, the ruins of this 14th-century rock relief form perhaps the most important and mysterious sculpture of the Middle Balinese Period. The carvings are enigmatic and stylistically unique, a 25-meter-long frieze of lifelike vignettes chiseled with an earthy, insightful touch. Yeh Pulu represents stories from the life of of Lord Krishna, one of Vishnu's reincarnations, though the only deity directly portrayed is Ganesh, the elephant-headed son of Shiva. Hike or ride your motorcycle to the extreme southeast corner of town, then walk 30 minutes through the ricefields; a good place to escape the tour buses.

Goa Gajah

A large car park packed with souvenir stalls and *warungs* marks the entrance to Bali's famous Elephant Cave. Formerly a monastery for both Hindu and Buddhists pilgrims, Goa Gajah centers around an enormous bulging-eyed demon who appears to be splitting and pushing the rock apart with his bare hands—Disney meets Balinese mythology. Below the baroque facade are bathing pools fed by well-endowed nymphs and a path which leads down to a small *candi* and Buddha statues sitting in the attitude of mediation. Visitors must be well dressed, pay an admission fee, and hire a scarf.

Gunung Kawi

Two km south of Tampaksiring, on the banks of the sacred Pakerisan River, is one of the more impressive historical sites of Bali: a blinding green watery canyon where two rows of ancient blackened tombs have been hewn out of a natural rock hillside as royal memorials. Equated with the Ellora Caves of India and the rock temples of Mamallapuram (near Madras), these temples preserve in stone the architectural styles otherwise destroyed by nature. Although built in the 10th century, the facade temples remain remarkably well preserved.

Tampaksiring

The sacred springs of Tirta Empul, situated in a valley beyond the last houses of Tampaksiring, provide the essential holy waters needed for religion and ritual. The complex features two rectangular bathing pools with 15 spouts that purify, cure illness, and bring immortality. Sadly, the entire place has degenerated into a messy collection of souvenir stalls filled with super-aggressive touts who plead, beg, and voraciously molest Western visitors: Bali gone bad.

GOA GAJAH

SOUVENIR STALLS & PARKING

TO UBUD

TO TAMPAKSIRING

HARITI & OTHER STATUES

ELEPHANT CAVE

BALE

BATHING PLACE

PURA TAMAN

MEDITATION NICHE

PETANU RIVER

BUDDHIST ANTIQUITIES

BUDDHA STATUES

NOT TO SCALE

© MOON PUBLICATIONS, INC.

BANGLI

Nestled on the slopes of Mt. Batur, Bangli is a friendly little town with enough potential to become a major travelers' center. Bangli became Bali's most powerful upland court in the late 19th century, largely as a reaction to the Dutch

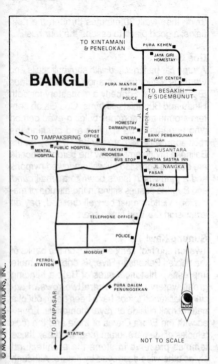

BANGLI

TO KINTAMANI & PENELOKAN
PURA KEHEN
JAYA GIRI HOMESTAY
ART CENTER
PURA MANTIK TIRTHA
TO BESAKIH & SIDEMBUNUT
POLICE
JL. MERDEKA
HOMESTAY DARMAPUTRA
POST OFFICE
TO TAMPAKSIRING
CINEMA
BANK PEMBANGUNAN DAERAH
PUBLIC HOSPITAL
BANK RAKYAT INDONESIA
MENTAL HOSPITAL
JL. NUSANTARA
ARTHA SASTRA INN
BUS STOP
JL. NANGKA
PASAR
PASAR
TELEPHONE OFFICE
POLICE
MOSQUE
PETROL STATION
TO DENPASAR
PURA DALEM PENUNGGEKAN
STATUE
MOON
NOT TO SCALE

© MOON PUBLICATIONS, INC.

presence in Buleleng. Today it slumbers along, largely ignored except for an occasional tour bus that deposits visitors at Pura Kehen. Bangli lacks the artistic temperament of Ubud, but it offers a rare chance to get off the beaten track and escape the tourist mentality that permeates much of modern Bali.

Attractions

Top draw is Pura Kehen, second largest and among the most impressive temples on Bali. Magnificently situated Pura Kehen was founded in the 11th century and consists of three levels connected by soaring flights of stairs. Gateways feature the splayed hands and hideous faces of *kala makara* demons whose function is to prevent malevolent spirits from entering the sacred grounds. Ornamentation on the highest temple is so overdone and uncontrolled that it's even rare for Bali—a stirring testament to the virtuosity of Bangli's stonecarvers.

Bangli Art Center, around the corner from Pura Kehen, occasionally sponsors art exhibits and performances of *kechak* and *wayang*. South of Bangli is the grotesque **Pura Dalem Penunggekan,** a Balinese Temple of the Dead carved with hellish scenes straight from Dante. Bangli also offers great hiking: three km west to Demulih Hill for views of Sanur, and a range of nine mountains named after the nipple-like *trompang* percussion plates in the *gamelan;* it's five km farther to Apuan, where the house of the *kepala desa* is as beautiful as a king's palace.

Accommodations

Bangli's rising popularity will bring more hotels, but for the present the best choice is the clean and comfortable Jaya Giri Homestay near Pura Kehen. Homestay Darmaputra near city center is ramshackle but adequate for an overnight. Better rooms are found at the Artha Sastra Inn where rooms with private bath start from US$5.

EASTERN BALI

A lovely region of terraced ricefields and soaring mountains, eastern Bali offers some of the finest scenery, weather, and beaches on the island. The entire region is dominated by mighty Gunung Agung, a sacred mountain which violently erupted during the closing years of the chaotic Sukarno regime in 1963. The final cataclysm postponed the Eka Dasa Rudra—an exorcism of evil which takes place only once every 100 years—until 1979, when the holy ceremony was finally completed. Today, the volcano quietly sleeps under the wary gaze of Balinese vulcanologists. Though rarely visited by Western tourists, eastern Bali offers enough natural beauty and history to waylay you for weeks.

KLUNGKUNG (SUKSESKAN)

After the Majapahit Empire of East Java fell to Muslim power in the 15th century, the royal court fled to Bali and reestablished itself at Gelgel, later transferring the capital to Klungkung in 1710. Of the eight Balinese rajadoms that ruled the island until conquest by the Dutch, it was the Gianyar and Klungkung empires that assumed the greatest territorial control. The reign of the Gelgel Dynasty was also the Golden Age of Bali, when the arts of dance, drama, music, and painting flourished as never before. In 1908 the Dutch mounted a military campaign against Klungkung in which the entire royal entourage chose collective suicide *puputan* rather than surrender.

Modern Klungkung is a dusty town without much character, though it merits a short visit to tour the Kerta Gosa and adjoining Royal Palace. Klungkung was renamed "Sukseskan" in 1992 to reflect its original title.

Attractions

Klungkung's greatest wonder is the ceiling of the Kerta Gosa, an ancient hall of justice first constructed in the late 1700s after the seat of power was transferred from Gelgel to Klungkung. Here, the all-powerful raja would sit with his Brahman elders to pass judgment in cases of murder, political conspiracy, and sacrilege. After the 1908 fire destroyed most of the palace

compound, the Dutch sponsored a series of renovations including a complete repainting on asbestos sheeting in the 1960s. Today the *bale's* walls and ceilings are covered in concentric murals, painted in the traditional *wayang* style, which depict the terrifying episodes due defendants after their deaths. The panels relate the fable of Bima and his two comical companions who venture into hell to rescue the soul of Bima's father. Panels toward the top describe heaven and discovery of the waters of immortality. For an exhaustive pictorial survey and discussion of each panel, refer to Idanna Pucci's landmark work, *The Epic of Life*. Paintings inside the adjacent Bale Kambang ("Floating Palace") show Balinese astrology and scenes from the tale of *Pan Brayut*.

Accommodations

Klungkung has three hotels and *losmen* scattered along the main road and near the bus terminal.

Ramayana Palace Hotel: Nine relatively clean rooms are found in the complex adjacent to the owner's house at the east end of Klungkung. Jl. Diponegoro, tel. (0366) 21044, US$5-8.

Hotel Wisnu: A much less attractive but survivable alternative if the Ramayana is filled. Jl. Rinjani, US$4-6.

BESAKIH

Besakih is the holiest site on Bali; the Mother Temple of Bali. Besakih dates from the 14th century and was built on a terraced site where prehistoric rites, ceremonies, and feasts once took place. The very complex architectural structure incorporates and venerates the holy Hindu trinity of Shiva, Vishnu, and Brahma through three main shrines, dozens of towering *merus,* and countless temples dedicated to all major figures in the Balinese pantheon.

Besakih lacks the architectural splendor of other Balinese temples, though the superb location and ungodly views are unforgettable. However, you must bring your change purse,

KLUNGKUNG (SUKSESKAN)

TO BESAKIH

JL. G. RINJANI

DAM

TO AMLAPURA

POLICE POST

BANK

HOTEL WISNU

MOSQUE

BUS STATION

PUPUTAN MONUMENT

BANK

JL. DIPONEGORO

HOTEL SUDIHATI

POLICE

KERTA GOSA

TELEPHONE

PASAR AREA

REST. SUMBER RASA

RAMAYANA PALACE MOTEL

CINEMA

POST OFFICE

PALACE

CINEMA

SUKSESKAN MUSEUM

TO GIANYAR

0   200 m

TO PURA BATU AND KLOTOK

© MOON PUBLICATIONS, INC.

as every device imaginable by which tourists may be separated from their *rupiahs* is in operation: a desperate scene of hustlers, touts, beggars, and barking vendors. Local guides such as Wayan Badere provide homestays and guide services to the summit of Mt. Agung.

NUSA PENIDA AND LEMBONGAN

Nusa Penida, Nusa Lembongan, and Nusa Ceningan—three islands situated just south of Kusamba and within sight of Sanur—guarantee a welcome relief from the mass tourism of mainland Bali. Nusa Ceningan is little more than barren rock with little of great note, but Lembongan and Penida offer the adventurous traveler a rich combination of stark natural beauty, friendly villagers who welcome overnighters into their homes, and excellent surfing, scuba diving, and fishing.

Transportation
Both Penida and Lembongan can be reached by boat from several different points. The journey is not recommended in small boats when the seas are rough.

From Padangbai: Four boats leave each morning from Padangbai for Buyuk on Nusa Penida. The fare is about US$2. From Buyuk, take a *bemo* to the government *losmen* in Sampalan, or head directly to Toyapakeh, from where small boats cross over to Nusa Lembongan.

From Kusamba: Small local boats called *jukung* also depart daily from Kusamba, cost US$2, and take 90 minutes to Toyapakeh on Nusa Penida. You'll be accompanied by villagers bearing rice, oils, and fresh vegetables.

From Sanur: Larger tourist boats depart daily from Sanur to Jungut Batu on Nusa Lembongan, take about 30 minutes, and cost US$10 per person.

Tours
Independent travelers who speak some Indonesian will have little trouble exploring Nusa Penida and Lembongan on their own. Visitors who would like guaranteed reservations or need dive arrangements can sign up for an organized tour in Kuta, Sanur, or Nusa Dua. Baruna Watersports Bali, the largest dive operator on Bali, has offices in many large hotels such as the Bali Hyatt, Bali Beach, Bali Sol, and Putri Bali. A full day of scuba diving including transportation, equipment, lunch, and two tanks or air costs US$60-80.

Nusa Penida
Clearly visible from Sanur Beach, Nusa Penida was once the Siberia of Bali, a penitentiary "demon" isle of banishment for criminals and undesirables from the kingdom of Klungkung. In Balinese mythology, the island is the home of the fanged giant Jero Gede Mecaling and is the origin of all plagues, famines, and invasions of rats. The island is a dry, hostile land of arid hills,

PADANGBAI

TO AMLAPURA

CEMETERY

RAI BEACH INN
KERTI BEACH INN
PADANG BAI BEACH INN

3 km TO MAIN RD.

TALIWAG MUSLIM WARUNG

RESTAURANT SUDI MAMPIR

CAFE SHOP DONA
HOTEL MADYA

WARUNG JAWA
WARUNG MUSLIM

BEMO PARK

TO KLUNGKUNG & DENPASAR

JOHNNY'S

POST OFFICE

LOMBOK FERRY TICKET OFFICE

PIER

TO PANTAI KECIL

MOSQUE

NOT TO SCALE

© MOON PUBLICATIONS, INC.

big succulents that resemble cacti, low trees, patches of green, and thorny bush, where a few marsupials live—or rather, survive.

Attractions: From Toyapakeh, ride on a tree-lined road along the sea three km west to Pura Ped, a temple complex dedicated to horrendous Mecaling. About one km north of Sewana, descend into Goa Karangasari, a vast limestone cave with deep, vaulted halls festooned with stalactites; still and silent like a hollow mountain. Sebuluh Waterfall near Batu Madeg and the natural springs near Sakti are also worth visiting.

Accommodations: Accommodations on Nusa Penida are currently limited to one beachfront *losmen* managed by local government officials in the town of Sampalan. Several international hotel groups have announced plans for major beach resorts.

Nusa Lembongan

Lembongan, not Penida, is the center of tourism for this small archipelago, largely because of the outstanding coral beds and almost iridescent blue-green waters which embrace the island. Tourism is on the rise, but for the near future, the economy continues to revolve around cultivation of seaweed, which is processed into crackers and chips and exported to Japan, France, and Southeast Asia.

Attractions: Seaweed farms are best seen at low tide when many of the island's 4,000 residents work the dank beds. Perhaps a more interesting sight is the cave at Jenggut Batu, curiously converted into an uninhabited house.

However, the chief draws on Lembongan are the superb snorkeling, big-game fishing, and consistent waves which crash madly down on Playground, Abration, and Shipwreck beaches just offshore from Jungut Batu.

Accommodations: Over 100 bungalow rooms are now located on the northern beach area around the principal town of Jungut Batu. Most are simple homestays where you eat with the family, but more formal places with clean rooms and private baths are now under construction.

Among the homestays under US$5 are Johnny's Inn, Losmen Wayan, and Tarsin Homestay. More expensive options from US$5-15 include Wayan Tarci, Agung Bungalows with rooms in all price ranges, and Nusa Lembongan Bungalows, which operates a reservation office on Jl. Pantai Legian in Kuta.

PADANGBAI

Padangbai is the port town for ferries to Lombok. Departures are daily at 0830 and 1330. A ticket office is right on the main street at Cafe Shop Dona. The perfectly shaped and protected bay is attractive, plus the Muslim town offers colorful one-eyed *prahus* (sailboats) and hikes through the adjacent hills.

Comfortable accommodations are found in the three beach bungalows located east of the pier. *Losmens* on the main road are scruffy to the extreme.

Goa Lawah, between Klungkung and Padangbai, is a bat cave considered one of Bali's nine most important temples and legendary home of a sacred dragon called Naga Basuki.

CANDIDASA

Candidasa takes its name from the local Shiva-Buddhist temple, established in 1181 and dedicated to Hatiri, the protector goddess of children. The east-coast alternative to Kuta is now an active mini-resort packed with *losmens*, seafood restaurants, and all other travelers' necessities. Though the fastest growing retreat on Bali, the beach itself is not wide enough to accommodate all the people who flock here, plus signs of creeping Kuta-ism are everywhere.

From town, you can climb the rolling hills for superb panoramas and then continue hiking back to Tenganan. Candidasa also makes a convenient base for exploring the temples and ricefields of eastern Bali.

Candidasa Accommodations

Candidasa is a one-street town lined with dozens of *losmen* and hotels in all price ranges. Owners are friendly and eager to please, most still naive about the tourist industry—a refreshing change. Cheaper hotels are located away from the beachfront; more expensive hotels with European toilets and gardens of hibiscus blossoms overlook the shoreline.

Homestay Ida: Many of Candidasa's better spots are located on the edge of town, removed from the hype and hustle that now engulfs the resort. A typical example is Homestay Ida, situated near a large lagoon and in the midst of a lovely coconut grove. And in a wise move, Ida employs bamboo and thatch for bungalow construction rather than the dreary concrete used elsewhere in Candidasa. US$12-20.

Homestay Lilaberata: A decent choice in the middle of Candidasa, Lilaberata is owned by Pak Lila, who speaks good English and often organizes Sunday tours to Amlapura, Tirtagangga, and other eastern Bali destinations. US$6-12.

Candi Dasa Beach Bungalows: Popular midrange destination with friendly management, attractive bamboo bungalows surrounded by gardens, and weekly *gamelan* performances. US$9-24.

Water Garden: The owners of TJ's Restaurant in Kuta opened their Candidasa escape several years ago after constructing a series of charming bungalows surrounded by streams, lily pools, and lush gardens. The result is one of the prettiest spots in town. P.O. Box 39, Amlapura, tel. and fax (0361) 35540, US$75-90.

Balina Beach Accommodations

Quieter bungalows in superior settings are several kilometers west of Candidasa. All are accessed by side roads off the highway near the Tenganan exit.

Balina Beach Bungalows: Six classes of rooms are available, from simple bungalows with common baths to luxurious chalets with a/c and Western toilets. Balina Beach serves as the scuba-diving center for the region, in-

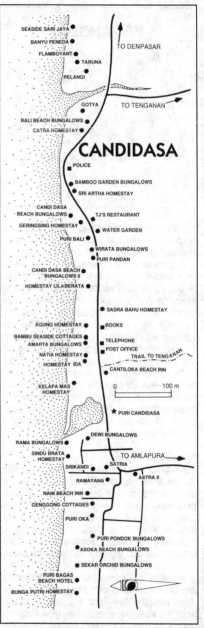

© MOON PUBLICATIONS, INC.

cluding offshore dives and visits to Nusa Penida and shipwrecks on the north coast. Balina Beach, tel. (0361) 88451, US$15-50.

Puri Buitan: Another upscale resort with oceanside pool and deluxe a/c chalets. Balina Beach, tel. (0361) 87182, US$35-55.

Amankila: Eastern Bali's final word in luxury is situated above a private beach near the village of Manggis. Accommodations include 35 luxury pavilions set among landscaped grounds; superior suites feature private saltwater swimming pools. P.O. Box 133, Klungkung 80701, tel. (0361) 71267, fax (0361) 71266, US$320-580.

TENGANAN

Tenganan is an original pre-Hindu settlement inhabited by the Bali Aga, aboriginal Balinese who settled the island long before the influx of immigrants from the decaying 16th-century Majapahit Empire. As with other megalithic towns, Tenganan is geometrically balanced with identical homes neatly facing each other across stone roads. Like Trunyan to the northwest, the village has attempted to preserve its culture and way of life against the onslaught of Westernization and mass tourism. The results have been mixed: the village is now plastered with signs marked, *Gamelan* Demonstration, Weaving Demonstration, and Please Come In. Yet the basic layout, totally different from that of any other community on Bali, remains, as do vestiges of their famous double-*ikat* textilework.

After paying your entrance fee and passing the souvenir shops, walk north past the wandering buffalo to visit *lontar* (palm-leaf script) artist Wratddhi Castra, and continue beyond the school to the path that leads six km to Candidasa. To reach Tenganan, take a *bemo* to the turnoff and continue on the back of a waiting motorcycle.

AMLAPURA

Amlapura (formerly called Karangasem) once served as seat of one of the richest kingdoms of Bali. Established during the waning days of the Gelgel Dynasty in the late 17th century, this rajadom rose to the pinnacle of its power in the 18th century. Amlapura was devastated during

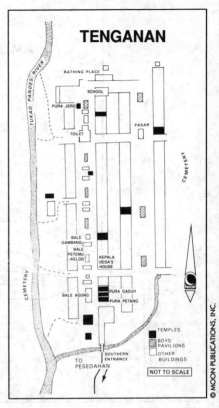

Agung's monthlong eruption in 1963; traces of the catastrophe are still visible today in the western part of town.

Attractions

Puri Kangiana: This enormous complex once functioned as the famous palace of the last raja. Inside, an air of slow-motion decay prevails. The fountains have stopped spouting and dragons and serpents sit stonily with wide-open mouths. A combination of European, Chinese, and Balinese architecture and interior design was used in this *puri's* construction. The largest and most striking pavilion is Bale London, with flourishing Edwardian decorations and long verandas set around the deserted courtyard.

Ujung Water Palace: Four km south of Amlapura, Ujung is the site of a majestic old mock-

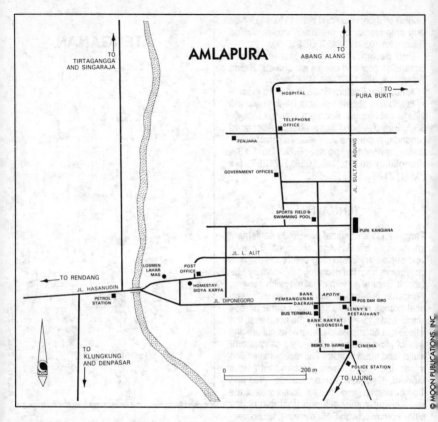

AMLAPURA

Map labels: TO TIRTAGANGGA AND SINGARAJA; TO ABANG ALANG; HOSPITAL; TO PURA BUKIT; TELEPHONE OFFICE; PENJARA; GOVERNMENT OFFICES; JL. SULTAN AGUNG; SPORTS FIELD & SWIMMING POOL; PURI KANGIANA; JL. L. ALIT; LOSMEN LAHAR MAS; POST OFFICE; TO RENDANG; JL. HASANUDIN; HOMESTAY SIDYA KARYA; PETROL STATION; BANK PEMBANGUNAN DAERAH; *APOTIK*; POS DAN GIRO; JL. DIPONEGORO; BUS TERMINAL; LENNY'S RESTAURANT; BANK RAKYAT INDONESIA; TO KLUNGKUNG AND DENPASAR; BEMO TO UJUNG; CINEMA; POLICE STATION; TO UJUNG; 0 — 200 m

© MOON PUBLICATIONS, INC.

European-style water palace surrounded by a moat. Most of the bungalows, statues, and fountains were destroyed by a 1979 earthquake. Today, children splash and farmers grow rice in the bathing pools: only your imagination can reconstruct the former glory. *Bemos* to Ujung leave from the south end of Amlapura.

TIRTAGANGGA

One of the prettiest and most relaxed places in all of Bali, Tirtagangga is a superb place to unwind and enjoy the splendid scenery that unfolds in all directions. Tirtagangga ("Water of the Ganges") is a water complex built with corvée labor on the site of a sacred spring by the old raja of Amlapura in 1947. With its shallow

pool, ornamental ponds, and pleasant weather, this is the perfect spot for family outings.

Attractions

Visitors are permitted to bathe in the ponds and in the formal swimming pool in the northwest corner, but come prepared for armies of exuberant schoolchildren. Much better is hiking through the fantastic scenery to remote villages almost completely untouched by the outside world. Simply pick a direction and go: north to Ababi, northwest to the Mahayana Buddhist colony at Budakling, west to the artist village of Abianjero, all the way around the coastline to Singaraja.

Bali's most spectacular scenery isn't found around Ubud or high in the mountains, but rather along the narrow road which winds west from Amlapura toward Rendang. No matter

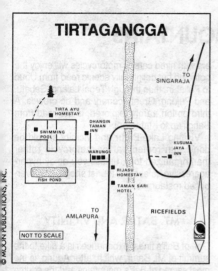

TIRTAGANGGA

TO SINGARAJA

TIRTA AYU HOMESTAY

DHANGIN TAMAN INN

SWIMMING POOL

WARUNGS

KUSUMA JAYA INN

RIJASU HOMESTAY

FISH POND

TAMAN SARI HOTEL

TO AMLAPURA

RICEFIELDS

NOT TO SCALE

© MOON PUBLICATIONS, INC.

how many photographs you've seen of the magical landscape, nothing prepares you for this journey. *Bemos* are extremely sporadic. The best strategy is to rent a motorcycle or car and allow as much time as possible. Highlights include the *salak* gardens at Sibetan, the almost-unbelievable views from Putung (Putung Bungalows has a comfortable restaurant and deserted units from US$8), and the postcard-perfect rice terraces around Iseh and Sideman.

Both Walter Spies and Swiss painter Theo Meier lived in Iseh. Sideman is a highly recommended place to *completely* escape the commercialism of Bali.

Accommodations

Tirtagangga—one of the finest and least touristy spots on Bali—offers some fabulous *losmen* with stunning views and perfect silence.

Taman Sari Hotel: *Bemos* from Amlapura stop at the intersection near the Taman Sari Hotel ("fresh water fish" in the restaurant) and Rijasa Homestay on the same side of the road. Both are ordinary but convenient. US$4-8.

Tirta Ayu Homestay: Better facilities and atmosphere are available in this four-room homestay, which overlooks the water palace and is managed by a descendant of the former raja. US$6-12.

Dhangin Taman Inn: A very attractive spot where you can sit in the sun and gaze across the rice paddies. The owner, Wayan, will draw a hiking map if you want to see the hillside village of Tanaharon, Tanah Lengis (known for its *angklung* orchestras), the Sivaite priests in remote Budakling, or the cattle-market town of Bebandam. Hiking around Tirtagangga is superb! US$4-10.

Kusuma Jaya Inn: Tirtagangga's top choice (literally), situated at the summit of a very steep stairway, offers good food and unforgettable views over endless ricefields. You'll never forget the sunset. US$5-15.

CENTRAL MOUNTAINS

Bali's spine of mountains is a popular escape from the hotter lowlands. The climate is fresh and brisk, and there are great walks through the volcanic crater of Mt. Batur. At night the air is so clear you can see the moon sail over the volcano.

The Batur region, unfortunately, has a reputation for money-hungry and aggressive people. Don't stop when people on the road try to flag you down to sell you tours or boat rides across the lake. Motorcycles should never be left unattended; store them with the *losmen* proprietor. *Losmens* charge whatever the market will bear; bargain hard.

PENELOKAN

Penelokan means "Place to Look." Perched at 1,450 meters, this cool but messy village has a collection of cheap *losmen* which offer spectacular views across the crater. Vegetables thrive in the cooler climate, so you'll be able to enjoy fresh greens and luscious strawberries. The imposing Puri Selera Restaurant is a good place to dine and escape the merchants who wave frantically from the road below.

Accommodations
Penelokan's dearth of decent hotels encourages most travelers to continue to Kintamani or spend the night down on the lake in the village of Toya Bungkah. Warm clothing and blankets are essential in the cheaper *losmen*.

Caldera Batur: The first *losmen* at the rim has simple rooms and a small cafe. US$5-10.

Lakeview Homestay: Very basic spot with claustrophobic cubicles and larger bungalows with private bath. US$4-10.

Losmen Gunawan: Excellent views, renovated rooms, and an ideal location about 500 meters past the road down to Kedisan make this the best choice in Penelokan. US$6-12.

Transportation
Most tour buses follow the main road via Tampaksiring, with pauses at the temples at Goa Gajah, Gunung Kawi, and Tirta Empul. Travelers with hired cars or motorcycles will enjoy the potholed but delightfully scenic road from Ubud to Peliatan, then through Tegal Lalang, Sebatu, and Pujung. Great scenery and no crowds. A third option, rarely explored, is the road from Bangli up to Kintamani.

Visiting Lake Batur and vicinity should be done with rented car or motorcycle rather than organized tour, unless you enjoy hyper-aggressive salesmen, tourist shops, and overpriced restaurants.

MT. BATUR AND VICINITY

One of Bali's finest experiences is a hike to the summit of Mt. Batur, which, after Agung, is the most sacred of Bali's mountains and the source of many Balinese myths. Batur is also an active volcano that still bellows and erupts, throwing out showers of volcanic debris and glowing red in the night. Batur's eruption of 1917 destroyed 65,000 homes and 2,500 temples and forced the relocation of Batur village to a safer site on the ridge.

Climbing Mt. Batur
Losmen operators in Penelokan, Kintamani, and Toya Bungkah lead climbs, but it's very simple to follow the signs and well-worn paths to the summit. Batur's bare slope is the easiest of Bali's volcanos to climb because you can drive to its base and you don't have to struggle through vegetation on your way to its three craters. There are several different approaches but the most popular is the stiff climb from Toya Bungkah and the shorter route from Purajati. After exploring the sandy middle crater and enjoying the panoramic views, return to Toya Bungkah or hike the back-side path toward Kintamani.

Accommodations
Simple *losmen* are in Kedisan, Toya Bungkah, and right at lakeside.

Kedisan: The village at the south end of Lake Batur has the Segara Homestay and the Buahan Losmen at the far end of town, but most travelers head directly to Toya Bungkah. Hikers

LAKE BATUR AND VICINITY

TO SINGARAJA

G. PENULISAN (1744 m)
T.V. TOWER & VIEWPOINT
TEMPLE
PENULISAN

TOYA MAMPEH

G. BATUR (1717 m)
3-HOUR ASCENT
2-HOUR ASCENT

KINTAMANI

BATUR

KUBUPENELOKAN

PURAJATI

SEKED

KALANGANYAR

TO UBUD

PENELOKAN
KEDISAN
BUAHAN

TO TEGAL LELANG & UBUD

TO TAMPAKSIRING & UBUD

TO BANGLI

TO RENDANG & BESAKIH

TO LUPAK

VIEWPOINT
SONGAN
TEMPLE

CEMETERY
TRUNYAN

TOYA BUNGKAH

BOAT TRIP

LAKE BATUR

ABANG

G. ABANG (2152 m)

0   2 km

© MOON PUBLICATIONS, INC.

with limited time should watch for the sign near Purajati which announces "Please follow white flag to Batur Volcano"; a quickie shortcut.

Toya Bungkah: Toya Bungkah (also called Tirtha) has a half-dozen *losmen* in the US$4-8 range including Norman Pangus Hot Springs ("no hassle!"), Mertha Losmen, Siki Inn, and Kardi's Mountain View.

Tirtha Yatra: A very basic but memorable *losmen* ideally located at the edge of the lake; a camper's delight. Bring all possible necessities. US$2-5.

Khamandalu: A newer *losmen* with clean rooms with attached bathrooms. Hot water, piped in from the nearby springs, is sporadic. US$12-15.

Balai Seni Art Center Guesthouse and Library: The "World Headquarters for the International Association for Art and the Future" offers gardens, a well-stocked library, and spacious bungalows managed by a professor from Jakarta. US$5-12.

Transportation

Private *bemo* drivers from Penelokan ask as high as Rp15,000 to take you down the paved road, but just wait patiently until a public *bemo* comes along and pay just Rp500. When the weather permits, a great alternative is to hike down to the lake in about two hours. The village of Toya Bungkah is another hour of hot, hard walking.

Trunyan And The Lake

Boat tours can be arranged from the fixed-price ticket office in Kedisan. Eight-man motorboats cost US$1 for a three-hour tour to Trunyan, the cemetery, the hot springs at Toya Bungkah, and back to Kedisan. Individuals can join large parties, often Indonesians on holiday. Alternatively, hike around the shore from Kedisan in three hours.

Trunyan is an ancient Bali Aga village nestled compactly under a precipitous crater wall. Trunyan's austere old temple—a fossilized relic of aboriginal Balinese architecture—features a gigantic megalithic image believed to be the largest on Bali.

The setting is spectacular and the village unique, but overall it's a horrible tourist trap filled with hyper-aggressive hustlers who demand outrageous fees for everything: arrival, photography, temple entrance, views of the statue, cemetery visits, etc.

KINTAMANI

Kintamani is a wind-blown market town spread haphazardly along the road which hugs the outer rim of Mt. Batur. Though the views are not as good, most travelers prefer to stay here instead of at Penelokan. Local villagers might remind you of the Newars of Nepal in the way they dress and stare—traditional, turbaned, and always carrying their *parang* (machetes). Kintamani is also known for vegetables and fruits not found elsewhere on Bali and the superb sunrise market held every three days.

Penulisan, eight km north, boasts the highest temple on Bali and spectacular views from the TV microwave station at the summit. Bring warm clothes for the bitter cold nights.

Accommodations

Most *losmen* along the main street offer cold, cubicle-like, damp-smelling rooms only suited for midget survivalists. Coming from Penelokan, you'll pass Pura Ulun Danu Batu before reaching the hotels in the center of town.

Hotel Miranda: On the left is a friendly but older *losmen* with rooms in all price ranges. Other inexpensive choices include Losmen Linggan Sari on the left and Losmen Kencana adjacent to the mosque. Losmen Sasaka on the right is slightly better. US$4-8.

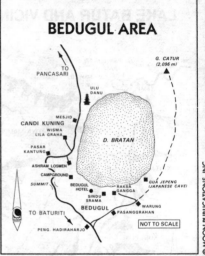

Hotel Puri Astina: Kintamani's only semi-luxurious hotel has spacious rooms with excellent views, but showers are icy cold and rates are sky high. Situated at the far end of town. US$18-28.

BEDUGUL AND LAKE BRATAN

Bedugul is a friendly lakeside resort located on the main road between Denpasar and Singaraja. Unlike Kintamani and Penelokan, Bedugul is a prosperous place with good hotels, warm restaurants, and outdoor activities from sailing to golf.

Attractions

From the *bemo* stop in Candi Kuning, walk down to Bratan Lake for photographs of picturesque Ulu Danu. This half-Hindu, half-Buddhist temple is dedicated to Dewi Danau, the water goddess of the Balinese religion. Boats can be hired near Wisma Lila Graha to paddle around the placid waters and visit caves dug by Indonesian slave laborers during WW II. Hikers might climb Mt. Catur and then return to circumnavigate the lake in the afternoon. Also visit the sprawling botanic gardens and orchid gardens at Lila Graha, only 500 meters from the market. Ten km north of Lake Bratan are Lake Buyan and Tamblingan, two lovely spots from where trails lead to Munduk and the north coast. Bedugul is a fine place to enjoy nature and escape the more common attractions on Bali.

Accommodations

Both Bedugul on the southern and Candi Kuning on the western shores of Lake Bratan have inexpensive *losmen* and more luxurious hotels. Top-end resorts are located in Pancasari, about 10 km north of the lake.

Mini Bali Losmen: This six-room *losmen* is the least expensive spot near the lake. Candi Kuning, US$4-6.

Ashram Losmen: A simple concrete hotel

with clean rooms facing the lake. The adjacent campground rents boats by the hour. Candi Kuning, US$8-12.

Wisma Lila Graha: A very comfortable and good-value hotel located across the road from the lake. Rooms with private bath face the water. Candi Kuning, US$18-35.

Bedugul Hotel: An older but still decent hotel which serves as the lakeside water-sports center. Bedugul, tel. (0361) 29593, US$10-28.

Bali Handara Country Club: The region's biggest splurge is this international hotel with tennis courts, restaurants, and an 18-hole championship golf course reported to be among the most scenic in Asia; the world's only course laid out inside an extinct volcanic crater. Pancasari, tel. (0361) 29984, US$60-120.

NORTHERN BALI

Northern Bali and the regency of Buleleng are a world apart from southern Bali. The sprawling region boasts secluded coastline, undeveloped beach resorts, an arid climate, coffee plantations rather than terraced ricefields, remote waterfalls and freshwater springs, untouched marine and forest reserves, and gaudily painted temples seething with baroque carved figures. Though not as classically rich as the Bali-Hindu southern half of the island, northern Bali boasts extravagant shrines carved from soft pink sandstone quarried near Singaraja and fanciful sculptures of plump Dutchmen cramped into motorcars, people copulating in the bushes, and a man riding a bicycle composed of leaves and flowers.

SINGARAJA

Bali's second largest city chiefly serves as a transit point for travelers heading west to the beaches at Lovina. With its suburban tree-lined avenues, rows of Chinese shophouses, and Muslim minarets, Singaraja still vaguely resembles a 19th-century colonial town and is populated by all of Bali's ethnic and religious minorities: Chinese, Bugis, Javanese, Malays, Hindus, and Arabs.

Attractions

Once the Dutch capital for all of Nusa Tenggara, Singaraja still boasts some fine old residences and colonial architecture of European design. One of the most noticeable is Kantor Bupati (formerly Hotel Singaraja), which loftily overlooks the whole city from the south end of Jalan Ngurah. Gudung Kirtya, a manuscript library just down the street from Kantor Bupati, holds thousands of rare and immensely valuable *lontar* epistles which relate the literature, mythology, medical science, folklore, religion, and history of Bali.

Transportation

Buses from Denpasar reach the terminal on the western edge of town, from where *bemos* continue out to Lovina, Gilimanuk, and finally, Surabaya. Buses from Kintamani and Lake Batur stop at the eastern terminal, from where *bemos* continue around the eastern coastline to Amlapura.

EAST OF SINGARAJA

Temples in the north are among the most spectacular on Bali. Blessed with a soft pliable sandstone, northern sculptors were able to create super-exuberant tableaux of *rakasas,* comic-strip panels, effusive wildlife, hilarious sidebars on mass tourism, and mischievous figures taken from Hindu-Balinese mythology. Northern architects employ terraced bases which lead to squat stone buildings, rather than the courtyards of *merus* common in the south. The following temples can be quickly reached by motorcycle; *bemos* from Singaraja's eastern terminal shuttle around the east coast toward Amlapura.

Sangsit

Pura Beji, located about 500 meters down a side street in Sangsit, is an extraordinarily lavish *subak* temple that provides a brilliant example of the northern rococo style of carving, swarming with carved demons, *naga* snakes, *leyak* guardians, and stone vegetation growing in and out of the spellbinding gateways and terraces.

Jagaraja

Jagaraja Pura Dalem and a number of other temples on the road to Sawan feature panels profusely carved with great humor: madcap scenes of bicyclists, Balinese flying kites, dog-fighting airplanes, fishermen hooking a whale, bats, tigers, crabs clinging to the walls, and a long-nosed Dutchman being held up by a bandit with a horse pistol.

Sawan

Pura Jagaraja, two km south of Jagaraja, proves the Balinese fondness for caricature, masterfully represented here in bas-reliefs of corpulent Europeans in vintage Model Ts being robbed by armed bandits, aircraft falling from the sky into the sea, Dutch steamers being attacked by sea monsters, and mammoth fish swallowing the canoe of a kite flier.

Kubutambahan

Pura Maduwe Karang, about one km beyond the Kintamani turnoff, is one of northern Bali's largest and most elaborately carved temples. Steps lead through the courtyard into a second, inner section dominated by a magnificent stone pyramidlike wall richly embellished with ghouls, noblemen, soft pornography, a riot of leaves and tendrils, horrifying renditions of Durga, battle scenes from the Ramayana, and—most famously—a one-meter-high relief of an official riding a floral bicycle!

East Coast

Beyond Kubutambahan the coast becomes dry, rough, and rather deserted. Yeh Sanih is a shady seaside spot with an enclosed natural swimming pool fed by underground springs. Tejakula, 35 km from Singaraja, is another bathing place with separate sections for *pria* and *wanita*. Both have simple *losmen* served by *bemos* which shuttle around the coast to Amlapura.

LOVINA BEACH

Lovina is the generic term for a number of small villages, beaches, and accommodations strung along the road west of Singaraja from Anturan to Temukus. The region lacks the hustle, fine sand, clear waters, and nightlife of Kuta, but it receives good comments from travelers who seek solitude and relaxation.

Anturan Accommodations

Compared to the *losmen* and hotels in southern Bali, those at Lovina are simple places without the hype or hustle of Kuta or Sanur. Budget huts and midpriced hotels are now plentiful from Anturan (the village nearest Singaraja) to Temukus, though the largest concentration fills the middle near Kalibukbuk.

Baruna Beach Inn: Comfortable cottages with private baths overlooking the beach. Continental breakfast is included in the room price. Recommended. P.O. Box 50, Tukad Munggah, tel. (0362) 41252, US$8-15.

Homestay Agung: One of the original backpackers' *losmen* is still among the friendliest places at the beach. P.O. Box 25, Anturan, US$4-7.

Sri Homestay: Simple bamboo bungalows in a striking location: adjacent to the ocean and surrounded by waving fields of rice. Anturan, US$3-6.

Jati Reef Bungalows: Good midpriced bungalows set in the ricefields slightly back from the beach. Owner/manager Simon also operates nearby Yuda's (formerly Simon's Seaside Cottages). Rooms are clean and roomy. P.O. Box 52, Tukad Munggah, tel. (0362) 21952, US$8-20.

Kalibukbuk Accommodations

Kalibukbuk, the main commercial center, has money changers, seafood restaurants, and a dozen *losmen* in the US$4-10 price range. *Bemos* from Singaraja stop at Nirwana Pub, near beachside bungalows and roadside hotels.

Janur's Dive Inn: About one km before Kalibukbuk proper is this small, homey, well-organized inn where owner/chef John (Made Janur) and his wife Rose serve as expert guides to the Gunung Batur region. They also take snorkeling groups to the nearby reefs. Kalibukbuk, US$4-6.

Banyualit Beach Inn: Both concrete and traditional bungalows with clean rooms, ocean views, plus friendly, helpful staff. Recommended. P.O. Box 17, Kalibukbuk, tel. (0362) 81101, US$15-20 fan, US$25-40 a/c.

Ayodaya Accommodations: Roadside location, but a pleasant and relatively short walk

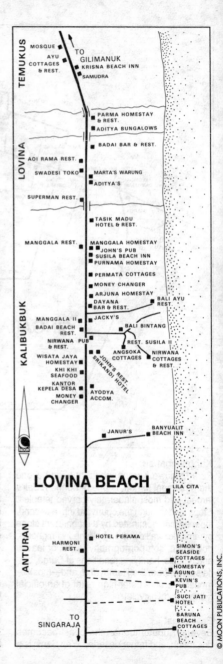

LOVINA BEACH

© MOON PUBLICATIONS, INC.

BOB RACE

A panel from the ceiling murals of the Kerta Gosa law court pavilion of Klungkung, painted in the wayang style, shows the horrors which await sinners. The scene to the left shows the punishment being inflicted on a man who tried to seduce his best friends' wives and his own sister; his genitals are being burned by a demon with a flaming torch. In the gory scene to the right, an enraged sow is savagely attacking a man who never married. Putting work above all human and spiritual values, he never had time for women, never married, and never had children—the most unpardonable sin of all. In vain, the man tries to tempt the sow away from his thigh by holding out nutmeg sprigs. These terrifying murals greatly influenced witnesses and defendants during hearings presided over by judges.

through the ricefields to the beach. Kalibukbuk, US$4-6.

Angsoka Cottages: Two-story bungalows on one of the few roads which connect the highway with the beach. A lovely setting surrounded by tropical gardens. Kalibukbuk, tel. (0362) 41841, US$8-10.

Nirwana Cottages: Seaside location, plus big, clean rooms spread around a refreshing garden. Kalibukbuk, tel. (0362) 41288, US$15-30.

Bali Lovina Beach Cottage: Top-end hotel with swimming pool, restaurant, bar, and 35 a/c rooms in two-story bungalows. Kalibukbuk, tel. (0362) 41385, US$45-65.

Lovina Accommodations

Just across a narrow stream is the small village of Lovina, namesake to the entire region.

Aditya's Bungalows: Literally seven meters from the beach, Aditya's offers older huts with common baths, plus newer bungalows with a/c, hot showers, and phones for room service. P.O. Box 35, Lovina, tel. (0362) 41059, US$4-28.

Samudra Beach Cottages: Quiet, remote, semiluxurious resort with both fan-cooled rooms and a/c bungalows just 10 meters from the beach. Good food in the breezy restaurant. P.O. Box 15, Temukus, tel. (0362) 41104, US$10-24.

NORTHWESTERN BALI

Northwestern Bali remains a region almost completely untouched by mass tourism, though a steady trickle of visitors is now exploring the region between Singaraja and Gilimanuk.

The major attractions of western Buleleng are mainly located in the first 25 km west of Singaraja and in the hills that flank the ocean. Top draw in the far west is the national park.

Waterfalls

Singsing Air Terjun ("Daybreak Waterfalls") and the higher-elevation Singsing Air Dua are signposted on the main road near Labuanhaji. Both are best visited during or immediately after the rainy season.

Brahma Arama Vihara

Bali's only Buddhist monastery, 18 km west of Singaraja and four km south of Banjar Tegeha, is where resident *bhikkus* teach Theravadic breathing technique (*pranayama*) and "slow-walking meditation." Nearby thermal hot springs can be reached on foot in an hour, or take a motorcycle taxi from the Banjar Tegeha intersection.

Pura Pulaki

Pulaki, 48 km west of Singaraja and two km off the main road, features a dramatic temple overrun with monkeys and Indonesian tourists who come to honor Nirartha, a saintly Javanese priest who migrated to Bali in the 16th century.

West Bali National Park

The extreme northwest corner of Bali boasts the 77,000-hectare aquatic and nature preserve of Taman Nasional Bali Barat, gazetted in 1984 as one of the 10 national parks in Indonesia. Visitors can explore the forested hills, scrub acacia near the coast, and unspoilt reef along Teluk Terima and eastern bays. Hiking and camping permits must be obtained at park headquarters offices in either Labuhan Lalang (12 km east of Gilimanuk) or Cekik, a few kilometers south of Gilimanuk. Mandatory guides cost US$2-5 per day.

Accommodations: Available in park shelters, but you must provide your own bedding, food, water, etc. Noncampers can find simple bungalows in Labuan Lalang and Gilimanuk.

Pulau Menjangan

This sanctuary island with its vast coral beds, just north of Bali Barat National Park, is considered Bali's premier scuba-diving and snorkeling locale. Dive shops in Kuta and Sanur organize tours to Menjangan as well as to coral reefs and submerged wrecks off the northwest coast. Independent travelers can also hire a boat from Labuan Lalang for about US$25 per half-day excursion. Food and simple lodgings are available in Labuan Lalang.

SUMATRA

The magnificent island of Sumatra—with great lakes, steamy jungles, wildlife reserves, spectacular waterfalls, and remote tribes—vies with Sulawesi as the third most popular tourist destination in Indonesia. Sumatra's name is a modified version of the Latin term meaning "black earth," referring to the island's dark, fertile soil, which produces a high crop yield. The island is physically characterized by an unbroken mountain wall which marches down the entire western aspect and includes 93 volcanic peaks, three of which are still active. Sumatra has long been renowned for its wildlife such as Indian elephants, tapirs, tigers, clouded leopards, civets, bearded pigs, sun bears, proboscis monkeys, Sumatran rhinoceros, and a large free-ranging population of orangutans, plus thick jungle which still covers much of the jagged island. Sumatra is also famed for its great diversity of tribes and numerous megalithic, aboriginal, and matriarchal societies—Southeast Asia's great ethnological goldmine.

SIGHTSEEING HIGHLIGHTS

All this makes Sumatra a magnificent destination for unhurried travelers.

Lake Toba: The largest lake in Southeast Asia, Lake Toba is famed for its pine-covered beaches, steep mountain slopes and cliffs, and traditional villages inhabited by the Batak. Sumatra's premier travel destination can be quickly reached from Penang via Medan; the best bet for travelers with limited time.

Bukittinggi: West Sumatra and the mountainous regions around Bukittinggi offer some of the most exciting scenery in Indonesia: peaks looming over deep canyons and splendid sheltered valleys, villages perched atop plunging ravines, great high plateaus, mountain lakes, and unique villages populated by the Minangkabau. Padang, the town closest to Bukittinggi, can be reached by air from Singapore, Jakarta, and Medan, though most travelers take a bus from Lake Toba or a ship from Jakarta.

Nias Island: Located off the west coast some 125 km southeast of Sibolga, Nias is a remote island famed for its megalithic stone altars and furniture, spectacular traditional architecture, and complex religious rites; a fascinating journey into the past. Nias can be reached by air from Medan or by boat from Sibolga.

Routes

Sumatra is an immense island which can be approached by air, sea, and land from many different directions. The northern approach begins with a 20-minute flight from Penang to Medan, followed by a short and scenic bus ride to Lake Toba. Most travelers then return to Medan and fly back to Penang. The bone-crushing overland journey south to Padang and Bukittinggi passes through one of the less touristy regions of Southeast Asia. From Padang, you can fly onward to Jakarta, Singapore, or Kuala Lumpur. Alternatives from Padang include the weekly Pelni boat to Jakarta, the marathon bus ride to Jakarta, and traveling by air or riverboat from Pekanbaru to Tanjung Pinang (an Indonesian island 60 km south of Singapore), and then, Singapore.

TRANSPORTATION TO SUMATRA

Because of visa restrictions and time-consuming travel conditions, Sumatra is best considered as a separate side trip from Malaysia or Singapore, rather than included in an all-inclusive two-month visit to Indonesia. A two-month whirlwind tour of Java, Bali, and Sumatra was a serious mistake made by this author in 1979. Never again!

Penang To Medan

Sumatra can be approached from a variety of directions, but the most convenient and popular option is to fly or ferry from Penang and then bus to Lake Toba and southward down to Bukittinggi.

Air: Malaysian Airlines's daily flight from Penang takes only 20 minutes and costs US$70 one-way or US$140 roundtrip. Sempati Air does the same flight at slightly lower cost. This inexpensive ticket is an excellent way to satisfy the "ticket out" requirement for an Indonesian visa.

SUMATRA

THAILAND

MALAYSIA

KUALA LUMPUR

MELAKA

SINGAPORE

TANJUNGPINANG

KEP. RIAU

P. LINGGA

P. SINGKEP

PANGKALPENANG

P. BANGKA

SABANG
BANDA ACEH
TANGSE
TAKENGON
MEULABOH
LHOKSEUMAWE
LANGSA
ACEH
BLANGKEJEREN
TAPAKTUAN
BINJAI
BRASTAGI
MEDAN
TEBINGTINGGI
TANJUNGBALAI
PENANG

NORTH SUMATRA

P. SIMEULUE
SINGKIL
D. TOBA
PRAPAT
SAMOSIR
SIBOLGA
GUNUNGSITOLI
RANTAUPRAPAT
DUMAI
BENGKALIS

P. NIAS
TELUKDALAM
PADANGSIDEMPUAN

P. BATU
PEKANBARU
RIAU
RENGAT

BUKITTINGGI
SOLOK
PADANG
MUARASIBERUT
P. SIBERUT
WEST SUMATRA
SUNGAIPENUH
JAMBI
JAMBI

KEP. MENTAWAI
P. SIPORA
PAGAI UTARA
PAGAI SELATAN
MUKOMUKO
BENGKULU
SOUTH SUMATRA
LUBUKLINGGAU
PALEMBANG
PRABUMULIH

BENGKULU
LAHAT
LAMPUNG
KOTABUMI

P. ENGGANO
BINTUAHAN
PANJANG
BELIMBING
SERANG

P. KRAKATOA
JAVA

0   100 km

© MOON PUBLICATIONS, INC.

Unused portions are refunded upon payment of a small service charge, often collected as the spread between exchange rates.

Sea: A fast hydrofoil, the *Gadis Langkasuka*, sails on Wed. and Fri. at 1430 from Penang to Belawan, Sumatra's port on the Malacca Straits. The journey takes five hours and costs US$45-60 depending on the class. The *bemo* from Belawan to Medan costs US$1, though this fare is often included in the price of the ferry.

Malacca To Dumai
Travelers bound directly for Bukittinggi can use the twice-weekly ferry from Malacca (Melaka) to Dumai, a sleepy port town 158 km east of Pekanbaru. The fare is about US$40. Buses continue east from Dumai to Pekanabaru and, eventually, Bukittinggi.

Note, however, that since Dumai is a "no visa" entry point, visitors *must* obtain a visa in advance from an Indonesian consulate.

Kuala Lumpur To Sumatra
Garuda and MAS fly twice weekly to Medan, Padang, and Pekanbaru.

Singapore To Sumatra
Singapore Air and Garuda fly daily to Medan and Pekanbaru, and three times weekly to Padang. Travelers heading to Sumatra from Europe or America should note that Singapore is closer than Jakarta to most Sumatran cities.

Riau Archipelago To Sumatra
Less expensive—but also more of a hassle—than direct air connections from Singapore are sea/land/air routes through the Riau Archipelago, the scattering of Indonesian islands immediately south of Singapore.

Singapore to Riau: There are dozens of routes, but the fastest is direct ferry from Singapore's Finger Pier on Prince Edward Rd. (tel. 336-0528) to either Sekupang (Batam Island) or Tanjung Pinang, the principal town on Bintan Island. Batam is the best bet for air transportation and boat connections to Sumatra. This trip takes three hours and costs US$20-30 depending on class.

A slower and cheaper approach is by ferry to Sekupang on Batam Island, where you proceed through Indonesian immigration. Boats leave three times weekly from Sekupang to Pekan-

baru on Sumatra. If you arrive on the wrong day, take a bus from Sekupang to Nagoya, a share taxi to Kabil, a ferry across to Tanjung Uban on Bintan Island, and finally (whew!) a bus to Tanjung Pinang, from where boats leave several times weekly for Pekanbaru. This route takes one day and costs about US$15.

Air: Garuda, Merpati, or Sempati fly daily from Batam Island and Tanjung Pinang to Medan (US$90), Padang (US$60), Palembang (US$60), and Pekanbaru (US$40). Batam has the larger airport and the largest number of departures, while smaller airlines use facilities on Bintam.

The main problem with flights from Riau to Sumatra or Jakarta is departure confirmation and, if you miss your flight, the high expense of hotels in Batam.

Sea: The most time-consuming but Conradesque route is from Sekupang (Batam Island) or Tanjung Pinang (Bintan Island) to Pekanbaru, via the town of Selat Panjang and up the Siak River. Two services are offered, a fast 24-hour express boat and a slower but identically priced boat which takes 40-50 hours depending on tides. Boats depart three times weekly from Sekupang, daily from the dock in Tanjung Pinang, and cost US$15-25 depending on class.

More information is under "Pekanbaru" and "Riau Archipelago."

Jakarta To Sumatra
Travelers can reach Sumatra from Jakarta by either air, land, or sea. Time permitting, buses up the Trans-Sumatra Hwy. are recommended as one of the quintessential travel experiences in Southeast Asia.

Air: Garuda, Merpati, and several private airlines fly daily from Jakarta to Jambi (US$65), Bengkulu (US$70), Pekanbaru (US$90), Padang (US$90), Medan (US$120), and Banda Aceh (US$180).

Sea: Pelni, the national steamship line, has four ships which depart Jakarta for various ports in Sumatra.

The most popular option is the 28-hour journey to Padang onboard the luxurious MV *Kerinci*, a fine way to avoid the grueling bus trip or the expensive flight. The ship departs Jakarta's Tanjung Priok Harbor on alternate Fridays at 1300 and arrives in Padang the following day around 1600. Fares run from US$20 deck class to US$60 in first class with private a/c cabins and all meals. Reservations are strongly recommended on this very popular line. You'll never forget the views of the Sumatran coastline, like a dream.

A second option is the comfortable a/c passenger vessel the KM *Lawit,* which sails alternate weeks between Jakarta and Medan with stops at Mentok (Bangka Island) and Tanjung Pinang (Bintan Island, near Singapore). Direct connections between Jakarta and Belawan, the harbor for Medan, are provided by the KM *Kambuna* and *Rinjani.* The Pelni office in Jakarta can confirm departures.

Bus: Improved road conditions and modern a/c buses now make overland travel across Sumatra a memorable and reasonably comfortable travel experience. Today, the entire Trans-Sumatra Hwy. has been paved and is in good condition except after severe storms, when mud-slides can be a problem.

Dozens of companies operate luxury a/c buses with reserved seats on the entire route from Jakarta to Lake Toba, though most travelers will spend a few days exploring other destinations such as Benkulu and Bukittinggi. Excellent service is provided by a company called ANS (Aman Nyamean Sejuk, an Indonesian name that means "Safe, Comfortable, Cool"). Sample fares and times from Jakarta: Bengkulu (US$10, 15 hours), Padang (US$25, 35 hours), Bukittinggi (US$28, 40 hours), Lake Toba (US$35, 56 hours), and Medan (US$40, 60 hours).

Tickets to all destinations can be purchased from agents in Jakarta or directly at private bus terminals. Alternatively, take a public bus from Kalideres bus terminal to Merak (three hours), from where ferries depart twice daily to Panjang at the southeastern tip of Sumatra.

The morning train from the Tanah Abang railway station connects with the afternoon ferry to Sumatra.

NORTHERN SUMATRA

North Sumatra (Sumatera Utara) is a land of craggy volcanos, high plateaus, plunging waterfalls, tropical jungle, rare wildlife, and Samosir Island in Lake Toba—one of Indonesia's major travel destinations. From the Dutch-built mountain resort of Brastagi you can visit traditional villages and climb two active volcanos. Orangutans can be seen in a rehabilitation center at Bukit Lawang, reachable from Medan. In the extreme north is Aceh, a staunchly Islamic town that ranks as one of the friendliest and least visited on the island. This rich mix of topography, wildlife, and ethnological traditions makes North Sumatra the most popular region on the island.

MEDAN

Sumatra's largest commercial center is the transportation hub which serves as the entry point for northern Sumatra. Medan is notorious among travelers for being noisy, dirty, and crowded—a crazy place of rubble-strewn streets and choking carbon-monoxide fumes. Most travelers simply arrive, make their way to the bus terminal, and leave immediately for Toba.

Attractions

Other than a sultan's palace and a mosque there is little to recommended in Medan. The tourist office on Jalan Palang Merah is poorly stocked, as is the information counter at the airport. Better-quality information can be had from travel agencies such as Nitour on Jalan Yamin and Pacto Tours on Jalan Palang Merah.

The Great Mosque, the largest in Sumatra, was built in a prewar Moroccan style by the same ruler who erected nearby Maimoon Palace (Istana Sultan Deli), an Italian-designed fantasy which incorporates an astounding mixture of Oriental, Middle Eastern, and Western architectural styles.

The Museum Sumatra Utara on Jalan Joni, in the southeast corner of town, features displays on the Sumatran tribals.

Surviving examples of Dutch-built rococo, art-deco, and art-nouveau architecture include Deli Maatschappij (now PPT Tobacco company),

White Society Club (now Bank Negara), Hotel de Boer (now Hotel Dharma Deli), Grand Hotel Medan (now a bank), Kesawan Shopping Center, an old Dutch church (Gareja Katedral), and Gubernoran, the imposing mansion of the former Dutch governor.

Budget Accommodations

Medan's *losmen* are hardly better than the town itself, though the scene is much improved from a decade ago.

Losmen Irama: The best spot for budget travelers is friendly, fairly clean, and conveniently located in an alley across from the Hotel Danu Toba International. The managers can help with travel arrangements across Sumatra, especially to their home island of Nias. 1125 Jl. Palang Merah, tel. (061) 326416, US$2-5.

Penginapan Tapian Nabaru: An excellent little place nicely located in an old Dutch home facing the Bobura River and adjacent to a public park and a Chinese temple. Quiet, clean, and only a 10-minute walk from the center of Medan. Recommended. 6 Jl. Hang Tuah, tel. (061) 512155, US$2-5.

Sigura Gura Hotel: Good location next to the Garuda office, but best considered a second choice after Irama and Tapian Nabaru. Look for the sign: Cheap Hotel. 2 Jl. Suprapto, tel. (061) 323991, US$2-5.

Moderate Accommodations

Many of the midpriced hotels are on Jl. Sisingamangaraja in the center of town.

Hotel Sumatera: A decent, renovated hotel some 400 meters from the Lake Toba bus terminal. The nearby Garuda and Dhaksina hotels have also been renovated. 21 Jl. Sisingamangaraja, tel. (061) 324807, US$10-15 standard, US$15-30 superior rooms.

Angkasa Hotel: A government-owned hotel with enormous a/c rooms, two swimming pools, and a popular Chinese restaurant. 61 Jl. Sutomo, tel. (061) 322555, US$30-45.

Wai Yat Hotel: A very popular hotel in operation for over 30 years. The Chinese owner and his Japanese-American wife (Wai Yat) are known for their hospitality and their exquisite Chinese

MEDAN

BUSES TO BELAWAN HARBOR
POST OFFICE
DHARMA DELI HOTEL
TRAIN STATION
ANGKASA HOTEL
JL. YAMIN
JL. VETERAN
CENTRAL MARKET
TO BRASTAGI
JL. GETAH
BUSES TO BOHOROK AND ACEH
JL. PARMAN
JL. HARYONO
JL. GAJAH MADA
HINDU TEMPLE
IRAMA LOSMEN
TOURIST OFFICE
JL. PANDU
WAI YAT HOTEL
HOTEL DANAU TOBA
MUSEUM
PELNI
JL. MUDA
JL. ARIFIN
SIGURA GURA HOTEL
GARUDA PLAZA HOTEL
HOTEL TIARA
DHAKSINA HOTEL
HOTEL SUMATERA
BUSES TO BRASTAGI
PENGINAPAN TAPIAN NABARU
POLONIA HOTEL
GARUDA HOTEL
JL. ABDULLAH LUBIS
MERPATI
PENANG FERRY OFFICE
MOSQUE
BUSES TO PADANG
BUSES TO BINJEI
SINGAPORE AIRLINES
MAIMOON PALACE
JL. IMAN BONJOL
JL. JUANDA
TO LAKE TOBA AND MAIN BUS TERMINAL (AMPLAS)
TO BRASTAGI
0   1 km
JL. KATAMSO
POLONIA AIRPORT
BUSES TO LAKE TOBA

© MOON PUBLICATIONS, INC.

restaurant. 44 Jl. Asia, tel. (061) 321683, US$6-10 fan, US$15-30 a/c.

Luxury Accommodations
Most of the following cater to foreign group tours and Indonesian businessmen.

Dharma Deli Hotel: Colonial charm can still be enjoyed in the foyer and restaurant of the former Hotel De Boer, an old Dutch hotel directly across from the historic post office. 2 Jl. Balai Kota, tel. (061) 327011, fax (061) 327153, US$30-50 in older rooms next to the pool, US$60-85 in the modern eight-story addition.

Danau Toba International Hotel: A four-star hotel and apartment complex in the heart of Medan, only five minutes from the airport, with 258 rooms, a Javanese restaurant, a fitness center, landscaped swimming pool, and banquet facilities. 17 Jl. Imam Bonjol, tel. (061) 327000, fax (061) 530553, US$80-150.

Tiara Hotel: Top spot in town with a swimming pool, a fitness center, and the largest convention facilities on Sumatra. Jl. Cut Mutiah, tel. (061) 516000, US$65-90.

Transportation
Taxis from the airport to city center cost about Rp2090. *Becak* drivers waiting at the airport entrance gate charge US$1 to any of the budget *losmens*. Or walk 30 minutes.

Medan's seaport is in Belawan, 26 km from town. Overpriced tourist buses shuttle travelers back and forth between the harbor and the ferry office just north of Maimoon Palace.

Medan has several bus terminals: Northwest Terminal off Jalan Subroto (Aceh and the Bohorok Orangutan Sanctuary), Brastagi Terminal on Jalan Iskander Muda (Brastagi), and the Prapat Bus Terminal at the south end of Jalan Sisingamangaraja (Lake Toba)—check the map. Amplas, a new main bus terminal, is located in south Medan on Jalan Pertahanan. Oplets into town cost Rp400. Private bus companies located on Jalan Sisingamangara have hourly departures to Lake Toba. Medan's two largest and best companies are ALS on Jalan Amuliun and ATS on Jalan Bintang. Both operate Mercedeses on scheduled routes. A *becak* from the airport to any bus terminal should cost about Rp1500.

BOHOROK ORANGUTAN CENTER

One of the world's two orangutan rehabilitation centers is located inside Gunung Leuser National Park, 80 km west of Medan near the towns of Bohorok and Bukit Lawang. The center serves to preserve wild orangutans and rehabilitate specimens confiscated from private collectors or captured from poachers. Visitors can watch feedings at 0800 and 1500 after obtaining a permit from the PPA office in Bukit Lawang, PPA headquarters in Medan, or the Medan tourist office. Just as alluring are the thick jungle and mountain trails which crisscross the national park. Guides can be hired for day treks and three-day journeys all the way to Brastagi.

Accommodations
Almost a dozen simple guesthouses are located along the riverbanks from Bukit Lawang to the cable-driven dugout which crosses the river to the orangutan sanctuary. The two original *losmen,* Wisma Leuser Sibayak (ask for Burhanuddin Rangkuti) and Wisma Bukit Lawang, are supplemented by newer upriver spots such as Yusman, Indah, Queen Paradise, and Bohorok River. All charge US$2-5 for simple rooms with common bath.

Transportation
Buses to Bukit Lawang take five hours from Medan's bus terminal on Jl. Sei Wampa. Direct buses via Medan are also available from Brastagi. Tours of the adjacent national park and hikes around Brastagi are arranged in Medan at Edelweiss on Jl. Irian Barat 49 and Jacky's Traveller's Center at Jl. Kediri 96.

Rafting The Alas River
Edelweiss Tours sponsors six-day rafting excursions down the Alas River, right through the heart of central Sumatra. Considered one of the more challenging rivers in Asia, the Alas runs through remote jungles, steep canyons, and narrow gorges, past a primate research center at Ketambe, and ends at the timber-mill town of Gelombang. Departures are scheduled monthly, leave on Saturdays, and cost around US$500 per person. Edelweiss and Jacky's Traveller's Centre also organize one-day excursions down the Wampu River, followed by a brief visit to the orangutan rehabilitation center.

BANDA ACEH

The northernmost province of Sumatra and westernmost province of Indonesia is rarely visited by travelers because of its isolation and undeserved reputation for religious extremism. The truth is that Aceh ranks as one of the friendliest and safest spots on the island, plus it offers historic architecture, superlative beaches, and picturesque rural areas.

Attractions
First visit the tourist office on Jl. Nyak Arief for maps, transportation details, and volunteer student guides.

Baitur Rahman Mosque: Aceh's premier attraction, in the center of town, was designed by an Italian architect and constructed 1879-81 by the Dutch to replace a mosque destroyed during the Aceh War. Behind the elaborate multiarched face, you'll see a splendid mixture of styles from Arabia, India, and Malaysia. Excellent views from the minarets.

Gunongan: Constructed in the 17th century for the wife of an Islamic sultan, Aceh's former Taman Sari, or Pleasure Garden, provides an odd, almost surrealistic contrast to the concrete drabness of modern Aceh.

Kerkhof: Final resting spot for some 2,200 Dutch and Indonesian soldiers who died during the 30-year Acehnese resistance movement. Like a 19th-century Dutch Vietnam Memorial, the names of thousands interred have been engraved on the commemorative wall of the wrought-iron art-nouveau entranceway.

Aceh State Museum: A large three-story museum filled with displays of local artifacts, handicrafts, ceremonial clothing, and a reconstructed *adat* Rumah Aceh, former home of an

Acehnese aristocrat. The museum is open Tues.-Sun. 0830-1800.

Colonial Architecture: Near Lapangan Merdeka ("Freedom Square") are several historic edifices, including the White Society Club, the Grand Hotel, and the Dutch Tobacco Company.

Weh (Sabang) Island

Pulau Weh—more often called Sabang after the main town—is a small but striking island blessed with beautiful beaches flanked with swaying palms, caves filled with bats and birds, outstanding snorkeling and scuba diving, hot springs, and a vast tropical game reserve known for its monkeys, reptiles, and flying foxes. The tourist office in Banda Aceh publishes a very helpful brochure about the island.

Accommodations: Four inexpensive *losmen* are in the principal town of Sabang, but most travelers stay at Hotel Pulau Jaya (tel. 0652-21344) on Jl. Umar, where clean rooms cost US$3-10. The owner can help with organized scuba-diving excursions, local treks, and homestays on other beaches.

Transportation: A local private airline called SMAC flies daily from Banda Aceh to Weh Island for about US$25.

Alternatively, take a *bemo* from Jl. Diponegoro to the port town of Pelabuhan Malahayati, 35 km from Banda Aceh. Boats leave every afternoon and take about two hours to Sabang Island.

Accommodations

Aceh has plenty of good *losmen* and hotels, though prices are somewhat higher than elsewhere in Indonesia.

Losmen International: Not the cheapest, but rooms are fairly clean and it's well located in Chinatown opposite the night market. 19 Jl. Achmad Yani, tel. (0651) 21834, US$3-8.

Aceh Hotel: An old colonial hotel built in ornate, gingerbread style and still trying to pretend that it is the prestigious first-class Dutch hotel that it ceased to be about 40 years ago. Despite the stained ceilings and peeling walls, the Aceh still sports more old-world atmosphere than most other Indonesian dives. Located just opposite the Baitur Rahman Mosque. 1 Jl. Mohammed Jam, tel. (0651) 21354, US$3-8.

Medan Hotel: Decent midpriced hotel with clean but simple rooms. 15A Jl. Yai, tel. (0651) 21501, US$5-20.

Sultan Hotel: Three-star hotel with 90 a/c rooms, a coffee shop, "banquet" facilities, and negotiable "grout" rates. Good value. 1 Jl. Panglima Polem, tel. (0361) 22469, fax (0361) 31770, US$25-60.

Kuala Tripa Hotel: Aceh's top-end hotel features the town's only disco, fitness center, and hotel swimming pool. 24 Jl. Mesjid Raya, tel. (0361) 21455, fax (0361) 21790, US$40-75.

BANDA ACEH TO TOBA

A fascinating journey can be made from Aceh to Lake Toba through the incredibly rugged topography of central Sumatra. Buses from Aceh reach Lake Tawar via Bureuen, though train enthusiasts might stop briefly in Sigli to view the colonial train station and its collection of antique locomotives.

Beautiful Lake Tawar and the town of Takingeun are great spots to unwind; inexpensive *losmen* are found near the marketplace and around the perimeter of the lake. Blangkejeren to the south offers longhouses which once served as ancestral homes of the Gayo, former headhunters who fiercely resisted Dutch rule. Another entrance to Gunung Leuser National Park is near Tanah Merah, two km north of Kutacane.

Kutacane, a small market town known for its rice and potent cannabis, marks the division line between the Gayo homelands and Batak country. Buses continue south from Kutacane to Brastagi and Lake Toba.

BRASTAGI AND VICINITY

Brastagi is a cool and refreshing Dutch-built hill resort that ranks as one of the highlights of the journey through Sumatra. The climb up to this town is like an elevator ride to almost 1,400 meters above sea level. The surrounding countryside offers great hiking, Batak and Karo villages with distinctive architecture, fields of European vegetables and fragrant flowers, and a pair of challenging volcanos.

Attractions

The only sight of note is the large market selling fresh fruits, flowers, and locally grown vegetables. However, while in Brastagi, try the

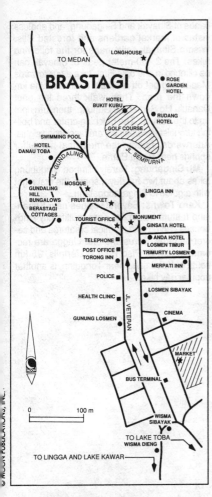

BRASTAGI

TO MEDAN
LONGHOUSE
ROSE GARDEN HOTEL
HOTEL BUKIT KUBU
RUDANG HOTEL
GOLF COURSE
SWIMMING POOL
HOTEL DANAU TOBA
JL. GUNDALING
JL. SEMPURNA
GUNDALING HILL BUNGALOWS
MOSQUE
FRUIT MARKET
BERASTAGI COTTAGES
LINGGA INN
TOURIST OFFICE
MONUMENT
GINSATA HOTEL
ANDA HOTEL
LOSMEN TIMUR
TELEPHONE
POST OFFICE
TORONG INN
TRIMURTY LOSMEN
MERPATI INN
POLICE
LOSMEN SIBAYAK
HEALTH CLINIC
JL. VETERAN
CINEMA
GUNUNG LOSMEN
MARKET
BUS TERMINAL
0 100 m
WISMA SIBAYAK
TO LAKE TOBA
WISMA DIENG
TO LINGGA AND LAKE KAWAR

refreshing vitamin-rich *marquisa* juice, buffalo-milk yogurt, hot spiced ginger milk, and *babi panggang,* a traditional Batak meal of roast pork and sauce.

A sensible way to explore the countryside and visit the traditional Karo Batak villages is to organize a party of four and hire a car for about US$40 per day. Guides from Rafflesia and Wisma Sibayak can help with jungle treks to Bukit Lawang, volcano climbs up Gunung Sibayak, and rafting expeditions down the Alas River.

The tourist office between the post office and the fruit market can help with additional information, as can the talented guides in the Rafflesia Tours Center opposite the post office.

Budget Accommodations

Backpackers generally stay in the inexpensive *losmen* and homestays on the main street, Jl. Veteran, while mid-market travelers and Dutch group tourists prefer the newer hotels on Gundaling Hill, west of town with great views of Mt. Sibayak.

Wisma Sibayak: Brastagi's backpackers' center is owned and operated by a fellow named Pelawi, a resident expert on Karo culture and an information goldmine on nearby hikes and histories. 1 Jl. Udara, US$2-5.

Losmen Sibayak Guesthouse: A main-road option that handles the overflow from Wisma Sibayak. Jalan Veteran, US$2-5.

Ginsata Hotel: Friendly, clean, cheap, and managed by Mr. Ginting, another local character and an information source on jungle treks and mountain climbs. Try the Nasi Padang restaurant downstairs. 79 Jl. Veteran, tel. (0628) 20901, US$2-5.

Moderate Accommodations

For a few dollars more, budget travelers can find better rooms with views up on Gundaling Hill.

Wisma Ikat: An old colonial villa with simple but clean rooms, plus a big garden with great views of Gunung Sibayak. Jl. Pendidikan, US$4-8.

Gundaling Hill Bungalows: Several other *losmen* and homestays on Gundaling Hill offer midpriced rooms with views of Mt. Sibayak. Karo Hill, BIB, Miranda, and Kaliaga Bungalows are recommended. Jl. Pendidikan and Jl. Gundaling, US$5-12.

Bukit Kubu Hotel: You'll feel like a Dutch colonialist at this gracious hotel, located one km before town amidst a nine-hole golf course, with tennis courts and tremendous views of nearby volcanos. Old-wing rooms are more romantic than new-wing additions. 2 Jl. Sempurna, tel. (0628) 20832, Medan tel. (061) 519636, US$15-30 standard rooms, US$45-65 bungalows.

International Sibayak Hotel: Brastagi's newest and biggest hotel has a swimming pool, a gym, a disco, tennis courts, and 120 a/c rooms overlooking landscaped gardens. Jalan

Merdeka, tel. (0628) 20928, fax (0628) 20459, US$60-95.

Transportation

Brastagi (also spelled Berastagi) nestles at the northern edge of the Karo Plateau, 68 km southwest of Medan at an elevation of 1,330 meters. From Medan, buses leave every 15 minutes from the depot on Jl. Iskandar Muda and take about two hours.

From Lake Toba, take a Medan-bound bus one hour to Siantar, then another bus three hours to Kabanjahe. A final minibus travels the last 12 km to Brastagi. The entire trip takes almost a full day, but the scenery is terrific.

Vicinity of Brastagi

Travelers often spend weeks exploring the tropical jungles, waterfalls, lakes, and volcanos near Brastagi.

Mt. Sibayak: First hike up Gundaling Hill for fantastic views over the town, the steaming volcanos of Sibayak and Singabung, and endless vistas of market gardens and forested hills. Wisma Sibayak sells maps for the following hikes. The 2,450-meter peak of Sibayak can be climbed in one day. First, take a bus towards Medan and get off at Daulu Junction, nine km down the road. Then walk three km past Danaulu I to Semangat Gunung, then turn right up to the summit. The belching crater and boiling turquoise-colored lake are fascinating sights. Afterwards, soak in the medicinal hot sulfur springs near Radja Berne.

Mt. Singabung: Rarely climbed Singabung takes about two full days; spend the first night with a guide in Singaranggalang.

Karo Towns: Several villages near Kabanjahe feature traditional Karo multifamily longhouses carved with mythical creatures and secret patterns. Barusjahe and Lingga are recommended. Si Piso Piso Waterfalls, 25 km south of Kabanjahe near Tongging, is another popular day hike.

LAKE TOBA

Lake Toba is one of the most spellbinding destinations in Indonesia. Surrounded on all sides by pine-covered beaches, steep mountain slopes, and forested hills, with Samosir Island sitting right in the middle, Toba is justifiably regarded as the chief draw of Sumatra and among the most idyllic and relaxing spots in the archipelago. Some of the charm has been lost to a new hydroelectric dam which lowered the lake level, and the arrival of Western touches such as videos and noisy motorcycles, yet Toba remains a great place to unwind and recover from the hardships of overland travel across Sumatra.

PRAPAT

Prapat is the main town on the lake and principal embarkation point for ferries to Samosir in the middle of the lake. Once the exile point for Sukarno during the war for independence, Prapat today has grown into a busy tourist resort that caters to upscale travelers and Indonesian weekenders.

The town is divided between shops and hotels along the busy Trans-Sumatran Hwy. and quieter places near the ferry terminal. A small tourist office is just under the Batak Welcome Gate at the central intersection. Prapat has a couple of banks which exchange traveler's checks at fair rates.

Warning: Prapat is a place where travel agents often sell worthless tickets and book nonexistent bus seats. Andilo Nancy Travel near the bus terminal and Bonanza Holiday in the Pago Pago Inn by the ferry dock are reliable. Bolok Silau Travel near the dock has also been recommended.

Accommodations
The is no reason to stay in Prapat unless you arrive late and miss the last ferry to Samosir. Budget *losmen* are down near the Samosir ferry dock and around the bus terminal on the Trans-Sumatran Hwy., handy for bus departures but two km from the ferry.

Andilo Travel: Three spots are conveniently located adjacent to the bus terminal. Andilo Nancy Travel, the oldest and most popular, also operates a small *losmen* near the ferry. Trans-Sumatra Hwy., tel. (0625) 41548, US$3-6.

Youth Hostel Melati: Another popular choice adjacent to the bus terminal. Trans-Sumatra Hwy., US$3-6.

Pago Pago Inn: The best budget spot near the ferry dock has clean, airy rooms plus good views of the lake. Their travel agency appears honest. 50 Jl. Haranggaol, US$3-6.

Prapat Hotel: Constructed by the Dutch in 1911, the oldest hotel at the lake offers clean and comfortable rooms overlooking the lake and a private beach. Batak singers entertain on weekends. 1 Jl. Marihat, tel. (0625) 41012, US$45-65.

Transportation
Until the airport is finished in a few years, Lake Toba will remain accessible only by overland transportation.

Buses leave hourly from the Amplas bus terminal in south Medan and from several private terminals such as the recommended ALS Bus Company on Jl. Amuliun. ALS and PMH, another good company, have offices in Prapat. Several other private bus companies are on Jl. Sisingamangaraja opposite the Grand Mosque. Express buses reach Lake Toba in about four hours, while ordinary buses can take six or eight. The direct route via Simalungun is quick, but the longer route through Brastagi is vastly more scenic, and a stopover in Brastagi is highly recommended.

Buses and minibuses from Bukittinggi take about 15 hours and usually stop at the main terminal two km from the ferry dock. *Oplet* continue down to the harbor. ALS and PMH provide the best bus service to Bukittinggi.

TOMOK

Ferries from Prapat generally go to Tomok, the main town on Samosir, before continuing up to Tuk Tuk. Most travelers head directly to Tuk Tuk and only visit Tomok on a hike or a shopping expedition.

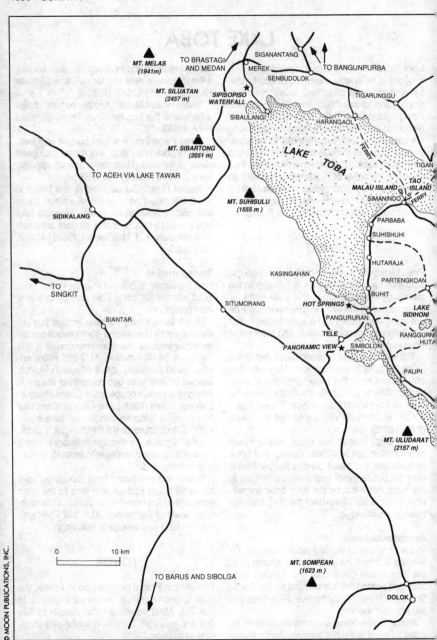

MT. MELAS
(1941m)

MT. SILUATAN
(2457 m)

TO BRASTAGI
AND MEDAN

SIGANANTANG

MEREK

SENBUDOLOK

TO BANGUNPURBA

SIPISOPISO
WATERFALL

TIGARUNGGU

SIBAULANGI

HARANGAOL

MT. SIBARTONG
(2051 m)

LAKE
TOBA

FERRY

TO ACEH VIA LAKE TAWAR

TIGAN

MALAU ISLAND

TAO
ISLAND

SIMANINDO

FERRY

MT. SUHISULU
(1555 m)

SIDIKALANG

PARBABA

SUHISHUHI

HUTARAJA

PARTENGKOAN

KASINGAHAN

TO
SINGKIT

SITUMORANG

BUHIT

HOT SPRINGS

LAKE
SIDIHONI

SIANTAR

PANGURURAN

RANGGURN
HUTA

TELE

SIMBOLON

PANORAMIC VIEW

PALIPI

MT. ULUDARAT
(2157 m)

© MOON PUBLICATIONS, INC.

0   10 km

MT. SOMPEAN
(1623 m)

TO BARUS AND SIBOLGA

DOLOK

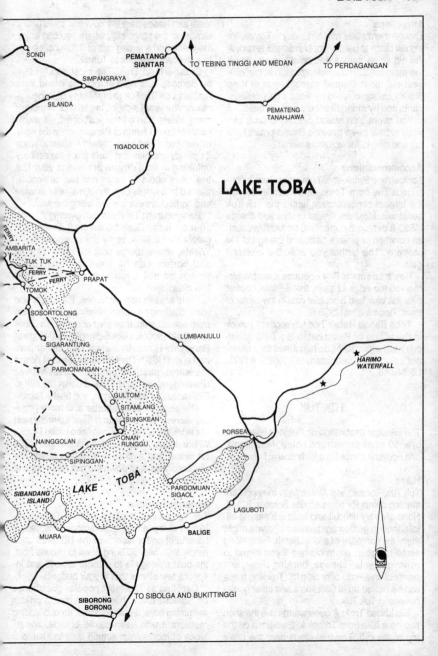

Attractions

Though there's little reason to stay in Tomok, it's a good place to bargain for handicrafts and view the old stone coffins and *adat* homes just off the main road. The chief attraction is the 200-year-old, boat-shaped sarcophagus of King Sidarbuta, surrounded by those of his descendants and by magnificent old banyan trees.

You might also attend Sunday church services to hear deep-throated Bataks praise Kristus and sing in full-volume strains.

Accommodations

Losmen and Batak-style homestays form a continuous line from Tomok to Ambarita, though the largest concentration flanks the Tuk Tuk peninsula. Most are similar in style and charge US$3-8 per room depending on facilities, such as common or private bath, and the age of the property. The farther you walk, the quieter it gets.

Roy's Losmen: Roy operates a simple *losmen* on the edge of town, three Batak houses near the lake, and a popular cafe in the center of town. Rooms cost US$3-6.

Toba Beach Hotel: Two km south of Tomok in the village of Parambatan is a fairly luxurious hotel with a lakeside restaurant for a pleasant splurge. Parambatan, tel. (0625) 41275, US$40-65.

TUK TUK

The principal destination on Samosir Island has over 50 small *losmen* and hotels, restaurants, and souvenir shops on a fairly scenic peninsula.

Hikes

Tuk Tuk, Tomok, and Ambarita to the north are starting points for hikes across Samosir Island. None are very difficult and trails are easy to follow, though guides are plentiful and you might enjoy the company of a local Batak. Bring along some raingear, warm clothes if you intend to overnight, small change, drinking water, and plenty of *kreteks* to offer as gifts. Trekking maps can be picked up at Carolina's and other guesthouses in Tuk Tuk.

Silakhosa Trek: A good warm-up is the short two-hour hike from Tomok to Silakhosa on the top of the cliff. The trail starts near the raja's tomb and heads past the souvenir stalls until it climbs up the steep cliff, where you can enjoy the views and a strong cup of Batak coffee before descending back to Tomok.

Cross-island Trek: The most popular trek on Samosir cuts right across the island from Ambarita or Tuk Tuk to the village of Pangururan on the west side of the island. Although many hikers start on the east coast, it's much better to take a *bemo* to Pangururan in the early morning and hike back toward Ambarita, since it's mostly downhill and you'll enjoy the scenery unfolding in front of you, not behind you! The trek takes about 10 hours and can be accomplished in a single day, though simple *losmen* and homestays are located along the way.

Pangururan: Trekkers can overnight in the 10-room Barat Guesthouse on Jl. Singamangaraja for US$2-4, or try the upmarket Hotel Wisata, where rooms cost US$4-15. Guides and porters can be hired in Pangururan, though the trail is relatively easy to follow in this direction.

There are two popular routes. The longer and more challenging option heads south along the main coastal road, then east about 16 km (three hours) past scenic Lake Sidihoni to the village of Ranggurni Huta. Homestays plus dinner here cost about US$2. The trail continues east across the island, past two primitive forest houses (Pasanggrahan I and II), and down the cliff to Sigarantung, Parmonangan, and finally Tomok.

The second route, shorter and more popular, leaves Pangururan and heads directly east to the village of Partungkoan (also called Dolok), where John's Accommodations charges US$2 for dinner and a room in a Batak chalet. The trail continues east down the mountain ridge to Ambarita.

Accommodations

Tuk Tuk peninsula offers the island's best selection of low-priced accommodations, plus a handful of better resorts in the US$8-25 price range. With over 50 bungalows to choose from, the best strategy is to wander around and inspect a few places that fit your budget.

Carolina's: The most popular guesthouse on Samosir Island has its own pier, a private swimming cove, a bulletin board, an outstanding restaurant with fresh-baked breads, and all types of rooms from simple huts to luxurious

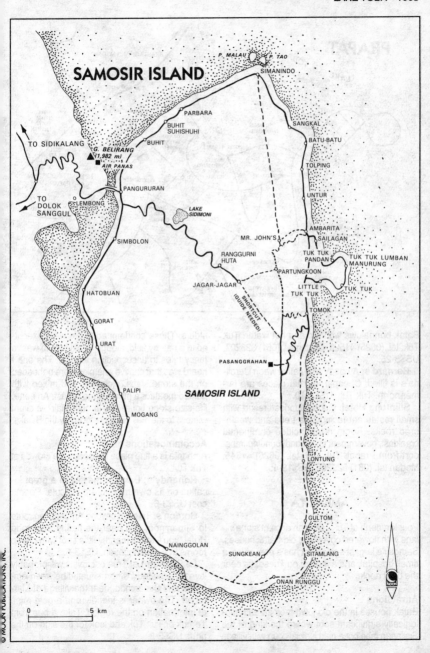

SAMOSIR ISLAND

TO SIDIKALANG

TO DOLOK SANGGUL

P. MALAU   P. TAO
SIMANINDO

PARBARA
BUHIT SUHISHUHI
BUHIT
G. BELIRANG
(1,982 m)
AIR PANAS
PANGURURAN
LEMBONG
SIMBOLON

SANGKAL
BATU-BATU
TOLPING
UNTUR

LAKE SIDIMONI

MR. JOHN'S
RANGGURNI HUTA
PARTUNGKOON
JAGAR-JAGAR
SHORTCUT (GUIDE NEEDED)

AMBARITA
SAILAGAN
TUK TUK PANDAN
TUK TUK LUMBAN MANURUNG
LITTLE TUK TUK
TUK TUK
TOMOK

HATOBUAN
GORAT
URAT

PALIPI

MOGANG

PASANGGRAHAN

SAMOSIR ISLAND

LONTUNG

GULTOM

NAINGGOLAN   SUNGKEAN   SITAMLANG
ONAN RUNGGU

0   5 km

MOON

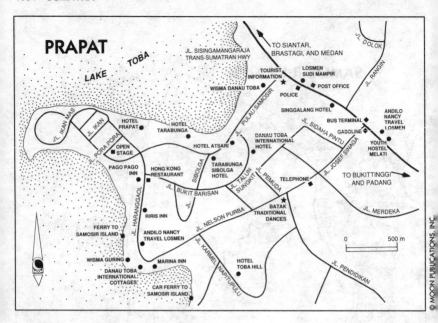

PRAPAT

© MOON PUBLICATIONS, INC.

Batak bungalows with a/c and hot water. Tuk Tuk, tel. (0625) 41520, Medan tel. (061) 326207, US$5-25.

Bernard's: A handy alternative when Carolina's is filled. Cheaper, quieter places are farther north. Tuk Tuk, US$6-10.

Silintong Hotel: Good midpriced resort with small restaurant facing pine trees and weathered rocks. Room rates include continental breakfast, government taxes, and roundtrip transport from Prapat. Tuk Tuk, tel. (0625) 41345, Medan tel. (061) 529265, US$18-45.

AMBARITA

Four km north of Tuk Tuk is an ancient stone village with flowered coves and old Batak houses. Samosir's largest settlement has a post office, a small hospital, and a market on Tuesdays near the boat dock.

Attractions

Batak houses in the old town face an archaeologically significant spot where the king of the Siallagan tribe once held judicial court with village elders. Those condemned to die were executed in a nearby field, though locals love to weave fancy tales to unsuspecting tourists. The one I heard was that captive enemies were beheaded on the stone slabs, diced up, and mixed with buffalo meat for a ritual village repast. An eerie, life-size stone figure sits in one chair—a silent witness to the rites once practiced by the Bataks.

Accommodations

Ambarita is a fine place to escape the crowds at Tuk Tuk.

Rohandy's: Batak homestay in a great location on its own miniature peninsula. Rooms cost US$3-6.

Gordon's: Two km beyond Ambarita en route to Simanindo, and near the flashy Sopotoba Hotel, you'll find a friendly little spot with cheap rooms in a quiet location. US$3-6.

Le Shangri-La: True escapists will probably love this isolated *losmen,* situated between Ambarita and Simanindo, near the village of Martahan. The owner is friendly and a gold mine of information on the region. Take a bus from Tomok or Tuk Tuk and look for the sign on the right. US$3-8.

SIMANINDO

Simanindo, a traditional village on the north tip of Samosir, 16 km from Ambarita, is chiefly visited for its boat building industry, offshore islands, and amazing Batak architecture.

Attractions

Superb examples of beautiful Batak homes are found all over the island, but none are as impressive as the former king's house in Simanindo, a large earthquake-proof structure which features elaborate carvings and sets of buffalo horns representing the 11 generations of the Sidarok rajas. Now a museum, the interior is filled with large Dutch and Chinese platters, spears, *kris,* carvings, witch-doctor charms, and *huda huda* horses once used in trance dances.

Flanking the king's residence are five large homes and smaller rice-storage barns which open onto a small pavilion of royal graves. Performances of life-size wooden puppets are given on weekends.

WESTERN SUMATRA

West Sumatra stretches from Sibolga in the north to Padang in the south—a region of isolated villages, towering mountain ranges, and vast jungle bisected by the infamous Trans-Sumatra Highway. So rugged and unpredictable is this winding road that one of the chief interests of West Sumatra is the journey through it. The legendary expedition has lost some of its horrors with improved highway maintenance, but overlanders must accept the inevitability of landslides, washed-out bridges, buses packed with everything from chickens to coffins, suicidal bus drivers, and endless Indonesian video movies played at full distorted volume. Medan to Padang takes 14 to 30 hours, depending on road conditions and how many times the driver stops for meals and *kreteks*. Overlanders generally overnight in Sibolga before continuing south. Aside from the journey itself, West Sumatra's chief attractions are the spectacular landscapes, Minangkabau culture around Bukittinggi, and the remote island of Nias.

SIBOLGA

Sibolga chiefly serves as the embarcation point for boats to Nias and as an overnight pit stop on the grueling journey from Toba to Bukittinggi. The eastern approach to the port town of Sibolga is dramatic: the bus rounds a corner and abruptly plunges down a series of hairpin turns to the coast. Buses often make this descent at sunset; travelers who have mounted themselves on the roof will enjoy a spectacular experience. Yet it is ironic that a town set in such a superb setting should turn out to be so uninspiring—Sibolga more closely resembles an exile point for political prisoners than a romantic ocean resort.

Accommodations
Self-appointed hotel touts and guides will appear at the *ekspres* bus terminal to direct you to the next available boat or one of Sibolga's famous *losmen,* which are grungy, noisy, and uniformly suffer from unpleasant owners.

Most travelers avoid Sibolga by catching the Nias boat, which departs nightly except Sundays around 2200. Tickets can be purchased until 2000 from the shipping office near the old harbor, but boats leave from the new harbor at the opposite end of town. On-board tickets are sold on a space-available basis.

Pandan and Kalangan beaches, eight and 14 km south of Sibolga, are pleasant alternatives when boats are delayed.

Hidap Baru: One of Sibolga's better hotels is more expensive than the dives near the dock but probably worth the money. 123 Jl. Suprapto, tel. (0642) 21957, US$5-15.

Losmen Bando Kanduang: Several inexpensive *losmen* are down near the Nias dock. 142 Jl. Horas, tel. (0642) 21149, US$4-6.

Hotel Tapian Nauli: Well-heeled or into Maughamesque colonial nostalgia? Try Sibolga's best hotel, in the north end of town. 5 Jl. Let Parman, tel. (0642) 21116, US$10-18.

NIAS ISLAND

With its famous megalithic stone altars and furniture, spectacular traditional architecture, and complex religious rites, a trip to this fascinating island, 125 km southwest of Sibolga, is a journey into the past. About the size of Bali, Nias boasts a magnificent megalithic heroic culture which flourished well into the 20th century; headhunting and human sacrifice were still practiced as late as 1935.

Nias today is known for its traditional culture—which remains largely intact despite a century of contact with the outside world—as well as its thick jungle, near-impassable roads, and beaches blessed with some of the finest surf between Australia and India.

Transportation
Gunung Sitoli, on the northern tip, is Nias's largest town and the only place where traveler's checks can be cashed at decent rates. A small tourist office is one block from the pier at 6 Jl. Sukarno.

However, since most of the megalithic monuments and beaches are located in the south, near the town of Teluk Dalam, it's best to take a boat from Sibolga directly to Teluk Dalam. The road which connects Gunung Sitoli with Teluk Dalam is primitive and barely passable in the wet season.

Air: Until an airport is constructed in the south, Nias's only air connection is on SMAC, which flies daily from Medan to Gunung Sitoli for about US$50.

Boat: Boats operate daily except Sundays from Sibolga to Gunung Sitoli, and three times weekly from Sibolga to Teluk Dalam. Departures are in the evenings around 2200 and take 10-12 hours.

Gunung Sitoli

The former Dutch administrative center and base for early German missionaries lacks charm but offers good walks to nearby villages with older homes. Traditional *rumah adat* with curious oval floor-plans still stand outside town in Hiliana and Hilimbawedesolo, 13 km south of Gunung Sitoli.

Accommodations: Local *losmen* are grungy but probably acceptable for one night. Hotel Wisata, just opposite the pier on Jl. Sirao, has clean and fairly comfortable rooms for US$4-8. Hotel Gomo, one block south of the pier, also has decent rooms in the same price range. Probably the best place is Wisma Soliga, two km outside town, where clean and spacious rooms cost from US$5.

Teluk Dalam

Teluk Dalam, second-largest town on Nias, chiefly serves as the access point for Lagundi Beach, 12 km west. Lagundi can be reached with a *bemo* or hired motorcycle for US$1. Traveler's checks can be exchanged in local stores, but only at very bad rates; bring a thick wad of small bills since nobody can change larger notes.

Accommodations: Wisma Jamburae has simple rooms from US$4, while Hotel Ampera has larger rooms from US$8.

Lagundi Beach

This horseshoe-shaped bay consists of two fishing villages, which together are the Kuta and

Legian of Nias, discovered by Australian and American surfers in the mid-1970s. Lagundi Bay served as the primary port of south Nias until the Krakatau eruption of 1883 wiped it out and the port was moved to Teluk Dalam (which means "Port of Peace"), leaving Lagundi to sleep on.

The surf here is almost legendary; much better than at Kuta, with waves breaking over three meters in hypnotically rhythmic patterns—an unreal world, like a dream. The best surf is a 15-minute walk to the point, where all the right-handers peel off, filled with wild sea turtles in the water.

Accommodations: Over 40 *losmen* flank the bay between the surfing spots on the west side and the less congested beaches in the east. All charge about US$1 per room but expect their guests to eat in their cafes to compensate for the low room rates.

Bawomataluo

The most important village architecturally in south Nias is renowned for its ancient homes festooned with superb carvings, high-roofed gables, and megalithic furniture scattered around the village courtyard. Top draw is the reconstructed *omo sebua* owned by the royal family but now converted into a museum raised on gigantic pillars and covered with exquisite wall carvings. Massive megaliths carved with great symbolism complete the scene. Touristy to the extreme (don't even *ask* about stone jumping), Bawomataluo remains the singular attraction of south Nias.

Bawomataluo is 14 km from Lagundi and best reached with hired motorcycle for about US$1.

Hilisimaetano

Sixteen km inland from Teluk Dalam on a good asphalt road is another traditional village with over 140 *adat* homes flanked by megaliths which line both sides of the broad stone-paved courtyard. Less popular than Bawomataluo; stone jumping is often performed for tourists on Saturday afternoons.

Bawomataluo-Hilisimaetano Hike

An outstanding one-day walk via a back path which passes through a number of traditional villages still filled with stone seats, memorial benches, and stairs of honor.

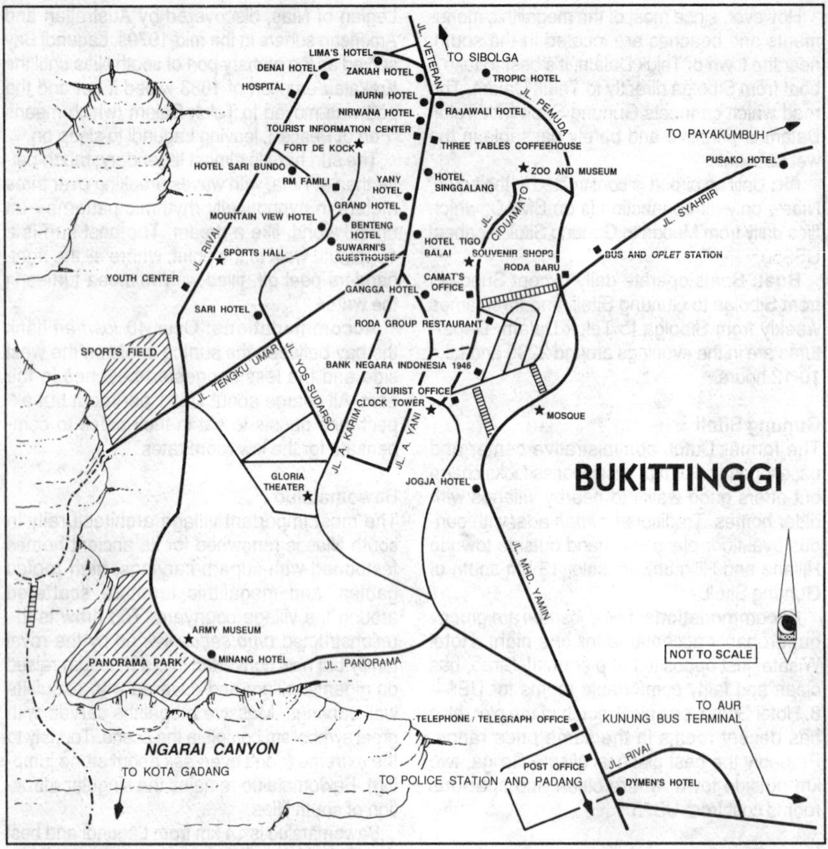

Map labels (BUKITTINGGI):

TO SIBOLGA
LIMA'S HOTEL
DENAI HOTEL
ZAKIAH HOTEL
TROPIC HOTEL
HOSPITAL
MURNI HOTEL
JL. VETERAN
JL. PEMUDA
NIRWANA HOTEL
RAJAWALI HOTEL
TOURIST INFORMATION CENTER
THREE TABLES COFFEEHOUSE
TO PAYAKUMBUH
FORT DE KOCK
ZOO AND MUSEUM
HOTEL SARI BUNDO
PUSAKO HOTEL
RM FAMILI
YANY HOTEL
HOTEL SINGGALANG
JL. SYAHRIR
MOUNTAIN VIEW HOTEL
GRAND HOTEL
JL. RIVAI
BENTENG HOTEL
HOTEL TIGO BALAI
JL. CIQUAMATO
SPORTS HALL
SUWARNI'S GUESTHOUSE
SOUVENIR SHOPS
RODA BARU
BUS AND OPLET STATION
YOUTH CENTER
GANGGA HOTEL
CAMAT'S OFFICE
SARI HOTEL
RODA GROUP RESTAURANT
SPORTS FIELD
BANK NEGARA INDONESIA 1946
JL. TENGKU UMAR
JL. YOS SUDARSO
TOURIST OFFICE
CLOCK TOWER
JL. A. KARIM
JL. A. YANI
MOSQUE
GLORIA THEATER
JOGJA HOTEL
BUKITTINGGI
JL. MHD YAMIN
NOT TO SCALE
ARMY MUSEUM
MINANG HOTEL
PANORAMA PARK
JL. PANORAMA
TELEPHONE / TELEGRAPH OFFICE
TO AUR KUNUNG BUS TERMINAL
NGARAI CANYON
TO KOTA GADANG
POST OFFICE
JL. RIVAI
TO POLICE STATION AND PADANG
DYMEN'S HOTEL

Orahill is the nicest town because of the relative absence of *"Allo Turi!"* Bawomataluo is best for tribal houses. Siwalawa is rather run-down. Onohondo is friendly, plus it has an inexpensive *losmen* for trekkers. Hilinawalo is the most traditional village, over 100 years old. Bawogosali is a pleasant and picturesque village, but Hilisimaetano is the worst for rascally kids. Just follow the stone path which connects all the villages on this 15-km walk. Highly recommended.

BUKITTINGGI

The administrative and cultural center for the Minangkabau people, Bukittinggi is one of the loveliest, friendliest, and most relaxed towns in Sumatra—a real oasis after the rugged bus ride from Toba or Jakarta. There are musical taxis, pompadoured horse-carts, veiled schoolgirls, flower markets, good restaurants, and a wide selection of reasonable accommodations. Bukittinggi is also an excellent base to explore the nearby canyons, caves, equatorial lakes, hot springs, and traditional villages centered around Minangkabau architecture.

It can't be overstressed how important proper dress is in West Sumatra. The Minangkabau regard many travelers as impoverished hippies because of their unkempt appearance, saying that they lack *baso basi*, "good manners." Women should *always* remain well covered and never expose their shoulders or knees. Men should dress in long pants and clean shirts, rather than shorts or muscle fatigues. Modesty and respectable dress will improve goodwill and make your trip much more enjoyable.

Attractions

The tourist office near the clock tower has maps, brochures, and schedules of upcoming cultural events, and can help with organized tours of the countryside. Information can also be picked up from local bookstores and travel agencies near Yany Hotel.

Clock Tower: In the center of town and overlooking the market is Bukittinggi's Big Ben, constructed by the Dutch in 1827.

Bukittinggi Museum: Minangkabau culture is featured in the cluster of traditional houses which comprise the oldest museum in West Sumatra. Inside the two rice barns and communal living house are exhibits of resplendent wedding costumes, headdresses, musical instruments, bronzework, costumed mannequins, and architectural models of current and obsolete villages. The adjacent zoo is deplorable.

Fort de Kock: Erected by the Dutch in 1825, this site is best visited at sunset when giant fruit bats come out, looking like birds without tails. The site now serves as a public water supply.

Ngarai Canyon: On the southeast edge of town lies a four-km-long chasm with sheer rocky walls plunging down to the riverbed below. A two-km trail leads down to the river past Japanese tunnels and across to the silversmith village of Kota Gadang.

Budget Accommodations

Bukittinggi's cheap *losmen* on Jl. Yani in the center of town charge US$2-5 for small but acceptable rooms. Be forewarned, however, that you are awakened each morning by the sounds of motorcycles, cars, and buses—ask for a room in the back.

Gangga Hotel: Walking down from the clock tower, the first rambling building on the right has decent rooms and sells inexpensive 10-day tours to Siberut Island. Proprietor Lala Iswandy is friendly and quite helpful. 70 Jl. Yani, tel. (0752) 22967, US$3-6.

Wisma Tigo Balai: Top-of-the-hill *losmen* with very basic rooms at rock-bottom prices. 100 Jl. Yani, tel. (0752) 21824, US$2-4.

Yany Hotel: An old colonial building with fairly clean rooms. The low-price cubicles are box-like, but the more expensive rooms include hot water and private bath. 101 Jl. Yani, tel. (0752) 22740, US$3-20.

Hotel Srikandi: Constructed in 1987 and still one of the newer lodges in the neighborhood. Clean rooms with private bath and a spacious veranda. 117 Jl. Yani, tel. (0752) 22984, US$5-8.

Moderate Accommodations

To beat the noise at somewhat higher prices, stay up near Fort de Kock.

Mountain View Hotel: Great views and pleasant atmosphere make this a real find. Suwarni's Guesthouse across the road and Hotel Benteng up the street are also highly recommended. 3 Jl. Benteng, tel. (0725) 21621, US$8-14.

Lima's Hotel: Older but very clean hotel removed from the traffic on Jl. Yani. Jalan Kesehatan, tel. (0752) 22763, US$12-25.

Hotel Pusako: The 1992 opening of this US$23-million-dollar Aerowisata-managed hotel finally provided Bukittinggi with first-class accommodations. Facilities in the 190-room hotel include three restaurants, a 350-person conference hall, tennis courts, and the area's only heated swimming pool. P.O. Box 69, tel. (0752) 22111, fax (0752) 21017, US$80-120.

Transportation

Bukittinggi's main bus terminal is located three km outside of town. Arrivals from Toba should get off in the center of town near the clock tower. Bus tickets to Toba and Jakarta should be purchased directly from ANS, ALS, or Enggano bus companies on Jalan Pemuda or out at the Aur Kuning *terminal bis.* Special minibuses now reach Lake Toba in about 14 hours with stops at hot springs and waterfalls.

VICINITY OF BUKITTINGGI

The countryside around Bukittinggi could keep you busy for weeks. Organized tours or chartered *bemos* are highly recommended—on your own you'll have long waits for public transport. Check with the travel agents in Yany and Singgalang hotels.

Lake Maninjau

Known for its culture, remoteness, and beauty, this huge crater lake 34 km west of Bukittinggi is among the largest in the world—a wonder in itself. The ride out is just as incredibly scenic as the 610-meter drop to the lakeshore. *Bemos* go direct from Bukittinggi, though a better alternative is to hike for six hours down from Lawang, a market village five km beyond Matur. Lake Maninjau has several inexpensive *losmen* and facilities for swimming, fishing, and boating.

Payakumbuh And Vicinity

Dozens of Minangkabau villages inhabited by traditional craftsmen and displaying horn-roofed homes are located outside Bukittinggi in countryside beautiful enough to stop your heart.

Payakumbuh, 33 km east of Bukittinggi, is larger than Bukittinggi and not as charming, but the surrounding landscape offers a spectacular blend of deep caves, icy waterfalls, broad canyons, blazing ricefields, megalithic stones carved by ancient peoples, and traditional villages largely unchanged by the 20th century.

Attractions: The village of Guguk, 13 km north of town, features an old village council house and over two dozen mysterious stone megaliths and menhirs profusely carved with symbolic figures. Grave sites? Magical talismans? Nobody knows.

Taram is a lovely traditional village just five km from Payakumbuh, while Balubus, 10 km from town, features a small museum and a long central avenue flanked by typical Minang housing. Nature lovers can also visit Harau Canyon (like a miniature Yosemite Valley, with four spectacular waterfalls and protected wildlife, a five-tiered waterfall at Burai, and limestone caves at Ngalan Indah).

Equator certificates (the equator is 37 km distant) are available from the local tourist office on Jl. Sudirman.

Accommodations: As a leading alternative to Bukittinggi, Payakumbuh now has several simple homestays and inexpensive hotels. Travelers usually stay at a cozy homestay called Mr. Wet's Place at 16 Jl. Lingkungan, about four blocks east of the bus stop. Mr. Wet rents bikes, leads treks, tells fairly good jokes, and performs "marvelous magic tricks."

Wisma Bougainville on Jl. Sudirman and Wisma Flamboyan at 73 Jl. Suryani have clean rooms for US$6-10.

Batusangkar And Vicinity

More attractive, and with greater attractions than Payakumbuh, is Batusangkar, 50 km southeast of Bukittinggi. Former capital of the Minangkabau nation and Dutch stronghold during their struggle against the Paderis, this town and its surrounding countryside are very special treasures—a real highlight of West Sumatra. The market is superb.

Attractions: Top draw is the famous Bali Janggo, a recently reconstructed Minangkabau royal palace filled with historical artifacts and valuable handicrafts. The palace is 10 km south of Batusangkar and adjacent to a striking modern mosque that almost floats in the heat. En route are two luxurious Minangkabau-style homes constructed by wealthy residents who now live in Jakarta.

Some of the oldest homes on Sumatra are still standing in the remote village of Balimbing; the best examples are down the side road behind the badly painted home at the town's entrance.

For a trip into the past, take a stroll through the ancient royal village of Pariangan on the slopes of Mt. Merapi, where people relax on the front steps as the volcano fumes above.

Mountaineers may want to climb Mt. Merapi starting from Sungai Puar on the southeast slope. This volcano is still deadly: two European tourists died in 1992 when the volcano suddenly began to spit lava and poisonous fumes.

Lake Singkarak, one hour west of Batusangkar, is commercialized and rather unattractive.

Accommodations: Batusangkar is a great place to escape the tourists in Bukittinggi. Hotel Yoherma, a few blocks north of town center, is a clean, modern hotel with upscale rooms priced US$4-12. Hotel Pagarruyng across the street and nearby Parma Hotel are slightly cheaper. Kiambang Homestay on the same street costs just US$3-8.

PADANG

The provincial capital and main gateway to West Sumatra, Padang chiefly serves as a transit spot between Bukittinggi and the deep south. The tourist office is helpful but closes at 1400 and is poorly located up Jalan Sudirman in the northern outskirts of town. Information about

THE PADANG HIGHLANDS

MANOGOPOH
SURABAYO
LUBURBASUNG
SIGIHUING
LUBURSAO
KOTO MUKO
MUKO MUKO
KOTO KECIL
LAWANG
MATUR

TO PANTAI RESERVE & BONJOL
TO MEDAN
SULIKI

KAMPUNG PISANG
SUNGAI JARING
BATANGPALUPUH
LIMBANANG
GUGUK
DANGUNG-DANGUNG

PANTAR
SIMPANG MALALAK
SIANOK
JAMBAK
LAMBAH
BARINGIN
NGLAU KAMANG

SUNGAILANDIR
BANCHAH
BAYUR
MALALAK
KOTA GADANG
BUKITTINGGI
TILATANG
SUNGAI JANIAH
UJUNGGUGUK
P. TARAB
PILADANG

SIGIRAN
TAMPUNIK
D. MANINJAU
MANINJAU VILLAGE
BALINGK
BASO
TO PEKANBARU

TIKU
BATUBASA
SUMEAIBATANG
MURMALINTANG
KOTOTUO
PADANGLUAR
RAO RAO
PAYAKUMBUH
TABAT PATAH

GASAN
SUNGAIGENANGGING
SUNGAITANANG
SUMANIK
G. SAGO (2,262 m)

SUNGAISARIK (MALAI)
BATAM
SUNGAILANDAI
SUNGAI BULUH
G. MERAPI
SUNGAITARAB

PAINGAN
G. SINGGALANG
PAGU PAGU
PADANGLAWAS
LINTAU

SUNGAILIMAU
KOTO BANGKO
G. TANDIKAT
TUJUH
PANDAI SIKET
KOTOBARU
T. SUNGAYANG
PAGARUYUNG
PALACE

PASIRBARU
KAMPUNGDALAM
KOTOLAWAS
GANTING
KAYUTANDUK
LIMAKAUM
BATUSANGKAR
SIMABUR
SITANGKAL

NARAS
SINGGALANG
LUBUK-MATAKUCING
PASARREBO
PARIANGAN
BALIMBING

MANGGUNG
the Anai Valley
PADANGPANJANG
KUBU KERAMBIL
SIKALADI
SUMPUR
SULIT AIR

PAUH BEACH
PARIAMAN
KUDU
P. ALAI
LIMAUPURUT
BARANGAN
AIRSANTOK
KANDANG
BATIPUH
BATU BERAGUNG
BARUH
BATUTEBAL
KUMBILAN
TIKALAK

KARANGAUR BEACH
BINASI BEACH
SUNUR
TANDIKAT
SAMPAN
AMPALU
PADANGSAGO
KOTO MAMBENG
KAYUTANAM
MALALO
D. SINGKARAK
SINGKARAK

KURAITAJI
SUNGAI SARIK
KEPALA ILALANG
PANINGGAHAN
SANING BAKAR
SOLOK

ULAKAN
PAUHKAMBAR
PAKAN DANGAN
SINTUK
SICHINCHIN
PARITMELINTANG
TO SAWAHLUNTO
SILUNGKANG

LUBUKALUNG
JAMBAK
MUARAPANAS
SELAYO
KOTOANAU

PASARUSANG
DUKU
CUPAK
BUKIT SILEH

LUBUK BUAYA
G. TALANG
LAKE DIATAS

LADANGPADI
SUKARAMI
LUBUK SELASIH
ALAHANPANJANG
LAKE DIBAWAH

TABING AIRPORT
AIRTAWAR
INDARUNG
BANDARBUAT

PADANG
LUBUK BEGALUNG
TELUK BAYUR HARBOR
BUNGUS BAY
BUNGUS
TELUKKABUNG

0 10 20 30 40km

PADANG

Map labels:

STRAITS OF MENTAWI

JL. PURUS III
NEW TIGA TIGA HOTEL
JL. PURUS II
JL. PURUS I
JL. VETERAN
JL. BANDAR PURIS
JL. PASIR IX
JL. KARTINI
ANGGEREK HOTEL
TO AIRPORT AND BUKITTINGGI
JL. JATI IV
JL. ABDULLAH MUIS
JL. JATI IV
JL. OLO LADANG
JL. YANI
JL. SUDIRMAN
ALDILLA HOTEL
WISMA MAYANG SARI
JL. RATULANGI
JL. TAN MALAKA
JL. OLO
HOTEL JAKARTA
HOTEL GARUDA
MARKET
GARUDA OFFICE
MERPATI OFFICE
TO SOUTH SUMATRA
JL. KOTO MABARK
TIGA TIGA HOTEL
MANDALA OFFICE
HOTEL CENDRAWASIH
JL. PEMUDA
JL. BANDAR OLO
JL. PASAR RAYA
JL. AZIZ CHAN
FEMINA HOTEL
HOTEL PADANG
HANG TUAH HOTEL
BUS TERMINAL
BEMO STATION
MARKET
POST OFFICE
CITY HALL
POLICE
JL. YAMIN
PADANG BEACH
JL. HANG TUAH
MACHUDUN HOTEL
AMUSEMENT PARK
SRIWIJAYA HOTEL
JL. PANCASILA
MARIANI HOTEL
JL. KANDUANG
JL. HILOGO
JL. IMAM BONJOL
JL. THAMRIN
CULTURAL CENTER
JL. DIPONEGORO
PROVINCIAL MUSEUM
HOTEL PANGERAN
TO SOLOK AND JAKARTA
JL. MONGISIDI
NATOUR MUARA HOTEL
KARIKA HOTEL
JL. DOBI
CHINATOWN
JL. GURUN
JL. COKROAMINOTO
POST OFFICE
CHINESE TEMPLE
JL. RAHMAN HAKIM
JL. BATIPUH
ESTUARY
JL. NIPAH
JL. KARAM
JL. KELENTENG
JL. ARAU
BATANG
ARAU RIVER
SITI NURBAYA PARK
PADANG HILL
BOATS TO SIBERUT ISLAND
FERRY
CHINESE CEMETERY
0   200 m

© MOON PUBLICATIONS, INC.

local sights can also be picked up from Pacto and Nitour.

Attractions

Adityawarman Museum offers informative exhibits on Minangkabau culture and the peoples of the Mentawai Islands. The adjacent cultural center occasionally sponsors dance and *pencak silat* performances. A popular walk leads south to the river and up Padang Hill via the Chinese cemetery; impressive views of the harbor. Farther south is Air Manis, a fishing village where boats can be hired to reach offshore islands.

The coastline south from Padang is extremely rugged and scenic, with pulse-stopping views from the highway as it twists over rocky ridges and curves past sandy coves. Travelers often escape Padang to spend a few days relaxing in the natural bay of Bungus, 23 km south or one hour by *oplet.* Bungus offers clean sand, bathtub-warm waters, and inexpensive *losmen:* the best reason to spend time in Padang.

Accommodations

Most travelers consider Padang simply a stepping-stone to Bukittinggi, but the town itself is surprisingly attractive and has decent hotels, professional travel services, and of course restaurants serving that famous Padang cuisine. Most of the hotels are in the center of town within easy walking distance of the bus terminal.

Tiga Tiga Hotel: Travelers usually stay in one of the simple hotels on Jl. Pemuda, directly across from the bus terminal and two blocks north of the Provincial Museum. The Tiga Tiga, one block north of the bus terminal, is simple, cheap, and has rooms in all price ranges. 31 Jl. Pemuda, tel. (0751) 22633, US$3-12.

Hotel Cendrawasih: Most travelers gravitate toward the Tiga Tiga, but right next door is a renovated hotel with better rooms at a slightly higher fare. 27 Jl. Pemuda, tel. (0751) 22894, US$4-15.

Hang Tuah Hotel: Nearly opposite the bus terminal is another convenient hotel with clean, spacious, and well-lighted rooms, plus a restaurant which includes continental breakfast in the room price. 1 Jl. Pemuda, tel. (0751) 22894, US$6-15.

Femina Hotel: Padang's best midpriced hotel is near the post office, Garuda, and the central market. Both fan-cooled and a/c rooms are available. 15 Jl. Bagindo Chan, tel. (0751) 21950, US$8-27.

Hotel Padang: A friendly place with tourists who sprawl over the lawn chairs, writing postcards and gazing at what might have been an English garden. 28 Jl. Bagindo Chan, tel. (0751) 31383, US$8-25.

Hotel Pangeran: The best hotel in the downtown area is popular with tour groups and the region's expatriate community. 3 Jl. Dobi, tel. (0751) 31233, US$22-45.

Pangeran Beach Hotel: The newest and most expensive hotel in Padang is on the northern end of town facing the beach. Facilities include a swimming pool, a bar, and a comfortable restaurant. 79 Jl. Juanda, tel. (0751) 31333, fax (0751) 51613, US$50-80.

Transportation

Padang—the transportation hub of West Sumatra—is halfway up Sumatra's west coast and three hours west of Bukittinggi.

Air: Garuda and Merpati fly daily from Jakarta, Medan, Palembang, and Pekanbaru, and three times weekly from Singapore, Kuala Lumpur, and Batam. Merpati flies once a week to Siberut Island.

Padang's Tabing Airport is nine km north of town. Taxis cost US$4 or walk to the road and hail an *oplet* or, better yet, a bus directly to Bukittinggi.

Sea: Pelni's KM *Kerinci* departs Jakarta's Tanjung Priok harbor every other Friday morning and arrives in Padang's Teluk Bayur Harbor on Saturday evening. Fares are US$22-55 depending on class. This boat is less exhausting than the bus—comfortable beds and hot showers are available. Deck-class passengers should grab a space early and be prepared to give English lessons to the friendly passengers.

The harbor is seven km south of town and served by *oplets.*

Bus: Padang's bus terminal is centrally located near the budget hotels and the Provincial Museum. Buses depart frequently in the mornings and take three hours to Bukittinggi, six hours to Pekanbaru, 12-16 hours to Lake Toba, and two to three days to Jakarta, depending on the service. Better long-haul companies include ANS and ALS.

MENTAWI ISLANDS

The Mentawi Archipelago—Siberut, Sipora, and North and South Pagai islands—comprises one of Indonesia's most complex geological, biological, and cultural puzzles. Separated almost a million years ago from the mainland of Sumatra, Mentawi has undergone a unique evolutionary divergence, giving rise to endemic forms of flora and fauna found nowhere else in Indonesia. And until quite recently, the people who lived in the jungles retained many of the stone-age traditions which disappeared generations ago from other regions of the nation.

Tourism, and deforestation in search of a fragrant resin called Gaharu, have transformed Mentawi to some degree, but much of the traditional lifestyles still survive in the villages away from the coastal plains.

Attractions

Siberut is the principal destination for all visitors to the Mentawi Archipelago. The two main towns on the island—Muara Siberut in the south and Sikabaluan in the north—have simple *losmen* or homestays geared to adventurous travelers. But the main activity is to take a river trip from Muara Siberut and then hike to several of the Mentawi villages. The most popular villages are Tiap, two hours upriver from Muara Siberut, and Rokdok (Rogdog), which is five hours distant. Treks from Rokdok usually head to Madobag and to Ugei the following day. Another destination is Siatanusa, a sago-producing village five hours away. Other typical villages include Madobak, six hours by boat, and Sakudai, two days of tough travel by boat and foot.

Tours

Tourism is on the rise. Government officials estimate that annual tourist arrivals to the principal island of Siberut rose from under 200 in 1988 to over 2000 by late 1992, and about ten percent of all visitors to Bukittinggi now take an organized tour of Siberut. Villagers are accustomed to Westerners and anxious to separate you from your *rupiah;* expect to pay a reasonable amount for lodging, photos, and entrance into old homes.

Nearly all visitors to Siberut join a scheduled tour from Bukittinggi. Ten-day tours, which cost US$100-125, include the boat from Padang, homestay accommodations, all meals, permits, and guide services. The Gangga Hotel in Bukittinggi appears to offer a good tour, but always check the credentials of your guide and his trekking and linguistic experience. Luxury tours are conducted by PT Nusa Mentawai on Jl. Batang Arau in Padang.

Independent travelers must pick up a *surat jalan* permit from the police station in Padang and then expect to pay fees for camping supplies, food and water, chartered boats from Muara Siberut, and the services of one of the guides who are invariably found awaiting the arrival of each boat from Padang.

Transportation

A small passenger boat departs Mon., Wed., Fri. at 2000 from Muara Harbor in Padang. Tickets can be purchased in advance from travel agents in Padang or directly at the harbor. The boat trip takes 10 hours, costs US$6-8, and terminates in Muara Siberut.

SOUTHERN SUMATRA

South Sumatra is a wild, underpopulated district known for its oil wealth, large sluggish rivers which flow through highland plains, and ambitious *transmigrasi* resettlement projects. Aside from a limited number of historical and archaeological sites, there's little of great interest here.

Transportation

To avoid the experience of your life riding up through the fetid swamplands of South Sumatra, simply fly from Jakarta to Padang for about US$110. Alternatives to this expensive flight include several days of hard bus travel, or the much more pleasant two-day sea journey with Pelni. Travel agents in Jakarta book reserved seats to Padang on modern Mercedes buses. There are many private bus companies, but the best are ALS and ANS. Direct service from Jakarta to Padang costs about US$20 and includes the ferry crossing from Java to Sumatra. Prices vary considerably; shop around. Consider breaking your journey for a rest stop in Bengkulu, or at any of the other towns on the Trans-Sumatran Highway. Sungai Penuh near Lake Kerinci is a popular choice.

Much more pleasant is the twice-monthly KM *Kerinci* which departs Jakarta on alternative Fridays and reaches Padang two days later. Costs range from simple deck class at US$20 to luxurious first-class for about US$50. The *Kerinci* is a modern ship with hot showers, restaurants, and comfortable lounges.

PEKANBARU

Capital of Riau Province and the main city of oil-rich Riau Daratan, Pekanbaru is a clean, modern, and well-laid-out town on the Siak River and serves as the gateway to Southeast Asia's largest and richest oil fields. However, it's not what you'd expect from an oil city: it's unexpectedly friendly and easygoing.

Unfortunately, from a tourist's point of view, Pekanbaru is an unappealing destination with little of great interest. Most travelers who visit this river port do so for one reason: to take the ferry up the river to Batam Island and, finally, Singapore.

Attractions

Grand Mosque: Pekanbaru's city mosque, with its bright onion dome, flanks the central church on Jl. Sheikh Burhanudin. Also, stroll around the fruit market and visit the sleazy harbor.

Siak Palace: The old royal palace at Siak Sri Indrapura was constructed in 1889 by the 11th of 12 sultans who ruled Siak from 1725 to 1945. From Pekanbaru, it's a two-hour downriver trip and three hours return by bus. A *losmen* at the jetty in Siak Sri Indrapura charges US$2-4.

Accommodations

The booming oil industry means Pekanbaru is somewhat expensive, though budget *losmen* are plentiful around the bus terminal on Jl. Nangka.

Hotel Linda: Penginapan Linda is probably the best spot near the bus terminal. 133 Jl. Nangka, US$4-8.

Sinda Hotel: A slightly better hotel near the bus terminal with both fan and a/c rooms. 73 Jl. Pepaya, tel. (0761) 23719, US$8-15.

Mutiara Pangheagar: Top hotel in Pekanbaru. 21 Jl. Yos Sudarso, tel. (0761) 23102, US$45-90.

Transportation

Pekanbaru is 175 km northeast of Bukittinggi and 310 km west of Singapore.

Air: Garuda, Merpati, or Sempati connect Pekanbaru on a daily basis with Jakarta, Medan, Padang, Palembang, Singapore, Tanjung Pinang, and Batam. The airport is 10 km outside town.

Bus: Buses and minibuses depart several times daily from Bukittinggi and take four to six hours to Pekanbaru. Buses from Jakarta take about 35 hours.

Boat: Though 18 meters deep, the Siak River can only be navigated by small and slow *kapal motor*. Tickets to Tanjung Pinang and Batam can be purchased at the harbor and from local travel agencies. Boats depart three times weekly; total cost is US$18 deck class and US$25 in a cabin.

The journey usually takes about 36 hours, though the complete crossing to Singapore can be made in under 24 hours with lucky connections. The night ferry which departs at 1700 arrives at 0600 in the town of Selat Panjang. Then, walk to one of the ferry terminals for the two-hour ride to Sekupang on Batam Island. It's best to find a boat that terminates next to the Immigration building on Batam to skip the expensive taxi ride across the island. The ferry to Singapore leaves every half hour from Sekupang and takes under one hour.

BENGKULU

Formerly known as Bencoolen, this historic coastal city of 70,000 has long been neglected by the tourism industry, largely because of its isolated location well off the Trans-Sumatran Highway.

History

Bengkulu, however, is a peaceful spot that once served as the center of British efforts to retain a toehold in Indonesia. The town was settled by the British in 1685 under the false impression that the best route to China was through the Sunda Straits. Bencoolen—a financial failure and "the most wretched place I ever beheld" according to Raffles, the final governor—was happily handed over to the Dutch in 1824, five years after Raffles fled Sumatra and founded Singapore. Today, it sleeps on.

Attractions

Fort Marlborough: Constructed from 1713 to 1719 by the British East India Company, Fort Marlborough remains the most formidable fort ever built by the British in the Orient. Other colonial reminders include a cupola-roofed memorial to a despised ex-governor and an old European cemetery dotted with the graves of British and Dutch sailors.

Sukarno's House: Sukarno, who distinguished himself early in his political career by his vocal opposition to colonial rule, was arrested by the Dutch on Java in 1933 and brought to Bengkulu in 1938, where he re-mained under house arrest until the Japanese arrived in 1941. His small house is open Tues.-Sun. 0800 to 1400.

Provincial Museum: Benkulu Museum Negeri, located south of town in an area called Padang Harapan, offers an extensive collection of prehistoric artifacts, bronze drums, traditional Engganese textiles, and most importantly, examples of highly regarded Bengkulu batiks called *kasin besuruh*.

Accommodations

Budget *losmen* are in Kampung Cina, while better hotels are at the beach some three km south of city center.

Penginapan Damia: Bengkulu's cheapest is reasonably clean but often hot and noisy. Penginapan Surya across the street is similar. 18 Jl. Abidin, tel. (0736) 32912, US$3-5.

Wisma Marlboro: Five minutes south of city center, with clean and spacious a/c rooms. 1 Jl. Hazarin, tel. (0736) 31004, US$9-12.

Hotel Asia: Spotless a/c rooms with private bath and hot water in the center of town. 922 Jl. Ahmad Yani, tel. (0736) 21901, US$12-25.

Nala Seaside Cottages: A pleasant set of cozy beachside chalets is three km south of town, near the expensive Pantai Nala Samudera Hotel. 133 Jl. Pantai Nala, tel. (0736) 21855, US$12-15.

Transportation

Bengkulu is 110 km west of Lubuk Linggau, a junction town on the Trans-Sumatran Highway.

Air: Merpati flies daily from Jakarta and Palembang. The airport, 14 km south of town, can be reached with chartered *bemo* for US$3. Merpati is in Hotel Asia on Jl. Ahmad Yani.

Bus: Buses approach Bengkulu from several directions, though most conveniently from Lubuk Linggau on the Trans-Sumatran Highway. Approximate bus times are five hours to Lubuk Linggau, 24 hours to Jakarta, and 28 hours to Padang via Muko Muka.

Bengkulu's long-distance bus terminal is nine km from the city center, but private bus operators have offices in and departures from downtown.

RIAU ARCHIPELAGO

Riau is a group of over 300 almost untouched islands that stretches south from Singapore across the South China Sea toward the giant landmasses of Sumatra and Kalimantan. Riau—most importantly the islands of Batam and Bintan—is a popular weekend getaway for the residents of Singapore and an intriguing stepping-stone en route to Sumatra and Java. The islands offer superb beaches, coral gardens and sunken freighters for scuba divers, small fishing *kampongs* mounted on rickety platforms, historical sights, seafood restaurants, and plentiful accommodations from simple *losmen* to five-star hotels. Batam and Bintan islands are abuzz with new projects: major hotels, marine clubs, dive operators, more golf courses, better ferry terminals, and expanded airports to handle the growing crowds.

Transportation

Modern air-conditioned hovercraft and slower ferries to Batam and Bintan leave frequently throughout the day from the Singapore Cruise Center at the World Trade Centre in Singapore. Most go to, and terminate at, the Indonesian immigration checkpoint at Sekupang on Batam Island. A limited number continue to Bintan. Hovercrafts cost S$25 and take only 30 minutes to reach Sekupang; clearing immigration can take almost as long.

Buses from Sekupang go to Nagoya, the principal town on Batam. Accommodations are available here, though most travelers prefer the beaches on the north coast. Taxis from Nagoya reach Kabil, from where a ferry crosses to Tanjunguban on Bintan Island. Buses continue onward to Tanjung Pinang, the commercial center of the archipelago. All this sounds complicated . . . but it isn't! Travel touts are everywhere to sell tickets and point the way.

Both Batam and Bintan have airports with flights to many destinations in Indonesia. Batam's recently extended Hang Nadim Airport handles connecting flights to Jakarta, Medan, Pekanbaru, and Pontianak. Batam to Jakarta costs about US$100; it's an economical way to reach Java from Singapore. Direct flights to Bali are expected soon. Merpati flies daily from Tan-

jung Pinang on Bintan Island to Pekanbaru and Jakarta.

A final alternative is the slow boat from either Sekupang or Tanjung Pinang to Pekanbaru. Costing under US$20 in deck class, this two-day journey passes remote islands, oil platforms, and fishing *kampongs,* then it's up the Siak River to Pekanbaru. Departures are usually in the late afternoon. More information under "Transportation to Sumatra" and "Penkanbaru."

BATAM ISLAND

An island about two-thirds the size of Singapore, Batam is now being developed as a major international tourist destination. After a 1987 United Nations survey recommended the island for marine tourism, domestic and foreign investors have flocked here to construct deluxe hotels, golf courses, and everything else desired by the overworked citizens of Singapore.

Sekupang

Hovercraft and ordinary ferries from Singapore dock at this minor port town. Controlled-price taxis are available from the harbor, while hotels often provide transfer in their own air-conditioned buses. Ordinary buses to Nagoya leave when filled.

Batam Fantasy Resort: This renovated and upgraded resort has 100 rooms with a restaurant, tennis courts, and a swimming pool. Tanjung Pinggir, tel. (0778) 322289, US$65-90.

Hilltop Hotel: Situated on a hilltop behind town is this aptly named 64-room hotel, popular with rich Singaporeans who haunt the karaoke club and disco. 8 Jl. Sutami, tel. (0778) 322482, US$60-100.

Nagoya

Nagoya is a new town built on reclaimed land less than a decade ago. Now the commercial and transportation hub of Batam, Nagoya is a slightly raucous place with modern hotels, dozens of excellent seafood restaurants, nightclubs, discos, massage parlors, duty-free shops, and hawker stalls that crowd the streets at night.

Accommodations in Nagoya are very expensive since most visitors are tourists, not travelers.

Budget Hotels: Inexpensive *losmen* under US$10 include several *penginapan* at Block C on Jl. Tenku Umar, about two km from town toward the post office. Penginapan Minang, Losmen Sederhana, and Penginapan Purnama are basic and badly overpriced compared to the average Indonesian dive.

Bukit Nagoya Hotel: The best midpriced hotel in the center of town offers 32 a/c rooms with private bath. 1 Jl. Sultan Abdul Rahman, tel. (0778) 352871, US$15-35.

Batam Jaya Hotel: A decent alternative to the Bukit Nagoya. Jalan Raja Ali Haji, tel. (0778) 358707, US$15-35.

Nongsa

Upmarket tourist developments are concentrated around the northeast corner of the island, where small fishing villages and groves of coconut palms face a beautiful sandy beach.

Packages with all transfers cost US$40-80 per night from travel agents in Singapore. Extensions cost US$30 per night at either hotel. Upscale plans are afoot farther along at Telok Mata Ikan ("Fish Eye Bay").

After a day of lazing on the beach, enjoy a sunset dinner in Batu Besar, a fishing village eight km from Nongsa.

Turi Beach Resort: The finest resort at Nongsa features 150 Balinese-style rooms with a huge swimming pool, a beach bar, and unlimited windsurfing, Hobie Cats, and snorkeling. Plus, you can see the lights of Singapore twinkling in the distance. P.O. Box 55, Batu Ampar, tel. (0778) 310078, fax (0778) 310042, Singapore tel. (065) 273-5055, US$110-165.

Batam View Beach Resort: Facilities at this 196-room hotel include a swimming pool with sunken bar, four tennis courts, three restaurants, a private beach with yacht harbor, and an adjacent 18-hole golf course. Jalan Hang Lakir, tel. (0778) 322281, fax (0778) 322735, Singapore tel. (065) 235-4366, US$110-165.

BINTAN ISLAND

Bintan is the largest and most populous island in Riau, containing the capital and chief port town of Tanjung Pinang. Situated on an important commercial sea lane, Bintan has long held strategic importance. Early kingdoms competed with the rulers of Temasek (Singapore) and Melaka for control of regional trade. The departure of the Portuguese from Melaka in the early 16th century marked the beginning of Riau's Golden Age: from 1530 to the end of the 18th century, Riau was the nucleus of the Malay civilization. Evidences of their glory can still be seen near Tanjung Pinang.

As on Batam, modern Bintan is also experiencing heady economic growth and enjoying a mini-tourism boom. An ambitious marine-tourism project has been announced by the Indonesian government.

Tanjung Pinang

Tanjung Pinang is a Malay-Chinese trading town which spreads between a surprisingly modern commercial center and an older fishing village erected on rickety stilts. Travelers tend to overnight here en route to other destinations, though the town can serve as a good base for exploring the nearby beaches, islands, and historical sights.

The markets, wharves, Chinese temples, mosques, and stilted houses at Pelantan 2 harbor are worth a look. Riau Kandil Museum, two km out of town on the road to Kijang, contains worthwhile collections of old *kris*, guns, antique brassware, genealogical charts, and most of the surviving *pusakas* (heirlooms) of the old Riau kingdoms.

Accommodations: Tanjung Pinang is a busy transit town with accommodations in all price ranges.

Budget travelers should look for signs marked Penginapan; the term *losmen* is not widely used in Riau. Homestays are also possible, but be extra cautious with your bags. Most of the inexpensive *penginapan* are in an alley between the wharf and the mosque.

Bung's Homestay: A very friendly homestay in the center of town, about two blocks from the ferry dock for Pekanbaru. 20 Lorong Bintan II, US$2-4.

Johnny's Guesthouse: Gregarious and helpful Johnny often greets arrivals at the ferry pier, armed with the latest tips on travel connections to Java and Sumatra. Nearby 3D Homestay handles the overflow. 22 Lorong Bintan II, US$2-4.

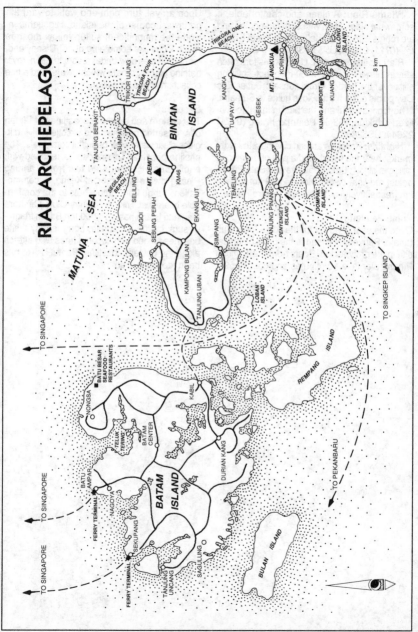

Wisma Riau: A clean and comfortable, if somewhat older, hotel with both fan-cooled and a/c rooms with private bath. Jalan Yusuf Kahar, tel. (0771) 21023, US$12-35.

Riau Holidays Indah: Upscale visitors often stay in this air-conditioned 50-room hotel built on stilts over the harbor. Great sunsets, but as Eric Oey points out in his fabulous guide to Sumatra, "The food is awful and the bar an insult to civilized drinking." 53 Jl. Pelantar II, tel. (0771) 22644, US$28-60.

Nightlife: Revolves around cinemas, the night market near the wharf, and a pair of renowned "villages of joy": Batu Duabelas and Batu Enambelas, red-light districts located 12 km and 16 km (respectively) outside town toward Kawai.

Pulau Penyenget

Once the seat of power for the Riau-Johor Sultanate, Penyenget Island is the chief historical site in the archipelago. Boats from the Tanjung Pinang pier take 10 minutes and cost Rp500. Upon arrival, turn right and walk toward the northwest corner of the island. Highlights include the magnificent sulfur-yellow mosque which looks like something out of Disneyland, former palaces now under reconstruction, royal bathing places, ornate watchtowers, and a fine collection of burial pavilions.

Beaches

The eastern and southern coastlines of Bintan offer deserted beaches and excellent diving in glass-clear water over beautiful coral reefs. The pristine beach at Trikora can be reached with public *bemo* or chartered taxi from Tanjung Pinang toward the airport at Kijang. Accommodations range from simple huts to the comfortable chalets at Trikora Country Club. Offshore Mantang Island has a 15,000-ton British freighter sunk by the Japanese. Long, sandy white beaches fringed with coconut trees also stretch along the eastern coastline; Pantai Brakit has been recommended.

NUSA TENGGARA

Stretching 1,500 km east from Lombok to Timor, Nusa Tenggara ("Southeastern Islands") offers the intrepid traveler a fascinating experience across three of Indonesia's most remote provinces: Nusa Tenggara Barat (Lombok and Sumbawa), Nusa Tenggara Timur (Komodo, Flores, the Solor and Alor archipelagoes, Sumba, and West Timor), and Timor Timur (East Timor).

Travel remains arduous and time-consuming, though Nusa Tenggara's lack of tourists and spectacular natural wonders ensure a welcome change from the commercialization of Bali and other Indonesian regions.

Warning: Malaria is a serious problem in Nusa Tenggara. Visitors are *strongly* advised to take malaria pills, use repellent, and stay well covered in the evenings.

SIGHTSEEING HIGHLIGHTS

Nusa Tenggara—also called the Lesser Sundas, in contrast to the Greater Sundas of western Indonesia—is home to hundreds of ethnic groups who speak scores of different languages and inhabit a landscape blessed with some of the most spectacular topography in all of Southeast Asia. Each island offers something unique.

Lombok
Long the neglected bridesmaid to Bali, Lombok has recently emerged from the shadows of its western neighbor to become one of the rising stars of Indonesian tourism. Although less than 100,000 Westerners visit the island annually, dozens of new hotels are on the drawing boards and all the accessible beach property has been zoned by Jakarta developers for the inevitable deluge. Yet you can still spend days traveling around the island without seeing another Westerner, and many of the spectacular beaches along the southern coastline remain characterized by simple *losmen* rather than five-star resorts.

Aside from a touch of Balinese culture and a beach resort near the main town, Lombok has three major attractions. Off the northwest corner

are the so-called Gili Islands—three small, lovely, and very popular islets blessed with white-sand beaches, inexpensive bungalows, and crystal-clear waters perfect for skin diving. Adventurous types can attempt a rugged climb to the summit of Mt. Rinjani—highest peak in Indonesia outside Irian Jaya. Other reasons to visit Lombok are the tremendous beaches and spectacular scenery along the southern coastline, from Kuta (Kute) Beach eight km east to the horseshoe-shaped bay at Tanjung Aan.

Sumbawa
Sumbawa is a rough and mountainous island often traversed in a single day by visitors bound for Komodo or Flores. However, West Sumbawa travelers who can endure rough roads or long hikes may want to visit the deserted beaches and idyllic fishing villages along the south coast or enjoy the game reserve and outstanding coral gardens surrounding Moyo Island in the northeast.

Surfers will certainly want to break the 250-km journey across the island and spend a few days at the up-and-coming surfer's paradise at Hu'u Beach, 40 km south of Dompu. Serious mountaineers can attempt to conquer 2,851-meter Mt. Tambora from the logging village of Calabai, six hours northwest of Soriutu on the Trans-Sumbawa Highway.

Komodo
One of Indonesia's unique wildlife regions, this small archipelago nestled between Sumbawa and Flores is home to the Komodo dragon, the sole survivor of carnivorous dinosaurs that thrived in tropical Asia 130 million years ago. Komodo can be reached by organized tour from Bali, twice-weekly Merpati service from Bali to Labuhanbajo on Flores, and ordinary ferry and chartered boat from Labuhanbajo and Sape (Sumbawa). Dragons are fed on Sundays and Wednesdays.

Komodo is best visited from March to June, a limited time period that avoids the Sept.-Dec. hot season, the Jan.-March rainy season, and the July-Sept. tourist season, when most of Ko-

NUSA TENGGARA

© MOON PUBLICATIONS, INC.

0   100 km

modo's 5,000 annual visitors compete for a limited number of beds.

Flores

One of Indonesia's most beautiful islands, Flores encompasses a fascinating ethnological region blessed with grandiose volcanos, high mountain lakes, stretches of savannah, and tropical deciduous forests. For many travelers, Flores is the highlight of their Nusa Tenggara excursion.

Although traces of indigenous culture survive in the more isolated towns, Flores is chiefly known for its natural wonders, such as the pristine beaches on the north coast and the magnificent spine of volcanos that dominates the 360-km-long island. Trekkable volcanos include 2,400-meter Gunung Ranaka near Ruteng, Gunung Meja near Ende, and the famous multi-colored lakes at the summit of Keli Mutu. Flores's finest sand and scuba diving are found at Waiara Beach, 13 km east of Maumere.

Hikers who wish to explore the countryside and visit traditional villages will have the best luck in the Bajawa Highlands, the Wolowaru re-gion just west of Keli Mutu, and the hills both south and west of Maumere. Flores has got it all.

Sumba

South of Flores and midway between Sumbawa and Timor lies one of the more culturally complex islands in Nusa Tenggara, famed as the source of some of the most handsome *ikat* fabrics in Indonesia. Sumba is also the breeding ground for the country's strongest horses and home to huge megalithic grave sites and spectacular rituals that reflect an ancient culture unaffected by the layers of Hinduism, Islam, and Christianity found elsewhere in Indonesia.

Most of the island's attractions are concentrated in West Sumba, where traditional villages, centuries-old festivals, and megalithic monuments have survived Sumba's entry into the modern world. The most impressive megalithic graves are in Tarung, just west of the commercial center of Waikabubak, and in Anakalang, 22 km east of Waikabubak. Fantastic beaches popular with Australian surfers are south of Waikabubak at Wanokaka and Rua.

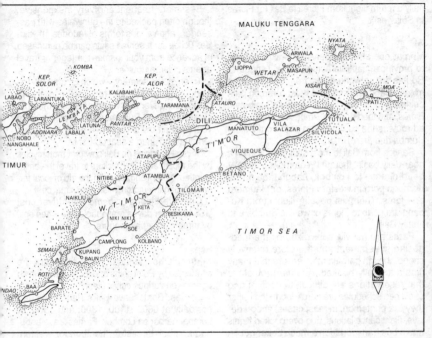

Timor

Timor, Nusa Tenggara's largest island, chiefly serves as an entry point from Australia or the end of the overland journey from Bali. Despite ongoing political problems which occasionally close the island to outsiders, a steady stream of mostly Australian travelers enters Timor from Darwin on one of the twice-weekly flights; a 60-day entry stamp is issued at Kupang's airport upon arrival. Visitors usually spend a few days exploring Kupang and snorkeling in the nearby bays before heading west toward Bali.

TRANSPORTATION

A decade ago, travel across Nusa Tenggara was a tiring and time-consuming experience due to the dearth of scheduled flights, abysmal roads which degenerated into muddy quagmires in the rainy season, and interisland boat service operated at the whim of the captain.

The situation has changed dramatically in recent years. Merpati and smaller airlines now link most of the provincial capitals with Bali, Jakarta, and other neighboring islands. Most of the roads have been surfaced (or resurfaced), and buses now race across the islands in record time. Pelni and other shipping lines operate boats between many ports and most islands are connected with dependable, daily interisland ferry service.

Delays are inevitable and travelers should be prepared for unpunctual boats and crowded buses, but the horror stories of earlier days are largely a thing of the past.

Time: Travelers intent on visiting all the major islands of Nusa Tenggara should allow the full two months granted on their tourist visa. Those with less time will probably need to limit their Nusa Tenggara experience to a few islands (Lombok, Komodo, and Flores are most likely) or utilize the services of Merpati to avoid lengthy overland travel.

A popular one-month itinerary is Bali to Lombok, a bus across Sumbawa, a side trip to see the dragons of Komodo, two weeks enjoying the beaches and volcanos on Flores, and finally a return flight from Flores to Bali (or Flores to Sulawesi).

Air

Merpati operates an extensive network of hops to provincial capitals across Nusa Tenggara. Routes are networked east from Bali and west from Kupang on Timor, the most common path being the route from Bali to Lombok, Sumbawa, Flores, and then down to Timor. A less-frequented route is the southeastern path from Bali to Sumba and then Timor.

Service from Bali to most destinations is on a near-daily basis, though Westerners generally head directly to Lombok, Labuhanbajo (the Komodo port) in western Flores, or Maumere on Flores. The most popular flights from Kupang are north to Flores or west to Sumba and finally Bali.

Fares are heavily subsidized by the Indonesian government and therefore relatively cheap, though bargain rates ensure that many flights are fully booked. Another problem is that reservations are difficult to confirm and published schedules are hardly worth the paper they are printed on. In most cases, airport delays, flight cancellations, and overbooked flights make bus transportation a much better bet on shorter routes.

Australia: Merpati flies twice weekly between Kupang on Timor and Darwin in Australia's Northern Territory, an excellent way to enter Indonesia and island-hop across Nusa Tenggara to Bali.

Kupang is a visa-free entry point and visitors arriving from Australia are automatically granted a 60-day visitor's permit. However, note that Australian visas are required of most nationalities going to Australia and Australian diplomatic offices are located only in Jakarta and on Bali, *not* on Timor.

Land

Travelers who stick to the main roads which cross Nusa Tenggara will have few problems, aside from portions of the Trans-Flores Hwy. which are still under construction and subject to flooding during the rainy season from Nov. to March. Otherwise, roads across Lombok, Sumbawa, Sumba, and Timor are fully surfaced and generally kept in good condition.

Buses are frequent and very inexpensive, though often packed to the gunwales with passengers and various forms of Indonesian wildlife. Tickets for reserved seats can be purchased in advance from your *losmen* manager or travel agents in larger towns.

To enjoy the scenery—which is, after all, the point of overland travel—request the front seat next to the driver or a window seat on the right side of the bus. Purchase these tickets from your *losmen* owner or arrive early at the bus terminal and snag a seat up front.

Several agencies on Bali now rent motorcycles by the month and allow visitors to travel the entire length of Nusa Tenggara with the aid of local ferries which carry motorcycles at minimal cost.

Chartered jeeps or *bemo* with driver cost US$40-60 per day, a reasonable fare when split by three or four passengers.

Sea

Nearly all the islands of Nusa Tenggara are connected by Pelni ships and local ferries which operate on various schedules.

Ferries: Boats leave Bali's Padangbai harbor daily at 0800, 1100, 1300, and 1530 for Lembar harbor on Lombok. Ferries leave Labuhan Lombok in eastern Lombok for western Sumbawa five times daily at 0800, 0930, 1200, 1500, and 1700. A ferry departs around 0800 from Sape in eastern Sumbawa to Labunhanbajo in western Flores three times weekly on Mon., Wed., and Sat., returning on Tues., Thurs., and Sunday. This service stops at Komodo in both directions. Roundtrip charter boats from Labuhanbajo to Komodo cost US$35-50 depending on your bargaining abilities.

Boat service from Flores to Sumba or Timor is very sporadic, though the situation is expected to improve soon. The most dependable way to reach Sumba is on a Merpati or Bouraq flight from Bali or Timor, though Merpati offers thrice-weekly service from Bima (Sumbawa) to Tambolaka on Sumba. Natrabu has announced plans to start a ferry service between Kupang and Flores, with stops in Savu, Roti, and Alor.

Pelni: The Pelni passenger ship *Kelimutu* circulates around Nusa Tenggara every two weeks on a circuitous path between Surabaya (Java), Benoa (Bali), Lembar (Lombok), Bima (Sumbawa), Waingapu (Sumba), Ende (Flores), Kupang (Timor), Dili (Timor), Maumere (Flores), and Ujung Pandang (Sulawesi), and then back to Surabaya on the reverse route. The most useful connections are to Sumba from Bima and Ende and the overnight passage from Maumere to Ujung Pandang.

Other Pelni ships include the *Awu,* which sails monthly from Bima to Ujung Pandang, and the *Tatamailau,* which connects Dili with Ujung Pandang and Ambon in Maluku. Schedules can be checked at Pelni offices in most provincial capitals and at the docks.

LOMBOK

Comparisons with Bali are almost inevitable. Lombok's size is almost identical with that of its more famous neighbor, but the landscape is drier and, aside from Gunung Rinjani, less spectacular. Lombok has a cultural connection— some 85,000 Balinese live on the island—but most of the population are Sasak Muslims whose art and lifestyles are quite distinct from those of their Hindu neighbors. Despite being called the "Bali of three decades ago," Lombok is a unique destination that compensates for its lack of rich culture and lush topography with excellent beaches and opportunities for outdoor adventure.

Lombok is also a curious study in momentum. Despite its sparkling beaches and soaring mountains, the island remained an isolated destination almost completely unaffected by mass tourism until the early 1990s. Today, the island is firmly established on the tourist trail that runs east from Bali to Komodo and Flores. As part of the Indonesian government's policy to move tourism away from Bali, Lombok has witnessed a surge of hotel construction and beach resorts under the watchful eye of the Lombok Tourism Development Corporation. Upcoming projects include an international airport in the Batujai/Penujak area (south of Praya near Kuta Beach) and a 600-hectare planned resort along the five beautiful beaches of south Lombok.

Fortunately, until these projects get off the ground, Lombok will remain a destination where you can spend days traveling without seeing another Westerner—especially in the southern and northeastern regions.

Principal destinations are Senggigi Beach, the Gili Islands off the northwest coast, a climb up Mt. Rinjani, and the beaches near Kuta on the south coast.

Transportation

Lombok can be reached in 25 minutes by air from Bali's international airport, and in about four hours by boat from Padangbai harbor.

Air: Merpati flies eight times daily from Bali to Lombok's Selaparang Airport, four km north of Mataram and six km east of Senggigi Beach. The one-way fare of US$25 is much higher than that of the ferry from Padangbai harbor, though many travelers take the plane to avoid the time-consuming *bemo* ride to Padangbai.

Bemo and taxis waiting outside Selaparang Airport go to Mataram, Senggigi Beach, and the dock for the Gili Islands. Kuta Beach can be reached by *bemo* or bus from the Sweta bus terminal in Cakranegara, though direct service may be offered by the time you arrive in Lombok.

Sea: Ferries depart Padangbai harbor daily at 0800, 1100, 1300, and 1530. One-way fares are US$3-4 and the crossing takes four or five hours depending on the weather. Morning ferries are recommended, since they dock at Lombok's Lembar harbor before nightfall; stay in Candidasa to make the early departures.

Lembar harbor, one hour south of Mataram, is served by *bemo* which rush you directly to your hotel or *losmen. Bemo* tickets are sold on the ferry. Special buses waiting at Lembar go to Labuhan Lombok, from where ferries continue east to Sumbawa.

Bus: Perama Transport offices in Kuta, Sanur, Ubud, Lovina, Candidasa, and Padangbai sell combination boat/bus tickets from Bali to most destinations on Lombok. These direct connections avoid overnighting in Mataram.

Getting Around: Attractions on Lombok are served by buses and *bemo* from the Sweta terminal. Official fares regulated by the local government are listed on a prominently displayed signboard.

An excellent alternative is to bring a motorcycle from Bali or rent one from any of the agents in Cakranegara. Motorcycles cost US$5-7 per day depending on condition and engine displacement.

AMPENAN, MATARAM, CAKRANEGARA, AND VICINITY

The population and commercial center of Lombok encompasses three contiguous towns that stretch nine km east from the old harbor at Ampenan to the main bus terminal at Sweta. Ampenan, a colorful and run-down port town with a popular *losmen,* blends into Mataram, the regional capital with big banks and modern government offices, which blends into Cakranegara, the main business and hotel area.

Although most travelers head directly to Senggigi, the Gili Islands, or Kuta Beach, the tri-city region features a good regional museum, a handful of Balinese-style temples, antique shops, handicraft factories, horse races, and a colorful cattle market.

Attractions

The West Nusa Tenggara government tourist office (tel. 0364-221730) at 70 Jl. Langko in Mataram has few brochures in English but is run by a helpful and very friendly staff.

Authentic homestays in the traditional villages of Jambianon, Krakas, and Godang (northwest coast) can be arranged with the Indonesian Environmental Forum (tel. 0364-23841) at 10B Jl. Pejanggik in Cakranegara.

West Nusa Tenggara Museum: A useful introduction to the history and ethnographic variety of both Lombok and Sumbawa.

Pura Meru: Constructed by a Balinese king in 1720 and still the largest Balinese temple on Lombok, Pura Meru is arranged around three royal courtyards filled with over 30 multiroofed *meru* shrines. The central plaza features three *meru* dedicated to Shiva, Vishnu, and Brahma.

Mayura Water Palace: Cakranegara's former Balinese court was constructed in 1744 around a huge ceremonial pond complete with floating pavilion, still accessible by a narrow causeway.

Selamet Riady Weaving Factory: One block north of Mayura is one of Lombok's last remaining *ikat* factories, best visited 0800-1200.

Antiques: Both authentic and instant antiques are sold at Sudirman's Antiques opposite the former *bemo* station in Ampenan. His collection of business cards testifies to his longevity and worldwide fame.

Lombok Asli near the University of Mataram is also recommended for quality crafts at reasonable prices.

Cattle Market: A completely authentic cattle market is held every Sunday just outside Cakranegara; a photographer's dream.

Selakalas Racetrack: Horse races, jockeyed by young boys aged 6-12, are held on Sundays on Jl. Gora, just north of the cattle market.

Gunung Sari: A small town six km north of Mataram famed for its production of low-priced instant antiques.

Gunung Pengsong

Some of Lombok's best panoramic views can be enjoyed from the Balinese temple constructed on this arid hill, about six km south of Mataram. Balinese festivals to honor rice goddess Dewi Sri are held here once each 210-day Balinese ceremonial calendar year.

Lingsar Temple

Lombok's most important temple—for both the Hindu Balinese and the local Sasaks who adhere to the Islamic Wetu Telu religion—was constructed in 1714 in a rich combination of Hindu, Balinese, and Islamic motifs. Both Balinese and Wetu Telu Sasaks worship together here, using different levels of the temple. Pura Lingsar is worn and faded but nevertheless the most impressive example of religious architecture on Lombok.

Lingsar is a few kilometers north of the main highway, midway between Cakranegara and Narmada. Direct *bemo* from Sweta terminal reach Lingsar and continue southeast to Narmada.

Narmada Water Palace

Constructed in 1805 by the Balinese raja of Mataram, the highly symbolic complex of Narmada, 10 km east of Cakranegara, encompasses a mixture of Balinese, Islamic, and Sasak architecture, combined with a miniature replica of the crater lake, Segara Anak, which fills the interior of Gunung Rinjani.

According to legend, the replica lake was constructed by the elderly king to more easily fulfill his religious obligations, but skeptics claim the old raja used the pools to spy on young maidens and select the loveliest to be his royal concubines.

Batu Kumbung

Four km north of Narmada is a small, rarely visited village known for its *gandrung* music ensemble and *kendang belek* dance groups. Some of the local women have revived the near-lost art of *ikat* weaving with backstrap looms. Pleasant walks can be made through the surrounding countryside. Villagers are shy but accustomed to Westerners.

Homestays are easy to find at US$3-4 per night; a rare opportunity to get off the tourist trail in Lombok.

Suranadi

One of the oldest and holiest temples on Lombok lies inside a pleasant garden noted for its restored Balinese-style baths and icy natural springs filled with sanctified eels. The temple can be combined with a hike through Taman Hutan Suranadi, a nature reserve and regional park located a few kilometers north en route to Sesaot.

Suranadi Hotel: Dutch visitors, perhaps seeking some colonial self-indulgence, often stay at this hotel, with its cracked tennis courts, dreary restaurant, and near-empty pool filled with gasping goldfish. Run-down nostalgia. P.O. Box 10, Narmada, tel. (0364) 23686, US$12-28.

Accommodations

Few visitors stay in town except to make onward travel connections and arrange a climb up Mt. Rinjani.

Wisma Triguna: The best budget *losmen* in the tri-city region features large three-bed rooms facing a noisy cobblestone courtyard. Proprietor Eddy Batubara rents cars, motorcycles, tents, and sleeping bags, and maintains an excellent information board and three-dimensional map of the Rinjani trek. Pak Eddy has arranged hundreds of all-inclusive three-day treks to the summit of Gunung Rinjani and helps with *bemo* to Lembar harbor (for Bali) and Labuhan Lombok (for Sumbawa). Other *losmen* in town such as Pabean and Zahir are dumpy and noisy. 76 Jl. Koperasi, Ampenan, tel. (0364) 21705, US$3-6.

Wisma Kertayoga: An older but very friendly hotel operated by a Balinese family in a good location midway between Ampenan and Cakranegara. 64 Jl. Pejanggik, Mataram, tel. (0364) 21775, US$6-12.

Srikandi Losmen: Attractive gardens, excellent location, and spotless rooms at reasonable rates make this a good choice for midlevel travelers. 2 Jl. Kebudayaan, Cakranegara, tel. (0364) 22747, US$6-15.

Granada Hotel: The tri-cities' top choice features 50 a/c rooms, a spacious restaurant, and a swimming pool surrounded by tropical jungle and a small zoo. Jalan Bung Karno, Mataram, tel. (0364) 22275, fax (0364) 23856, US$22-45.

SENGGIGI BEACH

Ten km north of Ampenan—past the horrendous Pertamina oil-storage tanks, delightful fishing boats with blue-checkered sails, a pink Balinese temple called Pura Segara, a smoking trash dump, and a weedy Chinese cemetery—lies Lombok's original beach resort.

Blessed with a long, curving stretch of sand and an expansive coral bed popular with skin and scuba divers, Senggigi is a great spot at which to relax and enjoy fabulous sunsets, despite the facts that the beach is somewhat narrow and covered with brownish sand and most of the clientele are upscale tourists on two-day escapes from Bali.

Senggigi hotels and *losmen* offer all possible amenities from money exchange to scuba packages and hiking programs up Rinjani. Batu Bolong temple, three km south of the beach, is the place for sunsets.

Accommodations

Most Senggigi hotels are aimed firmly at package tourists from Bali, though a handful of budget *losmen* are scattered along the highway near the south and north ends of the beach. After a decade of dormancy, Senggigi is exploding: 10 luxury hotels with over 6,000 rooms will open in the next few years, and by the turn of the century luxury hotels will probably line the entire highway from Batu Bolong to the town of Pemenang, over 20 km north.

Pondok Senggigi Losmen: Australian Ina and her Sasak husband, Tadjudin Nur, run

Senggigi's most popular travelers' center at the south end of the beach. The restaurant serves decent food and live entertainment is provided by local bands on weekends. Though often filled, Pondok Senggigi is a good place to start a search for other nearby *losmen*. Senggigi Beach, no phone, US$4-8.

Pondok Sederhana: Another good budget spot some 300 meters north of Senggigi Losmen. Rooms are simple and share a common bathroom but are well located on a hillside with views toward the beach. Senggigi Beach, US$4-8.

Lina Cottages: Just opposite Pondok Sederhana is an excellent midpriced choice situated directly on the beachfront with a/c rooms, a good restaurant, and friendly management. Senggigi Beach, US$12-18.

Rinjani Cottages: Back from the beach and just opposite the upscale Lombok Intan Laguna Hotel is another good choice for midlevel travelers featuring 15 bamboo cottages with fan or a/c, common or private bath. Senggigi Beach, US$8-18.

Bunga Beach Cottages: Four km beyond Senggigi Beach and directly facing the beach is a midpriced resort, opened in late 1991, with seven a/c cottages, a small pool, and almost no neighbors. Jalan Senggigi, Pemenang, Klui, tel. (0364) 93035, fax (0364) 93036, US$45-60.

Senggigi Beach Hotel: An Aerowisata-owned (Garuda subsidiary) hotel and Lombok's first resort features all possible water-sports facilities, restaurants, and a swimming pool amid 12 hectares of tropical gardens. Great location right near the promontory. P.O. Box 2, Mataram, tel. (0364) 93210, fax (0364) 93200, US$80-135.

Sheraton Senggigi Beach: International competition arrived in early 1992 with the opening of the first Sheraton east of Bali. P.O. Box 155, Mataram, tel. (0364) 27721, fax (0364) 27730, US$120-165.

GILI ISLANDS

Three of Lombok's prettiest islands lie in the clear waters just off the northwest corner of the main island. All of the coral-fringed islands—Gili Air, Gili Meno, and Gili Trawangan—sport clean beaches filled with fluffy white sand, skin diving over shallow coral gardens, and dozens of inexpensive *losmen* skirting the pancake-flat landscapes.

The Gilis' spectacular combination of beach and water has made them an overwhelmingly popular travelers' escape since the mid-1970s—comparable on a smaller scale to Samui in Thailand, Boracay in the Philippines, and Tioman in Malaysia.

And yet, perhaps too popular. Like many other small beach resorts in Southeast Asia developed without proper government supervision, none of the Gilis have adequate supplies of fresh water, decent trash collection, septic tanks, sewage-treatment facilities, or dependable sources of electrical power aside from noisy generators. And not all problems originate with tourists: Local fishermen have dynamited most of the once-pristine coral beds into oblivion.

Popularity has other pitfalls. From early June to late September, when thousands of backpackers descend on the islands, it's almost impossible to find a room after 1000, and hundreds of bewildered new arrivals are forced to camp on the beach and search for rooms the following morning. And in a mercenary attempt to check free enterprise among local *losmen* owners, village councils now enforce "recommended" price minimums for all island huts. No matter how beautiful the environment, six bucks for a rudimentary bamboo shack with outside toilet, no fan, and minimal furniture is a bad deal by anybody's standards.

Visitors should also remember that the Gilis are conservative Muslim enclaves where indecent dress and behavior are considered completely scandalous. Swimsuits and cutoff shorts are acceptable on the tourist beaches, but visitors venturing into town should respect local customs and remain well covered from knee to neck.

Now that I've talked you out of visiting the Gilis, allow me to reiterate that the islands are spectacular places blessed with many charms—a welcome escape from the calculated confines of Bali. Crowded, but otherwise a genuine tropical escape.

Transportation

The Bangsal dock for the Gilis is 30 km north of town. With lucky connections, you'll be relaxing on the sand in less than three hours.

Bemo from Sweta bus terminal in Cakrane-gara, Rembiga terminal a few kilometers north of Mataram, and the airport head 27 km north to the town of Pemenang, from where *cidomo* continue one km down the road to Bangsal harbor. Groups can charter direct *bemo* from Mataram or Senggigi for US$8-10. Shuttle buses to Bangsal are operated by Perama Tours in Mataram and Senggigi.

Bangsal harbor is a sleepy place with several cafes such as Toko Basuki and Kon Tiki Bungalows, plus an official ticket outlet which sells fixed-price boat tickets to each island. Departures start in the morning and finish around sunset, but it's best to start early to find a room. All-day charters which visit the three islands and allow time for skin diving cost US$20-25.

Unfortunately, there are no regular boat connections between the islands. For example, if you grow bored with Trawangan and want to experience Meno, you'll need to either charter a private boat to make the crossing or return to Bangsal and catch the next outbound ferry.

Another important note: Money-exchange facilities are almost nonexistent or offer poor rates. Bring plenty of small bills or expect to make frequent runs back to Mataram.

Gili Air

Which island to visit depends largely on whether you seek solitude or companionship, whether you prefer a large or a small island, and the importance of skin or scuba diving.

Gili Air, closest island to the mainland, is the smallest of the three Gilis (just 1.1 square km) but has the highest population: 1,000 people who make their living harvesting coconuts, fishing, raising livestock, and now through tourism. The island is perfectly flat and almost completely surrounded by a brilliant beach and a coral reef partially destroyed by dynamite.

Facilities on the island include a simple health clinic in the main village, a Perama office in Gili Indah Losmen that can help with travel plans and money exchange, and Boronang dive shop, which rents gear and runs scuba excursions to nearby reefs and submerged freshwater springs.

Accommodations: Most of the two-dozen *losmen* on Gili Air are scattered along the south coast near the harbor and the main fishing village. Most are similar in style—small rooms raised on stilts and sparsely furnished with two beds and rickety bamboo chairs—and charge US$5-8 depending on the number of included meals.

Two superior operations at higher price are Gili Indah on the southernmost tip and Hans Bungalows at the extreme northern end. The remaining *losmen* are almost completely identical aside from cafe fare and whatever ambience they might offer in their gardens.

Gili Meno

Midway between Gili Air and Trawangan is teardrop-shaped Gili Meno, the middle-sized (1.5 square km) but least populated (350) and least developed of the three islands.

Meno has the smallest number of *losmen* due to its shortage of fresh water. Though tough on tourism, high groundwater salinity has benefited some residents, who harvest salt during the dry season in the lake near the west coast.

Accommodations: Meno's lack of facilities and small number of *losmen* ensure a high degree of solitude at the cost of some minor inconveniences. Meno has about 10 bungalows scattered along the east coast and within walking distance of the pier at the southeastern corner.

Budget *losmen* cost US$5-8. Better facilities at higher prices include the Blue Coral Bungalows on the north coast (best spot for divers), midpriced Kontiki with attached bathrooms and a decent restaurant, and the upscale Indra Cemara, which has constructed a distillation plant to produce its own fresh water. Here, Balinese-style bungalows with a/c and private bathrooms cost US$30-45.

Gili Trawangan

Trawangan Island, the most distant and largest (3.5 square km) of the three islands, is home to over 700 fishermen who claim descent from the Bugis sailors of South Sulawesi. Trawangan briefly served as a penal colony in 1891 for some 350 Sasak rebels banished here by the raja of Lombok, and was later occupied during WW II by Japanese military forces who constructed two gun emplacements still standing on a southern hill.

Trawangan receives the most visitors for good reasons: plenty of *losmen* with decent facilities, spectacular beaches, and the best coral beds in the region. Other draws include watching sunrises over Gunung Rinjani (Lombok) and sunsets over Gunung Agung (Bali)—but be careful: sunburns will arise all over your body. Trawangan is an extremely hot island with very little shade; bring suntan lotion or expect to be finely roasted.

Scuba rentals and dive excursions are arranged at Albatros Scuba Adventures.

Accommodations: All of Trawangan's several-dozen *losmen* and homestays are on the east or northeast coast. As with Meno and Air, most are simple huts with common bath priced US$6-8 depending on meal arrangements. Better chalets with private bath are dearer, while huts without meals are somewhat less expensive.

Homestay owners wait for arrivals at the Trawangan pier. You can follow some engaging personality, take the recommendations of a previous visitor, or simply wander up the beach and inspect a few spots. Homestays in the middle sometimes have discos popular with singles, while couples often prefer the quieter places farther up the coast. Trawangan can be circumnavigated on foot in about five hours.

SOUTHWEST PENINSULA

Just south of Lembar harbor lie several excellent and completely untouched beaches, plus lovely coves dotted with tropical islands. Motorized outriggers from Lembar take you to Gili Genting and Gili Nanggu, where accommodations are available in simple bamboo bungalows. The village of Pelangan, 10 km west of Lembar, has another attractive beach and fairly good snorkeling.

Surfers often continue out to Bangko at the end of the road, where beach bungalows and simple *warungs* face the cliff and offshore breakers.

PRAYA AND VICINITY

Central and southern Lombok around the town of Praya form the island's tourist and handicraft center.

This is a journey through time, where entire villages of thatched palm have been constructed on hilltops to defend against human predators. Surrounding these Sasak villages are cultivated fields of *ubi kayu* and *ubi jalar,* types of

sweet potatoes. Hilltop graveyards of tiny upright stones, like gnarly black toothpicks, remind one of Torajaland except that these are Muslim graves and not animist/Christian.

Market days rotate between villages to encourage intracity commerce. Larger markets worth attending include Praya (Saturday), Sengkol (Thursday), and Kuta (Sunday).

Tour buses make daily stops in most of the following villages, though otherwise these are peaceful towns relatively unaffected by mass tourism. Shoppers should check prices in advance in Mataram to avoid being overcharged at the source.

Sukarara is an Islamic weaving center known for its production of traditional *songket, lambung* (black blouses), *sarung,* and *selendang* (shawls). Many of the homes here are old-style Sasak dwellings elevated on wooden platforms and covered with thatched roofs. The people are friendly and discreet photography is acceptable.

Penujak
Six km south of Praya is a small village known for its production of *gerabah* pottery made from red clays, decorated with lizard and frog images, and then fired in the late afternoon in traditional kilns. Sasaks arrive to purchase immense water containers while tourists usually pick up small souvenir items such as hand-painted flower vases and small water pitchers.

Pottery is also produced in several other nearby villages such as Kampung Tenandon, where more advanced firing equipment allows for greater delicacy in the pottery.

SADE (RAMBITAN)

Just south of Sengkol is a well-preserved Sasak village, which was declared a historic preservation area several years ago. Unlike many villages changed by modern improvements, Sade still has dozens of traditional homes constructed of thatch and bamboo, plus bonnet-capped *lumbung* (rice barns) which symbolize pre-Western Sasak culture.

Sade is now on every package tour, so expect some aggressive sales pitches from housewives and insistent young guides who demand a handful of *rupiah* for their services.

KUTA BEACH AND VICINITY

Kuta Beach is the somewhat confusing name given to the coastline that stretches eight km east from Kuta village to Tanjung Aan. Southeast from Tanjung Aan lies the village of Grupuk and an Australian surfer spot known as "Desert Point." The scenery is spectacular and the beaches rank among the best in eastern Indonesia.

Along with the superb beaches and dazzling landscapes, Kuta is also known for a weeklong festival called Bau Nyale held each year on the full moon of the second lunar month (usually late February or early March). The event revolves around the reproductive cycle of a bottom-dwelling sea worm which local Sasaks have woven into a romantic legend and public drama that retells the tragic story of Princess Nyale and her broken heart.

Kuta itself is a long, narrow town where you can pick up supplies and wait patiently for *bemo* back to Sweta. The coastal road heads east to the fabulous horseshoe-shaped bay at Tanjung Aan, where wealthy speculators from Jakarta have purchased most of the land in anticipation of a Balinese-style bonanza. But unlike the Balinese Kuta, the Lombok Tourism Development Corporation has organized a 600-hectare site near five contiguous beaches for the construction of almost 20 luxury hotels.

The road west from Kuta passes an amazing series of deserted beaches blessed with perfect sand and iridescent blue waters. After a few kilometers the road heads inland, but a side road leads south to the beach town of Air Goling and its offshore island of Nusa Tanjung.

West of Air Goling lie Mawun and Tampa, two fishing villages situated on arching bays of dazzling sand and crashing waves. The completion of the road from Tampa to Silungblanak will allow direct connection with the ferry harbor at Lembar.

Accommodations
Kuta has a good selection of budget *losmen* east of town, but many of the better beaches have been reserved for planned developments. While this sounds discouraging, tourism authorities have promised to monitor the hotels and keep major resorts at least 100 meters from the beach. In an unusual show of force several

years ago, the Lombok Tourism Development Corporation closed a foreign-funded hotel constructed just 25 meters from the beach and forced the owners to dismantle the beachside chalets and move them back from the water. It seems apparent that while nobody wants to reproduce the sterility of Nusa Dua, neither do they want to see the messy hodgepodge which typifies the Kuta of Bali.

Simple hotels are located in Kuta town, but most *losmen* are along the hot and barren road which heads east to Tanjung Aan. All are very similar—just simple wooden huts—and identically priced at US$4-8 depending on whether you need shared or private bath. New bungalows are opening quickly.

Several inexpensive bungalows and luxury hotels are under construction at Tanjung Aan and Grupuk, as well as west of Kuta toward Air Goling, Mawun, and Tampa.

Transportation
Direct *bemo* service from Sweta terminal to Praya is fairly frequent, though service south down to the beach remains sporadic, except during the high tourist seasons (summer and Christmas break). Local service from Praya to Kuta is now supplemented with private charters from the Praya *bemo* corner.

GUNUNG RINJANI

Famed for its great beauty and eerie isolation, Gunung Rinjani is the highest mountain in Indonesia outside Irian Jaya and the source of mystical inspiration for both the Muslim Sasaks, who sometimes follow a local religion called Wetu Telu, and the Balinese, who believe Rinjani to be the home of departed spirits and highest possible seat of the gods. Both groups hike the mountain several times yearly to bathe in the thermal springs, honor local gods, and throw ritualistic golden ornaments into Lake Segara Anak, though full-moon evenings are the most popular excuses to climb Rinjani.

Resembling a tropical moonscape with iridescent lakes and smoking hot springs, the amazing panorama which spreads across the summit includes Gunung Rinjani (3,726 meters) on the east, Gunung Senkereang Jaya (2,900 meters) and Plawangan (2,687 meters) to the north, Gunung Buanmangge (2,894 meters) just southeast of the lake, and Gunung Barujari (2,375 meters), which dominates the lakeside peninsula.

All these volcanos have erupted, collapsed, and showered sulfuric ash into multihued Segara Anak, a vast and impossibly elevated tropical lake which almost completely fills the inner caldera. These must have been memorable explosions: scientists estimate that the force necessary to create the half-dozen volcanos—as well as form the kidney-shaped crater lake which fills much of the six- by eight-km caldera—was equal to 274 Hiroshima-strength atomic bombs. The result is a tropical landscape you'll never forget.

Independent Travel Versus Group Tours
Local tourist officials estimate that well over 1,000 visitors annually hike toward the summit of Rinjani and spend a few days camping around and relaxing in the hot springs at Lake Segara. Although few trekkers bother to climb the actual summit (another tough day from the lake), the conquest of Rinjani remains one of Indonesia's unique experiences and certainly the most brilliant thing to do on Lombok.

Almost anybody in decent condition can make the climb, which is long and tiring but doesn't require any type of advanced mountaineering skills. Most hikers need three days and two nights for the roundtrip from Senaru (northern Lombok), including a descent to Lake Segara.

Escorted three-day tours from Wisma Triguna in Ampenan cost US$50-125 pp depending on the size of the party. Agencies in Mataram and Senggigi Beach such as Satriavi charge double. Even if you don't join a tour, Pak Eddy, the proprietor of Wisma Triguna in Ampenan, can help with trekking maps, advice, and fair-priced equipment rentals.

Most trekkers do Rinjani without the help of a guide, porter, or tour company, as the trail from Senaru is relatively easy to follow and dozens of other hikers are usually on the path. Though not absolutely necessary, guides are worth the modest expense since they know all the shortcuts, provide some entertaining insights, and help erect campsites and find fresh water. Guides and porters hired in Senaru charge US$4-6 per day, a reasonable fee that can be split among several hikers.

Rinjani should not be climbed during the Nov.-March rainy season or on full-moon evenings when hundreds of rowdy Indonesian teenagers crowd the lake. Bring along raingear, food, a flashlight, warm clothing, a sleeping bag or a thick blanket, a tent or a plastic tarp, a sleeping pad, fresh water, cooking equipment, matches, cigarettes for your guide, and a bottle of booze to warm the chilly evenings. Most supplies are available in Senaru but it's advisable to bring all possible provisions from Mataram.

The Trek
To Senaru: *Bemo* from Sweta terminal take three hours to reach the town of Anyar on the north coast of Lombok. From Anyar, it's three km east to the asphalted road which cuts off the main road and leads south to Batu Kok (four km) before terminating at Senaru (one more kilometer). The Anyar-to-Batu Kok hike—*very* long and tiring—should be avoided by flagging down a truck or finding a motorcycle taxi.

No need killing yourself before you even reach the mountain.

Batu Kok and Senaru: Your final night prior to the climb can be spent in the small town of Batu Kok, where friendly homestays provide cheap beds, hot meals, up-to-date trekking information, weather predictions, sleeping bag and tent rentals, packed lunches, extra food and drink, plus guides and porters at reasonable rates. All *losmen* will be filled with trekkers who have just returned from the summit—your best resource for last-minute tips.

Current favorites include the Rinjani Homestay, managed by the local conservation official; Guru Bakti, which charges US$4-5 for room and two meals; Pondok Senaru; and Raden's Palace, operated by a former schoolteacher from Batu Kok.

One km uphill is Senaru, a traditional Sasak village of two-dozen thatched-roofed huts neatly arranged behind protective walls in near-perfect lines. Just beyond this fascinating village lies the trail to Rinjani.

Day One: This is the toughest day. To minimize late-afternoon heat, start before dawn and set a steady pace to reach Base Camp (Pos 3) well before sunset. A series of markers helps keep track of distances: Marker 200 denotes the Rinjani rim.

From Senaru (600 meters), Pos 1 (920 meters) takes about two hours of moderate hiking. Pos 2 Campsite (1,550 meters) at Marker 114 three hours from Pos 1 has a rudimentary shelter and water supply. Pos 3 Base Camp (2,100 meters) at Marker 185, two hours beyond Pos 2, has a water supply and a roofed sleeping platform where most hikers spend the night. Depending on your stamina, Batu Kok to Base Camp takes five to nine hours.

Day Two: Another long day but not as strenuous as the first. Depart from Base Camp at dawn to beat the heat and ensure clear views from the crater rim, perhaps all the way west to Gunung Agung on Bali and Sumbawa to the east. From the crater rim, it's another four to six hours slowly winding down the narrow and dangerous path which descends into the caldera and then along the slippery trail which circumnavigates the lake to the hot springs.

Lakeside campsites are poorly maintained and often crowded with locals, but the hot springs are a godsend after two tough days of trekking, and the surrealistic atmosphere of Lake Segara Anak ("Child of the Seas") is something quite remarkable.

Day Three: Most hikers need about eight hours to retrace their steps back to Batu Kok. To *possibly* enjoy clear views from Rinjani summit, you must leave before dawn and hike a short portion the previous morning to familiarize yourself with the poorly marked trail. Roundtrip up Rinjani takes a full day.

Sembalun Lawang: An interesting alternative to the familiar Batu Kok return is the eastern departure to Sembalun Lawang, a remote village in a spectacular valley connected to the outside world by a terrible road. The situation has probably changed since my 1987 motorcycle visit, when the villagers stared at me like I was from Mars. Wisma Cemarasu in town has cheap rooms and can make arrangements with porters and guides.

TETEBATU AND VICINITY

Once a Dutch hill resort favored by overheated colonialists, Tetebatu still provides sweeping views over southern Lombok and the opportunity to hire a guide and climb Mt. Rinjani from a completely unique approach. The town is small and hardly spectacular, but within a few kilometers are several good waterfalls, a monkey forest, and handicraft villages such as Kotaraja (blacksmiths), Loyok (bamboo and palm-leaf weavings), Rungkung (pottery), and Pringgasela (Sasak weavings).

Tetebatu is 42 km east of Mataram and five km north of Kotaraja on the cool slopes of Mt. Rinjani. To reach Tetebatu, first take a *bemo* from Sweta terminal to Pomotong (Paokmotong), a second north to Kotaraja, and a final *bemo* or horse-cart up the rocky road to Tetebatu.

Accommodations
Wisma Soedjono: Tetebatu has several inexpensive *losmen* under US$5 (try Losmen Dewi Anjani), but most visitors stay at this old colonial-style house, formerly the home of a doctor from Jakarta. Facilities include a swimming pool, a cafe with rice-terrace views, car and motorcycle rentals, trekking information, and over 25 bungalows in various conditions and prices. Tetebatu, no phone, US$6-18.

Lendangnangka

Lendangnangka, a small but prosperous village seven km southeast of Tetebatu, is popular with backpackers who want to escape the standard tourist trail.

Radiah's Homestay: For over a decade, schoolteacher and town personality Haji Radiah has helped a steady stream of Westerners learn something about life in a traditional Sasak village by providing rooms, meals, maps, motorcycles, and cultural tidbits. Rooms with private bath and three good meals cost US$5-8.

LABUHAN LOMBOK

Labuhan Lombok is a sleepy Muslim town on a beautiful bay with fine views of Gunung Rinjani from the hill behind the harbor. Back in the days when boat service to Sumbawa was limited to a single early-morning departure, a steady stream of travelers would arrive in the late afternoon and spend the night in town.

Today, with five daily departures few travelers bother to explore the region or continue counterclockwise around the coast to the north shore. Actually, the most brilliant thing to do out here is the 16-km, five-hour hike from Pasugulan, north

of Aikmel on the main highway, to the remote and untouched Sasak farming village of Sembalunbumbung.

Accommodations

Two simple *losmen* here help out the traveler who arrives late and misses the last ferry to Sumbawa. Losmen Dian Dutaku is right on the main road across from the post office, while Munwar Losmen is slightly down the road toward the ferry port. Both are cheap and acceptable for the night.

Transportation

Labuhan Lombok is 73 km east and two hours by bus from Sweta terminal in Cakranegara. The harbor and ferry ticket office are about two km north of town.

Ferries to Potu Tanu on Sumbawa leave five times daily at 0800, 0930, 1200, 1500, and 1700. The crossing takes under two hours. Bus tickets are sold on the ferry for onward connections to Taliway (one hour), Alas (one hour), Sumbawa Besar (three hours), and Bima (10 hours).

Most travelers leave their *losmen* in Ampenan at 0530 to make the 0800 departure for Sumbawa. *Losmen* owners will wake you and deliver you to the first *bemo* for Labuhan Lombok.

SUMBAWA

Sumbawa—an island of rolling uplands, eroded foothills, and a volcanic mountain chain which extends east from Java all the way to Alor—divides itself into Sumbawa Besar in the west, where the locals speak a dialect of Sasak, and Bima in the east, where the language is closely related to those spoken on Flores and Sumba.

Most travelers hurry across the island and catch the first available ferry to Flores, though Sumbawa offers some stunning landscapes and a traditional culture largely undisturbed by mass tourism. Reset your watch: Sumbawa is one hour ahead of Java and Bali.

Transportation

Air: Merpati flies once daily from Denpasar to Sumbawa Besar for $35 and to Pale Belo airport south of Bima for $65. Merpati also flies to Bima from Bajawa, Ende, Labuhanbajo, and Ruteng (all on Flores), and to Tambolaka on Sumba.

Sea: Ferries depart Labuhan Lombok daily at 0800, 0930, 1200, 1500, and 1700, and take under two hours to reach Poto Tano, a fishing village 30 minutes south of Alas. *Bemo* waiting at the harbor reach Sumbawa Besar in two hours and Bima in about eight. Bus tickets can be purchased on the ferry from Lombok. Express bus companies on Lombok sell combination tickets from Sweta terminal to Sumbawa Besar, the town where most travelers spend their first nights.

LABUHAN ALAS

Labuhan Alas is a rather grubby town on a lovely little bay dotted with stilted homes. Since the ferry terminal was moved from Labuhan Alas to Poto Tano in 1989, few travelers overnight here, though a steady trickle of determined surfers heads south through Taliwang to the deserted beach at Malok. A rough track continues around the southern coastline before heading north to Sumbawa Besar.

Accommodations

Several simple *losmen* are located north of the bus terminal en route to Sumbawa Besar. **Los-**men Selamat** is an acceptable *losmen* about 100 meters north of the bus terminal. 7 Jl. Pahlawan, Rp4181-10,452.

Losmen Anda: Another decent place some 500 meters farther up the road. 14 Jl. Pahlawan, US$2-5.

SUMBAWA BESAR

West Sumbawa's largest town consists of little more than concrete shops, rough-looking *rumah makan,* and oversized government offices. Useful facilities include the Bank Negara on Jl. Kartini, a national-park office on Jl. Garuda (information on Moyo Island), and a Pelni office on Jl. Wahidan.

Attractions

Sumbawa Besar's only notable tourist attraction is the wooden palace of the sultan, constructed in 1885 and partially restored a few years ago. Up until the mid-1970s, the wrinkled 100-year-old former wife of the sultan lived here. Today the *istana* is slowly being converted into a local museum, though most of the old treasures are locked away in the Bala Kuning—the former home of the sultan's daughters. Dance rehearsals are held in the deserted palace on Sunday mornings.

Accommodations

The town is small enough to walk anywhere except to the harbor and to the airport. Several *losmen* are located on Jl. Hasanuddin, a five-minute walk south of the bus terminal and within earshot of the 0500 prayer call from the mosque.

Suci Losmen: Clean rooms and a pleasant courtyard make this the best *losmen* in town. The proprietor arranges bus tickets and advises on nearby beaches and islands. 57 Jl. Hasanuddin, tel. (0371) 21589, US$2-8.

Hotel Tambora: The best hotel in town is a 15-minute walk west from the bus terminal. Facilities include a Chinese restaurant, a travel agency, car rentals, local tours, and a small shop with local handicrafts. Managers are helpful to both group tours and backpackers, plus there's a useful map of Sumbawa mounted on the wall. 2 Jl. Kebayan, tel. (0371) 21555, fax (0371) 21624, US$4-8 fan, US$10-24 a/c.

Kencana Beach Inn: In 1992, the owners of Hotel Tambora opened a resort on a lovely beach 12 km west of Sumbawa Besar. Kencana Inn offers skin diving, horseback riding, fishing, and a good selection of Sumbawanese-style cottages—a fine place to escape the noise and dust of town. Pantai Karang Teruna, tel. (0371) 22555, US$8-24.

Transportation
Air: Brang Biji Airport is five minutes from the center of Sumbawa Besar. Merpati in the Hotel Tambora can help with daily departures to Bali, Jakarta, Ujung Pandang, and Banjarmasin.

Bus: Buses to Poto Tano (harbor for Lombok) depart three hours prior to boat departures (0700, 0800, 1200, 1400, and 1700) from the bus terminal on Jl. Diponegoro, just north of the budget hotels.

Buses to Bima depart from Stasiun Brang Bara every 30 minutes from 0700 to 1000 and take about seven hours on a very good highway. Best views are from the front seats near the driver and on the left side, which faces the northern coastline. Hotel Tambora and local travel agencies sell combination bus/boat tickets all the way to Bali and east to Komodo.

MOYO ISLAND

Pulau Moyo, a massive island slightly northeast of Sumbawa Besar, offers outstanding diving off the southern tip near Tanjung Pasir, plus an amazing array of wildlife, including almost 100 species of birds, wild deer and boar, megapodes, and miniature cattle called *banten.* Although most of the island is a protected nature reserve, hunting permits are granted by the police and expeditions are organized by an agency in Sumbawa Besar.

Accommodations
Simple huts operated by the nature-conservation office are at Tanjung Pasir and in several of the villages to the north. Local guards double as guides during the day and cooks in the evenings. Bring food and drink.

Transportation
Transportation can be arranged through the KSDA (Konservasi Sumber Daya Alam) office at 12 Jl. Garuda in Sumbawa Besar, near the western edge of town. Options include an expensive chartered boat from Sumbawa Besar harbor, the weekly cargo ship, and a motorcycle taxi to Air Bari, from where sailboats cost US$1 and take 30 minutes to reach Moyo Island.

GUNUNG TAMBORA

Bored with Indonesia? Need some excitement? Then climb one of the world's most dangerous volcanoes, Gunung Tambora. The massive 1815 eruption of Tambora—the most destructive and powerful in human history—was preceded for several years by dark, thick smoke which poured out of the crater. The rumblings and thundering grew more and more ominous. Finally, on 5 April, the volcano exploded with unbelievable fury: the blast shook Ternate and Surabaya, and in Batavia, 1250 km distant, Raffles marched his troops into the city to defend it against what he thought was a rebel attack.

The volcanic paroxysm reached its greatest magnitude the following week when the whole mountain turned into a body of liquid fire, creating thunder heard 1,775 km away on Sumatra and airborne ejecta which circled the globe and created the famous "year without summer" of 1816.

The human toll was staggering. Earthquakes, whirlwinds, and tsunamis caused by the collapse of the peak killed 12,000 people outright, while another 50,000 died of cholera, exposure, and starvation during the ensuing drought which devastated the whole of Nusa Tenggara. Tambora today is still considered a highly active and potentially deadly volcano.

Routes
The trail to the 2,851-meter summit of Gunung Tambora starts in the village of Pancasila, 15 km east of Calabai, a coastal logging town due west of the crater and opposite Moyo Island. Calabai can be reached by chartered boat from Sumbawa Besar or by bus from Soriutu, 20 km west of Dompu. Hikers must register with the police in Calabai and hire a guide in Pancasila for about US$3 per day, plus food. The round-trip hike takes two days.

HUU

Sumbawa's surfing scene centers on the village of Huu, 40 km south of Dompu on the southeast flank of Cempi Bay. Huu and its offshore breaks—Priscop, Nanga, Wall Peak, Lakey, the Pipes—were discovered in the late 1980s by Australian surfers who rode the empty waves and kept quiet about their newfound paradise.

In the early 1990s, however, several Australian surf companies constructed better lodges and organized surfing expeditions from Bali and Australia. Wealthy investors and hotel chains from Jakarta have recently sniffed around and purchased large tracts of land in anticipation of a major tourist boom. We'll see.

Huu is busiest during the southeast monsoons from June to September, when strong winds bring the largest waves. Take a bus from Dompu or Bima.

Accommodations

Budget *Losmen:* Almost a dozen simple *losmen* have been constructed at Huu. The US$6-8 daily charge includes three meals, drinks, and laundry services. Mona Lisa features a good restaurant, a volleyball court, and 28 rooms in various price ranges. US$4-12.

Lestari Cottages: Smaller and somewhat less expensive operation with a very popular restaurant and rooms with common or private bath. US$3-8.

BIMA-RABA

Sumbawa's principal commercial and transportation center is a handy pit stop crowded with horse-drawn carts called "Ben Hurs" and smiling Muslim schoolgirls dressed in long skirts and brightly colored *rimpu,* the wraparound headscarves required by the Islamic Muhammadiyah system. Residents are friendly but appreciate Western visitors who respect local etiquette and dress modestly.

Town facilities include Bank Negara Indonesia on Jl. Sultan Hasanuddin, the Merpati office on Jl. Sukarno Hatta, and Pelni on Jl. Pelabuhan at the port.

Attractions

Sultan's Palace: The town's principal sight is the former palace, constructed in 1927 and now a small museum with a desultory collection of royal regalia. Dance rehearsals are held on Sunday mornings.

Views: Two small hills are worth climbing for religious monuments and views over Bima. Behind the bus terminal in the southwest corner of town is a small hill capped with a Hindu temple. Better bets are the excellent views and the grave of Bima's first sultan, Abdul Kahir, at the top of Dana Taraha, east of the bus terminal and south of Hotel Parewa.

Accommodations

Losmen are concentrated in city center near the old sultan's palace.

Losmen Lila Graha: Bima's most popular *losmen* is run by Balinese Ibu Sarini and her cheerful, mustachioed sergeant-major husband. The hotel is fairly clean, very noisy, and centrally located just 10 minutes from the bus terminal. 20 Jl. Lombok, tel. (0371) 2645, US$3-8 fan, US$12-20 a/c.

Wisma Komodo: Much quieter and for many travelers a superior choice over the Lila Graha, this government-run hotel near the *istana* features enormous rooms with several beds and private bath. 5 Jl. St. Abrahim, tel. (0371) 2070, US$4-6 including breakfast.

Hotel Parewa: A popular midpriced hotel with a Chinese cafe, a helpful tour agency, and 24 spacious rooms adjacent to the main Merpati office. Their in-house Doro Parewa Makmur tour company arranges minibus tours of the region and charters the curiously named 50-ton ship, *Komodo Shalom,* for private tours of Komodo. 40 Jl. Sukarno Hatta, tel. (0371) 2652, US$7-10 fan, US$14-25 a/c.

Hotel Sanghyang: Opposite Wisma Komodo is supposedly the town's swankiest hotel, but nothing works and mosquitoes have taken over. However, the hotel's tour company operates a useful boat service to Komodo. 6 Jl. Hasanuddin, tel. (0371) 2788, US$18-40.

Transportation

Air: The Merpati office, on Jl. Sukarno Hatta adjacent to Hotel Parewa, sells tickets to Bali, Yogyakarta, Jakarta, Ujung Pandang, and Timor. The airport is 15 km south of town.

Bus: Bima-Raba has two bus terminals. Buses to Sumbawa Besar and other western destinations leave from the main terminal in the southwestern corner of the city. Departures are most frequent in the mornings before 1000 and in the evening from 1900 to 2000.

Buses to Sape, the harbor for Komodo and Flores, leave from Kumbe bus terminal in Raba, a 20-minute *bemo* ride east of Bima. It is difficult (often impossible) to find a bus which reaches Sape in time for the 0800 boat. Fortunately, hotels and *losmen* in Bima sell combination bus/boat tickets which do get you to Sape before the 0800 departure.

SAPE

Sape is a pleasant fishing village three km from the pier for Komodo and Flores. People here are friendly—a million "Hello Misters!"—and even the police smile at you. The PHPA office, about two km down the road toward the harbor, has little information on Komodo aside from some old weather charts and topographical maps. Sape has a post office but no bank; exchange plenty of money in Bima.

Accommodations

Many travelers overnight in one of Sape's three *losmen* to guarantee a seat on the 0800 boat.

Losmen Give: Tiny, primitive rooms but free tea and a pleasant back garden. US$2-4.

Losmen Ratna Sari: Friendly management and larger rooms with either common or public bath. US$2-8.

Losmen Friendship: Sape's only decent hotel has budget rooms with common bath and better digs with a/c and private bath. US$2-10.

Transportation

Ferries to Labuhanbajo in Flores depart at 0800 on Mon., Wed., and Sat. from Pelabuhan Sape, three km down the road. Note: *Only the Saturday boat stops at Komodo.* The crossing takes six hours to Komodo and another four hours to Flores. Allow eight hours for the direct crossing. Boat charters to Komodo are substantially cheaper in Labuhanbajo than in Sape.

The ferry departure schedule:
Sape-Komodo-Labuhanbajo: Sat. at 0800
Sape-Labuhanbajo: Mon. and Wed. at 0900
Labuhanbajo-Komodo-Sape: Sun. at 0800
Labuhanbajo-Sape: Tues. and Thurs. at 0900

KOMODO

One of the great wildlife regions of the world, this small archipelago nestled between Sumbawa and Flores is home of the Komodo dragon, perhaps a distant relative of carnivorous dinosaurs that thrived in tropical Asia 130 million years ago.

The giant monitor lizards—largest on Earth—remained a myth until the turn of this century when a Dutch army officer and curator of the Bogor Zoological Museum arrived to document the existence of *Varanus komodoensis*. Inhabiting the windswept island without any serious competing scavengers or predators, this solitary carnivore has achieved optimal size—up to three meters long with fearsome-looking jaws, forked tongue, sharp claws, and muscular legs to support the heavy body. The dragons have claimed several human victims, including an 84-year-old Swiss tourist in 1979, a 12-year-old boy in 1987, and Tony Wheeler in 1993 (just kidding).

Dragon Spotting

Komodo Island, part of the Indonesian national-park system, is administered by the KDSA from its office in Loh Liang. Visitors must register with the KDSA and pay a series of fees for entry permits, photography, and guides. Fees for dragon food—goats or small deer—can be shared among the entire party. Hauling a putrefying goat from Sumbawa or Flores is not necessary or sensible; neither will a heap of stinking fish make you popular with the KDSA.

Komodo now attracts over 5,000 visitors annually, who generally arrive during the busy tourist months from June to September. The best time to visit is during the low season from April to June, or during the end of the dry season from Sept. to Dec., when the dragons are the hungriest. Note: Dragons are fed only on Sundays and Wednesdays.

Dragon spotting is a fascinating but very commercialized affair tightly controlled by the KDSA. Guides lead you to the dragon-watching site at Banu Nggulung, about two km north of Loh Liang, string up a goat or a deer, and patiently wait until several of the beasts arrive for their af-

ternoon feasts. Visitors can safely click away from a safe distance or climb down a ladder to photograph the dragons—locally called *ora*.

Afterward, guides can be hired to explore the interior of the island and climb up Gunung Arab. Boats to offshore islands and isolated coral beds can be chartered from the KDSA.

Accommodations

The KSDA administrative site of Loh Liang, a 30-minute walk north of Kampung Komodo, has several clean and spacious cabins with both dormitory and double rooms priced at US$3-5 per person. The KSDA cafe serves extremely basic food and drink at high prices; bring extra supplies or survive on a steady diet of *nasi goreng* and *mee goreng*.

Transportation

Expensive guided tours are sold by the travel agents in Jakarta and Bali, but an overland trip isn't tough—it just requires an appreciation of *jam karet* ("rubber time").

Air: Hurried visitors can reach Komodo quickly with the twice-weekly Merpati flight from Bali to Labuhanbajo on the western tip of Flores. The flight costs US$90 and takes about three hours including a brief stop in Bima.

Alternatively, take a Friday flight from Bali to Bima and then local transportation to Sape, from where ferries depart for Komodo at 0800 on Saturday morning.

Sea: The Sape-Komodo-Labuhanbajo ferry departs at 0800 on Saturday, returning at 0800 on Sunday.

Otherwise, you can find some fellow passengers and charter a boat for the one-way or roundtrip journey. Labuhanbajo is the better choice since boats from Sape take eight hours to cover the somewhat dangerous 150 kilometers. Ten-person boats from Labuhanbajo reach Komodo in about three hours and charge US$30-35 for a day visit, US$40-50 for an overnight excursion, and up to US$80 for faster, more comfortable boats. The Bajo Beach Hotel in Labuhanbajo charges US$50 for its 10-person boat.

FLORES

One of Indonesia's highlights, Flores is a remarkable island blessed with grandiose volcanos, high mountain lakes, stretches of savannah, tropical deciduous forest, superb beaches, great scuba diving, and some of the finest ethnological regions in the archipelago. This alluring combination—traditional culture and great natural beauty—has made Flores *the* upcoming star of Indonesian tourism and the highlight of any visit to Nusa Tenggara.

History
Prior to the arrival of Western powers in the 16th century, Flores was occasionally visited by trading ships from China and the Majapahit Empire of Central Java. In 1544, a Portuguese explorer named Cabot arrived en route to the Spice Islands and christened the easternmost peninsula "Cabo das Flores" or "Cape of Flowers," though ironically the island has few flowers and was known to Javanese sailors as "Stone Island." Dominican priests sent by the Portuguese profoundly influenced local culture, and today many of the islanders have Portuguese names, practice old Portuguese customs and dances, and even *look* Portuguese. Flores, however, offered little of economic value to the Iberians aside from its function as a convenient stopover to the sandalwood forests of Timor.

The Portuguese era ended in 1859 when Dutch forces took over the island and brought in Jesuit and Franciscan priests who introduced other Christian denominations. Today, Flores is almost entirely Catholic. A native rebellion was crushed by the Dutch in 1907, but it wasn't until 1936 that they considered the island safe enough to be transferred from military to civilian control.

In December 1992, an earthquake measured at 7.5 on the Richter scale struck Flores and destroyed most of Maumere and Larantuka, killing over 3,000 Indonesians in a matter of minutes. The devastation was worst on the nearby island of Babi, where a gigantic, boiling hot, 20-meter tsunami swept over the island, leaving bodies hanging in trees and corpses floating in the once-tranquil bays.

Flores has begun reconstruction, though it will be years before Maumere and other eastern towns fully recover from the quake of '92.

Transportation
Flores is a few hours by air from Bali, or several days of overlanding by bus and boat. The center of tourism on Flores is Maumere; visitors bound for Komodo should fly to Labuhanbajo.

Air: Merpati flies daily to Maumere from Bali (US$100), Ujung Pandang in Sulawesi (US$75), Kupang in Timor (US$45), and Bima in Sumbawa (US$50). Bouraq also flies from Bali to Maumere.

Merpati's flight from Bali to Labuhanbajo is difficult to book due to high demand, infrequent flights, small planes, and the unimproved landing field. Reserve early and reconfirm often. Merpati also serves Ruteng, Bajawa, and Larantuka from Ende, with connections to most towns in Indonesia.

Sea: The ferry schedule between Sape in Sumbawa and Labuhanbajo in Flores is listed above under "Sape." Pelni's *Kelimutu* sails every other Sat. from Ende to Kupang in Timor, and every other Mon. from Ende to Waingapu in Sumba.

Ferries depart Larantuka for Kupang on Tues. and Fri. afternoons. Several of the ferries make brief stops in the Solor and Alor archipelagoes.

Land: Decades ago, few roads in Indonesia could compare with the Trans-Flores Highway, a 700-km nightmare of destroyed bridges, horrific mountain passes, and muddy quagmires which could delay you for several weeks.

Today, the Trans-Flores Hwy. has been almost completely paved and, except during the rainy season from Nov. to April, can be covered by bus in a few days. The only problem area is the stretch from Moni (Keli Mutu) to Maumere, which washes out during the rainy season and demands a long detour via the north-coast town of Kota Baru.

The scenery across Flores is absolutely gorgeous. To best enjoy the vistas, ask your *losmen* owner to reserve a front seat next to the driver or a window seat on the south side of the bus. Travel distances and approximate times:

Labuhanbajo-Ruteng	127 km	4 hours
Ruteng-Bajawa	131 km	6 hours
Bajawa-Ende	128 km	5 hours
Ende-Moni	50 km	2 hours
Moni-Maumere	99 km	4 hours
Maumere-Larantuka	138 km	4 hours

LABUHANBAJO AND VICINITY

Labuhanbajo is a small fishing village perfectly situated on a lovely bay at the western tip of Flores. The town chiefly serves as the departure point for Komodo, though the beautiful islands and beaches are worth exploring in their own right.

Once well off the beaten track, Labuhanbajo is now visited by hundreds of Western tourists during the high season from June to September. Facilities include a Bank Rakyat Indonesia, a post office, a Merpati office at the airport, a health center, and a KSDA office for information on Komodo and Rinca islands.

Attractions

Snorkeling and sunbathing can hardly be recommended in Labuhanbajo, but within a few kilometers are deserted islands and superb beaches with clean white sand. Scuba dives are organized at Baruna Water Sports and the Bajo Beach Club on the main road near the post office. Owner Pak Hendrik Chandra also conducts tours to a nearby cave (Batu Cermin or "Stone Mirror Cave"), whip fights in Kapar village (five km north), and a southern hillside sprinkled with petrified wood.

Small outriggers charge a few dollars to the following spots:

Bidadari Island: Serious divers head to the more distant islands of Tatawa, Sebayur Kecil, and Sebolan, but skin diving and lazing on the beach are recommended on Pulau Bidadari, just 20 minutes from Labuhanbajo.

Waecicu Beach: Twenty minutes by boat north of town is a long and clean beach with coral beds, several *losmen,* and the upscale Waecicu Beach Hotel.

Batugosok Beach: Another excellent beach just 20 minutes from town. Take the Batugosaok Hotel boat.

Accommodations

Almost a dozen *losmen* and homestays line the main road, plus several midmarket hotels have been constructed on sandy beaches outside town.

Bajo Beach Hotel: The largest hotel in town arranges transportation to Komodo, scuba dives, and local tours, and has plenty of rooms in all price ranges, but bargain hard for the best prices. US$3-10 fan, US$12-20 a/c.

Mutiara Beach Hotel: Opposite the Bajo Beach Hotel and directly on the water is another favorite with clean rooms and harbor views from its popular cafe. Leo rents vehicles and arranges trips to Komodo but will try to squeeze every *rupiah* out of you. US$3-8.

Waicicu Beach Hotel: Twenty minutes north of town by boat is a fine beach with several good *losmen* constructed in a simple but attractive Sumbawanese style. Waicicu also arranges tours to Komodo and might rent diving equipment. US$4-6 includes three meals.

Batugosok Beach Hotel: Another beach escape about 20 minutes from town with hotel boat. A recommended escape. US$4-6 includes three meals.

RUTENG AND VICINITY

Ruteng is a cool, neat, overwhelmingly Catholic town set amidst the scenic hills and network of valleys which comprise the Manggarai district, the rice bowl of Flores and one of the largest coffee-growing regions of indonesia. The local Manggarai people speak a language unintelligible to other Floresians and still follow a few traditional rites such as whip fighting (*caci*), an ancient homage to ancestral spirits often performed at Catholic weddings.

Facilities in Ruteng include the Bank Rakyat Indonesia on Jl. Sudarso, the post office on Jl. Baruk, and Merpati on Jl. Pertiwi.

Attractions

Ruteng is great for hiking—endless views of beautiful lush-green *sawah* (ricefields), hills, mountains, and valleys.

Golo Curu: Excellent early-morning panoramas over Ruteng are best enjoyed from this hill about one km north of town, just past Wisma Agung I.

Gunung Ranaka: Southeast of Ruteng is an active volcano (2,400 meters) that can be climbed in about four hours from Robo. Alternatively, take a jeep to the top and hike the eight km down to Robo.

Lambaleda: A traditional Manggarai weaving village located 50 km northwest of Ruteng.

Pagal: Most Manggarai weaving villages are 21 km north of Ruteng near the village of Pagal on the road to Reo. The weaving season in Cibal Timur, two hours east of Pagal, is from May to October, while the weaving season in Compang, a few kilometers west of Golongorong (just north of Pagal), is from October to March. Samples of Manggarai *songket* and black *sarung* are sold in the Ruteng market.

Pongkor and Todo: Manggarai culture once centered on the traditional villages of Pongkor and Todo, 45 km southwest of Ruteng. Home to the last Manggarai rajas, these small villages still have a few circular conelike homes in the circular village, surrounded by circular ricefields divided into pie-shaped sections.

Accommodations

Wisma Dahlia: A clean and comfortable 30-room *losmen* with a popular cafe and friendly management, just north of the bus terminal. Jl. Kartini, US$3-15.

Hotel Sindha: Four blocks northeast from the bus terminal and just opposite Bank Rakyat is one of Ruteng's best *losmen*. The Chinese owners run a good cafe but sometimes overcharge for their rooms. Bargain. Jl. Yos Sudarso, US$4-10.

Wisma Agung II: The downtown *losmen* affiliated with Agung I is, unfortunately, overpriced and located near the mosque—very noisy in the morning. Jl. Motang Rua, US$5-8.

Wisma Agung I: A decent spot run by a proprietor who spent eight years in Canada before returning to run his two *losmen*, a local bakery, a road-construction crew, and a thriving porn business. Quiet location north of town on the road to Reo. 10 Jl. Wae Cos, US$3-6.

Transportation

Air: Merpati flies daily to Ende (US$35), Bima (US$48), Kupang (US$65), and Bali (US$95).

Bus: Buses leave 0700-1000 to Labuhanbajo (four hours), Bajawa (six hours), and Ende (10-14 hours). Purchase tickets at the bus terminal, your *losmen,* or from the Bis Agogo travel agency adjacent to Losmen Ranaka.

BAJAWA AND VICINITY

The most traditional areas of Flores and among the great natural wonders of Nusa Tenggara, Bajawa and the Bajawa Highlands are home to the Ngada people, who have retained many of their animistic beliefs despite conversion to Christianity in the early 20th century.

Sadly, most travelers hurry through the region on their way to Maumere and miss the richness of local culture and the spectacular scenery: brooding volcanos looming over verdant *sawah,* stone megaliths abandoned in thick jungle, and male sacrificial posts (*ngadhu*) and accompanying female fertility shrines (*bhaga*) still honored in many villages.

Tradition also permeates many local festivals such as the Soa planting festival in September, the sacrificial Umamoni event in the fall, and the six-day celebration of Reba held in late December. Also, watch for boxing matches in which just the middle knuckles are used and partners steer their fighters from behind, like puppeteers.

Bajawa is a great place to learn about pre-Islamic, pretourism Indonesia.

Attractions

Buses from Ruteng pass through a spectacular array of immense volcanos before arriving in the scenic but often chilly hill town of Bajawa.

Ancestral Poles: According to Ngada tradition, the *ngadhu,* a carved wooden post crowned by a conical roof, and the *bhaga,* a little thatched house that represents female fertility, must always be aligned with the village cult house, royal tombs, and other megalithic structures. Two ancestral poles stand on Jl. Satsuitubu, in the south end of town.

Langa: Seven km south of Bajawa and just before Bena at the base of magnificent Gunung Inerie (2,245 meters) lies Langa, home to the six-day Reba ceremony and almost a dozen *ngadhu* and *bhaga.*

Bena: The finest traditional village near Bajawa features totem figures and megaliths in the town square, surrounded by Ngadanese bamboo dwellings and ritual houses topped by warriors wielding spears and *parangs*. Visitors must register and pay a small fee and can overnight in a simple guesthouse.

Gunung Inerie is an all-day expedition from Bena.

Wogo: The road from Bena continues clockwise through Jerebuu and Were to the *adat* village of Wogo, where the nearby village of Wogo Tua ("Old Wogo") features several large megaliths surrounded by grasses and bamboo.

Soa: Soa, 26 km north of Bajawa and constructed around a huge amphitheater with tiers of great megaliths, is known for its unusual festivals, annual deer hunts, and traditional boxing called *sagi*. Best visited for the colorful market held on Sunday evenings and Monday mornings.

Boawae: Forty-one km east of Bajawa lies the most famous *ikat*-weaving village in central Flores.

Accommodations

Bajawa has over a half-dozen *losmen* near the bus station, but in different directions.

Hotel Kambera: Bajawa's travelers' center, three blocks southwest of the bus terminal, compensates for its small rooms with a good restaurant, a useful wall map, and reliable information on nearby villages. 9 Jl. El Tari, tel. (0383) 166, US$3-6.

Hotel Johny: A small and friendly *losmen* that handles the overflow from Hotel Kambera. Jl. Gajah Mada, tel. (0383) 79, US$3-5.

Hotel Virgo: A newer place with clean rooms just one block north of the Hotel Kambera. Jalan Mayjen Dipanjaitan, tel. (0383) 61, US$3-6.

Hotel Kembang: A somewhat upscale 12-room *losmen* three blocks southwest of the bus terminal. 12 Jl. Diponegoro, tel. (0383) 72, US$4-8.

ENDE

Ende—the commercial center, political headquarters, and largest town on Flores—principally serves as a stopover en route to Keli Mutu and nearby *ikat*-weaving villages.

Attractions

Ende itself has little of great interest aside from the old port area and views of nearby volcanos: Ebulobo to the west, Meja to the southeast, Ipi farther to the south.

Sukarno's House: Now a national shrine and museum, this cream-colored building on Jl. Dewantara was Sukarno's home during his exile in the 1930s.

Harbor: The new harbor, Pelabuhan Ipi, southeast of town past the airport, is where the Pelni ship *Kelimutu* departs every other week. More intriguing are the docks and back alleys of Pelabuhan Ende, west of city center, where Bugis immigrants continue traditional boatbuilding techniques.

Nuabosi: Excellent views, a traditional clan house with sacrificial altar, and a gracious Dutch guesthouse can be enjoyed in this mountain town 10 km north of Ende.

Gunung Ipi: Ende's most impressive volcano can be climbed from the volcanology station in Tentandara, eight km south of town.

Accommodations

Ende has almost a dozen inexpensive *losmen* and several decent hotels. Many are clean and comfortable but subject to wake-up calls from town mosques.

Losmen Ikhlas: This curiously named *losmen* some 350 meters west of the airport is Ende's most popular travelers' center and information resource on local tours, bus schedules, sights, maps, and flights. Owner Djamal speaks good English and German. Jalan Ahmad Yani, tel. (0383) 21695, US$2-6.

Losmen Safari: A clean and well-organized *losmen* adjacent to the Ikhlas. 3 Jl. Ahmad Yani, tel. (0383) 21499, US$2-6.

Nirwana Hotel: Ende's best midpriced *losmen,* just west of the Protestant church, has small but clean rooms with private bath and more luxurious rooms with a/c and TV. 29 Jl. Pahlawan, tel. (0383) 21199, US$3-6 fan, US$8-12 a/c.

Dewi Putra Hotel: Ende's largest and most luxurious hotel has over 40 spotless rooms with either fan or a/c. This hotel and many other *losmen* arrange daily roundtrip tours of Keli Mutu, plus visits to *ikat*-weaving villages. Jalan Dewantara, tel. (0383) 21465, US$5-8 fan, US$10-15 a/c.

Transportation

Ende is second only to Maumere for transportation connections.

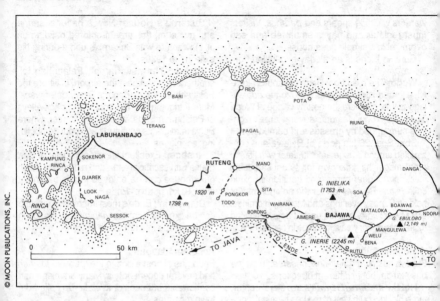

Air: Merpati stops daily in Ende on its Trans-Nusa Tenggara flight from Bali to Timor, with other stops in Mataram (Lombok), Bima (Sumbawa), Labuhanbajo, Ruteng, and Bajawa. The Bali flight takes just two hours over a distance that might require over a week by bus and boat. Reservations and reconfirmations are absolutely necessary. Merpati is on Jl. Nangka two blocks north of the airport.

Boat: Every other Saturday, the Pelni ship *Kelimutu* departs from Pelabuhan Ipi (new harbor) to Kupang in Timor. After returning from Timor, the *Kelimutu* leaves the following Monday to Waingapu in Sumba.

Smaller, unscheduled ferries depart weekly for Sumba, Timor, and various towns on the south coast of Flores. Inquire at Pelabuhan Ende (old harbor) from March to October, and at the new harbor between October and March. Pelni is on Jl. Pabean near the old harbor.

Bus: Buses west to Bajawa leave from the downtown terminal on Jl. Hatta, while buses east to Keli Mutu and Maumere depart from Terminal Ende in the north end of town. Most *losmen* sell bus tickets which include pick-up from the *losmen*.

KELI MUTU

Keli Mutu is one of the more otherworldly sights in all of Indonesia, a volcanic cone filled with three lakes with different-colored waters and in constant state of flux as minerals leach in from the earth. Legend claims all three lakes are abodes of the dead: souls of sinners and sorcerers in the maroon lake, virgins and the pure of heart in the green, elderly in the blue.

Keli Mutu is a popular destination accessed by paved road from Moni (Mone), 52 km west of Maumere. Guides are unnecessary, though it's important to reach the summit at dawn before the clouds roll in and ruin the views.

Transportation

The most convenient way to reach the crater is with minibuses and the Catholic mission truck, which departs at 0400 from Moni. Tickets are sold the previous night from most *losmen*. Other options from Moni include a tough 11-km hike, uncomfortable horseback rides, and expensive jeep rentals. Bring warm clothing, a flashlight, hot drinks, snacks, and a sense of patience; the lakes are obscured by clouds over half the time.

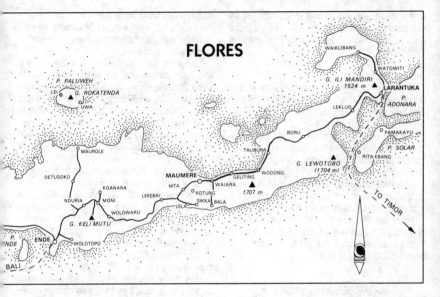

After (hopefully) viewing the lakes, hike around the perimeter to escape the crowds, then hike down to Moni via the shortcut and continue to Maumere or Ende by bus.

MONI (MONE) AND VICINITY

One of the finer aspects to Keli Mutu is an overnight in the nearby village and Catholic mission of Moni, 14 km north of the volcano. Blessed with the constant sound of running water and fantastic views of surrounding volcanos, Moni provides a welcome relief from the monotonous towns of central Flores. The Tuesday-morning market attracts many of the local Lio people.

Attractions

Several traditional weaving villages are southeast of Moni and due south of Wolowaru. Take a morning truck or hike from Moni or Wolowaru. The 20-km roundtrip trek between Wolowaru and Nggela can be done in a single day.

Wolowaru: Twelve km east of Moni is a small town often used as a base for visits to the southern weaving villages. A cluster of old-style *rumah adat* with their high, steeply pitched roofs stands at the town entrance. The weekly market is on Saturday. Inexpensive *losmen* and homestays in Wolowaru include Losmen Kelimutu, Losmen Setia, and Losmen Hidaya. All charge US$2-4 for small rooms with common bath.

Jopu: Five km south of Wolowaru is an old-style Florinese village with steep-roofed *adat* houses and a distinctive Flemish-looking church, secluded in a valley with magnificent volcanos on all sides. Weavers in Jopu produce a limited number of attractive *sarung ikat* but also inferior weavings colored with artificial dyes.

Wolonjita: Four km south of Jopu is another village with better *sarung* at slightly lower prices.

Nggela: Nggela is a well-known *ikat*-weaving village at the end of a terrible dirt road on a high cliff with views over the Sawu Sea. Nggela is famous for its use of hand-spun thread and natural dyes, though artificially dyed and mass-produced items are also sold by many of the 1,300 inhabitants.

The quality *ikat* and superb location perhaps compensates for the highly aggressive saleswomen who charge for photos and constantly wave their wares in your face. Approximate prices with firm bargaining are US$15-20 for an *ikat* shawl (*selendang*) and US$30-80 for an *ikat* sarong. Before arrival, check prices in Ende and at the Jawa Timur handicraft shop in Wolowaru.

Accommodations

The tourism boom on Flores has brought the linear village of Moni almost a dozen *losmen* and homestays which uniformly charge US$2-4 for rooms with common bath.

Market Hotels: On the main road, just opposite the market, are Homestay Daniel, Homestay Amina Moe, Homestay John, Homestay Friendly, and Losmen Nusa Bunga.

Wisma Kelimutu: Owned by and adjacent to the local Catholic mission is another popular spot with large, clean rooms and a good cafe.

Moni Sao Ria Wisata: Moni's top-end choice is about 1.5 km west of town on the road to Ende, near the turnoff to Keli Mutu. Rooms with private bath cost US$6-9.

MAUMERE AND VICINITY

Within easy range of Maumere—the principal tourist destination on Flores—are superb beaches, some of the finest scuba diving in the country, traditional weaving villages, and spectacular topography from volcanos to arid peninsulas.

Once the shining star of regional tourism, Maumere was almost completely destroyed in December 1992 by an earthquake that took over 3,000 lives and significantly altered the array of tourist services. Most facilities will probably be back in business by the mid-1990s, though town planners intend to realign some of the streets and relocate many of the *losmen* and other tourist facilities.

Maumere Attractions

Cathedral: Prior to the earthquake, Maumere's principal attraction was its large Catholic church filled with paintings of the Twelve Stations of the Cross, executed by a local artist in a distinctive Indonesian style. The cathedral was badly damaged in 1992 but may be reconstructed by local church authorities.

Market: A good place to search for thick Maumere blankets, but don't purchase ivory jewelry carved from old tusks—ivory cannot be imported to most Western countries.

Attractions Near Maumere

Villages south and west of Maumere can be reached with local *bemo* or, better yet, rented motorcycles and cars.

Ladelero: Ladelero, 22 km southwest from Maumere on the road to Ende, is known for its large Catholic seminary and attached museum crammed with rare Florinese *ikat* from Sikka and Jopu, Chinese ceramics, old swords, and artifacts from other regions of Indonesia. The museum is open daily until 1400. A market is held two km past Ladelero at Nita until 1000 on Thursdays.

Sikka: An idyllic seaside location 27 km southwest of Maumere and a long tradition of distinctive Sikkanese *ikat* weaving make Sikka the most visited village near Maumere. Here, practically every house owns a primitive loom that spins popular motifs such as Dutch-influenced designs, plants, and cubist lizards—fertility symbols on Flores. Prices, however, are steep, and the saleswomen are both aggressive and mercenary. Sikka also has a fine church constructed by the Portuguese, who controlled most of Flores until the mid-18th century.

Geliting: Kewapandai district's largest market is held on Fridays in this seaside village, some 10 km east of Maumere on the road to Larantuka.

Accommodations

Many of the following *losmen* and hotels were destroyed in the quake but will probably have been reconstructed or relocated by the time you arrive.

Losmen Wini Rae: An old favorite located slightly outside town and midway between the bus terminal and harbor. Choices include common or private bath, fan or a/c. Jalan Gajah Mada, tel. (0383) 388, US$3-8 fan, US$10-15 a/c.

Wisma Flora Jaya: Small quarters but friendly atmosphere, excellent food, and convenient location in the center of town just two blocks from the market: you'll have a great time with Mama Jo. Jalan Raja Don Thomas, tel. (0383) 333, US$3-8 fan, US$12-20 a/c.

Permata Sari Inn: Visitors arriving by air or with private transportation often stay at the Permata Sari, one km from the airport and two km outside city center. Clean rooms, friendly managers, seaside cafe, and excellent sunsets over a sandy black beach. 1 Jl. Sudirman, tel. (0383) 171, US$4-8 fan, US$10-15 a/c.

Losmen Beng Goan III: Prior to the earthquake, the Beng Goan operated two successful *losmen* near the market, plus a quieter, cleaner place two blocks south. Jalan Slamet Riyadi, tel. (0383) 283, US$3-8.

Gardena Hotel: A quiet and popular place three blocks east of the market and two blocks back from the bay. All rooms have attached baths and include complimentary breakfast. Guide services are available from Marsel Mitak. 5 Jl. Patirangga, tel (0383) 21489, US$4-8 fan, US$12-16 a/c.

Maiwali Hotel: Maumere's best hotel has tennis courts, a bar, Chinese seafood restaurant, and a tour office that arranges *bemo* charters and escorted tours to Keli Mutu and nearby weaving villages. Jalan Raja Don Thomas, tel. (0383) 220, US$6-12 fan, US$15-25 a/c.

Transportation

Air: Merpati has daily flights to and from Bali (US$110), Kupang (US$40), Bima (US$60), and Ujung Pandang (US$70), with connections to Yogyakarta, Surabaya, and Jakarta.

Maumere's Wai Oti Airport, three km from town, is served by taxis and *bemo* from the Maumere-Larantuka road, about 600 meters from the airport.

Bus: Buses west to Ende leave from the Ende terminal, about 1.5 km south of city center. Buses east to Larantuka leave from the Waioti terminal, some three km east of town just past the airport turnoff. Departures are most frequent before noon and *losmen* owners can arrange pick-up at your hotel.

Sea: Pelni's *Kelimutu* leaves every other week for Ujung Pandang before returning to Maumere and heading east to Kalabahi (Alor) and, finally, Dili (Timor). Check with the Pelni office on Jl. Slamet Riyadi or with the harbormaster down at the dock.

Smaller shipping lines also sail to Timor, Alor, Solor, and Ujung Pandang.

WAIARA BEACH

Maumere's most popular beach resort and dive destination is 12 km east of town on the road to Larantuka. According to dive professionals, Maumere Bay—with its detached coral reefs, great diversity of ocean life, and world-class drop-offs—offers some of the finest diving in Indonesia. Diving, not the mediocre black-sand beach, is the main draw of Waiara.

Scuba Diving

The best visibility is during the dry season from March to November. Local dive operators have identified several dozen sites within the 40-km expanse of Maumere Bay, including over a dozen fairly good shore dives, superior coral gardens off Pulau Besar, cave diving near Pulau Babi, and best of all, the perfect corals and unlimited sealife at Pomana Besar Island and Gosong Bone Atoll.

Prior to the earthquake of Dec. 1992, Waiara Beach had two dive operators that provided rental equipment and dive boats. Both resorts were destroyed by the quake and tidal wave but intend to rebuild their properties and resume business by early 1994.

Sao Wisata: The most professional services were provided by Flores Sao Resort (Sao Wisata), a private company owned by a local politician who was granted guardianship over the local marine reserve. Sao Wisata operates a two-star hotel, conducts five-day NAUI certification courses, and runs a 25-knot catamaran and a live-aboard dive boat. All-inclusive dive packages (airport pick-up, accommodations, meals, and two dives per day) cost US$80-120 per day depending on room choice. Four-day eight-dive packages cost from US$300.

Sea World: Diving in Maumere began in the early 1970s after an Italian couple arrived to establish the first local dive club, then called Waiara Cottages. The operation was taken over several years ago by a local Roman Catholic foundation, which attempted to maintain the dive boat and scuba equipment in working condition. Sea World closed down after the earthquake but intends to reopen in the near future.

Accommodations

Waiara was leveled by the earthquake, though the two principal dive resorts will probably return, as will several of the inexpensive beachside bungalows that once lined the bay.

Sao Wisata: The premier dive operator has all-inclusive dive packages (described above), and less expensive packages for nondivers that cost from US$20 per day. 18 Jl. Don Thomas, Maumere, tel. (0383) 342. Jakarta headquarters: Borobudor Hotel, room 68, Jl. Lapangan, Banteng Selatan, Jakarta 10710, tel. (021) 380-5555, fax (021) 359741.

Sea World Resort: Sea World has always been the less-expensive alternative to Sao Wisata and will probably remain so after rebuilding. P.O. Box 3, Jl. Nai Noha, KM 13, Maumere, tel. (0383) 570, US$12-20.

LARANTUKA

Larantuka is an old Portuguese trading center where traces of the colonial era remain evident in old stone and stucco houses, in the large-boned, Latin-featured inhabitants, in family names such as Monteiros and da Silva, and even in place-names such as Posto (the town's center). Strategically situated on sea routes used by Portuguese seeking sandalwood from Timor, the Portuguese-Catholic heritage also survives in its prayers recited in unintelligible Portuguese, Christmas and Good Friday processions, and much of the Iberian church architecture that survived the quake of 1992.

Larantuka chiefly serves as the embarkation point for the twice-weekly ferry to Timor and boats to the islands of the Solor and Alor archipelagoes. Town facilities include a Bank Rakyat that *doesn't* provide exchange services, a post office and tourist information center several kilometers north of town, and a Merpati office diagonally opposite the church.

Accommodations

Larantuka was badly damaged in the big quake, but the following *losmen* will probably be back in business by the time you arrive.

Rulies Hotel: The most popular travelers' place in town has good vibes and rooms with common or private bath. 40 Jl. Yos Sudarso, tel. (0383) 21198, US$3-8.

Trisna Hotel: A larger and slightly more luxurious spot adjacent to the Rulies. 38 Jl. Yos Sudarso, US$3-10.

Transportation

Air: Merpati flies once weekly to and from Kupang with a stop on the island of Lembata.

Sea: Ferries to Kupang leave twice weekly on Tues. and Fri. afternoons and return from Kupang on Mon. and Thurs., the day after the flight arrives from Darwin.

Boats depart almost daily for the islands of the Solor archipelago. Check with the *syahbandar* office at the harbor or with the Pelni representative on Jl. Niaga. The new ferry dock is five km from town on the road to Maumere.

SOLOR AND ALOR ARCHIPELAGOES

Separated from the larger islands by swift and narrow straits, the islands off the east coast of Flores are among the most traditional and untouched regions of Indonesia; a welcome escape from the tidal wave of mass tourism.

The Solor Archipelago includes Solor, Adonara, and Lembata, while the Alor Archipelago includes Pantar and Alor islands. Lembata and Alor—the two principal islands and the only ones with tourist facilities—receive a steady trickle of visitors throughout the year, but Western travelers should be prepared for tough travel conditions and rudimentary meals and accommodations. The rewards are friendly people, lovely scenery, and a fascinating travel experience for anyone interested in traditional Indonesian culture.

Visitors should bring along plenty of small bills since the entire region has only one exchange facility, in Kalabahi on Alor.

Transportation

Air: Merpati flies once weekly to Lewoleba (Lembata) from Larantuka and Kupang, before returning directly to Kupang. Merpati also flies several times weekly between Kupang and Kalabahi (Alor).

Sea: Ferries connect nearly all the islands on a daily basis. Boats from Larantuka head east to the nearby islands of Solor and Adonara. Boats continue from Waiwerang (Adonara) to Lewoleba. A weekly boat from Lewoleba reaches Kalabahi with overnight stops in Waiwerang and Balauring (northeast Lembata). A final ship continues from Kalabahi down to Kupang.

Pelni's *Kelimutu* sails every other week from Kalabahi to Maumere before returning to Kalabahi and continuing east to Dili and Kupang.

Adonara

Adonara is a Catholic island settled in the early 16th century by the Portuguese, though many of the residents still follow animist practices and worship nature spirits under the firm gaze of Gunung Boleng (1,650 meters), which soars above the scrubby island.

Waiwerang: Boats from Larantuka cross the narrow channel to Wailebe or go directly to Waiwerang, largest town on the island. Market days are Monday and Thursday. Losmen Taufik and Losmen Tresna on the main road near the pier have rooms under US$3.

Solor

Once the rendezvous point for Portuguese sandalwood traders, and home to Dominican monks who built an impressive stone fortress, Solor today is a sleepy and rarely visited island known for its whaling village of Lamalera on the east coast and fortress ruins near Lohajong in the northeast corner. The principal township of Rita Ebang is served by boats from Larantuka.

Lembata

Lembata is a striking island of scrub grasslands, inland stands of eucalyptus trees, and open savannahs, inhabited by people with distinct dialects, customs, and beliefs in animism despite their conversion to Christianity. The main attractions are market day in the main town of Lewoleba, a climb up Gunung Ile Ape from the north coast, and the traditional whaling village of Lamalera in the far south.

Lewoleba: Served by boats from Larantuka, Lewoleba is best visited for the Monday market, which attracts thousands of people from across the archipelago. Losmen Rejeki is a friendly spot run by a young Chinese manager who can help with maps and advise on island walks. Motorcycles and cars can be rented here.

Gunung Ile Ape: North of Lewoleba is the most traditional region of the island: the towering pinnacle of Mt. Ile Ape (1,450 meters) can be climbed with local guides from the village of Lamaguete. Travelers can overnight by contacting the *kepala desa*.

Lamalera: Lamalera is one of the final whaling villages in Indonesia and among the last places on earth where people hunt whales from rudimentary boats, constructed without nails and propelled with sails of *gewang* palm. Unfortunately, whales are rare; only a dozen are speared each whaling season from May to October. A beachside house provides inexpensive rooms and meals.

Alor

Alor, 60 km north of Timor, has a population sharply divided between Islamic peoples living in the relatively narrow lowlands and a large number of indigenous ethnolinguistic groups residing in the mountainous interior. Chiefly known for its unique forms of *ikat* and bronze kettle drums called *moko,* Alor receives a grand total of about 30 tourists per year, mostly in July and August.

Kalabahi: Alor's main town serves as a base for visits to traditional villages such as Tapkala, 13 km east on a paved road, and Atimelang, described by Cora Dubois in her two-part ethnological tome, *The People of Alor.* An excellent three-km white-sand beach is found at Mali, 18 km north of Kalabahi.

Three *losmen* are in Kalabahi. Adi Dharma Hotel on the waterfront is run by an English teacher who is a goldmine of information about Alor. Nearby Hotel Melati, also on the waterfront, handles the overflow. Overflow? On Alor?

SUMBA

Outlying, dry, mostly barren Sumba is one of the most fascinating islands of Nusa Tenggara. Internationally known as the source of some of the most handsome *ikat* fabrics in Indonesia, Sumba is also famed as the breeding ground for the country's strongest horses, and for its ritual tribal life, flawlessly built high-peaked thatch-roofed villages, and mammoth sculptured stone tombs. Here you find an authentic ancient culture with none of the layers of Hinduism, Islam, or Christianity found elsewhere in Indonesia.

Sumba's premier tourist district is in the west near Waikabubak, where traditional culture remains apparent in megalithic gravesites, old homes covered with thatched roofing rather than galvanized steel, and age-old rituals, such as tribal war games (*pasola*) held every spring.

East Sumbanese highlights include textile villages south of Waingapu and deserted beaches with good surf.

Transportation

Situated south of Flores and midway between Sumbawa and Timor, Sumba is off the beaten path and somewhat removed from the standard Bali-to-Timor route. The most convenient access is by air from Bali, Kupang, or Bima. Aside from sea transport, Merpati from Bima is the least expensive way to reach the island.

Air: Sumba has two airports; the larger one is Mauhau Airport, six km outside Waingapu in East Sumba, and the other is Tambolaka airport, 42 km from Waikabubak in West Sumba.

Merpati flies daily to Waingapu from Bali (US$80) and Kupang (US$60), and three times weekly to Tambolaka from Bima (US$30) and Waingapu (US$28). The thrice-weekly Merpati schedule is Denpasar-Bima-Tambolaka-Waingapu-Kupang-return. Bouraq flies three times weekly Denpasar-Waingapu-Kupang-return.

Sea: Pelni's *Kelimutu* calls twice monthly at Waingapu on its Nusa Tenggara circuit: Padangbai-Lembar-Bima-Waingapu-Ende-Kupang-Dili-Kalabahi-Maumere-Ujung-Pandang-return. Smaller ships also sail from Ende to Waingapu.

Bus: Buses and minibuses take five or six hours to cover the 137-km paved road between Waingapu and Waikabubak. Outlying villages are served by a slow and crowded *bemo* network.

The ideal solution is a motorcycle (US$6) or chartered jeep (US$35-40) rented from any *losmen* or hotel. The jeep cost can be split between four or five passengers.

The *Pasola*

Sumba's premier event is a ritualistic tribal war held by hundreds of horsemen in various villages during February and March, shortly after the full moon and coinciding with the harvesting of a strange, multihued sea worm called the *nyale*. Essentially a violent and primeval jousting match between teams of horsemen brandishing long wooden spears and shields, the sometimes deadly *pasola* now attracts large crowds and even a few tour groups brought to the island specifically to witness the event. Exact dates and locations can be checked from any Indonesian tourist office.

Ikat

Visitors to Sumba are invariably met by hordes of *ikat* salesmen who quickly become tiresome with their insistent hawking of sarongs and Sumba blankets. Before opening your wallet, be patient and learn all you can about the process.

Fine *ikat* represents a colossal amount of human labor, and even in a poor society such as Sumba fabrics woven with fine threads and natural dyes rightly command stratospheric prices. Cylinder skirts for women (*lau*) and the sarong and shoulder mantle worn by men (*hinggi*) should cost US$25-100 if quickly woven with imported colored thread, synthetic dyes, and larger designs. However, fine ceremonial skirts woven with supplementary warp (*lau pahudu*) and blue-and-rust mantles (*hinggi kombu*) repeatedly dipped to ensure deep, saturated colors often cost US$250-1000.

Visit the handicraft shop in the Sandlewood Hotel and weaving villages near Waingapu before you begin negotiations. Many salesmen start at two or three times the correct price, so bargain firmly but keep your sense of humor.

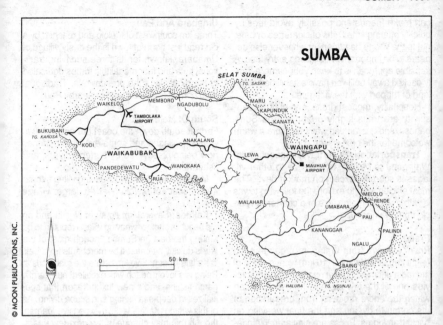

Prices are about the same, but the selection is larger in Waingapu than in the nearby weaving villages.

WAINGAPU

Waingapu, principal port and district capital of East Sumba, is a sprawling commercial center of little note, but it's a useful base from which to explore the traditional weaving villages to the south and purchase East Sumbanese *ikat,* the finest in Nusa Tenggara.

Facilities include a Bank Rakyat with exchange services, a Merpati office on Jl. Ahmad Yani in the Elim Hotel, and a Pelni office down at the port.

Accommodations

Waingapu has two inexpensive *losmen* in the northern district near the harbor and four *losmen* one km south of the harbor near the bus terminal and the bank.

Hotel Lima Saudara: A popular spot near the waterfront; all rooms include private bath. 2 Jl. Wangametei, tel. 83, US$3-8.

Hotel Surabaya: An acceptable if noisy spot just opposite the bus terminal and supermarket. Motorcycle rentals cost US$6 per day. 2 Jl. El Tari, tel. 125, US$3-8.

Elim Hotel: An old but excellent-value hotel adjacent to the Merpati office and two blocks northeast of the bus terminal. All rooms include private bath. 73 Jl. Ahmad Yani, tel. 232, US$4-7 fan, US$12-20 a/c.

Sandlewood Hotel: Waingapu's best is this strangely misspelled hotel with a good restaurant and the largest selection of *ikat* on the island. All rooms include breakfast. 23 Jl. Panjaitan, tel. 199, US$5-8 fan, US$12-20 a/c.

VILLAGES NEAR WAINGAPU

Traditional East Sumbanese weaving villages are found near Waingapu, 65 km south near the town of Melolo, and along the southeastern coastline between Melolo and Baing.

Village Etiquette: Many villages now expect a donation of 1000-2000 *rupiah* to look around and take photographs. Independent travelers can make friends and possibly avoid fees by quickly offering small gifts of cigarettes or betel nut to the village headman, or whoever else appears to be important or collecting entry fees. A sensible approach is to keep your camera firmly packed away until you have established some kind of rapport with the villagers.

Hospitality, modest dress, and cultural sensitivity are traits highly prized by the Sumbanese, and guaranteed ways to insure a warm welcome for the next visitor.

Transportation: *Bemo* travel frequently from Waingapu to Melolo, but service to other villages is sporadic except on market days. The most efficient way to explore the following towns is with a rented motorcycle or a chartered vehicle from Waingapu.

Praliu

Praliu (two km from Waingapu), Lambanapu (eight km), and Kwangu (10 km) weave some of the most outstanding *ikat* on the island and provide one of the few places where visitors can watch the entire process, from preparation of the cotton to dyeing and the final weaving on backstrap looms. Prices are similar to Waingapu's and bargaining is essential.

Melolo

Melolo is a small town, 65 km southeast of Waingapu, at the end of a savannahlike plain pitted with deep craters and muddy pools; the bus twists and lurches the whole way. Visitors heading to nearby villages must often change *bemo* here.

LD Gah Homestay: Outside of Waingapu, the only places to sleep in East Sumba are homestays with the *kepala desa* and here in Melolo in this primitive four-room *losmen*. The Timorese owners prepare simple meals and rent motorcycles for exploring the nearby villages.

Rende

The finest megalithic funerary sculptures in East Sumba are here in Rende, a small raja village seven km south of Melolo. The largest tomb was constructed for a former ruler with four massive menhirs and elevated tablets richly carved with animal effigies and sacrificial deities.

Rende also contains traditional clan houses whose thatched roofs have unfortunately been covered with corrugated tin. *Ikat* produced in Rende is top quality but very expensive.

Umabara And Pau

Three km southwest of Melolo and reached by a dirt road just north of town is the dusty village of Umabara, known for its three surviving traditional huts and four megalithic tombs dedicated to the relatives of the present raja. Traditional *adat* homes are also found in nearby Pau.

South Of Melolo

Farther south down the coast are several *ikat*-weaving villages and some excellent beaches now being discovered by surfers, divers, and fishermen.

Mangili: A well-known weaving village some 40 km south of Melolo near the larger village of Ngalu.

Kaliuda: Several km south of Ngallu and on the beach is another weaving village reputed to be among the best on Sumba, though most of the *ikat* is quickly purchased by merchants from Bali.

Kailala Beach: Five km before the road ends at Baing is a lovely beach with excellent surf, terrific game fishing, and a new luxury resort that specializes in deep-sea fishing and scuba diving. As of this writing, Kailala lacks inexpensive *losmen,* though this may change in the next few years; check with the *losmen* owners in Waingapu.

WAIKABUBAK

Waikabubak, capital and commercial center of West Sumba, is composed of a small business district surrounded by several hilltop villages with tall houses and ancestral graves. Waikabubak serves as the tourist center of Sumba—an excellent place from which to visit the nearby villages and learn something of traditional culture.

Attractions

Surprisingly, several villages on the outskirts of Waikabubak offer some of the finest architecture and megalithic monuments anywhere on Sumba.

Tarung: First stop should be this hilltop village, one km west of city center, which serves as the spiritual center of the local Marapu religion and ceremonial site of the annual Wula Padu festival. Tarung features almost a dozen old homes covered with thatch, plus some of West Sumba's most impressive gravesites. Many tombs are carved with crosses (symbolizing Christan conversion) and older ornaments such as buffalo heads (power), horses (a safe trip to heaven), and dogs (faithfulness).

Bondomaroto: Three km southeast of Waikabubak is another traditional village known for its strange megalithic carvings of sacred buffalo, and *ikat* weaving with backstrap looms.

Praijing: The trail opposite Bondomaroto leads to this lovely five-terraced village at the summit of a small hill. As elsewhere on Sumba, Praijing was constructed on a hilltop for defensive reasons and to resist the slave traders who frequently raided the island from Timor and Flores. Also, tombs are not built in remote graveyards outside town, but right in the center of the village; people here *live* with their dead.

Accommodations

Hotel Aloha: Waikabubak's travelers' center has clean rooms with complimentary breakfast, a popular cafe, motorcycle rentals, and plenty of current information on Sumbanese attractions. Jalan Gajah Mada, tel. 24, US$4-9.

Losmen Pelita: The cheapest place in town is near the mosque and somewhat noisy but acceptable for a short stay. 2 Jl. Achmad Yani, tel. 104, US$2-6.

Hotel Manandang: A clean and relatively new hotel with budget rooms with common bath and better facilities with private bath and a/c. 4 Jl. Pemuda, tel. 197, US$6-10 fan, US$14-20 a/c.

Mona Lisa Hotel: Waikabubak's top-end choice has a fine restaurant and rooms fashioned after Sumbanese clan houses in an isolated location about three km northwest of city center. Jalan Adhyaksa, tel. 174, US$30-45.

Transportation

The easiest way to reach Waikabubak is by bus from Waingapu. Visitors arriving at the Tambolaka airport, about 42 km north of Waikabubak, can reach town with Merpati shuttle buses for US$1 or with chartered taxis that cost US$15-20.

EAST OF WAIKABUBAK

Anakalang

Twenty-two km east and one hour by *bemo* lies a busy village (Pasunga) known for its massive gravesite and oft-photographed tomb, conveniently situated right on the roadside. A paved road just opposite leads south to the next village.

Kabunduk

Beyond the central pathway is a small megalithic tomb topped by two carved horsemen, and an immense 30-ton slab (Resi Moni) under which the final raja of the Anakalang kingdom was buried in 1939.

Entrance fees paid to the *kepala desa* in Kapunduk (Matakakeri) should include admittance and photography of all nearby tombs. Visitors can overnight in the traditional house that faces the central altars; a rare opportunity to experience traditional Sumbanese life.

Lai Tarung

A dirt path west of Kapunduk heads up the hill to another village with numerous old graves and an elevated slab on which corpses once laid in state.

Gulabakul (Prai Bokul)

Two km south of Kapunduk is Sumba's largest and heaviest megalith, Umbu Sawola, a 70-ton monster erected in 1971 over the burial spot of Anakalang's richest raja.

SOUTH OF WAIKABUBAK

Wanokaka and Lamboya, two traditional regions south of Waikabubak, are famed for their annual *pasola,* stone tombs, and wonderful beaches popular with surfers and foreign hotel developers.

Paigoli

Just before Wanokaka Beach, where village priests sometimes gather *nyale* sea worms on *pasola* day, is a huge grave (Watu Kajiwa) fronted by one of the most famous tombstones on Sumba. Perhaps the oldest monument on the island, Watu Kajiwa is spectacularly carved with primitive yet powerful images of men, women, and nature.

Rua Beach

The long and sparkling beaches near Rua village and Tanjung Karosa to the west have been earmarked by the government for new hotels and other commercial enterprises. As of this writing, only the American-managed three-star Sumba Reef Lodge has opened, though surfers and backpackers can stay at several simple *losmen* owned by local fishermen.

The road continues west to an almost unending series of deserted beaches blessed with brilliantly pure white sand. Beyond Marosi Beach is Lemandunga, where *nyale* worms are gathered for the Labmoya *pasola,* followed by a surfers' spot at Pantai Patiala and a deserted beach called Pantai Dasang. The road to the following west-coast beaches may be completed by the time you arrive.

WEST OF WAIKABUBAK

Kodi is the westernmost district of Sumba, and Bonodokodi (Kodi), several kilometers east of the ocean, is the largest town. Spectacular beaches on the west coast are attracting a steady stream of travelers, who arrive to surf, dive, and enjoy the unhurried pace of life.

Pero

Also called Redakapal ("Ship Lookout"), Pantai Pero serves as the Australian surfers' center for Sumba. The sand is great and the water is clear, plus there are plenty of other superb (and deserted) beaches to the south and to the north.

Accommodations: Several inexpensive *losmen* operated by Muslim fishermen are located at Pantai Pero. All charge US$4-6 for a room plus three meals. An Australian firm has started construction on what appears to be a fairly luxurious resort.

Transportation: Buses direct to Pero can be booked from most *losmen* in Waikabubak. Some buses stop in Kodi, from where you can hike down to Pantai Pero.

Pronobaroro

Two km south of Pero is a traditional village with the highest peaked roofs in all of Sumba, plus megalithic tombs and elaborate homes decorated with pig jaws and buffalo horns.

Ratenegaro

Three km south of Pronobaroro lies another intriguing hamlet separated by the Bonodokodi River from the tapered roofs of Wainyapu. Both villages face a fine beach blessed with sparkling waters and swaying palms.

TIMOR

After a long period of isolation, Timor once again receives a steady stream of visitors, mostly Australians, who enter via Kupang from Darwin. After picking up a 60-day entry stamp upon arrival at the airport, and a short holiday sightseeing around Kupang, most travelers then island-hop westward across Nusa Tenggara or fly directly to Bali.

Timor still suffers from lingering political disruptions, though most of the island is secure and visitors can travel safely from Kupang to Dili.

Warning: Malaria is an extremely serious problem, not only on Timor, but on all other islands in Nusa Tenggara. Visitors are *strongly* urged to take malaria pills, use repellent, and stay well covered in the evenings.

Transportation
Kupang is the transportation hub for the island and arrival point for visitors from Australia.

International Air: Merpati flies from Darwin in Australia's Northern Territory to Kupang on Wed. and Sat. for A$220 one-way, A$380 return. No visa is required, as Kupang is now an official entry point, and travelers with sufficient funds do not need an onward ticket.

Note: Most travelers flying from Kupang to Darwin need an Australian visa, and Australian diplomatic offices are only located in Bali and Jakarta. Be sure to obtain your Australian visa *before* you begin the long journey from Bali to Timor.

Regional Air: A popular way to explore Nusa Tenggara is to fly from Bali to Kupang and then overland back to Bali. Merpati flies daily between Kupang and Dili (US$40), Maumere (US$40), Waingapu (US$60), Bajawa (US$65), Ujung Pandang (US$90), Bali (US$110), and Jakarta (US$200). Merpati also flies on a weekly basis to Tamboldka Airport, Sumba (US$85), Alor (US$50), Lembata (US$45), Roti (US$25), and Savu (US$40).

Ship: Kupang's Tanau Harbor, seven km from the *bemo* terminal, is home base for two Pelni ships. The *Kelimutu* departs every two weeks on a Kupang-Dili-Kalabahi-Maumere-Ujung Pandang and return route. The *Kelimutu* then sails Kupang-Ende-Waingapu-Bima-Lombok-Bali-Surabaya-Banjarmasin and return.

More exotic ports are served by Pelni's newest ship, the *Tatamailau,* which sails monthly from Dili to Ambon and Banda (both in Maluku) before stopping at six ports in Irian Jaya; an inexpensive yet comfortable way to tour Indonesia's most remote provinces. The *Tatamailau* then returns to Dili and sails west to Ujung Pandang, Surabaya, Banjarmasin, Cirebon, and Pontianak. Schedules and fares can be checked with the Pelni office on Jl. Pahlawan in Kupang, opposite Fort Concordia.

Smaller ferries depart once or twice weekly to Roti, Savu, Kalabahi, and other remote islands in the Solor and Alor archipelagoes. The most useful service is the twice-weekly ferry from Kupang to Larantuka on Flores; this boat leaves the day after the flight arrives from Darwin. Contact Perum shipping agency on Jl. Cak Doko.

KUPANG AND VICINITY

Kupang, the largest town in Nusa Tenggara, lies just 485 km from the coast of Australia—closer to Darwin than to Jakarta. Christianity is the dominant religion, but small minorities of Muslims, Hindu Balinese, and Chinese also live in Kupang, along with a veritable rainbow of races: Atoni, Rotinese, Savunese, Florinese, Kisarese, Adonese, Solorese, Ambonese, Javanese, Eurasians.

The Portuguese arrived on Timor in 1515, only three years after their conquest of Malacca, chiefly to harvest sandalwood and extract its aromatic oil. Seven years later, the survivors of Magellan's crew (Ferdinand was killed by Lapu Lapu in the Philippines) anchored off the island. The Dutch East Indies company seized Kupang in 1653 and established its military headquarters at Fort Concordia, while the Portuguese ran off and took East Timor. A final curious note was the arrival in 1789 of Captain Bligh after the disgruntled crew of the *Bounty* mutinied and forced Bligh to sail his rowboat from the Tongas to Kupang, across 3,816 nautical miles of open seas.

Kupang is a booming commercial center with all possible facilities, including a tourist office on Jl. Sukarno near the central *bemo* station, several banks, Garuda on Jl. Kohsasi, and Merpati on Jl. Sudirman adjacent to Hotel Flobamor.

Attractions

The historical Kupang described above has largely disappeared and been replaced with a messy assortment of concrete buildings and roads filled with the most nerve-wracking traffic east of Bali.

Museum: An excellent place to learn something about the complex history of Nusa Tenggara, though inconveniently located several kilometers east of city center; take *bemo* no. 4 from the downtown terminal. Open daily until 1600 except Fridays and Sundays.

Lasiana Beach: Pantai Lasiana, 11 km east of Kupang, is a deserted two-km-long beach with excellent sand and vendors on weekends.

Semau Island: Pulau Semau, a 45-square-km island visible from Kupang, offers some good snorkeling, decent beaches, an inland swimming pond, and a midpriced hotel owned by Teddy's Bar in Kupang. Room, board, and transportation cost US$20-35.

Accommodations

Kupang has over a dozen inexpensive *losmen* widely spread across town, four one-star hotels, and a new three-star hotel opened in early 1993. *Losmen* touts waiting at the airport and harbor provide free transportation to many of the following hotels.

Backpackers: Kupang's most popular *losmen* is very basic but friendly and a good source of travel information, plus there's a natural swimming pool nearby. Located four km south of city center; take a no. 3 (three-lamp) *bemo* from the downtown terminal. 38 Jl. Kancil, US$2-3.

Eden Homestay: Another popular guesthouse just opposite the Backpackers. 6 Jl. Kancil. tel. (0391) 21921, US$2-3.

Fatuleu Homestay: A quiet, clean, and mosquito-free place with a beautiful garden and a friendly owner who speaks English and leads tours. Conveniently located in the center of town, just past the three-star Orchid Garden Hotel. 1 Jl. Fatuleu, tel. (0391) 31374, US$3-8.

Sea Breezes Homestay: Simple *losmen* in an excellent waterfront location adjacent to Teddy's Bar and just across from the downtown terminal. Jalan Ikan Tongkol, US$3-5.

Teddy's Bar: Although the proprietor no longer rents rooms, Teddy's—a hangout for expats—is an excellent place to arrange tours, find out about surfing packages to Roti, overnight on one of those gigantic fishing platforms (*bagan*) outside town, or just rent a motorcycle or a minivan. Jalan Ikan Tongkol, tel. (0391) 21142.

Clara's Hotel: Recommended seaside hotel operated by a former soldier (now a preacher) who speaks good English and leads tours for Natrabu. Great views and good food in the second-floor restaurant. Located about 1.5 km west of town toward Tenau harbor. Jalan Pahlawan, tel. (0391) 22580, US$5-8 fan, US$12-16 a/c.

Hotel Flobamor II: Decent one-star hotel in the center of town next to the Merpati office. Popular with foreign project workers and long-term businessmen. 23 Jl. Sudirman, tel. (0391) 21346, US$25-50.

Orchid Garden Hotel: A three-star hotel with all possible amenities such as a pool, a business center, and a health club. 2 Jl. Fatuleu, tel. (0391) 21707, fax (0391) 31399, US$55-80.

Transportation

Air: Kupang's airport is 15 km east of city center and served by taxis for about US$4 per person. Arrivals can also hike 500 meters from the terminal and flag down a *bemo*.

Bus: Kupang's local bus and *bemo* terminal (Terminal Kota Kupang) is on the waterfront in the center of town. However, long-distance buses to Atambua, Dili, and other East Timor destinations depart from the Oebufu/Walikota Terminal in the east part of town near the museum. Take *bemo* no. 10.

Most travelers going to Dili overnight in Atambua, near the old border, about eight hours from Kupang. The most comfortable buses are operated by Natrabu on Jl. Gunung Mutis, two blocks southeast of Teddy's Bar.

Boat: Ships to Flores, Savu, Roti, Alor, and Sumba depart from the port of Tenau, eight km west of Kupang, reachable with *bemo* nos. 12 or 13 from the downtown "Terminal."

ROTI

Roti is a small but fascinating island known for its lontar cultivation and traditional culture, situated just 20 minutes by air west of Timor. Although not a part of Timor province, Roti is included here as a recommended side trip from Kupang.

The island is beautiful and almost completely untouched by tourists, except when the P&O Spice Island Cruise ship *Island Explorer* stops and disgorges several dozen wealthy foreign passengers. Aside from this scheduled disruption, the only visitors to bother with Roti are a handful of Australian surfers who have discovered the waves off southwest Roti. Surfing season is from April to October.

Transportation

Merpati's twice-weekly flight from Kupang to Baa takes just 20 minutes and costs US$24. Ferries depart Kupang for Olafulihaa (northeast corner) several times weekly and take about four hours. Both services are unreliable, disorganized, and subject to sudden cancellations.

Baa

The largest town on Roti has two mosques, a church, some government offices, no bank, and a colonial-style home once inhabited by a local raja.

Accommodations: Ricky's is a friendly spot with motorcycle rentals, tours, cold beer (order in advance), and simple but decent rooms for US$3-6. Two other joints handle the overflow.

Namberala (Dela)

Surfers' paradise is located at the southern end of Roti, where the road ends at Tanjung Bua. Waves are largest during the summer months when lefts break over an outside reef. Several simple *losmen* here charge US$4-6 per day with three meals. Alcohol is expensive; bring an ample supply from Kupang.

Papela

Papela harbor in the far northeast corner is a spectacular combination of brilliant blue waters and an arching bay filled with bobbing boats. Fishermen here survive by gathering mother-of-pearl and sea cucumbers from the Australian coast; a fine place to relax for a few days.

Accommodations: Papela has several inexpensive *losmen* and homestays which cater to a steady trickle of international travelers. Best of the lot is Vonny's Homestay, operated by a Tasmanian lady who can help with tours, boat rentals, and travel tips on Roti.

SOE

Back to Timor. Most travelers overnight in Atambua, though chilly Soe, four hours and 110 km east of Kupang, might be an interesting stop if you have some extra time. Bill Dalton—mentor, guru, literary genius, and consummate bullshit artist—claims this is the richest area for travelers in West Timor.

Attractions

Traditional architecture survives in conical, steeply pitched homes called *lopo,* though the government encourages the Timorese to live in more modern styles. Market days provide the regional highlights: Niki Niki (Wednesday), Batu Putih (Sunday), and Oenlasi (Tuesday), the largest market in Soe District. Sandalwood carvings are produced in a small factory near Bank Rakyat.

Accommodations

Believe it or not, Soe has a half-dozen *losmen* and hotels.

Hotel Anda: An inexpensive place run by a multilingual couple from Roti who can help with local details. 5 Jl. Kartini, US$2-4.

Mahkota Plaza Hotel: Soe's best, just opposite the bus terminal, has a good restaurant and 20 clean rooms with private bath. Jl. Suharto, US$4-15.

ATAMBUA

Atambua is the largest town in central Timor and a useful place to overnight between Kupang and Dili.

Accommodations

Losmen Minang: An inexpensive and somewhat clean *losmen* near the bus terminal. 12

Jl. Sukarno, tel. (0391) 135, US$3-6 including breakfast.

Nusatara Hotel: Best value in town but often full. All rooms have attached bath and include breakfast. 22 Jl. Sukarno, tel. (0391) 117, US$4-8.

DILI

Dili and East Timor—"Tim Tim" or "Timor Timor"—were closed to international tourism from 1976 to 1989, until the Indonesian government thought it safe enough to open this former Portuguese colony to the outside world.

Dili made international headlines in 1989 when Pope John Paul II visited the town, and again in Nov. 1991 when overzealous government troops fired on student demonstrators and killed dozens in a horrific bloodbath universally condemned by human-rights organizations.

Dili has a tourist office on Jl. Kaikoli, several banks with exchange facilities, and a Merpati/Garuda office on Jl. Avenida Bispo Medeiros. Indra Kelana agency on Jl. Kolmera is the local expert and the leading tour operator in East Timor.

Attractions

Dili will never win any awards for civic beauty, though the crumbling old stores near the waterfront and remnants of the Portuguese empire impart a vaguely Mediterranean atmosphere.

Liberation Monument: The spirit of Sukarno and Stalinist Realism survives in an aesthetically horrendous monument near the crafts center, dedicated to the annexation of East Timor into the Republic of Indonesia.

Catholic Cathedral: Another monument—largest church in all of Southeast Asia—constructed for and blessed during the 1989 visit of the Pope. Attend Sunday services, then lay a flower at the nearby graveyard.

Accommodations

Hotels in Dili are plentiful, though more expensive than elsewhere in Nusa Tenggara.

Wisma Taufiq: Decent budget place in a central location just one block back from the bay. Jalan Americao Thomas, tel. (0391) 22151, US$4-6.

Hotel Dili: An older hotel east of city center and facing the beach with acceptable rooms in the midpriced level. Called "best value" or "run down" depending on the guidebook. 25 Jl. Sada Bandeira, tel. (0391) 21871, US$8-18.

Hotel Mahkota Timor: New three-story 100-room seafront hotel with upscale restaurant and business facilities. Jalan Alves Aldea, tel. (0391) 21283, US$32-55.

SULAWESI

Sit and stare at a large wall map of Sulawesi for a while and you'll see dragons, giraffes, spiders, orchids, even a headless octopus. Lying between Kalimantan and the Maluku Islands, Sulawesi (formerly known as Celebes) is Indonesia's third largest and second most popular tourist destination. An amazing diversity of societies exists here, with a distinct separation of old and new, traditional and modern within the many cultures themselves. Sulawesi also boasts some of the most remote jungle areas in the archipelago, with unusual flora and fauna and nearly unknown tribes.

Most travelers limit their visits to the Tana Toraja culture region in the south-central leg and the necessary stop in Ujung Pandang. The island's second most popular region is North Sulawesi (Sulawesi Utara), a beautiful land of vast coconut and clove plantations, active volcanos, lakes, hot springs, ancient burial sites, picturesque villages, white-sand coral islands, and outstanding snorkeling and diving—considered some of the finest in Southeast Asia. For complete details, read Bill Dalton's *Indonesia Handbook*.

TRANSPORTATION

Getting There
Ujung Pandang (formerly Makassar) on the tip of the southwest peninsula is the major port of call and gateway to Sulawesi.

Air: Garuda and Merpati fly daily to Ujung Pandang from Jakarta, Surabaya, Denpasar, and other towns such as Balikpapan and Biak. Popular with travelers is the flight from Bali to Ujung Pandang and a return to Surabaya. Another option is traveling overland through Central Sulawesi to Manado, then flying back to Surabaya or east to Maluku or Irian Jaya.

Sea: All seven of the Pelni boats that shuttle around the archipelago stop in Ujung Pandang. The most popular choices are the MV *Rinjani* and the MV *Kerinci*. Both ships sail every other week from Surabaya and cost less than half the airfare.

Getting Around
The tortuously shaped island of Sulawesi can be toured by air, sea, or overland transportation.

Land: The southwest and northern peninsulas of Sulawesi have the best road systems, though one can now travel overland the whole length of the island. Roads are kept in good condition except during the monsoon season, when the route through Central Sulawesi turns into a muddy quagmire.

Air: Flying is the most expedient (though expensive) way to get around. Tana Toraja—the most popular destination on Sulawesi—can be reached direct three times daily from Jakarta, twice daily from Surabaya, and once daily from Biak, Denpasar, Medan, and Manado with Garuda International. Bouraq flies weekly from Balikpapan. These direct flights avoid having to spend a night in Ujung Pandang. Alternatively, Merpati has direct connections from Ujung Pandang to Tator (Tana Toraja) three times weekly from Ujung Pandang for about US$60 roundtrip. Flights land in Rantetaya, 14 km west of Makale and 32 km south of Rantepao; taxis and *bemos* continue into town.

Sea: Sulawesi has perhaps the best shipping services in all of Indonesia. Pelni's modern seacraft continually circle the island, stopping at Ujung Pandang, Pantoloan (Palu's port), Toli Toli, Kwandang, and Bitung (Manado's port). Sea connections are also made between Sulawesi and Kalimantan, Surabaya, Bali, Lombok, Sumbawa, and Maluku; see the Pelni route map in the Indonesia introduction.

SOUTHERN SULAWESI

This remarkable province offers spectacular limestone mountains, an almost endless coastline, huge shallow lakes, hot springs, caves and waterfalls, rare and exotic flora and fauna, Dutch fortress ruins, the age-old practice of *prahu* building, and fascinating cultures rich with unequaled ceremonies and festivals. The southern coastline and fishing villages are inhabited by the Muslim Bugis and Makassarese, while the interior mountains are home to the Christian Torajas, whose culture and architecture are the primary reasons to visit the island.

UJUNG PANDANG

Formerly known as Makassar, this bustling commercial, shipping, and government center constitutes a major air-sea crossroads between western and eastern Indonesia—the largest and busiest mercantile center in the eastern archipelago for almost 500 years. Ujung Pandang is a chaotic city that chiefly serves travelers as a transit point for Tana Toraja, though you will enjoy the sailing *prahus* and spectacularly beautiful sunsets over Makassar Bay.

Attractions

The tourist office (tel. 21142) is inconveniently located four km southeast of town. Tours around town and Tana Toraja can be arranged from Ramayana Travel on Jalan Anuang and from Pacto on Jalan Sudirman. Pacto also offers unique expeditions to the beaches of Southeast Sulawesi and the megaliths of Bada Valley in Central Sulawesi.

Fort Rotterdam: Within the walls of this once-crumbling fort are some of the finest examples of 17th-century Dutch colonial architecture in all of Indonesia. The spacious La Galigo Museum covers the ethnology of the region, with exhibits of ceramics, weaving technology, and miniature houses fashioned with extraordinary detail. The historical museum across the yard has fascinating photos, the famous Silkendang Buddha image, and a whole section devoted to the cultural heritage of the Goa Kingdom.

Dance rehearsals take place in the nearby Conservatory of Performing Arts.

Boat Harbor: Ujung Pandang's finest sight is the row of handsome Bugis schooners docked in the harbors north of city center. Pelabuhan Paotere, north of Sukarno Harbor, has a handful of traditional *pinsis* whose designs haven't changed since the days of Genghis Khan.

Clara Bundt House: A refreshing escape from the squalor of Ujung Pandang can be found among the seashells and orchids inside the home of Clara and her German father.

Budget Accommodations

Hotels in the cheapest category around the port area tend to be either full or extremely barebones. The information counter at the airport has a list of hotels in all price ranges.

Ramayana Satrya Hotel: A popular if somewhat pricey 52-room hotel conveniently located on the road from the airport, near the Merpati office and the Liman Express bus stop and about two km east of the beach. The owners provide direct bus service to Wisma Maria in Rantepao. *Bemo* from the airport pass this hotel. 121 Jl. Bawakaraeng, P.O. Box 467, tel. (0411) 22165, US$7-16.

Hotel Purnama: A decent midtown hotel located just to the south of Fort Rotterdam. Like all other hotels in Ujung Pandang, the Purnama is overpriced, but it's well located for sunsets and inner-city explorations. 3 Jl. Pattimura, tel. (0411) 33830, US$5-10.

Hotel Nusantara: Good location in the north of town, but rooms are extremely simple. Hotel Murah across the street is also cheap but only survivable for one night. 103 Jl. Sarappo, tel. (0411) 33163, US$3-6.

Fortune Home: The former manager of the once-popular Mandar Inn has moved his operation one km south of Losari Beach, just below the city stadium. 19 Jl. Gagak, tel. (0411) 851496, US$4-8.

Moderate Accommodations

Pasanggrahan Makassar Hotel: A seaside hotel with 25 clean, breezy rooms and an ex-

SULAWESI

LAUT CELEBES

KEP. SANGIHE

SULAWESI UTARA

MANADO
LIKUPANG
BITUNG
TONDANO

SELAT MAKASSAR

BORNEO

SANTIGI
TOLI-TOLI
LANU
BIAU
PIMPI
LOMBAGIN
KOTAMOBAGU

KUANDANG
GORONTALO
TILAMUTA
TALUDAA
DUMOGA
MARISA

SIBOA
TOMINI
TINOMBO

SULAWESI
TENGAH

MAPAGA
TORIBULU

TEL. TOMINI

KEP. TOGIAN

LAUT MALUKU

SELAT WALEA
MALIK
TEKU

TG. KARANG
DONGGALA

PARIGI
PALU
AMPANA
BOALANG
LUWUK

PASANGKAYU

LORE LINDU
RESERVE

TOJO
BATUI

PALAM
P. PELENG

KEP. SULA

KAROSA
GIMPU
POSO
MOROWALI
RESERVE

KEMBANI

P. TALIABU

SULAWESI
SELATAN

D. POSO
TENTENA

P. BANGKULU

TEL. TOLO
KEP. BANGGAI

PENDOLO
KOLONDALE

MESAMBA
SAROAKO
D. MATANA
SOKITA

MAMUJU
BONEBONE
MALILI
D. TOWUTI
LABOTA

TALAPANG
RANTEPAO
PALOPO
TOLALA

MAMASA
MAKALE
G. RANTEKOMBOLA
(3455 m)

CENRANA
POLEWALI
MONDEODO
SULAWESI TENGGARA

MAJENE
ENREKANG

PINRANG
SIWA

PANGKAJENE
SENGKANG SOPPENG
KENDARI
MONSE

PARE PARE
D. TEMPE
KOLAKA
BENUA
SELAT WOWONI

SUMPANGBINANGAE
WATANGSOPPENG
BAULA

BARU
WATAMPONE (BONE)
TOWARI

PANGKAJENE
SAMAK
RAHA

UJUNG
PANDANG
MAROS
BALANGNIPA
SINJAI
P. MUNA
BONE
P. BUTON

MALINO
TANETTE
PISING
PASARWAJO

TAKALAR
BULUKUMBA
P. KABENA
KEP.
TUKANGBESI

BANTAENG
BIRA
MAWASANGKA

JENEPONTO

BENTENG
P. SELAYAR
P. BATUATA

0   200 km

P. TANAHJAMPA
P. KALAOTOA
LAUT BANDA

© MOON PUBLICATIONS, INC.

UJUNG PADANG

TO PRAHU HARBOR AND MAIN HARBOR

JL. SERAM UJUNG

IMMIGRATION

JL. BUTUNG

JAMESON SUPERMARKET

HOTEL MURAH

HOTEL NUSANTARA

JL. BANDA

JL. BURU

SOEKARNO HARBOR

JL. SANGIR

DIPONEGORO TOMB

JL. LEMBE

J L. DIPONEGORO

JL. K.H. HASYIM

JL. NUSANTARA

JL. MARTADINATA

JL. SULAWESI

JL. RACAN

PELNI OFFICE

MAIN BEMO STATION

CENTRAL MARKET

JL. TIMOR

HATTA HARBOR

JL. BALI

JL. K.H. RAMLI

JL. SUMBA

LIMAN EXPRESS BUSES

JL. SERUI

JL. H.O.S. COKROAMINOTO

JL. ANDALAS

JL. VETERAN

JL. TINUMBU

0   500 m

BOATS TO KAYANGAN ISLAND

CHINESE TEMPLE

JL. RIBURANE

JL. A. YANI

TAXIS

MANDALA AIRLINES

HOTEL SENTRAL

JL. MESJID RAYA

JL. IRIAN

JL. BULUL SERAUNG

HOTEL AMAN

GARUDA

JL. UJUNG PANDANG

FORT ROTTERDAM

POST OFFICE

JL. SLAMET RYADI

JL. BALAI KOTA

POLICE

JL. KATAOLADINO

SPORTS FIELD

BANK INDONESIA

BEMOS TO AND FROM AIRPORT

RAMAYANA SATRYA HOTEL

MERPATI AIRLINES

BENTENG HOTEL

JL. SUPRAATMAN

JL. THAMRIN

JL. KARTINI

JL. G. BAWAKARAENG

HOTEL MARLIN

LIMAN EXPRESS BUSES (MAIN OFFICE)

JL. PASAR IKAN

LOSARI BEACH INN

JL. PATTIMURA

HOTEL PURNAMA

MARANNU CITY HOTEL

JL. AMANAGAPPA

TO TOURIST OFFICE AND AIRPORT

MAKASSAR GOLDEN HOTEL

JL. SOMBA OPU

JL. BAUMASEPE

JL. INCE NURDIN

JL. JEND. SUDIRMAN

JL. SALAHUTU

LOSARI BEACH GUESTHOUSE

JL. ALI MALAKA

JL. KHAIRIL ANWAR

JL. PENGHIBUR

JL. MOKTHAR LUFTHI

JL. SAMIUN

JL. SAWER GADING

PANTAI LOSARI

CLARA BUNDT ORCHID GARDENS

JL. HASANUDDIN

JL. SOETOMO

SEMPATI AIRLINES

THR AMUSEMENT PARK

JL. LATIMOJONG

JL. VETERAN

JL. DATUMUSENG

JL. DR.

JL. EMMY SAELAN

© MOON PUBLICATIONS, INC.

cellent restaurant. Front rooms offer beautiful views of the harbor. Good value. 297 Jl. Somba Opu, tel. (0411) 85421, US$25-35.

Makassar Golden Hotel: Perfect waterfront location plus swimming pool, nightclub, and unforgettable sunsets from the Toraja-style terrace restaurant. The best in town. 52 Jl. Pasar Ikan, tel. (0411) 22208, US$65-90.

Transportation

Ujung Pandang's Hasanuddin Airport has all the usual facilities and is located 23 km from town. Taxis cost about US$5-8, or simply walk (or take a *becak* for Rp200) 500 meters to the main road, then flag down a *bemo* and pay Rp1000 all the way to main *bemo* station on Jalan Cokroaminoto near the Central Market.

Pelni docks at Pelabuhan Hatta, close to city center. Tickets to Surabaya, Kalimantan, and North Sulawesi can be purchased directly at the Pelni office, or from shipping agents which charge a small commission but save chasing around.

Within the city you can walk, bargain with a *becak* driver, attempt to decipher the *bemo* routes, or rent a taxi for US$40 per day.

Large buses from Ujung Pandang to Tana Toraja cost about Rp10,000, leave daily at 0700, 1400, and 1900, and take 10-12 hours along a well-surfaced road. Liman Express is the best service; tickets can be purchased from the Marlin Hotel, opposite the Ramayana.

OTHER SOUTHERN DESTINATIONS

Few Westerners visit the following towns, though all provide an easy escape from the standard tourist trail between Ujung Pandang and Tana Toraja. Travel throughout the region is surprisingly easy along well-maintained roads that cut across spectacular landscapes. Buses to towns north and east of Ujung Pandang depart from Terminal Panaikan, a few kilometers outside town on the road to the airport. Buses to towns south of Ujung Pandang leave from Perumnas Todopuli Terminal, two km east of the tourist office.

One interesting route is south from Ujung Pandang along the southern coast to Bulukumba, then north to Watampone (Bone) and Sing-

kang nestled in the foothills overlooking Lake Tempe, and finally Palopo, from where a spectacular road heads southwest up to Tana Toraja. All these towns have simple hotels.

The Gowa Empire

Gowa and Tallo were two small kingdoms which united in the 16th century to form the powerful Makassar empire, which ruled much of southern Sulawesi until defeat by the Dutch and Bugis in 1669.

Remnants of royal tombs, graves, and palaces can be visited at Old Gowa (eight km southeast of Ujung Pandang), Tallo (three km north), and Sombaopu (seven km south), where a reconstructed former royal palace now serves as a museum and storehouse for recent excavations.

Bantimurung Falls

A deep limestone canyon, 41 km northeast of Ujung Pandang, attracts visitors for its spectacular waterfalls, lush tropical vegetation, and brilliantly colored butterflies once collected by the famous British naturalist Alfred Russel Wallace. Take a *bemo* to Maros, then another east toward Bone.

Five km west of Bantimurang are a series of limestone caves covered with rare and valuable prehistoric paintings dating back some 5,000 years. Both Bantimurang and the caves at Taman Purbakala Leang Leang are well signposted and charge modest admission fees.

Malino

On the lower slopes of Mount Bawa Kareng, 70 km southeast of Ujung Padang, lies a former Dutch hill resort with a great Sunday flower market and hikes to nearby waterfalls, river valleys, and, possibly, the summit of Mount Bawa Kareng. Bring warm clothing; at 1050 meters Malino can get chilly.

Bulukumba And Tana Beru

Traditional shipbuilding has declined dramatically since the early 1980s, though massive vessels are still constructed entirely by hand in several villages along the southern coastline.

Tana Beru, 174 km from Ujung Pandang and 28 km east of Bulukumba, is your best bet during the dry season from April to October. The nearby town of Bira, once the boatbuilding center for the region, now serves as the departure point for boats to Selayar Island. Ships are also constructed in the village of Ara, 13 km north of Bira.

Losmen Sinar Jaya: An inexpensive *losmen* in Bulukumba. Bira also has a cheap *losmen* near its stunning white-sand beach. 4 Jl. Saw-erigading, US$2-4.

Selayar Island
Once an important island for its strategic location on the spice trail, Selayar is now visited for its beaches on the north side and a famous Dong Son drum kept at Bontobangun, three km south of the principal town of Benteng.

Ferries depart Bira daily at 1400, or take the 0700 bus from Ujung Pandang's Terminal Panaikan, which connects directly with the af-ternoon ferry.

Hotel Berlian: A Benteng hotel. US$4-6.

Watampone (Bone)
Once the strongest of all Bugis kingdoms, Watampone ruled much of the region until the late 17th century when British and Dutch de-stroyed the city in an effort to support the Ma-kassarese empire.

Now a sleepy town some 180 km northeast of Ujung Pandang, Watampone is chiefly noted for its simple royal palace constructed in the 1930s to house the reinstated raja of Bone, an informative museum on the town square, and limestone caves at Gua Mampu (34 km north), considered the largest and most spectacular in South Sulawesi.

Wisma Bola Ridie: Watampone has plen-ty of decent hotels under US$10, including this rambling Dutch colonial structure, owned and operated by a descendant of the last raja of Bone. 6 Jl. Merdeka, tel. (0421) 412, US$4-8.

Wattansoppeng (Soppeng)
Another former capital of the Bugis kingdom, Soppeng today is a very attractive town famous for its profuse orchid gardens, silk factories, to-bacco cured with palm sugar, cacao planta-tions, and millions of fruit bats which live peace-fully in the town's trees.

Hotel Makmur: Clean spacious rooms with private bath. 104 Jl. Kemakmuran, US$4-8.

Singkang
Singkang, 192 km northeast of Ujung Pandang, is a sleepy town in a great hillside location over-looking shallow Lake Tempe.

Top draws are the views from the govern-ment resthouses across the square from the mosque, a thriving silk industry modeled on Thai techniques, and Bugis traditions such as dance and weddings recently revitalized by a determined local princess.

Wisma Ayuni: Clean, spacious, high-ceilinged rooms in an old Dutch home. Jalan Puang Ri Maggalatung, US$2-4.

Hotel Apada: Somewhat expensive but the best place to experience traditional Bugis at-mosphere as promoted by a local aristocrat. Hotel Apada is one km from the lake. Jalan Durian, US$10-18.

Palopo
Palopo, 389 km northeast of Ujung Pandang but only three hours by bus from Rantepao, once served as the linchpin of the powerful Lawu kingdom. Also, it's the port from which en-chained Torajan slaves were sold and shipped out to Java and Siam.

Palopo is noted for the various types of *prahu* docked to the long pier, magnificent panora-mas across expansive Bone Bay, an ancient mosque opposite the post office, and a small museum in the house of a former raja of Luwu.

Wisma Kumda Indah: The most popular hotel in town has both fan-cooled and a/c rooms at reasonable rates. Jalan Opu Tosapaille, US$6-12

Palopo Hotel: Adjacent to the bus terminal. Rooms are ratty but acceptable for a single night. 11 Jl. Kelapa, US$3-8.

Pare Pare
Second-largest city and seaport of South Su-lawesi, 155 km north of Ujung Pandang, Pare Pare serves as a transportation center and stopover spot between Ujung Pandang and Tana Toraja.

Aside from the small Museum of Ethnology on the highway to Rantepao, most visitors stop here only to catch the daily boat to a Kalimantan port (Nunukan, Tarakan, Samarinda, or Balik-papan), or the thrice-weekly service to north-ern Sulawesi (Donggala, Toli Toli, and Manado). The latter services spare you the ordeal of overland travel across Central Sulawesi. In fact, the awful condition of roads through Central Sulawesi makes taking a boat to the northern peninsula an attractive proposition; many travelers backtrack from Tana Toraja simply to avoid the journey.

Travel agents and shipping companies are plentiful near the bus terminal, at the harbor, and on the main street just up from the waterfront.

Hotel Gandaria: A clean and comfortable hotel with friendly, helpful managers, just five minutes from the bus terminal. Ask to see the proprietor's valuable collection of ritual objects and wedding costumes obtained from royal families. 171 Jl. Bau Masepe, tel (0421) 21093, US$6-12.

Majene

Majene is a small, peaceful fishing and boat-building village on a stunning moon-shaped bay about 80 km northwest of Pare Pare. The main activity is walking along the bay in the morning and exploring the nearby towns in the afternoon: Pangali-Ali, Cilallang, the ancient graveyards at Ondongan and Salabose, and the silk-weaving villages of Tinamburng, Luaor, and especially Pambusuang. Ibu Darmi Masud can help with directions.

Ibu Darmi Masud Homestay: Better than the rough *losmen* in the center of town is this friendly homestay near the harbor. 12 Jl. Amanna Wewang, Ujung Pandang reservations tel. (0411) 22482, US$3-6.

TANA TORAJA

The second most popular tourist destination in Indonesia, Tana Toraja is one of the country's most ruggedly magnificent regions—a high, fertile plateau buffered by green mountains which have protected traditional patterns of life and customs. The district is inhabited by proto-Malay peoples who, though largely Christianized in the early 20th-century by Dutch missionaries, continue to honor their ancestors through a religion called Aluk Todol. Similar to the Batak and Minangkabau of Sumatra, the Torajans are noted for their remarkable architecture, which features ship-shaped flying roofs and large panels elaborately ornamented with geometric and animal motifs. But it is their frequent and highly ritualistic religious ceremonies—including rites of birth, marriage, and death—that attract increasing numbers of foreign visitors; Torajan funerals are considered among the most spectacular in Asia. This is a destination that deserves 10 days to two weeks to fully appreciate.

The principal towns of Rantepao and Makale serve as bases for extended multiday hikes in the surrounding countryside. Tana Toraja is best visited during the dry season from April to October, when most of the burial and harvest festivals occur. Monsoons which sweep across the land from November to March ruin the roads but provide an opportunity to escape the European and Japanese tour groups which flood the area in late summer. Funeral observers should dress conservatively, photograph with discretion, and bring along small gifts of cigarettes or rice for village dignitaries.

Attractions

Tana Toraja can be touristy in the busy summer months, but once you're just a kilometer outside town, you're in a tropical Xanadu, peaceful and beautiful. People ask you in for coffee and cigarettes, invite you to attend their ceremonies, and sometimes offer a room to overnight. Travelers should return the favor with a small present of food, betel nut, antibiotics, or cigarettes. Please don't give out candy; Torajans can hardly afford dental bills!

Villages near Rantepao can be reached with public *bemos* or hiked in a single day. *Bemos*, minibuses, and jeeps rented from *losmens* and the market cost about US$20-25 per day; a good deal for groups of people with limited time. Self-appointed guides can be hired everywhere at about US$5 per day, though their services are unnecessary for nearby hikes. Professional guides for multi-day treks can be hired from the tourist office for US$10-20 per day for small groups.

Virtually anywhere in Torajaland you can spend the night in the *tongkonan,* or ask the *kepala kampung* (village chief) for help with accommodations. Always give the lady of the house US$2-3 for food and bring along small gifts for the village headman.

TANA TORAJA

NOT TO SCALE

Getting There

Liman Express buses leave from their office on Jalan Laiya and pause near the Ramayana Hotel in Ujung Pandang daily at 0700, 1400, and 1900. Advance tickets can be purchased at the Hotel Marlin, just opposite the Ramayana.

Merpati flies three times weekly to the airport near Rantepao.

An interesting five-day journey is from Ujung Pandang to Pare Pare, Polewali, Mamasa, Bittuang, and Rantepao. This adventurous route requires three days of hiking from Mamasa to Bittuang, from where buses continue to Makale.

MAKALE AND VICINITY

Makale, an administrative center built by the Dutch in 1925, is the second-largest town in Tana Toraja. Few tourists stay here, though Makale—like Rantepao—can serve as a base for outstanding hikes.

Liman Express buses stop near the mosque in the middle of town. Minibuses up to Rantepao take about 45 minutes. Merpati flies from Ujung Pandang to Pongtiku Airport (12 km northwest of Makale) on Tuesday, Thursday, and Saturday.

Attractions

Guides can be picked up from the *losmen,* or simply orient yourself with the wall map in the Bupati Daerah building (2.5 km north of town) and wander off in any direction. Villagers throughout Tana Toraja are friendly, helpful, and accustomed to lost Westerners, though a basic understanding of Bahasa Indonesia will help. Buy a phrasebook and learn to use it!

East from Makale you'll find a row of *tau tau* effigies near Tondon (one km from Makale), caves with elaborately carved coffins near Suaya (six km), a king's *tongkonan* (house) that doubles as a museum in Buntukalando (8 km), minibuses to Makale at Sangalla (10 km), and hot springs at Makula (13 km).

Hikes west from Makale tend to be very long, but the scenery is spectacular and it's highly unlikely you'll see any other Westerners. First, take a *bemo* or walk to Rembon (12 km northwest), the swimming hole at Seseng (20 km), and finally to the market town of Bittuang (42 km). Both short and multi-day treks start from Bittuang. The 58-km trail to Mamasa takes three

days, with luscious scenery of valleys, mountains, villages, and rice terraces. Another possibility is an eight-day trek from Bittuang back to Makale via the townships of Ponding, Pana, Nosu, Simbuang, Petarian, and Sanik.

Accommodations

Makale is a clean and pleasant town with a good selection of hotels on the half-dozen streets which form the city center.

Losmen Indra: Just south of the bus stop is a friendly spot, but prepare yourself for early-morning calls from the nearby mosque. Several other inexpensive *losmen* are along the main road. 11 Jl. Merdeka, tel. (0423) 22022, US$4-8.

Wisma Bungin: A modern hotel with spotlessly clean rooms at very fair prices. Recommended. 35 Jl. Pongtiku, tel. (0423) 22255, US$4-8.

Losmen Martha: At the far north end of Makale is a pleasant family-run place with cheap, quiet rooms. 75 Jl. Pongtiku, tel. (0423) 22011, US$3-6.

Marannu City Hotel: Tour groups usually stay at this hotel, five minutes from Makale and 15 minutes from the airport. Facilities include a swimming pool, tennis courts, and a 24-hour restaurant. 116 Jl. Pongtiku, tel. (0423) 22028, fax (0423) 22028, US$44-65.

RANTEPAO AND VICINITY

Rantepao is a cool and pleasant town that serves as the focal point for tourism in Tana Toraja. Despite all the visitors who inundate it, and the heady air of rampant commercialism, Rantepao has remained a mellow town with lots of atmosphere. The tourist office on Jalan Pontigu offers useful hand-drawn maps, has schedules on upcoming funeral ceremonies, and can help arrange guides and charter *bemos*. Bank Rakyat near the town square cashes traveler's checks at good rates. Rantepao also has a post office, a long-distance phone center open 24 hours, a Merpati office, travel agencies, countless souvenir shops, and a fascinating market that peaks every six days.

Budget Accommodations

Rantepao offers dozens of budget *losmen* geared to travelers and a good selection of upscale hotels aimed at group tours. Rooms are scarce and reservations recommended from July to September; otherwise, they're plentiful and deeply discounted for longer stays.

Rantepao's cheapest places are on the main avenue of Jl. Mappanyuki near the mosque and the bus terminal. However, better and certainly quieter *losmen* and homestays are 10-15 minutes by *bemo* from the center of town. A sensible strategy is to follow a hotel tout from the bus terminal or wander the side streets and inspect a few places.

Wisma Maria I: An old favorite just two blocks from the center of town. Nice garden, boiled water, and direct service provided by Liman Express from Ujung Pandang—very convenient. Jalan Ratulangi, tel. (0423) 21165, US$5-15.

Wisma Monika: A travelers' special run by friendly folks with clean and quiet rooms. Jalan Ratulangi, tel. (0423) 21216, US$5-8.

Wisma Rosa: Perhaps the oldest *losmen* in town, with quiet rooms facing ricefields and a pleasant garden. North of town across the Sadan River, a 10-minute walk from the bus terminal. Recommended. Jalan Pahlawan, tel. (0423) 21075, US$4-10.

Wisma Surya: Good place managed by Mrs. Ross Boby, tourist official at the Rantepao information center. Her brother leads tours at reasonable cost. 36 Jl. Kostan, tel. (0423) 21312, US$4-8.

Moderate Accommodations

Monton Guesthouse: Opened in July 1992 and highly recommended by many travelers, Monton is slightly outside town and just west of Wisma Irama. All rooms include private bath with hot showers. Proprietor Parubak once worked at the local tourist office and can help with trekking details. 14 Jl. Abdul Gani, tel. (0423) 21675, fax (0423) 21500, US$9-14.

Wisma Irama: A very beautiful and quiet hotel, which ranks among the better deals in town, offers both budget fan-cooled rooms and luxurious a/c rooms with private bath and hot showers. 18 Jl. Abdul Gani, tel. (0423) 21371, US$8-20.

Hotel Indra: Well run and conveniently located with three separate operations: economic Indra I with fan-cooled rooms, midpriced Indra City Hotel, and upscale Indra II with a/c chalets

facing a lovely garden and the Sadan River. 63 Jl. Landorundun, tel. (0423) 21163, fax (0423) 21500, US$6-32.

Pia's Poppies: Trendy Toraja-style resort with late-night disco, French restaurant, and great views over ricefields and mountains. South of town in Karassi. 27 Jalan Pongtiku, tel. (0423) 21156, US$10-25.

Luxury Accommodations

Top-end hotels are outside town toward Makale or Palopo.

Toraja Cottages: Four km northeast of Rantepao and near the Wednesday market is an upscale resort with a swimming pool, Torajan-style chalets, and the most popular nightclub in town. The luxury extension is called Toraja Prince. 4 Jl. Pakubalasalu, tel. (0423) 21089, fax (0423) 21369, US$40-60.

Missiliana Hotel: Three km south on the road to Makale is a 120-room two-star property designed for package tours, especially for European clients of Insatra and Ramayana Tours. Jalan Batukangsi, tel. (0423) 21234, fax (0423) 21212, US$42-85.

Transportation

Rantepao is 328 km and eight hours by bus north of Ujung Pandang.

Air: Merpati departs daily from Ujung Pandang at 0900 and arrives at 0945 at the Rantetayo airport near Makale, 24 km south of Rantepao. Flights cost US$35 and depart daily, weather permitting, from Rantetayo at 1015. Merpati provides bus service into Rantepao.

Bus: Buses from Ujung Pandang take about eight hours and depart daily from the Panaikan bus terminal at 0700, 1300, and 1900. Tickets can be purchased in advance from several agencies such as Liman Expres on Jalan Laiya and Litha Company on Jl. Gunung Merapi. You can also take the next available bus or minibus from Panaikan bus terminal.

South Of Rantepao

Many of the following sites are within walking distance, but those closest to Rantepao can be super-touristy and thronged with kids asking for money and candy. Solo travelers will find themselves harassed less than those who join group tours. Distances from Rantepao are noted in kilometers.

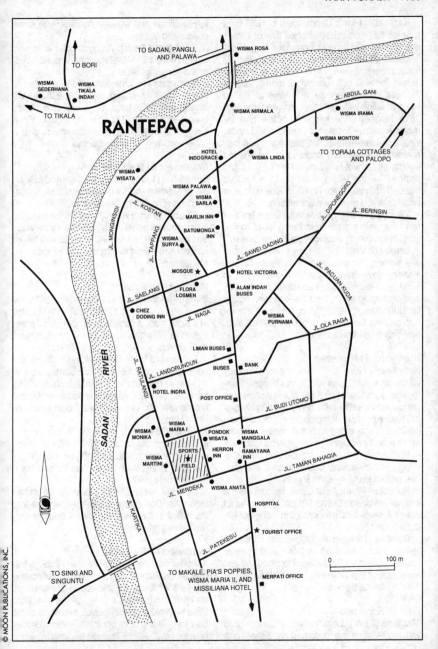

RANTEPAO

TO SADAN, PANGLI, AND PALAWA

TO BORI

TO TIKALA

WISMA SEDERHANA

WISMA TIKALA INDAH

WISMA ROSA

WISMA NIRMALA

JL. ABDUL GANI

WISMA IRAMA

WISMA MONTON

HOTEL INDOGRACE

WISMA LINDA

TO TORAJA COTTAGES AND PALOPO

WISMA WISATA

WISMA PALAWA

JL. KOSTAN

JL. TAPPANG

JL. MONGINSIDI

WISMA SARLA

MARLIN INN

BATUMONGA INN

WISMA SURYA

JL. SAWEI GADING

JL. DIPONEGORO

JL. BERINGIN

MOSQUE ★

HOTEL VICTORIA

JL. PACUAN KUDA

JL. SAELANG

FLORA LOSMEN

ALAM INDAH BUSES

CHEZ DODING INN

JL. NAGA

WISMA PURNAMA

JL. OLA RAGA

LIMAN BUSES

JL. LANDORUNDUN

BUSES

BANK

SADAN RIVER

JL. RATULANGI

HOTEL INDRA

POST OFFICE

JL. BUDI UTOMO

WISMA MARIA I

WISMA MONIKA

PONDOK WISATA

WISMA MANGGALA

SPORTS FIELD

HERRON INN

RAMAYANA INN

JL. TAMAN BAHAGIA

WISMA MARTINI

JL. MERDEKA

WISMA ANATA

JL. KARTIKA

HOSPITAL

★ TOURIST OFFICE

TO SINKI AND SINGUNTU

JL. PATEKESU

TO MAKALE, PIA'S POPPIES, WISMA MARIA II, AND MISSILIANA HOTEL

MERPATI OFFICE

0   100 m

© MOON PUBLICATIONS, INC.

Karasbik (1 km): Constructed in 1983 for a funeral, this horseshoe-shaped row of *rumah adat* is arranged around a group of megaliths.

Londa (8 km): Aside from their spectacular funeral ceremonies, Tana Torajans are also known for their cliff burial sites (*liang*), carved wooden coffins (*erong*), and rows of lifelike wooden effigies (*tau tau*) that represent the spirits of departed ancestors. Two of the more famous sites are located at Lemo and Londa, where the interconnecting passages and natural amphitheaters are stacked with old wooden coffins strategically arranged with skulls and bones. Guides with gaslamps take visitors through both caves for Rp1000; kids hold your hand until you give them something.

Tilanga (12 km): A beautiful three-km trail from the main road or from Lemo leads to this natural swimming pool with cool, clear water.

Lemo (12 km): The hanging graves at Lemo are among the best known in Tana Toraja. Peering down from the balconies are rows of wide-eyed *tau tau,* silent spectators best seen and photographed in the early-morning hours. Unfortunately, theft for the primitive art market has caused families to remove most effigies, and only a few figures remain.

Southeast Of Rantepao
Keta Kesu (4 km): En route to the most touristy village near Rantepao you'll pass through Buntupune, a traditional enclave of *tongkonan,* rice barns, and the noteworthy home of Pong Maramba. Keta Kesu is a restored and highly commercialized village with handicraft shops, effigies, and a rotted wooden sign proclaiming Coffins.

Sullukang (6 km): A very old and secluded village with megaliths around a *rante* and statues seated in a run-down shack.

Palatoke (9 km): As at Lemo, Palatoke has a cliffside burial site, but no *tau tau.* This beautiful out-of-the-way site is tricky to find: consider hiring a young guide.

Buntao (16 km): A village with a *patane* (grave house) reached by infrequent truck or full-day hike from Rantepao. No signs, so just keep asking the way. Return via Nanggala or hike to Makale through Sangalla.

East Of Rantepao
Marante (6 km): Located just off the road to Palopo, Marante is a mixture of traditional Torajan dwellings and wooden houses, with some coffins and *tau tau.*

Tandung (17 km): A spectacular area with pine forests, 18-meter-high stands of bamboo, and a gorgeous lake.

Nanggala (15 km): Situated in an area of pretty ricefields, Nanggala is a traditional village known for its large *tongkonan* and 14 rice barns—the best you'll see in Torajaland. From Nanggala, walk south over mountains past a coffee-growing region to Buntao.

Southwest Of Rantepao
Singki Hill (1 km): Cross the river and hike up the overgrown trail for good views over Rantepao and surrounding landscapes.

Siguntu (6 km): A traditional village featuring a nobleman's house with remarkable carvings and handsome rice barns. Adventurous hikers can continue west to Bittuang via Langda and Mandanan.

North Of Rantepao
Pangli (8 km): Pangli is known for its house grave with a stone statue carved in the likeness of a dead man, a substitute for cliff burial sites. Pangli is also the source of a famous *tuak* (homemade beer).

Palawa (13 km): This traditional village has numerous *tongkonan* and rice barns decorated with *kerbau* horns. Palawa, built on rising terraces, reminds you of the spires of Gothic cathedrals. Also visit Palawa's Stonehenge-like circle of stones.

Sadan (16 km): Hyped as the weaving center of Torajaland, the cultural significance of Sadan is greatly exaggerated, though you might enjoy the palm toddy, *tuak sissing biang,* one bamboo full for Rp1500.

Deri (14 km): Clinging to the side of the mountain, Deri offers a hawk's-eye view into the valley and a mammoth black boulder with two carved graves.

Northwest Of Rantepao
A six-day roundtrip trek can be made through seldom-visited villages using a combination of walking and vehicle transport. Rantepao to Batutumonga via Tikala and Pana is an 11-km full-day hike. Near Pana is an old set of cliff graves with some of the best *rante, liang,* and *tau tau* in Toraja. Graves here are painted black (representing death), yellow

(life and blessings from the gods), white (purity), and red (human life). Near Batutumonga, visit the circle of 56 stones arranged amphitheater-fashion and the smithy fashioned from two huge bamboo bellows. A schoolteacher maintains a room in his house for travelers. From Batutumonga, hike to Pulu Pulu via Lokomata and Pangala or use the rugged trail past Gunung Sesean, highest mountain in Tana Toraja. The walk to Lokomata is recommended for its panoramic views—considered some of the best trekking in the region. Pulu Pulu to Awan is a 33-km 14-hour hike with a swim at Sulutallang, midway between Baruppu and Awan. Awan to Bittuang is another full day, with swimming in Bolokan. Return to Rantepao by truck or hike to Mamasa in three days.

CENTRAL SULAWESI

The mountainous province of Sulawesi Tengah offers beautiful scenery, primitive tribes, ancient megaliths, sleepy port towns, vast stretches of coastline, fantastic diving on coral reefs, and unusual natural phenomena. Until recently this province was isolated, but now, with the completion of the Trans-Sulawesi Highway, a steady stream of determined adventurers are slowly wandering from Tana Toraja to Palu and onward to the northern town of Manado.

Sightseeing Highlights

Aside from the journey itself, the main attractions of Central Sulawesi are Lake Poso—perhaps the next Lake Toba—and the megaliths of the Bada, Besoa, and Napu valleys, some 40 km east of Lake Poso. Pendolo, a lovely town hugging the southern shores of Lake Poso, ranks as among the most idyllic and scenic destinations on Sulawesi. Also of interest is Lore Lindu National Park on the southern end of Palu Valley.

The rugged journey essentially ends in the town of Palu, the administrative capital and transportation hub for Central Sulawesi, from where you can reach northern Sulawesi by bus, boat, or plane. Many travelers simply visit Lake Poso and then return to Ujung Pandang.

Transportation

The Trans-Sulawesi Hwy. between Ujung Pandang and Palu was essentially finished in 1992, though some sections remain little more than muddy paths closed during the rainy season by landslides and the ever-encroaching jungle.

Rantepao to Lake Poso (245 km): The road from Rantepao to Wotu is fully surfaced and served by a steady stream of buses and minitrucks. The road deteriorates starting from Mangkutana, a few kilometers north of Wotu, and remains a muddy track strangled by jungle until it reaches Pendolo on the southern shore of Lake Poso. This is the worst, near-legendary, section of the highway.

During the dry season, Bina Wisata bus company in Rantepao operates twice-weekly bus service to Pendolo. The journey takes about 12 hours in favorable conditions but up to 30 hours during the rainy season. Alternatively, take a *bemo* from Rantepao to Palopo, another *bemo* to Mangkutana via Wotu, and a third *bemo* north to Pendolo. Simple *losmen* are located in all these towns.

Pendolo to Tentena (40 km): Although a fairly good road connects these two towns, most travelers take the ferry *Pamona,* which departs at 0600 and arrives in Tentena around 1100.

Tentena to Poso (57 km): As Tentena lacks the charm of Pendolo, most visitors immediately take a bus north to the small port town of Poso on the shores of Tomini Bay. Tentena to Poso takes two hours by bus.

Tentena to Bada Valley (60 km): The megaliths in Bada Valley are just 60 km west of Tentena, but the journey can take anywhere from eight hours to five days depending on road conditions. Jeeps leave from Tonusu, 10 km north of Tentena.

However, during bad weather an easier approach is from Gimpu, 99 km south of Palu along a surfaced road. Gimpu to Gintu (the main town in Bada Valley) takes two days by foot or on horseback.

Poso to Palu (220 km): Buses and minibuses from Poso to Palu take about eight hours on a decent road. Alternatively, exhausted travelers bound for Manado can take one of the thrice-weekly ships from Poso to Gorontalo in North Sulawesi. The journey takes two days with stops at various ports and in the Togian Islands. The bus from Gorontalo to Manado takes one day.

Palu to North Sulawesi: Garuda, Merpati, and Bouraq fly several times weekly to Gorontalo (US$60) and Manado (US$85). Pelni liners, the *Kerinci* and the *Kambuna,* sail weekly from Palu to various ports in North Sulawesi, plus other destinations such as the east coast of Kalimantan and Pare Pare in South Sulawesi.

The bus from Palu to Gorontalo takes almost two days on very rough roads. Gorontalo to Manado is another full day of bone-crunching travel.

MANGKUTANA

Mangkutana, a small village several kilometers north of Wotu, serves as the launching point for the ridiculously treacherous journey north to Lake Poso.

Toyota Land Cruisers leave when filled and take just six hours to Pendolo during the dry season. Wet-season delays such as destroyed bridges, landslides, and muddy trenches—which gladly swallow jeeps—can make this a two- or three-day journey.

Accommodations
Losmen in Mangkutana, such as Penginapan Sumber Urip and Penginapan Melati Mekar, charge US$2-3 per night. Several of the travel agencies will let you sleep for free in their *warung* if you are traveling with them the following day.

PENDOLO AND LAKE POSO

Pendolo, on the southern shore of Lake Poso, ranks as the most attractive and memorable destination in Central Sulawesi. Flanked by a wonderful lake surrounded by brilliant green hills, Pendolo has the potential to become the next Lake Toba, which almost certainly will happen once the road from Wotu is fully surfaced. For the present, however, Pendolo and Lake Poso remain sleepy paradises visited annually by only a few hundred backpackers.

Attractions
Lake Poso, called the "second-clearest lake in the world," guarantees a wonderful reward after the long and rough journey from Rantepao or Palu. Measuring about 37 km long and 13 km

wide, Danau Poso is known for its indigenous fish species (especially the huge eels, which reach over two meters in length) and white sandy beaches which cover almost 75% of the coastline. The lake is also quite deep (440 meters) and situated at a refreshing elevation of 515 meters.

Boats can be chartered to visit Taipa village on the western shore, from where you can hike up to a promontory viewpoint and to lakeside Bancea Orchid Reserve, which raises over 50 plant species. A primitive track follows the western shore, but public transportation remains sporadic.

Accommodations
Almost a dozen simple *losmen* now line the lakeside. Losmen Wisata Masamda is typical, with simple rooms with shared bath for US$2-3 and rooms with private bath for US$4-5. Similar facilities are offered at Pondok Wisata Victory and the slightly more expensive Danau Poso Hotel farther up the lake.

TENTENA

Tentena is a small town in a lovely location on the north shore of Lake Poso. Once the home of headhunters, Tentena was Christianized in the early part of the 20th century by a Dutch Reformed Church missionary named Albertus Kruyt. Today, almost all the highland peoples are Christians who attend Sunday services in the whitewashed chapel.

The Pamona people who live around Lake Poso are distant relatives of the Torajans, but eastern Torajan culture is now extinct here. In fact, except for the enigmatic monoliths near Gintu and burial caves around Tentena, little remains in Central Sulawesi of pre-Christian culture.

Balai Buku, one-half km north of the docks, has books in Bahasa Indonesia about early missionary work in Sulawesi.

Attractions
Boat rides and caving are the main activities near Tentena. Among the more accessible caves is a rocky overhang just five minutes behind the church and Latea Caves, some 20 minutes behind town. Pamona Caves, near the

Theological Institute and Poso River, has been cleared of skeletons but remains a pleasant place to relax and enjoy the views.

Accommodations

Tentena is more developed than Pendolo, with almost a dozen *losmen* and midpriced hotels. The budget places are near the bus station or dock, while better hotels are nicely situated near the river and in the hills.

Penginapan Wisata Remaja: A decent place near the dock with simple but clean rooms. US$2-5.

Losmen Rio: Near the bus terminal, this rudimentary dive is only acceptable for one night. The Adjacent losmen is just as bad. US$2-3.

Pamona Indah Hotel: A lakeside hotel with a good restaurant and near-luxury rooms with private bath. US$6-18.

Hotel Nusantara: Overlooking the river and lake, the Nusantara offers fine rooms in all price categories. Budget rooms US$2-3, standard US$6-9, private bungalows US$9-12.

Panorama Hotel: Two km from the boat dock and up on the hill. Not only superb views, but Ibu feeds you like her long-lost starving child—the food is plentiful, fresh, and delicious. US$3-8.

POSO

A busy port town on the southern shore of Tomini Bay, Poso today serves mostly as a transit point for travelers heading northwest to Palu or sailing northeast to Gorontalo in North Sulawesi.

Accommodations

Most hotels and *losmen* are just north of the Poso River, which empties into Tomini Bay.

Anugrah Inn: Conveniently located near the bus terminal in the southern part of town, but far removed from the beach and the central business district. 1 Jl. Samosir, tel. (0451) 21820, US$5-8.

Penginapan Sulawesi: Basic but fairly clean rooms just north of the river. Friendly management. Jalan Salim, tel. (0451) 21294, US$2-3.

Hotel Bambu Jaya: The best in town is nicely situated right on the seashore just opposite Penginapan Sulawesi. Rooms are clean and comfortable. 105 Jl. Agus Salim, tel. (0451) 21570, US$6-8 fan, US$12-20 a/c.

Transportation

Those who depart Tentena very early in the morning can lunch in Poso, then catch an afternoon bus to Palu, arriving in the late evening. Along parts of this fairly well-surfaced road you might think you're in Bali—you pass Balinese *transmigrasi* villages filled with Balinese statues and rice offerings to Dewi Sri.

Pelni ships sail to Gorontalo in North Sulawesi every few days—a great way to avoid the long and painful bus journey. Schedules can be checked at the harbormaster's office on Jl. Pattimura and in the nearby Pelni office.

PALU

Palu is a rapidly growing commercial center and transportation hub in an attractive location at the south end of Palu Bay.

Attractions

Get maps and help with organizing a Bada Valley excursion from the Central Sulawesi Tourist Office on Jl. Cik Ditiro, five blocks east of the northernmost bridge.

Central Sulawesi Museum: Get a good introduction to the pre-Christian history of the region on Jl. Sapiri, six blocks southwest of the river. Exhibits include replicas of Bada Valley megaliths, bark cloth, and rare *ikat,* including the only Indonesian double *ikat* produced outside of Tenganan, Bali.

Traditional Dance: Live performances of local dance and theater are occasionally given in the Gedung Olah Seni (GONI) building on Jl. Muhammed Yamin in the eastern part of town.

Accommodations

Most of Palu's *losmen* and hotels are in the center of town just east of the Poso River. The noise can be ferocious; ask for a room in the rear.

Purnama Raya Hotel: Centrally located hotel with small but clean rooms. All include private bath. 4 Jl. Wahidin, tel. (0451) 23646, US$4-6.

Karsam Hotel: Fifteen minutes north of city center and about 100 meters from the beach is another acceptable hotel with decent rooms. 15 Jl. Suharso, tel. (0451) 21776, US$3-5.

New Dely Hotel: Good-value hotel near the tourist office and a 10-minute walk east from city center. 17 Jl. Tadulako, tel. (0451) 21037, US$7-9 fan, US$12-25 a/c.

Hotel Palu Beach: Palu's top-end hotel has gone to seed but compensates somewhat with sweeping views over the magnificent bay. Ask for a discount. 22 Jl. Raden Saleh, tel. (0451) 21126, US$20-30.

Transportation

Palu is a major transport hub for Central Sulawesi, with planes, boats, and buses to all possible destinations in Indonesia.

Air: Garuda, Merpati, and Bouraq fly to other destinations on Sulawesi (Ujung Pandang and Manado), plus Kalimantan (Balikpapan and Banjarmasin), Java (Jakarta, Yogyakarta, and Surabaya), and eastern Indonesia (Maluku and Irian Jaya).

Boat: Three ports are north of Palu, but most departures are from Pantoloan, 35 km north of Palu. The Pelni ship *Kambuna* departs every other week from Pantoloan for Toli Toli and Bitung, the port for Manado. The ship then returns to Pantoloan and heads west to Kalimantan. Service to Kalimantan and Ujung Pandang is also provided by the *Tidar*. Pick up current schedules and tickets at the Pelni office on Jl. Gajah Mada.

Bus: All buses leave from the Besusu Terminal on Jl. Wahidin. Travel times are eight hours to Poso, two days to Gorontalo, and three days to Manado.

DONGGALA

Superb beaches are north of Palu near the town of Donggala. Once a powerful center of maritime trade, Donggala lost most of its importance when the regional capital was shifted to Palu after WW II and the shipping industry was transferred across the bay to Pantoloan.

Accommodations

Milano Beach Cottages: North of town on a great beach, this is a pleasant place with scuba-diving facilities, sailboat rentals, and rooms, plus meals. The German owner can be contacted via Milano Ice Cream shop on Jl. Hasanudin in Palu. US$7-12.

Wisma Rame: Back in town you'll find a clean place run by a very helpful Muslim. US$2-4.

LORE LINDU PARK AND BADA VALLEY MEGALITHS

Some 55 km south of Palu lies an immense national park chiefly visited for its ancient and utterly mysterious megalithic monuments, whose origins continue to baffle archaeologists. Carved from stone and eerily resembling the megaliths of Easter Island, these enigmatic monuments date back over 1000 years and provide a connection with megalithic cultures which once flourished on Nias and Sumba.

The tourist office and the PHPA office on Jl. Parman in Palu have information.

Transportation

Today, some two-dozen megaliths can be seen near the principal town of Gintu, a small village located just outside the southern boundary of the park. To reach Gintu, first take a bus or a taxi 100 km south from Palu to Gimpu, where a simple *losmen* is located on the main street.

From Gintu it's a two-day hike or horseback ride south to Gintu with an overnight stay at Moa. Gintu accommodations are limited to local homestays. Most of the monuments can be visited in a single day, though a local guide will be necessary to find the widely scattered stones.

What a place: no English speakers, and except for occasional groups of Germans with a guide from Palu, no tourists. Real adventure in the heart of Sulawesi.

NORTH SULAWESI

A beautiful land of vast coconut and clove plantations, active volcanos, lakes, hot springs, ancient burial sites, picturesque villages, white sand, coral islands, and outstanding snorkeling and diving, Sulawesi Utara comprises one of the most prosperous and spectacular regions in Indonesia.

The area has been embraced by scuba divers—who acclaim the diving as among the best in the world—but otherwise remains well off the beaten track for most Western travelers.

MANADO AND VICINITY

The capital of North Sulawesi is a destination almost completely unlike any other in Indonesia: prosperous, progressive, and Protestant, a legacy of several centuries of Portuguese and Dutch domination. Right away you'll notice the strength of the middle class and the almost complete absence of extreme poverty. Manado typifies modern, upwardly mobile Indonesia—a jolt after all the squalor of the major islands; even the outlying towns are paradigms of order and cleanliness.

Attractions

Manado itself has little of great interest aside from its spectacular location around a broad bay flanked by three towering volcanos. Most of the sights are located outside town in the mountains and designated nature reserves.

The tourist office (tel. 64299), unfortunately, is difficult to find, senselessly hidden away in an alley in the south of town off Jl. 17 Agustus. Try the tourist information center in the Bunaken Souvenir Shop on Jl. Sam Ratulangi.

Bunaken Sea Gardens: Top draw in North Sulawesi is the world-famous sea gardens located near Bunaken Island, some 30 minutes by boat north of Manado. Underwater walls, spectacular coral formations, deep caves, and a tremendous array of sealife attract a steady stream of divers from throughout the world.

Dives can be arranged at Murex, Nusantara Diving Center (the oldest in town), and Tirta Satwa Dive Resort in Malalayang. All provide dive masters, equipment, PADI courses, and accommodations in nearby beach chalets at very reasonable cost. Public boats at US$1 and inexpensive charters from US$12 leave from Toko Samudera Jaya in the Kuala Jengki market. Western dive operators such as Sea and See in San Francisco also conduct dive tours to Manado.

Sawangan Monuments: The most extensive collection of *waruga*, old pre-Christian tombs of ancestral Minahasans, is found in this small mountain town, 22 km southeast of Manado and three km south of Airmadidi. Hewn from single blocks of limestone, *waruga* are shaped like small Chinese temples with enormous roof-shaped covers, often lavishly decorated with intricate animal and anthropomorphic carvings. Colts leave from Manado's Paal 2 Terminal.

Mount Klabat: Just behind the police station in Airmadidi lies a well-worn trail that leads to the summit of Mt. Klabat, a dormant volcano that ranks as the highest peak (1,995 meters) in North Sulawesi. Summit climbs require almost 12 hours, so come prepared with enough gear to overnight or simply do half the mountain and enjoy the views.

Lake Tondano: The road continues south from Sawangan, past the unique Javanese-style Alfalah Mosque and Japanese caves used in WW II, until it reaches Tondano, an administrative center on the northern shore of Danau Tondano. Around the lake you'll find restaurants, boat rentals, hot springs, and a pottery village.

Tomohon and Mount Lokon: Next, head east to the hilltop village of Tomohon ("City of Flowers"), saddled between the twin volcanos of Lokon on the northwest and Mahawu on the northeast. Explore the vegetable and flower markets and continue a few kilometers north to Kakaskasan, from where a two-hour hike leads to the summit of Mt. Lokon. Guides are unnecessary, but you'll need to register with the local *kepala desa*.

Kawangkoan Caves: More caves used by the Japanese during WW II are located three km north of Kawangkoan. Colts leave from Pasar Karombasan (Wanea Terminal) in Manado.

MANADO

TELUK MANADO

JL. JUANDA

JL. LEMBANG

TERMINAL
CALACA

WARUNG
VENDJE

JL. LEKATAMSO

JL. HUSNI THAMRIN

JL. PANJAITAN

JL. TENDEAN

PASAR 45

KAWANUA
CITY HOTEL

ANGKASA
HOTEL

GUNUNG
WENANG
HOSPITAL

JL. HASANUDIN

WISMA
MUSTIKA

PELNI OFFICE

JL. KARTINI

HOTEL KAWANUA

JL. YOS SUDARSO

AHLAN
CITY HOTEL

TO BITUNG &
MAPANGET
AIRPORT

POST OFFICE

GARUDA OFFICE

METROPOLE
DEVRA EXPRESS

JL. MAHAKEREH

BOURAQ
OFFICE

JL.
MAENGKET
TELEPHONE
OFFICE

JL. KUMARAKA

JL. MARTADINATA

TERMINAL
PAAL 2

HOTEL
NEW QUEEN

JL. DIPONEGORO

JL. MIANGAS

JL. TIKALA

TO
RACETRACK

JL. IMAM BONJOL

MERPATI
OFFICE

JL. S. RATULANGI

JL. 14 PEBUARI

HOTEL
MINAHASA

GELANGGANG
REMAJA

JL. A. YANI

JL. PEMUDA

JL. 17 AGUSTUS

TOURIST
OFFICE

JL. POMOROUW

IMMIGRATION
OFFICE

JL. W. MOGINSIDI

JL. ARILASUT

JL. W. R. SUPRATMAN

JL. TELING

CEMETERY

TERMINAL FOR BUSES
TO GORONTALO,
PALU, POSO, ETC.

TO TASIK RIA RESORT
AND MANADO BEACH HOTEL

STADION
KLABAT

TO
TOMOHON

NOT TO SCALE

© MOON PUBLICATIONS, INC.

Budget Accommodations

Manado is a progressive city with a good selection of hotels but only a limited number of budget *losmen*.

Hotel Kawanua: The best deal in town is often confused with the much more expensive Kawanua City Hotel, two blocks away. Ask for *"kecil"* (small) and you'll probably find this place. Clean, comfortable, and very friendly. Highly recommended. 40 Jl. Sudirman, tel. (0431) 63842, US$5-15.

Jakarta Jaya: Unlike most budget dives in Manado, this *losmen* is relatively clean and only a few blocks from the water, en route to the Ahlan Hotel. Room rates include a small breakfast. 25 Jl. Hasanudin, tel. (0431) 64330, US$3-4.

Moderate To Luxury Accommodations

Panorama Ridge: Somewhat outside town, but spotless rooms and fabulous views over Manado Bay make this good value for mid-level travelers. Jalan Tomohon Raya, tel. (0431) 51158, US$12-20.

Hotel Minahasa: Warm atmosphere in an old Dutch mansion. Highly recommended for the friendly vibes and helpful management. 199 Jl. Sam Ratulangi, tel. (0431) 62059, US$9-18.

Manado Beach Hotel: Manado's most luxurious resort is situated on beachfront property in Tasik Ria, a planned community 18 km south of Manado. Opened in late 1992, facilities at the 250-room resort include several restaurants, convention halls, tennis courts, and two pools facing a dazzling beach. P.O. Box 1030, tel. (0431) 67001, fax (0431) 67007, US$90-150.

Transportation

Manado is an international gateway city where entry-free visas can be approved on arrival.

Air: Manado has international connections via Jakarta with many European cities, plus Guam, Hong Kong, Tokyo, and Manila. Garuda and Merpati serve Jakarta, several cities on Kalimantan, and the remote islands of Maluku. Manado airport is seven km from town. Taxis cost US$4 or take an *oplet* to the center of town.

Boat: Manado's main port is located at Bitung, 47 km east of town. Pelni has two ships, the *Kabuna* and the *Umsini,* which sail from Jakarta via Surabaya, Ujung Pandang, and Pan-

toloan near Palu. Pelni boats from Poso terminate in Gorontalo, from where buses continue east to Manado.

Bus: Certainly the most challenging way to reach Manado is by bus from Palu along the Trans-Sulawesi Highway. Although the highway has been "completed," it's difficult to connect with the far northeast tip of this rugged peninsula. The journey takes about two days from Palu to Gorontalo and another tough day to Manado along rough but passable roads.

Five bus and *bemo* terminals are scattered around Manado. Pasar 45 is the main *bemo* station. Calaca, just north of Pasar 45, serves the airport. Gorontalo Bus Terminal has buses to Gorontalo and Palu. Pasar Paal 2 has Colts to Bitung and Airmadidi. Pasar Karombasan serves Tondanao and Kawangkoan.

GORONTALO AND VICINITY

Gorontalo, the second-largest city in North Sulawesi, is an attractive destination nicely situated at the confluence of Lake Limboto and three rivers that flow into the ocean.

Attractions

Gorontalo's varied mix of European history can be seen in splendid old Dutch architecture, such as the Hotel Saronde and the old public hospital, and Portuguese fortresses situated outside town.

Lake Limboto: Five km northwest of town in a fertile rice-growing area lies an immense yet incredibly shallow lake. Hire a *prahu* from boys to visit small lakeside fishing villages.

Otanaha Fortress: Exhilerating views over Lake Limboto compensate for the sad ruins of this old Portuguese fort.

Kwangdung: Some 65 km north of Gorontalo lies the sleepy hamlet of Kwangdung, the primary port for Gorontalo. The ruins of two Portuguese forts still stand on the outskirts of town, Benteng Ota Mas Udangan, which once faced the sea before the waters receded, and Benteng Oranje ("Orange Fort"), northeast of town on the road to Manado.

Accommodations

Most of Gorontalo's hotels and tourist services are concentrated in city center at the north end of town.

Penginapan Teluk Kau: A Dutch-built home with gigantic canopied double beds and high ceilings. Standards have fallen and the place badly needs renovation, but it's acceptable for one night. 42 Jl. Jenderal Parman, tel. (0435) 21511, US$4-6.

Hotel Wisata: Excellent-value hotel near the Merpati office with both fan and a/c rooms. 23 Jl. 19 Januari, tel. (0435) 21736, US$5-18.

Hotel Saronde: Another Dutch colonial villa converted into a hotel with large, comfortable rooms. 17 Jl. Walanda Maramis, tel. (0435) 21735, US$6-10 fan, US$12-16 a/c.

Hotel Saronde II: Attached to the old colonial building is the most upscale hotel in town. All rooms are a/c with private bath and hot water. 17 Jl. Walanda Maramis, tel. (0435) 21735, US$20-35.

Transportation

Air: Merpati and Bouraq fly daily to Manado and Palu, with same-day connections to Maluku, Kalimantan, Jakarta, Surabaya, and Bali. The Merpati office is in the Hotel Wisata on Jl. 19 Januari.

Bus: Buses from the central terminal on Jl. Ratulangi take about 12 hours to Manado and almost two days on a bad road to Palu.

Boat: Pelni's *Umsini* departs every other Monday morning for Bitung (Manado) and every other Monday for Ujung Pandang and Surabaya. Pelni and Gapsu, a smaller shipping line, have offices in town and at the Kwangtung harbor.

For every traveller who has any taste of his own, the only useful guide-book will be the one which he himself has written.

—Aldous Huxley,
Along the Road

All travel is circular.

Paul Theroux,
The Great Railway Bazaar

INDEX

Page numbers in **boldface** indicate the primary reference. *Italicized* page numbers indicate information in captions, charts, illustrations, maps, or special topics.

THE METRIC SYSTEM

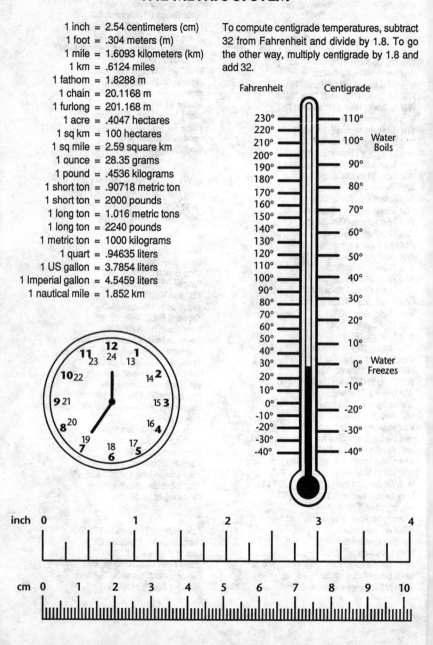

1 inch	= 2.54 centimeters (cm)
1 foot	= .304 meters (m)
1 mile	= 1.6093 kilometers (km)
1 km	= .6124 miles
1 fathom	= 1.8288 m
1 chain	= 20.1168 m
1 furlong	= 201.168 m
1 acre	= .4047 hectares
1 sq km	= 100 hectares
1 sq mile	= 2.59 square km
1 ounce	= 28.35 grams
1 pound	= .4536 kilograms
1 short ton	= .90718 metric ton
1 short ton	= 2000 pounds
1 long ton	= 1.016 metric tons
1 long ton	= 2240 pounds
1 metric ton	= 1000 kilograms
1 quart	= .94635 liters
1 US gallon	= 3.7854 liters
1 Imperial gallon	= 4.5459 liters
1 nautical mile	= 1.852 km

To compute centigrade temperatures, subtract 32 from Fahrenheit and divide by 1.8. To go the other way, multiply centigrade by 1.8 and add 32.

Fahrenheit — Centigrade

Water Boils

Water Freezes

inch 0 1 2 3 4

cm 0 1 2 3 4 5 6 7 8 9 10

READER PROFILE

Knowing a bit about you and your travel experiences will help me improve this book. I'll collect the results—including your picks for Southeast Asia's top-10 lists—and report my findings in the next edition. Include suggestions on guesthouses, restaurants, and transportation secrets that might help the next traveler. Use extra paper if necessary. Please send the following survey, plus your comments and recommendations, to:

Carl Parkes
Moon Publications
P.O. Box 3040
Chico, California 95927
U.S.A.

1. Gender: ❑ male ❑ female
2. Age: ❑ under 25 ❑ 25-30 ❑ 30-35 ❑ 35-40 ❑ 40-50 ❑ 50+
3. Status: ❑ single ❑ married
4. Income: ❑ under $20K ❑ $20-30K ❑ $30-40K ❑ $40-50K ❑ $50K+
5. Occupation:_____
6. Education: ❑ high school ❑ some college ❑ college grad ❑ post grad
7. Travel style: ❑ budget ❑ moderate ❑ luxury
8. Vacations: ❑ once yearly ❑ twice yearly ❑ 3+ yearly
9. Why do you travel?_____
_____
10. What's best about travel?_____
_____
11. What's worst about travel?_____
_____

12. This journey:
    Length of time:_____
    Countries visited:_____
    _____

    Expenses:
    1. Total _____
    2. Average daily expenses_____
    3. Average hotel price _____
    4. Average meal price _____
    5. Total airfare _____
    6. Shopping expenses _____

13. Favorites (also include a list of your *least* favorites)
    1. Best countries (in order of preference)_____

    2. Hotels and guesthouses (address, price, description)_____

    3. Restaurants (address, price, favorite dishes)_____

    4. Airline_____

    5. Cuisine_____

    6. Nightspots_____

    7. Cultural events_____

    8. Outdoor adventures_____

    9. Temples or historical sites_____

    10. Beaches_____

    11. People_____

    12. Travel moments_____

14. This book:
Strongest points:_____

Weakest points:_____

How accurate did you find the information?_____

Favorite introduction section (history, government, etc.; none)____

Suggestions for improvements:_____

15. Name and Address_____
_____
_____

MOON HANDBOOKS—THE IDEAL TRAVELING COMPANIONS

Open a Moon Handbook and you're opening your eyes and heart to the world. Thoughtful, sensitive, and provocative, Moon Handbooks encourage an intimate understanding of a region, from its culture and history to essential practicalities. Fun to read and packed with valuable information on accommodations, dining, recreation, plus indispensable travel tips, detailed maps, charts, illustrations, photos, glossaries, and indexes, Moon Handbooks are ideal traveling companions: informative, entertaining, and highly practical.

To locate the bookstore nearest you that carries Moon Travel Handbooks or to order directly from Moon Publications, call: (800) 345-5473, Monday-Friday, 9 a.m.-5 p.m. PST.

THE PACIFIC/ASIA SERIES

BALI HANDBOOK by Bill Dalton
Detailed travel information on the most famous island in the world. 428 pages. **$12.95**

BANGKOK HANDBOOK by Michael Buckley
Your tour guide through this exotic and dynamic city reveals the affordable and accessible possibilities. Thai phrasebook. 214 pages. **$10.95**

BLUEPRINT FOR PARADISE: How to Live on a Tropic Island by Ross Norgrove
This one-of-a-kind guide has everything you need to know about moving to and living comfortably on a tropical island. 212 pages. **$14.95**

FIJI ISLANDS HANDBOOK by David Stanley
The first and still the best source of information on travel around this 322-island archipelago. Fijian glossary. 198 pages. **$11.95**

INDONESIA HANDBOOK by Bill Dalton
This one-volume encyclopedia explores island by island the many facets of this sprawling, kaleidoscopic island nation. Extensive Indonesian vocabulary. 1,000 pages. **$19.95**

JAPAN HANDBOOK by J.D. Bisignani
In this comprehensive new edition, award-winning travel writer J.D. Bisignani offers to inveterate travelers, newcomers, and businesspeople alike a thoroughgoing presentation of Japan's many facets. 950 pages. **$22.50**

MICRONESIA HANDBOOK: Guide to the Caroline, Gilbert, Mariana, and Marshall Islands by David Stanley
Micronesia Handbook guides you on a real Pacific adventure all your own. 345 pages. **$11.95**

NEW ZEALAND HANDBOOK by Jane King
Introduces you to the people, places, history, and culture of this extraordinary land. 571 pages. **$18.95**

OUTBACK AUSTRALIA HANDBOOK by Marael Johnson
Australia is an endlessly fascinating, vast land, and *Outback Australia Handbook* explores the cities and towns, sheep stations, and wilderness areas of the Northern Territory, Western Australia, and South Australia. Full of travel tips and cultural information for adventuring, relaxing, or just getting away from it all. 355 pages. **$15.95**

PHILIPPINES HANDBOOK   by Peter Harper and Evelyn Peplow
Crammed with detailed information, *Philippines Handbook* equips the escapist, hedonist, or
business traveler with thorough coverage of the Philippines's colorful history, landscapes, and
culture. 600 pages.   **$17.95**

SOUTHEAST ASIA HANDBOOK   by Carl Parkes
Helps the enlightened traveler discover the real Southeast Asia. 873 pages.   **$21.95**

SOUTH KOREA HANDBOOK   by Robert Nilsen
Whether you're visiting on business or searching for adventure, *South Korea Handbook* is an
invaluable companion. Korean glossary with useful notes on speaking and reading the
language. 548 pages.   **$14.95**

SOUTH PACIFIC HANDBOOK   by David Stanley
The original comprehensive guide to the 16 territories in the South Pacific. 740 pages.   **$19.95**

TAHITI-POLYNESIA HANDBOOK   by David Stanley
All five French-Polynesian archipelagoes are covered in this comprehensive guide by
Oceania's best-known travel writer. 235 pages.   **$11.95**

THAILAND HANDBOOK   by Carl Parkes
Presents the richest source of information on travel in Thailand. 568 pages.   **$16.95**

THE HAWAIIAN SERIES

BIG ISLAND OF HAWAII HANDBOOK   by J.D. Bisignani
An entertaining yet informative text packed with insider tips on accommodations, dining, sports
and outdoor activities, natural attractions, and must-see sights. 350 pages.   **$13.95**

HAWAII HANDBOOK   by J.D. Bisignani
Winner of the 1989 Hawaii Visitors Bureau's Best Guide Award and the Grand Award for
Excellence in Travel Journalism, this guide takes you beyond the glitz and high-priced hype and
leads you to a genuine Hawaiian experience. Covers all 8 Hawaiian Islands. 879 pages.   **$15.95**

KAUAI HANDBOOK   by J.D. Bisignani
Kauai Handbook is the perfect antidote to the workaday world. Hawaiian and pidgin glossaries.
236 pages.   **$9.95**

MAUI HANDBOOK   by J.D. Bisignani
"No fool-'round" advice on accommodations, eateries, and recreation, plus a comprehensive
introduction to island ways, geography, and history. Hawaiian and pidgin glossaries. 350 pages.
$11.95

OAHU HANDBOOK   by J.D. Bisignani
A handy guide to Honolulu, renowned surfing beaches, and Oahu's countless other diversions.
Hawaiian and pidgin glossaries. 354 pages.   **$11.95**

THE AMERICAS SERIES

ALASKA-YUKON HANDBOOK   by Deke Castleman and Don Pitcher
Get the inside story, with plenty of well-seasoned advice to help you cover more miles on less money. 384 pages.   **$14.95**

ARIZONA TRAVELER'S HANDBOOK   by Bill Weir
This meticulously researched guide contains everything necessary to make Arizona accessible and enjoyable. 505 pages.   **$14.95**

BAJA HANDBOOK   by Joe Cummings
A comprehensive guide with all the travel information and background on the land, history, and culture of this untamed thousand-mile-long peninsula. 356 pages.   **$13.95**

BELIZE HANDBOOK   by Chicki Mallan
Complete with detailed maps, practical information, and an overview of the area's flamboyant history, culture, and geographical features, *Belize Handbook* is the only comprehensive guide of its kind to this spectacular region. 263 pages.   **$14.95**

BRITISH COLUMBIA HANDBOOK   by Jane King
With an emphasis on outdoor adventures, this guide covers mainland British Columbia, Vancouver Island, the Queen Charlotte Islands, and the Canadian Rockies. 381 pages.
$15.95

CANCUN HANDBOOK   by Chicki Mallan
Covers the city's luxury scene as well as more modest attractions, plus many side trips to unspoiled beaches and Mayan ruins. Spanish glossary. 257 pages.   **$12.95**

CATALINA ISLAND HANDBOOK: A Guide to California's Channel Islands
by Chicki Mallan
A complete guide to these remarkable islands, from the windy solitude of the Channel Islands National Marine Sanctuary to bustling Avalon. 245 pages.   **$10.95**

COLORADO HANDBOOK   by Stephen Metzger
Essential details to the all-season possibilities in Colorado fill this guide. Practical travel tips combine with recreation—skiing, nightlife, and wilderness exploration—plus entertaining essays. 416 pages.   **$17.95**

COSTA RICA HANDBOOK   by Christopher P. Baker
Experience the many wonders of the natural world as you explore this remarkable land. Spanish-English glossary. 574 pages.   **$17.95**

IDAHO HANDBOOK   by Bill Loftus
A year-round guide to everything in this outdoor wonderland, from whitewater adventures to rural hideaways. 275 pages.   **$12.95**

JAMAICA HANDBOOK   by Karl Luntta
From the sun and surf of Montego Bay and Ocho Rios to the cool slopes of the Blue Mountains, author Karl Luntta offers island-seekers a perceptive, personal view of Jamaica. 230 pages.
$14.95

MONTANA HANDBOOK by W.C. McRae and Judy Jewell
The wild West is yours with this extensive guide to the Treasure State, complete with travel practicalities, history, and lively essays on Montana life. 393 pages. **$13.95**

NEVADA HANDBOOK by Deke Castleman
Nevada Handbook puts the Silver State into perspective and makes it manageable and affordable. 400 pages. **$14.95**

NEW MEXICO HANDBOOK by Stephen Metzger
A close-up and complete look at every aspect of this wondrous state. 375 pages. **$14.95**

NORTHERN CALIFORNIA HANDBOOK by Kim Weir
An outstanding companion for imaginative travel in the territory north of the Tehachapis. 765 pages. **$19.95**

OREGON HANDBOOK by Stuart Warren and Ted Long Ishikawa
Brimming with travel practicalities and insiders' views on Oregon's history, culture, arts, and activities. 461 pages. **$15.95**

PACIFIC MEXICO HANDBOOK by Bruce Whipperman
Explore 2,000 miles of gorgeous beaches, quiet resort towns, and famous archaeological sites along Mexico's Pacific coast. Spanish-English glossary. 428 pages. **$15.95**

TEXAS HANDBOOK by Joe Cummings
Seasoned travel writer Joe Cummings brings an insider's perspective to his home state. 483 pages. **$13.95**

UTAH HANDBOOK by Bill Weir
Weir gives you all the carefully researched facts and background to make your visit a success. 445 pages. **$14.95**

WASHINGTON HANDBOOK by Dianne J. Boulerice Lyons and Archie Satterfield
Covers sights, shopping, services, transportation, and outdoor recreation, with complete listings for restaurants and accommodations. 433 pages. **$13.95**

WYOMING HANDBOOK by Don Pitcher
All you need to know to open the doors to this wide and wild state. 495 pages. **$14.95**

YUCATAN HANDBOOK by Chicki Mallan
All the information you'll need to guide you into every corner of this exotic land. Mayan and Spanish glossaries. 391 pages. **$14.95**

THE INTERNATIONAL SERIES

EGYPT HANDBOOK by Kathy Hansen
An invaluable resource for intelligent travel in Egypt. Arabic glossary. 522 pages. **$18.95**

MOSCOW-ST. PETERSBURG HANDBOOK by Masha Nordbye
Provides the visitor with an extensive introduction to the history, culture, and people of these two great cities, as well as practical information on where to stay, eat, and shop. 260 pages. **$13.95**

NEPAL HANDBOOK   by Kerry Moran
Whether you're planning a week in Kathmandu or months out on the trail, *Nepal Handbook* will take you into the heart of this Himalayan jewel. 378 pages.   **$12.95**

NEPALI AAMA   by Broughton Coburn
A delightful photo-journey into the life of a Gurung tribeswoman of Central Nepal. Having lived with Aama (translated, "mother") for two years, first as an outsider and later as an adopted member of the family, Coburn presents an intimate glimpse into a culture alive with humor, folklore, religion, and ancient rituals. 165 pages.   **$13.95**

PAKISTAN HANDBOOK   by Isobel Shaw
For armchair travelers and trekkers alike, the most detailed and authoritative guide to Pakistan ever published. Urdu glossary. 478 pages.   **$15.95**

STAYING HEALTHY IN ASIA, AFRICA, AND LATIN AMERICA
by Dirk G. Schroeder, Sc D, MPH
Don't leave home without it! Besides providing a complete overview of the health problems that exist in these areas, this book will help you determine which immunizations you'll need beforehand, what medications to take with you, and how to recognize and treat infections and diseases. Includes extensively illustrated first-aid information and precautions for heat, cold, and high altitude. 200 pages.   **$10.95**

TIBET HANDBOOK: A PILGRIMAGE GUIDE
by Victor Chan
This remarkable book is both a comprehensive trekking guide to mountain paths and plateau trails, and a pilgrimage guide that draws on Tibetan literature and religious history. 1104 pages.
$30.00

MOONBELTS

Made of heavy-duty Cordura nylon, the Moonbelt offers maximum protection for your money and important papers. This all-weather pouch slips under your shirt or waistband, rendering it virtually undetectable and inaccessible to pickpockets. One-inch-wide nylon webbing, heavy-duty zipper, one-inch quick-release buckle. Accommodates traveler's checks, passport, cash, photos. Size 5 x 9 inches. Black.   **$8.95**

**New travel handbooks may be available that are not on this list.
To find out more about current or upcoming titles,
call us toll-free at (800) 345-5473.**

IMPORTANT ORDERING INFORMATION

FOR FASTER SERVICE: Call to locate the bookstore nearest you that carries Moon Travel Handbooks or order directly from Moon Publications:

(800) 345-5473 • **Monday-Friday** • **9 a.m.-5 p.m. PST** • **fax (916) 345-6751**

PRICES: All prices are subject to change. We always ship the most current edition. We will let you know if there is a price increase on the book you ordered.

SHIPPING & HANDLING OPTIONS: 1) Domestic UPS or USPS first class (allow 10 working days for delivery): $3.50 for the first item, 50 cents for each additional item.

Exceptions:
- **Moonbelt** shipping is $1.50 for one, 50 cents for each additional belt.
- Add $2.00 for same-day handling.
- UPS 2nd Day Air or Printed Airmail requires a special quote.
- International Surface Bookrate (8-12 weeks delivery):
  $3.00 for the first item, $1.00 for each additional item. Note: Moon Publications cannot guarantee international surface bookrate shipping.

FOREIGN ORDERS: All orders that originate outside the U.S.A. must be paid for with either an International Money Order or a check in U.S. currency drawn on a major U.S. bank based in the U.S.A.

TELEPHONE ORDERS: We accept Visa or MasterCard payments. Minimum order is US$15.00. Call in your order: (800) 345-5473, 9 a.m.-5 p.m. Pacific Standard Time.

ORDER FORM

Be sure to call (800) 345-5473 for current prices and editions or for the name of the bookstore
nearest you that carries Moon Travel Handbooks • 9 a.m.–5 p.m. PST
(See important ordering information on preceding page)

Name: _____ Date: _____

Street: _____

City: _____ Daytime Phone: _____

State or Country: _____ Zip Code: _____

QUANTITY	TITLE	PRICE

Taxable Total_____

Sales Tax (7.25%) for California Residents_____

Shipping & Handling_____

TOTAL_____

Ship: ☐ UPS (no PO Boxes) ☐ 1st class ☐ International surface mail

Ship to: ☐ address above ☐ other _____

_____

_____

Make checks payable to: **MOON PUBLICATIONS, INC**. P.O. Box 3040, Chico, CA 95927-3040
U.S.A. We accept Visa and MasterCard. **To Order**: Call in your Visa or MasterCard number, or send
a written order with your Visa or MasterCard number and expiration date clearly written.

Card Number: ☐ **Visa** ☐ **MasterCard**

☐ ☐ ☐ ☐ ☐ ☐ ☐ ☐ ☐ ☐ ☐ ☐ ☐ ☐ ☐ ☐

Exact Name on Card: _____

expiration date:_____

signature_____

S/94

ABOUT THE AUTHOR

Carl Parkes, author of *Southeast Asia Handbook,* was born into an American Air Force family and spent his childhood in California, Nebraska, Alabama, and Japan, where his love of Asia first began. After graduating from the University of California at Santa Barbara, Carl traveled throughout Europe and later returned to work in Hawaii, Lake Tahoe, Aspen, Salt Lake City, and finally, San Francisco. But childhood memories of Asia continued to pull him eastward. After a 12-month journey across Asia, Carl returned to San Francisco to work as a stockbroker and plan his escape from the nine-to-five world. A chance encounter in Singapore with Bill Dalton offered a more intriguing option: research and write a travel guidebook to Southeast Asia.

Carl fervently believes that travel is an immensely rewarding undertaking that affirms the basic truths of life. "Travel is much more than just monuments and ruins. It's an opportunity to reach out and discover what's best about the world. Travel enriches our lives, spreads prosperity, dissolves political barriers, promotes international peace, and brings excitement and change to our lives."

Besides travel writing, Carl enjoys straight-ahead jazz, photography, Anchor Steam beer, opera, art openings, poetry readings, and samba nightclubs in his favorite city of San Francisco. The author also gives travel slide shows and leads adventure expeditions to Southeast Asia. Future plans include a summer of motorcycling around Europe and more books on his favorite destinations.

ABOUT THE ILLUSTRATOR

Terra Muzick is one of America's premier illustrators of children's books, calendars, and toys. Her career began with Hallmark Cards soon after graduation from art school in Ohio. In 1980 she moved to San Francisco, where she drew Snoopys before going freelance the following year. Since then, Terra has rafted in Thailand, enjoyed a massage on Kuta Beach, and kept busy with gallery openings, Cacophony capers, and the Art Deco Society.